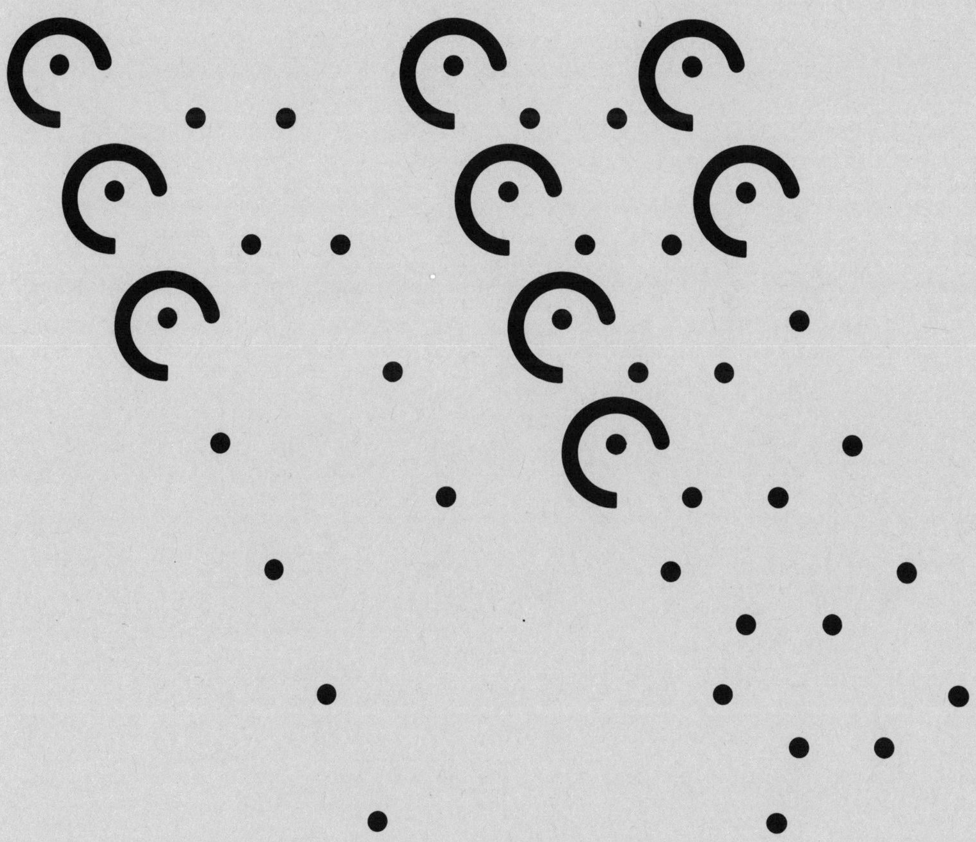

Hermeneia
—A Critical
and Historical
Commentary
on the Bible

Amos

A Commentary on the
Book of Amos

by Shalom M. Paul

Edited by
Frank Moore Cross

Fortress
Press

Minneapolis

Amos

A commentary on the Book of Amos

Cover and interior design by Kenneth Hiebert
Production management by Publishers' WorkGroup
Typesetting on an Ibycus System at Polebridge Press

Library of Congress Cataloging-in-Publication Data

Paul, Shalom M.
Amos : a commentary on the book of Amos / by Shalom M. Paul ; edited by Frank Moore Cross.
p. cm. — (Hermeneia—a critical and historical commentary on the Bible)
Includes bibliographical references and index.
ISBN 0-8006-6023-4 :
1. Bible. O.T. Amos—Commentaries. I. Cross, Frank Moore.
II. Bible. O.T. Amos. English. 1991. III. Title. IV. Series.
BS 1585.3.P38 1991
224'.8077—dc20 90-45137
CIP

∞™

The paper used in this publication meets the minimum requirements of American National Standard for Information Sciences—Permanence of Paper for Printed Library Materials, ANSI Z329.48–1984.

Manufactured in the U.S.A. AF 1-6023

02 01 99 98 2 3 4 5 6 7 8 9 10

TO–

YONA

MICHAL • YAEL • BENZI

TAL • TAMAR • DROR

ZIV • ROTEM

Psalm 128:3, 6

Contents
Amos

The name *Hermeneia,* Greek ἑρμηνεία, has been chosen as the title of the commentary series to which this volume belongs. The word *Hermeneia* has a rich background in the history of biblical interpretation as a term used in the ancient Greek-speaking world for the detailed, systematic exposition of a scriptural work. It is hoped that the series, like its name, will carry forward this old and venerable tradition. A second, entirely practical reason for selecting the name lies in the desire to avoid a long descriptive title and its inevitable acronym, or worse, an unpronounceable abbreviation.

The series is designed to be a critical and historical commentary to the Bible without arbitrary limits in size or scope. It will utilize the full range of philological and historical tools, including textual criticism (often slighted in modern commentaries), the methods of the history of tradition (including genre and prosodic analysis), and the history of religion.

Hermeneia is designed for the serious student of the Bible. It will make full use of ancient Semitic and classical languages; at the same time, English translations of all comparative materials—Greek, Latin, Canaanite, or Akkadian—will be supplied alongside the citation of the source in its original language. Insofar as possible, the aim is to provide the student or scholar with full critical discussion of each problem of interpretation and with the primary data upon which the discussion is based.

Hermeneia is designed to be international and interconfessional in the selection of authors; its editorial boards were formed with this end in view. Occasionally the series will offer translations of distinguished commentaries which originally appeared in languages other than English. Published volumes of the series will be revised continually, and eventually, new commentaries will replace older works in order to preserve the currency of the series. Commentaries are also being assigned for important literary works in the categories of apocryphal and pseudepigraphical works relating to the Old and New Testaments, including some of Essene or Gnostic authorship.

The editors of *Hermeneia* impose no systematic-theological perspective upon the series (directly, or indirectly by selection of authors). It is expected that authors will struggle to lay bare the ancient meaning of a biblical work or pericope. In this way the text's human relevance should become transparent, as is always the case in competent historical discourse. However, the series eschews for itself homiletical translation of the Bible.

The editors are heavily indebted to Augsburg Fortress for its energy and courage in taking up an expensive, long-term project, the rewards of which will accrue chiefly to the field of biblical scholarship.

Frank Moore Cross
For the Old Testament
Editorial Board

Helmut Koester
For the New Testament
Editorial Board

This commentary is a product of several decades of research into and teaching of the Book of Amos. The important volume of F. I. Anderson and D. N. Freedman, *Amos*, AB 24a (Garden City, N.Y.: Doubleday, 1990) appeared too late for me to incorporate its exegetical insights into my work.

In the notes, when an author's name appears, followed by a page number, the reference is to that author's commentary volume, listed in the bibliography, pp. 299–303.

It is a great pleasure to express my appreciation to Frank Moore Cross for his invitation to me to contribute this volume for the Hermeneia series, for his thorough and critical reading of my typescript, and for his enlightening suggestions, which are duly noted in the commentary. I am also extremely grateful to Beth La Rocca for her unstinting devotion and labor in editing the entire typescript.

I was proud to dedicate my previous book to my wife, Yona, and to our three children, Michal, Yael, and Benzi. It is with great joy that I can now dedicate this volume also to my two lovely granddaughters, Tal and Tamar.

January 1990

Shalom Paul
Jerusalem

Reference Codes

1. Sources and Abbreviations

α'	Aquila
AASOR	Annual of the American Schools of Oriental Research
AB	Anchor Bible
AbB	Altbabylonische Briefe in Umschrift und Übersetzung
ABL	R. E. Harper, *Assyrian and Babylonian Letters*
AcAn	*Acta Antiqua*
AcOr	*Acta Orientalia*
ADAJ	*Annual of the Department of Antiquities of Jordan*
AfO	*Archiv für Orientforschung*
AHw	W. von Soden, *Akkadische Handwörterbuch*
AION	*Annali dell'Instituto Universitario Orientale di Napoli*
AJSL	*American Journal of Semitic Languages and Literatures*
AKA	E. A. W. Budge and L. W. King, *The Annals of the Kings of Assyria*
AMT	R. C. Thompson, *Assyrian Medical Texts*
AnBib	Analecta Biblica
ANEP	*The Ancient Near East in Pictures* (ed. J. B. Pritchard)
ANESTP	*Ancient Near East: Supplementary Texts and Pictures* (ed. J. B. Pritchard)
ANET	*Ancient Near Eastern Texts* (ed. J. B. Pritchard)
AnOr	Analecta Orientalia
AnSt	Anatolian Studies
Anton	*Antonianum*
AO	Der Alte Orient
AOAT	Alter Orient und Altes Testament
AOB	Altorientalische Bibliothek
AOS	American Oriental Series
AOS Essays	American Oriental Society Essays
AOTU	Altorientalische Texte und Untersuchungen
ARM	Archives Royales de Mari
ArOr	*Archiv Orientální*
ASKT	P. Haupt, *Akkadische und sumerische Keilschrifttexte*
ASTI	*Annual of the Swedish Theological Institute*
ATANT	Abhandlungen zur Theologie des Alten und Neuen Testaments
ATD	Das Alte Testament Deutsch (Göttingen)
ATR	*Anglican Theological Review*
AuS	G. Dalman, *Arbeit und Sitte in Palästina*
AusBR	*Australian Biblical Review*
AUSS	*Andrews University Seminary Studies*
AWAT	*Archiv für wissenschaftliche Erforschung des AT* (ed. E. O. A. Merx)
BA	*Biblical Archaeologist*
BAR	*Biblical Archaeology Review*
BASOR	*Bulletin of the American Schools of Oriental Research*
BASP	*Bulletin of the American Society of Papyrologists*
BBB	Bonner biblische Beiträge
BBR	H. Zimmern, *Beiträge zur Kenntnis der babylonischen Religion*
BBSt	L. W. King, *Babylonian Boundary-Stones*
BC	*Biblischer Commentar über das Alte Testament*
BDB	F. Brown, S. R. Driver, and C. A. Briggs, *A Hebrew and English Lexicon of the Old Testament*
BE	The Babylonian Expedition of the University of Pennsylvania
BeO	*Bibbia e Oriente*
BEvT	Beiträge zur Evangelischen Theologie
BFCT	Beiträge zur Förderung christlicher Theologie
BH^3	Biblia Hebraica (ed. R. Kittel)
BHH	Biblisch-historisches Handwörterbuch
BHS^4	Biblia Hebraica Stuttgartensia (ed. K. Elliger and W. Rudolph)
BHT	S. Smith, *Babylonian Historical Texts*
Bib	*Biblica*
BibLeb	*Bibel und Leben*
BibOr	Biblica et Orientalia
BIES	*Bulletin of the Israel Exploration Society* (Heb.)
BiTod	*The Bible Today*
BJRL	*Bulletin of the John Rylands Library*
BK	*Bibel und Kirche*
BKAT	Biblischer Kommentar: Altes Testament
BLe	H. Bauer and P. Leander, *Historische Grammatik der Hebräischen Sprache*
BM	*Beth Miqra*
BMT	Tablets in the Collections of the British Museum
BN	Biblische Notizen
BO	*Bibliotheca Orientalis*
BoSt	*Boghazköi Studien*
BRL	K. Galling, *Biblisches Reallexikon*
BRM	Babylonian Records in the Library of J. Pierpont Morgan
BT	*The Bible Translator*
BTB	*Biblical Theology Bulletin*
BTS	*Bible et Terre Sainte*
BVC	*Bible et Vie Chrétienne*
BWANT	Beiträge zur Wissenschaft vom Alten und Neuen Testament
BWL	W. Lambert, *Babylonian Wisdom Literature*
BZ	*Biblische Zeitschrift*

BZAW	Beihefte zur Zeitschrift für die Alttestamentliche Wissenschaft
CAD	*The Assyrian Dictionary of the Oriental Institute of the University of Chicago*
CAT	Commentaire de l'Ancien Testament
CB	*Cultura Bíblica*
CBQ	*Catholic Biblical Quarterly*
CIS	*Corpus Inscriptionum Semiticarum*
CML	G. R. Driver, *Canaanite Myths and Legends*
CollB	Collationes Brugenses et Gandavenses
CollNam	*Collationes Namurcenses*
CRAIBL	*Comptes rendus de l'Académie des inscriptions et belles-lettres*
CRRA	Comptes Rendus de la . . . Rencontre Assyriologique Internationale
CT	Cuneiform Texts from Babylonian Tablets in the British Museum
CTA	*Corpus des tablettes en cunéiformes alphabétiques à Ras Shamra-Ugarit de 1929 à 1939* (ed. A. Herdner)
CTM	*Concordia Theological Monthly*
CurTM	*Currents in Theology and Mission*
CuW	*Christentum und Wissenschaft*
DBAT	Dielheimer Blätter zum Alten Testament
DBSup	*Dictionnaire de la Bible, Supplément*
DISO	C. F. Jean and J. Hoftijzer, *Dictionnaire des Inscriptions Sémitiques de l'Ouest*
DJD	Discoveries in the Judaean Desert
DTT	*Dansk Teologisk Tidsskrift*
EA	J. A. Knudtzon, *Die El-Amarna Tafeln*
EBib	Études Bibliques
EM	*Encyclopaedia Miqraith = Encyclopaedia Biblica* (Heb.)
EncJud	*Encyclopaedia Judaica*
EphCarm	*Ephemerides Carmeliticae*
EstBíb	*Estudios Bíblicos*
ETL	*Ephemerides Theologicae Lovanienses*
ETR	*Études Théologiques et Religieuses*
EvQ	*Evangelical Quarterly*
EvT	*Evangelische Theologie*
ExpTim	*The Expository Times*
FRLANT	Forschungen zur Religion und Literatur des Alten und Neuen Testaments
FuF	*Forschungen und Fortschritte*
G	Septuagint
GKC	*Gesenius' Hebrew Grammar* (ed. E. Kautzsch)
GTT	Gereformeerd Theologisch Tijschrift
HAR	*Hebrew Annual Review*
HAT	Handbuch zum Alten Testament
HBD	*Harper's Biblical Dictionary*
HKAT	Handkommentar zum Alten Testament
HL	*Hittite Laws*
HS	Die Heilige Schrift des AT (ed. F. Feldmann and H. Herkenne)
HSAT	Die Heilige Schrift des AT (Kautzsch) (ed. A. Bertholet)
HSM	Harvard Semitic Monographs
HSS	Harvard Semitic Series
HTR	*Harvard Theological Review*
HTSt	*Hervormde Teologiese Studies*
HUCA	*Hebrew Union College Annual*
ICC	International Critical Commentary
IDB	*Interpreter's Dictionary of the Bible*
IDBSup	*Interpreter's Dictionary of the Bible, Supplement*
IEJ	*Israel Exploration Journal*
Int	*Interpretation*
ITQ	*Irish Theological Quarterly*
JANESCU	*Journal of the Ancient Near Eastern Society of Columbia University*
JAOS	*Journal of the American Oriental Society*
JBL	*Journal of Biblical Literature*
JCS	*Journal of Cuneiform Studies*
JEOL	*Jaarbericht van het Vooraziatisch-Egyptisch Gezelschap (Genootschap). Ex Oriente Lux*
JETS	*Journal of the Evangelical Theological Society*
JJS	*Journal of Jewish Studies*
JNES	*Journal of Near Eastern Studies*
JNSL	*Journal of Northwest Semitic Languages*
JPOS	*Journal of the Palestine Oriental Society*
JQR	*Jewish Quarterly Review*
JR	*Journal of Religion*
JRAS	*Journal of the Royal Asiatic Society*
JSOT	*Journal for the Study of the Old Testament*
JSS	*Journal of Semitic Studies*
JTS	*Journal of Theological Studies*
KAH	*Keilschrifttexte aus Assur historischen Inhalts*
KAI	H. Donner and W. Röllig, *Kanaanäische und Aramäische Inschriften*
KAR	E. Ebeling, *Keilschrifttexte aus Assur religiösen Inhalts*
KAT	Kommentar zum Alten Testament (ed. E. Sellin)
KB	L. Köhler and W. Baumgartner, *Hebräisches und Aramäisches Lexikon zum Alten Testament*
KBib	*Keilinschriftliche Bibliothek, Sammlung von assyrischen und babylonischen Texten in Umschrift und Übersetzung*
KBo	*Keilschrifttexte aus Boghazköi*
KD	*Kerygma und Dogma*
KS	Kleine Schriften
KTU	M. Dietrich, O. Loretz, and J. Sanmartín, *Die Keilalphabetischen Texte aus Ugarit*
KUB	*Keilschrifturkunden aus Boghazköi*
LD	Lectio Divina
Leš	*Lešonenu*
LH	*Laws of Hammurapi*
LIH	L. W. King, *The Letters and Inscriptions of Hammurabi*

LKA	E. Ebeling, *Literarische Keilschrifttexte aus Assur*
LuVitor	*Lumin Vitoria*
MDP	*Mémoires de la Délégation en Perse*
MGWJ	*Monatsschrift für Geschichte und Wissenschaft des Judentums*
MIO	Mitteilungen des Instituts für Orientforschung
MRŠ	*Mission de Ras Shamra*
MSL	Materialien zum Sumerischen Lexikon
MT	Masoretic Text
MUSJ	*Mélanges de l'Université Saint-Joseph*
NEB	*New English Bible*
NGTT	Nederuitse Gereformeede Teologiese Tydskrif
NJPS	*New Jewish Publication Society Translation of the Bible*
NKZ	*Neue Kirchliche Zeitschrift*
NorTT	*Norsk Teologisk Tidsskrift*
NovT	*Novum Testamentum*
NV	Nova et Vetera
OIP	Oriental Institute Publications
OLP	Orientalia Lovaniensia Periodica
OLZ	*Orientalistische Literaturzeitung*
Or	*Orientalia*
OrAnt	*Oriens Antiquus*
OTL	Old Testament Library
OTS	*Oudtestamentische Studiën*
PAAJR	*Proceedings of the American Academy for Jewish Research*
PBS	*Publications of the Babylonian Section, University Museum, University of Pennsylvania*
PEFQS	*Palestine Exploration Fund, Quarterly Statement*
PEQ	*Palestine Exploration Quarterly*
PG	J.-P. Migne, *Patrologia Graeca*
PL	J.-P. Migne, *Patrologia Latina*
PRU	*Le Palais Royal d'Ugarit*
PSBA	*Proceedings of the Society of Biblical Archeology*
1QH	*Hôdāyôt*, Qumran Cave 1
R	*Cuneiform Inscriptions of Western Asia* (ed. H. C. Rawlinson)
RA	*Revue d'Assyriologie et d'Archéologie Orientale*
RArch	*Revue Archéologique*
RB	*Revue Biblique*
RE	*Realencyklopädie für protestantische Theologie und Kirche*
ReBi	Religion och Bibel
REJ	*Revue des Études Juives*
ResQ	Restoration Quarterly
RevExp	*Review and Expositor*
RevQ	*Revue de Qumran*
RevScRel	*Revue des Sciences Religieuses*
RevSém	*Revue Sémitique*
RevT	*Revista Teológica*
RGG	*Die Religion in Geschichte und Gegenwart*
RHPR	*Revue d'Histoire et de Philosophie Religieuses*
RHR	*Revue de l'Histoire des Religions*
RIDA	*Revue International des Droits de l'Antiquité*
RivB	*Rivista Biblica*
RLA	*Reallexikon der Assyriologie*
RŠ	Signatur für Texte aus Ras Shamra
RSO	*Rivista degli Studi Orientali*
RSR	*Recherches de Science Religieuse*
RTL	*Revue théologiques de Louvain*
RTP	*Revue de Théologie et de Philosophie*
σ'	Symmachus
S	Syriac Version, Peshiṭta
SANT	Studien zum Alten und Neuen Testament
SAT	*Die Schriften des Alten Testaments*
SBFLA	*Studii Biblici Franciscani Liber Annuus*
SBJ	*La Sainte Bible de Jerusalem*
SBLASP	Society of Biblical Literature Abstracts and Seminar Papers
SBLDS	Society of Biblical Literature Dissertation Series
SBLMS	Society of Biblical Literature Monograph Series
SBLSBS	Society of Biblical Literature Sources for Bible Study
SBT	Studies in Biblical Theology
ScEs	*Science et esprit*
SCR	*Studies in Comparative Religion*
ScrB	*Scripture Bulletin*
SDAWPH	*Sitzungsberichte der Deutschen Akademie der Wissenschaften*
SEÅ	*Svensk Exegetisk Årsbok*
Sem	*Semitica*
Shnaton	*Shnaton, An Annual for Biblical and Ancient Near Eastern Studies* (ed. M. Weinfeld)
SJLA	Studies in Judaism in Late Antiquity
SJT	*Scottish Journal of Theology*
SL	*Sumerian Laws*
SMSR	*Studi e Materiali di Storia delle Religioni*
SOTSMS	Society for Old Testament Study Monograph Series
SR	*Studies in Religion*
ST	*Studia Theologica*
StGen	Studium Generale
SThU	Schweizerische Theologische Umschau
SThZ	Schweizerische Theologische Zeitschrift
STT	O. R. Gurney, J. J. Finkelstein, and P. Hullin, *The Sultantepe Tablets*
StudOr	Studia Orientalia
SVT	Supplements to Vetus Testamentum
SWJT	*Southwestern Journal of Theology*
SymBu	Symbolae Biblicae Upsalienses
Θ'	Theodotion
T	Targum Jonathan (to the Prophets)
TBei	Theologische Beiträge

TBl — Theologische Blätter
TBü — Theologische Bücherei
TCL — Musée du Louvre. Département des Antiquités Orientales, Textes Cunéiformes
TDNT — *Theological Dictionary of the New Testament*
TDOT — *Theological Dictionary of the Old Testament*
TGl — *Theologie und Glaube*
THAT — *Theologisches Handwörterbuch zum Alten Testament* (ed. E. Jenni and C. Westermann)
ThSt — *Theologische Studien*
ThT — *Theologische Tijdschrift*
TLZ — *Theologische Literaturzeitung*
TQ — *Theologische Quartalschrift*
TRu — *Theologische Rundschau*
TS — *Theological Studies*
TSK — *Theologische Studien und Kritiken*
TTKi — *Tidsskrift for Teologi og Kirke*
TTZ — *Trierer Theologische Zeitschrift*
TV — Theologica Vida
TWAT — *Theologisches Wörterbuch zum Alten Testament* (ed. G. J. Botterweck and H. Ringgren)
TWNT — *Theologisches Wörterbuch zum Neuen Testament*
TZ — *Theologische Zeitschrift*
UET — Ur Excavations, Texts
UF — *Ugaritische Forschungen*
Ug — *Ugaritica*
UT — C. H. Gordon, *Ugaritic Textbook*
UUÅ — *Uppsala Universitets Årsskrift*
V — Vulgate
VAB — Vorderasiatische Bibliothek
VAS — *Vorderasiatische Schriftdenkmäler der Königlichen Museen zu Berlin*
VC — *Vigilae Christienae*
VD — *Verbum Domini*
VS — Verbum Salutis
VSpir — *La Vie Spirituelle*
VT — *Vetus Testamentum*
WMANT — Wissenschaftliche Monographien zum Alten und Neuen Testament
WO — *Die Welt des Orients*
WuD — *Wort und Dienst*
WVDOG — *Wissenschaftliche Veröffentlichungen der Deutschen Orient-Gesellschaft*
WZKM — *Wiener Zeitschrift für die Kunde des Morgenländes*
YNERS — Yale Near Eastern Research Series
YOS — Yale Oriental Series, Babylonian Texts
ZA — *Zeitschrift für Assyriologie*
ZAW — *Zeitschrift für die Alttestamentliche Wissenschaft*
ZDMG — *Zeitschrift der Deutschen Morgenländischen Gesellschaft*
ZDPV — *Zeitschrift des Deutschen Palästina-Vereins*
ZNW — *Zeitschrift für die Neutestamentliche Wissenschaft*
ZTK — *Zeitschrift für Theologie und Kirche*
ZWT — *Zeitschrift für Wissenschaftliche Theologie*

2. Short Titles of Studies and Articles Often Cited

Alter, *Art*
R. Alter, *The Art of Biblical Poetry* (New York: Basic Books, 1985).

Amsler, "Amos"
S. Amsler, "Amos, prophète de la onzième heure," *TZ* 21 (1965) 318–28.

Avishur, "Construct State"
Y. Avishur, "Pairs of Synonymous Words in the Construct State (and in Appositional Hendiadys) in Biblical Hebrew," *Sem* 2 (1971–1972) 17–81.

Avishur, "Forms"
Y. Avishur, "The Forms of Repetition of Numbers Indicating Wholeness (3,7,10)—in the Bible and in Ancient Semitic Literature," *Beer-Sheva* 1 (1973) 1–55 (Heb.).

Avishur, "Patterns"
Y. Avishur, "Patterns of the Double Rhetorical Question," in *Zer Li-Gevurot. The Zalman Shazar Jubilee Volume: A Collection of Studies in Bible, Eretz Yisrael, Hebrew Language, and Talmudic Literature* (ed. B. Z. Luria; Jerusalem: Kiryat Sepher, 1973) 421–64 (Heb.).

Avishur, *Phoenician Inscriptions*
Y. Avishur, *Phoenician Inscriptions and the Bible: Studies in Stylistic and Literary Devices and Selected Inscriptions* (2 vols.; Jerusalem: E. Rubinstein, 1979) (Heb.).

Avishur, "Word Pairs"
Y. Avishur, "Word Pairs Common to Phoenician and Biblical Hebrew," *UF* 7 (1975) 13–47.

Bach, *Aufforderungen*
R. Bach, *Die Aufforderungen zur Flucht und zum Kampf im alttestamentlichen Prophetenspruch* (WMANT 9; Neukirchen-Vluyn: Neukirchener Verlag, 1962).

Bach, "Gottesrecht"
R. Bach, "Gottesrecht und weltliches Recht in der Verkündigung des Propheten Amos," in *Festschrift für Günther Dehn* (ed. W. Schneemelcher; Neukirchen-Vluyn: Verlag der Erziehungsvereins, 1957) 23–34.

Balla, *Die Droh*
E. Balla, *Die Droh-und Scheltworte des Amos* (Leipzig: Edelmann, 1926).

Barstad, *Religious Polemics*
H. M. Barstad, *The Religious Polemics of Amos* (SVT 34; Leiden: Brill, 1984).

Bartlett, "Land of Seir"
J. R. Bartlett, "The Land of Seir and the Brotherhood of Edom," *JTS* 20 (1969) 13–18.

Baumann, *Der Aufbau*
E. Baumann, *Der Aufbau der Amosreden* (BZAW 7; Giessen: Töpelmann, 1903).

Baumann, "Einzelheit"
E. Baumann, "Eine Einzelheit," *ZAW* 64 (1952) 62.

Beek, "Religious Background"
M. A. Beek, "The Religious Background of Amos 2:6–8," in *OTS* 5 (Leiden: Brill, 1948) 132–41.

ben Saruq, *Maḥberet*
M. ben Saruq, *Sepher HaMaḥberet* (ed. Y. Philipawaski; Yadenburg, 1854) (Heb.).

Benson, "Mouth of the Lion"
A. Benson, "From the Mouth of the Lion: The Messianism of Amos," *CBQ* 19 (1957) 199–212.

Bentzen, "Ritual Background"
A. Bentzen, "The Ritual Background of Amos i 2—ii 16," in *OTS* 8 (Leiden: Brill, 1950) 85–99.

Berridge, "Intention"
J. M. Berridge, "Die Intention der Botschaft des Amos. Exegetische Überlegungen zu Amos 5," *TZ* 32 (1976) 321–40.

Blau, "Homonyme"
J. Blau, "Über Homonyme und angeblich Homonyme Wurzeln I," *VT* 6 (1956) 242–48; II, *VT* 7 (1957) 100–101.

Borger, *Inschriften*
R. Borger, *Die Inschriften Asarhaddons Königs von Assyrien* (*AfO* Beiheft 9; Graz: Selbstverlag des Herausgebers, 1956).

Botterweck, "Authentizität"
G. J. Botterweck, "Zur Authentizität des Buches Amos," *BZ* 2 (1958) 176–89.

Brin, "Visions"
G. Brin, "The Visions of Amos (7:1—8:3): Studies in Structures and Ideas," in *Isac Leo Seeligmann Volume, Essays in the Bible and the Ancient World* (ed. A. Rofé and Y. Zakovitch; 3 vols; Jerusalem: E. Rubinstein, 1983) 2.275–90 (Heb.).

Brunet, "Vision"
G. Brunet, "La vision de l'étain, réinterpretation d'Amos VII,7–9," *VT* 16 (1966) 387–95.

Budde, "Amos"
K. Budde, "Zum Text und Auslegung des Buches Amos," *JBL* 43 (1924) 46–131; 44 (1925) 63–122.

Cassuto, *Biblical*
U. M. D. Cassuto, *Biblical and Oriental Studies* (tr. I. Abrahams; 2 vols.; Jerusalem: Magnes, 1973, 1975).

Cazelles, "L'arrière-plan"
H. Cazelles, "L'arrière-plan historique d'Amos 1:9–10," *Proceedings of the Sixth World Congress of Jewish Studies* (3 vols.; Jerusalem: World Union of Jewish Studies, 1977) 1. 71–76.

Cazelles, "Problem"
H. Cazelles, "The Problem of the Kings in Osée 8:4," *CBQ* 11 (1949) 14–25.

Christensen, "Prosodic Structure"
D. L. Christensen, "The Prosodic Structure of Amos 1—2," *HTR* 67 (1974) 427–36.

Christensen, *Transformation*
D. L. Christensen, *Transformation of the War Oracles in Old Testament Prophecy: Studies in the Oracles against the Nations* (Missoula, MT: Scholars, 1975).

Clay, *Epics*
A. T. Clay, *Epics, Hymns, Omens, and Other Texts* (BRM 4; New Haven: Yale University, 1923).
Cohen, "Amos"
S. Cohen, "Amos *Was* a Navi," *HUCA* 32 (1961) 175–78.
Coote, "Amos 1:11"
R. B. Coote, "Amos 1:11 *RḤMYW*," *JBL* 90 (1971) 206–8.
Cowley, *Aramaic Papyri*
A. E. Cowley, *Aramaic Papyri of the Fifth Century B.C.* (Oxford: Clarendon, 1923).
Crenshaw, *Hymnic Affirmation*
J. L. Crenshaw, *Hymnic Affirmation of Divine Justice: The Doxologies of Amos and Related Texts in the O.T.* (SBLDS 24; Missoula, MT: Scholars, 1975).
Crenshaw, "Influence"
J. L. Crenshaw, "The Influence of the Wise upon Amos—The 'Doxologies of Amos' and Job 5:9–16; 9:5–10," *ZAW* 79 (1967) 42–52.
Crenshaw, "Theophanic Tradition"
J. L. Crenshaw, "Amos and the Theophanic Tradition," *ZAW* 80 (1968) 203–15.
Cross, "Aramaic Stele"
F. M. Cross, "A New Aramaic Stele from Taymā'," in *A Wise and Discerning Heart: Studies Presented to Joseph A. Fitzmyer, S.J., in Celebration of His Sixty-fifth Birthday* (ed. R. E. Brown and A. A. Di Lella) = *CBQ* 48 (1986) 387–94.
Cross, *Canaanite Myth*
F. M. Cross, *Canaanite Myth and Hebrew Epic: Essays in the History of the Religion of Israel* (Cambridge: Harvard University, 1973).
Cross, "Divine Warrior"
F. M. Cross, "The Divine Warrior in Israel's Early Cult," in *Biblical Motifs: Origins and Transformations* (ed. A. Altmann; Studies and Texts 3; Cambridge: Harvard University, 1986) 11–30.
Crüsemann, *Studien*
F. Crüsemann, *Studien zur Formgeschichte von Hymnus und Danklied in Israel* (WMANT 32; Neukirchen-Vluyn: Neukirchener Verlag, 1969).
Delekat, "Wörterbuch"
L. Delekat, "Zum hebräischen Wörterbuch," *VT* 14 (1964) 7–66.
Dion, "Le message moral"
P. E. Dion, "Le message moral du prophète Amos s'inspirait-il du 'droit de l'alliance'?" *ScEs* 27 (1975) 5–34.
Dossin, "Une révélation"
G. Dossin, "Une révélation du dieu Dagan à Terqa," *RA* 42 (1948) 316–20.
Driver and Miles, *Babylonian Laws*
G. R. Driver and J. C. Miles, *The Babylonian Laws: Edited with Translation and Commentary* (2 vols.; Oxford: Clarendon, 1952).
Duhm, "Anmerkungen"
B. Duhm, "Anmerkungen zu den Zwölf Propheten, 1. Buch Amos," *ZAW* 31 (1911) 1–18.
Dürr, "Recht"
L. Dürr, "Altorientalisches Recht bei den Propheten Amos und Hosea," *BZ* 23 (1935–1936) 150–57.
Ehrlich, *Mikrâ*
A. B. Ehrlich, *Mikrâ ki-Pheschutô* (3 vols.; New York: Ktav, 1969) (Heb.).
Ehrlich, *Randglossen*
A. B. Ehrlich, *Randglossen zur Hebräischen Bibel* (7 vols.; Leipzig: Hinrichs, 1912).
Farr, "Language"
G. Farr, "The Language of Amos, Popular or Cultic?" *VT* 16 (1966) 312–24.
Feliks, *Plant World*
J. Feliks, *The Plant World of the Bible* (Ramat-Gan: Bar Ilan University, 1968) (Heb.).
Fensham, "Common Trends"
F. C. Fensham, "Common Trends in Curses of the Near Eastern Treaties and *Kudurru*-Inscriptions Compared with Maledictions of Amos and Isaiah," *ZAW* 75 (1963) 155–75.
Fensham, "Treaty"
F. C. Fensham, "The Treaty between the Israelites and the Tyrians," in SVT 17 (Leiden: Brill, 1969) 71–87.
Fey, *Amos und Jesaja*
R. Fey, *Amos und Jesaja, Abhändigkeit und Eigenständigkeit des Jesaja* (WMANT 12; Neukirchen-Vluyn: Neukirchener Verlag, 1963).
Fishbane, "Treaty Background"
M. Fishbane, "The Treaty Background of Amos 1,11 and Related Matters," *JBL* 89 (1970) 313–18.
Fitzmyer, *Sefîre*
J. A. Fitzmyer, *The Aramaic Inscriptions of Sefîre* (BibOr 19; Rome: Pontifical Biblical Institute, 1967).
Galling, "Bethel und Gilgal II"
K. Galling, "Bethel und Gilgal II," *ZDPV* 67 (1944–1945) 21–43.
Gaster, "Hymn"
T. H. Gaster, "An Ancient Hymn in the Prophecies of Amos," *Journal of the Manchester University Egyptian and Oriental Society* 19 (1935) 23–26.
Gese, "Beiträge"
H. Gese, "Kleine Beiträge zum Verständnis des Amosbuches," *VT* 12 (1962) 417–38.
Gese, "Komposition"
H. Gese, "Komposition bei Amos," SVT 32 (Leiden: Brill, 1981) 74–95.
Gibson, *Aramaic Inscriptions*
J. C. L. Gibson, *Textbook of Syrian Semitic Inscriptions; Volume II: Aramaic Inscriptions Including Inscriptions in the Dialect of Zendjirli* (Oxford: Clarendon, 1975).
Gibson, *Hebrew and Moabite Inscriptions*
J. C. L. Gibson, *Textbook of Syrian Semitic Inscriptions; Volume 1: Hebrew and Moabite Inscriptions* (Oxford: Clarendon, 1971).

Ginsberg, *Israelian Heritage*
H. L. Ginsberg, *The Israelian Heritage of Judaism* (Texts and Studies of the Jewish Theological Seminary of America 24; New York: Jewish Theological Seminary of America, 1982).

Gitay, "Study"
Y. Gitay, "A Study of Amos's Art of Speech. A Rhetorical Analysis of Amos 3:1–15," *CBQ* 42 (1980) 293–309.

Glueck, "Three Notes"
J. J. Glueck, "Three Notes on the Book of Amos," *Studies in the Books of Hosea and Amos: Die Ou Testamentiese Werkgemeenskap in Suid Afrika: 7th and 8th Congresses* (Potchefstroom: Rege–Pers Beperk, 1964–65) 115–21.

Goetze, *Omen Texts*
A. Goetze, *Old Babylonian Omen Texts* (YOS 10; New Haven: Yale University; London: Cumberledge, 1947).

Gordis, "Composition"
R. Gordis, "The Composition and Structure of Amos," *HTR* 33 (1940) 239–51.

Gordis, "Studies"
R. Gordis, "Studies in the Book of Amos," in *American Academy for Jewish Research Jubilee Volume (1928–29 / 1978–79)* (ed. S. A. Baron and J. E. Barzilay; *PAAJR* 46–47; New York: American Academy for Jewish Research, 1980) 201–64.

Gössmann, *Planetarium*
F. Gössmann, *Planetarium Babylonicum oder Die Sumerisch-Babylonischen Stern-Namen* (ed. P. A. Deimel; Sumerisches Lexikon, IV/2; Rome: Pontifical Biblical Institute, 1950).

Gottlieb, "Amos und Jerusalem"
H. Gottlieb, "Amos und Jerusalem," *VT* 17 (1967) 430–63.

Gottwald, *Kingdoms*
N. K. Gottwald, *All the Kingdoms of the Earth: Israelite Prophecy and International Relations in the Ancient Near East* (New York and London: Harper & Row, 1964).

Greenfield, "Marzeaḥ"
J. C. Greenfield, "The *Marzeaḥ* as a Social Institution," *AcAn* 22 (1974) 451–55.

Greenfield, "Scripture"
J. C. Greenfield, "Scripture and Inscription: The Literary and Rhetorical Element in Some Early Phoenician Inscriptions," in *Near Eastern Studies in Honor of William Foxwell Albright* (ed. H. Goedicke; Baltimore and London: Johns Hopkins University, 1971) 253–68.

Greenfield, "Stylistic Aspects"
J. C. Greenfield, "Stylistic Aspects of the Sefire Treaty Inscriptions," *AcOr* 29 (1965) 1–18.

Gressmann, *Der Messias*
H. Gressmann, *Der Messias* (FRLANT 43; Göttingen: Vandenhoeck & Ruprecht, 1929).

Gressmann, *Prophetie*
H. Gressmann, *Die älteste Geschichtschreibung und Prophetie Israels (Von Samuel bis Amos und Hosea)* (*SAT* 2/1; Göttingen: Vandenhoeck & Ruprecht, ^{2}1921).

Gruber, *Aspects*
M. I. Gruber, *Aspects of Nonverbal Communication in the Ancient Near East* (Studia Pohl 12/1–2; Rome: Pontifical Biblical Institute, 1980).

Gunneweg, "Erwägungen"
A. H. J. Gunneweg, "Erwägungen zu Amos, 7,14," *ZTK* 57 (1960) 1–16.

Hallo, "Qarqar"
W. W. Hallo, "From Qarqar to Carchemish: Assyria and Israel in the Light of New Discoveries," *BA* 23 (1960) 34–61; reprinted in *The Biblical Archeologist Reader* (ed. E. F. Campbell and D. N. Freedman; Garden City, NY: Doubleday, 1962) 2.152–88.

Haran, *Ages and Institutions*
M. Haran, *Ages and Institutions in the Bible* (Tel Aviv: Am Oved, 1972) (Heb.).

Haran, "Amos"
M. Haran, "Amos," *EM* 6 (1971) 271–87 (Heb.).

Haran, "Biblical Studies"
M. Haran, "Biblical Studies: The Literary Applications of the Numerical Sequence x/x+1 and Their Connections with the Patterns of Parallelism," *Tarbiz* 39 (1970) 109–36 (Heb.) = "The Graded Numerical Sequence and the Phenomenon of 'Automatism' in Biblical Poetry," in SVT 22 (Leiden: Brill, 1972) 238–67.

Haran, "Observations"
M. Haran, "Observations on the Historical Background of Amos 1:2—2:6," *BIES* 30 (1966) 56–69 (Heb.) = *IEJ* 18 (1968) 201–12.

Haran, "Rise and Decline"
M. Haran, "The Rise and Decline of the Empire of Jeroboam ben Joash," *VT* 17 (1967) 266–97; translation of "The Rise and Fall of the Empire of Jeroboam II," *Zion* 31 (1966–1967) 18–38 (Heb.).

Haran, *Temples*
M. Haran, *Temples and Temple Service in Ancient Israel: An Inquiry into the Character of Cult Phenomena and the Historical Setting of the Priestly School* (Oxford: Clarendon, 1978).

Hasel, *Remnant*
G. F. Hasel, *The Remnant: The History and Theology of the Remnant Idea from Genesis to Isaiah* (Andrews University Monograph Studies in Religion 5; Berrien Springs, MI: Andrews University, 1972).

Hayes, "Usage"
J. H. Hayes, "The Usage of Oracles against Foreign Nations in Ancient Israel," *JBL* 87 (1968) 81–92.

Hentschke, *Stellung*
R. Hentschke, *Die Stellung der vorexilischen Schriftspropheten zum Kultus* (BZAW 75; Berlin: Töpelmann, 1957).

Hesse, "Amos 5"
F. Hesse, "Amos 5:4–6, 14f.," *ZAW* 68 (1956) 1–17.
Hillers, "Amos 7:4"
D. R. Hillers, "Amos 7:4 and Ancient Parallels," *CBQ* 26 (1964) 221–25.
Hillers, *Treaty Curses*
D. R. Hillers, *Treaty Curses and the Old Testament Prophets* (BibOr 16; Rome: Pontifical Biblical Institute, 1964).
Hoffman, "Amos"
Y. Hoffman, "Did Amos Regard Himself as a Nabi?" *VT* 27 (1977) 209–12.
Hoffman, *Doctrine of Exodus*
Y. Hoffman, *The Doctrine of Exodus in the Bible* (Tel Aviv: Tel Aviv University, 1983) (Heb.).
Hoffman, *Prophecies*
Y. Hoffman, *The Prophecies against Foreign Nations in the Bible* (Tel Aviv: HaKibbutz HaMeuhad, 1977) (Heb.).
Hoffmann, "Versuche"
G. Hoffmann, "Versuche zu Amos," *ZAW* 3 (1883) 87–126, 279f.
Horst, "Doxologien"
F. Horst, "Die Doxologien im Amosbuch," *ZAW* 47 (1929) 45–54; reprinted in idem, *Gottes Recht: Studien zum Recht im Alten Testament* (ed. H. W. Wolff; München: Kaiser, 1961) 155–66.
Horst, "Visionsschilderungen"
F. Horst, "Die Visionsschilderungen der alttestamentlichen Propheten," *EvT* 20 (1960) 193–205.
ibn Ganaḥ, *Haschoraschim*
Y. ibn Ganaḥ, *Sepher Haschoraschim* (ed. W. Bacher; Berlin: H. Itzkowski, 1896) (Heb.).
Ikeda, *Kingdom*
Y. Ikeda, *The Kingdom of Hamath and Its Relations with Aram and Israel* (diss.; Jerusalem University, 1977) (Heb.).
Jastrow, *Dictionary*
M. Jastrow, *Dictionary of the Targumim, the Talmud Bavli and Yerushalmi, and the Midrashic Literature* (2 vols.; New York: Putnam, 1950).
Kapelrud, *Central Ideas*
A. S. Kapelrud, *Central Ideas in Amos* (Skrifter utgitt av det Norske Videnskaps—Akademi i Oslo 2; Oslo: Aschenoug, 1956, ²1961).
Kapelrud, "New Ideas"
A. S. Kapelrud, "New Ideas in Amos," in SVT 15 (Leiden: Brill, 1966) 193–206.
Katzenstein, *Tyre*
H. J. Katzenstein, *The History of Tyre: From the Beginning of the Second Millennium B.C.E. until the Fall of the Neo-Babylonian Empire in 538 B.C.E.* (Jerusalem: Schocken Institute, 1973).
Kaufmann, *Toledoth*
Y. Kaufmann, *Toledoth Ha-Emunah Ha-Yisrealith* (Jerusalem and Tel Aviv: Dvir, 1957) 8 vols., 6.56–92 (Heb.).
Kimchi, *Radicum Liber*
D. Kimchi, *Radicum Liber* (= *Sepher Haschorachim*; Berlin: G. Bethge, 1847; reprinted Jerusalem, 1967) (Heb.). Photocopy.
Kutsch, "'Trauerbräuche'"
E. Kutsch, "'Trauerbräuche' und 'Selbstminderungsriten' im Alten Testament," in *Drei Wiener Antrittsreden* (ThSt 78; Zürich: EVZ-Verlag, 1965) 25–42.
Kutscher, *Language*
E. Y. Kutscher, *The Language and Linguistic Background of the Isaiah Scroll* (Jerusalem: Magnes, 1959) (Heb.); English translation (Leiden: Brill, 1974).
Kutscher, *Words*
E. Y. Kutscher, *Words and Their History* (Jerusalem: Kiryat Sepher, 1968) (Heb.).
Landsberger, *Fauna*
B. Landsberger, *The Fauna of Ancient Mesopotamia* (*MSL* 8; 2 vols.; Rome: Pontifical Biblical Institute, 1962).
Lehming, "Erwägungen"
S. Lehming, "Erwägungen zu Amos," *ZTK* 55 (1958) 145–69.
Limburg, "Sevenfold"
J. Limburg, "Sevenfold Structure in the Book of Amos," *JBL* 106 (1987) 217–22.
Lindblom, *Prophecy*
J. Lindblom, *Prophecy in Ancient Israel* (Philadelphia: Fortress, 1965).
Lipiński, *La Royauté*
E. Lipiński, *La Royauté de Yahwé dans la Poésie et le Culte de l'Ancien Israël* (Bruges: Paleis der Academiën, 1968).
Loewenstamm, *Tradition of the Exodus*
S. E. Loewenstamm, *The Tradition of the Exodus in Its Development* (Jerusalem: Magnes, 1965) (Heb.).
Löhr, *Untersuchungen*
M. Löhr, *Untersuchungen zum Buch Amos* (BZAW 4; Giessen: Töpelmann, 1901).
Long, "Reports"
B. O. Long, "Reports of Visions among the Prophets," *JBL* 95 (1976) 353–66.
Luckenbill, *Annals*
D. D. Luckenbill, *The Annals of Sennacherib* (*OIP* 2; Chicago: University of Chicago, 1924).
Maag, *Text*
V. Maag, *Text, Wortschaft und Begriffswelt des Buches Amos* (Leiden: Brill, 1951).
Malamat, "Arameans"
A. Malamat, "Arameans," in *Peoples of Old Testament Times* (ed. D. W. Thomas; Oxford: Clarendon, 1973) 134–55.
Margulis, *Studies*
B. B. Margulis, *Studies in the Oracles against the Nations* (diss.; Brandeis University, 1967).

Markert, *Struktur*
L. Markert, *Struktur und Bezeichnung des Scheltworts: Eine gattungskritische Studie anhand des Amosbuches* (BZAW 140; Berlin: de Gruyter, 1977).

Marzal, *Gleanings*
A. Marzal, *Gleanings from the Wisdom of Mari* (Studia Pohl 11; Rome: Pontifical Biblical Institute, 1976).

Melamed, "Break-up"
E. Z. Melamed, "Break-up of Stereotype Phrases as an Artistic Device in Biblical Poetry," in *Studies in the Bible* (ed. C. Rabin; Scripta Hierosolymitana 8; Jerusalem: Magnes, 1961) 115–63; reprinted in *Studies in the Bible Presented to Professor M. H. Segal* (ed. J. M. Grintz and J. Liver; Publications of the Israel Society for Biblical Research 17; Jerusalem: Kiryat Sepher, 1964) 188–219 (Heb.).

Milgrom, "Missing Thief"
J. Milgrom, "The Missing Thief in Leviticus 5:20ff.," *RIDA* 3e série 22 (1975) 71–85.

Miller, *Divine Warrior*
P. D. Miller, Jr., *The Divine Warrior in Early Israel* (HSM 5; Cambridge: Harvard University, 1973).

Miller, "Fire"
P. D. Miller, Jr., "Fire in the Mythology of Canaan and Israel," *CBQ* 27 (1965) 256–61.

Moran, "Background"
W. Moran, "The Ancient Near Eastern Background of the Love of God in Deuteronomy," *CBQ* 25 (1963) 77–87.

Morgenstern, "Amos Studies IV"
J. Morgenstern, "Amos Studies IV: The Addresses of Amos—Text and Commentary," *HUCA* 32 (1961) 295–350.

Morgenstern, "Jerusalem"
J. Morgenstern, "Jerusalem 485 B.C.," *HUCA* 28 (1957) 42–43.

Muffs, *Studies*
Y. Muffs, *Studies in the Aramaic Legal Papyri from Elephantine* (Studia et documenta ad iura orientis antiqui pertinentia 8; Leiden: Brill, 1969).

Na'aman, "Letter"
N. Na'aman, "Sennacherib's 'Letter to God' on His Campaign to Judah," *BASOR* 214 (1974) 25–39.

Neher, *Amos*
A. Neher, *Amos. Contribution à l'étude du prophètisme* (Paris: Vrin, 1980, ²1981).

Neubauer, "Erwägungen"
K. W. Neubauer, "Erwägungen zu Amos 5:4–15," *ZAW* 78 (1966) 292–316.

Niditsch, *Vision*
S. Niditsch, *The Symbolic Vision in Biblical Tradition* (HSM 30; Chico, CA: Scholars, 1983).

Oettli, "Amos und Hosea"
S. Oettli, *Amos und Hosea. Zwei Zeugen gegen die Anwendung der Evolutionstheorie auf die Religion Israels,* BFCT 5/4 (Gütersloh: Bertelsmann, 1901).

Oort, "Amos"
H. Oort, "De profeet Amos," *ThT* 14 (1880) 114–58.

Oppenheim, *Interpretation*
A. L. Oppenheim, *The Interpretation of Dreams in the Ancient Near East* (Transactions of the American Philosophical Society 46/3; Philadelphia: American Philosophical Society, 1959).

Paul, "Amos III 15"
S. M. Paul, "Amos III 15—Winter and Summer Mansions," *VT* 28 (1978) 358–60.

Paul, "Concatenous"
S. M. Paul, "Amos 1:3—2:3: A Concatenous Literary Pattern," *JBL* 90 (1971) 397–403.

Paul, "Euphemism"
S. M. Paul, "Euphemism and Dysphemism," *EncJud* 6.959–61.

Paul, "Hosea 8:8–10"
S. M. Paul, "מַשָּׂא מֶלֶךְ שָׂרִים: Hosea 8:8–10 and Ancient Near Eastern Royal Epithets," in *Studies in Bible and the Ancient Near East, Presented to Samuel E. Loewenstamm on His Seventieth Birthday* (ed. Y. Avishur and Y. Blau; Jerusalem: E. Rubinstein, 1978) 309–17 (Heb.); English translation in *Studies in the Bible* (ed. S. Japhet; Scripta Hierosolymitana 31; Jerusalem: Magnes, 1986) 193–204.

Paul, "Literary Reinvestigation"
S. M. Paul, "A Literary Reinvestigation of the Oracles against the Nations of Amos," in *De la Tôrah au Messie: Études d'exégèse et d'herméneutique bibliques offertes à Henri Cazelles* (ed. J. Doré, P. Grelot, and M. Carrez; Paris: Desclée, 1981) 189–204.

Paul, "Prophets"
S. M. Paul, "Prophets and Prophecy," *EncJud* 13 1150–75.

Perles, *Analekten*
F. Perles, *Analekten zur Textkritik des Alten Testaments* (Leipzig: Engel, 1922).

Pfeifer, "Ausweisung"
G. Pfeifer, "Die Ausweisung eines lästigen Ausländers. Amos 7:10–17," *ZAW* 96 (1984) 112–18.

Pfeifer, "Denkformenanalyse"
G. Pfeifer, "Denkformenanalyse als exegetische Methode, erläutert an Amos 1,2—2,16," *ZAW* 88 (1976) 56–71.

Pope, *Song of Songs*
M. Pope, *Song of Songs: A New Translation with Introduction and Commentary* (AB 7c; Garden City, NY: Doubleday, 1977).

Porten, *Archives*
B. Porten, *Archives from Elephantine: The Life of an Ancient Jewish Military Colony* (Berkeley and Los Angeles: University of California, 1968).

Power, "Note"
E. Power, "Note to Amos 7:1," *Bib* 8 (1927) 87–92.

Priest, "Covenant"
J. Priest, "The Covenant of Brothers," *JBL* 84 (1965) 400–406.
Reisner, *Hymnen*
G. A. Reisner, *Sumerisch-babylonische Hymnen nach Thontafeln griechischer Zeit* (Berlin: W. Spemann, 1896).
Renaud, "Genèse"
B. Renaud, "Genèse et Théologie d'Amos 3, 3–8," in *Mélanges Bibliques et Orientaux en l'Honneur de M. Henri Cazelles* (ed. A. Caquot and M. Delcor; AOAT 212; Neukirchen-Vluyn: Neukirchener Verlag, 1981) 353–72.
Reventlow, *Amt*
H. G. Reventlow, *Das Amt des Propheten bei Amos* (FRLANT 80; Göttingen: Vandenhoeck & Ruprecht, 1962).
Roth, "Numerical Sequence"
W. M. W. Roth, "The Numerical Sequence *x/x+1* in the Old Testament," *VT* 12 (1962) 300–311.
Salonen, *Fischerei*
A. Salonen, *Die Fischerei im alten Mesopotamien nach sumerisch-akkadischen Quellen* (Annales Academiae Scientiarum Fennicae B 166; Helsinki: Suomalainen Tiedeakatemia, 1970).
Salonen, *Hausegeräte*
A. Salonen, *Die Hausegeräte der alten Mesopotamier nach sumerisch-akkadischen Quellen* (Annales Academiae Scientiarum Fennicae B 139 & B 144; Helsinki: Suomalainen Tiedeakatemia, 1965–1966).
Salonen, *Die Möbel*
A. Salonen, *Die Möbel des alten Mesopotamien nach sumerisch-akkadischen Quellen* (Annales Academiae Scientiarum Fennicae B 127; Helsinki: Suomalainen Tiedeakatemia, 1963).
Salonen, *Wasserfahrzeuge*
A. Salonen, *Die Wasserfahrzeuge in Babylonien nach šumerisch-akkadischen Quellen* (StudOr 8/4; Helsinki: Societas Orientalis Fennica, 1939).
Sasson, *Military Establishments*
J. M. Sasson, *The Military Establishments at Mari* (Studia Pohl 3; Rome: Pontifical Biblical Institute, 1969).
Schmidt, "Redaktion"
W. H. Schmidt, "Die deuteronomistische Redaktion des Amosbuches," *ZAW* 77 (1965) 168–93.
Seeligmann, "History"
I. L. Seeligmann, "On the History and Nature of Prophecy in Israel," in Eretz Israel 3 *(Dedicated to the Memory of U. M. D. Cassuto 1883–1951;* ed. J. W. Hirschberg and others; Jerusalem: Israel Exploration Society, 1954) 125–32 (Heb.).
Seeligmann, "Terminologie"
I. L. Seeligmann, "Zur Terminologie für das Gerichtsverfahren im Wortschatz des biblischen Hebräisch," in *Hebräische Wortforschung: Festschrift zum 80. Geburtstag von Walter Baumgartner* (ed. B. Hartmann and others; SVT 16; Leiden: Brill, 1967) 251–78.
Seidel, "Four Prophets"
M. Seidel, "Four Prophets Who Prophesied at the Same Time," in idem, *Ḥiqrê Mikra* (Jerusalem: Mosad HaRav Kook, 1978) 195–238 (Heb.).
Seierstad, *Offenbarungserlebnisse*
I. P. Seierstad, *Die Offenbarungserlebnisse der Propheten Amos, Jesaja und Jeremia: Eine Untersuchung der Erlebnisvorgänge unter besonderer Berücksichtigung ihrer religiössittlichen Art und Auswirkung* (Oslo: Dybwad, 1946, [2]1965).
Seux, *Épithètes*
M.-J. Seux, *Épithètes Royales Akkadiennes et Sumériennes* (Paris: Letouzey & Ané, 1967).
Sievers and Guthe, *Amos*
E. Sievers and H. Guthe, *Amos, metrisch bearbeitet* (Abhandlungen der Philologisch-historischen Klasse der Königl. Sächsischen Gesellschaft der Wissenschaften 23/3; Leipzig: Teubner, 1907).
Simons, *Handbook*
J. Simons, *Handbook for the Study of Egyptian Topographical Lists Relating to Western Asia* (Leiden: Brill, 1937).
Sinclair, "Courtroom Motif"
L. A. Sinclair, "The Courtroom Motif in the Book of Amos," *JBL* 85 (1966) 351–53.
Sister, "Types"
M. Sister, "Die Typen der prophetischen Visionen in der Bibel," *MGWJ* 78 (1934) 399ff.; reprinted and translated as "Types of Prophetic Visions in the Bible," in *LeToldoth HaḤevrah VeHasifruth Bitqufath HaMiqra'* (Tel Aviv: Seminar HaKibbutzim, 1962) 135–43 (Heb.).
Snaith, *Text of Amos*
N. H. Snaith, *Notes on the Hebrew Text of Amos* (2 vols.; London: Epworth, 1945–1946).
Speier, "Bemerkungen"
S. Speier, "Bemerkungen zu Amos," *VT* 3 (1953) 305–10.
Tawil, "Lexicographical Note"
H. Tawil, "Hebrew צלח/הצלח, Akkadian *ešēru/šūšuru*. A Lexicographical Note," *JBL* 95 (1976) 405–13.
Terrien, "Amos and Wisdom"
S. Terrien, "Amos and Wisdom," in *Israel's Prophetic Heritage: Essays in Honor of James Muilenburg* (ed. B. W. Anderson and W. Harrelson; New York: Harper & Brothers, 1962) 108–15; reprinted in *Studies in Ancient Israelite Wisdom* (ed. J. L. Crenshaw; New York: Ktav, 1976) 448–55.
Thureau-Dangin, *Une relation*
F. Thureau-Dangin, *Une relation de la huitième campagne de Sargon* (TCL 3; Paris: Guethner, 1912).
Tur-Sinai, *HaLashon*
N. H. Tur-Sinai, "King and Princes—Amos and His Prophecy against the Nations," in idem,

HaLashon VeHasefer (Jerusalem: Bialik, 1954) vol. 1, 81–91 (Heb.).
Tur-Sinai, *Peshuṭo*
N. H. Tur-Sinai, *Peshuṭo shel Miqra* (6 vols.; Jerusalem: Kiryat Sepher, 1967) 3/2, 450–77 (Heb.).
Uffenheimer, "Amos and Hosea"
B. Uffenheimer, "Amos and Hosea—Two Directions in Israel's Prophecy," in *Zer Li-Gevurot. The Zalman Shazar Jubilee Volume: A Collection of Studies in Bible, Eretz Yisrael, Hebrew Language, and Talmudic Literature* (ed. B. Z. Luria; Jerusalem: Kiryat Sepher, 1973) 284–320 (Heb.); translated and abridged in *Dor LeDor* 5 (1976) 101–10.
de Vaux, "Remnant"
R. de Vaux, "The Remnant of Israel According to the Prophets," in idem, *The Bible and the Ancient Near East* (tr. J. McHugh; Garden City, NY: Doubleday, 1971) 15–30.
Vesco, "Amos"
J.-L. Vesco, "Amos de Téqoa, défenseur de l'homme," *RB* 87 (1980) 481–513.
Vollmer, *Rückblicke*
J. Vollmer, *Geschichtliche Rückblicke und Motive in der Prophetie des Amos, Hosea und Jesaja* (BZAW 119; Berlin: de Gruyter, 1971).
von Rad, *Theology*
G. von Rad, *Old Testament Theology* (tr. D. M. G. Stalker; 2 vols.; New York and Evanston: Harper & Row, 1962/1965).
Wagner, "Überlegungen"
S. Wagner, "Überlegungen zur Frage nach den Beziehungen des Propheten Amos zum Südreich," *TLZ* 96 (1971) 653–70.
Ward, *Amos*
J. M. Ward, *Amos and Isaiah: Prophets of the Word of God* (Nashville and New York: Abingdon, 1969).
Watson, *Hebrew Poetry*
W. G. E. Watson, *Classical Hebrew Poetry* (*JSOT* Supplement Series 26; Sheffield: JSOT, 1984).
Watts, "Old Hymn"
J. D. W. Watts, "An Old Hymn Preserved in the Book of Amos," *JNES* 15 (1956) 33–39.
Watts, *Vision*
J. D. W. Watts, *Vision and Prophecy in Amos* (Leiden: Brill, 1958).
Weinfeld, "Balaam"
M. Weinfeld, "The Balaam Oracle in the Deir ʿAlla Inscription," *Shnaton* 5–6 (1981–1982) 141–47 (Heb.).
Weinfeld, "Concept"
M. Weinfeld, "The Concept of the Day of the Lord and the Problem of Its *Sitz im Leben*," in *Studies in the Minor Prophets* (ed. B. Z. Luria; Jerusalem: Kiryat Sepher, 1981) 55–76 (Heb.).
Weinfeld, "Covenant Terminology"
M. Weinfeld, "Covenant Terminology in the Ancient Near East," *JAOS* 93 (1973) 190–99.
Weinfeld, *Deuteronomy*
M. Weinfeld, *Deuteronomy and the Deuteronomic School* (Oxford: Clarendon, 1972).
Weinfeld, "Divine Intervention"
M. Weinfeld, "'They Fought from Heaven'—Divine Intervention in Ancient Israel and in the Ancient Near East," in Eretz Israel 14 (*H. L. Ginsberg Volume;* ed. M. Haran and others; Jerusalem: Israel Exploration Society, 1978) 23–30 (Heb.) = "Divine Intervention in War in Ancient Israel and in the Ancient Near East," in *History, Historiography and Interpretation. Studies in Biblical and Cuneiform Literature* (ed. H. Tadmor and M. Weinfeld; Jerusalem: Magnes, 1983) 121–47.
Weinfeld, "Mesopotamian Prophecies"
M. Weinfeld, "Mesopotamian Prophecies of the End of Days," *Shnaton* 3 (1979) 263–76 (Heb.).
Weinfeld, "Worship"
M. Weinfeld, "The Worship of Molech and the Queen of Heaven and Its Background," *UF* 4 (1972) 133–54.
Weippert, "'Heiliger Krieg'"
M. Weippert, "'Heiliger Krieg' in Israel und Assyrien: Kritische Anmerkungen zu Gerhard von Rads Konzept des 'Heiligen Krieges' im alten Israel," *ZAW* 84 (1972) 460–93.
Weiser, *Profetie*
A. Weiser, *Die Profetie des Amos* (BZAW 53; Giessen: Töpelmann, 1929).
Weiss, "Days"
M. Weiss, "These Days and the Days to Come According to Amos 9, 13," in Eretz Israel 14 (*H. L. Ginsberg Volume;* ed. M. Haran and others; Jerusalem: Israel Exploration Society, 1978) 69–73 (Heb.).
Weiss, *HaMiqra*
M. Weiss, *HaMiqra Kidmuto* (Jerusalem: Bialik, 1967, ³1987) 71–74, 262–263; (³1987) 180–186 (Heb.) = *The Bible from Within: The Method of Total Interpretation* (Jerusalem: Magnes, 1984) 102–6, 417–21.
Weiss, "Methodologisches"
M. Weiss, "Methodologisches über die Behandlung der Metapher, dargelegt an Amos 1:2," *TZ* 23 (1967) 1–25.
Weiss, "Numerical Sequence"
M. Weiss, "The Pattern of Numerical Sequence in Amos: For Three . . . and for Four," *Tarbiz* 36 (1967) 307–18 (Heb.) = "The Pattern of Numerical Sequence in Amos 1—2. A Re-Examination," *JBL* 86 (1967) 416–23.
Weiss, "Origin"
M. Weiss, "The Origin of the 'Day of the Lord'—Reconsidered," *HUCA* 37 (1966) 29–72.
Weiss, "Pattern"
M. Weiss, "The Pattern of the 'Execration Texts' in the Prophetic Literature," *IEJ* 19 (1969) 150–57.

Weiss, "Prophets"
M. Weiss, "'And I Raised Up Prophets from amongst Your Sons'—A Note about the History and Character of Israelite Prophecy," in *Isac Leo Seeligmann Volume: Essays in the Bible and the Ancient World* (ed. A. Rofé and Y. Zakovitch; 3 vols.; Jerusalem: E. Rubinstein, 1983) vol. 1, 257–74 (Heb.).

Weiss, "Traces"
M. Weiss, "On the Traces of a Biblical Metaphor," *Tarbiz* 34 (1964–1965) 107–28, 211–23, 303–18 (Heb.).

Weiss, *MiShuṭ*
R. Weiss, *MiShuṭ BaMiqra* (Jerusalem: E. Rubinstein, 1977) (Heb.).

Westermann, *Basic Forms*
C. Westermann, *Grundformen prophetischer Rede* (München: Kaiser, 1960) = *Basic Forms of Prophetic Speech* (tr. H. C. White; Philadelphia: Westminster, 1967).

Willi-Plein, *Vorformen*
I. Willi-Plein, *Vorformen der Schriftexegese innerhalb des Alten Testaments. Untersuchungen zum literarischen Werken der auf Amos, Hosea und Micha zurückgehender Bücher im hebräischen Zwölfprophetenbuch* (BZAW 123; Berlin and New York: de Gruyter, 1971).

Wiseman, *Chronicles*
D. J. Wiseman, *Chronicles of Chaldaean Kings (626–556 B.C.) in the British Museum* (London: The British Museum, 1956).

Wiseman, "Vassal Treaties"
D. J. Wiseman, "The Vassal-Treaties of Esarhaddon," *Iraq* 20 (1958) i–ii, 11–99; plates 1–12, 1–53.

Wolff, *Amos the Prophet*
H. W. Wolff, *Amos the Prophet: The Man and His Background* (tr. F. R. McCurley; Philadelphia: Fortress, 1973).

Wolff, *Zitat*
H. W. Wolff, *Das Zitat im Prophetenspruch* (BEvT 4; München: Kaiser, 1937); reprinted in *Gesammelte Studien zum Alten Testament* (TBü 22; München: Kaiser, 1964) 36–129.

Würthwein, "Amos-Studien"
E. Würthwein, "Amos-Studien," *ZAW* 62 (1950) 10–52; reprinted in idem, *Wort und Existenz. Studien zum Alten Testament* (Göttingen: Vandenhoeck & Ruprecht, 1970) 68–110.

Würthwein, "Kultbescheid"
E. Würthwein, "Kultpolemik oder Kultbescheid?" in *Tradition und Situation. Studien zur alttestamentlichen Prophetie: Festschrift für A. Weiser* (ed. E. Würthwein and O. Kaiser; Göttingen: Vandenhoeck & Ruprecht, 1963) 115–31.

Yadin, *Art of Warfare*
Y. Yadin, *The Art of Warfare in Biblical Lands in the Light of Archaeological Study* (2 vols.; New York, Toronto, and London: Weidenfeld & Nicolson, 1963).

Zakovitch, *For Three*
Y. Zakovitch, *"For Three . . . and for Four": The Pattern of the Numerical Sequence in the Bible* (2 vols.; Jerusalem: Mekor, 1979) (Heb.).

Editor's Note

With the publication of Shalom Paul's *Amos*, a second commentary on Amos in the *Hermeneia* series, the editors have begun to make good our promise to commission new works on biblical books that have already appeared in our series. Our desire as we expressed it was to preserve the currency of the series and also to present commentaries written by scholars with different fields of special competence or different methods of approach to critical and historical issues. Shalom Paul's commentary is very different from Wolff's. Both will long continue, we believe, to be useful to the serious student of Amos.

The endpapers to this volume display fragments of a leather scroll of Amos, dated paleographically to the first century C.E., from Qumran Cave 5 (5QAm): the largest of the fragments attests portions of five lines from Am 1:3–5. The fragments are reproduced, with the permission of the publisher, from M. Baillet, J. T. Milik, and R. de Vaux, O.P., *Les 'Petites Grottes' de Qumran: Exploration de la falaise, Les grottes 2Q, 3Q, 5Q, 6Q, 7Q à 10Q, Le rouleau de cuivre,* DJD 3/Planches (Oxford: At the Clarendon Press, 1962), pl. xxxvi/4.

I. General Introduction to the Book of Amos

The Book of Amos is the third book in the collection of the so-called Twelve Minor Prophets (the designation refers to their brevity and not to their importance) appearing in the Masoretic Hebrew canon between the writings of the prophets Joel and Obadiah. The order was most likely influenced both by the striking similarities between Joel 4:16a and Amos 1:2 and between Joel 4:18a and Amos 9:10b and by the reference in Amos 9:12 to Edom, the nation that constitutes the primary subject of the oracle of Obadiah (compare in particular Obad 19 and Amos 9:12). In the Septuagint, however, where the books are arranged according to their length, Amos appears between Hosea and Micah. The Book of Amos constitutes the earliest collection of oracles that have been preserved as an independent literary work. Although it comprises only nine chapters and altogether a mere 146 verses, it has been the subject of voluminous literature.[1] If in 1959 a scholar could write, "Amos-studies are already on the way to becoming a small library on their own,"[2] how much more so thirty years later—as the extensive and comprehensive bibliography in this volume readily attests.

Amos, by vocation a sheep and cattle herder and dresser of sycamore trees (Amos 1:1; 7:14), was called to prophecy from his home in Tekoa, a town in the highlands of Judah on the edge of the Judean desert, identified with Khirbet Teqūʿ approximately five miles south of Bethlehem, sometime during the reigns of Jeroboam II, king of Israel (789–748), and Uzziah, king of Judah (785–733).[3]

During this period, the Silver Age of Israelite history, Israel reached the summit of its material power and economic prosperity as well as the apogee of its territorial expansion, comparable only to the era of David and Solomon, the Golden Age. Although the exact duration of Amos's prophetic call cannot be dated, he must have completed his mission prior to 745, for his oracles make no reference to the dramatic reversal in domestic political affairs after the death of Jeroboam II, nor is there any indication of the westward territorial expansion of Assyria under the reign of Tiglatpileser III, which took place during this period. Assyria, moreover, is never mentioned in his prophecies, and the nation that is referred to several times in the book (for example, 3:11; 6:14) as God's agent for punishing Israel remains anonymous. Whatever information may be culled from the oracles against the foreign nations (1:3—2:3) also alludes to events either contemporaneous to the initial stages of Jeroboam II's reign or, more likely, to historical events prior to the time of the prophet—but by all accounts, pre-Assyrian.

During the extensive reign of Jeroboam II, neither the Arameans, who had previously engaged Israel in repeated battles and had conquered and subjugated extensive territory of the northern kingdom, nor Assyria constituted any danger to the nation. Although the ascendancy and power of the Arameans were terminated by the Assyrian king Adadnirari III (810–783), who subjugated Damascus,[4] after his death, the Assyrians themselves suffered internally from a series of extremely

1 All the issues discussed in the Introduction are dealt with in detail with a complete bibliography in the commentary. Only representative references are cited here.

2 J. L. Mays, "Words about the Words of Amos. Recent Study of the Book of Amos," *Int* 13 (1959) 259.

3 Chronology is a very complicated subject, and the dates given by historians for the various regnal years are often at variance. For convenient references reflecting the differing opinions pertaining to the reigns of the kings of this period, consult the charts of H. Tadmor, "Chronology," *EM* 4.261–62 (Heb.); J. Bright, *A History of Israel* (3d ed.; Philadelphia: Westminster, 1981) 470–71; J. M. Miller and J. H. Hayes, *A History of Ancient Israel and Judah* (Philadelphia: Westminster, 1986) 296; and J. A. Brinkman, "Appendix: Mesopotamian Chronology of the Historical Period," in A. Leo Oppenheim, *Ancient Mesopotamia: Portrait of a Dead Civilization* (Chicago: The University of Chicago, 1964) 347.

4 For the problems relating to the dating of the submission of Damascus, see W. T. Pitard, *Ancient Damascus* (Winona Lake, IN: Eisenbrauns, 1987) 162–67. Whereas most scholars date the event ca. 802, Pitard opts for 796.

ineffectual and weak kings (Shalmaneser IV, 782–773; Asshur-dan III, 772–755; and Asshur-nirari V, 754–745) and were also threatened externally on their northern border by the expansionistic policies of the kingdom of Urartu, especially under the reign of Sardur III (810–743).

Israel, which enjoyed peaceful relations during this era with Judah under the prosperous and benign reign of Uzziah, was able to reassert itself and witnessed an unparalleled resurgence in all areas of life. Through military conquests, the territories east of the Jordan were recovered and annexed (Amos 6:13), and the northern border was extended to Lebo-Hamath (2 Kgs 14:25). This geographical expansion, accompanied by thriving commerce and trade, resulted in an affluent society composed of a small, wealthy upper class. Their vast accumulation of wealth led to a luxurious life style that also expressed itself in an inordinate edifice complex climaxed by magnificent building projects adorned with lavish furnishings (Amos 3:15; 5:11; 6:4–6)—vividly attested to by the archaeological excavations at Samaria. This opulence was accompanied by a panoply of pomp and ceremony and by an intensive and zealous religious life that was concretized both in a lavish cult and in elaborate rites that took place at the main northern shrines (Amos 4:4–5; 5:21–23). For the Israelites all signs pointed to God's unlimited beneficial favor. His protection was assumed to be unconditional, and thus they felt totally secure in the present and thoroughly confident in their future.

Blinded by their boundless optimism, which was posited on false premises, they were oblivious to the clouds of wrath and recompense swiftly gathering all about them. Amos, however, a keen and acute observer of their modus vivendi, was not bedazzled or beguiled by the economic, political, or religious state of affairs. He was well aware of the burrowing worm of decay and corruption that was undermining the society's ethical and moral foundations. He constantly and consistently called the upper class to task for their bribery and extortion, for their corruption of the judiciary, for perversion and dishonesty, for injustice and immorality, for exploitation of the impoverished and underprivileged, for resolute dissolute behavior, for pampered prosperity and boisterous banquetry, for greed and arrogant security, for self-indulgence and a life of carpe diem, and for pride and prejudice. He unremittingly threatened that terminal consumption would undermine their conspicuous consumption. According to Amos, the wealthy minority who practiced a careless life style, who could not care less for the poor majority (6:6), and who took advantage of the plight of the poor to advance their own selfish ends were actually accelerating the Day of the Lord, which paradoxically would be one of "darkness and not light" (5:18–20). His defiant words were aimed not only at braggarts and bacchanalian behavior but also at all those who exchanged the upkeep of shrines, sanctuaries, and sacrifices for God's true desire of honesty, justice, and righteousness. He seriously questioned and sarcastically lampooned their theology and ideology, their beliefs and practices. He polemicized unsparingly against their popular misconceptions. They who had not fulfilled their part of the covenantal obligations would not be spared on the Day of the Lord.

Amos delivered a devastating diatribe against the nation's distorted concept of the wholesale panacea of the cult—the opium of the masses. For him, as for many of the other classical prophets, cultic zeal could neither engender public weal nor atone for infringements upon the moral law. Ritual can never be a surrogate for ethics. "God requires devotion, not devotions," right more than rite.[5] When the cult became a substitute for moral behavior, it was severely denounced and condemned. Amos, unlike his audience in the northern kingdom, did not view religion as the mere practice of a cultivated cult. For the prophet, religion was identified with a person's everyday life style. Thus any ritual act performed by a worshiper whose moral character was blemished was categorically criticized. The acceptance of the cult became conditional upon the moral acceptability of the worshiper. Obviously, such a "radical" understanding of God's will would inevitably lead to a head-on confrontation with the official representatives of the religious establishment, the priests, who maintained and supported the paramount importance of the rich display of the cult (Amos 7:10ff.; compare Jer 20; 29:25ff.). Never-

5 S. Spiegel, *Amos Vs. Amaziah* (Essays in Judaism 3; New York: Jewish Theological Seminary, 1957) 43.

theless, even at the point of dire danger to their own lives, the prophets, led by Amos, who was the first to introduce this novel idea of the supremacy of morality, relentlessly declared that justice, integrity, honesty, faithfulness, kindness, compassion, and righteousness were God's primary and ultimate demands and requirements of Israel. Because Israel was the one and only people with whom the Lord contracted a covenant, it alone was held responsible for all its social transgressions (Amos 3:2).

Amos then added yet another dimension to this unique concept. Morality was not only of supreme importance but also the decisive factor in determining the ultimate destiny of the nation. This, too, was a radical shift from the basic outlook expressed in the Torah literature and in the Former Prophets, where the sin of idolatry was considered the primary transgression leading to the decline and fall of the nation. Except on two possible occasions (5:26; 8:14—and the latter is highly improbable; see commentary), Amos never cites the worship of idols in his oracles. According to him, moral rectitude alone determined the destiny of Israel.[6]

Because the foundations of the society were corrupt at the core, the nation was doomed to an impending and imminent calamitous catastrophe. Amos, intoning a death knell for the living (5:2), reiterated a resounding and radical no to the major current public thoughts. The Day of the Lord would not be one of light for Israel but darkness (5:18–20). Victory, prosperity, and the elaborate cult were all mocked and no longer equated with divine favor (compare 4:4–5; 5:5, 21–25; 6:13–14). Election did not automatically imply divine protection. Indeed, Israel did not even have the exclusive rights to exodus. In a powerful and ironic outburst, the prophet boldly equated Israel's exodus tradition with those of two of her main adversaries, the Philistines and Arameans (9:7). Only the covenant relationship remained unique to Israel (3:1), and when the nation did not live up to its obligations it was threatened with extinction.

Amos's message of doom was delivered primarily in the first-person address of the Lord of Israel and, at times, in the third person, in the name of the Deity (for example, 2:13–16; 3:14–15; 6:11; 9:1). Yahweh, the Creator of the world and its sole Sovereign, is also the Lord of history (1:3—2:16; 6:14; 9:7) and nature (2:13; 8:9) who judges all guilty nations (1:3—2:3, 9; 9:8a). However, first and foremost he takes Israel to task for its repeated everyday transgressions. Amos was the first prophet to threaten the entire nation with destruction. As the instrument of his punishment, the Deity may also employ a foreign nation, which would lay siege to Israel and conquer it in a military encounter (3:11; 4:2–3; 5:3; 6:7, 14; 7:17). Israel would ultimately suffer deportation and exile (4:2–3; 5:27; 6:7; 7:17).

In addition to these imminent historical calamities, Israel had already suffered a series of natural catastrophes that had decimated the nation (4:6–11). His message was so harsh and unsparing that in some of his oracles he actually envisaged no survivors remaining after the holocaust (6:9–10; 9:2–4).

Very rarely did Amos foresee any glimpse of hope, and then only for a mere remnant (5:3, 15; 9:9). Herein lies the paradoxical plight of the prophet. While denouncing the nation and threatening it with dire punishment and frightful maledictions, he nevertheless, at times, pleaded with Israel to seek God that they might live (5:4, 14). Because divine plans were not always absolute and unchangeable, repentance could tip the scales of justice and mercy: "Perhaps the Lord, the God of Hosts, will show favor to the remnant of Joseph" (5:15). This valiant attempt to arouse the population from its lethargic stupor proved in vain, however, as the litany of divine frustration so painfully attests (4:6–11).

When censure, admonishment, and historical and natural calamities proved to no avail, the prophet had one more avenue of approach. If the people refused to repent, maybe God himself would recant and relent. The messenger of God then became the intercessor for his people. Amos had worthy predecessors—Abraham (Gen 18:25; 20:7), Moses (Exod 32:11–14; Num 14:13–20), and Samuel (1 Sam 7:5–9; 12:19, 23; 15:11)—and followers—Jeremiah (for example, Jer 14:1ff.; 15:1, 11; 18:20; compare also 7:16; 11:14; 14:11–13) and Ezekiel (Ezek 9:8; 11:13; compare Ezek 22:30; Ps 106:23)—who fulfilled but rarely succeeded in this arduous task. (The major exception was Moses; see previous citations.) In his

6 See Y. Kaufmann, *The Religion of Israel* (tr. M. Greenberg; Chicago: The University of Chicago, 1960) 365–67.

role as an intercessor, which was an integral part of the true prophet's mission, Amos pleaded the case of his people before God in a desperate effort to offset their impending doom.[7] Twice, in his first two visions (7:1–3, 4–6), he was partially successful. Although he was unable to abrogate the divine verdict, he was successful at least in delaying and postponing it. A moment comes, however, when even God's "long suffering" and patience becomes exhausted. When the Deity finally decided to exercise his attribute of justice at the expense of his attribute of mercy, intercession was in vain. All that remained was one final and ultimate calamitous confrontation: "Prepare to meet your God, O Israel!" (4:12).

Amos, while introducing several new ideas into the theology of early Israel, was still very much rooted in the religious, cultural, and literary traditions of his predecessors, to whom and with whom he felt intimately linked (2:12; 3:7–8). Both the concepts of God as Ruler of history and nature and Israel as God's chosen people ("my people," 7:8; 8:3; 9:10) were not novel. As God's messenger he cast his oracles in traditional formulae and styles: compare כֹּה אָמַר ה' ("Thus said the Lord"), the messenger or herald formula, as in 1:3, 6, 9, 11, 13; 2:1, 4, 6; 3:11, 12; 5:3, 4, 16; and 7:17; נְאֻם ה' in 2:11, 16; 3:10, 15; 4:3, 5, 6, 8, 9, 10, 11; 6:8, 14; 8:3, 9, 11; and 9:7, 8, 12, 13; אָמַר ה', as in 1:5, 8, 15; 2:3; and 5:17; שִׁמְעוּ ("Hear"), 3:1, 13; 4:1; 5:1 (7:16); and 8:4; הוֹי ("Woe"), 5:18 and 6:1; and כֹּה הִרְאַנִי ה' ("This the Lord showed me"), 7:1, 4, 7 and 8:1. He also was heir to the literary and historical traditions of his people—Sodom and Gomorrah (4:11), the plagues in Egypt (4:10), the exodus from Egypt (2:10; 3:1; 9:7), the forty-year trek through the wilderness (5:25), the conquest of Canaan (2:9), the past chastisements of the nation (4:6–11), and the relation of David and musical creativity (6:5)—and was well acquainted with covenant laws.[8]

Amos was also influenced by the psalm (for example, the doxologies, 4:13; 5:8–9; 9:5–6) and wisdom genres of literature. The extent of the latter, however, is the focus of a great deal of dispute. After scholars proposed and propounded a hypothetical cultic office for Amos and conjectured that he was initially a cultic prophet, that is, a prophet of salvation *(Heilsprophet)* who after his second vision became a prophet of doom *(Unheilsprophet)*,[9] a well-deserved reaction set in that sought his intellectual roots in sapiential circles. Specific words, expressions, numerical formulations, didactic rhetorical questions, woe sayings, and exhortations were all traced back to and said to have been shaped by one commonly assumed source, tribal wisdom *(Sippenweisheit)*.[10] However, subsequent investigation has shown that most of the arguments are either nonexistent, inconclusive, or altogether too general. (Each of these is dealt with in detail in its appropriate place.) As this commentary will show, Amos was heir to many variegated literary influences and poetic conventions and formulae, which he employed with creative sophistication to propound and expound his divinely given message.

Amos blended his new teaching with time-honored traditions in a very polished and artistic fashion. His extensive array of literary genres includes judgment speeches, dirges, disputation sayings, exhortations,

7 See S. M. Paul, "Prophets and Prophecy," *EncJud* 13.1169–71.

8 For some possible examples, see R. Bach, "Gottesrecht und weltliches Recht in der Verkündigung des Propheten Amos," in *Festschrift für Günther Dehn* (ed. W. Schneemelcher; Neukirchen: Verlag des Erziehungsvereins, 1957) 23–34.

9 See especially E. Würthwein, "Amos-Studien," *ZAW* 62 (1950) 10–52; reprinted in idem, *Wort und Existenz* (Göttingen: Vandenhoeck & Ruprecht, 1970) 68–110; and H. G. Reventlow, *Das Amt des Propheten bei Amos* (FRLANT 80; Göttingen: Vandenhoeck & Ruprecht, 1962).

10 See S. Terrien, "Amos and Wisdom," in *Israel's Prophetic Heritage: Essays in Honor of James Muilenburg* (ed. B. W. Anderson and W. Harrelson; New York: Harper & Brothers, 1962) 108–15; reprinted in *Studies in Ancient Israelite Wisdom* (ed. J. L. Crenshaw; New York: Ktav, 1976) 448–55; and H. W. Wolff, *Amos the Prophet: The Man and His Background* (tr. F. R. McCurley; Philadelphia: Fortress, 1973). For a critique of this view, see J. L. Crenshaw, "The Influence of the Wise upon Amos—The 'Doxologies of Amos' and Job 5:9–16; 9:5–10," *ZAW* 79 (1967) 42–52.

admonitions, vision reports, narratives, and eschatological promises. He exhibited a great finesse in rhetorical forms and dynamic oratory skills. His rich imagery was influenced by his profession and by his acquaintance with nature (2:13; 3:4–5, 8, 12; 4:1; 5:11, 17, 19; 6:12; 7:1–2, 4, 14; 8:1; 9:9). His metaphors and similes are abundant (2:9; 3:12; 5:2, 7, 19, 24; 6:12; 9:9), and he had a penchant for paronomasia (5:5b; 6:1, 6, 7; 8:2). He also adeptly and effectively employed the literary convention of irony (5:20; 6:12; 9:4, 7) and sarcasm (3:12; 4:4–5; 6:1). He skillfully polemicized against popular concepts by personally confronting his audience and citing their own words as self-accusations (2:12; 4:1; 5:14b; 6:13; 7:16; 8:5, 14; 9:10). He also favored rhetorical didactic questions (2:11; 3:3–6, 8; 5:18, 25; 6:12; 8:8).

The prophet, moreover, had a decided predilection for delivering his oracles seriatim. The book commences with a catalogue of six prophecies against foreign nations, each formulated in a set literary pattern: the messenger or herald formula, "Thus said the Lord"; the staircase numerical pattern, "for three transgressions of . . . and for four . . ."; the absolute irrevocability of the divine decision; the mention of the specific crime(s) committed; and finally the verdict pronounced by the Deity in the first person, condemning each nation to punishment by fire, along with other chastisements. Then the seventh oracle, against Judah, which follows the same literary pattern, is climaxed by the eighth and final oracle, the surprise denunciation of Israel. Other oracles presented in a series are the litany of punishments with a repetitive refrain ("Yet you did not return to me, declares the Lord," 4:6–11) and the sequence of visions in chapters 7 and 8. Also note 3:3–8, in which the prophet draws his audience slowly but surely into the vortex of his seemingly innocuous examples of cause and effect derived from everyday life in order to reach his cardinal point—the irresistibility of prophecy.

Amos with great dexterity often invoked surprise finales in order to express a dramatic denouement (such as the eighth oracle against Israel and the eight questions in 3:3–8) or to upset firmly established popular beliefs and ideas (such as 3:2; 5:18; 9:7). Several of his oracles are constructed in a cohesive concatenous pattern whose sequential ordering is determined by the literary mnemonic device of catchwords, phrases, and ideas common to the contiguous units (see comments to Amos 1:3—2:3; 3:3–8).

He also had a great fondness for expressing completeness in heptads: the seven oracles in 1—2, climaxed by the eighth and final one against Israel; the seven rhetorical questions in 3:3–8, culminating in the eighth one referring to prophecy; and the inescapability and paralysis of the seven units of the Israelite army in 2:14–16 (compare also 2:6–8; 4:4–5, 6–11; 5:8–9, 21–23; 6:1–6; 9:1–4). The prophet, furthermore, had a preference for another very much overlooked numerical pattern, that of the pentad. Compare the five kindnesses God had bestowed upon Israel during its early history in 2:9–11; the fivefold negative לֹא in 2:14–16; the pentad litany refrain "Yet you did not return to me, declares the Lord," 4:6–11; the five cosmic acts of the Deity hailed in the doxologies of 4:13 and 5:8; the five vision reports, 7—9; the pentad of curses heaped upon the priest Amaziah, 7:17; and the fivefold repetition of the particles אִם and מִשָּׁם in the pericope describing the total inability to escape wherever and whenever from the grasp of the Deity, 9:2–4b.

Amos also employed "futility curses" (5:11), as well as the principle of talionic punishment: because Moab was accused of burning the bones of an Edomite king, its ramparts would be destroyed by conflagration (2:1–2); because Israel had heaped up its ill-gotten gains in אַרְמְנוֹת ("fortresses," 3:10), these very fortresses would be destroyed (3:11); because they multiplied the din of their songs (5:23), their songs would be turned into dirges (8:10); because they had "turned" (הפך) justice to gall (5:7), God would "overturn" (הפך) their festivals to mourning (8:10). Another literary characteristic of Amos is the didactic repetition of his thought, expressed first positively and then negatively: "Seek me so that you may live; but do not seek . . ." (5:4–5); the Day of the Lord will be one of "darkness and not light, gloom with no glimmer" (5:20); "I will cast a famine . . . , not a famine for bread but . . ." (8:11). In addition, several pericopes are encased within a literary inclusio: 1:3—2:3, וְהִכְרַתִּי; 2:9–10, הָאֱמֹרִי; 3:2, אֶפְקֹד עַל, 3:14, פָּקְדִי—וּפָקַדְתִּי עַל; 3:4, הֲיִשְׁאַג אַרְיֵה, 3:8, אַרְיֵה שָׁאָג; 6:1, רֵאשִׁית הַגּוֹיִם, 6:7, בְּראשׁ גֹּלִים; 9:1, בַּחֶרֶב אֶהֱרֹג, 9:4, הַחֶרֶב וַהֲרָגָתַם.

Most studies of Amos seriously question the integrity of the book. Exegetes have attempted to divide the book into a series of multiple strata, dating from the actual words of the prophet, that is, from the middle of the eighth century, to the early fourth or third century.[11] The most often cited hypothesis is that of Wolff,[12] who as a result of his form-critical and redactional criticism postulated that the book underwent a lengthy process of oral and literary transmission, comprising six independent layers: the first two from the time of Amos (the first, 3—6, is the oldest kernel; the second includes the oracles against the nations [excluding Tyre, Edom, and Judah] and the visions in 7:1–8; 8:1–2; 9:1–4); the third stage is designated Amos's school of disciples and is dated between 760 and 730; the fourth, the Bethel redaction, is related to the time of Josiah; the fifth is the assumed Deuteronomistic redaction;[13] and the sixth is the postexilic eschatology of salvation, which includes several stray verses as well as the conclusion of the book (9:11–15). This scissors-and-paste method is to be seriously questioned. The cautious criticism of Bright, written in response to Wolff's conjecture of multilayers of redaction, soberly appraises the limits of this approach:

> But do the tools at our disposal really allow us anything like the precision in describing this process that we find here? In so small a book as Amos do we have a broad enough field of evidence to entitle us to say that this stylistic tract, this line of thought, this formal characteristic, could not have been employed by the prophet, but must be assigned to some later stratum tradition?[14]

So, too, Hammershaimb: "On the contrary, there is little against accepting that almost all the book goes back to Amos himself."[15] In the present commentary, these issues are dealt with in situ as they arise. Almost all of the arguments for later interpolations and redactions, including a Deuteronomistic one, are shown to be based on fragile foundations and inconclusive evidence.[16] When each case is examined and analyzed on its own, without preconceived conjectures and unsupported hypotheses, the book in its entirety (with one or two minor exceptions) can be reclaimed for its rightful author, the prophet Amos. The results of the investigation support the integrity of the book.

The book itself is a composite of independent collections with a well-organized structure arranged according to common literary genres. It commences, after the superscription and introductory motto (1:1–2), with six stereotypically structured and concatenously patterned oracles against foreign nations: Arameans, Philistines, Phoenicians, Edomites, Ammonites, and Moabites, followed by one against Judah, and culminating with an oracle against Israel (1:3—2:16).[17] The next section (3:1—5:17) is formally grouped together by the introductory phrase "Hear this word" (3:1; 4:1; 5:1). These oracles are characterized by reprimands and reproofs that focus on the ethical and moral sins of the affluent and opulent upper classes of Samaria. Here is found the unique series of rhetorical questions of the irresistible sequence of cause and effect that served as the justification and legitimization of the prophet's commission (3:3–8). It is also highlighted by a litany of wasted opportunity that reiterates that Israel, although often chastised, refused to return to the Lord (4:6–12). Only

11 For example, S. Jozaki, "The Secondary Passages of the Book of Amos," in Kwansei Gakuin University Annual Studies 4 (Nishinomiya: Kwansei Gakuin University, 1956) 25–100.

12 H. W. Wolff, *Joel and Amos* (tr. W. Janzen, S. Dean McBride, Jr., and C. A. Muenchow; ed. S. Dean McBride; Hermeneia—A Critical and Historical Commentary on the Bible; Philadelphia: Fortress, 1977) 106–13. I have omitted the various minute details of the verses, half verses and phrases that Wolff assumes to be characteristic of the four last stages of his conjectured hypothesis. They can be found in his work just cited.

13 W. H. Schmidt, "Die deuteronomistische Redaktion des Amosbuches," *ZAW* 77 (1965) 168–93.

14 J. Bright, "A New View of Amos," *Int* 25 (1971) 357.

15 E. Hammershaimb, *The Book of Amos: A Commentary* (tr. J. Sturdy; Oxford: Blackwell, 1970) 14.

16 See S. M. Paul, "A Literary Reinvestigation of the Authenticity of the Oracles against the Nations of Amos," in *De la Tôrah au Messie: Études d'exégèse et d'herméneutique bibliques offertes à Henri Cazelles* (ed. J. Doré, P. Grelot, M. Carrez; Paris: Desclée, 1981) 189–204.

17 S. M. Paul, "Amos 1:3—2:3: A Concatenous Literary Pattern," *JBL* 90 (1971) 397–403.

in this section is there a call to repentance, a call to seek the Lord that they may live (5:4, 6, 14–15).

Next come two הוֹי "woe" oracles (5:18–27; 6:1–7; for the possibility of another such oracle commencing at Amos 5:7, see the commentary). The first contains the "Day of the Lord" prophecy, in which Amos reverses the popular concept prevalent in his time and states that, rather than a time of light and salvation, a time of darkness and disaster awaits them (5:18–20). The second contains a vivid and unparalleled description of the hedonistic life style of the northern kingdom bon vivants whose luxurious living habits have desensitized them to the tragedy of their people (6:1–7).

It is followed by a series of five visions (7:1–3, 4–5, 7–9; 8:1–3; 9:1–4), interspersed with a biographical narrative (7:10–16) and a collection of independent oracles that enlarges upon the theme of judgment (8:4–14; 9:7–10). In the first two visions (a swarm of locusts and a judgment by fire), the prophet successfully intercedes and the Lord withholds punishment. The next two, whose symbolic significance the prophet does not immediately grasp (the Lord standing by a wall with an instrument in his hand—not a plumb line as commonly interpreted—and a basket of summer fruit), foreshadow the divine decision to execute judgment upon Israel. The last vision, which is seen as taking place by "the altar" (probably at Bethel), represents the final demise of Israel, from which no escape is possible. The biographical narrative recounts the confrontation of Amos with Amaziah, the priest of Bethel, who denounces the prophet to King Jeroboam II, accuses him of sedition, and banishes him from the northern kingdom. Amos affirms that he is not a professional prophet but was summoned from tending his flocks by the Lord in order to deliver these oracles against Israel. The pericope concludes with a devastating fivefold curse against Amaziah, his family, and the entire nation. In 9:7–10, the prophet declares that Israel has no unique claim for exclusivity or favoritism. The Lord will punish any and every nation guilty of transgression.

The final literary unit, 9:11–15, contains a prophecy of comfort and consolation, blessing and salvation, describing the glorious future of Israel, which will be reunited as in the days of old and blessed with unfailing abundance and fertility, never again to be uprooted from the land.

Deeply rooted in earlier traditions, Amos, with his innovative ideas, distinctive literary style, and polemics against popular current beliefs, inaugurated a new epoch in the religious life of Israel. He became the first of a series of major prophets who over the next three centuries played major roles in the theological, ideological, cultural, and historical development of the nation.

II. Introductory Material concerning the "Oracles against the Nations"

1. Literary Origins

Oracles against foreign nations are found in many of the prophetic books. Form-critical research of this literary genre began with the works of Gunkel[18] and primarily Gressmann, the latter as part of two separate studies: *Der Ursprung des israelitisch-judäischen Eschatologie* and *Der Messias.*[19] In his earlier work Gressmann concluded (as did Gunkel) that these oracles were the oldest *Gattung* of prophetic literature. They were dated to the period prior to the rise of classical prophecy and were said to be representative of pre–eighth-century Israelite eschatology. They were authored assumedly by *Heilspropheten* within a royal court setting and were distinguished from

18 H. Gunkel, *Die Propheten* (Göttingen: Vandenhoeck & Ruprecht, 1917); idem, "Propheten II: Seit Amos," *RGG*[1] 4.1866–86. This article was reprinted in *RGG*[2] 4.1538–54 and translated into English as "The Israelite Prophecy from the Time of Amos," in *Twentieth Century Theology in the Making* (tr. R. A. Wilson; ed. J. Pelikan; New York: Harper & Row, 1969) 48–75.

19 H. Gressmann, *Der Ursprung des israelitisch-judäischen Eschatologie* (FRLANT 6; Göttingen: Vandenhoeck & Ruprecht, 1905); idem, *Der Messias* (FRLANT 43; Göttingen: Vandenhoeck & Ruprecht, 1929). For criticism, see C. Westermann, *Basic Forms of Prophetic Speech* (tr. H. C. White; Philadelphia: Westminster, 1967) 23–34; Y. Hoffman, *The Prophecies against Foreign Nations in the Bible* (Tel Aviv: HaKibbutz HaMeuhad, 1977) 11ff. (Heb.).

classical prophecy by the notable absence of ethical motivations. In his later study, Gressmann drew a literary distinction between what he called *Heidenorakel* and *Völkerorakel.* In the former, the foreign nation was specifically designated by name and was the subject of an oracle of *Unheil,* with an implicit understanding of *Heil* for Israel. In the latter, the nations were not designated by name, and there was an explicit message of *Heil* for Israel. He contended that both threat and promise were originally a literary unity, and only with Amos was the threat separated from the promise and directed to Israel. He also made a connection between this literary form and the prophecies known as the Day of the Lord.

Bentzen,[20] too, proposed an early date (before the rise of classical prophecy) for these oracles but incorrectly concluded that the prophecies in Amos were somehow modeled after the ritual of the early-second-millennium Egyptian execration texts relating to foreign princes and peoples. He postulated, furthermore, a cultic ceremony in Israel that presumably took place during an assumed enthronement ritual during a conjectured annual New Year festival. He, in turn, was followed, among others, by Fohrer, who extended the investigation to encompass additional units of prophetic oracles against the nations.[21]

Reventlow, in two studies,[22] also accepted a ritual background for these oracles but assumed their *Sitz im Leben* to be in *Völkerritual* ("folk ritual"), which supposedly took place as part of an institutionalized ritual of maledictions during an alleged covenant renewal festival. The nations were assumed to be subject to covenant law, and the prophet was viewed as the successor to the covenant mediator of the premonarchial tribal confederation.[23]

Another possibility as to their origin was alluded to by Fensham,[24] who suggested a possible association with the curse clauses found in extrabiblical treaty literature: "A remarkable agreement between Sefire-curses and maledictions against foreign nations exists."[25] "The calamities predicted against the foreign nations must have developed out of these (i.e., anti-Israel) maledictions."[26] Hillers[27] continued this trend of thought and, after referring to a "high proportion of expressions with parallels in treaty curses," raised the intriguing query, "Is the implication present in some cases that these nations have broken treaties with Israel?"[28]

Haran, Seeligmann, and Kaufmann, three Israeli scholars, presented a different view altogether. Similar to Gunkel and Gressmann, they interpreted the oracles against the nations as part of the literary heritage of preclassical prophecy. However, they understood this genre as being a development of the so-called ancient *Mošlim* literature. Haran, in a study of Isaiah 15—16 and Jeremiah 48, concluded that both oracles were elaborations of the "Song of the *Mošlim*" (Num 21) and were the result of a continuous literary creativity.[29] Seeligmann, in his study of the influence of mantic prophecy upon classical prophecy,[30] interpreted these oracles as fragments of a national prophetic literature and related them to "war prophecy."[31] He also noted the absence of moral categories in this literary genre.[32] Kaufmann,[33] who divided these oracles into different literary types,

20 A. Bentzen, "The Ritual Background of Amos 1:2—2:16," in *OTS* 8 (Leiden: Brill, 1950) 85–99. For a criticism of this study, see S. M. Paul, "Amos 1:3—2:3: A Concatenous Literary Pattern," *JBL* 90 (1971) 398–99.

21 G. Fohrer, "Prophetie und Magie," *ZAW* 78 (1966) 40–44; reprinted in idem, *Studien zur alttestamentliche Prophetie* (BZAW 99; Berlin: Töpelmann, 1967) 257–59.

22 H. G. Reventlow, *Das Amt des Propheten bei Amos* (FRLANT 80; Göttingen: Vandenhoek & Ruprecht, 1962; idem, *Wächter über Israel: Ezechiel und seine Tradition* (BZAW 82; Berlin: Töpelmann, 1962) 134–47.

23 See Reventlow, *Amt,* 62–75.

24 F. C. Fensham, "Common Trends in Curses of the Near Eastern Treaties and *Kudurru*-Inscriptions Compared with Maledictions of Amos and Isaiah," *ZAW* 75 (1963) 155–75.

25 Ibid., 167. Compare G. E. Wright, "The Nations in Hebrew Prophecy," *Encounter* 26 (1965) 225–37.

26 Fensham, "Common Trends," 172–73.

27 D. R. Hillers, *Treaty Curses and the Old Testament Prophets* (BibOr 16; Rome: Pontifical Biblical Institute, 1964).

28 Ibid., 88–89.

29 M. Diman (Haran), "An Archaic Remnant in Prophetic Literature," *BIES* 13 (1946–1947) 7–16 (Heb.).

30 I. A. Seeligmann, "On the History and Nature of Prophecy in Israel," in Eretz Israel 3 (*Dedicated to the Memory of M. D. U. Cassuto 1883–1951;* ed. J. W. Hirschberg and others; Jerusalem: Israel Exploration Society, 1954) 125–32 (Heb.).

also concluded that they belonged to the preclassical literary heritage whose origins were in the *Mošlim* tradition and connected them with the early Israelite eschatology of the Day of the Lord.

Margulis[34] suggested, as well, that the literary and ideological origins of these oracles were rooted in the secular war traditions of the preclassical period.[35] He examined the various motifs associated with this genre (which he designated as "proto-oracles-against-the-nations") such as fire, exile, and captivity, which, according to him, also pointed to the *Mošlim* literature.[36] The motifs of theophany and the Divine Warrior were, in his view, a "literary contamination" of the Day of the Lord prophecies upon the oracles against the nations.[37] He further noted that the *Begründung* of these oracles is of a political-militaristic nature.[38] No reference is made to the internal behavior of the people condemned; moral categories are absent; the crimes referred to are political offenses of a nonmoralistic, secular character. (The "gradual moralization of the *Begründung* concepts and motifs" came later under the influence of classical prophecy.)[39] However, as regards Israel, "the actions are defined and evaluated within a context of covenant ideology with pronouncement of doom conceived as punishment for covenant violations."[40]

Yet another stage of research into this prophetic form has also connected the oracles against the nations with war oracles. Hayes, first in an unpublished dissertation[41] and then in a short study,[42] regarded "warfare as the original *Sitz im Leben* for the Israelite oracles against the foreign nations."[43] He based this concept on both the dominant military imagery and the holy war ideology in these oracles and further suggested parallels from other ancient Near Eastern cultures. He rooted them, however, in a royal cultic setting and connected them with national psalms of lament.[44] Christensen, in a comprehensive study of the subject,[45] suggested that with Amos these oracles became a "literary mode, a vehicle of divine judgment," with the central motif of God as the "Divine Warrior."[46] According to him, the war oracle itself by the ninth century (even before the time of Amos) was already in the form of a judgment speech.[47] He interpreted 1 Kgs 20:28 as constituting the basic background framework of the oracles in Amos: a message formula, an indictment, and an announcement of punishment.[48] Moreover, according to Christensen, "the innovation of

31 Ibid., 130.
32 Ibid., 125.
33 Y. Kaufmann, *Toledoth Ha-Emunah Ha-Yisrealith* (8 vols.; Jerusalem and Tel Aviv: Dvir, 1956) 3.40–48, 415ff. (Heb.). For others who interpret them as an early literary type, compare, for example, N. H. Tur-Sinai, "Kings and Princes—Amos and His Prophecy against the Nations," in idem, *HaLashon VeHasepher* (3 vols.; Jerusalem: Bialik, 1954) 1.81–85 (Heb.); B. Uffenheimer, "Amos and Hosea—Two Directions in Israelite Prophecy," in *Zer Li-Gevurot: The Zalman Shazar Jubilee Volume: A Collection of Studies in Bible, Eretz Yisrael, Hebrew Language, and Talmudic Literature* (ed. B. Z. Luria; Jerusalem: Kiryat Sepher, 1973) 286 n 2 (Heb.); and N. K. Gottwald, *All the Kingdoms of the Earth: Israelite Prophecy and International Relations in the Ancient Near East* (New York: Harper & Row, 1964) 47–49.
34 B. B. Margulis, *Studies in the Oracles against the Nations* (Unpub. PhD diss., Brandeis University, 1967) 566.
35 Ibid., 67.
36 Ibid., 22ff.
37 Ibid., 67.
38 Ibid., 241–42.
39 Ibid., 30.
40 Ibid., 241.
41 J. H. Hayes, *The Oracles against the Nations in the Old Testament: Their Usage and Theological Importance* (Unpub. ThD diss., Princeton Theological Seminary, 1964).
42 J. H. Hayes, "The Usage of Oracles against Foreign Nations in Ancient Israel," *JBL* 87 (1968) 81–92.
43 Ibid., 84.
44 Ibid., 87–90.
45 D. L. Christensen, *Transformation of the War Oracle in Old Testament Prophecy: Studies in the Oracles against the Nations* (Missoula, MT: Scholars, 1975).
46 Ibid., 17. See also F. M. Cross, "The Divine Warrior in Israel's Early Cult," in *Biblical Motifs: Origins and Transformations* (Studies and Texts 3; ed. A. Altmann; Cambridge: Harvard University, 1966) 11–30; P. D. Miller, Jr., *The Divine Warrior in Early Israel* (HSM 5; Cambridge: Harvard University, 1973).
47 Christensen, *Transformation,* 32.
48 Ibid.

Amos is that Yahweh's holy war is now directed not only against Israel's ancient foes, but against Israel as well."[49] He concluded that Amos took "the earlier speech form of a war oracle in the form of a judgment speech against a specific nation or people and transformed it into a judgment speech against Israel."[50] The prophet thus molded an older historical and literary tradition into a new literary form.

The most recent and most fully developed investigation of this genre was made by Hoffman.[51] He likewise located the origin of this prophetic form in the war oracles, which he designated "oracles-before-battle."[52] Before engaging in battle, a cultic-liturgic procedure was conducted in which the seers promised victory over Israel's enemies. An analysis of these war oracles yielded the following characteristics: (1) the name of the nation and the ensuing calamity are both stated; (2) in many, the messenger formula "Thus said the Lord" is present; (3) and, in a few, the sin that accounts for the impending doom is also designated. Moreover, salvation for Israel is implicit, for the name of Israel, the victorious nation, is always cited. These oracles are seen as the immediate predecessors of the oracles against the nations that, according to Hoffman, developed organically from them.

When the oracles-before-battle gradually went out of existence (with the decline in importance of the popular prophets of the Elijah and Elisha type), they were absorbed into this new literary form in the oracles of the classical prophets, of whom Amos was the first. Their framework, however, was preserved, and a degree of similarity in both structure and basic elements was maintained. In common with the oracles in Amos are the messenger formula, the designation of the foreign nation by name, and the imminent punishment of the offending nation. Nevertheless, despite the obvious literary continuity, two major differences come to the fore. Whereas in the earlier oracles-before-battle the sin for which the impending doom is threatened is only occasionally recorded, in the oracles of Amos it becomes a constant feature. The reason for this first difference is that the oracles-before-battle basically anticipate salvation for Israel, a salvation that is not dependent upon the behavior or deeds of the foreign nation. Its behavior and its doom have no specific connection. When the sin is stated, it is always against Israel or its God (compare, for example, 1 Sam 15:2; 1 Kgs 20:28) and thus constitutes the formal justification for Israel's victory. In Amos, however, the sin for which the nation is to be punished is always clearly specified, although whether or not it was committed against Israel is irrelevant. Punishment of the foreign nation also does not imply salvation for Israel. The nation is doomed for its sin alone. That Israel will not benefit from the other's downfall is obvious because Israel itself is about to experience a similar catastrophe. Furthermore, whereas the identity of the nation that is to carry out the punishment is always made explicit in the oracles-before-battle, in Amos it is never mentioned. The punishment of the offending nation is a consequence of its own actions and is not for the sake of Israel. Only the name of the nation destined to be defeated is recorded and not the name of the victor.

Amos may now be seen as creatively investing an older

49 Ibid., 70.

50 Ibid., 71. He goes on to conclude, "Taking the Davidic Empire as an ideal type, Amos composed an oracle of judgment against each of its member nations, including Israel. Yahweh, the Divine Warrior, was about to punish each of these nations for breach of covenant. Yahweh, the suzerain of these nations, will punish his disobedient vassals through military defeat, no doubt at the hands of resurgent Assyria" (71–72). F. M. Cross (*Canaanite Myth and Hebrew Epic: Essays in the History of the Religion of Israel* [Cambridge, MA: Harvard University, 1973] 174) is of like opinion: "The context is the declaration of war against the nations of the Davidic empire who have breached covenant." Compare also 228–29, 345 n 5. He further states (in a written communication) "that all the nations except Tyre were in treaty or subject to Israel during the United Empire, and Tyre was in a parity treaty *(aḫḫūtu).*" Because of the unique selection of this nation alone, along with the absence of Assyria from the oracles against the nations, he "doubts that Jerusalem ever gave up claims of suzerainty over these nations, nor forgave them for violations of stipulations of treaty—against Israel/Judah—and against each other as treaty partners with Israel, i.e., Jerusalem."

51 Hoffman, *Prophecies,* 21–66, 267–306; see his brief English summary, pp. i–iv; and idem, "From Oracle to Prophecy: The Growth, Crystallization and Disintegration of a Biblical Gattung," *JNSL* 10 (1982) 75–81.

52 Num 21:27–30; 24:15–22; 1 Kgs 20:28; 2 Kgs 3:15–19; Isa 7:3–9; 2 Chr 20:15–29.

literary form with new content. The designation of the sin, which formerly was not primary, becomes an essential and integral element in his oracles. Concomitantly, he eliminates explicitly, as well as implicitly, all references to the salvation or victory of Israel. Just the opposite will take place, for Israel itself is now included in the catalogue of the accused, judged, and doomed. "A non-prophetic, nationalistic, non-moralistic *Gattung* of salvation was transformed into a prophetic *Gattung,* bearing a deep moral and theological message about the universality of God, about His omnipotence and absolute justice as revealed in history."[53]

2. Sequential Ordering

Amos 1:3–2:3

Commentators on the Book of Amos have had to come to grips with the historical, chronological, and literary problems of the first six oracles against the nations of Aram, Philistia, Tyre, Edom, Ammon, and Moab.[54] Are the historical events alluded to here contemporaneous with the prophet Amos,[55] or do they represent heinous crimes of the past, that is, are they pre-Jeroboam II?[56] Are the oracles against Tyre, Edom, and Judah original or secondary?[57] If secondary, are they exilic or post-exilic? Were these prophecies originally independent, self-contained units,[58] or were they from the very outset a single literary unit?[59] The majority of scholars have so concentrated their attention on these admittedly weighty issues that an important literary problem has gone largely unnoticed: Are the first six oracles against the foreign nations ordered in any recognizably logical fashion? The most cited solution to this problem was offered by Bentzen, according to whom the prophecies were "modelled on a cultic pattern, resembling the ritual behind the Egyptian Execration texts," in which the nations are enumerated in a fixed order culminating in the mention of Egypt.[60] His thesis, which has gained only a limited number of adherents—and even then with serious reservations[61]—has been refuted by both Wolff and Weiss.[62] The latter has shown that (1) the constant order in the execration texts—south (Nubians), north (Asiatics), west (Libyans), and lastly Egypt—is not unique to these texts but is the conventional sequence in which these nations are listed in all Egyptian documents, magical or otherwise; (2) this fixed order was not due to

53 Hoffman, "From Oracle to Prophecy," 81.

54 See Paul, "Concatenous," 397–403.

55 See, for example, M. Haran, "Observations on the Historical Background of Amos 1:2—2:6," *IEJ* 18 (1968) 203–7; idem, "The Rise and Decline of the Empire of Jeroboam ben Joash," *VT* 17 (1967) 266–97; K. N. Schoville, "A Note on the Oracles against Gaza, Tyre and Edom," in SVT 26 (Leiden: Brill, 1974) 55–63; Wolff, 149ff.

56 See Kaufmann, *Toledoth,* 6.63.

57 Most commentators view them as secondary. See discussion later.

58 For example, E. Sievers and H. Guthe, *Amos, metrisch bearbeitet* (Abhandlungen der Philologisch-historischen Klasse der Königl. Sächsischen Gesellschaft d. Wissenschaften 23/3; Leipzig: Teubner, 1907) 72; Robinson-Horst, 76; Osty; S. Mowinckel, *Prophecy and Tradition: The Prophetic Books in Light of the Study of the Growth and History of the Tradition* (Oslo: Dybwad, 1946) 57; E. Würthwein, "Amos-Studien," *ZAW* 62 (1950) 57 n 7.

59 Compare G. J. Botterweck, "Zur Authentizität des Buches Amos," *BZ* 2 (1958) 178; Reventlow, *Amt,* 58.

60 A. Bentzen, "Ritual Background," 85–99; see also idem, *Introduction to the Old Testament* (2 vols.; 2d ed.; Copenhagen: Gad, 1952) 2.140–41.

61 H. Ringgren, *Israelite Religion* (tr. D. E. Green; London: SPCK, 1969) 263; A. S. Kapelrud, *Central Ideas in Amos* (Skrifter utgitt av det Norske Videnskaps—Academie: Oslo 2; Oslo: Aschenoug, 1961) 19–20; idem, "New Ideas in Amos," in SVT 15 (Leiden: Brill, 1966) 197ff.; Fohrer, "Prophetie," 40–42; idem, *Introduction to the Old Testament* (tr. D. E. Green; London: SPCK, 1970) 434. Compare Reventlow, *Amt,* 64; F. C. Fensham, "The Treaty between the Israelites and the Tyrians," in SVT 17 (Leiden: Brill, 1969) 82.

Compare the remarks of Amsler, 170, who accepts the cultic framework of the oracles but points out that (1) the feature of a particular motivation for the punishment of each nation, as found in Amos, is absent from the Egyptian texts; (2) when evil acts are enumerated in those texts, the purpose is to protect the country magically and not to condemn it; (3) the verdict of condemnation is lacking in the execration texts. In place of the sympathetic magical act of breaking vases or figurines bearing the names of the enemies, the prophetic oracles substitute an explicit word that announces the personal intervention of God. Magic gives way to theology. He concludes that Amos used a ritual style proper for a liturgical ceremony, but with a new purpose.

62 Wolff, 145–47; M. Weiss, "The Pattern of the 'Execration Texts' in the Prophetic Literature," *IEJ*

"any inherent magical design but to the fact that it was the natural expression of the Egyptian outlook," that is, Egypt was south oriented because its whole existence was dependent upon and influenced by the course of the Nile, which flowed from the south to the north; and (3) the directional order of the nations in Amos—northeast (Aram), southwest (Philistia), northwest (Tyre), southeast (Edom, Ammon, Moab), and finally Judah and Israel—is entirely different from that in the Execration texts—south, north, west, and then Egypt. Fohrer, who accepts Bentzen's thesis that the "sequence of the nations themselves is determined by the model of the Egyptian Execration texts" but who admits that it is hardly likely that the Egyptian ritual was imitated, eliminates the Tyre and Edom oracles and winds up with a geographical sequence of north, west, east, and center, which obviously does not dovetail with the order of south, north, west, and center in the Execration texts.[63]

Kaufmann proposed, in turn, that the order of the nations was to be understood as an alternating listing of the enemies of Israel and Judah respectively.[64] The sequence begins with the Arameans, the classic enemy of *Israel* during that period; proceeds to the Philistines, the foes of *Judah;* and continues with the Phoenicians, the enemy of *Israel;* the Edomites, the enemy of *Judah;* the Ammonites, the enemy of *Israel;* and finally the Moabites, who attacked Edom (the supposed allies of *Judah*).[65] This north-south orientation is correct, but (1) it presupposes that all the oracles are of national significance, that is, that the crimes were committed against Israel or Judah, an assumption that is very problematic[66] and that still leaves the final oracle concerning the conflict of Moab against Edom (and not against Judah) extremely difficult to reconcile;[67] and (2) the Philistines, in this specific case, may possibly be described as attacking Israel and not Judah, thus disrupting the assumed alternating sequence.

However, none of these scholars has discerned the systematic and coherent literary ordering that underlies these oracles.[68] What is stressed here is their *literary* sequence, for attempts at a historical and geographical ordering made by a few commentators have yielded some partially positive results. Thus the coupling of the first two, Aram and Philistia, is also found in Amos 9:7b, "Did I not bring Israel up from the land of Egypt and the Philistines from Caphtor and the Arameans from Kir?" Historically speaking, however, the importance of the interrelationship of these two nations is realized only when the influence of Amos 4:10–12 upon Isa 9:7ff. is taken into account. This penetrating insight was made by Ginsberg, who pointed out that the former verses served as the historical backdrop for Isaiah's review of past punishments against Israel and that in Isa 9:11 the Arameans and the Philistines are coupled in a mutual

19 (1969) 150–57. Weiss also rejects Wolff's points of criticism. See, too, Hoffman, *Prophecies,* 155ff.

63 Fohrer, "Prophetie," 40. Compare Weiss's criticism of this study as well, "Pattern."

64 Kaufmann, *Toledoth,* 6.63.

65 Compare also Haran, "Rise and Decline"; Weiser, *Profetie,* 112.

66 See Reventlow, *Amt,* 68ff.; Gottwald, *Kingdoms,* 107 n 24. So, too, J. A. Soggin, *The Prophet Amos* (tr. J. Bowden; London: SCM, 1987) 45.

67 The interpretation of Tur-Sinai (*HaLashon,* 1.84ff.) of מֶלֶךְ אֱדוֹם (Amos 2:1) as a reflex of the Punic expression מלך אדם ("a human sacrifice"), which is based upon the study of O. Eissfeldt (*Molk als Opferbegriff im Punischen und Hebräischen und das Ende des Gottes Moloch* [Halle: Niemeyer, 1935]), has been refuted by M. Weinfeld ("The Worship of Molech and the Queen of Heaven and Its Background," *UF* 4 [1972] 133–54).

68 This problem is entirely ignored by almost all commentators previously cited. Sievers and Guthe, *Amos,* 72, refer in passing to the "Verwandtschaft des Inhalts" ("the contextual relationship") but do not explicate. Schmidt ("Redaktion," 178 n 29) posits a north-south grouping, but only after he omits Tyre and Edom as Deuteronomistic redactions. R. K. Harrison (*Introduction to the Old Testament* [Leicester: Inter-Varsity, 1969] 888) links the last three nations together as blood relations to Israel (compare also Theis, 114) but is silent as to the others. Kaufmann (*Toledoth,* 6.63) sees an alternating grouping of the enemies of Israel and Judah respectively, but he does not explain the specific internal ordering itself. Weiser (*Profetie,* 86) suggests that the order was psychologically arranged, starting with the mightiest and most important nations. Compare the criticism of Wolff, 175. This may very well explain the primary importance of Aram, but how can one fathom the specific descending order of the others? For a geographical ordering of events in Assyrian annals, see H. Tadmor, "The Campaigns of Sargon II of Assur: A Chronological-Historical Study," *JCS* 12 (1958) 36.

attack against Israel.[69]

The next two nations, Philistia and Tyre, are in close proximity on the Mediterranean littoral, and they are often cited together (Jer 47:4; Ezek 25:15—26:2ff.; Joel 4:4–8; Zech 9:3–6; Ps 83:8). Haran pointed out this close relationship and added that this traditional coupling helps to prove that the oracle against Tyre was an integral part of the original prophecy and not a later addition.[70] As for the argument advanced by those who consider the Tyre oracle a late interpolation because it contains an almost literal repetition of the crimes listed against Philistia, he counters that this is a natural way to express complicity in a similar crime.[71] (Note that in Joel 4:4–8 the two are again accused of the same crime of selling slaves, this time to the Greeks.) Furthermore, according to Haran, no later editor would have accused Tyre of a breach of covenant because during the time of the destruction of the First Temple Tyre did not make peace with Nebuchadrezzar (compare Ezek 26:7ff.; 29:17–18; Josephus, *Antiquities,* X.11. 1; *Against Apion,* 1.21).[72]

As for the grouping of the three southeastern nations, Weiss has pointed out that the three are bound by geographical proximity, historical relationships, and consanguineous and ethnic ties to Israel.[73] Compare the mention of the three together in Deut 23:4–8; Isa 22:14; Jer 48—49; Ezek 25:2–14; and Dan 11:41; and of Ammon and Moab in Gen 19:37–38; Zeph 2:8–11; and Neh 13:1ff.

These important insights, however, did not lead to any further understanding of the overall literary pattern Amos employed in his presentation of the oracles. The question may still be posed: Why does Philistia come immediately after Aram, and why is it followed by Tyre, which is succeeded, in turn, by Edom, Ammon, and Moab? Despite the correctness of the historical and geographical couplings just mentioned, the internal order of nations could still have been rearranged in other ways, such as Edom-Moab-Ammon (compare Isa 11:14; Dan 11:41); Moab-Ammon-Edom (Jer 48—49); or even Ammon-Moab-Edom (Ezek 25:2–14).[74]

Nevertheless, an internal literary order can be discerned that weaves the various units into a coherent whole. Each link in this chain of oracles can be shown to be tied to one another by an indissoluble bond characterized by the well-known literary mnemonic device of the concatenation of similar catchwords, phrases, or ideas shared only by the two contiguous units.

First, a few remarks about the general literary traits common to all six of the oracles:[75] (1) They are all introduced by the well-known *Botenformel* ("messenger [or] herald formula") כֹּה אָמַר ה' ("Thus said the Lord"). (2) This opening address is followed by the staircase numerical pattern[76] עַל־שְׁלֹשָׁה פִּשְׁעֵי . . . וְעַל־אַרְבָּעָה ("for

69 H. L. Ginsberg, "From Isaiah's Diary," in *ʿOz LeDavid: Collected Readings in Bible Presented to David ben Gurion on His Seventy-seventh Birthday* (ed. Y. Kaufmann and others; Jerusalem: Kiryat Sepher, 1964) 347–48 (Heb.).

70 Haran, "Observations," 203–7. Compare O. Eissfeldt, "Philister und Phönizer," AO 34 (1936) 21–26.

71 Haran, "Observations."

72 Ibid. Haran also suggests reading אֲרָם ("Aram") instead of אֱדוֹם ("Edom") in both v 6 (Philistia) and v 9 (Tyre). Although many commentators have accepted the emendation of אֲרָם for אֱדוֹם in the oracle against Tyre, with the sole exception of P. Haupt ("Scriptio Plena der emphatischen *LA*- im Hebräischen," *OLZ* 10 [1907] 308; "Was Amos a Sheepman?" *JBL* 35 [1916] 288–90), Haran is alone in suggesting it in the oracle against Philistia.

73 Weiss, "Pattern," 151; Harrison, *Introduction to the Old Testament,* 888.

74 Note that Moab and Ammon are always linked together and are never separated by Edom.

75 Compare Amsler, 169; Schmidt, "Redaktion," 174; Reventlow, *Amt,* 56–58; H. Frey, *Das Buch des Ringens Gottes um seine Kirche. Der Prophet Amos* (Die Botschaft des Alten Testament 23/1; Stuttgart: Calwer, 1965) 41–42; Werner, 43–58; Wolff, 135–39. See also R. P. Knierim, "'I will not cause it to return' in Amos 1 and 2," in *Canon and Authority: Essays in Old Testament Religion and Theology* (ed. G. Coates and B. Long; Philadelphia: Fortress, 1976) 169.

76 See H. L. Ginsberg, "Towards the History of the Graded Number Sequence," in *Minḥa LeDavid: Jubilee Volume Dedicated to David Yellin* (Jerusalem: Vaʿad HaYovel, 1935) 78–81 (Heb.); U. Cassuto, *Biblical and Oriental Studies* (2 vols.; tr. I. Abrahams; Jerusalem: Magnes, 1975) 2.27–29; W. M. W. Roth, "The Numerical Sequence *x/x+1* in the Old Testament," *VT* 12 (1962) 300–311; S. Gevirtz, *Patterns in the Early Poetry of Israel* (Studies in Ancient Oriental Civilization 32; Chicago: University of Chicago, 1963) 15–24. For a reexamination of this particular numerical sequence in Amos, see M. Weiss, "The Pattern of Numerical Sequence in Amos

three transgressions of [the specific nation] and for four"), with only the name of the nation varying in each case. (3) Thereupon follows the announcement of the absolute irrevocability of the divine decision, לֹא אֲשִׁיבֶנּוּ ("I shall not revoke it" [that is, the punishment]). (4) The particular heinous crime of each is then introduced by the particle עַל. (5) The oracles conclude with a final verdict in which the Deity, speaking in the first person, condemns each nation to punishment by fire: וְשִׁלַּחְתִּי אֵשׁ (1:4, 7, 10, 12; 2:2), or its variant, וְהִצַּתִּי אֵשׁ (1:14).

In addition to these common denominators, specific agglutinant elements link the nations together in a cohesive pattern and create the sequential arrangement of these oracles. The pattern is as follows:

	verses	
והכרתי יושב מ(בקעת־און) ותומך שבט מ(בית עדן)	5	ארם
והכרתי יושב מ(אשדוד) ותומך שבט מ(אשקלון)	8	עזה
על־הגלותם גלות שלמה להסגיר לאדום	6	
על־הסגירם גלות שלמה לאדום	9	צור
ולא זכרו ברית אחים	9	
אחיו	11	אדום
על־רדפו בחרב אחיו ושחת רחמיו	11	
על־בקעם הרות הגלעד	13	עמון
בתרועה, (v 14) מלכם, שריו (v 15)	14–15	
מלך־ (v 1), בתרועה (v 2), שריה (v 3)	2:1–3	מואב

One of the punishments against Damascus (v 5) is וְהִכְרַתִּי יוֹשֵׁב מִ(בִּקְעַת־אָוֶן) וְתוֹמֵךְ שֵׁבֶט מִ(בֵּית עֶדֶן), a threat that is literally repeated (except for the obvious change in sites) only in the next unit, the oracle against Gaza (v 8): וְהִכְרַתִּי יוֹשֵׁב מֵ(אַשְׁדּוֹד) וְתוֹמֵךְ שֵׁבֶט מֵ(אַשְׁקְלוֹן). Furthermore, "exile" is mentioned in both: for Aram, the punishment (v 5); for Gaza, the crime (v 6); compare also Tyre, v 9. The prophet's accusation against Gaza, in turn, עַל־הַגְלוֹתָם גָּלוּת שְׁלֵמָה לְהַסְגִּיר לֶאֱדוֹם (v 6) is almost precisely the same as the one leveled against the next nation, Tyre (v 9), עַל־הַסְגִּירָם גָּלוּת שְׁלֵמָה לֶאֱדוֹם. The oracle against Tyre then continues with the charge of the breach of a "brotherly" political covenant (v 9), וְלֹא זָכְרוּ בְּרִית אַחִים, which, by its key word, "brother," leads to the next oracle against Edom, which also mentions a major offense against its "brother" (v 11), עַל־רָדְפוֹ בַחֶרֶב אָחִיו.[77] Note also that after the mention of Edom in the oracles against both Gaza and Tyre, the following oracle is directed against Edom itself. The link between Edom and Ammon is admittedly the only one that does not contain an exactly identical word or phrase. However, the common denominator between the two, which led to their present juxtaposition, is very likely the nature of the crimes involved: both were committed with a sword. The former pursued its "brother" with a "sword" (v 11); the latter ripped open the bellies of pregnant women, obviously with a sword (v 13). (חֶרֶב in v 11 and לְהַרְחִיב in v 13 may also have a "sound" link.) Moreover, yet another connection between the two may be contained within the phrase וְשִׁחֵת רַחֲמָיו (v 11).[78] The fact that a concrete noun would be expected to parallel אָחִיו ("his brother") rather than an abstract one, "affection,"[79] coupled with the untenability of the prevalent translation of שִׁחֵת ("he stifled/suppressed")—which offers an otherwise unattested meaning for this verb forced upon it by the difficulty of the passage[80]—leads one to suspect that רַחֲמָיו does in truth refer to a certain part of the

1—2: A Re-Examination," *JBL* 86 (1967) 416–23. See also G. Sauer, *Die Sprüche Agurs* (BWANT 84; Stuttgart: Kohlhammer, 1963) 24–91; M. Haran, "The Graded Numerical Sequence and the Phenomenon of 'Automatism' in Biblical Poetry," in SVT 22 (Leiden: Brill, 1972) 238–67, esp. 244–45, 257–61; H. P. Rüger, "Die gestaffelten Zahlensprüche des Alten Testaments und aram. Achikar 92," *VT* 31 (1981) 229–34. For additional literature, see n 168.

77 See J. Priest, "The Covenant of Brothers," *JBL* 84 (1965) 400–406.

78 Compare Jer 13:14 and Ps 78:38 for very interesting analogies. The verb appears there, however, in the *hiph'il*.

79 Both G (*μήτραν*) and Jerome (in his commentary, *vulvam eius*) interpret the word concretely as "womb." See also ibn Ezra; M. Rahmer, *Die Hebräischen Traditionen in den Werken des Hieronymus 2 Theil: Die Commentarien zu den XII Kleinen Propheten III. Amos* (Berlin: Poppelauer, 1902); Y. Zakovitch, *"For Three . . . and for Four": The Pattern of the Numerical Sequence in the Bible* (2 vols.; Jerusalem: Mekor, 1979) 1.179–84 (Heb.). On the basis of this, both Döderlein and Dathe (compare J. C. W. Dahl, *Amos* [1795] 82–83) interpreted the word to mean *"in mulieres gravidas"* ("in pregnant women") by synecdoche. N. H. Snaith, *The Book of Amos* (2 vols.; London: Epworth, 1946) 2.25–26, opined that it was a very late Hebrew word for "his friends." Compare G. A. L. Baur (*Der Prophet Amos erklärt* [Giessen, 1847] 243–44), who translated it "Brüdervolk" ("brother nation").

80 Heb. שִׁחֵת almost always appears in connection with the destruction of human beings and not with expressions of emotions or inanimate objects.

population that was "destroyed" (שִׁחֵת) by the Ammonite enemy. The problem, however, with the suggested translation, "his allies," for רַחֲמָיו[81] is that it is based on an incorrect analogy with the Akkadian verb *ra'āmu.* The interdialectal equivalent of Heb. רחם is Akk. *rêmu* and not *ra'āmu,* and *rêmu* is not the verb used in extrabiblical treaty contexts to denote love, that is, fidelity.[82]

This linguistic dilemma can be solved by realizing that the substantive רַחֲמָיו is the same as that found in Judg 5:30, רַחַם רַחֲמָתַיִם, meaning "young women."[83] This same word is also attested in the Moabite Mesha inscription (lines 15–17):

ואחזה . ואהרג . כל[ה] . שבעת . אלפן . ג[ב]רן . ו[גר]ן .
וגברת . ו[גר]ת . ורחמת . כי . לעשתר . כמש . החרמתה,

"So I captured it [Nebo] and slayed all, seven thousand men . . . , and women . . . , and maid-servants/girls,[84] for I had devoted them to destruction for (the god) Ashtar-Chemosh." Furthermore, *rḥm* is also well known in Ugaritic and is synonymous with Ugar. *btlt,* which means a "young woman." Compare *rḥm ʿnt* to *btlt ʿnt.*[85] This then adds another link to the mutual crimes of Edom and Ammon: both wielded the *sword* in order to kill the *female* population.[86]

The last two nations, Ammon and Moab, are once again linked by key phrases that appear nowhere else in the other oracles: בִּתְרוּעָה (1:14; 2:2); שָׂרָיו (1:15) and שָׂרֶיהָ (2:3); מַלְכָּם (1:15) and מֶלֶךְ (2:1). The entire unit is also tied together by one grand inclusio, beginning and ending with וְהִכְרַתִּי (1:5; 2:3).

As a final note, whether such a sequential, concatenous pattern is a product of originally independent units welded together by Amos or by a later editor or is explained as a single literary composite, the process of an internal associative patterning provides the key to its correct interrelationship.[87]

Compare, for example, Gen 6:17; 9:15; 1 Sam 26:15; 2 Sam 1:14. The sole exceptions are Ezek 28:17; Mal 2:8.

81 M. Fishbane, "The Treaty Background of Amos 1:11 and Related Matters," *JBL* 89 (1970) 313–18.

82 For a study of the concept of love implying fidelity in treaty literature, see W. Moran, "The Ancient Near Eastern Background of the Love of God in Deuteronomy," *CBQ* 25 (1963) 77–87. See also R. B. Coote, "Amos 1:11: *RḤMYW,*" *JBL* 90 (1971) 206–8; Y. Muffs, *Studies in the Aramaic Legal Papyri from Elephantine* (Studia documenta ad iura orientis antiqui pertinentia 8; Leiden: Brill, 1969) 132 n 2; G. Schmuttermayr, "*RḤM*—Eine lexikalische Studie," *Bib* 51 (1970) 499–532.

83 See already Y. ibn Ganaḥ, *Sepher Haschoraschim* (ed. W. Bacher; Berlin: H. Itzkowski, 1896) 477 (Heb.). Compare Y. Kaufmann, *The Book of Judges* (Jerusalem: Kiryat Sepher, 1962) 145–46 (Heb.). This is mentioned by Fishbane ("Treaty Background," 313), who also cites the Mesha inscription but immediately discounts it. It is very possible that this same word appears in Isa 49:15, מֵרַחֵם. See M. Dahood, "Denominative רחם, 'to conceive, enwomb,'" *Bib* 44 (1963) 204. Compare M. Gruber, "'Will a Woman Forget Her Infant?' Isa 49:15," *Tarbiz* 51 (1981–1982) 491–92 (Heb.); R. Gordis, "On מרחם בן בטנה in Isa 49:15," *Tarbiz* 53 (1983–1984) 137–38 (Heb.).

84 *KAI,* I.33; *ANET,* 320. Compare S. Segert, "Die Sprache der moabitischen Königsinschrift," *ArOr* 29 (1961) 244. J. C. L. Gibson (*Textbook of Syrian Semitic Inscriptions: Vol. I: Hebrew and Moabite Inscriptions* [Oxford: Clarendon, 1971] 76) translates "female slaves."

85 *CTA* 6:ii:27. Compare also the divine name *rḥmy, CTA* 23:16; *CTA* 15:ii:6.

86 H. Gese, "Komposition bei Amos," in SVT 32 (Leiden: Brill, 1981) 80, notes that in Ammon there is also "eine polarer Zusammenordnung vorgebürtlich-nachtodlich" ("a polarized juxtaposition, prenatal–postmortem").

87 Gese, "Komposition," unfortunately did not take into account that the literary mnemonic device of concatenation does not refer only to actual words, but, as stated previously, also to "ideas shared *only* by the two contiguous units." Both D. L. Christensen ("The Prosodic Structure of Amos 1—2," *HTR* 67 [1974] 427–36) and G. Pfeifer ("Denkformenanalyse als exegetische Methode, erläutert an Amos 1:2—2:16," *ZAW* 88 [1976] 56–71) either overlooked the significance of this literary device or somewhat misunderstood it. For an example of a concatenous pattern in the legal material of the Book of the Covenant in Exodus, see S. M. Paul, *Studies in the Book of the Covenant in the Light of Cuneiform and Biblical Law* (SVT 18; Leiden: Brill, 1970) 106–11.

3. Authenticity

Additional literary criteria can be supplied to demonstrate the basic unity and originality of these oracles.[88] First, however, the question of whether any of these oracles is a secondary, later interpolation must be considered.

1. The Oracle against the Philistines (Gaza)[89]

(1) The prime reason for doubting the originality of this oracle is the absence of Gath[90]—the only city of the Philistine pentapolis not mentioned in this pericope. The underlying assumption is that this oracle must have been added later, that is, after 712 B.C.E., when the city was captured by the Assyrian king Sargon II. However, no oracle against Philistia anywhere in *prophetic* literature records all five names of the Philistine cities.[91] In 2 Sam 1:20, only Gath and Ashkelon appear; in Jer 47:5 only Gaza and Ashdod; and in Jer 25:20; Zeph 2:4; and Zech 9:5–7, Gath alone is again conspicuous by its absence. Compare also 2 Chr 26:6. (For possible reasons, see further.) Obviously, none of these oracles was meant to be all-inclusive.

(2) Gath was not the only Philistine city that fell in Sargon II's western campaign. The Assyrian king, on his way to quell a revolt that broke out in Ashdod, captured "Ekron" *(am-qa-[ar]-nu-na)* and a couple of other cities that had joined the rebellion.[92] He then recounts, *$^{\bar{a}l}$Asdudu $^{\bar{a}l}$Gimtu $^{\bar{a}l}$Asdudimmu alme akšud,* "The cities of Ashdod, Gath, and Ashdod-Yam I besieged (and) conquered."[93] Thus, at least for consistency's sake, those who explain the absence of Gath due to its capture should logically expect to find Ekron and Ashdod also missing from this oracle.[94] Yet, they are clearly present.

(3) Even more significant is the fact that the city was not wiped off the face of the Philistine map as a result of being captured. Sargon goes on to declare, "I restored those cities [Ashdod, Gath, and Ashdod-Yam], and I settled therein people of the lands my hands had conquered." Gath, although annexed by Sargon to the newly established province of Ashdod,[95] was no longer of any major political significance (which was true even before it became subsidiary to Ashdod), but it nevertheless continued to exist and was even repopulated.

(4) As for the arguments that deny its originality based on style and contents—its similarity to the preceding oracle against Aram—that this similarity is intentional and deliberate and constitutes the specific literary reason for its present position after Damascus has already been noted.[96]

(5) As for the contention that this oracle upsets an assumed geographical order and thus must be a later addition, the question may be asked, Whose geographical order? Not only have various scholars superimposed their own preconceived arrangement[97] but this argu-

88 See Paul, "Literary Reinvestigation," 189–204.

89 Most commentators today do not question the authenticity of this oracle. For earlier opinions, see Marti, 160; Nowack, 123.

90 For different opinions as to the identity of biblical Gath, see B. Mazar, "Gath and Gittaim," *IEJ* 4 (1954) 227–35; reprinted in idem, *Cities and Districts in Eretz-Israel* (Jerusalem: Mosad Bialik, 1975) 101–9 (Heb.); H. E. Kassis, "Gath and the Structure of the 'Philistine' Society," *JBL* 84 (1965) 259–71; A. F. Rainey, "The Identification of Philistine Gath," in Eretz Israel 12 (*Nelson Glueck Memorial Volume;* ed. B. Mazar and others; Jerusalem: Israel Exploration Society, 1975) 63*–76*; K. A. Kitchen, "The Philistines," in *Peoples of Old Testament Times* (ed. D. J. Wiseman; Oxford: Clarendon, 1973) 62–63.

91 Compare Kaufmann, *Toledoth,* 6.61 n 11; Mays, 33. The satirical allusion to Gath in Mic 1:10 "shows that such a proverb as 'Tell it not to Gath' had long since taken root in Israelite oral and written tradition" (Rainey, "Identification," 74).

92 H. Tadmor, "The Assyrian Campaigns to Philistia," in *The Military History of the Land of Israel in Biblical Times* (ed. J. Liver; Jerusalem: Israel Defence Forces Publishing House, 1964) 274–75 (Heb.). See idem, "Campaigns of Sargon II," 33–39; idem, "Philistia under Assyrian Rule," *BA* 29 (1966) 86–102.

93 For the Display Inscription, see H. Winckler, *Die Keilschrifttexte Sargons* (Leipzig: Pfeiffer, 1889) pl. 33 lines 104–7.

94 Compare Hoffman, *Prophecies,* 166; M. Haran, *Ages and Institutions in the Bible* (Tel Aviv: Am Oved, 1972) 294 (Heb.); Rudolph, 132.

95 H. Tadmor, "Assyrian Campaigns," 275. Compare A. Alt, "Neue Assyrische Nachrichten über Palästina," in idem, *Kleine Schriften zur Geschichte des Volkes Israel* (3 vols.; München: C. H. Beck, 1953) 2.238–41. See also N. Na'aman, "Sennacherib's 'Letter to God' on His Campaign to Judah," *BASOR* 214 (1974) 25–39.

96 Paul, "Literary Reinvestigation," 190.

97 Marti; B. Duhm, "Anmerkungen zu den Zwölf Propheten. I: Buch Amos," *ZAW* 31 (1911) 1–18.

ment may work both ways. Thus for Bentzen[98] this precise geographical slot reserved for Philistia is part of the evidence (according to his theory) that the oracle is original![99] Nevertheless, as has just been shown, geography is only one—and not the most decisive—factor in determining the order of Amos's roll call of nations.

Why then is Gath absent from the list? Several solutions have been offered by those who do not deny this oracle's authenticity: "probably an accident";[100] Gath is implied in the concluding phrase "the remnant of the Philistines";[101] it probably was no longer independent, having come under Aramean rule when Hazael expropriated it during the latter part of the ninth century from the Judeans as part of his campaigns in the west (2 Kgs 12:17–18);[102] it was under Judean control when Uzziah recaptured the city (2 Chr 26:6);[103] or it may already have been subservient to Ashdod before 712.[104] Of course, the solution selected is determined by the historical dating of the oracle, but no matter when that may be the city was obviously no longer of any major significance[105] and thus could easily be omitted. Nevertheless, clearly there is no reason on chronological or any other grounds to deny the authenticity of the oracle to Amos, for "it would have been very strange of Amos himself had he not included the Philistines in his threats against the surrounding peoples."[106]

2. The Oracle against Tyre[107]

(1) The authenticity of this oracle has been doubted on the grounds of its being a mere "echo of the one against Gaza"[108] (which, as noted, was considered by some to be a repetition of the oracle against Damascus!). This "almost verbatim" similarity is deemed to be inconsistent with Amos's skill in poetic variation, thus marking the Tyre oracle as secondary. Here, too, as demonstrated previously, the literary and contextual similarity is intentional and produced by the mnemonic device of associative reasoning, which lends conclusive weight in

98 Bentzen, "Ritual Background," 90, as well as the oracles against Tyre and Edom.

99 So correctly Hoffman, *Prophecies.*

100 Mentioned as a possibility by Kaufmann, *Toledoth,* 6.61; and Hammershaimb, 29.

101 Suggested by Hammershaimb, 29–30; and Rudolph.

102 Compare Mays.

103 Compare Rainey, "The Identification of Philistine Gath," 63*–76*; Mays; and also listed as a possibility by Wolff, 158; and Rudolph.

104 Compare Haran, *Ages and Institutions,* 293–94.

105 Ibid., 293.

106 Hammershaimb, 30. Compare Mays: "Its absence here is hardly serious evidence against the authenticity of the saying"; and Rudolph.

107 The authenticity is doubted by many. In addition to Harper, cxxxi–cxxxii, 28; Nowack, 123–24; Marti, 160; Mays, 34; and Wolff, 140, the following may be added (without pretensions of being all-inclusive): Wellhausen, 69–70; M. Löhr, *Untersuchungen zum Buche Amos* (BZAW 33; Giessen: Töpelmann, 1903) 87–88; Kapelrud, *Central Ideas,* 24; Schmidt, "Redaktion," 174–78; G. Fohrer, "Zehn Jahre Literatur zur alttestamentlichen Prophetie (1951–1960) Fortsetzung," *TRu* 28 (1962) 61; and J. Morgenstern, "Jerusalem 485 B.C.," *HUCA* 28 (1957) 42–43. See also H.-P. Müller, "Phönizien und Juda in exilisch-nachexilischer Zeit," *WO* 6 (1971) 189–204; Gese, "Komposition," 88; G. Pfeifer, "Denkformenanalyse," 56–71.

In contrast there is a growing list of those who tend to accept its originality; compare, for example, Driver; Sellin, 165; H. Gressmann, *Die älteste Geschichtsschreibung und Prophetie Israels (von Samuel bis Amos und Hosea)* (2d ed.; SAT 2/1; Göttingen: Vandenhoeck & Ruprecht, 1921), 333–36; Robinson-Horst, 76; Cripps, 127–28; Amsler, 173–74; Cramer, 190; van Gelderen, 20ff.; A. Neher, *Amos: Contribution à l'étude du prophètisme* (Paris: Vrin, 1980); Schmidt, "Redaktion," 43; Hammershaimb, 35 ("It is a bad principle to lay down rules for what verse patterns and strophe formations Amos could have used. He varies the verses freely as he wishes to, and not according to the rules of European metre"); V. Maag, *Text, Wortschaft, und Begriffswelt des Buches Amos* (Leiden: Brill, 1951) 120. Compare also O. Eissfeldt, "Philister und Phönizer," 8; K. Budde, "Zum Text und Auslegung des Buches Amos," *JBL* 43 (1924) 61; A. Carlson, "Profeten Amos och Davidsriket," *Religion och Bibel* 25 (1966) 57–58; M. A. Beek, "The Religious Background of Amos 2:6–8," in *OTS* 5 (Leiden: Brill, 1948) 132–41; Priest, "Covenant," 400–401; Botterweck, "Authentizität," 179–80; Fensham, "Treaty," 71–87, esp. 80–83; Schoville, "Note on the Oracles," 55–63; and the works of Kaufmann and Haran cited in nn 91 and 94. H. Cazelles ("L'arrière-plan historique d'Amos 1:9–10," in *The Proceedings of the Sixth World Congress of Jewish Studies* [3 vols.; Jerusalem: World Union of Jewish Studies, 1977] 1.71–76) dates the oracle to the second half of the Syro-Ephraimite war.

108 Mays, 34; Wolff, 140, 158. Nevertheless, a new and significant point is made in the second half of v 9.

favor of its originality.[109] Furthermore, its almost literal repetition of the charge against Philistia is of singular importance; that is, it specifically expresses complicity in a similar crime.[110]

(2) Its originality is further contested on the basis of its being a "pale generalization" in comparison to the other oracles. Even though this contention itself may be called a "pale generalization"—for specific charges are leveled against Tyre—the question may be raised of why this imaginary latter-day interpolator wished to leave matters so "vague." He obviously could have been as specific as he desired, even given the circumscribed framework in which he worked.[111]

(3) Tyre's guilt is engaging in slave trade, and this accusation reappears only in exilic or postexilic texts (Ezek 27:13; Joel 4:6–7); ergo, here, too, a reflection of later times is contended.[112] Obviously, this argument may also be reversed, for Amos is actually providing here the earliest evidence of a "business practice" that became a Tyrian profession for hundreds of years. Its traffic in slaves need not have started after the fall of the Temple.[113]

(4) An often repeated argument is the form-critical one: the literary formulation here, on the one hand, is rather different from those oracles that are undisputedly authentic, and, on the other hand, it is similar to the oracles against Edom and Judah, whose originality is, in turn, sorely contested on this and other grounds (see further). The five literary traits shared by all the oracles have been noted. However, whereas the infinitival clause referring to the crimes is elaborated by one (1:9) or more (1:11; 2:4) verbal clauses, thus expanding upon the indictment (unlike the other four "original" oracles), the announcement of punishment is greatly abbreviated, being reduced to merely the stereotypic judgment by fire (again unlike the others, whose list of punishments is much more detailed). Furthermore, the concluding formula ("said the (my) Lord (God)") is omitted.[114]

The commentators who attempt to defend the originality of this oracle have mostly overlooked or not contended with this form-critical argument. Although Reventlow makes note of it, his claim for "uniformity of form" is based upon his own prior assumption that the charge as well as the punishment in each oracle originally comprised a single sentence. This assumption, in turn, leads him to make a large number of emendations and deletions,[115] which, as correctly stated by Wolff, is "too high a price to pay for the uniformity in form of all the individual oracles."[116] As is shown later, these variations in form are explainable on other grounds. However, the basic proposition itself—if so much is similar, then any variation from the pattern necessarily and obviously reveals a later hand—must be decisively rejected. Here Rudolph's observation made first in connection with the minor variations evidenced in several of the so-called authentic oracles should be recalled: "Wir stehen hier vor der grundsätlichen Frage, ob ein Prophet, der bei einer bestimmten Gelengenheit das, was er sagen will, nach einem bestimmten Schema ordnet, verpflichtet ist, keinen Schritt vom Schema abzuweichen, oder ob er sich bei aller Bindung an eine allgemeine Rahmenordnung im einzelnen Freiheiten erlauben kann, m.a.W.: Überschreitet die formgeschichtliche Betrachtung nicht ihre Kompetenz, wenn sie einen Propheten in einer Zwangsjacke steckt? Die Antwort kann nicht schwerfallen, und dass sich der Prophet nicht sklavisch bindet, lässt sich beweisen. . . . haben wir es hier mit einer willkürlichen Ausdrucksvariation zu tun. . . . Kurz: Amos schematisiert nicht." ("Here we confront the fundamental question whether a prophet, who on a specific occasion arranges what he has to say according to a specific model, is obliged not to deviate one step from this model or, in spite of being bound by a general framework, can allow himself liberties in details. In other words, does the form-critical way of thinking not overstep its competence when it places a straitjacket upon the prophet? The answer is not difficult, and it can be demonstrated that the prophet is not slavishly bound. . . . We are dealing here with an

109 Paul, "Literary Reinvestigation," 191.

110 Haran, "Observations," 201–7; and Rudolph, 120 (who also calls attention to the similarity of Amos 1:3 and 1:13).

111 Hoffman, *Prophecies*, 166–67.

112 Compare, for example, Mays, 34.

113 Compare the comments of Y. M. Grintz, "'Because They Exiled a Whole Exile to Deliver to Edom,'" *BM* 32 (1967) 24–26 (Heb.).

114 For example, Harper, 28; Wolff, 140.

115 Reventlow, *Amt*, 62.

116 Wolff, 140; compare Rudolph, 120.

arbitrary variation of expression. In short, Amos does not schematize.") Then in reference to the form-critical differences of these oracles, he writes: "Ebenso muss man ihm die Freiheit zubilligen, sich beim Schuldaufweis und bei der Strafankündigung bald knapper, bald ausführlicher zu äussern. So besteht rein vom Formellen her kein Anlass, die Echtheit der drei genannten Sprüche unzuzweifeln." ("Similarly one must allow him the freedom, in both the demonstration of guilt and the announcement of punishment, to express himself at times more briefly, at other times more fully. Thus from a purely formal point of view there is no reason to question the authenticity of the three oracles referred to.")[117] (For further considerations relating to this point, see later.)

(5) Another reason for its being considered a later addition is the alleged Deuteronomistic vocabulary in this oracle, especially the expression זָכַר בְּרִית ("to remember the covenant"), which is argued to be "unattested in pre-exilic material but is relatively frequent in the priestly work." Thus the conclusion is that "the whole sentence corresponds to the theological and salvation-historical language and thought of circles trained in the Deuteronomistic tradition."[118] However, as Cazelles correctly noted, Wolff's remarks pertain to the theological concept of בְּרִית but not to the unique phrase בְּרִית אַחִים ("a brotherly covenant"), which, as has been often observed, is an adaptation of a Mesopotamian political expression signifying a parity treaty and has nothing to do with the unique Israelite concept of a covenant made between God and Israel.[119]

3. The Oracle against Edom[120]

(1) For the form-critical arguments, see 2(4). "The variation in the patterns of strophes is not a criterion against their genuineness."[121]

(2) The primary contention made here by almost all scholars is the supposed postexilic background of the oracle. Their reasoning is that throughout the period of the monarchy Israel was in control of Edom with the exception of a brief period when, under the reign of King Joram, the Edomites rebelled and installed a king of their own (2 Kgs 8:20–22). So how and when could Edom have persecuted Israel?[122] It supposedly had its revenge only with the fall of Jerusalem: "In this period alone are there supporting statements elsewhere."

---

117 Rudolph, 119–20; so, too, Hammershaimb, 35. See also Priest, "Covenant," 405 n 21; Fensham, "Treaty," 81; Gordis, "Composition," 242 n 10; Pfeifer, "Denkformenanalyse," 61 n 17. Compare R. Alter, "Biblical Type-Scenes and the Uses of Convention," *Critical Inquiry* 5 (1978) 368: "The process of literary creation . . . is an uneasy dialectic between the necessity to use established forms in order to be able to communicate coherently and the necessity to break and remake those forms because they are arbitrary restrictions and because what is merely repeated automatically no longer conveys a message."

118 Wolff, 159–60.

119 Cazelles, "L'arrière-plan," 74; Fensham, "Treaty," 81. See esp. Priest, "Covenant."

120 For those who deny the authenticity of this oracle, see n 107. In addition, the following may be added: M. Haller, "Edom im Urteil der Propheten," in *Vom Alten Testament: Karl Marti zum siebzigsten Geburtstag* (BZAW 41; ed. K. Budde; Giessen: Töpelmann, 1925) 112; J. Rieger, *Die Bedeutung der Geschichte für die Verkündigung des Amos und Hosea* (Giessen: Töpelmann, 1929) 20, 29; Fosbroke, 782; J. Morgenstern, "Jerusalem," 115 n 38; idem, "Amos Studies IV: The Addresses of Amos—Text and Commentary," *HUCA* 32 (1961) 340–41; Mays, 36; Budde, "Amos," 57–59, 65–66; R. H. Pfeiffer, *Introduction to the Old Testament* (New York: Harper, 1948) 579; Bentzen, *Introduction,* 2.141.
To the few who interpret it as original, add F. Buhl, *Geschichte der Edomiter* (Leipzig: Edelmann, 1893) 66–67; Botterweck, "Authentizität," 181. Compare the comments of Margulis, *Studies,* 116 (on Edom and Tyre): "Why should the alleged interpolator(s) be capable of doing what Amos allegedly could not have done? There are, moreover, no anachronisms, no self-contradictions, indeed no serious implausibilities which rule out Amosian authorship of these oracles." Cazelles ("L'arrière-plan," 76) dates it to the first half of the Syro-Ephraimite war. See also Reventlow, *Amt,* 57, 113.

121 Mays, 38.

122 Hammershaimb, 37. Compare J. R. Bartlett, "The Land of Seir and the Brotherhood of Edom," *JTS* 20 (1969) 13–18; idem, "The Brotherhood of Edom," *JSOT* 4 (1977) 2–27.

(Compare Isa 34:5–17; 63:1–6; Jer 49:7–22; Ezek 25:12–14; 35:5; Joel 4:19; Obad 10–14; Mal 1:4; Ps 137:7; Lam 4:21–22.) Thus "only in this later period was it especially appropriate to expect that 'pity' might be shown by Edom."[123]

However, as others have correctly noted, this reservation against its authenticity is highly dubious, to say the least. Because skirmishes between Israel and Edom must have occurred for hundreds of years before Amos, "there could have been circumstances which would justify Amos in using language like that of these verses."[124] The inability to identify specifically the event referred to here is no reason for assuming that the oracle is necessarily late. The scholar must confess, "wie spärlich die Quellen sind" ("how meager the sources are")[125] and realize what is so patently clear, that we do not have a complete history of the relations between these two nations. Even if the statement were correct that national enmity between Edom and Israel was unknown before the destruction of the First Temple,[126] should Amos, if he did have some harsh words to utter against that nation, have moderated his tone because in a couple of hundred years Edom would be worthy of an even sharper invective?[127] However, scholars have made some suggestions for a possible earlier dating of this oracle.[128] Moreover, recall that Amos in all of his charges and indictments is citing concrete incidents and specific episodes and is not reviewing entire periods.[129] Such an episode could obviously have occurred innumerable times. Finally, if the event referred to was during the sixth century, two characteristic elements of that period are lacking here: (1) there is no hint of Edom's aiding in the destruction of Judah, as is specifically stated in the undeniably late passages referred to previously in the other biblical books; and (2) there is no reference to Edom's appropriation of territory and domination of southern Judea after its collapse.[130] Furthermore, Edom as the only one of the traditional triad of Edom, Moab, and Ammon to be missing from this series would indeed be strange.

4. The Oracle against Judah[131]

Most scholars are in agreement that the oracle against Judah (in its entirety or at least the second part of v 4) does not belong to the original series. They adduce the following reasons to support their case:

(1) Amos was summoned to prophesy only against Israel (7:15) and is otherwise unconcerned with the crimes and fate of Judah. (The problem of the other references to Judah in 1:2; 6:1; 7:12; and 9:11 is discussed in situ.) To this it may be reasonably countered that the prophet also was not commissioned to level indictments against the foreign nations.[132] Even if the few other brief references to Judah are spurious (which is

123 Wolff, 160.

124 Hammershaimb, 38.

125 Rudolph, 134, thinks, however, that the end of v 11 is a later interpolation added after the fall of Jerusalem. See especially the general statement of J. Vollmer, *Geschichtliche Rückblicke und Motive in der Prophetie des Amos, Hosea und Jesaja* (BZAW 119; Berlin: de Gruyter, 1971) 7.

126 M. Haller, "Edom im Urteil der Propheten," in *Vom Alten Testament: Karl Marti zum siebzigsten Geburtstag* (ed. K. Budde; BZAW 41; Giessen: Töpelmann, 1925) 112, and the studies of Morgenstern, "Jerusalem" and "Amos Studies IV."

127 Hoffman, *Prophecies,* 168.

128 For example, Cripps, 282–83; Haran, "Observations," 207–12; Kaufmann, *Toledoth,* 6.61.

129 Hoffman, *Prophecies,* 168.

130 Ibid.

131 Among those who maintain its authenticity are Haran, "Rise and Decline," 274; Cripps; Driver; Kaufmann, *Toledoth,* 6.61; Hoffman, *Prophecies,* 168; Hammershaimb; Gordis, "Composition," 240–43; idem, "Studies in the Book of Amos," in *American Academy for Jewish Research Jubilee Volume, 1928–29/1978–79, PAAJR* 46–47 (ed. S. W. Baron and I. E. Barzilay; New York: American Academy for Jewish Research, 1980) 203–5; Botterweck, "Authentizität," 181; Rudolph, "Die angefochtenen Völkersprüche in Amos 1 und 2," in *Schalom. Studien zu Glaube und Geschichte Israels: Alfred Jepsen zum 71. Geburtstag* (ed. K.-H. Bernhardt; Arbeiten zur Theologie 1/46; Stuttgart: Calwer, 1971) 45–49, and in his commentary (except for the second half of v 4); S. Wagner, "Überlegungen zur Frage nach den Beziehungen des Propheten Amos zum Südreich," *TLZ* 96 (1971) 665–68; F. H. Seilhamer, "The Role of Covenant in the Mission and Message of Amos," in *A Light unto My Path: Old Testament Studies in Honor of Jacob M. Myers* (ed. H. N. Bream, R. D. Heine, and C. A. Moore; Gettysburg Theological Studies 6; Philadelphia: Temple University, 1974) 437–38. Compare also the hesitancy of Soggin, *Amos,* 45–46.

132 Compare Hammershaimb, 45–46.

highly doubtful), clearly the Book of Amos is almost completely devoid of other descriptions relating to the nations as well. Moreover, were he to have omitted an accusation against Judah, "so wäre bei dem ganzen tour d'horizon die Auslassung von Juda befremdlich gewesen; sie hätte gar zu leicht bei den nordisraelitischen Hörern den Eindruck nationalistischer Parteilichkeit erweckt." ("The omission of Judah from the entire *tour d'horizon* would have been strange. It would too easily have aroused the impression of a nationalistic bias in the northern Israelite audience.")[133] By not sparing even his own fellow Judean citizens from severe reproach, his denunciation becomes all the more poignant.

(2) It is further argued that an oracle against Judah would have led his hearers to anticipate and suspect a forthcoming one against Israel and thereby would have weakened his *pièce de résistance* and left it as a mere anticlimax. According to Wellhausen, the surprise is weakened when "das Gewitter schliesslich in Israel selbst einschlägt" ("the thunderstorm finally smashes into Israel itself").[134] Here, too, this psychological presupposition can best be countered with the words of Rudolph: "So ist das nicht stichhaltig, weil die ephraimitische Hörerschaft die Bescheltung und drohende Bestrafung Judas sicher mit derselben Genugtuung vernahm wie die Worte gegen die Fremdvölker." ("It is not valid, because the Ephraimite audience surely heard the accusation and threatened punishment of Judah with the same satisfaction as they did the words against the foreign nations.")[135]

(3) "Nor can we say that, because the formula is filled out in a different way from the majority of the oracles, the Judah oracle is spurious. The statistics show four long forms (Damascus, Gaza, Ammon, Moab) against three short (Tyre, Edom, Judah); out of seven only one type could have the majority. And who can be certain that Amos was bound to a rigid consistency of form?"[136]

(4) The oracle is also questioned on the grounds of its uniqueness: no moral or ethical crimes against human beings are listed, only those of a religious nature, that is, the rejection of God's laws and the worship of idols. However, a religious denunciation per se obviously does not certify lateness. This conceptual argument and the following literary arguments are nevertheless linked together by most scholars, pointing to a single later source—the Deuteronomic school. The combination of the repudiation of God's instructions and the following of other gods is certainly typical and characteristic of this school (for example, Deut 11:18; 2 Kgs 17:15). However, the possibility must also be reckoned with that, according to Amos, apostasy was actually the cardinal sin of Judah.[137] Furthermore, although the indictment is of a general theological character and does not cite specific wrongs (as in the other oracles), this accusation "das Übel in seiner Wurzel aufdeckt, und alle Sünden, auch die auf dem sittlichen und sozialen Gebiet, in sich schliesst" ("exposes the evil in its root and encompasses in it all the sins, including those in the moral and social realm").[138]

(5) The above point is reinforced by recourse to the unique vocabulary and phraseology of this literary unit, which are characteristic of the Deuteronomistic school.[139] Yet here again Rudolph's comments are insightful: "Natürlich haben wir hier Ausdrücke, die auch der deuteronomistischen Literatur geläufig sind . . . , aber der deuteronomische Stil war ja nicht eines Tages plötzlich da, sondern hat sich entwickelt." ("Naturally we have here expressions that are frequent also in the Deuteronomistic literature. . . . However, the Deuteronomic style did not spring up suddenly overnight, but itself underwent development.")[140] The style that later became the hallmark of the Deuteronomist had precedents and does appear occasionally in earlier sources (although, admittedly, not in a concentrated form).

133 Rudolph, 121.
134 Wellhausen, 71, quoted by Rudolph, 121 n 9.
135 Rudolph, 121; Schmidt, "Redaktion," 177 n 28.
136 Mays, 41, who nevertheless doubts its authenticity.
137 So Rudolph, 121, who also compares van Gelderen, 30, and Botterweck, "Authentizität," 181.
138 Rudolph, 121.
139 Almost all commentators following B. Duhm, *Die Theologie der Propheten als Grundlage für die innere Entwicklungsgeschichte der israelitischen Religion* (Bonn: Marcus, 1875) 119. See especially, Schmidt, "Redaktion," 174–77.
140 Rudolph; compare G. Farr, "The Language of Amos, Popular or Cultic?" *VT* 16 (1966) 318.

A review of the most often cited expressions is nevertheless in order:

(a) תּוֹרַת ה׳ ("the instruction of the Lord") is also found in Isa 5:24; 30:9, verses that are neither considered to be secondary nor under any Deuteronomistic influence. (Compare, too, Isa 1:10, תּוֹרַת אֱלֹהֵינוּ.) Furthermore, not only does the expression not appear in Deuteronomy but it is not even considered to be characteristic of the Deuteronomic style. תּוֹרָה in this verse is not, as it is in later literature, the written "Torah" of Moses but rather "instructions." (Compare also Josh 24:26; Isa 1:10.)

(b) The verb שׁמר along with the plural noun חוקים appears very frequently in Deuteronomy (for example, Deut 4:6; 6:24; 16:12) and in Deuteronomic passages, but it is also found in other verses that are definitely not related to this literature.[141]

(c) Another expression characteristic of this school is הָלַךְ אַחֲרֵי ("to follow [foreign gods]"), but here, too, it is attested in pre-Deuteronomic literature (such as Hos 2:7, 15; 5:11; 11:10). Weinfeld has further pointed out that "Deuteronomy and deuteronomic literature abound with terms originating in the diplomatic vocabulary of the Near East."[142] As an example he cites the cognate semantic and etymological Akkadian expression *arki . . . alāku* ("to follow after"), a phrase that clearly predates the Deuteronomic school.

(d) כְּזָבִים ("lies") is a cacophemism employed here for "false gods/idols." The expression is similar to other denigrating terms for idols known from this school, such as הֶבֶל ("vanity"; Deut 32:21; 1 Kgs 16:13, 26; 2 Kgs 17:15; Jer 2:5; 8:19; 14:22), שִׁקּוּצִים ("detestable things"), גִּלּוּלִים ("fetishes"), תּוֹעֵבָה ("abomination"), and תֹּהוּ ("nothingness").[143] Nevertheless, this specific dysphemism for idolatry is unique to Amos and unattested anywhere else in the Bible.[144] Caution is in order regarding far-reaching conclusions based on such a singular term.

In sum, the overall phraseology does resemble this later school of literature and has even been termed "proto-Deuteronomistic,"[145] but when the terms are examined individually the results are far from conclusive. The cautious remark of Hammershaimb bears repeating: "Finally, it is not certain that Amos is dependent on Deuteronomy in these verses."[146] Moreover, even a later Deuteronomic touch here or there does not mean that the oracle per se is not basically an integral part of the original series.

(6) Finally, a few argue, somewhat similarly to point 2 previously addressed, that without the oracle on Judah there would be a total of seven prophecies, with Israel being the seventh, a symbolic number representing climax, totality, and completion.[147] However, if Judah were included in the original pattern, then the oracle against Israel would be number eight, a number of seemingly no symbolic significance, and thereby upset the well-documented pattern of a repeated sixfold series reaching its culmination in the seventh round.[148] Furthermore, other sections in the book clearly show that Amos has a great fondness for expressing himself in literary patterns that comprise a heptad.[149]

However, an alternative numerical scheme, well attested in the Bible and in Ugaritic, serves the same purpose. In the pattern of seven-eight, eight functions as the paired number with seven in an ascending staircase parallelism[150] and, similar to seven, may even express the concept of culmination or climactic finish. Compare the following few examples:

(a) The period of ordination of Aaron took place for seven days: "You shall not go outside the Tent of Meeting for seven days. . . . For your ordination will require

141 For a list, see M. Weinfeld, *Deuteronomy and the Deuteronomic School* (Oxford: Clarendon, 1972) 336.

142 Ibid., 83, 332.

143 Ibid., 323.

144 In contrast to Farr, "Language," 318, who cites Ps 40:5.

145 Haran, *Ages and Institutions,* 291.

146 Hammershaimb, 46.

147 Compare F. Hehn, "Zur Bedeutung der Siebenzahl," in BZAW 41 (Giessen: Töpelmann, 1925) 128–36.

148 See the many examples collected by Y. Avishur, "The Forms of Repetition of Numbers Indicating Wholeness (3, 7, 10)—in the Bible and in Ancient Semitic Literature," *Beer-Sheva* 1 (1973) 1–55 (Heb.).

149 Compare, for example, Amos 2:6–7, 14–16; 3:3–8; 4:4–5, 6–11; 5:8–9, 21–23; 9:2–4. See Gordis, "Composition," 242–43, who accepts the authenticity of all the oracles, and idem, "The Heptad as an Element of Biblical and Rabbinic Style," *JBL* 62 (1943) 17–26. See Weiss, "Numerical Sequence," 420, for a list of studies.

150 One of the few to take note of this alternate numerical pattern is S. E. Loewenstamm (*The Tradition of the Exodus in Its Development* [Jerusalem: Magnes,

seven days" (Lev 8:33–35); and immediately thereafter, "on the eighth day. . . . For today the Lord will appear to you" (Lev 9:1–4).

(b) "You shall do the same with your cattle and your flocks; seven days it shall remain with its mother; on the eighth day you shall give it to me" (Exod 22:29). Compare also Lev 22:27.

(c) "Seven days you shall bring offerings by fire to the Lord. On the eighth day you shall observe a sacred occasion . . .; it is a solemn gathering" (Lev 23:36). Compare Lev 14:9–10; 15:13–14; 23:39; Num 6:9–10; 29:12–35; Neh 8:18; 2 Chr 7:9. Note also that the rite of circumcision takes place on the eighth day (Gen 17:12).

(d) In a noncultic framework, according to 1 Sam 16:10–11; 17:12, David was the eighth and youngest of his family—unlike 1 Chr 2:13–15, where he is presented as being the seventh.[151]

The eight in all these passages represents the climax. Moreover, it and its multiples also function as the consecutive numerical parallel counterpart to seven and its multiples, thereby representing a totality:

(a) Mic 5:4: "We shall raise against him [= Assyria] seven shepherds, eight princes of men."

(b) Eccl 11:2: "Distribute portions to seven or even[152] to eight."

(c) Ps 90:10: "Seventy years is the span of our life, and, given the strength, eighty years" *(NJPS)*.

(d) 1 Kgs 5:29 = 2 Chr 2:1, 17: "Seventy thousand porters and eighty thousand quarriers" (of Solomon).

This graduated sequential literary pattern is frequent in the literature of the ancient Near East. Compare the following examples from Ugaritic poetry:

(a) *šbʿ. šnt yṣrk. bʿl. / / ṯmn. rkb ʿrpt.*, "For seven years Baal failed; the rider in the clouds for eight" (*CTA* 19:i:42–44).

(b) "The house of a king is destroyed," *ḏšbʿ [ʾa]ḫm. lh. / / ṯmnt. bn ʾum*, "that had seven [bre]thren; eight mother's sons" (*CTA* 14:i:8–9).

(c) *tld. šbʿ. bnm. lk / / wṯmn tṯtmnm*, "She shall bear seven sons unto thee; yea eight shall she produce" (*CTA* 15:ii:23–24).

(d) *škb ʿmnh. šbʿ. lšbʿm / / tš[ʿ]ly. ṯmn. lṯmnym*, "He did lie with her seven and seventy (times); she was mounted eight and eighty (times)" (*CTA* 5:v:19–21).[153]

It is also attested in Akkadian: "The goddess . . . wept, whose seven brothers were killed *(7 aḫḫēšu dīku)*, whose eight brothers-in-law were laid out" *(8 ḫatānšu šunullu)*;[154] in Phoenician:[155] שבע צרתי ושמנה אשת בעל,

1965] 33 n 31 [Heb.]), who cites a few examples and also refers to C. H. Gordon, "Ugarit as a Link Between Greek and Hebrew Literature," *RSO* 29 (1954) 168. Compare, too, Roth, "Numerical Sequence," 300–311; and Y. Avishur (*Phoenician Inscriptions and the Bible: Studies in Stylistic and Literary Devices and Selected Inscriptions* [2 vols.; Jerusalem: E. Rubenstein, 1979] 1.53–54 [Heb.]), who lists the recent studies on staircase parallelism on p. 53 n 48. See also J. Limburg ("Sevenfold Structure in the Book of Amos," *JBL* 106 [1987] 220–21), who, however, does not bring any of the evidence presented here.

151 Compare the remarkable resemblance to this in an excerpt from the Sumerian Lugalbanda epic. See C. Wilcke, *Das Lugalbandaepos* (Wiesbaden: Harrassowitz, 1969) 49–50: "Damals waren es sieben (imin), waren es sieben. . . . (lugal.ban.da 8-kam.ma.ne.ne) Lugalbanda, der achte von ihnen." ("At that time there were seven, there were seven. . . . Lugalbanda (was) the eighth one of them.") (This text was brought to my attention by Dr. Victor Hurowitz.)

152 H. L. Ginsberg (*Koheleth Interpreted: A New Commentary on the Torah, the Prophets and the Holy Writings* [Tel Aviv and Jerusalem: Newman, 1961] 126 [Heb.]) suggests the possibility of reading here the verb וְגַמֵּל ("and render") instead of וְגַם, thereby creating a direct parallelism.

153 For other examples, see Avishur, *Phoenician Inscriptions*, 1.54. See also his article, "Word Pairs Common to Phoenician and Biblical Hebrew," *UF* 7 (1975) 29–30. For the reverse order in Akkadian, eight-seven, compare *EA* 84:4–6; and in Ugaritic, *CTA* 23:19–20.

154 A neo-Babylonian lament republished by W. G. Lambert, "A Neo-Babylonian Tammuz Lament," in *Studies in Literature from the Ancient Near East, by Members of the American Oriental Society Dedicated to Samuel Noah Kramer* (ed. J. M. Sasson) = *JAOS* 103/1 (1983) 211–15. The passage is found in reverse, line 7.

155 *KAI*, I.27:17–18, p. 6 (read *ṣrty*, not *ṣrsy*; compare vol. II, p. 46); Avishur, *Phoenician Inscriptions*, 2.254. T. H. Gaster, in his study of this incantation from Arslan Tash ("A Canaanite Magical Text," *Or* 11

"His seven co-wives and eight wives of Baal"; and in sixth-century C.E. Aramaic incantation texts from Nippur:[156] בשיבעא איסרין די לא מישתרין ובתמניה חתימין די לא מיתברין, "With the seven spells which may not be loosed; and the eight seals which may not be broken."

In sum, Amos may very well have resorted to this alternative literary pattern for two complementary reasons. First, it, too, expressed finality and climactic culmination. Because the more usual scheme ended with seven, however, his captive northern audience, who must have been enjoying every minute of his diatribe, would psychologically be in a state of mind that would lead them to believe that he had reached the climax of his fulmination with his oracle against Judah. The moment he continued with his eighth, the last and least expected oracle—for him the sole purpose of this extended prolegomenon—they would have been taken completely unaware.[157] Amos, who delights over and over again in making use of surprise endings,[158] thus forcefully and compellingly makes his final indictment.

Additional literary form-critical analysis helps to substantiate the authenticity of all the oracles.

Additional Literary and Form-Critical Criteria

(1) In a study of the repetition of numbers indicating wholeness, Avishur examined the formal phenomenon of having schemes, formulae, phrases, expressions, words, and particles repeated three, seven, or ten times in biblical and ancient Near Eastern literature.[159] Although each number by itself represents a totality, the smaller ones may also appear within the larger patterns. He correctly observes that emphasis on these repetitions has implications for the formal aspects of the literary units. As one of his examples, he presents Amos 1:3—2:5. His analysis of the numerical patterns is followed, along with his diagrammatic presentation of the literary units, in the table below. This artful interweaving of the repetition of a threefold pattern within a larger sevenfold pattern provides an additional literary criterion for determining the structural integrity and wholeness of this entire pericope.

The authenticity of all these oracles can be investigated, from a literary point of view, in yet another way. One of the reasons often given in commentaries against the originality of some of the units is that they exhibit variations in structure, phraseology, or style, and deviation from a formal scheme is assumed to imply different authorship. However, an examination of those oracles that, according to all scholars, are accepted as "original" —Damascus, Gaza,[160] Ammon, and Moab—discloses

7	ושלחתי אש	ושלחתי אש	והצתי אש	ושלחתי אש	ושלחתי אש	ושלחתי אש	ושלחתי אש
3			בחומת רבה		בחומת צר	בחומת עזה	
3	ביהודה	במואב		בתימן			
7	ואכלה	ואכלה	ואכלה	ואכלה	ואכלה	ואכלה	ואכלה
3			ארמנותיה		ארמנתיה	ארמנתיה	
3	ארמנות	ארמנות		ארמנות			
	ירושלם	הקריות		בצרה			
3		והכרתי שופט				והכרתי יושב	והכרתי יושב
3		מקרבה				מאשדוד	מבקעת־און
3/4		אמר ה׳	אמר ה׳			אמר אדני ה׳	אמר ה׳

[1942] 41–79), also cites a Mandean amulet with this same literary scheme (p. 63).

156 J. A. Montgomery, *Aramaic Incantation Texts from Nippur* (Philadelphia: University of Pennsylvania Museum, 1913) 195–200 and 105.

157 Compare E. M. Good (*Irony in the Old Testament* [Philadelphia: Westminster, 1965] 34): "The irony lies in the shock of the climax which is surely not intended to be noticed until too late."

158 Note that this is one of the literary characteristics of the style of Amos; compare Amos 3:2.

159 Avishur, "Forms," 12–13.

160 Because the oracle against the Philistines is accepted as original by most scholars today and because formally it is constructed similarly to the other three (and thus different from Tyre, Edom, and Judah), it is included here as authentic.

many internal and structural variations among themselves:

(a) The direct object of the fire:

Damascus: "I will release fire against the house of Hazael" (1:4).
Gaza: "I will release fire against the wall of Gaza" (1:7).
Ammon: "I will set fire to the wall of Rabbah" (1:14).
Moab: "I will release fire against Moab" (2:2).

Note that in the oracle against Damascus, the fire is directed against the house (that is, the kingdom); in Gaza and Ammon, against the capital city; and in Moab, against the country itself. Furthermore, whereas in Gaza and Ammon the fire attacks the *walls* of the city, in Damascus it is ignited against the *house,* and neither of these two is mentioned in Moab. The verb for "setting fire" also varies:[161] three times וְשִׁלַּחְתִּי is employed (Amos 1:4, 7; 2:2) and once וְהִצַּתִּי (Amos 1:14).

(b) The fire in two instances (Gaza and Ammon) devours "her fortresses," that is, those of the nation; in Damascus the object is the fortresses of the dynasty, and in Moab the fortresses of a leading city designated by name:

Damascus: "and it shall devour the fortresses of Ben-hadad."
Gaza: "and it shall devour its fortresses."
Ammon: "and it shall devour its fortresses."
Moab: "and it shall devour the fortresses of Kerioth."

(c) The introduction to the oracles against these four nations also differs:

Damascus: "For three transgressions of Damascus," that is, the capital of Aram.
Gaza: "For three transgressions of Gaza," that is, a leading Philistine city.
Ammon: "For three transgressions of the Ammonites," that is, the people.
Moab: "For three transgressions of Moab," that is, the country.

(d) In three of the four oracles, the reason or motivation of the crime is cited and is introduced by the particle ל or לְמַעַן:

Gaza: "They exiled an entire population (לְהַסְגִּיר) to deliver up to Edom."
Ammon: "They ripped open the pregnant women of Gilead (לְמַעַן) in order to enlarge their own territory."
Moab: "He burned the bones of the king of Edom for (לְ) lime."[162]

However, in the oracle against Aram, such a result clause is absent.

(e) The indictment is worded three times in the plural (Damascus, "because they threshed"; Gaza, "because they exiled"; Ammon, "because they ripped open") and once in the singular (Moab, "because he burned").

(f) The concluding formula also slightly varies: three times it is "said the Lord" (Damascus, Ammon, and Moab), but once it is "said my Lord God" (Gaza).

(g) Only in Moab are those to be punished not the subject of the final clause but the object: "I will cut off the ruler from its midst and slay all its officers along with him." Contrast this to:

Damascus: "And the people of Aram shall be exiled to Kir."
Gaza: "And the remnant of the Philistines shall perish."
Ammon: "Their king and his officers shall go into exile together."

(h) As part of the punishment, in three of the oracles (Damascus, Gaza, Moab) the verb וְהִכְרַתִּי ("I will cut off") is found; this verb is absent, however, in the oracle against Ammon.

The point here is that not one of the four assumedly "authentic" oracles is worded exactly the same as the others. The prophet has obviously set for himself a fixed literary framework, but within this framework he is at liberty to make minor stylistic changes. Although these variations do not alter the intent or meaning, they do succeed in offsetting a monotonous verbatim repetition of each oracle.[163] This feature of internal variations within a schematic pattern is also a well-known literary

161 Variation only for avoidance of monotony; the meaning remains the same. Compare Margulis (*Studies,* 85): "The variations—especially those of a 'lexical' nature—do serve, however, an important function, viz. to define the 'limits' of 'stereotypness.' The most highly-stereotyped expression may be said to coexist with a number of stylistic variants, in which form it is transmitted in tradition."

162 There are difficulties involved in translating "to lime" as many commentators do. When understood as a result clause, however, it makes perfect sense and is structurally similar to the other two oracles. See the commentary.

163 See also the pertinent remarks of D. N. Freedman ("Deliberate Deviation from an Established Pattern of Repetition in Hebrew Poetry as a Rhetorical

device in ancient Near Eastern literature.[164] In sum, variety in form does not necessarily point to different authorship and must not be used here as a yardstick for assuming lateness in some of the oracles.

Then again, were some of these oracles actually introduced later, one would naturally expect them to be stylistically harmonized among themselves, as well as with the "authentic" oracles. Yet here, too, differences crop up:

(a) The oracle against Tyre is against the city-state, whereas those against Edom and Judah are directed against the country proper.

(b) The punishments display minor stylistic variations:

Tyre:	"I will release fire against the wall of Tyre, and it will devour its fortresses" (1:10).
Edom:	"I will release fire against Teman, and it will devour the fortresses of Bozrah" (1:12).
Judah:	"I will release fire against Judah, and it will devour the fortresses of Jerusalem" (2:5).

(c) One of the crimes of Tyre is "because *they* handed over an entire population" (1:9); and of Judah, "because *they* have spurned" (2:4). However, the indictment against Edom is worded in the singular: "because *he* pursued his brother" (1:11).

If a later editor were responsible for these additional oracles, he naturally could have harmonized the differences and produced a literary unity. The stylistic variations are an integral part of the original corpus, however, and thus are not to be used as a criterion here for determining interpolations. Note, too, that some of the variations of the supposedly "interpolated" oracles are exactly the same as those of the "authentic" ones.

Another form-critical argument most often resorted to as a criterion for establishing the lack of authenticity of these three oracles is that their overall construction is decidedly different from the other four. This observation is correct and basic. However, in addition to the points made above, how else can one explain that, on the one hand, only in these three are multiple indictments made instead of the one charge found in the other four; and, on the other hand, the announcement of punishment is reduced to the basic formula ("to set fire against") instead of the descriptive enlargement that characterizes the threats against the other four?

First, "it is not probable that any Hebrew prophet wrote with the fear of the standards of German literary criticism before his eyes."[165] Thus he should not be put into a preconceived literary straitjacket. Furthermore, even this specific deviation can be explained as part of an intentional literary device employed by the prophet. Ward[166] suggests a "perfectly patterned alternation between two similar forms," which he designates "type A and type B." Type A oracles are those whose accusation contains one line and whose announcement of punishment contains three lines, along with the concluding formula. Type B oracles are those whose accusation consists of two lines and whose announcement of punishment is one line, without the concluding formula. Therefore, two oracles, Damascus and Gaza, belonging to type A, are followed by two, Tyre and Edom, that are type B; upon which again are found two type A oracles, Ammon and Moab, followed by two type B, Judah and Israel (the latter he designates "expanded type B"). There is no compelling reason, or even a convincing one, to doubt the originality of this alternating pairing of similarly styled oracles.[167]

This conclusion may be restated in other terms that once again point to an intentional pattern for the internal formulation of these oracles. Amos alternated his accusations from emphasis on the punishment to emphasis on the crimes. Thus he commences by elaborating on the punishment twice, continues with a descriptive expansion of the crimes of the next two nations, follows with two expanded threats, and concludes with an extensive listing of the crimes committed by Judah and Israel.

Device," in *Proceedings of the Ninth World Congress of Jewish Studies: Division A: The Period of the Bible* [Jerusalem: World Union of Jewish Studies, 1986] 1.45–52), who also cites two other examples of "deliberate deviations" from heptads in Amos 4:5 and 6:4. See also n 117 above.

164 See Avishur, "Forms," n 148 above.

165 W. F. Lofthouse, cited by Cripps, 282.

166 J. M. Ward, *Amos and Isaiah: Prophets of the Word of God* (Nashville and New York: Abingdon, 1969) 98–99. Compare Gordis, "Studies," 203.

167 Unfortunately V. Fritz ("Die Fremdvölkersprüche des Amos," *VT* 37 [1987] 26–38) still considers most of the oracles not to be original. This "nihilistic" approach denies Amos's authorship to almost everything related to the oracles against the nations

Variety thus is the spice of Amos's style. The pericope in toto should once again be recognized as the unique creation of the first of the literary prophets, whose poetic devices and rhetorical skill are ever a source of admiration.

4. The Graded Numerical Sequence

The pattern of the graded numerical sequence, commonly referred to as x/x+1, is a stylistic device well known from the literature of the Bible and the ancient Near East.[168] It can be employed in two different ways: to refer to an indefinite or approximate number, whether large or small; or to refer to a specific number, in which case the number appearing in the second colon, which functions as the poetic parallel to the first one, is the determining number. Both of these approaches have been applied to the introductory eightfold repetition of the three-four pattern in the oracles against the nations. Some exegetes interpret the ascending numbers to have an indefinite or approximate value, that is, for several transgressions or for approximately three or four;[169] others place the entire emphasis upon the final number, for four transgressions or for the fourth transgression.[170]

Weiss has convincingly shown, however, that the numerical pattern in Amos is sui generis, unique both stylistically and structurally.[171] When the graduated numbers are meant to signify an indefinite figure, no example or illustration is delineated;[172] however, in Amos specific transgressions are always enumerated. In contrast, when the literary device is employed to indicate a definite number (that is, the last one), it is always immediately illustrated by that very number of examples;[173] but in Amos there is no listing of four transgressions for any of the nations (at least from Damascus through Moab). Weiss further points out that all the other cases of this poetic device are constructed in "complete" or "incomplete" parallelism. If "complete," predicates are found in both halves of the parallel verse; if "incomplete," the sole predicate always appears in the first colon, which thereby constitutes "a complete unit in both syntax and thought."[174] This structure contrasts, however, with the pattern in the oracles of Amos, where the predicate appears only in the second colon, and the first part of the verse is thus left as an incomplete sentence. He also remarks that the sentence bears no evidence of parallelism, save for the two numbers themselves. In the light of these deviations from the standard pattern, Weiss reaches a novel solution. Because a well-known "compositional rule of poetry [is the] break-up of compound linguistic stereotypes into their two components, placing one in the first half of the verse and the

(p. 37).

168 This stylistic device has been repeatedly investigated. See Roth, "Numerical Sequence," 300–311; idem, *Numerical Sayings in the Old Testament* (SVT 13; Leiden: Brill, 1965); S. Gevirtz, *Patterns of the Early Poetry of Israel* (Studies in Ancient Oriental Civilization 32; Chicago: University of Chicago, 1963) 16–24; G. Sauer, *Die Sprüche Agurs* (BWANT 84; Stuttgart: Kohlhammer, 1963) 24–91; M. Weiss, "Numerical Sequence," 416–23; H. P. Rüger, "Die gestaffelten Zahlensprüche," 229–34. In addition, the following Hebrew articles should be noted: H. L. Ginsberg, "Towards the History of the Graded Number Sequence," in *Minḥa LeDavid: Dedicated to David Yellin* (Jerusalem: Vaʿad HaYovel, 78–82 [Heb.]; M. H. Segal, "On the Poetical Form of Biblical Poetry," *Tarbiz* 1 (1930) 16ff. (Heb.); idem, "A Study of the Forms of Biblical Poetry," *Tarbiz* 18 (1947) 142–45 (Heb.); Cassuto, *Biblical*, 2.18–29; S. E. Loewenstamm, "Studies in the Stylistic Patterns of Biblical and Ugaritic Literature," *Leš* 32 (1968) 27–36 (Heb.); Haran, "Biblical Studies," 109–36. See also Loewenstamm's note, "The Phrase '*X* (or) *X* Plus One' in Biblical and Old Oriental Laws," *Bib* 53 (1972) 543. Examples are also attested in Sumerian, Akkadian, Hittite, Aramaic, Greek, and especially Ugaritic literature.

Many scholars locate the provenance of this literary scheme in (folk) wisdom literature. However, influence of the wisdom genre upon Amos has been highly exaggerated.

169 For this interpretation, found in ancient Christian and medieval Jewish commentators, see Weiss, "Numerical Sequence," 416 n 2.

170 Ibid., 416 n 3. Haran ("Biblical Studies," 123–25) attempts to find rare examples where the determining number is the first one.

171 Weiss, "Numerical Sequence." The following is a summary of his presentation.

172 For example, 1 Sam 18:7; Mic 5:4; Ps 91:7.

173 Compare Prov 6:16; 30:15, 18, 21, 29; Job 5:19. See, too, Eccl 23:16; 25:7; 26:28; 50:25; Ahiqar lines 92–93.

174 Weiss, "Numerical Sequence," 417.

other in the second,"[175] he concludes that three and four are the two "most natural components of the number seven."[176] This then was the numerical figure the prophet had in mind, that is, because of *seven* transgressions, divine punishment would be immediately forthcoming. Seven, the well-known typological number symbolizing completeness and finality (which does appear elsewhere several times in Amos in literary units of heptads),[177] signifies "the whole, full sin. Judgment is pronounced on each nation because of its complete sin."[178] As further proof, Weiss contends that the oracle against Israel contains an exact enumeration of seven sins.[179] He is aware that his suggestion is an ad hoc exegesis because no other example of such a numerical pattern in the Bible or in the ancient Near East functions in this way, that is, that the total number is broken up into two of its component parts. Nevertheless, he counters by referring to a somewhat similar usage in which the "wholeness of a thing is demonstrated by two of its components and by two numbers" (for example, Judg 12:14; Job 1:3). He also supports his suggestion by referring to the phenomenon of hendiadys, by which two different components express a totality. Third and "most importantly, the novelty of expression is due to the poetic creativity of the prophet."[180]

However, there is no clear-cut indication in the other verses to which Weiss refers that the author intended to write a typological number that he subsequently broke down into two of its component parts. When he wished to write seventy, he wrote seventy, and thus there is no need to assume that he expressed seventy by forty and thirty. Of greater importance is the fact that there is no example of hendiadys that is structured stylistically like the three-four pattern in these oracles. Hendiadys, the literary device of "one by means of two," is a figure of speech whereby a "complex idea is expressed by two words connected by a complete conjunction," but it need not represent the sum total.[181]

Weiss's ad hoc solution has been further subjected to severe criticism by Zakovitch.[182] The latter first argues that the absence of a predicate in the first colon is no reason to deny the pattern of the graduated number scheme here. Amos is at liberty to make such changes. The fact that the verb is missing in the first colon, although unique to this specific graduated number scheme, is not unusual in biblical poetry, which provides many instances of parallel cola in which the predicate (either subject, object, or a combination of the two) is present only in the second colon but is understood to apply to the first colon as well by "backward attraction" (compare, for example, Pss 6:14; 145:5; Prov 7:6, 12; 8:2, 3).[183] The verse, moreover, does have a further indication of being poetical in design and thus parallel in purpose because it repeats the particle עַל in both stichs. As for the exact number of transgressions enumerated in the oracle against Israel, Zakovitch opts for four and not seven as Weiss opined.[184] He thus concludes that there is no reason to accept Weiss's interpretation that three-four originally was meant to imply the number seven. Instead, he connects the numerical scheme of three and four to the prophet's similar use of seven and eight (referring to the complete number of oracles against the nations and

175 See E. Z. Melamed, "Break-up of Stereotype Phrases as an Artistic Device in Biblical Poetry," in *Studies in the Bible* (ed. C. Rabin; Scripta Hierosolymitana 8; Jerusalem: Magnes, 1961) 115–53; reprinted in *Studies in the Bible, Presented to Professor M. H. Segal* (ed. J. M. Grintz and J. Liver; Publications of the Israel Society for Biblical Research 17; Jerusalem: Kiryat Sepher, 1964) 188–219 (Heb.).

176 Weiss, "Numerical Sequence," 419. He also notes (419 n 15) that this is the interpretation of Luther and Calvin. Compare also C. Stuhlmueller, "Amos, Desert-Trained Prophet," *BiTod* 1 (1962/63) 229; J.-L. Vesco, "Amos de Téqoa, défenseur de l'homme," *RB* 87 (1980) 488 n 15.

177 Compare, for example, Amos 2:6–7, 14–16; 4:4–5, 6–12; 5:8–9, 21–23; 9:1–4. See also Limburg ("Sevenfold," 217–22), who thinks that Weiss's suggestion is "worth reconsidering" (p. 222).

178 Weiss, "Numerical Sequence," 420.

179 See, however, n 184 below and the comments to Amos 2:6–8.

180 Weiss, "Numerical Sequence," 421–23.

181 Weiss's approach has also been criticized by Haran, "Biblical Studies," 128.

182 Zakovitch, *For Three,* 179–84. For a brief English summary, see pp. xiii–xiv.

183 Haran ("Biblical Studies," 127) suggests several other examples, including 2 Sam 1:22; Jer 47:3; Ps 12:6.

184 Among others who enumerate four transgressions in the oracle against Israel, compare, for example, Segal, "Poetical Form," 16–17; idem, "Study of Forms," 144; Weiser, *Profetie,* 106; Gottwald, *Kingdoms,* 113; Farr, "Language," 320. However, others maintain that even though several transgres-

Israel). Both are intended as climax couplets. Three-four thus indicates a complete accumulation of sins. Although the Deity may have been initially ready to relent, when the accounting finally reached the peak of three-four, he no longer was willing to withhold or revoke his retributive punishment.[185]

Zakovitch here is partially influenced by the unique approach to this problem offered by Seeligmann.[186] The latter suggested that the first four visions of Amos (7—8), which, according to his interpretation, chronologically precede the oracles against the nations, provided the ideological background for this novel numerical pattern. The prophet, drawing from his own personal experience based on his visions, concluded that God was ready to forgive Israel once or twice (the first two visions) but not a third or fourth time (the second two visions). So here, as well, as soon as the individual nation acquired a debit of three or four transgressions, the wrath of God could no longer be placated.

First of all, however, is a serious question of whether Seeligmann's basic assumption is correct, that is, whether the visions are to be understood chronologically prior to the oracles against the nations. Because no convincing proof exists for this conclusion, there is no reason to assume that Amos created this literary pattern based on his own prior personal experience. Even if the visions did precede the oracles, Rudolph's doubts are still in order: "Nur kann man fragen, ob diese einmalige Erfahrung in bezug auf Israel für den Propheten ausreichte, um daraus ein allgemeines Gesetz des göttlichen Handelns zu machen, das auch auf die Heidenwelt anwendbar war." ("One can only ask whether this single experience in reference to Israel was sufficient for the prophet to formulate from it a general law of divine action which was applicable to the pagan world as well.")[187]

Another view, popular among medieval Jewish commentators (with some representatives yet today),[188] should also be noted but rejected. According to this interpretation, the prophet actually intended to say the following: "For three sins of (the specific nation) I will forgive; *but* for four (that is, the fourth) I shall not." The *waw* in וְעַל is understood as an adversative, and the parallelism of the verse becomes antithetical. However, the prophet says "four" and not "fourth." Furthermore, as Haran has shown, in all cases of the ascending numerical pattern, the parallelism is of a synonymous nature whereby the second number expresses an identical concept and not an opposite one or, as stated previously, is the natural numerical parallel to the first number and, as such, complements and climaxes it.[189]

What then is the purpose and meaning of the three-four pattern here? Weiss's statement that "this type of composition, not being a creation *ex nihilo*, was yet an *ad hoc* one"[190] is correct. Amos wanted to state as poignantly as possible that the transgression(s) enumerated was (were) the most vile, abominable, and despicable of all, thereby causing God to intervene directly and execute punishment. It thus was in a real sense the "complete" sin. However, it is neither "the last of four crimes, the one which tips, indeed, overloads the scale,"[191] nor does it imply that Amos "does not itemize the first three

sions are listed, because only one is introduced by the particle עַל, only one crime is originally intended; compare Cassuto, *Biblical*, 27 n 19. Compare also Haran ("Biblical Studies," 128–30), who denies the organic connection of vv 7ff. with the original oracle against Israel. See comments to Amos 2:6–8.

185 Zakovitch, *For Three*, 175–79.

186 Seeligmann, "History," 129.

187 Rudolph, 129.

188 This interpretation, found already in Rabbinic literature (compare Babylonian Talmud, Yoma 86b) was common in medieval Jewish commentaries (many of which actually enumerated the specific occasions of the transgressions); for example, Saadiah Gaon (as quoted, but not accepted, by Ibn Ezra); Rashi; Joseph Kara; Kimchi; Abarbanel; Eliezer Beaugency. So, too, the Karaite commentators, Daniel al-Ḳumissi, *Commentarius in Librum Duodecim Prophetarum* (Jerusalem: Mekize Nirdamim, 1957) 32; and Yefet ben ʿAli, who refers it to the fourth generation. A few moderns also adopted this interpretation; compare Tur-Sinai, *HaLashon*, 1.82; and B. K. Soper, "For Three Transgressions and for Four: A New Interpretation of Amos 1:3, etc.," *ExpTim* 71 (1959–1960) 86–87. Compare, as well, G. Richter, *Erläuterungen zu dunkeln Stellen in den kleinen Propheten* (Gütersloh: Bertelsmann, 1914) 66f.

189 Haran, "Biblical Studies," 135–36.

190 Weiss, "Numerical Sequence," 423.

191 Wolff, 138. See, too, his study *Amos the Prophet*, 34–44. Compare also J. Lindblom, "Wisdom in the Old Testament Prophets," in *Wisdom in Israel and in the Ancient Near East: Presented to Prof. H. H. Rowley by the Society for Old Testament Study* (ed. M. Noth and D. W.

crimes but rather jumps to the fourth."[192] Rather, it is to be understood as a novel poetical way by which the prophet expresses the concepts of totality and climax. He resorts to the use of the typological number three and its functional parallel four, in order to signify completion. This numerical pattern of three-four is also well attested elsewhere as designating a climactic nature.[193] Other biblical examples that display such a threefold repetition climaxing on the fourth round include Jotham's parable, Judg 9:8–15; the seduction of Samson, Judg 16:6–20; the ordination of Samuel, 1 Sam 3:4–15; and the tragedies of Job, Job 1:14–19. Note, too, that Noah first sends out a raven and then three times a dove. On the fourth occasion, the bird does not return to the ark (Gen 8:7–12).[194] Compare also the Balaam episode in Num 22:22ff. Amos is thus employing the literary scheme three-four in the same manner as he uses seven-eight (the number of oracles), that is, both three and seven are typologically complete numbers,[195] for which four and eight provide the complementary numerical parallelism and also add a climactic dimension.

One additional aspect to the selection of this specific pattern has been all but overlooked.[196] The choice of these two specific numbers, עַל־שְׁלֹשָׁה וְעַל־אַרְבָּעָה, may have been influenced, in an associate imitative manner, by the phrase עַל־שִׁלֵּשִׁים וְעַל־רִבֵּעִים (not as a literal adaptation "for the third and fourth generations," but as a literary midrashic one; note the repetition of the particle וְעַל preceding both of them), which in all its occurrences (Exod 20:5; 34:7; Num 14:8; Deut 5:9) expresses the length and finality of God's retributive justice and punishment.[197] It would thus by extension in Amos serve as a fitting introductory formula explicating the forthcoming imminent action of God against those nations who have completely overstepped the bounds of all humanity by grievously offending against their fellow human beings.

Thomas; SVT 3; Leiden: E. J. Brill, 1955) 202–3; S. Terrien, "Amos and Wisdom," 109–10; Haran, "Biblical Studies," 135; Driver, 132–33; Tur-Sinai, *HaLashon,* 1.83; and idem, *Peshuṭo shel Miqra* 3/2 (Jerusalem: Kiryat Sepher, 1967) 450 (Heb.).

192 Mays, 24.

193 See Zakovitch *(For Three),* who has studied this phenomenon in great detail. Compare also S. Talmon, "The Book of Daniel" in *The Literary Guide to the Bible* (ed. R. Alter and F. Kermode; Cambridge, MA: Collins, 1987) 347–49.

194 It has been almost entirely overlooked that this stylistic device functions also in Mesopotamian literature. The Cuthean legend of Naram-Sin relates that on the first, second, and third years he sent out myriads of troops, "but none of them returned alive." Then, when "the New Year Festival of the fourth year [arrived] . . ." *(ša rebūti šatti [ina kašādi]).* See O. R. Gurney, "The Sultantepe Tablets IV: The Cuthean Legend of Naram-Sin," *Anatolian Studies* 5 (1955) 93–113. The pertinent lines are on p. 103: 84–87 and p. 105:104.

Another example may be brought from the Atrahasis epic. Enlil resolved three times (by plague, famine, and drought) to reduce the number of humankind that had multiplied and whose noise disturbed his sleep. However, as he failed (actually he was thwarted by different means), he finally decided to wipe out the entire human race by a flood. See W. G. Lambert and A. R. Millard (*Atra-Ḫasis: The Babylonian Story of the Flood* [Oxford: Clarendon, 1969]), and compare also the Gilgamesh epic, IX:146–56. For the seven-eight climax, see C. Wilcke, *Das Lugalbandaepos* (Wiesbaden: Harrassowitz, 1969) 49–50.

195 See Avishur ("Forms," 3–11), who brings multiple examples. Avishur also occasionally remarks on the climactic dimension of the three-four and seven-eight numerical patterns. See his remarks on pp. 8–10.

196 With the exception of Zakovitch (*For Three,* 175–228), who also studies this pattern in connection with the concept of retribution. For an English summary, see pp. xiii–xv.

197 Compare likewise the words of God to Abraham when he contracts a covenant with him. He informs him that his offspring will "be enslaved and oppressed four hundred years. . . . And they shall return in the fourth generation, for the iniquity of the Amorites will not be fulfilled until then" (Gen 15:16).

Amos

1 Superscription and Motto

1 The words of Amos, one of the sheep breeders
from Tekoa, who prophesied concerning
Israel during the reigns of Uzziah king of
Judah and Jeroboam son of Joash king of
Israel, two years before the earthquake.
2 He proclaimed:
The Lord roars from Zion
And thunders from Jerusalem.
The shepherds' pastures dry up
And the summit of Carmel withers.

■ **1** The introductory title to the book supplies a wealth of information: the prophet's name, his professional occupation, his home, and the time of his prophetic activity. Most exegetes, however, consider the superscription to be the product of two stages,[1] that is, an original introduction: "The words of Amos from Tekoa who prophesied[2] concerning Israel two years before the earthquake"; and a later expansion: "who was one of the sheep breeders . . . during the reigns of Uzziah king of Judah and Jeroboam son of Joash king of Israel." This analysis is based on the two relative clauses (אֲשֶׁר), which may refer to two different antecedents, as well as the two different dates cited at the end of the verse, with the synchronistic one credited to a Deuteronomic editor.[3] The final product supplies the reader with the most complete superscription to be found in all of prophetic literature.

The verse begins, "The words of Amos" (דִּבְרֵי עָמוֹס). Such an introduction is also found at the beginning of wisdom collections (דִּבְרֵי חֲכָמִים, Prov 22:17; דִּבְרֵי אָגוּר, Prov 30:1; דִּבְרֵי לְמוּאֵל, Prov 31:1; דִּבְרֵי קֹהֶלֶת, Eccl 1:1), historical works (דִּבְרֵי שְׁלֹמֹה, 1 Kgs 11:41; דִּבְרֵי נְחֶמְיָה, Neh 1:1), and a prophetic book (דִּבְרֵי יִרְמְיָהוּ, Jer 1:1).[4]

His name: The prophet's name appears without a patronymic,[5] similar to the superscriptions to the prophetic collections of Obadiah, Micah, Nahum, Habbakuk, Haggai, and Malachi. The *qatul*-form[6] of the name, עָמוֹס, is attested in several other personal names in the Bible; compare, for example, עָכוֹר, Josh 7:24; זָנוֹחַ, Josh 15:34; צָדוֹק, 2 Kgs 15:33; אָמוֹן, 2 Kgs 21:18ff.; אָמוֹץ, Isa 1:1; עָמוֹק, Neh 12:7, 20.[7] Although the name עָמוֹס appears only as the name of the prophet (Amos 1:1; 7:8, 10–12; 8:2), the root עמס is found affixed to a theophoric element in the personal name עֲמַסְיָה, 2 Chr 17:16. (Compare similarly the hypocoristic pattern צָדוֹק alongside צִדְקִיָּה, for example, 1 Kgs 22:11 and Jer 27:12; צִדְקִיָּהוּ, 1 Kgs 22:24; 2 Kgs 24:17; Jer 29:21; 36:12; and יְהוֹצָדָק, for example, Hag 1:1.) The same stem appears in the proper names עֲמָשָׂא; 2 Sam 17:25; עֲמָשַׂי, 1 Chr 6:10; and עֲמַשְׁסַי, Neh 11:13.[8] The name is also documented extrabiblically on two seals (Phoenician? Transjordanian?) עמסאל,[9] as well as in personal names: Phoenician and Punic (עמס, עמסמלך, מלקרתעמס, בעלעמס,

1 Compare, for example, Harper, 1–2; Mays, 18; Hammershaimb, 19; Wolff, 117; Rudolph, 109–10, who analyze the respective component parts in detail.

2 According to Rudolph (110), even the phrase אֲשֶׁר חָזָה, which he interprets absolutely as "welcher schaute = als Seher auftrat" ("who saw = he appeared as a seer"), is secondary. For further references, compare p. 110 n 3. Amos is also called a חֹזֶה by the priest Amaziah (7:12).

3 Compare Wolff, 121.

4 Compare also 2 Sam 20:17; Job 31:40.

5 This in no way needs to be interpreted as being of "lowly birth"; contrast Koehler, 35; Terrien, "Amos and Wisdom," 114 n 13.

6 *BLe* 466n‴.

7 See M. Noth, *Die israelitischen Personennamen im Rahmen der gemeinsemitischen Namengebung* (BWANT 3/10; Stuttgart: Kohlhammer, 1928) 38, 178f.

8 M. Noth (*Die israelitischen Personennamen*, 253b) correctly interprets the name as a conflation of two variant spellings, one with a *samech* (ס) and the other with a *sin* (שׂ).

9 See N. Avigad, "Some Unpublished Ancient Seals," *BIES* 25 (1961) 241 (Heb.), לנדבאל בן עמסאל; and

אשמנעמס),[10] Amorite (*Yaḫmus-AN* [= *EL*/*IL*]),[11] and Ugaritic (*bn* ʿ*ms*).[12] The basic meaning of the verb עמס is to "carry," that is, "to protect, preserve, save."[13] Thus עָמוֹס means "carried, protected [by the Lord]."[14]

His occupation: Amos is described here as being one of the נֹקְדִים.[15] That a נוֹקֵד is not identical with an ordinary רוֹעֶה ("shepherd") is evident from 2 Kgs 3:4, where King Mesha of Moab is reported to be a נוֹקֵד who "used to pay as tribute to the king of Israel (the wool of) a hundred thousand lambs and the wool of a hundred thousand rams."[16] The reference is to a "herdsman/a breeder of cattle and sheep."[17] This profession is amply documented in Mesopotamian sources from Old Babylonian to neo-Babylonian times (Akk. *nāqidu*)[18] and is found as well in Ugaritic, *nqdm.* In both there is also evidence of an "overseer of the herdsmen" (Akk. *rab nāqidī*;[19] Ugar. *rb nqdm*[20]). Despite the appearance of the latter alongside a *rb khnm* ("chief of priests") as well as the listing of *nqdm* in a series of vocational groups before the classes of *khnm* and *qdšm,*[21] there is no reason to conclude that such an individual was a cultic functionary (who practiced augury)[22] or belonged to the temple personnel.[23]

---

idem, "A Group of Hebrew Seals," in Eretz Israel 9 (*W. F. Albright Volume;* ed. A. Malamat; Jerusalem: Israel Exploration Society, 1968) 8 (Heb.), לאלתמך בן עמסאל. He dates the seals between the eighth and seventh centuries B.C.E. For the latter (found in Amman), compare also F. Vattioni, "I Sigilli Ebraici," *Bib* 50 (1969) 380 no. 201; and S. H. Horn, "A Seal from Amman," *BASOR* 205 (1972) 43–45.

10 See F. L. Benz, *Personal Names in the Phoenician and Punic Inscriptions* (Rome: Pontifical Biblical Institute, 1972) 72–73, 97, 141, 172, 173.

11 See H. B. Huffmon, *Amorite Personal Names in the Mari Texts: A Structural and Lexical Study* (Baltimore: Johns Hopkins University, 1965) 198. Compare also Noth, "Remarks on the Sixth Volume of Mari Texts," *JSS* 1 (1956) 325; reprinted in idem, *Aufsätze zur biblischen Landes- und Altertumskunde* (2 vols.; Neukirchen: Neukirchener Verlag, 1971) 2.237.

12 *UT* 2021:3 = *KTU* 4.335,3. For such lists without patronymics, see A. Alt, "Menschen ohne Namen," in idem, *Kleine Schriften zur Geschichte des Volkes Israel* (3 vols.; München: C. H. Beck, 1959) 3.198–213.

13 For studies of the root עמס in Hebrew, Ugaritic, Phoenician, and Punic, see M. Held, "The Root *ZBL*/*SBL* in Akkadian, Ugaritic and Biblical Hebrew," in *Essays in Memory of E. A. Speiser* (ed. W. W. Hallo; New Haven: Yale University, 1968) = *JAOS* 88 (1968) 94 n 89; J. C. Greenfield, "Scripture and Literature: The Literary and Rhetorical Element in Some Early Phoenician Inscriptions," in *Near Eastern Studies in Honor of William Foxwell Albright* (ed. H. Goedicke; Baltimore and London: Johns Hopkins University, 1971) 260–63; Y. Avishur, "Word Pairs," 27; and especially J. J. Stamm, "Der Name des Propheten Amos und sein sprachlicher Hintergrund," in *Prophecy: Essays Presented to Georg Fohrer on His Sixty-fifth Birthday, 6 September 1980* (ed. J. A. Emerton; BZAW 150; Berlin and New York: de Gruyter, 1980) 137–42.

14 Stamm ("Der Name des Propheten Amos," 142) remarks that since the *qatul*-form, although usually a passive, can also bear an active sense, the name of the prophet may have a double sense: "Der (von Jahwe) Getragene" ("he who is carried/supported [by Yahweh]") and "Der Träger" ("the carrier/supporter"). In Rabbinic literature the name of the prophet was usually interpreted as "encumbered, weighted" and explained as his having a speech defect, that is, heavy tongued, lisping, stutterer. This interpretation, in turn, is then related to some assumed anomalies in his speech that appear in Amos 5:11, בּוֹשַׁסְכֶם, and 7:14, בּוֹלֵס. Compare, for example, Lev Rab 10:2; Eccl Rab 1:2.

15 Hebrew בַּנֹּקְדִים; compare 1 Sam 10:11, 12, הֲגַם שָׁאוּל בַּנְּבִיאִים ("Is Saul too among the prophets?").

16 Reconstructing the word in the partially broken section at the end of the Moabite Mesha inscription, lines 30–31, has also been suggested: "I lead [my נקדי there in order to tend the] sheep." See *KAI,* II.179.

17 Compare the various ancient versions that relate the word to cattle and sheep herdsmen: α', ἐν ποιμνιοτρόφοις ("among shepherds"); σ', ἐν τοῖς ποιμέσιν ("among the shepherds"); other Greek versions, ἐν τοῖς κτηνοτρόφοις ("among the cattle-keepers"). S translated it by the same root, נקדא, and T rendered מָרֵי גִתִּין ("owners of herds, cattlemen").

18 See *CAD, N,* I.333–35. Sumerian *na.gada* is a loanword from the Akkadian. For an example of a "shepherd" (*rē*ʾ*û*) being subordinate to a *nāqidu* in a neo-Babylonian text, see M. San Nicolò, "Materialien zur Viehwirtschaft in den neubabylonischen Tempeln," *Or* 17 (1948) 284f. Compare, too, the Arabic *naqada,* which defines a particular kind of sheep, and *naqqādu,* one who watches over this type of sheep, that is, a shepherd. In a Sumerian lexical list, Izi G 254–55, the word also defines a "lead ox."

19 *CAD, N,* I. 335.

20 *CTA* 6:vi:55.

21 *CTA* 71:71. For a review of the various opinions held in Ugaritic, see T. Yamashita, "Noqed," in *Ras Shamra Parallels: The Texts from Ugarit and the Hebrew Bible* (ed. L. R. Fisher; AnOr 50; Rome: Pontifical

Amos himself later states (7:14) that he was a בּוֹקֵר ("cattle breeder") who was in charge of flocks of "sheep and goats" (צֹאן).[24] This is similar to Akkadian sources in which the *nāqidu* is also said to be in charge of both cattle and sheep and goats. Compare, for example, "If a man hires a herdsman (*nāqidu*) to herd cattle or sheep and goats (*ana alpī u ṣēnī re'îm*)."[25]

His place: Tekoa, about five miles south of Bethlehem, on the border of the cultivated land to the west and the wilderness to the east[26] (called the "wilderness of Tekoa," 2 Chr 20:20, which was part of the wilderness of Judea) was well suited as a residence for Amos's secular profession.[27]

His period: There is a double dating for the period when Amos "prophesied (חָזָה) concerning Israel" (יִשְׂרָאֵל).[28] The first is the common synchronistic dating[29] by the reigns of the kings of Judah (Uzziah, 785–733) and Israel (Jeroboam ben Joash,[30] 789–749). The second, however, is unique. It records his activity in relation to a cataclysmic event in nature: "two years before the earthquake" (הָרָעַשׁ).[31] Most exegetes relate this earthquake to the one attested at stratum VI of Hazor and dated to around 760 B.C.E.[32] Because earthquakes are not rare in Israel and have occurred at all times,[33] this one must have been extremely violent and unparalleled; it not only was used for dating this prophetic book but also was referred to hundreds of years later by the prophet Zechariah (Zech 14:4–5): "On that day, he [the Lord] will set his feet on the Mount of Olives, near Jerusalem on the east; and the Mount of

Biblical Institute, 1975) 2.63–64; M. Dietrich and O. Loretz, "Die ugaritische Berufsgruppe der *NQDM* und das Amt des *RB NQDM*," *UF* 9 (1977) 336–37; and P. C. Craigie, "Amos the *nōqēd* in the Light of Ugaritic," *SR* 11 (1982) 29–33. Craigie concludes that the word in Ugaritic and in Amos refers to a "manager of sheep herds."

22 In contrast to M. Bič ("Der Prophet Amos—Ein Häpatoskopos?" *VT* 1 [1951] 293–96), who defines Amos as a hepatoscoper. This interpretation was totally refuted by A. Murtonen ("The Prophet Amos—A Hepatoscoper?" *VT* 2 [1952] 170–71 [responded to by Bič, "*Maštîn Beqîr*," *VT* 4 (1954) 413–15]); H. J. Stoebe, "Der Prophet Amos und sein bürgerlicher Beruf," *WuD* 5 (1957) 160–81; S. Segert, "Zur Bedeutung des Wortes *Nōqēd*," in *Hebräische Wortforschung: Festschrift zum 80. Geburtstag von W. Baumgartner* (ed. B. Hartmann and others; SVT 16; Leiden: Brill, 1967) 279–83; J. Wright, "Did Amos Inspect Livers?" *AusBR* 23 (1975) 3–11.

23 In contrast to Kapelrud, *Central Ideas*, 5–7, 69.

24 Compare Rudolph, 114, "Damit wäre auch geklärt, warum *noqed* sowohl Rinder- als auch Schafhalter bedeuten kann." ("This would also explain why *noqed* can mean not only a cattle owner but also a sheep owner.")

25 *LH* 261:21–24. For further examples, see *CAD, N*, I.333–35.

26 For Tekoa, today *Ḫirbet Teqūʿa*, see *EM* 8.924–26 (Heb.); V. R. Gold, "Tekoa," *IDB* 4.527–29. Both the place name and the gentilic appear seven times apiece in the Hebrew Bible (and once more in G's addition to Josh 15:59).

27 There is no need to attempt to find a northern location for Tekoa, as was already suggested by Kimchi in medieval times (compare his comments to this verse); H. Schmidt, "Die Herkunft des Propheten Amos," in *Beiträge zur alttestamentliche Wissenschaft: Karl Budde zum siebzigsten Geburtstag* (ed. K. Marti; BZAW 34; Giessen: Töpelmann, 1920) 158–71; S. Speier, "Bemerkungen zu Amos," *VT* 3 (1953) 305–6. Compare also L. Randellini, "Ricchi e Poveri nel Libro del Profeta Amos," *SBFLA* 2 (1951–1952) 9 n 8.

28 G, Ιερουσαλημ ("Jerusalem") is probably a scribal error based on an abbreviation; compare Harper, 2; Maag, *Text*, 1; Wolff, 116.

29 This is the usual way in which prophetic superscriptions are worded. For the various different opinions as to the regnal dates, consult the chart provided by H. Tadmor, "Chronology," *EM* 4.262 (Heb.).

30 The patronymic is added so as to distinguish this king (Jeroboam II) from the founder of the northern dynasty, Jeroboam ben Nebat (Jeroboam I).

31 Compare, for example, Ezek 38:19; Zech 14:5.

32 See Y. Yadin, *Hazor II: An Account of the Second Season of Excavations, 1956* (Jerusalem: Magnes, 1960) 24–26, 36–37. J. A. Soggin ("Das Erdbeben von Amos 1:1 und die Chronologie der Könige Ussia und Jotham von Judah," *ZAW* 82 [1970] 117–21) also relates this to the tradition found in Josephus, *Antiquities* IX. 222–27, who connects the earthquake with the cultic transgression of Uzziah, king of Judah, and the beginning of the coregency of Jotham.

33 See D. H. Kallner-Amiran ("A Revised Earthquake Catalogue of Palestine," *IEJ* 1 [1950–1951] 223–46 and *IEJ* 2 [1952] 48–65) for data relating to earthquakes in Israel for the last two thousand years.

Olives shall split from east to west, and one part of the Mount shall shift to the north and the other to the south, [forming] a huge gorge. And the Valley in the Hills shall be stopped up . . .;[34] it shall be stopped up as it was stopped up as a result of the earthquake in the days of King Uzziah of Judah."[35] The occurrence of this earthquake, which was interpreted as a fulfillment of some of his prophetic oracles,[36] most probably authenticated his being accepted as a true prophet and thus was cited in the introduction to his book.

■ **2** Verse 2,[37] consisting of two bicola narrating an audition of the Lord[38] and its concomitant effects, is often referred to as the motto of the Book of Amos.[39] Its authenticity, nevertheless, has been challenged on the basis of the mention of both "Zion"[40] and "Jerusalem" (which do not appear together elsewhere in the oracles of Amos). It is usually ascribed to a Judean redactor who, it is assumed, was responsible for including a few interpolations pertaining to Judah in this prophetic book whose message is otherwise directed entirely to northern Israel.[41] However, several indications point to the originality of the passage.[42] The vocabulary, as well as the

34 Reading וְנִסְתַּם ("shall be stopped up") along with T and G, ἐμφραχθήσεται instead of Masoretic וְנַסְתֶּם ("you shall flee").

35 According to J. Milgrom ("Did Isaiah Prophesy during the Reign of Uzziah?" *VT* 14 [1964] 178–82), Isaiah drew upon this very earthquake for his description of the eschatological quake of Isa 2:10ff.

36 Compare, for example, Amos 9:1.

37 The verb וַיֹּאמַר ("he proclaimed") serves as the transitional link between the superscription of the book and this verse; compare Deut 33:2; 2 Sam 22:2; Hos 1:2; Ps 18:2.

38 Yahweh, the personal name of the Lord of Israel, is significantly and emphatically the first word uttered by the prophet. Compare similarly in other theophanies: Deut 33:2; Judg 5:4; Mic 1:3; Hab 3:3; Ps 68:8.

39 For a thorough and comprehensive study of this verse and its manifold implications, as well as its relation to the variant formulations in Jeremiah and Joel, see M. Weiss, "On the Traces of a Biblical Metaphor," *Tarbiz* 34 (1964–1965) 107–28, 211–23, 303–18 (Heb.); idem, "Methodologisches über die Behandlung der Metapher, dargelegt an Amos 1,2," *TZ* 23 (1967) 1–25. For its origin in Amos, see M. Weinfeld, "The Change in the Conception of Religion in Deuteronomy," *Tarbiz* 31 (1962) 13 and n 49 (Heb.).

Among those who have designated the verse as the motto of the entire book (or of the following oracle), see, for example, Hammershaimb, 19; Harper, 9; Fosbroke, 777; Ward, *Amos,* 19 n 4; Rudolph, 117; Pfeifer, "Denkformenanalyse," 70; or as the overture to the book, see, for example, Harper, 9–10; Cripps, 115; Marti, 157; Robinson-Horst, 75; Weiser, *Profetie,* 85–86; Mays, 21; Schmidt, "Redaktion," 171 n 9; Botterweck, "Authentizität," 177–78.

A few exegetes connect this verse directly with v 1; compare, for example, Marti, 157, and A. B. Ehrlich, *Randglossen zur Hebräischen Bibel* (7 vols.; Leipzig: Hinrichs, 1912) 5.227. Many interpret it as an introduction to the oracles against the nations; see, for example, Wellhausen, 67; Nowack, 121; J. Lindblom, *Prophecy in Ancient Israel* (Philadelphia: Fortress, 1965) 116; Bentzen, "Ritual Background," 95–96; Kapelrud, *Central Ideas,* 17–18; Farr, "Language," 313–14; O. Eissfeldt, *The Old Testament: An Introduction* (tr. P. R. Ackroyd; New York and Evanston: Harper & Row, 1965) 398; Tur-Sinai, *HaLashon,* 1.82; Kaufmann, *Toledoth,* 3.70 n 1; Haran, "Rise and Decline," 272; idem, "Biblical Studies," 129.

For those who view it as a self-contained entity, see Neher, *Amos,* 11–14; Maag, *Text,* 3–4; Robinson-Horst, 75; Weiss, "Traces," 109. For other possible interpretations, see K. Budde, "Amos 1:2," *ZAW* 30 (1910) 37–41; idem, "Amos," 50–54; Sellin, 196–97.

For various views of the literary function of the verse, see Weiss, "Traces," 305. For the different opinions of the relationship between the first and second halves of the verse as well as the interpretation of the metaphor as the sound of thunder, a thunderstorm, an earthquake, a sirocco, or a combination of all the above, see Weiss, "Traces," 109–10, 126 n 117. Note should also be made of the literary association between the רַעַשׁ in v 1 and the "roaring" in this verse.

40 For the appearance of God from Zion, compare Ps 50:2. Herein the centrality and preeminence of Zion/Jerusalem are highlighted.

41 Compare, for example, the arguments of Wolff, 121.

42 Among those who claim the originality of the verse, see van Hoonacker; Duhm, "Anmerkungen," 7; Sellin, 197; Robinson-Horst, 75; Deden, 123–24; I. P. Seierstad, "Erlebnis und Gehorsam beim Propheten Amos," *ZAW* 52 (1934) 25; Neher, *Amos,* 11–12; Maag, *Text,* 4; Kapelrud, *Central Ideas,* 117–18; Snaith, *Text of Amos,* 2.9ff.; H. Frey, *Das Buch des Ringens Gottes um seine Kirche. Der Prophet Amos* (Die Botschaft des Alten Testaments 23/1; Stuttgart: Calwer, ²1965) 36–39; Reventlow, *Amt,* 16, 113; H. Gottlieb, "Amos und Jerusalem," *VT* 17 (1967)

theme itself, is characteristic of other undisputed passages of the prophet. The verb שׁאג is found both in Amos 3:4,[43] where it is parallel, as here, to the expression נָתַן קוֹל,[44] and in Amos 3:8, where the roaring of a lion is likened to the overwhelming effect of the Word of God upon the prophet. Furthermore, the indication that the effects of the "roaring" of God reach from Jerusalem as far north as the Carmel (mentioned again in 9:3) is an extremely fitting prelude to the prophetic message of one who was sent from Judah to northern Israel to announce the Lord's sovereignty over the entire nation. Moreover, the description of the desiccation of the "shepherds' pastures" flows naturally from the mouth of the prophet who draws many of his images from his very own realm of experience as a sheep breeder (compare 1:1; 7:14).[45]

Rudolph correctly warns against too hasty a decision for the excision of "Jerusalem" from the verse based on the example of Isaiah, whose sharp critique against the cult did not diminish his veneration for the Temple in Jerusalem where the Lord appeared to him (Isa 6): "Was dem Judäer Jesaja recht ist, sollte für den Judäer Amos billig sein, wenn er in Jerusalem den Ausgangspunkt für die Offenbarung Jahwes auch für das Nordreich sieht." ("What is correct for the Judean Isaiah should be right for the Judean Amos, if he views Jerusalem as the starting point for the revelation of Yahweh for the northern kingdom as well.")[46]

452–53.

43 This is the usual verb to describe the roar of a lion. Roaring is an integral part of the strategy and battle tactics of a lion, for it paralyzes or frightens away all who are within audible range. Here it refers to the frightening and overwhelming effect of the audible manifestation of the God of Israel (compare Job 37:4). Compare Rudolph, 116–17: "Die Metapher vermittelt den unmittelbaren Eindruck des Unheimlichen, Beängstigenden, Grausigen der Kundmachung Jahwes, wo das Gefühl der volligen Ohnmacht und Preisgegenbenheit bei einem Erdbeben oder der durch keine Willensanstrengung zu unterdrückende Furchtschauer, wenn man plötzlich den Löwen brüllen hört, einen vergleichbaren Massstab abgibt." ("The metaphor provokes the immediate impression of the sinister, terrifying, dreadful elements of the proclamation of Yahweh for which a comparable criterion is provided by the feeling of absolute impotency and surrender during an earthquake, or the terrifying horror that one cannot suppress by any exertion of will when one suddenly hears the roaring of a lion.") See also Weiss, "Traces," 306–7. Compare also Ezek 19:7, ". . . the land and all that was in it were appalled at the sound of his roaring" (מִקּוֹל שַׁאֲגָתוֹ)—that is, the king of Judah. The verb also appears in Ugar., *ṯ'g*, *UT* 2627, in connection with the "neighing" or "bellowing" of a bull (*'ibr*).

44 So, too, in Jer 2:15. It is a well-known stylistic device in biblical and Rabbinic literature to have the shorter word or expression (here, the single word יִשְׁאָג) appear in the first stich and the longer one (here, two words, יִתֵּן קוֹלוֹ) in the second. (Note also the present and durative tenses of these verbs.) Compare, too, the precedence of צִיּוֹן ("Zion"), consisting of two syllables, to יְרוּשָׁלַיִם ("Jerusalem"), five syllables. For a study of this phenomenon, also called the "law of increasing numbers," see S. Y. Friedman, "Law of Increasing Numbers in Mishnaic Hebrew," *Leš* 35 (1971) 117–29, 192–206 (Heb.).

For the roar (נָתַן קוֹל) of lions and the desolation of the land, cf. Jer 2:15. This expression when applied to the Deity usually refers to the roaring sound of thunder. Compare, for example, 2 Sam 22:14; Isa 30:30–31; Joel 2:11; 4:6; Pss 18:14; 46:7b; 68:34; 77:18; 104:7; Job 37:4–5.

45 Although these considerations are weighed by Wolff, 121–22, he nevertheless concludes that the words "Zion" and "Jerusalem," as well as the entire verse, are the result of a later Judean redaction. See also Schmidt, "Redaktion," 171 n 9.

46 Rudolph, 117. So, too, Snaith, *Text of Amos*, 2.9ff. Robinson-Horst, 75; Deden, 123–24. Compare Botterweck, "Authentizität," 177: "Der Vers . . . bezeugt nur, dass ein aus Juda stammender Prophet sich die bedeutende Residenz Jerusalem als wahren Sitz Jahwes vorstellen konnte." ("The verse . . . attests only that a prophet who comes from Judah can conceive of the important capital of Jerusalem as the true residence of Yahweh.") Compare Ehrlich (*Randglossen*, 5.227), who notes that the Lord's roar goes forth from Zion and Jerusalem and not from Samaria and Bethel.

For those who interpret this verse as an "overture to a liturgical reading of Amos traditions" or as a "fragment taken from a cultic hymn" serving a cultic purpose in "liturgical language,"[47] Rudolph's criticism again should be noted. He remarks that it is most decisive that the impending judgment is against the Lord's own land, thus contradicting the traditional view that the Lord's abode in Jerusalem guarantees the safety of the entire land and its people.[48]

The *Sitz im Leben* of this hymnic verse is rather to be sought in another literary genre, widespread throughout the literature of the ancient Near East. This genre is the motif of the manifestation of the Deity and the resultant catastrophic effects upon the cosmos and nature.[49] The awesomeness of the appearance of the overwhelming grandeur, majesty, and power of God wreaks havoc throughout the land and leads to the convulsion of the heaven, earth, sea, and all therein. A vivid narration of such a theophany is given in detail in Nah 1:3–5: "The Lord . . . travels in a whirlwind and storm. . . . He rebukes the sea and dries it up, and he makes all rivers fail; Bashan and Carmel languish, and the blossoms of Lebanon wither. The mountains quake because of him, and the hills melt. The earth heaves before him, the world and all that dwell therein."[50] As has been shown, the origin of this description lies in the image of the Deity as a warrior god.[51] Similarly devastating effects upon the elements of nature are reported as a consequence of the theophanies of warrior gods in Mesopotamia (for example, Enlil, Marduk, Ishtar, Adad—but significantly not Shamash, who is never pictured as a "man of war"), as well as in the majestic appearance of the king of Assyria on the battlefield.[52]

Further investigation[53] into the various topoi of the theophany of the divine warrior demonstrates that the imagery of the convulsion of nature is also similarly worded in the literature of Mesopotamia, Canaan, Egypt, and Greece,[54] that is, "the voice (= thunder) of the deity shakes the heaven and earth."[55] Compare the following two descriptions in Akkadian: *ša ina zikir pîšu šamû irubbu erṣetu inarruṭu itarruru ḫuršāni* ("At the sound of his voice, heaven trembles; the earth convulses; the hills shake with fear")[56]; *ša iddin rigmašu ina šamê kīma Adad u targub gabbi māti ištu rigmīšu* ("Who gives forth his voice in heaven like Adad, and all the earth shakes from his voice").[57] And in Ugaritic: "Ba[al gives] forth his holy

47 See Wolff, 122; Lindblom, *Prophecy*, 116; Farr, "Language," 313. For other cultic interpretations, compare Bentzen, "Ritual Background"; Kapelrud, *Central Ideas*, 17–18; Weiser, *Profetie*, 77f.; Robinson, 75; Ward, *Amos*, 99–100.

48 Rudolph, 117.

49 See the basic study of J. Jeremias, *Theophanie. Die Geschichte einer alttestamentlichen Gattung* (WMANT 10; Neukirchen-Vluyn: Neukirchener Verlag, 1965) esp. 75–87, 142–57. Compare Wolff, 118. See also the very perceptive comments of Cross (*Canaanite Myth*, 145–94) on the two types of theophany in Canaanite myths. He concludes that "the language of theophany in early Israel was primarily language drawn from the theophany of Baʿl."

50 Compare also Exod 19:18; Deut 33:2–3; Judg 5:4–5; 2 Sam 22:8; 1 Kgs 19:11ff.; Isa 24:18–20; 28:6; 63:19; 64:2; Mic 1:3–4; Joel 2:2–3; 4:15; Hag 3:3ff.; Pss 29; 50:1; 97:4–5; 104:32. Compare also the inscription from Quntillet ʿAjrud, ובזרח אל . . . וימסן הרם ("When El appears [lit., "shines"], the mountains melt"). See M. Weinfeld, "Further Remarks on the ʿAjrud Inscriptions," *Shnaton* 5–6 (1978–1979) 238 (Heb.).

51 S. E. Loewenstamm, "The Shaking of Nature at the Time of the Manifestation of the Lord," in *ʿOz LeDavid: Collected Readings in Bible Presented to David ben Gurion on His Seventy-seventh Birthday* (ed. Y. Kaufmann and others; Jerusalem: Kiryat Sepher, 1964) 508–20 (Heb.). For the different verbs employed to describe the upheaval and convulsion of the earth, see 510–11.

52 Loewenstamm, "Shaking," 514ff. See also M. Weippert, "'Heiliger Krieg' in Israel und Assyrien: Kritische Anmerkungen zu Gerhard von Rads Konzept des 'Heiligen Krieges' im alten Israel," *ZAW* 84 (1972) 460–93.

53 M. Weinfeld, "Divine War in Israel and the Ancient Near East," in *Studies in the Bible and the Ancient Near East, Presented to Samuel E. Loewenstamm on His Seventieth Birthday* (ed. Y. Avishur and Y. Blau; Jerusalem: E. Rubinstein, 1978) 171–81 (Heb. vol.); idem, "Divine Intervention in War in Ancient Israel and in the Ancient Near East," in *History, Historiography and Interpretation. Studies in Biblical and Cuneiform Literature* (ed. H. Tadmor and M. Weinfeld; Jerusalem: Magnes, 1983) 121–47.

54 Weinfeld, "Divine Intervention," 121ff.

55 Compare Joel 2:11.

56 E. Ebeling, *Die akkadische Gebetsserie 'Handerhebung'* (Berlin: Akademie Verlag, 1953) 104:8–9. (See, however, *CAD, N*, I.348, *narāṭu*, 1b.) Compare also Ebeling, *Die akkadische*, 98: [*ša ina rigim*] *pîšu nišē ušḫarra* [*itarraru*] *qerbētu iḫîlu ṣēru* ("[At whose

voice (*qlh qdš*); the high places of the ea[rth] quake."[58]

An added dimension in this verse is the figure of speech portraying the warrior God with the sound imagery of a lion. The description of a deity likened to a lion is also known from the Bible (for example, Hos 5:14; 11:10–11; 13:7–8)[59] as well as from Egyptian[60] and Mesopotamian sources,[61] with many of the verbs designating the sound of the roaring common to the "roar" of the gods as well as to the "roar" of lions.[62]

In sum, the shattering sound of the voice of the warrior Deity produces a cataclysmic reverberation and destructive upheaval in the world. In the present passage in Amos, this result is expressed by the desiccation of all of nature.[63] The wrath of the Lord that culminates in a drought is a frequent biblical motif (compare, for example, Amos 4:6–8; 7:4; Isa 5:6; 19:17; 42:15; Jer 12:4). The awesome, spine-chilling roar reverberating from Jerusalem to "the summit of Carmel" (רֹאשׁ הַכַּרְמֶל)[64] results in a devastating and desiccating drought that sears all vegetation from "the pastures of the shepherds" (נְאוֹת הָרֹעִים) to the heights of the forests. The two verbs employed here to describe the "drying up" of

thund]ering the people fell silent; the fields [tremble]; the plain shakes"). Compare also: *ša ina rigimšu ḫuršāni inuššu* ("[Adad] at whose roar the mountains quake") in J. V. Kinnier-Wilson, "The Kurba'il Statue of Shalmaneser III," *Iraq* 24 (1962) 93:6.

57 *EA* 147:14–15. See, however, the note in *CAD, N,* I.54 and 94, both under *rigmu.* For the rare verb *ragābu,* see Weinfeld, "Divine Intervention," 121 n 5; and *AHw* 2.941. Note the similarities between this passage and both Joel 4:16, when "the Lord gives forth his voice (יִתֵּן קוֹלוֹ = *iddin rigmašu),* the heaven and earth quake" (וְרָעֲשׁוּ [שָׁמַיִם] וָאָרֶץ = *targub gabbi māti*), and Jer 25:30, "The Lord roars from on high" [that is, from heaven] (מִמָּרוֹם יִשְׁאָג . . . יִתֵּן קוֹלוֹ = *ša iddin rigmašu ina šamê*).

58 *CTA* 4: vii:29–35. Compare also *CTA* 4 (= *UT* 51), v:70, *w⟨y⟩tn.qlh.b'rpt* ("[Baal] gives forth his voice in the clouds"). Ugar. *ytn ql* = Heb. יִתֵּן קוֹל. Compare Cassuto, *Biblical,* 1.16, 77, and Ps 99:1.

59 For the imagery of the Deity as a lion as well as the employment of lions as an instrument of divine punishment, see W. E. Staples, "Epic Motifs in Amos," *JNES* 25 (1966) 109; J. Hempel, "Jahwegleichnisse bei israelitischen Propheten," *ZAW* 42 (1924) 88ff.; A. Benson, "From the Mouth of the Lion: The Messianism of Amos," *CBQ* 19 (1957) 199–200.

60 For Egyptian examples, see H. Gressmann, "Hadad und Baal nach den Amarnabriefen und nach ägyptischen Texten," in BZAW 33 (Giessen: Töpelmann, 1918) 198ff.; and J. Spiegel, "Der 'Ruf' des Königs," *WZKM* 54 (1957) 191–203, esp. 201.

61 For deities compared to lions in Mesopotamian literature, see T. Jacobsen, (*Toward the Image of Tammuz and Other Essays on Mesopotamian History and Culture* [ed. W. Moran; HSS 21; Cambridge: Harvard University, 1970] 339 n 27): "Because its roar, the thunder, is like the roar that issues from the lion's mouth, it [^{d}Im-dugud^{mušen}] was imagined with the head of a lion." For other Sumerian examples, see Weinfeld, "'Rider of the Clouds' and 'Gatherer of the Clouds,'" in *The Gaster Festschrift* (ed. D. Marcus; *JANESCU* 5; New York: Columbia University, 1973) 423; M. Weinfeld and S. N. Kramer, "Sumerian Literature and the Book of Psalms—An Introduction to Comparative Research," *BM* 57 (1974) 145–46 (Heb.). For Akkadian citations (*labbu,* "lion"), compare *utta'ar kî labbi leqi uz[za]* ("He [Anzu] roared like a lion, filled with rage") in E. Reiner, "Deux Fragments du Myth de Zû," *RA* 48 [1954] 147 i 38); *ina erṣeti labbāku* ("On earth I [the god] am a lion") in L. Cagni, *The Poem of Erra: Sources from the Ancient Near East* (Malibu: Udena, 1977) I:107. For other examples, see *CAD, L, labbu,* 24–25. For *nēšu* ("lion"), see *CAD, N,* II.196; and *AHw,* 2.783. Compare also *šumma Ereškigal ikkillaša kima nēši iddi erṣet māti inaddi* ("If Ereškigal roars like a lion, the territory of the country will fall into ruin"; note the paronomasia *iddi . . . inaddi*), in R. C. Thompson, *The Reports of the Magicians and Astrologers of Nineveh and Babylon* (2 vols.; Luzac Semitic Text and Translation Series 6 and 7; London: Luzac, 1900; vols. 1 and 2.267:10. See also E. Lipiński, *La Royauté de Yahwé dans la Poésie et le Culte de l'Ancien Israël* (Brussels: Paleis der Academiën, 1968) 109, 112, 140–41.

62 Compare the following Akkadian words for "roaring": *na'āru, CAD, N,* I.6–7; *nā'iru* (adjective), *CAD, N,* I.150–51; *ramāmu, AHw,* 2.949; *šagāmu, AHw* 3.1125–26; and the noun *šāgimu, AHw* 3.1127. Thunder was conceived as the roar that issued from the lion's mouth. For the roaring of lions, compare also Jer 2:14–15; Ezek 19:6–7.

63 Metaphors do not have to follow the laws of logic; Rudolph, 116 n 28; and Weiss, "Methodologisches," 10ff.

64 Hebrew ראשׁ designates the "top, summit" of a mountain (compare Gen 8:5; Exod 19:20; 24:17; 34:2; Num 14:40, 44; Isa 2:2; 30:17; Ps 72:16) as does its cognate and semantic Akkadian equivalents *rēštu* (*AHw* 2.972) and *rēšu* (*AHw* 2.974). Compare also Syr. רישׁי טוריא and Arab. *rā's al-jibāli.* It does

nature, אבל[65] and יבש,[66] are also coupled together in Jer 12:4; 23:10. The Carmel,[67] which is the northern mountain range of Israel, is distinguished by its lush and bountiful vegetation, pasture land, and forests (compare, for example, Isa 33:9; 35:2; Jer 50:19; Amos 9:3; Nah 1:4; 2 Chr 26:10). It represents the polar opposite of "wilderness" (Isa 32:15–16; Jer 4:26; 50:19) and "brush" (Isa 29:17; 32:15),[68] and its withering signifies a major calamity (Isa 33:9; Nah 1:4). In Amos the reference to the Carmel is important both for its fertile areas, which are doomed, and for its northern location, which signifies the extension and application of the prophetic word to the northern kingdom of Israel. The unusual expression "shepherds' pastures"[69] (found elsewhere only in Jer 33:12) is a variant of the more familiar phrase נְאוֹת (הַ)מִּדְבָּר ("the desert pastures"; see Jer 9:9; 23:10; Joel 1:19–20; 2:22; Ps 65:13).[70] It most likely was selected here to describe the effect of the roar of God upon the shepherds themselves.[71] The withering of the pastureland forebodes the end of their own sustenance. This phrase well befits the prophet Amos, who was a shepherd by profession (7:15) and who draws upon his own personal experience for his vivid imagery (compare 3:12). Together, the "pastures of the shepherds" and the "summit of Carmel" constitute a merism, implying the total devastation of all fertile places.[72]

The image of roaring that results in the shriveling up and withering away of nature is also attested in Sumerian and Babylonian literature.[73] A Sumerian hymn states that when the goddess Inanna, who is portrayed as riding

not mean here, as some have suggested (for example, Kimchi), "the best," as in Exod 30:23; Jer 22:6; Ezek 27:22; Cant 4:14. For רֹאשׁ הַכַּרְמֶל, see also Amos 9:3.

65 Hebrew אבל is the interdialectal semantic and etymological equivalent of Akk. *abālu*, B ("to dry up, dry out"); see *CAD, A*, I.29–31. It is not to be confused with its homonym, אבל ("to mourn"). It is correctly translated יִצְדּוֹן in T. See also Rashi, Kimchi. Compare, too, Isa 24:4, 7; 33:9; Hos 4:3; Joel 1:10. For studies of this verb and its homonym, see G. R. Driver ("Confused Hebrew Roots," in *Occident and Orient. Being Studies in Semitic Philology and Literature, Jewish History and Philosophy and Folklore in the Widest Sense. In Honor of Haham M. Gaster's Eightieth Birthday* [ed. A. Marmorstein and B. Schindler; London: Taylor's Foreign Press, 1936] 73–75); and E. Kutsch ("'Trauerbräuche' und 'Selbstminderungsriten' im Alten Testament," in *Drei Wiener Antrittsreden* [ThSt 78; Zürich: EVZ Verlag, 1965] 35–36), who suggests that both verbs derive from one common root meaning "to diminish."

66 Because יבש ("to be dry") is parallel to אבל, it is incorrect to repoint the verb יָבֵשׁ, from the root בוש, as suggested by Duhm ("Anmerkungen"), followed by Sellin, 161, and preferred by Rudolph, 109, 116.

67 For the Carmel mountain, see Z. Kallai, "Carmel," *EM* 4.324–29 (Heb.); G. W. Van Beek, "Carmel, Mount," *IDB* 1.538; M. C. Astour, "Carmel, Mount," *IDBSup* 141.

68 So most commentators. See Weiss, "Traces," 121, who comments that if it were merely a matter of geography, the parallel expression would be "Sharon," "Bashan," or "Lebanon."

69 The singular נָוֶה signifies the pastureland, where the shepherds graze their flocks; compare, for example, 2 Sam 7:8; 15:25; Jer 23:3; 49:20; Ps 23:1–2; Job 18:15. For its Akkadian interdialectal cognate *nawûm*, in Old Babylonian ("flocks"), and in Middle and Late Babylonian ("pastureland"), see D. O. Edzard, "Altbabylonisch *nawûm*," *ZA* 53 (1959) 168–73. See *CAD, N*, I.249–51. Compare also A. Malamat, "Mari and the Bible," *JAOS* 82 (1962) 146; Lipiński, *La Royauté*, 141 n 3.

70 Compare also G, V, and S to Zeph 2:6. For the parallelism of נְאוֹת מִדְבָּר and הָרִים, compare Jer 9:9; and נְוֵה–הַר, Jer 31:22.

71 So, too, Duhm, "Anmerkungen"; Weiss, "Traces," 123; and followed by Rudolph, 116. However, the רוֹעִים here, as well as רֹאשׁ, have no allegorical significance and do not refer to the leaders of the people, as interpreted by T ("the dwellings of the kings") and followed by Kapelrud, *Central Ideas*, 19 ("leaders of foreign nations" and "the king of Israel").

72 Although most exegetes interpret the expressions as constituting a merism, they differ on the exact connotation of the two polar opposites. Suggestions range from "south to north" (Hoffman, *Prophecies*, 156; Nowack, 120; J. Morgenstern, "Amos Studies I," *HUCA* 11 [1936] 138 n 144; Cripps, 116); "Judah-Israel" (Robinson-Horst, 75; G. A. Danell, *Studies in the Name Israel in the Old Testament* [Uppsala: Appelbergs, 1946] 113–14 n 14); "low and high" areas (Weiser, *Profetie*, 79); "pastures/meadows to forests" or "summits" (Hammershaimb, 20; Buttenweiser, *The Prophets of Israel from the Eighth to the Fifth Century: Their Faith and Their Message* [New York: Macmillan, 1914] 212; Wolff, 125); to "minimal/scant to maximal/fertile" vegetation (Sellin, 161; Weiss, "Traces," 121). Nevertheless, all agree that the intention of the prophet is to express the completeness of the devastation; compare Wolff, 125.

73 For Egyptian and Greek examples, see Weinfeld,

on a lion, "roars at the earth like thunder, no vegetation can stand up to you."[74] In the Babylonian "Fable of the Fox," the dog—a disputant against the fox and the wolf—is described as praising his own strength in the following terms: "The dog opened his mouth as he bayed, fearful to them was his bellow. Their hearts were so overcome that they secreted gall. 'My strength is overcoming; I am a claw of the Zu-bird, a very lion. At my terrible bellow the mountains and the rivers dry up'" (*ana rigmīja danni etanabbala šadû u nārū*).[75] Note here the same connection of the roaring of an animal, who is compared to "a very lion," and the "drying up" (*abālu*,[76] the Akkadian interdialectal semantic and etymological equivalent of Hebrew אבל found in Amos) of the elements of nature.

Even though the imagery is not unique to the Bible, Amos nevertheless employs it in his own novel way. The verse functions here as a prologue to the impending and imminent judgment of God against the foreign nations. As such it is also found in two other variant formulations in Jer 25:30ff. and Joel 4:16.[77] In all three contexts the purpose of the juxtaposition is the same: the Lord, the divine warrior, whose majestic roar so mightily convulses nature, comes to initiate or culminate action against foreign nations.[78] Amos, chronologically the first of these three prophets, adds, moreover, yet another unexpected and surprising dimension by including in his roll call of the accused both Judah and Israel.

Thus, this hymnic verse, which vividly portrays the effects of the wrath of God upon nature and introduces

"Divine Intervention," 122–23. For an example from Horace, see *Odes*, III, 5:1: *Caelo tonantem credidmus Iovem regnare* ("In the heaven when he roars, we believe that Jupiter reigns").

74 W. W. Hallo and J. J. A. van Dijk, *The Exaltation of Inanna* (YNERS 3; New York and London: Yale University, 1968) 14:10. Weinfeld ("'Rider of the Clouds' and 'Gatherer of the Clouds,'" in *The Gaster Festschrift* [ed. D. Marcus; New York: Columbia University, 1973] 423) already noted this and the following comparison.

75 M. Lambert, *Babylonian Wisdom Literature* (Oxford: Clarendon, 1960) 192:14–18 and note on p. 334. This imagery was discussed by Weiss in the German version of his study of this verse ("Methodologisches," 19–23), but he rejected the analogy. See, however, S. E. Loewenstamm's counterarguments in favor of this comparison in "Some Remarks on Biblical Passages in the Light of Their Akkadian Parallels," in *Bible Studies. Y. M. Grintz in Memoriam* (ed. B. Uffenheimer) = *Teʿuda* 2 (1982) 189ff. (Heb.). Neither scholar took note of the fact that here, as well, the image of a lion is found.

76 See n 65 above.

77 For a thorough study of the relationship between this verse in Amos and the analogous ones in Jeremiah and Joel, see Weiss, "Traces," 211–23, 316–18. See, too, Hoffman, *Prophecies*, 177 n 1.

Scholars are divided as to whom to attribute the original metaphor. Among those who favor Amos are Wellhausen, 67; Nowack, 121; Duhm, "Anmerkungen," 1, 100; Sellin, 197–98; Ehrlich, *Randglossen*, 5.227; Cramer, 102–3; Maag, *Text*, 4; Neher, *Amos*, 11; Weiss, "Traces," 304; Rudolph, 118. Among those who opt for Joel are Marti, 157; Harper, 9–10; Cripps, 115; Morgenstern, "Amos Studies I," 137 n 144; P. Volz, *Die vorexilische Jahweprophetie und der Messias* (Göttingen: Vandenhoeck & Ruprecht, 1897) 20; A. Lods, *Histoire de la littérature Hebräique et Juive: de puis les origines jusqu'à la ruine de l'état juif* (Paris: Payot, 1950) 235. For Jeremiah, see G. Fohrer, "Zion-Jerusalem im Alten Testament," in idem, *Studien zur alttestamentlichen Theologie und Geschichte: 1949–1966* (BZAW 115; Berlin: Töpelmann, 1969) 224. By contrast, some credit none of the three as its ultimate source but interpret the verses as variant formulations of a popular or literary expression; compare, for example, M. Buttenweiser, *Prophets of Israel*, 228f.; R. Kittel, *Geschichte des Volkes Israel. 3 Bd. Die Zeit der Wegführung nach Babel und die Aufrichtung der neuen Gemeinde* (3 vols.; Stuttgart: Kohlhammer, 1923) 2.375 n 2; Tur-Sinai, *HaLashon*, 1.83; Botterweck, "Authentizität," 177; and Kaufmann, *Toledoth*, 6.70 n 1.

According to Mays, 21, it is derived from the cult. K. Budde ("Amos 1:2," *ZAW* 30 [1910] 38) maintains that the verse comes from the editor of the Twelve Minor Prophets. It has been overlooked that in the very verse in which Joel cites this "motto" (Joel 4:16), there also appears the very same root, רעשׁ (וְרָעֲשׁוּ שָׁמַיִם וָאָרֶץ) which appears in the superscription to the Book of Amos. This could very well indicate that Joel already creatively employed the first two verses of Amos. In Jer 25:31 in place of רַעַשׁ there is found its synonym, שָׁאוֹן.

78 Others have also noted that it serves as an appropriate introduction to God's action against the nations; compare, for example, Mays, 21; Bentzen, "Ritual Background," 95–96. Volz (*Der Prophet Jeremiah* [KAT 10; Leipzig: Deichert, 1928]) even combines this verse with the oracles against the nations in Jer 46ff.

the forthcoming indictments, should be seen as an authentic, alarming, and terrifying overture to the following oracles against the nations. The paradox here is that the manifestation of the Lord that formerly signaled aid and salvation for his people[79] now presages the forthcoming judgment and punishment of Judah and Israel, along with the other nations.[80]

79 In theophanies (biblical as well as Mesopotamian), the manifestation of the deity is usually for the aid of his people. See Weippert, "'Heiliger Krieg,'" and Weinfeld, "Divine Intervention," 121. Compare Deut 33:2ff.; Judg 5:4ff.; Pss 46:6ff.; 68:7ff.

80 For God's coming to punish, compare Ibn Ezra (second comment); Kimchi; Abarbanel; and among moderns, R. Fey, *Amos und Jesaja: Abhändigkeit und Eigenständigkeit des Jesaja* (WMANT 12; Neukirchen: Neukirchener Verlag, 1963) 41. For his coming to render judgment, compare Bentzen, "Ritual Background"; Kapelrud, *Central Ideas*, 18; and H. H. Krause, "Der Gerichtsprophet Amos: Ein Vorläufer des Deuteronomisten," *ZAW* 50 (1932) 226. For an expression of his wrath, compare Schmidt, "Redaktion," 172 (continuation of n 9 from 171). Compare also J. A. Soggin, "The Prophets on Holy War as Judgment against Israel," in idem, *Old Testament and Oriental Studies* (BibOr 20; Rome: Pontifical Biblical Institute, 1975) 67–71.

1

Oracles against the Nations

3 Thus said the Lord:
For three transgressions of Damascus
And for four, I will not revoke it;
Because they threshed Gilead
With threshing-sledges of iron.
4 So I will release fire against the house of
Hazael,
And it shall devour the fortresses of Ben-
hadad.
5 I will break the gate bar of Damascus,
And cut off the ruler from the valley of Aven
And the scepter-bearer from Beth-eden.
And the people of Aram shall go in exile to
Kir
—said the Lord.
6 Thus said the Lord:
For three transgressions of Gaza
And for four, I will not revoke it;
Because they exiled an entire population,
Delivering them over to Edom.
7 So I will release fire against the wall of Gaza,
And it shall devour its fortresses.
8 And I will cut off the ruler from Ashdod
And the scepter-bearer from Ashkelon.
I will turn my hand against Ekron,
And the remnant of the Philistines shall
perish
—said my Lord God.
9 Thus said the Lord:
For three transgressions of Tyre
And for four, I will not revoke it;
Because they delivered over an entire
population to Edom,
And they did not remember the covenant of
brotherhood.
10 So I will release fire against the wall of Tyre,
And it shall devour its fortresses.
11 Thus said the Lord:
For three transgressions of Edom
And for four, I will not revoke it;
Because he pursued his brother with the
sword,
And destroyed his womenfolk.
His anger seethed ceaselessly,
And his fury raged incessantly.
12 So I will release fire against Teman,
And it shall devour the fortresses of Bozrah.
13 Thus said the Lord:
For three transgressions of the Ammonites
And for four, I will not revoke it;
Because they ripped open the pregnant
women of Gilead
In order to enlarge their own territory.
14 So I will set fire to the wall of Rabbah,
And it shall devour its fortresses,
Amid battle cries on the day of combat,
In a whirlwind on the day of tempest.
15 And their king shall go into exile,
He and his officers together
—said the Lord.

2

1 Thus said the Lord:
For three transgressions of Moab
And for four, I will not revoke it;
Because he burned the bones of the king of
Edom for lime.
2 So I will release fire against Moab,
And it shall devour the fortresses of Kerioth.
And Moab shall perish amid the uproar,
Amid battle cries with the blare of the horn.
3 I will cut off the ruler from its midst,
And all its officers I will slay with him
—said the Lord.
4 Thus said the Lord:
For three transgressions of Judah
And for four, I will not revoke it;
Because they have spurned the instruction
of the Lord,
And his laws they have not observed.
Their delusions led them astray,
Those that their fathers followed.
5 So I will release fire against Judah,
And it shall devour the fortresses of
Jerusalem.
6 Thus said the Lord:
For three transgressions of Israel
And for four, I will not revoke it;
Because they have sold for silver the
innocent,
And the needy for a hidden gain.
7 They who trample the heads of the poor into
the dust of the ground,
And thrust the humble off the road.
A man and his father cohabit with the same
young woman,
Thereby profaning my holy name.
8 Upon garments seized in distraint
They stretch themselves out beside every
altar,
And the wine of the fined they drink in the
house of their God.
9 Yet it was I who destroyed the Amorites
before them,
Whose height was as lofty as the cedars
And whose strength was like that of the
oaks.
I destroyed his boughs above and his trunk
below.
10 It was I who brought you up from the land of
Egypt
And led you through the wilderness forty
years
To possess the land of the Amorites.
11 And I raised some of your sons to be prophets
And some of your young men to be
Nazirites.
Is this not so, children of Israel?
—declares the Lord.
12 But you made the Nazirites drink wine,
And the prophets you ordered, "Do not
prophesy!"
13 Thus I will hamper your movements,
As a wagon is hindered when full of cut
grain.

14 Flight shall fail the swift,
The strong shall be unable to exert his strength,
The brave shall not be able to save his own life.
15 The archer shall not hold his ground,
The fleet-footed shall not escape,
Nor shall the horseman save his own life.
16 Even the most stouthearted of warriors
Shall flee stripped of arms on that day
—declares the Lord.

■ **1:3** The root פשע, which introduces these oracles, is a central term in the vocabulary of Amos. The plural noun appears ten times—Amos 1:3, 6, 9, 11, 13; 2:1, 4, 6; 3:14; 5:12—and the verb twice, in 4:4.[1] It encompasses crimes of one nation against another, of a nation against God (Amos 2:4), and of the people of Israel against one another (Amos 2:6ff.). Its specific connotation here is neither moral-ethical, as it is when it appears alongside the analogous terms חֵטְא and עָוֹן (for example, Exod 34:7; Num 14:18),[2] nor is it cultic (for example, Lev 16:16, 21), nor does it reflect the prophet's "familiarity with the realm of the oral clan-tradition."[3] In the present context it belongs to the "language of politics"[4] and means "to revolt, rebel, cast off allegiance to authority," whether of an overlord or the Overlord.[5] See, for example, the verbal form in 1 Kgs 12:19; 2 Kgs 1:1; 3:5, 7; 8:20, 22; Isa 1:2; 2 Chr 10:19; 21:8, 10. In Ezek 20:38 and Lam 3:42, it stands in parallelism with the verbs מרד and מרה ("to revolt"); in Hos 8:1 with עבר בְּרִית ("to transgress the covenant"); and in Isa 59:13 with כחש ("to act unfaithfully [to the Lord]") and נָסוֹג מֵאַחַר ("to turn away [from our God]"). Compare the analogous Akkadian expression, *ina adê ḫaṭû* (= Heb. פשע ב) ("to break a treaty").[6]

Why was this specific term chosen to describe the military atrocities committed by these foreign nations? Against whom did they rebel? Although it has been suggested that the attacks were upon the Israelites,[7] this accusation cannot apply to all the nations, especially not to the one against Moab. The nationalistic interpretation is not, as will be seen, as predominant as most exegetes suggest. Thus the use of פשע should not be interpreted unilaterally as referring to revolts against prior treaty agreements with Israel and Judah.

The revolt implied here can better be understood as one against God.[8] This universalistic concept of the God of Israel is also clearly evidenced in Amos 9:7: "Amos kenne dagegen einen universalen Gott, dessen Machtbereich sich über alle Völker erstreckt.[9] . . . Die Völker werden wie Israel selbst grundsätzlich unter die gleiche Ordnung des in weltweitem Rahmen geltenden Jahwewillens gestellt." ("Amos, on the contrary, is cognizant of a universal God whose sphere of influence extends over all the nations. . . . The nations, as Israel itself, are subordinated essentially to the same order of the will of Yahweh, which is valid within a universal framework.")[10]

1 The word *pšʿ* is also attested in a Ugaritic text, *CTA* 17:vi:43–44, where it appears in parallelism to *gʾn* ("haughtiness, arrogance").
2 In Amos 4:4, the accusation is leveled against Israel's ritual practice. As Bach ("Gottesrecht," 111) comments, "fulfilling the demands of the cult has displaced fulfilling the demands of God."
3 Wolff, 153.
4 G. von Rad, *Old Testament Theology* (2 vols.; tr. D. M. G. Stalker; New York and Evanston: Harper & Row, 1962) 1.263; Mays, 28.
5 So most commentators; for example, Cripps, 118; Mays, 30; Hammershaimb, 22; Kapelrud, *Central Ideas*, 22.
6 For a comparative lexical study of treaty terminology in Israel and Mesopotamia, see M. Weinfeld, "Covenant Terminology in the Ancient Near East," *JAOS* 93 (1973) 190–99; idem, "בְּרִית," *TWAT* I (1972) 781–808.
7 Würthwein, "Amos-Studien," 38. Compare Weiser, *Profetie*, 103.
8 Reventlow, *Amt*, 70. Compare Robinson-Horst, 76–77.
9 Reventlow, *Amt*, 70.
10 Ibid., 75. This idea is not related, however, to his concept of a "Bundesfest" ("covenant festival").

All of mankind is considered the vassal of the Lord whose power, authority, and law embrace the entire world community of nations. His sovereignty is not confined merely to the territorial borders of Israel and Judah.[11] Offenses against him are punished directly, wherever they are committed and whoever the guilty party may be.[12] The Lord enforces the law he authors and imposes punishments against his rebel vassals. His law binds all peoples, for the God of Israel is the God of all the nations.[13]

Nevertheless, the prophet still makes a clear-cut distinction between the nature and essence of the transgressions of the nations and those of Judah and Israel. Because the latter are bound by an intimate covenant relationship (Amos 3:1–2), they are specifically indicted for infractions of a religious-moral-ethical nature.[14] The foreign nations, however, flout divine authority whenever they commit major acts of barbarity and atrocity against fellow nations. For such crimes they are found guilty of revolting against the Lord of history, who, in turn, holds them directly accountable[15] and executes punitive action against them. As a king "musters his troops when his vassal rebels (2 Kgs 3:5b–6), so God musters troops when his vassal disobeys laws."[16]

Many different suggestions have been offered to unravel the precise nuance of the verb אֲשִׁיבֶנּוּ (*hiphʿil* of שׁוּב) and its proleptic suffixal pronoun "it." The Deity, speaking in the first person, announces the irrevocability and irreversibility of his judgment, but what is the exact significance of his ominous declaration?[17]

According to Wolff, "it" refers to the recalling of the "Word" of Yahweh, and he cites as further examples Num 23:20; Isa 45:23; 55:11.[18] The latter two passages, however, employ the verb in the *qal* and also contain a specific reference to the "Word" (דָּבָר) of the Deity. This is not the case in Amos. In Num 23:20, where the *hiphʿil* does occur, there is also a direct antecedent: "My message was to bless; when he blesses, I cannot reverse it" (that is, the blessing).[19] However, in Amos, there is no direct or implied antecedent. Wolff further resorts to Akkadian texts[20] that employ the verb *enû* ("to change, revoke, retract")[21] in similar contexts always specifically mentioning the "command" or "word" of the Deity that cannot be reversed. Compare *ša amat qibitišu mamman la innû* ("[Marduk] whose word, once spoken, nobody can reverse").[22] This, as just stated, does not apply to the verse in Amos. Unacceptable also are the suggestions to interpret the verb "to rest" ("I shall not let it rest")[23] or "to make requital."[24]

The correct exegesis, as noted by many commentators, is to translate the verb here "to cancel/annul/revoke/retract/recall" (for example, Num 23:20; Isa 43:13; Esth 8:5, 8) and to relate the suffix "it" to the punishment that is *subsequently* to be announced.[25] "It" is *anticipatory*.

11 Compare, for example, Pfeifer, "Denkformenanalyse," 56–71; J.-L. Vesco, "Amos de Téqoa, défenseur de l'homme," *RB* 87 (1980) 481–513.

12 Compare Gottwald, *Kingdoms,* 109: "The nation wronged is immaterial, for it is the cruelty and barbarity of nation versus nation which Yahweh condemns." See, too, p. 110; Kapelrud, *Central Ideas,* 22–26; Beek, "Religious Background," 132–33.
The innovation here is that Amos is sent not to chastise individuals, as his predecessors did, but entire nations. Nevertheless, this specific form of prophetic speech is a development of the announcement of judgment against an individual. See Westermann, *Basic Forms,* 169–70.

13 Compare A. J. Heschel, *The Prophets* (Philadelphia: Jewish Publication Society, 1962) 32: "Justice is a divine concern."

14 Bach ("Gottesrecht," 107) comments that in reference to Israel, פשע refers to behavior contrary to the apodictic law. For the prophet, "law was part of a covenant, whose form was that of a treaty" (p. 106).

15 Reventlow, *Amt,* 69. Compare M. Buber, *The Prophetic Faith* (New York: Harper & Brothers, 1960) 97–98.

16 Bach, "Gottesrecht," 149–50.

17 Rudolph has successfully refuted many of the earlier proposals.

18 Wolff, 128. R. P. Knierim ("'I will not cause it to return' in Amos 1 and 2," in *Canon and Authority. Essays in Old Testament Religion and Theology* [ed. G. W. Coats and B. O. Long; Philadelphia: Fortress, 1977] 163–75) refers "it" to an assumed אַפִּי ("my wrath").

19 *NJPS.*

20 Wolff, 154.

21 See *CAD, E,* 173ff. For a reflex of this verb in a biblical text, see S. M. Paul, "Unrecognized Biblical Legal Idioms in the Light of Comparative Akkadian Expressions," *RB* 86 (1979) 231–35.

22 *AMT* 93, 9:5.

23 R. Gordis, "Some Hitherto Unrecognized Meanings of the Verb *Shub,*" *JBL* 52 (1933) 153–62; and idem, "Studies," 202–3.

Wolff's reservation that a female suffix would be expected "in view of the regularly recurring use of [the feminine] אֵשׁ, 'fire'"[26] overlooks the fact that "fire" is not the only impending punishment but often is merely one of several imminent threats against the accused nations.

Both Sellin[27] and Rudolph have correctly understood the intention of this neutral suffix. Quoting the latter, "es ist absichtlich geheimnisvoll zur Erhöhung der Spannung." ("'It' is intentionally full of mystery in order to heighten the tension.")[28] This rhetorical device of frightening and suspense-ridden anticipation reappears later in Amos and should be noted as characteristic of his finely developed artistic style.[29] It is one of the many literary devices employed by the prophet to capture, maintain, and sustain his audience's attention. Tension mounts as the forthcoming punishment is initially left ambiguously undefined, only to be explicated after the intervening description of the crime. No matter what the exact nature of the ominous punishment may be, "it" is irrevocable. The first-person declaration of the Deity is a decree of absolute finality.

In the first oracle, directed against Damascus, the prophet employs the agricultural imagery of threshing[30] to describe the barbaric atrocity committed by the Arameans against Gilead.[31] It is metaphorically used to portray that nation's cruel and inhumane treatment of the land as well as its occupants.[32] For similar figurative usages depicting extremely harsh cruelty in warfare, compare 2 Kgs 13:7; Isa 41:15; Mic 4:13; Hab 3:12.

The cognate Akkadian verb *dâšu*[33] is also found in Assyrian royal inscriptions referring to both the "threshing" of a country and a people. For countries, compare *Bit-Amukkani kīma dajašti adiš* ("I [Tiglatpileser III] threshed [the country] Bit-Amukkani as [with] a threshing sledge").[34] For people, compare *dâ'iš kullat nākirī* ("[Assurnaṣirpal] who threshes all the enemies").[35] Such brutal and brutish treatment is also listed among the curses of the Assyrian vassal treaties of Esarhaddon: *ina epinni ša parzilli ālīku[nu nagêkunu] lu[ ]* ("May [Shamash] [ ] with an iron threshing-sledge your

24 D. N. Freedman, "The Burning Bush," *Bib* 50 (1969) 246. (Compare already Graetz, "vergelten, heimzahlen.") Freedman further suggests that "in all likelihood" לֹא is to be interpreted as an emphatic *lamed*—see also W. F. Albright, *Yahweh and the Gods of Canaan: A Historical Analysis of Two Contrasting Faiths* (Garden City, N.Y.: Doubleday, 1968) 216 n 23—and translates, "I will surely make requital." (Note that the suffix is glossed over.) H. M. Barstad (*The Religious Polemics of Amos* [SVT 34; Leiden: Brill, 1984] 12–13) also omits the suffix in his translation, "I will not be indulgent."

25 For example, Wellhausen; Cripps, 119; Mays, 25; Kaufmann, *Toledoth*, 6.63 n 13 (Heb.).

26 Wolff, 128. Although some Greek manuscripts translate *αὐτήν*, fem. sing. (compare V, *eam*), and others *αὐτούς*, masc. pl., most accord with the Hebrew text, *αὐτόν*, masc. sing. See Rudolph, 126.

27 Sellin.

28 Rudolph, 130.

29 Compare, for example, Amos 4:12. Compare also A. Alt's comments on the "Unbestimmtheit" ("indefiniteness") as to the identification of the enemy, Amos 2:14f.; 3:11; 5:3, 6, 7; 8:4, in his *Kleine Schriften zur Geschichte des Volkes Israel* (3 vols.; München: Beck, 1959) 2.165 n 3.

30 On threshing, see Dalman, *AuS* III.14; S. Yeivin, "Work," *EM* 4.1016; idem, "Agriculture," *EM* 6.35 (Heb.); H. N. Richardson, "Threshing," *IDB* 4.636.

31 For the Arameans being the first nation to be indicted, see previous comments relating to the order of the nations.

32 For example, Hammershaimb, 26; Rudolph, 130. See T, יָתְבֵי אֲרַע גִלְעַד ("the inhabitants of Gilead"). Compare also the commentaries of ibn Ezra and Kimchi. G, *τὰς ἐν γαστρὶ ἐχούσας τῶν ἐν Γαλααδ* ("the pregnant women who were in Gilead"), accepted as the original text by Tur-Sinai (*Peschuṭo*, 3/2.451), and now attested at Qumran, 5QAm (4) 1 הרו[ת] הגלע[ד] (M. Baillet, J. T. Milik, and R. de Vaux, *Les "Petites Grottes" de Qumran* [DJD 3/1; Oxford: Clarendon, 1962] 173, plate xxxvi, line 4), is an example of internal textual harmonization based on Amos 1:13. It may also have been added because of the difficulty of the indefiniteness of the object, "Gilead." Compare T, which added "the dwellers (of Gilead)."

33 See *CAD, D*, 121, b) metaphoric.

34 A. H. Layard, *Inscriptions in the Cuneiform Character from Assyrian Monuments* (London: Longman & Pickering, 1851) 17:11; compare P. Rost, *Die Keilschrifttexte Tiglat-Pilesers III* (Leipzig: Pfeiffer, 1893) pl. 29:12.

35 *AKA* 214:4.

cities [and your districts]").[36] Although the exact restoration of the verb in question is still in doubt,[37] it is clearly stated that the threatened curse will be executed with an "iron threshing-sledge." This Akkadian expression, *epinnu ša parzilli,* is the interdialectal equivalent of the Hebrew חֲרֻצוֹת הַבַּרְזֶל, employed by Amos in his analogous figure of speech.[38]

The crime itself was committed in Gilead,[39] first marked as the border between Laban (= Aram) and Jacob (= Israel) (Gen 31:25, 44ff.), which became the residence of the two and a half tribes constituting the Israelite settlement in Transjordan (Josh 22:9, 15). In the south it extended to the Arnon River and in the north to the Yarmuk River. Bordering on Aramean territory, it was the first to suffer from military incursions, which from the mid-ninth century on became extremely severe (2 Kgs 10:33). By the beginning of the eighth century, however, the Aramean attacks terminated with the resurgence of Assyrian power under Adadnirari III. Israel then was able to slowly recuperate and restore its hegemony over the area (compare 2 Kgs 13:5 and the inscription of Adadnirari) until it reached its maximal strength under Jeroboam II, who occupied Damascus and Hamath (2 Kgs 14:25, 28). It was finally captured in 732 B.C.E. by Tiglatpileser III, who deported its inhabitants (2 Kgs 15:20 = 1 Chr 5:26).

The actual time when this barbaric event took place is very much debated. Many refer it to the last half of the ninth century when the Arameans under Hazael and his son, Ben-hadad, invaded Gilead during the reigns of Jehu (2 Kgs 8:12; 10:32–33) and his son, Jehoahaz (2 Kgs 13:3, 7; note that the latter verse employs the same verb as here, לָדוּשׁ). However, both Wolff[40] and Rudolph[41] suggest a date contemporaneous to Amos and relate the cruelty described here as occurring toward the end of the rule of Jeroboam II. According to their suggestion, the Arameans allegedly witnessed an upsurgence of power and renewal of strength during the second quarter of the eighth century, while the Assyrians were occupied to the north, combating the Urartians. Haran also dates the event to the time of Amos, but toward the beginning of the rule of Jeroboam II.[42]

■ **1:4** The pronouncement of punishment by fire reappears as a stereotypic refrain in each of the oracles except for Israel.[43] The fire motif, which is integral to the stock language of war oracles, can ultimately be traced to Num

36 D. J. Wiseman, "The Vassal-Treaties of Esarhaddon," *Iraq* 20 (1958) vii:545–46 (p. 69). This was also noted by Fishbane, "Treaty Background," 317–18.

37 Wiseman ("Vassal Treaties," 69, line 546) suggested reading *lu-[q]u-ki[t?]* ("cut up"); E. A. Speiser (oral suggestion), *lu-[ša-am-]qi[t]* ("overthrow"); and R. Borger ("Zu den Asharhaddon Verträgen aus Nimrud," *ZA* 54 [1961] 192), *lu-[šá-b]al-ki[t]* ("overturn"), comparing line 574.

38 This form is a hapax legomenon. Compare also חָרִצֵי הַבַּרְזֶל, 2 Sam 12:31. The singular, חָרוּץ ("threshing-sledge"), occurs in conjunction with the verb for threshing also in Isa 28:27 and in Isa 41:15 (where an analogous term, מוֹרַג, also appears). The חָרוּץ was a heavy wooden sledge, bent upward at the front, with sharpened iron props or stones on the underside, drawn by oxen in order to chop up ears of grain. See Dalman, *AuS* III.14, 83, 88; *BRL,* 137–39; Driver, 227. Compare the description of the leviathan in Job 41:22.

39 See M. Noth, "Gilead und Gad," *ZDPV* 75 (1959) 14–73, esp. 60–61, reprinted in *Aufsätze zur biblischen Landes-und Altertumskunde* (2 vols.; ed. H. W. Wolff; Neukirchen-Vluyn: Neukirchener Verlag, 1971) 1.489–543, esp. 532–33; S. Yeivin and S. E. Loewenstamm, "Gilead," *EM* 2.512–16 (Heb.); S. Cohen, "Gilead," *IDB* 2.397–98. For Ammonite incursions in this area during the eleventh century, see F. M. Cross, "The Ammonite Oppression of the Tribes of Gad and Reuben: Missing Verses from 1 Samuel 11 in 4QSamuel," in *The Hebrew and Greek Texts of Samuel* = (Proceedings of IOSCS—Vienna; ed. E. Tov; Jerusalem: Academon, 1980) 105–19.

40 Wolff.

41 Rudolph, 130–31. Compare S. Cohen, "The Political Background of the Words of Amos," *HUCA* 36 (1965) 153–60; Fensham, "Treaty," 83.

42 Haran, "Rise and Decline," 266–97, esp. 276ff. See also J. A. Soggin, "Amos VI:13–14 und I:3 auf dem Hintergrund der Beziehungen zwischen Israel und Damaskus im 9. und 8. Jahrhundert," in *Near Eastern Studies in Honor of William Foxwell Albright* (ed. H. Goedicke; Baltimore and London: Johns Hopkins University, 1971) 433–41.

43 Cross, "Divine Warrior," 167. Note the predominance of this motif outside of the oracles: Amos 3:6; 5:6, 17; 7:4, 9—altogether some eleven times. Compare also Hos 8:14; Jer 17:17; 21:14; 49:27; 50:32; Lam 4:11. Haran (*Ages and Institutions,* 288) assumes that this refrain also appeared in the oracle against Israel but was somehow eventually omitted from the text.

21:27–30, where, as here, fire is said to destroy enemy cities, which are recorded by name. (In the latter, however, there is no evidence of any divine agency at work; fire, in its prestereotypic version, is still a "self-moved force.")[44] The theme of conflagration coupled with a theophany is part and parcel of the vocabulary of the Deity's Holy War[45]—a divine fire that executes judgment upon the condemned nation by consuming its defenses as well as its land. The Lord is pictured here as a military leader, the Divine Warrior,[46] who employs an all-devouring fire as one of his weapons of war.

This motif of a divine fire in battle often appears in the mythology of the ancient Near East[47] (for example, the storm god who bears his weapon of lightning),[48] as well as in the Bible, specifically in the context of military assaults. Thus Deut 9:3: "Know then this day that none other than the Lord your God is crossing at your head, a devouring fire; it is he who will wipe them out." Compare also 2 Sam 22:8ff.; Isa 29:6; 30:27, 30; 66:15–16; Pss 18:9, 13; 50:2–3; 104:4. Here, too, in Amos the image does not refer to any human agency (such as an anticipated attack of Assyria),[49] but is rather "a dramatic portrayal of the revival of Holy War brought off by the theophanic manifestation of Yahweh."[50]

The image itself is rooted, of course, in the reality of warfare, in which conflagration accompanies the capture and destruction of enemy cities and citadels (compare, for example, Josh 6:24; 8:8; 11:11; Judg 1:8), as is so often confirmed by archaeological excavations. See especially the plate of the capture of Thebes by Ashurbanipal's army, where the central gate of the city is set on fire by a lighted torch held by one of the Assyrian soldiers.[51]

Many examples can also be drawn from extrabiblical literary sources. Compare, for example, the Aramaic curse in Sefire I A 35–36, איך זי תקד שעותא זא באש כן תקד ארפד ו[בנתה ר]בת, ("Just as this wax is burned by fire, so may Arpad be burned and [her gr]eat [daughter cities]").[52] So, too, the multiple citations found in the Mesopotamian literary and omen texts.[53] Note, as well, the Akkadian semantic and partial etymological equivalent of Heb. שִׁלַּח אֵשׁ,[54] *išāta nadû* (literally, "to throw fire"); for example, *ana ekallātišu išāta addi* ("I set fire to his palaces");[55] *ina napḫar mātātiki išātu iddima* ("[The enemy] has set fire to all your countries").[56]

Because fire, by its very nature, "consumes" (Heb. אכל = Akk. *akālu*), compare the analogous use of the Akkadian verb with fire. For example, *išāta ultaqmu . . . ultākil išātu* ("[Cyrus] set fire (to the temples) and had them consumed by fire").[57] For the employment of fire in the total devastation of a city, compare *dūršu ekallašu u nišišu ina išāti iqtali* ("He burnt down his walls, his palaces, and his people").[58] So, too, in the initial penetration into the city: *nakru ana dalat abullīya išāta inaddima ana libbi āli*

44 Margulis, *Studies*, 88.

45 For the use of fire in the battles of the gods in the mythology of the ancient Near East, see P. D. Miller, Jr., "Fire in the Mythology of Canaan and Israel," *CBQ* 27 (1965) 256–61; idem, *Divine Warrior*, 31ff.; Weinfeld, "Divine Intervention," 131ff.

46 See H. Fredriksson, *Jahwe als Krieger: Studien zum alttestamentlichen Gottesbild* (Lund: Gleerup, 1945) 93–94.

47 *ANEP*, 490ff. Compare D. R. Hillers, "Amos 7:4 and Ancient Parallels," *CBQ* 26 (1964) 221–25.

48 Compare Miller ("Fire" and *Divine Warrior*) for many examples. Compare *CTA* 2:i:32 (referring to the messengers of Yam), *'išt. 'ištm ḥrb lṭšt* ("a fire, two fires . . . a sharpened sword"). Compare also R. S. Hendel, "'The Flame of the Whirling Sword': A Note on Genesis 3:24," *JBL* 104 (1985) 671–74.

49 Against Rudolph, 31.

50 Mays, 25.

51 Y. Yadin, *The Art of Warfare in Biblical Lands in the Light of Archaeological Study* (2 vols.; New York, Toronto, London: Weidenfeld & Nicolson, 1963) 2.462. See also p. 421 for Sargon's assault and setting fire to the city of Kisheim.

52 J. A. Fitzmyer, *The Aramaic Inscriptions of Sefîre* (BibOr 19; Rome: Pontifical Biblical Institute, 1967) 14.

53 *išātu, CAD, I*, 229a, 230–31, 2', a', b'.

54 The verb שִׁלַּחְתִּי also appears in Amos 4:10; 8:11.

55 3 *R* 8 ii 89 (G. Smith, *The Cuneiform Inscriptions of Western Asia* [ed. H. C. Rawlinson; London: The British Museum, 1870]), recorded by Shalmaneser III in his conquest of Hamath.

56 3 *R* 19 No. 3:7–8; Smith, *Cuneiform Inscriptions*.

57 *BHT*, pl. 10 VI 24. Just as נצת (v 14) is a variant of שִׁלַּח אֵשׁ, so, too, compare the various Akkadian verbs that alternate with *išāta nadû* ("to set afire") (*CAD, N*, I.93); for example, *šarāpu, qalû, qamû*. Compare, too, Ugar. *šyt 'išt b* and *'ikl išt, CTA* 4:vi:22ff.

58 D. J. Wiseman, *Chronicles of Chaldean Kings (626–556 B.C.) in the British Museum* (London: The British Museum, 1956) 74:19.

irruba ("The enemy will set fire to the door of my city gate and enter the city").[59] Note how this last citation also confirms the sequence of the action described in Amos: the setting on fire precedes the actual entrance into the city, thereby obviating the proposal of some scholars to transpose the respective cola in this verse.[60]

The use of the verbs in the first-person singular in the description of the successive stages of the attack and destruction of a city is very reminiscent of the style of Mesopotamian war annals, in which the king similarly boasts in the first person of his assault and conquest of enemy sites.

The fire the Deity is sending is directed against "the house of Hazael" and will consume "the fortresses[61] of Ben-hadad." Both Hazael and Ben-hadad are names of Aramean rulers.[62] Three kings bearing the name Ben-hadad are known from Aramean history.[63] Ben-hadad I, the son of Tabrimmon, ruled during the beginning of the ninth century. First a treaty partner with Baasha, king of Israel, he later switched allegiance to Asa, king of Judah (1 Kgs 15:18–20). Ben-hadad II (also known by his Aramean name, Bar-hadad, and called in Assyrian inscriptions Adad-idri/Hadad-ʿezer),[64] the former's son or grandson, ruled during the mid-ninth century and was the major adversary of Ahab, king of Israel (1 Kgs 20:1–34; 2 Kgs 6:24; 8:7, 9). He also led the coalition of Syrian kings against the Assyrian monarch Shalmaneser III in 853, 848, and 845 B.C.E. He was eventually assassinated by a usurper, Hazael (2 Kgs 8:15). Ben-hadad III, the son of Hazael (2 Kgs 13:3, 24), is also mentioned in the Aramaic Zakir stele from Hamath.[65] He was a contemporary of Jehoash, king of Israel; Joash, king of Judah; and the Assyrian ruler Adadnirari III. The latter, in the fifth year of his reign, besieged Damascus[66] and aided Jehoash in defeating the Aramean king three times. As a consequence of these battles, Israel retrieved from Aramean control the cities Hazael had previously captured from Jehoahaz, the father of Jehoash (2 Kgs 13:24–25).

Hazael (843–796), the usurper and assassin of Ben-hadad II (1 Kgs 19:15–17; 2 Kgs 8:7–15), founded a new dynasty. Although Shalmaneser III was still powerful enough in his last campaign (his twenty-first year) to launch an attack against the cities of Hazael "in the land of Damascus," Assyrian might and pressure were sinking rapidly. During the reign of the next Assyrian king, Shamshi-Adad V, Hazael was at liberty to lead an attack against northern Israel in which he seized Transjordan up to the Arnon River. Israel thereby lost "all the land of the Gilead" (2 Kgs 10:32–33; 13:7). He even succeeded in making an incursion into Judah, reaching as far as Gath, and received tribute from Joash (2 Kgs 12:18–19). During his reign, Aram attained the pinnacle of its power.

Even though both royal names are amply documented, it is nevertheless suggested here that Amos is not referring to two respective Aramean kings but rather to two dynastic titles for the kingdom of Aram per se.[67] The practice of designating a kingdom by the name of the founder of a dynasty can be documented from Assyrian sources. Adadnirari III refers to Menahem, king of Israel, as belonging to *bīt Ḫumri*, "the house/dynasty of

59 *KAR* 148:6, 16.

60 Marti; Morgenstern, "Amos Studies IV," 300, 314; Mays, 29.

61 For אַרְמוֹן ("fortress"), see S. M. Paul, "Cuneiform Light on Jer 9, 20," *Bib* 49 (1968) 374. For the parallelism between בַּיִת and אַרְמְנוֹת, compare 1 Kgs 16:18; 2 Kgs 15:25.

62 For these kings, see S. E. Loewenstamm, "Ben-hadad," *EM* 2.155–58 (Heb.); idem, "Hazael," *EM* 3.87–88 (Heb.); R. A. Bowman, "Ben-hadad," *IDB* 1.381–82; idem, "Hazael," *IDB* 2.538; R. M. Talbert, "Ben-Hadad," *IDBSup* 95. See A. Malamat, "Arameans," in *Peoples of Old Testament Times* (ed. D. W. Thomas; Oxford: Clarendon, 1973) 134–55.

63 The existence of yet another king bearing this name, Ben-hadad IV (ca. 806 B.C.E.), has been suggested by F. M. Cross, Jr., "The Stele Dedicated to Melcarth by Ben-hadad of Damascus," *BASOR* 205 (1972) 36–42.

64 See the Aramaic inscription from el-Breǧ, *KAI*, I. 201, 1–3; 202, A 4; II.203f. For the Assyrian name, compare, for example, D. D. Luckenbill, *Ancient Records of Assyria and Babylonia: Historical Records of Assyria from Sargon to the End* (2 vols.; Chicago: University of Chicago, 1926) 1. no. 681.

65 *KAI*, I.202, A 4.

66 *ANET*, 281.

67 Compare the designation of King Jehu as *mār Ḫumri* ("son of Omri") in the Black Obelisk of Shalmaneser III, even though the former destroyed the Omri-line; *ANET*, 280; *ANEP*, 355.

Omri (= Israel)."[68] Tiglatpileser III also declares,[69] "The widespread [land of *bīt*] *Ḫaza'ili* (= Beth Hazael = Aram Damascus) in its entirety from Mou[nt Leb]anon as far as the town of [Ramoth] Gilead and the town of Abel-Beth-Maacah which are on the borderland of the land of *bīt Ḫumria* (= Beth Omri = Israel), I restored to the territory of Assyria."[70]

Even more significant is the appearance of the exact title *bīt Ḫaza'ilu* (= בֵּית חֲזָאֵל, "the dynasty of Hazael") in this inscription as a designation for the kingdom of Aram Damascus—the kingdom being called after the name of the founder of the dynasty.[71] Similarly the recurrent throne name, Ben-hadad, is also used as a title for the Aramean kingdom, as is evidenced by the almost exact passage in Jer 49:27, where "the wall of Damascus" is paralleled by the phrase "the fortresses of Ben-hadad," the latter obviously representing an epithet for Aram.[72] Thus the verse in Amos is most likely pertaining to the destruction of the kingdom of Aram[73] and not to the dynasties of its individual kings.[74]

Verse 4 is structurally different from the other oracles against the nations in that it combines two different stylistic patterns: with Amos 1:7, 10, 14, it shares the initial direct reference to a city, country, or kingdom, indicated by two words bound by the construct state; and with Amos 1:12; 2:2, 5, it shares the expression "the fortresses of *X*," which appears in the second stich.

■ **1:5** First the Lord declares, "I shall break (וְשָׁבַרְתִּי)[75] the bars" of the city gates of "Damascus" (בְּרִיחַ דַּמֶּשֶׂק).[76] This marks a decisive stage in the ultimate defeat of the city,[77] for it is then totally exposed to the onslaught from without (compare Jer 51:30; Lam 2:9).

Several exegetes have suggested the transposing of v 5a after v 5bβ in order to achieve a bicola parallelism similar to Amos 1:8.[78] This conjecture, however, is unsupported by any textual evidence and is unnecessary. For the sequence of setting fire (v 4) and then breaking the bars of the city (v 5), see also Jer 51:30[79] (compare Nah 3:13).[80]

After the gates are broken, the entire population is subject to severe punishment. The first one to be "cut off" (וְהִכְרַתִּי)[81] is the יוֹשֵׁב. This term does not refer to the inhabitants,[82] who are specifically mentioned at the end of the verse as being sent out into exile, but rather, literally, to the "one who sits [on the throne]," that is, the ruler. יוֹשֵׁב is one of several epithets employed by Amos

68 *ANET*, 284. See S. Parpola, *Neo-Assyrian Toponyms* (AOAT 6; Neukirchen-Vluyn: Neukirchener Verlag, 1970) 82–83.

69 See D. J. Wiseman, "A Fragmentary Inscription of Tiglath-Pileser III from Nimrud," *Iraq* 18 (1956) 120–21, 125.

70 See H. Tadmor ("The Southern Border of Aram," *IEJ* 12 [1962] 114–22) for the reconstructed text.

71 Compare Wiseman, "Haza'el," *RLA*, 4.238; Malamat, "Arameans," 145.

72 Compare also B. Maisler, "Phoenician Inscriptions from Byblos," *Leš* 14 (1946) 181 (Heb.); idem, "A Study of Biblical Personal Names," *Leš* 15 (1947) 43 (Heb.); B. Mazar, *The Kingdoms of Israel and Judah* (ed. A. Malamat; Jerusalem: Israel Exploration Society, 1961) 139 n 20 (Heb.).

73 Compare also P. Höffken ("Eine Bemerkung zum 'Haus Hasaels' im Amos 1:4," *ZAW* 94 [1982] 413–15), who reaches a similar conclusion.
W. G. E. Watson (*Classical Hebrew Poetry* [*JSOT* Supplement Series 26; Sheffield: JSOT Press, 1984] 133) brings this as an example of "epithetic word pairs . . . PN_1 // son of PN_2." However, in all the other examples cited—Judg 5:12, בָּרָק // בֶּן־אֲבִינֹעַם; 2 Sam 20:1, דָּוִד // בֶּן־יִשַׁי; Num 23:18, // בְּנוֹ צִפֹּר בָּלָק; Ugar. *bʿl* // *bn dgn*, *CTA* 14:ii:77–79—the breakup of each one of these stereotypic phrases refers to the same individual. Thus structurally there is a connection but not contextually.

74 Against Wolff, 156; this does not mean that Amos is referring to contemporary events.

75 For the analogous use of Akk. *šebēru* (= Heb. שׁבר) with bolts and locks (Akk. *sikkūru, šigaru*), see *AHw* 3.1206; and A. Salonen, *Die Türen des alten Mesopotamien* (Annales Academiae Scientiarum Fennicae B-124; Helsinki: Suomalainen Tiedeakatemia, 1961) 83–86, 86–88. Compare *amaḫḫaṣ daltu sikkūru ušabbir* ("I will smash the door and break the bolt") CT 15,45:17.

76 For bars made out of bronze, 1 Kgs 4:13.

77 Compare Judg 16:3.

78 Marti; Morgenstern, "Amos Studies IV," 300, 314; Mays, 29.

79 "Her dwellings are set afire; her bars are broken" (נִשְׁבְּרוּ בְרִיחֶיהָ).

80 Compare the Assyrian inscription cited previously, n 59.

81 In Amos 1:5, 8, and 2:3, the "cutting off" of the ruler is expressed by the same verb in the first person, וְהִכְרַתִּי, thereby creating a literary inclusio for all the oracles against the foreign nations.

82 Against G, κατοικοῦντας ("the inhabitants," a plural), and T, יָתֵיב, S, V, and many modern exegetes (a collective singular).

to designate various types of rulers; compare תּוֹמֵךְ שֵׁבֶט (here and v 8, again parallel to יוֹשֵׁב) and the analogous terms שׁוֹפֵט and שָׂרִים (2:3). Although Wolff and Rudolph interpret יוֹשֵׁב correctly, their reference to the use of this expression in Isa 10:13 is incorrect. There the substantive, which appears in the plural, does refer to the inhabitants of the city who are to be exiled and not to the rulers.[83] The comparison, however, to the Deity who sits enthroned in heaven is an apt one;[84] compare Pss 2:4; 9:8; 29:10.[85] Compare, too, the identical term in Ugar., *il yṯb bʿṯtrt il ṯpṭ bhdrʿy* ("El sits enthroned in Ashtaroth; El rules in Edrei").[86] Note here, as well, the parallel terms *yṯb* (= יוֹשֵׁב) and *ṯpṭ* (= שׁוֹפֵט). In Akkadian, the ruler is similarly called *āšib parakki* ("one who sits on a dais"); *āšib kussî* ("one who sits on the throne").[87] Compare, in particular, the title of Yahdunlim, king of Mari, *wāšib Mari* ("enthroned [= ruler] of Mari")[88] and the cognate expression in Aramaic, יתב בכרסאה.[89]

Paralleling the "enthroned" ruler is another appellation for royalty, תּוֹמֵךְ שֵׁבֶט, literally, "the one who holds a scepter." The exact semantic analogue of this title appears in the Aramaic inscription of Panammu I, king of Sam'al, from the first half of the eighth century: יאחז חטר ביאדי ("He who holds the scepter in Ya'di [= Sam'al]";[90] Aram. יאחז חטר = Heb. תּוֹמֵךְ שֵׁבֶט).[91] Note also the continuation of this inscription: וישב על משבי וימלך ("who sits on my throne and rules"), where, similar to Amos, the verb ישב is employed in conjunction with the ruler. Furthermore, in lines 8–9 the terms are juxtaposed: ישבת על משב אבי ונתן הדד בידי חטר ("I sat on the throne of my father and Hadad put a scepter in my hand"). Both Heb. תּוֹמֵךְ שֵׁבֶט and Aram. אחז חטר, moreover, are themselves reflexes of an earlier Mesopotamian royal title: *tāmiḫ ḫaṭṭi* ("he who holds the scepter"),[92] first attested in the inscriptions of the Assyrian king Aššur-reš-iši I (1133–1116).[93] Amos may have selected this specific epithet here, which is documented in an Aramaic inscription, because he was addressing his oracle directly to Damascus.[94]

The rulers are to be cut off from both בִּקְעַת־אָוֶן and בֵּית עֶדֶן. The first location, "the vale of Aven," is a cacophemism[95] referring to a deity (most likely Baal) worshiped in that region. Compare בֵּית־אֵל ("Bethel"), which is also designated בֵּית אָוֶן ("Beth-aven" = "house of iniquity") in Josh 7:2; 18:12; 1 Sam 13:5; 14:23; Hos 4:15; 5:8; 10:5. Although G (confirming the consonants

83 Compare *NJPS*.

84 Rudolph, 126. For the correspondence of royal and divine epithets, see S. M. Paul, "משא מלך שרים: Hosea 8:8–10 and Ancient Near Eastern Royal Epithets," in *Studies in the Bible* (ed. S. Japhet; Scripta Hierosolymitana 31; Jerusalem: Magnes, 1986) 202.

85 Compare also 1 Kgs 22:19 = 2 Chr 18:18; 2 Kgs 19:15 = Isa 37:16; Pss 80:2; 99:1; Lam 5:19. M. I. Gruber ("The Many Faces of Hebrew נשא פנים, 'Lift Up the Face,'" *ZAW* 95 [1983] 257 n 25) suggests the same meaning in Job 22:8: "The man of violence owns the earth and the man who is an object of favoritism is enthroned therein" (יֵשֶׁב בָּהּ).

86 RŠ 24.252 in *MRŠ*, XVI. See B. Margalit, "A Ugaritic Psalm (RŠ 24.252)," *JBL* 89 (1970) 292:2–3. For another interpretation of this passage, see Cross, *Canaanite Myth,* 21. According to Cross, the translation should be "'El is enthroned with ʿAṯtart ⟨of the field⟩; 'El sits as judge with Haddu his shepherd" (reading *bi-Haddi rāʿiyi*). But he, too, translates Ugar. *yṯb* as "enthroned." Compare also his translation of the expression *bʿl yṯb:* "Baʿl sits enthroned," in *Ugaritica* V, 3 (RŠ 24.245) and his reference to Ps 29:10 (*Canaanite Myth,* 148, 155 n 43. See also p. 130, n 65). Compare also *yṯb lksi mlk, CTA* 6.vi.33; 76.iii.14; 127:23. For the place names, see Josh 12:4.

87 See *CAD, A,* II.430.

88 G. Dossin, "L'inscription de fondation de Iaḫdun-Lim, roi de Mari," *Syria* 32 (1955) 1–27, col. 1, line 36.

89 See A. E. Cowley, *Aramaic Papyri of the Fifth Century B.C.* (Oxford: Clarendon, 1923) 6:2. Compare Greenfield ("Scripture," 255), who refers to the inscription of Panammu I, king of Samal. See also W. B. Barrick ("The Meaning and Usage of *RKB* in Biblical Hebrew," *JBL* 101 [1982] 491–92 and nn 60–61) for additional bibliographical references.

90 See *KAI,* I.214:15, 20, 25. Compare also the Phoenician inscription of Kilamuwa, *KAI,* I.24:13–14: "If one of my children who shall sit in my place [= reign after me] . . ." (ומי . בבני אש . ישב . תחתן). See *ANESTP,* 654.

For the "scepter" and the "chair" as signs of kingship, see Greenfield, "Scripture," 255–57.

91 Compare the Babylonian inscription *ušatmiḫ rittuššu ḫaṭṭu išartu* ("He [Nabu] caused [Nebuchadrezzar] to hold the just scepter in his hands"); *PSBA* 20.157, r. 18. Akk. *ḫaṭṭu išartu* = Phoen. חטר משפט (*KAI,* I.1:12) = Heb. שֵׁבֶט מִישֹׁר (Ps 45:7).

92 See M.-J. Seux, *Épithètes Royales Akkadiennes et Sumériennes* (Paris: Letouzey & Ané, 1967) 337–39.

93 For the royal epithets *nāš(i)/tāmiḫ ḫaṭṭi,* see Seux, *Épithètes,* 204, 337.

94 This literary device of employing native vocabulary

of the Masoretic text) transliterates אָוֶן in Amos as Ων, which has been identified, in turn, with Baalbeq (= *bqʿt bʿl,* "the valley of Baal"), called Heliopolis by Greek and Roman authors[96] (compare Ezek 30:17, אָוֶן, where G translates ʿΗλίου), the valley referred to here is most likely the fertile area between the Lebanon and anti-Lebanon mountains, called בִּקְעַת הַלְּבָנוֹן (Josh 11:17; 12:7), that is, Coele Syria, which today is known as *ʾel Beqâʿ* ("the Valley").

The other site, "Beth-eden,"[97] known from Assyrian sources as *Bīt Adini,* was an Aramean city-state on the banks of the Euphrates, whose capital Tel Barsip (today, *Tel ʾAḥmar*) was located some two hundred miles north-northeast of Damascus.[98] Founded in the tenth century B.C.E., by the first half of the following century it had become one of the most important of all the Aramean states. Shalmaneser III, in three successive campaigns (857–855) captured Tel Barsip along with its ruler, Aḫuni, renamed it Kar-Shalmaneser, and annexed it as an Assyrian province. During most of the eighth century, it was ruled by an Assyrian governor, Shamshi-ilu, who was in charge of the western regions of Aram-Naharaim (which included Beth-eden) and whose dated documents span some three decades (780–752). During his incumbency Assyria was experiencing an interval of political weakness under the reigns of Shalmaneser IV (782–773), Asshur-dan III (770), and Asshur-nirari V (752), which enabled Shamshi-ilu to "virtually rule the empire as *turtānu* (commander-in-chief)."[99] His role is evidenced by the fact that he inscribed his own monuments in a quasi-royal style and, in a totally unprecedented fashion, omitted the name of the Assyrian king from his inscriptions.[100] This situation prevailed until the ascendancy of Tiglatpileser III, who changed the "sixteen districts of the land of Damascus" into four Assyrian provinces.[101] He thereby dissolved the various semi-autonomous Assyrian proconsulships and deprived their governors of their autonomous sovereign power.[102]

Because Shamshi-ilu was such a well-known personality and power in his own day and because he was a contemporary of Amos, it has been suggested that he is the one referred to here as the "bearer of the scepter" in Beth-eden.[103] This identification, however, raises the problem as to why Amos would refer to an area that at the time was both under Assyrian rule and administered by an Assyrian governor as part of his oracle against Aram.

---

when addressing foreign nations demands a thorough study. For a possible example, see C. Rabin, "An Arabic Phrase in Isaiah 21:11–12," in *Studi sull'Oriente e la Bibbia offerti al P. Giovanni Rinaldi* (ed. G. Buccellati; Genova: Ed. Studio e Vita, 1967) 303–9. Note that the sole appearance in prophetic literature of the Phoenician word for "gold" (חָרוּץ) is found in Zechariah's oracle against Tyre, Zech 9:3. (This substantive, which is derived from Akkadian, also appears in Ps 68:14; Prov 3:14; 8:10, 19; 16:16.) See also the brief remarks of A. Hurvitz, "The Chronological Significance of 'Aramaisms' in Biblical Hebrew," *IEJ* 18 (1968) 236–37: "The usage of what seems to be Aramaisms in such context [in the description of foreign nations and foreign peoples] may well reflect the use of peculiar expressions characteristic of a foreign language." See the examples he brings in n 14.

95 For examples of cacophemy, see S. M. Paul, "Euphemism and Dysphemism," *EncJud* 6.959–61.

96 For Baalbek and the god (Gad) worshiped there, see O. Eissfeldt, "Die älteste Bezeugungen von Baalbek als Kultstätte," *FuF* 12 (1936) 51–53; idem, *Ras Schamra und Sanchunjaton* (Halle: Niemeyer, 1939) 34. Compare also Cross, *Canaanite Myth,* 7 n 13. See, however, S. E. Loewenstamm ("בקעה," *EM* 2.311 [Heb.]) and Hammershaimb (27), who do not accept the identification.

97 The site also appears in the Hebrew Bible simply as עֶדֶן; compare 2 Kgs 19:12 = Isa 37:12; Ezek 27:23.

98 See F. Thureau-Dangin and M. Dunand, *Til-Barsib* (Bibliothèque Archaeologique et Historique 23; Paris: Guethner, 1936).

99 W. W. Hallo, "From Qarqar to Carchemish: Assyria and Israel in the Light of New Discoveries," *BA* 23 (1960) 34–61, esp. 44 (reprinted in *The Biblical Archaeologist Reader* [ed. E. F. Campbell and D. N. Freedman; vol. 2; Garden City, N.Y.: Doubleday, 1962] 152–88).

100 A. Malamat, "Amos 1:5 in the Light of the Tel Barsip Inscriptions," *BASOR* 129 (1953) 25–26.

101 *ANET,* 283.

102 Hallo, "Qarqar," 48.

103 See n 100. According to Hallo ("Qarqar," 38–39), the reference here is to Aḫuni, the Aramean-Hittite ruler of Beth-eden during the time of Shalmaneser III (857–855), some one hundred years earlier than Amos: "The fate of Beth-Eden still served Assyria as an intimidating example another fifty years later (2 Kgs 19:12 = Isa 37:12)."

Furthermore, it should be reiterated that the allusions to events and personalities in these prophecies are not necessarily contemporaneous with Amos himself. Moreover, the title "scepter-bearer" reappears as an appellative in the oracle against the Philistines, in which again it represents the epithet of the ruler in general but not necessarily the present holder of the office.

In an attempt to avoid this problem the conjectured reading מִבְּנֵי עֶדֶן ("from the people of Eden") has been suggested, "alluding to the offshoots of the Aramean ethnic grouping which had spread outside the confines of Mesopotamia and were subservient to the state of Damascus, rather than to the 'homeland' of this grouping which had long since been transformed into an Assyrian province."[104] According to this interpretation, the oracle is to be dated to the beginning of Jeroboam II's reign, prior to his reconquest of Transjordan, when Aram still maintained its control over Gilead. If, however, as stated previously, the oracles are not perforce reflexes of contemporary events, this conclusion based on a conjectured reading is doubtful.

A more probable solution is to understand the reference here as reflecting an earlier period when בִּקְעַת־אָוֶן[105] and בֵּית עֶדֶן represented the two polar extremes of Aram, thus comprising a geographical merism: from Lebanon to Beth-eden on the Euphrates, that is, the entire kingdom of Aram from west to east, is destined for destruction.

Finally, the "people of Aram" (עַם־אֲרָם)[106] will be exiled to Kir. Exile and deportation are predominant motifs throughout the Book of Amos;[107] they appear ten times in both the *Begründung* and *Ankündigung* sections of his oracles. (For the verb גלה, see Amos 1:5, 6; 5:5, 27; 6:7; 7:11, 17; and for the nouns גּוֹלָה and גָּלוּת, see Amos 1:15 and 1:6, 9, respectively.) It is very significant that the threat of wholesale deportation of conquered populations is unattested in the Bible prior to the time of Amos, who employs it as a recurring refrain in his oracles.

Nevertheless, assuming that Amos was familiar with the highly developed system of Tiglatpileser III, who implemented the punishment of mass deportations as a regular policy against his conquered foes, is unnecessary. The practice of the deportation of rebellious leaders, their families, and entire populations is amply documented prior to this Assyrian king. Compare, for example, the statement recorded in the treaty of the Hittite king Suppiluliuma with his Mitannian vassal Mattiwaza from the fourteenth century B.C.E.: "I reached Wassukanni (the capital of the Mitanni empire on the upper Habur River). The inhabitants of the provincial center Suta together with their cattle, sheep, (and) horses, together with their possessions, and together with their deportees, I brought to Hittite land. . . ."[108] Note, too, an Urartian deportation of some fifty thousand people.[109] Assyrian annals also occasionally document large deportations. Compare the statement of Ashurnaṣirpal II (mid-ninth century) of having deported fifteen thousand Aḫlamu-Arameans from Bīt-zamani and two thousand from Bīt-adini to Calah.[110]

This mass punishment, however, was used only sporadically up until the time of Tiglatpileser III, who

---

104 See Haran, "Rise and Decline," 276–77 n 3. His reading is partially based on G, ἐξ ἀνδρῶν χαρραν = מִבְּנֵי חָרָן ("the people of Haran"). For various explanations of this translation, see S. Talmon, "Synonymous Readings in the Textual Traditions of the Old Testament," in *Studies in the Bible* (ed. C. Rabin; Scripta Hierosolymitana 8; Jerusalem: Magnes, 1961) 346; Wolff, 129. According to Malamat ("Arameans"), the reason is that Shamshi-ilu actually resided in Haran.

105 There is no need to look for another location for Beth-eden as does Gottwald, *Kingdoms*, 95–96 n 2. There is also no documentation for Wolff's conjecture (156) that, under Shamshi-ilu, Beth-eden may have been annexed to the Aramean empire because of the Urartu pressure upon the Assyrian empire.

106 Note the heavy tone of the repetition of the letter *mem* in the two consecutive words עַם־אֲרָם.

107 According to Margulis, *Studies*, 105ff., this theme is an expansion of the captivity motif from Num 21:27ff.

108 E. F. Weidner, *Politische Dokumente aus Kleinasien. Die Staatsverträge in akkadischer Sprache aus dem Archiv von Boghazköi* (Leipzig: Hinrichs, 1923) 6–15. See also *ANET*, 318.

109 A. Goetze, *Kleinasien* (2d ed.; München: Beck, 1957) 128, 196.

110 D. J. Wiseman, "The New Stela of Aššur-naṣir-pal II," *Iraq* 14 (1952) 25–27. For another example, see W. Schramm (*Einleitung in die Assyrischen Königsinschriften. Zweiter Teil, 934–722 v. Chr.* [Leiden and Köln: Brill, 1973] 65 [bottom]) for Shalmanessar III, who also deported many from Bīt-adini. For Tiglatpileser I, see R. Borger, *Keilschrifturkunden*.

institutionalized it as part of his political policy. He introduced, moreover, an entirely new dimension to this system—the repopulation of the vacated area by the relocation there of other groups of exiles. This programmatic exchange of populations, interspersed far and wide among the various conquered regions, led to a permanent system of colonization and, in addition, helped to quell potential sparks of revolt.[111] Conquered peoples were also relocated at times in formerly uninhabited areas, thereby extending and expanding the outlying arable regions of Assyria.[112]

There is, however, no indication that Amos, who does not mention Assyria even once in his prophecies and whose oracles most probably preceded Tiglatpileser's campaign to the west, was aware of this Assyrian king or of his innovatory practice.[113] Therefore, although he does bring to prominence for the first time the threat of exile that hangs as a sword of Damocles over the foreign nations as well as Israel, there is no need to posit a knowledge of the Assyrian monarch's practice for the dating of this motif.

The exact location of the place to where they will be exiled, Kir, which is mentioned three other times in the Bible (Amos 9:7; 2 Kgs 16:9; Isa 22:6), is still uncertain. However, on the basis of Isa 22:6, which lists it alongside of Elam, it has been sought in the vicinity of that country.[114] This threat of exile for the people of Aram was fulfilled within a generation, when Tiglatpileser III captured Damascus (732 B.C.E.) and deported its inhabitants to Kir (2 Kgs 16:9). Because קִיר is missing from the verse in 2 Kings in several G manuscripts, some exegetes interpret it there as a later interpolation into the Masoretic text based on the present verse in Amos.[115] Unfortunately, the section pertaining to the Assyrian king's conquest of Damascus in 732 is missing from his annals, so ascertaining the veracity of this point of information is impossible from his records.

The significance of Amos's threat of exile to Kir becomes clear when it is juxtaposed to Amos 9:7, where this site is stated to be the original homeland of the Arameans. Thus, what the prophet is actually implying is that the Arameans are about to experience a reversal of their history by being sent back to their ultimate place of origin. Amos, "almost one half a millennium after the beginning of Aramean settlements in Syria," was still aware of a "national account of the Aramean migration, much like the chronicle of the Israelite exodus from Egypt." It further highlights "the historical consequences of Aramean 'misbehavior,' leading to their return to their ancestral homeland—reminiscent of the threat to a disobedient Israel (Deut 28:68; Hos 8:10)."[116]

Because this threat clearly spells out the "abrogation of the proud political history of the Arameans,"[117] there is no need to emend to מִקִּרְיָה ("from [their] homeland"; compare Mic 4:10)[118] or to add the phrase אֲשֶׁר הֶעֱלֵיתִים מִשָּׁם, based on Amos 9:7, which has no textual support whatsoever.[119] Unnecessary, as well, are the suggestions that Kir ("city") is the Aramean name for Ur, or that one *mem* was accidentally deleted from the text due to haplography and that the original reading was מְקַיָּרָה = *'el-Muqajjar,* the modern name for Ur.[120]

The threatened punishment thus encompasses not

Einleitung in die Assyrischen Königsinschriften. Erster Teil: Das Zweite Jahrtausend vor Chr. (Leiden and Köln: Brill, 1964) 108ff. See also the references cited in *CAD, N,* II.3–4, under the entry *nasāḫu* ("to deport"). See in general H. W. F. Saggs, *The Might That Was Syria* (London: Sidwick & Jackson, 1984) 48–49, 62, 125–29, 134–35, 263–64. On p. 128, he states, "Deportation of conquered peoples was already practiced by Assyrian kings of the thirteenth century, but it became a major feature of state policy from the ninth century."

111 Gottwald, *Kingdoms,* 98, 100,

112 See especially B. Oded (*Mass Deportation and Deportees in the Neo-Assyrian Empire* [Wiesbaden: Ludwig Reichert, 1979]) for a comprehensive study of this Assyrian king's policy of deportation and its various motives: as a form of punishment, liquidation of rival powers, loyalty to empire, military conscription, source for craftsmen and unskilled laborers, and program of colonization, as well as population of urban centers and strategic sites.

113 So, too, Gottwald, *Kingdoms,* 102.

114 For קִיר, see *EM* 7.177 (Heb.); C. H. Gordon, "Kir, 2," *IDB* 3.36.

115 For example, Marti, Nowack, Mays, Hammershaimb (28); compare also Rudolph, 132.

116 Malamat, "Arameans," 139.

117 Wolff, 157.

118 Ehrlich, *Randglossen,* 5.228.

119 Budde, "Amos," 568.

120 P. Haupt, "Ur of the Chaldees," *JBL* 36 (1917) 99; followed by E. G. H. Kraeling, *Aram and Israel: Or the Arameans in Syria and Mesopotamia* (Columbia University Oriental Studies 13; New York: AMS,

only the geographical borders of the kingdom but the entire population as well, from the rulers (יוֹשֵׁב and תּוֹמֵךְ שֵׁבֶט) to the masses of Aram (עַם־אֲרָם). The Lord is portrayed here as the Divine Warrior who is about to bring on the imminent catastrophe and total defeat of the Arameans.

■ **1:6** Gaza,[121] the southernmost of the Philistine pentapolis,[122] represents, by metonymy, the entire Philistine realm, just as Damascus, the leading city of the Aramean kingdom, symbolizes that empire. It was selected either because it was the foremost city of the Philistines at the time of the incident referred to in the oracle or because of the leading role it played as a center of the slave trade, being situated on the crossroads of the caravan routes that led to both Edom and Arabia.[123]

For the possible reasons for the absence of Gath from this oracle, see above.[124] The city is also missing from the prophecies found in Jer 25:20; Zeph 2:4; Zech 9:5–7. Moreover, note that whereas rulers for the four other Philistine cities are documented extrabiblically throughout this period[125]—Gaza: Ḫanunu, Ṣil-Bel; Ashkelon: Mitinti, Rukbitu, Šarruludani, Sidqa, Mitinti; Ashdod: Azuri, Aḫimatu, Iamani, Mitinti, Aḫimilku; Ekron: Padi, Ikausi—there is no record of any king ruling in Gath after the time of Achish (last mentioned in 1 Kgs 2:39–40). Gath itself is not mentioned again in cuneiform sources[126] until the time of Sargon II, when it most likely was incorporated into Ashdod (712 B.C.E.).[127] Its absence therefore cannot be used for dating this oracle one way or another.

Gaza is indicted for having "exiled an entire population (גָלוּת שְׁלֵמָה)[128] which they delivered (לְהַסְגִּיר) to Edom."[129] Most medieval and modern commentators correctly interpret גָלוּת שְׁלֵמָה as an "entire/complete/mass exile" (compare also Jer 13:19).[130] So, too, the ancient versions, with the exception of G, which mistakenly transliterated the letters שלמה as (τοῦ) Σαλωμων, the personal name "Solomon" (also in v 9). The other interpretation, favored by a few exegetes,[131] "a peaceful exile," that is, a nation with whom they formerly had amicable relations (compare Gen 33:18), is not appropriate here.

The wholesale deportation of populations was for the economic gain that occurred through slave traffic (compare Ezek 27:13; Joel 4:6–7). The sale of human booty on the slave market was a well-known practice that became a profitable by-product for the victors in war.[132]

Conspicuous by its absence is any indication as to the specific people or region affected by this action of the Philistines (unlike Amos 1:3). The reason, as already noted,[133] is that the prophet is not inveighing here against an incursion into Judean territory per se (if at all) but is rather indicting the inhumanity and cruelty of the forceful traffic in human beings, who are thereby abused

1918) 16; Budde, "Amos," 56; Sellin; van Gelderen.

121 For a review of the history of Gaza, see I. Ephʿal, "Gaza," *EM* 4.116–22 (Heb.); W. F. Stinespring, "Gaza," *IDB* 2.357–58.

122 Gen 10:19; compare Judg 6:4; 1 Kgs 5:4; 2 Kgs 18:8. For the pentapolis, see Josh 13:3; 1 Sam 6:17.

123 For the various opinions, compare Snaith, *Text of Amos;* Fosbroke; Driver, 104; Cripps, 124; Wolff, 157; Rudolph, 132.

124 See p. 17. For Gath, see *EM* 2.571–72 (Heb.); W. F. Stinespring, "Gath," *IDB* 2.355–56; compare, in general, H. E. Kassis, "Gath and 'Philistine' Society," *JBL* 84 (1965) 259–71. Gath was captured by Hazael, king of Damascus, during the time of Joash (2 Kgs 12:18). According to the Chronicler, it was recaptured by Uzziah (2 Chr 26:6).

125 See the respective entries in *RLA*.

126 It is mentioned, however, in Amos 6:2.

127 The only other reference to Gath in cuneiform sources after the conquest of Sargon II (according to *RLA* 3.376) is *EA* 290:9.

128 For גָּלוּת ("exile = exiled people"), see Amos 1:9; Isa 20:4; 45:13; Jer 24:5; 28:4; 29:22; 40:1; Obad 20 (twice).

129 Note the sixfold recurrence of the letter ל in the Hebrew verse: על־הגלותם גלות שלמה להסגיר לאדום.

130 Compare also the translations of T, G, V, and S to this verse.

131 For example, Harper; Deden; Neher, *Amos;* Haran, "Rise and Decline." The suggested proposal of Y. M. Grintz ("Because They Exiled a Whole Exile to Deliver to Edom," *BM* 32 [1967] 25 [Heb.]; reprinted in idem, *Moṣaʾey Doroth* [Tel Aviv: Tel Aviv University, 1969] 354–56 [Heb.]) is very forced. For another proposal, "they exiled an ally," see Christensen, "Prosodic Structure," 427–36, based on the notes of J. Nougayrol, "Guerre et paix à Ugarit," *Iraq* 25 (1963) 110; W. F. Albright, "A New Archaeological Interpretation," *BASOR* 163 (1961) 52 n 75; M. Dahood, *Psalms, I:1–50, Introduction, Translation and Notes* (AB 16; Garden City, N.Y.: Doubleday, 1966) 42.

132 See I. Mendelsohn, *Slavery in the Ancient Near East: A Comparative Study on Slavery in Babylonia, Assyria,*

and debased to mere numbers and objects of merchandise. Note also that the two nations located on the Mediterranean coast are guilty of complicity in the same crime—slave trade.[134]

Because the Edomites, who are designated as the ones to whom the mass exile was "delivered" (הסגיר),[135] most likely employed the captives as slave labor in their copper and smelting operations on the eastern side of *Wādī-'el-ʿArabah*, near *Feinān*,[136] or functioned as middlemen in a transit station for other potential buyers of slaves in Africa or Southern Arabia,[137] the objection as to how Edom could have utilized so much forced labor—which led, in turn, to the emendation of the text to "Aram"—is not convincing.[138] A continual supply of manpower was a constant necessity because of the severe impositions of working in the copper mines. Moreover, the exact number of this "mass exile" is not recorded; it could have amounted altogether to the entire deportation of only a town or a city.

Another proposal to cope with the assumed problem of "Edom" in this oracle is also totally unwarranted. According to this suggestion,[139] אֱדוֹם is a Hebraism for אדון, which is assumed to be identical with אדן ("Adana"), the land of Azitawadda, king of the Danunites, who are identified with the Greeks.[140] First, that such an alleged "Hebraism" crept into the text not once but twice (also in Amos 1:9) is highly improbable. Furthermore, when the prophet Joel refers to similar slave trade practice actually conducted by the Greeks (Joel 4:6), he refers to them as בְּנֵי הַיְּוָנִים ("the Ionians"; compare also Ezek 27:13) and not as אדן.[141]

According to another line of exegesis, the reading לֶאֱדוֹם is correct, but the particle ל is interpreted as the accusative ל: "for their [that is, the Philistines and, in v 9, the Phoenicians] turning over Edom into exile."[142] This reading would then supply the otherwise missing identification of the victims of the transaction. However, besides the fact that the ל-accusative is rare in biblical Hebrew,[143] this interpretation misconstrues the intent of the prophet. He leaves the name of the invaded country unmentioned to place the emphasis upon the very act itself and thereby brands it as part of man's inhumanity to man, regardless of the ultimate identification of the victims.

■ **1:7-8** Following the stereotypic punishment of fire, which will "devour" both the "wall (חוֹמָה) of Gaza" and "its fortresses" (אַרְמְנֹתֶיהָ) in v 7,[144] the oracle continues with the identical words employed against Damascus: the

Syria, and Palestine from the Middle of the Third Millennium to the End of the First Millennium (New York: Oxford University, 1949) 1ff., 92ff., 121. See also Driver, 134; Cripps, 124; Mays, 32.

133 See above, p. 12.

134 See Haran, "Rise and Decline."

135 For the verb הסגיר as signifying a commercial transaction, see Deut 32:30 (where it is parallel to מכר, "to sell"); Obad 14. Compare Gordis, "Studies," 209–10. The verb also appears in Amos 6:8. See also pp. 60–61.

136 Compare, for example, Wolff, 157; Rudolph, 133.

137 Compare, for example, Gottwald, *Kingdoms,* 28–29.

138 See Haran, "Observations," 209ff.; idem, *Ages and Institutions,* 307. So, too, P. Haupt, "Scriptio Plena des emphatischen *la-* im Hebräischen," *OLZ* 10 (1907) 308; idem, "Was Amos a Sheepman?" *JBL* 35 (1916) 288–90.

139 See Y. M. Grintz, "Because They Exiled a Whole Exile to Deliver to Edom," 24–26.

140 See *KAI,* I.5–6; II.39–50.

141 So, too, in all the other biblical references; compare Gen. 10:2, 4; Isa 66:19; Zech 9:13; Dan 8:21; 10:20; 11:2; 1 Chr 1:5, 7. The first two words in Ezek 27:19 should be read דַּנֵּי יַיִן ("casks of wine") and thus do not refer to the Greeks.

142 Gordis, "Studies," 207, who also cites as another example Amos 5:6, לְבֵית־אֵל.

143 See, for example, 1 Sam 23:10; 2 Sam 3:30; Job 5:2. However, the few examples are usually understood to be under the influence of Aramaic. See P. K. McCarter, Jr., *II Samuel: A New Translation with Introduction and Commentary* (AB 9; Garden City, N.Y.: Doubleday, 1984) 110.

144 For the coupling of חוֹמָה and אַרְמְנוֹת, see also Amos 1:10, 14. In Jer 49:27, an oracle against Aram, there reappears the identical refrain as here but with the verb הִצַּתִּי, as in Amos 1:14. Lamentations 2:7 also contains the two substantives along with the verb הִסְגִּיר: "He has *handed over* to the foe the walls of the citadels" (חוֹמֹת אַרְמְנוֹתֶיהָ).

For a similar reference to the destruction of walls, palace (= fortresses), and population by fire in a Babylonian inscription, compare *dūršu ekallašu u*

rulers (יוֹשֵׁב and תּוֹמֵךְ שֵׁבֶט) of Ashdod and Ashkelon shall be cut off.[145] The Deity then says, "I will turn my hand against Ekron." This same idiomatic expression, לְהָשִׁיב יָד עַל, appears in Isa 1:25; Jer 6:9; Zech 13:7; and Ps 81:15, where it is parallel to the verb אַכְנִיעַ ("I shall subdue"). The Lord himself is about to wreak vengeance upon Ekron[146] by striking it with repeated blows.[147]

Finally, "the שְׁאֵרִית of the Philistines shall perish" (אָבְדוּ). Several alternative interpretations have been offered to explain the exact nuance of שְׁאֵרִית[148] in this verse:

1. "Rest" (that is, all those left unmentioned in the oracle, especially Gath; compare Jer 39:3; Neh 7:72)[149]
2. "The very last man" (of the Philistines)[150]
3. "The remnant" (of the Philistines, wherever they may be)[151]

The meaning nevertheless is clear: Not one of the Philistines will escape the forthcoming judgment. All those who have escaped punishment so far[152] will shortly meet their fate and face annihilation.[153]

For a similar verse that employs several of the same punishments, see Ezek 25:7, the oracle against Ammon:

---

nišīšu ina išātu iqtali ("He burnt his wall, his palace, and his people"); Wiseman, *Chronicles,* 74:19.

145 Note the repeated occurrence of the letter שׁ throughout v 8.

146 Just as in the first oracle, in which other regions of Aram are under attack and not just Damascus, so, too, here three other Philistine cities along with Gaza will suffer the direct punishment of the God of Israel. For Ekron see S. Ahitub, "Ekron," *EM* 6.339–43 (Heb.); W. F. Stinespring, "Ekron," *IDB* 2.69.

147 See Rashi to this verse; and Ehrlich, *Randglossen,* 4.8 to Isa 1:25. Could there be an intended paronomasia of the verb וַהֲשִׁיבוֹתִי with the oft-repeated refrain, אֲשִׁיבֶנּוּ?

148 For other references to שְׁאֵרִית, compare Babylonia (Isa 14:22; Jer 50:26), Aram (Isa 17:3), Ashdod (Jer 25:20), Moab (Isa 15:9; 16:4), Edom (Amos 9:12), Philistines (Isa 14:13), and Joseph (= Israel) (Amos 5:15).

149 Compare H. J. Katzenstein, *The History of Tyre: From the Beginning of the Second Millennium B.C.E. until the Fall of the Neo-Babylonian Empire in 538 B.C.E.* (Jerusalem: Schocken Institute, 1973) 197 n 24; Rudolph, 132.

150 For example, Wellhausen, 69; Ewald; Nowack; Mays, 32; Hammershaimb, 31. However, this is usually expressed by the Heb. אַחֲרִית; compare Amos 4:2; 8:10; 9:1. See H. Gese, "Kleine Beiträge zum Verständnis des Amosbuches," *VT* 12 (1962) 436–37.

151 Harper, 27. Both Harper and Gese ("Beiträge," 436–37) base their interpretations on Ezek 36:3, 4.

For a study of the root, see G. F. Hasel, "Semantic Values of Derivatives of the Hebrew Root *Š'R,*" *AUSS* 2 (1973) 152–59. He points out that on the basis of cognates in Ugaritic, Aramaic, Palmyrene, Nabatean, Arabic, and Syriac, the root is of a common West Semitic origin, designating "the residual part which is left over or remains after the removal of the balance of a small part, half, or larger whole." It is also frequently employed with groups of people. See also his book *The Remnant: The History and the Theology of the Remnant Idea from Genesis to Isaiah* (Andrews University Monograph Studies in Religion 5; Berrien Springs, MI: Andrews University, 1974) 50–134, where he discusses the remnant motif in Sumerian, Akkadian, Hittite, Ugaritic, and Egyptian texts. See also R. de Vaux, "The Remnant of Israel According to the Prophets," in idem, *The Bible and the Ancient Near East* (tr. D. McHugh; Garden City, NY: Doubleday, 1971) 15–30. Compare also the comparable Akkadian term, *šittu,* which refers to "that or those which remain over" (from other punishments); *AHw* 3.1033 e. See *Iraq* 25 (1963) 54ff., *šittat ummanātešunu;* and E. Weidner, *Die Inschriften Tukulti-Ninurtas I und seiner Nachfolger* (AfO Beihefte 12; Graz: im Selbstverlag, 1959) 3 No. 1 iii 45, *šittat ummanātešunu ina šal[lat]i amnu* ("The rest of their soldiers I numbered in my booty"). Compare, esp., 5 *R* 4 92–93: T. G. Pinches, *The Cuneiform Inscriptions of Western Asia* (ed. H. C. Rawlinson; London: The British Museum, 1909): "I showed mercy to the rest of the sons (*šitti mārê*) who had escaped the punishment of slaughter and famine"; and *šittat nišē ša ana šūṣû napišti ipparšidu* ("The remainder of the men who escaped to save their lives"), *TCL* 3:146 = F. Thureau-Dangin, *Une relation de la huitième campagne de Sargon* (TCL 3; Paris: Guethner, 1912).

For another term for "remnant," *riḫtu,* see Hasel, *Remnant,* 83ff.

152 For example, Cripps, 126; Driver, 136; Wolff, 158. For the same use of שְׁאֵרִית, compare Amos 5:15; 9:12; Jer 8:3; 25:20; 47:4 (the last two also in reference to the Philistines).

153 For Heb. אבד, compare its Akkadian interdialectal semantic and cognate equivalent, *abātu* ("to destroy, ruin," in reference to people), *CAD, A,* I.43, and *ubbutu,* 43–44. Compare, too, its use in both Moabite, Mesha Stele, line 7, "And Israel perished" (אבד אבד); and in the Aramaic of Sefire II C 4–6, "I shall destroy the inscriptions . . . I shall destroy KTK

"Assuredly, I will stretch out my hand against you (נָטִיתִי אֶת־יָדִי עָלֶיךָ = וַהֲשִׁיבוֹתִי יָדִי עַל־) . . .; I will cut you off (וְהִכְרַתִּי = וְהִכְרַתִּיךָ) from among the people and wipe you out (וְאָבְדוּ = וְהַאֲבַדְתִּיךָ) from among the countries and destroy you." Even more analogous is another oracle against the Philistines, Ezek 25:16: "Assuredly, thus said the Lord God (אָמַר אֲדֹנָי ה׳ = אָמַר אֲדֹנָי ה׳), I will stretch out my hand (וַהֲשִׁיבוֹתִי יָדִי עַל־ = נוֹטֶה יָדִי עַל־) against the Philistines and cut off (וְהִכְרַתִּי = וְהִכְרַתִּי) the Cherethites[154] and wipe out (וְאָבְדוּ = וְהַאֲבַדְתִּי) the last survivors (שְׁאֵרִית = שְׁאֵרִית) of the sea coast."

The oracle concludes with the words אֲדֹנָי ה׳. This is the most common title for the God of Israel in the Book of Amos, occurring twenty times. This epithet, although absent from G,[155] is present in T and V and is also found in the Qumran scroll of Amos from Murabbʿât, Mur XII (88) 3.25.[156]

■ **1:9-10** Unlike the first two oracles, which list several cities or territories, the oracle against the Phoenicians is represented solely by Tyre, without any reference to Sidon.[157] "We can say with certainty that from the time of Ethbaal[158] (887–856 B.C.E.), until the end of the eighth century, the city of Sidon with its dependencies was an integral part of the kingdom of Tyre, at first perhaps as a vassal state, but eventually as part and parcel of the Tyrian empire."[159]

The charge here is similar to that leveled against the Philistines and yet is still a bit different. The Phoenicians are accused of acting as agents in slave commerce by delivering people to the Edomites. For Phoenician participation in slave trade, compare Ezek 27:13; Joel 4:6–7.[160] There is no need, however, to identify the "exiled population" as consisting of Israelites.[161]

Many commentators favor the slight graphic emendation of לֶאֱדוֹם ("to Edom") to לַאֲרָם ("to Aram") in order to solve the geographical problem of the distance between Phoenicia and Edom.[162] One exegete[163] accepts both the correction "to Aram" and G's reading, *τοῦ Σαλωμων* ("of Solomon"),[164] and emends the text to לַאֲרָם גְּבוּל שְׁלֹמֹה, "(for handing over) the border of Solomon to Aram," referring to the twenty Galilean towns Solomon surrendered to Hiram of Tyre (1 Kgs 9:11b–13); he assumes, based on his own emendations here, these towns were later handed over by Tyre to Aram. These readings and conjectures, however, are entirely unwarranted and unnecessary.[165] The reading "Edom" is definitely in order.[166] The juxtaposition of the oracles against the Philistines and the Phoenicians, predicated upon their geographical proximity and

and its king" (אהאבד ספר[י]א . . . אהבד אית כתך ואית מלכה); Fitzmyer, *Sefîre*, 82.

154 Note the paronomasia, וְהִכְרַתִּי אֶת־כְּרֵתִים.

155 It may have been lost by haplography; Rudolph, 126. There is no reason to view אֲדֹנָי as a later expansion, as does Wolff, 130.

156 P. Benoit, J. T. Milik, and R. de Vaux, *Les grottes de Murabbʿât* (DJD 2/1; Oxford: Clarendon, 1961) 186.

157 For the history of Tyre, see especially Katzenstein, *Tyre;* and idem, "Tyre," *EM* 6.698–707 (Heb.); A. S. Kapelrud, "Tyre," *IDB* 4.721–23.

158 See 1 Kgs 16:31.

159 Katzenstein, *Tyre,* 132, who adds that Sidon disappears from all inscriptions from Tiglatpileser III until Sennacherib, except for administrative documents during the time of Sargon II. In Assyrian inscriptions, when both cities appear, Tyre always precedes Sidon. Compare Zech 9:2.

160 Compare also Homer, *The Odyssey* (tr. A. J. Murray; Loeb Classical Library; 2 vols.; Cambridge: Harvard University; London: Heinemann, 1960) 2:XV:415ff.

161 Compare Budde, "Amos," 65; Driver, 137; Cripps, 128. See already Wellhausen, "Dass die גלות aus Israeliten besteht, ist durchaus nicht notwendig." ("It is not at all necessary that the גלות consists of the Israelites.")

162 Compare, for example, Oettli, *Amos und Hosea*; Budde, "Amos," 64; Nötscher; Amsler; Robinson-Horst, 75; Maag, *Text,* 7; Botterweck, "Authentizität," 179–80; Katzenstein, *Tyre,* 196; Haran, "Observations," 206.

163 Sellin², 205; compare Botterweck, "Authentizität," 179, "sehr ansprechend" ("very appealing").

164 Also found in G, v 6.

165 See also Rudolph's objections (126 n 9) to R. H. Smith, ("Abram and Melchizedek [Gen 14:18–20]," *ZAW* 77 [1965] 144), who interprets the root שלם as a "vassal relationship."

166 See Paul, "Concatenous," 397–403. One must also keep in mind the far-reaching trade relations that Tyre maintained as a leading commercial center (compare Ezekiel 26—28). Compare also Reventlow, *Amt,* 68–69: "Aber Tyrus war eben eine typische phönizische Handelsstadt, und dass bei diesen

complicity in a similar crime, is also based upon their contextual and verbal similarities.[167] Moreover, Edom, after being cited in both these literary units, then becomes the subject of the very next oracle. This is yet another link in the literary concatenation previously described.[168]

Haran's thorough study[169] of the various meanings of the verb הסגיר leads him to the correct conclusion that, in a nonpriestly context, the common denominator is "to hand over to one stronger (Deut 32:30; Amos 6:8; Ps 31:9); a victim to his victor (Obad 14; Job 16:11; Ps 78:48); a refugee to his pursuers (Josh 20:5; 1 Sam 23:11–12, 20); a slave to his owners (Deut 23:16; 1 Sam 30:15)." Because the "mass deportation [is] handed over" to Edom, he therefore concludes that Edom here is the stronger of the two. Since he assumes that the oracles all pertain to crimes committed against Israel or Judah and because, according to him, there was no identifiable time when Edom did have the upper hand, he, too, suggests that Edom (אֱדוֹם) must be a scribal mistake for Aram (אֲרָם).[170] However, note that such a border raid or military incursion could have taken place innumerable times in the long and complex history of Judah/Israel and Edom, the greater part of which is still unknown. Even more important is the fact that the presupposition that the oracles against the nations are entirely based on offenses committed against either Israel or Judah is unfounded.[171] The identity of the victimized nation is left unmentioned in this oracle.[172]

The verb הסגיר, with this same technical meaning, is also attested in extrabiblical sources. In the Phoenician inscription of Ešmunʿazōr, king of Sidon,[173] it appears in the *yiphʿil* (= Heb. *hiphʿil*) as a "technical term for 'handing over' slaves, prisoners, escapees and . . . for forced deportation"[174] (exactly the same as the verse in Amos): lines 9–10: ויסגרנם האלנם הקדשם את ממלכ⟨ת⟩ אדר אש משל בנם לקצתנם ("And may the holy gods *deliver* them to a mighty ruler who might rule them, in order to cut them down"). So, too, lines 21–22: לם יסגרנם אלנם הקדשם אל ויקצן הממלכת הא ("Lest these holy gods *deliver* them and cut down that ruler").

Its etymological cognate, סגר, is found in Aramaic, in the *paʿel*, in the Genesis Apocryphon 22:16–17, where it replaces the Hebrew verb מִגֵּן of Gen 14:20: ויברך אל עליון די סגר שנאיך בידך ("Blessed be the Most High God who has *delivered* your enemies into your hand").[175] Its alloform, סכר,[176] also appears in Aramaic in Sefire III 2–3, again in the causative *hapfʿel* tense: הסכר תהסכרהם בידי וברך יהסכר לברי ועקרך יסכר לעקרי ועקר [חד מ]לכי ארפד יהסכרן לי, (["Whoever speaks against me] you must *hand them over* into my hands and your son must *hand* (*them*) *over* to my son and your offspring must *hand (them) over* to my offspring and the offspring of [any of the ki]ngs of Arpad must *hand them over* to me").[177] (Note

Geschäften der Sklavenhandel eine grosse Rolle gespielt haben mag, ist nicht verwunderlich." ("But Tyre was precisely a typical Phoenician commercial city, and it is not surprising that the slave trade may have played a large role in these transactions.")

167 Compare Ward, *Amos,* 99 n 4: "The similarity in the accusation of Tyre to that of Philistia may be due to historical facts rather than editorial imitation."

168 Note also the "roll call" of nations in Ps 60:10–11: "*Moab* would be my washbasin; on *Edom* I would cast my shoe; acclaim me, O *Philistia!* Would that I were brought to עִיר מָצוֹר (the bastion)! Would that I were led to *Edom!*" If, however, the *mêm* in מָצוֹר is interpreted as an enclitic, belonging to the end of the previous word (that is, עִירָם צוֹר)—see H.-J. Kraus, *Psalmen 1—63* (BKAT XV/1; Neukirchen-Vluyn: Neukirchener Verlag, 1972) 430—then the reference here would be to "Tyre" (צוֹר). If so, the order of the last three would be the same as in Amos: Philistia, Tyre, Edom.

169 Haran, "Observations," 210–12; idem, *Ages and Institutions,* 307.

170 See n 162.

171 See comments previously.

172 The prophet does not say, עַל הַסְגִּירְכֶם ("for handing *you* over") but עַל הַסְגִּירָם ("for handing *them* over")—the nation is left (intentionally?) unidentified.

173 *KAI,* I.14; J. C. L. Gibson, *Textbook of Syrian Semitic Inscriptions. Vol. 3. Phoenician Inscriptions, Including Inscriptions in the Mixed Dialect of Arslan Tash* (Oxford: Clarendon, 1982) 108; for translation, see F. Rosenthal, *ANET,* 505. See also Z. Harris, *A Grammar of the Phoenician Language* (AOS Essays 8; New Haven: American Oriental Society, 1936) 126.

174 Compare Greenfield, "Scripture," 263–64, who does not make reference, however, to Amos; idem, "Stylistic Aspects of the Sefire Treaty Inscriptions," *AcOr* 29 (1965) 9.

175 J. A. Fitzmyer, *The Genesis Apocryphon of Qumran Cave I* (BibOr 18A; Rome: Pontifical Biblical Institute, 1971) 22:17, p. 72.

176 For Heb. סכר ("to hand over, deliver") in the *piʿel,* see Isa 19:4.

177 Fitzmyer, *Sefîre,* III:2–3, p. 96.

that here, as in Amos, the verb is followed three times by the particle ל, indicating the party to whom they are being handed over.)[178]

The Phoenicians are further accused of "ignoring בְּרִית אַחִים." This phrase, "a covenant of brotherhood," is a hapax legomenon, and both the covenant alluded to and the treaty partner are left unidentified. Most commentators,[179] however, assume that Amos is referring to a treaty contracted between the Phoenicians and the Israelites, which is first alluded to during the time of David and Hiram (2 Sam 5:11; 1 Kgs 5:15b; 1 Chr 14:1) and clearly stated during the reigns of Solomon and Hiram (1 Kgs 5:15a, 26; 2 Chr 2:2ff.). The possibility of a treaty existing between the former two is also predicated on the technical use of אָהַב (literally, "to love") in 1 Kgs 5:15b: "for Hiram had always been an אֹהֵב of David."[180] This Hebrew root is the interdialectal semantic equivalent of Akk. *ra'āmu* ("to love"), which, within the lexicon of treaty terminology, connotes faithfulness and loyalty.[181] Compare, for example, the stipulation in the vassal treaties of Esarhaddon, *kî napšātkunu la tara'amani* ("You will love [Ashurbanipal] as yourselves").[182] Compare, too, the Amarna letter of Tushratta to Amenhopis IV: "Should my brother increase tenfold the friendship [*ra'amūta*] and brotherliness [*aḫḫūta*] (between us) over (that maintained by) his father, then we will love each other very very much" [*nirtana'am*].[183]

The treaty (בְּרִית) relations between Solomon and Hiram, moreover, are specifically mentioned in 1 Kgs 5:26 and are further alluded to by the term "my brother" (אָחִי), employed by Hiram when addressing Solomon (1 Kgs 9:13). The Hebrew אָח, as well as its Akkadian cognate, *aḫu*,[184] is a well-documented technical term for treaty partners. This treaty relationship was renewed and strengthened by the marriage of Ahab, king of Israel, to Jezebel, the daughter of Ethbaal, king of Phoenicia (1 Kgs 16:31), but was subsequently terminated by the murder of the royal family by Jehu and the wholesale destruction of the temple of the Tyrian Baal along with all its prophets and priests (2 Kgs 10:19).

It is impossible to say whether the prophet has in mind any one of these treaty relations that existed in the past or whether he is alluding to an unattested assumed renewal of the ties between the two nations during the reign of Jeroboam II.[185] Nor is there any conclusive indication that Amos is referring to bonds of kinship between Israel and Edom.[186] Once again the referent is left unidentified[187] to place the emphasis upon the deplorable act itself rather than upon the specific party affected. Thus, although the prophet may have had Israel in mind, his indictment does not preclude the possibility that he was actually referring to another nation. In the long run the nation itself is inconsequential. "It is the right common to humanity at large which he [Amos] vindicates and defends."[188]

What is patently clear, however, is the technical, political treaty terminology employed by the prophet. The Hebrew אַחִים (most likely an abstract plural) is the interdialectal semantic and etymological equivalent of

178 For הַסְגִּיר בְּיַד, 1 Sam 23:11, 12, 20.
179 See, for example, J. R. Bartlett, "The Brotherhood of Edom," *JSOT* 4 (1977) 2–27; idem, "Land of Seir," 13–18.
180 Compare 1 Sam 18:1, 3.
181 See especially Moran, "Background," 77–87, esp. 78. Compare Fishbane, "Treaty Background," 314–15.
182 Wiseman, "Vassal Treaties," IV:268, p. 49.
183 *EA* 29:166.
184 For multiple examples, see *CAD, A*, I.200ff. For the title "brother" in treaty relations among the Hittites, see H. Goetze, *Kleinasien* (Handbuch der Altertumswissenschaft 3/1.3 [Kulturgeschichte des Alten Orients] 3.1; München: Beck, ²1957) 97–98.
185 So Rudolph, 104, in order to make the reference contemporaneous to the time of Amos. Compare Katzenstein, *Tyre*, 132, citing B. Mazar, "The Philistines and the Rise of Israel and Tyre," *Proceedings of the Israel Academy of Sciences and Humanities* 1/7 (1967) 16.
186 Already assumed by Wellhausen, 69–70; Nötscher; Fosbroke; M. Noth, "Edomites," *RGG*³ 2.309; and Wolff, 159, who adds that the prophet's intentions were "not to one particular treaty but to the paradigm of all treaties." There is also no need to posit here Neher's reference (*Amos*, 62f.) to the Noahide covenant of nations in Gen 9.
187 Compare, for example, Amos 6:14.
188 Driver, 137. Compare also Gottwald, *Kingdoms*, 105; Ehrlich, *Mikrâ*, 3.402; idem, *Randglossen*, 6.229.

Akk. *aḫḫūtu,* which refers not only to a "brotherly relationship" but also to a "brotherhood (referring to a political relationship), between peoples and rulers of an equal status."[189] This term can be traced all the way back to pre-Sargonic times: *nam.šeš.e.aka* ("brotherhood pact").[190] It is also very frequently found in Akkadian texts to express a parity treaty. See, for example, the Amarna text just cited above. Among the multiple examples which can be documented, compare RN_1 *u* RN_2 *ana aḫḫūti ana aḫāmiš raksu* ("RN_1 and RN_2 [two royal names] are on a status of equality by mutual agreement").[191] Compare also "Two great countries have become one country, and two great kings [Hattusilis III and Ramses II] have become brothers" (*ana ištēt aḫḫūti;* literally, "have become one brotherhood alliance").[192] That is why treaty partners are called "brothers," Heb. אָח (for example, 1 Kgs 9:13; 20:32; compare Gen 26:29–31) and Akk. *aḫu* (plural, *aḫḫū*). For example, "When your father and I made the alliance and when we became loving brothers (*aḫḫū*), we did by no means become brothers (*ana aḫḫī*) for a day";[193] "Egypt and Hatti are at peace and brothers (*aḫḫū*) forever, like (the two of) us."[194]

Finally, the observance of a covenant or a treaty is often expressed by the verb "to remember" (Heb. זכר, Akk. *ḫasāsu*).[195] For the former, compare Gen 9:15; Exod 2:24; 6:5; 32:13; Lev 26:42, 45; Jer 2:2; Ps 98:3.[196] For the latter, *ḫasāsu* with the treaty terms of *adê* and *ṭābti,* compare, for example, *la nāṣir adê la ḫāsis ṭābti* ("[He] who does not keep the sworn agreement, does not remember the good relations").[197]

This technical use of זכר and its semantic analogue in Mesopotamian political terminology completely invalidates the suggestion of interpreting the verb as a witness to Deuteronomistic traditions.[198] Furthermore, the sin of Tyre does not lie "in breaking their 'brother-treaty' by not returning an 'exile' to their ally"[199] but, as previously cited, in their immoral traffic in human beings for

189 Both *aḫḫūtum, CAD, A,* I.187–88, 193, and *atḫūtu, CAD, A,* II.493, represent such a relationship. For references, see J. M. Munn-Rankin, "Diplomacy in Western Asia in the Early Second Millennium B.C.," *Iraq* 18 (1956) 68–110; Priest, "Covenant," 400–406; E. Gerstenberger, "Covenant and Commandment," *JBL* 84 (1965) 40–42; Fensham, "Treaty," 71–87; Fishbane, "Treaty Background," 314–15; Moran, "Background"; idem, "A Note on the Treaty Terminology of the Sefîre Stelas," *JNES* 22 (1963) 175 n 22. For covenant terminology, see F. Vattioni, "La terminologia dell'alleanza," *Biblos Press* 6 (1965) 112–16; and especially M. Weinfeld, "Covenant Terminology," 190–99; idem, "בְּרִית," *TWAT* I (1972) 781–808, reprinted and tr. *TDOT* II.253–97; idem, "הַבְּרִית וְהַחֶסֶד," *Leš* 36 (1972) 85–105 (Heb.). For Heb. אַחֲוָה = Akk. *aḫḫūtu,* compare Zech 11:14 (with v 10). See, in general, P. Kalluveettil, *Declaration and Covenant: A Comprehensive Review of Covenant Formulae from the Old Testament and the Ancient Near East* (AnBib 58; Rome: Pontifical Biblical Institute, 1982); D. J. McCarthy, *Treaty and Covenant: A Study in Form in the Ancient Oriental Documents and the Old Testament* (AnBib 21a; Rome: Pontifical Biblical Institute, 1978).

190 E. Sollberger, *Corpus des inscriptiones 'royales' présargoniques de Lagaš* (Geneva: Droz, 1956) 43, 45:ii:10. Compare now the brotherhood statement in Ebla: an.tá.šeš *ú* an.na.šeš ("You [are my] brother and I [am your] brother"). See G. Pettinato, *The Archives of Ebla* (Garden City, NY: Doubleday, 1981) 97–98; W. H. Shea, "The Form and Significance of the Eblaite Letter to Hamazi," *OrAnt* 23 (1984) 143–58; M. Weinfeld, "Initiation of Political Friendship in Ebla and Its Later Developments," in *Wirtschaft und Gesellschaft von Ebla* (Heidelberger Studien zum Alten Orient. Band 2; ed. H. Hauptmann and H. Waetzoldt; Heidelberg: Heidelberger Orientverlag, 1988) 345–48.

191 *KBo* 1.1: r. 27 in *WVDOG* 30/I (Leipzig, 1930).

192 *KUB* 3 24+59:8.

193 *KUB* 3 72 (also *KBo* 1 10): 7–8.

194 *KBo* 1 7:21. See Weinfeld, "Covenant Terminology," 193, for citations.

195 Compare W. Schottroff, *"Gedenken" im alten Orient und im alten Testament: Die Wurzel zakar im semitischen Sprachkreis* (WMANT 15; Neukirchen-Vluyn: Neukirchener Verlag, 1964) 157ff..

196 For the opposite, שָׁכַח בְּרִית ("to forget [= to disregard] the covenant"), see Deut 4:23, 31; Prov 2:17 (and compare the note on this last verse by Ehrlich, *Randglossen,* 6.18).

197 R. Borger, *Die Inschriften Asarhaddons, Königs von Assyrien* (AfO Beiheft 9; Graz: im Selbstverlag des Herausgebers, 1956) 46 ii 41. For Akk. *ṭā/ūbtu* and Aram. טבתא ("friendship, good relations, amity established by treaty"), see Moran, "A Note on the Treaty Terminology of the Sefîre Stelas," *JNES* 22 (1963) 173–76; and Fitzmyer, *Sefîre,* 74, for additional citations, bibliography, and biblical analogies. For the analogies, see also D. R. Hillers, "A Note on Some Treaty Terminology in the Old Testament," *BASOR* 176 (1964) 46–47.

198 Against Wolff, 159–60.

slave purposes, thereby abrogating their "brotherhood" relationship.

The oracle concludes once again on the theme of punishment by fire, this time against the wall of Tyre and its fortresses (v 10).

■ **1:11** The oracle against Edom introduces the first of the three nations that had traditional ethnic ties with Israel. The use of אָחִיו ("his brother") may refer to this kinship because Edom and Israel (Esau and Jacob) are often referred to as "brothers" (for example, Gen 25:19ff.; 27:40–41; Num 20:14; Deut 2:4; 23:8; Obad 10, 12). The crime would then be interpreted as a "violation of the customary ethos of kinship obligations."[200]

Strained relations between the two nations are already reflected in the Jacob-Esau narratives in Genesis. Although Edom was subjugated to the domination of the first kings of Israel (compare, for example, 1 Sam 14:47; 2 Sam 8:13–14; 1 Kgs 11:15–17; 22:48), they rebelled toward the end of the reign of Solomon (1 Kgs 11:21ff.) and eventually attained their independence during the time of Jehoram, king of Judah, in the mid-ninth century (2 Kgs 8:20–22), from which time some scholars date the historical incident referred to here in Amos.[201] Some sixty years later Amaziah defeated them in the Valley of Salt, captured Sela, and incorporated it into Judah (2 Kgs 14:7; 2 Chr 25:11–12). Most scholars assume that with their defeat Edom once again came entirely under the rule of Judah. They apparently only regained their freedom during the reign of Ahaz, who was severely pressured by Rezin, king of Aram (2 Kgs 16:6; read לֶאֱדוֹם ["to Edom"] and וַאֲדוֹמִים ["and the Edomites"] for לַאֲרָם ["to Aram"] and וַאֲרָמִים ["and the Arameans"]). When Ahaz finally became subservient to the Assyrian monarch Tiglatpileser III,[202] Elath (Eloth), which formerly had been rebuilt and restored to Judah under Uzziah (2 Kgs 14:22; 2 Chr 26:2), also came under Assyrian influence. Thus it is argued that because during the reign of Jeroboam II, that is, during the time of Amos, Edom was still within Judah's control, the crime of which they are accused in this oracle must belong to the later exilic or postexilic period.[203] For after the conquest of Jerusalem, Edom is derogatorily singled out for both acting with extreme vengeance against the refugees and for appropriating Judean territory (compare Ezek 25:12–14; 35:5; Obad 10–14; Lam 4:21–22).

Haran, however, is of the opinion that Amaziah's capture of Sela did not necessarily imply his total control over Edom.[204] He suggests that only Sela was incorporated into Judah and that only Elath was rebuilt by Uzziah.[205] Nowhere, according to him, is there any other indication that Edom in its entirety fell again under the rule of the kings of Judah. Furthermore, Sela itself, in all likelihood, is not to be identified with Petra (in southern Edom) but with the site *es-Sela*, which is located on the northern border of Edom.[206] Therefore, the atrocity described here could very well be dated to the early years of the reign of Jeroboam II, or even before he became king of Israel. Because documentary sources are so sparse, however, definitively dating this affair is impossible. It may refer to a very cruel border raid, which could have occurred at any one of several different intervals in the strained relations between the two nations.[207]

This brief historical review is entirely predicated upon the understanding of אָחִיו ("his brother") as referring to the kinship relations that existed between Israel and Edom. It should be added, however, that the word "brother" has also been interpreted by some in a political, diplomatic sense, that is, as a treaty partner, similar to the expression בְּרִית אַחִים discussed previously (v 9).[208] In

199 Against Fishbane, "Treaty Background," 318, comparing Sefire III 4ff.
200 Mays, 35.
201 See Hoffman, *Prophecies*, 167.
202 *ANET*, 282.
203 So, for example, Wolff, 160.
204 Haran, "Observations," 209–12; S. Cohen, "The Political Background of the Words of Amos," *HUCA* 36 (1965) 159 n 17. For another approach, see R. Gordis, "Edom, Israel and Amos: An Unrecognized Source for Edomite History," in *Essays on the Occasion of the Seventieth Anniversary of the Dropsie University, 1909–1979* (ed. A. I. Kautsch and L. Nemoy; Philadelphia: Dropsie University, 1979) 109–32.
205 Compare Mazar, "Gē-HaMelech," *EM* 2.479–80 (Heb.).
206 For Sela, see Mazar, "Sela," *EM* 5.1050–51 (Heb.). Excavations at the site clearly indicate that Petra was not inhabited until much later than the time of Jeroboam II. See P. C. Hammond, "New Light on the Nabataeans," *BAR* 7 (1981) 22–41.
207 Compare also Rudolph, 134. See Bartlett, "Land of Seir," 13–18.
208 Compare Fishbane, "Treaty Background," 315, 317.

this case, the injured party referred to would be unknown. Nevertheless, the frequent references to Edom as a "brother" of Judah tend to favor the ethnic rather than the political interpretation.

Two possible allusions to the earlier Jacob-Esau narrative may be noted here.[209] Esau is promised in his blessing that he will live by the "sword" (עַל-חַרְבְּךָ תִחְיֶה; Gen 27:40), and here, in Amos, Edom (= Esau) pursued and persecuted his brother Judah (= Jacob) by the "sword."[210] Rebekah, in turn, thought that Esau's wrath (אַף, חֵמָה) would only be temporary (Gen 27:44–45); here, however, Amos states that it (אַף, עֶבְרָה) endures for all time.[211]

Edom is also accused of having שִׁחֵת רַחֲמָיו. The usual interpretation of this expression, "he stifled his mercy," abounds in difficulties. The meaning "stifle/suppress" for the verb שִׁחֵת is a makeshift one and is totally unattested in connection with human emotions.[212] Moreover, as a parallel to the substantive אָחִיו, one would expect רַחֲמָיו to represent a concrete noun rather than an abstract one, "affection, mercy." Although it has been suggested that the substantive may mean "allies,"[213] this proposal is based on an incorrect analogy to the Akkadian verb *ra'āmu* ("to love"). The interdialectal equivalent of Heb. רחם is Akk. *rêmu*, not *ra'āmu*, and *rêmu* is not the term used in extrabiblical treaty contexts to denote love, that is, covenant/treaty fidelity.[214]

The problem is solved once רַחֲמָיו is related to the very same word that appears in Judg 5:30, רַחַם רַחֲמָתַיִם ("young women").[215] Cognates are also attested in the

209 Another oblique possibility also should be considered. Heb. רדף in its figurative sense of "persecute, harass" may be a veiled reflex to Gen 27:41, where it is said that Esau וַיִּשְׂטֹם Jacob and planned to kill him. Although the root שׂטם is usually translated "to bear a grudge," N. H. Tur-Sinai (*The Book of Job* [Tel Aviv: Javneh, 1954] [Heb.]), 126, relying on Aramaic and Syriac, has pointed out that originally it meant "to hunt, persecute." (Compare also M. Jastrow, *Dictionary of the Targumim, the Talmud Bavli and Yerushalmi, and the Midrashic Literature* [2 vols.; New York: Putnam, 1950] 2.1554.) Compare the translation of this verb in *NJPS* to Ps 55:4; Job 16:9; 30:21 (all rendered "harassed"). See also Gen 49:23; 50:15; compare Hos 5:2.

210 The expression לִרְדֹּף בַּחֶרֶב also appears in Jer 29:18.

211 Edom became the symbol for the paradigmatic enemy of Israel in late biblical and talmudic times. See Y. Hoffman, "Edom as the Symbol of Wickedness in Prophetic Literature," in *Bible and Jewish History: Studies in Bible and Jewish History Dedicated to the Memory of Jacob Liver* (ed. B. Uffenheimer; Tel Aviv: Tel Aviv University, 1972) 76–89 (Heb.).

212 Otherwise, it is only attested with חָכְמָה ("wisdom"), Ezek 28:17, and בְּרִית ("covenant"), Mal 2:8. See D. Vetter, "שׁחת, *šḥt* pi./hi. 'verderben,'" *THAT* II.892, "language of combat."

213 Fishbane, "Treaty Background," 313–18, and partially accepted (although not etymologically) by Coote, "Amos 1:11," 206–8, "he spoiled his covenant mercy." See, too, Barstad, *Religious Polemics*, 13; M. L. Barré, "Amos 1:11 Reconsidered," *CBQ* 47 (1985) 420–27. Fishbane, in an additional note ("Additional Remarks on *Rḥmyw*," *JBL* 91 [1972] 391–93), supports his suggestion by bringing examples of the root *rḥm* in Aramaic (compare Sefire III 8; Genesis Apocryphon 21:21). However, this does not mean that the same semantic range applies to Hebrew. G. Baur (*Der Prophet Amos erklärt* [Giessen, 1847] 243–44) translated "Brüdervolk" ("brother nation"). Compare Snaith, *Text of Amos*, 25–26, "his friends." Rudolph, 125, "Brüderlichkeit" ("brotherliness"); Gordis, "Studies," 211, "friends, kinsmen," relating the word to Aram. רחם, "friend."

214 See Paul, "Concatenous," 402–3. For additional studies of this root, see Y. Muffs, *Studies*, 132 n 2; G. Schmuttermayr, "*RḤM*—Eine lexikalische Studie," *Bib* 51 (1970) 499–532.

215 Paul, "Concatenous," 402–3. See already Y. ibn Ganaḥ, *Haschoraschim*, 477. Compare also Y. Kaufmann, *The Book of Judges* (Jerusalem: Kiryat Sepher, 1962) 145–46 (Heb.). A variant of this same word is most likely found in Isa 49:15. See M. Dahood, "Denominative *riḥḥam*, 'to conceive, enwomb,'" *Bib* 44 (1963) 204. Compare Y. Avishur, "Patterns of the Double Rhetorical Question," in *Zer Li-Gevurot: The Zalman Shazar Jubilee Volume: A Collection of Studies in Bible, Eretz Yisrael, Hebrew Language and Talmudic Literature* (ed. B. Z. Luria; Jerusalem: Kiryat Sepher, 1973) 439 n 67 (Heb.); M. I. Gruber, "'Will a Woman Forget Her Infant?' Isa 49:15," *Tarbiz* 51 (1982) 491–92 (Heb.), who also draws attention to 1QH 9:36, מרחמת. See Y. Licht, *The Thanksgiving Scroll: A Scroll from the Wilderness of Judea* (Jerusalem: Bialik, 1957) 149 (Heb.). Compare also Gordis, "Studies in the Relationship of Biblical and Rabbinic Hebrew," in *Louis Ginzberg Jubilee Volume: On the Occasion of His Seventieth Birthday* (ed. S. Lieberman, L. Zeitlin, S. Spiegel, and A. Marx; New York: American Academy for Jewish Research, 1946), Eng. section, 186; idem, "Studies," 210 n 21.

Mesha Moabite inscription רחמת[216] and in Ugaritic *rḥm*, where it appears as a synonym to *btlt* (compare *rḥm ʿnt* = *btlt ʿnt*), "a young woman."[217] The indictment here is that Edom "destroyed" (שִׁחֵת) the female population of his adversary. For the employment of the verb שִׁחֵת in the *piʿel*, designating the destruction of human beings, see Gen 6:17; 9:15; Num 32:15; 1 Sam 26:15; 2 Sam 1:14. The choice of this unique phrase creates the contextual literary link between the crimes committed by Edom and Ammon: both nations wielded the *sword* in order to kill *womenfolk*.[218] Furthermore, just as Ammon is accused of having "split open the (wombs) of pregnant women" (v 13), רַחֲמָיו, which metonymically means "women," literally refers to the very "womb" itself (רֶחֶם).[219] The prophet thereby creates a merism by accusing Edom of having persecuted both the males (אָחִיו) and the females (רַחֲמָיו); that is, the entire element of the population was subjected to their brutal and atrocious attacks.

Amos may very well have selected this rare Hebrew noun, moreover, in order to effect a double entendre or Januslike construction.[220] He continues his accusation against Edom by condemning their incessant, never-ending wrath and fury, which obliquely implies that the nation had indeed subdued all sparks of "mercy" (רַחֲמִים) whatsoever. The word then is pivotal, primarily meaning "young women," but, by secondary anticipatory allusion to the continuation of the verse, also implying "mercy."[221] That this latter association is possible and would be understood by his audience is demonstrated by the combination of these very two roots, רחם and שחת, in other passages. Compare Jer 13:14: וְלֹא אֲרַחֵם מֵהַשְׁחִיתָם ("No *mercy* will stop me from *destroying* them"). See especially Ps 78:38, which actually contains no fewer than three of the key terms in this verse (within, of course, an entirely different setting): וְהוּא רַחוּם . . . וְלֹא יַשְׁחִית וְהִרְבָּה לְהָשִׁיב אַפּוֹ וְלֹא־יָעִיר כָּל־חֲמָתוֹ ("But he being *merciful* . . . and would not *destroy;* he restrained his *wrath*

216 For the Mesha inscription, *KAI*, I.30; compare S. Segert, "Die Sprache der Moabitischen Königsinschrift," *ArOr* 29 (1961) 244. The noun appears in line 17.

217 *CTA* 6:ii:26–27.

218 Paul, "Concatenous," 397–403.

219 Both G (μήτραν) and Jerome (in his commentary, *vulvam eius*) translated the noun concretely as "womb." Based on this, both Döderlein and Dathe (*apud* J. C. W. Dahl, *Amos* [1795] 82–83) interpret the word by synecdoche as "*in mulieres gravidas*" ("in pregnant women"). See also Zakovitch ("*For Three,*" 186 n 49), who accepts Paul ("Concatenous," 402–3) but suggests the vocalization רְחָמָיו ("wombs") for רַחֲמָיו. According to him, the Masoretes misunderstood the meaning of the noun and assumed it meant "mercy."

Rudolph accepts as an alternative suggestion the emended reading (by Wutz) of G (ἐλυμήνατο μήτραν) ἐπὶ γῆς ("upon the ground") to ἐπ' ἴσης or ἐπίσην ("und schändete den gleichen (d.h. gemeinsamen) Mutterschoss"; "he violated the same, i.e., common, womb"). However, ἐπὶ γῆς ("upon the ground") is clearly influenced by the expression in Gen 38:9, וְשִׁחֵת אַרְצָה (G, ἐξέχεεν ἐπὶ τὴν γῆν; "he poured out on the ground") and not, as Wolff (130) suggests, "perhaps to correspond to place designations in 1:3b and 13b?" Thus the suggestion of Christensen ("Prosodic Structure," 431) to read *wĕ-šiḥet* ⟨*'Edôm*⟩ *raḥmâw* ("[Edom] violated his obligations of kinship") is also completely untenable.

220 For the literary phenomenon of "Janus parallelism," see C. H. Gordon ("New Directions," *BASP* 15 [1978] 59–60), on Cant 2:12; idem, "Assymetric Janus Parallelism," in Eretz Israel 16 [*Harry M. Orlinsky Volume;* ed. B. A. Levine and A. Malamat; Jerusalem: Israel Exploration Society, 1982] 80*–81*), who defines the phenomenon as "when a polyseme parallels what precedes it with one meaning and what follows it with a different meaning . . .; it looks both ways but with different faces." He further adds that the "spirit of punning allows a modicum of phonetic liberty." See also G. Rendsburg, "Janus Parallelism in Gen 48:26," *JBL* 99 (1980) 291–93; D. T. Tsumura, "Janus Parallelism in Nah 1:8," *JBL* 102 (1983) 109–11; E. Zurro, "Disemia de *brḥ* y paralelismo bifronte en Job 9:25," *Bib* 62 (1981) 546–47. Although not all of the cited examples in these articles are convincing, the phenomenon does exist and merits a special investigation. See also Watson (*Hebrew Poetry*, 159), who suggests an example from Ugaritic, *CTA* 3 B ii 24–26, and Jer 2:14–15. For a comprehensive study of this literary phenomenon, see now S. M. Paul, "Polysensuous Polvalency in Poetic Parallelism," in *"Sha'arei Talmon": Studies in the Bible, Qumran, and the Ancient Near East Presented to Shemaryahu Talmon* (Winona Lake, IN: Eisenbrauns, 1991) 147–63.

221 By employing this poetic substantive, there now appear four consecutive words each containing the Hebrew letter ח: בחרב אחיו ושחת רחמיו.

time and again, and did not give full vent to his *fury*"). (A fourth term, חֲמָתוֹ ["fury"], is here equivalent to עֶבְרָתוֹ in Amos.)

The prophet continues by denouncing their relentless anger and fury. Although the expression טָרַף אַף appears once again in Job 16:9, אַפּוֹ טָרַף וַיִּשְׂטְמֵנִי ("In his anger he tears and persecutes me"),[222] most exegetes favor emending the verb in Amos from וַיִּטְרֹף to וַיִּטֹּר[223] (from the root, נטר), "he guards, keeps," thereby creating a complementary parallel to שְׁמָרָה in the following stich. Edom is then assumed to be the subject of the verse "Edom maintained his anger continuously."[224] The pair of verbs נטר and שמר are also found together in Jer 3:5: הֲיִנְטֹר לְעוֹלָם אִם־יִשְׁמֹר לָנֶצַח. Held, however, has suggested a new line of interpretation.[225] He accepts the standard emendation but relates the two verbs, שמר/נטר, to a pair of Akkadian statives, *šamāru* and *nadāru*,[226] meaning "to rage, to be furious," which are totally unrelated to the transitive homonyms, נצר (נטר)/שמר ("to guard, to watch"). Jeremiah 3:5 is then translated, "Does one hate for all time? Does one rage forever?" Thus in Amos the synonymous pair of nouns, "wrath" (אַף) and "fury" (עֶבְרָה),[227] would then function as the subject of the verbs and not as their objects: "His anger raged unceasing;[228] his fury stormed unchecked."[229]

The parallelism of these two cola is chiastic with עֶבְרָתוֹ ("his fury") being placed at the beginning of the second stich for the sake of emphasis. (The construction is usually interpreted by most commentators as an example of *casus pendens,* as the noun was mistakenly understood

222 Compare somewhat similarly Job 18:4: טֹרֵף נַפְשׁוֹ בְּאַפּוֹ ("You who tear yourself to pieces in anger"). There is no reason, however, to interpret this as a "sapiential idiom"; against Terrien, "Amos and Wisdom," 113.

223 Ever since J. Olshausen, *Die Psalmen erklärt* (Leipzig: Hirzel, 1853) 397 on Ps 103:9. Compare S, נטר and V, *tenuerit* ("he maintained").

224 Observe, however, that although the expression נָטַר אַף is otherwise unattested, a similar idiom referring to the Deity is found in Mic 7:18: לֹא־הֶחֱזִיק לָעַד אַפּוֹ ("He has not maintained his wrath forever").

225 See M. Held ("Rhetorical Questions in Ugaritic and Biblical Hebrew," in Eretz Israel 9 [*W. F. A. Albright Volume;* ed. A. Malamat; Jerusalem: Israel Exploration Society, 1969] 73 n 19; idem, "Studies in Biblical Homonyms in the Light of Akkadian,' *JANESCU* 3 [1970/71] 46–55) for multiple examples. This suggestion was already offered by G. R. Driver ("Studies in the Vocabulary of the Old Testament, 2, 3," *JTS* 32 [1931] 361–63), who does not refer to Amos in his study. J. A. Bewer's similar comment ("Lexical Notes," *AJSL* 17 [1900–1901] 168) has gone all but unnoticed. Compare, too, P. Haupt, "Eine alttestamentliche Festliturgie für den Nikanortag," *ZDMG* 61 (1907) 284–85.

226 For *šamāru,* see *AHw* 3.1154; for *nadāru, CAD, N,* I.59–61.

227 See Y. Avishur ("Pairs of Synonymous Words in the Construct State [and in Appositional Hendiadys] in Biblical Hebrew," *Sem* 2 [1971/72] 22–23) for examples. The usual order, אַף followed by עֶבְרָה, is reversed in Isa 14:6.

228 The mistranslation of G, εἰς μαρτύριον (= Heb. לְעֵד, "for a testimony, proof") for לָעַד ("forever") is related, in turn, to its misinterpreting Heb. נֶצַח, in the second stich, as an Aramaism, εἰς νεῖκος ("strife, dispute"). See Rudolph, 127. The opposite error crept into the Masoretic Hebrew text in Zeph 3:8, where the same letters were mispointed לָעַד ("for eternity") instead of לְעֵד, as found in G, εἰς μαρτύριον (compare also S), "For the day when I arise as an accuser."

229 Compare also *NEB:* "And his anger seethed forever, his fury stormed unchecked." How can one then explain the present Masoretic reading, וַיִּטְרֹף, supported by G, ἥρπασεν ("to ravish"); α', ἠγρεύσεν ("to grow wild")? Compare also σ' and θ'. According to Coote ("Amos 1:11," 208 n 13), who cites W. Moran, orally (compare M. Dahood, *Psalms II:51–100, Introduction, Translation, and Notes* [AB 17; Garden City, NY: Doubleday, 1968] 68, 201; Christensen, "Prosodic Structure," 62ff.; M. L. Barré, "Amos 1:11 Reconsidered," *CBQ* 47 [1985] 422 n 12), the last letter of the verb is due to the "unfamiliarity" of the scribe with the Ugaritic conjunction *pa* ("and, but"), which is allegedly found elsewhere in the Bible. This suggestion is totally unfounded, and thus the proposed reading, ויטר פלעד, which was assumed to be subsequently misdivided, is totally inadmissible. The פ in וַיִּטְרֹף may be due to a back-formation, influenced by the פ in אַף. For an analogous form of contamination, compare Job 21:23, שַׁלְאֲנַן וְשָׁלֵיו, where the ל, which is part of the root שָׁלֵו, actually entered by error into the first word, שַׁאֲנָן, creating the ghost word, שַׁלְאֲנַן. So, too, the addition of the מ in the adjective נְמִבְזָה, which was influenced by the following נָמֵס in 1 Sam 15:9. Then again, it may simply be a scribal mistake influenced by the similar idiom found in Job. Compare also the expression in Ps 50:22.

as the object of the verb.) The verb accordingly should be vocalized שָׁמְרָה, third-person feminine singular, and not שָׁמָרָה, second-person masculine singular with tonal retraction.[230]

There is no need to add a ל before נֶצַח (that is, לָנֶצַח), parallel to לָעַד (for example, Ps 9:19), because the ל in the first stich services the adverbial accusative of time in the second stich as well—a common trait in biblical poetry. For נֶצַח, compare, for example, Jer 15:18; Pss 13:2; 16:11; 74:3.[231]

The two sites cited for destruction by conflagration are Bozrah and Teman. Bozrah, today *'el-Buṣeirah* (a diminutive form), thirty miles southeast of the Dead Sea, was the chief city in northern Edom (compare, for example, Isa 34:6; 36:1). Teman, a city or district in Edom (compare Ezek 25:13), is a common metonymic appellation for the entire country (compare Jer 49:7, 20; Obad 9; Hab 3:3). If Teman refers specifically to a city or a region here, then the two geographical sites would represent the entirety of Edom, as in Ezek 25:13, in which Dedan replaces Bozrah: "I will stretch out my hand against Edom—from Teman to Dedan they shall fall by the sword." (Compare also Jer 49:7–8, in which both Teman and Dedan [southwest of Edom, in the Ḥijāz, identified with the oasis of *'el-ʿUlā*] are mentioned.) If, however, Teman designates all of Edom, then the verse would be similar to the oracles against Moab and Judah, in which first the country and then the leading city are cited: Moab—Keriyot, Judah—Jerusalem.[232] Note, too, that only in the oracles in which the reference is first to the country is there no addition of any object (that is, wall), as there is when a city is cited (compare vv 7, 10, 14). Either way the intention remains the same: All of Edom is destined for destruction.

■ **1:13** Although in cuneiform sources the usual designation for the Ammonites[233] is *bīt Ammāna,* occasionally accompanied by the determinative for a "city" or for the "land," in an Assyrian letter from Nimrud (Calah), from the second half or the end of the eighth century, there appears the term *^{māt}Ba-an-am-ma-na-aia,* "(the land) of the Ammonites," whose representatives, along with those from Egypt, Gaza, Judah, and Moab, came to Calah to bring horses and tribute to the king of Assyria.[234] Because this same epithet is also found in a native Ammonite inscription (Tel Siran, lines 1, 2, 3), *bn ʿmn*[235] (= Heb. בְּנֵי־עַמּוֹן), the prophet very likely commenced his oracle against the Ammonites by employing their own

230 For recessive tone, see *GKC,* 29de. Those who interpret the stich as a *casus pendens* vocalize שָׁמָרָהּ with a *mappiq* in the final ה, referring to the feminine subject, עֶבְרָה.

231 See, for example, Ehrlich, *Randglossen,* 6.229; Rudolph, 127; Wolff, 131. For the adverbial accusative of time, see *GKC,* 118k. Compare also עוֹלָם for לְעוֹלָם in Pss 10:16; 48:15; 89:38.
There is, of course, no reason to interpret this entire stich as being secondary, against, for example, Wolff; Rudolph.

232 For Teman, see S. Ahitub, "Teman," *EM* 8.524–25 (Heb.); V. R. Gold, "Teman," *IDB* 4.534–35. The identification of Teman with *Tawilan* in the vicinity of Petra (in southern Edom) has been accepted by many atlases, historical geographies, and dictionaries. However, R. de Vaux ("Teman, ville ou région d'Edom?" *RB* 76 [1969] 379ff.) seriously questioned this suggestion. Later archaeological excavations (starting in 1968) have shown that *Tawilan* was occupied during the eighth and sixth centuries B.C.E. but was not fortified and therefore would not be a fitting urban site comparable to Bozrah, the capital of Edom. He concludes that Teman here refers to the entire country of Edom. See, however, the several references to יהוה תמן from Kuntillet ʿAjrūd, which point to southern Edom. Compare also Hab 3:3.

233 For Ammon, see B. Oded, "Ammon, Ammonites," *EM* 6.254–71 (Heb.); G. M. Landes, "Ammon, Ammonites," *IDB* 1.108–14; S. H. Horn, "Ammon, Ammonites," *IDBSup* 20–21.

234 See H. W. F. Saggs, "The Nimrud Letters—II: Relations with the West," *Iraq* 17 (1955) 134–35. The expression appears in line 35. For geographical names of this type, see *RLA,* 2.33ff.

235 H. O. Thompson and F. Zayadine, "The Tell-Siran Inscription," *BASOR* 212 (1973) 5–11. The inscription is dated about 600 B.C.E. In each of the first three lines in which the expression appears, it refers to the names of Ammonite kings. For another possible occurrence of this name, see R. W. Dajani, "The Ammonite Theatre Fragment," ADAJ 12–13 (1967–1968) 65–67 (second line in the fragment). This inscription is also dated ca. 600 B.C.E.

indigenous expression to designate their ethnic group.[236]

Amos condemns the Ammonites for barbarities perpetrated in the course of border warfare. The brutal atrocity they committed as part of their territorial expansion into Gilead was "ripping open" (בִּקְעָם)[237] the bellies of "pregnant women" (הָרוֹת).[238] This heinous act of cruelty is attested three other times in the Bible: 2 Kgs 8:12, when the prophet Elisha predicts that the Arameans led by Hazael would act in a similar fashion against Israel; 2 Kgs 15:16, when Menahem, king of Israel, executes this inhumane torture during his attack upon a neighboring town; and Hos 14:1, when the prophet threatens the doom of Samaria.[239] In all four passages the same Hebrew verb בקע ("to rip open") appears, either in the *piʿel* (2 Kgs 8:12; 15:16), *puʿal* (Hos 14:1), or *qal* (Amos 1:13). This verb, in the *piʿel,* also describes the activity of bears (2 Kgs 2:24) and other animals (Hos 13:8), who rend apart human beings. Compare, too, its Ugaritic interdialectal semantic and cognate equivalent *bqʿ*: *tiḫd bn.ilm.mt.bḥrb tbqʿnn* ("She [Anat] seized Mot son of El, ripped him open with a sword").[240] Note that Ugar. *bqʿ* describes the ripping apart of a body with a sword (Ugar. *ḥrb*)—the instrument of destruction implied in the biblical passages as well.[241]

There are, moreover, a couple of rare extrabiblical references to this horrendous action committed in battle. A Middle-Assyrian hymn composed to extol the conquests of Tiglatpileser I (ca. 1114–1076) records: *ušerriṭi libbi arâti unappil lakûti ša dannūtišunu unakkis kišādāti* ("He slit the wombs of the pregnant women, he gouged out the eyes of the infants, he cut the throats of their strong men").[242] A Neo-Babylonian lament includes: *īnāya la immar . . . nukkusu šatur ummāti* ("My eyes cannot look on . . . the ripping of the mother's wombs").[243]

In two of the biblical verses cited above, 2 Kgs 8:12 and Hos 14:1, alongside of the slitting of the wombs of pregnant women, mention is also made of the dashing to pieces (רטש) of babies (Heb. עוֹלָלִים = Assy. *lakûti,* "suckling children"). For Tiglatpileser I, such behavior was worthy of heroic adulation; for Amos, it was an example of a brutal act of savage and unforgivable cruelty committed against defenseless human beings—all for the sake of Lebensraum (לְמַעַן הַרְחִיב אֶת־גְּבוּלָם).[244]

The Ammonites, in turn, similar to the other nations,

236 For the employment of vocabulary native to the foreign nation addressed, see previous comments and notes to Amos 1:5, תּוֹמֵךְ שֵׁבֶט.

237 For the vocalization בִּקְעָם, see *GKC,* 61a. For the *qal,* see also 2 Chr 21:17; 32:1. Thus there is no need to vocalize בקע here as a *piʿel.* The verb, by extension, comes to designate the breaching and conquering of a besieged town; compare, for example, 2 Sam 23:16; Isa 7:6; Ezek 26:10; 30:16; 1 Chr 11:18; 2 Chr 21:17; 32:1.

238 Heb. הָרוֹת is not a variant of הָרִים ("mountains"), against Sadiah, Kimchi, ibn Ezra, and some modern commentators. See already ibn Ganaḥ, *Sefer HaRiqmah* (2 vols.; Jerusalem: Academy for the Hebrew Language, 1964) 1. רמ״ג, 12, and n 8; idem, *Haschoraschim,* 123–24. The substantive הָרוֹת was incorrectly added by harmonization to Amos 1:3 (where Gilead is also mentioned) in G and in the Qumran scroll, 5QAm (4)1. See previous comments to that verse. For the suggestion that it may be an example of polysemy, see G. Rendsburg, "Janus Parallelism," 292–93, n 5.

The suggestion of J. Reider ("Etymological Studies in Biblical Hebrew," *VT* 4 [1954] 279) to interpret the noun as a "stony tract" completely misinterprets the verse, besides confusing Heb. ה with Arab. ح..

239 This expression of heartless murder does not appear before the time of Elisha nor after Hosea and Amos. Linguistically it is chronologically circumscribed to the last generations of Samaria.

240 *CTA* 6:ii:30–32.

241 Compare also Homer, *Iliad* VI:57–58; XXII:163f. See Harper's note on p. 36 citing Wellhausen for additional Arabic sources.

242 E. Ebeling, "Ein Heldenlied auf Tiglatpileser I," *Or* 18 (1949) 35, reverse 3–4. See E. Ebeling, F. Köcher, and L. Rost, *Literarische Keilschrifttexte aus Assur* (Berlin: Akademie Verlag, 1953) 62. This comparison was also made independently by M. Cogan, "'Ripping Open Pregnant Women' in Light of an Assyrian Analogue," *JAOS* 103 (1983) 755–57.

243 W. G. Lambert, "A Neo-Babylonian Tammuz Lament," in *Studies in Literature from the Ancient Near East, by Members of the American Oriental Society Dedicated to Samuel Noah Kramer* (ed. J. M. Sasson) = *JAOS* 103/1 1983) 211–15 rev. line 19.

244 Fishbane ("Treaty Background") assumes that the act committed here was an infringement of a boundary treaty. Usually, however, such encroachments upon neighboring territory are described by the Hebrew verb לְהַסִּיג/לְהַשִּׂיג; compare, for example, Deut 27:17; Prov 22:28; Job 24:2. For לְהַרְחִיב ("to enlarge") in the context of the expansion of territory,

will first be subject to punishment by fire. In this case, however, Amos employs the variant expression וְהִצַּתִּי אֵשׁ rather than וְשִׁלַּחְתִּי אֵשׁ, which appears in all the other oracles.[245] If one assumes[246] that the present text in Amos is based on a subsequent correction influenced by the oracle against Ammon in Jer 49:2 (in which the verb is also derived from the root נצת, תִּצַּתְנָה), why then was not Amos 1:4 also revised in the light of the similar oracle against Aram in Jer 49:27, in which the verb וְהִצַּתִּי appears and not וְשִׁלַּחְתִּי? Obviously, no revision is involved here, for this is yet another example of an "internal variation within a schematic pattern."[247] "Amos eben die Freiheit nahm, auch einmal vom Schema abzuweichen, wenn es ihm passt" ("Amos took the liberty to deviate once again from the pattern when it suited him.")[248]

The conflagration will destroy the wall and fortresses of רַבָּה. Rabbah, "the great," the capital city of the Ammonites (2 Sam 11:1 = 1 Chr 20:1; 2 Sam 12:27, 29), was located on the upper course of the Jabbok River (2 Sam 12:27, "the water city"). In Hellenistic times it was called Philadelphia, after Ptolemy II Philadelphus, and today is known as Amman, the capital of Jordan.[249] Its fuller biblical name, רַבַּת בְּנֵי עַמּוֹן ("Rabbah of the Ammonites"; 2 Sam 12:26), distinguished it from other cities that were also called רַבָּה,[250] for example, הָרַבָּה in Judah, Josh 15:60; חֲמַת רַבָּה, Amos 6:2; צִידוֹן רַבָּה, Josh 11:8; 19:28.[251] As the capital city, it naturally would be circumvallated by fortifications.

The assault will take place "amid battle cries (בִּתְרוּעָה) on a day of battle (בְּיוֹם מִלְחָמָה), in a whirlwind on a day of tempest" (בְּסַעַר בְּיוֹם סוּפָה). תְּרוּעָה denotes the shouting and din of the battle cry raised by the attacking troops, accompanied by the sounds of the blowing of horns and trumpets. It is part and parcel of the *rite de bataille de guerre*.[252] For the same expression, see Jer 4:19: "the blare of horns (קוֹל שׁוֹפָר), alarms of war" (תְּרוּעַת מִלְחָמָה). Compare, too, תְּרוּעַת מִלְחָמָה, which is found in

compare, for example, Exod 34:24; Deut 12:20; 19:8; 33:20. Its Akkadian interdialectal semantic equivalent, *ruppušu*, is also employed in similar contexts, for example, "I appointed governors over Egypt." *ša Aššur šar ilāni urappiša kisurrûš*, "I thus enlarged the territory of Assur, king of the gods"; *ZDMG* 72 (1918) 178:13; *murappiš miṣri u kudurri* ("who enlarges the territory and region"); AOB 1 50:15; 63:24, 27, 32, in E. F. Weidner, *Die Inschriften der altassyrischen Könige* (Leipzig, 1926). So, too, Akk. *šurbû* ("to make large"), for example, *mušarbû miṣir māt Aššur* ("who enlarges the territory of Assyria"); D. G. Lyon, *Keilschrifttexte Sargon's Königs von Assyrien (722–705 v. Chr.)* (Leipzig: Hinrichs, 1883) 5:30.

245 There is no need to engage in harmonization here, against Wolff (161), who corrects the Masoretic text to וְשִׁלַּחְתִּי. See Paul, "Literary Reinvestigation," 198–200, esp. 198. Compare also S. Segert ("A Controlling Device for Copying Stereotype Passages? [Amos I 3—II 8, vi 1–6]," *VT* 34 [1984] 481–82), who also cites a paper of D. N. Freedman. On the interchange of similar verbs in Akkadian, see n 57.

246 Wolff.

247 Paul, "Literary Reinvestigation," 199.

248 Rudolph, 127.

249 See E. Stern, "Rabbah, Rabbath Ammon," *EM* 7.315–19 (Heb.); G. M. Landes, "Rabbah," *IDB* 4.1–3; idem, "Rabbah," *IDBSup* 724. Compare, for example, Josh 13:25; Ezek 25:5; for "Rabbah of the Ammonites," compare Deut 3:11; 2 Sam 12:26; 17:27; Jer 49:2; Ezek 21:25.

250 Compare also הָרַבִּית, Josh 19:20.

251 Compare, similarly, Akk. *Ṣidunnu ṣiḫru* ("Little Sidon") and *Ṣidunnu rabû* ("Great Sidon") in D. D. Luckenbill, *The Annals of Sennacherib* (OIP 2; Chicago: University of Chicago, 1924) 29 ii 41; and *ʿrd rbt* ("Great Arad") in the inscription of Shoshenq I (lines 107–9); J. Simons, *Handbook for the Study of Egyptian Topographical Lists Relating to Western Asia* (Leiden: Brill, 1937) 178–86; K. A. Kitchen, *The Third Intermediate Period in Egypt, 1110–650 B.C.* (Warminster: Aris & Phillips, 1973) 432–47. There is also mention of a *rbt* in the Shoshenq inscription (no. 13) and in the list of cities captured by Thutmose III (no. 105). For the latter, see Simons, *Handbook*, 109–22. Compare also the references to the city of *Rubata*, *EA* 289:13; 290:11, discussed by J. A. Knudtzon, *Die El-Amarna-Tafeln* (2 vols.; Vorderasiatische Bibliothek 2/2; Aalen: Otto Zeller, 1964) 2.1342. For other cuneiform citations of *rabû* with places and lands, see *AHw* 2.937. See also Amos 6:2, חֲמַת רַבָּה, and comments there.

252 For תְּרוּעָה, see P. Humbert, *La "terouʿa": Analyse d'un rite biblique* (Neuchâtel, 1946). Compare, for example, Num 10:9; Josh 6:5, 20; Judg 7:21; 1 Sam 4:5–6; 17:20, 52; Isa 15:4; Jer 4:19; 20:16; 49:2; Hos 5:8; Amos 2:2; Mic 4:9.

Jeremiah's oracle against Ammon (Jer 49:2).[253] For the shouts of battle preceding the actual attack, compare Ezek 21:27: "to set battering rams . . . to raise battle shouts (קוֹל בִּתְרוּעָה), to set battering rams against the gates, to cast up mounds, to erect towers"; and Isa 42:13: "The Lord goes forth like a warrior; like a fighter he whips up his rage. He yells (יָרִיעַ), he roars aloud, he charges upon his enemies."

The "day of combat" (יוֹם מִלְחָמָה)[254] and the day of "whirlwind storms and tempests" (סַעַר, סוּפָה)[255] are variant expressions for the "Day of the Lord."[256] They characterize in military and theophanic terms the attack of the Divine Warrior, armed with the forces of nature,[257] against his enemies.

Storm metaphors in the description of battles are also well documented in Akkadian sources, for example, *kīma tīb mehê šamri ana nakri azīq* ("I blew against the enemy like the onrush of a raging storm");[258] *kīma tīb šāri ezzeqe(!) kīma anhulli (= imhulli) šitmurāku* ("I blow like the onrush of a wind; I rage like a [destructive] evil wind").[259] For the Akkadian cognate expression to בְּיוֹם סוּפָה, Akk. *ūm(i) mehê*, compare *ša kīma ūmi mehê ramû uggassu* ("who is clad in anger like a stormy day").[260]

The final doom and disaster of the Ammonite kingdom will be the sending of their political leadership, "their king"[261] (מַלְכָּם) and "officers" (שָׂרָיו), into exile.[262] Only twice does Amos employ this threat—once against Damascus and here against Ammon—both of whom perpetrated barbaric atrocities against Gilead.[263] For both, deportation will follow their nation's demise in battle. However, whereas in the oracle against Aram, the masses (עָם) are destined to be exiled (Amos 1:5), in the oracle against Ammon only the leading officials of the nation will suffer this punishment, meted out measure for measure: those who expanded their territorial borders at the expense of a neighboring country shall themselves be driven out of their own country.

This very same verse is repeated in Jer 49:3 in the oracle against Ammon, with one significant change—in place of הוּא, "he" (= the king), there appears כֹּהֲנָיו, "his priests":

Amos 1:15: וְהָלַךְ מַלְכָּם בַּגּוֹלָה הוּא וְשָׂרָיו יַחְדָּו
Jer 49:3: כִּי מַלְכָּם בַּגּוֹלָה יֵלֵךְ כֹּהֲנָיו וְשָׂרָיו יַחְדָּיו

In both passages the Masoretic pointing of מַלְכָּם refers to "their king." However, in G's translation of Jeremiah (MT Jer 49:3 = G Jer 30:19), the word is transliterated

253 Compare the analogous Akkadian expression, *rigim tāhāzi* ("battle cry"); for example, AOTU 1.304, 25 in B. Meissner, *Assyriologische Forschungen* (AOTU 1/1; Leiden: Brill, 1918) 1. For the roaring of an army accompanying a battle attack, compare, for example, *rigim ummāniya galtu kīma Adad ušašgim* ("I [Sargon] made the roar of my army as frightful as that of thunder"); TCL 3:343 = Thureau-Dangin, *Une relation.*

254 Similar expressions appear in 1 Sam 13:22; Hos 10:14; Prov 21:31; Job 38:23. Compare also the inscription found at Kuntillet ʿAjrud, where the expression בים מלח(מת) appears twice, once in connection with Baal and once with El. See M. Weinfeld, "Further Remarks on the ʿAjrud Inscriptions," *Shnaton* 5–6 (1978–1979) 238 (Heb.).

255 Note the asyndeton construction of the sentence (compare Amos 2:2), as well as the assonance of the Hebrew letter *samech.* This pair of substantives appears in various types of grammatical constructions, for example, סוּפָה וּסְעָרָה, Isa 29:6; Nah 1:3; or reversed (as in Amos), בְּסַעֲרֶךָ וּבְסוּפָתְךָ, Ps 83:16. See Y. Avishur, "The Construct State of Biblical Synonyms Employed in Early Hebrew Poetry," *BM* 66 (1976) 430 (Heb.); reprinted in idem, *The Construct State of Synonyms in Biblical Rhetoric: Studies in the Stylistic Phenomenon of Synonymous Word Pairs in the Construct State* (Jerusalem: Kiryat Sepher, 1977) 159 (Heb.). G misunderstood סוּפָה as סוֹפָהּ (συντελείας αὐτῆς, "her end").

256 Compare Ezek 13:5.

257 Compare Isa 29:6; 40:24; 41:16; 66:15; Jer 23:19; 30:23; Ezek 13:13; Hos 8:7; Nah 1:3; Ps 83:15, 16.

258 OIP 2.45:77; compare 83:44 in Luckenbill, *Annals.*

259 *KAH*, 2.84:19–20, in O. Schroeder, *Keilschrifttexte aus Assur historischen Inhalts* (*WVDOG* 37; Leipzig: Hinrichs, 1922). Compare Borger, *Inschriften,* 58:16, *kima ezzi tib mehê* ("Like a raging storm [I tore up their roots]"). See also *CAD, M,* II.6.

260 *BWL*, 343:5. See also *MSL* 14, 328, 61; *AHw*, 3.1420.

261 G translates: οἱ Βασιλεῖς αὐτῆς ("her kings").

262 It should also be added that מֶלֶךְ and שָׂרִים are a well-documented pair of nouns often appearing together. See Avishur, *Phoenician Inscriptions,* 1.46.

263 Could these two crimes be the ones specifically perpetrated against Israelite territory?

Μελχομ, that is, Milcom, the name of the patron deity of the Ammonites (1 Kgs 11:5, 33; 2 Kgs 23:13).[264] (Compare also G's translation of מַלְכָּם in 2 Sam 12:30; 1 Chr 20:2; and the Lucianic recension of Zeph 1:5.) Because the noun מלכם also appears in Jer 49:1 (G 30:17) in a context that most likely refers to their god and not to their king (and is transliterated as such by G, V, and S)—"Has Israel no sons, has he no heir? Then why has Milcom (מַלְכָּם) dispossessed Gad, and why have his people settled in his [Gad's] towns?"—most commentators defend the reading of Milcom in Jer 49:3 as well: "For Milcom shall go into exile, together with his priests and officials." In such a context the reading "his priests," that is, the priests of this god, is definitely in place. Compare the analogous passage in Jer 48:7: "And Chemosh [the national god of Moab] shall go forth into exile, together with his priests and officials."

Because "Milcom" (Μελχομ)[265] and "his priests" (οἱ ἱερεῖς αὐτῶν)[266] are also found in several of the Greek translations of the Book of Amos, some commentators suggest, in harmonization with Jeremiah, to emend הוּא to כֹּהֲנָיו and to revocalize מַלְכָּם to מִלְכֹּם. In Amos, however, this exegesis is unfounded. In all of the oracles against the foreign nations, the prophet clearly reiterates that the Lord is going to war against the respective nations themselves and not against their gods. Only the human antagonists, who have committed these heinous transgressions, are his adversaries. These oracles have no references to gods or idolatry. Consequently there is no need to introduce here either the name of the deity or "his priests." Nevertheless, the choice of the substantive מַלְכָּם, which appears only here in the oracle against Ammon, is obviously intentional, producing a subtle double entendre on the name of their national deity.[267]

■ **2:1** Although some commentators relate this barbarity to the event recounted in 2 Kgs 3:4–27, when Joram king of Israel and Jehoshaphat king of Judah aligned themselves with Edom in a campaign against Moab (where, however, no mention whatsoever is made of the crime recounted here), the sparsity of documentation concerning the relations of these two rival nations should warn one not to translate conjecture into historical fact. The hostilities that must have characterized the history of these two border nations are almost entirely unknown to us, and it is simply poor method to draw such a definitive conclusion from a rare and exceptional incident that

264 The deity's name is documented in an actual Ammonite inscription, the Amman Citadel Inscription, line 1. For studies of this inscription, see S. H. Horn, "The Amman Citadel Inscription," *BASOR* 193 (1969) 2–13; F. M. Cross, "Epigraphic Notes on the Amman Citadel Inscription," *BASOR* 193 (1969) 13–19; W. F. Albright, "Some Comments on the Amman Citadel Inscription," *BASOR* 198 (1970) 38–40; R. Kutscher, "A New Inscription from ʿAmman," *Qadmoniot* 17 (1972) 27–28 (Heb.); E. Puech and A. Rofé, "L'inscription de la citadelle d'Amman," *RB* 80 (1973) 531–41. It also appears on two Ammonite seals dated to the seventh and sixth century B.C.E. See N. Avigad, "Seals of Exiles," *IEJ* 15 (1965) 222–28; G. Garbini, "Un nuovo sigillo aramaico-ammonita," *AION* 17 (1967) 251–56. In an Ammonite seal impression dated to about the sixth century, there appears the first occurrence of the divine name Milcom as the theophoric element in a personal name: למלכמאור ("Belonging to Milcomor"). See L. G. Heer, "The Servant of Baalis," *BA* 48 (1985) 169–72. See also G. C. Heider (*The Cult of Molek—A Reassessment* [JSOT Supplement 43; JSOT Press, 1985] 301–10) for a review of the problems. Compare also *mlkm* in a god list from Ugarit; A. Herdner, *Corpus des tablettes en cunéiform alphabétiques découvertes à Ras Shamra-Ugarit de 1929 à 1939* (Paris: Geuthner, 1963) 1.109–10, no. 29.

265 For "Milcom," see G (Lucianic recension), α', θ', σ', V, S. For an attempt to defend this reading, see E. Puech, "Milkom, le dieu ammonite en Amos I, 15," *VT* 27 (1977) 117–25. For another approach to the Greek translation, see J. de Waard, "A Greek Translation—Technical Treatment of Amos 1:15," in *On Language, Culture and Religion: In Honor of Eugene A. Nida* (ed. M. Black and W. A. Smalley; Approaches to Semiotics 56; The Hague: Mouton, 1974) 111–18.

266 For "his priests," see G, α', θ', σ', S. T and V support the Masoretic text.

267 Elsewhere the prophet refers to תּוֹמֵךְ שֵׁבֶט, יוֹשֵׁב (Amos 1:5, 8), שׁוֹפֵט, and שָׂרֶיהָ (Amos 2:3). In the last verse, שׁוֹפֵט replaces מֶלֶךְ; instead of מַלְכָּם and שָׂרָיו, there appear שׁוֹפֵט and שָׂרֶיהָ.

happens to be preserved in the Bible.[268] What is of primary significance, however, is that the atrocity recorded here was committed by one foreign nation against another and does not involve Israel or Judah at all.[269] This is the best proof that the oracles of Amos against the foreign nations are intended to denounce the barbaric act of inhumanity itself, no matter by whom or against whom it was perpetrated. Such a crime is a direct offense against the Lord, whose moral laws operate and are binding within the international community of nations. He who flouts the will of the God of Israel will be punished directly by the Judge of all the nations.

Moab is accused of acting in a reprehensible fashion by desecrating a human corpse: He "burnt the bones of the king of Edom," most likely after they were disinterred.[270] The only question is the exact significance of the particle ל in the final word, לְשִׂיד. It can mean "to lime," which then implies the totality of the destruction of the corpse. The bones were burnt so completely that the "ashes became as fine and white as powdered chalk."[271] Although this interpretation is favored by some commentators[272] and has the support of V, "*usque ad cinerem*" ("entirely unto ashes"), it nevertheless is problematic. First, לְשִׂיד can not mean "to ashes" but only "to lime." If the former were intended, it would have been expressed either by Heb. עָפָר, אֵפֶר, or דֶּשֶׁן. The semantic development implied here—from "lime" to "ashes"—is totally undocumented and unprecedented. Second, the ל preceding the noun is more probably to be understood as the ל "of purpose"[273] and thus would be analogous to the other purpose clauses found in Amos 1:6 (לְהַסְגִּיר) and 1:13 (לְמַעַן).

Therefore, the second line of interpretation, "for lime," is preferable. As outrageous as it appears, Moab burnt the bones of the Edomite king in order to obtain lime for the purpose of plastering and whitewashing—be it stones[274] or houses. This "seems to reflect a practice of calcinating human skeletons to acquire lime."[275] Compare already T: עַל דְאוֹקִיד גַרְמֵי מַלְכָּא דֶאֱדוֹם וְסַדִּינוּן כְּגִירָא בְּבֵיתָא ("Since he burnt the bones of the king of Edom and whitewashed [with] them his house like with plaster/lime").[276]

The proposed emendations לַשֵּׁד ("to a demon")[277] or לְשׁוֹד ("for violence")[278] are conjectural and unwarranted. The former is based on Ps 106:37, in which reference is made to the sacrifice of children to demons. However, there is no indication whatsoever that such a practice is being alluded to in Amos. This interpretation, moreover, is based on the incorrect understanding of the phrase מֶלֶךְ־אֱדוֹם as designating a "human sacrifice" (see later). Furthermore, Amos is continuing here his *moral* indictment against the barbarities and atrocities of the nations. None of the charges is related to the *cultic* sphere. The latter, לְשׁוֹד, is also dependent upon the

268 Rudolph, 138. Compare, too, Wolff, 162. Hostilities between the two may be alluded to in the concluding lines of the Mesha inscription; see *KAI,* II.179.

269 The forced conjecture that Edom was an ally of Judah at the time of the oracle against Moab—forced because it is resorted to only in order to maintain an assumed nationalistic background for all of these oracles (see previously, p. 12)—is to be rejected; against Weiser, *Profetie,* 112; Würthwein, "Amos-Studien," 36; Haran, "Rise and Decline," 273; Kaufmann, *Toledoth,* 6.63; Gottwald, *Kingdoms,* 107 n 24 and 109 n 27.

270 The curse and practice of the removal of the bones of the dead from their graves is also well known from Assyrian military inscriptions.

271 R. Gradwohl, *Die Farben im Alten Testament: Eine Terminologische Studie* (BZAW 83; Berlin: Töpelmann, 1963) 86–87.

272 For example, Kimchi; R. J. Forbes, *BHH,* 2.921f.; Hammershaimb, 41.

273 See also Y. ibn Ganaḥ, *Sepher HaRiqmah* (2 vols.; Jerusalem: Academy for the Jewish Language, 1964) 58:10–14 (Heb.).

274 Deut 27:2, 4.

275 Gottwald, *Kingdoms,* 109.

276 Followed by Rashi and partially by Kimchi, who offers both explanations. Compare also Ehrlich, *Randglossen,* 5.230 (referring to 2 Kgs 23:16 and Isa 33:12), who translates, "um Tünche zu gewinnen" ("in order to obtain lime"), noting that the word is vocalized לַשִּׂיד and not לְשִׂיד.

277 W. F. Albright, *Yahweh and the Gods of Canaan: A Historical Analysis of Two Contrasting Faiths* (Garden City, NY: Doubleday, 1968) 240. This suggestion was already made by Tur-Sinai in *HaLashon,* 1.84–89; idem, *Peshuṭo,* 3/2.453; M. Dahood, *Psalms III:101–150, Introduction, Translation and Notes* (AB 17a; Garden City, NY: Doubleday, 1974) 74.

278 See Harper, 38, 41; and Tur-Sinai, *HaLashon,* 1.89.

incorrect interpretation of מֶלֶךְ־אֱדוֹם and has been subsequently discounted even by the scholar who originally made the suggestion.[279]

This then leads to the aforementioned, now disproved, explanation of מֶלֶךְ־אֱדוֹם. Tur-Sinai,[280] expanding upon the study of Eissfeldt on Phoenician and Punic inscriptions pertaining to sacrifices,[281] suggested that the words מלך־אדום are to be identified with the expression *mlk ʾdm,* which appears there and which Eissfeldt had translated literally as a "human sacrifice." Relating this to the verse in Amos, Tur-Sinai rendered the passage: "for he burnt a human sacrifice for violence." Weinfeld,[282] however, in a comprehensive study of the problem, attempted to show that this specific phrase in the Phoenician-Punic inscriptions does not designate human sacrifices or vows but means "king of mankind" and is to be understood as a divine epithet or a theophoric personal name.[283] Although most scholars still support the former view—for example, F. M. Cross, "sacrifice of kindred" (written communication)—clearly its application to this verse in Amos is not justified.

■ **2:2** The destruction of Moab by fire is a paradigmatic example of a "Spiegelstrafe"—as they committed the crime of "burning," so will the Lord retaliate by "sending fire" into their country.[284] This conflagration will destroy the fortresses of הַקְּרִיּוֹת.[285] Not recognizing that the reference here is to a proper place name, G translated τῶν πόλεων αὐτῆς ("her cities" = Heb. קריותיה). (Compare also T, כְּרַכָּא, "the city.")[286] Most commentators,[287] however, correctly interpret הַקְּרִיּוֹת as the name of one of the principal cities of Moab, mentioned in Jer 48:24: "Judgment has come upon . . . Kerioth (קְרִיּוֹת) and Bozrah—upon all the towns of the land of Moab, far and near." It is also mentioned in Jer 48:41: "Kerioth (הַקְּרִיּוֹת) shall be captured and the strongholds shall be seized."[288] In the Moabite Mesha inscription (lines 12–13), it features as the site of the sanctuary of Chemosh, the chief god of the Moabites: "I brought back from there [Ataroth] . . . and dragged it [the booty] before Chemosh at Kerioth" (בקרית).[289] It also appears in the Genesis Apocryphon, 21:29:[290] "They destroyed . . . the Emim [who were in] Shaveh HaKerioth" (בשוה הקריות), which corresponds to the biblical place name שָׁוֵה קִרְיָתָיִם ("the plain of Kiryathaim"), located in the area of Moab (Gen 14:5). Kerioth is modern *ʾel-qureiyāt (Qurēyāt ʿAlēyān),* four miles northeast of Dibān and thirteen miles south of Madeba in *Wādi*

279 Tur-Sinai, *Peshuṭo,* 453.

280 Tur-Sinai, *HaLashon,* 1.84ff.

281 O. Eissfeldt, *Molk als Opferbegriff im Punischen und Hebräischen und das Ende des Gottes Moloch* (Halle: Niemeyer, 1935) 12. See, however, Christensen ("Prosodic Structure," 342 n 32), who accepts both Albright's and Tur-Sinai's suggestions.

282 Weinfeld, "Worship," 133–54, esp. 137–40. Compare also the criticism of M. Smith ("On Burning Babies," *JAOS* 95 [1975] 477–79) and the rejoinder of Weinfeld ("Burning Babies in Ancient Israel," *UF* 10 [1978] 411–16).

283 Compare also Weinfeld ("Worship," 133–54) for the related expressions, *mlk ʾmr* and *mlk bʿl.*

284 Compare Cripps, 136, and Rudolph, 136.

285 Compare Isa 25:2 and Prov 18:19, where קִרְיָה and אַרְמוֹן appear in parallel cola.

286 V and S, however, correctly render the Hebrew proper name. On the definite article preceding a place name, compare הַיַּרְדֵּן, הַגִּלְגָּל; *GKC,* 126e.

287 See K.-H. Bernhardt, "Beobachtungen zur Identifizierung moabitischen Ortslagen," *ZDPV* 76 (1960) 136–58, esp. 143–44 (and map, p. 137); B. Oded, "Keriyot," *EM* 7.269–70 (Heb.); A. Kuschke, "Zweimal *Ḳrjtn,*" *ZDPV* 77 (1961) 24–34; idem, "Horonaim and Qiryathaim: Remarks on a Recent Contribution to the Topography of Moab," *PEQ* 99 (1967) 104–5. Rudolph equates this city with קִיר מוֹאָב in Isa 15:1.

288 Some commentators, however, translate the word here as "towns"; compare J. Bright, *Jeremiah: Introduction, Translation and Notes* (AB 21; Garden City, NY: Doubleday, 1965); Rudolph, *Jeremia* (HAT 1/12; Tübingen: Mohr, 1958) 262. It should be noted, nevertheless, that הַקְּרִיּוֹת appears only in Amos and Jeremiah.

289 See *KAI,* II.176; Gibson, *Hebrew and Moabite Inscriptions,* 80. Yet even here it has been suggested that it may simply mean "city" (= Dibon), comparing קִיר in line 11; compare H. Reviv, *A Commentary on Selected Inscriptions from the Period of the Monarchy in Israel* (Jewish Historical Sources 1; Jerusalem: The Historical Society of Israel, 1975) 22 (Heb.).

290 Fitzmyer, *Genesis Apocryphon,* 165.

'el-Buṭm, in the eastern part of the plateau of *'el-Belqā*.[291]

The literary structure of the name of a country followed by a principal city or cities is also found in the oracles against Edom (Amos 1:12) and Judah (2:5).

The tumult and pandemonium, din and clangor of the battle onslaught are all inherent in the word שָׁאוֹן.[292] Compare, for example, in similar military contexts, Isa 13:4; 66:6; Jer 25:31; Hos 10:14; Ps 74:23.[293] Of the many substantives that express the fury and fanfare of war, Amos intentionally selected this one because of its additional overtones. In Jer 48:45, בְּנֵי שָׁאוֹן functions as the parallel phrase to "Moab": ". . . For fire went forth from Heshbon, flames from the midst of Sihon, consuming the brow of Moab, the pate of the people of Shaon" (בְּנֵי שָׁאוֹן). שָׁאוֹן thus is none other than an archaic appellation for Moab, and by employing the term here Amos creates a very effective double entendre[294] to describe the attack of the Divine Warrior upon that nation—the שָׁאוֹן of arms shall "disarm" the people of שָׁאוֹן.[295]

The stentorian sound of the blare and blasting of the horns[296] is also characteristic of the uproar of war. Both תְּרוּעָה and שׁוֹפָר appear in various parallel constructions throughout the Bible; compare, for example, Lev 25:9; 2 Sam 6:15; Jer 4:19; Zeph 1:16; Ps 47:6; 1 Chr 15:28. Compare within a battle context Job 39:25: "As the trumpet (שׁוֹפָר) sounds, he says, 'Aha!' From afar he smells the battle, the roaring and shouting (תְּרוּעָה) of the officers." For the sounding of the שׁוֹפָר prior to an attack, see, for example, Num 10:6; Josh 6:4ff.; Judg 3:27; Jer 4:19; Amos 3:6; Zeph 1:16; Job 39:25. For קוֹל and תְּרוּעָה, compare 1 Sam 4:6; Jer 4:19; Ezek 21:27; Ps 27:6–7; 2 Chr 15:14.

■ **2:3** For the concluding refrain, וְהִכְרַתִּי, forming a literary inclusio with the opening oracle against Damascus, see previous comments.[297]

For שׁוֹפֵט alternating with other nouns signifying political leadership, see previous remarks.[298]

The feminine suffix in מִקִּרְבָּהּ ("from her midst") and שָׂרֶיהָ ("her officers") is usually explained as referring to the city of Kerioth in the preceding verse or to the land of Moab, treated as a feminine substantive.[299] Others harmonize and emend to the masculine מִקִּרְבּוֹ and שָׂרָיו, but the textual correction is entirely unnecessary.[300]

Both the masses (v 2, מוֹאָב) and the political leaders of Moab are doomed to extermination (compare Amos 1:5, 8).

■ **2:4** For the originality of this oracle, see previous comments.[301]

The indictment against Judah is entirely different from the previous oracles against the nations and the forthcoming oracle against Israel. Judah is not accused of a breach of the moral law but is charged with the "spurning of the teachings of the Lord."[302] For the expression

---

291 There is no need to emend the noun to קִיר מוֹאָב, against, for example, Meinhold; Weiser, *Profetie;* Sellin, 168; J. Morgenstern, "Amos Studies IV," 315; or to בְּעָרֵי מוֹאָב, Procksch, *BHK*.

292 For שָׁאוֹן and קוֹל, compare Isa 13:4; 66:6; Jer 51:55. Compare Avishur, "Construct State," 59–60, no. 135.

293 For other passages that refer to the panic caused in battle by the Deity, compare, for example, Josh 10:10; Judg 4:15; 7:22; 1 Sam 14:15, 20.

294 This was already suggested by G. Hoffmann, "Versuche zu Amos," *ZAW* 3 (1883) 97, who thought it was an old title for the acropolis of Moab. See also Rudolph, 136 n 33.

295 For the theophanic background, see Farr, "Language," 317.

296 In Mari there is also evidence that a horn was added to the soldier's armament. See J. M. Sasson, *The Military Establishments at Mari* (Studia Pohl 3; Rome: Pontifical Biblical Institute, 1969) 30; see also A. Parrot, *Mission archéologique de Mari, II, Le Palais, vol. 2: Peintures murales* (Paris: Geuthner, 1958) 100, pl. xxiii, 1, 2, color pl. C.

297 See p. 51 n 8.

298 See pp. 51–52. The שׁוֹפֵט here designates the ruler (ibn Ezra). Compare, for example, 2 Kgs 15:5; Mic 4:14; Ps 2:10. See W. Richter, "Zu den 'Richtern Israels,'" *ZAW* 77 (1965) 40–72; J. A. Soggin, "Osservazioni sulla radice *špṭ* e sul termine *šōpᵉṭīm* in ebraico biblico," *OrAnt* 19 (1980) 57–59; and Cross (*Canaanite Myth*, 119–20 n 3), who also refers to Amorite *šāpiṭum*, Ugaritic *ṯāpiṭu*, and Phoenician and Punic *šūpēṭ*. For שׁוֹפֵט paired with שַׂר, see Exod 2:14; Mic 7:3; Zeph 3:3; Ps 148:11; Prov 8:16. For its employment in a hendiadys, see Melamed, "Break-up," 200–201 (Heb.).

299 Compare Kimchi; Amsler; Hammershaimb, 43; Wolff, 132; Rudolph, 128.

300 Against many commentators following Wellhausen. Cross suggests reading מִקִּרְבֹּה with preexilic orthography, *ōh* ⟨ *uh*, with שָׂרֶיהָ then being attracted to it secondarily (written communication).

301 See pp. 20–24. Amos most likely added the oracle against Judah to the catalogue of oracles against the nations, which he may have received en bloc. For the

מָאַס תּוֹרַת ה', see Isa 5:24.[303]

The Akkadian interdialectal semantic and etymological equivalent of מאס,[304] *mêšu (mêsu),* also means "to despise, to have contempt for, to disregard."[305] It, too, is employed in reference to disregarding the gods and their rites. For example, *pillud ê ili lumēš parṣī lukabbis* ("I will despise [my] god's [cultic] regulations and trample on [his] rites");[306] *kīnūte mēsī ištari tētiq temēši*[307] ("You transgressed (and) disregarded the proper rites of the goddess").[308]

The expression שָׁמַר חֻקִּים,[309] although prevalent in Deuteronomic and Deuteronomistic literature,[310] need not necessarily have originated there nor be limited to that genre. Note the chiastic formulation of the first two cola. The two terms תּוֹרָה and חֻקּוֹת/חֻקִּים/חֹק appear in several different types of parallel construction.[311]

The action of the parents becomes paradigmatic to their children. The sons follow their parents in being led astray by idol worship.[312] The Heb. כְּזָבִים ("delusions, lies") is one of several cacophemistic[313] words employed in the Bible to describe idolatry. Compare, for example, הֶבֶל, הֲבָלִים ("vanity, vanities") in Deut 32:21; 1 Kgs 16:13, 26; Jer 2:5; שֶׁקֶר ("lie") in Jer 10:14–15; אֱלִיל ("nothingness") in Lev 19:4; אָוֶן ("delusion") in Isa 66:3; תּוֹעֵבָה ("abomination"); שִׁקּוּצִים ("detestable things"); גִּלּוּלִים ("pellets of dung" per Cross); תֹּהוּ ("worthless").[314] This term, however, should not be prejudged as being a Deuteronomic surrogate for idols because it is otherwise totally unattested with such a meaning.[315] The verbal form תעה ("to lead astray") is also nowhere else directly and unequivocally employed in connection with idol worship.[316] Thus there is no compelling reason to deny this expression to the prophet.

The following of idols,[317] of course, directly follows from the spurning of the Lord's teachings. The idiom הָלַךְ אַחֲרֵי ("to follow after"), which expresses loyalty (to God or gods), is extremely common in Deuteronomic and Deuteronomistic phraseology but appears also in pre-Deuteronomic literature.[318] Its Akkadian interdialectal semantic and etymological equivalent, *arki . . . alāku* ("to follow after"), is part of the diplomatic vocabulary of the ancient Near East and refers to the concept of loyalty in a political context.[319] It, too, moreover, appears within a religious context. Compare *rē'û māt Aššur ālik arkiki* ("The shepherd of Assyria who follows

---

sequence of the country followed by its capital city or cities, compare Amos 1:12; 2:2. For a bibliography of vv 4–5, see G. Pfeifer, "'Ich bin im tiefe Wasser geraten, und die Flut will mich ersäufen' (Psalm LXIX.3)—Anregungen und Vorschläge zur Aufarbeitung wissenschaftlicher Sekundarliteratur," *VT* 37 (1987) 327–29.

302 Note that the reference to the Lord is in the third person.

303 Thus there is no need to interpret the phrase as uniquely Deuteronomistic. For תּוֹרַת אֱלֹהֵינוּ, see Isa 1:10.

304 For the use of the מאס, see also Amos 5:21, מָאַסְתִּי חַגֵּיכֶם. For the verb with חֻקִּים, compare Lev 26:16.

305 See *CAD, M,* II.41–42 for the use of the verb with oaths, commands, and cultic rites. Compare similarly the use of the Hebrew verb in 1 Sam 15:23, 26; 2 Kgs 17:15; Jer 6:19; Ezek 20:24; Prov 3:11; Job 5:17. See now the extensive study of this verb in Akkadian by M. Held ("Studies in Biblical Lexicography in the Light of Akkadian, Part II," in *Studies in Bible Dedicated to the Memory of U. Cassuto on the 100th Anniversary of His Birth* [Jerusalem: Magnes, 1987] 114–26 [Heb.]), who relates it only to Zech 3:9 and Job 23:12.

306 *BWL,* 78:135. Compare Isa 5:24, where Heb. מאס . . . נאץ are contextually analogous to the pair of verbs in the Akkadian quote.

307 *BWL,* 76:81.

308 See also M. Weinfeld, "Desecrating, Treading Down and Trampling," in *Hebrew Language Studies Presented to Professor Ze'ev Ben-Hayyim* (ed. M. bar Asher, A. Dothan, D. Tene, and G. B. Ṣarfati; Jerusalem: Magnes, 1983) 195–200 (Heb.).

309 Compare also the Akkadian interdialectal semantic equivalent, *naṣāru* ("to obey commands, to observe laws, decrees"), *CAD, N,* II.42–43.

310 See Weinfeld, *Deuteronomy,* 77 n 6 and p. 336.

311 For the pair תּוֹרָה and חֻקִּים, see also Exod 18:16; Hos 4:6; 8:1. See Avishur, "Construct State," 28, no. 16.

312 For similar accusations against idolatry, see Jer 2:5; Ezek 2:3–4.

313 See S. M. Paul, "Euphemism," 959–61.

314 For references, see Weinfeld, *Deuteronomy,* 323.

315 Contrary to most commentators. It should also not be interpreted as an interpolation (Rudolph, 125) or as a gloss (Harper, 44).

316 See, however, in a somewhat similar context, Jer 23:13, 32. This verb is definitely not Deuteronomistic.

317 G adds ἃ ἐποίησαν ("which they made").

318 See Weinfeld, *Deuteronomy,* 320, 332. For a closely analogous comparison, see Jer 9:12–13.

319 Weinfeld, *Deuteronomy,* 83, 332.

you [Ishtar]");[320] *arki Ištar italluku ṭāb* ("It is good to follow Ishtar").[321]

■ **2:5** Once again, and for the final time, the recurring refrain of destruction by fire is repeated—now devastating Judah and the fortresses of Jerusalem.

Introductory Comments, 2:6–16

The oracle against Israel is the culmination of the fulmination of the prophet against the nations.[322] The previous oracles serve as one grand prolegomenon to his final surprise indictment against Israel.[323] After capturing his audience within the web of his first seven pronouncements, he adds his eighth and final one,[324] the grand finale and raison d'être of his prophetic commission. It is to Israel that Amos was specifically sent (Amos 7:15), and thus this concluding prophecy contains the most detailed list of charges and accusations. The extensive and elaborate series of wrongdoings is spelled out precisely because Israel has benefited from the ongoing kindnesses of the Lord. Israel is not arraigned for crimes committed as a consequence of military belligerency (as were the foreign nations) or for idolatry (as was Judah) but for transgressions committed within the social sphere. Israel's guilt lies within the domain of the everyday oppressive behavior of its citizens toward one another. Its unethical and immoral actions signify the breaking of the covenant[325] and thus lead to its inextricable punishment. Amos, the first of the classical prophets, gives expression here to the new prophetic concept of the "supremacy of morality."[326] The destiny of the people of Israel is now determined by their moral behavior and not by religious infidelity. Unethical actions, and not idolatry, which is hardly mentioned in his prophecies, will ultimately bring about the destruction of the nation.[327]

No consensus yet exists as to the exact number of charges cited by the prophet. Some commentators count four crimes;[328] others opine for a list of seven.[329] As the following comments to the verses attempt to demonstrate, Amos most likely enumerates seven offenses—all within the social sphere.[330]

The beginning of the oracle is fashioned in the standard stylistic pattern of the preceding seven. It then continues with a detailed catalogue of accusations, but unlike the others it does not conclude with the same formulaic punishment. It is yet another example of the breakup of a stereotypic pattern upon reaching the climactic crescendo conclusion.[331] Just as the account of creation in Genesis 1 is formulated with a recurrent final refrain at the end of each of the six days, culminating with the account of the Shabbat on the seventh day, which omits this repetitive refrain,[332] so, too, the first seven oracles (with all their internal variants) are ordered according to a preconceived pattern, which is deliber-

320 J. A. Craig, *Assyrian and Babylonian Religious Texts* (4 vols.; Leipzig: Hinrichs, 1895) 1.54, IV, 19 (= *Beiträge zur Assyriologie* 5, 628).

321 *LKA*, 29d, 8; also *STT* 52:29′.

322 In addition to most commentaries, see also Weiser, *Profetie*, 86, 110; Würthwein, "Amos-Studien," 38; H. Junker, "Amos, der Mann, den Gott mit unwiderstehlicher Gewalt zum Propheten machte," *TTZ* 65 (1956) 321–28; Botterweck, "Authentizität," 178. For the literary unit, Amos 2:6–16, see J. Vollmer, *Rückblicke*, 20–29.

323 Compare Weiser (*Profetie*, 107), who describes the oracle against Israel, "wie ein Blitz aus heiterem Himmel" ("like a bolt from the blue").

324 See previous introductory comments.

325 Compare P. Buis, "Les formulaires d'alliance," *VT* 16 (1966) 410.

326 Kaufmann, *Toledoth*, 6.71–81.

327 Later prophets reintroduce the offense of religious disloyalty and idol worship.

328 For example, Weiser, *Profetie*, 106; Gottwald, *Kingdoms*, 113; Zakovitch, *For Three*, 183–84; Gese, "Komposition," 89–90.

329 For example, Weiss, "Pattern," 150–57. See also Vesco, "Amos," 488.

330 For other heptads in the book, compare Amos 2:6–8, 14–16; 4:4–5, 6–11; 5:8–9, 21–23; 6:1–6; 9:1–4. For the relationship of the crimes enumerated here and Israel's legal tradition, compare, for example, Würthwein, "Amos-Studien," 10–52; Beek, "Religious Background," 134–41; Bach, "Gottesrecht," 23ff., 28ff.; idem, *Aufforderungen*, 109ff. The last counts five actions here contrary to apodictic law. According to him, Amos's accusations all refer to the breach of apodictic laws and are all covenant related. Thus God "acts to enforce the law," 84–85.

331 See Avishur, "Forms," 1–55, esp. 14.

332 "And it was evening and it was morning, the X day." There is no need, therefore, to assume that the formulaic ending was also originally attached to the oracle against Israel, as does Haran ("Biblical Studies," 109–36, esp. 128–30), who suggests that vv 7ff. were not originally part and parcel of this oracle against Israel.

ately altered when the climax of the prophecy is reached —the oracle against Israel.

■ **2:6** The first accusation[333] has been explained in two different ways: Some exegetes relate it to the bribery of judges,[334] others to the illegal action of creditors selling debtors into slavery.[335] According to the first interpretation: "They [the judges] have sold for silver those whose cause was just." The judges are reproached for accepting bribes (בַּכֶּסֶף, "for [the price of] silver")[336] from the guilty parties, as a result of which the צַדִּיק ("he whose cause is just")[337] is "sold," that is, colloquially speaking, "sold out." Justice has been perverted, and the innocent become the victims of a distorted, "paid for," bribed verdict.

The main problem with this line of interpretation is that the judges do not "sell" the accused.[338] Moreover, nowhere in the Bible is the verb מכר employed in the context of bribery. Amos 5:12, in which similar charges are leveled against Israel and the צַדִּיק again appears in parallel to אֶבְיוֹנִים, specifically states that "bribes are taken" (לֹקְחֵי כֹפֶר). Compare, too, 1 Sam 12:3; Isa 1:23; 5:23; Mic 3:11; Ps 15:5.

The other suggestion is that the צַדִּיק, who is either the "innocent guiltless party" or, in a nonforensic sense, an "honest man,"[339] has been sold in order to satisfy creditors demanding their monetary compensation from the debtors, בַּכֶּסֶף ("for/on account of silver"), which they owed and could not pay. Alternately, an innocent individual has been sold into slavery on the false charge of owing money, that is, בַּכֶּסֶף ("on account of silver").[340] Another suggestion is that the individual has been sold "for silver," that is, for a paltry debt too insignificant to justify such an action. According to all these latter interpretations,[341] the charge is sale into slavery to pay a real or assumed debt; the party sold is otherwise guiltless.

The צַדִּיק is not the only one who suffers from such unscrupulous behavior. Another victim—the second offense—is the defenseless אֶבְיוֹן ("the needy")[342] who have no means whatsoever at their disposal to protect themselves from being sold into debt slavery.[343] (Those who interpret the first stich as referring to the bribery of judges naturally continue the same line of exegesis here as well.)

The major problem centers around the exact meaning of the substantive נַעֲלָיִם. According to the Masoretic pointing, the noun refers to "a pair of sandals," which is then understood to denote a trifling sum—the debtors are sold into slavery for a very small debt.[344] The question arises, however, of why such an idea is expressed by means of a "pair of sandals." Nowhere else in the Bible does this image symbolize a paltry sum. One manner of phrasing this concept would be the way found in Gen 14:23, where a שְׂרוֹךְ־נַעַל ("shoe latchet") and a

333 For מִכְרָם (instead of the usual מָכְרָם), similar to בִּקְעָם (Amos 1:13), compare Neh 13:15. Compare also 2 Sam 1:10, נִפְלוֹ, with 1 Sam 29:3, נָפְלוֹ. See *GKC*, 119p.

334 Bribery: for example, ibn Ezra; Sellin²; Robinson-Horst; Hammershaimb, 46; compare Cripps, 140.

335 Debt slavery: for example, Ehrlich, *Randglossen*, 5.230; Harper, 49; Wolff, 165; Mays, 46; Rudolph, 138, 141–42; D. N. Freedman, "Prolegomenon" to G. B. Gray, *The Forms of Hebrew Poetry* (New York: Ktav, 1972) xxix. For references to the selling into slavery, compare Exod 21:7ff.; Lev 25:39; Deut 15:12; 2 Kgs 4:1; Isa 50:1; Neh 5:8.

336 For ב-*pretii*, compare Amos 8:6; see *GKC*, 119p.

337 Compare Exod 23:7.

338 Rudolph, 138.

339 Ibid.

340 For ב ("on account of"), compare Isa 50:1.

341 Wolff, 165. See Bach, "Gottesrecht," 23–24. Compare Vesco, "Amos," 489, "Il peut être débiteur insolvable mais il n'a rien fait illégal. Son seul tort est de ne pas avoir d'argent" ("He may be an insolvent debtor, but he has done nothing illegal. His only wrong is not having money.")

342 Compare Ugar. *'abynt*, *CTA* 17:i:17. Compare, too, *abiyānum* in Mari, ARM X 37:23; 44:10; 55:10, which W. von Soden ("Zur Herkunft von hebr. *'ebjōn*, 'arm,'" MIO 15 [1969] 322–26) suggests is an Old Amorite word. For אֶבְיוֹן, see G. J. Botterweck, "*'bywn*," *TWAT* I (1973) 38–43.

343 For the parallelism of צַדִּיק and אֶבְיוֹן, see Amos 5:12. Compare the related terms צֶדֶק and עֲנָוָה, Zeph 2:3; Ps 45:5. In Amos 8:6 the parallelism is between the common pair דַּלִּים and אֶבְיוֹן.

344 Almost all commentators; for example, Harper, 49; Mays, 47; Cripps, 140; Rudolph, 141. The sole example known to me of the employment of shoes and/or sandals to indicate a very meager amount of money is found in *ABL* 1285, rev. 27–28, where an exorcist complains to the king, "I cannot afford a pair of sandals or the wages of a tailor," *ammar sēni ammar igri ša* LÚ.TÚG.KA.KÉŠ. The text has been collated and re-edited by S. Parpola, "The Complaint of a Forlorn Scholar," in *Language, Literature, and History:*

חוט ("thread") compose a merism, inferring that Abraham took nothing at all from Abimelech.[345] However, here, neither a latchet nor a thread is mentioned, but rather, supposedly, a pair of sandals. Moreover, the assumption that sandals must have been so cheap and so insignificant an item that they eventually became synonymous for any extremely small amount of money is completely an ad hoc interpretation. The entire line of reasoning is totally without any foundation and has misguided most exegetes.

Speiser, by contrast, suggested that "sandals" were meant to be interpreted literally. Basing himself on two other passages where sandals are employed in a legal context, Deut 25:9 and Ruth 4:7, he concluded that a practice developed to use sandals "to validate arrangements by circumventing legal obstacles. . . . We have here a proverbial saying which refers to the oppression of the poor by means which may be legal but do not conform to the spirit of the law."[346] However, these passages do not warrant such conclusions and are not in any way related to what is being described by the prophet.

The key to the correct interpretation of the substantive נעלים lies in the realization that the present vocalization of the word is based on a misunderstanding of its original meaning.[347] The hapax legomenon singular noun נעלם, derived from the root עלם ("to hide"), was confused with the dual and/or plural form נַעֲלָיִם ("sandals") and was repointed accordingly, the final *mem* being mistakenly understood as the masculine plural suffix rather than the third radical of the stem.[348] This rare substantive develops semantically from the basic root meaning of that which is "hidden" to a "(hidden) gift" or "payoff." Other nouns that share a similar development from analogous stems are also attested in Hebrew.[349]

This noun, although appearing only here and in Amos 8:6, is also reflected indirectly in G, 1 Sam 12:3. According to the Masoretic text, the farewell speech of Samuel reads as follows: "Here I am! Testify against me (עֲנוּ בִי) in the presence of the Lord and in the presence of his anointed one. Whose ox have I taken, or whose ass have I taken? Whom have I defrauded or whom have I robbed? From whom have I taken a bribe (לָקַחְתִּי כֹפֶר) to look the other way (וְאַעְלִים עֵינַי בּוֹ)? I will return it to you." The Hebrew text as reflected in the end of this verse according to G is, however, significantly different. Instead of the corrupt Heb. עֵינַי בּוֹ,[350] G has ἀποκρίθητε κατ᾽ ἐμοῦ (= Heb. עֲנוּ בִי, "testify against me"), thereby creating a literary inclusio, for the sentence then commences and concludes with the same words, עֲנוּ בִי. As for Heb. וְאַעְלִים, G translates ὑπόδημα ("a pair of sandals"), reflecting the Heb. נַעֲלָיִם. This same reading is once again evidenced in Sir 46:19, where, in his summary fashion of succinctly recapitulating the career of the great personalities of the past, he says of Samuel, "And

Philological and Historical Studies Presented to Erica Reiner (ed. F. Rochberg-Halton; New Haven, CT: American Oriental Society, 1987) 264, lines 27–28. For a study of shoes and sandals in Mesopotamia, see A. Salonen, *Die Fussbekleidung der alten Mesopotamier nach sumerisch-akkadischen Quellen* (Helsinki: Suomalainen Tiedeakatemia, 1969).

345 For another image of a paltry sum, see Ezek 13:19.

346 E. A. Speiser, "Of Shoes and Shekels (I Samuel 12:3; 13:21)," *BASOR* 77 (1940) 18, reprinted in *Oriental and Biblical Studies: Collected Writings of E. A. Speiser* (ed. J. J. Finkelstein and M. Greenberg; Philadelphia: University of Pennsylvania, 1967) 155. Compare T and Kimchi. This interpretation is also accepted by R. de Vaux, *Ancient Israel: Its Life and Institutions* (tr. J. McHugh; New York: McGraw-Hill, 1961) 169; Mays, 45. See, however, Vesco, "Amos," 490.

347 See Gordis, "*Naʿalam* and Other Observations on the Ain Feshka Scrolls," *JNES* 9 (1950) 44–47; idem, "Studies," 213–15. Compare also Tur-Sinai, *Peshuṭo*, 454–55. Gordis noted that S, קורבנא interpreted נעלם as a "gift, bribe." He also compared the hapax legomenon נַעֲלָמִים in Ps 26:4 (parallel to מְרֵעִים) and translated "men of bribes, corrupt men." The substantive appears in parallelism with נעזבים in 1QH 3:28; compare also 1QH 4:13f.

348 Suggestions for vocalization are נַעֲלָם, נֶעֱלָם, or נַעֲלֹם.

349 Compare (1) Heb. מַטְמוֹן ("hidden treasure/secret hoard") from טמן ("to hide"), parallel to אוֹצָר ("treasure"), Isa 45:3; and to כֶּסֶף ("silver/money"), Gen 43:23; Jer 41:8; Job 3:21; Prov 2:4. (2) מַצְפּוּן ("secret treasures") from צפן ("to conceal"), Obad 6, "How ransacked his hoards" (מַצְפֻּנָיו). (Compare the analogous verse in Jer 49:10.) The verb then develops the meaning "to store up"; compare Hos 13:12; Pss 31:20; 119:11; Prov 2:1, 7; 7:1; 10:14; Job 10:13; 21:19; Cant 7:14. Similarly צְפוּנִי ("my treasured, cherished place") = Jerusalem in Ezek 7:22; compare also Pss 17:14; 83:4, "treasured ones."

350 The correct Hebrew would have been וְאַעְלִים עֵינַי מִמֶּנּוּ ("And I shall hide my eyes from him").

while he rested on his bed, he had the Lord and his anointed testify, 'A bribe (כֹּפֶר) and נעלם from whom have I taken.' And no man witnessed against him" (עָנָה בוֹ). Although G also reads here ὑπόδημα ("a pair of sandals"; probably a supercorrection based on G to Samuel), the Hebrew spelling נעלם without a *yod* is correct. Once again, as in the Book of Samuel, the nouns כֹּפֶר and נעלם are parallel to one another, as are כֶּסֶף and נעלם in Amos. All three are to be interpreted as different types of gift payments. Thus, a lost Hebrew word is no longer "hidden" from sight.

In sum, the indictment boils down to the "Erbarmungslösigkeit und Verachtung der Menschenwürde" ("the lack of pity and contempt for human dignity").[351]

For the use of בַּעֲבוּר ("on account of," "for the sake of"), compare 1 Sam 12:22; 2 Sam 6:12; 9:7; Jer 14:4; Mic 2:10; Pss 106:32; 132:10. It also parallels the particle ב in Amos 8:6, as in the present verse.[352]

■ **2:7** This verse does not begin a new oracle.[353] The participial formulation followed by verbs in the imperfect[354] expands the indictment and further delineates (after the past crimes listed in the former verse) the ongoing offenses for which Israel is found guilty. The accusations, unlike the oracles against the foreign nations that enumerate only past transgressions, are in the present and reflect the social situation current at the time of the prophet himself.

His third charge relates to the oppression of the poor who are trampled upon as though they were the dust of the ground.[355] Although the intent is clear, the exact wording of the verse presents several difficulties. The form and meaning of שֹׁאֲפִים must first be clarified. This verb is not to be confused with its homonym, שאף ("to gasp, pant after"); it is a biform of שוף ("to crush, trample upon").[356] It also appears (outside the analogous verse in Amos 8:4) in Ezek 36:3;[357] Pss 56:2, 3; 57:4;[358] and in postbiblical literature.[359] Here G correctly understood the meaning of this verb and translated τὰ πατοῦντα, from the verb πατέω ("to tread (on), trample").[360] The א in the verb does not represent, as some thought, a rare mater lectionis (compare דאג, Neh 13:16 and several examples in 1QIs^a, for example, יאכה, Isa 30:31; גמלאם, Isa 63:7)[361] but preserves a variant writing of the participial form of ע"ו verbs.[362] From these metaplastic forms, new verbs were created that preserved the א. Compare the roots קאם, Hos 10:14, alongside the common קום; לאט, 2 Sam 19:5, alongside לוט; and ראם, Zech 14:10, alongside רום. Here, then, the א is not to be deleted but is to be understood as another example of this rare by-formation from the ע"ו verb, שוף, and should be vocalized הַשָּׁאפִים.

Because all other examples of this verb just cited are followed by the direct object without any particle, the ב in בְּרֹאשׁ דַּלִּים ("the heads of the poor") is problematic and has been explained in various ways: as analogous to other

351 Rudolph, 141.

352 This parallel between בַּעֲבוּר and ב lends support to the interpretation of the particle ב as "on account of" and not as the ב-*pretii*. עֲבוּר, however, does not mean "produce" here as suggested by Hoffmann, "Versuch," 99.

353 Against, for example, Reventlow (*Amt,* 57–58) and Haran ("Biblical Studies," 128–30), there is no reason to assume that the stereotypic ending וְשִׁלַּחְתִּי אֵשׁ was also once present here. The oracle is intentionally constructed in a different fashion. See Wolff, 141.

354 Compare Amos 6:1b, 3–6. Compare Wolff, 133, 141. For a participial construction continued by the imperfect, compare Amos 6:6a.

355 See Rudolph, 138, for a list of suggested interpretations, which he correctly rejects. See also I. Zolli, "Note esegetiche (Amos 2,7a)," *RSO* 16 (1936) 178–83. Compare the common Akkadian expression of belittlement, *anaku epru ištu šupāl šēpē šarri* ("I am the dust from under the sandals of the king"); for example, *EA* 149:4–5.

356 See *BDB,* שאף II.983. Compare Gen 3:15; Job 9:17.

357 Compare W. Zimmerli, *Ezekiel, II* (Philadelphia: Fortress, 1979) 228.

358 Compare H.-J. Kraus, *Psalmen 1—63* (BKAT xv/1; Neukirchen-Vluyn: Neukirchener Verlag, 1972) 412.

359 See H. Yalon, *Studies in the Hebrew Language* (Jerusalem: Bialik, 1971) 17 (Heb.); and S. Lieberman's note to B. Mandelbaum's edition of *Pesikta de Rav Kahana* (New York: Jewish Theological Seminary of America, 1961) 139–40 (Heb.).

360 So, too, V, *conterunt,* from *contero* ("destroy, wear away, trample underfoot"); S, דדישין; compare T, דְּשַׁיְטִין from שוט ("to despise, reject"); Jastrow, *Dictionary,* 1531. T translates the Hebrew roots דכא, Ps 72:4; כתת, Ps 29:24; שטח, Exod 32:20, all by the verb שוף.

361 See E. Y. Kutscher (*The Language and Linguistic Background of the Isaiah Scroll* [Jerusalem: Magnes, 1959] 120 [Heb.]) for further examples.

362 Similar to Aramaic and Arabic. See ibid., 121 n 74.

verbs, which may take either a direct object or an object introduced by a particle;[363] as the ב -*pretii* ("at the cost of");[364] as the ב of means;[365] or as a scribal error that should be deleted.[366] Notwithstanding these difficulties, the prophet is referring to the rights of the poor, which are trampled upon and crushed into עֲפַר־אֶרֶץ ("the dust of the ground"). Many exegetes have explained these last two words as a doublet or hybrid reading and have therefore omitted one or the other or even both, assuming that the colon is too long for metrical symmetry with the second colon.[367] However, a study[368] of the various appearances of these two interchangeable nouns shows no need to excise them as a gloss. They appear in all different types of parallel formations and, what is more important, appear together in the same stich. Compare 2 Sam 22:43, וְאֶשְׁחָקֵם כַּעֲפַר־אָרֶץ ("I pounded them like dust of the earth"). (In the parallel verse in Ps 18:43 only כְּעָפָר appears.) In Job 14:19, תִּשְׁטֹף סְפִיחֶיהָ עֲפַר־אָרֶץ ("Torrents [vocalizing, סְפִיחָה] wash away the dust of the earth"). Note that in these examples taken from poetic passages אֶרֶץ appears without the demonstrative ־ה. For עֲפַר הָאָרֶץ, see Gen 13:16; 28:14; Exod 8:12; Isa 40:12.

For the pair דַּל[369]/עָנִי, compare, for example, Isa 10:2; 26:6; Zeph 3:12; Prov 22:22. For עָנָו–דַּל, see Isa 11:4; אֶבְיוֹן–עָנִי/עָנָו, Isa 29:19; Jer 22:16; Ps 70:6; and אֶבְיוֹן–דַּל, Amos 4:1; 8:6; Ps 72:13.[370]

For similar expressions of abusing the poor and depriving them of their legal rights, compare Isa 3:15: מַלָּכֶם תְּדַכְּאוּ עַמִּי וּפְנֵי עֲנִיִּים תִּטְחָנוּ ("How dare you crush my people and grind the faces of the poor"); and Prov 22:22: אַל־תִּגְזָל־דָּל כִּי דַל־הוּא וְאַל־תְּדַכֵּא עָנִי בַשָּׁעַר ("Do not rob the wretched [דָּל] because he is wretched; do not crush the poor man [עָנִי] in the gate").

The Akkadian verb *kabāsu* ("to step upon purposely, trample, crush") is employed in a similar fashion.[371] Compare the following example of the D-stem, *kubbusu*: *ekdūtija kima qaqqaru lukabbis* ("May I step on those who are insolent toward me as upon the ground").[372] The verb also develops the meaning "to treat with contempt."[373]

So, too, here in Amos:[374] They step upon the heads of the poor as though they were stepping upon the ground beneath them, that is, they treat the underprivileged with contempt and abuse.[375]

The expression לְהַטּוֹת דֶּרֶךְ is usually interpreted as a

363 For example, Mays, 41, comparing the Hebrew verbs פגש and פגע, which appear both with a direct object and with the particle ב.

364 See Beek ("Religious Background," 134–35), comparing 1 Chr 12:19. See the criticism of Rudolph, 138, who translates "gegen" ("against"). So, too, Wolff, 133.

365 R. Gordis (*The Book of Job: Commentary, New Translation and Special Studies* [Moreshet 2; New York: Jewish Theological Seminary, 1978] 175), who compares Isa 5:14 with Job 16:10, and Ps 22:8 with Job 16:4. See also his remarks, "Studies," 215.

366 Many commentators simply delete or avoid in translation.

367 For example, Wellhausen; Marti, 167; Sellin, 199; Weiser, *Profetie*, 134; Wolff, 133; Rudolph, 138. But the words do appear in G.

368 See Avishur, "Construct State," 44 n 45.

369 Hebrew (דַּל(ים appears also in Amos 4:1; 5:11; 8:6. Compare similarly Ugar. *dl*, Gordon, *UT*, 664 (p. 384); and Akk. *dallu*, *CAD, D*, 52, "small, inferior"; *dullu*, 173, "misery, hardship"; *dullulu*, 178, "wronged, oppressed."

370 Avishur, "Construct State," 160. For דַּל and עָנִי, see J. van der Ploeg, "Les pauvres d'Israël et leur piété," in *OTS* 7 (Leiden: Brill, 1950) 237–40. Fey (*Amos und Jesaja*, 62–63) sees here a dependency of Isaiah upon Amos.

371 See *CAD, K*, 10.

372 L. W. King, *The Seven Tablets of Creation: Or the Babylonian and Assyrian Legends Concerning the Creation of the World and of Mankind* (Luzac's Semitic Text and Translation Series 13; London: Luzac, 1902) 2 pl. 84:97.

373 For similar imagery, compare *ša annam appa[lu] Šamaš ana dinān eperi ša takbusu liddin* ("Should I say, 'Yes,' let Shamash treat me as if I were the dust upon which you have stepped"), in G. Dossin, *Lettres de la première dynastie babylonienne* (TCL 18; Paris: Geuthner, 1934, 85:15).

374 There are some who view the initial ה as a remnant of an original הוֹי ("Ah"). See *NJPS*.

375 See M. Weinfeld, "Desecrating," 195–200; and compare the Rabbinic idiom פּוֹסֵעַ עַל־רָאשֵׁי עַם קוֹדֶשׁ ("stepping on the heads of a holy people"); for example, Babylonian Talmud Megillah 27b; Sanhedrin 7b. Because, as seen before, נעלים is actually a noun meaning a "gift payment," could there be a muted double entendre here implying that the poor are trampled upon by "sandals"?

legal phrase meaning to "pervert justice," דֶּרֶךְ being understood as a synonym for מִשְׁפָּט ("justice"); compare לְהַטּוֹת אָרְחוֹת מִשְׁפָּט ("to pervert the course of justice"), Prov 17:23.[376] However, in every other passage where לְהַטּוֹת means legally "to pervert," it is always followed by a direct object that indicates its juridical content; compare, for example, מִשְׁפָּט ("justice"), Exod 23:6; Deut 16:19; צַדִּיק ("he who is legally in the right"), Isa 29:21; Prov 18:5; דִּין ("legal cause"), Isa 10:2.[377] As for the suggestion that דֶּרֶךְ is synonymous with מִשְׁפָּט, this is possible only when the context and vocabulary are explicitly within the legal sphere (for example, Jer 5:4, 5).

The fourth accusation, therefore, does not pertain to the perversion of judicial procedures. Its intention becomes clear, however, once it is compared with the almost identical passage in Job 24:4, יַטּוּ אֶבְיֹנִים מִדָּרֶךְ ("They push the needy off the roads"). The indictment here makes the similar charge that the needy are "turned aside" (יַטּוּ), that is, pushed off the road.[378] This figuratively expresses the same idea that the underprivileged class[379] is bullied and oppressed by the wealthy, who deprive and block them from obtaining the privileges and prerogatives to which they are naturally entitled.

Many have thought that the next accusation, the fifth, is one of cultic prostitution or of orgiastic practices and immoral actions that take place at the various shrines.[380] However, the female involved is not called a קְדֵשָׁה ("cultic prostitute") but rather a נַעֲרָה ("young woman"), a term without any cultic connotations whatsoever.[381] Moreover, the wrongs committed by the shrines are referred to only in the next verse, and there they are devoid of all sexual overtones and implications. Furthermore, no law in the Bible forbids a father and son from having intimate relations with one and the same unmarried young woman. A man may not have sexual intercourse with his wife's daughter (Lev 18:17; 20:14), nor a son with the wife of his father (Lev 18:8; 20:11; Deut 23:1; 27:20) nor a father with the wife of his son (Lev 18:15; 20:12). However, this specific prohibition is not mentioned in any of the biblical legal collections.[382] Moreover, in all of his charges, Amos is not denouncing cultic rites and wrongs but rather the lack of basic moral conduct.

Amos appears to be actually proscribing a deed that went beyond the existing law. The employment of the

---

376 For example, Kimchi; Deden; Maag, *Text,* 88, 151, 229; Mays, 46; Cripps, 141; Wolff, 133; I. L. Seeligmann, "Zur Terminologie für das Gerichtsverfahren im Wortschatz des biblischen Hebräische," in *Hebräische Wortforschung: Festschrift zum 80. Geburtstag von Walter Baumgartner* (ed. B. Hartmann and others; SVT 16; Leiden: Brill, 1967) 269 n 2; A. Kuschke, "Arm und Reich im Alten Testament, mit besonderen Berücksichtung der nachexilischen Zeit," *ZAW* 57 (1939) 49–50; Vesco, "Amos," 491; Soggin, *Amos,* 48.

377 Correctly, Rudolph, 138–39.

378 Many exegetes add the particle מ to (מ)דֶּרֶךְ in Amos and thereby create an even more identical parallel to Job. See Sellin; Ehrlich, *Randglossen,* 5.231; H. L. Ginsberg, "Some Notes on the Minor Prophets," in Eretz Israel 3 (*M. D. U. Cassuto Memorial Volume;* ed. B. Mazar and others; Jerusalem: Israel Exploration Society, 1954) 83 (Heb.). Ginsberg transposes אֶרֶץ from the first stich to here and reads, וּמִדֶּרֶךְ יַטּוּ עַנְוֵי־ אָרֶץ. However, as D. N. Freedman remarks upon this verse ("Isaiah 42:13," *CBQ* 30 [1968] 226 n 3), "the omission of the preposition in poetry is not uncommon." See also the comments of M. H. Pope (*Job: Introduction, Translation and Notes* [AB 15; Garden City, NY: Doubleday, 1973] 176) on this verse.

379 For עֲנָוִים as a plural of עָנִי, see L. Delekat, "Zum hebräischen Wörterbuch," *VT* 14 (1964) 44–46. For the vocabulary and study of the poor in the Bible, see M. Schwantes, "Das Recht der Armen," in Beiträge zur Biblischen Exegese und Theologie 4 (Bern and Frankfurt: Peter Lang, 1977). See also, H. M. Orlinsky and M. Weinberg, "The Masorah on עֲנָוִים in Amos 2:7," *Estudios Masoréticos (V Congreso de la IOMS). Dedicados a Harry M. Orlinsky* (ed. E. F. Tejero; Textos y Estudios "Cardenal Cisneros" 33; Madrid: Institut "Arias Montano," 1983) 25–35.

380 For example, Robinson-Horst, 79; Weiser, *Profetie,* 141; Cripps, 142; Hammershaimb, 48–49; Pfeifer, "Denkformenanalyse," 67.

381 See also Gordis, "Studies," 216; Bach, "Gottesrecht," 30–33; Robinson-Horst, 79; Weiser, *Profetie,* 141. Barstad (*Religious Polemics,* 17–36) concludes that the נַעֲרָה here is none other than a "*marzeaḥ* hostess"!

382 This act of misconduct is also not related to the law in Exod 21:7–11.

unique expression "a man and his father" is most probably meant to indicate both the continuity of the act involved (father setting the example for his son), as well as the lack of shame and promiscuity involved when a father and son both "go to the (same)[383] young woman." The Heb. expression יֵלְכוּ אֶל, furthermore, has a special nuance, as already noted by Ehrlich:[384] "Uebrigens ist יֵלְכוּ hier wahrscheinlich nicht vom blossen Gange zu verstehen, denn הלך kann auch heissen, sich mit jemandem einlassen; vgl. zu Num 22,13 und Pr 1,11. Hier ist das Verbum speziell vom Einlassen des Mannes mit einem fremden Weibe gebraucht; vgl. Midrasch rabba Num. Par. 10, wo zu lesen ist: הנואף הזה הולך[385] אל אשת איש והיא מתעברת ממנו = der Ehebrecher lässt sich mit dem Weibe des Nächsten ein, und sie wird von ihm schwanger." ("Moreover, יֵלְכוּ here probably does not refer to mere motion, for הלך can also signify having dealings with someone; cf. Num 22:13 and Prov 1:11. Here the verb is specifically employed with reference to the intercourse of a man with a foreign woman. Cf. Num Midrash Rabba, paragraph 10, 'The adulterer has relations with his neighbor's wife and she became pregnant by him.'") He then goes on to bring other analogies for "'gehen' mit 'zu' konstruiert, den unehelichen Verkehr des Mannes mit einem Weibe" ("'to go' construed with 'to' [to mean] extramarital intercourse").

His exegetical insight can now be corroborated from Akkadian, where the expression *ana . . . alāku*,[386] the interdialectal semantic and cognate equivalent of Heb. הָלַךְ אֶל, has the same idiomatic meaning, "to have sexual intercourse." Note the following passages: *šumma amēlu ana sinništi ina alāki ikkal* ("If a man eats during intercourse"); *ana sinništi alāka muṭṭu* ("He is incapable of having intercourse"); *ana* NIN.DINGIR *ilīšu lu illik* ("If he had intercourse with the priestess of his god"). A final reference can be made to Middle Babylonian dream omens: *šumma amēlu ana* SAL.TUR *ill[ik]* ("If a man has intercourse with a SAL.TUR").[387] The various Akkadian equivalents of Sumerian SAL.TUR—*ṣiḫirtu* ("girl"), *ṣuḫārtu* ("young woman"), and *batūltu* ("adolescent")[388]—are all fitting chronological analogues to the age group into which הַנַּעֲרָה would very well fit. The same semantic development is also attested in Aramaic, in which the expression אֲזַל אֶל/עַל (= Heb. הָלַךְ אֶל) is employed in Talmudic and Geonic literature for sexual intercourse.[389]

Another reason why the prophet may have selected this unique term containing the verb הלך may have been in order to connect it (verbally but not contextually) with his previous accusation against Judah. There, in the course of his indictment, he declared: "They are beguiled by the delusions after which their *fathers went*" (הָלְכוּ אֲבוֹתָם); and here again, "[A man] and his *father go*" (וְאָבִיו יֵלְכוּ).[390]

In the Hittite laws it is permissible for the two to have sexual intercourse with the same woman: "If father and son sleep with (the same) slave girl or harlot, there shall be no punishment."[391] However, as mentioned previously, the female referred to in Amos is not a harlot or a slave,[392] but just a "young woman" who belongs to the same category as that of the דַּלִּים and עֲנָוִים previously mentioned—just one more member of the defenseless

383 For example, Cramer; Ehrlich, *Mikrâ*, 3.403; idem, *Randglossen*, 5.232; Weiser, *Profetie;* Amsler, 181; Wolff; Rudolph. See also Gottwald, *Kingdoms*, 113. Among those who stress the moral aspect of the crime are L. Dürr, "Altorientalisches Recht bei den Propheten Amos und Hosea," *BZ* 23 (1935–1936) 150–57; Beek, "Religious Background," 135–37; Würthwein, "Amos-Studien," 45–46; Bach, "Gottesrecht," 30–33.

384 Ehrlich, *Mikrâ*, 3.403; *Randglossen*, 5.232.

385 Although the standard editions of this midrash have the reading אֵצֶל and not אֶל, the interpretation remains the same.

386 Compare *CAD, A*, I.321, 7′, for the following two examples and other citations. See S. M. Paul, "Two Cognate Semitic Terms for Mating and Copulation," *VT* 32 (1982) 492–94.

387 V. Scheil, *MDP*, p. 14.55 iii 9.

388 For discussion, see *CAD, B*, 174; *Ṣ*, 185; and B. Landsberger, "Bemerkungen zu San Nicolò und Ungnad, Neue Babylonische Rechts- und Verwaltungsurkunden, Bd. II.2," *ZA* 39 (1929–1930) 290–91.

389 N. M. Bronznick ("More on *HLK 'L*," *VT* 35 [1985] 98–99), who cites also S. Abramson, "On the Hebrew in the Babylonian Talmud," in *Archive of the New Dictionary of Rabbinic Literature* (ed. M. Z. Kaddari; Ramat-Gan: Bar-Ilan University, 1974) 2.12–13 (Heb.). Compare Babylonian Talmud, Ḥullin 69a.

390 Compare also the "two walking together" in Amos 3:2.

391 *HL*, II, 194. See *ANET*, 196; J. Friedrich, *Die Hethitischen Gesetze* (Documenta et Monumenta Orientis Antiqui 7; Leiden: Brill, 1959) par. 80 and

and exploited human beings in northern Israel.[393]

Although the expression חִלֵּל אֶת־שֵׁם קָדְשִׁי ("to profane my holy name") is found in the language of Ezekiel (for example, Ezek 20:39; 36:20–22) and the Holiness Code (Lev 20:3; 22:2, 32), there is no reason whatsoever to consider it a late interpolation or redaction here.[394] As Rudolph correctly states, the elimination of the phrase would be a "bedauerliche Amputation" ("a regrettable amputation")[395] . . . "und selbst wenn Amos ihn geschaffen haben sollte, was spricht dagegen? Passt er nicht genau zu seiner Verkündigung?" ("and even if Amos should have created it, what speaks against it? Does it not precisely suit his message?")[396]

Because there is no compelling reason to doubt the originality of the phrase in Amos, the only question that remains is the significance of its position at the end of this verse. Is it to be understood as belonging solely to the last (fifth) accusation, or does it function as a summation of the previous five indictments? The latter appears to be more correct and herein lies another innovation in the *Weltanschauung* of the prophet. By employing a phrase (which otherwise almost always appears in the context of cultic and sacral transgressions)[397] within a list of moral offenses, Amos endows it with a new dimension, hereby declaring that *every moral* infringement is an act of profanation of God's name. "Alle Missachtung und Misshandlung der Schwachen und Wehrlosen ist letzlich eine Missachtung Jahwes selbst." ("Every contempt and abuse of the weak and defenseless is ultimately a contempt of Yahweh himself.")[398] לְמַעַן here indicates the consequence of the action;[399] by acting immorally they flout the divine will.

Its specific position within the pericope may have yet another connection. Just as it appears after the accusation of immoral cohabitation, so, too, does a very similar expression appear in Leviticus 18 after a long list of forbidden sexual relationships (Lev 18:21).[400]

■ **2:8** The sixth charge is one of distraints for unpaid debts. The unique expression בְּגָדִים חֲבֻלִים is interpreted by most commentators to mean "garments taken in pledge" as security or pawn when a loan is granted by a creditor.[401] However, several studies have clearly shown that both in a juridical context (Exod 22:25; Deut 24:6, 17) and in wisdom literature (Prov 13:13; 20:16; 27:13; Job 24:9) the verb חבל applies to distraints—persons as well as property—that take place only when the loan falls due and the debt is defaulted.[402] Compare, for example,

p. 85.

392 Against Wellhausen, 72–73; Cripps, 142; Weiser, *Profetie*, 91–93; Beek, "Religious Background," 135–37; Dürr, "Recht," 153; Maag, *Text;* Mays, 175–76; Robinson-Horst, 79; Hammershaimb, 44–45. Compare Rudolph (142–43), who connects it incorrectly with Exod 21:7, as do A. Alt, as cited in K. Galling, "Bethel und Gilgal II," *ZDPV* 67 (1944) 37; Würthwein, "Amos-Studien," 45–46; Amsler; Vesco, "Amos," 492. Compare P. E. Dion, "Le message moral du prophète Amos, s'inspirait-il du 'droit de l'alliance'?" *ScEs* 27 (1975) 17–18.

393 See Beek, "Religious Background," 136; Maag, *Text*, 175; Würthwein, "Amos-Studien," 102; Rudolph, 142–43.

394 Against Wolff, 134; Vollmer, *Rückblicke*, 22.

395 Rudolph, 144; against Wolff.

396 Rudolph, 144. See also Gese ("Komposition," 92 n 55), who states that its occurrence in Ezekiel and the Holiness Codes is only a relative argument: "da wir wenig altes sakralrechtliches Material haben. . . . Dieser Terminus der Profanierens ist vordeuteronomisch natürlich auch vorauszusetzen, vgl. Gen. XLIX 4, wohl auch Ex. XX 25" ("as we have little material relating to the ancient sacral law. . . . This term of profanation is also naturally presumed to be pre-Deuteronomic; cf. Gen 49:4; probably also Exod 20:25").

397 Compare, however, Jer 34:16, where it is employed for the resubjugating of liberated slaves.

398 Rudolph, 143. Compare Beek, "Religious Background," 136; Dürr, "Recht," 150–54. See also Würthwein ("Amos-Studien," 46), who states that it is "eine Entweihung des heiligen Jahwenamens, weil es gegen Jahwes offenbarten Willen verstösst" ("a desecration of the holy name of Yahweh, because it offends against the revealed will of Yahweh"). For חלל, see F. Maass, "*ḥll*," *THAT* 1 (1975) 570–75; W. Dommershausen, "*ḥll*," *TWAT* II (1977) 972–81.

399 For example, Cripps, 142; Hammershaimb, 49; Rudolph, 139; Soggin, 48.

400 Compare Weinfeld, *Deuteronomy*, 187–88.

401 See almost all commentaries.

402 Primarily J. Milgrom, "The Missing Thief in

Job 24:9: "They snatch (יַגְזְלוּ) the orphan from the breast; the suckling [reading עַל for עֹל][403] of the poor they seize" (יַחְבֹּלוּ). "The seizure of children can hardly take place at the time of a loan but only as a distraint for non-payment."[404] For the seizure of persons in distraint, see 2 Kgs 4:1; Isa 50:1. In biblical Hebrew the antithesis of חבל is expressed by the verb שלם[405] (Prov 13:13; compare Sir 8:13); that is, if payment is not received (שלם) from the debtor, if the loan is defaulted, his property is confiscated (חבל). The creditor may seize whatever he desires except what is essential to life. However, the distraint pledge does not remain within his jurisdiction forever but must be returned upon payment of the loan.

Extrabiblical evidence brought by Milgrom[406] also confirms that the seizure of property is for distraint. Compare Josephus, *Antiquities* IV. 8.28,[407] and Mishnah, Baba Meṣia 9:13: "If one man made a loan to another [and he was not repaid at the end of the specified time], he may only exact a distraint from him (יְמַשְׁכְּנוּ) with the consent of the court, but he may not enter his house to take his distraint." (The Mishnah goes on to detail what may and may not be taken after the debt falls due.)

In the Aramaic papyri from Elephantine the creditor's right of distress is also deferred until the time that the loan falls due.[408] This is learned from two of the Aramaic documents: Cowley 10[409] and Kraeling 11.[410] Both refer to the issue that the debtor can take no legal steps against the seizure of pledges. Cowley 10 states: "And I shall not be able to complain against you before a governor or a judge because you have taken a pledge from me, while this document is in your hand." Kraeling 11 states that if the debtor dies before paying and his children do not repay the debt, the creditor has "power to confiscate from his house enough to pay the above debt—he is given blanket authority over his slaves, utensils, both of copper and iron, clothing and grain." As Yaron concludes, "the purpose of such distraint . . . is to put pressure on the defaulting debtor."[411]

So, too, in Mesopotamian sources: "E. Neufeld[412] citing Koschaker on Nuzi and Middle Assyrian mortgage documents and Driver-Miles on Hammurabi's laws, makes a convincing case that in Mesopotamian law the seizure of pledges took place only after default."[413] As Driver and Miles summarize, "If the debtor fails to pay his debt when it has fallen due, the creditor is entitled, apparently without recourse to a court, 'to levy a distress' (Bab. *nepûm*). . . . In several documents the distress (Bab. *nipûtum*) is seized as a pledge to ensure or compel either repayment of a debt or the return of property to its rightful owner . . . and the creditor is said 'to release' (Bab. *uššurum*) it on the repayment of the loan, when the owner is said 'to take away' (Bab. *tabālum*) his distress."[414]

Leviticus 5:20ff.," *RIDA*³ 22 (1975) 77ff.; idem, *Cult and Conscience: The Asham and the Priestly Doctrine of Repentance* (SJLA 18; Leiden: Brill, 1976) 95ff. See also M. David, "Deux anciens termes bibliques pour la gage," *OTS* 2 (1943) 79–86; Z. W. Falk, *Hebrew Law in Biblical Times* (Jerusalem: Wahrmann, 1964) 101; S. E. Loewenstamm in his review of R. de Vaux, *Les institutions de l'Ancien Testament, I* (Paris, 1958), in *Kiryat Sepher* 34 (1958) 48 (Heb.). Compare also Falk, "Zum jüdischen Bürgschaftsrecht," *RIDA*³ 10 (1963) 43ff.; and I. L. Seeligmann, "Lending, Pledge, and Interest in Biblical Law and Biblical Thought," in *Studies in Bible and the Ancient Near East, Presented to S. E. Loewenstamm* (ed. Y. Avishur and J. Blau; Jerusalem: E. Rubinstein, 1978) 183–205, esp. 191–95 (Heb).

403 So most commentators.

404 Milgrom, "Missing Thief," 79.

405 Ibid., 81.

406 Ibid. Compare also the Hebrew ostracon from Yabneh Yam, where the seized garment may also have been a distraint. See Gibson, *Hebrew and Moabite Inscriptions*, 26–30.

407 "If the debtor acts without shame regarding the repayment, it is forbidden to enter his (the debtor's) house to seize a pledge before judgment can be given regarding it."

408 R. Yaron, "Notes on Aramaic Papyri, II," *JNES* 20 (1961) 127–30; idem, *Introduction to the Law of the Aramaic Papyri* (Oxford: Clarendon, 1961) 96–97; idem, *The Law of the Elephantine Documents* (Jerusalem: Mifʿal HaŠichpul, 1968) 48 (Heb.).

409 Cowley, *Aramaic Papyri*, ll. 12–14, pp. 33–31.

410 E. G. Kraeling, *The Brooklyn Museum Aramaic Papyri: New Documents of the Fifth Century B.C. from the Jewish Colony at Elephantine* (New Haven: Yale University, 1935) 259–65.

411 Yaron, *Introduction*, 96–97; compare also p. 35.

412 E. Neufeld, "Inalienability of Mobile and Immobile Pledges in the Laws of the Bible," *RIDA* 9 (1962) 33–44; see esp. 35 n 4.

413 Ibid., 35 n 5. Both cited by Milgrom, "Missing Thief," 80–81.

414 G. R. Driver and J. C. Miles, *The Babylonian Laws:*

Hammurabi's laws, however, forbid the distraint of a debtor's corn (LH 131) or his ox (LH 241), the latter under the penalty of paying a fine. "The evident purpose of the lawgiver in either case is to safeguard the owner's only means of subsistence, just as the Hebrew law [Deut 24:6, 10–13; compare Job 24:3, where taking the widow's ox for a pledge is cited as an extreme example of harsh conduct] forbids a creditor to seize a debtor's cloak or hand-mill."[415]

Compare further the following examples taken from Babylonian letters for persons taken as distress (Akk. *nipûtu*):[416] "I am under pressure (for payment) and my people were taken as distress"; "We just paid the silver but he (still) raises claims against us (and) our women were taken as distress."[417]

The Akkadian etymological equivalent of Heb. חבל, *ḫabālu* (verb) and *ḫubullu* (noun), however, does not mean to take as a pledge or distraint. The verb means "to borrow, to acquire on credit, basically to assume a financial obligation."[418] The noun *ḫubullu,* referring to a "debt, obligation," is attested in Old Akkadian, Old Babylonian, and Old and Middle Assyrian and develops the meaning "interest" in Middle and Neo-Babylonian.[419] Thus, one may conclude that the Heb. verb חבל in legal contexts is actually the semantic equivalent of Akk. *nepû* ("to take persons [mostly women] or animals as distress, pledge, to distrain"), and the noun / חֲבֹל חֲבֹלָה[420] is equivalent to Akk. *nipûtu* ("distress").

In sum, חבל in all instances pertains

> to the seizure of property of the debtor who has not paid his debt on time. [If the laws pertained to a pledge taken at the time of a loan], it would mean that the Torah limits the permission of the borrower to receive a pledge at the time of the loan, but does not recognize any restriction of permission to seize items of the borrower who does not repay his debt. But ever since the law of Hammurapi (241) until today there are many laws which for social reasons restrict the right of the creditor to confiscate the property of the borrower who did not pay on time, without limiting the right of the creditor to receive a pledge at the time of the loan, whereas there is no support for the existence of the opposite situation.[421]

Thus, Amos is inveighing here against the confiscation of clothing as distraint for an unpaid debt, a situation already prohibited by law in Exod 22:25–26 with a special reservation: "If you take your neighbor's garment in distraint (חָבֹל תַּחְבֹּל), you must return it to him before the sun sets; it is his only clothing, the sole covering for his skin. In what else shall he sleep? Therefore, if he cries out to me, I will pay heed, for I am compassionate." Deuteronomy 24:17 says, "You shall not take a widow's garment in distraint" (תַחֲבֹל).

Amos is not alone in indicting elements of the population for such immoral behavior. Compare the words of the prophet Ezekiel, who uses the seizing or returning of a distraint as one of his criteria for distinguishing between a righteous and wicked man (Ezek 18:7, 12, 16; 33:15). Job three times refers to the same theme in his catalogue of iniquities committed by the people: "They lead away the donkeys of the fatherless and seize the widow's bull as a pledge" (יַחְבְּלוּ), Job 24:3. (Compare the prohibition in LH 241, which forbids the distraint of a debtor's ox.)[422] Moreover, significantly this accusation in Job is directly followed in the next verse (v 4) by "They chase the needy off the roads," thereby providing a similar juxtaposition of charges against the wealthy, as is found in Amos 2:7–8. In this very same chapter (Job

Edited with Translation and Commentary (2 vols.; Oxford: Clarendon, 1952) 2.210.

415 Ibid.

416 See *CAD, N,* II.249–51.

417 Compare also Gen 47:18–19, 23–24; and Neh 5:5.

418 See *CAD, Ḫ, ḫabālu* B, 6–7; *ḫubullu* A, 216–18.

419 Except for isolated instances in Elam, Ras Shamra, and Nuzi. For *nepû, CAD, N,* II.171–72.

420 For the noun חֲבֹל, Ezek 18:12, 16; 33:15; Neh 1:7; and חֲבֹלָה, Ezek 18:7.

421 S. E. Loewenstamm, "Review," 48.

422 For donkeys taken as distraint, note the following letter from Mari: *nipûssu 1 ANSE išdud* ("As his distress he led away one donkey"); ARM IV 58:14. (Akk. *šadādu* is the interdialectal equivalent of Heb. נהג found in Job 24:3.) And as for oxen, compare *3 alpēja ittepi* ("He distrained three of my oxen"); TCL 1, 2:19, in F. Thureau-Dangin, *Lettres et contrats de l'époque de la première dynastie babylonienne* (Paris: Guethner, 1910).

24:9), he also accuses them of taking human beings as a distress, a practice well known from Mesopotamian sources (as noted previously). In Job 22:6, the taking of a distraint appears, as in Amos, in connection with the confiscating of garments: "You exact a distraint (תַּחְבֹּל) from your fellows without reasons, and leave them naked, stripped of their clothes."

In Amos's denunciation, moreover, these wealthy creditors add insult to injury, for not only do they violate a law that is intended to provide protection for the poor but they also take these very garments and "יַטּוּ by every altar." The verb, derived from the root נטה ("to stretch, spread out"), is vocalized in the *hiphʿil* and is to be interpreted as a reflexive: "they stretch themselves out."[423] For a similar reflexive *hiphʿil* construction, compare the later Mishnaic usage יַטּוּ וְיִקְרְאוּ ("they stretch themselves out and recite the *Shemaʿ*"); הִטֵּיתִי לִקְרֹא ("I stretched myself out to recite the *Shemaʿ*"). Thus there is no need to revocalize[424] the verb as a *qal*, יִטּוּ, or to emend to יַצִּיעוּ ("they spread out [the garments]").[425] The preposition עַל[426] makes clear that not the garments are being spread out but that they are stretching themselves "upon" (עַל) these very garments. The choice of the verb יַטּוּ, moreover, was intentionally selected to provide a verbal link with the preceding verse—with, of course, two entirely different meanings. Even at the cultic shrines themselves, the wealthy remain insensitive to the illegal and immoral acts they commit against the destitute. Amos, by stating that this action takes place "by every altar"[427] and by expressing this offense by the use of imperfect verbs in both stichs, clearly indicates that the taking of basic necessities for reclining and feasting was extremely widespread at this time, thereby poignantly emphasizing how abhorrent their action was.[428] Even if their behavior were within the letter of the law, as long as the poor are made to suffer, the practice is denounced as being totally reprehensible.[429]

Amos now states his seventh charge against the wealthy, indicting them for another immoral act that is culminated within the environs of a cultic setting. This time, moreover, he adds a sarcastic note: "They drink יֵין עֲנוּשִׁים in the house of their God" (בֵּית אֱלֹהֵיהֶם)[430]—"*their* God," not "our God"; "*their* shrines," not "my shrine."

The expression יֵין עֲנוּשִׁים appears only here.[431] The root, ענשׁ, refers in the Bible to monetary fines and indemnity: for the verb, see, for example, Exod 21:22; Deut 22:19; 2 Chr 36:3; for the noun, compare, for example, 2 Kgs 23:33. The grammatical form עֲנוּשִׁים has been interpreted by some exegetes as an abstract substantive similar to, for example, מְגוּרִים (Gen 17:8; 28:4; 47:9) and נְעוּרִים (Gen 8:21; Isa 54:6; Ps 127:4).[432] It was also understood by G as ἐκ συκοφαντιῶν ("to extort by false information") and by T as אוֹנְסָה ("compulsion, force"). Note that both missed the monetary nuance of the word. It is preferable, however, to view it as a passive participle, paralleling the previous חֲבֻלִים, and to translate "wine obtained by mulcting," that is, wine bought with money received from exacting fines from the poor.[433] It is impossible to know whether these fines were legal or not and whether the parties were actually guilty. Whatever the case, fines are not to be exacted in

423 Already correctly noted by ibn Ganaḥ, *Haschorashim*, 301, and Kimchi. The Mishnaic references are found in Mishnah Ber, 1:3.

424 Rudolph, 139, draws attention to Isa 30:11.

425 For proposed emendations, see Harper.

426 Heb. עַל is neither to be deleted (against H. Oort, "De profeet Amos," *ThT* 14 [1880] 114–58; Sellin; Wolff, 134); nor connected to מִכְרָם, Harper, 52; nor interpreted as an apocope for עַל־עֲפַר הָאָרֶץ, Rudolph, 139.

427 This expression and the following, בֵּית אֱלֹהֵיהֶם, are not late additions to the text; against Wolff.

428 There is absolutely no reference here to pagan cultic practices or orgies practiced by the shrines. Bach ("Gottesrecht") consummately remarks that their "culpability is compounded by hybris—their behavior is not only contumacious, but contumelious."

429 The suggestion of M. Dahood ("'To Pawn One's Cloak,'" *Bib* 42 [1961] 359–66) to connect v 8 with v 7b, by relating the "pledged garments . . . to those which the clients who, unable to pay cash, would place in pawn with the [sacred] prostitute until they could make the necessary payment," has been correctly criticized by Rudolph, 145 n 25.

430 The Hebrew expression appears in two other passages, Judg 9:27 and 1 Chr 10:10 (but not within the same context). Compare the analogous Akkadian, *bit ili* ("temple").

431 Compare Prov 4:17: "They drink the wine of lawlessness" (יֵין חֲמָסִים).

432 So Rudolph, 139.

433 There is also no support in biblical Hebrew for Barstad's translation (*Religious Polemics*, 15): "They

order to allow the wealthy to indulge their appetites, feasting and drinking by the shrines. This is "entweder der Gipfel der Frechheit oder das Zeichen eines abgestumpten Gewissens" ("either the height of insolence or the sign of a blunted conscience").[434] Obviously, then, the two cultic locations should not be deleted from the text.[435] The irony is that precisely at the very places of worship, they act in a way that is condemned by the God of Israel. Once again Amos deplores and denounces actions that go beyond the actual prescriptions of the law.

■ **2:9** Now comes a dramatic reversal introduced by an emphatic וְאָנֹכִי.[436] Roles are reversed and Israel becomes the object. By means of a series of emphatic first-person pronouns and verbs, Amos contrasts the deeds of the God of Israel with those of Israel. Whereas they are singled out and reprimanded for their exploitation and deprivation of the needy, the Lord reminds them that he, for his part, had constantly come to their aid when they were in need.[437] Their immoral and unethical treatment of those who are unable to defend themselves is juxtaposed here to his protective treatment throughout their early history when they were unable to defend themselves. The acts of kindness of God stand as a stark antithesis to their persistent deeds of disobedience.[438]

These verses should also be understood against a covenant-*rib* background.[439] Amos lists the past and present beneficent acts that the ruler has performed for his vassals. By such deeds the overlord establishes his claim to the loyalty and obedience of those who must submit to his rule. Yet despite all these goodnesses and despite the fact that Israel owes its very existence and preservation to the Lord, they have remained faithful only to their own infidelity. They are guilty of major infractions of covenant law. They have flouted the will of their Sovereign to whom they owe absolute allegiance.

The first act of the Lord's kindness was his total decimation of the Amorites. Once again the imagery of the military prowess of the Divine Warrior is drawn upon but this time in a context favorable to Israel. The "Amorites" here are a collective title for the inhabitants of Canaan during the time of the conquest.[440] The use of this term to describe the population annihilated[441] at the time of Joshua is pre-Deuteronomic but is not necessarily rooted solely in the E-tradition.[442]

"Yet it was I who destroyed the Amorites מִפְּנֵיהֶם." The third-person plural suffixal ending is constructed similarly to the third-person plural address of vv 6–8 (compare בֵּית אֱלֹהֵיהֶם, v 8) and should not be emended to the second-person masculine plural מִפְּנֵיכֶם.[443] It serves as a transition to the direct address of the accused, which commences with the next verse and continues through v 13. This style is characteristic of the prophet who, similar to the oracles against the nations in which he directly addresses Israel only at the very end, so, here as well, also begins with a nonpersonal third-person address and only subsequently accuses them directly in the second person.

The word מִפְּנֵיהֶם may be interpreted in a double sense,[444] both geographically ("from before them"; compare, Exod 23:30; 34:11, 24; Lev 18:24; Deut 8:20) and causatively ("on account of," that is, "for their behalf, for their sake"); compare Josh 2:10; 4:23; Isa 63:12.

drink the wine given as rates" (as he himself admits).

434 Rudolph, 145.

435 Against Wolff, 134, 167.

436 For the emphatic אָנֹכִי, see *GKC*, 135a. The conjunctive introduces a *casus pendens*, "as for me, I. . . ."

437 Rudolph, 146; Wolff, 168.

438 For other references to the early history of Israel in Amos, see Amos 3:1; 5:25; 9:7.

439 J. Bright (*Covenant and Promise: The Future in the Preaching of the Preexilic Prophets* [London: SCM, 1977] 84) explains "his attack [as] deeply rooted in theology . . . against the backdrop of the events of exodus and giving of land." See also Weinfeld, *Deuteronomy*, 138 n 2. Such a review of the Lord's past actions is attested only in connection with Israel, for only they have been selected for such a covenantal relationship.

440 Gen 48:22; Josh 24:15; Judg 6:10; 2 Sam 21:2.

441 The tradition of a complete annihilation is found only in the Book of Joshua, especially 1—14, but not in Judges. For the idealized concept of the former and its rationale, see M. Weinfeld, "The Period of the Conquest and of the Judges as Seen by the Earlier and the Later Sources," *VT* 17 (1967) 93–113.

442 So Rudolph, 146, following Noth, "Der Gebrauch von אמרי im alten Testament," *ZAW* 58 (1940–1941) 184f.; in contrast to Schmidt, "Redaktion," 180; and Wolff, 168.

443 Many commentators, following Duhm, "Anmerkungen," 4. The shift to direct address is not the result of an assumed inserted section; against Wolff, 134.

444 See also Rudolph, 139, and Wolff, 134.

For the use of the verb השמד along with מִפְּנֵיכֶם/מִפְּנֵי/מִפְּנֵיהֶם in the context of descriptions of conquest, compare, for example, Deut 2:12, 21–22; Josh 24:8; 2 Kgs 21:9; compare, too, its employment with reference to the Amorites and their height and strength, for example, Deut 1:27–28. This verb denoting "total annihilation" is repeated for emphasis in this verse (הִשְׁמַדְתִּי . . . אַשְׁמִיד).[445] Compare also Amos 9:8, where the negative formulation states that the annihilation will not be total, כִּי לֹא הַשְׁמֵיד אַשְׁמִיד. In Amos 2:9 the characteristic verbal sequence of *qatal-yaqtul* is followed.[446]

There may also be a veiled allusion here. Just as the Lord destroyed the Amorites, so, too, may he also destroy the Israelites who now behave as oppressors themselves.[447]

The Amorites are described here as a nation of gigantic stature and prowess. For the overwhelming size of the original inhabitants of Canaan, compare the traditions preserved in Num 13:28; Deut 1:28; 2:10, 21; 9:2; Josh 14:12, 15; 15:14. Amos expands upon this description of mammoth proportions to include the entire preconquest population of Canaan. His point is clear: The Israelites would never have been able to enter the promised land and annihilate the powerful inhabitants without the aid of their Deity.

For other references to these two trees—אֲרָזִים ("cedars") and אַלּוֹנִים ("oaks")[448]—compare Isa 2:13, again in the context of their stately and lofty height; Isa 44:14; Ezek 27:5–6; Zech 11:1–2. For the comparison of another nation to a lofty cedar, see Ezek 31:3: "Assyria was a cedar in Lebanon . . . of lofty stature." (Compare also Ezek 17:22.) The preponderant height of the cedar tree is contrasted to its polar opposite[449] in 1 Kgs 5:13: "He [Solomon] discoursed about trees, from the cedar in Lebanon to the hyssop that grows out of the wall." The cedar tree (Akk. *erēnu*) is similarly renowned for its height and might in Mesopotamian sources: *erēnī ṣirūti* ("tall cedars"); *erēnī . . . dannūti šiḫūti paglūti* ("mighty, tall, thick cedars"); *gišmaḫḫē erēni . . . išiḫuma ikbiru* ("cedar trunks . . . grown high and thick").[450]

The oak (אַלּוֹן), because of its strength, was employed in the making of oars (Ezek 27:6). Its might is also alluded to in the following description of a god taken from a Mesopotamian document (where *allānu* appears as the Akkadian interdialectal etymological and semantic equivalent of Heb. אַלּוֹן): *[karā]nu damūšu allānu idāšu* ("His blood is wine, his arms are oak").[451] An אַלּוֹן is also one of the trees listed in Isa 44:14 from which idols are constructed.

The word חָסֹן appears only one other time in scriptures, in Isa 1:31, again in connection with trees, this time the "terebrinth" (אֵלָה).[452] It has been suggested, however, that its meaning there may refer to "stored wealth," relating חָסֹן to the verb חסן ("to store"; Isa 23:18) and the noun חֹסֶן ("treasure"; Isa 33:6; Jer 20:5; Ezek 22:25; Prov 15:6; 27:24).[453] חֲסִין, with the meaning "strength, power," also occurs in Ps 89:9, describing the might of the Lord, and appears twice in biblical Aramaic (Dan 2:37; 4:27), as well as in extrabiblical Aramaic sources.[454]

The arboreal imagery employed by Amos to portray

445 The repetition adds to the forcefulness and emphasis of the total annihilation.

446 For a study of the *qatal-yaqtul* sequence in Ugaritic and Hebrew, see M. Held, "The *YQTL-QTL* (*QTL-YQTL*) Sequence of Identical Verbs in Biblical Hebrew and in Ugaritic," in *Studies and Essays in Honor of Abraham A. Neuman* (ed. M. ben Horin, B. D. Weinryb, and S. Zeitlin; Leiden: Brill, 1962) 281–90.

447 Compare Vollmer, *Rückblicke*, 28: "Mit der Tradition begründet Amos das Ende der Tradition" ("with the tradition Amos establishes the end of the tradition").

448 For these two trees, see J. Feliks, *Plant World of the Bible* (Ramat Gan: Bar Ilan University, 1968) 76–78, 107–8 (Heb.). See also Ugar., *'rz* ("cedar").

449 Compare also 2 Kgs 14:9, for another example of the merism cedar-thorn.

450 See *CAD, E*, 274, for citations.

451 See *CAD, A*, I.354.

452 See S. D. Luzatto's commentary to Isaiah, *Il Profeta Isaia* (Padova: Bianchi, 1867 [Heb.]).

453 See *NJPS:* "Stored wealth shall become as tow." For etymological equivalents in other Semitic languages, see *KB*, I, 324. For yet another interpretation of the word in this passage based on Rabbinic Hebrew, "semiprocessed flax," see M. Tsevat, "Isaiah I 31," *VT* 19 (1969) 261–63; and S. E. Loewenstamm's rejoinder, "Isaiah I 31," *VT* 22 (1972) 246–48.

454 See *DISO*, 93.

the Amorites continues with his description of their extirpation as the "destroying of his boughs above (פִּרְיוֹ מִמַּעַל) and his trunk below" (וְשָׁרָשָׁיו מִתָּחַת)—a merism depicting total extermination. These paired polar opposites, פְּרִי and שֹׁרֶשׁ, are found several times in the Bible: 2 Kgs 19:30; Isa 14:29; 37:31; Ezek 17:9; Hos 9:16. There are, in addition, several alternate substantives for פְּרִי: שֹׁרֶשׁ-קָצִיר in Job 14:8–9; 18:16; 29:19; שֹׁרֶשׁ-פֻּארָה in Isa 10:33—11:1; שֹׁרֶשׁ-עָנָף in Mal 3:19; שֹׁרֶשׁ-דָלִית in Ezek 17:6; 31:7 (compare Num 24:7).[455] The expression is also found in Phoenician:[456] *l' ykn lm šrš lmṭ wpr lmʿl* ("May they have no trunk below nor boughs above"), again in the context of total annihilation.[457]

Amos, however, unlike all these examples in both Hebrew and Phoenician, reverses the conventional order by citing first the top of the tree and not its bottom. This change is most likely intentional and due to his previous imagery, which also commenced with the height of the tree.[458] "By emphasizing at the end of the retrospect Yahweh's total judgment upon the land's former inhabitants, Amos anticipated the sentence which is to be passed on its present population."[459] Thus this verse foreshadows not only the forthcoming punishments but also Amos 9:8, where the prophet declares that "the Lord God has his eye upon the sinful kingdom: 'I will wipe it off (וְהִשְׁמַדְתִּי) the face of the earth.'"

Note the repetitive appearance of the root letters על (in מִמַּעַל), which also link the particle עַל in vv 6, 7, and 8 with the following verb הֶעֱלֵיתִי in v 10.

455 Compare H. L. Ginsberg, "'Roots Below and Fruits Above' and Related Matters," in *Hebrew and Semitic Studies Presented to G. R. Driver* (ed. D. W. Thomas and W. D. McHardy; Oxford: Clarendon, 1963) 72–76; idem, "Contributions to Biblical Lexicography," in *Hanoch Yalon Jubilee Volume: On the Occasion of His Seventy-fifth Birthday* (ed. S. Lieberman and others; Jerusalem: Kiryat Sepher, 1963) 167–70 (Heb.). (See also Avishur, "Word Pairs," 41–42.) Ginsberg, in these studies, has demonstrated that שֹׁרֶשׁ refers to the trunk of the tree and not merely to its roots, and פְּרִי, to its boughs and not merely to its fruits. Note, too, that קָצִיר, פֻּארָה, עָנָף, and דָלִיּוֹתָיו, all meaning "branches" and "boughs," may replace פְּרִי in the idiom. Compare also the instructions of Lev 23:40 with Neh 8:15.

456 *KAI,* I.14:11–12. This is part of the curse formula found in the fifth-century Ešmunʿazōr inscription. Several of the biblical passages are also in the context of a total annihilation. For an example from Ugaritic literature of a city, personified as a plant, being cursed, see *CTA* 3:iii:159–60, where both "root" (*šrš*) and "top" (*r'iš*) are to perish.

457 Analogous word pairs expressing the same merism appear in Mesopotamian sources: (1) *šuršu* ("root")—*pir'u* ("fruit"). Thus in the Erra Epic: *ša iṣi šurussu lipparima la išammuḫ piri'šu* ("Let the *root* of the tree be cut [var., "I shall cut"] so that it will bear no *fruit*"). See F. Gössmann, *Das Era-Epos* (Würzburg: Augustinus, 1955) IV:125; L. Cagni, *L'Epopea Di Erra* (Roma: Istituto di Studi del Vincino Oriente, 1969) 118. (2) *išdu* ("foundation, foot, root")—*qimmatu* ("crown"); for example, "sacred tree—whose root(s) (*išissu*)—its crown" (*qimmassu*); F. Gössmann, *Das Era-Epos,* 14–15, 98–99. (3), *šuršu—artu* ("foliage"); for example, *šaplānu šuršišu E[a . . .] elēnu artašu urab[bi]* ("Below Ea[. . .ed] its roots, above [gr]ew its foliage"); *BBR,* No. 80, rev. 8 and duplicate 81:9. For other similar expressions, *šuršu—qarnu,* see F. Küchler, *Beiträge zur Kenntnis der assyrische-babylonischen Medizin* (Assyriologische Bibliothek 18; Leipzig: Hinrichs, 1904) 8–9; *šuršu—qimmatu,* see F. Köcher, "Ein spätbabylonischer Hymnus auf den Tempel Ezida in Borsippa," *ZA* 53 (1959) 236–40. For the suggested connection between these and the concept of a "Weltbaum," see B. Margulis (Margalît), "Weltbaum und Weltberg in Ugaritic Literature: Notes and Observations on RŠ 24, 245," *ZAW* 86 (1974) 6–8.

458 It has been suggested by A. Ḥacham in his commentary on Amos in *Minor Prophets* (Daʿat Miqra 10; Jerusalem: Mosad HaRav Kook, 1973 [Heb.]) that the prophet selected the term אֱמֹרִי ("Amorites") rather than "Canaanites" in order to create a paronomasia with Heb. אָמִיר ("topmost branch"); compare Isa 17:6. Note further that although אָמִיר appears again in Isa 17:9, G translates it "Amorites" (Αμορραῖοι).

The word for "below" in all these passages is לְמַטָּה, except for Amos and Job 18:16, where מִתַּחַת is employed. The Akkadian equivalents of "from above and below" are *šaplānu—elēnu* ("below . . . above"); see *CAD, E,* 84; and *eliš u šapliš* ("above and below"), that is, everywhere; ibid, 96. For further parallels, see S. Gevirtz, "West-Semitic Curses and the Problem of the Origins of Hebrew Law," *VT* 11 (1961) 150 n 2.

459 Wolff, 169.

■ 2:10 The Deity's second act of kindness toward his people in the past is also introduced by an emphatic וְאָנֹכִי.[460] Here, however, he directly confronts his audience and addresses them for the first time in the second-person plural (אֶתְכֶם), which continues through v 13.[461] The very existence of the people of Israel was predicated upon their being redeemed from Egypt, from the house of bondage.[462]

In the Bible two different verbs are employed to describe the Lord's delivery of his people from Egypt: העלה and הוציא. According to many exegetes, the use of העלה here is indicative of a Deuteronomistic redaction. (הוציא, in contrast, is usually assigned to P.) However, a study of the occurrences of the verb העלה[463] shows that it also appears in pre-Deuteronomic literature[464] and is, moreover, the one and only way Amos depicts the exodus from Egypt; compare Amos 3:1; 9:7. That it is an "old conventional formula for the Exodus"[465] is evidenced by Mic 6:4. Furthermore, were it a later interpolation, the redactor would obviously not have inserted it at this spot, for it creates a blatantly erroneous chronological sequence: v 10 contextually should precede v 9; the exodus and the forty years of wandering in the wilderness were historically antecedent to the extermination of the Amorites in Canaan.

The problem of explaining this anomaly, nevertheless, still exists. Many commentators resolve it by simply reversing the order of the two verses to create an accurate temporal sequence.[466] Others avoid the difficulty by asserting that the prophet does not intend to present a historical survey and thus places no importance upon the chronological sequence of events.[467] If the passages are not reversed, however, a literary method in this descriptive "madness" may be discerned. The present order now produces a fine example of inclusio, for the prophet both begins (v 9) and concludes (v 10) with the theme of the Amorites. Furthermore, as noted previously, the initial reference to the Amorites affords

460 Whereas the first וְאָנֹכִי is employed for what God did *against* the Amorites and was introduced by an adversative *waw*, the second introduces that which he did *for* Israel.

461 Once again Amos confronts the people directly in the second person after beginning his summary remarks in the third person (v 9).

462 There is no contradiction here with Amos 9:7 (see there); against Wolff. For an analysis of the three citations of the exodus from Egypt in Amos (2:10; 3:1; 9:7), see Y. Hoffman, *The Doctrine of the Exodus in the Bible* (Tel Aviv: Tel Aviv University, 1983) 32–38 (Heb.). All three appear in polemical passages that conclude with the punishment of Israel. "Until the destruction of Samaria, 720 B.C., the Exodus was the main theological doctrine in the Northern Kingdom, whereas in Jerusalem it did not gain the same importance. . . . Amos . . . makes light of this Exodus tradition and treats it in a rather argumentative and polemical manner" (p. 233).

463 See P. Humbert, "Dieu fait sortir," *TZ* 18 (1962) 357–61; J. Wijngaards, "הוציא and העלה: A Twofold Approach to the Exodus," *VT* 15 (1965) 91–102. See also T. R. Hobbs ("Amos 3:1b and 2:10," *ZAW* 81 [1969] 384–87), who considers the verb secondary but assigns it to the disciples of Amos rather than to a Deuteronomistic redactor. Note, moreover, that the verb is not found at all in Deuteronomy in connection with the exodus motif. Wijngaards ("Twofold Approach," 100) assumes that it is a pre-Deuteronomic phrase replaced in Deuteronomy by הוציא.

464 Against Wolff, 169, who interprets vv 10–12 as the work of a Deuteronomistic redactor. So, too, Weiser, *Profetie*, 93ff.; Schmidt, "Redaktion," 180; Vollmer, *Rückblicke*, 24–25; L. Markert, *Struktur und Bezeichnung des Scheltworts: Eine gattungskritische Studie anhand des Amosbuches* (BZAW 140; Berlin: de Gruyter, 1977) 73–74; R. F. Melugin, "The Formation of Amos: An Analysis of Exegetical Method," in SBLASP 1 (ed. P. J. Achtemeier; Missoula, MT: Scholars, 1978) 384–85. Compare the counter remarks of Rudolph, 146; S. Lehming, "Erwägungen zu Amos," *ZTK* 55 (1958) 149 n 2; T. W. Overholt, "Commanding the Prophets: Amos and the Problem of Prophetic Authority," *CBQ* 41 (1979) 517–32; Mays, 44–45. See already K. Galling, *Die Erwählungstradition Israels* (BZAW 48; Giessen: Töpelmann, 1928) 10 n 1.

465 Mays, 51. Compare J. Bright (*The Future in the Preaching of the Preexilic Prophets* [London: SCM, 1977] 84 n 7): "I am unable to agree that 2:10–12 is to be assigned on form-critical grounds to a later stratum of Amos traditions." See also Amsler, "Amos," 319 n 4; Hoffman, *Doctrine of Exodus*, 33–34.

466 For example, Harper, 45.

467 For example, Hammershaimb, 51. Compare also Gordis, "Studies," 216–17.

the prophet the opportunity of contrasting God's benevolent actions to Israel in the past, when they were in need, with their present actions toward others who now are in need.[468]

The prolonged perambulation of forty years in the wilderness is viewed here positively[469] (and not as a punishment for disobedience) and serves as the third demonstration of the Lord's acts of grace to Israel in the past. For the same two motifs expressed in the identical sequence by the same two verbs, see Jer 2:6: "They never asked themselves, 'Where is the Lord, who brought us up (הַמַּעֲלֶה) from the land of Egypt, who led us through (הַמּוֹלִיךְ) the wilderness . . .?'" Compare, for the other side of the picture, Jer 2:2: "I accounted to your favor the devotion of your youth, your love as a bride—How you followed me in the wilderness, in a land not sown," where the extensive trek through the wilderness is witness of Israel's fidelity to the Lord.

The verb הוליך ("to lead"), furthermore, has overtones of leading and guiding with care;[470] compare, for example, Deut 8:2, 15; 29:4; Josh 24:3; Isa 42:16; 48:21; 63:13; Jer 2:6, 17; Hos 2:16; Pss 106:9; 136:16. The point that is being made is that the Lord did not merely lead them through the wilderness but did so with provident care and solicitude.[471]

The contention, often repeated, that the motif of a forty-year wandering in the wilderness is unattested prior to Deuteronomy and Deuteronomistic literature is simply unfounded. It reappears in Amos 5:25, a verse that bears no marks of Deuteronomic or Deuteronomistic influence, and is found in other early traditions and sources as well; compare Exod 16:35; Num 14:33–34; 32:13; Josh 5:6; Ps 95:10. The theme is obviously a *Gemeingut der Tradition* ("common property of the tradition"), and it is therefore totally unwarranted to interpret it as being dependent upon Deuteronomy and thus to deny its authenticity in Amos.[472]

The goal of the exodus and the journey through the wilderness was ultimately "to possess the land of the Amorites."[473] Thus the fourth in the series of God's favors to his people: the gift of land. All four of these events are inexorably and intrinsically linked together, for the redemption from Egypt was only the first stage in the grand master plan—the bestowal of a permanent settlement.

For the expression "to dispossess the Amorites" (לְהוֹרִישׁ אֶת־הָאֱמֹרִי), compare, for example, Num 21:32; 32:39; for "to possess the land" of the Amorites (לָרֶשֶׁת אֶת־אַרְצוֹ),[474] usually occurring in the context of the Amorite settlements in Transjordan, see, for example, Num 21:35. Compare the similarity in wording together with the identical sequence of events in Josh 24:5–8: ". . . I freed you (הוֹצֵאתִי) . . . from Egypt. . . . After you had lived a long time in the wilderness, I brought you to the land of the Amorites (אֶרֶץ הָאֱמֹרִי) who lived beyond the Jordan. . . . You took possession of their land (וַתִּירְשׁוּ אֶת־אַרְצָם) after I annihilated them for you" (וָאַשְׁמִידֵם מִפְּנֵיכֶם). Compare also Judg 11:19–22.

■ **2:11** God's care and concern for his people, moreover, did not terminate with their settling in the land of Canaan. He maintained his protection up until the present by his fifth act of beneficence[475]—sending

468 Compare Amsler ("Amos," 319 n 4), who comments that the prior mentioning of the Amorites was "pour ruiner l'orgueil militaire qu'Israël prétendait tirer de ses propres victoires" ("in order to destroy the military arrogance which Israel claimed to infer from its own victories"). He also adds quite correctly, "Un glossateur n'aurait pas manqué de respecter l'ordre chronologique" ("A glossator would not have failed to respect the chronological order").

469 See also Hos 2:16; 13:5. For the different biblical traditions concerning the wilderness motif and Israel's wandering in the wilderness, see R. Adamiak, *Justice and History in the Old Testament: The Evolution of Divine Retribution in the Historiographies of the Wilderness Generation* (Cleveland: John T. Zubal, 1982), and S. Talmon, "The 'Desert Motif' in the Bible and in Qumran Literature," in *Biblical Motifs: Origins and Transformations* (ed. A. Altmann; Studies and Texts 3; Cambridge: Harvard University, 1966) 31–63.

470 Compare Ehrlich, *Randglossen*, 5.232.

471 Compare also its Akkadian interdialectal semantic equivalent, *abālu*, which means "to bring" and also "to support persons"; *CAD, A*, I. *abālu* A, 1, pp. 11ff., 23.

472 Against Wolff, 170. See also Rudolph, 146.

473 For the infinitive with ל, expressing purpose, see *GKC*, 114f.

474 The expression לָרֶשֶׁת אֶת־הָאָרֶץ is also characteristic of Deuteronomic and Deuteronomistic literature, for example, Deut 2:31; 9:4; 11:31; Josh 1:11; 18:3; Judg 2:6; 18:9; but is not limited to it. See Hoffman, *Doctrine of Exodus*, 34.

475 For the recurring phenomenon of pentads in Amos, see also the fivefold refrain in Amos 4:6–11; the

spiritual leaders in the form of prophets and Nazirites. The line of prophetic messengers following Moses (compare, for example, Samuel, Nathan, Gad, Ahijah, Jehu, Elijah, Elisha, Michaiah, Jonah, and many other anonymous messengers of God)[476] created a continual chain of constant communication between God and Israel. Amos is now the latest link in this prophetic continuum. For other references linking the prophetic activity to the period following the exodus, see Judg 6:8–10; 2 Kgs 17:7–14; Jer 7:22–26; Hos 12:10–11, 14; Mic 6:4.

The use of קום in the *hiphʿil* (וָאָקִים), "I raised up prophets" ("from among your sons"—מִבְּנֵיכֶם; for the partitive ־מ, compare Exod 17:5) in connection with prophets, see, for example, Deut 18:15, 18; Jer 6:17; 29:15; and other charismatic spiritual and political leaders—judges, Judg 2:16, 18; saviors, Judg 3:9, 15; priests, 1 Sam 2:35; kings ("shepherds"), 1 Kgs 14:14; Jer 23:4–5; 30:9; Ezek 34:23; Mic 5:4; Zech 11:16—is a common figure of speech[477] that signifies the appointment and induction[478] of these individuals into their respective offices and positions.[479]

As for the Nazirites,[480] this is the only place in the Bible where their selection is described as indicative of God's favor and goodness to Israel.[481] They are mentioned here alongside the prophets (who were selected and elected by the Deity) because by their own voluntary strict ritual behavior and vows they, too, exemplify the will of God. Their personal manner of living highlights another form of dedication to God.[482] In the narrative accounts of the only two known Nazirites, Samson (Judg 13:5, 7; 16:17) and Samuel (1 Sam 1:11), the prohibition of the cutting of the hair is specifically enjoined.[483] Here, similar to the laws in Num 6:3–4, they are characterized by their abstinence from wine. Wine may be the key literary reason why the Nazirites, so rarely mentioned in the biblical books, are singled out for distinction, because one of the charges listed dealt

fivefold curse in 7:17; the five visions in 7—9; and the pentad describing inescapability in 9:2–4.

476 For the references to these named prophets, see the concordances. For unnamed prophets, compare, for example, Judg 6:8; 1 Kgs 13:1; 20:35; 2 Kgs 16:13.

477 In later biblical Hebrew, the verb לְהָעִיר designates such an election to office. See, for example, Isa 41:2; 45:13; Ezra 1:1. Compare the analogous use of Akk. *šutbû*, from *tebû* ("to arouse"), *AHw*, 3.1343.

478 See also Weinfeld, "Ancient Near Eastern Patterns in Prophetic Literature," *VT* 27 (1977) 181 n 23. There is no reason whatsoever to view this verse as a Deuteronomistic addition; against Wolff; Schmidt, "Redaktion," 181–82; Vollmer, *Rückblicke*, 25; or to delete it for other sundry reasons; against Gressmann, *Prophetie*, 338; Weiser, *Profetie*, 95. Note that in Deut 18:15, 18, and Jer 29:15, the expression is a bit different, לְהָקִים לְ.

479 H. Bardtke ("Der Erweckungsgedanke in der exilisch-nachexilischen Literatur des Alten Testaments," in *Von Ugarit nach Qumran. Beiträge zur alttestamentlichen und altorientalischen Forschung. Otto Eissfeldt zum 1 September 1957* [ed. J. Hempel and L. Rost; BZAW 77; Berlin: Töpelmann, 1958] 12–15) points out that the activity of לְהָקִים is always inspired by God. Compare also 2 Sam 12:11; 1 Kgs 11:14, 23; Amos 6:14 for other examples.

480 The particle מ in וּמִבַּחוּרֵיכֶם ("and from some of your young men" [to be Nazirites]) is another example of the partitive מ. For Nazirites, see M. Haran, "Nazirites," *EM* 5.795–99 (Heb.); J. Milgrom, "Nazirites," *EncJud* 12.907–9; J. C. Rylaarsdam, "Nazirite," *IDB* 3.526–27. See also Z. Wiseman, "The Institution of the Nazirites in the Bible," *Tarbiz* 36 (1967) 207–20 (Heb.); Y. Amit, "Nazirites for Life—The Evolution of a Motif," in *Studies in Judaica* (ed. M. A. Friedman and M. Gil) = *Teʿudah* 4 (1986) 23–36 (Heb.).

481 Compare ibn Ezra; Kimchi; Abarbanel; Budde, "Amos," 43.

482 There is no hint here, however, that the Nazirites are dedicated from birth, as were Samson and Samuel. The Qumran scroll from Cave IV specifically mentions that Samuel was a נְזִיר עוֹלָם ("a Nazirite for life"). See F. M. Cross, "A New Qumran Biblical Fragment Related to the Original Hebrew Underlying the Septuagint," *BASOR* 132 (1953) 26; P. K. McCarter, *I Samuel: A New Translation with Introduction, Notes and Commentary* (AB 8; Garden City, NY: Doubleday, 1980) 53–54. This is not a divine election but a vow taken by the mother of Samuel. The tradition is also found in Sir 46:13; Josephus, *Antiquities* V.10.3; and Mishnah Nazir 9:5.

483 There is no reason to connect the Nazirites and the prophets with charismatic martial activity in the present context. For a study of this verse, see M. Weiss, "'And I Raised Up Prophets from Amongst Your Sons': A Note about the History and Character of Israelite Prophecy," in *Isac Leo Seeligmann Volume: Essays in the Bible and the Ancient World* (3 vols.; ed. A. Rofé and Y. Zakovitch; Jerusalem: E. Rubinstein, 1983) 1.257–74 (Heb.). There is also no reason to relate the Nazirites to the Rechabites (Jeremiah 35). See Weiss, "Prophets," 268.

precisely with wine (v 8). The class of individuals who are usually mentioned alongside the prophets, the priests, are notable by their absence. Perhaps it may have something to do with the prophet-priest conflict that begins at the time of Amos (Amos 7:12–17).

All of this is followed up by a challenging question leveled squarely at the populace, demanding their response to confirm the facts and thereby involving them directly in the prophetic disputation. This polemical device of the rhetorical question, so favored by Amos,[484] forcibly brings home his main point: "Will anyone deny these facts?" It applies to all the statements from v 9 through v 11a.[485] By its present position, it functions both as a conclusion to the manifold benefactions of the Deity and as an introduction to his next accusation: This is what the Lord has done for you, and see how you persist in acting!

The thrust of his remarks all center about the constant care and concern God has displayed from the beginning of the history of his people up until the present, that is, salvation history. However, Amos, in his usual penchant and predilection for reversing commonly expected conclusions, employs the motif of salvation history not as a guarantee for further divine dispensation and protection, as the people so ardently assume and presume (for example, Amos 5:14, 18; 9:10), but rather as an indictment. "Salvation history is proclaimed as judgment history."[486]

The use of the emphatic particle אַף (for example, Gen 3:1; 18:13, 23; Job 9:14; 19:4; 34:17; 40:8) gives special stress to the following negative אַיִן.

The concluding formula נְאֻם־ה׳ appears some 357 times in the Bible.[487]

■ **2:12** By an effective use of chiastic parallelism with the preceding verse, Amos refers first to the people's corrupting the Nazirites (mentioned last in v 11) and then to their silencing the prophets (mentioned first in v 11). The Nazirites, who are coerced into drinking wine, are thereby forced to break their vows of abstinence. By such impudent action, the populace establishes its own rules of behavior, which run counter to the will of the Deity. Once again they are charged with oppressing a class of people who are unable to defend themselves. However, the present indictment does not refer to offenses committed against the ordinary, underprivileged citizens, but against those who dedicate their lives in consecration to God. The Nazirites, moreover, are not alone in suffering from their dictatorial and impertinent misbehavior; the prophets feel their sting as well.

On many other recorded occasions, the prophets encountered both popular and royal resistance that attempted to terminate their prophetic mission; compare 1 Kgs 13:4; 18:4; 19:2, 10; 22:26–27; 2 Kgs 1:9ff.; 6:31; Isa 30:10 ("Who said to the seers, 'Do not see,' to the prophets, 'Do not prophecy truth to us.'"); Jer 2:30; 11:21 ("Assuredly, thus said the Lord of Hosts concerning the men of Anathoth who seek your life and say, 'You must not prophesy (לֹא תִנָּבֵא) any more in the name of the Lord, or you will die by our hand.'"); 18:18; 20:10; 26:23. Thus, there is no reason whatsoever to cast any doubt on the originality of this verse.[488] The second-person plural accusation[489] creates a smooth transition

484 For other examples of rhetorical questions in Amos, see 3:3–8; 5:18, 25; 6:12; 8:8; 9:7.

485 Several commentators think that the question logically should stand at the end of v 12; for example, Harper, 54, 57; Cripps, 146.

486 Wolff, 170.

487 There again is no need to view this as a Deuteronomistic redaction; against Wolff, 170. For the formula, see F. Baumgärtel, "Die Formel *nᵉʾum jahwe*," *ZAW* 73 (1961) 227–90.

488 For example, Ehrlich, *Randglossen*, 5.232–33; Marti; Duhm, "Anmerkungen"; Weiser, *Profetie*, 95; Fosbroke; Sellin; Amsler; Rudolph, 147. See also H. Schmidt, *Der Prophet Amos* (Tübingen: Mohr, 1917) 32; Gressmann, *Prophetie*, 338; E. Balla, *Die Droh— und Scheltworte des Amos* (Leipzig: Edelmann, 1926) 20; Lehming, "Erwägungen," 151; Schmidt, "Redaktion," 180–83; Vollmer, *Rückblicke*, 24–25. See, however, Weiss, "Prophets," 264ff.

489 For this literary device, see H. W. Wolff, *Das Zitat im Prophetenspruch* (BEvT 4; München: Kaiser, 1937); reprinted in idem, *Gesammelte Studien zum Alten Testament* (TBü 22; München: Kaiser, 1964) 36–112. It serves as a polemical self-incrimination whereby the actual words of the accused are cited against him. Compare also Amos 4:1; 6:13; 8:14; 9:10.

between the list of the acts of kindnesses of God and the introduction of divine punishment (v 13). This specific charge serves as a literary foreshadow of the forthcoming pericope (3:3–8) and most likely reflects a personal experience in the life of the prophet himself, who was similarly confronted by the priest Amaziah and ordered to cease prophesying in the north (Amos 7:12–13, 16; לֹא תִנָּבֵא). By silencing the prophet, they silence the source of communication between the Lord and his people.

■ **2:13** Now comes the announcement of punishment for their multiple transgressions.[490] It is introduced by the same key emphatic first-person pronoun, אָנֹכִי, which appears here for the third and climactically last time. Its repetition is deliberate: The same אָנֹכִי, which destroyed the Amorites (v 9) and brought Israel out of Egypt (v 10), shall now render judgment upon his people.[491]

The exact nature of the threatened imminent chastisement depends upon the understanding of the rare verb מֵעִיק, for which several different interpretations have been suggested.[492] Some derive it from a medial *waw* root עוק and relate it to the Arabic عاق, عوقا ("to hamper, hinder") (عوقا, "hindrance") and translate "I shall hamper/hinder/slow your movements as a wagon/threshing-sledge is slowed/comes to a halt [read תֵּעוֹק, *niphal?*], when. . . ." Compare G (Alexandrinus), κωλύω ("to hinder"). Others assume the verb to be derived from the geminate root עקק, cognate of Arabic عقّ ("to cut in pieces"), and render "I shall cut you up in pieces as a wagon/threshing-cart cuts up . . . ," referring to the rifts and rills in the earth caused by an earthquake. Another suggestion is to relate the verb to a medial *yod*, עיק, equivalent to the Arabic عاق(ي) ("to groan"), that is, "I will make it groan beneath you just as a wagon/threshing-cart groans"—the allusion once again being to an earthquake. This is supported by α', τριξήσω (⟩ τρίξειν) and V, *stridebo* (⟩ *stridere*), "creak/groan." Other commentators interpret עוק as an Aramaism for צוק ("to press," comparing Pss 55:4, עָקָה; 66:11, מוּעָקָה): "I shall press you just as a . . . is pressed. . . ." This exegesis is supported by T and S.[493] Yet another meaning for the root עוק has been proposed on the basis of postbiblical עוּקָה ("cavity, trough, pit") and Arabic عقّة ("deep excavation"); عقيق ("channel," based on an unattested عقّ, "to hollow out").[494] This image again would refer to the effects of an earthquake. Finally, some follow G's translation κυλίω (⟩ κυλίειν), "to turn, roll, rotate," which would likewise infer a similar punishment.

Although problems exist with almost all of these suggestions, the basic presupposition of most commentators that the meaning of the verb is somehow related to a punishment by an earthquake[495] does not follow from the vivid description in the ensuing verses of the total incapacitation and immobility of the armed forces of Israel.[496] In the light of the detailed summary of the paralysis of all units of the army, it seems preferable to accept the interpretation that most graphically serves as a fitting introduction to this situation, that is, the first one mentioned here. The movements of Israel shall be "hampered, hindered" and thereby come haltingly to a stop. In line with this explanation, תַּחְתֵּיכֶם would mean "in your place" (T, בְּאַתְרְכוֹן), that is, where you are; compare Exod 16:29; 2 Sam 2:23; Job 40:12. They shall become totally transfixed.

Amos selects an agricultural image[497] to portray the terror of the awesome oncoming attack of the Deity, which will leave the people totally helpless and incapacitated. The employment of similes to "graphically portray the magnitude of punishment awaiting transgressors of the covenant"[498] is very common in the Bible as well as

490 For הִנֵּה introducing the punishment, compare Amos 6:11, 14; 9:9. From vv 6–12, the Deity appears as the plaintiff; from vv 13–16, as the judge.

491 This אָנֹכִי, unlike the preceding two, is followed by the present tense, indicating the imminence of the forthcoming punishment.

492 For a study of the various interpretations and their criticism, see also Gese, "Beiträge," 417–24; and H.-P. Müller, "Die Wurzeln *ʿyq, yʿq* und *ʿwq*," *VT* 21 (1971) 556–64. Compare also the discussions of Harper, 62; Hammershaimb, 54; Rudolph, 139, 148–49.

493 So ibn Ganaḥ, *Haschoraschim,* 301; ben Saruq; Rashi; ibn Ezra; Kimchi.

494 This is Gese's ("Beiträge") own suggestion.

495 Against Rudolph, 148.

496 Compare, already, ibn Ezra; Ehrlich, *Mikrâ,* 3.404, which is not repeated in *Randglossen,* 5.233. Both, however, opt for another etymology than the one accepted here.

497 For other agricultural images in Amos, compare, for example, 1:3; 7:1; 8:2; 9:9.

498 Weinfeld, *Deuteronomy,* 134. See also Hillers, *Treaty Curses,* 18–26.

in the ancient Near East. In Hebrew they are introduced by כַּאֲשֶׁר; see Amos 3:12; 5:19; 9:9; and, for example, Deut 1:44; 28:29, 49; 1 Kgs 14:10, 15; 2 Kgs 21:13; in Aramaic by אֵיךְ זִי;[499] and in Assyrian by *kī ša*.[500]

An עֲגָלָה can mean either a "wagon/cart" (for example, Gen 45:19, 21, 27; 46:5; 1 Sam 6:7ff.)[501] or a "threshing-sledge" (Isa 28:27–28). If the former, the intention would be that the sheer overwhelming weight of the עָמִיר[502] ("cut grain") brings the vehicle to a standstill. If the latter, the picture is one of the threshing-sledge being clogged by the cut grain and thus unable to move.[503] The first interpretation seems preferable[504] because the עָמִיר ("cut grain") consists of the harvested ears of grain that are brought by wagon from the fields to the threshing floor.[505] Compare Jer 9:21, "like cut grain (עָמִיר) behind the reaper," and Mic 4:12, "He has gathered them like the cut grain (עָמִיר)."

The imagery actually is paradoxical. The reason the cart comes to a halt is that it is overloaded, which is precisely a reflection of the abundance and prosperity of the accused. Compare similarly the use of the term "cows of Bashan" in Amos 4:1.

Introductory Comments, 2:14–16

The ensuing series of seven examples[506] exemplifies the immobility and helplessness of the entire Israelite army. All the various divisions and categories of the troops are threatened with total impotence in time of war. The section is very artistically composed, as the following diagram and remarks demonstrate:

1. וְאָבַד מָנוֹס מִקָּל
2. וְחָזָק לֹא־יְאַמֵּץ כֹּחוֹ
3. וְגִבּוֹר לֹא־יְמַלֵּט נַפְשׁוֹ
4. וְתֹפֵשׂ הַקֶּשֶׁת לֹא יַעֲמֹד
5. וְקַל בְּרַגְלָיו לֹא יְמַלֵּט
6. וְרֹכֵב הַסּוּס לֹא יְמַלֵּט נַפְשׁוֹ
7. וְאַמִּיץ לִבּוֹ בַּגִּבּוֹרִים
   עָרוֹם יָנוּס

The pericope begins and ends with three key roots: נוס (v 14, מָנוֹס, noun; v 16, יָנוּס, verb); אמץ (v 14, יְאַמֵּץ, verb; v 16, אַמִּיץ, noun); and גבר (v 14, גִּבּוֹר; v 16, גִּבּוֹרִים), creating a manifold internal inclusio and a partial chiastic structure. It includes, moreover, the twice-repeated phrase לֹא יְמַלֵּט נַפְשׁוֹ (vv 14, 16) and the twice-repeated noun/adjective קַל (vv 14, 15).

There is, in addition, an internal stylistic development. The subjects of v 14 all consist of one word (חָזָק, קַל, גִּבּוֹר); v 15, of two words (תֹּפֵשׂ הַקֶּשֶׁת, קַל בְּרַגְלָיו, רֹכֵב הַסּוּס); v 16, of three words (אַמִּיץ לִבּוֹ בַּגִּבּוֹרִים). Note, too, that the phrase לֹא יְמַלֵּט appears three times (twice with נַפְשׁוֹ). The only two stichs that do not contain the negative לֹא, which is repeated five times, are the first and last.[507]

The announcement of the forthcoming catastrophe is directed entirely against the army of Israel, the army in which the people took such pride during this period of

499 For example, Sefire I, A:35–42 in Fitzmyer, *Sefire*.

500 For example, Wiseman, "Vassal Treaties," lines 526–659, pp. 67–79.

501 The objection that such carts were unknown in ancient Israel is unwarranted in the light of the biblical verses cited and the actual reliefs from that period. Compare, for example, *ANEP*, 128, no. 367, and Gese, "Beiträge," 419. Compare also the use of wagons and carts in Mesopotamia (Akk. *eriqqu*) to carry various types of freight. For example, *ina eriqqi tibna kî azbila* ("I brought straw on the wagon"); BE 17 34:39 in H. Radau, *Letters to Cassite Kings from the Temple Archives of Nippur* (Philadelphia: University of Pennsylvania, 1908).

502 Compare also Jer 9:21; Mic 4:12; Zech 12:6; IQM XI,10. Could there be an allusive paronomasia between עָמִיר and אֱמֹרִי, vv 9–10?

503 This was already proposed by J. G. Wetzstein ("Briefliche Bemerkungen von Consul Dr. J. G. Wetzstein," *ZAW* 3 [1883] 278–79), who contrasts this image with the one in Ps 18:37 and also cites evidence from Bedouin songs.

504 According to either interpretation, לָהּ is an ethical dative; see *GKC*, 119s. The definite article with the descriptive participle, הַמְלֵאָה, serves as a relative clause.

505 See *AuS* 3.52, 58; Feliks, *Plant World*, 140.

506 For other heptads, compare, for example, Amos 2:6–8, 14–16; 4:4–5, 6–11; 5:8–9, 21–23; 6:1–6; 9:1–4.

507 The suggestion of R. Rendtorff, "Zu Amos 2:14–16," *ZAW* 85 (1975) 226–27, accepted by Vesco, "Amos," 489, to transpose several of the stichs, thereby reconstructing the unit, unnecessarily disrupts the internal pattern of the original literary composition.

military resurgence (compare Amos 6:13). There is furthermore an additional dimension of terror and horror within the threat, for the prophet does not spell out from whom they will be unable to flee and against whom they will be powerless to fight. All that is stated is that the defenders of the people will be incapable of employing those qualities and skills for which they are distinguished.[508] This description is not one of panic caused by destruction in the wake of an earthquake but of the impotency of all segments of the fighting forces to act—they are stymied in motion or, at most, flee from battle unarmed.

■ **2:14** There will be no escape from the impending punishment.[509] That on which soldiers rely—swiftness, strength, weaponry—all shall be of no avail. In this macabre scenario of absolute inescapability, Amos describes the malfunctioning of all the various battle units that comprised the Israelite army.

First is the infantry. One of the outstanding characteristics of this military corps is its swiftness; compare 2 Sam 2:18ff.; Lam 4:19; 1 Chr 12:8; (Eccl 9:1); and especially Jer 46:6, which is almost an exact reflex of the verse in Amos, אַל־יָנוּס הַקַּל וְאַל־יִמָּלֵט הַגִּבּוֹר ("Let not the swift get away; let not the warrior escape").[510] But in Amos, "There shall be no flight/place of escape (מָנוֹס)[511] for the swift." (For the use of אָבַד מִ־ with מָנוֹס, see also Jer 25:35; Ps 142:5; Job 11:20.)

For a similar situation drawn from an Assyrian historical text, compare *ēdu ul ipparšid multaḫṭu ul ūṣi ina qātēja* ("Not a single one could flee; not one survivor escaped my hands").[512]

So, too, the "strong will be unable to exert his strength." For the verbal expression אַמֵּץ כֹּחַ, compare Nah 2:2; Prov 24:5. For the nominal form, אַמִּיץ כֹּחַ, compare Isa 40:26; Job 9:4, 19. For the pair of verbs חזק and אמץ, compare, for example, Deut 3:28; 31:6, 7, 23; Josh 1:6, 7, 9, 18; Isa 35:3; Pss 27:14; 31:25; 1 Chr 22:13; 28:20.[513]

Even the "mighty, brave warrior will be unable to save his own life."[514] For the pair of verbs נוס and מלט, compare, for example, Amos 9:11; Jer 48:19. For מַלֵּט נֶפֶשׁ, compare 1 Sam 19:11; 1 Kgs 1:12; Ezek 33:5; Ps 89:49; and here again in Amos 2:15.[515]

■ **2:15** Neither shall the "archers" provide any protection. They, too, "will be unable to hold their own ground" (לֹא יַעֲמֹד) in battle. תֹּפֵשׂ הַקֶּשֶׁת (literally, "one who holds

508 Compare the similar theme in Ps 33:16–17: "Kings are not delivered by a large force; warriors (גִּבּוֹר) are not saved by great strength (כֹּחַ). Horses (הַסּוּס) are a false hope for deliverance; for all their great power they provide no escape (לֹא יְמַלֵּט)."

509 For the theme of inescapability in Amos, see also 5:18–20; 9:1–4.

510 This was seen independently by Z. Weisman ("Stylistic Parallels in Amos and Jeremiah: Their Implications for the Composition of Amos," *Shnaton* 1 [1975] 129–49 [Heb.]) in his list of comparisons between Amos and Jeremiah.

511 מָנוֹס may indicate "flight" as well as "place of flight, refuge," *KB*, 568. Compare T, בֵּית עֵירוֹקֵי. See also *GKC*, 85e, מ of place.

512 For examples, see *CAD, N,* I.283–84, and *AHw* 2.735, *naparšudu.* Note that in Mari there was an army contingent called *ṣābum qallatum* ("light troop"), that is, lightly armed contingent, "which was the counterpart of the *ṣābum kalibbitum,* 'heavily-armed contingent.'" For example, "Now send a lightly-armed group and have it ambush the enemy force," ARM 2, 22, 13. See Sasson, *Military Establishments,* 17–18. For *ṣābum qallatum,* see ARM I 60:16; II 22:13. For *ṣabum kibittum,* see ARM II 22:6; 130:22. Compare ARM IV 49:7. The terms are limited, however, to Mari. When *qallu* (= Heb. קַל) refers to a single person and not to a group in Mari, it designates a courier or messenger; for example, *2 awīli qallūtim,* "Two swift men (messengers)," ARM I 39:r. 17′. Compare Isa 18:2, "Go swift (קַלִּים) messengers."

513 Compare the idiom "to exert/employ one's full strength" in Akkadian: *emūqija lugammir* ("I will exert all my strength"); *CAD, G,* 30e.

514 Wolff (134–35) also did not perceive the artistry of the section and thus deleted this as well as other stichs. His statement that "the 3-fold repetition of לֹא יְמַלֵּט (נַפְשׁוֹ) would be unusual for Amos" is unusual indeed.

515 For analogous Akkadian expressions formed with *napištu* (= Heb. נֶפֶשׁ), compare *napištam eṭēru* and *napištam šūzubu* ("to save one's life"). See *CAD, E,* 402 (*eṭēru*), 425 (*ezēbu*); *N,* I.298. Akkadian *ezēbu,* similar to Heb. מַלֵּט (v 15), may also appear absolutely without the accompanying *napištu* = נֶפֶשׁ; see *CAD, E,* 424. Hebrew מַלֵּט may very well be cognate to Akk. *bulluṭu* ("to keep alive"); see *CAD, B,* 59–62.

the bow"), an expression that appears only here, designates one who is skilled as a bowman. Words signifying "holding and grasping" in Hebrew as well as in Akkadian develop the meaning "to be skilled or trained in" their respective fields. For תפש, compare תֹּפֵשׂ כִּנּוֹר וְעוּגָב ("skilled in playing the lyre and the pipe," Gen 4:21); תֹּפְשֵׂי הַמִּלְחָמָה ("skilled in battle," Num 31:27); תֹּפְשֵׂי הַתּוֹרָה ("those skilled in the teaching," Jer 2:8); similar to here, תֹּפְשֵׂי דֹּרְכֵי קָשֶׁת ("archers," Jer 46:9); תֹּפְשֵׂי מָשׁוֹט ("oarsmen," Ezek 27:29); and תֹּפְשֵׂי חֲרָבוֹת ("swordsmen," Ezek 38:4). Compare also Heb. אחז ("to hold"): אֲחֻזֵי חֶרֶב ("trained, skilled in warfare," Cant 3:8); אֹחֵז רֹמַח וְצִנָּה ("skilled in spear and shield," 2 Chr 25:5).[516]

Similar Akkadian expressions are formed with the verbs *aḫāzu*, *ṣabātu*, and *tamāḫu* ("to seize, hold, grasp"). For the exact cognate of Heb. תֹּפֵשׂ קֶשֶׁת, compare Akk. *tāmeḫ qašti.*[517] In Akkadian texts, the "bowman" (Akk. *qaštu* = Heb. קֶשֶׁת) is referred to also as *awīl qašti, ša qašti, ṣāb(ē) qašti, nāš(i) qašti.*[518]

For the idiom of "standing one's ground" in battle (לַעֲמֹד), compare Ezek 13:5, לַעֲמֹד בַּמִּלְחָמָה. Compare also the use of לַעֲמֹד לְפָנֵי/לִפְנֵי ("to hold one's own against/withstand") in Judg 2:14; 2 Kgs 10:4; Dan 8:7. For עמד alone, see Jer 46:15; Dan 11:25.

Neither shall the "fleet-footed" (קַל בְּרַגְלָיו; compare 2 Sam 2:18) flee. There is no need to revocalize the *piʿel* verb יְמַלֵּט to the *niphʿal*, יִמָּלֵט,[519] or to supply the noun נַפְשׁוֹ in order to harmonize with the twice-repeated expression.[520] The verb is used here absolutely ("shall not escape")[521] and is yet another example of the prophet's penchant to vary slightly his phrases of speech in order to avoid verbatim repetition.[522]

The immobility of the fleet-footed seems to duplicate what was already stated in v 14a. Could the reference be to yet another military unit?[523] (Compare Akk. *lasāmu*, "to run fast, to serve as a runner," from which is derived the noun, *lāsimu*, "express messenger, [military] scout.")[524] However, the prophet, in order to formulate a series of seven units and thereby indicate completeness, may simply have partially repeated himself, but nevertheless in a somewhat varied fashion.[525] One other faint possibility may be considered. Perhaps "fleet-footed" refers not to the soldiers themselves but, as the next stich specifically indicates, to horses. For the use of קַל to refer to horses, compare Isa 30:16: "'No,' you declared, 'We shall flee on steeds' (עַל־סוּס נָנוּס [note the paronomasia]); therefore you shall flee! 'We shall ride on swift mounts' (קַל)—therefore your pursuers shall prove swift!" (יִקַּלּוּ).[526]

Nor shall the cavalry fare any better. It is incorrect to state that "mounted cavalry began only in Persian times"[527] and therefore to interpret רֹכֵב הַסּוּס ("horsemen") as "chariot warriors."[528] They probably did not

516 This idiom has also been noted in passing by Weinfeld, *Deuteronomy,* 163 n 4. For an interesting cognate equivalent of Heb. תֹּפְשֵׂי הַתּוֹרָה, Jer 2:8, compare Akk. *šūḫuz ṣibitte* ("to teach correct instruction"). See S. M. Paul, "Sargon's Administrative Diction in 2 Kgs 17:27," *JBL* 88 (1969) 73 n 3.

517 See *AHw*, 3.1312. Compare also the Middle Babylonian curse, *ina tāḫāzi qāssu la iṣabbat* ("He shall not hold his bow in battle"); *BBSt* 8 IV, 24, s. 29. For *aḫāzu,* see *CAD, A,* I.447, 4a.

518 See *CAD, Q,* 147ff. For archers in the Israelite army, see H. G. May, "Archer," *IDB* 1.208. For the Assyrian army, see Yadin, *Art of Warfare,* 2.295–96.

519 For example, Harper, 60, and others based on G, διασωθῇ; T, יִשְׁתֵּיזִיב; V, *salvabitur;* and S.

520 Compare Hammershaimb, 55.

521 Compare Rudolph, 140; and see n 515 above.

522 See previous comments on the oracles against the nations.

523 This is hinted at by Rudolph, 149 n 31, but without any definitive answer.

524 *CAD, L,* 104–7.

525 There is no need, therefore, to delete the stich.

526 See ibn Ezra. In Akkadian as well, the adjective *lāsimu* describes swift horses. See *CAD, L,* 106–7. Compare *[m]ūru ša [tulli]di kî jāti lu lāsim* ("Let the colt which you bear be a swift runner like me [the horse]"), *BWL* 218 IV 17; *mūr nisqika lu lāsim* ("May your thoroughbred be a swift runner"), *JRAS* (1920) 566:17. See *CAD, M,* II.215–16.

527 Wolff, 172.

528 For רֹכֵב, see K. Galling, "Der Ehrenname Elisas und die Entrückung Elias," *ZTK* 53 (1956) 131; and S. Mowinckel, "Drive and/or Ride in O.T.," *VT* 12 (1962) 278–99. The latter maintains that the reference here is to chariot warriors (p. 286). Compare also the Akkadian interdialectal semantic and etymological equivalent, *rākib sisê,* E. Ebeling, *Die akkadische Gebetsserie "Handerhebung"* (Berlin: Akademie Verlag, 1953) 116, 5; and *ina sisê la irakkab* ("He does not ride on horseback"); ARM VI 76:22, 24.

play an important part in the Israelite army of the eighth century, as one can learn from the sarcastic jibe of Rabshakeh: "Come now, make this wager with my master, the king of Assyria. I'll give you two thousand horses if you can produce riders to mount them" (Isa 36:8 = 2 Kgs 18:23). Nevertheless, they are known to have been introduced into the Assyrian army already by the time of Assurnaṣirpal II (883–859)[529]—Akk. *pitḫallu* ("cavalry").[530] Compare, for example, *narkabāti pitḫallu zūku ša GN issija asseqe* ("I [Assurnaṣirpal II] incorporated into my [army] the chariotry, cavalry, and infantry of Carchemish.")[531] By neo-Assyrian times, chariotry was one of the mainstays of the Assyrian army, along with the infantry. Compare the following statements taken from the annals of Sargon: *50 narkabāti 200 pitḫallu 300 zūk šēpē ina libbišunu akṣur* ("I formed a unit consisting of fifty chariots, two hundred mounted men, and three hundred foot soldiers"); *ina 1 narkabtija u līm pitḫal šēpēja šitmurti zūk šēpēja li[ʾūt t]āḫāzi* ("with only me on my chariot, and one thousand of my own shock cavalry and my own battle-experienced foot soldiers").[532]

There is therefore no need to totally deny the existence of a cavalry corps in Israel at this time, even if it might not have been as many as the two thousand as Sennacherib's commander in chief insultingly chides. Nevertheless, even they will not escape with their lives.

■ **2:16** Even the "most stouthearted warrior"[533] will find himself in a desperate state of panic and rout on that day of battle. This superlative expression is a hapax legomenon and functions as an intensified variant of יְאַמֵּץ כֹּחוֹ, v 14. The verbal expression אַמֵּץ לֵב ("be of good courage") is found twice in Pss 27:14; 31:25.[534] The substantive לֵב means here "courage"; compare, too, Gen 42:28; 1 Sam 17:32; 2 Sam 17:10; Jer 4:9; Ezek 21:12; Ps 40:13. (The expression אַמִּיץ לֵב is a variant of the analogous אַמִּיץ כֹּחַ, Isa 40:26; Job 9:4, 19.) Compare similarly the Akkadian cognate *libbu* ("heart, courage"): *ša libbi išû u emūqu la išû anāku* ("I am one who has courage but no strength").[535]

"On that day[536] the courage of the heartiest warrior" will fail him, and he "shall flee naked" (עָרוֹם).[537] This expression, as has been correctly interpreted by T, עַרְטִילָא דְלָא זַיִן, and some medieval commentators,[538] means to "flee unarmed."[539] Compare similarly the following account of the onslaught of the Assyrian army under Ashurbanipal and its identical consequences upon the enemy: *tib tāḫāzija danni ēdurma mērânuššu innabit* ("He became afraid of the attack of my heavy fighting force and fled naked").[540] Such a situation arises when the panic-stricken army drops its weapons and flees for its life. Compare *ina kakkī ummānum idurma kakkīša itabbak* ("As to the war, the troops will become frightened and throw away their weapons");[541] *ummānka ana pani ummān nakrika kakkīša itabbak* ("Your army will drop its

529 For illustrations of the Assyrian cavalry, see J. Wiesner, *Fahren und Reiten in Alteuropa und in alten Orient* (AO 38/2–4; Leipzig: Hinrichs, 1939) 70. See also Yadin, *Art of Warfare,* 297.

530 See *AHw*, 2.888.

531 *AKA* 367 iii 69.

532 See *CAD, Z, zūku,* 153; and *AHw, pitḫallu,* 2.888.

533 See *GKC*, 133g.

534 G, καὶ εὑρήσει (= Heb. וְיִמְצָא; "he will find") is due to a metathesis of the letters of the first Hebrew word. For other internal Greek corrections, see Wolff, 135; Rudolph, 140.

535 BRM 4, 6:11 in A. T. Clay, *Epics, Hymns, Omens, and Other Texts* (New Haven: Yale University, 1923). Compare also BRM 4, 13:52: "The courage (*libbu*) of my army will be taken away by the gods."

536 This is not an eschatological term here; correctly, Rudolph, 150.

537 Could this be a veiled retribution to their crime of distraining clothes, v 8?

538 For example, Rashi; Kimchi refers it to clothing rather than to weapons.

539 Ehrlich (*Mikrâ*, 3.404) adduced a similar semantic comparison from the Greek γυμὸς, which also means "naked, unarmed, defenseless." (He changed his mind, however, in his comments in the *Randglossen*, 5.233.)

540 R. C. Thompson, *The Prisms of Esarhaddon and Ashurbanipal Found at Nineveh, 1927–1928* (London: The British Museum, 1931) pl. 16 IV 42. Compare M. Streck, *Assurbanipal und die letzten assyrischen Könige bis zum Untergang Nineveh's* (VAB 7; Leipzig: Hinrichs, 1916) 48 V 112.

541 A. Goetze, *Old Babylonian Omen Texts* (YOS 10; New Haven and London: Yale University, 1947) 24:42.

weapons in the face of the army of your enemy").[542] Discretion in such cases becomes the better part of valor.

This chapter, similarly to all the following (with the sole exception of chapter 9), concludes on the note of destruction (and/or exile).

542 Ibid., 50:6–7.

3 Divine Election and Judgment

1 **Hear this word that the Lord has spoken**
concerning you, O children of Israel,
concerning the entire family which I
brought up from the land of Egypt.
2 **You alone have I chosen from all the families**
of the earth.
That is why I shall call you to account for all
your iniquities.

■ **1** The second section of the book[1] is characterized by a series of independent prophecies introduced by the second-person plural imperative, שִׁמְעוּ ("Hear"). Compare Amos 3:1, (9), 13; 4:1; 5:1.[2]

Most commentators agree that v 1 contains editorial expansions,[3] but opinions are divided as to what is original and what is secondary. The words אֲשֶׁר דִּבֶּר ה׳ ("which the Lord has spoken") are definitely not a later interpolation[4] because this deletion would leave the continuation of the verse "syntactically cumbersome"[5] and also destroy the overall inclusio of the pericope: Amos 3:1 (דִּבֶּר ה׳) and 3:8 (ה׳ דִּבֶּר). A more reasonable assumption is that the second half of the sentence beginning with עַל may be secondary, functioning as an explanatory gloss to make clear that his reference to Israel (יִשְׂרָאֵל[6] עֲלֵיכֶם בְּנֵי) applies to Judah (עַל) as well, that is, "the whole family that I brought out of Egypt."[7] This explanation is further supported by the fact that, on the one hand, Amos 3:1a is a complete sentence in itself, and, on the other, the additional stich would contain a repetition of the addressee and a change of person.[8] Furthermore, although לֵאמֹר does appear three more times in the book (2:12; 7:10; 8:5), it never introduces a divine address but only precedes the quoted words of the people themselves. However, even if 3:1b is an editorial prose addition, it is, nevertheless, not to be ascribed to a Deuteronomic redaction.[9]

Although a new section of the book formally starts with this chapter, within the first two verses a sort of minirecapitulation of some of the main motifs and ex-

1 Compare also the second section of Hosea, beginning with chapter 4; Rudolph, 152.

2 For the various usages of שמע in oracles, see Y. Hoffman, "Two Opening Formulae in Biblical Style," *Tarbiz* 46 (1977) 157–80 (Heb.). See also M. O'Rourke-Boyle, "The Covenant Lawsuit of the Prophet Amos: III:1—IV:13," *VT* 21 (1971) 338–62.

3 The threefold Hebrew introduction, עֲלֵיכֶם, בְּנֵי יִשְׂרָאֵל, עַל כָּל הַמִּשְׁפָּחָה ("against you, children of Israel, against the whole family"), may be somewhat compared to Gen 12:1: מֵאַרְצְךָ, וּמִמּוֹלַדְתְּךָ, וּמִבֵּית אָבִיךָ ("from your country, from your kindred, from your father's house") and Gen 22:2: אֶת־בִּנְךָ, אֶת־יְחִידְךָ, אֲשֶׁר אָהַבְתָּ ("your son, your favored one, whom you love"), but the syntactical construction is much more difficult in Amos.

4 For example, M. Löhr, *Untersuchungen zum Buch Amos* (BZAW 4; Giessen: Töpelmann, 1901); J. Morgenstern, "Amos Studies IV," 319–20; Marti.

5 Wolff, 174, who adds that the vocative normally follows directly upon an imperative expression. Compare Amos 4:1a; 8:4a; against, for example, Harper, 65, 66, who considers בְּנֵי יִשְׂרָאֵל a gloss, unnecessary after עֲלֵיכֶם.

6 G (οἶκος Ισραηλ) and some Hebrew manuscripts read בֵּית יִשְׂרָאֵל ("house of Israel") for בְּנֵי יִשְׂרָאֵל ("children of Israel"). Compare Jer 10:1. For this phenomenon of the interchange of בְּנֵי/בֵּית, see S. Talmon, "Synonymous Readings in the Textual Traditions of the Old Testament," in *Studies in the Bible* (ed. C. Rabin; Scripta Hierosolymitana 8; Jerusalem: Magnes, 1961) 346–48. T and V support the Masoretic text. The phrase בְּנֵי יִשְׂרָאֵל is also another link between chapters 2 and 3. See 2:11.

7 Compare Bach (*Aufforderungen*, 155), who contends that Amos refers to two "Israels": "the nation = northern Israel, (and) a people with a history . . . two repositories of Israel—Israel and Judah" (Amos 3:1, 2; 5:25; 9:7).

8 Compare Harper, 65; Wolff, 174; Rudolph, 152. See, however, the reservations of Cripps, 150–51, even if it is an interpolation.

9 Against Wolff, 175. See also T. R. Hobbs, "Amos 3:1b and 2:10," *ZAW* 81 (1969) 384–87; and Rudolph, 152.

pressions of the first two chapters can be discerned.[10] Just as Israel climaxes the catalogue of oracles against the nations, here, too, they are singled out within the context of all the other "families of the earth." Both chapters 2 and 3 mention the goodness of God toward Israel (2:9–11; 3:2a) and its corresponding iniquities (2:6–8, 12; 3:2b). In 2:10 and 3:1 the exodus from Egypt is cited as one of the kindnesses of God and is identically formulated in both verses. So, too, in both 2:11 and 3:1, there is a direct address to "the children of Israel."

For the motif of the exodus from Egypt as a guarantee for the salvation of the people in a current crisis, compare Num 24:8; Judg 6:13; 1 Kgs 8:51–53[11]—a guarantee that Amos presently proceeds to contradict.[12] Amos differentiates between the significance of the exodus motif, predominant in the northern kingdom,[13] which he downplays, and the election motif, which he reinterprets. Salvation history connected with the exodus and the wilderness trek, although playing a major role in the theology of the north, was not central to the belief then predominant in Judah. Amos goes even one step further by reacting to and refuting the unwarranted assumption of impunity that they incorrectly drew from these former acts of God's kindness.[14]

■ **2** Herein lies the special relationship of the Lord with his people. Other nations, too, have had their history determined by the Lord of Israel, who, once in the past, brought them out from one country to another (Amos 9:7). Israel's distinction does not lie, however, in the past, in its exodus from Egypt, for in this it is no more than on a par with others. It is rather based on the fact that of all the nations of the world only they were selected and elected as God's chosen people. Moreover, its election remains operative up until the present time.

The election formula here, רַק אֶתְכֶם יָדַעְתִּי מִכֹּל מִשְׁפְּחוֹת הָאֲדָמָה, is distinct from the terminology of the Deuteronomic election theology, רַק . . . וַיִּבְחַר . . . בָּכֶם מִכָּל הָעַמִּים ("He only . . . chose you from among all peoples"; Deut 10:15).[15] It does contain, however, an expression found elsewhere only in the patriarchal blessings and most likely alludes to this tradition: "All the families of the earth (כֹּל מִשְׁפְּחוֹת הָאֲדָמָה) shall bless themselves by you" (Gen 12:3; 28:14). Most significant is the way in which the tie between Israel and the Lord is expressed, יָדַעְתִּי. The verb ידע signifies an emotional and experiential relationship between the two and has the meaning "to select, to choose." Compare, for example, Gen 18:19; Exod 33:12, 17; Deut 9:24; Jer 1:5; Hos 13:5. "Only you" (רַק אֶתְכֶם)—note the placing of the direct object before the verb for emphasis—"have I chosen."

Moreover, in the light of studies on covenantal terminology,[16] the verb ידע can now be interpreted with an additional connotation. In the vassal treaties of the

10 Chapter 2 completes the first section of the book formally and contextually—the oracles against all the nations are concluded. Nevertheless, as a result of editorial activity, the beginning of chapter 3, although not the conclusion of 2:13–16, as Budde ("Amos," 75–76) and Maag (*Text,* 8–9, 13) contend, does contain several of the motifs present in the former chapter. Key words appearing in chapter 3 are אֲדָמָה (vv 2, 5); אֶרֶץ (vv 1, 9, 11, 14; twice, מִצְרַיִם); שְׁתֵּי/שְׁנַיִם (vv 3, 12); אַרְמְנוֹת (vv 9 [twice], 11); בֵּית (vv 13, 14, 15 [four times]).

11 See also Loewenstamm, *Tradition of the Exodus,* 21–22.

12 For another approach, see Hoffman (*Doctrine of Exodus,* 35), who emphasizes the possibly ironical but definitely polemical character of this verse by interpreting it as a citation of the popular theology. The prophet frequently cites his adversaries in his polemics; compare, for example, 4:1; 5:14; 6:13; 8:5; 9:10.

13 See Hoffman, *Doctrine of Exodus,* 32–38; compare G. Pfeifer, "Amos and Deuterojesaja denkformenanalytisch verglichen," *ZAW* 93 (1981) 440.

14 See H. L. Ginsberg, *The Israelian Heritage of Judaism* (Texts and Studies of the Jewish Theological Seminary of America 24; New York: Jewish Theological Seminary of America, 1982) 1, 26–27, 33. See also Amos 9:7.

15 See Th. C. Vriezen, *Die Erwählung Israels nach dem Alten Testament* (ATANT 24; Zurich: Zwingli, 1953) 62ff., 90; idem, "Erwägungen zu Amos 3:2," in *Archäologie und Altes Testament: Festschrift für K. Galling* (ed. A. Kuschke and E. Kutsch; Tübingen: Mohr, 1970) 255–58. See also M. Sekine, "Vom Verstehen der Heilsgeschichte," *ZAW* 75 (1963) 152–53.

16 See H. B. Huffmon, "The Treaty Background of Hebrew *Yāda*ʿ," *BASOR* 181 (1966) 31–37; H. B. Huffmon and S. Parker, "A Further Note on the Treaty Background of Hebrew *Yāda*ʿ," *BASOR* 184 (1966) 36–38. See also L. A. Sinclair, "The Courtroom Motif in the Book of Amos," *JBL* 85 (1966) 351–53; D. R. Hillers, *Covenant—The History of a Biblical Idea* (Baltimore: Johns Hopkins University, 1969) 121–22. These studies bring a list of biblical

ancient Near East, the cognate verbs, in Akkadian *idû*[17] and in Hittite *šak* ("to know"), also have a technical legal meaning: to recognize as a legitimate suzerain or vassal and to recognize treaty stipulations as binding. Thus what is actually implied here is that the Lord has made a covenant with the people of Israel, who alone are recognized as his sole legitimate covenant partners: "Only you have I selected as my covenant partner." Their distinction and dignity stem not merely from a one-time act in history, the exodus from Egypt, but also from the permanent covenant relationship that permanently binds them to their God.

Then one of Amos's surprise, unanticipated climactic conclusions follows immediately.[18] One would assume that election and covenant relations would imply and guarantee special benefits and protection. Amos's contemporaries mistakenly took this for granted. The popular inference based on their unique position was "Never shall the evil overtake us or come near to us" (Amos 9:10). They felt at ease and confident (6:1), for they thought that the Lord was truly with them (5:14). Reveling in their economic prosperity (4:1; 6:4–6) and exulting in their military victories (6:13), they firmly believed that the "Day of the Lord" would be for them one of light and salvation (5:18). In other words, God was unconditionally on their side.

Now comes the poignant shock of Amos's words. Unexpectedly upsetting their popular opinions (which he may have been actually alluding to in his initial words),[19] the prophet draws a totally different conclusion from that of his contemporaries. He contends that election and covenantal ties on the part of the Lord are actually only one side of the picture. This relationship is predicated upon a reciprocity, which demands complete obedience to the commands of the Deity. Precisely because Israel has been covenantally elected, it is held responsible for all its actions.[20] The imminent judgment is predicated upon their very election. Here the prophet employs for the third and climactic time the word כָּל. Because he is addressing *all* of Israel, and because he has chosen and legally bound them from *all* the nations of the world, he shall now execute punishment upon them for *all* their iniquities.[21] Other nations are indicted for grave atrocities and barbaric actions, but only Israel is taken to task for *every one* of its moral-ethical infractions (Amos 2:6ff.). It, which holds a unique position among the nations of the world, shall also be judged in a unique fashion. The election of Israel is not unconditional and does not grant immunity. Punishment is required wherever and whenever covenantal demands are not met.

Amos in his characteristic fashion deliberately leaves the nature of the punishment unspecified[22] and thereby adds a dimension of tension and terror to his words (compare Amos 4:12). He ominously declares that the Lord "will call them to account (אֶפְקֹד עַל) for all of their transgressions," but he does not explicate the how or when of this threat. By the use of the expression פקד על ("call to account, punish"),[23] the chapter now begins (3:2—אֶפְקֹד עַל) and concludes (3:14—וּפָקַדְתִּי עַל) on the same note, forming thereby one grand literary inclusio.

Note, too, the contrast between 3:1–2 and 9:7ff., both

citations supporting this technical interpretation. Bach (*Aufforderungen*, 155) cites several other verses, including Isa 1:3.

17 See *CAD, I, idû*, 23, 32, "to select, choose."

18 For other surprise conclusions that upset popular theology, see, for example, 5:18–20; 9:7. See also Loewenstamm, *Tradition of the Exodus*, 21–22, and Weiser, *Profetie*, 123: "Antithese und Paradoxie sind die Form seiner Gedankenführung" ("Antithesis and paradox are the model for his train of thought").

19 Amos may very well be ironically echoing their own familiar slogans: "God is with us"; "Only with us has God selected/entered into covenant relations." He also may be responding to their objections to his equating Israel with all the other nations. Compare Rudolph, 151; Amsler, 186. See also Weiser, *Profetie*, 120; Balla, *Die Droh*, 27–28; Vollmer, *Rückblicke*, 31–32.

20 Compare Cripps, 152: "The greater your privileges so much the more your responsibility." See also J. J. Collins, "History and Tradition in the Prophet Amos," *ITQ* 41 (1974) 125–26.

21 The word עֲוֺנֹתֵיכֶם ("your iniquities") is found only here in Amos. For עָוֺן (and חֵטְא) as denoting violation of treaty, see Weinfeld (*Deuteronomy*, 111 n 5), and his reference there to M. Tsevat's article ("The Neo-Assyrian and Neo-Babylonian Vassal Oaths and the Prophet Ezekiel," *JBL* 78 [1959] 199–204) on Ezek 21:28–29.

22 Compare, similarly, Amos 4:12.

23 For פקד על ("to call to account"), see, for example, Exod 20:5; Jer 5:9, 29; Hos 1:4. See especially the comments to 3:14.

of which refer to the exodus motif. In the former, Amos commences with the idea of chosenness in order to explicate the reason for the imminent punishment. In the latter he begins with their "unchosenness" and concludes with the future restoration (see later). In both cases he starts off with the opposite of what he is leading up to.

3 The Irresistible Sequence of Cause and Effect

3 **Do two walk together**
without having met?
4 **Does a lion roar in the forest**
if he has no prey?
Does a beast growl from his lair
without having caught something?
5 **Does a bird swoop down upon a ground trap**
if there is no bait for it?
Does a trap spring up from the ground
if it has not made a catch?
6 **Can a ram's horn be sounded in a town**
and the people not be startled?
Can disaster befall a town
if the Lord has not caused it?
7 **Indeed, my Lord God does nothing without**
revealing his counsel to his servants the
prophets.
8 **A lion has roared,**
Who is not terrified?
My Lord God has spoken,
Who will not prophesy?

■ **3–8** The next pericope consists of a series of rhetorical questions characterized by analogies drawn from common experience and well-known empirical phenomena. The prophet employs this literary expression in order to draw his unexpecting audience logically and skillfully into the flow of a persuasive and penetrating presentation of the inextricable relationship of all events and happenings.[1] This didactic device, which is commonly assumed to be drawn from folk wisdom, is anchored in the premise that every event has its immediate cause, and every cause, in turn, leads to its own concomitant result. Once the people are cognizant of the fact that nothing is accidental, and that there is an indissoluble and inevitable interrelationship between cause and result in both the animal and human spheres of existence, they would then be unable to deny that an identical sequence exists between the direct command of God to the prophet to speak (the cause) and the ensuing words of the prophet (the result)—a necessary conclusion that thus applies and expands the law of causality from the natural and social realms to the religious sphere. Amos is hereby presenting an "apologia" for his (and every prophet's) calling. He

1 For a rhetorical analysis of chapter 3, with special emphasis placed upon this pericope, see Y. Gitay, "A Study of Amos's Art of Speech: A Rhetorical Analysis of Amos 3:1–15," *CBQ* 42 (1980) 293–309. He views the entire chapter as one literary whole whose individual component parts are mutually related as part of a single discourse (p. 295). B. Renaud ("Genèse et Théologie d'Amos 3,3–8," in *Mélanges Bibliques et Orientaux en l'Honneur de M. Henri Cazelles* [ed. A. Caquot and M. Delcor; AOAT 212; Neukirchen-Vluyn: Neukirchener Verlag, 1981] 353–72) proposes an artificial reconstruction of the unit in three stages: vv 4–5, 6b, and v 8 are assumed to be two independent sections representing the original unity, to which were later added vv 3 and 6a, and subsequently v 7—each with its own supposedly different theological outlook. See already Gressmann (*Prophetie,* 339f.), who divided the section into two separate entities. The criticism of Weiser (*Profetie,* 12), applied to the latter, is equally cogent for the former, "Eulen nach Athen tragen" ("It's like carrying coals to Newcastle"). For other studies, see Zakovitch, *For Three,* 195–99; Uffenheimer, "Amos and Hosea," 287; S. Mittmann, "Gestalt und Gehalt einer prophetischen Selbstfertigung (Amos 3:3–8)," *TQ* 151 (1971) 134–45; Markert, *Struktur,* 89–94.

justifies and legitimizes his prophetic commission[2] by explaining its authority and authenticity as well as its absolute force and necessity. By such compelling and commanding reasoning, Amos responds to the attacks and protests that must have been leveled against him and his message.[3] His (as well as other prophets') right to speech had been challenged (2:12) and his words and ideas impugned. In defense of his previous oracle announcing impending punishment of the elected people (3:1–2), he forcefully and cogently argues that prophecy is not a self-generating act; rather, the prophet is irresistibly compelled to deliver God's words: "A lion has roared, who is not terrified? My Lord God has spoken, who will not prophesy?" (3:8).

Although, as has been often assumed, Amos adopted and adapted the style of the wisdom teacher in this pericope,[4] his composition nevertheless remains unique in both its form and content as well as in its comprehensive presentation and internal development. Note at the outset that Amos has a decided predilection for delivering his oracles seriatim. The book commences with a catalogue of prophecies against foreign nations, and in the ensuing chapters further examples are clearly attested.[5] This formal literary device, moreover, is skillfully used by him here and in chapters 1 and 2 for an additional psychological purpose. He first attracts the attention of his listeners by deftly drawing them into his orbit of thinking by means of statements they can readily and favorably accept, and then suddenly and dramatically he confronts his already captive audience with a totally unexpected and climactic finale. The literary genre of the prophecies against foreign nations aptly served him as a prelude to his surprise denunciation of Israel.[6] Now, by employing another genre, this time drawn from the sphere of wisdom literature, he gradually yet persuasively leads his opponents step by step into the vortex of a seemingly innocuous reasoning process. He commences by bringing an example from an everyday normal occurrence, and then he carefully continues to describe crisis situations that take place in both the animal and human worlds—all of which merely serve as a cohesive prolegomenon to his essential and final point: The phenomenon of prophecy is likewise a product of this same irresistible sequence of cause and effect.

Another literary similarity exists between his use of these two different genres (in chapters 1 and 2 and here). Not only are they presented in a series, but also in both he skillfully employs the well-known pattern of the graduated ascending number scheme, 7/8, in which the eighth oracle and the eighth rhetorical question (and not the seventh) bring the respective pericopes to their unexpected conclusion.[7] The first seven oracles as well as the seven rhetorical questions serve as an effective decoy for his ultimate trap; they are preclimactic. His audience, who most probably assumed that the seventh oracle (against Judah)[8] and the seventh question ("Can disaster befall a town if the Lord has not caused it?") would be the final one, is thus completely caught off guard when the prophet adds his eighth and final thrust. The effect is even more poignant in light of Amos's literary penchant for expressing himself also in heptads (see 2:6–8, 14–16;

2 For example, Hammershaimb, 57; Mays, 89; Wolff, 183; Rudolph, 154; Fey, *Amos und Jesaja,* 41; Ward, *Amos,* 39.

3 Compare Reventlow, *Amt,* 27; W. Baumgartner, "The Wisdom Literature," in *The Old Testament and Modern Study: A Generation of Discovery and Research* (ed. H. H. Rowley; Oxford: Clarendon, 1951) 211; Rudolph, 151; Wolff, 181. See, too, R. F. Melugin, "The Formation of Amos: An Analysis of Exegetical Method," in SBLASP 1 (Missoula, MT: Scholars, 1978) 381. For the appeal to reason and method of analogy, see Gitay, "Study," 298.

4 Compare J. Lindblom, "Wisdom in the Old Testament Prophets," in *Wisdom in Israel and in the Ancient Near East: Presented to Prof. H. H. Rowley by the Society for Old Testament Study* (ed. M. Noth and D. W. Thomas; SVT 3; Leiden: Brill, 1955) 201; Gese, "Beiträge," 424–27; Terrien, "Amos and Wisdom," 111–15; Reventlow, *Amt,* 27–30; Ward, *Amos,* 40; Amsler, 187; Mays, 60; Rudolph, 154; Wolff, 93, 183; idem, *Amos the Prophet.*

5 For other literary units presented in a series, compare the litany of punishments with their stereotypic refrain, Amos 4:6–11, and the sequence of visions in Amos 7—8.

6 See Paul, "Concatenous," 397–403; idem, "Literary Reinvestigation," 189–204.

7 See Paul ("Literary Reinvestigation," 196–97) for examples from Ugaritic and the Bible.

8 For a discussion of the originality of this oracle, see Paul, "Literary Reinvestigation," 196–97.

4:4–5, 6–11; 5:8–9, 21–23; 9:1–4)[9] and upon noting that the personal name of the God of Israel, YHWH, appears for the first time specifically in the seventh question—two impressive reasons that would naturally lead to the conclusion that the prophet had reached the apogee of his presentation with his seventh pronouncement. It is all the more startling, then, that he immediately confounds his by now unsuspecting listeners with his dramatic denouement. Such surprise finales are yet another literary device this prophet utilizes with great dexterity in order to upset and reverse firmly established beliefs and principles held by the people of Israel; compare, for example, 3:2; 5:18; 9:7.

The internal logical development of the subject matter itself is also well designed. After a general and logical all-inclusive introductory question (v 3, see later), he proceeds at first with a pair of examples drawn exclusively from the animal world—a lion and its victim (v 4)—and then continues by presenting two rhetorical questions rooted in the antagonistic relationship between the animal (birds) and human world—the latter which sets traps for the former (v 5). Thereupon he progresses to the interpersonal realm, where human hostility is directed against other humans (v 6a), and then finally he ascends to the human–divine sphere of interaction—catastrophes on earth are divine doings (v 6b). Then, and only then, after all areas of existence are acknowledged to fall within the same preconceived pattern of cause and result, does he add his last link, that is, the unique causal relationship between the prophet and the Lord (v 8b).

An additional emotional dimension in this literary unit (after the first innocuous introductory question) is the ominous feeling of no exit, no escape. The examples all depict the parties involved as being in situations in which they are ensnared or overpowered by some stronger force, be it animal, human, or divine. This physical or psychological entrapment provides a very fitting analogue to the end of the previous chapter, where Amos described the imminent defeat of Israel in terms of complete and total inescapability. With the aid of a heptad to express completeness, he powerfully portrayed the paralysis of all the military units and divisions of the Israelite army (2:14–16). This theme of total inescapability also recurs in 9:1–4.

Another unique facet of this pericope, which has all but escaped the attention of commentators, is the novel way in which Amos employs the literary device of the double rhetorical question.[10] The particle אם that introduces v 6 is not, as some have thought, a more intensive form of the question but rather the standard correlative and complement of the interrogative particle הֲ, which is employed in the three previous verses. Despite the some dozen different ways of posing and composing double questions in biblical Hebrew,[11] this

9 See R. Gordis, "The Heptad as an Element of Biblical and Rabbinic Style," *JBL* 62 (1943) 17–26; idem, "Studies," 128. Zakovitch (*For Three,* 195) sees here a pattern of 3–4 (actually, one question followed by three pairs of questions) within a larger pattern of 6–7, and brings examples from biblical and ancient Near Eastern literature (p. 547). Although he does not accept the originality of vv 7 and 8, he correctly interprets the internal structural and contextual order of the literary unit leading up to the seventh question (pp. 198–99). For another extended series of rhetorical questions, see Mic 6:6–7.

10 For other rhetorical questions in Amos, see 5:25; 6:2, 12; 8:8. This technique is also usually associated with wisdom literature. See Wolff, *Amos the Prophet,* 6–16. Compare, however, Crenshaw, "Influence," 44. The purpose of the question is to draw an example from the natural or human world in order to inculcate a moral or pragmatic teaching. Actually in Amos (and elsewhere) it is employed in order to convince and persuade; it is a literary polemical device. See also Gitay, "Study," 296, 302; and J. L. Crenshaw ("Impossible Questions, Sayings, and Tasks," in *Gnomic Wisdom* [ed. J. D. Crossan; Semeia 17; Chico, CA: Scholars, 1980] 19–34), who, however, does not place this literary device within the realm of polemics.

For an analogous rhetorical question from Mesopotamian literature, see *BWL* 241, lines 40–42: *ina la nâkimi erâtme, ina la akâlime kabrat* ("Has she become pregnant without having had intercourse? Has she become fat without eating?").

11 See Avishur, "Patterns," 421–64. See also M. Held, "Rhetorical Questions in Ugaritic and Biblical Hebrew," in Eretz Israel 9 (*W. F. Albright Volume,* ed. A. Malamat; Jerusalem: Israel Exploration Society, 1969) 71–79.

specific pattern—five consecutive questions introduced by הֲ followed by two introduced by אִם[12]—is unparalleled and can be attributed to the innovative literary creativity of the prophet himself.

Once this literary device is recognized, seeing whether it can be pursued yet one step further is intriguing. Biblical Hebrew also has several different ways of formulating a triple question. The two most attested are . . . הֲ מַדּוּעַ . . . אִם (for example, Jer 2:14, 31; 8:4–5; 16:19; 49:1; compare Isa 50:2) and כִּי . . . אִם . . . הֲ (for example, Num 11:12; Isa 66:8; Jer 18:14–15; 31:20; [48:27]; Amos 6:12; Mic 4:9; Hab 3:8; Job 7:12; 10:5–6; and a possible conflate of both forms in Jer 8:22). In the latter form, the particle כִּי introduces the logical conclusion of the two preceding אִם . . . הֲ questions.[13] This very tripartite pattern is also attested once in the Book of Amos, 6:12. Thus is it only merely a coincidence that in this unit directly after the double אִם . . . הֲ questions in vv 3–6, v 7 begins with כִּי, the particle that so often functions as the introduction to the third part of this conventional literary pattern? If this verse is a later interpolation, as most[14]—but not all[15]—modern commentators think (see later), at least formally and externally (if admittedly not contextually) the addition conforms to the distinctive style of the biblical formulation of the triple question.

A further point: In the first five questions, all of which are introduced by the interrogative הֲ, the result or effect precedes the cause: "Do two walk together" (result) "without having met?" (cause). "Does a lion roar in the forest" (result) "if he has no prey?" (cause). "Does a beast growl from his lair" (result) "without having caught something?" (cause). "Does a bird swoop down upon a ground trap" (result) "if there is no bait for it?" (cause). "Does a trap spring up from the ground" (result) "if it has not made a catch?" (cause).

In the first half of v 6, however, the prophet deliberately reverses his train of thought and states the cause prior to the result:[16] "Can a ram's horn be sounded in a town" (cause) "and the people not be startled?" (result). At this juncture, the change of formal presentation coincides with a change of formulation, for precisely here the prophet introduces his rhetorical question for the first time with the interrogatory particle אִם. Change of order of reasoning with a change of formal expression is a delicate additional literary touch. Then, in v 6b, he once again employs the אִם particle but reverts to his original pattern of result preceding cause: "Can disaster befall a town" (result) "if the Lord has not caused it?" (cause). By thus alternating the cause–result sequence (v 6a) with the immediately preceding and following result–cause sequence (vv 5b and 6a), the prophet artfully varies a stereotypic formal pattern and creates thereby a very effective chiastic word order.

One more feature accompanies this stylistic formal change from הֲ to אִם. In the first five הֲ-questions, the subject matter remains the same in the single or double cola (that is, individuals, lions and prey, birds and traps). In v 6 (when he leaves the realm of the animal world), however, two אִם-questions appear, consisting of two different subjects or themes in each of the separate cola:

---

12   For other examples of two consecutive interrogatives introduced by אִם, see Jer 48:27 and Job 6:12.

13   See Avishur ("Patterns," 421–64) for the distinction between מַדּוּעַ and כִּי. For כִּי after two initial series of rhetorical questions, see Job 10:4–6 (and, partially, Hab 3:8). Zakovitch (*For Three*, 199) also remarks upon the particle כִּי in this rhetorical sequence but negates the originality of v 7.

14   For it being a later literary addition, for example, compare the commentaries of Marti, Nowack, Sellin, Weiser, Wolff, and Rudolph. See also Duhm, "Anmerkungen," 5; Löhr, *Untersuchungen*; E. Baumann, "Eine Einzelheit," *ZAW* 64 (1952) 62; Lehming, "Erwägungen," 145–69; Schmidt, "Redaktion," 168–93; Gese, "Beiträge," 424–27; Ward, *Amos*, 15.

15   Compare the commentaries of Harper, Theis-Lippel, Robinson-Horst, Cripps, and Hammershaimb. See,

too, Maag, *Text*, 14; Gressmann, *Prophetie;* Reventlow, *Amt*, 27–28; Terrien, "Amos and Wisdom," 112; and K. Cramer, *Amos: Versuch einer theologischen Interpretation* (BWANT 3/15; Stuttgart: Kohlhammer, 1930) 16. Gitay ("Study," 304–5) bases the verse's authenticity on its rhetorical function.

16   Although this point was seen by many commentators, for example, Cripps, 155; Wolff, 183; Rudolph, 154, they neither indicate that it is an intentional reversal of the train of thought, nor, for the most part, connect it with the change in the rhetorical formulation.

the sounding of a "ram's horn" (v 6a) and a "disaster" in the city (v 6b). The former makes the people tremble; the latter is the Lord's doing.

Note also that in his application of the process of cause and effect, Amos relies on the senses of both seeing and hearing—and these two are employed in an alternating pattern.[17] One naturally reaches the obvious conclusion when one *sees* two walking together (v 3), when one *hears* the growl of a lion (v 4), when one *sees* a bird swooping down or caught in a trap (v 5), and when one *hears* the blast of a ram's horn (v 6a). All these *sights*[18] and *sounds* together demonstrate the inevitable connection between cause and effect.

An internal literary pattern characterized by symmetry and concatenation is also discernible within this section:

הֲיֵלְכוּ שְׁנַיִם יַחְדָּו בִּלְתִּי אִם־נוֹעָדוּ

בִּלְתִּי אִם־לָכָד	הֲיִתֵּן כְּפִיר קוֹלוֹ מִמְּעֹנָתוֹ	וְטֶרֶף אֵין לוֹ	הֲיִשְׁאַג אַרְיֵה בַּיַּעַר
וְלָכוֹד לֹא יִלְכּוֹד	הֲיַעֲלֶה־פַּח מִן הָאֲדָמָה	וּמוֹקֵשׁ אֵין לָהּ	הֲתִפּוֹל צִפּוֹר עַל־פַּח הָאָרֶץ
וַה׳ לֹא עָשָׂה	אִם־תִּהְיֶה רָעָה בְּעִיר	וְעָם לֹא יֶחֱרָדוּ	אִם־יִתָּקַע שׁוֹפָר בְּעִיר
	כִּי אִם־גָּלָה סוֹדוֹ אֶל־עֲבָדָיו הַנְּבִיאִים		כִּי לֹא יַעֲשֶׂה אֲדֹנָי ה׳ דָּבָר
מִי לֹא יִנָּבֵא	אֲדֹנָי ה׳ דִּבֶּר	מִי לֹא יִירָא	אַרְיֵה שָׁאָג

1. The negative expression בִּלְתִּי אִם ("if . . . not") appears before a verb only twice in the entire Bible, and these two sole occurrences are in the consecutive vv 3 and 4b.[19] Note also the alternating formulations of בִּלְתִּי אִם (v 3), הֲ . . . וְ (v 4a), הֲ . . . בִּלְתִּי אִם (v 4b), הֲ . . . וּ (v 5a), followed once by הֲ . . . לֹא and twice by אִם . . . לֹא. (Interestingly enough, the word אִם itself is employed in three different ways in these series of questions: as part of a negation [vv 3, 4b], as the correlative of הֲ in a double rhetorical question [v 6], and simply as a particle [v 7]).

2. In addition to בִּלְתִּי אִם, there are several other negative formulations, all of which appear in set pairs:

a.	וְטֶרֶף אֵין לוֹ	(v 4a)	וּמוֹקֵשׁ אֵין לָהּ	(v 5a);
b.	וְעָם לֹא יֶחֱרָדוּ	(v 6a)	וַה׳ לֹא עָשָׂה[20]	(v 6b);
c.	מִי לֹא יִירָא	(v 8a)	מִי לֹא יִנָּבֵא	(v 8b).

3. The verb לכד ("catch, capture") appears in two consecutive final cola, vv 4b and 5b.

4. Because in vv 4–6 the place or instrument in question is always specifically mentioned in both cola, and because the same word, בְּעִיר ("in a town"), is twice repeated in v 6, more caution should be taken before concluding (as most commentators do) that the word פַּח ("trap") in v 5a is a so-called redundant intrusion from v 5b. (See later for further evidence for the originality of this word in v 5a).

5. Verse 7a is directly linked to the immediately prior v 6b by the identical three words, ה׳ לֹא עָשָׂה . . . לֹא יַעֲשֶׂה ה׳ ("[if] the Lord has not done it" . . . "the Lord does not do . . ."), which are arranged chiastically.

6. Verse 8, in turn, contains two specific features that link it directly with v 7: (1) Three identical words אֲדֹנָי ה׳ דָּבָר (v 7a) and אֲדֹנָי ה׳ דִּבֶּר (v 8b). (Of course, דָּבָר in v 7a is a noun, and דִּבֶּר in v 8b a verb; however, the appearance of this base root twice in conjunction with the rare expression אֲדֹנָי ה׳ is very striking and most likely intentional.) (2) Only in these two verses is there a specific mention of prophets, הַנְּבִיאִים ("the prophets"; v 7b), and their prophecy, יִנָּבֵא ("he will . . . prophesy"; v 8b). (For the significance of these last two points, 5 and 6, in determining the originality of v 7, see further.)

7. A chiastic inclusio exists between הֲיִשְׁאַג אַרְיֵה ("does a lion roar . . ."; v 4a) and אַרְיֵה שָׁאָג ("a lion has roared"; v 8a).

8. Another (editorial) inclusio can also be detected in the phrase דִּבֶּר ה׳ ("the Lord has spoken"; v 1) and אֲדֹנָי ה׳ דִּבֶּר ("my Lord God has spoken"; v 8). (Although the first two verses of chapter 3 are an independent literary unit, they formally serve as the contextual background for the ensuing justification of the prophet's mission.)[21]

9. Finally, as a literary aside, attention should also be drawn to the chapter's overall embracive inclusio: שִׁמְעוּ . . . אֶפְקֹד ("Hear . . . I will call to account"; vv 1–2) and שִׁמְעוּ . . . פָּקְדִי . . . וּפָקַדְתִּי ("Hear . . . [when] I make an accounting . . . I will bring them to account"; vv 13–14).

17 Compare Uffenheimer, "Amos and Hosea," 287.

18 Compare Renaud, "Genèse," 365: "L'effet visible permet de remonter à la cause invisible" ("The visible result allows one to go back to the invisible cause").

19 In both Gen 47:18 and Judg 7:14, בִּלְתִּי אִם is employed before a substantive. For extrabiblical occurrences of Northwest Semitic cognates to Heb. בִּלְתִּי, see Phoen. בלת in the Tabnit Inscription, line 5, שכב בלת אנך ("Only I am lying [in this coffin]"), *KAI*, I.13:5; and Ugar., *blt*, C. Gordon, *UT*, 466, 479. See also C. J. Labuschagne, "Ugaritic *BLT* and *BILTÎ* in Isa X 4," *VT* 14 (1964) 97–99.

20 The לֹא-negation is already introduced in v 5b.

21 Gitay, "Study," 295, suggests that a rhetorical analysis of the various literary units of this chapter reveals their being "mutually related" and "are part of a

■ **3** "Do two walk together (יַחְדָּו)[22] without having met?" Doubt has been cast by some commentators on the authenticity of this verse in relation to the entire literary unit.[23] The main arguments are: (1) This verse is the only one in the composition that lacks a complementary poetic colon. (2) A plural verb is found only in this sentence. (3) Unlike all the other verses, the image portrayed here is a peaceful one, bearing no overtones of a threatening situation. However: (1) Because the pericope consists of a heptad of introductory questions, and because seven is an odd and not an even number, one verse by necessity must contain only a single and not a double question. (2) The plural verb is necessitated by the subject שְׁנַיִם ("two"). Moreover, the anonymity of "two walking together" makes this theme an appropriate continuation of the cause-and-effect dual relationship just described between Israel and God (vv 1–2),[24] on the one hand, and serves, in addition, as a convenient all-purpose introduction to the remaining six questions of "bilateral" relations, on the other. (3) The citing of a "neutral" or "normal" life situation and not one that alludes to a specific threat or crisis is intentional, in order to lure the audience into the prophet's train of thought. By bringing his example, however, in the form of a rhetorical question and not a statement, he rationally compels his listeners to frame his intended answer. It serves as a "coexpression of the speaker's conviction."[25] By capturing their attention with such a banal and everyday event with which they can readily concur, Amos "socratically" and psychologically weaves the first thread in the web that will eventually bind them to his own preplanned conclusion. Linguistically, too, this verse bears a distinctive "trademark" of Amos; that is, the expression בִּלְתִּי אִם preceding a verb, as noted previously, appears only in this book.

The verb נוֹעָדוּ here means merely "to meet," without any overtones of by plan or by design.[26] Neither does it imply meeting by agreement or by making an appointment. People naturally bump into one another by chance without prearranging either the time or the place of the liaison.[27] Were the prophet to have asked whether two people walk together only by predesignation, he would have defeated his purpose from the very outset, for the answer to such a question is that of course they do; sometimes two individuals do walk together by chance. However, his examples are geared toward an absolute nega-

single discourse." See also p. 306.

22 Compare the striking similarity to Gen 22:6, 8. Note, too, the iterative or frequentative force of most of the verbs in this pericope. The prophet draws here, as he does so often throughout his oracles, upon his own personal experiences for most of his examples.

23 For example, Nowack; Marti; Gese, "Beiträge," 425; Schmidt, "Redaktion," 183; Renaud, "Genèse," 357–59. Gese ("Beiträge," 424–27) and Marti attach this verse to vv 1–2 and consider it to be a gloss supplying the motif for the punishment announced in 3:2b. See also H. J. Stoebe, "Überlegungen zu den geistlichen Voraussetzungen der Prophetie des Amos," in *Wort-Gebot-Glaube Beiträge zur Theologie des Alten Testaments* (*Walther Eichrodt zum 80. Geburtstag*) (ed. H. J. Stoebe; ATANT 59; Zürich: Zwingli, 1970) 217ff.; and W. Eichrodt, "Die Vollmacht des Amos. Zu einer schwierigen Stelle im Amosbuch 3:3–8," in *Beiträge zur Alttestamentlichen Theologie: Festschrift für Walther Zimmerli zum 70. Geburtstag* (ed. H. Donner; Göttingen: Vandenhoeck & Ruprecht, 1977) 124–31. However, according to Wolff (184): "Verse 3 belongs to the original series of questions, even though this sentence differs in tone from those that follow." See also his note *b* on pp. 180–81: "Verse 3 gives the impression of being a preface." See also Weiser, *Profetie;* S. Mittmann, "Gestalt und Gehalt einer prophetischen Selbstfertigung (Amos 3:3–8)," *TQ* 151 (1971) 135–37.

24 Compare Gitay, "Study," 295, and Koch, *Amos*, 2.16. Renaud, "Genèse," 354, also observes that the first two verses, which are the words of Yahweh, pertain to the election of Israel, whereas vv 3–8, which are the words of the prophet, concern his own election.

25 Gitay, "Study," 306.

26 For יעד ("to meet") compare the frequent expression אֹהֶל מוֹעֵד ("the Tent of Meeting"); and for the verb in the *niphʿal*, for example, Exod 25:22, וְנוֹעַדְתִּי; Exod 30:6, 36, אִוָּעֵד, to describe the meeting of Moses with God. These examples do not imply, however, that in Amos the verb bears "une portée théologique" ("a theological import") or "une allusion à l'experience de Möise" ("an allusion to the experience of Moses"), against Renaud, "Genèse," 359, or that there is an allusion here to the covenant; Stoebe, "Überlegungen," 221.

27 See Rudolph, 151 n 3a, with additional bibliographical references and discussion, especially to Gese, "Beiträge," 425. See also Tur-Sinai, *Peshuṭo,* 488. G, ἐὰν μὴ γνωρίσωσιν ἑαυτούς (= Heb. נוֹדְעוּ; "unless they knew one another"), is a metathesis, most probably influenced by the verb ידע in v 2a. So Rudolph, 151 n 3a, and Wolff, 179 n *a*, against Marti; Nowack; Cripps. D. W. Thomas ("Note on נועדו in Amos

tive response without room for any exception, and so disagreeing with him is impossible for what he describes is so self-evident. If two people are seen walking together, it is clearly because they have met. *Quod erat demonstrandum.* As Rudolph so correctly comments on this verse, "Je unbestreitbarer seine Beispiele sind, desto brauchbarer für die Absicht, die er mit ihnen verfolgt"[28] ("The more incontestable his examples are, the more useful they are for the purpose which he achieves with them").

■ **4** "Does a lion roar in the forest if he has no prey? Does a beast (כְּפִיר)[29] growl from his lair without having caught something?"

These two rhetorical questions most likely refer to two different stages in the hunt. The initial roar of the lion[30] issues *from the forest* (בַּיַּעַר),[31] when it has first located and confronted its prey, but before it has made the kill. The second growl is the sound of victory and contentment it emits *from its den* (מִמְּעֹנָתוֹ),[32] after it has successfully captured and consumed its victim.[33] For other references to roars before or after the catch, see, for example, Isa 5:29; 31:4; Pss 22:14; 104:21. Compare also Ezek 22:25, in which the same three themes (אַרְיֵה, שׁאג, טרף) appear in the same consecutive order.

■ **5** "Does a bird[34] swoop down upon a ground trap (אֶרֶץ)[35] if there is no bait for it? Does a trap spring up from the ground (אֲדָמָה) if it has not made a catch?"

The two antithetical verbal expressions in the separate cola, נפל על and עלה מן, also represent two different stages in the capture of a bird, before and after it is trapped. The meaning of נפל על is not the same as נפל ב; only the latter means "fall into" (a trap into which most translators and exegetes have themselves inadvertently fallen here). נפל על, as the preposition itself indicates, means to "swoop" or "plunge down upon."[36] Amos is rhetorically posing the following question: Does a bird swoop down upon a ground trap (פַּח) unless there is a מוֹקֵשׁ? The only problem is what exactly is meant by a

III:3," *JTS* 7 (1956) 69–70) follows G but derives the root from an Arabic cognate, *wdʿ* ("was still, quiet, at rest"), which in the third and sixth forms means "to be reconciled, to make peace"—thereby misunderstanding the intention of the question. The Masoretic text is independently confirmed by two other Greek translations, α', συντάξωνται ("agree to come together") and θ', συνέλθωσιν αλλήλοις ("meet one another"), as well as by V, *convenerit eis* ("they have agreed") and T, אִזְדַּמְנוּ ("they met"). In some passages, however, a prearranged agreement or meeting is being referred to; see, for example, Job 2:11; Neh 6:2.

28 Rudolph, 155.

29 For כְּפִיר as "great (lion) beast," rather than its usual translation, "young lion," see Ezek 19:3: "She raised up one of her cubs; he became a great beast" (כְּפִיר). For the roar of a כְּפִיר אֲרָיוֹת, see Judg 14:5.

30 Compare Amos 1:2; 3:8. The lion is also mentioned in 3:4, 8, 12. Soggin, 57, following C. Houtman ("De jubelzang van de struiken der wildernis in Psalm 96:12b," in *Loven en geloven: Festschrift N. H. Ridderbos* [Amsterdam: Franeker, 1975] 164–72), translates יַעַר ("scrub").

31 For other examples of an אַרְיֵה ("lion") in the יַעַר ("forest"), see Jer 5:6; 12:8.

32 The מְעֹנָה or מָעוֹן is the "den" of lions; see Nah 2:12–13; Ps 104:21–22; Job 38:39–40; Cant 4:8; jackals, Jer 9:10; 10:22; 49:33; 51:37; and other wild animals, Job 37:8. The noun has not been added but, as becomes obvious from a comparison of the comparable place names in the other cola, is original; against Cripps, 154; Wolff, 180.

33 For the interpretation of two different stages in the catch, compare Nowack, 152; Sellin, 214; Theis-Lippel, 120; Hammershaimb, 58; Cripps, 153; Rudolph, 155. See especially J. Braslavi ("Does a Lion Roar in the Forest When He Has No Prey," *BM* 30 [1967] 12–16 [Heb.]), who also refers to W. Kahle, *Der Kleine Brehm: Das gesamte Tierreich in allgemeinverständlicher Darstellung* (Berlin: Vögels, 1933) 1.586. See also Braslavi, "The Lions of the Desert of Tekoa in the Book of Amos," *BM* 32 (1967) 56–64 (Heb.). Note that here, too, as in v 3, the theme of "meeting" is continued (Cross, written communication).

34 For the sequence of a צִפּוֹר ("bird") following a אַרְיֵה ("lion") in a totally different context, see Hos 11:10–11.

35 For the word pair אֶרֶץ . . . אֲדָמָה, see R. Weiss, *Studies in the Text and Language of the Bible* (Jerusalem: Magnes, 1981) 138 (Heb.).

36 This nuance has been almost entirely overlooked. For a rare exception, see E. Vogt, "'Ihr Tisch werde zur Falle' (Ps 69:23)," *Bib* 43 (1962) 80. "Fall upon" by extension comes to mean "attack," for example, Isa 16:9; Jer 48:32. Compare also the Akkadian interdialectal semantic equivalent, *ana X maqātu* ("to fall upon" and "to attack"). See *CAD, M,* I.240ff.

מוֹקֵשׁ. Because it is usually assumed that מוֹקֵשׁ is synonymous with פַּח, and because, to further compound and confound the issue, G reflects a reading עַל (ἐπὶ [τὴν γῆν]) "upon" and omits פַּח, many commentators conclude that the noun פַּח in the first colon has been incorrectly repeated from the second colon and consequently should be deleted.[37] The few commentators who defend the correctness of the Masoretic text and who also make a distinction between the nouns פַּח and מוֹקֵשׁ conclude that a מוֹקֵשׁ refers to either a "throwing stick/boomerang"[38] or to a "striker," that is, the moveable part of a trap that strikes and paralyzes the ensnared bird.[39] However, these same commentators unfortunately overlooked the correct nuance of Heb. נפל על and themselves "fell into" a translation trap. What is being described in this verse is the *cause* of a bird's sudden and swift descent. Why does a bird swoop down upon a trap? It swoops because of the מוֹקֵשׁ, which is obviously none other than the "bait" or "decoy" that is attached to the trap.[40] For this meaning of מוֹקֵשׁ, compare 1 Sam 18:21: "Saul thought, 'I will give her [Michal] to him [David]; let her be the bait that lures him [מוֹקֵשׁ] to his death at the hands of the Philistines.'" (By *pars pro toto,* מוֹקֵשׁ, which is the "bait" of a trap, comes to signify primarily the "trap" itself.) The bait or decoy first lures the unsuspecting bird to plunge down from on high (v 5a), and then the trap itself springs up to ensnare its victim (v 5b).[41]

■ **6** "Can a ram's horn be sounded in a town and the people not be startled?[42] Can disaster befall a town if the Lord has not caused it?"

Here the locus changes, and the focus is on events that take place within a town or city (בְּעִיר).[43] The questions are introduced by the interrogative אִם (see previously), and in v 6a the cause precedes the result (see previously).[44] This sequence not only produces its own literary effect but also is contextually necessary, for many possible reasons would result in a people's taking

37 So most commentators, for example, Wolff, 180 n *d.* Some, however, accept G as original and interpret פַּח as a corruption of פְּנֵי; so Ehrlich, *Randglossen,* 5.234; Harper, 69, following F. Perles, *Analekten zur Textkritik des Alten Testaments* (Leipzig: Engel, 1895).

38 Thus Wolff, 185, who refers to M. F. von Oppenheim, *Der Tell Halaf: Eine neue Kultur im ältesten Mesopotamien* (Leipzig: Brockhaus, 1931) 93–94, and plates 9b, 17b. Hammershaimb, 58, derives his evidence from A. Erman and H. Ranke, *Ägypten und ägyptisches Leben im Altertum* (Tübingen: J. C. B. Mohr [Siebeck], 1923) 264.

39 See G. R. Driver, "Reflections on Recent Articles," *JBL* 73 (1954) 131–36. (Driver's Akkadian equivalents, however, are very questionable.) On the subject of traps and snares, see G. Gerleman, "Contributions to the Old Testament Terminology of the Chase," *Bulletin de la Société Royale des Lettres de Lund* (Kungl. Humanistiska Vetenskapssamfundet I Lund Årsberattelse 1945–1946; Lund: Gleerup, 1946) 4.79–90 (on p. 81, מוֹקֵשׁ, "manned clap net"; p. 82, פַּח, "automatic bird trap"); and L. E. Toombs, "Traps and Snares," *IDB* 4.687–88. For the combination of צִפּוֹר ("bird") and פַּח ("trap"), see Ps 124:7; Prov 7:23; Eccl 9:12; for פַּח and מוֹקֵשׁ, see Josh 23:13; Isa 8:14; Pss 69:23; 141:9. See, too, Ugaritic *yqšm* ("bird watchers"). Compare Hos 9:8, פַּח יָקוֹשׁ; Pss 91:3, פַּח יָקוּשׁ; 124:7, פַּח יוֹקְשִׁים.

40 For the meaning "bait," see Driver, "Reflections," 131–36; Harper, 71; Cripps, 144–54; Vogt, "Ihr Tisch," 80; and Rudolph (151 n 5a), who also cites van Hoonacker, van Gelderen, Robinson, Snaith, and Amsler. Both Vogt and Rudolph also note Ps 69:23. See, too, H. Heller, "New Biblical Interpretations," in *Zvi Karl Memorial Volume* (ed. A. Weiser and B. Z. Luria; Jerusalem: Kiryat Sepher, 1960) 51 (Heb.); D. Ashbel, "Notes on the Prophecy of Amos—'Does a Bird Swoop Down upon a Ground Trap If There Is No Bait for It?'" *BM* 25 (1966) 103–4 (Heb.); and Toombs, "Traps and Snares," 687–88. Interestingly enough, T translates Heb. מוֹקֵשׁ by Aram. צֵיד ("provision, game").

41 For an Assyrian text referring to a bird (Heb. צִפּוֹר = Akk. *iṣṣūru*) being caught (Heb. לכד = Akk. *ṣabātu*) in a trap or decoy, see the curse found in Wiseman, "Vassal Treaties," 73, line 582: *kî ša iṣṣūru ina tu-ba-qi iṣṣabatuni* ("just as a bird is caught in a ?"). For the problematic Akk. *tubāqu,* see Wiseman, "Vassal Treaties," 73, "trap"; *CAD, I,* 209, *iṣṣūr tubāqi,* "decoy"; *AHw,* 3.1364, *tubāqu,* "ein Gebusch?" ("a thicket"?). Compare Akk. *arru* ("bird used for decoy") and *arrutu* ("used as decoy"), *CAD, A,* II.305–6. See also A. Salonen, *Vögel und Vogelfang im alten Mesopotamien* (Annales Academiae Scientiarum Fennicae B180; Helsinki: Suomalainen Tiedeakatemia, 1973) 29–48.

42 For the use of עָם ("people") with a plural verb, see, for example, Exod 19:8, 10.

43 By the locus now being the "city," the prophet "progressively zeroes in on the world of experience of his hearers [in Samaria]," Wolff, 186.

44 See n 16. There is no reason either to reverse the two stichs, as suggested by W. Baumgartner ("Amos 3:3–8," *ZAW* 33 [1913] 78–80), or to interpret v 6a

alarm.[45] Here, however, the alarm is specifically caused by the ram's horn heralding the imminent danger of an approaching enemy.[46]

The second half of v 6 returns to the result–cause sequence, thereby creating an internal chiastic order. In v 6b, the finale to his interrogatory overture, Amos indulges in yet another polemic, this time against the popular belief that the Lord will not bring any misfortune or catastrophe (רָעָה)[47] upon his chosen people. Having been elected and selected, they naively believed that their God, the God of Hosts, was truly with them (Amos 5:14), and that the Day of the Lord would be one of light for them (5:18). They therefore feel secure enough to boast confidently, "Never shall the evil (הָרָעָה) overtake us or come near to us" (9:10).[48] Amos here, as elsewhere, demolishes these popular sentiments and time-honored beliefs and reaches completely opposite conclusions.[49]

■ **7** "Indeed,[50] my Lord God does nothing[51] without having revealed his counsel[52] to his servants the prophets."

Most commentators regard this verse as a later interpolation.[53] It is a prose, didactic, declarative, dogmatic assertion (not a rhetorical question) that is contended to be "reminiscent of Deuteronomistic history writing"[54] or a "Deuteronomic cliché."[55] Although the expression עֲבָדָיו הַנְּבִיאִים ("his servants, the prophets") is typical of that school (for example, 2 Kgs 9:7; 17:13, 23; 21:10; 24:2; Jer 7:25; 25:4; 26:5; 29:19; 35:15; 44:4; compare Ezek 38:17; Zech 1:6; Dan 9:6, 10; Ezra 9:11), that the

as "une intervention rédactionnelle" ("a redactional intervention"), against Renaud, "Genèse," 359.

45 Compare Rudolph, 156, "weil hier die Fortsetzung des bisherigen Schemas zu Unrichtigkeiten geführt hätte: Das Erschrecken der Menschen kann vielerei Anlässe haben nicht nur den hier genannten" ("because here the continuation of the pattern up to now would have led to an inaccuracy: The terror of humans may have many causes, not only those mentioned here"). See also Kimchi, relying on the additional words supplied by T.

46 For example, Jer 6:1, 17; Ezek 33:3; Hos 5:8; 8:1; Joel 2:15. For a similar alarming effect of such a blast upon the people—within the context of the Sinaitic theophany—see Exod 19:18–19.

47 For רָעָה ("misfortune, calamity") in Amos, see 6:3; 9:4, 10. See also Deut 32:23; 1 Sam 6:9; 2 Kgs 6:33; Isa 45:7; Jer 1:14; 18:8; Ezek 7:5; Job 2:10. For the expression לַעֲשׂוֹת רָעָה that appears here, see Exod 32:14. The interpretation "das Böse der Israel getan" ("the evil which Israel did") is not correct here; against M. J. Mulder ("Ein Vorschlag zur Übersetzung von Amos iii:6b," *VT* 34 [1984] 106–8), who translates the end of the verse (incorrectly), "and shall Yahweh not react?"

In Akkadian the same semantic development also occurs: *lemnu* ("morally bad, evil" = Heb. רַע); *lemuttu* ("misfortune" = Heb. רָעָה). See *CAD, L,* 128. Compare the example, *Enlil lemutta ina māti išakkan* ("Enlil will inflict a calamity upon the country"). For the cognate Akkadian expression to Heb. לַעֲשׂוֹת רָעָה, *lemuttam epēšu* ("to do evil"), see *BWL* 240 ii 18–19.

48 For similar arrogant sentiments, see Mic 3:11: "The Lord is in our midst; no calamity (רָעָה) shall overtake us"; and Jer 5:12: "No misfortune (רָעָה) shall come upon us."

49 See Gitay, "Study," 296–97; Kapelrud, "New Ideas," 198.

50 Heb. כִּי is asseverative. Note, moreover, the use of כִּי twice in this verse corresponding to the double אִם and הֲ in the former verses.

51 For Heb. לֹא . . . דָּבָר ("anything, nothing"), see Exod 9:4; 1 Kgs 5:7; 10:3; Isa 39:2; and especially Amos's ironic use of this expression as a double entendre in 6:13. For the Akkadian interdialectal semantic equivalent of לַעֲשׂוֹת דָּבָר, *amatu epēšu* ("to perform an act"), see *CAD, E,* 202.

52 For Heb. גִּלָּה סוֹד (in both the *piʿēl* and *qal*), see Prov 11:13; 20:19; 25:9. Wolff, 187, agrees that "the expression, 'to reveal a plan,' is otherwise at home in proverbial wisdom," yet he does not interpret it by "reference to its wisdom background"; against Terrien, "Amos and Wisdom," 112–15. Compare Jer 23:18, 22.

53 See n 14. Compare Wolff, 181: "It can be asserted with considerable assurance that 3:7 is a later literary addition." See, too, Renaud, "Genèse"; and I. Willi-Plein, *Vorformen der Schriftexegese innerhalb des Alten Testaments: Untersuchungen zum literarischen Werden der auf Amos, Hosea und Micha zurückgehenden Bücher im hebräischen Zwölfprophetenbuch* (BZAW 123; Berlin: de Gruyter, 1971) 21–23.

54 Compare, for example, Weiser, *Profetie,* 128; Lehming, "Erwägungen," 152; Fey, *Amos und Jesaja,* 42; Mays, 61; Wolff, 187; and Rudolph, 107 (with certain reservations). See especially Schmidt, "Redaktion," 185–88.

55 W. Zimmerli and J. Jeremias, *The Servant of God* (SBT 20; London: SCM, 1957) 22–23.

prophet could not have expressed himself in this manner does not inevitably and absolutely follow. "The fact that the representation of the prophets as the servants of YHWH occurs especially in Jeremiah and the later prophets is not sufficient proof that Amos could not have used this image."[56] As succinctly stated by Rudolph in another connection, "Natürlich haben wir hier Ausdrücke, die auch deuteronomistischen Literatur geläufig sind, . . . aber der deuteronomische Stil war ja nicht eines Tages plötzlich da sondern hat sich entwickelt"[57] ("Of course we have here expressions which are also familiar from the Deuteronomistic literature . . . the Deuteronomic style, however, did not spring up overnight, but itself underwent development"). It is obviously more than a bit exaggerated to declare that the "theology seems very unlike the thinking of Amos."[58] The notion expressed here is intrinsically rooted in the biblical concept of prophecy. The prophet stands in the presence of God (Jer 15:1, 19), is privy to the divine council (Isa 6; Jer 23:18, 22), and as the spokesman for the Deity is apprised in advance as to the plans of his God. The institution of prophecy is founded on the basic premise that God makes his will known to chosen individuals, as is already clearly stated in Gen 18:17.

If the verse is a later interpolation, the great adroitness and artistry with which it was inserted must be admitted. As was demonstrated previously, v 7a is chiastically interrelated to v 6b by the identical phrase, לֹא יַעֲשֶׂה ה'/ ה' לֹא עָשָׂה, and is related to v 8b by the words דִּבֶּר אֲדֹנָי ה'. Verse 7b is also connected to v 8b by the common theme of prophecy. Furthermore, as noted previously, the formal literary framework is the כִּי . . . אִם . . . הֲ pattern, even though the particle כִּי here serves a different function. Thus Hammershaimb's cautious comment (reached without the aid of the above literary connections) is definitely in order: "Verse 7 can, however, be interpreted as a far from superfluous element in the context."[59] This verse firmly establishes the credibility of the prophet per se.

■ **8** "A lion has roared, who is not terrified?[60] My Lord God has spoken, who[61] will not prophesy?"

Amos finally reaches the climax and ultimate purpose of his presentation. Literarily, as seen previously, the first two words form a chiastic inclusio with v 4.[62] The style of this verse is also distinct:[63] a declarative statement of fact followed by a rhetorical question. The prophet thereby artfully concludes his thought in the same stylistic manner with which he began, that is, by employing the device of a rhetorical question to express a consequential relationship. The staccatolike effect of the entire sentence highlights and emotionally reflects his own existential situation. The prophet acts under divine compulsion. "A prophet does not choose his profession but is chosen, often against his own will. . . . A prophet does not elect to prophesy but is selected by God and is irresistibly compelled to deliver his message."[64] Thus,

56 Hammershaimb, 60.

57 Rudolph, 121. Nevertheless, he still considers the verse secondary.

58 Mays, 61–62. So, too, Renaud, "Genèse," 355.

59 Hammershaimb, 59. Compare Gitay, "Study," 299.

60 Some exegetes consider this verse as an independent oracle. Compare the argument based on meter by D. K. Stuart, *Studies in Early Hebrew Meter* (Missoula, MT: Scholars, 1976) 201. See, too, Renaud, "Genèse," 350. See, however, Wolff, 181–82, and Rudolph, 154 n 13.

61 See O. R. Schwarzwald, "Complementary Distribution and Shift in the Syntax of 'Who' Abstract," *BM* 24 (1979) 81–88 (Heb.).

62 For other examples of literary units that begin and end with the same root words, see Amos 2:14, 16 (אמץ, גִּבּוֹר, נוס) and 9:1, 4 (הרג, חֶרֶב).

63 Gitay ("Study," 306) suggests that the prophet "breaks the stylistic pattern in order to attract attention. The usage of mixed 'genres' in 3–6, 7, 8 . . . is effective." See also p. 299, in which he calls the verse "apologetic . . . establishing a relationship between the prophet and the audience."

64 Paul, "Prophets," 1151–52. See also Cripps, 157–58; Rudolph, 156. Compare Jer 20:7–9.

for the populace to demand or even threaten him to remain silent is useless (2:12).[65] The prophet speaks when commanded but, once commanded, must speak.[66]

65 See Weiser, *Profetie,* 131; Reventlow, *Amt,* 28.

66 See Paul, "Prophets," 1151–52. Compare Rudolph, 156: "Une wie man da nicht überlegen kann: soll ich zittern oder soll ich nicht zittern?—man zittert eben—, genauso ist es, wenn der Ruf Jahwes ergeht" ("And as one cannot reflect, Should I tremble or should I not tremble?—one just trembles—so exactly does it happen when the call of Yahweh goes forth"). Compare H. Junker, "'Leo rugit, quis non timebit? Deus locutus est, quis non prophetabit?' Eine textkritische und exegetische Untersuchung über Amos 3:3–8," *TTZ* 59 (1950) 4–13.

3 Witnesses to Samaria's Outrages and Oppression

9 Proclaim over the fortresses of Ashdod
And over the fortresses of the land of Egypt,
And say, "Assemble upon the hills of Samaria!
Look at the manifold outrages within her
And the oppression in her midst!
10 For they are incapable of doing what is right
—declares the Lord,
Those who store up violence and rapine in their fortresses."
11 Therefore, thus said my Lord God:
An enemy shall surround the land,
He shall strip you of your strength,
And your fortresses shall be sacked.
12 Thus said the Lord:
As the shepherd rescues out of the mouth of a lion
Two shank bones or a tip of an ear,
So shall the Israelites dwelling in Samaria be rescued,
Only with the head of a bed
Or the foot* of a couch.

***Hebrew obscure**

■ **9** This new oracle, beginning with הַשְׁמִיעוּ ("proclaim"),[1] is directed against the wealthy class of Samaria to whom witnesses are sent to bear evidence against their crimes and outrageous oppression. With the announcement of punishment pronounced against them, the oracle comes to an end.

The pericope begins with an invocation of the prophet giving "instruction to heralds"[2] to summon witnesses from the "fortresses" (אַרְמְנוֹת)[3] of both Ashdod and Egypt. The key word, אַרְמְנוֹת, appears four times in the next three sentences. The witnesses who come from their respective אַרְמְנוֹת are to get a firsthand view of what the aristocracy of Samaria has hoarded up in their אַרְמְנוֹת, leading eventually to the plundering of these very same אַרְמְנוֹת. Measure for measure: where the evidence for their crime is found, there will the punishment be executed. As they have amassed their wealth through plunder, so shall they, in turn, be plundered. Samaria's aristocracy shall be judged by their counterparts.

In accordance with Israelite law (for example, Deut 17:6; 19:15; compare 1 Kgs 21:10), two witnesses are summoned forth to bear eyewitness testimony to the acts of injustice committed in the north. Once they testify, the final judgment will be given. The two selected to corroborate the situation are Ashdod (representing the Philistines) and Egypt, both of whom in the past have had their own history of oppressing Israel. Therefore, they both can be considered, in an ironic fashion, to be independent, expert, experienced, and competent witnesses.[4] It is well known that G reads here ἐν

1. See the introduction for the literary division of the Book of Amos. In this section the oracles begin with imperatives derived from the root שמע. Note that here, too, the interplay of sound (הַשְׁמִיעוּ, "hear") and sight (רְאוּ, "see") links this passage with the former pericope.
2. See Wolff, 191, following F. Crüsemann, *Studien zur Formgeschichte von Hymnus und Danklied in Israel* (WMANT 32; Neukirchen-Vluyn: Neukirchener Verlag, 1969) 54, 229–30.
3. אַרְמְנוֹת is a favorite key word in the Book of Amos; compare its multiple usage in chapters 1 and 2. For the meaning "fortress," see S. M. Paul, "Cuneiform Light on Jer. 9,20," *Bib* 49 (1968) 374.
4. Just as the nations are held accountable for dire infringements of the basic moral law (Amos 1—2), so, too, can they be called to act as witnesses when Israel trespasses its moral imperatives.

’Ασσυρίοις (“Assyria”; אַשּׁוּר) for “Ashdod” (אַשְׁדוֹד). Because these two classical enemies of Israel, Assyria and Egypt, often occur together in the Bible (for example, Isa 7:18; Hos 11:5), some exegetes tend to favor the Greek. However, even though this is the only passage in which Ashdod appears alongside Egypt, the Masoretic “Ashdod” is still to be preferred. The reading אַשּׁוּר was produced either by a faulty metathesis of letters and a graphic error of ד and ר or by a scribal reflex based on the predominance of Assyria as one of the major enemies of Israel, thereby creating a parallel country comparable to the major empire of Egypt. If “Assyria” were the original reading, no scribe would have mistaken it for “Ashdod,” a mere component of the Philistine pentapolis. Neither in size nor in historical importance did Ashdod ever vie with Assyria. Thus Ashdod could never substitute for Assyria, but the latter could very easily replace the former. Furthermore, whereas Assyria is never cited by name anywhere in the entire Book of Amos because most, if not all, of his prophecies were completed prior to the westward expansion of the neo-Assyrian empire under Tiglatpileser III,[5] Ashdod is mentioned once as part of the oracle against the Philistine cities (1:8). The reading “Ashdod,” moreover, is attested to by other Greek translations, ἐν ἀζώτῳ, as well as by T and V. As will be seen later, Amos creates a very ingenious paronomasia on the names of the two countries in vv 10 and 11, one of which is based on the very word Ashdod.

The heralds are commanded to direct their proclamation “to/over/or concerning[6] (הַשְׁמִיעוּ עַל־) the fortresses of Ashdod (אַרְמְנוֹת בְּאַשְׁדּוֹד) and Egypt” (אַרְמְנוֹת בְּאֶרֶץ מִצְרָיִם). (For the use of a construct state before the preposition, אַרְמְנוֹת בְּ־, see, for example, 2 Sam 1:21, הָרֵי בַגִּלְבֹּעַ; Isa 9:2, שִׂמְחַת בַּקָּצִיר; Ps 136:8, בַּיּוֹם לְמֶמְשֶׁלֶת.)[7] Fortresses, that is, the inhabitants of the fortresses, will come to witness what is taking place in the similar fortresses of Samaria.

The dual command הַשְׁמִיעוּ . . . וְאִמְרוּ (“proclaim . . . and say”) is apparently a *terminus technicus* to messengers and appears several other times in the Bible; see Isa 48:20; Jer 4:5 (where in the list of following imperatives הֵאָסְפוּ [“gather”] also appears as in Amos); 31:7; 46:14; 50:2.[8]

The witnesses are commanded to “gather on[9] the hills of Samaria” (הָרֵי שֹׁמְרוֹן) in order to get a direct view of the events in that city. G, ἐπὶ τὸ ὄρος (= Heb. עַל הַר; “on the hill [of Samaria],” singular, not plural) is in accord with two other passages in Amos, 4:1 and 6:1, and complies with the geography of that area in that Samaria is atop a single hill (1 Kgs 16:24).[10] However, the plural reading is still preferable. In its favor are T (עַל טוּרֵי) and V *(in montibus),* which both support the Masoretic text, and the similar use of the plural, הָרֵי שֹׁמְרוֹן, in Jer 31:4. Nevertheless, what the prophet most likely has in mind is not the mountain of Samaria per se but the hills that surround that city. Because he is rhetorically inviting representatives from the two nations, much room will be needed to accommodate them all.[11] Moreover, the mountaintops surrounding Samaria are higher in altitude[12] and thereby provide an excellent vantage point from which they can look down into Samaria to gather their eyewitness reports.

They are to witness the many מְהוּמֹת and עֲשׁוּקִים within Samaria. The first substantive, מְהוּמָה, is found only twice in the plural, here and 2 Chr 15:5,[13] both times with the same adjective, רַבּוֹת (“many”), indicating intensification.[14] It usually designates the confusion, tumult, and panic associated with divine judgment or the effect caused by the Deity in battle.[15] However, it also is

5 See Kaufmann, *Toledoth,* 6.87.

6 Although it has been suggested that הַשְׁמִיעוּ עַל (also in Jer 4:16; 51:27; Ezek 27:30) is a variant of הַשְׁמִיעוּ אֶל (Isa 62:11; Jer 49:2; 50:29; Ezek 36:15), for example, Soggin, 60, within the present literary context, “proclaim over” seems preferable.

7 See *GKC,* 130a.

8 Thus there is no reason to delete וְאִמְרוּ, as does Harper, 75.

9 For הֵאָסְפוּ עַל, see also 2 Sam 17:11; Ezek 39:17. The verb אסף, as well as its Akkadian semantic equivalent, *puḫḫuru* (“to assemble”), is also employed to designate the concentration of troops. See Lipiński, *La Royauté,* 251–52 n 1.

10 Favored by most commentators.

11 Compare Wolff, 190.

12 Wolff, 190, for comparative measurements of the hills. Nevertheless, Wolff still favors the reading in the singular. Compare also Rudolph, 159.

13 See also 1QH 3:25.

14 *GKC,* 124e.

15 Wolff, 193. See 1 Sam 5:9; 14:20; Isa 22:5; Zech 14:13.

associated with human actions. Compare, for example, Ezek 22:5: "Both the near and far shall scorn you, O besmirched of name, O laden with מְהוּמָה" (רַבַּת הַמְּהוּמָה—note again the use of the same adjective); Prov 15:16 (where the noun אוֹצָר ["treasure"] also appears; see Amos 3:10); and 2 Chr 15:5 (cited previously), where it signifies the opposite of שָׁלוֹם: "At those times no wayfarer was safe (שָׁלוֹם) for there was much tumult (מְהוּמוֹת רַבּוֹת) among all the inhabitants of the lands." In Amos it is a general, all-inclusive term for the great fear and confusion within the society due to the outrages committed by the wealthy.

The second substantive, עֲשׁוּקִים, is an abstract plural[16] (see also Job 35:9; Eccl 4:1a) designating the manifold "oppression" of the downtrodden masses, at whose expense the upper class increases its ill-gotten gains.

■ **10** They are simply "incapable of doing[17] right." The abstract noun נְכֹחָה designates that which is "straight," that is, "straightforward, honest, just, correct."[18] It appears again in Isa 59:14: "Because honesty (אֱמֶת) stumbles in the public square and uprightness/integrity (נְכֹחָה) cannot enter." Its occurrence in some sapiential passages[19] has led several exegetes to refer to it as one of the influences of the wisdom realm upon the prophet, his "geistige Heimat."[20] The entire theory, however, is seriously open to question.[21]

The expression נְאֻם־ה' is considered by many as secondary.[22] However, it may be authentic, functioning here as a deliberate "delaying tactic"[23] before revealing the identity of the guilty party, who, as yet, has been left unnamed.

The accused are the members of the upper class of Samaria who "pile up and store away (הָאֹצְרִים) in their fortresses" both חָמָס and שֹׁד. Both terms are well-known substantives, often occurring together (see, for example, Isa 60:18; Jer 6:7; 20:8; Ezek 45:9; Hab 1:3; 2:17), representing the lawlessness and corruption of the society.[24] חָמָס ("violence, lawlessness") usually pertains to crimes committed against persons[25] and also appears alongside דָּמִים ("[bloody] crimes").[26] שֹׁד, commonly paired with שֶׁבֶר,[27] refers primarily to crimes against property.[28]

Amos's choice of terms, moreover, is very clever. By employing the verb אֹצְרִים, he deftly alludes to מִצְרָיִם; and שֹׁד, in turn, is an alliterative wordplay upon אַשְׁדּוֹד. Thus he skillfully composes a paronomasia on the names of the very two countries who are invited to witness the current crimes of Samaria.[29] The representatives of these foreign אַרְמְנוֹת are to bear testimony concerning the crimes committed against people and property, the proceeds of which are stored away in the אַרְמְנוֹת of Samaria.

16 Many commentators, for example, Ehrlich, *Randglossen*, 5.235; Hammershaimb, 61; Rudolph, 159; Wolff, 190. See also Milgrom, "Missing Thief," 76–77. Note that three key words link this pericope with Amos 4:1: הַר שֹׁמְרוֹן; הָעֲשֻׁקוֹת–וַעֲשׁוּקִים; שִׁמְעוּ–הַשְׁמִיעוּ–הָרֵי שֹׁמְרוֹן.

17 For other examples of the infinitive (here עֲשׂוֹת) as object of the verb, see, for example, 1 Kgs 3:7; Isa 1:14. See *GKC*, 114c. Cross interprets לֹא יָדְעוּ as "willful ignorance" (written communication).

18 Compare the Akkadian adjective *išaru* ("normal, regular, straight"), which also comes to mean "fair, just, correct"; *CAD, I*, 224.

19 The masculine plural appears in 2 Sam 15:3; Prov 8:9; 24:26; and the feminine plural in Isa 26:10; 30:10.

20 See Terrien, "Amos and Wisdom," 112–13; Fey, *Amos und Jesaja*, 39–40; and especially Wolff, *Amos the Prophet*, 56–59. This term coined by Wolff, which literally means "spiritual or intellectual homeland," is, according to Wolff, best translated "cultural background." See the editor's introduction to Wolff's work just cited, p. vii.

21 See the criticisms of Crenshaw ("Influence," 46, 49), who refers to 2 Sam 15:3; Isa 26:10; 30:10; 57:2; 59:14; idem, "Method in Determining Wisdom Influence upon Historical Literature," *JBL* 88 (1969) 132–33; idem, "Prolegomenon," in *Studies in Ancient Israelite Wisdom* (ed. J. L. Crenshaw; New York: Ktav, 1970) 9; H. H. Schmidt, "Amos. Zur Frage nach des 'geistigen Heimat' des Propheten," *WuD* 10 (1969) 90.

22 For example, Sellin; Wolff, 190; Maag, *Text*, 15; but it already appears in G, λέγει κύριος.

23 See also Amos 1:3ff., לֹא אֲשִׁיבֶנּוּ; 4:12.

24 See Seeligmann, "Terminologie," 257–59.

25 Compare Wolff, 194.

26 For example, Ezek 7:23; 9:9; Hab 2:8, 17.

27 Seeligmann, "Terminologie," 257–59.

28 For example, Hos 9:6; 10:14; Obad 5; Mic 2:4.

29 Paronomasia of place-names is frequent in the Bible; see Mic 1:10–15 for several examples. See, in general, R. Weiss, *MiShuṭ BaMiqra* (Jerusalem: Rubinstein, 1977) 162–89 (Heb.).

■ **11** For the introduction of the punishment by לָכֵן, see also Amos 5:11, 16; 6:7; 7:17. The first word following the messenger/herald formula, צַר, has been interpreted in several different ways: G and α' translated Τύρος (צֹר = "Tyre"), thereby identifying the assumed foe. However, T, עָקָא; S, אֻלְצָנָא; and σ', πολιορκία, all reflect צַר = צָרָה ("straits, distress"); see also V, *tribulabitur* ("be in distress"). However, in the light of the context of the continuation of the verse, clearly the substantive refers to the oppressor, that is, צַר = "enemy" (compare, for example, Gen 14:20; Num 10:9; Deut 32:27; 2 Sam 24:13; Isa 9:10; Esth 7:6).

The difficulty of the *waw* preceding the next word, וּסְבִיב, has brought forth several suggestions.[30] Some emend to מִסָּבִיב on the basis of G, κυκλόθεν: "An adversary round about the land!"[31] However, in light of V, *circumietur* ("be encompassed"), it seems preferable to read יְסוֹבֵב[32] or סוֹבֵב[33] ("shall surround," that is, "lay siege"): "An enemy shall encircle the land." (Compare also S.) Just as the witnesses "gathered" around to bear testimony, so shall the enemy—but this time in order to attack!

Note that the identification of the attacking adversary is not given. The enemy remains anonymous here as well as throughout the entire book, because Amos did not yet know who would personify God's "rod of wrath." His prophecies are pre-Assyrian. There is always the possibility that he may have thought that one of the eyewitnesses would, in turn, become the executor of judgment: "Let the hands of the witnesses be the first against him to put him to death" (Deut 17:7). Be that as it may, by purposely selecting the noun צַר to designate the "enemy," he cleverly effected yet another wordplay on the nation, מִצְרַיִם. Note in addition the assonance of the repeated sibilants in these three words, צַר סָבִיב הָאָרֶץ.[34]

First the seige and then the plunder. The punishment is in the form of *lex talionis* or an "Entsprechungsstrafe: Was sie durch Raub an sich gerissen haben, wird ihnen durch Raub entrissen" ("Matching punishment: What they had seized for themselves by pillage will be seized from them by pillage").[35] The location of their crime (אַרְמְנוֹת) shall become the place of their punishment (אַרְמְנוֹתֵיהֶם). There is no mention of the destruction of the land or the decimation of the population. Only the fortresses in which they amassed their ill-gotten wealth are destined to be despoiled.

The anonymous, unspecified enemy, after laying siege to the country, shall enter and וְהוֹרִד ("strip"; literally, "take down") עֻזֵּךְ. The substantive עֹז has two meanings: "strength, might," referring to "strongholds" (see, for example, Pss 28:7, 8; 46:2; 59:10, 18; Prov 14:26)[36] and "glory" (see, for example, Ps 29:1; Prov 31:25).[37] Maybe both are intended here, for the "glory" of Samaria was the wealth stashed away in its "strongholds." There is no need, however, to change the tense of the active verb וְהוֹרִד (see also G, κατάξει) to the passive וְהוּרַד (so T, וִיבַטֵּל; and V, *detrahetur*, "be taken away") in order to harmonize it with the next passive verb, נָבֹזּוּ, "shall be plundered,"[38] for the active-passive combination of verbs is a familiar phenomenon in biblical Hebrew. Thus the enemy "shall strip you of your glory/strongholds"[39] and "your fortresses shall be plundered."[40] With the fourth

---

30 The Masoretic text expresses an exclamation: "An enemy, and all about the land!" See Rudolph, 159, and *NJPS*.

31 See H. S. Pelser, "Amos 3:11—A Communication," in *Studies in the Books of Hosea and Amos: Die Ou Testamentiese Werkgemeenskap in Suid Afrika—7th and 8th Congresses* (Potchefstroom: Rege-Pers Beperk, 1965) 154. He attempts to justify further the change from *waw* to *mem* on the basis of a phenomenon known from Akkadian. However, this simply does not apply to the Hebrew here.

32 Already Wellhausen and many modern commentators.

33 Favored by Ehrlich, *Randglossen*, 5.236. For this usage, in the *qal*, see, for example, 2 Kgs 6:15; and in the *pi'el*, see, for example, Ps 7:8. Compare similarly the Akkadian verb *lamû* ("to surround, besiege"),

CAD, L, 73–75; for example, *nakrum ālam ilawwî* ("The enemy will lay seige to the city"), J. Nougayrol, "Textes hépatoscopiques d'époque ancienne conservés au musée du Louvre," *RA* 38 (1941) 84 r., 33.

34 This is an example of the "calamity" referred to in v 6a. The choice of צַר, rather than another word for "enemy," was also influenced by the intention to imply that there would be a מָצוֹר ("seige") around the city.

35 Rudolph, 164.

36 For example, Cripps, 161; see M. Dahood (*Psalms I:1—50; Introduction, Translation and Notes* [AB 8; Garden City, N.Y.: Doubleday, 1966] 50) on Ps 8:3. See especially Prov 21:22, ". . . and brought down its mighty stronghold" (וַיֹּרֶד עֹז מִבְטֶחָה). See also Maag, *Text*, 16, 91, 183.

37 See Ehrlich, *Mikrâ*, 3.405; idem, *Randglossen*, 5.236.

and climactic reference to the catchword אַרְמְנוֹת (which, additionally, produces an inclusio, vv 9a and 11b), the prophet pronounces the retaliation that is to overtake Samaria. What they have plundered shall be plundered in return.

■ **12** Although this verse commences with the traditional herald formula that begins a new oracle,[41] it still continues the theme of the plunder of the wealthy of Samaria, as will be seen. Amos, drawing upon his own pastoral experience as a shepherd, conveys his verdict of judgment in a very powerful image of the attacking lion.[42] This time his message has legal overtones. If a shepherd can produce evidence that an animal under his care was torn to pieces by beasts, he is absolved from paying any penalty: "If it [the animal] was torn by beasts, he shall bring it as evidence. He need not replace what has been torn by beasts" (Exod 22:12; see also Gen 31:39; 1 Sam 17:34, 35). Livestock devoured by wild beasts is also dealt with in Mesopotamian law: SL 8, New Sumerian Law Fragments III 9′–11′[43] and LH 244, 266,[44] by a lion, and HL 75,[45] by a wolf. In the latter two, the one in charge acquits himself by taking an exculpatory oath; in Exod 22:12, acquittal is achieved by bringing the torn animal as evidence to the owner.[46]

This is the legal background of the image employed here by Amos.[47] Once again the motif, as previously in v 9, is that of bearing testimony based on visual evidence. The shepherd, in order to verify his innocence, must prove that the animal under his care was killed by an attack of a ravenous beast and that there was no negligence on his part. This he does by "snatching away" (יַצִּיל) from the very "mouth of the lion" (מִפִּי הָאֲרִי)[48] any small remains of the devoured animal. Amos mentions first שְׁתֵּי כְרָעַיִם, "two shank bones." The substantive, כְּרָעַיִם, always relates to part of the leg of an animal; see Exod 12:9; 29:17; Lev 1:9, 13; 4:11; 8:21; 9:14; 11:21. So, too, its Akkadian interdialectal semantic and etymological equivalent, *kurītu,* which designates the "part of (hind) leg of an animal which is between knee and fetlock."[49] The other remnant is בְּדַל־אֹזֶן, a hapax legomenon, which T translates חַסְחוּס, "cartilage forming the ear"—similar to Pseudo-Jonathan's translation of תְּנוּךְ אֹזֶן in Exod 29:20. It is usually understood to be an "ear-lap" or "tip of the ear."[50] Amos selected these very two parts of the animal's body to create a merism, that is, from top (ear) to bottom (leg), almost nothing whatsoever will be saved.

The verb "to rescue" (יַצִּיל) literally means to "snatch, take away" (see Amos 4:11).[51] For the expression "to snatch from one's mouth," see Ezek 34:10: "Thus said

38 For the form, see *GKC,* 67t; *BLe,* 431i. For other forms of the passive with the same meaning, see Isa 24:3; Jer 50:37.

39 For עֹז in connection with the verbal root ירד, see Ezek 26:11; Prov 21:22.

40 For בזז in oracles against Israel, see, for example, Isa 24:3; 42:24; Jer 20:5; 30:16.

41 The entire verse is an independent oracle and should not be concluded with the words בְּנֵי יִשְׂרָאֵל; against Gressmann, *Prophetie;* Weiser, *Profetie,* 145; Nötscher; Maag, *Text,* 17; Amsler. See Wolff, 197. See also Rudolph, 164, for the connection with the former pericope.

42 See Amos 3:4, 8; 5:19.

43 See M. Civil, "New Sumerian Law Fragments," in *Studies in Honor of Benno Landsberger on His Seventy-fifth Birthday, April 21, 1965* (ed. H. G. Güterbock and T. Jacobsen; Assyriological Studies 16; Chicago: University of Chicago, 1965) 7, and his comments on p. 8.

44 See Driver and Miles, *Babylonian Laws.*

45 J. Friedrich, *Die hethitischen Gesetze* (Documenta et Monumenta Orientis Antiqui 7; Leiden: Brill, 1959).

46 See S. M. Paul, *Studies in the Book of the Covenant in the Light of Cuneiform and Biblical Law* (SVT 18; Leiden: Brill, 1970) 94.

47 Note also the use of Heb. אוֹ ("or"), which appears very often in legal contexts; see, for example, Exod 21:33, 37; 22:9. Check concordances for multiple references.

48 Compare a similar description in Akkadian, *CAD, L,* a), 24; see n 53.

49 *CAD, K,* 560.

50 According to ibn Ganaḥ (*Haschoraschim,* 58) and ibn Ezra, it refers to a "single ear."

51 The same semantic development is also evidenced by the Akkadian interdialectal equivalent, *eṭēru* ("to take something away [from somebody], to take out, to save a person"). See *CAD, E, eṭēru,* A, 401. See the comments on p. 404: "The two spheres of *eṭēru,* 'to take away' and 'to save,' can be connected if we interpret 'to save' as to take away from disaster, death, etc.; that a semantic connection exists is shown by the logograms KAR and SUR, which are common

the Lord God: I am going to deal with the shepherds! I will demand a reckoning of them for my flock, and I will dismiss them from tending the flock. The shepherds shall not tend themselves anymore; for I will snatch away my flock from their mouths (וְהִצַּלְתִּי מִפִּיהֶם), and it shall not be their prey!"[52] For the shepherd snatching away an animal from the mouth of a lion, see also 1 Sam 17:35. For a similar image, compare the Epic of Erra: *ina pī labbi* [= Heb. מִפִּי הָאֲרִי] *nāʾiri ul ikkimu šalamtu* ("They cannot snatch a carcass from the mouth of a savage lion").[53]

Playing on this dual meaning of the verb, Amos ironically and sarcastically declares that "just so shall the Israelites living in Samaria escape" (יִנָּצְלוּ)[54] the divine judgment.[55] For all practical purposes only a few small worthless parts shall remain.[56] The deliverance of Israel[57] will be similar[58] to the animal whose sparse remains serve as testimony for his having been entirely devoured and destroyed. The proof that is brought is actual evidence for the total loss.[59]

Although in biblical Hebrew the expression ישב ב־ almost always refers to the place in which one "dwells" (for example, הַיֹּשְׁבִים בְּשֹׁמְרוֹן), it never occurs in connection with the object upon which a person "sits." The verb ישב ("to sit") in such cases appears with the prepositions עַל, עִם, לְ, אֶל.[60] Thus the translation "So shall the Israelites escape who dwell in Samaria *on* or *at* the . . ." is incorrect.[61] It can mean only "So shall the Israelites escape who dwell in Samaria *with*. . . ."[62] Because the entire context of this verse and the previous ones, vv 9–11, refers to the plundering of Israel and its illegal gains and not to the destruction of Israel per se, the reference to the parts of the bed are meant to indicate the paltry pieces of property that the wealthy Israelites will barely manage to save,[63] this and no more. The focus, sarcastically, is on the insignificant character of what will remain of the vast wealth of Samaria (compare also v 15). The choice of the image of their beds is opportune, for it was upon them that they were accustomed to while away their time in feasting and carousing (6:4ff.).

The two meager parts of their surviving property are פְּאַת מִטָּה and דְּמֶשֶׁק עָרֶשׂ. The second word in each expression, מִטָּה—עָרֶשׂ, constitutes parallel terms for a "bed"[64] (see Amos 6:4; Ps 6:7),[65] and the first word in both describes the specific part of the bed itself. Hebrew פֵּאָה ("corner, side")[66] may refer to the corner of a table (Exod 25:26; 37:13), a field (Lev 19:9; 23:22), a face

to both spheres."

52 See also Ps 119:43.

53 L. Cagni, *L'epopea di Erra* (Studi Semitici 34; Rome: Instituto di Studi del Vincino Oriente, 1969) V.11. The Akkadian verb here is *ekēmu*, "to take away (by force)"; *CAD, E*, 64ff.

54 This is another instance of the use of active-passive sequence of verbs in Amos. See v 11.

55 Herein is another example of "Can disaster befall a town if the Lord has not caused it?" (Amos 3:6).

56 See Nowack, 135: "Nur ein kümmerliche Rest wird aus dem Gericht übrig sein" ("Only a pitiful remnant will remain after the judgment").

57 This is not a remnant in the positive sense, as, for example, Amos 5:15; 9:8b. See Hasel, *Remnant*, 179–81, 472: "The 'rescued' remnant is meaningless for Israel's national existence." Compare O. Loretz, "Vergleich und Kommentar in Amos 3:12," *BZ* 20 (1976) 122–25. For the concept of "remnant," see de Vaux, "Remnant," 526–39.

58 For the correlatives כַּאֲשֶׁר . . . כֵּן ("as . . . so"), see Exod 1:12; Isa 52:14–15.

59 See Amsler ("Amos," 319): "Ces oracles [3:12; 5:3; 6:10] tournent en ridicule l'espoir de ceux qui croient encore pouvoir échapper à la ruine" ("These oracles turn to ridicule the hope of those who believe that they still would be able to escape destruction"). See also p. 320. Compare Benson, "Mouth of the Lion," 200; H. A. Moeller, "Ambiguity of Amos 3:12," *BT* 15 (1964) 31–34; Cripps, 162; Weiser, *Profetie*, 147–48. See also G. Pfeifer, "'Rettung' als Beweis der Vernichtung (Amos 3,12)," *ZAW* 100 (1988) 269–77.

60 Check dictionaries and concordances.

61 Against, for example, Wolff, 196; Rudolph, 158. It is also incorrect to interpret בְּנֵי יִשְׂרָאֵל ("children of Israel") as a vocative beginning an address that is followed by the imperative שִׁמְעוּ ("hear") in the next verse; against Hoffmann, "Versuche," 102; Koehler; Gressmann, *Prophetie;* Weiser, *Profetie*, 145; Maag, *Text*, 16–17. Hebrew שִׁמְעוּ in v 13 begins a new oracle.

62 Compare M. L. Margolis, "Notes on Some Passages in Amos," *AJSL* 17 (1900–1901) 170–71. For ב meaning "only with," see, for example, Gen 32:11: "Only with my staff (בְּמַקְלִי) I crossed this Jordan."

63 So, too, for example, Ehrlich, *Mikrâ*, 3.405–6; Sellin; van Gelderen; Cramer, 4

64 For Heb. מִטָּה, compare Ugar. *mṭt*, *CTA* 14:30. For Heb. עֶרֶשׂ, compare Akk. *eršu*, *CAD, E*, 317, and Ugar. *ʿrš*, *UT*, 461–62, no. 1927.

65 See likewise the pair עֶרֶשׂ . . . מִשְׁכָּב, Ps 41:4; Prov 7:16–17; Job 7:13.

66 Compare Ugar., *pʾat.mdbr*, *UT*, 641.

(Lev 13:41), or, as here, to the corner of a bed.[67] Thus in the present context the פְּאַת מִטָּה most likely indicates the corner at the head of the bed. This meaning can also be corroborated by its Akkadian interdialectal equivalent, *pūtu* ("forehead, front side"),[68] which also occurs in connection with a part of the bed (Akk. *eršu* = Heb. עֶרֶשׂ): for example, *pūtu ša erši* ("the front of the bed"),[69] which may also mean the "head of the bed." Compare *eršašu pūtu u amarta rukusma* ("Tie [white thread] to the head and the side of his bed").[70]

The major *crux interpretum* is the word דְּמֶשֶׁק. When not emended, it is usually related to the Hebrew word דַּמֶּשֶׂק and translated as the "Damask linens" of the bed. This interpretation, however, is totally unacceptable on many counts. First, the word is spelled with a שׁ and not a שׂ and the ד is pointed with a *shewa*, דְ, and not a *pataḥ*, דַ; דְּמֶשֶׁק is simply not דַּמֶּשֶׂק ("Damascus"). Second, the word is not a place-name parallel to Samaria, as some contend based on the transliteration of the versions,[71] but complements the other part of the bed in the paired parallel phrases. Third, it is most unlikely—and no proof exists—that Damascus (even if one repoints דַּמֶּשֶׂק) was a center of the well-known textile industry at this time. Most damaging to this line of exegesis, however, is the fact that the word "damask" does not derive from Damascus at all, but is a Greek word, μέταξα (Old Latin, *metaxa*), which entered into Syriac as *mīdaqs, mītaqs,* Talmudic Aramaic, מְטַכְסָא, and then into Arabic as a loan word in the form *midaqs,* which was metathesized to *dimaqs.*[72] Thus this word simply did not exist at the time of Amos. Many emendations have been offered to solve this hapax legomenon: compare, for example, וּבַד מִשּׁק, "a part from the foot" (based on a different division of the letters of the word;[73] however, Heb. שׁוֹק never refers to the "foot" of a bed); and וּבְמִקְרָשׁ, "on the edge," a word unattested in the Bible.[74] The most commonly

67 There is no need to emend to צְפִית, based incorrectly on Isa 21:5, as do Marti, Sellin; or to derive פֵּאָה from the root יפה ("beautiful"), *KB,* 750; Maag, *Text,* 185–86. It also appears in parallel to קָדְקֹד ("pate") with the meaning "brow" in Jer 48:45; and most likely in Num 24:17, reading קָדְקֹד for קַרְקַר.

68 See *AHw,* 2.884. For the vocabulary of beds and their parts in Mesopotamia, see A. Salonen, *Die Möbel des alten Mesopotamien nach sumerisch-akkadischen Quellen* (Annales Academiae Scientiarum Fennicae B 127; Helsinki: Suomalainen Tiedeakatemia, 1963) 148–51. For pictures of beds from this period, see *ANEP,* 451, 658, 660; Salonen, *Die Möbel,* pl. XLIV. See also S. Mittmann ("Amos 3:12–15 und das Bett der Samarier," *ZDPV* 92 [1976] 149–67), who relates it (with many examples) to a special back of an ottoman kind on which one reclines.

69 Salonen, *Die Möbel,* 152; B. Landsberger, *The Series Ḫar-ra=ḫubullu Tablets, I–IV* (*MSL* 5; Rome: Pontifical Biblical Institute, 1957) 166.

70 *ASKT,* 90–91:56.

71 Thus G, ἐν Δαμασκῷ and α', σ', θ', T, V, S; followed by Weiser, *Profetie,* 145; C. H. Gordon, *Introduction to Old Testament Times* (Ventnor, NJ: Ventnor Publications, 1953) 214; O. Eissfeldt, *Kleine Schriften zum Alten Testament* (6 vols.; Tübingen: Mohr, 1968) 4.114 n 1. G also had difficulty understanding the Heb. עֶרֶשׂ, which it transliterated as ἱερεῖς ("priests") instead of ιερες = עֶרֶשׂ; see Rudolph, 159. See also Wolff, 196–97. J. F. A. Sawyer ("Those Priests in Damascus: A Possible Example of Anti-Sectarian Polemic in the Septuagint Version of Amos 3:12," *ASTI* 8 [1970–1971] 123–30) assumes this transcription to be intended as an attack against the priests of Qumran. See, however, for this phenomenon, that is, transliterations corrupted to similar-looking Greek words, E. Tov, "Loan-Words, Homophony, and Transliterations in the Septuagint," *Bib* 60 (1979) 235–36.

72 See already S. Fränkel, *Die Aramäischen Fremdwörter im Arabischen* (Leiden: Brill, 1886) 40, 288. Compare Y. Kutscher, *Words and Their History* (Jerusalem: Kiryat Sepher, 1961) 95–96 (Heb.). So, too, correctly, Hammershaimb, 62; Rudolph, 160.

73 I. Rabinowitz ("The Crux at Amos 3:12," *JBL* 67 [1948] 145–48), who did realize, however, that the prophet was referring to the remaining property and not to the people: "All that will be left of the Israelites in Samaria will consist of just enough pieces of debris to afford mute evidence of their utter destruction" (p. 229). So, too, J. Reider ("דמשק in Amos 3:12," *JBL* 67 [1948] 245–48), who, however, imaginatively invents an unattested Hebrew word, דעם ("pillar, support"), which he thinks was then glossed by the assumed synonym, שֹׁק. See also H. A. Moeller, "Ambiguity of Amos 3:12," *BT* 15 (1964) 31–34; Willi-Plein, *Vorformen,* 23–24. For the reading שׁוֹק (interpreted as parallel to פֵּאָה), see also one of the several interpretations of Kimchi.

74 G. R. Driver, "Difficult Words in the Hebrew Prophets," in *Studies in Old Testament Prophecy Presented to Professor Theodore H. Robinson* (ed. H. H. Rowley; Edinburgh: T. & T. Clark, 1950) 69; idem, "Linguistic and Textual Problems: Minor Prophets

cited suggestion[75] is based on Akk. *amartu* ("sideboard [of a bed]"), which in Neo-Babylonian and Late Babylonian appears as *amaštu,* from which is derived the emendation אֲמֶשֶׁת for דְּמֶשֶׁק.[76] However, the form *amaštu* apparently does not appear in Neo-Assyrian sources contemporary to Amos.[77] Even if it did, it is extremely difficult, if not well-nigh impossible, to explain דמשק as a graphic corruption of *amaštu.* Moreover, those who accept the ghost word אמשת still translate it incorrectly; *amartu* / *amaštu* is not the head or "headboard" but the "sideboard" of a bed.[78]

Even though the etymology and meaning of the word are still unknown, most likely it refers to another part of the bed. In the light of the first half of the verse, in which the prophet uses the imagery from bottom (legs) to top (ear) to create an anatomical merism, it stands to reason that here, too, he names chiastically the two opposite sides of the bed, from top to bottom: פֵּאָה ("front/head") and דְּמֶשֶׁק, which in the present context would then represent the "rear/foot" of the bed. Only the meager polar opposites will be saved; all the rest will be destroyed.

II," *JTS* 39 (1938) 262. For the reading וּבְקֶרֶשׂ עֶרֶשׂ ("on a board of a bed"), see Daniel al-Ḳūmissi, *Commentarius in Librum Duodecim Prophetarum* (ed. I. D. Markin; Jerusalem: Meqiṣey Nirdamim, 1957) 34.

75 For other proposed emendations: דִּבֶשֶׁת (Marti); מִשְׁכָּב (Sellin); שְׂמִכַת (Graetz, Nowack); רֹאשׁ (Robinson-Horst); see Gese, "Beiträge," 428. Rudolph, 160, however, reconstructs a totally unattested reading. The suggestion of A. Guillaume ("Hebrew Notes: Amos 3,12," *PEQ* 79 [1947] 42–44) is patently unacceptable.

76 See Gese ("Beiträge," 428), followed by several exegetes such as Wolff, 196, 198, and K. Deller, in his review of Salonen, *Die Möbel,* in *Or* 33 (1964) 102.

77 See *CAD, A,* II, 4, *amartu* (compare p. 5, *amaru* B, "sideboard of a bed," Neo-Assyrian). See also Salonen, *Die Möbel,* 148–51; and R. Borger, "Die Aussprache des Gottesnamens Ninurta," *Or* 30 (1961) 203.

78 Salonen, *Die Möbel,* 148–51.

3 Judgment upon Altars and Ostentatious Buildings

13 **Listen and warn the house of Jacob**
—declares my Lord God, the God of Hosts:
14 **That when I call Israel to account for its transgressions,**
I will wreak judgment on the altars of Bethel,
And the horns of the altar shall be hewn off
And shall fall to the ground.
15 **I will demolish the winter house**
Along with the summer house.
The houses of ivory shall be destroyed
And the great houses terminated
—declares the Lord.

■ **3:13–15** This next pericope, vv 13–15, commences with the imperative שִׁמְעוּ ("hear"; see 3:1; [3:9]; 4:1; 5:1). As in 3:9, there is no indication as to whom the command is directed. The identification of the parties involved is dependent upon the understanding of the following imperative, הָעִידוּ בְּ.[1] This verbal expression has been interpreted, however, in two different ways: as a denominative of עֵד ("witness") meaning "to witness against"[2] (see, for example, Deut 4:26; 30:19), or "to warn"[3] (see, for example, Gen 43:3; Exod 19:23; 2 Kgs 17:13; Jer 11:7). Those exegetes who favor the first translation relate it to the foreign parties mentioned in v 9. Both passages would then refer to their witnessing against Israel: In the former they serve as witnesses of the crime, and in the latter for the punishment.[4] According to the second interpretation (which seems to be preferable), the prophet's intention here is not to bear witness to what has already happened,[5] but "to warn" Israel about the forthcoming punishment for their actions. Those who serve this warning may be court heralds. Interestingly, the procedure of warning (v 13) prior to punishment (vv 14–15) becomes standard in Rabbinic literature; compare אֵין עוֹנְשִׁין אֶת הָאָדָם עַד שֶׁמַּזְהִירִין אוֹתוֹ ("One does not punish someone unless he has first given him warning").[6]

The expression בֵּית יַעֲקֹב ("House of Jacob") refers to the northern kingdom of Israel (see 9:8b). Elsewhere in the book (6:8; 7:2, 5) the term יַעֲקֹב ("Jacob") appears. The fuller phrase is intentionally employed here, as will be seen. The expanded epithet of the God of Israel, אֲדֹנָי ה׳ אֱלֹהֵי הַצְּבָאוֹת, appears in this word order only here.[7] For the same four words in another sequence, see 5:16. For other titles, see ה׳ אֱלֹהֵי[8](הַ)צְּבָאוֹת (4:13; 5:14, 15, 27; 6:14); אֲדֹנָי ה׳ הַצְּבָאוֹת (9:5); אֲדֹנָי ה׳ (3:7, 8; 9:5).

■ **14** The crimes of northern Israel[9] are so grave that the Lord himself will destroy the two foci of the nation's very existence: both the religious (v 14) and the secular (v 15). The altar(s) of Bethel[10] are first singled out because this sacred spot, some ten miles north of Jerusalem, was one

1 For the pairing of the initial two verbs in this verse, see also Pss 50:7; 81:9. For the opposite order, see 2 Kgs 17:13–14; Jer 6:10; 11:7.
2 For example, Wolff, 200–201; Rudolph, 158; Soggin, 64.
3 For example, Hammershaimb, 63. See Seeligmann, "Terminologie," 265–66.
4 Compare Rudolph, 165.
5 One bears witness for past and present events but not for future ones.
6 For example, Sifre Deut., קע״ג (Eng. equivalent is p. 173). See *Siphre ad Deuteronomium*, ed. L. Finkelstein (New York: Jewish Theological Seminary, 1969) 220.
7 Most commentators consider various elements of this expanded theophoric epithet as being due to later expansions. Contrast, for example, Wolff, 199; Rudolph, 160.
8 The form הַצְּבָאוֹת appears once in Hos 12:6; three times in Amos, 3:13; 6:14; 9:5; and one more time in 1 Chr 27:3 (in a secular context).
9 For כִּי (which introduces this verse) following הֵעִיד בְּ, see, for example, Deut 4:26; 8:19; 31:28–29.
10 For Bethel, see Galling, "Bethel und Gilgal II," 26–43; C. A. Keller, "Über einige alttestamentliche Heiligtumslegenden I," *ZAW* 67 (1955) 162–68; W. J. Dumbrell, "The Role of Bethel in the Biblical Narratives," *Australian Journal of Biblical Archaeology* 2 (1974) 65–76.

of the prime religious centers of northern Israel during the time of Amos (see 4:4; 5:5, 6; 7:10, 13; [9:1]) and functioned as a royal sanctuary (7:13). According to traditions preserved in Genesis, both Abraham and Jacob erected altars in Bethel (Gen 12:8; 35:7). For the altar at Bethel and the elevation of this site as one of the two national shrines in the north (along with Dan) during the time of Jeroboam I, see 1 Kgs 12:28–33; 13:1–2. For other references to this cultic center during this period, compare also Hos 4:15; 10:5, 8, 15; 12:5.[11] The altar was finally demolished by King Josiah as reported in 2 Kgs 23:15.

The altar had a dual function: It served as an asylum—he who grasped its horns[12] was immune from punishment (see Exod 21:13–14; 1 Kgs 1:50; 2:28)—and was also the site where the blood of sacrifices was spilled, where expiation and atonement could be attained (see Lev 4:7ff.; 16:18; Ezek 43:20). Thus the destruction of the altar and its horns[13] actually symbolizes the end of the sanctuary, immunity, and expiation for the people. The threatened punishment is totally devastating to the religious life of northern Israel.[14]

For another description of the execution of punishment within a sacral setting, see Amos 9:1ff. In a paradoxical fashion and contrary to all popular expectations, the end of Israel's cultic existence would be brought about by their very own God.[15]

Because all the other biblical passages mention only one altar in Bethel, some commentators suggest reading here מִזְבַּח ("altar") for מִזְבְּחוֹת ("altars").[16] This may be explained by a possible backward contamination (dittography) from the following word בֵּית—the letters ית being repeated as וֹת at the end of מזבח, thereby creating a plural.[17] There is, however, no convincing reason to deny the existence of multiple altars in Bethel, even if it had only one central sanctuary.[18]

Note the extensive use of the key word בַּיִת ("house") in this unit: v 13, בֵּית יַעֲקֹב ("house of Jacob"), which is most likely the reason why יַעֲקֹב ("Jacob") alone, the common name for northern Israel in Amos, is not used, but rather בֵּית יַעֲקֹב; v 14, בֵּית־אֵל; and v 15, בֵּית־הַחֹרֶף, בֵּית הַקָּיִץ, בָּתֵּי הַשֵּׁן, בָּתִּים רַבִּים ("winter house, summer house, houses of ivory, great houses")—four times!

It is most interesting to compare the language of this verse, בְּיוֹם פָּקְדִי (פשעי־ישראל עליו) ("When I make an accounting [that is, "punish" Israel for its transgressions], I will bring to account [that is, "wreak punishment on"]), with Exod 32:34, וּבְיוֹם פָּקְדִי . . . וּפָקַדְתִּי עֲלֵיהֶם (חטאתם) ("And when I make an accounting [that is, "punish"], I will bring them to account [that is, "wreak judgment" for their sins]"). These passages are the only two in the Bible that contain the phraseology בְּיוֹם פָּקְדִי . . . וּפָקַדְתִּי עַל. The similarity in expression, moreover, may also allude to the similarity of context. In Exodus the punishment

11 For references to the god Bethel in the Bible (see Jer 48:13) and in Elephantine, see O. Eissfeldt, *Kleine Schriften zum Alten Testament* (6 vols.; Tübingen: Mohr, 1962–1979) 1.206–33. For its possible occurrence in Hosea, see H. L. Ginsberg, "Hosea's Ephraim, More Fool Than Knave. A New Interpretation of Hosea 12:1–14," *JBL* 80 (1961) 339–47.

12 For horned altars, see Y. Ahroni, "Tel Beersheba," *IEJ* 23 (1973) 254–56; idem, "The Horned Altar at Beersheba," *BA* 37 (1974) 2–6; A. Biran, "An Israelite Horned Altar at Dan," *BA* 37 (1974) 106–7, fig. 15; see idem, "Tell er-Ruqeish to Tell er-Ridan," *IEJ* 24 (1974) 262. See also *ANEP*, 575. See, in general, F. J. Stendebach, "Altarformen im kanaanäisch-israelitischen Raum," *BZ* 20 (1976) 180–96.

13 For the verb גדע ("to cut/hew off") in connection with קֶרֶן ("horn" and, by extension, "strength"), see Jer 48:25; Ps 75:11; Lam 2:3. For the verbal sequence גדע and נפל, see Isa 22:25; and for the reverse order, Isa 9:9; 14:12.

14 Some exegetes interpret this as a reference to an earthquake; see, for example, Sellin, Fosbroke, Amsler, Rudolph.

15 This is yet one more of the polemical attacks that Amos levels against popular beliefs.

16 See Hammershaimb, 64.

17 For a possibly similar backward contamination, see Hos 10:5, לְעֶגְלוֹת בֵּית אָוֶן. Because the reference here is generally assumed to be the golden calf, עֵגֶל (singular), the plural suffix וֹת of עֶגְלוֹת may have been caused by the dittography of the letters ית in the next word, בֵּית.

18 See, a bit differently, Cripps, 163. According to Rudolph, 160, the singular, מִזְבַּח, following the plural מִזְבְּחוֹת, is to be interpreted in a distributive sense. See *GKC*, 124p.

refers to the golden calf incident, and in Amos the threat is leveled against the central altar of Bethel, where Jeroboam I had also set up a golden calf. The sins of the past, which abide in the present, will once more be extirpated.

Another significant theological concept also present in this verse is that of delayed punishment: "When I make an accounting, I will punish Israel for its transgressions; I will. . . ." "*When* I make an accounting"—divine punishment is not always executed immediately upon the sinner directly, or even upon the sinner's generation, but may be delayed to a later period. This doctrine of "vertical retribution," found also in the ancient Near East, is dominant in biblical literature.[19] The prophet Ahijah proclaims that the punishment for the sins of Jeroboam I will fall upon his son Abijah (1 Kgs 14:14–18); Jehu, the son of Hanani, declares that Elah will pay for his father's (Baasha's) sins (1 Kgs 16:1–4). Although this doctrine was subsequently modified in Deuteronomy (7:10; 24:16) and opposed by the prophet Ezekiel (chapter 18),[20] the concept nevertheless was well known and accepted in Israel and here is clearly espoused by Amos. Divine punishment, although presently delayed, will nevertheless be executed in the future.[21] Then, it will take into account all of Israel's sins.

Verses 13–14, along with vv 1–2, comprise one grand redactional inclusio of the entire chapter: see שִׁמְעוּ (v 1) and אֶפְקֹד עֲלֵיכֶם (v 2), with שִׁמְעוּ (v 13) and . . . פָּקְדִי וּפָקַדְתִּי עַל (v 14).[22]

■ **15** Not only will the sacred precincts be destroyed, but so, too, the secular ones as well. The splendid residences of the wealthy upper-class residents of Samaria are also destined for demolition.[23] They who enjoy the present life of pomp, pleasure, and prosperity (see 6:4–6) shall soon witness the demise of their self-indulgent life style.

The winter (see also Jer 36:22) and summer mansions refer to the two separate pleasure estates between which the opulent residents of the northern capital divided their time.[24] Similar dwelling places are documented in the inscription of Barrakub, the Aramean king of Sam'al, who was an approximate contemporary of Amos:[25] "My fathers, the kings of Sam'al, had no good house [palace]. They had the house [palace] of Kilamuwa, which was their winter house [palace] (בית שתוא) and also their summer house [palace] (בית כיצא). But I have built this house."[26] Cuneiform sources from the Middle[27] and Late Babylonian[28] periods provide

19 See Exod 20:5; 34:6–7; Lev 26:39–40; 2 Sam 12:13–14; 1 Kgs 17:18; 21:29; 2 Kgs 22:19–20; Isa 14:21; Zech 8:14; Lam 5:6; Neh 9:2; see also Jer 18:21; Job 27:14.

20 See M. Greenberg, "Some Postulates of Biblical Criminal Law," in *Yehezkel Kaufmann Jubilee Volume: Studies in the Bible and Jewish Religion Dedicated to Yehezkel Kaufmann on the Occasion of his 70th Birthday* (ed. M. Haran; Jerusalem: Magnes, 1960) 20–27; idem, *Ezekiel, 1–20: A New Translation with Introduction and Commentary* (AB 22; Garden City, NY: Doubleday, 1983) 337–40.

21 See J. Milgrom, "Vertical Retribution: Ruminations on *Parashat Shelaḥ*," *Conservative Judaism* 34 (1981) 11–16.

22 Note that three key phrases connect this pericope with Amos 4:4: זִבְחֵיכֶם—מִזְבְּחוֹת; לִפְשֹׁעַ/וּפִשְׁעוּ—פִּשְׁעֵי; בֵּית־אֵל (in both units).

23 For the use of the verbal form הכה with בַּיִת, see also Amos 6:11; see, too, Amos 9:1.

24 See S. M. Paul, "Amos III 15—Winter and Summer Mansions," *VT* 28 (1978) 358–60. The two mansions do not refer to two different parts of the same house (see Judg 3:20) but to two separate dwelling places in different regions of northern Israel; they function as a merism. Both Wolff and Rudolph drew attention to the preposition עַל, which connects the two Hebrew terms in the verse and has the force of "together with." See Gen 28:9; 32:12.

For the two residences of Ahab—his "winter palace" in the warmer Jezreel Valley (1 Kgs 21:1) and his other one in Samaria (1 Kgs 21:18)—see B. D. Napier, "The Omrides of Jezreel," *VT* 9 (1959) 366. See also the various statements in the Midrash referring to the "two palaces of Ahab's sons, one for winter days and one for summer days," Esther Rabbah I, 12, and the additional references cited there.

25 See *KAI*, I.40, no. 216:16–20; II.232–34; Gibson, *Aramaic Inscriptions*, 87–92. The translation follows F. Rosenthal in *ANET*², 501.

26 Until Barrakub built his new palace, obviously the one built by Kilamuwa had to suffice for both his winter and summer residence. See B. Landsberger, *Sam'al: Studien zur Entdeckung Ruinenstätte Karatepe* (Ankara: Turkische historische Gesellschaft, 1948) 71–72 n 89.

27 BE 14, 124:5–7 in A. T. Clay, *Documents from the Temple Archives of Nippur Dated in the Reigns of Cassite Rulers* (Philadelphia: University of Pennsylvania, 1906).

28 *VAS* 15, 24:3, 9, 10 in O. Schroeder, *Kontrakte der Seleukidenzeit aus Warka* (Leipzig: Hinrichs, 1916); and BRM 2 36:9 in A. T. Clay, *Legal Documents from*

independent evidence for a *bīt kuṣṣi* ("winter house") and *ekal kuṣṣi* ("winter palace").[29] Cyrus, king of Persia, is also reported to have had separate capitals and palaces in Susa, Ecbatana, and Babylon—all befitting the various climatic seasons.[30]

"Houses of ivory" (בָּתֵּי הַשֵּׁן) refer to luxury manor houses whose walls and furniture were adorned and decorated with ivory.[31] First Kgs 22:39 has a reference to the "ivory palace" (בֵּית הַשֵּׁן) of Ahab, king of Israel, and Ps 45:9 mentions "ivoried palaces" (הֵיכְלֵי שֵׁן).[32] Compare also the "beds of ivory" (מִטּוֹת שֵׁן) in Amos 6:4.[33] Excavations at Samaria have unearthed the opulence of these buildings with their plethora of ivory inlays.[34] The conspicuous consumption of the voluptuaries of the north, whose faith resided in their wealth, shall soon be terminated, and their luxury villas demolished (אָבְדוּ).[35]

The usual translation, "and many houses shall be destroyed" (וְסָפוּ בָּתִּים רַבִּים), providing a summary description of the wholesale destruction of the houses in Samaria, is inadequate here[36] because the invective of Amos is specifically directed against the nobility and the wealthy elite residing in that city and not against the population in general. There is also no necessity to resort to the forced emendations of בָּתֵּי הָבְנִים ("houses of ebony"; see Ezek 27:15)[37] or בָּתֵּי בְּרוֹמִים ("the many-colored woven curtains of the houses"; see Ezek 27:24).[38] Hebrew בָּתִּים רַבִּים may simply mean "great houses."[39] For רַב (and רַבָּה) ("great"), see, for example, Gen 6:5; 7:11; Isa 51:10; Amos 7:4; Pss 36:7; 48:3; Lam

Erech Dated in the Seleucid Era, 312–65 B.C. (New York: privately printed, 1913). For contents and translation of the three texts, see Paul, "Amos III 15," 358–60.

29 R. Koldeway (in R. Koldeway and F. Wetzel, *Die Königsbürgen von Babylon, 2 Teil: Die Hauptburg und der Sommerpalast Nebukadnezars im Hügel Babil* [*WVDOG* 55; Leipzig: Hinrichs, 1932] 41–58) coined the expression "summer palace" to describe Nebuchadrezzar's palace in the northeastern corner of Tell Babel. See especially p. 157. See also Koldeway and Wetzel, *Die Königsburgen von Babylon 1 Teil* (*WVDOG* 54; Leipzig: Hinrichs, 1931) 28; O. E. Ravn, *Herodotus' Description of Babylon* (tr. M. Tovborg-Sensen; Copenhagen: NYT Nordisk, 1942) 291; G. Roux, *Ancient Iraq* (London: Allen & Unwin, 1964) 355–56.

30 See Xenophon, *Cyropaedia*, VIII, vi 22 in *Cyropaedia II* (tr. W. Miller; Loeb Classical Library; New York and London: Heinemann, 1914). See, too, Xenophon, *Anabasis*, III, v 15 in *Anabasis I–VII* (tr. C. L. Brownson; Loeb Classical Library; New York and London: Heinemann, 1922). See also A. T. Olmstead, *History of the Persian Empire (Achaemenid Period)* (Chicago: University of Chicago, 1948) chapter 12, "The Three Capitals: Ecbatana, Babylon, and Susa," pp. 162–71.

31 Compare T: בָּתִּין דִּמְכַבְּשִׁין בְּשֵׁן דְּפִיל ("houses which they inlay with ivory"). So, too, in Amos 6:4.

32 Solomon also had a כִּסֵּא־שֵׁן גָּדוֹל ("a large throne of ivory"), 1 Kgs 10:18 = 2 Chr 9:17. Mention is also made of an "ivory tower" (מִגְדַּל הַשֵּׁן) in Cant 7:5.

33 See similarly in Akkadian, *1 eršu šinni* ("one bed of ivory"), TCL 3, 388 (Sargon) in Thureau-Dangin, *Une relation.* For other references to "beds of ivory," see OIP 2 34 iii 43 (Sennacherib) in Luckenbill, *Annals; AKA* 364 iii 61 (Assurnaṣirpal).

34 For the excavations at Samaria, see J. W. Crowfoot and G. M. Crowfoot, *Early Ivories from Samaria: Samaria-Sebaste 2* (London: Palestine Exploration Fund, 1938); idem, *Samaria-Sebaste III: The Objects from Samaria* (London: Palestine Exploration Fund, 1957); A. Parrot, *Samaria: The Capital of the Kingdom of Israel* (tr. S. H. Hooke; Studies in Biblical Archeology 7; New York: Philosophical Library, 1958) 53–71; P. R. Ackroyd, "Samaria," in *Archeology and Old Testament Study: Jubilee Volume for the Society for Old Testament Study 1917–1967* (ed. D. N. Thomas; Oxford: Clarendon, 1967) 343–54; N. Avigad, "Samaria," in *Encyclopedia of Archaeological Excavations in the Holy Land* (4 vols.; ed. M. Avi-Yonah and E. Stern; London: Oxford University, 1978) 4.1039; idem, "Shomron," *EM* 8, 148–62 (Heb.). For a list of ivories from Samaria, see C. Decamps de Mertzenfeld, *Inventaire commenté des ivoires phéniciens et apparentés, découverts dans la proche orient* (Paris: de Boccard, 1954) 62–75.

For the excavations at Tirṣah *(Tell el-Farah)*, a few kilometers north of Samaria, see R. de Vaux, "El-Farʿa, Tell, North," *Encyclopedia of Archaeological Excavations in the Holy Land* 2 (4 vols.; ed. M. Avi-Yonah and E. Stern; Oxford: Oxford University, 1975–1978) 395–404.

35 The Akkadian interdialectal etymological and semantic equivalent, *abātu,* is also used in connection with the destruction of buildings. See *CAD, A,* I, *abātu,* 42; *ubbutu,* 43.

36 Against, for example, Driver; van Hoonacker; Guthe; Weiser; Harper, 78; Wolff, 199.

37 Marti; Robinson; Maag, *Text,* 17; Osty; Nowack. Sellin proposed reading יָרָבְעָם, "Jeroboam."

38 H. Donner, "Die soziale Botschaft der Propheten im

1:1. The "great houses" would then refer to the large estates of the upper class. Compare Isa 5:9: "Surely great houses (בָּתִּים רַבִּים) shall lie forlorn; spacious and splendid ones (גְּדֹלִים וְטוֹבִים) without occupants."[40] Another possible suggestion is to read בָּתֵּי(ם) רַבִּים (enclitic *mem* attached to first word) and translate, "the houses of the nobles."[41] For רַב, a common title affixed to the names of important officials, see Jer 39:9, 13; 41:1; it is also found in Aramaic,[42] Ugaritic,[43] and Akkadian.[44]

The verb סָפוּ, derived either from the root סוף ("come to an end, cease") or from ספה ("sweep away, destroy"), which usually indicates the decimation of humans or animals, refers only in this passage to the destruction of building structures.[45] Many commentators interpret this once again as an allusion to a calamity caused by an earthquake.

Lichte der Gesellschaftsordnung in Israel," *OrAnt* 2 (1963) 237 n 19. See the objections of Wolff, 199.

39 See already ibn Ganaḥ, *Haschoraschim,* 465. Compare Deden; Cripps, 164–65; Rudolph, 160. The reading רַבִּים is supported by G, ἕτεροι πολλοί ("many other"); T, סַגִּיאִין ("numerous"); V, *multae* ("many"). Harper, 80, suggested comparing Akk. *bitu rabû,* the ideographic equivalent of *ekallu,* derived from Sum. É.GAL ("great house"). See also Akk. *bitu rabitu* ("great house"), HSS 5 71:5, 13, 33; 72:10, 14 in E. Chiera, *Excavations at Nuzi I. Texts of Varied Contents* (Cambridge: Harvard University, 1929). For *rabû* ("large") describing buildings, see *AHw* 2.937, 4. Compare also in Aramaic, Cowley, *Aramaic Papyri,* 42:6, ביתא (ר)בא ("the large house").

40 See Gordis, "Studies," 219. See also the second commentary of Kimchi.

41 G. S. Glanzman ("Two Notes: Am 3:15 and Hosea 11:8–9," *CBQ* 23 [1961] 227–33) revived the suggestion of E. Baumann, *Der Aufbau der Amosreden* (BZAW 7; Giessen: Töpelmann, 1903) 34. Compare possibly 2 Kgs 25:9: "He burnt the House of the Lord, the king's palace, and all the houses of Jerusalem; he burned down the house of every notable person" (בֵּית גָּדוֹל). So *NJPS,* even though it is noted there that the translation of the Hebrew is uncertain. Here, too, the meaning might be "great mansion."

42 See Sefire I A 39; II B 3, רבוה ("his nobles").

43 See, for example, Ugar. *mlk rb,* the equivalent of Akk. *šarru rabû* ("great king"), *CTA* 64:13, 26; *rb khnm,* "chief of the priests," *CTA* 87:54–55; *rb qrt,* "chief of the town = mayor," *UT* 1024: rev. 3; and *bt ilm rbm,* "the house of the great gods," *PRU* II 57 90:1–2. For a discussion of the first term with much additional evidence, see Paul, "Hosea 8:8–10," 333–40.

44 See *AHw, rabû,* 2.938.

45 For both possibilities, see commentaries and also dictionaries under the two respective entries.

4 Condemnation and Punishment of the Uppity Upper-Class Women

1 Hear this word, cows of Bashan
On the hill of Samaria,
Who oppress the poor,
Crush the destitute,
Who order their lords,
"Bring so that we may imbibe!"
2 My Lord God swears by his holiness:
Behold, days are coming upon you
When you shall be transported in baskets,
And the very last one of you, in fishermen's pots.
3 Through the breaches each of you shall be brought straight out,
And you will be thrown . . .*
—declares the Lord.

*Hebrew obscure

■ **1** This new section, which is an oracle of judgment,[1] continues the series of oracles that commence with the imperative, שִׁמְעוּ ("hear"; Amos 3:1, [9], 13; 5:1). It is related to the above pericope Amos 3:9ff. by both its references to "the hill of Samaria" (3:9; see also Amos 3:12, "Samaria") and by the key theme of "exploitation" (עשק, 3:9; 4:1) of the poor.[2] On this occasion, however, the prophet's condemnation is leveled specifically against the uppity upper-class women of northern Israel,[3] who, by their incessant demand upon their husbands to provide for their gluttonous needs to carouse and feast, are responsible for goading them on to impoverish even further the poor. These women are charged not only with complicity and collusion but also are indicted as the ultimate cause of the exploitation of the underprivileged classes.

Amos, the sheepherder, picturesquely draws a unique image to describe this female elite class by calling them "the cows of Bashan," פָּרוֹת הַבָּשָׁן.[4] Bashan, a fertile plain in Transjordan located on both sides of the middle and upper Yarmuk River, was famous for its plush pastures and robust cows (for example, Deut 32:14; Ezek 39:18;

1 See G. M. Tucker, "Prophetic Speech," *Int* 32 (1978) 40–45.

2 Further connections are the roots פשע, זבח, in relation to בֵּית־אֵל in Amos 3:14 and 4:4. Note also that the substantive הַר(ים) ("mount[ains]") begins (v 1) and concludes (v 13) the chapter, creating a literary inclusio.

3 For other attacks against women, this time the elite of Jerusalem, see Isa 3:16ff.; 32:9ff.

4 This is the only passage where women are compared to cows. (See, however, for the same imagery in connection with menfolk, Jer 31:17; Hos 4:16.) For the comparison to a mare, see Cant 1:9. This indictment is not an attack against any supposed Canaanite fertility cult and New Year festival, as has been suggested by H. M. Barstad, "Die Basankühe in Amos IV:1," *VT* 25 (1975) 286–97; idem, *Religious Polemics,* 37ff., where he makes an imaginative connection with the *mrzḥ* ceremony. See also A. J. Williams, "A Further Suggestion about Amos IV:1–3," *VT* 29 (1979) 206. P. F. Jacobs ("'Cows of Bashan'—A Note on the Interpretation of Amos 4:1," *JBL* 104 [1985] 109–10) follows the suggestion made by K. Koch (*The Prophets* [tr. M. Kohl; Philadelphia: Fortress, 1983] 46) that Amos is referring to a "cultic name the women gave themselves, since they imagined themselves to be the worshippers of the mighty bull of Samaria (Hos 8:5f.), a North Israelite manifestation of Yahweh." In light of the drawing of figures with bovine features found in Pithos No. 1 from Kuntillet ʿAjrud, Jacobs attempts to find additional evidence for this proposal and suggests that these women fancy themselves to be none other than the "imitators/partakers of the feminine counterpart of Yahweh, bull of Samaria"—referring to their immoral behavior. This conjecture, as well as the above, is totally unfounded. Speier ("Bemerkungen," 306–7) interprets this term as a double entendre based on a supposed derived use of Arabic, *baṯne*/*baṯane,* meaning "ein üppig gebautes Mädchen" ("a voluptuously built girl"). See also Soggin, 70, who translates "prosperous." For animal names employed metaphorically to denote dignitaries and various classes of people in Hebrew and Ugaritic, see F.

Ps 22:13; see also Jer 50:19; Mic 7:14).[5] By making reference to these well-fed, healthy, and pleasantly plump bovines,[6] he once again introduces an element of surprise into his oracle. These pedigreed "cows" represent none other than the pampered leading ladies of Samaria, whose main purpose in life is to tend to their own self-indulgence, irrespective of the cost—to others.

The three appositional participles (הָעֹשְׁקוֹת,[7] הָרֹצְצוֹת,[8] הָאֹמְרוֹת), which signify the ongoing repetitive nature of their oppressive and exploitative actions and injustice against the poor, conclude with a direct quotation,[9] directed to their husbands: "Bring so that we may imbibe!"[10] The use of אָדוֹן ("lord") to signify their spouses is rare in the Bible (see Gen 18:12; Judg 19:26; Ps 45:12); the substantive usually employed for "husband" is בַּעַל or אִישׁ.[11] The reason this specific term was selected may very well be due to the intention of the prophet to relate אֲדֹנֵיהֶם[12] ("their lords") with the following verse, where in contrast the true "Lord" (אֲדֹנָי) appears.

Although G (ἐπίδοτε), V *(afferte)*, and S (איתו) all render the verb "bring" in the plural, the cohortative singular (הָבִיאָה)[13] has here a distributive sense. Each woman makes the same nagging demands upon her own husband.

■ 2 The irrevocability and irrefutability of the forthcoming divine punishment is emphasized by an oath formula in which the "Lord God[14] swears by[15] his holiness" (בְּקָדְשׁוֹ), that is, by the attribute of his very own being. Such an oath is found in only one other verse, in Ps

Rosenthal, "Rescensiones," *Or* 16 (1947) 401–2. See also M. Dahood, "The Value of Ugaritic for Textual Criticism," *Bib* 40 (1959) 160–70; P. D. Miller, Jr., "Animal Names as Designations in Ugaritic and Hebrew," *UF* 2 (1970) 177–86; and K. J. Cathcart, *Nahum in the Light of Northwest Semitic* (BibOr 26; Rome: Pontifical Biblical Institute, 1973) 109.

5 For Bashan, see S. Cohen, "Bashan," *IDB* 1.363–64; *EncJud* 4.291–93.

6 See Rudolph, 167.

7 For the meaning of the verb, see Milgrom, "Missing Thief," 76–77, 82, "nonfurtive, product of open force."

8 For the parallelism of the pair of verbs רצץ and עשק, see Deut 28:33; 1 Sam 12:3–4; Hos 5:11. Note the asyndeton construction of the three participles. For other examples of an imperative second person masculine plural (here, שִׁמְעוּ) introducing a feminine plural (here, הָעֹשְׁקוֹת, הָרֹצְצוֹת, הָאֹמְרוֹת), see Isa 23:1 (הֵילִילוּ אֳנִיּוֹת, "Howl, you ships [of Tarshish]!") and Isa 32:11 (חִרְדוּ שַׁאֲנַנּוֹת, "Tremble, you carefree ones!"). See *GKC*, 144a. For the parallelism of דַּל ("poor") and אֶבְיוֹן ("needy"), see Amos 8:6 (and Amos 2:6–7); Prov 14:31. For עשק in connection with (דַּלִּים), see Prov 14:31; 22:16; 28:3. For רצץ and דַּלִּים, see Job 20:19.

9 For other direct quotations of the people, see Amos 2:12; 5:14; 6:13; 8:5; 9:10.

10 There is no reason to conclude from this that reference is being made to a certain breed of pampered cows who demand of their herdsmen to bring them drinking water, as interpreted by Ehrlich, *Mikrâ*, 3.406; idem, *Randglossen*, 5.237–38; Dalman, *AuS* VI.176; Wolff, 206. The prophet deftly alludes to his intended meaning in 4:1b, when he refers to their "masters" by the word אָדוֹן ("lord"). The owner of an animal in biblical Hebrew is called בַּעַל (see Exod 21:28) or קוֹנֶה (Isa 1:3) but never אָדוֹן.

11 For the former, for example, Exod 21:3, 22; for the latter, for example, Lev 20:10; 22:12; Deut 24:3; Hos 2:9, 18.

12 For the masculine ending instead of the expected female one, see Ruth 1:8.

13 For the form, see *GKC*, 72y. Note that the same verb, הָבִיאוּ ("bring"), is found in the first verse (v 4) of the next literary unit, forming a concatenous tie. The root שתה ("to drink") is also repeated in v 8. For a similar verbal sequence in Aramaic (אמטי . . . נשתי; "bring . . . and we will drink") in the context of a polemic against the cult, see M. Weinfeld, "The Aramaic Text (in Demotic Script) from Egypt on Sacrifice and Morality and Its Relationship to Biblical Texts," *Shnaton* 9 (1987) 181, lines 5–6 (Heb.).

14 See Amos 3:7, 8, 11, 13; 4:2, 5. There is no reason, therefore, to delete אֲדֹנָי; against Wolff, 200. Both names appear also in the oath formula in Amos 6:8.

15 For other oath formulae introduced by נִשְׁבַּע בְּ־ ("swear by"), see, for example, Deut 6:13; Josh 2:12; Isa 62:8. The בְּ serves as the particle of means or instrument. See the similar use of Arab. بـ in oaths; W. Wright, *A Grammar of the Arabic Language* (Cambridge: Kaisler, 1951) 2, par. 62. For studies on oaths, see F. Horst, "Der Eid im AT," *EvT* 17 (1957) 370–73, repr. in *Gottes Recht: Studien zum Recht im Alten Testament* (ed. H. W. Wolff; TBü 22; München: Kaiser, 1961) 298–301; M. Greenberg, "The Hebrew Oath Particle *ḤAY/ḤĒ*," *JBL* 76 (1957) 34–39; idem, "Oaths," *EncJud* 12.1295–98; S. E. Loewenstamm, "Oath," *EM* 7.479–91 (Heb.); M. Pope, "Oaths," *IDB* 3.575–77. In Mishnaic times oaths were also taken in the name of God, the temple, cult, altar, and other sacred objects. See S.

89:36, נִשְׁבַּעְתִּי בְקָדְשִׁי ("I have sworn by my holiness").[16] Additional oath formulas appear in Amos 6:8 and 8:7.

For the construction כִּי ... נִשְׁבַּע, in which the כִּי particle acts as an asseverative introduction to the contents of the actual oath, compare Gen 22:16; 1 Kgs 1:13, 17, 30; Isa 45:23; Jer 22:5; 49:13.[17]

The "days which are coming upon you" (יָמִים בָּאִים)[18] is an expression often used in eschatological descriptions; compare Amos 8:11; 9:13. It serves as an introduction to an entirely new period of time; compare 1 Sam 2:31; 2 Kgs 20:17; Jer 7:32; 9:24; 16:14. Note the irony: in lieu of the demands of the bon vivants upon their "lords" (אֲדֹנֵיהֶם), the days are coming when the oath of the "Lord" (אֲדֹנָי ה׳) will be executed.[19]

The remainder of this verse abounds in lexical difficulties that have given rise to varied suggestions that attempt to understand the prophet's vivid—yet problematic—description of the impending doom of Samaria's privileged class. A review of the interpretations will demonstrate the perplexities of the passage.[20] The first crux is צִנּוֹת:

1. "Shields"[21]—compare צִנָּה (for example, 1 Kgs 10:16; Ezek 23:24; 38:4; Pss 5:13; 91:4); צִנּוֹת (2 Chr 11:12). Thus α', Θυρεοῖς ("with shields"); T, עַל תְּרֵיסֵיהוֹן ("upon their shields"); and then by extension, G, ἐν ὅπλοις, and S, בזינא ("with weapons"). See, too, V, *in contis* ("on pikes"). Among modern commentators this solution is favored by Snaith and Driver;[22] the latter, in addition, makes reference to an alleged Akk. *ṣinnatu* that occurs in Mari, ARM II, 50 r. 9,[23] which he translates as "shields." Note at the outset, however, that the meaning of the Akkadian word is still very much in dispute.[24] Whereas Sasson[25] weighs the possibility of translating "shields" in one or two of the Mari texts, Frankena[26] definitely decides in its favor. However, these very same occurrences of the word are translated "lance" by von Soden, *CAD* (both with a question mark),[27] Birot,[28] and Dossin.[29] More decisive is the fact that this substantive is

Lieberman, *Greek in Jewish Palestine: Studies in the Life and Manners of Jewish Palestine in the 2nd–4th Centuries C.E.* (New York: Jewish Theological Seminary of America, 1942) 132ff.

16 Two other passages that may reflect this same type of oath are Pss 60:8 and 108:8, אֱלֹהִים דִּבֶּר בְּקָדְשׁוֹ ("God promised by his holiness"), which, however, may also be translated "God promised in his sanctuary." In Akkadian there is an oath called *māmīt asakki* ("the oath of taboo"). Akkadian *asakku* ("something set apart [for god or king, a taboo]"; *CAD, A,* II, 326–27) corresponds semantically at times with Heb. קֹדֶשׁ. This correspondence was already seen by M. Weinfeld ("The Royal and Sacred Aspects of the Tithe in the Old Testament," *Beer-Sheba* 1 [1973] 123 n 6 [Heb.]), who compared the oath in ARM VIII, 16:6′–8′, *asak Iaḫdunlim u Zimrilim izkurū* ("They swore by the *asakku* of I. and Z").

17 *GKC,* 157b.

18 It appears once in Isa 39:6 and many times in Jeremiah, for example, Jer 7:32; 9:24.

19 Is there yet another ironic overtone in the use of the root בוא? They say הָבִיאָה ("bring"), and the prophet responds, "days are coming" (בָּאִים).

20 See the study by S. M. Paul, "Fishing Imagery in Amos 4:2," *JBL* 97 (1978) 183–90.

21 Compare also the medieval exegetes, Menahem ben Sarug, *Sepher HaMaḥberet* (ed. Y. Philipawaski; Yadenburg, 1854) 150, entry צן, second division (Heb.), and D. Kimchi, *Radicum Liber* (Berlin: G. Bethge, 1847) 315 (Heb.), and his Hebrew commentary to this verse.

22 G. R. Driver, "Babylonian and Hebrew Notes," *WO* 2 (1954) 20–21.

23 ARM II, 106. For further references in Mari, see ARM XV, 270.

24 Initially according to *CAD, Ṣ,* 201, the references in Mari were read *gizinnatu* (and not ^gi^*ṣinnatu*), which "refers to a metal object used for both agricultural and military purposes. . . . It is possible that the word *gizinnatu* represents a W. Sem. form of *haṣṣinnu,* 'ax,' which appears in Heb. as *garzen.*" Nevertheless, note that *haṣṣinnu* does appear in Mari, for example, ARM II, 139, 15–16; VII, 249, several times, and that *CAD* does not have a separate listing for the word *gizinnatu.* Note, too, G. Dossin's comment in ARM XIII, 166, "Mais l'absence de ce déterminatif dans notre text [56, line 4] (comme dans ARM I, 62, line 20) permet d'écarter la lecture *gizinnatum* suggérée dans *CAD*" ("But the absence of this determinative in our text [as in ARM 1.62:20] allows one to discard the reading *gizinnatum* suggested in *CAD*"). See, too, his remarks on p. 172 to line 32 of letter 144. Now, however, in *CAD, S,* 285–86, the word is read *sinnatu.* See, similarly, *AHw,* 2.1047.

25 Sasson, *Military Establishments,* 27, 67 n 136.

26 R. Frankena, "Some Remarks on a New Approach to Hebrew," in *Travels in the World of the Old Testament: Studies Presented to M. A. Beek on the Occasion of His Sixty-fifth Birthday* (ed. N. S. H. G. Heerma von Voss, Ph. H. J. Houwinkten, N. A. vam Uchelen; Studia Neerlandica 16; Assen: van Gorcum, 1974) 43–44.

27 *AHw,* 2.1047. See also *CAD, S, sinnatu,* 285–86: "He made (the army) throw down its equipment and lances(?) (in surrender)."

now read *sinnatu* and not *ṣinnatu,* which, of course, automatically invalidates any cognate relationship with the Hebrew. Furthermore, there is no precedent in the ancient Near East for Driver's imaginative interpretation of captives being "lifted on shields for the mockery of a brutal and licentious soldiery." Thus Rudolph's criticism that this image "ist allzu phantasievoll" ("is far too fanciful") and Wolff's "highly unlikely" are definitely in place. Moreover, were this the picture the prophet had in mind, the proper preposition with the verb נשא should have been עַל and not בְּ.[30] (Compare T above and Exod 19:4; Deut 32:11; Ps 91:12.) This proposed solution for the first hemistich would be somewhat incongruous with the remaining half of the verse. The mistranslation and misunderstanding were most likely due to the familiar Hebrew idiom נֹשֵׂא צִנָּה ("shield bearer"; see 1 Sam 17:7, 41; 1 Chr 12:24; 2 Chr 14:7).

2. "Ropes"—This translation was suggested by Schwantes based on his interpretation of G, ὅπλα and further supported by his recourse to an Akk. noun, *ṣinnatu* ("halter, nose-rope").[31] However, as Rudolph perceptively observed, ὅπλα is never used elsewhere in G with the meaning "ropes" but is employed as the translation of צִנָּה in Pss 5:13 and 91:4, where the Hebrew word clearly has the meaning "shield" and not "rope." Furthermore, the alleged Akkadian counterpart, *ṣinnatu,* is a rare word appearing in vocabulary lists alongside *ṣerretu* ("nose-rope") and may be a phonetic variant of the latter.[32] In a literary context it is attested only once, in a difficult line of a Neo-Babylonian letter,[33] and there its meaning is highly doubtful. (Interestingly enough, the word appears in that letter in connection with *embūbu,* "flute," and both words occur together in another difficult cuneiform text.)[34] Thus the proposed portrayal of captives being led in single file with ropes fastened to rings drawn through their lips, although attested in Mesopotamian pictorial representations,[35] is not what the prophet has in mind here.[36]

3. "Thorns"—Ibn Ezra (also Rudolph) compared צִנּוֹת to צְנִינִים ("thorns"; Num 33:55; Josh 23:13) and צִנִּים (Prov 22:5). From this meaning it is only a short step to the most favored of interpretations, "hooks" (so, for example, Harper, Sellin, Nötscher, Weiser, Maag, Robinson, Cripps, Hammershaimb, Tur-Sinai). For the semantic development from "thorn" to "hook," compare חוֹחַ ("thorn";[37] for example, 2 Kgs 14:9; Isa 34:13; Hos 9:6; Cant 2:2), which also denotes "hook" when used in connection with a captured marine creature (Job 40:26) and human captives (2 Chr 33:11). Compare, too, חָח ("hook"; see 2 Kgs 19:28 = Isa 37:29; Ezek 19:4; 29:4; 38:4). However, except for this verse, there is no evidence to attach either such a basic or derived meaning to צִנּוֹת,[38] and the use of the verb נשא would also exacerbate

28 ARM XIII, 78, letter 56:4.
29 ARM XIII, 165–66, letter 56:4.
30 See Eliezer Ben Iehuda, *Thesaurus totius hebraitatis et veteris et recentioris* (Jerusalem: Ben Yehuda Hemda, 1908–1951) 11.5541 n 2.
31 S. J. Schwantes ("Note on Amos 4:2b," *ZAW* 79 [1967] 82–83), who unnecessarily goes on to emend the verse. This interpretation was accepted by Wolff and Vesco, "Amos," 496.
32 *CAD, Ṣ,* 201, *ṣinnatu* B. See, too, *AHw,* 2.1103.
33 A. T. Clay, *Neo-Babylonian Letters from Erech* (YOS 3; New Haven: Yale University, 1919) 142:34.
34 For reference, see *CAD, Ṣ,* 201, *ṣinnatu* A, in a late Babylonian text found in E. Ebeling, F. Köcher, and L. Rost, *Literarische Keilschrifttexte aus Assur* (Berlin: Akademie Verlag, 1953) 2:7–8.
35 G. Rawlinson, *The Five Great Monarchies* (New York: 1881) 243.
36 The prophet is also not referring to prisoners bound to one another by the neck; see H. Gressmann, *Altorientalische Bilder zum Alten Testament gesammelt und beschrieben* (Berlin/Leipzig: de Gruyter, 1927) pls. xv:39; xxxvii:86; lvi:128; and *ANEP,* 4:7, 8, 9; 107:325, 326. For that image, see Isa 52:2.
37 See also Akk. *ḫaḫinu* ("thorny plant") *CAD, Ḫ,* 30; *ḫiḫinû, CAD, Ḫ,* 184; and *ḫaḫḫu,* which is an Aramaic loan word in Akkadian; see W. von Soden, "Aramäische Wörter in nA, nB, und spB Texten. Ein Vorbericht I," *Or* 35 (1966) 9. The conjectured references to the myth of a chaos monster assumed here by A. J. Williams ("A Further Suggestion about Amos IV 1–3," *VT* 29 [1979] 206–11) are totally unfounded.
38 For the borrowing of the word צִן into late Egyptian, see W. A. Ward, "Notes on Some Semitic Loan Words and Personal Names," *Or* 32 (1963) 419, 435–36.

the difficulty in such a case (Tur-Sinai). For further criticism, see further.

4. “Baskets”—Thus ibn Ganaḥ,[39] ibn Balʿam,[40] and Eliezer Beaugency[41] (first interpretation), who compares Heb. צִנְצֶנֶת (“jar”; Exod 16:33).[42] Note, moreover, should also be made of Aram. צְנָא (“basket”). Compare צנא דמלאי תמרי (“a basketful of dates”; Babylonian Talmud, Taʿanith 9b) and צנא דמלאי ספרי (“a basketful of books”; Babylonian Talmud, Megillah 28b), the latter being a metaphor for a learned individual. Related Aramaic forms of this substantive are צִינָא (Targum Yerushalmi to Deut 23:25), pl. צִינַיָּא (Targum Yerushalmi to Deut 26:3), and צִינָיָת (Midrash Lam 1:52 on Lam 1:17). These words are all related to Aram. צִינָא, צִינְתָא, צִנָּה (“palms”).[43] From these well-documented usages is derived the next meaning.

5. “Boats”—in the form of baskets (Rashi, Metṣudat Zion; compare Abarbanel) or shields (Kimchi)[44] made from palms (Luria),[45] an interpretation that was obviously influenced by his (incorrect) understanding of the following סִירוֹת as “boats” (see later). Although both Luria and Zolli[46] (see later), have the *guffa*-boat in mind,[47] it is hardly likely that the prophet conceived of a deportation by boat for the inhabitants of Samaria. All of his veiled references to future exile point to the east (thus overland) and not to the west, or overseas (Amos 5:27; 7:17; 9:4, 9). Because Assyria is nowhere specifically mentioned by name in the entire book,[48] a forced crossing of the Tigris and Euphrates rivers on boat is surely not within the purview of the prophet (contrary to Luria).

Three principal suggestions have been offered for the next crux, סִירוֹת דּוּגָה (whether or not דּוּגָה, itself a hapax legomenon, is interpreted as a mere gloss, for example, Sellin, Weiser, Maag, Amsler).

1. “Thorns”—thus Daniel al-Ḳumissi[49] and ibn Ezra. Then, by extension, the entire phrase is understood by most moderns to mean “fishhooks” (for example, Harper, Nötscher, Maag, Cripps, Hammershaimb, Tur-Sinai, Rudolph). This interpretation would then complement the assumed parallel development of צִנּוֹת, that is, “thorns” ⟩ “hooks.” Here, too, note first that the meaning “hook” is otherwise unattested for this word. Furthermore, the plural of סִיר, “thorn,” always appears elsewhere in the masculine, סִירִים (Isa 34:13; Hos 2:8; Nah 1:10[?]; Eccl 7:6), and never in the feminine סִירוֹת, as here.[50] Naturally, once the meaning “hooks” for צִנּוֹת is excluded, the similar meaning for סִירוֹת would also be precluded. Moreover, a further difficulty to this interpretation is based on realia. Fishing hooks were all but unknown in Mesopotamia, at least from the third millennium on.[51] Different methods and implements were employed for the catching of freshwater and marine fish. For the latter, spears, pikes, harpoons, and nets were used.[52] For the former, the most common device was weir baskets.[53] Fishing hooks, however, are never mentioned. Among the widely attested and documented technical terms for fishing equipment in Mesopotamia, no word apparently even exists for fishing hooks.[54] Salonen even goes so far as to suggest that the fishing hook was replaced at a very early date by the weir basket in freshwater fishing.[55] Furthermore, in Egypt, where

39 ibn Ganaḥ, *Haschoraschim*, 433.

40 Judah ibn Balʿam, cited by Poznański (see n 41), 147 n 2.

41 Eliezer aus Beaugency, *Kommentar zu Ezechiel und den XII Kleinen Propheten* (ed. S. Poznański; Warsaw: H. Eppelberg, 1914) 147 n 2 (Heb.).

42 See, too, ben Iehuda, *Thesaurus totius hebraitatis et veteris et recentioris* (Jerusalem: Ben Yehuda Hemda) 11.5541 (Heb.).

43 But it is not related to Heb. טֶנֶא (“small wicker basket”; Zolli, see n 46), which is an Egyptian loan word *(dnjt)* in Hebrew. See T. O. Lambdin, “Egyptian Loan Words in the Old Testament,” *JAOS* 73 (1953) 159.
For Talmudic references, see Jastrow, *Dictionary*.

44 Kimchi, *Radicum Liber*, 315.

45 B. Z. Luria, “Amos 4:2,” *BM* 30 (1967) 10–11 (Heb.).

46 E. Zolli, “Amos 4:2b,” *Anton* 30 (1955) 188–90.

47 But see further on the rarity of the *guffa*-boat in antiquity.

48 Kaufmann, *Toledoth*, 6.87.

49 Daniel al-Ḳumissi, *Commentarius in Librum Duodecum Prophetarum* (Jerusalem: Meqiṣey Nirdamim, 1957) 34.

50 This was already pointed out by Ehrlich, *Randglossen*, 5.238.

51 A. Salonen, *Die Wasserfahrzeuge in Babylonien* (StudOr 8/4; Helsinki: Societas Orientalis Fennica, 1939) 38.

52 A. Salonen, *Die Fischerei im Alten Mesopotamien nach sumerisch-akkadischen Quellen* (Annales Academiae Scientiarum Fennicae B166; Helsinki: Suomalainen Tiedeakatemia, 1970) 51ff.

53 See B. Landsberger, *The Fauna of Ancient Mesopotamia* (MSL 8; 2 vols.; Rome: Pontifical Biblical Institute,

hooks were in use, baskets were still considered the "simplest method" for catching fish.[56]

Wolff and Rudolph, basing themselves on Dalman,[57] comment that here the prophet has "harpoons" in mind and not "fishhooks" (already suggested by Osty). However, such a meaning is totally undocumented, and Dalman's comments refer to חוֹחַ and not to סִירוֹת.

2. "Boats"—So Rashi, Kimchi[58] (see Abarbanel), and Zolli. Compare Isa 18:2, where T translates Heb. כְּלֵי־גֹמֶא ("papyrus boats") by Aram. דּוּגְּגִין, and the conjectured restoration [ובדגו]גין די נונין ("fishermen's boats") in 11QtgJob to Job 40:31.[59] No one, as yet, has made reference to what would appear at first glance to be the most likely semantic counterpart to the Hebrew expression, that is, Sum. giš.ma$_2$.su.ku$_6$ = Akk. *elip bā'iri* ("fisherman's barge, skiff").[60] Compare also Sum. giš.ma$_2$.ku.[61] However, these boats in Mesopotamia were never made out of palms (as Luria contends) but of reeds, rushwood, or skins.[62] Furthermore, the *guffa*-boat,[63] to which Zolli and Weiser specifically refer and for which Luria brings a pictorial representation,[64] is rare in Mesopotamia. It appears as a hapax legomenon in the Sargon legend, *quppu ša šūri* ("a basket of cut reeds").[65] (Rare, too, is its Neo-Babylonian synonym, *elippu ḫallatu*.)[66] Seldom does it show up pictorially.[67] Mention should be made of a section in Herodotus 1:194, who describes "the boats which ply down the Euphrates to the city. These boats are circular in shape and made of hides (κυκλοτερέα πάντα σκύτινα). They build them in Armenia to the northward of Assyria, where they cut withies and make the frames, and then stretch skins on the under side of the craft. They are not fined-off or tapered in any way at bow or stern, but quite round like a shield (ἀσπίδος). . . . It is quite impossible to paddle the boats upstream because of the strength of the current, and that is why they are constructed of hide instead of wood." As has been noted, the description given by Herodotus actually represents a combination of different types of boats.[68]

In sum, a naval deportation does not fit the geographical ideational outlook of the prophet.[69]

3. "Pots"—סִיר (Exod 16:3; 2 Kgs 4:38, 39, 41; Ezek 11:7); plural סִירוֹת (Exod 27:3; 38:3; 1 Kgs 7:45; 2 Kgs 25:14; Jer 52:18, 19; Zech 14:20; 2 Chr 4:11, 16; 35:13): so G, εἰς λέβητας ("kettles, cauldrons"); V, *in ollis* ("earthenware jars, pots"); S, בקסדא ("pots"). Thus it is understood by Menahem ben Saruq,[70] Eliezer Beaugency (first interpretation),[71] and, among moderns, Ehrlich,[72] Cramer, Maag, and Driver,[73] as "fish pots." The advantage of this interpretation is that the Hebrew word for a metal pot, סִיר, always appears with a feminine plural (see references previously).

1962) 2.79–80.

54 Salonen, *Fischerei*, 55.

55 Ibid.

56 Ibid., 52.

57 Dalman, *AuS* 6.360; see Vesco, "Amos," 496.

58 Kimchi, *Radicum Liber*, 238. See Babylonian Talmud, Baba Bathra 73a.

59 M. Sokoloff, *The Targum to Job from Qumran Cave XI* (Bar Ilan Studies in Near Eastern Language and Culture; Ramat-Gan: Bar-Ilan University, 1974) 96 col. XXXV:10. On 163, he states, "This conjectured restoration is based on G*: ἐν πλοίοις ἁλιέων, 'in boats of fishermen.'"

60 For cuneiform references, see Salonen, *Wasserfahrzeuge*, 37–38; idem, *Fischerei*, 71–72; and *CAD, E*, 95, 6'.

61 Salonen, *Wasserfahrzeuge*, 34.

62 Ibid., 5, 138, 144–45.

63 Ibid., 13.

64 Luria, "Amos," 11.

65 Salonen, *Wasserfahrzeuge*, 71–74. See *CAD, Q*, *quppu*, "a wicker basket, wooden chest"; and B. Lewis, *The Sargon Legend* (Cambridge, MA: American Schools of Oriental Research, 1980) 45.

66 Salonen, *Wasserfahrzeuge*, 74. See *CAD, Ḫ*, *ḫallatu* B, 44, "a kind of basket."

67 For representations from the time of Sennacherib, see Salonen, *Wasserfahrzeuge*, pls. XX:1 and XXII:1, and idem, *Fischerei*, XV:2.

68 Salonen, *Wasserfahrzeuge*, 72, who also cites Delitzsch, in *Festschrift E. Sachau* (Berlin, 1915) 90ff. See also Salonen's comments on pp. 73–74.

69 The Hebrew word סִירָה ("boat") is a later addition to the vocabulary, based on this interpretation of the medieval commentators.

70 Menahem ben Saruq, *Sepher HaMaḥberet* (ed. Y. Philipawski; Yadenburg, 1854) 128, second division of סר (Heb.).

71 Poznański, *Kommentar*, 147 n 2.

72 Ehrlich, *Mikrâ*, 407.

73 Ehrlich (*Mikrâ*, 407), who comments that the image of being packed tight as fish in baskets is similar to the English expression "like sardines in a tin."

After all the possibilities have been reviewed, clearly the fewest difficulties are attached to the interpretation of צִנּוֹת and סִירוֹת as "baskets" and "pots," respectively. The former is well attested by its cognates, cited previously, and the latter is well documented in the Bible itself. The image of the prophet is most likely to be understood in the light of the common practice of catching, packing, and transporting fish in such receptacles.[74] That baskets were predominantly employed for such purposes is amply documented in Mesopotamian sources. "Their freshwater fishermen's main device . . . was the weir or the sa.numun$_2$ . . . which was made of rushes and which served for taking the fish from the water and for transporting them overland."[75] For other types of fish receptacles,[76] see, for example, Sum. bugin$_2$.šu.ḫa (= Akk. *buginnu ša bā'iri*),[77] *lamaqartu / lamaqurtu (ša nūni),*[78] and references to the *pisannu*-receptacle[79] in which great quantities of different types of fish were all packed into the same container.[80]

Moreover, a picturesque description of captives in a fisherman's basket is found in one of the "prophetic" texts from Mari.[81] The god Dagan, in the course of delivering his message through a "prophet" to the king Zimrilim, states, *u šarrā[ni ša Binî]amina ina sussul bā'i[ri . . .]š-ši-il-šu-nu-ti-ma maḫrika [lušku]nšunūti* ("Then I, Dagan, will make the Benjaminite sheiks wriggle/writhe[82] in a fisherman's basket[83] and deliver them in front of you").[84]

Thus the proposed translation for this difficult verse in

74 Salonen, *Fischerei,* 51, 55ff.

75 Landsberger, *Fauna,* 79–80. For sa.numun$_2$ ("weir baskets"), see Salonen, *Fischerei,* 57–60. On p. 57 he states, "sa.numun$_2$ = sa.ZI.ZI.NIGIN$_2$ wörtlich eine runde (Reuse) aus numun$_2$-Pflanze" (". . . literally a round [weir basket] out of numun-plants").

76 Salonen, *Wasserfahrzeuge,* 75–79.

77 Salonen, *Fischerei,* 75; idem, *Die Hausgeräte der Alten Mesopotamier nach sumerisch-akkadischen Quellen* (Annales Academiae Scientiarum Fennicae B 139; Helsinki: Suomalainen Tiedeakatemia, 1965) I, s.v.; *CAD, B,* 31, "pail"; 306, "trough, bucket."

78 Salonen, *Fischerei,* 77; idem, *Hausgeräte,* II.336–37; *CAD, L,* 60.

79 Salonen, *Fischerei,* 77–79; idem, *Hausgeräte,* I, s.v.; *AHw,* 2.867–68.

80 Salonen, *Fischerei,* 79.

81 Dossin, "Une révélation," 130, lines 37–38. See, too, W. von Soden, "Verkündigung des Gotteswillens durch prophetisches Wort in den altbabylonischen Briefen aus Mari," *WO* 1/5 (1947–1952) 398, lines 37–38, and *AHw,* 2.1063–64 (*sussullu,* "Kasten" ["box"]).

82 Three suggestions have been offered for the restoration of the reading of the verb:

a. *[lu-pa-á]š-ši-il-šu-nu-ti-ma,* Dossin, "Une révélation," 130, whose translation "j'emménerai" ("I will lead away") is followed by J.-G. Heintz, "Oracles prophétiques et 'guerre sainte' selon les archives royales de mari et l'ancien Testament," in SVT 17 (Leiden: Brill, 1968) 129–30, "tirer, traîner" ("to draw, drag"), from the verb *pašālu;* but, as stated later, a verb with this meaning is undocumented.

b. *[lu-ša-a]b-ši-il-šu-nu-ti-ma* ("I will have them cooked"), a *shaph'el* of *bašālu / šubšulu* ("to cook a meal"). This interpretation by A. Malamat ("Prophecy in the Mari Documents," in Eretz Israel 4 [*Yitzak Ben-Zvi Volume;* Jerusalem: Israel Exploration Society, 1956] 82, note to lines 37–38 [Heb.]) is accepted by W. L. Moran in *ANET,* 623 n 6, and is offered as one of two possible translations by A. Marzal, *Gleanings from the Wisdom of Mari* (Studia Pohl 11; Rome: Pontifical Biblical Institute, 1976) 57, 88 n 97.

c. *[lu-ša-a]p-ši-il-šu-nu-ti-ma,* from *pašālu* ("creep, crawl"), used in connection with enemy captives, *AHw,* 2.841, 1064. Von Soden translates the *š*-form here "zappeln lassen" ("to make writhe/wriggle"), both in *WO* 1/5 (1947–1952) 398, and in *AHw.* His reading and translation are cited by Marzal, *Gleanings,* 57–58, and are followed by H. Schmökel, "Gotteswort in Mari und Israel," *TLZ* 76 (1951) 53; F. Ellermeier, *Prophetie in Mari und Israel* (Herzberg am Harz: Jungfer, 1968) 27; and A. Finet, "Citations littéraires dans la correspondence de Mari," *RA* 68 (1974) 41 n 5, "je les ferai frétiller" ("I will make them wriggle"). This last interpretation is the one accepted here because (1) *pašālu* with the meaning "to lead away" is undocumented in *AHw* and (2) one does not boil or roast *(bašālu)* or cook a meal *(šubšulu)* in a fisherman's wooden basket. See also *CAD, S,* 418 b).

83 Akk. *sussul bā'iri.* Salonen, *Fischerei,* 79; idem, *Hausgeräte,* I.244ff.; *AHw,* 1.96, 2.1063g; *CAD, B,* 32. So, too, Schmökel, "Gotteswort," 53; Ellermeier, *Prophetie,* 27; J.-G. Heintz, "Oracles prophétiques," 129–30; A. Finet, "Citations littéraires," 41 n 5, "la nasse" ("the weir net"). Marzal, *Gleanings,* 58, compares this image with that of the divine "net" found in other Mari texts: "In this method of fishing a basket with a wicket is placed opposing the current of water; when the fish have entered it, they are entrapped and unable to get out." Dossin ("Une révélation," 130)

Amos—"And you will be transported[85] in baskets, and the very last one of you[86] (אַחֲרִיתְכֶן), in fishermen's pots"—now adds a further image to the other symbols for the catching of fish employed in connection with captive Israel (compare Jer 16:16; Hab 1:14).[87]

■ **3** After the destruction of the city, the "breaches" (פְּרָצִים)[88] in the walls of the city will be so numerous that each inhabitant "shall be brought straight out" (reading תְּצֶאנָה),[89] straight ahead through the breach directly "in front of her" (אִשָּׁה נֶגְדָּהּ).[90] For this idiom, compare Joshua's attack upon Jericho when the soldiers marched into the city, each one "straight in front of him" (אִישׁ נֶגְדּוֹ), Josh 6:5, 20.[91] The intention of the prophet is not that the residents of the city will escape by the shortest and fastest route but that they will be carried off (in their baskets) as captives without any difficulty. The enemy will not have to make any detour. The Akkadian inter-dialectal semantic and etymological equivalent of Heb. הוֹצִיא (*hiphʿil* of יצא), *šuṣû*, "to make leave, send off/away"[92] *(shaphʿel* of *aṣû)*, is similarly used in historical texts for the removal of both the population and their possessions from a city. For example, "They removed *(ušēṣû)* the citizens of Babylon to Seleucid";[93] "I took out *(ušēṣâ)* their images, their possessions, their prisoners, and burned that city."[94]

The next stich, however, contains a perplexing crux, הַהַרְמוֹנָה, which still baffles the exegetes' resourcefulness. The inventive proposals for solving the difficulty can be divided roughly into two different categories—those that interpret the word (with or without emending it) as a

read *ṣuṣṣulu* instead of *sussulu*, which he translated "harpoon," and compared Job 40:31. Moran (*ANET*, 623 n 7) accepted this reading, translated "fisherman's spit" (so, too, Marzal, *Gleanings*, 57), and interpreted it as an instrument for cooking (again with A. Malamat, "Prophecy," 82). However, the word is unattested in Akkadian.

84 Another example of the use of this container for the transportation of fish is found in a late Babylonian text: *kî nūnē . . . ina sussullu indaṭû* ("should there be a shortage of fish in the basket"); A. Tremayne, *Records from Erech, Time of Cyrus and Cambyses (538–521 B.C.)* (YOS 7; New Haven: Yale University, 1952) 90:15. See *CAD, B*, 270–71; *M*, I, *maṭû*, 2a, 433; *S*, 418 b). In *CAD, B* and *S*, the translation is a "shortage of fish"; in *M*, "fish of poor quality."

85 Heb. נִשָּׂא can be either *nipḥʿal* or *piʿēl*, *GKC*, 75 oo. For its use as a *niphʿal* with אֶת, see *GKC*, 121 a–b. This is the interpretation accepted in the commentary.

86 See Amos 8:10; 9:1. See Gese, "Beiträge," 436–37. Compare Rudolph (168), who interprets it along with Amos 8:10 and 9:1 as "nur eine rhetorische Figur, um die Totalität der Katastrophe zu veranschaulichen" ("only a rhetorical figure of speech to illustrate the totality of the catastrophe"). For a discussion of this term and various proposals for its translation, see Hasel, *Remnant*, 181–83. He (along with Sellin, 216; Driver, 168; Cripps, 167; Weiser, 150; and Wolff) understands it to mean "remnant/residue," and refers it to the women of Samaria themselves. The medieval commentators, Rashi, ibn Ezra, and Kimchi, refer it to the progeny.

87 For the similar image in Mesopotamian texts, see *CAD, N*, II, 339–40 h).

88 See, for example, Amos 9:11 for the reverse picture (positive) of Israel's destiny. See also, for example, 1 Kgs 11:27; Neh 6:1. For a חוֹמָה פְּרוּצָה ("breached wall"), see Neh 2:13 (plural); 2 Chr 32:5; for a עִיר פְּרוּצָה ("a breached city"), see Prov 25:28. See also Akk. *parāṣu* ("to breach a wall"), *AHw*, 2.832, and the noun *pelirṣu*, "Durchbruch" ("breach"), *AHw*, 2.855. See also Ugar. *prṣ*. The use of פְּרָצִים and not בִּפְרָצִים (against Ehrlich, *Mikrâ*, 407) is an example of the accusative of direction. Thus Wolff, 204, and Rudolph, 161; see *GKC*, 118h. There is no need whatsoever to resort here to a change in vocalization—against J. J. Glück, "The Verb פרץ in the Bible and in Qumran Literature," *RevQ* 5 (1964–1965) 124–25, פְּרָצִים, an abstract plural; or to emendation—Marti, עֲרֻמִּים ("naked"), based on an inner Greek scribal error in G (see Wolff and Rudolph); or מַרְפְּתִים ("from the stalls"), Sellin², Maag, *Text*, 19.

89 Following G, καὶ ἐξενεχθήσεσθε ("you shall be brought forth"), and accepted by most modern commentators.

90 For the function of אִשָּׁה as a distributive pronoun, see *GKC*, 139b. For נֶגְדּוֹ, see also Jer 31:39.

91 See Rashi; Ehrlich, *Randglossen*, 5.408.

92 See *CAD, A*, II, 374ff.

93 BMT, pl. 18, r. 17.

94 *AKA* 59 iv 3. For an example of the forced exit from a city after a breach had been made, see *ABL*, 460, r. 9: "After they had cut a breach *(niksu kî [ik]kisu)*, they made him go out" *(ultēṣûniš)*.

place-name to where the deported people will be exiled, and those that emend it to refer not to a geographical site but rather to some other location. Among the former are G, *εἰς τὸ ὄρος τὸ Ρεμμαν*, which divides the Hebrew word into two independent substantives, הָהָר רִמּוֹן ("the mountain Remman"); σ', *ἀρμένιαν*, and T, טוּרֵי חַרְמִינֵי ("[mountains of] Armenia"); α', *ἔρμωνα*, who merely transliterates the letters החרמונה (so, too, the reading of T according to Rashi, טוּרֵי חַרְמוֹנֵי);[95] and V, *Armon* ("[Mt.] Hermon"; see Deut 3:8, 9). For additional conjectures, see הַר מִנִּי, "to Mt. Minni" (see Jer 51:27), that is, Mannai, a place name in Assyria; הַר אֲמָנָה, "to Mt. Amana," in Lebanon (Cant 4:8); or simply "to Harmon," which, as has been suggested, is to be identified with Hermal in the vicinity of Kadesh on the Orontes in north Syria.[96] As for the latter, proposed emendations are הָאַרְמוֹנָה ("to the stronghold"); הַחֲרִימָנָה ("to the harem"); הַמַּחֲרָאָה or הַמַּדְמֵנָה ("to the dung heap").[97] Ingenious suggestions are not wanting; only a suitable solution is still wanted.

Accepting G's translation, *ἀπορριθήσεσθε* (compare V, *proiciemini*), which reflects the passive וְהָשְׁלַכְתֶּנָה[98] ("and you will be thrown"),[99] the image conjures up two different possibilities. It may refer to the throwing out of dead bodies; see Amos 8:3 (reading הָשְׁלַךְ, and placing the pause under this word, רַב הַפֶּגֶר . . . הָשְׁלַךְ); and, for example, 1 Kgs 13:24–25; Isa 34:3; Jer 14:16. Akkadian likewise employs the verb *nadû* ("to throw")[100] to refer to the "throwing out of a corpse" in the expressions *šalamtam nadû* and *pagram nadû* (the equivalent of Heb. לְהַשְׁלִיךְ פֶּגֶר). However, in the light of the theme of deportation that is so common in the book and as a continuation of the allusion already made in the previous verse, it is more reasonable to explain the activity referred to here as the "throwing out," that is, the exiling and deporting of the population.[101] This interpretation finds support in the employment of the verb השליך in connection with the exile of King Jehoiakin of Judah in Jer 22:28; and in Deut 29:27, referring to the exile of Israel.[102]

Note that the identity of the invading enemy who will cast out Israel remains unspecified, as it does throughout the oracles of Amos. Furthermore, this allusion is the first in Amos to the recurring motif of punishment by deportation; see Amos 5:5, 27; 6:7; 7:11, 17. In the previous chapter, Amos 3:11, 15, the power, pride, glory, and security of the people were all attacked and threatened with imminent attack and destruction. Here the people themselves are the direct target of the anonymous enemy's onslaught. Amos is threatening the population of northern Israel with tragic consequences.

95 In A. Sperber's edition, *The Bible in Aramaic: Based on Old Manuscripts and Printed Texts* (Leiden: Brill, 1959).

96 For the suggestion, Harmon = Hermal, see D. N. Freedman and F. I. Andersen, "Harmon in Amos 4:3," *BASOR* 198 (1970) 41, followed by Vesco, "Amos," 496. An additional problem with this as well as with all the other proposals that make reference to a specific place-name is that Amos otherwise leaves the exact site of deportation unidentified throughout all his oracles. He is unaware of the ultimate location and can merely point to the general area. See Amos 5:27.

97 For all these and sundry others, see Harper, 85. See also Tur-Sinai (*Peshuṭo*, 460), who relates it to חֵרֶם (see, for example, Ezek 32:3; Hab 1:15) and translates "a fishing net." Many of the suggestions and emendations lack textual support as well as a proper philological basis.

98 The final ה ַ of the verb is a bit difficult. It may have been caused by analogy with וּתְצֶאנָה, or the ה may merely be a case of dittography from the following word.

99 Thus complementing the passive reading of the first verb; see above, n 89.

100 See *CAD, N*, 73–74.

101 Compare T, וְיַגְלוֹן יַתְהוֹן ("And they shall exile you").

102 See also the "casting away/out," that is, rejection of personified Israel in Ezek 16:5. For the semantic development of השלך and its Akk. cognate, *nadû* ("to throw/cast ⟩ to reject, abandon, expose"), see M. Cogan, "A Technical Term for Exposure," *JNES* 27 (1968) 133–35; C. Cohen, "The Legend of Sargon and the Birth of Moses," *JANESCU* 4 (1972) 49. For the identical sequence of action in an Assyrian text relating to the "taking and throwing out" (Akk. *šuṣû . . . nadû*) of bones outside the city (Akk. *kamâti*), see Streck, *Assurbanipal und die letzten assyrisichen Könige bis zum Untergang Ninevah's* (VAB 7; Leipzig: Hinrichs, 1916) 38, iv, line 81.

4

Castigating Chastisement of the Cult and Futile Punitive Retribution

4 Come to Bethel and transgress!
To Gilgal, transgress even more!
Bring your sacrifices on the morn!
Your tithes on the third day!
5 Burn a thank-offering of leavened bread!
And proclaim freewill offerings aloud!
For you love that, O Israelites
—declares my Lord God.
6 I, for my part, have given you
Cleanness of teeth in all your towns
And lack of food in all your settlements.
Yet you did not return to me
—declares the Lord.
7 I also withheld the rain from you,
While there were yet three months to the harvest.
I would make it rain on one town,
But on another town I would not bring rain.
One field would be rained upon
And another field on which it did not rain would wither.
8 Then two or three towns would stagger
To another town to drink water,
But they could not quench their thirst.
Yet you did not return to me
—declares the Lord.
9 I struck you with blast and blight.
Repeatedly your gardens and vineyards,
Your fig trees and olive trees the locust devoured.
Yet you did not return to me
—declares the Lord.
10 I released against you pestilence
In the manner of Egypt.
I slew with the sword your elite troops
Together with your captured horses.
And I made the stench of your army camps
Rise up into your very nostrils.
Yet you did not return to me
—declares the Lord.
11 I overturned you, as God overturned Sodom and Gomorrah,
So that you were like a brand snatched from the fire.
Yet you did not return to me
—declares the Lord.
12 Therefore, thus I am about to do to you, O Israel:
Because this is what I will do to you—
Prepare to meet your God, O Israel!
13 For lo:
He who formed the mountains
And created the wind,
And declares to man what his intention is*,
Who turns blackness into glimmering dawn

And treads upon the heights of the earth,
The Lord, the God of Hosts, is his name!

***Hebrew obscure**

■ 4 This next pericope, which introduces a new theme, is not restricted to the upper classes of northern Israel but is directed against the entire population en masse.[1] The prophet addresses a satirical invitation to the people to continue to perform their customary rites at the customary places and at the customary times—all of which paradoxically and bewilderingly exacerbates and epitomizes their transgressions.

Amos singles out two of the major cult sites in northern Israel,[2] Bethel[3] and Gilgal.[4] The former, some ten miles north of Jerusalem, was founded by Jeroboam I (1 Kgs 12:28–33) and became one of the chief sanctuaries of the northern kingdom. Its roots, however, can be traced back to much earlier periods (compare Gen 28:11–22; Judg 20:18). The latter, the first encampment of the Israelites west of the Jordan in Canaan, is also well known as a sacred site from the time of the conquest of Canaan up until the time of the prophet (compare Josh 4:19–20; 5:2–10; 15:7; 1 Sam 7:16; 10:8; 11:15; 15:12; Hos 4:15; 9:15; 12:12). Both sanctuaries are coupled together once again in Amos 5:5 (see also 1 Sam 7:16; Hos 4:15).

The paradoxical summons, "come and sin" (. . . בֹּאוּ וּפִשְׁעוּ), which has been called "a parody of a priestly Torah,"[5] is another example of Amos's employment of the element of surprise.[6] The people are invited to come to their favorite cultic centers in order to sin and to "transgress even more" (הַרְבּוּ לִפְשֹׁעַ)![7] Note once again the employment of the root פשע.[8] Throughout Amos 1:3—2:3 this key term characterized crimes against

1 Rudolph, 172, has drawn attention to the analogous structure of Amos 2:6–16 and 4:4–12. Both are divided into three parts: the disclosure of the crime, the unsuccessful nature of the acts of God, and the announcement of punishment. Although the middle sections differ (Amos 2:9–12; 4:6–11)—the former recounting the acts of God's grace and the latter, the divine curses that plagued Israel—nevertheless, both recount the fact that the divine purpose was not achieved. See also the function of וְאָנֹכִי, Amos 2:9, 10; וְגַם אֲנִי, Amos 4:6; and וְגַם אָנֹכִי, Amos 4:7, which introduces the contrast between the people's behavior and God's actions.

2 In Hebrew, Bethel and Gilgal are both accusative of direction; see *GKC*, 118d.

3 For Bethel, see K. Galling, "Bethel und Gilgal," *ZDPV* 66 (1943) 140–55; idem, "Bethel und Gilgal II," 21–43; A. Alt, "Die Wallfahrt von Sichem nach Bethel," in idem, *Kleine Schriften zur Geschichte des Volkes Israel* (3 vols.; München: Beck, 1968) 1.79–88. See also comments on Amos 3:14.

4 For Gilgal, see H.-J. Kraus, "Gilgal. Ein Beitrag zur Kultusgeschichte Israels," *VT* 1 (1951) 181–99; J. Muilenburg, "The Site of Ancient Gilgal," *BASOR* 140 (1955) 11–27; O. Bächli, "Zur Lage des alten Gilgal," *ZDPV* 83 (1967) 64–71; F. Langlemet, *Gilgal et les récits de la traversée du Jourdain* (Cahiers de la Revue Biblique 11; Paris: Gabalda, 1969).

5 See J. Begrich, "Die priesterliche Tora," in *Werden und Wesen des Alten Testaments* (ed. P. Volz, F. Stummer, and J. Hempel; BZAW 66; Berlin: Töpelmann, 1936) 77; reprinted in idem, *Gesammelte Studien zum Alten Testament* (TBü 21; München: Kaiser, 1964) 247–48, followed by many, for example, Wolff, 211; Rudolph, 175. Compare the priestly imperative invitation (בֹּאוּ) to visit cultic sites, Pss 96:8; 100:2, 4; Rudolph, 175. For examples of the employment of בוא as referring to the entrance of pilgrims into a sanctuary, see Wolff, 218.

Note also the use of the root בוא, which links together the two consecutive literary units: v 1, הָבִיאָה; v 2, בָּאִים; v 4, הָבִיאוּ/בֹּאוּ. See also the key phrases linking this verse with 3:14: פשע, בֵּית־אֵל, זְבָחִים/מִזְבְּחוֹת.

6 For other surprise endings, see Amos 3:1–2; 9:7–8.

7 For the expression הַרְבּוּ לִפְשֹׁעַ, see Ezra 10:13; for the form, see 2 Chr 36:14. See *GKC*, 114n, note 2. For the same root, appearing as הַרְבּוֹת, see v 9.

Note the sixfold use of the second-person masculine plural throughout these two verses (to be contrasted immediately with the first-person Yahweh address) to indicate that the cult per se was not at fault, only the people performing it.

8 On פשע, see R. Knierim, "*pšʿ*," *THAT* 2 (1972) 488–95.

humanity; here it appears in the context of a crime against the divine sphere. Both are "rebellions," for both flout the divine will. But what precisely is the nature of the transgression and rebellion in this passage?

The prophet is obviously not berating them for practicing their cultic rites at sanctuaries outside Jerusalem because the Deuteronomic law of the centralization of the cult was not yet in effect. He also is not accusing them of offering illegitimate sacrifices or of being involved in idol worship, as these play hardly any role whatsoever in his condemnations.[9] Nevertheless, he is unequivocally declaring that the more they attend the cultic sites and the more zealous they are in performing the manifold attendant rites, the more they continue to offend and transgress. Herein lies one of the major innovations in prophetic religion.

The relationship of the prophets to the cult has gone through several different stages of interpretation in modern research. One of the basic axioms of biblical scholarship was the alleged fundamental and irreconcilable opposition and antagonism between prophet and priest. The prophets were said to be the authors of "ethical monotheism" and were responsible for the deritualization of religion. Thus the inevitable conflict between the "word-possessed" prophet and the "cult-possessed" priest, between the former, who brought God's word to humanity, and the latter, who raised humanity's sacrifice to God. With the development of form-critical studies, a partial reevaluation took place. Many scholars began to stress the basic positive attitude of the prophets toward the ritual. Prophets were understood to be associated with the cult, actually functioning members of the cultic personnel. Their oracles were considered to be liturgically fixed as an integral component of Israelite worship.

Although both extreme views are seriously open to question, undeniably the prophetic attacks against the cult did introduce a new dimension into the religion of Israel. The essence of God's demand, according to their outlook, is not to be found in the cult but in the moral and ethical spheres of life. Whereas Samuel demanded the "primacy of obedience" over sacrifice (1 Sam 15:22), Amos and many of the other classical prophets stressed the "primacy of morality." For them worship and ritual were means; justice and righteousness were ends. "God requires devotion, not devotions," right rather than rite. When the cult became a substitute for moral behavior, it was condemned. Any cultic act performed by a worshiper whose moral character was not beyond reproach was deemed unacceptable. This new standard of priorities eventually led to a head-on clash with the acknowledged heads of the religious establishment, the priests (compare Amos 7:10ff.; Jer 20; 29:24ff.). Although the prophets devaluated the intrinsic significance of ritual, they were no more absolutely opposed to the cult than they were to song and psalm (Amos 5:23) or to prayer, festival, and Sabbath (Isa 1:13–15). Isaiah's prophetic call came from within the Temple (Isa 6), and both the exilic (Isa 44:28; 52:11; 66:20–24; Jer 33:11, 18; Ezek 20:40–44; 22:8, 26; 40—48) as well as the postexilic prophets (Haggai and Zechariah) had positive attitudes toward the Temple and cult and advocated the rebuilding of the sanctuary, the restoration of sacrificial worship, and the reinstitution of ceremonial law. Only when the cult became a substitute and surrogate panacea for religion itself did the prophets inveigh so heavily against it. They adamantly opposed the absolutization of the cult and stressed instead God's ultimate concern with proper personal behavior. Principal among the Deity's demands were justice, kindness, righteousness, integrity, honesty, and faithfulness (for example, Isa 1:16–17; Jer 9:22–23; 22:15–16; Hos 6:6; Amos 5:15, 24; Mic 6:8).

The prophets went one ideological step further. Morality, which for them was of ultimate significance, also became the decisive factor in determining the national destiny of Israel. Herein was a shift from the older traditions expressed in the Torah literature and in the preclassical prophetic writings, according to which the primary transgression that would determine the ultimate fate of the nation was the sin of idolatry. With the emergence of classical prophecy, a new criterion became operative, that of moral rectitude. The destiny of Israel was henceforth intrinsically determined by its basic moral posture; immorality and unethical behavior would ultimately lead to the doom of the nation.[10]

9 Against Barstad, *Religious Polemics*, 56ff.

10 For the exemplary treatment of this entire subject, see Kaufmann, *Toledoth*, 6.71–81. See also Paul, "Prophets," 1172–73.

A note of irony rings clearly when Amos emphatically states "*your* sacrifices" (זִבְחֵיכֶם) and "*your* tithes" (מַעְשְׂרֹתֵיכֶם). These offerings may be important to the people, but for the prophet they epitomize the very basis of his indictment. The cult has become an anthropocentric staff of life, but theocentrically it is void of all substance.

Amos now spells out the details of his ironic summons. After startling them by his invitation to come to the leading sanctuaries and . . . sin, he sarcastically bids them to continue to practice their elaborate cultus by offering all of their customary sacrifices at these very sanctuaries.[11] לַבֹּקֶר has been interpreted in two different ways. Several commentators regard the ל as distributive ("every morning"),[12] thereby heightening his taunt: "Bring your sacrifices[13] morningly." Others have suggested that what is being referred to here reflects an otherwise unattested custom of offering a sacrifice on the morning after the arrival of the worshiper at the sanctuary.[14] Rites characteristic of northern Israel may be reflected in these verses.

The expression לִשְׁלֹשֶׁת יָמִים has also received two similar explanations. If the ל is distributive, the meaning would be "every three days," which, of course, could only be meant sarcastically, for tithes were never offered at such frequent intervals.[15] The other proposal is "on the third day." However, the presentation of tithe payments two days after the arrival of the pilgrim at the sanctuary is unattested elsewhere (unless, again, some peculiar northern Israelite custom is alluded to here). In either case, Amos is critically and cynically urging them to punctiliously follow their own established rites.

The origin of the offering of tithes at the sanctuary of Bethel is traced back by E to Jacob, the *hieros eponymos* of the northern tribes (Gen 28:22). Yet another tradition traces tithing back to Abraham and Jerusalem (Gen 14:20). Both have a common etiological purpose: the explanation of the origin of the practice of offering tithes in both Israel and Judah.

As some have correctly noted, the practice of tithing was originally of a voluntary nature (see, for example, Gen 14:20; 28:20–22) and not a compulsory annual obligation as it later became in accordance with Deuteronomic legislation (Deut 14:22–29; 26:12).[16] Note that here, too, it is cited in proximity to "freewill offerings" (v 5).

Once again Amos resorts to one of his favorite literary devices, the employment of a heptad. Note the seven imperative verbs in vv 4–5.[17] Attention should also be drawn to the threefold use of "three," which constitutes a key word in this chapter, linking two literary units: שְׁלֹשֶׁת, v 4; שְׁלֹשָׁה, v 7; שָׁלֹשׁ, v 8.

■ **5** The cutting chastisement and castigation continues as he parodies additional cultic prescriptions. In P the verb

11 For the sacrificial cult in general, see R. Rendtorff, *Studien zur Geschichte des Opfers im Alten Israel* (WMANT 24; Neukirchen-Vluyn: Neukirchener Verlag, 1967); R. de Vaux, *Les sacrifices de l'Ancien Testament* (Cahiers de la Revue Biblique 1; Paris: Gabalda, 1964); M. Haran, *Temples and Temple Service in Ancient Israel: An Inquiry into the Character of Cult Phenomena and the Historical Setting of the Priestly School* (Oxford: Clarendon, 1978).

12 For example, Kimchi; Harper, 94; Cripps, 170; Robinson; L. Delekat, "Zum hebräischen Wörterbuch," *VT* 14 (1964) 8; see *GKC,* 123d. When the intention is distributive, the plural is usually used; see Isa 33:2; Pss 73:14; 101:8; Job 7:18; Lam 3:23. See, however, Jer 21:12. In later biblical Hebrew, distribution is also expressed by the repetition of the singular; compare, for example, 1 Chr 9:27; and throughout the Book of Esther. See *KB,* I.145.

13 For זבח, see J. Bergman, H. Ringgren, and B. Lang, "*zbḥ,*" *TWAT* II (1977) 509–31.

14 Wellhausen; Weiser, *Profetie,* 162; Hammershaimb, 67; Wolff, 219; Rudolph, 176. See also the comments on tithes at the end of the verse.

15 See Deut 14:22, 28; 26:12 for the setting aside of the tithe every year or every third year. The attempt to interpret the word יָמִים ("days") as "years" in order to harmonize this verse with the Deuteronomic injunction is artificial; against Kimchi; van Hoonacker; Ridderbos; Neher, *Amos,* 86; Deden; Robinson-Horst.

16 For the institution of tithes, see M. Haran, "Tithe," *EM* 5.206–8 (Heb.); M. Weinfeld, "Tithes," *EncJud* 15.1156–62; and Kaufmann, *Toledoth,* 1.148–54 (Heb.). For the practice in the Bible and the ancient Near East, see M. Weinfeld, "The Royal and Sacred Aspects of the Tithe in the Old Testament," *Beer-Sheba* 1 (1973) 122–31, esp. 123–26 (Heb.); idem, *Deuteronomy,* 213–15. See also J. Milgrom, *Studies in Levitical Terminology I: The Encroacher and the Levite, the Term ʿAboda* (University of California Publications in Near Eastern Studies 14; Berkeley and Los Angeles: University of California, 1970) 67 n 246, in connection with Lev 27:30.

17 The fifth verb, קַטֵּר (v 5), is an infinitive absolute,

קטר[18] is employed for the offering of incense and appears in the *hiphʿil.* However, outside P it means "to offer a meal offering," occurring occasionally in the *hiphʿil,* but mainly in the *piʿel.*[19] Amos chidingly comments, "offer (קַטֵּר) a sacrifice of thanksgiving (תּוֹדָה) of that which is leavened" (מֵחָמֵץ),[20] that is, the meal-offering accompanying the thanksgiving sacrifice "which in the non-Priestly custom probably might take the form of leavened bread and even be offered up on the altar."[21] Although leavened bread was forbidden on the altar with blood sacrifices (Exod 23:18; 34:25; Lev 2:11), according to Lev 7:13, "This offering, with cakes of leavened bread (חָמֵץ) added, he shall offer along with his thanksgiving sacrifice (תּוֹדָה) of well-being."[22] One who brought a sacrifice of well-being as a תּוֹדָה could offer unleavened cakes in addition to the animal sacrifice. Even if this specific Levitical prescription is to be dated later than the time of Amos, the sacrifice to which Amos is referring is nevertheless a legitimate one that most likely was customary in northern Israel. The sacrifices themselves are proper; only the people offering them are acting improperly.

For the pairing of the verbs זבח (v 4) and קטר, see, for example, 1 Kgs 22:44; 2 Kgs 12:4; 14:4; Isa 65:3; Hos 4:13; 11:2; Hab 1:16. The former refers to any animal sacrifice; the latter refers to a cereal offering.

The "freewill offering" (נְדָבָה) was a voluntary spontaneous nonprescribed offering that usually appears alongside a "vow" (נֶדֶר); see Lev 7:16; 22:18, 21; 23:38; Num 15:3; 29:39; Deut 12:6, 17. (The verb נדר may even be employed with the substantive נְדָבָה; see Deut 23:24.) Three of the offerings mentioned here—זֶבַח, מַעֲשֵׂר, and נְדָבָה—are also listed together in Deut 12:6. Once again the prophet resorts to ridicule by telling them to "proclaim . . . aloud" (קִרְאוּ . . . הַשְׁמִיעוּ) and publicly their freewill offerings for all to hear. According to Amos, the entire panoply of cultic worship can never replace or be a surrogate for morality. The externalities of the ritual cannot take the place of correct ethical behavior. The cult fulfills their needs—"For *you* love that, O Israelites"[23]—not the Lord's. It is what *they* love to do; not what God desires them to do.

■ **6ff.** In Amos 2:6–16 the people's immoral and unethical behavior was contrasted to God's goodness and grace toward them throughout their history *(Heilsgeschichte).* Here, however, their cultic and ritual behavior is followed by a section that delineates the Deity's punitive and retributive actions[24] *(Unheilsgeschichte).* For their meticulous cultic observance, they expected commensurate blessings of bounty and fertility. Instead, they were struck by curses and maledictions. The two pericopes, vv 4–5 and 6–13, are related by contrast.[25] The opening

which functions as an imperative. See *GKC,* 113bb. This once again illustrates Amos's penchant for stylistic deviation. See comments on chapters 1 and 2 and 6:1–6, and D. N. Freedman, "Deliberate Deviation from an Established Pattern of Repetition in Hebrew Poetry as a Rhetorical Device," in *Proceedings of the Ninth World Congress of Jewish Studies* (Jerusalem: World Union of Jewish Studies, 1986) 1.45–52. For other heptads, see Amos 2:6–8, 14–16; 4:6–11; 5:8–9, 21–23; 9:1–4.

18 Because the infinitive absolute functions here as an imperative (see *GKC,* 133bb), there is no reason to emend to the imperative form, וְקַטְּרוּ; against, for example, Ewald; H. Oort, "De profeet Amos," *ThT* 14 (1880) 144; Wellhausen, 79; Vollmer, *Rückblicke,* 10. For the verb, see also D. Edelman, "The Meaning of *qiṭṭar,*" *VT* 35 (1985) 395–400.

19 Compare Akk. *quṭṭuru* ("to cause something to smoke, to make an incense offering), *CAD, Q,* 166–67. The use of the Akkadian verb in both the *D-* and *Š*-forms disproves the assumption that the verb קטר in the *piʿel* is older than that of the *hiphʿil.*

20 The מ here is partitive not privative, contrary to Robinson-Horst; Snaith, *Text of Amos.* For Heb. חָמֵץ, compare its Akkadian cognate, *emṣu* ("sour"), *CAD, E,* 152–53, c)′ "of bread made with sour dough." See also D. Kellerman, "*ḥmṣ,*" *TWAT* II (1977) 1061–68.

21 For the basic study, see M. Haran, "The Uses of Incense in the Ancient Israelite Ritual," *VT* 10 (1960) 116ff. The quote here is from p. 117. See also idem, *Temples,* 234.

22 See the commentaries to Leviticus. See also Lev 23:17 and D. Z. Hoffmann, *Leviticus* (2 vols.; Jerusalem: Mosad Harav Kook, 1966) 1.174 (Heb.).

23 See Jer 5:31. According to Watson (*Hebrew Poetry,* 307), Heb. כֵּן should be translated here "proper": "You love what is proper," thereby exacerbating the irony. This, however, is a very forced interpretation. See also G. R. Driver cited in Robinson-Horst; Maag, *Text,* 20, 157; Rudolph.

24 See Rudolph, 172.

25 Many commentators make a clear distinction between this pericope and the former one. See already A. Winter, "Analyse des Buches Amos," *TSK* 83

emphatic adversative, וְגַם אֲנִי ("I, for my part"; see Amos 2:10), introduces an antithesis to that which preceded,[26] an antithesis that contrasts that which the people have brought to God in the cult to that which God has brought them for breaking the covenant. Because the existence of Israel is predicated upon a covenant relationship with God, when faithful they are granted their just rewards and blessings for their fidelity.[27] When they abrogate the covenant stipulations, however, divine punishment inexorably takes its course and exacts its damaging toll in fulfillment of the covenant curses,[28] exemplified by pernicious plagues.[29]

Amos presents here in an "*atemberaubenden Rhythmus*" ("breathtaking rhythm")[30] a review and catalogue[31] of

(1910) 323–74, esp. 341f.; Balla, *Die Droh*, 18–19; L. Köhler, "Amos," *Schweizeriche Theologische Zeitschrift* 34 (1917) 10–21, 68–79, 145–57, 190–208, esp. 72; Weiser, *Profetie*, 160, 165–66; Reventlow, *Amt*, 76. J. Meinhold (*Studien zur israelitischen Religionsgeschichte I: Der heilige Rest 1. Elias, Amos, Hosea, Jesaja* [Bonn: Weber's, 1903] 38–39); and Marti, 180, interpret the connection ironically. Vollmer (*Rückblicke*, 9–20) correctly treats Amos 4:4–12a as one unit. For the interconnection between vv 4–5 and vv 6–12, see pp. 13–15: "Der Jahwekultus war den Israeliten heilig. Wenn Amos ihn als Frevel bezeichnet, muss er dies begründen" (pp. 14–15). "Mit dem Rückblick legt Amos dar, warum die Kultteilnehmer Frevler sind: Sie sind Abtrünnige, die trotz wiederholter Mahnungen Jahwes in Form von Katastrophen nicht bis zu ihm umgekehrt sind" (p. 15). ("The cult of Yahweh was sacred to the Israelites. When Amos designates it as a sacrilege, he has to substantiate the charge. With his retrospect Amos explicates why the participants in the cult are impious. They, who, despite the repeated warnings of Yahweh expressed in the form of catastrophes, do not return to him, are apostates.") Others who also regard it as a single unit include Marti, 180–81; Procksch, 74ff.; Duhm, "Anmerkungen," 6–7; Harper, 90; Sellin, 181ff. Barstad (*Religious Polemics*, 59) regards all of chapter 4 as "a consistent coherent speech unit," but he relates it to non-Yahwistic or Yahwistic/syncretistic cults.

See also J. L. Crenshaw ("A Liturgy of Wasted Opportunity [Amos 4:6–12; Isa 9:7–10; 5:25–29]," *Semitics* 1 [1970] 27–37) for the strophic structure of vv 6–12.

26 See also Jer 13:26; Ezek 16:43; 20:25; Mic 6:13; Mal 2:9. See Kimchi; C. J. Labuschagne, "The Emphasizing Particle גם and Its Connotations," in *Studia Biblica et Semitica: Theodoro Christiano Vriezen qui munere professoris theologiae per XXV annos functus est* (Wageningen: Voenman & Zonen, 1966) 193–206; see p. 199. Because this is a well-attested linking design that introduces the Deity's reaction to the nation's misbehavior, there is no reason to call it a "secondary linking device," against Wolff, 213. See Sellin, 221; Marti, 180; Cripps, 171. As stated previously, the entire pericope is structured in the same pattern as Amos 2:6–16. Moreover, Amos 4:6, וְגַם אֲנִי, is analogous to Amos 2:9, וְאָנֹכִי. See also Vollmer, *Rückblicke*, 10.

27 See, in general, D. R. Hillers, *Covenant: The History of a Biblical Idea* (Baltimore: Johns Hopkins University, 1969); D. J. McCarthy, *Treaty and Covenant: A Study in Form in the Ancient Oriental Documents and the Old Testament* (AnBib 21a; Rome: Pontifical Biblical Institute, 1978).

28 The first well-documented investigations of this subject with corresponding references to the literature of the ancient Near East were made by Fensham, "Common Trends," 155–75, and D. R. Hillers, *Treaty Curses*. For other studies specifically related to Amos, see Bach, "Gottesrecht," 23–34; W. Brueggemann, "Amos 4:4–13 and Israel's Covenant Worship," *VT* 15 (1965) 1–15; P. E. Dion, "Le message moral du prophète Amos s'inspirait-il du 'droit de l'alliance'?" *ScEs* 27 (1975) 5–34; M. O'Rourke-Boyle, "The Covenant Lawsuit of the Prophet Amos: 3:1—4:13," *VT* 21 (1971) 338–62; F. H. Seilhamer, "The Role of Covenant in the Mission and Message of Amos," in *A Light unto My Path: Old Testament Studies in Honor of Jacob M. Myers* (ed. H. N. Bream, R. D. Heim, and C. A. Moore; Gettysburg Theological Studies 6; Philadelphia: Temple University, 1974) 435–52; L. A. Sinclair, "The Courtroom Motif in the Book of Amos," *JBL* 85 (1966) 351–53; W. Zimmerli, "Das Gottesrecht bei den Propheten Amos, Hosea, und Jesaja," in *Werden und Wirken des Alten Testaments: Festschrift für Claus Westermann zum 70. Geburtstag* (ed. R. Albertz, H.-P. Mueller, H. W. Wolff, and W. Zimmerli; Göttingen: Vandenhoeck & Ruprecht, 1980) 235–66.

29 See Reventlow, *Amt*, 75–90, esp. 86–87 (see the criticism of Vollmer, *Rückblicke*, 18); R. Mayer, "Sünde und Gericht in der Bildersprache der vorexilischen Prophetie," *BZ* 8 (1964) 22–44, esp. 28ff.

30 Weiser, *Profetie*, 162; compare also p. 172.

31 The prophet resorts again to one of his favorite literary devices of presenting a theme in seriatim. See Amos 1—2 and the sequence of visions in Amos 7—8. The purpose of the series is to set the stage and give the reason for the final dénouement in Amos 4:12. Once more Amos employs a logical development, drawing upon the people's experience, in

the treaty maledictions that have befallen the nation in the past.[32] They are all introduced directly by a verb in the first-person singular, signaling God's direct intervention into the rebellious history of Israel. The seven calamities are also highlighted by a fivefold recurring refrain,[33] וְלֹא שַׁבְתֶּם עָדַי ("Yet you did not return to me").[34] This "bolerolike" iteration has its own overwhelming cumulative effect, culminating in v 12.[35] The prophet does not merely announce the *Vernichtungsgericht* ("judgment of extermination"); he psychologically prepares his audience for it by leading them disaster by disaster to the inevitable logical conclusion.

Amos employs the curse genre here in a novel fashion.[36] Maledictions, whether in treaties, legal collections, boundary stones, or elsewhere, are always future oriented. The people are warned and threatened in advance by a series of curses for any infringement upon what is demanded of them.[37] Here, however, the curses relate not to the future but rather to the past history of Israel. Whereas the maledictions in Leviticus (chapter 26) and Deuteronomy (chapter 28) are prospective and foretell what *will* happen, Amos relates retrospectively what *has* happened. The threatened ominous results have already occurred. The manifold disasters that have overtaken the people are none other than the very implementation and actualization of these curses.

The paradox, however, is that they have not achieved their intended effect. Israel has neither learned nor "returned," despite the plagues God has visited upon them. Over and over again, they have been severely reprimanded, yet they remain insolently and indifferently aloof, disregarding the demands of the Deity who has inflicted their affliction. Herein lies the essence of the futility of punishment.[38] God has both threatened and executed his threat for breach of the covenant obligations. The people nevertheless remain unmoved. They have become immune to all forms of punition. The strategy and tactics of chastisement and chastening have misfired. The aim of disciplinary punishment was not meant to be merely retributive and deterrent but also, and primarily, to lead to reform. Frustratingly enough (for the Deity), all past encounters have been to no avail. The only result they may have had, ironically, was to lead the people to accelerate their cultic activity. This series has been aptly and adeptly called both "ein Parodie zur Heilsgeschichte" ("a parody on salvation history")[39] (relating to Amos 2:9–10) and an "Unheilsgeschichte" ("disaster history"). As God has worked his wonders in history for Israel, so here the prophet recalls God's curses, which have wrought havoc in the realms of both nature and history. His ultimate purpose of restoring Israel, however, has not been successful.

---

order to reach the inevitable conclusion. Compare Amos 3:3–8. This is another example of Amos's employment of a heptad followed by a climactic (eighth) conclusion; cf. Amos 1—2; 3:3–8; 5:21–24.

32 These punishments need not refer merely to the immediate past. Thus there is no reason to deny their authenticity on the grounds that they do not fit the period of Jeroboam II. See Weiser, *Profetie,* 167; Sellin, 220–21. See, moreover, Vollmer, *Rückblicke,* 19: "Er ist nicht Historiker, der ein Interesse an der Geschichte als solcher hätte, sondern eher Geschichtstheologe" ("He is not a historian who had an interest in history per se, but rather a theologian of history").

33 Sufficient note has not been made of Amos's employment of the pentad. It is also to be found in Amos 7:17; 9:2–4; and the five visions of chapters 7—9. Pentads are also a familiar phenomenon in Rabbinic literature. For multiple examples, see C. Y. Kasovsky, *Thesaurus Mishnae* (4 vols.; Jerusalem: Jewish Theological Seminary of America, 1957) 2.709–10. See also the refrain in Isa 9:11, 16, 20; 10:4, in a similar context. For repetitive phrases and the employment of the typological number, seven, in the Sefire treaties, see Weinfeld, *Deuteronomy,* 125 and n 3. For other heptads in the book, see Amos 2:6–8, 14–16; 4:4–5; 5:8–9, 21–23; 9:1–4. See also Limburg, "Sevenfold," 217–22.

34 For an attempt to discern a progressive intensification in the curse plagues, see Gese, "Komposition," 85–86; Gordis, "Studies," 221.

35 See also Mays, 80–81.

36 See n 28.

37 For a chart comparing Amos with Lev 26, Deut 28, and 1 Kgs 8, see Wolff, 213.

38 See Paul, "Prophets," 1174. Compare Isa 1:5ff.; 9:12ff.; Jer 2:30; 5:3; Ezek 20.

39 See Vollmer, *Rückblicke,* 20; G. von Rad, *Theologie des Alten Testaments* (2 vols.; München: Kaiser, 1960) 2.187; J. Begrich ("Die priesterliche Torah" in *Werden und Wesen des Alten Testaments* [ed. P. Volz, F. Stummer, and J. Hempel; BZAW 66; Berlin: Töpelmann, 1936] 77; reprinted in idem, *Gesammelte Studien zum Alten Testament* [TBü 21; München:

■ 6 The first in the series of seven covenant curse plagues was famine. In the initial colon, it is figuratively described by a euphemistic hapax legomenon, "cleanness of teeth" (נִקְיוֹן שִׁנַּיִם),[40] and in the second colon by the expression "lack of food" (חֹסֶר לֶחֶם). When one has nothing to bite into or chew upon, one's teeth remain "clean." The extent of this famine covered the entire land: "all your towns" (בְּכָל־עָרֵיכֶם) and "all your settlements" (בְּכֹל מְקוֹמֹתֵיכֶם).[41]

The purpose of inflicting the famine[42] was twofold: to punish the people for breaking the covenant and to make them repent. Yet they did not "return to" God. They remained obdurate and obstinate, to the utter frustration of the Deity. The nuance of the phrase שׁוּב עַד may be a bit more intense than the usual שׁוּב אֶל,[43] in that the latter indicates direction "toward" (אֶל), in general, whereas the former signifies, in addition, the actual attainment of purpose (עַד, "unto") and is expressly limited to references to a return to God (for example, Deut 4:30; 30:2; Isa 9:12; 19:22; Hos 14:2; Joel 2:12; Job 22:23; Lam 3:40).

■ 7 The second plague was a calamitous drought. The harvest season, first barley and then wheat, takes place during the months of May and June.[44] Because the latter rains[45] were held back (מנע)[46] some three months prior to the harvest, that is, in March and April, the total yield of crops for that year failed. The results were disastrous for the entire population.

Compare the repetitive refrain of (אֲנִי) וְגַם אָנֹכִי here and in v 6 with the similar refrain אַף אָנֹכִי in the curse list of Lev 26. The recurrence of this expression is not an indication of its being secondary[47] but is rather the way Amos emphatically stresses the divine origin of the disaster.

By stating that "one town" (עִיר אֶחָת) would repeatedly be rained upon but another not,[48] Amos is further accentuating the divine source of the natural disaster, for "selective" raining is against nature. The people should

Kaiser, 1964] 247–48) termed it a "parody of a priestly Torah."

40 Some of the versions read here (שִׁנַּיִם) קִהָיוֹן ("blunting of teeth"; compare Jer 31:29–30; Ezek 18:2) instead of נִקְיוֹן; see G, *γομφιασμὸν ὀδόντων*; T, אַקְהָיוּת; S, קהיות; V, *stuporem*. α', and θ', *καθαρισμόν*, in contrast, along with the parallel colon "lack of bread," all support the Masoretic text. There is nothing to support M. D. Goldman's suggested translation, "falling out of teeth," *AusBR* 4 (1954–1955) 55. Compare another figurative expression, נִקְיוֹן כַּפַּיִם ("cleanness of hands"), Gen 20:5; Pss 26:6; 73:13.

For another description of a famine, see Amos 8:11–12.

41 Not "houses" as interpreted by M. Dahood, "Hebrew-Ugaritic Lexicography," *Bib* 48 (1967) 431.

42 For the plague of famine throughout the land, see, for example, 1 Kgs 17:1; 2 Kgs 4:38; 8:1. See also Gen 12:10; 26:1; 41:54; 2 Sam 21:1; Ruth 1:1.

Famine is also featured in Mesopotamian treaty curses with a wide variety of synonyms, including *sunqu* ("want"), *bubūtu* ("famine"), *ḫušaḫḫu* ("scarcity"), *nibrītu* ("hunger"), *dannatu* ("famine"), and *arurtu* ("famine," ensuing from a drought). See the ample documentation under the respective entries in *CAD* and *AHw*. For an analogue to Heb. חֹסֶר לֶחֶם ("lack of bread"), see *ina bubūti ša akalim lu la amât* ("May I not die for want of bread"), *ABL* 756, r. 5.

43 Because Barstad (*Religious Polemics*, 63–66) incorrectly refers the verb here to a "missionary" usage rather than a "covenantal" one, he (mis)translates, "turn to" and not "return to." For a study of שׁוּב, see W. L. Holladay, *The Root ŠÛBH in the Old Testament with Particular Reference to Its Usages in Covenantal Contexts* (Leiden: Brill, 1958). See also H. W. Wolff, "Das Thema 'Umkehr' in der alttestamentlichen Prophetie," in *Gesammelte Studien zum Alten Testament* (TBü 22; München: Kaiser, 1964) 130–52; and J. A. Soggin, "*šūb*," *THAT* (1976) 2.884–91.

44 See Dalman, *AuS*, 1.132; 3.4–6. See the Gezer Calendar, lines 4–5, ירח קצר שערם ירח קצר ("month of barley harvest, month of [wheat] harvest"), *KAI*, I.34.

45 For גֶשֶׁם as the general term for both the former and latter rains, see Joel 2:23: "He makes the rain (גֶשֶׁם) fall as formerly—the early rain (מוֹרֶה) and the late" (מַלְקוֹשׁ).

46 See Jer 3:3. The verb מנע in connection with rain appears only in these two verses. See P. Raymond, *L'eau, sa vie et sa signification dans l'Ancien Testament* (SVT 6; Leiden: Brill, 1958).

47 Against Wolff, 209. So, too, there is no need to consider the rest of the verse as a gloss due to the fact that the plague of drought is treated at such length; against Marti, 182; Fosbroke, 807; Weiser, *Profetie*, 153.

48 Heb. וְהִמְטַרְתִּי is a frequentative: "I have repeatedly made it rain." For the noun מטר, compare Ugar. *mṭr*, *UT* 1466; Aram. מטרא. It also appears as a West Semitic loanword in the Akkadian of Ras Shamra, *miṭar; MRŠ* VI, 47; RŠ 16.150:12. See also *CAD, M*, II.144.

have realized that something peculiar was occurring that could not be accounted for by the natural order.[49] So, too, when only "one field" (חֶלְקָה אַחַת) would be "rained upon" (תִּמָּטֵר) while another "on which it did not rain"[50] (אֲשֶׁר־לֹא־תַמְטִיר) "would wither" (תִּיבָשׁ).

Note that the noun עִיר appears in three consecutive verses, vv 6, 7, 8; in the latter two, it appears twice. Whereas v 6 expresses the concept of totality by the combination of עִיר-מָקוֹם, here the phrase is עִיר-חֶלְקָה. Because חֶלְקָה[51] is synonymous with שָׂדֶה ("field"), this is none other than a variant of the common merism, "city/town–field."

In Mesopotamian curse lists, drought and famine are also usually coupled together. Compare, for example, *ūmē arurti šanāti ḫušaḫḫi* ("days of drought, years of scarcity").[52] The motif of a god withholding rain to fulfill a curse is also found in Mesopotamian literature. Compare, for example, *Adad . . . zunni ina šamê liṭeršu . . . māssu ina ḫušaḫḫim u bubūtim liḫalliq* ("May Adad . . . deprive him of rain from the sky . . . [and] cause his land to perish from hunger and famine").[53] When rains are scarce, the harvest naturally fails; see, for example, *ina muḫḫi zunni ša šatti anniti imṭûni ebūru la inneppešuni* ("On account of the rains that were scarce this year, nothing can be harvested").[54]

■ **8** The drought spelled disaster not only for the farmer but for the residents in the cities and towns as well. Owing to the lack of rain, the wells and cisterns had dried up, causing people from several different towns to search for drinking water in other places—but they were unable to quench their thirst. "Two or three towns" (שְׁתַּיִם שָׁלֹשׁ עָרִים) is an example of the well-known staircase numerical parallelism. In this case 2/3 represents an indefinite small number, that is, "several."[55]

Their search for water[56] is described by the verb נוע,[57] which in several passages in the Bible appears in conjunction with both the nominal and verbal forms of שכר ("to be drunk"; Isa 24:20; 29:9; Ps 107:27). In these as well as many other verses, the correct nuance of the verb is "to reel, to stagger," describing the tipsy tottering of a drunkard.[58] Here in Amos they are portrayed as taking a zigzag course not because of drunkenness but due to dehydration, unable to find adequate water sources to slake their thirst. For the use of שבע in reference to water or the quenching of thirst, see Ps 107:9; Prov 30:16.[59]

Yet here, too, the drought, which normally would result in prayer and repentance (see Jer 14), was of no avail, for "they did not return to me."[60] Israel simply does not learn from bitter experience (see Hos 7:9).[61]

The motif of the futile searching for food is found both in biblical and extrabiblical sources. Compare Pss 59:16 (where the same verbs, נוע and שבע, both appear); 109:10; Job 15:23; and figuratively in Amos 8:11–13. In

49 Compare the plagues in Egypt that did not affect the territory of Goshen, Exod 8:18–19; 9:26; 10:23. Note the chiastic structure of this hemistich.

50 Heb. תַּמְטִיר, a third-person feminine singular, is to be understood impersonally as a neuter form. So, for example, Hammershaimb, 72; Wolff, 209; Rudolph, 170. Compare similarly, for example, נִשְׂעֲרָה ("it stormed"), Ps 50:3; תַּשְׁלֵג ("it snowed"), Ps 68:15. There is thus no need to emend to the passive, תִּמָּטֵר, as suggested by H. Graetz, *Emendationes in plerosque Sacrae Scripturae Veteris Testamenti libros*, fasc. 2 (ed. G. Bacher; Breslau: Schottlaender, 1893); or to the first-person masculine singular ("I will send rain") as reflected in G, βρέξω, and V, *plui.* The root מטר appears four times in this verse.

51 For Heb. חלק(ה) ("field"), see, for example, Gen 33:19; 2 Sam 14:30; 2 Kgs 9:10. See its cognates Akk. *eqlu* and Aram. חַקְלָא.

52 *BBSt* 4 IV 9. See also *sunqu bubūtu arurtu ḫušaḫḫu* ("want, famine, drought, scarcity"), *KAH* 1.3 r. 7. For the cognate expression "holding back of rain" in Akkadian, see *arḫu zunnu ukâl* ("[This] month will hold the rain back"), *CAD, Z,* 161–62.

53 *LH* XLII:68, 71.

54 *ABL* 1391, r. 2.

55 For studies of the staircase parallelism, see Roth, "Numerical Sequence," 300–311. For a list of studies subsequent to Roth, see Avishur, *Phoenician Inscriptions,* 1.53 n 48.

56 Their search is for a place that has cisterns and a better water supply; Marti, 183; Vollmer, *Rückblicke,* 10.

57 See Amos 8:12; 9:9.

58 See, for example, Ps 109:10; Lam 4:14. There is no reason to accept here the suggestion of O. Eissfeldt, "*NUAḤ,* sich vertragen," in idem, *Kleine Schriften zum Alten Testament* (6 vols; Tübingen: Mohr, 1966) 3.124–28, "to make an agreement."

59 See also ibn Ezra. Compare, for example, also Akk. *šebû* ("to be sated") in connection with drinking, *AHw,* 3.1207; and Aram. שבע, in Sefire, I A 21–23.

60 See Isa 9:12.

61 See S. M. Paul, "The Image of the Oven and the Cake in Hosea VII 4–10," *VT* 18 (1968) 114–20, esp.

extrabiblical records, compare the Aramaic Sefire inscription, I A:24: "May his seven daughters go looking for food, but not. . . ."[62]

The topos of the previous lines in Sefire, I A:21–23 is also lack of satiation: "[And should seven nurses] anoint [their breasts and] nurse a young boy, may he not have his fill; and should seven mares suckle a colt, may it not be sa[ted; and should seven] cows give suck to a calf, may it not have its fill; and should seven ewes suckle a lamb, [may it not be sa]ted." The Aramaic verb is also שׂבע.

All the above are part of a literary genre called "futility curses." See, for example, Lev 26:26; Deut 28:30–31, 38–40; Hos 4:10; 5:6; 9:12, 16; and Amos 5:11.[63]

An extensive list of such curses appears in the Akkadian-Aramaic bilingual statue from Tell Fekherye, lines 30–36: "May he sow but let him not reap. May he sow a thousand but get one *sūtu* in return./ May he sow a thousand measures but get one *parisu* in return. May one hundred ewes not satiate a lamb./ May one hundred ewes suckle a lamb but let it not be sated. May one hundred cows not satiate a calf./ May one hundred cows suckle a calf but let it not be sated. May one hundred mothers not satiate a child./ May one hundred women suckle a child but let it not be sated. May one hundred baking-women not fill an oven./ May one hundred women bake bread in an oven but let them not fill it."[64]

■ **9** The third scourge in this inventory was one that struck the cereal crops: blast and blight. The first of the two, שִׁדָּפוֹן, denotes a desiccation caused by the sirocco,[65] whereas the second, יֵרָקוֹן,[66] refers to the brownish yellow withering color of the grain.[67] These two blights are also coupled together in the same order in other lists of curses: Deut 28:22; 1 Kgs 8:37 (= 2 Chr 6:28); Hag 2:17.[68] Interestingly enough, in the catalogue of maledictions in Deuteronomy (Deut 28:21) the plagues of "pestilence" (דֶּבֶר) and "sword" (חֶרֶב) are listed before blast and blight (Deut 28:22), whereas in Amos the two follow in the very next verse (Amos 4:10). In 1 Kgs 8:37 (= 2 Chr 6:28), "famine" (רָעָב) and "pestilence" (דֶּבֶר) precede "blast and blight" and are followed by the attack of "locusts" (אַרְבֶּה, חָסִיל). The order is similar to Amos, in which the two plagues upon the crops are preceded by famine and then followed by "locusts" (גָּזָם). These series are all based upon traditional listings and couplings of well-known plagues.[69]

Next in line were the locusts (גָּזָם),[70] who devoured

118–19.

62 See Fitzmyer (*Sefire*, 43–44) for the problems of this line. See also Weinfeld, *Deuteronomy*, 125–26, and notes.

63 Hillers, *Treaty Curses*, 28–29.

64 For the translation here (first the Akkadian followed by the variants from the Aramaic version after the oblique stroke), see J. C. Greenfield and A. Shaffer, "Notes on the Akkadian-Aramaic Bilingual Statue from Tell Fekherye," *Iraq* 45 (1983) 113. See also their joint study, "Some Observations on the Akkadian-Aramaic Bilingual from Tell-Fekherye," *Shnaton* V–VI (1978–1979) 119–29 (Heb.). For the editio princeps, see A. Abou-Assaf, P. Bordreuil, and A. R. Millard, *La statue de Tell Fekherye et son inscription bilingue assyro-araméenne* (Études Assyrologiques 7; Paris: Editions Recherche sur les civilisations, 1982).

65 See Gen 41:6: "But close behind them sprouted seven ears of grain, thin and scorched (שְׁדוּפֹת) by the east wind."

66 For the color ירק, see A. Brenner, *Colour Terms in the Old Testament* (*JSOT* Supp. Ser. 21; Sheffield: JSOT, 1982) 150–51, 189–90; R. Gradwohl, *Die Farben im Alten Testament: Eine Terminologische Studie* (BZAW 83; Berlin: Töpelmann, 1963) 31ff. Compare Ugar. *yrq* ("gold"), *UT* 1160; and Akk. *arāqu* ("to become green or yellow, to turn pale"), *CAD, A,* II.231–32, and its derivatives. In Akkadian this word is employed in connection with the face, similar to Jer 30:6.

67 See Dalman, *AuS*, I.158, 326; II.333f. Brenner (*Colour Terms*, 257) notes that E. Hareuveni ("Studies in the Names of the Flora of Israel," *Leš* 2 [1929] 176–83 [Heb.]) suggests another relationship between these two: "Too much rain causes יֵרָקוֹן . . . while little or no rain together with drying wind causes שִׁדָּפוֹן."

68 In Deut 28:22 and Hag 2:17, the two are also introduced by the verbal stem נכה ("to strike"). The Akkadian verb *maḫāṣu* ("to hit, strike"), which is the interdialectal semantic equivalent of Heb. נכה, is also employed in the similar context of ruining a harvest. See *CAD, M,* I.77.

69 S adds here a third blight, ברדא ("hail"), similar to the series in Hag 2:17.

70 See *AuS* I.394; IV.170. For locust attacks, see, for example, Joel 1:4–7. For גָּזָם, see Joel 1:4; 2:25. For the locust *(erbu)* as a plague devouring the country's harvest in Mesopotamian sources, see the references in *CAD, E,* 257.

their gardens,[71] vineyards, and fig and olive trees, all of which, along with the grain crops just mentioned, constituted the most important agricultural products of the land. The only difficulty here is the word הַרְבּוֹת. Although many commentators tend to accept the emendation הֶחֱרַבְתִּי ("I have dried up"[72] [your gardens, etc.]), the Masoretic text is supported by many of the ancient versions.[73] If correct, this infinitive *hiphʿil* construct may be interpreted either as an adverb, "frequently, repeatedly," or as an adjective referring to the sum total of the crops, that is, your "many" gardens and the like. For the latter, see Prov 25:27: "It is not good to eat much (הַרְבּוֹת) honey."

■ **10** The next plague, pestilence (דֶּבֶר), also occurs as a traditional punishment; see, for example, Lev 26:25; Num 14:12; Deut 28:21; 2 Sam 24:15; Ezek 14:19. The verbal expression שִׁלַּח דֶּבֶר בְּ־ ("to cast/inflict/set loose a pestilence") appears in Lev 26:25; Isa 9:7 (revocalizing Hebrew דָּבָר to דֶּבֶר with G, *θάνατον*, "death"); and Ezek 28:23. Compare likewise the similar use of the Akkadian verb *nadû* ("to cast"), the interdialectal semantic equivalent of Heb. שׁלח, in lists of curses from Mesopotamia, for example, *sunqa bubūta ḫušaḫḫu mūtānu ana mātišu liddî* ("May he [Adad] inflict [literally, "cast"] hunger, famine, want, [and] pestilence on his land").[74] Akkadian *mūtānu ana (mātišu) liddî* is the exact equivalent of Heb. וְשִׁלַּח בָּ(כֶם) דֶּבֶר.

This blight was inflicted בְּדֶרֶךְ מִצְרַיִם (a phrase also found in Isa 10:24, 26), which alludes to the similar disaster that struck both the livestock (Exod 9:3–7) and the population of Egypt (Exod 9:15) during the Israelite sojourn in Egypt. Although the Masoretic text בְּדֶרֶךְ ("in the manner/way of") is supported by G, ἐν ὁδῷ ("in [the] way"), many exegetes still prefer the emended reading כְּדֶרֶךְ[75] ("like the manner of [Egypt]"). Either way the intended paronomasia between דֶּבֶר and דֶּרֶךְ still remains. For בְּדֶרֶךְ with the meaning "(in the) manner/custom of," see Gen 19:31; 31:35; 1 Kgs 16:26; Jer 10:2.

The scourge of pestilence was considered so severe that both G, *θάνατον*,[76] and V, *mortem*, translate it as "death."[77] The connection is even more poignant in Akkadian, in which the word for "epidemic, pestilence, plague" is *mūtānu*,[78] which is derived from the verb *mātu* ("to die").[79]

---

71 Heb. גַּנּוֹתֵיכֶם, plural of גַּנָּה (Isa 61:11), may also refer to "vegetable gardens" (גַּן יָרָק), Deut 11:10; 1 Kgs 21:2. Compare Akk. *gannu/gannatu* (pl.), *CAD, G*, 41; *AHw*, 1.280, "(vegetable) garden," which is probably a loanword in Neo-Babylonian from Aramaic.

72 Most commentators following Wellhausen; for example, Sellin; Tur-Sinai, *Peshuṭo*, 461; Hammershaimb, 72; Cripps, 275; Vollmer, *Rückblicke*, 11. Similarly, but preferring the *piʿel*, חֵרַבְתִּי, are van Hoonacker; van Gelderen; Rudolph, 170. This form, however, does not appear in biblical Hebrew. It should also not be overlooked that the verb חרב is never used elsewhere in connection with the desiccation of crops or produce. Ehrlich's suggestion (*Randglossen*, 5.238), followed by Cramer, to read תַּרְבּוּת, with a proposed meaning of "Ertrag" ("produce"), is forced and unattested.

73 So σ' and θ', τὸ πλῆθος; V, *multitudinem;* T, סַגְיוּת. Note, too, the use of הַרְבּוּ in v 4. G translates ἐπλεθύνατε ("you have multiplied"), reflecting Heb. הִרְבֵּיתֶם.

74 *AKA* 108 VIII 86.

75 For כְּדֶרֶךְ, see, for example, Maag, *Text;* Sellin, 223. For a discussion of whether or not Rashi had the textual reading כְּדֶרֶךְ, see S. Speier, "Had Rashi Another Vorlage in Amos 4,10 Than Is Found in the Usual Edition?" *Leš* 33 (1968–1969) 15–16 (Heb.). Nowack, 139; Marti, 183; Sievers and Guthe, *Amos*, 23; Weiser, *Profetie*, 153; Cripps, 174; Vollmer, *Rückblicke*, 11, unnecessarily delete בְּדֶרֶךְ as a dittography of דֶּבֶר. O. Procksch, *Die kleinen prophetischen Schriften vor dem Exil* (Stuttgart: Deichert [Scholl], 1910); Morgenstern, "Amos Studies IV," 318; and Fey, *Amos und Jesaja*, 92, favor the emendation כְּדֶבֶר ("like [the] plague").

76 Compare also G to Exod 5:3; 9:3, 15; Lev 26:25; Num 14:12; Deut 28:21.

77 α' translates literally λοιμόν ("plague, pestilence").

78 See *CAD, M*, I.296.

79 Compare also (possibly) Ugar. *dbr* ("death"), *CML*, 154b. In Late Babylonian there also appears a substantive *dibiru* ("a calamity"). However, this is most likely a Sumerian loanword and is not to be connected with Heb. דֶּבֶר. See *CAD, D*, 134–35. Thus the reference in *KB*, 203, is misleading.

This plague is followed in turn by the one of "sword" (חֶרֶב),[80] that is, war. For the sequence of these two in other catalogues of punishments, see Lev 26:25; Ezek 5:17; 14:16–19.

In the course of a disastrous military carnage, the elite troops (בַּחוּרִים)[81] were put to death by the sword[82] "together with your captured horses" (עִם שְׁבִי סוּסֵיכֶם). Because the root שׁבה almost always refers to human beings, Heb. שְׁבִי is often emended to צְבִי ("beauty, pomp")[83] of the horses. However, despite the difficulty of the proposed emendation—not only graphically but also contextually, for this adjective never appears in connection with a description of animals—there actually is one passage where the root שׁבה is employed in relation with animals: "If a man gives to his neighbor an ass, or a sheep, or any beast, to keep and it dies or is injured or is captured (נִשְׁבָּה) . . ." (Exod 22:9). The emendation is therefore unwarranted. As to his purport, could the prophet be alluding to the worthlessness of human life, which was "on the same par as" (עִם)[84] captured horses,[85] and thus similarly and summarily dispatched? For the sequence of חֶרֶב and שְׁבִי (referring, however, to humans), see, for example, Ezra 9:7; Dan 11:33.

The next execration that was executed may be interpreted in two different ways. If one follows the Masoretic pointing, בְּאשׁ is a substantive, derived from the root באשׁ, meaning "stench":[86] "I have made the stench of מַחֲנֵיכֶם rise in your very nostrils." מַחֲנֶה in this context would refer to the "army"[87] (see, for example, Deut 23:10; Josh 8:13; 10:5; 11:4; Judg 4:15, 16; 7:1, 8–11; 8:10–12; 1 Sam 17:46; 1 Kgs 22:36; 2 Kgs 3:9; Joel 2:11), whose corpses, lying unburied in the fields, foul the air with their rancid smell.[88] Compare Isa 34:3, "Their slain shall be cast out, and the stench of their carcasses shall rise up" (יַעֲלֶה בָאְשָׁם). The idiom עלה באשׁ is also found in Joel 2:20.

However, in light of G, ἐν πυρὶ ("in fire"), many exegetes favor revocalizing the word to בָּאֵשׁ: "I shall make מַחֲנֵיכֶם go up in fire unto your very nostrils."[89] The reference then would be to the smoke of the burning camps (מַחֲנֶה) that entered one's nostrils.[90]

Despite this calamitous martial catastrophe, they still did not return to the Lord.

■ **11** The most dire and disastrous of all the plagues was the seventh and last one: a major earthquake comparable in proportion to that which destroyed the proverbial

80 There is no reason to delete this plague as being a case of dittography; against Rudolph, 171. For דֶּבֶר and חֶרֶב, see Fey, "Amos und Jesaja," 93. For the recurring motif of חֶרֶב, רָעָב, and דֶּבֶר, see Y. Avishur, "Breakup of Stereotype Phrases as a Literary Stylistic Pattern in Biblical Poetry," in *Studies in Rabbinic Literature, Bible, and the History of Israel, Dedicated to Prof. E. Z. Melamed* (ed. Y. D. Gilat and others; Ramat Gan: Bar-Ilan University, 1982) 37–38 (Heb.).

81 See 1 Sam 9:2; Isa 9:16. Compare also Mari Akkadian, *bēru* B ("elite troops"), *CAD, B,* 211–12. See Sasson, *Military Establishments,* 22–24 nn 63–64.

82 There is no reason to delete this stich or to view it as a gloss; against Nowack, 139; Marti, 183; Sievers and Guthe, *Amos,* 37; Vollmer, *Rückblicke,* 11; Amsler. Compare Jer 11:22.

83 Ever since H. Zeijdner, "Bijdragen tot de Tekstkritiek op het O. T.," *ThSt* 4 (1886) 196–204; idem, *ThSt* 6 (1888) 247ff., followed by Sellin, 223; Robinson-Horst, 86; Maag, *Text,* 21f.; Amsler, 198. Ehrlich (*Randglossen,* 5.239) emends to טֹבִי ("the best of" [the horses]). (In his earlier Hebrew commentary, p. 458, he maintains the Masoretic reading.) There is also no reason to regard this stich as a later addition; against, for example, Harper, 100; Procksch, 75; Cripps, 174; Fosbroke, 807.

84 For the meaning of עִם ("on a par with"), see S. M. Paul, "Psalm 72:5—A Traditional Blessing for the Long Life of the King," *JNES* 31 (1972) 351–52, and accompanying notes. See Ehrlich, *Mikrâ,* 3.408.

85 For an example of horses taken as booty in Assyrian sources, see H. Winckler, *Die Keilschrifttexte Sargons* (Leipzig: Pfeiffer, 1889), pl. 32, 68:12, *sisû la mīnam* ("horses without number"). See *CAD, S,* 332, for additional examples.

86 See the Akkadian cognate *bu'šu* ("stench"); *CAD, B,* 352–53.

87 See *BDB,* 334, 2c; *KB,* 540:3. See similarly Akk. *karašu,* which means both "camp" and "army"; *CAD, K,* 210–12. So, too, מחנתה in the Aramaic Zakir inscription, line 5: ברהדד ומחנתה וברגש ומחנתה ("Barhadad and his army, Bargush and his army"), followed by the names of several other kings and their "armies"; *KAI,* I.37, text 202.

88 For the image, compare the following Late Babylonian passage: *Adad ina māti ikkalma mātu pūssu uṣṣan* ("Adad will wreak havoc in the country, till the whole surface of the country stinks [with the dead]"), *CT* 39,14:18. The Akk. verb here is *eṣēnu* / *uṣṣunu* ("to smell bad"); *CAD, E,* 344–45.

89 For example, van Hoonacker; Sellin; Cripps, 175.

90 According to both interpretations, however, the *waw* in וּבְאַפְּכֶם remains problematic. Many simply delete it

twin cities of evil, Sodom and Gomorrah. The root הפך, which also appears in that narrative (Gen 19:25, 29), signifies a radical change[91] and is frequently employed to describe an immediate and complete upheaval and annihilation. The point of comparison between the tale in Genesis and the verse here is the suddenness and thoroughness of the destruction.[92] The description of the disaster is further intensified by adding to the infinitival construct מַהְפֵּכַת[93] the name of the Deity, אֱלֹהִים (see Isa 13:19), which here, as in other passages, expresses not only the source of the catastrophe but also its incomparable enormity and immensity.[94]

Throughout the Bible are comparable descriptions of the punishment of various lands and cities in an analogous way, that is, just as Sodom and Gomorrah were overturned. The expression became paradigmatic for the completeness of the destruction.[95] Compare, for example, for Israel, Deut 29:22; (Isa 1:9); 13:19; Edom, Jer 20:16; 49:18; Babylon, Jer 50:40; Hos 11:8; Moab and Ammon, Zeph 2:9. This is the only incident from patriarchal times that is referred to so frequently in later sources. Because some of these later passages occur in the context of the violation of treaty agreements,[96] one "may legitimately assume that the overthrow of Sodom and Gomorrah was conceived as the classic punishment of the breach of covenant with the Deity, and the Deity was conceived as employing the conventional means of punishing treaty violators (i.e., by destroying the land with brimstone and salt . . .)."[97]

Continuing his analogy of an earthquake accompanied by the eruption of a conflagration[98] (drawn from Gen 19), Amos compares the survivors to a "brand (אוּד)[99] plucked from the burning," thereby indicating that they were severely scorched and were rescued only at the very last moment.[100] The prophet again resorts to one of his recurrent themes, destruction by fire. For a similar image, see Zech 3:2. Even this disaster, however, did not have a sobering effect, for they remained unmoved and did not return to the Lord.

■ **12** The prophet reaches the climax[101] of his *catalogus calamitatum*[102] with a culminating catastrophe, which resounds even the more intimidating and terrifying because of its indefinite and unspecified nature.[103] This is another example of how Amos heightens the awesome

with the versions. Others view it as either an emphatic or explanative particle. See *GKC*, 154a (n 1b). See also Gordon, *UT* 101 n 1, drawing an analogy from Ugaritic. Tur-Sinai, *Peshuṭo*, 462, emends to בְּאַגַּפֵּיכֶם ("your troops"). Rudolph, 171, rejects A. Weiser's suggestion ("Zu Amos 4:6–13," *ZAW* 46 [1928] 56) to accept G manuscripts' reading ἐν τῇ ὀργῇ μου ("in my anger" = בְּאַפִּי), placing the word at the beginning of the next verse.

Whichever pointing is favored can be directly related to a similar theme in the immediate context. If בְּאֵשׁ, then compare שְׂרֵפָה ("conflagration"), v 11; if בָּאשׁ, compare the plague of pestilence, דָּבֶר, in this very same verse.

91 See Greenfield, "Stylistic Aspects," 11; idem, "The Background and Parallel to a Proverb of Ahiqar," in *Hommages à André Dupont-Sommer* (ed. A. Dupont-Sommer and M. Philonenko; Paris: Adrien-Maisonneuve, 1971) 51–52. Compare Akk. *abāku*, B ("to turn upside down"), *ubbuku* ("to overturn"), *CAD, A*, I.9, and *abiktu* ("decisive defeat, massacre, carnage") *CAD, A*, I.52. For example, "The king (variant, "the gods") will overthrow all the countries in a decisive defeat"; R. C. Thompson, *The Reports of the Magicians and Astrologers of Nineveh and Babylon* (2 vols.; Luzac's Semitic Text and Translation Series 6 & 7; London: Luzac, 1900) 270:8.

For the root הפך in Amos, see also 5:7, 8; 6:12; 8:10.

92 That the destruction was not absolutely total is indicated by the use of the partitive בָּכֶם. The prophet is not referring to the destruction of northern Israel; against Wolff, 222.

93 See *GKC*, 115d.

94 For the intensive, superlative use of the name of the Deity, see, for example, 1 Sam 14:15. For examples, see *BDB*, 43, 2; *KB*, 52e.

95 See Hillers (*Treaty Curses*, 74–76), who calls this image a "parade example for sudden destruction," p. 75.

96 See also the use of Aram. הפך in Sefire, I C 19–24.

97 Weinfeld, *Deuteronomy*, 111. See Deut 29:22.

98 See Hammershaimb, 73.

99 In Isa 7:4 the imagery of an אוד (in the plural) is employed to express contempt.

100 Compare the similar motif of a remnant (but with different imagery) in Amos 3:12; 5:3.

101 The use of לָכֵן to introduce a dramatic climax is also found in Amos 5:11, 13; 6:7.

102 Rudolph, 180. According to Weiser (*Profetie*, 54), the oracle may have been intentionally patterned after the cultic procedure of reciting the saving deeds of the Lord, but in reverse.

103 See Weiser, *Profetie*, 57; Procksch; Harper, 103;

suspense of his audience by alluding to some enigmatic horror yet to come.[104]

The verse, however, abounds in difficulties, both textual and contextual.[105] The reduplication of two phrases, both of which end with the same two words, אֶעֱשֶׂה־לְּךָ ("I am about to do to you"), has raised doubts about the nature of this passage. Some exegetes assume that it indicates a doublet or conflation[106] of two variant readings: לָכֵן כֹּה אֶעֱשֶׂה־לְּךָ יִשְׂרָאֵל and עֵקֶב כִּי־זֹאת אֶעֱשֶׂה־לָּךְ. (There are those, too, who incorrectly assume that the entire verse is not original. However, this would totally undermine the thrust of the prophet's message, for all that would remain would be a list of curses fulfilled in the past without any indication of what the future harbors for the people of Israel.) Others suggest that the original text was either[107] עֵקֶב כִּי[108] זֹאת עָשִׂיתָ לָכֵן כֹּה אֶעֱשֶׂה־לְּךָ יִשְׂרָאֵל, or[109] לָכֵן כֹּה אֶעֱשֶׂה־לְּךָ יִשְׂרָאֵל עֵקֶב כִּי־זֹאת עָשִׂיתָ (תַּעֲשֶׂה).[110]

Nevertheless, the text may very possibly be perfectly in order, and the correct interpretation of the reduplication can perhaps be understood only by envisioning that the prophetic threat "von irgendeiner drohenden Gebärde begleitet wurde"[111] ("was accompanied by some kind of a threatening gesture"). Such a threatening hand movement does not necessarily imply that the prophet was pointing to any specific object in the vicinity (for example, the sanctuary).[112] It may merely be a symbolic and very dramatic gesture whereby Amos wished to reinforce the impression of the finality of his predicted punishment.

The expression כֹּה אֶעֱשֶׂה־לְּךָ ("this is what I will do to you") reminds one of the beginning of the classical oath-curse formula: כֹּה יַעֲשֶׂה־לִּי אֱלֹהִים ("So may God do to me . . ."; for example, 1 Kgs 2:23), where the demonstrative adverb כֹּה refers to an empirical demonstration (for example, Gen 15:5; and the use of כָּכָה, for example, Deut 25:9; Josh 10:25).[113] Compare especially the ceremony described in 1 Sam 11:7. The phrase here is apparently an apocopated form of this threatening curse formula.[114]

With the change of address from the plural (in the preceding verses) to the singular, the impending chastisement is now addressed individually to each member of the nation. Because Israel has not "returned" to the Lord,[115] that is, has not mended its ways and has not taken the necessary steps toward a reconciliation, Amos

Amsler, 201; Cripps, 175; Robinson-Horst, 87; Driver, 176; Vollmer, *Rückblicke*, 13. There is no reason to assume that the original words of the prophet were lost; against Nowack, 140; Harper, 102.

104 See Ehrlich, *Mikrâ*, 3.409; Rudolph, 181. Compare the comments on לֹא אֲשִׁיבֶנּוּ, Amos 1:3.

105 Many commentators delete one or the other of these two stichs. For example, Oort, "Amos," 117; Elhorst; Wellhausen, 80; Marti, 180, 184–85; Nowack, 140; Robinson-Horst, 87; Nötscher; Harper, 102–3; Duhm, "Anmerkungen," 7; Vollmer, *Rückblicke*, 12. See B. J. Weingreen, "Rabbinic-Type Glosses in the Old Testament," *JSS* 19 (1957) 159. Baumann (*Der Aufbau*, 15) suggests that Amos 5:21–27 is the conclusion of Amos 4:12a. This, of course, is totally unfounded.

106 See S. Oettli, "Amos und Hosea. Zwei Zeugen gegen die Anwendung der Evolutionstheorie auf die Religions Israels," BFCT 5/4 (Gütersloh: Bertelsman, 1901); Tur-Sinai, *Peshuṭo*, 462; Gordis, "Studies," 222–23.

107 Oettli, "Amos und Hosea"; Budde, "Amos."

108 The phrase עֵקֶב כִּי appears only one other time, 2 Sam 12:10. For the variant עֵקֶב אֲשֶׁר, see Gen 22:18; 26:5; 2 Sam 12:6.

109 Sellin²; Morgenstern, "Amos Studies IV," 318.

110 Instead of כֹּה, some read כָּלָה ("destruction"), that is, "I will destroy you, Israel." So Rudolph, "Gott und Mensch bei Amos: Anmerkungen zu Weiser's *Amosbuch*," in *Imago Dei: Beiträge zur theologischen Anthropologie: Gustav Krüger zum siebzigsten Geburtstag* (ed. H. Bornkamm; Giessen: Töpelmann, 1932) 31 n 3 (who subsequently changed his mind; see Rudolph, 171).

111 Ehrlich, *Mikrâ*, 3.409; idem, *Randglossen*, 5.239. See Cramer, 43, 90–95; Hammershaimb, 74.

112 Wolff, 222. The clause, contrary to Wolff, does not refer to Josiah's action at Bethel.

113 See M. R. Lehmann, "Biblical Oaths," *ZAW* 81 (1969) 74–79, esp. 81–82; Cripps, 175; Harper, 103. For the syntactical structure of oaths and vows, see M. Z. Segal, ("On the Structure of Oaths and Vows in Hebrew," *Leš* 1 [1928–1929] 215–27 [Heb.]); for a variant, see Jer 5:13: "The prophets shall prove mere wind, for the Word is not in them. Thus-and-thus shall be done to them!" (כֹּה יֵעָשֶׂה לָהֶם).

114 See the introduction to the long lists of curses in Lev 26:16: אַף־אֲנִי אֶעֱשֶׂה־זֹּאת לָכֶם ("I in turn will do this to you . . .").

115 Note the use of both אֱלֹהֶיךָ ("your God") and יִשְׂרָאֵל ("Israel")—echoes of the covenantal formula. The combination of אֱלֹהֶיךָ יִשְׂרָאֵל, in which יִשְׂרָאֵל serves as a vocative, is also found in another context in Exod 32:4; 1 Kgs 12:28—in connection with the golden calf.

now declares that the Lord himself shall take matters into his own hands. Israel repeatedly has had opportunities to learn from its past calamities. The curses were inflicted not merely to punish them, not merely to exact retribution for their immoral ways, but also to goad them on to final repentance. Because they refused to take the past lessons to heart, they no longer will be plagued by an additional warning. God's patience has worn thin. Frustrated over and over again, the Deity declares that the final hour of reckoning is at hand. The opportunity to repent has passed. For another dramatic example of such an abrogation of repentance, compare the series of plagues executed upon Pharaoh in Exodus. Because he, too, did not take the successive punishments to heart and did not relent, but instead consistently "hardened his own heart," the hour eventually came when the Lord no longer offered him the opportunity to repent. As measure for measure, God "hardened Pharaoh's heart."[116]

This menacing warning of forthcoming punishment is coupled with another of the prophet's favorite literary devices.[117] The catalogue of past calamities is composed of seven plagues: (1) famine (v 6); (2) drought (vv 7–8); (3) agricultural blights (v 9a); (4) locusts (v 9b); (5) pestilence (v 10a); (6) sword, that is, military defeat (v 10b); and (7) earthquake (v 11). The last one, the seventh, was so disastrous that it was compared to the overturn of Sodom and Gomorrah; only a sparse remnant remained alive. Because finality and completeness is usually expressed by the number seven, the people could very well conclude that with the seventh curse, the most all-encompassing, Israel had finally witnessed the end of its multiple hardships. At this very dramatic junction, Amos once again employs his unexpected ploy of adding an eighth pronouncement to climax the former seven.[118] Moreover, this eighth and crowning catastrophe is to be executed not by one of the "agents" of the Lord, that is, by one of his many plagues, but by Yahweh himself!

Thus comes the terrifying exhortative, "Prepare to meet your God, O Israel!" Clearly the prophet is not making an ultimate call to repentance, nor is he inviting Israel by means of a liturgical formula to a covenant renewal ceremony.[119] The imperative הִכּוֹן, which appears elsewhere only in Ezek 38:7, represents a summons to a final battle. Whereas in the Ezekiel passage

116 This dramatic change takes place after the fourth plague, Exod 10:1; as contrasted to Exod 8:11, 28; 9:7, 35. This was already seen by Maimonides in his *Laws of Repentance* 6:3. See also Kaufmann's comments in *Toledoth,* 1.451–55, on Isa 6:9–10.

117 Compare also the conclusion of the fivefold אִם ("if")—lack of escape clauses, which also ends with a summary finale, Amos 9:4b.

118 See Paul, "Literary Reinvestigation," 196–97, relating to the oracles against the nations, Judah, and Israel in Amos 1—2.

119 This is the classical Jewish interpretation. See, for example, Kimchi (but not accepted by ibn Ezra). See also Harper, 103–4; J. D. W. Watts, *Vision and Prophecy in Amos* (Leiden: Brill, 1958) 52ff. Those who interpret the passage as a call to repentance usually rely on G, τοῦ ἐπικαλεῖσθαι ("to call upon"), reflecting לִקְרֹא אֶת, instead of the Masoretic לִקְרַאת. So, too, S. This suggestion has been presented anew in great detail by W. Brueggemann ("Amos 4:4–13 and Israel's Covenant Worship," *VT* 15 [1965] 1–15), who interprets הִכּוֹן and לִקְרַאת in the light of the Sinai covenant tradition reflected in Exodus 19 and 34 (already suggested in passing by Marti; Cripps; Nowack; F. Horst, "Die Doxologien im Amosbuch," *ZAW* 47 (1929) 53 n 3, reprinted in idem, *Gottes Recht: Studien zum Recht im Alten Testament* (ed. H. W. Wolff; TBü 12; München: Kaiser, 1961) 155–66. This is a "liturgic formula of preparation for covenant-making or renewal which includes both threat and call to repentance. . . . The climax of the curse recital is not destruction, but an invitation to Israel that she may repent . . . and thereby confront the God of Sinai and remake the covenant which she has dissolved by disobedience" (p. 2). Brueggemann, however, did not interpret correctly either the intention of the prophet or the series of executed curses. Because Israel has constantly not learned from its past, the Lord will now take matters into his own hands and prepare the final judgment day.

All the chapters in Amos (except the last one) end on a threat of exile or destruction and not on a call to repentance. The doxologies, furthermore, follow directly upon verses describing the forthcoming punishment of Israel. Thus a call to repentance simply does not fit into the structure of Amos's literary unit here. For the relationship between this unit and this doxology, see Watts, *Vision,* esp. 52–53; idem, "An Old Hymn Preserved in the Book of Amos," *JNES* 15 (1956) 33–39; Horst, "Doxologien," 45, 48; Maag, *Text,* 25; Reventlow, *Amt,* 77.

Note should also be made of the study by W. E. Staples, "Epic Motifs in Amos," *JNES* 25 (1966) 106–12. He makes the interesting suggestion that there is

Gog is summoned to be an agent of the Lord, here Israel is to "prepare itself" for the final blow to be delivered directly by the Lord himself. Judgment day is near at hand; the terminal encounter is imminent. Because all the other agents of divine punishment proved ineffectual, Israel[120] must now confront its God verily in person![121]

Excursus: The Doxologies in the Book of Amos

■ **13** Amos concludes his threat of an imminent, awesome, final confrontation with the Deity by a doxology. It is the first of three short doxologies (4:13; 5:8–9; 9:5–6), all of which have been subject to multiple investigations. The problems as to whether these three are original or secondary, whether they once comprised one hymn that was subsequently divided into three or were originally three independent short hymns, and what their ultimate *Sitz im Leben* was have engaged the minds of all those who have written extensively on the Book of Amos. As the following brief survey demonstrates, scholarly disagreement still abounds.

In general, doubt is cast upon the authenticity of the doxologies primarily on the basis that they supposedly interrupt the context in which they are found. They are also said to contain an elevated theology, assumed to be the product of the exilic or postexilic period, and are purportedly characterized by late Hebrew.[122]

There is also very little agreement as to their "life setting." Sellin attributed them to a postexilic editor who added them as a polemic against the alleged idolatrous cult practiced at Bethe!.[123] Wolff also interpreted Amos 4:6–13 as a struggle against a syncretistic cult at Bethel, but he assumed it to have taken place during the period of Josiah.[124] He, in turn, accepted the hypothesis advanced by Horst[125] and Crenshaw,[126] who characterized them as a "doxology of judgment." Crenshaw related them to the oath as part of sacred law and suggested that the prophetic *rib*-lawsuit provided the best background for an understanding of these hymns: "In a time when the destruction of the Temple and the subsequent Babylonian exile seemed to indicate Yahweh's impotence, the doxologies were an expression of faith in Yahweh."[127]

Many other suggestions have been brought forward in an attempt to unravel these doxologies. Guthe proposed that they originally served as conclusions to the collections of the prophet's oracles, comparing a similar literary phenomenon present in the Book of Psalms.[128] Weiser assumed that they were inserted to

---

an archetypal literary pattern for destruction. The ultimate catastrophe is preceded by a series of disasters that ultimately are of no avail. There then follows the final calamity, from which a remnant usually remains. He brings as a comparison the plagues preceding the deluge in the Atrahasis myth. See already H. Gressmann (*Der Ursprung der israelitisch-jüdischen Eschatologie* [FRLANT 6; Göttingen: Vandenhoeck & Ruprecht, 1905] 169ff.), who mentions a preprophetic scheme that "das verschiedene Plagen chronologisch aneinanderreihte, bis die Katastrophe eintritt" ("arranges the different plagues chronologically one after the other, until the catastrophe takes place"). He lists as examples Isa 5:25–30; 9:7—10:4; the plagues in Egypt; and Babylonian parallels.

For other studies of the verse, see G. W. Ramsey ("Amos IV: 12. A New Perspective," *JBL* 89 [1970] 187–91), who incorrectly interprets אֱלֹהֶיךָ as a plural, "your gods"; and R. Youngblood ("לקראת in Amos 4:12," *JBL* 90 [1971] 98), who accepts Ramsey's "Prepare to call your 'gods,' O Israel!" but reads לִקְרֹא אֶת. His suggested "gods" is totally out of place in this context.

120 "Israel" is twice repeated for emphasis in this verse.

121 Applying the title of the article of Amsler ("Amos, prophète de la onzième heure," 318–28), it appears that the clock now seems to be striking the very last minute before midnight!

122 The first to question their authenticity was B. Duhm, *Die Theologie der Propheten als Grundlage für die innere Entwicklungsgeschichte der israelitischen Religion* (Bonn: Marcus, 1875) 119. See also Horst, "Doxologien," 45–54. For the various criteria to determine lateness and a thorough investigation of the doxologies, see J. L. Crenshaw, *Hymnic Affirmation of Divine Justice: The Doxologies of Amos and Related Texts in the Old Testament* (SBLDS 24; Missoula, MT: Scholars, 1975).

123 Sellin, 193.

124 Wolff, 215–17, 224.

125 Horst, "Doxologien," 165–66.

126 Crenshaw, *Hymnic Affirmation,* 121ff.

127 Ibid., 143. Rudolph, 200, who accepts the authenticity of the first and third hymns, objects to Crenshaw's postexilic dating. See, in turn, Crenshaw's rejoinder, *Hymnic Affirmation,* 154. See, in addition, G. von Rad, "Gerichtsdoxologie," in *Schalom: Studien zu Glaube und Geschichte Israels. Alfred Jepsen zum 71. Geburtstag dargebracht von Freunden Schülern und Kollegen* (Arbeiten zur Theologie 1/46; ed. K.-H. Bernhardt; Stuttgart: Calwer Verlag, 1971) 28–37; reprinted in idem, *Gesammelte Studien zum Alten Testament* (TBü 48; München: Kaiser, 1973) 2.245–54.

close sections read as part of the liturgy to demonstrate the way humans submitted to divine judgment.[129] According to Budde, they were employed to fill in for lost speeches of Amos.[130] Frost suggested that they were "asseverations of thanksgiving."[131] Watts conjectured that these verses reflected themes from an autumn new year festival and interpreted them as a ritual polemic sung by a choir against Baal worship.[132] Gaster proposed that they constituted an ancient hymn to Yahweh of Hosts and that they were probably remnants of earlier literature.[133] Their relationship to the "participial hymn" was stressed by Gunkel[134] and Crüsemann.[135] The wisdom dimension of the doxologies as well as an underlying theophanic tradition was advanced by Crenshaw.[136] Brueggemann, by contrast, understood the hymn to be "a doxology on creation to motivate repentance and covenant renewal."[137]

Although the doxologies are usually assumed to be later additions, many scholars nevertheless favor an early dating, and some even attribute the hymns to Amos himself.[138] The following comments to individual verses attempt to demonstrate that the first and third of these hymns are related to their respective contexts and that therefore there is no need to assume that they are later interpolations. (For the problem of the exact position of the second hymn, see the comments to Amos 5:8–9.) The present doxology, Amos 4:13, styled in participial fashion, follows naturally upon the previous verses by emphasizing the power and might of the omnipotent God of creation whom Israel is about to confront in final judgment.

■ **13** The doxology begins[139] by extolling the acts of God in creation. For the sequence of the same three participial verbs for "creation" (יוֹצֵר,[140] בֹּרֵא,[141] עֹשֵׂה) in

128 H. Guthe, *Der Prophet Amos* (ed. E. Kautzsch and A. Bertholet; HSAT 2/4; Tübingen: Mohr, 1923) 37.

129 Weiser, *Profetie,* 156–57, 164, 181. See also S. Jozaki, "The Secondary Passages of the Book of Amos," in Kwansei Gakuin University Annual Studies 4 (Nishinomiya: Kwansei Gakuin University, 1956) 25–100, esp. 26.

130 Budde, "Amos," 106.

131 S. B. Frost, "Asseverations by Thanksgiving," *VT* 8 (1958) 380–90.

132 Watts, "Old Hymn," 33–39; idem, *Vision,* 51–67.

133 T. H. Gaster, "An Ancient Hymn in the Prophecies of Amos," *Journal of the Manchester University Egyptian and Oriental Society* 19 (1935) 23–26.

134 H. Gunkel, *Einleitung in die Psalmen. Die Gattungen der religiösen Lyrik Israels* (Göttingen: Vandenhoeck & Ruprecht, 1953) 44ff.

135 Crüsemann, *Studien,* 95, 102–6. He interprets the doxologies as an independent hymn, probably of northern provenance, that was added by a redactor prior to the exile. On pp. 136–50, 223–24, he adds suggested analogues to extrabiblical literature.

136 Crenshaw, "Influence," 41–52, esp. 49–50; idem, "Amos and the Theophanic Tradition," *ZAW* 80 (1968) 203–15. See also J. Jeremias, *Theophanie: Die Geschichte einer alttestamentlichen Gattung* (WMANT 10; Neukirchen-Vluyn: Neukirchener Verlag, 1965). For the wisdom genre, see W. Zimmerli, "Ort und Grenze der Weisheit im Rahmen der alttestamentlichen Theologie," in idem, *Gottes Offenbarung: Gesammelte Aufsätze zum Alten Testament* (TBü 19; München: Kaiser, 1963) 300–315; Terrien, "Amos and Wisdom," 454; Wolff, 215–17.

137 Brueggemann, "Amos 4:4–13," 11. For yet other interpretations, see W. Berg, *Die sogenannten Hymnenfragmente im Amosbuch* (Europäische Hochschulschriften 23/45; Bern and Frankfurt: M. Lang, 1974); K. Koch, "Die Rolle der hymnischen Abschnitte in der Komposition des Amos-Buche," *ZAW* 86 (1974) 504–37; P. Carny ("Amos 4:13—A Doxology?" in *HaZvi Yisrael: Studies in Bible Dedicated to the Memory of Israel and Zvi Brodie,* [ed. J. Licht and G. Brin; Tel Aviv: Tel Aviv University, 1976] 143–50 [Heb.]), who considers this verse as a dire threat to Israel, emphasizing God's destructive activities.

138 See Cramer, 92: "I am of the opinion that we may have genuine material of Amos in the doxologies." He suggests that they were among the most important parts of Amos's message, which were sung by the prophet (p. 93). See Maag, *Text,* 24f., 56–58; Watts, "Old Hymn," 33–39; van Hoonacker, 240, 279; Robinson-Horst, 87, 89–90, 105–6; Botterweck, "Authentizität," 186; Haran, "Amos," *EM* 6.278 (Heb.); Hammershaimb, 74, 133; Rudolph, 181–83. See also R. Vuilleumier-Bessard, *La tradition cultuelle d'Israël dans la prophétie d'Amos et d'Osée* (Cahiers Théologiques 45; Neuchâtel and Paris: Delachaux & Niestlé, 1960) 88–90.

139 Heb. כִּי is used as a "linking device"; see Wolff, 215.

140 For a study of the verb יצר ("to form"), denoting the plastic shaping of a craftsman, see P. Humbert, "Emploi et portée bibliques du verbe *yāṣar* et de ses dérivés substantifs," in *Von Ugarit nach Qumran: Beiträge zur Alttestamentlichen und Altorientalischen Forschung* (ed. J. Hempel and L. Rost; BZAW 77; Berlin: Töpelmann, 1958) 82–88. For the use of participles in the doxologies, see F. Foresti, "Funzione Semantica dei brani participiali di Amos: 4:13, 5:8s., 9:5s.," *Bib* 62 (1981) 169–84.

141 For a study of the verb ברא, which connotes an extraordinary divine creation, see P. Humbert, "Emploi et portée du verbe *bārā* (créer) dans l'Ancien

another doxology (with distinct polemical overtones), see Isa 45:7 (compare also the triad of verbs in another order in Isa 43:7; 45:18). These very same verbs, which are found in the two independent accounts of cosmogony in Gen 1—3,[142] represent the comprehensive creative powers of the Lord.[143]

Because the creation of "mountains" (הָרִים) and "wind" (רוּחַ)[144] does not refer to parallel natural phenomena, some scholars[145] favor G's translation of the first phrase (ἐγὼ στερεῶν) βροντήν = הָרַעַם (יוֹצֵר): "(It is) I who creates the thunder. . . ." Although "thunder" and "wind" appear to be a complementary pair, and the assumed loss of the ע in הָרַעַם (which allegedly caused the remaining letters הרם to be read הָרִם) may be attributed to an aural error, all other ancient versions substantiate the Masoretic Hebrew text. Furthermore, nowhere else is the creation of thunder cited as one of the marvels of God's creations. Moreover, note also that "thunder" and "wind" never occur coupled together in the Bible. There is thus no need to correct the text, which is highlighting various aspects of the cosmic power of the Creator.[146] For the mention of mountains as part of God's creative activities, compare, for example, Isa 40:12; Ps 65:7; Prov 8:25.[147] Rudolph's comment here provides further insight into the choice of these two elements of nature: "Wenn Jahwe der Schöpfer der Berge und des Windes ist, so ist damit das Festeste und das Beweglichste, zugleich das Nichtzuübersehende und das Niesichtbare nebeneinandergestellt. Die Zusammenfügung von Gegensätzen drückt aber immer die Totalität aus . . ., somit bezeichnen die beiden ersten Partizipialsätze Jahwe also den Schöpfer des Alls." ("If Yahweh is the creator of the mountains and the wind, namely, the most stable and the most moveable, then at the same time are juxtaposed that which cannot be overlooked and that which is invisible. The combination of opposites, however, always expresses the totality. . . . Thus the first two participial phrases denote Yahweh as the creator of everything.")[148]

The next clause still defies a satisfactory explanation because of the enigmatic hapax legomenon שֵׂחוֹ. The Masoretic text is reflected in almost all of the ancient versions: α', τίς ἡ ὁμιλία αὐτοῦ ("what his instruction [is]"); σ', τὸ φώνημα αὐτοῦ ("his utterance"); θ', τὸν λόγον αὐτοῦ ("his word"); V, *eloquium suum* ("his expression of thought"). Thus most commentators interpret this substantive as a by-form of Heb. שִׂיחַ (compare 1 Kgs 18:27; 2 Kgs 9:11; Pss 55:3; 64:2; 104:34; Prov 23:29) and translate "And he tells man what his wish/thoughts/plans are."[149] (The problem would still remain, however, as to whom the pronominal suffix "his" refers—to man or to God.) G translates τὸν χριστὸν αὐτοῦ ("his anointed one") by reading the exact same letters (מה שחו) but rendering them as one word, not two: מְ(ה)שִׂחוֹ. T, by contrast, explicates that the creation of the mountains

Testament," *TZ* 3 (1947) 401–22; reprinted in idem, *Opuscules d'un Hébraïsant* (Neuchâtel: Secrétariat de l'Université, 1958) 146–65.

142 See W. H. Schmidt, *Die Schöpfungsgeschichte der Priesterschaft* (WMANT 17; Neukirchen-Vluyn: Neukirchener Verlag, 1967) 164–67, 200.

143 This, of course, does not mean that the terminus ברא (or its ideology) is late. See H. Gunkel, *Genesis* (Göttingen: Vandenhoeck & Ruprecht, 1969) 102: "Die uns bekannte alttestamentliche Literatur ist viel zu dürftig, als dass auf das mehr oder minder zufällige Vorkommen oder Nichtvorkommen eines solchen Ausdrucks allzuviel zu bauen wäre" ("The Old Testament literature known to us is all too scanty to build so much on the more or less accidental presence or absence of such an expression"). See Humbert, "Verbe *bārā*," 404, 416.

Both of the above are cited favorably by Rudolph, 182 n 23.

144 In the present context of creative cosmic activities, רוּחַ refers to "wind" and not to "breath" (G, πνεῦμα); against Wolff, 223.

For רוּחַ ("wind") in the creation account of P (Gen 1:2), see K. Galling, "Der Charakter der Chaosschilderung in Gen 1:2," *ZTK* 47 (1950) 154; H. M. Orlinsky, "The Plain Meaning of *Ruaḥ* in Gen 1:2," *JQR* 58 (1957) 174–82.

145 For example, Nowack, 141; Driver, 177.

146 Note that each of the four words—יוצר, הרים, ברא, רוח—contains the letter ר. Furthermore, there is a graduated lengthening of the clauses of the doxology. Here the initial praises consist of two words apiece. In addition, הָרִים creates, along with הַר in v 1, a literary inclusio for the entire chapter.

147 For an Akkadian parallel, see the epithet *pātiqu ḫuršāni* ("He who fashioned the mountains"), *Beiträge zur Assyriologie* 5 (1906) 652:15. In the *Enuma Elish* epic of creation, Marduk is credited with the creation of the various winds: *ušēṣâmma šārē ša ibnû sibittišunu* ("He released the seven winds which he had created"), tablet IV, 47.

148 Rudolph, 182.

149 See Ps 94:11. Heb. שִׂיחַ, however, usually means "plea/complaint/prayer." See Crenshaw (*Hymnic*

and the wind was "to declare to man what his works are" (מָא עוֹבָדוֹהִי = Heb. מַעֲשֵׂהוּ) —a late aural error after the weakening of the laryngeals.[150] However interpreted, this clause adds to God's praise from within the context of his contact with humankind.[151]

The theme of the doxology returns to the praise of God as revealed in nature. The following phrase is translated by almost all commentators as "He who makes the dawn (שַׁחַר) [into] darkness (עֵיפָה)."[152] This is the standard meaning of שַׁחַר[153] (compare, for example, Gen 19:15; Cant 6:10) and is the commonly accepted interpretation of עֵיפָה (compare Job 10:22). However, as ibn Ganaḥ[154] already pointed out, the latter never denotes darkness but is connected to the root עיף, a metathesized form of יפע that means "brightness, glimmer."[155] In light of this, the sense of both nouns should be reversed: עֵיפָה is actually the "glimmering dawn," and שַׁחַר refers to "blackness."[156] For this meaning, see also Joel 2:2: "A day of darkness and gloom, a day of densest cloud, spread like soot (שַׁחַר) over the hills." The Deity is extolled here as "He who turns blackness into daybreak," similar to Amos 5:8.

The Deity also is extolled as the one who "treads on (דֹּרֵךְ עַל)[157] the high places of the earth" (בָּמֳתֵי אָרֶץ),[158] that is, the hills; compare Deut 32:13; Isa 58:14; Mic 1:3. With this expression of God's power, drawn from the

Affirmation, 122) for an interpretation based on his understanding of the doxologies as part of a prophetic lawsuit.

150 Accepted by Ehrlich, *Mikrâ,* 3.409; and *Randglossen,* 5.239; and by Budde, "Amos." See also ibn Ezra and Kimchi.

151 S, תשבוחתה ("his glory"), obviously read שִׁבְחוֹ. See Rudolph, 171. Several forced emendations have been offered in an attempt to relate all of the praises of the Deity to the realm of nature. A. Vaccari ("Hymnus Propheticus in Deum Creatorem," *VD* 9 [1929] 184–88, esp. 187), followed by B. N. Wambacq (*L'épithète divine Jahvé Seba'ôt* [Bruges: de Brouwer, 1947] 188 n 3), emends the text to the un-Hebraic, וּמַגִּיר לַאֲדָמָה מֵי שַׁחוֹ ("He pours the inundating waters upon the land"). For yet another improbable suggestion, see Horst, "Doxologien," 49. In contrast, see Gaster ("Hymn," 24–25), who suggests the reading וּמַגְדִּיל לַאֲדָמָה שִׂיחָהּ ("and he maketh her foison [= abundance] to grow upon the earth"). See also H.-P. Müller, "Die Hebräische Wurzel *śiaḥ,*" *VT* 19 (1969) 361–71, esp. 367, 369.

152 G, *ὄρθρον καὶ ὁμίχλην* ("dawn and darkness")," which presupposes a *waw* between the two substantives (וְעֵיפָה), is preferred by Cripps, 177. Otherwise, see Rudolph, 170: "der zum Morgenlicht die Dunkelheit macht" ("he who turns darkness into dawn"); see Amos 5:8.

153 L. Köhler, "Die Morgenröte im Alten Testament," *ZAW* 3 (1926) 56–59. See also Akk. *šēru,* "Morgen," *AHw,* 3.1219. *Šahar* is also the name of the deity of dawn who appears in several Ugaritic texts, especially in *KTU* 1.23, which describes the birth of this god along with his brother, *Šalim.*

154 Ibn Ganaḥ, *Haschoraschim,* 360. See also H. L. Ginsberg, "An Unrecognized Allusion to Kings Pekah and Hosea of Israel (Isa 8:23)," in Eretz Israel 5 (*Benjamin Mazar Volume;* ed. M. Avi-Yonah; Jerusalem: Israel Exploration Society, 1958) 64* par. r. See Job 10:22: "A land whose light (עֵפָתָה) is like darkness, all gloom and disarray, whose light (וַתֹּפַע) is like darkness." Job 11:17: "You will shine (תָּעֻפָה); you will be like the morning." This is also the meaning of the root in Job 3:9: "May it not see the glimmerings (עַפְעַפֵּי) of the dawn." Note that in this last phrase (and in Job 41:10) both substantives are similar to those in Amos. Could he have intended a double entendre here?

155 See *KB,* 405. See also Akk. *apû* ("to become visible, appear"); *šūpû* ("to make manifest"); *šutāpû* ("to shine forth"); *CAD, A,* II.201ff.

156 It is related, of course, to the adjective שָׁחוֹר ("black"), Lev 13:31, 37; Zech 6:2, 6; Cant 1:5; 5:11; and the verb שחר ("blackened"), Job 30:29: "My skin, blackened (שָׁחַר), is peeling off me. . . ."

157 For דֹּרֵךְ עַל ("tread upon"), see Deut 33:29; 1 Sam 5:5; Mic 1:3; Ps 91:13; Job 9:8.

158 For the form, see *GKC,* 87s. For Heb. בָּמָה = Ugar. *bmt* ("back"), see W. F. Albright, "The High Place in Ancient Palestine," in SVT 4 (Leiden: Brill, 1957) 256. (Compare also Akk. *bamtu,* B ["chest"], *CAD, B,* 78.) See also Deut 33:29; Hab 3:19. When the Deity is the subject, the context is that of the theophanic tradition of the covenant lawsuit. When Israel is the subject, it is within the context of victory over their enemies. For a study of the various meanings of בָּמָה, see P. H. Vaughan, *The Meaning of "Bāmâ" in the Old Testament: A Study of Etymological, Textual and Archaeological Evidence* (SOTSMS 3; Cambridge: Cambridge University, 1974).

imagery of a mighty conqueror, the hymn ends.[159] By beginning and concluding the panegyric of God with reference to the mountains and hills, the prophet creates a poetic inclusio.

The refrain ה׳ אֱלֹהֵי־צְבָאוֹת שְׁמוֹ,[160] which concludes the doxology in Amos 4:13 (see ה׳ שְׁמוֹ in the middle of the second doxology, Amos 5:8, and at the end of the third doxology, Amos 9:6),[161] has also been the subject of multiple investigations.[162] There is no reason, however, to cast doubt upon its originality[163] or to attribute it to some conjectured polemic against the sanctuary in Bethel.[164]

---

159 See U. Devescovi, "Camminare sulle Altare," *RivB* 9 (1961) 235–42; and J. L. Crenshaw, "*Wᵉdōrēk ʿal-bāmŏtê ʾāreṣ,*" *CBQ* 34 (1972) 39–53. He points out that although the phrase has a Canaanite mythological background, it should be understood in the Bible as a metaphor for the imagery of victory and security. See also Lipiński, *La Royauté,* 138–39 (including notes), who refers to the Baal stele in C. F.-A. Schaeffer, "Les fouilles de Minet-el-Beida et de Ras Shamra. Quatrième campagne," *Syria* 14 (1933) 123–24, pl. XVI, for a possible visual image of the expression.

160 The epithet ה׳ צְבָאוֹת is found nine times in various combinations in the Book of Amos: אֲדֹנָי ה׳ אֱלֹהֵי הַצְּבָאוֹת, Amos 3:13 (unique to Amos); אֲדֹנָי ה׳ הַצְּבָאוֹת, Amos 9:5 (unique to Amos); ה׳ אֱלֹהֵי צְבָאוֹת אֲדֹנָי, Amos 5:16 (unique to Amos); ה׳ אֱלֹהֵי הַצְּבָאוֹת, Amos 6:14 (otherwise only in Hos 12:6); ה׳ אֱלֹהֵי־צְבָאוֹת, Amos 4:13; 5:14, 15, 27; 6:8 (otherwise found nine times in 2 Sam; 1 Kgs; Jer; Ps).

For a proposed Ugaritic comparison, *ršp ṣbʾi,* see W. J. Fulco, *The Canaanite God Rešep* (AOS 8; New Haven: American Oriental Society, 1976) 42.

161 This refrain may very well have originally ended this hymn as well. See the comments on Amos 5:8.

162 For studies of the phrase, see E. Kautzsch, "*ṣᵉbāʾôth,*" Pauly's *Realencyclopädie der classischen Altertumswissenschaft* 3, Aufl., XXI (1908) 620–27; V. Maag, "Jahwäs Heerscharen," *Festschrift für Ludwig Köhler zu seinen 70. Geburtstag* (ed. W. Baumgartner; Bern: Schweizerische Theologische Umschau, 1950) 28–29, 49; O. Eissfeldt, "Jahwe Zebaoth," in idem, *Kleine Schriften zum Alten Testament* (6 vols.; Tübingen: Mohr [Siebeck], 1966) 3.103–23; J. L. Crenshaw ("*YHWH Ṣᵉbāʾôt Šᵉmô:* A Form-Critical Analysis," *ZAW* 81 [1969] 156–75; idem, *Hymnic Affirmation,* 15–23, 75–114), who interprets the cultic refrain as a polemic against false oaths. The most exhaustive study was made by B. N. Wambacq, *L'épithète divine. Jahvé Sebaʾôt.* It was reviewed by W. F. Albright, *JBL* 67 (1948) 377–81; see also Crüsemann, *Studiens,* 83–154.

For the phrase in the context of the "holy war," see Isa 31:4; Zech 4:6. See also B. W. Anderson, "Hosts, Host of Heaven," *IDB* 1.654–56. For a suggested explanation for the absence of this title in later works, see W. Kessler, "Aus welchen Gründen wird die Bezeichnung 'Jahweh Zebaoth' in der späteren Zeit gemieden?" in *Gottes ist der Orient: Festschrift für Otto Eissfeldt zu seinen 70. Geburtstag am 1. September 1957* (Berlin: Evangelische Verlag, 1959) 79–83.

See also J. A. Emerton, "New Light on Israelite Religion: The Implications of the Inscriptions from Kuntillet ʿAjrud," *ZAW* 94 (1982) 2–20.

163 As do most commentators. For an exception, see Rudolph, 182 n 22.

164 Against Wolff, following Sellin, but see the objections of Rudolph, 182. Nonetheless, it may at times carry some overtones of a polemical character. See Crenshaw, "Influence," 51; idem, "Theophanic Tradition," 211–12; Rudolph, 182: "einem Hieb gegen die konkurrierenden heidnischen Schöpferungsgötter" ("a cutting remark against the competing pagan gods of creation").

5 Funerary Dirge over the Nation and a Ray of Hope

1 Hear this word that I intone over you—
A dirge, O house of Israel:
2 Fallen, no more to rise,
Is Maiden Israel.
Abandoned on her own soil,
With none to lift her up.
3 For thus said my Lord God
About the house of Israel*:
The town that marches out a thousand strong
Shall have but a hundred left.
And the one that marches out a hundred strong
Shall have but ten left.
4 Indeed, thus said the Lord to the house of Israel:
Seek me so that you may live!
5 But do not seek Bethel!
Nor go to Gilgal!
Nor cross over to Beer-sheba!
For Gilgal shall go into galling exile,
And Bethel shall become a nullity.
6 Seek the Lord so that you may live!
Lest he flare up like fire against the house of Joseph
And consume Bethel with none to quench it.
7 They who turn justice into wormwood
And hurl righteousness to the ground.
8 He who made the Pleiades and Orion,
Who turns pitch-darkness into dawn
And darkens day into night,
Who summons the waters of the sea
And pours them out upon the face of the earth,
The Lord is his name!
9 It is he who brings** ruin upon the strong(holds)
And brings devastation upon the fortresses.
10 They hate the arbiter in the gate,
And the one who pleads honestly they loathe.
11 Therefore,
Because you levy a straw tax on the poor
And exact a grain tax from him,
You have built houses of hewn stone,
But you shall not dwell in them.
You have planted delightful vineyards,
But you shall not drink their wine.
12 For indeed I know how numerous are your transgressions
And how countless your sins.
You persecutors of the innocent,
Takers of bribes,
Who subvert the cause of the needy in the gate.

13 Therefore, at such a time the prudent one moans,
For it is a time of misfortune.
14 Seek good and not evil,
That you may live.
So that the Lord, the God of Hosts,
Will really be with you as you claim!
15 Hate evil and love good!
And set up justice in the gate!
Perhaps the Lord, the God of Hosts,
Will show favor to the remnant of Joseph.
16 Therefore, thus said the Lord, the God of Hosts, my Lord:
In all the city squares there shall be lamentation,
And in all the streets they shall cry, "Alas, alas."
They shall call the farmhand to mourning
And to lamentation those skilled in wailing.
17 Even in all the vineyards, lamentation,
When I pass through your midst
—said the Lord.

*transposed from end of verse
**Hebrew obscure

Introductory Comments to the Literary Unit, 5:1–17

The first major literary section in chapter 5 consists of vv 1–17. It is a composite collection of independent short prophetic oracles that are structured according to an overall chiastic pattern.[1] Verses 1–3 are a dirge, in which the word יִשְׂרָאֵל ("Israel") is repeated three times. This is followed by the unit vv 4–6, an oracle that consists of the twice-repeated call to "seek the Lord that you may live" (דִּרְשׁוּנִי/דִּרְשׁוּ אֶת־ה׳ וִחְיוּ), which creates a dramatic contrast to the dirge. Internally, these verses are also structured on a chiastic pattern: v 4, דִּרְשׁוּנִי וִחְיוּ (a); v 5, וְאַל־תִּדְרְשׁוּ בֵּית־אֵל (b); וְהַגִּלְגָּל לֹא תָבֹאוּ (c); וּבְאֵר שֶׁבַע לֹא תַעֲבֹרוּ (d); כִּי הַגִּלְגָּל גָּלֹה יִגְלֶה (c′); וּבֵית אֵל יִהְיֶה לְאָוֶן (b′); v 6, דִּרְשׁוּ . . . וִחְיוּ (a′). The next pericope, vv 7, 10–12, 13, expounds both the iniquities of the population, emphasizing the absence of justice and righteousness, and the corresponding punishments. Verses 7, 10, and 11 are themselves also patterned chiastically (see commentary). The prophet then returns to further define the exhortation of "seeking God" (see vv 4–6), which is explained as "seeking the good," דִּרְשׁוּ־טוֹב, in

1 This overall pattern was seen independently by J. de Waard, "The Chiastic Structure of Amos 5:1–17," *VT* 27 (1977) 170–77. Our conclusions are almost entirely identical. For further details about the individual verses, see his comments and references to other studies. J. de Waard and W. A. Smalley (*A Translator's Handbook on the Book of Amos: Helps for Translators* [New York: United Bible Societies, 1979] 195) also attempt to find an overall chiastic pattern for the entire Book of Amos, which, in turn, is broken down into smaller chiastic literary units. A "revised structuration" of their pattern was presented in a lecture by T. Bulkeley, "The Structure of the Book of Amos and the Day of the Lord," at the 1986 International Meeting of the Society of Biblical Literature, 18–20 August, held in Jerusalem. His suggestion, however, to relate the doxologies as well as the oracles against the foreign nations to the Day of the Lord is untenable. See also J. M. Berridge, "Die Intention der Botschaft des Amos. Exegetische Überlegungen zu Amos 5," *TZ* 32 (1976) 321–40; and N. J. Tromp, "Amos 5:1–17. Towards a Stylistic and Rhetorical Analysis," in *Prophets, Worship and Theodicy* (*OTS* 23; Leiden: Brill, 1984) 56–84. Once one recognizes the chiastic structure here, there is no need to transpose some of these independent literary units, as is usually done, for example, Rudolph. See also C. Coulot, "Propositions pour une structuration du livre d'Amos au niveau rédactionnel," *RevScRel* 51 (1977) 169–86, esp. 179–80; Markert, *Struktur*, 125–53.

order to survive, vv 14–15. At this point two key terms, דרש and חיה, appear for the climactic third time. Finally the literary pendulum swings back to the theme of the funeral dirge, vv 16–17, containing a threefold repetition of a מִסְפֵּד ("lamentation") uttered בְּכָל ("in all") of three different localities, representing the total encircling of northern Israel in one grand dirge. The passage can be diagrammatically presented:

1–3:	a
4–6:	b
7, 10–12, 13:	c
14–15:	b′
16–17:	a′

For the problem of vv 8–9, 13 and additional literary devices employed within the smaller units themselves,[2] see the commentary.

■ **1** This oracle (vv 1–3), similar to Amos 3:1 and Amos 4:1, also begins with the formal summons, שִׁמְעוּ אֶת־הַדָּבָר הַזֶּה ("Hear this word"). The call here, similar to Amos 4:1, is to hear the words of the prophet, which are followed by the words of the Lord (Amos 4:2; 5:3). The theme for the first time is a funerary lament.[3] This dirge follows well upon the end of the last chapter, where Israel is warned that it is about to experience the full wrath of the Lord in a theophanic confrontation. After this encounter nothing will be left except to intone dirges upon fallen Israel. The setting of this oracle is most likely in a cultic center where the people have congregated for some festival.[4] Once again Amos confronts a "captive" audience. On such festive occasions the worshipers were expecting to hear and participate in words of joy. Amos in his usual fashion paradoxically overwhelms them with the unexpected.[5] He commences on a neutral tone, "Hear this word that I intone." However, that "word" (דָּבָר) immediately turns out to be the mournful sounds of "lamentation" (קִינָה, see Amos 8:10).[6] The shocked audience then actually hears the prophet's recitation of the threnody delivered in the traditional rhythmic pattern of the dirge. First he recites his own elegy over fallen Israel, which is followed by the lament of the Lord himself.

Amos is the first to utter a dirge for the entire nation. His funerary lament is ever so more the shocking when it is realized that he is actually mourning the death of his listeners themselves! The audience is summoned to hear their own keening while yet alive.[7]

2 For example, the threefold repetition of בֵּית יִשְׂרָאֵל, vv 1, 3, 4 (and again in v 25); בֵּית־אֵל, vv 5 (twice), 7; שַׁעַר, vv 10, 12, 15; ה' אֱלֹהֵי־צְבָאוֹת, vv 14, 15, 16; מִסְפֵּד and בְּכָל, vv 16 (twice), 17, along with יִשְׂרָאֵל, דרש, and חיה mentioned previously.

3 For another dirge over the nation introduced by שִׁמְעוּ, see Lam 1:18. For vv 1–3 as a "Totenklage" ("dirge"), see K. W. Neubauer, "Erwägungen zu Amos 5:4–15," *ZAW* 78 (1966) 294. G introduces this lament with the name of the Deity, "(Hear) the word of the Lord," τὸν λόγον κυρίου; see Amos 3:1. The Masoretic text, however, is more similar to Amos 4:1. Variations in style are common throughout the book.

4 See Hammershaimb, 76; Rudolph, 187. See Amos 9:1ff.

5 See Maag, *Text*, 27f.; Amsler, 203 n 2.

6 The expression נשׂא קִינָה עַל ("to intone a dirge over") appears here for the first time in the Bible. See Jer 7:29; 9:9; Ezek 19:1; 26:17; 27:2, 32 (אֶל instead of עַל); 28:12; 32:2. The Akkadian substantives for "dirge" *(ṣirḫu, ṣiriḫtu)* and "lament" *(bikītu)* are similarly employed with the cognate verb *našû*. See *ṣiriḫtu nissāti u bikīti ana Sin ina antalî našû* ("while they sang dirges, wailings, and laments for Sin during the eclipse") BRM 4, 6:44 in Clay, *Epics;* Akk. *ṣiriḫtu / bikītu ana X našû* = Heb. נָשָׂא קִינָה עַל. See also Akk. *mudê ṣirḫi* = Heb. יוֹדְעֵי נֶהִי ("skilled in wailing"), Amos 5:16. See *CAD, Ṣ*, 206.

For a study of the "dirge," see J. Tigay, "Dirge," *EM* 7.125–44 (Heb.).

7 See E. Sellin and G. Fohrer, *Introduction to the Old Testament* (tr. D. E. Green; Nashville and New York: Abingdon, 1968) 276, who describe prophetic elegies as depicting future laments in the past tense in order to intensify the threat of the catastrophe. In the prophets' eyes, the forthcoming destruction is already a past event. See also O. Eissfeldt, *The Old Testament: An Introduction* (tr. P. R. Ackroyd; New York and Evanston: Harper & Row, 1965) 95–96: "For the 'prophetic' political dirge is older, a lament, that is to say, over something still in the future, but represented as the downfall, already in the past, of the people or of some other community. This can only be understood as the taking over of an already existing 'non-prophetic' political dirge into prophetic use. We find it first in Amos. . . . This proclamation of the catastrophe . . . must have had a terrifying effect upon the crown, and this was its intention."

■ **2** There now follow the words of the prophet's funeral dirge. The nation of Israel (called בֵּית יִשְׂרָאֵל, "house of Israel,"[8] in vv 1, 3, 4) is here personified as "Maiden Israel" (בְּתוּלַת יִשְׂרָאֵל)[9] for the first time in the Bible. The choice of this description is very poignant. Israel, still enjoying its vibrant political, economic, and military vitality and yet in the flower of youth, is about to come to a premature end. Its early demise before achieving adult maturity makes its situation ever so more tragic.

The lament is intoned in the perfect tense: נָפְלָה, נִטְּשָׁה. For Amos the die has been cast, and the destruction has already been determined. For him it is a fait accompli, and so he bewails Israel's fatal collapse. Both verbs are followed, in turn, by a circumstantial clause, and together they describe the total helplessness and inability of Israel to recover. Israel has so "fallen" (נָפְלָה)[10] that she is "no more to rise" (לֹא־תוֹסִיף קוּם).[11] She has been cast down and "abandoned" (נִטְּשָׁה),[12] "with none to lift her up" (אֵין מְקִימָהּ).[13] Her fall is so great that she can neither raise herself by her own power, nor is there anyone else to lift her. She is completely powerless and shattered.[14] The irony, of course, is that normally the Lord himself would help her to rise and recover.[15] Compare Amos 9:11, in which the Lord says, "I will raise up (אָקִים) the fallen (נֹפֶלֶת) tabernacle of David." The tragedy is further intensified by the fact that the dénouement of Israel will take place not on foreign territory but on "her own soil" (עַל־אַדְמָתָהּ).[16]

■ **3** The words of the Lord,[17] following those of the prophet, explicate and clarify the reason for the dirge.[18]

---

8 G, οἶκος Ισραηλ (questionably) and V, *domus Israhel* (definitely) attach בֵּית יִשְׂרָאֵל ("the house of Israel," which appears at the end of v 1) to v 2 as its subject. This division is incorrect, and it destroys the characteristic dirge meter. Moreover, the similar construction, שִׁמְעוּ אֶת־הַדָּבָר הַזֶּה אֲשֶׁר . . . בֵּית יִשְׂרָאֵל ("Hear this word which . . ., O house of Israel"), also appears in Amos 3:1 and 4:1.

9 See S. M. Paul ("Virgin, Virginity," *EncJud* 10.160–61) for other occurrences and references to this epithet personifying countries and nations; for example, Isa 23:12 (Sidon); Isa 47:1 (Babylon); Jer 46:11 (Egypt). The symbolic expression בְּתוּלַת יִשְׂרָאֵל ("Maiden Israel") appears elsewhere in Jer 18:13; 31:4, 21. In Deut 22:19 it is used literally.

There is no reason to refer this expression to capital cities, against J. J. Schmitt, "The Virgin of Israel: Meaning and Use of the Phrase in Amos and Jeremiah," in his abstract and lecture presented at The XII Congress of the International Organization for the Study of the Old Testament, Jerusalem, 1986.

10 For נפל in connection with nations, see, for example, Isa 21:9; Jer 51:8; and with individuals, see, for example, 2 Sam 1:19, 25, 27; 3:34; Isa 14:12; Jer 9:21; Ezek 29:5; Lam 2:21—all these passages in the context of dirges—"fallen," usually in battle. See also the Akkadian cognate, *maqātu* ("to fall"), meaning "to suffer a downfall, fall in battle, to suffer a defeat," *CAD, M*, I.243.

11 See Ehrlich, *Randglossen*, 5.239. For the exact same expression, see Isa 24:20; Amos 8:14. For a similar variant, see Jer 9:21; Ezek 29:5. Compare also the reverse picture of Israel's destiny employing the same two verbs, Amos 9:11.

12 For נטש parallel to עזב, see 1 Kgs 8:57; Isa 32:14; Jer 12:7; Ps 27:9; and for נטש along with נפל, see Ezek 29:5. For a similar semantic development from "cast down/out" to "abandoned," see Heb. הִשְׁלִיךְ. See M. Cogan, "A Technical Term for Exposure," *JNES* 27 (1968) 133–35; and C. Cohen, "The Legend of Sargon and the Birth of Moses," *JANESCU* 4 (1972) 49 (for עזב). See also Amos 4:3. For the antithetical structure, so characteristic of Amos, see Amos 5:14, 18, 20; 8:11; 9:4.

13 See Lam 1:14.

14 For the motif of inescapability, see also Amos 2:14–16; 5:18–20; 9:1–4.

15 See, for example, 1 Sam 2:8; Hos 6:2.

16 Compare Kimchi. The prophet most likely envisions a devastating attack by an enemy in the land of Israel itself. See Wolff, 236; Rudolph, 188. Seeligmann ("History," 125–32) relates this and the following verse to the literary genre of war oracles.

17 There is no reason to view אֲדֹנָי as an addition, contrary to Wolff, 227, because Amos very often varies his stylistic formulae. However, the suggestion of many commentators to transpose the last two words, לְבֵית יִשְׂרָאֵל, to follow the introduction, is very possible; see similarly Amos 5:4. For other opinions, see Harper, 106.

18 Against those who deem it a gloss, for example, Oort, "Amos," and those who consider it a misplaced saying, for example, Koehler; Robinson-Horst, 88; Fosbroke, 810. See also Weiser, *Profetie*, 170–80; and Wellhausen, 81, "der Grund der Klage" ("the basis of the lament").

Israel will suffer an overwhelmingly resounding military defeat (see also Amos 2:14–16; 4:10; 7:11) from which only a tenth of its troops will survive. Of an army contingent of one thousand men (see Exod 18:21; Deut 1:15; 1 Sam 10:19; 1 Chr 27:1; 2 Chr 25:5) that "marches out" (הַיּוֹצֵאת),[19] from "each town" (הָעִיר),[20] only one hundred shall be "left" (תַּשְׁאִיר);[21] of a detachment of one hundred soldiers (see Judg 7:16; 1 Sam 22:7; 2 Sam 18:1, 4), only ten shall be "left" (תַּשְׁאִיר).[22] The thought here that only a mere remnant shall remain after a ninety percent decimation of the army is similar to Amos 3:12.[23] This scanty residue is meaningless for the future of the nation.[24] Thus Amos once again denounces their present ill-founded hopes of national immunity and false sense of security. Israel is on the brink of almost total destruction, no matter how much they rely on their armed forces.

For comparative curse imagery drawn from the Mesopotamian sphere, compare *1 līm bitāti ana 1 bīti litūr* ("May a thousand horses turn into one horse"); *1000 maškunū ana 1 maškini litūr* ("May [a camp of] a thousand tents turn into [one with] a single tent").[25]

■ **4** Nevertheless, the next literary unit,[26] vv 4–6, presents a ray of hope; the final death statement has not been signed. There is yet a chance for survival if Israel only "seeks" the Lord.[27] The expressed call for life (opening with the messenger formula and followed by two imperatives) can cancel out the above funeral lament; the divine judgment is not yet irrevocable. Salvation is conditional.

Does this not stand in contradiction with the previous verses? Some commentators resolve the problem by contending that the words of the prophet are meant to be ironical,[28] or that Amos is addressing the masses and not the official religious and political leadership as previously.[29] There is, however, no reason to hear tones of irony here. The imperative call is serious and is

19 For the verb יצא ("to march out to battle"), see 2 Sam 18:2–4, 6; 2 Kgs 5:2. Compare also Isa 42:13. See the expressions יוֹצֵא צָבָא (Num 1:3, 45; 26:2; 2 Chr 25:5); הַיֹּצְאִים בַּצָּבָא (Num 31:36); יֵצֵא בַּצָּבָא (Deut 24:5), all referring to "soldiers." The Akkadian interdialectal cognate and semantic equivalent, *waṣû,* also carries this same technical military nuance. For examples, see *CAD, A,* II.359–60; 363–64. Compare "They marched out *(ūṣû)* of Babylon and attacked the army of Assyria," Wiseman, *Chronicles,* 50:12. So, too, *āṣitu* ("expeditionary force"), *CAD, A,* II.355. The same is also true of the verb in Ugaritic, *yṣ'*. Compare *wyṣi' trḫ ḥdṯ* ("Let the newly wed march forth"), *CTA* 14:ii:100–101. See M. Lichtenstein, "A Note on the Text of I Keret," *JANESCU* 2 (1970) 94–100.

20 For הָעִיר, meaning *"each and any"* town or city, see also בַּמַּמְלָכָה, Amos 9:8. See *GKC,* 126n. For the organization of the Israelite army, see R. de Vaux, *Ancient Israel: Its Life and Institutions* (tr. J. McHugh; New York, Toronto, and London: McGraw-Hill, 1961) 214ff. For army units numbering a "thousand" *(līmu)* and a "hundred" *(meat)* in Mesopotamia, see the respective entries in *CAD, L,* 197–98; and *M,* II.1.

21 Ehrlich (*Randglossen,* 5.239), Sellin, and Tur-Sinai (*Peshuṭo,* 463) suggest vocalizing in the *niph'al,* תִּשָּׁאֵר. The technical term שְׁאֵרִית ("a remnant") is derived from this verb.

22 For the number 10 in conjunction with the decimation of Israel, compare also Amos 6:9. For the number 100, see A. Frisch, "The Number One Hundred in the Bible," *BM* 102 (1985) 435–40 (Heb.).

23 For other descriptions of decisive military defeats, see Amos 2:14–16; 4:10.

24 See Hasel, *Remnant,* 187–90. On p. 189 he comments, "The popular notion that Israel as a whole will remain on the day of battle is transformed by Amos into a threat against the national existence of Israel. The number of the surviving remnant will be so small that Israel as a nation will be unable to recuperate from the disaster. . . . Only a remnant of Israel will remain but not Israel as a remnant."

25 Taken from the treaty between Asshur-nirari V and Mati'ilu of Arpad. See E. F. Weidner, "Der Staatsvertrag Aššurnirâris VI. von Assyrien mit Mati'ilu von Bît-Agusi," *AfO* 8 (1932–1933) 17ff., rev. vi:3–5. For similar curses, see above. For the corresponding blessing, see Isa 60:22.

26 The כִּי is an emphatic particle. For this unit, see also J. Lust, "Remarks on the Redaction of Amos V, 4–6, 14–15," in *Remembering All the Way* (ed. A. S. van der Woude; *OTS* 21; Leiden: Brill, 1981) 129–54.

27 Chapter 5 is the only chapter in the book in which the prophet directly calls for a return and promises salvation. Wolff (*Amos the Prophet,* 30ff.) calls this a "Mahnrede" ("exhortation speech") and refers it to the wisdom tradition.

28 See Weiser, *Profetie,* 190–92; T. M. Raitt, "The Prophetic Summons to Repentance," *ZAW* 83 (1971) 30–49, esp. 35 n 16. Compare, in contrast, Würthwein, "Amos-Studien," 38; F. Hesse, "Amos 5:4–6, 14f.," *ZAW* 68 (1956) 7–10.

29 A. Alt, *Kleine Schriften zur Geschichte des Volkes Israel* (3

emphatically repeated three times (vv 4, 6, 14). As for the conjectured distinction between the judgment leveled against the leaders as contrasted to the potential salvation of the masses, it simply is not present in these units. Both vv 1–3 and vv 4ff. are addressed to the entire corporate body of Israel. The assumed difficulty disappears when one bears in mind the main thrust of prophetic thought. According to the prophets, the decision of God is very often subject to change, but the change is dependent and contingent upon the people's return. See especially Jer 18:18ff. Repentance has the power to abrogate the death sentence for the individual as well as for the entire nation.

This section (vv 4–6), as mentioned previously, is structured on a chiastic pattern. (Note also that just as vv 1–2 are the words of the prophet followed by v 3, the words of the Lord, so, conversely, vv 4–5 are the words of the Lord, followed by v 6, those of the prophet.) Amos first exhorts the people to seek the Lord so that they may live (וִחְיוּ).[30] He then explicates how and where *not* to seek him (v 5); and then concludes with the exhortation to seek the Lord in order to remain alive (v 6a), thus creating a literary inclusio.

The key word, דרש, is a *terminus technicus* that has several connotations in earlier literature when pertaining to the Deity. It may pertain to frequenting a sanctuary[31] or to inquiring the will of the Lord through oracles delivered by men of God.[32] Amos, in another of his ongoing disputations with the people, totally rejects these commonly held ideas. He employs this cultic language, but for a novel purpose—to oppose and reject that very cult. He wants—rather he demands—that the people seek the Lord directly and not the pilgrim sites. What "seeking the Lord" specifically means will be spelled out later. For the moment the people must have been shocked, for they have always frequented cultic places, and for them the pilgrimage was identical to seeking the Lord. Was he not to be found there? Where and how were they to "seek him"?[33] Amos now defines this issue as a matter of life or death.

■ **5** The imperative (v 4) followed (or preceded) by a negative prohibitive (v 5) is typical of sapiential literature, for example, Prov 4:5–6; 9:8; 19:18; 20:13, 22; 24:21; 30:7–8.[34] The employment of the negative אַל in the first stich (rather than לֹא as in the next two) was most likely intentional, in order to create a paronomasia upon

vols.; München: Beck, 1953–1959) 2.269. However, see the correct criticism of Wolff, 238, who remarks that nowhere else is such a distinction made, and even more significantly, this oracle is obviously directed against the very same audience previously addressed.

Note the threefold repetition of the verb חיה, vv 4, 6, 14. Each time it is the hoped-for result of "seeking" the Lord. The sentences themselves, upon repetition, become longer.

30 For the same imperative, see, for example, Gen 42:18; Jer 27:17. See *GKC*, 110f. For the construction, see Hesse, "Amos 5," 4 n 22; Neubauer, "Erwägungen," 309. For other studies, see Amsler, "Amos," 318–28; Berridge, "Intention," 321–40; O. Keel, "Rechttum oder Annahme des drohenden Gerichts?" *BZ* 21 (1977) 200–218.

31 See, for example, Deut 12:5; 2 Chr 1:5 (according to Cripps, 180, but not accepted by Wolff, 238). See, however, Rudolph, 190. See also M. Weinfeld, "Instructions for Temple Visitors in the Bible and in Ancient Egypt," in *Egyptological Studies* (ed. S. Israelit-Groll; Scripta Hierosolymitana 28; Jerusalem: Magnes, 1982) 236.

32 See, for example, Gen 25:22; 1 Kgs 22:5; 2 Kgs 22:13. See C. Westermann, "Die Begriffe für Fragen und Suchen im Alten Testament," *KD* 6 (1960) 2–30, reprinted in idem, *Forschung am Alten Testament: Gesammelte Studien* (TBü55; München: Kaiser, 1974) 2.162–90. See also Kapelrud, *Central Ideas*, 36, who argues that דרש in vv 4, 6, 14 is used differently from that in v 5, which refers to seeking the Lord in Jerusalem. This is a totally unsupported contention. See also the remarks of Weiser, 810–11. See, too, Ps 24:6. For דרש, see G. Gerleman and E. Ruprecht, "*drš*," *THAT* 1 (1975) 460–67; S. Wagner, "*drš*," *TWAT* II (1977) 313–29.

33 For an interesting occurrence of the themes of "seeking" and "life" in Mesopotamian literature in a completely different context, see *Gilgamesh* XI:198, *balaṭa ša tuba'û tuttā atta* ("You may find the life you are seeking"). Observe the interesting comment in the Babylonian Talmud, Makkoth 24b, where Rabbi Simlai states, "The 613 commandments that were given to Moses were reduced by David to eleven (Ps 15). Isaiah reduced them to six (Isa 33:15); Micah reduced them to three (Mic 6:8); Isaiah further reduced them to two (Isa 56:1); finally Amos came and reduced them all to one" (Amos 5:4).

34 See Wolff, *Amos the Prophet*, 44–53.

the place-name אֵל (בֵּית־) ("Bethel"). It is the only time that this negative particle appears in the oracles. The verse commences on a chiastic pattern: אַל־תִּדְרְשׁוּ בֵּית־אֵל ("Do not seek Bethel"), verb followed by cultic site; וְהַגִּלְגָּל לֹא תָבֹאוּ ("Nor go to Gilgal"), cultic site followed by verb.

Amos now lists the three most frequented sanctuaries[35] where the people are exhorted *not* to go, for the Lord is neither to be sought nor to be found there. Unlike vv 4 and 6, this passage is not conditional. It is an outright directive to avoid these three cultic sites. Bethel, listed first, was the main center in northern Israel. It also appears in Amos 3:14, 4:4,[36] and twice in the dramatic confrontation with Amaziah, the priest of Bethel, Amos 7:10, 13. Ironically, in the latter passage the priest forbids Amos himself from appearing in Bethel—but for entirely different reasons! Gilgal is also coupled with Bethel in Amos 3:14. For the employment of the verb בוא in conjunction with visiting sanctuaries, see, for example, Exod 34:34; Isa 1:12; Hos 4:15; Joel 1:13; Pss 95:6; 96:8; 100:2.[37]

The third site, Beer-sheba, is mentioned again in a cultic context in Amos 8:14. It was a popular southern sanctuary going back to traditions associated with the patriarchs, especially with Abraham and Isaac.[38] From this passage one learns that even as late as the middle of the eighth century, worshipers from northern Israel continued to cross the border (תַעֲבֹרוּ)[39] into Judah in order to frequent this ancient cultic site.

The prophet now employs a very clever geographic paronomasia: *nomen est omen.*[40] By means of alliterative reiteration, Amos first declares that "Gilgal" (הַגִּלְגָּל) "shall go into galling exile" (גָּלֹה יִגְלֶה). By the repetition of the verb, whose first two root letters are גל, Amos skillfully draws attention to the duplication of these very two letters in the name of Gilgal (גִל־גָל).[41] However, now they are redefined to anticipate and foreshadow the forthcoming deportation of the inhabitants of that site.[42]

35 For a comprehensive study of these sanctuaries, see H.-J. Kraus, *Gottesdienst in Israel: Grundriss einer Geschichte des alttestamentlichen Gottesdienstes* (München: Kaiser, 1962) 172–202.

36 Wolff, *Amos the Prophet,* 44–53. This is not a polemic against the deity Bethel (see Jer 48:13); against Crenshaw, *Hymnic Affirmation,* 125–26.

37 Wolff, 218–19, 239 n 65. Gilgal goes back to the time of Joshua (Josh 5:9). The exact same phrase appears in Hos 4:15 in reverse order, אַל־תָּבֹאוּ הַגִּלְגָּל ("do not go to Gilgal").

38 For example, Gen 21:14, 32–33; 22:19; 26:23–25, 31–33; 28:10; 46:1. Compare also 1 Kgs 19:3; 2 Kgs 23:8. Compare Alt, *Kleine Schriften zur Geschichte des Volkes Israel,* 1.53. See W. Zimmerli, *Geschichte und Tradition von Beersheba im Alten Testament* (Giessen: Töpelmann, 1932).

39 There is no reason to seek an alleged northern location for this site. For עבר with this connotation, see 1 Sam 14:1; 2 Kgs 8:21; and esp. Amos 6:2. Compare also the Akkadian interdialectal semantic equivalent, *etēqu* (= Heb. עבר), with the meaning "to cross boundaries," *CAD, A,* II.388.

For the Israelite sanctuary at Beersheba, see Y. Yadin, "Beer-sheba, the High Place Destroyed by King Josiah," *BASOR* 222 (1976) 5–17; Z. Herzog, A. F. Rainey, and Sh. Moskowitz, "The Stratigraphy of Beer-sheba and the Location of the Sanctuary," *BASOR* 225 (1977) 49–58; Z. Herzog, "Israelite Sanctuaries at Arad and Beer-Sheba," in *Temples and High Places in Biblical Times* (ed. A. Biran; Jerusalem: Keter, 1981) 120–22. Cross notes that "Israel must have been fond of patriarchal shrines, including Beer-sheba. Note the pilgrimages to the Mt. of God in the South, Horeb-Teman: Elijah narrative and Kuntilat ʿAjrūd shrine. The connections of ʿAjrūd and the North are palpable in script, names (in *-yaw*), and references to Yahweh of Teman and Samaria" (written communication).

40 According to Rashi, לְפִי שְׁמוֹ קִלְלָתוֹ ("According to its name, its curse").

41 The alliterative pun is difficult to reproduce in other languages. For several "playful" attempts, compare "Gilgal wird Galle weinen" ("Gilgal shall weep gall," Ewald); "Gilgal giltig entgilt es" ("Gilgal shall compensate commensurately," Baur); "Die Rollstadt rollt von dannen" ("The rolling city shall rock and roll," von Orelli); "Gilgal shall go into galling captivity" (Mitchell); "Gilgal wird zum Galgen gehn" ("Gilgal will go to the gallows," Wellhausen); "Gilgal shall taste the gall of exile" (G. A. Smith), (each, my trans.), all cited in Harper, 111–12 nn. For another paronomastic explanation of the name Gilgal, see Josh 5:9.

42 For other paronomastic puns on names of cities, see, for example, 2 Sam 1:20; Isa 10:29, 30; 15:9; Jer 6:1; Hos 12:12; Mic 1:10–15; Zeph 2:4.

The threat of exile, one of the major recurring themes throughout his oracles (for example, Amos 4:2–3; 5:27; 6:7; 7:11, 17) is strikingly stressed here. (In the last two verses גָּלֹה יִגְלֶה also appears for emphasis.)

Following his chiastic pattern, Amos returns to Bethel, which was mentioned first in the initial half of the verse. By declaring that בֵּית־אֵל will become אָוֶן ("nullity"), Amos is subtly relating the root און ("that which is naught") to the letters אל, which compose the final part of the compound place-name בֵּית־אֵל. However, he reinterprets them as אַל ("not") rather than אֵל ("god"). *Beth-el,* that is, *Beth-al* ("house of Nothingness"), will become nothing more than a nullity. For אָוֶן with this meaning, compare the string of synonymous nouns in Isa 41:29: אָוֶן, אֶפֶס, רוּחַ, תֹהוּ, all referring to that which is null and void. G correctly understood this clever pun and translated אָוֶן not as "wickedness," as many moderns have, but as ὡς οὐχ ὑπάρχουσα ("like that which is not").[43] This pun on the name of Bethel[44] became so popular that Hosea a bit later refers three times to the very site as בֵּית אָוֶן (Hos 4:15; 5:8; 10:5).[45]

Amos, after this twofold paronomasia relating to the destiny of the two northern centers, does not continue with a similar doom oracle against the third sanctuary, Beer-sheba. The reason that this site was passed over was most likely not because of any difficulty in inventing a corresponding wordplay,[46] for he could have predicted, even nonparonomastically, a suitable tragic end for this cultic center. There is also no reason to delete it from the beginning of the verse on the pretext of its being a later Judean interpolation.[47] He omitted it because his main thrust throughout the oracles centered upon northern Israel, its leaders, populace, and cultic sites, and not upon a southern locale,[48] for which it sufficed merely to sound the warning against its popular significance.[49]

This oracle not to frequent these traditional sanctuaries must have come as a great shock to the people. For them it would be a total absurdity and paradox to declare that the centrality of the sanctuary and all its rites and ceremonies were odious to the Deity.[50]

■ **6** The chiastic literary pattern of vv 4–6, structured on the pattern of an inclusio, ends on the identical words with which it started. This time, however, it is the prophet who reiterates the words of the Lord and exhorts the people to "seek the Lord so that you may live."[51] Survival is still possible; however, it is precondi-

43 So, too, S. See also ibn Ezra.

44 See also the following attempts to catch the wordplay: "Bethel wird des Teufels werden" ("Bethel shall go to the devil," Wellhausen); "Bethel ist einen Bettel wert" ("Bethel is worth waste," Rudolph).

45 See also M. Garsiel, *Midrashic Name Derivations in the Bible* (Ramat-Gan: Revivim, 1987) 131 (Heb.). For a site בֵּית אָוֶן next to Bethel, see Josh 7:2; 18:12; 1 Sam 13:5; 14:23. For אָוֶן, see, too, Amos 1:5. Compare also, Hos 12:12.

46 Against Rosenmüller; Neubauer, "Erwägungen," 310 n 86.

47 Against, for example, Maag, *Text,* 344–45; Morgenstern, "Amos Studies IV"; Wolff, 228, 239; Kapelrud, *Central Ideas,* 36; Willi-Plein, *Vorformen,* 31ff.

48 So, too, for example, Hitzig, Keil, van Gelderen, Ridderbos, Rudolph, 191.

49 For other examples of this phenomenon, see Zakovitch, *For Three,* 417–19 (Heb.), who argues for the authenticity of this cultic site on the basis of the literary pattern of the section.

50 Behind this oracle is the real issue of Amos's message, the supremacy of morality. See p. 139. It is not a matter of cult or amphictyonic law, contrary to Hesse, "Amos 5," 12; Bach, "Gottesrecht," 23–34; Würthwein, "Amos Studien," 43–50; J. Harvey, "Le '*rib*-pattern,' réquisitoire prophétique sur la rupture de l'alliance," *Bib* 43 (1962) 172–96.

51 Wolff, 240, once again unnecessarily deletes the entire verse as a later addition. Compare also Weiser, *Profetie,* 183ff.; Neubauer, "Erwägungen," 309; Hesse, "Amos 5," 5ff. Although clearly these are the words of the prophet, they may have already begun in the prior verse. See H. W. Hertzberg, "Die prophetische Botschaft vom Heil," *NKZ* 43 (1932) 518, "Es mache sachlich keinen Unterscheid, ob sie von Jahwe in der 3. Person sprechen oder ihn in der 1. Person reden lassen." ("It makes no essential difference whether they speak of Yahweh in the third person, or let him talk in the first person.") Rudolph, 189, is followed by Hesse, "Amos 5," 1–17. For other studies on the subject, see T. M. Raitt, "The Prophetic Summons to Repentance," *ZAW* 83 (1971) 30–49; Berridge, "Intention," 321–40; J. Vermeylen, "Prophètes de la conversion et traditions sacrales," *RTL* 9 (1978) 5–32.

tioned not upon their cultic observance but upon their returning to the Lord. They must seek the Lord, not the sanctuaries. If not, they will be consumed by the wrath of the Lord—execution by fire (compare Amos 1:4, 7, 10, 12, 14; 2:2, 5; 7:4).

The major problem in this verse is the meaning of the verb צלח. Because it must somehow refer to the act of burning—see G, ἀναλάμψῃ ("flame up"); V, *conburatur* ("burn up"); T, יִדְלַק ("to kindle")[52]—scholars were prone to suggest emendations such as יִשְׁלַח[53] ("to send"), יַצִּית[54] ("to set on fire"), יַשְׁלִיךְ[55] ("to cast"), יְלַחֵךְ ("to lick").[56] Rudolph, on the other hand, defended the Masoretic reading and connected the verb with Akkadian *ṣelû* ("to burn"),[57] which, however, refers to the burning of incense and is attested only in Late Babylonian texts.[58] Its Hebrew interdialectal semantic and etymological equivalent, moreover, is צלה and not צלח, and the former is used only in connection with the roasting of meat.[59]

Recent investigations show that the verb צלח[60] need not be emended, for it conveys the exact sense demanded by the context, that is, burning.[61] In Akkadian and in Hebrew, several verbs of movement that express the action of "speeding" and "rushing" also refer to the activity of "burning."[62] Compare Akk. *ḫamāṭu* ("to hurry/hasten" and "to burn");[63] *ṣarāḫu* ("to dispatch quickly" and "to heat/scorch");[64] Heb. בער ("to burn," but in the *piʿel* [and *hiphʿil*] "to sweep away/wipe out");[65] and דלק ("to pursue hotly"[66] and "to burn/kindle").[67] So, too, צלח, which means "to proceed/pass/go ⟩ advance ⟩ progress ⟩ prosper ⟩ succeed," also means "to burn, flare up."[68]

The Lord's wrath, which will "flare up like fire" (יִצְלַח כָּאֵשׁ), will be directed against בֵּית יוֹסֵף ("the house of Joseph"), that is, the northern kingdom.[69] This epithet (and its shorter form, יוֹסֵף, "Joseph," in Amos 5:15; 6:6),[70] refers originally to the Joseph tribes of Ephraim

52 So, too, S.

53 For example, Graetz; Wellhausen; Sellin, 227; Ehrlich, *Mikrâ*, 3.409; Maag, *Text*, 21. Several of these commentators are then forced to emend the particle כ to ב (כָּאֵשׁ).

54 For example, Nowack, יַצִּית כָּאֵשׁ; Oettli, *Amos und Hosea*, יַצֵּת כָּאֵשׁ.

55 For example, Budde, "Amos," 107; Harper, 112–13.

56 For example, J. Reider, "Contributions to the Scriptural Text," *HUCA* 24 (1952–1953) 95; Tur-Sinai, *Peshuṭo*, 463, יְלַחֵךְ כָּאֵשׁ. The verb means "to lick." See 1 Kgs 18:38.

57 For example, Sellin; J. Blau, "Über Homonyme und angeblich Homonyme Wurzeln II," *VT* 7 (1957) 100–101; A. Guillaume, *Hebrew and Arabic Lexicography I* (Leiden: Brill, 1963) 33; Rudolph, 189.

58 See *CAD, Ṣ*, 124.

59 See 1 Sam 2:15; Isa 44:16, 19.

60 This verb must not be confused with its Aramaic homonym, צלח ("to split, cleave"). See Blau ("Homonyme"), who distinguishes between צלח I ("to split ⟩ succeed"), which he relates to Aram. צלח; and צלח II ("to burn") in Amos 5:6, which he equates with Syr. *ṣrḥ*.

61 The verb also appears in connection with fire in Sir 8:10. See already F. Perles, "Ergänzungen zu den 'Akkadischen Fremdwörten,'" *OLZ* 21 (1918) 70; and M. Margolis, "Notes on Some Passages in Amos," *AJSL* 17 (1900–1901) 171. See E. Puech, "Sur la racine *ṣlḥ* en hébreu et en araméen," *Sem* 21 (1972) 5–17; N. Waldman, "Words for 'Heat' and Their Extended Meanings," in *Gratz College Annual of Jewish Studies* 3 (ed. I. D. Passow and S. T. Lachs; Philadelphia: Gratz College, 1974) 43–49, esp. 46–47 n 34; H. Tawil, "Hebrew צלח/הצלח, Akkadian *ešēru*/*šūšuru*: A Lexicographical Note," *JBL* 95 (1976) 405–13.

62 Tawil, "Lexicographical Note," 412–13.

63 *CAD, Ḫ*, 62–65. Although there are different thematic vowels, the two are interrelated. See *CAD, Ḫ*, 65 n.

64 *CAD, Ṣ*, 98–99; 100–101. Here again they are listed as homonyms but are apparently interrelated. N. Waldman ("Words for 'Heat,'" 46–47) relates Heb. צלח to Akk. *ṣarāḫu* by the interchange of *l*/*r* and brings several examples of this interchange in Akkadian and Hebrew. Perles (*Analekten*, 94) already equated the two.

65 For example, 1 Kgs 14:10; 16:3; 21:21. Compare Tawil ("Lexicographical Note," 412), who also cites Ugar. *bʿr* ("to lead"), I Keret 101–2; 190–91; II AB IV:16–17; and "burn, kindle," VAB IV:69–70 in S. H. Langdon, *Die neubabylonischen Königsinschriften* (Leipzig: Hinrichs, 1912).

66 For example, Gen 31:36; 1 Sam 17:53; Isa 5:11; Lam 4:19.

67 For example, Ezek 24:10; Obad 18; Prov 26:23.

68 Tawil, "Lexicographical Note," 412.

69 See, for example, Obad 18; Zech 10:6.

70 See, for example, Ezek 37:16, 19; Ps 78:67.

and Manasseh and then by extension to all of northern Israel.

The Hebrew text continues by stating that the fire will "consume לְבֵית־אֵל, with none to quench it" (וְאֵין־מְכַבֶּה).[71] Although the reading Bethel is confirmed by most of the ancient translations (α', θ', σ', T, V), several exegetes[72] still favor G, τῷ οἴκῳ Ισραηλ = בֵּית יִשְׂרָאֵל ("the house of Israel"), assuming that the first three letters of יִשְׂרָאֵל were inadvertently omitted, that is, בֵּית (יִשְׂרָ)אֵל. Thus, "the house of Israel" would parallel "the house of Joseph." The Masoretic reading, nevertheless, is still to be favored not only because it is attested by almost all of the early versions but also because this specific literary unit revolves around the key theme of בֵּית־אֵל, which now is mentioned for the third time; see v 5 (twice). Thus, it is neither to be deleted nor emended. Against this central northern cultic site, God's anger is directly centered.

■ **7** Amos proceeds to explicate how the Israelites have not sought the Lord by delineating his charges against them, which are the explicit reason for the imminent punishment.[73] The list of accusations, which commences with a chiastic pattern (a) הַהֹפְכִים ("who turn") (b) מִשְׁפָּט ("justice") (b') וּצְדָקָה ("and righteousness") (a') הִנִּיחוּ ("hurl down"), begins with a definite plural participle followed by a finite verb (see similarly Amos 2:7).[74] Many exegetes assume, however, that this verse begins an entirely new oracle and that the first ה in the participle הַהֹפְכִים is actually the remnant of an original הוֹי ("woe"-cry), which would then initiate the first of three such oracles that follow this same literary pattern (Amos 5:18; 6:1).[75] However, in light of the introductory note to chapter 5 that demonstrated a chiastic literary pattern to vv 1–17, there is no reason to emend the Masoretic text.[76]

The judges are charged with having "turn[ed] (הַהֹפְכִים) justice (מִשְׁפָּט)[77] into wormwood" (לְלַעֲנָה)[78]—into a bitter plant with a repulsive taste—and having "hurl[ed] (הִנִּיחוּ)[79] righteousness (צְדָקָה) to the ground."

71 For example, Isa 1:31; Jer 4:4; 21:12. Compare אֵין מְקִימָהּ, Amos 5:2. For the לְ, see *GKC,* 119s; *KB,* 465, no. 19. It may also be a לְ-accusative. Ehrlich (*Randglossen,* 5.240) calls the expression "einen parenthetischen Umstandssatz" ("a parenthetical circumstantial clause").

72 For example, Nowack; Marti; Ehrlich, *Randglossen,* 5.240; Cripps, 183; Tur-Sinai, *Peshuṭo,* 463; Gordis, "Studies," 229. See also Hos 10:15, where G reads οἶκος τοῦ Ισραηλ ("the house of Israel") for Heb. בֵּית־אֵל. Others omit Bethel as a gloss, for example, Wellhausen, 86; Maag, *Text,* 26; Robinson-Horst, 88. For the theme of "fire" and "Bethel," see 2 Kgs 23:15. For similar threats, see Jer 4:4; 21:12. For fire as a divine punishment in Amos, see, for example, 1:4, 7, 10, 12, 14; 2:2, 5; 7:4.

73 See *GKC,* 116x, for examples.

74 So, for example, Ehrlich, *Mikrâ,* 3.410; idem, *Randglossen,* 5.240; Cripps, 183.

75 Since G. A. Smith (1896) and accepted by many, for example, Weiser, *Profetie,* 163, 194ff.; Sellin, 229; Maag, *Text,* 30; Wolff, 228–29; Rudolph, 194–95; Gordis, "Studies," 229; Soggin, 88–89. See also E. Gerstenberger, "The Woe-Oracles of the Prophets," *JBL* 81 (1962) 252, 254; Wolff, 242–45. Some commentators (for example, van Hoonacker, 245; Wolff) simply transfer v 7 after vv 8–9 in order to establish the direct link with v 10. See, however, Hammershaimb, 80. Cross suggests that the "initial ה should be interpreted as an interrogative referring to the House of Joseph and Bethel, a use in lament parallel to אֵיכָה; see 2 Sam 1:19" (written communication).

76 G's translation, κύριος ὁ ποιῶν εἰς ὕψος κρίμα καὶ δικαιοσύνην εἰς γῆν ἔθηκεν ("The Lord [it is] who renders judgment on high and has established justice on earth"), constitutes an introduction to the following two hymnic verses and obviates the difficulty of the separation of v 7 from vv 10–11. For a very forced rendering of the supposed Hebrew original underlying the Greek translation, see J. D. W. Watts, "Note on the Text of Amos 5:7," *VT* 4 (1954) 215–16; and idem, *Vision,* 54–57. For several arguments in favor of the Masoretic text, see Wolff, 229, n *s.*

77 For הפך ל ("to turn to the opposite"), see also Amos 6:12; 8:10. J. Greenfield ("The Background and Parallel to a Proverb in Ahiqar," in *Hommages à André Dupont-Sommer* [ed. A. Caquot and M. Philonenko; Paris: Adrien-Maisonneuve, 1971] 57 n 3) compares the expression הָפַךְ מִשְׁפָּט to Akk. *dinam nabalkatum* ("to overthrow justice"). See *CAD, N,* I.17, 2e, "to pervert law and justice." Compare also the Akkadian cognate *abāku, CAD, A,* I.9, "to turn upside down, to upset," which also means "to reverse, to overthrow a treaty," and esp. with *dinu,* "to overthrow a legal decision." For references, see *CAD.*

78 For לַעֲנָה ("wormwood"), see M. Zohari, *Plant Life of Palestine: Israel and Jordan* (New York: Ronald, 1962) 134; Feliks, *Plant World,* 200–201. In addition to one other passage in Amos 6:12, the plant appears six other times in the Bible: Deut 29:17; Jer 9:14; 23:15; Prov 5:4; Lam 3:15, 19; and once in Sir 31:49. It often occurs in parallelism with רֹאשׁ ("poison weed"), as in Amos 6:12; Deut 29:17; Jer 23:15; Lam 3:19.

Compare his similar charge in Amos 6:12: "You have turned (הֲפַכְתֶּם) justice (מִשְׁפָּט) into poison weed (לְרֹאשׁ) and the fruit of righteousness (צְדָקָה) to wormwood" (לְלַעֲנָה).[80] Because מִשְׁפָּט and צְדָקָה[81] (both personified)[82] have been hurled down, he later exhorts them, in contrast, to "set up (הַצִּיגוּ) justice" (5:15) so that justice and righteousness will well up like water and an unfailing stream (Amos 5:24).[83]

The direct continuation of these charges is found in vv 10ff.[84]

■ 8 The second of the three short hymnic praises of God in Amos is admitted by almost all commentators to be out of place because it interrupts the prophet's arraignment of Israel that began in v 7 and continues in v 10.[85] It is commonly agreed, however, that this doxology was attracted to its present position by the catchphrase הפך ל-, which appears in both v 7 and v 8.[86] Israel was accused of having turned justice into (הַהֹפְכִים ל-) wormwood. Now it will have to face the Lord, the Creator and ruler, who among his many formidable feats turns pitch-darkness into (הפך ל-) dawn. This hymn is a declaration of affirmation and asseveration of the power and majesty

The plant is usually identified with the species *Artemisia absinthium*. *KB* (506) refers to Akk. *karān lāni* in its entry to לַעֲנָה. See, however, *CAD, K,* 201, which identifies this plant as "a kind of vine and the wine made of its fruit."

For G, εἰς ὕψος ("on high"), read לְמַעְלָה. This is accepted, for example, by H. Oort, "Het Vaderland van Amos," *ThT* 25 (1891) 121–25; Budde, "Amos," 108–9; Maag, *Text,* 30. Although the expression הפך למעלה ("to turn upside down") is found in Judg 7:13 and is attested indirectly in Sefire I:C, 19–23, there is no need to accept the proposed reading here; compare Amos 6:12 and the comments to the text.

79 For the expression, see Isa 28:2, ". . . shall be hurled with force to the ground" (הִנִּיחַ לָאָרֶץ בְּיָד). Then, of course, it will be "trampled underfoot" (v 3). Compare, for the image, Dan 8:12, וְתַשְׁלֵךְ אֱמֶת אַרְצָה ("it hurled truth to the ground").

There may be an indirect connection here between this and the former oracle. Israel "has fallen" (Amos 5:2) because it has hurled justice to the ground.

80 Weinfeld, *Deuteronomy,* 91 n 2, comparing Amos 6:12 and Hos 10:4, assumes that the prophets were making a pun on the idea of צֶמַח צְדָקָה ("the sprout of righteousness"), known from biblical and Phoenician sources: "Instead of the sprout of צְדָקָה there comes out the sprout of poison."

81 "Justice" and "righteousness" are central themes in the oracles of Amos; for example, 5:24; 6:12. Wolff, 245, locates these as well within the realm of wisdom literature, based on Prov 1:3; 2:9; 8:20; 16:8; 21:3. Its legal background, however, is patently clear.

82 See their counterparts in Akkadian, *kittu* and *mēšaru;* H. Cazelles, "De l'idéologie royale orientale," in *The Gaster Festschrift* (*JANESCU* 5; ed. D. Marcus; New York: Columbia University, 1973) 59–73.

83 For the king's responsibility in both Israel and Mesopotamia for setting up justice and righteousness, see Weinfeld, *Deuteronomy,* 152ff.; and idem, "Mesopotamian Prophecies of the End of Days," *Shnaton* 3 (1979) 263–76, esp. 266–67 (Heb.). The innovative idea in Amos, however, is that what formerly was considered the duty of the king now becomes the responsibility and obligation of every one of the citizens.

For a thorough study of these concepts, see M. Weinfeld, *Justice and Righteousness in Israel and the Nations: Equality and Freedom in Ancient Israel in Light of Social Justice in the Ancient Near East* (Jerusalem: Magnes, 1985) (Heb.).

84 So most commentators.

85 There is no consensus, however, as to its original setting. Some place it after v 20 or at the end of the chapter; others suggest attaching it to Amos 4:13 or after Amos 5:17. Several exegetes opt for Amos 9:5a as the original setting for Amos 5:9. For different opinions and suggestions, see the commentaries. Watts (*Vision,* 54–57) does not think that the doxology severs the literary unit and includes vv 6–7 in the hymn itself. In this he follows the lead of G, which interprets Amos 5:7 as part of the doxology. This solution, however, is entirely unwarranted. See also Farr, "Language," 322–23.

Note the employment of seven verbs in the doxology, yet another example of the heptad in Amos; see, for example, 2:6–7, 14–16; 4:4–5, 6–11; 5:21–23; 9:1–4.

86 For example, Weiser, *Profetie,* 202; Gese, "Beiträge," 434; Wolff, 241. Unfortunately, Crenshaw (*Hymnic Affirmation,* 127 n 48) thinks that the catchword principle does not play a significant role in the text of Amos. See the comments on the oracles against the nations in chapters 1—2.

of the Lord, who will bring the threatened punishment upon those who defy his will. Those who are guilty of social inversion shall now witness and suffer cosmic inversion.

This doxology celebrates the power of the Deity in his manifold acts of creation. The prophet first declares that the Lord made both the constellations of כִּימָה and כְּסִיל.[87] These two are similarly juxtaposed in Job 9:10 with the identical verb for creation, עֹשֶׂה, and appear once again in parallel stichs in Job 38:31. The former, כִּימָה, is usually identified with the Pleiades, the constellation of seven stars;[88] and the latter, כְּסִיל, with Orion.[89]

Because the Pleiades and Orion are associated with the New Year (Nisan) and thus with the change of the winter and summer seasons,[90] the Lord, the Creator of the natural order, is praised here as the one who regulates the times and seasons of the year. There may also be here a muted polemic against heathen astral worship. The stars and constellations are not divine but are God's creations.[91]

The next two contrasting praises are structured chiastically: The Lord both "turns pitch-darkness (צַלְמָוֶת)[92] into dawn and darkens day into night"[93] (see Amos 4:13). He changes not only the annual seasons but also the daily alternation of day and night. This foreshadows the pericope of the Day of the Lord—note יוֹם in both units, here and vv 18, 20—which also will be a time of darkness.

This feat of majestic power is often found in Sumerian and Akkadian literature. See, for example, *ša urri ana mūši taškunu* ("You who have changed the day into night");[94] *ša ūmu namru ana ikleti taškunu* ("You who turned the bright day into darkness").[95] It is also part of stock curses: *ūmu namrum da'ummatam līwīšum* ("May the bright day turn into darkness for him");[96] *ūmam ana mūšim litēršum* ("May he [the god] turn day into night for him").[97]

From the Lord's control of time and his works in heaven, the prophet continues by exalting his power as evidenced in acts performed on earth. He "summons (הַקּוֹרֵא)[98] the waters of the sea and pours them out upon the face of the earth" (see Amos 9:6). This has been interpreted as referring either to the inundations of floods, to the regulation of the rainfall, or as an allusion to the Deluge.[99]

Because the phrase ה׳ שְׁמוֹ concludes the other two

87 See especially the study of S. Mowinckel, *Die Sternnamen im Alten Testament* = *NorTT* 29 (1928) 5–75, esp. 45ff. See also Dalman, *AuS,* I.497ff.; *EM* 4.103 (Heb.).

88 So, for example, Mowinckel, *Die Sternnamen,* 45–51. See Akk. *kimtu* ("family"). So, too, in Ethiopic, *kîma* / *kêma* = Pleiades. Other less likely suggestions have been Sirius (for example, Hoffmann, "Versuche," 107ff.; Robinson-Horst), Hyades (see V to Job 9:9), or Arcturus (see G to Job 9:9; and V to Amos 5:5).

89 Some, however, interpret כְּסִיל as Sirius (the dog of Orion); see Dalman, *AuS,* I.14, 39, 497–501. For mythological traditions associated with Orion, see Cripps, 185 n 4; Maag, *Text,* 159; T. H. Gaster, *Myth, Legend, and Custom in the Old Testament* (New York and Evanston: Harper & Row, 1969) 790. For mention of both in Homer, see *Iliad* XVIII, 486–89; XXII, 26–30; *Odyssey* V, 272–74. The two are also coupled together in Mesopotamian texts: Orion = *šidallu* / *šitaddalu* / *sitaddaru;* and Pleiades = *zappu.* See, for example, G. Meier, "Die zweite Tafel der Serie *bīt mēseri,*" *AfO* 14 (1941) 142:47. See *CAD, Z,* 50. See also F. Gössmann, *Planetarium Babylonicum, oder: Die sumerisch-babylonischen Stern-Namen* (ed. P. A. Deimel; Sumerisches Lexikon IV/2; Rome: Pontifical Biblical Institute, 1950) nos. 348, 393.

90 See G. Fohrer, *Das Buch Hiob* (KAT 16; Gütersloh: Gerd Mohn, 1963) 216. The beginnings of seasons, in turn, regulate the plantings and the harvests.

91 For example, Rudolph, 200, and many others.

92 For צַלְמָוֶת, see S. M. Paul, "*ṣlmwt,*" *EM* 6.735–36 (Heb.). For the opposite, see Job 24:17: "For all of them morning (בֹּקֶר) is darkness" (צַלְמָוֶת).

93 For the construction, see *GKC,* 117ii. There is no need to add a ל to לילה. Note the merism in these two stichs.

94 G. A. Reisner, *Sumerisch-babylonische Hymnen nach Thontafeln grieschischer Zeit* (Berlin: W. Spemann, 1896) 77:18–19, including its Sumerian equivalent.

95 Reisner, *Hymnen,* 77:20–21, including its Sumerian equivalent.

96 *RA* 46 (1972) 92:68. See *LKA,* 1:16.

97 *LH* XXVII:88–89. See also *Gilgamesh* XI:106, *[mim]ma namru ana eṭûti uttirru* ("[Adad] who turned to blackness all that had been light").

98 Resorting to the Arabic root *qry* ("to gather [water]") is not necessary to explain the imagery here; against I. Eitan, "Biblical Studies: II—Stray Notes to Minor Prophets," *HUCA* (1939) 6 (comparing Prov 27:16); Speier, "Bemerkungen," 307; Gordis, "Studies," 229–30.

99 See Harper, 116. The last interpretation is favored by only a few, for example, Robinson-Horst, 89–90;

hymns, Amos 4:13 (ה' אֱלֹהֵי־צְבָאוֹת שְׁמוֹ) and Amos 9:6, probably here, too, it should come at the end of the doxology. Therefore, it has been suggested that either vv 8 and 9 be transposed (which, however, would separate the immediate proximity of the catchword הפך) or that the last two words, ה' שְׁמוֹ, be transposed to the end of v 9.

■ **9** The Lord controls not only the laws of nature (v 8) but also determines the destiny of nations. For this characteristic juxtaposition of God's control over nature as well as history, see, for example, Isa 40:22–23; 45:12–13.

This chiastically structured verse bristles with difficulties: the rare verb בלג; the repetition of שׁד in both stichs; the possible dual meaning of עָז; and the ancient versions' pointing of the final verb as a causative. First, the verb בלג. The other occurrences of this verb (Ps 39:14; Job 9:27; 10:20) are of no aid in unraveling its meaning here. (Some commentators, deriving the verb from Arab. بلج ["to be bright"],[100] suggest the unlikely translation "to burst or flash forth.")[101] G, ὁ διαιρῶν ("he who divides, distributes") may be based on a reading such as הַמַּפְלִיג/הַמְפַלֵּג, which, however, is untenable in this context. The other ancient versions were also at pains to provide a suitable solution; see T, דִּמְגַבַּר ("who strengthens");[102] V, *qui arridet* ("who laughs at"); so, too, α', ὁ μειδιῶν ("who smiles"); σ', τὸν ποιοῦντα καταγελάσαι ("who makes ridiculous")—all these are most likely derived from the Arabic root just cited, which also means "to be cheerful, merry, smiling." Other proposals have been to relate this verb to Arab. بلغ ("to bring about");[103] Judaeo-Arabic بلق ("to reach, attain to");[104] or Syr. *b^elaq* ("to make suddenly come").[105] Yet another possibility would be to connect the verb with the root פלג, which in Mishnaic Hebrew also means "to set loose."[106] A completely satisfactory solution has yet to be found.

The repetition of שׁד in both cola has disturbed many commentators. Relying on G's two different translations of the noun in this verse, συντριμμὸν ("fracture, destruction") and ταλαιπωρίαν ("affliction"), they emend the first שׁד to שֶׁבֶר and create the common parallel pair of שֶׁבֶר/שׁד.[107] The repetition of the same noun, however, is not so rare as would appear at first sight, even for Amos himself. Compare Amos 3:9a (אַרְמְנוֹת) and 9:5b (יְאֹר). However, G need not have been based on a variant Hebrew version but may merely have resorted to two different translations for its own internal stylistic reasons.

Neher, *Amos*, 70; Crenshaw (*Hymnic Affirmation*, 28), who bases his suggestion on the supposed violent nature of the verb שׁפך ("to pour"). However, the other two occurrences of the verb with "water" are not related to any violent activity. See Exod 4:9; 1 Sam 7:6. Note that the Akkadian interdialectal cognate equivalent, *šapāku (AHw*, 3.1168), also appears with clouds, rains, and water.

T's paraphrase here, "He who commands to gather great armies (מְשִׁרְיָן סַגִּיאָן) like the waters of the sea" (כְּמֵי יַמָּא), recalls a similar image from an inscription of Cyrus, "His extensive troops *(ummānišu rapšāti)* whose number, like water in a river *(ša kima mê nāri)* cannot be discerned," in T. G. Pinches, *The Cuneiform Inscriptions of Western Asia* (ed. H. C. Rawlinson; V; London: The British Museum, 1909) 35:16.

100 *KB*, 126: "Arab. *balağa*, hervorbrechen (Morgenröte) ('the breaking forth [of dawn]'); *baliğa*, frölich, heiter sein ('to be cheerful, happy')." Compare *BDB*, 114, "cause to burst or flash."

101 For example, Cripps, 187; Hammershaimb, 81.

102 So, similarly, Menahem ben Saruq, *Maḥberet*, 45; Rashi; Kimchi.

103 J. J. Glueck, "Three Notes on the Book of Amos," in *Studies in the Books of Hosea and Amos: Die 7th–8th OT Werkgemeenskap in Suid-Afrika 1964–1965* (Potchefstroom: Rege-Pers Beperk, 1965) 115–16. See also the note of Tur-Sinai in E. ben Iehuda, *A Complete Dictionary of Ancient and Modern Hebrew* (16 vols.; Jerusalem and Tel Aviv: La'Am, 1980) 1.544 n 2 (Heb.). See, too, D. Yellin, "Forgotten Meanings of Hebrew Roots," *Leš* 1 (1928–1929) 9 (Heb.).

104 Gaster, "Hymn," 23–26. Gaster also cites S. von Grünberg's suggestion of deriving the verb from Arab. *'aflaga* (أفلج), "to conquer, subdue."

105 *KB*, 126.

106 See Oort, "Amos," 118; Sellin. Maag (*Text*, 25) translates: "He who makes destruction (שֶׁבֶר) break in upon stronghold(s)."

107 For example, Ewald; Hitzig; Oort, "Amos," 118; Graetz; Smith; Nowack; Oettli, *Amos und Hosea;* Harper; Sellin; Maag, *Text*, 25. See, however, the pertinent criticism of L. Zalcman, "Astronomical Illusions in Amos," *JBL* 100 (1981) 53–58. He, in turn, considers v 9b as a quotation and translates, "Who flashes forth destruction on the strong as 'Destruction shall come on the fortress,'" referring to Isa 13:6; Joel 1:15; and Job 5:21.

There is no compelling reason, therefore, to support any emendation or change here.

The noun עָז[108] may refer to nations or individuals, "powerful/strong" (see Num 13:28; Deut 28:50; Isa 19:4), so, for example, V, *robustum,* and T, תַּקִּיפִין; or to "strongholds" (variant of עֹז, see Ps 46:2, and also מָעוֹז),[109] thus paralleling מִבְצָר in the second stich (see Amos 3:11; note, too, the appearance of שֹׁד in Amos 3:10).

All the ancient versions[110] support the pointing of the verb as a causative, יָבִיא ("brings"), rather than the Masoretic *qal,* יָבוֹא ("comes"), thereby maintaining the Lord as the subject of both stichs. Thus,[111] "It is he who brings (suddenly)/sets loose (?) ruin upon the strong(holds) and brings devastation upon the fortresses."[112] The hymn praises the might of the Deity above and beyond all human power and powerholds. "Alle menschliche Stärke und alle menschlichen Macht- und Schutzmittel kommen gegen Jahwe nicht auf, eben weil er der allmächtige Schöpfer ist" ("All human strength and all human means of might and protection cannot prevail against Yahweh, precisely because he is the omnipotent creator").[113]

■ 10 Following the preceding hymnic interpolation, this chiastically structured verse continues the prophet's arraignment, which concludes in v 12.[114] The literary unit of vv 10–12 forms, moreover, an inclusio, beginning and ending with the catchword שַׁעַר (which appears yet a third time in v 15).

The שַׁעַר ("gate") of the city was the spot where public

108 There is no reason to emend to עִ(י)ר, "city," against K. Koch, "Die Rolle der hymnischen Abschnitte in der Komposition des Amos-Buches," *ZAW* 86 (1974) 522 n 74.

109 *KB,* 577. For עָז as a variant spelling of עֹז, see Exod 15:13; Isa 26:1; Pss 21:2; 74:13 (but not necessarily with the meaning "stronghold"). See also the expressions מִגְדַּל־עֹז (Judg 9:51; Ps 61:4; Prov 18:10), עִיר עָז (Isa 26:1), קִרְיַת־עֹז (Prov 18:11, 19).

110 See G, ἐπάγων; V, *affert;* T, מַשְׁלִיט.

111 The exegetical tradition of interpreting this passage astronomically and thus connecting it contextually with the beginning of v 8 began with Hoffmann, "Versuche," 111. He suggested reading שׁוֹר ("the Bull = Taurus") for the first and second שֹׁד; עֵז ("She-Goat = Capella") for עָז; and מַבְצִיר (others, מְבַצֵּר; "the Vintager = Vindemiator [= Vindemiatrix]") for מִבְצָר and thus translated: "He who makes Taurus to rise hard on (the rising of) Capella and causes Taurus to set hard on (the rising of) Vindemiator." Because Taurus rises in May to June (and sets in October to November), Capella in April to May, and Vindemiator in September (which inaugurates the בָּצִיר, "wine gathering"), this verse was supposedly describing the Deity's complete control of the entire year by means of astronomical imagery. He was followed by Duhm ("Anmerkungen," 1–18 [esp. 9–10]), who, in order to support the conjectured interpretation and readings, made a further emendation. Basing himself on G's translation of the second שֹׁד, ταλαιπωρίαν, a substantive that is usually employed to render Heb. שֶׁבֶר (see Isa 51:19; 59:7; 60:18; Jer 48:3), he posited that the assumed Heb. שֶׁבֶר was a corruption of yet another noun, שְׁבוֹ, a jewel mentioned in Exod 28:19; 39:12, which he identified with the star Gemma. He, in turn, translated the verse as: "Who bids Taurus and Capella rise; who bids Gemma with Arcturus set." This translation was accepted by Nowack, 144–45, and Gressmann, *Prophetie,* 347. Next came G. R. Driver ("Two Astronomical Passages in the Old Testament," *JTS* 4 [1953] 208–12), who further added his own astronomical emendation, מְבַצֵּר (for מִבְצָר), which he identified as Virgo. See also Maag, *Text,* 26; Watts, *Vision,* 56–57; Cripps, 297–99. For objections, see Rudolph, 201.

Apparently underlying all these attempts at stargazing was the unproven assumption that a doxology cannot contain references to God's punishing the guilty. However, "It is not in the stars!" Some other commentators, who did not hold such presuppositions, nevertheless also resorted to emendations; for example, Gaster ("Hymn"): "He who maketh destruction (שֶׁבֶר—based on G) to come upon (Judaeo-Arabic, *balaqa,* "to reach/attain to") men's strongholds (Arab. *ʿawadha,* "to seek refuge") and bringeth (יָבִיא) ruin on their fortresses." Otherwise, Horst ("Doxologien," 45–54): "He who leaps over (הַמְדַלֵּג) the strong wall" (שׁוּר מָעוֹז).

112 See Hos 10:14.

113 Rudolph, 201. See Wellhausen, 81–82; Weiser, *Profetie,* 164; Sellin, 228–91; Crenshaw, *Hymnic Affirmation,* 128.

114 Most commentators connect vv 10ff. with v 7. See also J. de Waard, "The Chiastic Structure of Amos V, 1–18," *VT* 27 (1977) 170–77.

legal hearings took place and where justice was administered.[115] The person in charge of dispensing this justice, the מוֹכִיחַ ("the arbiter, judge"),[116] had become, however, the object of the people's hate (שָׂנְאוּ).[117] For the "arbiter at the gate," and the dangers to which he was exposed, see Isa 29:21: "Who cause men to lose their lawsuits (דָּבָר), laying a snare for the arbiter at the gate (לַמּוֹכִיחַ בַּשַּׁעַר) and wronging (וַיַּטּוּ) by falsehood him who was in the right" (צַדִּיק).[118]

Likewise detested and abominated (יְתָעֵבוּ) was the דֹּבֵר תָּמִים. תָּמִים is an adverb[119] describing the manner in which the person involved presents his case.[120] The construction is similar to the expression הוֹלֵךְ תָּמִים ("he who walks with integrity";[121] see Ps 15:2; Prov 28:18). So, too, דֹּבֵר תָּמִים ("he who pleads with integrity and honesty")[122] is the one who is most detested by the populace.[123] Amos accuses them of despising and abhorring those who both practice and dispense justice.

■ **11** Many commentators regard v 11 as the work of a redactor and thus not an integral part of the original oracle.[124] It is true that the expression לָכֵן יַעַן is a hapax legomenon and that both the theme of the reproach (taxes exacted from the poor) and the manner of the address itself (here, second-person plural, as contrasted to vv 7, 10, third-person plural) are different. These considerations nevertheless need not weigh against its authenticity. The uniqueness of the expression does not negate its having been coined by Amos. As for the change of person, this is such a common stylistic feature of prophetic denunciations and so widely attested that it actually becomes a characteristic aspect of oracles in general. Furthermore, even though the nature of the charge has changed, it still remains part and parcel of the prophetic condemnation of the immoral behavior of the population. The accusations leveled against the Israelites cover many different aspects and dimensions of their unethical way of life.[125]

However, this is the only place in the book in which

115 For the central role of the שַׁעַר in legal proceedings, see L. Koehler, *Hebrew Man* (tr. P. R. Ackroyd; London: Akademie Verlag, 1956) 149ff. See, for example, Deut 21:19–20; 22:15; 25:7; Ruth 4:1ff.; Lam 5:14. For the corruption of justice at the gate, see Prov 22:22. So, too, in Mesopotamia. See the entries *bābu, bābtu, CAD, B,* 19–20. Similarly, in Ugaritic, the *ṯǵr* ("gate") was the place of popular assembly and judgment. See M. Astour, "Un texte d'Ugarit récemment découvert et ses rapports avec l'origine des cultes bachiques grecs," *RHR* 164 (1963) 1–15. Dan'el dispensed justice by the gate; see *CTA* 17:v:4–8.

116 For מוֹכִיחַ, see H. J. Boecker, *Redeformen des Rechtslebens im Alten Testament* (WMANT 14; Neukirchen-Vluyn: Neukirchener Verlag, 1963) 45ff.; Seeligmann, "Terminologie," 266ff.; W. Richter, *Recht und Ethos: Versuch einer Ortung des weisheitlichen Mahnspruches* (SANT 15; München: Kösel, 1966) 166–86; and R. Wilson, "An Interpretation of Ezekiel's Dumbness," *VT* 22 (1972) 91–104. See Ezek 3:26; Prov 24:25; 25:12; 28:23; Job 9:33; 32:12. For the connection of שׂנא and תּוֹכַחַת, see Prov 12:1; 15:10.

117 Note that the root שׂנא is a key word in this chapter, vv 10, 15 (the people are the subject), and v 21 (God is the subject).

118 There is a remarkable collocation here of the very same key terms found in Amos 5:10, 12. This was already noted by M. Seidel, "Four Prophets Who Prophesied at the Same Time," in idem, *Ḥiqrē Mikra* (Jerusalem: Mosad HaRav Kook, 1978) 195–238 (Heb.).

119 See *GKC,* 118n.

120 For other forms connected with דָּבָר, see *KB,* 201.

121 Compare the Akkadian interdialectal cognate equivalent of this expression, *alāku / atalluku šalmiš* ("to perform one's duties perfectly/faithfully"). See Muffs (*Studies,* 203–4), who compares Mal 2:6.

122 This may be the judge, for example, Hammershaimb, 82; the witnesses, for example, Weiser, *Profetie,* 197; Neubauer, "Erwägungen," 314 n 104; Wolff, 246; Rudolph, 198; or "anyone whose plea is just." It does not refer here to "one who pleads the case of the innocent," against Marti; Riessler; Maag, *Text,* 103. The Akkadian semantic equivalent of Heb. דבר, *dabābu,* also means "to plea in court, to litigate"; see *CAD, D,* 8–10.

123 For the coupling of שׂנא and תעב, see Deut 12:31.

124 For example, Weiser, *Profetie,* 197; Robinson-Horst; Neubauer, "Erwägungen," 313; Wolff. Many, however, also argue for it being a direct continuation of vv 7, 10, for example, Sellin; Maag, *Text,* 103; Amsler.

125 See H.-J. Kraus, "Die prophetische Botschaft gegen das soziale Unrecht Israels," *EvT* 15 (1955) 295–307; Kapelrud, *Central Ideas,* 48–50.

לָכֵן does not introduce the direct words of the punishment. Again, Amos appears to be using a "delaying tactic" before leveling his final threat of punishment.

Amos once more turns his attention to the theme of the exploitation of the poor[126] at the hands of the wealthy. The sole problem here is the exact meaning of the hapax legomenon בּוֹשַׁסְכֶם. The verb is commonly assumed to be a hybrid form of בּוֹשְׁכֶם and בּוֹסְכֶם, derived from the root בוס/בסס ("to trample down"; for example, Isa 14:25; 63:6; Ps 60:14).[127] The unusual writing of this verb with a שׁ (which, if correct, would be its sole attestation, for in all the other biblical passages the verb appears only with a ס) supposedly led to its being mispointed as a שׁ. Another suggested solution is that this is a conflate reading of two different verbs, בוס and שסה, both meaning "to plunder." Although both these verbs always govern a direct object in Hebrew and never appear with the preposition עַל, evidence for such a possible construction has been adduced from a Ugaritic text. The passage in *CTA* 16:vi:48, *ṯšm ʿl dl*, originally translated "those who prey upon the poor," appears, at first glance, to be identical to the phrase in Amos. One scholar even went one step further.[128] By equating Heb. עַל דָּל with Ugar. *ʿl dl* and revocalizing Heb. עַל to על ("child"), he translated the passage in Amos: "because of your despoiling the child of the poor." Because the first morpheme of the Hebrew root ב, however, was missing in the Ugaritic verb, he assumed that the ב was not part of the root but was actually the preposition ב, meaning "on account of." Because such a nuance is rare in Hebrew (for example, Deut 9:4, 5; Jer 51:46), he further conjectured that it, in turn, was glossed by the more common יַעַן and that this gloss was then incorporated into the text. First, serious doubt exists as to the above interpretation of the Ugaritic text itself.[129] There is no need, moreover, to resort to either of these assumed conflate readings or to such complex exegesis. The solution is much simpler. This extremely rare Hebrew verb, attested only here, is none other than the interdialectal cognate of Akk. *šabāšu* ("to gather, collect a [grain] tax"), from which was derived the noun *šibšu* ("a [grain] tax").[130] Detailed investigation into this Akkadian word has fully documented its employment as a tax on many different agricultural products, but primarily it refers to a straw tax.[131] The Hebrew verb בשס, a metathesized form of its Akkadian etymological cognate *šabāšu* / *šabāsu*, should be

126 For דָּל, see H.-J. Fabry, "*dal*," *TWAT* II (1977) 221–44.

127 See, for example, Harper, 118. The suggestion of Wellhausen, בּוֹסְכֶם, was accepted by many commentators. Ehrlich (*Randglossen*, 5.240–41), however, already raised the objection that בוס never appears with the preposition עַל (see Jer 12:10; Zech 10:5).

128 T. Fenton, "Ugaritica-Biblica," *UF* 1 (1969) 65–66. He interpreted the verb as being the infinitive construct of *šss* with the preposition *b* and vocalized *bešussekem*. He, in turn, was followed by Dion ("Le message moral," 25 nn 81–82).

129 See H. L. Ginsberg, *The Legend of King Keret—A Canaanite Epic of the Bronze Age* (BASOR Supplementary Studies 2–3; New Haven: Yale University, 1946) 49. M. Held ("The Root *ZBL* / *SBL* in Akkadian, Ugaritic, and Biblical Hebrew," in *Essays in Memory of E. A. Speiser* [ed. W. W. Hallo; New Haven: Yale University, 1968] = *JAOS* 88 [1968] 93 n 66) translates the Ugaritic passage as "You do not chase away those that prey on the poor." Ginsberg, however, now interprets the *m* in Ugar. *ṯšm* as a root letter and also relates this verb to the Akk. *šabāšu* / *šabāsu* by means of metathesis and attested phonological change. This oral communication is reported in H. R. Cohen, *Biblical Hapax Legomena in the Light of Akkadian and Ugaritic* (SBLDS 37; Missoula, MT: Scholars, 1978) 94 n 262.

130 This was already suggested by H. Torczyner, "Presidential Address," *JPOS* 16 (1936) 6–7; see also idem (Tur-Sinai), *Peshuṭo*, 463. He first suggested a reading of בְּשָׁסְכֶם or בְּשׁוֹסְכֶם, and then שְׁבָסְכֶם. Wolff, 230, basing himself on Torczyner (Tur-Sinai), suggests that the verb be interpreted as a *qal* infinitive construct with a suffix, שְׁבָסְכֶם or שׁוֹבְסְכֶם. The present form "was revocalized after the first two consonants of the form had been transposed." See also Vesco, "Amos," 498; Soggin, 89.

131 Subsequent to Torczyner's (Tur-Sinai's) insight, much new documentation of this Akkadian verb and noun has been published. This is all referred to in Cohen's study of the hapax legomena; see n 129; and Cohen's nn 262–68 on pp. 94–96. For a discussion of *šibšu* from the Old Akkadian through Late Babylonian periods, see M. de J. Ellis, *Agriculture and the State in Ancient Mesopotamia: An Introduction to Problems of Land Tenure* (Occasional Publications of the Babylonian Fund I; Philadelphia: University Museum, 1976).

pointed בְּשָׁסְכֶם (שָׁבְסְכֶם)—a *qal* infinitive with a second-person suffix; it refers to the exacting of a "grain tax."

Taxes were regularly collected in Mesopotamia from cultivated land and harvests. In addition to *šibšu*, other well-documented taxes were *miksu*, *nusāḫū*, and *biltu*.[132] Corresponding to one of the latter, Amos next refers to another "grain tax" (מַשְׂאַת־בַּר);[133] for מַשְׂאֵת as a technical term of taxation, see also 2 Chr 24:6, 9. This noun (derived from the root נשׂא, "to lift up, carry, take away"; compare its Akkadian interdialectal equivalent, *biltu*, derived from *wabālu*, "to bring, carry") may also refer to a "gift" or "ratio/allotment" (see Gen 43:34; 2 Sam 11:8; Jer 40:5; Ezek 20:40; Esth 2:18) and is the etymological cognate to Punic *mś't*.[134] The "term reflects the graphics of both the politico-economic and cultic situations, whereby a gift is presented by lifting it up, or whereby a tax is 'carried away' from persons."[135] The verb employed here, לקח, is also related to this same sphere of activity. Compare its interdialectal etymological and cognate equivalent, Akk. *leqû* ("to take"), which is applied to the taking of taxes, customs, and duties.[136] Thus Amos is inveighing against the unfair, if not illegal, taxation of the indigent classes. The underprivileged are made to finance the indulgence of the wealthy by paying taxes collected at harvest time.

The prophet proceeds to pronounce a retaliatory punishment in the form of a "futility curse,"[137] that is, a curse that describes the reversal of one's expectations. Because the upper class has enlarged its property and wealth at the expense of the poor, its very own possessions will be taken from it. The people of the upper class will not enjoy the fruits of their own labor. They will neither dwell in the luxuriously expensive "houses of hewn stone" (בָּתֵּי גָזִית)[138] that they have built,[139] nor will they drink the wine of the "delightful vineyards" (כַּרְמֵי־חֶמֶד)[140] that they have planted. Interestingly enough, because they have profited by the taxation of the agricultural produce of the poor, they will be punished by a curse against their very own plantations. For similar threats combining house and vineyard, see Deut 28:30; Zeph 1:13. For the positive side of the picture, that is, the blessings of house and vineyards, see Isa 65:21–22 and Amos himself in 9:14, where he reverses this very curse for the future.[141]

132 For *nusāḫū*, see J. N. Postgate, *Neo-Assyrian Royal Grants and Decrees* (Studia Pohl: Series Maior 1; Rome: Pontifical Biblical Institute, 1969) 14; idem, *Taxation and Conscription in the Assyrian Empire* (Studia Pohl: Series Maior 3; Rome: Pontifical Biblical Institute, 1974) 174, 175, 187–89. See also *CAD, N*, II.351–52, *nusāḫū*, "tax on agricultural produce, especially barley." See *šibše nusāḫē kî ša āli iddan* ("He pays straw taxes and barley taxes like [the rest of] the village"); cited in *CAD, N*, II.352. For *miksu*, see *CAD, M*, II.63–65, and M. de J. Ellis, "Taxation in Ancient Mesopotamia: The History of the Term *miksu*," *JCS* 26 (1974) 234–46. For *biltu*, see *CAD, B*, 232–34. For detailed descriptions of the latter two, see also Ellis, cited in n 131.

133 For בַּר, see also Amos 8:5–6; and Gen 42:3, 25; Ps 72:16; Prov 11:26. See Dalman, *AuS*, III.161. Wolff, 247 n 130, notes that Akk. *bāru*, III, also means "tax, tribute" (referring to *AHw*, 1.108; see now *CAD, B*, 120) and "thus corresponds precisely to מַשְׂאֵת, "levy, tribute." However, this word appears only in Late Babylonian texts and is actually an Old Persian loanword. See *CAD, B*, 120. The correct etymological cognate to Heb. מַשְׂאֵת is, as noted in the text and in the following note, Punic *mś't*.

134 See the Marseilles Tariff, *KAI*, I,69:3, 6, 10, 17, 18, 20, 21; see also 75:2; 119:5; and in the plural, 74:1. *KB*, 605, refers to Akk. *maššitu*, but this noun, which is derived from *našû* (= נשׂא), means "delivery." See *CAD, M*, I.389–90. Comparison should also be made with Heb. מַשָּׂא ("tribute"), Hos 8:10; 2 Chr 17:11; and Akk. *biltu*. See Paul, "Hosea 8:8–10," 197.

135 B. Levine, *In the Presence of the Lord: A Study of Cult and Some Cultic Terms in Ancient Israel* (SJLA 5; Leiden: Brill, 1974) 17 n 40.

136 For multiple examples, see *CAD, L*, 141, 3a 4′; 142, 3b 5′.

137 For the genre of "futility curses," see Hillers, *Treaty Curses*, 28–29.

138 This specific expression appears only here in the Bible. Compare the vaunting of the inhabitants of Samaria in Isa 9:9: "Bricks have fallen—we'll rebuild with dressed stone."

139 See a similar Akkadian curse, *bît ippušu libêl šanûmma* ("The house which he builds let another person take over"), *BBSt* no. 6, ii:53.

140 See Isa 27:2 (according to some mss. and ancient versions), כֶּרֶם חֶמֶד ("vineyard of delight"). Similarly Isa 32:12: "Lament . . . for the pleasant fields (שְׂדֵי־חֶמֶד), for the spreading grapevines." The interdialectal etymological and cognate equivalent of Heb. חמד appears in Ugar. *ḥmd*, *UT*, 872; and in *EA* 138:126, *ḫamūdu*, as a West Semitic gloss for *jāpu*.

141 Note that in this verse, Amos 5:11, and in Amos 9:14

■ **12** This verse, too, should not be interpreted as a later addition or as a new oracle[142] but as an integral part of the prophet's detailed description of the offenses of the wealthy class against the defenseless population of northern Israel. Structurally its originality is evidenced by the literary inclusio pattern that it creates with v 10, beginning and ending on the theme of the perversion of justice at the שַׁעַר (the "city gate").

Amos continues his arraignment of the upper class with an emphatic (כִּי) first-person all-embracing *j'accuse* of their "manifold" (רַבִּים פִּשְׁעֵיכֶם)[143] and "multiple" (עֲצֻמִים חַטֹּאתֵיכֶם)[144] offenses. He then specifically spells out a few of their cardinal crimes[145]—each one pertaining to their devious and corrupt juridical practices.

The first charge of injustice is that they are "enemies"/"persecutors" (צֹרְרֵי)[146] of the one who is "innocent" (צַדִּיק).[147] The second is that they "take[148] bribes" (לֹקְחֵי כֹפֶר) and thereby distort justice. כֹּפֶר is not a bribe "to overlook or disregard an offence, but rather a payment made for the purpose of erasing or 'wiping away' [כפר] guilt incurred by the offence. . . . As is often the case with terms connoting a payment or gift, *kôper* appropriates less respectable applications. It may be synonymous with 'bribe' or with unjust gain (cf. 1 Sam 12:3; Prov 6:35; Job 36:18)."[149] In this connection *leqû*, the Akkadian interdialectal etymological and semantic equivalent of Heb. לקח, should be cited as also employed within the context of accepting gifts and bribes.[150] Compare, in reference to people, in general, *awīlû ša ṭātam ilqû* ("the men who have accepted bribes"), and for judges, in particular, *dajānu ṭātu u kadrâ ileqqēma* ("the judge who shall take a bribe and gift").[151]

Last, the prophet, returning to his original third-person address (v 7), accuses the judges of turning aside, that is, "subvert[ing] (הִטּוּ)[152] the cause of the needy (אֶבְיוֹן)[153] at the gate." The poor and underprivileged are continually the victims of the local judiciary, who victimize them at the very place (שַּׁעַר) where justice should be

appears the identical sequence of four verbs: בנה, ישב, נטע, and שתה. For the Ugaritic interdialectal semantic and etymological equivalents of Heb. ישב and שתה, *ytb* and *šty* in a similar parallel structure, see T. Yamashita, "Professions," in *Ras Shamra Parallels: The Texts from Ugarit and the Hebrew Bible* (ed. L. R. Fisher; AnOr 50; Rome: Pontifical Biblical Institute, 1975) 16.

142 Against, for example, Wolff, 248.

143 For the parallelism of פשע and חטא, see, for example, Isa 59:12. For the set pair of adjectives רב and עצום, see, for example, Exod 1:9; Deut 7:1; Isa 8:7; 53:12; Mic 4:3; Zech 8:22; Ps 135:10; Prov 7:26. See also עָצְמוּ חַטֹּאתָיִךְ ("Your sins were so many"), Jer 30:14, 15, parallel to רֹב עֲוֹנֵךְ ("Your iniquity was so great"). See Avishur, *The Construct State of Synonyms in Biblical Rhetoric: Studies in the Stylistic Phenomenon of Synonymous Word Pairs in the Construct State* (Jerusalem: Kiryat Sepher, 1977) 127, 128, 145 (Heb.).

144 Ever since Wellhausen, חַטֹּאתֵיכֶם has been emended to חַטָּאֵיכֶם because of the following plural masculine adjective, עֲצֻמִים. However, it has not been noted that whenever the substantive פֶּשַׁע appears, it is always coupled with the corresponding feminine forms: חַטָּאָה, Exod 34:7; Lev 16:16; Ezek 33:10; Mic 1:5; Ps 25:7; חַטָּאת, Gen 31:36; Dan 9:24; or חֲטָאָה, Ps 32:1. The lack of correspondence is due to the influence of the preceding masculine forms, רַבִּים פִּשְׁעֵיכֶם. See also Wolff, 230.

145 Ehrlich, *Randglossen,* 5.241.

146 Note the assonance of the letter צ, צֹרְרֵי צַדִּיק. They act as a צַר ("enemy"), Amos 3:11. See *KB,* 990, צרר, II, for references. Compare the interdialectal cognates in Ugar. *ṣrrt, UT,* 2200; and Akk. *ṣerru, CAD, Ṣ,* 137–38. Others have connected the verb with its homonym, צרר ("to press"), *KB,* 990.

147 See T, זַכָּאָה ("he who is innocent"). For צַדִּיק, see K. Koch, "*ṣdq,*" *THAT* 2 (1976) 507–30.

148 For Heb. לקח in the context of accepting bribes and gifts, see, for example, 1 Sam 8:3; 12:3–4; 2 Kgs 5:15, 16, 20, 23, 26; Ezek 18:13, 17; Ps 15:5.

149 B. H. Levine, *In the Presence of the Lord: A Study of Cult and Some Cultic Terms in Ancient Israel* (SJLA 5; Leiden: Brill, 1974) 61–62.

150 See *CAD, L,* 139, for this and other examples. See also n 148.

151 See W. G. Lambert, "Nebuchadnezzar King of Justice," *Iraq* 27 (1965) 5, col. II, line 7. For other terms for presents and gifts that develop the meaning of a bribe, see Greenfield, "Stylistic Aspects," 10; and idem, "Some Aspects of Treaty Inscriptions in the Bible," *Fourth World Congress of Jewish Studies* 1 (Jerusalem: World Union of Jewish Studies, 1967) 119; J. J. Finkelstein, "Middle Assyrian *Šulmānu* Texts," *JAOS* 72 (1952) 77–81.

For judges and bribes, see *BWL,* 132:97–100: "You give the unscrupulous judge . . . Him who accepts a present and yet lets justice miscarry, you make bear his punishment. As for him who declines a present *(ṭāti)* but nevertheless takes the part of the weak, it is pleasing to Shamash, and he will prolong his life." See also *BWL,* 320, nn 98–99.

152 This is an elliptical expression for the subverting of מִשְׁפָּט, as several of the other verses indicate.

dispensed.[154] This is the exact opposite of how these leaders should behave. Compare Exod 23:6, לֹא תַטֶּה מִשְׁפַּט אֶבְיֹנְךָ בְּרִיבוֹ ("Do not subvert [תַטֶּה] the cause of your poor in his litigation"; see Deut 16:20; 24:17). For similar accusations, see Isa 10:2, "to subvert (לְהַטּוֹת) the cause of the poor"; Mal 3:5, "who subvert (מַטֵּי) [the cause of] the widow, orphan, and stranger"; Prov 17:23, "The wicked man draws a bribe (שֹׁחַד) out of his bosom to pervert (לְהַטּוֹת) the course of justice"; and Prov 18:5, "who subvert (לְהַטּוֹת) the innocent in judgment." Compare also Isa 29:21.

■ **13** Verse 13 is generally interpreted as either a late wisdom[155] or apocalyptic[156] gloss or is assumed to be misplaced in its present position,[157] for לָכֵן in the oracles of Amos always serves as an introduction to the actual punishment.[158] (For an exception, however, see comments to Amos 5:11.) A further vexing problem is the meaning of מַשְׂכִּיל.[159] If the מַשְׂכִּיל refers, as some think,[160] to Amos, why would he, of all people, be silent?[161] If it refers to the "prudent one"[162] in general, for what reason need he keep silent: to protect his own skin?[163] Or is it merely the cautionary wisdom of not questioning God's actions?[164] Does מַשְׂכִּיל refer to the "prudent one" at all? Some have related it to the same word that appears as a superscription to several (wisdom?) Psalms[165] to connote a type of hymn (Pss 32:1; 42:1; 44:1; 45:1; and also in Ps 47:8).[166] According to this line of interpretation, at that "time of misfortune" (עֵת רָעָה; see Mic 2:3),[167] such hymns will be silent.

In light of such divergent exegesis, yet another suggestion might be offered for consideration. The symmetrical chiastic structure of the composite pericope of vv 1–17 has been noted previously. The second and fourth sections begin on the similar note "to seek" the Lord and/or good (vv 4, 14). The fourth section then terminates with a public lamentation (vv 16–17). Thus it is also possible that the second section, followed by the third, which delineates the punishments, could also conclude on a similar mournful tone. Further support for this suggestion may be adduced if יִדֹּם is derived not from the verb דמם ("to keep silent")[168] but from the homonymous root דמם ("to mutter, moan, groan, sigh"). This verb has been recognized in several biblical verses;

153 See Kapelrud, "New Ideas," 193–206. For Heb. אֶבְיוֹן, compare Ugar. *'bjnt, UT*, 24.

154 For a similar accusation leveled in Mesopotamian literature against corrupt judges, see the Hymn to Shamash, II:41–47, *ANET*³, 388.

155 For example, Weiser, *Profetie,* 211; Maag, *Text;* Neubauer, "Erwägungen," 294; Rudolph, 185.

156 For example, Nowack; Sellin; Cripps, 189.

157 For example, Wolff, 249–50, who would place it after vv 16–17, but nevertheless interprets it as a later addition written by a disciple of Amos. See Ehrlich, *Randglossen,* 5.241; idem, *Mikrâ,* 3.410 n 2; Hammershaimb, 84, however, regards vv 10–13 as a single unit.

158 Rudolph, 185.

159 For מַשְׂכִּיל, see *KB,* 605.

160 For example, Amsler, "Amos," 326. See also V. Maag, "Zur Übersetzung von *Maśkil* in Amos 5.13, Ps 47.8, und in den Überschriften einiger Psalmen," SThU 12 (1943) 108–15; Cramer, 85f.

161 Rudolph, 185.

162 For example, Budde, "Amos," 110; Ridderbos; van Gelderen. Gordis ("Studies," 232) translates, "Therefore, he who understands that time will remain silent," interpreting the particle ב and מַשְׂכִּיל as governing עֵת. For this construction, he compares Pss 32:8; 101:2.

163 Harper, 123. Other suggestions are that it reflects his inability to tell others how to avoid punishment or implies that his speech will not accomplish anything.

164 Wolff, 249–50.

165 Sellin², 239–40 (who transfers the verse to follow v 26), followed by I. Engnell, "The 'Ebed Yahweh Songs and the Suffering Messiah in Deutero-Isaiah," *BJRL* 31 (1948) 76 n 2; Kaufmann, *Toledoth,* 6.60 n 9. See also Maag, *Text;* Ginsberg (*Israelian Heritage,* 33) translates "song of adoration," and suggests that the verse should perhaps be inserted between vv 17 and 18.

166 See S. Mowinckel, *Psalmenstudien: Die technischen Termini in den Psalmenüberschriften* (6 vols.; Kristiania: Dybwad, 1923) 4.5ff. See *KB,* 605; H.-J. Kraus, *Psalmen 1—63* (BKAT XV/1; Neukirchen-Vluyn: Neukirchener Verlag, 1972) xxii–xxiii. See, however, V. Maag, "Zur Übersetzung von *Maśkil,*" 108–15.

167 See Jer 2:27, 28; 15:11; Ps 37:19; Eccl 9:12. Rudolph, 185, correctly criticizes those who refer the "time of disaster" to the present. It is future oriented. Compare the use of Akk. *lemnu* ("ill-boding, unhappy, fateful") with nouns designating time, *CAD, L,* 122–23. For יוֹם רָעָה ("time of misfortune"), see Eccl 7:14; 12:1 (יְמֵי הָרָעָה).

168 See, however, E. Y. Kutscher, "Mittelhebräisch und

compare Isa 23:2 (where it parallels the verb הֵילִילוּ, "wail," of v 1); Ps 4:5.[169] It is cognate both to Ugar. *dmm,* which appears in parallel to *bky* ("to cry"),[170] and to Akk. *damāmu* ("to mourn, moan, groan").[171] If correct, then this section would also end on the same mournful note: "At such a time the prudent one (?) moans."

■ **14** Once again (see v 4) the prophet holds out the option for life.[172] Once again the message remains the same: survival is conditioned upon "seeking." This is the third and climactic occurrence of the verb דרשׁ. This time, however, Amos explicates and defines what the exhortation "Seek me/the Lord" (vv 4, 6) actually means. Previously he clarified how not to seek the Lord—not through the channel of the cult (v 5). Now he expresses himself in a positive vein: "Seek the Lord" equals "Seek good," that is, the answer is to be found in the moral-ethical life. Moreover, just as he continued with the negative אַל in v 5, "But do not seek," so here as well he continues with the same vetitive[173] in antithetical parallelism:[174] "(Seek the good)[175] and not (וְאַל) evil, so that you may survive."[176] For Amos, "seeking" signifies a total dedication to and concern with[177] the "good" (טוֹב). One finds the Lord, according to the prophet, not in the observance of ritual, but in one's undivided devotion to the moral dimension of human relations (compare Mic 6:8).

For a similar development of the same theme—first stated in a general fashion and then expounded in ethical terms—see Zeph 2:3: "Seek (בַּקְּשׁוּ) the Lord. . . . Seek righteousness, seek humility." Note, too, that in this passage survival is also dependent upon correct moral behavior: "perhaps you will find shelter on the day of the Lord's anger."

Then follows one of the rare occasions in prophetic literature in which the reader overhears the words of the people themselves (cited by the prophet).[178] It is characteristic of Amos's polemical style to mention the sentiments of the people or even to quote their popular

Jüdisch-Aramäisch im neuen Köhler-Baumgartner," in *Hebräisch Wortforschung. Festschrift zum 80. Geburtstag von Walter Baumgartner* (ed. B. Hartmann and others; SVT 16; Leiden: Brill, 1967) 158–75, especially 167. Cross notes, "If the point is surprise and not lament, then the translation might be 'struck dumb, astonished'" (written communication).

169 For example, G. R. Driver, "A Confused Hebrew Root (דום, דמה, דמם)," in *Sepher Tur-Sinai* (ed. M. Haran and B. Z. Luria; Jerusalem: Kiryat Sepher, 1960) 1*ff.; M. Dahood, "Textual Problems in Isaiah," *CBQ* 22 (1960) 400ff. See also Lev 10:3; Ezek 24:17; Pss 31:18; 107:29; Lam 2:10. See *KB*, 217, דמם, II. See also Arab. *damdama* ("to mutter, murmur"). See also J. J. Jackson, "Amos 5:13 Contextually Understood," *ZAW* 98 (1986) 434–35.

170 *UT*, 674. See *tbkn.wtdm.ly* ("Let her mourn me and let her bewail me"), *CTA* 16:i:30.

171 *CAD, D*, 59–61; *dumāmu* B, 179.

172 There is no need to deny these words to Amos, contrary to Weiser, *Profetie*, 183–94; Cripps, 191 n 1; Snaith, *Book of Amos*, 93; Nowack, 145 (v 15); Robinson-Horst (v 14b); Wolff, 234, 250. Furthermore, once one recognizes the overall pattern of this literary unit, there is no reason to transpose vv 14–15 to follow vv 4–6, against Hammershaimb, 84; Rudolph, 189, 191–92. Many, however, do accept their authenticity; see Cramer, 40–43; Maag, *Text*, 28–29, 32; Hesse, "Amos 5," 1–17; Neubauer, "Erwägungen," 292–316; Gottlieb, "Amos und Jerusalem," 451–54; Mays, 99–102; Rudolph, 193; Hasel, *Remnant*, 190–91. See also G. Lust, "Remarks on the Redaction of Amos V:4–6, 14–15," in *Remembering All the Way* (ed. A. S. van der Woude; *OTS* 21; Leiden: Brill, 1981) 129–54.

173 *GKC*, 152 f, g.

174 For the antithesis of the two, see also Amos 9:4. This is characteristic of Amos's style (see Amos 5:18, 20; 8:11) and has been associated with the genre of sapiential literature; see, for example, Prov 24:21; 25:9; and see Wolff, *Amos the Prophet*, 67–69; and his commentary, 250. (See, however, Rudolph, 193.) The pair are found, however, also in narrative (Gen 31:24; Num 24:13), legal (Lev 27:10, 12, 14; Deut 30:15), and in Psalm literature (Pss 34:17; 37:27; 52:5). For the prophets, see Isa 5:20; Jer 42:6; Mic 3:2. For a note on such antithetical pairs, see M. Held, "The Action-Result (Factitive-Passive) Sequence of Identical Verbs in Biblical Hebrew and Ugaritic," *JBL* 84 (1965) 282 n 71.

175 The expression דִּרְשׁ טוֹב appears elsewhere only in Esth 10:3, but compare similarly Prov 11:27: "He who earnestly seeks what is good (שֹׁחֵר טוֹב) . . .; he who is bent on evil (וְדֹרֵשׁ רָעָה)." For a discussion of Amos's understanding of טוֹב, see Hasel, *Remnant*, 196–98.

176 Although this is characteristic of Deuteronomic phraseology, for example, Deut 4:1; 5:30; 8:1; Jer 35:7, it is not limited to this literature.

177 For the verb דרשׁ ("to be concerned with, devoted to") see, for example, Deut 11:12; Isa 1:17; 16:5. For other examples, see *KB*, 223.

178 For a study of quotations in prophetic literature, see Wolff, *Zitat*.

conceptions, in order to contradict them (for example, Amos 5:18; 8:5; 9:10). In this instance, however, he avidly wishes that what the people say were true; but, according to him, it would become an actuality only if they followed his exhortation. For if they "seek good and not evil," then "the Lord, the God of Hosts,[179] will really[180] be with you as you claim." This popular catch phrase or slogan,[181] "The Lord is with us" (see Isa 7:14; 8:8), has its roots in the good fortune, prosperity, and military and economic success of the northern kingdom. The Israelites believed that only because the Lord was with them were they able to reach the pinnacle of success that characterized the period of Jeroboam II. The prophet, however, makes this state of affairs entirely contingent. God's help and continued presence are conditioned solely on their behavior. The "good" is obtained not from within the cult. Salvation and survival are posited entirely on the ethical-moral dimension of life.

■ **15** Amos continues to expand upon what devotion to good and not evil truly demands of the individual. In this verse, chiastically parallel to v 14 (רָע, טוֹב–טוֹב, רָע), the prophet declares that they must "hate evil" (שִׂנְאוּ־רָע)[182] with the same passion as they presently "hate (שָׂנְאוּ) the arbiter at the gate" (v 10). Conversely, concern and devotion to good is not sufficient; they must sincerely "love good" (אֶהֱבוּ טוֹב).[183] "Love good" is then practically interpreted to mean a way of life that is counter to their present manner of behavior. They who are in the habit of "overthrowing" (הַהֹפְכִים) and "hurling down" (הִנִּיחוּ) justice and righteousness (v 7) must rectify their actions and "set up (הַצִּיגוּ)[184] justice in the gate."

Then, and only then, "perhaps (אוּלַי) the Lord, the God of Hosts, will show favor (יֶחֱנַן)[185] to the remnant of Joseph." The act implied in the verb חנן is the bestowal of pardon and favor by one in a superior position upon one

179 There is no reason to delete אֱלֹהֵי־צְבָאוֹת as a later addition, against, for example, Sellin, 231; Weiser, *Profetie*, 188; Wolff, 251. See, however, Robinson-Horst, 90; Maag, *Text*, 32; Amsler, 205. It appears in three consecutive verses, 14, 15, 16, and then in v 27; see also Amos 4:13. See the comments of Neubauer ("Erwägungen," 306 n 72), who also claims its originality based on the cultic context. So, too, von Rad, *Theology*, 1.18–21. The phrase is used intentionally in order to be reinterpreted.

180 כֵּן is used here emphatically and not with the meaning "recht, richtig"; against Maag, *Text*, 32, 157–58; and Neubauer, "Erwägungen," 305. For the correlatives, כֵּן . . . כַּאֲשֶׁר, see Gen 18:5; and for the reverse sequence, Exod 1:12; Isa 52:14–15; Amos 3:12.

181 See Deut 20:4; Mic 3:11; Ps 46:8, 12. See also Num 14:43; 23:21; Judg 6:13. For a thorough study of this "*terminus technicus*," its typology, and examples, see Neubauer ("Erwägungen," 295–302), who posits here an anticultic polemic (p. 316), utilizing a formulation that stems from the sphere of oracles of salvation. The cult is not the way toward salvation as the people believe and practice. See Crenshaw, *Hymnic Affirmation*, 43.

182 See also Ps 97:10; Prov 8:13; and in parallel cola, Ps 109:5; Prov 26:26. There is no need to view these phrases as part of any influence of wisdom literature upon Amos, contrary to Wolff, *Amos the Prophet*, 69–70. See also the pertinent remark by A. Hurvitz, "Wisdom Vocabulary in the Hebrew Psalter: A Contribution to the Study of 'Wisdom Psalms,'" *VT* 38 (1988) 49 n 24. The two expressions also appear together in Phoenician; see *KAI*, I,26 A III.17–18. For a comparative parallel from Akkadian, see *lemutta zērma kitta rā[m]* ("Hate what is evil; love what is right"), BE 1/1, no. 83, r. 24 in H. V. Hilprecht, *Old Babylonian Inscriptions Chiefly from Nippur* (Philadelphia: University of Pennsylvania, 1893). For the opposite, see *MDP* 10, pl. 11 iii, 10 in V. Scheil, *Textes élamites-sémitiques* (Paris: Leroux, 1908); *UET* 1, 165 ii 7 in C. J. Gadd and L. Legrain, *Ur: Royal Inscriptions*, vol. 1 (2 vols.; London: The Trustees of the Two Museums, 1928).

183 See the exact opposite in Mic 3:2: "But you hate good (שֹׂנְאֵי טוֹב) and love evil" (וְאֹהֲבֵי רָעָה), which follows immediately upon v. 1, "For you ought to know what is right" (מִשְׁפָּט). For the collocation of these themes, see also Ps 37:27–28: "Shun evil (רָע) and do good (טוֹב) . . . For the Lord loves what is right" (מִשְׁפָּט). See Seidel, "Four Prophets," 195–238.

184 This is the only instance in the Bible where the verb יצג in the *hiphʿil* is followed by an abstract object, "Justice" (מִשְׁפָּט), which is once again personified; as it has been "overturned," so must it be "set up" again.

185 See the standard dictionaries and concordances. Compare its Akkadian cognate, *enēnu* ("to pray, ask for mercy"), *CAD, E*, 162–63. Neubauer ("Erwägungen," 302–4), basing himself on the multiple occurrences of this verb in psalms of lament (see Pss 4:2; 6:3; 9:14; 25:16; 30:11; 31:10; 41:5, 11; 51:3; 56:2; 57:2; 86:3, 16; 119:58, 132), relates its use here to the cult by interpreting the words of Amos (as previously vv 4–6) as "eine bewusste Anspielung des Amos auf kultische Verhältnisse" ("a conscious

who is dependent upon him.[186] The operative and decisive word here is אוּלַי ("perhaps").[187] Repentance in and of itself is a sine qua non, but it does not operate absolutely or automatically. It cannot be resorted to as a magical device or opted for as a guarantee to change the will of God. Complete certainty of its acceptance or rejection is never really known, for the final decision is always reserved for God alone.[188] "Vielmehr wird durch dieses Vielleicht die absolute Souveränität und Freiheit Jahwes sichergestellt: Reue und Busse auf der menschlichen Seite ist zwar unabdingbare Voraussetzung für die göttliche Vergebung, aber erzwingen lässt sie sich auch dadurch nicht, es steht ganz bei Jahwe, ob er Gnade walten lassen will oder nicht." ("Rather the absolute sovereignty and freedom of Yahweh are secured by this 'perhaps.' Repentance and atonement by humans are indeed an irrevocable presupposition for divine forgiveness, but they cannot by these means coerce him. It depends entirely upon Yahweh whether he will show mercy or not.")[189] Israel's ultimate destiny depends on the Lord's reaction to their response. Salvation is conditional upon God's will, even after repentance.[190] If, however, God does accept their reformed behavior and actions, he may respond by extending his pardon to the "remnant[191] of Joseph" (שְׁאֵרִית יוֹסֵף).[192]

■ **16** This section[193] now brings to an end the series of oracles on the very same dire note on which they began (Amos 5:1–3): the tones and sounds of lamentation.[194] Once again לָכֵן introduces the announcement of judgment (see Amos 3:11; 4:12; 5:11; 6:7; 7:17)—the "city

allusion to cultic situations") (p. 304). See, too, Rudolph, 193 n 11.

186 See 2 Sam 12:22.

187 See Babylonian Talmud, Hagigah, 4b, "When Rabbi Ashi reached this verse, he would begin crying, 'All this and (only) "Perhaps"!'" (כּוּלֵּי הַאי וְאוּלַי).

188 See Hasel, *Remnant,* 203–4. See Neubauer, "Erwägungen," 307: "Selbst wenn ihr das alles tut, selbst dann ist euch das Heil Jahwes noch lange nicht sicher!" ("Even if you do everything, even then Yahweh's salvation is still not quite certain for you!"). For similar theological statements, see Joel 2:14; Jonah 3:9; Zeph 2:3; Lam 3:29.

189 Rudolph, 193. He also correctly criticizes both Wolff's relating this thought to the influence of wisdom literature and his regarding the entire passage as being a later interpretation of the "prophet's disciple" (p. 251).

See also Weiser, *Profetie,* 162: "Gott ist nicht an das Volk gebunden, wohl aber ist das Volk an Gott gebunden" ("God is not tied to the people, but rather the people are tied to God"). See also E. K. Dietrich, *Die Umkehr im Alten Testament und im Judentum* (Stuttgart: Kohlhammer, 1936) 51.

190 Hasel, *Remnant,* 206: "Yet for Amos human action cannot be a substitute for God's action, nor can God's action be a substitute for human action. Each has its proper sphere."

191 For this as yet "embryonic" concept of a remnant, see also Amos 3:12; 4:11; 5:3; 9:9. For a study of the term, see R. de Vaux, "Remnant," 15–30, especially 18, where de Vaux states that the idea of a "remnant" was already well established by the time of Amos and suggests that "the words of Amos would arouse in them mixed feelings of hope and fear . . . fear tempered by hope." For the antiquity of the concept, see H. Gressmann, *Der Ursprung der israelitisch-jüdischen Eschatologie* (FRLANT 6; Göttingen: Vandenhoeck & Ruprecht, 1905) 229–38.

192 The northern tribes are once again referred to as "Joseph"; see Amos 5:6; 6:6. There is no reason whatsoever to deny the originality of this term to Amos, against Wolff, 251. See Hasel (*Remnant,* 199–202) for a discussion of this concept. He is of the opinion that the term preceded Amos, was taken from popular Israelite belief, and "was probably connected with the tradition of the house of Jacob which was rather predominate in the Northern Kingdom" (p. 200). See also S. Herrmann, *Die prophetischen Heilserwartungen im Alten Testament: Ursprung und Gestaltwandel* (BWANT 85; Stuttgart: Kohlhammer, 1965) 119.

Hasel (*Remnant,* 201) says that the term cannot refer to the contemporary northern kingdom, against Wellhausen, 82; Gottwald, *Kingdoms,* 115, among others. Israel at this time was in a very prosperous state. He thus understands it as a "future entity," citing many other scholars (202 n 286; 205 n 293; 473). "In Amos the remnant is an entity of eschatological expectation. Thus in Amos we encounter for the first time a connection of the remnant motif with eschatology" (205 and n 295).

193 For the present section, see also M. Gruber, *Aspects of Nonverbal Communication in the Ancient Near East* (Studia Pohl 12/1–2; Rome: Pontifical Biblical Institute, 1980) 434–56.

194 The sequence of the divine names here is unique; compare Amos 3:13.

squares" (רְחֹבוֹת) and "streets" (חוּצוֹת)[195] will resound with the mournful cries of wailing. Note the threefold occurrence of מִסְפֵּד ("lamenting")[196] in this and the next verse. This emphatic repetition, together with the statement that the dirges and elegies will extend to both town and country as well as to the fields and vineyards (v 17), poignantly expresses the overwhelming dimension of the mourning rites that will encompass all elements of the population as well as all populated areas.

For further examples of mourning ceremonies taking place in the open squares and public places, compare, for example, Isa 15:3; Jer 48:38. In postbiblical Mishnaic times, public prayers during fast days were also recited in the main square of the city.[197]

To make his point even more poignant, Amos pronounces the actual plaintive cry of the mourners, הוֹ־הוֹ.[198] Other well-known wails of woe in the Bible[199] are אוֹיָה, הוֹי, אוֹי, אֲבוֹי, אֲהָהּ, וַי, הָהּ, הָהּ.[200]

Although commentators all interpret אִכָּר[201] as a collective noun,[202] they are not in agreement as to whether these "farmhands" are the subject[203] or the object of the verb. The latter seems to be the preferable:[204] They are the ones called upon to mourn.[205] This, in turn, leads one to transpose the preposition אֶל in the second stich to precede מִסְפֵּד, reading וְאֶל־מִסְפֵּד יוֹדְעֵי נֶהִי "and to lamentation those skilled in wailing [shall also

195 For the parallel pair of רְחוֹב and חוּץ, see, for example, Jer 9:20; Nah 2:5; Prov 1:20; 7:12; 22:13.

196 M. I. Gruber, in *Aspects of Nonverbal Communication in the Ancient Near East* (Studia Pohl 12/1–2; Rome: Pontifical Biblical Institute, 1980) 444, translates "funeral oration." Compare the Akkadian interdialectal semantic and etymological cognate, *sipdu, sipittu* ("mourning"), *CAD, S,* 299–300; *sapādu* ("to beat oneself/the breast, to mourn"), *CAD, S,* 150–51. For example, *[ina muḫḫi bī]ti isappid ū'i iqabbima* ("He performs the wailing for the temple, says 'Woe!'"); F. H. Weissbach, *Babylonische Miscellen* (WVDOG 4; Leipzig: Hinrichs, 1903) No. 12:18. Note that in this passage there is the same sequence of words as in the Amos verse: Akk. *sapādu* = Heb. מִסְפֵּד; Akk. *ū'i qabû* = Heb. יֹאמְרוּ הוֹ־הוֹ. This was also seen by M. Held, "Studies in Biblical Lexicography in the Light of Akkadian," in Eretz Israel 16 (*Harry M. Orlinsky Volume;* ed. B. A. Levine and A. Malamat; Jerusalem: Israel Exploration Society, 1982) 83 n 50.

197 Mishnah, Taanith, chapter 2.

198 This specific cry appears only here. See Kutscher, *Language,* 173 n 42 (Heb.); 299 n 47 (Eng.).

199 Check concordances for citations.

200 For similar cries of lamentation in Akkadian, *ū'a, ū'i, ūja,* see *AHw,* 3.1398. See, similar to the sequence in Amos, the following passage: *u₈-a ul iqbima ul iṣr[uḫ sipitta]* ("He did not say 'Woe!' and did not perform [the customary mourning]"); Borger, *Inschriften,* 110, 71: obv. 3. See, too, 43:57; *BWL* 274:15–16; *ANET,* 384:66; 461:299ff. See also n 196.

For lamentations, wailings, dirges, and mourning in Mesopotamian literature, see the respective entries in *CAD* and *AHw: bikītu, girrānu, ikkillu, ṣirḫitu, ṣirḫu, sipittu.*

201 Heb. אִכָּר is a loanword from Akk. *ikkaru* ("farm laborer, plowman"), *CAD, I,* 54, which is a loanword from Sum. engar (which itself may be derived from a pre-Sumerian stratum; see S. A. Kaufman, *The Akkadian Influences on Aramaic* [Assyriological Studies 19; Chicago and London: University of Chicago, 1974] 58). It later entered Aram. אִכָּר, Mandean *ikkārā,* Syr. *akkāra,* and Arab. *ikkār.* For a study of the meaning of אִכָּר, see Gese ("Beiträge," 432–36), who translates "Grundbesitzloser Landarbeiter" ("a farmhand without landed property"), 342–33. The funereal interpretation "gravedigger," derived from the root כרה, proposed by Glueck ("Three Notes," 116–19), is to be totally rejected.

202 See *GKC,* 145b.

203 See, for example, Harper; Guthe; Sellin; Hammershaimb, 86; Rudolph, 196.

204 As traditionally understood. See Isa 22:12: "My Lord God of Hosts summoned on that day to weeping and lamenting" (וַיִּקְרָא . . . לִבְכִי וּלְמִסְפֵּד . . .). There is no need to emend the noun to the plural אִכָּרִים and then interpret it as the subject of וְקָרְאוּ, against Sellin.

205 The "farmhands" (אִכָּר) were most likely called out because they were the ones accustomed to raise their voices in joy. Compare likewise in Akkadian literature, *ikkarišu ina ṣēri aj ilsa alāla* ("His farm worker [who violates the oath] shall never sing the harvest song in the field"), *CAD, I,* 52. Conversely, "the cattle trampled the meadow, the sustenance of the land; the farmer cries bitterly over his [plot of land]" *(ikkaru ina muḫḫi [irm]ūšu ibakki ṣarpiš);* F. Gössmann, *Das Era Epos* (Würzburg: Augustinus Verlag, 1955) I:138, 84. For the theme of the lamenting farm laborer, see Jer 14:4; Joel 1:11 (who also mentions vinedressers).

be called]."[206] Guilds of professional mourners[207] were very common in ancient Near Eastern cultures and included both females (Jer 9:16–17, 19; Ezek 8:14; 32:16)[208] and males (Eccl 12:5; 2 Chr 35:25; in the latter verse females are also mentioned).[209] These experts, "skilled in (the craft of) wailing" (יוֹדְעֵי נֶהִי)[210] had their (etymological, semantic, and professional) counterparts in Mesopotamian society: *mudē ṣirḫi* ("those who are well versed in dirges").[211]

■ **17** In another example of the use of vivid contrast, Amos declares that lamentation will spread even to the vineyards, the very place where rejoicing is usually the greatest (compare Judg 9:27; 21:20–21; Jer 48:33). This site par excellence of joy will turn into a place of mourning. For a similar description (this time applied to Moab), see Isa 16:10: "Rejoicing and gladness are gone from the farm land; in the vineyards (כְּרָמִים)[212] no shouting or cheering is heard. No more does the treader tread wine in the presses. I have silenced the shouts." Thus the entire country—city and town, country and fields (note the third mention of בְּכָל)—will be inundated with the sounds of keening, threnodies, and funeral requiems (third mention of מִסְפֵּד).

This sad and sorrowful scenario will take place "when[213] I pass through your midst" (אֶעֱבֹר בְּקִרְבְּךָ). The language here is strongly reminiscent of Exod 12:12, 23.[214] Just as the Lord "went through" (עבר בּ־) Egypt and struck down all their firstborn, so now he is again about to "pass through"—but this time the object of his attack is Israel. Amos, however, once more leaves the

206 See V, *et ad planctum eos qui sciunt plangere* ("and to lamentation those who know to bewail"); see also S. So, too, several medieval commentators, for example, ibn Ganaḥ, Kimchi, and most exegetes ever since Wellhausen.

For the parallelism of אֵבֶל and מִסְפֵּד, see Jer 6:26; Mic 1:8.

207 For mourning practices, see Kutsch, "'Trauerbräuche'," 25–42; M. Gruber, "Mourning," *EncJud* 10.485–87. See also H. Jahnow, *Das hebräische Leichenlied im Rahmen der Völkerdichtung* (BZAW 36; Giessen: Töpelmann, 1923).

208 See also 2 Sam 1:24; Jer 49:3; Ezek 32:16; Zech 12:11–14; but not necessarily professional mourners. See also Mishnah, Nedarim 9:10. See, too, Ugar. *bkyt* ("weeping women") parallel to *mšspdt* ("mourning women"), *CTA* 19:iv:171–72, 183.

209 See Rabbinic Hebrew, סַפְּדָנִים ("professional mourners"); for example, Babylonian Talmud, Berachoth, 62a.

210 For נְהִי, see Jer 9:9, 17, 18, 19; 31:15; Mic 2:4. This specific expression is unique to Amos.

211 Both male and female professionals are also attested in Mesopotamia; see *CAD, Ṣ*, 206, *ša ṣirḫi; B*, 35, *bakkītu*. See, too, *ANEP*, 210 (638).

212 Gese's proposal ("Beiträge," 433–34), וּבְכָל־הַכֹּרְמִים ("and among all the vinedressers"), already suggested by Hoffmann ("Versuche," 112), is unnecessary. See also Gruber (*Aspects*, 446), who reads כּוֹרִם in the former verse: "The farmer will summon the funeral orators (סוֹפְדִים), the vinedresser (כּוֹרִם), the expert in elegy." See, correctly, Wolff, 249; and Rudolph, 196. For אִכָּרִים and כֹּרְמִים, see Isa 61:5; Joel 1:11; 2 Chr 26:10. The emphasis is upon all the places where the lamentation will take place. The prophet is also setting into contrast their actions—planting "pleasant vineyards" (v 11)—with what will actually take place in those very vineyards.

213 כִּי here should be translated "when," and not "for"; against, for example, Cripps, 192; Wolff, 231.

214 See Crenshaw, "Theophanic Tradition," 206–7. For עבר בּ־ ("to invade"), see Nah 2:1. For the Akkadian cognate expression, *ina libbi etēqu* (= Heb. לַעֲבוֹר בְּקֶרֶב), see *AHw*, 1.261 1a). The exact nuance of Heb. עבר here and in several other biblical passages (for example, Ezek 9:5) has not been adequately defined. Its import becomes clear when compared with its Akkadian cognate and semantic equivalent, *bâ'u*, which, in addition to its basic meaning, "to go through, to pass over," also refers to "sweeping over destructively." See *CAD, B*, 180, c, for examples.

It is unnecessary to give this phrase a cultic setting (especially within the New Year festival), when, according to this interpretation, the appearance of God would bring destruction upon Israel's enemies and judgment upon Israel's own sinners. See A. Weiser, "Zur Frage nach den Beziehungen der Psalmen zum Kult: Die Darstellung der Theophanie in den Psalmen und im Festkult," in *Festschrift Alfred Bertholet zum 80. Geburtstag* (ed. W. Baumgartner and others; Tübingen: Mohr, 1950) 513–31; H.-P. Müller, "Die kultische Darstellung der Theophanie," *VT* 14 (1964) 183–91; M. J. Hauan, "The Background and Meaning of Amos 5:17B," *HTR* 79 (1986) 337–48.

Amos is clearly alluding to an ancient tradition in order to highlight a dramatic reversal. This time when the Lord "passes through," it will not be to destroy Israel's enemies, but rather Israel itself!

exact nature of the imminent and ominous catastrophic confrontation (בְּקִרְבְּךָ, "in your midst") between the Deity and Israel unstated and unspecified in order to heighten its threatening and terrifying effect (see, for example, Amos 4:12).

5 The "Day of the Lord"

18 Woe to you who yearn for the Day of the Lord!
What avail will the Day of the Lord be for you?
It shall be darkness, not light!
19 As when a man flees from a lion
And a bear confronts him,
Or when he reaches home
And leans his hand on the wall
A snake bites him!
20 Surely the Day of the Lord shall be darkness, not light,
Gloom, not gleam!

Introductory Comments to the "Day of the Lord"

The next literary section, containing the words of the prophet (vv 18–20), is followed by another pericope accenting the words of the Lord (vv 21–27).[1] They are connected, however, by a common ideological denominator. Both highlight a total reversal of popular beliefs—one concerning the "Day of the Lord," the other, the prevalent attitude toward the cult. Amos by attacking and denouncing these two major pillars of popular theology—one ideological and the other of practical daily significance—may also, in turn, be reacting and responding to the harsh criticism leveled against him by the people of the north. (For other reversals of popular notions, see, for example, Amos 3:2; 5:14; 6:1ff.; 9:7.)

Although there is no direct contextual reason for the juxtaposition of this section (vv 18–20) to the previous one, it may have been occasioned by two complementary reasons. First is the likely literary tie: The initial הוֹי "woe" cry (v 18) is related to the הוֹ־הוֹ cry of v 16. Second is a conceptual linkage, for here, too, the prophet abrogates another commonly held idea, as he did in Amos 5:14, "God is with us." Because their present state of affairs was flourishing as evidenced by their economic prosperity and military successes, God must be on their side. They thus had no reason at all to doubt that this situation would continue to prevail in the future. How then could the prophet threaten dire punishment for the chosen people? This present pericope, artfully constructed of a "woe"-oracle,[2] a rhetorical question, and a dramatic simile, comes to upset their misconceptions about what lies in store for the future of the northern nation.

The "Day of the Lord" (יוֹם ה'), an expression that appears for the first time in biblical literature in the Book of Amos,[3] is a theme that has been subjected to extensive investigations. Only a brief survey of the leading views

1 Both sections also contain rhetorical questions, v 18 and vv 20, 25.

2 For the literary genre of the הוֹי oracles, see E. Gerstenberger ("The Woe-Oracles of the Prophets," *JBL* 81 [1962] 249–63), who concludes that the *Sitz im Leben* of these oracles is to be located in the lament over the dead. However, he roots them ultimately in the wisdom of the clan, a theory that Wolff (*Amos the Prophet,* 23ff.; and his commentary, 243–45) supports and attempts to further substantiate. See also R. J. Clifford, "The Use of *HÔY* in the Prophets," *CBQ* 28 (1966) 458–64; W. Janzen, "*AŠRÊ* and *HÔI* in the Old Testament," *HTR* 62 (1970) 432ff.; and idem, *Mourning Cry and Woe Oracle* (BZAW 125; Berlin: de Gruyter, 1972); H. J. Zobel, "*HÔY,*" *TDOT* 3 (1978) 359–65. See, however, the criticism of Crenshaw, "Influence," 47–48; and G. Wanke, "אוֹי und הוֹי," *ZAW* 78 (1966) 215–18. One must clearly distinguish between the use of אוֹי and הוֹי; that הוֹי never appears in wisdom literature is of decisive significance.

Westermann (*Basic Forms,* 190–98) and, even earlier, Mowinckel (*Psalmenstudien: Segen und Fluch in Israels Kult und Psalmdichtung* [6 vols.; Kristiania: Dybwad, 1924] 5.119ff.) have presented the case for the origin of this cry within the curse genre.

For the connection with public laments, see Barstad, *Religious Polemics,* 103–8. For other studies, see the references in Wolff, 242 nn 99–100.

3 Amos may well have coined the exact term although the concept itself antedated him. See יוֹם מִדְיָן, Isa 9:3; יוֹם יִזְרְעֶאל, Hos 2:2; יוֹם יְרוּשָׁלָיִם, Ps 137:7; יוֹם מִצְרַיִם, Ezek 30:9.

concerning its *Sitz im Leben* is possible here.[4] Gressmann, who was the first to study the concept in detail, noted its common ancient Near Eastern motifs of cosmic catastrophe and placed the Day of the Lord within a popular eschatological framework.[5] Mowinckel, however, posited a cultic origin, anchoring it within an assumed annual New Year ritual celebrating the coronation of the Lord, who was about to destroy his enemies and bring forth national salvation for Israel.[6] The most well-received theory was advanced by von Rad who, basing himself upon the predominant martial imagery in the description of the Day of the Lord, concluded that its roots were to be found in sacral war traditions. The Day of the Lord was the time of the Lord's "holy war," when he went forth to fight and conquer his (= Israel's) enemies.[7] A very serious and poignant criticism was leveled against this position by Weiss, who, noting the absence of war imagery from Amos 5 and Isaiah 2, suggested that the proper context for the concept was to be found in the biblical descriptions of a theophany.[8] Cross, in turn, combined some of the basic results of both Mowinckel's and von Rad's studies and concluded that the Day of the Lord was both the day of the Lord's victory in battle and the day of his festivities.[9] Yet another proposal related the concept to covenant traditions and the execution of treaty curses.[10] Everson, who wrote in terms of the "Days of the Lord," placed more emphasis upon its historical setting and related five of its occurrences to past events: Isa 22:1–14, the campaign of Sennacherib against Jerusalem in 701 B.C.E.; Jer 46:2–12, the defeat of the Egyptian army at Carchemish by the Babylonians in 605; Ezek 13:1–9; and Lam 1:12; 2:1, the fall of Jerusalem to the Babylonians in 587/6.[11] The study of the "holy war" theme was also expanded into neighboring cultures by Weippert, who, in a critique of von Rad, clearly demonstrated that "profane" and "holy" wars cannot be distinguished in the ancient world and that cultic preparations prior to war and a deity's intervention on behalf of its

4 The notes refer only to the most representative studies on the subject. For an ample bibliography, see Barstad (*Religious Polemics,* 106–8), who relates the concept to public laments.

5 H. Gressmann, *Der Ursprung der israelitisch-jüdischen Eschatologie* (FRLANT 6; Göttingen: Vandenhoeck & Ruprecht, 1905) 143ff. See also idem, *Der Messias.*

6 S. Mowinckel, *Psalmenstudien: Das Thronbesteigungsfest Jahwäs und der Ursprung der Eschatologie* (6 vols.; Kristiania: Dybwad, 1922) 2.248, 272, 318–19; and idem, "Jahwes dag," *NorTT* 59 (1958) 1–56, 209–29. For a list of others who preceded and followed this line of interpretation, see Barstad, *Religious Polemics,* 90 n 71.

7 G. von Rad, "The Origin of the Concept of the Day of Yahweh," *JSS* 4 (1959) 97–108; and idem, *Theology,* 2.119–25. For those who preceded him, see Barstad, *Religious Polemics,* 92 n 85; and for those who followed his interpretation, *Religious Polemics,* 92 n 87.

8 M. Weiss, "The Origin of the 'Day of the Lord'—Reconsidered," *HUCA* 37 (1966) 29–60.

9 Cross, "Divine Warrior," 11–30. See R. W. Klein, "The Day of the Lord," *CTM* 39 (1968) 517–25. M. Weinfeld ("Aspirations for the Kingdom of God in the Bible and Their Reflection in Jewish Liturgy—The Essence of the Concept of the 'Day of the Lord,'" in *Messianism and Eschatology: A Collection of Essays* [ed. Z. Barag; Jerusalem: Zalman Shazar Center, 1983] 73–96 [Heb.]) also sees a "kernel of truth" in combining the two, for the "Day of the Lord," according to him, is related to the expectation of the kingship as well as to the idea of God coming in battle to judge and punish the wicked (p. 23). For an English adapted version of this study, see idem, "The Day of the Lord: Aspirations for the Kingdom of God in the Bible and Jewish Liturgy," in *Studies in the Bible* (ed. S. Japhet; Scripta Hierosolymitana 31; Jerusalem: Magnes, 1986) 341–72. See, too, idem, "The Concept of the Day of the Lord and the Problem of Its *Sitz im Leben,*" in *Studies in the Minor Prophets* (ed. B. Z. Luria; Jerusalem: Kiryat Sepher, 1981) 55–76 (Heb.).

10 See F. J. Hélewa, "L'origine du concept prophétique du 'Jour de Yahvé,'" *EphCarm* 15 (1964) 3–36; F. C. Fensham, "A Possible Origin of the Concept of the Day of the Lord," *Biblical Essays: Die Ou Testamentiese Werkgemeenskap in Suid Afrika—9th Congress* (Potchefstroom: Rege Pers Beperk, 1966) 90–97; C. van Leeuwen, "The Prophecy of the *Yôm YHWH* in Amos V: 18–20," in *Language and Meaning* (*OTS* 19; Leiden: Brill, 1974) 113–34.

11 A. J. Everson, "The Days of Yahweh," *JBL* 93 (1974) 329–37; and idem, "Day of the Lord," *IDBSup,* 209–10.

own nation were common motifs throughout the ancient Near East, as documented in Mari, Hittite, and especially neo-Assyrian sources.[12]

It can be safely concluded, nevertheless, that the term the "Day of the Lord" (יוֹם ה׳),[13] which occurs primarily in oracles against foreign nations, does not refer literally to a "day" per se but rather to a "time" or a "period,"[14] when, according to popular belief, the Lord will appear (or has appeared) in order to render judgment and destroy his enemies. As is common in the literary conventions of theophanies in the Bible and the ancient Near East, this war is described as having concomitant cosmic upheavals.[15] In Amos the people are described as eagerly yearning for this Day of the Lord, when the Deity will revenge himself upon their enemies, thereby bringing salvation and redemption to Israel. The prophet, in another of his dramatic reversals of popular ideology,[16] states that the Day of the Lord will indeed be a time of judgment, but this time the judged will be Israel. The Lord shall appear, this time not in order to save Israel, but rather to punish them, because they now are accounted among his enemies.[17]

■ **18** The first of the two "woe"-oracles (see Amos 6:1)[18] is ironically directed against those who earnestly believe in and "yearn for" (הַמִּתְאַוִּים)[19] the "Day of the Lord" (יוֹם ה׳),[20] a term that is repeated three times within these verses, Amos 5:18a, 18b, 20. Although Amos is the first to employ this expression in the Bible,[21] by the force of his polemic, obviously the popular conception of victory and salvation that will be brought about by the Lord's

12 Weippert, "'Heiliger Krieg,'" 460–93.

13 For the biblical references to this and closely related expressions (for example, יוֹם חָרוֹן, יוֹם אַף־ה׳, יוֹם נָקָם, יוֹם לַה׳, יוֹם עֶבְרַת ה׳, אַפּוֹ), see Weiss, "Origin," chart following p. 60. Most scholars tend to agree that the concept can be described even without the employment of the word יוֹם. The determining factor is the content of the oracle itself. See, for example, V. Eppstein, "The Day of Yahweh in Jer 4:23–28," *JBL* 87 (1968) 93–97. Many also relate the term בַּיּוֹם הַהוּא to the "Day of the Lord." For a study of this expression, see Y. Hoffman, "'אחרית הימים' and 'ביום ההוא'—Their Relation to Eschatological Passages in the Bible," *BM* 71 (1978) 438–44 (Heb.).

14 For a study of יוֹם, see E. Jenni, *"yôm,"* *THAT* 1^2 (1975) 711ff. For the use of the word in connection with "Day of the Lord," see Weinfeld, "Concept," 58–59. The employment of the Akkadian equivalent, *ūmu* ("day"), with the name of a deity, for example, *ūm(i) Enlil, Bēl,* or *ūm ili* ("day of the god"), refers to cultic festivals in honor of these deities. See Barstad, *Religious Polemics,* 99–100; *BWL* 38:16.

15 See Weinfeld, "Concept" and his other articles cited in n 9. See also his studies on descriptions of theophanies: "'They Fought from Heaven'—Divine Intervention in Ancient Israel and in the Ancient Near East," in Eretz Israel 14 (*H. L. Ginsberg Volume;* ed. M. Haran; Jerusalem: Israel Exploration Society, 1978) 23–30 (Heb.); and idem, "Divine Intervention," 171–81.

16 See, for example, Amos 3:1–2; 5:4–6; 9:7.

17 See also G. Fohrer ("Der Tag JHWHs," in Eretz Israel 16 [*Harry M. Orlinsky Volume;* ed. B. A. Levin and A. Malamat; Jerusalem: Israel Exploration Society, 1982] 43*–50*); and Wolff (33–34) for the development of the term. For additional studies, see K. D. Schnunk, "Strukturlinien in der Entwicklung der Vorstellung vom 'Tag Yahwehs,'" *VT* 14 (1964) 319–30; C. Carniti, "L'espressione 'Il Giorno di JHWH': Origine ed Evoluzione Semantica," *BeO* 12 (1970) 11–25; and K.A.D. Smelik, "The Meaning of Amos V:18–20," *VT* 36 (1986) 129–45 (who relates the issue to the preaching of "false" prophets).

18 If, of course, one does not follow the suggestion to read הוי in Amos 5:7.

19 The *hithpaʿel* of אוה appears fifteen times in the Bible; check concordances for references. See also המתאוים ליום ישעך ("those who yearn for the day of thy salvation") in Qumran; J. A. Sanders, *The Psalms Scroll of Cave 11 (IIQPs)* (DJD 4; Oxford: Clarendon, 1981) col. xxii:4. For the plural participle followed by the second-person plural finite verb, cf. Amos 6:3.

20 Outside the prophetic texts, the phrase appears only once, Lam 2:22, בְּיוֹם אַף־ה׳ ("on the day of the wrath of the Lord").

From among the vast literature on the Day of the Lord, see also L. Černý, *The Day of Yahweh and Some Relevant Problems* (Práce Z Vědeckých Ústavů 53; V Praze: University Karlovy, 1948); G. von Rad, "The Origin of the Concept of the Day of Yahweh," *JSS* 4 (1959) 97–108; Weiss, "Origin," 29–60; Weinfeld, "Concept"; H. D. Preuss, *Jahweglaube und Zukunftserwartung* (BWANT 87; Stuttgart: Kohlhammer, 1968) 170–79; H.-P. Müller, *Ursprünge und Strukturen alttestamentlicher Eschatologie* (BZAW 109; Berlin: Töpelmann, 1969) 69–85; Y. Hoffman, "The Day of the Lord as a Concept and a Term in the Prophetic Literature," *ZAW* 93 (1981) 37–50.

21 For the problem of whether or not the phrase was known prior to the time of Amos, see Weiss, "Origin," 46.

defeating the enemies of Israel was well established and central to their thoughts. Thus once again Amos directly confronts, challenges, and dramatically reverses another pillar of popular belief and hope (see, for example, Amos 3:1–2; 5:4–6; 9:7). Contrary to the prevailing and predominating opinion, it will be a time of defeat and disaster for Israel and not one of victory and salvation. The Lord will wreak judgment and vengeance upon them and will not save them. When the Lord appears, it is to strike down the sinning kingdom (any sinning kingdom, 9:7), which includes first and foremost his own elected people (3:2). Past salvation is not an unlimited guarantee for future life insurance.

By abruptly changing the tone and the address to a second-person plural, Amos directly confronts his audience with the charge, "What avail will [it] be for you" (לָמָּה־זֶּה לָכֶם)?[22] For this "Day of the Lord" will be one of "darkness, not light" (הוּא־חֹשֶׁךְ וְלֹא־אוֹר), that is, one of disaster, not salvation.[23] The motif of darkness, literally (8:9) and figuratively (see Isa 9:1), becomes a vivid part of the description of the "Day of the Lord" in prophetic literature (see, for example, Isa 13:10; Ezek 30:3; Joel 2:1–2; Zeph 1:15). Here the contrasting "darkness, not light," comes to emphasize[24] the doom and calamity[25] in store for Israel. By repeating the phrase in v 20, Amos creates a very effective inclusio.[26]

For the cognate expression in Akkadian literature, usually appearing in curses, compare *iklet la nawārim . . . ana šimtim lišimšum* ("May [the gods] make never-brightening darkness his fate").[27] Akkadian *iklet la nawārim* = Heb. חֹשֶׁךְ (וְ)לֹא־אוֹר. Compare similarly to Amos 8:9, *ūmu namrum da'ummatum līwīšum* ("May the bright day turn into darkness for him");[28] *šapāt ikletumma ul ibašši nūru* ("The darkness is dense, there is no light").[29]

■ **19** Amos once again resorts to a simile drawn from his own background experience to dramatize forcefully and picturesquely his message.[30] In order to express one of his favorite themes, the inescapability from impending punishment (see 2:14–16; 9:1–4), he draws upon the

22 For the expression לָמָּה־זֶּה לָכֶם, see Gen 25:32: "I am at the point of death, so of what use is my birthright to me?" (לָמָּה־זֶּה לִי); see also Gen 25:22. Similarly, Gen 27:46, "What good will life be to me?" (לָמָּה לִּי חַיִּים); Job 30:2, "Of what use to me (לָמָּה לִּי) the strength of their hands?" In all four לָמָּה לִּי means "what good, to what avail." For the construction לָמָּה־זֶּה, see *GKC,* 136c. It appears twenty-three times in the Bible, and זֶה functions as an emphatic intensification of the interrogative. See *KB,* 254, no. 15. Both G, *ἵνα τί αὕτη ὑμῖν*, and V, *ad quid eam vobis* ("to what [purpose] is this to you?") misinterpreted זֶה as a demonstrative pronoun. V also incorrectly connected the phrase יוֹם ה׳ with the following: *dies Domini ista tenebrae et non lux* ("the Day of the Lord is darkness and not light"); followed by Harper; van Hoonacker.

23 See Rudolph, 203. According to B. Margalit ("The Early Israelite Epic and the Origin of Biblical Eschatology," in *Ḥeqer VeIyyun BeMadaei HaYahaduth: Sifruth Miqra VeLashon* [Haifa: University of Haifa, 1976] 175 [Heb.]), however, the motif of darkness in connection with the Day of the Lord does not refer metaphorically to disaster but represents a "theophanic darkness," which is one of the strategic ways in which the Lord wages his war against his enemies. According to Margalit, "the tradition of the Day of the Lord represents a futurization of the epic past *(Urzeit)* of the people of Israel."

For studies on light and darkness, see S. Aalen, *Die Begriffe 'Licht' und 'Finsternis' im Alten Testament, im Spätjudentum und im Rabbinismus* (Oslo: Dybwad, 1951); W. von Soden, "Licht und Finsternis in der sumerischen und babylonisch-assyrischen Religion," StGen 13 (1960) 647–53.

24 Compare similarly, Isa 50:10, "Though he walk in darkness and have no light" (הָלַךְ חֲשֵׁכִים וְאֵין נֹגַהּ לוֹ); Lam 3:2, "Me he drove on and on in darkness without light" (חֹשֶׁךְ וְלֹא־אוֹר). Such antithetical constructions are very much a part of the style of the oracles of Amos; see 5:4–5, 14, 20; 8:11; 9:4.

25 For an Akkadian substantive meaning both "darkness" and "calamity," see *CAD, A,* I.126, *adirtu.*

26 This shows that there is no need to delete the expression as a "premature denouement," against Wolff, 253, following Löhr, *Untersuchungen,* 19; Duhm, "Anmerkungen," 10; Procksch; Sellin. Rudolph, 203, has also drawn attention to the preponderance of the "dumpfe *o*-Laute" in this verse and v 20, reminiscent of the הוֹ־הוֹ of v 16.

27 *LH* XLII:68.

28 *RA* 46 (1972) 92:68.

29 *Gilgamesh,* Tablet IX:iii:11; iv:48; v:30, 33, 36.

30 See Amos 2:13; 3:3–6, 12; 6:12; 9:9.

image of the onslaught, one after the other, of a lion (הָאֲרִי) and a bear (הַדֹּב),[31] whose attacks[32] are ferocious and usually fatal (for example, 1 Sam 17:34, 36, 37; 2 Kgs 2:24; Hos 13:7–8; Prov 28:15). Even if a man extricates himself from the frightening consecutive attacks of both of these fearsome animals and successfully manages to reach[33] home alive, nevertheless, the very moment he leans his hand against the wall for a moment's respite, he would be fatally bitten by yet another threatening menace, a snake (הַנָּחָשׁ).[34] Misfortune strikes when least expected. The point is very clear: Momentary success is only illusionary. Even if Israel has escaped with its life intact in all previous encounters with its enemies,[35] this time deliverance will not be forthcoming. Precisely when Israel feels itself secure, more than ever will the deadly "bite" of the "Day of the Lord" take place.

■ **20** Thus ends the chiastic inclusio, which began in v 18,[36] on the same somber, dark tones. Here, however, there is an intensification[37] heightened by a parallel repetition and reiteration of a series of synonyms for darkness,[38] that is, calamity and catastrophe: חֹשֶׁךְ ("darkness"), לֹא־אוֹר ("not light"), אָפֵל ("blackest night"),[39] לֹא־נֹגַהּ ("without a glimmer").[40] For these same four words in another verse, see Isa 59:9: "We hope for light (אוֹר), and lo! there is darkness (חֹשֶׁךְ); for a gleam (לִנְגֹהוֹת), and we must walk in gloom" (בַּאֲפֵלוֹת).

Note the effectively subtle recurrent repetition of the syllable *lô:* twice negative, לֹא; once interrogative, הֲלֹא; and finally the personal preposition with the third-person

31 For the use of the definite article, see *GKC,* 126q, r.

32 For Heb. פגע, see Exod 5:3.

33 Heb. בא ב means "to enter."

34 For the dangerous, if not deadly, bite of a snake, see Num 21:6, 9; Jer 8:17; Amos 9:3; Prov 23:32; Eccl 10:8, 11. This is also a common theme in Akkadian texts, for example, *šumma amēlu ṣēru iššikšu* ("If a snake bit a man"), *AMT* 92, 7:6; *šumma ṣēru ina bīt amēli iqnun* ("If a snake nests in a man's house"), *KAR* 386:56. See also Goetze, *Omen Texts,* 18:64; Heb. נשך = Akk. *našāku* = Ugar. *ntk,* "to bite." Heb. נחש = Ugar. *nḥš,* "snake." For Ugar. *ntk* referring to a snakebite, see *RŠ* 24.244 (= *KTU* 1.100); and see B. A. Levine and J. M. de Tarragon, O.P., "'Shapshu Cries Out in Heaven': Dealing with Snake Bites at Ugarit (*KTU* 1.100, 1:107)," *RB* 95 (1988) 481–518.

35 Compare similarly the impossibility of escape from danger in the following passage noted for its alliteration, Isa 24:17–18: "Terror, and pit, and trap (פַּחַד וָפַחַת וָפָח). . . . He who flees at the report of the terror shall fall into the pit; and he who climbs out of the pit, shall be caught in the trap." (See Jer 48:43–44.) Note that here, as well, three items are mentioned. Compare the Latin saying, *"incidit in Scyllam, qui vult vitare Charybdim"* ("He who wishes to escape Charybdis falls into Scylla") cited in Harper, 133. For a variant of this expression—*incidis in Scillam, cupiens vitare Charibdim* ("Desiring to escape Charybdis, you fall into Scylla")—see the twelfth-century Latin poet Galterus de Castellione or Walther of Châtillon in his epic *Alexandreis,* book V, line 301. See Galteri de Castellione, *Alexandreis* (ed. M. L. Colker; Padova: Antenore, 1978) 133. Compare also the English phrase "out of the frying pan into the fire."

36 There יוֹם ה' followed by חֹשֶׁךְ; here חֹשֶׁךְ, then יוֹם ה'.

37 Heb. הֲלֹא functions here as an emphatic element, but it also has polemical overtones; see Amos 9:7; Mal 2:10.

38 For the parallelism of חֹשֶׁךְ and אָפֵל, see Isa 29:18: "And the eyes of the blind shall see even in darkness and obscurity" (וּמֵאֹפֶל וּמֵחֹשֶׁךְ). (In IQIs[a] the reading is אפלה.) See also Exod 10:22; Joel 2:2; Zeph 1:15; Prov 7:9. For חֹשֶׁךְ and נֹגַהּ, see Isa 50:10: ". . . Though he walk in darkness and have no light (חֲשֵׁכִים וְאֵין נֹגַהּ לוֹ). . . ." For the contrasting description, see Isa 9:1: "The people that walked in darkness (בַּחֹשֶׁךְ) have seen a brilliant light (אוֹר). On those who dwelt in a land of glory, light has dawned" (אוֹר נָגַהּ). Note other examples of antithetical parallelism, so characteristic of Amos, in 5:4–5, 14, 18; 8:11; 9:4.

39 אָפֵל is a hapax legomenon. Many commentators repoint וְאֹפֶל (already suggested by Ehrlich, *Randglossen,* 5.241). אֹפֶל and אֲפֵלָה are the two attested forms; see concordances for references, and see n 38. This repointing (supported by the versions) would heighten the staccato effect of yet another substantive containing the *o* sound. See n 26.

40 For the various nominal parallel combinations of נֹגַהּ and אוֹר, see also Hab 3:4, 11; Prov 4:18; and for the corresponding verbal parallelism, see 2 Sam 22:29 = Ps 18:29: "The Lord, my God, lights up my darkness" (יַגִּיהַּ חָשְׁכִּי). Heb. נֹגַהּ = Ugar. *ngh.* For נֹגַהּ, see F. Schnutenhaus, "Das Kommen und Erscheinen Gottes im Alten Testament," *ZAW* 76 (1964) 1–22, especially 9–10. Compare also the Balaam inscription from Deir ʿAlla, line 7: כי שם חשך ואל נגה ("For he let there be darkness and not brightness"). See Weinfeld ("Balaam," 141–43) for a bibliography on the inscription from the years 1976 to 1980.

pronominal suffix, לוֹ—all having one grand cumulative auditory effect upon the listeners. This is further heightened by the fact that the expression לֹא־אוֹר/נֹגַהּ appears here (along with v 18) for the third and climactic time, לֹא־אוֹר (twice) and לֹא־נֹגַהּ (once).

5

Ritual Praxis without Moral Practice

21 **I hate, I despise your festivals,**
I take no delight in your solemn assemblies.
22 **Even if you offer me burnt offerings and your meal offerings,**
I will not accept them.
And the gift offerings of your fatlings
I will not look upon favorably.
23 **Remove from me the din of your hymns!**
And to the melody of your lutes I will not listen.
24 **But let justice roll on like water,**
And righteousness like an ever-flowing stream.
25 **Did you offer me sacrifices and meal offerings**
Those forty years in the wilderness,
O house of Israel?
26 **And you shall carry off**
Sikkuth, your king,
And Kiyyun, your astral god,
Your images that you have made for yourselves.
27 **As I drive you into exile beyond Damascus**
—said the Lord, the God of Hosts, is his name.

Introductory Comments to 5:21-27

The link between this oracle and the former one[1] is the common theme of contrast and dramatic reversal.[2] Amos, responding to the popular beliefs of his day, vehemently and boldly refutes their significance and importance. Here he levels his most uncompromising attack against the lavishness of the official monotheistic cult.[3] He upbraids in no uncertain terms Israel's extensive ritual praxis, rejecting it in toto: holidays, festal gatherings, and sacrifices, along with their accompanying hymns, melodies, and musical instruments. His intention is to destroy all of their "idle worship." To all of this ritual mayhem (v 23, הֲמוֹן) he replies that God demands justice and morality and not the minutiae of the cult: Not rite but right is demanded; devotion not devotions.[4]

The direct address of the deity in vv 21–22 is commonly interpreted as a free adaptation and parody of the practice of delivering cultic decisions at a sanctuary, where a spokesman for the cult (priest or prophet) would issue an oracle from the Lord in answer to a plea.[5] The oracle here was most likely uttered at one of the major

1 This is not a continuation of Amos 5:18–20 (against, for example, S. Mowinckel, *He That Cometh* [tr. G. W. Anderson; Oxford: Blackwell, 1956] 132; Kapelrud, *Central Ideas,* 71, 74–75; E. Würthwein, "Amos 5,21–27," *TLZ* 72 [1947] 150) but an originally independent oracle; see, for example, Amsler, 212 n 3; Rudolph, 208; Wolff, 260.

2 See Rudolph, 208, who interprets the connection with the above as Amos's reaction to the protests of the people who refuse to accept his interpretation of the Day of the Lord as a time of calamity. They point to their punctilious performance of the cult to justify their correct behavior. The prophet counters in order to destroy their illusions.

3 The entire attack here is leveled against the established authorized cult and not against any pagan practices. The only exception in the entire book is Amos 5:26, and possibly Amos 8:14; see later for respective comments. For similar attacks, see, for example, Isa 1:10–17; Jer 6:19–21; Hos 6:6; 8:13; Mal 1:10; 2:13. See also Amos 9:1.

Note the extended use of the second-person plural. It is not the cult per se that is under attack, but its practitioners.

4 See especially Kaufmann, *Toledoth,* 6.71–81; S. Spiegel, *Amos Vs. Amaziah* (New York: Jewish Theological Seminary, 1957).

5 J. Begrich ("Die priestliche Thora," in *Werden und Wesen des Alten Testaments* [ed. P. Volz, F. Stummer, and J. Hempel; BZAW 66; Berlin: Töpelmann, 1936] 73ff.) interprets this section as a "prophetischen Nachahmungen priesterlicher Tora" ("prophetic imitation of a priestly Torah"). Würthwein ("Amos Studien," 43–52) suggests another "Gat-

official sanctuaries in the north at the time of a religious holiday. It has even been suggested that "one must probably imagine that Amos interrupted the discourse of a cultic spokesman at the sanctuary,"[6] in order to render a negative cultic decision.

Some have noted the thematic and ideological ties between this pericope and Isa 1:11–15. What has been overlooked, however, is the remarkable similarity of vocabulary employed in both units. Compare the following: Amos 5:21: שָׂנֵאתִי, Isa 1:14 (נַפְשִׁי) שָׂנְאָה; v 21: עַצְּרֹתֵיכֶם, Isa 1:13, עֲצָרָה; v 22: עֹלוֹת, Isa 1:11, עֹלוֹת; v 22: מִנְחֹתֵיכֶם (also Amos 5:25), Isa 1:13 (שָׁוְא)־מִנְחַת; v 22: מְרִיאֵיכֶם, Isa 1:11, מְרִיאִים; v 23: הָסֵר מֵעָלַי, Isa 1:16 הָסִירוּ . . . (מִנֶּגֶד עֵינָי); v 23: לֹא אֶשְׁמָע, Isa 1:15, אֵינֶנִּי שֹׁמֵעַ; v 25: זְבָחִים, Isa 1:11, זִבְחֵיכֶם. Compare also v 21: חַגֵּיכֶם ("your festivals") and Isa 1:14, חָדְשֵׁיכֶם וּמוֹעֲדֵיכֶם ("your new moons and fixed seasons"); v 22: לֹא אַבִּיט ("I shall not look") and Isa 1:15, אַעְלִים עֵינַי ("I shall hide my eyes"); v 22: לֹא אֶרְצֶה ("I do not want") and Isa 1:11, לֹא חָפָצְתִּי ("I have no delight").

■ **21** With forceful, unequivocal vehemence, the Deity addresses his next impassioned attack against the cult by commencing with two verbs juxtaposed asyndetically in a first-person address: "I hate (שָׂנֵאתִי),[7] I despise (מָאַסְתִּי)[8] your festivals." (The use of the verb שׂנא in a cultic context is also found in Deut 16:22 and Isa 1:14.) The direct object of this outpouring of detestation and abhorrence is "your festivals" (חַגֵּיכֶם). The substantive חַג is the technical term originally employed as the name for the three pilgrimage festivals (see Exod 23:14–16; 34:22, 25).[9]

"I take no delight (וְלֹא אָרִיחַ) in your solemn assemblies" (בְּעַצְּרֹתֵיכֶם). The Heb. לְהָרִיחַ בְּ־, a term originally applied to the "smelling,"[10] that is, "receiving favorably," of sacrifices (for example, Gen 8:21; Exod 30:38; Lev 26:31; 1 Sam 26:19) is here extended to apply to the disfavor of the Lord toward Israel's "festal gatherings" (עַצְּרֹתֵיכֶם),[11] which were popular assemblies for the

tung," that of the oracle. See also idem, "Kultpolemik oder Kultbescheid?" in *Tradition und Situation: Studien zur alttestamentlichen Prophetie, Festschrift für A. Weiser* (ed. E. Würthwein and O. Kaiser; Göttingen: Vandenhoeck & Ruprecht, 1963) 115–31; followed by many, including Wolff, 261–62; Rudolph, 208.

6 Wolff, 206. For other negative responses, compare Isa 1:10–17; Jer 6:19–21; Mal 1:10; 2:13.

7 Compare also the Ugaritic interdialectal semantic and cognate equivalent, *šn'*, in the context of hating sacrifices; *ṯn dbḥm šna' bʿl* ("Baal hates two sacrifices") *CTA* 4:iii:17.

8 Heb. מאס appears elsewhere in the context of the spurning of God or his teachings. Check various references in the concordance. Its Akkadian cognate, *mêšu* ("to despise, have contempt for, disregard"), refers occasionally to cultic behavior; see *CAD, M*, II.41f. See also M. Held, "Studies in Biblical Lexicography in the Light of Akkadian, Part II," in *Studies in Bible Dedicated to the Memory of U. Cassuto on the 100th Anniversary of His Birth* (ed. S. Loewenstamm; Jerusalem: Magnes, 1987) 114–26.

9 Heb. חַג also refers, at times, to the "festal sacrifice" itself (so, too, here Kimchi); see Exod 23:18; Mal 2:3; Ps 118:27. It also becomes the designation for the holiday of Tabernacles, Sukkoth, for example, 1 Kgs 8:65; Ezek 45:23; 2 Chr 7:8, 9. For חַג, see G. J. Botterweck and B. Kedar-Kopfstein, "*ḥag*," *TWAT* II (1977) 730–44; M. Haran, *Temples and Temple Service in Ancient Israel* (Oxford: Clarendon, 1978) 289ff.

10 Note that the rejection of the entire panoply of the cult is expressed by its not being acceptable to several of the different senses—smell, v 22; sight, v 23; hearing, v 23. God's disgust is completely "sensible."

11 Two forms of the substantive exist: עֲצָרָה, 2 Kgs 10:20; Isa 1:13; Joel 1:14; 2:15; and עֲצֶרֶת, Lev 23:36; Num 29:35; Deut 16:8; Neh 8:18; 2 Chr 7:9; (and Jer 9:1—in a secular sense of "assembly"). For the *dagesh* in the צ of עַצְּרֹתֵיכֶם, see *BLe*, 212k; *GKC*, 20h. This is the sole occurrence of the noun in the plural.

עֲצֶרֶת becomes the technical expression for the seventh day of Passover (Deut 16:8) and for the eighth day of Sukkoth (Lev 23:36). In Second Temple times, the word was employed as a synonym for the holiday of "Weeks," Shavuoth, for example, Mishnah, Halah 4:10.

For a study of the biblical root, see E. Kutsch, "Die Wurzel *ʿṣr* im Hebräischen," *VT* 2 (1952) 57–69. See also Haran, *Temples*, 286 n 14, "But the *ʿaṣeret* differs from the *ḥag* in that it did not necessarily involve merrymaking (on the contrary, it may be synonymous with fast, as in Joel), nor does it involve the obligation of pilgrimage and 'appearing before Yahweh.'"

purpose of prayer and sacrifice during holidays or times of trouble; see Lev 23:36; Num 29:35; Deut 16:8; 2 Kgs 10:20; Isa 1:13; Joel 1:14; 2:15; Neh 8:18.

■ **22** In this verse the Lord categorically rejects all sacrifices,[12] three of which are specifically mentioned by name: עֹלָה, מִנְחָה, and שֶׁלֶם. He declares that, "Even if you offer me burnt offerings (תַּעֲלוּ־לִי עֹלוֹת)[13] and your meal offerings (מִנְחֹתֵיכֶם), I will not accept them" (לֹא אֶרְצֶה). There is no reason to reject the first five words of this verse[14] or to assume that a colon fell out after v 22a.[15] Inveighing against the former are the following considerations: Although מִנְחָה[16] does serve at times as a general description for sacrifices (compare, for example, Gen 4:3–5; Isa 1:13), it does not necessarily follow that here it is used in such a comprehensive fashion and that the other term, עוֹלוֹת, is therefore superfluous. When these two sacrifices appear together, מִנְחָה has the specific meaning of a "meal offering"; compare Lev 23:37; Num 29:16; Josh 22:23; Jer 14:12. Furthermore, the fact that the phrase כִּי אִם ("unless, except") after a negative (v 21) usually has a concessive function (see Amos 3:7) does not mean that here these two words must be interpreted in such a fashion. The Heb. כִּי can very well represent the emphatic כִּי ("Even if/when . . .").[17] Although the expression העלה עולה is frequent in the late work of the Chronicler, it is also documented in earlier sources, for example, Josh 22:23; 1 Sam 7:9; Jer 14:12. As for the latter contention, many of those who regard the first stich as being authentic claim that a colon must have dropped out of the Masoretic text, and so they arbitrarily supply, without any supporting evidence, various complementary clauses: לֹא אֶשְׂמַח ("I will not rejoice");[18] לֹא אֶנָּחֵם ("I will not be consoled");[19] לֹא אֶקָּחֶנָּה מִידֵיכֶם ("I will not accept them from your hands");[20] הִנֵּה בְּעֵינַי רָעוֹת ("They are evil in my eyes").[21] All of these suggestions are totally unfounded and unwarranted once it is realized that the suffix of מִנְחֹתֵיכֶם also applies to עוֹלוֹת and functions as a double-duty suffix.[22] Thus, "Even if you offer me (your) burnt offerings and your meal offerings," all of these sacrifices are "unacceptable" (לֹא אֶרְצֶה). רצה is the official, most frequently employed technical term for the favorable (or unfavorable) acceptance of an animal sacrifice; see, for example, Lev 1:3–4; 19:7; 22:23, 25, 27; Jer 14:12; Ezek 20:41; Hos 8:13; Mal 1:10; 2:13; Ps 51:18.[23]

The root נבט ("to look at"), however, is not attested elsewhere in a cultic context, but here it, too, clearly refers to the unacceptability of the sacrifice in question: "I will not take note of/take no heed/not look favorably upon." Compare the similar employment of the root שעה ("to look at")[24] in Gen 4:4–5, also with reference to the (non)acceptance of sacrifices.[25]

The third offering rejected here is שֶׁלֶם מְרִיאֵיכֶם. מְרִיא (a "fatling") is a well-known term for a type of animal

12 For the institution of sacrifices, see Y. Licht and J. Milgrom, "Sacrifices," *EM* 7.222–51 (Heb.); A. Rainey, "Sacrifice," *EncJud* 14.599–607; T. H. Gaster, "Sacrifices and Offerings, OT," *IDB* 4.147–59; R. de Vaux, *Les sacrifices de l'Ancien Testament* (Paris: Gabalda, 1964); R. Rendtorff, *Studien zur Geschichte des Opfers im Alten Israel* (WMANT 24; Neukirchen-Vluyn: Neukirchener Verlag, 1967). See also J. Milgrom, "Sacrifices and Offerings, OT," *IDBSup* 763–71.

13 Compare the Akkadian cognate *šūlû* (from *elû*), "to offer or dedicate (something) to a deity," *CAD, E,* 130, 9c.

14 Against Wolff, 259.

15 Against Würthwein, "Kultbescheid," 117.

16 Compare Ugar. *mnḥ,* "gift, tribute," *UT,* 1500; Phoen. and Pun. מנחת, *DISO,* 159; Aram. מנחה, *DISO,* 159.

17 For אִם ("when") see, for example, Gen 38:9; Num 36:4. See Hammershaimb, 89; and Rudolph, 206. For כִּי אִם, see 1 Sam 21:6; Job 42:8. Note, too, G, which also did not understand the expression as a concessive.

18 Budde, "Amos," 115.

19 Sellin².

20 Morgenstern, "Amos Studies IV," 302, 319.

21 Rudolph, 206.

22 Already G and V. For this linguistic phenomenon in Psalms, see M. Dahood (*Psalms III: 101–150, Introduction, Translation and Notes* [AB 17a; Garden City, NY: Doubleday, 1970] 429–34), and the bibliography attached to the individual verses cited in the respective Psalms.

23 See Würthwein, "Kultbescheid," 122–23; Rendtorff, *Studien,* 253–58.

24 See its Akkadian etymological cognate, *šeʾû* ("to look at"), *AHw,* 3.1222–24. See also Akkadian *palāsu/naplusu* ("to look at," "to look favorably"), *AHw,* 2.814–15.

25 See Isa 17:7.

presented as a sacrifice; see, for example, 2 Sam 6:13; 1 Kgs 1:9, 19, 25; Isa 1:11; 11:6; Ezek 39:18.[26] Compare its cognates in Ugar. *mr'*[27] (as an adjective and noun), and Akk. *mīru* ("fattened animal"),[28] derived from *marû* ("to fatten");[29] see also *mīrtu* ("cow") and *mīru* ("young bull").[30] These "fatted beasts" are offered here as a שֶׁלֶם.[31] Although this is the only occasion in the Bible in which the familiar שְׁלָמִים sacrifice appears in the singular, there is no need to doubt its authenticity or to emend it to the plural שַׁלְמֵי.[32] The singular is documented several times in the Punic tariffs from Marseilles (dated to the fourth or third century B.C.E.), as *šlm kll.*[33] The plural is also well attested in Ugaritic: *šrp (w)šlmm* ("a burnt offering [and] a *šlmm*-offering").[34]

Although the שְׁלָמִים sacrifice is attested in the early cult (see Exod 20:21; 24:5), and references to it are found in very early monarchic times (see, for example, 1 Sam 10:8; 11:15; 2 Sam 6:17–18; 24:25), it does not appear in any of the prophetic works, except for Amos, until the time of Ezekiel 40—48.[35] Because it is listed here alongside the two major sacrifices (עוֹלָה and מִנְחָה), it may be that it played a predominant role specifically in the cult of northern Israel.

■ **23** The accusation of the Deity that began in the second-person plural (vv 21–22) continues with a singular imperative, confronting each one directly and individually.[36] Attention is now focused upon the songs and music that were part and parcel of their festal gatherings.[37] He demands and commands that each one "remove [the burden] from me" (הָסֵר מֵעָלַי)[38] of all hymns of praise (שִׁיר),[39] which are actually no more than one grand cacophonous "din" (הֲמוֹן).[40] The singing of God's praises as a component part of these holiday rites is also referred to in the parallel context of Amos 8:10: "I will turn your festivals (חַגֵּיכֶם) into mourning and all your songs (שִׁירֵיכֶם) into dirges."

26 See S. E. Loewenstamm, "מריא," *EM* 5.455–56 (Heb.), for a discussion of this term and its possible identifications.

27 *UT*, 1544.

28 *CAD, M,* II.110.

29 *CAD, M,* I.307–8. The verb also appears in biblical Hebrew, Isa 11:6; for וּמְרִיא, read יִמְרְאוּ ("will feed"). See IQIs^a, ימרו, and G, Βοσκη Θήσονται ("will feed"). It is also documented in Rabbinic Hebrew. See M. Jastrow, *Dictionary,* 2.842.

30 *CAD, M,* II.110.

31 See Rendtorff, *Studien,* 253–58, and especially B. A. Levine, *In the Presence of the Lord: A Study of Cult and Some Cultic Terms in Ancient Israel* (SJLA 5; Leiden: Brill, 1974) 8–9, 45–46, 118–22. He argues, contrary to the other scholars, that the singular has not been definitely attested in Ugaritic, but suggests that it may occur in a Hebrew ostracon from Arad. See *IEJ* 19 (1969) 49–50. See also W. Eisenbeis, *Die Wurzel šlm im Alten Testament* (BZAW 113; Berlin: de Gruyter, 1969) 72–73.

32 See Rashi; Tur-Sinai, *Peshuṭo,* 465.

33 *CIS* 1.165.

34 *UT,* 612:9–10; 613:15–16; see also 609:9–10; 611:9–10.

35 See Levine, *Presence,* 45–46.

36 Several commentators find the transition from the second-person plural to the singular imperative disturbing. Thus it has been suggested that הָסֵר was originally meant to be an infinitive absolute (see קַטֵּר, Amos 4:5) which was "misinterpreted" as a singular imperative and thus led to the change of the assumed original plural suffixes of the nouns to the singular. See Würthwein, "Kultbescheid," 117; Rudolph, 206. The versions, however, have singular suffixes and thus help to confirm the Masoretic text. Moreover, the transition from the plural to the singular need no longer be considered so anomalous because multiple examples exist throughout prophetic literature. It does not have to be explained on the basis of a different genre, contrary to Wolff, 259, 261–63.

37 Compare Isa 30:29: "For you there shall be singing (שִׁיר) as on a night when a festival is hallowed."

38 Ehrlich, *Randglossen,* 5.242, caught this nuance of מֵעָלַי very well. Compare also Hammershaimb, 90: "so that they do not weigh upon him like a burden." For another example, see Gen 33:13: "My lord knows that the children are frail and that the flocks and herds, which are nursing, are a care/burden to me (עָלָי); if they are driven hard a single day, all the flocks will die." See also Isa 1:14. For the expression הָסֵר מֵעָלַי, see Ps 39:11.

For a similar contextual and syntactical construction of this and the next verse, compare Ezek 45:9.

39 See, for example, Pss 33:3; 57:8; 96:1; 98:1; 108:2; 144:9; see Wolff, 264.

40 Of course, there may be a clever double entendre intended here: הֲמוֹן שִׁרֶיךָ, "the multitude of your songs" and "the noise of your songs" (see ibn Ezra). For the latter, see, for example, 1 Sam 4:14; 14:19; Isa 13:4; 31:4; 33:3; Jer 10:13. The expression reappears in Ezek 26:13: "I will put an end to the din of your songs (הֲמוֹן שִׁירַיִךְ) and the sound of your lyres shall be heard no more" (וְקוֹל כִּנּוֹרַיִךְ לֹא יִשָּׁמַע עוֹד).

Not only is their singing revolting to the Lord but, he further adds in the chiastically structured second colon, "And to the melody of your lutes (זִמְרַת נְבָלֶיךָ) I will not listen" (לֹא אֶשְׁמָע). The root זמר refers to music accompanied by an instrument,[41] here the נֵבֶל, variously identified as a harp, lute, or lyre.[42] For a similar parallel construction of שִׁיר and נֵבֶל, along with the verb זמר, see Ps 144:9: "O God, I will sing you a new song (שִׁיר), sing a hymn to you with a ten-stringed harp" (בְּנֵבֶל עָשׂוֹר אֲזַמְּרָה־לָּךְ).

Note that this total disavowal of the cult is expressed anthropomorphically by the Lord's shutting off, so to speak, several of his own senses: smell (v 21, לֹא אָרִיחַ), sight (v 22, לֹא אַבִּיט), and hearing (v 23, לֹא אֶשְׁמָע).[43] This last in the series of the Deity's rejection of their cult brings the list of verbs to the culminatory number of seven (שָׂנֵאתִי, מָאַסְתִּי, לֹא אָרִיחַ, לֹא אֶרְצֶה, לֹא אַבִּיט, הָסֵר, לֹא אֶשְׁמָע)—a heptad of negation representing a complete and comprehensive repudiation.[44]

In sum their cultic ceremonial behavior is found to be as totally repugnant as their secular living habits, which are also accompanied by the very same songs and playing of musical instruments. Compare Amos 6:5, where both נֵבֶל and שִׁיר reappear.

■ **24** The prophet does not go on to contrast the present cult with any proposals for reform. Ritual per se, with all its paraphernalia and panoply, simply cannot substitute for the basic moral and ethical actions of humans.[45] When these are lacking, religious life, with all its ritual accoutrements, becomes a sham. What is required above all else is justice and righteousness.[46] The proper divine-human relationship is based upon a correct human-human relationship: "But[47] let justice (מִשְׁפָּט) roll on (וְיִגַּל)[48] like water, and righteousness (צְדָקָה) like an ever-flowing stream" (כְּנַחַל אֵיתָן).[49] (Note again the chiastic construction of the verse.) By once again drawing upon the imagery of the open country[50] so well known to the prophet and his listeners, Amos likens his demand for

Note that here, too, the second colon contains the verb שמע.

41 Heb. זמר = Ugar. *zmr* (*UT*, 823) = Akk. *zamāru* (*CAD*, *Z*, 35–38).

42 For the various suggested identifications of the נֵבֶל, see C. H. Kraeling, "Music in the Bible," in *Ancient and Oriental Music* (New Oxford History of Music; 2 vols.; ed. E. Welles; London: Oxford University, 1954) 1.283–312 (esp. 296). (See pl. viii a and *ANEP* 200, for an instrument with ten strings; see Pss 33:2; 144:9.) See also B. Bauer, "Music in the Bible," *EncJud* 12.559–66; idem, "Nebel," *EM* 5.767–71 (Heb.); idem, "The Biblical *Nebel*," *Yuval* 1 (1968) 89–161.

43 See also Wolff, 264; Rudolph, 209.

44 For other heptads, see Amos 2:6–8, 14–16; 4:4–5, 6–11; 5:8–9; 9:1–4. Here, too, the heptad is followed by a climactic eighth statement (v 24); see Amos 1—2; 3:3–8; 4:6–12.

45 See Kaufmann (*Toledoth*, 6.71–81) on the "supremacy of morality." See R. Hentschkė, *Die Stellung der vorexilischen Schriftspropheten zum Kultus* (BZAW 75; Berlin: Töpelmann, 1957).

46 For מִשְׁפָּט and צְדָקָה, see Amos 5:7; 6:12. This theme is maintained throughout the various sections of this chapter, Amos 5:7, 15, 24. See Jer 22:3, 15–16. For the analogous terms, Phoen. *ṣdq mšr* and Akk. *kittum u mīšarum*, see M. Weinfeld, "'Justice and Righteousness' in Ancient Israel against the Background of 'Social Reforms' in the Ancient Near East," in *Mesopotamien und seine Nachbarn* (ed. H.-J. Nissen and J. Renger; Berlin: Deitrich Reimer, 1982) 491–519; the terms represent the concept of social justice. See also idem, *Justice and Righteousness in Israel and the Nations* (Jerusalem: Magnes, 1985) (Heb.). In the surrounding cultures, the two are the concern of the king, who sponsored social reforms in order to implement social justice. The innovation in Amos is that he demands such action on the part of the entire population.

47 The *waw* of וְיִגַּל is adversative. Those who interpret the *waw* as consecutive misconstrue the force of the contrast, for example, H. Cazelles, "À propos de quelques textes difficiles relatifs à la justice de Dieu dans l'Ancien Testament," *RB* 58 (1951) 159–88; J. P. Hyatt, "The Translation and Meaning of Amos 5, 23–24," *ZAW* 68 (1956) 17–24.

48 There is a very interesting play on words here. For Heb. גלל, I, see *KB*, 186. The words for "wave," גַּל; "fountain," גַּל (Cant 4:12); and "spring," גֻּלָּה (Josh 15:19; Judg 1:15) are all derived from the Hebrew root גלל. The connection between the latter and the verse in Amos was already suggested by ibn Ezra, and Ehrlich, *Mikrâ*, 3.411 (Heb.). Hebrew יִגַּל is a *niphʿal* middle. Note, too, the paronomasia based on two different Hebrew roots, גלל and גלה—since justice does not "roll on" (וְיִגַּל), the Lord will eventually "roll" them out to exile (וְהִגְלֵיתִי), v 27.

49 For נַחַל אֵיתָן ("a wadi with a perennial stream"), see also Deut 21:4; Sir 40:13; similarly נַהֲרוֹת אֵיתָן ("rivers of steady flow"), Ps 74:15. For the opposite figure, (נַחַל) אַכְזָב ("a disappointing stream"), see Jer 15:8. For a poetic description of such a stream, see Job 6:15–20; and see also the wordplay in Mic 1:14.

ever-streaming justice and righteousness to a riverbed that never fails.[51] Their moral actions may be compared to a wadi (נַחַל), often dried up. Just as a field becomes desiccated without a constant supply of water, so, too, a society must be "watered" by justice and righteousness in order to survive.

For a similar juxtaposition of an attack against the cult and a demand for ethical actions, compare Isa 1:11–15 with vv 16–17.

■ **25** To further reinforce the polemic against the people that sacrifice is not the essence of the Lord's demand upon Israel, evidence is brought from a historical precedent: the forty-year sojourn in the wilderness. Precisely during this time Israel enjoyed divine grace and benefited from God's protection (Amos 2:10). Yet all of this care and concern was not in any way linked to, or posited upon, any conditions or obligations of cultic worship or fulfillment of ritual prescriptions. Once again a rhetorical question[52] is resorted to in order to press the issue: "Did[53] you offer[54] me[55] sacrifices and meal offerings[56] (הַזְּבָחִים וּמִנְחָה הִגַּשְׁתֶּם־לִי) those forty years in the wilderness?"[57] The expected answer is, of course, "No." Nevertheless, the absence of an established cult did not impinge upon or restrict the relationship of the Lord toward Israel, for he continued to guide them through the barren wilderness with full watch and ward. Ergo, the divine-human relationship is not contingent upon the existence of, or obedience to, any elaborate sacrificial system, but solely and uniquely upon an absolute inviolable commitment to an ethical-moral way of life.

Obviously the underlying assumption of this rhetorical question is a tradition that sacrifices were not the hallmark of the wilderness period,[58] and that the people knew and readily acknowledged this fact. Otherwise, the effect of the argument would be negated by the people's contradiction of the basic presupposition. Compare Jer 7:22–23: "For when I freed your fathers from the land of Egypt, I did not speak with them or command them

---

50 See Amos 2:13; 3:3–6, 12; 6:12; 9:9.

51 J. P. Hyatt ("The Translation and Meaning of Amos 5:23–24," *ZAW* 68 [1956] 17–24) incorrectly relates the qualities of justice and righteousness here to the Deity. Soggin, 97, cites others who interpret this verse as an introduction to the judgment pronounced in v 27 and translate: "But judgment will flow down like water, justice like an ever-flowing stream." This, however, does not fit the intended contrast with vv 22–23. For a similar image, see Isa 48:18: "If only you would heed my commands! Then your prosperity would be like a river (כְּנָהָר), and your triumph (וְצִדְקָתְךָ) like the waves of the sea" (כְּגַלֵּי הַיָּם).

Comparison to this image has been made by M. C. Astour ("Two Ugaritic Serpent Charms," *JNES* 27 [1968] 13–36), referring to *RŠ* 24.244, lines 68–69 (p. 15): "His vitality *(ḥt)* became strong like a torrent *(km.nḥl)*; it streamed like a stream" *(tplg.km.plg)*.

52 For other polemical rhetorical questions, see Amos 2:11; 3:3–8; 5:18; 8:8; 9:7.

53 For the use of the interrogative ־הַ with a *patach* followed by a *dagesh* in the next letter, see Num 13:19, הַבְּמַחֲנִים. Thus there is no need to vocalize the text here with a *ḥateph-pathaḥ*, הֲ. See also *GKC*, 150d. There is also no reason to harmonize both nouns in the singular, הַזֶּבַח וּמִנְחָה, positing a dittography; against Ehrlich, *Randglossen*, 5.242; Budde, "Amos," 116; Cramer. Rudolph weighs the idea favorably, along with the other possibility of reading מְנָחֹת—thus harmonizing both in the plural.

54 For Heb. הגיש in connection with various sacrifices, see Exod 32:6; 1 Sam 13:9 (שְׁלָמִים); Lev 2:8; 1 Kgs 5:1; Mal 2:12; 3:3 (מִנְחָה); Lev 8:14; 2 Chr 29:23 (חַטָּאת); 1 Sam 13:9 (עוֹלָה).

55 See H. W. Hertzberg, "Die prophetische Kritik am Kult," *TLZ* 75 (1950) 219–60, especially 223. It has been suggested that if the intent of the passage was to contrast לִי ("to me") with the other deities mentioned in the next verse, the word order would have been הַהִגַּשְׁתֶּם־לִי זְבָחִים וּמִנְחָה.

56 The two terms זֶבַח and מִנְחָה are comprehensive expressions for animal and vegetable offerings.

57 See S. Talmon, "The 'Desert Motif' in the Bible and in Qumran Literature," in *Biblical Motifs, Origins and Transformation* (ed. A. Altmann; Studies and Texts 3; Cambridge: Harvard University, 1966) 31–63. See also Marti, 196; Weiser, *Profetie*, 228; R. Hentschke, *Stellung*, 83; R. Knierim, "Das erste Gebote," *ZAW* 77 (1965) 31.

For forty years equaling one generation in biblical tradition, see S. Talmon, "*Har* and *Midbār:* An Antithetical Pair of Biblical Motifs," in *Figurative Language in the Ancient Near East* (ed. M. Mindlin, M. J. Geller, and J. E. Wansbrough; London: School of Oriental and African Studies, 1987) 136–37.

58 Compare already the insightful comments of the medieval exegetes, Rashi, ibn Ezra, and Kimchi.

concerning burnt offerings or sacrifice. But this is what I commanded them: Do my bidding, that I may be your God and you may be my people. Walk only in the way I enjoin upon you, that it may go well with you." According to the early traditions found in JE, Israel engaged in some form of cultic activity (including the offering of sacrifices) before they left Egypt (Exod 12:21–27) and while at Mt. Sinai (Exod 3:12; 17:15; 24:4–8; 32:5–6), but not during the wilderness period. Relying on this tradition rather than the one reflected in P, whereby the obligatory cult was already inaugurated at Sinai,[59] does not mean that Moses could not have issued cultic prescriptions but that they did not come into effect until the entry into Canaan. One must also take into consideration that during this period in the wilderness sacrifices must have been severely limited by the circumstances and conditions of Israel's sojourn and wanderings.[60] Amos is thus contrasting the lavish and excessive ritual practice of his day with the frugal one that may have existed during those forty years.[61] Nevertheless, that period was still, in his view, the ideal period of Israel's history (see also Hos 2:16; 9:10; Jer 2:2).[62]

■ **26** This verse, beginning with a verb in the perfect consecutive future,[63] is linked with the following one, which concludes the chapter on the theme of exile.[64] It describes a procession in which the people are carrying the effigies of two deities. But because idolatry is otherwise not mentioned in any of the other oracles (with the dubious exception of Amos 8:14), and because at least one of the two gods mentioned, Sikkuth (סִכּוּת), is supposed to have been introduced into Israel only after the Assyrian conquest (2 Kgs 17:30),[65] many commentators attempt to excise these references from the text or dissociate them from Amos. They either surmise that the verse is a later interpolation,[66] revocalize the nouns in question and thereby "de-astralize" the passage,[67] or accept the presence of two deities but assume that they are other than the ones referred to in the Masoretic

59 See Ehrlich, *Mikrâ,* 3.411; idem, *Randglossen,* 5.242–43; Hammershaimb, 91–92; Haran, "Amos," 284–85, who also note that there is almost a complete lack of sacrificial prescriptions in the earliest compilation of biblical legal material, Exod 21—23.

60 See also Orelli, van Gelderen, Ridderbos, Deden, and Cripps for the view that both the necessary animals and agricultural produce were lacking.

61 See Kaufmann, *Toledoth,* 6.71 n 24; Rudolph; Soggin, 100–101.

62 It is incorrect to assume that v 26 is the continuation of the question of v 25; against Guthe, 40; Marti, 197; Robinson-Horst, 93; Sellin²; Maag, *Text,* 35; Würthwein, "Amos-Studien," 48; idem, "Kultbescheid," 117; Amsler; Tur-Sinai, *Peshuṭo,* 465; Wolff, 260. See also Fosbroke, 822; H. Pfeiffer, "The Polemic against Idolatry in the Old Testament," *JBL* 33 (1924) 232, 237. So, too, it is totally unwarranted to assume that both these verses are a later addition from the hand of a Deuteronomistic redactor; against Schmidt, "Redaktion," 188–91; Wolff, 259–60, 264–65. Sellin¹ and Weiser (*Profetie,* 172–74) suggest reversing vv 24 and 25.

63 See also Gen 45:19. See *GKC,* 112x. There is no need to change the vocalization to the *niphʿal,* וְנִשֵּׂאתֶם: "You will be carried along with," against Hentschke, *Stellung,* 87; Sellin²; Weiser, *Profetie.*

64 See the connection already made in the *Damascus Covenant* 7:13–19: "I will send into exile Sakkût, your king, and Kêwān, your images, beyond the tents of Damascus. . . ." (Heb. מֵהָלְאָה, "beyond," was metathesized to מֵאָהֳלֵי, "beyond the tents of.") For translation, see C. Rabin, *The Zadokite Documents* (2d ed.; Oxford: Clarendon, 1958) 29, 31; see also J. Murphy O'Connor, "The Essenes of Palestine," *BA* 40 (1977) 100–124; P. von der Osten-Sacken, "Die Bücher der Tora als Hütte der Gemeinde—Amos 5.26f. in der Damaskusschrift," *ZAW* 91 (1979) 425–35.

65 Heb. סִכּוּת בְּנוֹת. For the first element of the composite name, see E. Lipiński, "*SKN* et *SGN* dans le sémitique-occidental du nord," *UF* 5 (1973) 191–207, especially 202–4. He compares it to Ugar. *sknt* ("aspect, image"; *CTA* 4:i:43) and translates, "Vous avez porté l'image de votre roi" ("You have carried the image of your god"). He is followed by W. W. Hallo ("New Moons and Sabbaths: A Case-Study in the Contrastive Approach," *HUCA* 48 [1977] 15). For the second element, related to Akk. *bānitu* (from *banû,* "to create"), see J. R. Tournay, "Un cylinder babylonien découvert en Transjordanie," *RB* 74 (1967) 248–54; A. Haldar, "Tradition and History," *BO* 31 (1974) 34–35.

66 See Wellhausen, 84. See Wolff, 259–60, following Schmidt, "Redaktion," 190, who concludes that it is a postexilic Judean gloss; so, too, Rudolph, on v 26b.

67 See the tortuous exegesis of S. Gevirtz ("A New Look at an Old Crux: Amos 5:26," *JBL* 87 [1968] 267–76), who translates: "But you carry [vocalizing the verb in the *piʿel,* וְנִשֵּׂאתֶם, 'to bring to/supply'; see 1 Kgs 9:11; Esth 9:3; Ezra 8:36, and interpreting אֶת as serving a dative function, equivalent to אֶל] (these things = sacrifices) to the shrine [following G, σ', α', V, and S, משכנה] of your (god) *MLX* [following G and V], and to the abode [by equating the forms *qittûl* and

text.[68] Thus סכּוּת is converted by some to סֻכַּת ("hut, booth")[69] and מַלְכְּכֶם ("your king") to מֹלֶךְ ("Moloch") or מִלְכֹּם ("Milcom")[70] based on G, τὴν σκηνὴν τοῦ Μολοχ ("the tent of Moloch"), and V, *tabernaculum Moloch vestro* ("tabernacle of your Moloch"), and כִּיּוּן is revocalized to כַּוָּן, that is, a "*kamānu*-cake," associated with the cult of the queen of heaven, Ishtar.[71]

These tortuous ways of resolving the assumed difficulties inherent in the verse, as attractive as they may be, are completely unnecessary and superfluous. Both of these two deities have a long "history" behind them. The first, סכּוּת, is the Hebrew transliteration of ^{d}SAG.KUD, an astral deity known from Mesopotamian sources[72] and also found in a list of gods from Ugarit.[73] There he is identified with Ninurta (and thus secondarily with the planet Saturn), one of the leading gods in the Mesopotamian pantheon. The epithet מַלְכְּכֶם ("your king"), following the deity's proper name, is a hierarchical device for ranking gods in Mesopotamia[74] and is indicative of the supreme rank of this deity in the cult the prophet is satirizing.

---

mqtl, סכּוּת = מַסֶּכֶת, translated 'shrine,' and כִּיּוּן = מָכוֹן, 'abode'] of your images—the hosts [Arab. *kaukabun,* 'quantity/mass' (of an army)] of your gods that you have made for yourselves." Kaufmann (*Toledoth,* 6.73 n 24) also emends away any reference to astral deities by reading מַסְּכוֹת, which he relates to נֶסֶךְ ("libations") and כַּוָּנִים ("*kamānu* cakes"). For both together in a single passage, see Jer 44:19. The fanciful erotic interpretation of H. H. Hirschberg ("Some Additional Arabic Etymologies in Old Testament Lexicography," *VT* 11 [1961] 375–76), who discovers here symbols of a fertility cult, equating two of the key words, סכּוּת and כִּיּוּן, with the masculine and feminine sexual organs, needs no refutation. Maag (*Text,* 34–36) translates the verse as a question: "And did you bear the tabernacle of your king, the pedestal of your gods, which you made, O Israel?" For "pedestal," see also Amsler.

68 See Weinfeld ("Worship," 149–50), who, by comparing an Assyrian text (*ABL,* 1212, r. 1–10) that mentions a booth in which the image of Ishtar, the queen of heaven, was carried, accepts the ancient versions' translation of סכּוּת = סוּכָּה ("a booth") and relates the references to the "image of your king," Hadad-Adad, and to the symbol of the queen, Ishtar, which was a star. This then is taken as "evidence for the worship of the host of heaven, especially the King and Queen of heaven, in Israel as early as the days of Jeroboam II." (See later for partial confirmation.)

69 See also σ', τὴν σκηνὴν (same as G) and S, משכנא ("tent"). So, too, Amsler; C. D. Isbell, "Another Look at Amos," *JBL* 97 (1978) 97–99. This verse (along with the former and following ones as well) is quoted in Acts 7:43: "Yes, you took up the tabernacle of Moloch, and the star of your god Rephan, images which you made to worship."

70 For Milcom, see α' Μολχόμ and S; for Moloch, see G and V; θ' and σ' follow MT.

71 See Jer 7:18; 44:19. For *kamānu* cakes, see *CAD, K,* 110–11, from *kamû/kawû,* B ("to bake, roast"), *CAD, K,* 131. See also H. Hoffner, *Alimenta Hethaeorum: Food Production in Hittite Asia Minor* (AOS 55; New Haven: American Oriental Society, 1974) 174; M. Held, "Studies in Biblical Lexicography in the Light of Akkadian," in Eretz Israel 16 (*Harry M. Orlinsky Volume;* ed. B. A. Levine and A. Malamat; Jerusalem: Israel Exploration Society, 1982) 76–77.

72 For סכּוּת, see T. L. Fenton, "Sikkuth," *EM* 5.1037 (Heb.); P. Artzi, "Sikkuth and Chiun," *EncJud* 14.1531. For textual references, see A. Deimel, *Pantheon Babylonicum* (Rome: Pontifical Biblical Institute, 1914) 231; E. F. Weidner, "Altbabylonische Götterlisten," *AfO* 2 (1924–1925) 1–18; idem, "Eine Beschreibung des Sternenhimmels aus Assur," *AfO* 4 (1927) 78; K. L. Tallqvist, *Akkadische Götterepitheta* (StudOr 7; Helsinki: The Academic Bookshop, 1938) 421, 424, 440; H. Zimmern, *Beiträge zur Kenntnis der babylonischen Religion* (Leipzig: Hinrichs, 1901) 10, line 179; F. Gössmann, *Planetarium Babylonicum, oder: Die sumerische-babylonischen Stern-Namen* (ed. P. A. Deimel; Sumerisches Lexikon IV/2; Rome: Pontifical Biblical Institute, 1950) 124; S. Langdon, *Babylonian Liturgies: Sumerian Texts from the Early Period and from the Library of Ashurbanipal* (Paris: Guethner, 1913) 124–30. Ninurta had a secondary association with the planet Saturn; see references in Tallqvist and Gössmann. See also O. Loretz, "Die babylonischen Gottesnamen Sukkut und Kajjamanu. Ein Beitrag zur jüdischen Astrologie," *ZAW* 101 (1989) 286–89.

73 For the "An" god list, see J. Nougayrol, "Textes Suméro-Accadiens des Archives et Bibliothèques Privées d'Ugarit," in *Ug V* (ed. C. F. A. Schaeffer and others; Mission de Ras Shamra 16; Paris: Guethner, 1968) 214:44.

74 See Artzi, "Sikkuth and Chiun," *EncJud* 14.1531. See, for example, *Anum šarrum ittaṣâ ṣalam banû* ("Anu, the king, has risen, the beautiful constellation"); F. Thureau-Dangin, *Rituels accadiens* (Paris: Leroux, 1921) 119:17.

כִּיּוּן,[75] however, is the Hebrew equivalent of Akk. *kajamānu* (literally, "the steady one"),[76] which is one of the appellations of the star god, Saturn.[77] Note that Amos appropriately adds כּוֹכַב אֱלֹהֵיכֶם ("the star of your god") to this deity's name.[78] These two deities, SAG.KUD and Kajamānu, were assumed to appear alongside one another in astrological lists and in *Šurpu* II:179–80. However, the recent collation of this text has shown that the editors have erred in their reading.[79]

Amos in his parody of these gods, whose names are cacophonously vocalized on the pattern of Heb. שִׁקּוּץ ("detestable things"),[80] further denigrates them satirically, "your images (צַלְמֵיכֶם)[81] that you have made for yourselves" (עֲשִׂיתֶם לָכֶם). The expression (ל) עשה is often

75 G's transliteration, Ραιφαν (compare also Acts 7:43, cited in n 69 above), is usually regarded as an inner-Greek error for Καιφαν. The intervocalic *m* in *kajamānu* comes to be pronounced like *w*. See S. A. Kaufman, *The Akkadian Influence on Aramaic* (Assyriological Studies 19; Chicago and London: University of Chicago, 1974) 143: "It is well known that in NB/LB intervocalic *m* represents *w*, both in the case of original *w* and original *m*. That is to say that *w* is the allophone of *m* occurring in intervocalic position." He then brings a list of words with etymological *m* appearing as *w* in Aramaic, which were borrowed from Babylonian. According to M. Pope ("Notes on the Rephaim Texts from Ugarit," in *Essays on the Ancient Near East in Memory of Jacob Joel Finkelstein* [ed. M. Ellis; Hamden, CT: Archon Books, 1977] 170), "The collocation of MLK and RPU . . . is significant in the light of the Ugaritic association of RPU and MLK." This relationship is simply not to be found, however, in the text of Amos.

76 *CAD, K,* 36, 38. See also Gössmann, *Planetarium,* No. 313; *ABL,* 1401 r. 6; S. H. Langdon, *Die neubabylonischen Königsinschriften* (VAB 4; Leipzig: Hinrichs, 1912) 278 vii, 1. Since Saturn was the most distant of the planets known to the Mesopotamians, and hence its movements were the slowest and steadiest, it is described by the epithet "the steady one."

77 Already noted by ibn Ezra, "The word *kijjun* is known from Arabic and Persian, i.e., *kaiwan* is Saturn" (Heb. שַׁבְּתַאי); and Kimchi.

78 For כּוֹכָב = Akk. *kakkabu* ("star"), affixed to names of deities, see *Nannaru kakkabišu uštēpâ* ("He made the moon, his star, come forth"), *Enuma Elish,* V:12; see also VII:126, where it is attached to *Nēberu* ("Jupiter"). It is also a very familiar epithet of Ishtar. See *CAD, K,* 47.

79 E. Reiner (*Šurpu: A Collection of Sumerian and Akkadian Incantations* [*AfO* Beiheft 11; Graz: Selbstverlag des Herausgebers, 1958] 18), following H. Zimmern (*Die Beschwörungstafeln Šurpu* [Leipzig: Hinrichs, 1896]), read dSAG.KUD and dSAG.UŠ. The correct reading, however, is d*Sag-kud* dUŠ, the first deity being SAG.GUD and the second *Nita* and not *Kajamānu.* This collation was made by R. Borger ("Amos 5,26, Apostelgeschichte 7,43 und Šurpu II,180," *ZAW* 100 [1988] 70–81), who demonstrates that Zimmern was mistakenly influenced by the passage in Amos! The name *Kiyyun* also occurs on an Aramaic magic bowl, alongside other Babylonian deities such as Šamaš and Sin. See C. D. Isbell, *Corpus of the Aramaic Incantation Bowls* (SBLDS 17; Missoula, MT: Scholars, 1975) 138, bowl 62:3, כיון. See also Nabatean, כונא, *CIS,* II, 199. See, too, J. Obermann, "Two Magic Bowls: New Incantation Texts from Mesopotamia," *JAOS* 57 (1940) 1–31.

80 See 1 Kgs 11:5; 2 Kgs 23:13. For this linguistic phenomenon called "cacophony" or "dysphemism," see Paul, "Euphemism," 959–61. For another explanation, see Fenton, "Sikkuth," *EM* 5.1037.

81 See E. A. Speiser, "Note on Amos 5:26," *BASOR* 108 (1947) 5–6 (Heb. צֶלֶם = Akk. *ṣalmu*): "*ṣalmu,* 'figure,' is familiar in Babylonian and Assyrian astronomy, where it is reserved for astral bodies which were pictured in human form. . . . In such cases the name of the constellation (*kakkab* X) is followed in the text by *ṣalmu,* introducing the particular image which the constellation is said to represent."

Hammershaimb, 94, by contrast, relates צֶלֶם to an Aramaic/Arabic god, *Ṣalm,* known from inscriptions from Tema, *KAI,* I.228:2, 3ff.; 229:3, whom some identify with Saturn; see *KAI,* II.279. See also Gibson, *Aramaic Inscriptions,* 148–51: "The deity named *ṢLM* was probably Mesopotamian in origin. His name also appears as a component of a priest's personal name, *ṢLMŠZB*"; see also p. 149, lines 9, 11, 21. See *CAD, Ṣ,* 79, which also refers to a "constellation." See also *KUB,* 37, 54:2 in F. Köcher, *Literarische Texte in akkadischer Sprache* (Berlin: Akademie Verlag, 1953); R. Frankena, *Tākultu. De sacrale maaltijd in het assyrische ritueel* (Leiden: Brill, 1954) 95 no. 101; 112 no. 199. See, too, F. M. Cross ("A New Aramaic Stele from Taymā'," in *A Wise and Discerning Heart: Studies Presented to Joseph A. Fitzmyer, S.J., in Celebration of His Sixty-fifth Birthday* [ed. R. E. Brown and A. A. DiLella;=*CBQ* 48 (1986)] 392–93), who draws attention to the name of the god in Mesopotamian personal names but concludes that the deity is "not yet clearly identified."

used in the context of making idols; see Exod 20:4; 1 Kgs 14:9; 2 Kgs 17:29–31; Hos 8:4, 6; 13:2; and for the specific phrase עשׂה צְלָמִים ("make images"), see Ezek 7:20; 16:17. So, too, in Akkadian compare the interdialectal semantic and partial etymological equivalent, *ṣalmam epēšu* ("to make an image"); for example, *ēpiš ṣalam Aššur u ilāni rabûti* ("The one who made the image of [the god] Assur and the [other] great gods").[82]

The verse as it now stands is thus definitely in order. Nevertheless, two suggestions for a minor rearrangement and emendation of the words may be considered:

וּנְשָׂאתֶם אֵת סִכּוּת מַלְכְּכֶם
וְאֵת כִּיּוּן כּוֹכַבְכֶם צַלְמֵי אֱלֹהֵיכֶם . . .

"And you shall bear aloft Sikkuth, your king, and Kiyyun, your star, the graven images of your gods which you have made for yourselves."[83] Or,

וּנְשָׂאתֶם אֵת סִכּוּת מַלְכְּכֶם
וְאֵת כִּיּוּן כּוֹכַב אֱלֹהֵיכֶם
צַלְמֵיכֶם אֲשֶׁר עֲשִׂיתֶם לָכֶם

"And you shall carry off Sikkuth, your king, and Kiyyun, the star of your god—your images which you have made for yourselves."[84] Both readings have the advantage of appending כּוֹכָב ("star") directly to the star god, Kiyyun = Saturn.

Amos is ridiculing the great cult processionals, when statues of gods were carried triumphantly on high by their worshipers.[85] Here, however, he has another processional in mind—one of deportation. They will carry their idols—but into exile (see Isa 46:1–2, 7).[86]

There is no reason to suspect this verse of being introduced by a later redactor after the Assyrian conquest of Israel. During the very period of the oracles of Amos, Jeroboam II extended his conquests over Damascus and Hamath into northern Syria (2 Kgs 14:28). Israel then came into contact—politically, commercially, and culturally—with sections of Aramean territory that formerly had been influenced by Mesopotamian culture. Most likely, then, preserved here in the Book of Amos is a rare glimpse of a Mesopotamian astral cult that through Aramean intervention penetrated northern Israel.[87] To all this zealous foreign cultic affiliation (supplementing their own devout cult listed previously), the prophet derisively responds, "You will carry your effigies—but off into exile!" Furthermore, those who assume it to be an interpolation also miss the ironic poignancy of the words of the prophet in their present

82 OIP 2, 150 No. X 2 in Luckenbill, *Annals.* Compare also *šarrum ṣalmam ippuš* ("The king will make an image"), *RA* 44 (1972) 42:45. See also H. Tadmor, "Fragments of a Stele of Sargon II from the Excavations of Ashdod," in Eretz Israel 8 (*E. L. Sukenik Memorial Volume;* ed. N. Avigad and others; Jerusalem: Israel Exploration Society, 1967) 156 r. 13.

83 H. Cazelles, "The Problem of the Kings in Osée, 8:4," *CBQ* 11 (1949) 20 and n 22.

84 C. D. Isbell, "Another Look at Amos 5:26," *JBL* 97 (1978) 97–99, who reconstructs the text on the basis of G: "You will take up the tabernacle of Milcom; the star of your god [which is] Kiyyun, your images which. . . ."

85 Cazelles, "Problem," 21. See Akk. *našû* ("to lift up," "to carry") = Heb. נשׂא, in this context.

For gods going into exile, see Jer 48:7; 49:3. See Ehrlich, *Randglossen,* 5.243: "Nach dem Abfall aber bleiben Israel nur seine Götzen, die es auf dem Wege ins Exil wird tragen müssen, statt von ihnen getragen zu werden, vgl. Ex, 19:4 und sieh zu Jes, 46:1." ("But after the apostasy Israel will be left only with its idols, which they will have to carry on the road to exile instead of being carried by them; compare Exod 19:4 and see Isa 46:1.") Weiser (*Profetie,* 172–74) interprets the verse in terms of northern Israelite cultic processions—one last "grotesque festival procession."

86 Contrary to the interpretation of Cazelles, "Problem," and Isbell, "Another Look." This is an ironic punishment based on talion—because they are so devoted to this cult, they will go off into exile actually carrying these effigies. This connection with the cult (foreign) may be the reason why this verse was attached to the above, where, too, a passion for the cult (monotheistic) was described.

87 This idea has been alluded to by both J. W. McKay (*Religion in Judah under the Assyrians 732–609 B.C.* [SBT 2/26; London: SCM, 1973]), in a single line on p. 68, and M. Cogan (*Imperialism and Religion: Assyria, Judah, and Israel in the Eighth and Seventh Centuries B.C.E.* [SBLMS 19; Missoula, MT: Scholars, 1974] 104), who correctly dates this oracle prior to the advent of Tiglatpileser III and thus criticizes those who "unjustly suspect" it of being written after 722 B.C.E.: "Israel's reassertion of political domain over Damascus and Hamath during the final years of Jeroboam II exposed Israel anew to mid-eighth century Aramean culture, a culture suffused with Mesopotamian elements." (In n 41, he notes the invoking of at least five pairs of Mesopotamian deities and other West-Semitic deities in the Aramaic Sefire treaties.) "We suspect that astral cults popular in Northern Syria penetrated Israelite practice through Aramean mediation as was the case a century later in

context. The people will be driven into exile by "The Lord, the God of hosts" (v 27), that is, the Lord of all the *astral* hosts will deport them along with their *astral* deities!

■ **27** The oracle now reaches its climax with the announcement of the imminent punishment of exile, a theme often repeated throughout the book.[88] All the basic props and supports of the nation will utterly fail them: Neither their lavish cult (Amos 5:21ff.), nor their extensive wealth (Amos 6:1–6), nor even their military successes (Amos 6:13) will offset their destined fate of deportation.

But to where precisely will Israel be exiled? What exactly did Amos intend by using such an ill-defined geographical term as "beyond Damascus" (מֵהָלְאָה לְדַמָּשֶׂק)?[89] Most commentators assume that the prophet was alluding to Assyria—and such a fate did overtake northern Israel within the next couple of decades (2 Kgs 17:6). However, if Amos did have Assyria in mind, why need he refer to it so indirectly as "beyond Damascus"? Moreover, keep in mind that Assyria is never once referred to in the oracles of Amos and is most probably not within his political purview.[90]

The answer is to be sought in one of Amos's characteristic literary traits. He deliberately at times leaves his exact intent unspecified or anomalously vague in order to exacerbate the psychological tension upon the people (for example, 4:12).[91] Nevertheless, his allusion here can be comprehended in ironic tones. Israel, during this period, had extended its boundaries by means of victories in the battlefield as far as Damascus (2 Kgs 14:28). Well, now they shall go even farther, "beyond Damascus"—not in victory, but in exile! Exiled by "the Lord, the God of hosts, is his name."[92]

Judah." See his reference to H. Tadmor ("Jeroboam, Son of Joash," *EM* 3.777 [Heb.]) for a similar reflection. For the impact of Aramaic and Arameans on the Assyrian empire, see F. M. Fales, "Accadico e aramaico: livelli dell' interferenza linguistica," *Vicino Oriente* III (1980) 243–67; and H. Tadmor, "The Aramization of Assyria: Aspects of Western Impact," in *Mesopotamien und seine Nachbarn: Politische und Kulturelle Wechselbezeihungen im Alten Vorderasien* (ed. H.-J. Nissen and J. Renger; Berliner Beiträge zum Vorderen Orient 1; *CRRA XXV;* Berlin: Dietrich Heimer, 1982) 2.449–70.

According to Ginsberg (*Israelian Heritage,* 41 n 57): "To judge by the silence of Deutero-Hosea, the Sakkut-Kaiwan cult was no longer of any importance in Israel after the fall of the Omri dynasty and the loss of Damascus."

See also G. C. Heider, *The Cult of Molek. A Reassessment* (*JSOT* Supplement Series 43; Sheffield: JSOT, 1985) 308–9.

88 See Amos 6:7; 7:11, 17; 9:4, 9; and in the oracles against the nations, 1:5, 15.

89 Heb. מֵהָלְאָה לְ־ appears two more times in conjunction with place names, Gen 35:21; Jer 22:19.

90 See previously. Compare Wellhausen (84), it is not "clear that Amos has the Assyrians in mind"; Wolff, 266.

91 See also Gottwald, *Kingdoms,* 97: "The primary force of the designation is not precisely geographical but rather psychological." He, however, goes on to reach a different conclusion, that is, that Israel will now "face an enemy more distant and dangerous than the customary Damascus."

92 See Crenshaw ("*YHWH Ṣ^{e}ba'ôt Š^{e}mô:* A Form Critical Analysis," *ZAW* [1969] 156–75, especially 162 n 34) for a long list of those who reject the authenticity of the refrain. Compare, however, the final comment to the previous verse.

6 Indictment of Conspicuous Consumption

1 **Woe, you who are carefree in Zion**
And secure on the hill of Samaria,
The notables of the choicest of nations*
To whom the house of Israel comes.
2 **Cross over to Calneh and look,**
And go from there to Hamath Rabbah;
Then go down to Gath of the Philistines.
Are (you) better than these kingdoms?
Or is their territory larger than yours?
3 **You who thrust off the day of disaster,**
But bring near the seat of violence.*
4 **Who lie upon beds of ivory,**
Sprawled out on their couches,
Who dine on lambs from the flock
And on calves from the feeding stall.
5 **Who improvise melodies to the tune of the lute,**
Like David, they invent for themselves* musical instruments.
6 **Who imbibe from bowls of wine,**
And anoint themselves with the choicest of oils,
But remain unconcerned over the ruin of Joseph.
7 **Therefore, they now shall go into exile at the head of the exiles,**
And spent will be the sprawlers' spree.

***Hebrew obscure**

■ **1** This woe oracle (6:1–7) is structured similarly to the preceding one (5:18ff.): Both commence with הוֹי, are followed by a participle introducing the prophetic accusation, and conclude on the same threatened punishment, that of exile.[1] They also contain two identical words, שִׁיר and נֵבֶל (5:22; 6:5), and a similar theme, יוֹם ה׳ (5:18) and יוֹם רָע (Amos 6:3). Thus they were juxtaposed: Both religious and secular celebrations are abominable if morality is absent.

The first major problem in this verse is the reference to "Zion" (צִיּוֹן). Because it is commonly assumed that Amos never addressed the population of his southern homeland of Judah, and because his commission orders were to prophesy in the north (7:15), exegetes have expended much effort on proposed emendations to create a substantive that would provide a "better" parallel pair with "Samaria" in the adjoining colon.[2]

1 Compare the similar structure and contents of the הוֹי-oracles in Isa 5:11–13.

2 For example, Sellin[1], בָּעִיר ("in the [capital] city"), but in his second and third editions he left it unemended; Cheyne (cited in Harper, 141), בְּתִרְצָה ("in Tirzah"); so, too, Budde, "Amos," 121–23, and see Maag, *Text,* 37; Ehrlich, *Randglossen,* 5.243, בְּגָאוֹן ("in pride"); Riessler, בְּצִיּוֹן ("in the rock")—Arab. *ṣuwwa* (but see Rudolph); Rudolph, 215, בְּבִצָּרוֹן ("in the fortress"). For the latter, see Zech 9:12, where בִּצָּרוֹן may be an epithet of שֹׁמְרוֹן, "Samaria." Others simply assume that צִיּוֹן ("Zion") was inserted by a later Judean glossator; for example, Marti; Fosbroke; Wolff, 270. Otherwise, G. Fohrer, "Zion-Jerusalem in the Old Testament," *TDNT* 7.295; Oettli, "Amos und Hosea," 72. So, too, Gottwald (*Kingdoms,* 107), although the word "Judah [is] debatable . . . there is no conclusive reason for deleting it." See Gordis ("Composition," 241–42; idem, "Studies," 237), where he remarks that if it were a postexilic addition it "would be consolatory not minatory"; Hammershaimb, 96. Haran ("Biblical Studies," 114–15), however, maintains the reading צִיּוֹן but does not think that the prophet was directing his oracle also

Here, however, the words of Oettli still ring true: "Why should not Amos, a Judean, be allowed in the course of his address to touch on his own homeland?"[3] As has been demonstrated, moreover, there is no reason whatsoever to negate the authenticity of the prophecy against Judah (2:3–4).[4]

Furthermore, if Amos is assumed to have been limited to uttering oracles only against northern Israel, how can the first six oracles against the foreign nations be explained? Even those who relegate several of these oracles to a later redaction do not deny that the core still contains the words of Amos. In sum, unless irrefutable evidence can be brought to bear against these few sparse references to Judah, there is no reason to delete them facilely based on some unfounded preconceived notions of modern exegesis. The prophet's condemnation and accusation apply equally as well to Zion.

Nevertheless, he does concentrate his main indictment against the elite upper-class circles of Samaria (see 3:12, 15; 4:1), the crème de la crème.[5] They are those who, similar to their counterparts in Zion, are living at ease in a "carefree" manner (הַשַּׁאֲנַנִּים), totally confident and "secure" (הַבֹּטְחִים בְּ־) in their life style.[6] Amos calls these proud, vain, and insolent officials, "notables (נְקֻבֵי)[7] of the choicest of nations" (רֵאשִׁית הַגּוֹיִם).[8] He gives sardonic and sarcastic expression to the manner in which these prominent celebrities actually think and speak about themselves. They are securely ensconced in their arrogance as the acknowledged, distinguished leaders of Samaria. They are the chosen of the choicest nations. All's right in their world; no harm can come to them! (Yet as the oracle will conclude, on still another ironic tone forming a literary inclusio [v 7], these רֵאשִׁית will be deported at the "head" [רֹאשׁ] of the exiles!)

The last colon still remains an enigma: וּבָאוּ לָהֶם בֵּית יִשְׂרָאֵל. It, too, has been the object of multiple emendations,[9] and even when the Masoretic text is kept intact it is considered by some as a later Deuteronomistic redac-

---

against Judah: "He recalls Zion in the first stich only in order to balance the verse and to preserve poetic parallelism. 'Zion-Samaria' is a variant of the pair, 'Samaria-Zion', which is a set pair in the Bible: cf. Mic 1:5; Jer 23:13–14; Ezek 23:4; etc. According to the rule Samaria, which is the larger and more important, should have been mentioned first. It is possible that the order was reversed in order to end with Samaria, against which he is solely directing his oracles." His view is followed by Watson, *Hebrew Poetry,* 139. Note, however, that all these commentators overlook the assonance of "Zion" and "Samaria" in the Hebrew: הַשַּׁאֲנַנִּים בְּצִיּוֹן וְהַבֹּטְחִים בְּהַר שֹׁמְרוֹן.

3 In situ.

4 See previous comments to this oracle.

5 Rudolph's choice expression, 218.

6 For the parallelism of שאנן and בטח, see also Isa 32:9: "You carefree (שַׁאֲנַנּוֹת) women . . . you confident (בֹּטְחוֹת) ladies"; and v 11, "Tremble, you carefree ones (שַׁאֲנַנּוֹת); quake, O confident ones" (בֹּטְחוֹת); and v 18. Compare also Prov 1:33.

For the expression בטח ב־, see Isa 47:10: "You were secure in your wickedness" (וַתִּבְטְחִי בְרָעָתֵךְ). See S. D. Luzzato's commentary to Isaiah, *Il profeta Isaia* (Padova: Bianchi, 1867) 510–11 (Heb.).

Note that Amos describes these ebullient, carefree, socially secure Israelites six times throughout this pericope with the definite article הַ followed by a plural participle. A seventh occurrence of the ה, this time an interrogative הֲ־, also followed by a plural participle, appears in v 2. There is one more plural participle describing their pampered existence, וְאֹכְלִים, in v 5; however, this one is without a definite article, illustrating Amos's tendency for variation within a set pattern. Compare comments on the style of chapters 1—2.

7 These distinguished prominent officials are those who are "designated by name" (נִקְּבוּ בְּשֵׁמוֹת), Num 1:17. See also 1 Chr 12:31; 2 Chr 28:15; and compare Isa 62:2. Compare Arab. *naqib* ("leader, prince"). For the root נקב, see *KB,* 678–79: "durchboren" ("to perforate"), "punktieren" ("to puncture"), "bezeichnen" ("to designate"). See similarly Rudolph, 215, "gezeichnet = ausgezeichnet" ("marked = distinguished").

8 For this expression, compare also Num 24:20: "A leading nation (רֵאשִׁית גּוֹיִם) is Amalek." For רֵאשִׁית ("choice, chief part"), see, for example, Deut 33:21; 1 Sam 15:21; Jer 49:35; Ps 111:10; Prov 1:7; 4:7; Dan 11:41; and again in Amos, 6:6. Note the sarcastic pun on this expression in v 7. Compare Akk. *ašaridu* ("first in rank, foremost"), *CAD, A,* II.416–17; Seux, *Épithètes,* 47f.

9 For example, Oettli, "Amos und Hosea," 72: וְכֵאלֹהִים הֵם בְּבֵית יִשְׂרָאֵל ("and like gods they are in the house of Israel," followed by Robinson-Horst, Maag, *Text,* 37); and instead of the verb וּבָאוּ ("they come"), it has been suggested to read וְאָבוּ, "and they desire," Sellin²; Rudolph, 216 (the latter offers an entirely different emendation, following Oettli, "Amos und Hosea," 72). For another impossible emendation, see W. L. Holladay, "Amos VI 1b: A Suggested Solution," *VT* 22 (1972) 107–10. G interprets יִשְׂרָאֵל

tion.[10] If the text is in order, the words וּבָאוּ לָהֶם apparently conceal some sort of idiomatic expression, implying that the Israelites (or delegations from other cities) "come to" these preeminent notables either for advice or in order to petition them against injustice.[11] The problem, however, has yet to be resolved.

■ **2** This verse is almost unanimously attributed to a later disciple or redactor of Amos. The prevalent general assumption is that the historical references here are to the destruction of the three named kingdoms—Calneh, Hamath Rabbah, and Gath of the Philistines—which took place after the time of Amos. The people are sarcastically reminded that because their kingdom of Israel is no better, stronger, or larger than the other three,[12] all of which were conquered by the Assyrians, the same dread fate awaits them. This commonly accepted thesis, however, should be reexamined.

"Cross over[13] to Calneh[14] and look" (עִבְרוּ כַלְנֵה וּרְאוּ).[15] Biblical Calneh, mentioned also in Isa 10:9 as "Calno" (כַּלְנוֹ), is to be identified with Akk. *Kullani(a)* (identical with *Kunalia* / *Kinallua*), the capital city of *Pattin* / *Ḫattin* (alternately known in Assyrian as *Unqi*, and

בֵּית ("house of Israel") as a vocative beginning the next verse.

10 So Wolff, 271.

11 So, for example, Sellin; Ehrlich, *Mikrâ*, 3.411 (but otherwise in *Randglossen*, 5.243, where he vocalizes וּבֹאוּ [an imperative] and refers לָהֶם to the preceding "nations": "Go to them, house of Israel!"). For בא אֶל/ עַד in legal contexts, see Exod 18:16; 2 Sam 15:4.

On the other hand, H. L. Ginsberg suggests that the idiom means "to pin their hopes upon," based on the expression בָּא עַד in Isa 45:24; Ps 65:3; Job 6:20 (oral communication). See also *NEB*: "you to whom the people of Israel resort."

12 Once again Amos resorts to the technique of a rhetorical question (compare 2:11; 3:3–8; 5:18, 25; 8:8; 9:7), this time a double one (הֲ . . . אִם). Although the pronominal subject is omitted in the first part of the question, it is self-understood that it refers to those previously mentioned: "Are [you] better than these kingdoms? Or is their territory larger than yours?" For similar rhetorical questions, also beginning with טוֹב מִ־, see Judg 11:25: "Are you any better than Balak (הֲטוֹב טוֹב אַתָּה מִבָּלָק) son of Zippor, king of Moab?"; and Nah 3:8: "Were you any better than No-Amon . . ." (הֲתֵיטְבִי מִנֹּא אָמוֹן)?

Some, however, relate "those kingdoms" (הַמַּמְלָכוֹת הָאֵלֶּה) not to the three previously mentioned foreign nations but to the kingdoms of Judah and Israel referred to in the first verse: "Are they [that is, the three] any better than those kingdoms [Judah and Israel]?" See Gordis, "Composition," 244; idem, "Studies," 240–41. Similarly some emend the second stich by transferring the preposition or the suffixes: אִם־רַב מִגְּבוּלָם גְּבֻלְכֶם ("Is your territory larger than their territory?") or אִם־רַב גְּבוּלְכֶם מִגְּבֻלָם ("Is your territory larger than their territory?"). See A. Geiger, *Urschrift und Übersetzungen der Bibel* (Frankfurt: Verlag Maada, ^{2}1928) 96–97. However, the Masoretic text is perfectly sound and in order, without need of these minor corrections. For those who suggest that this is a quotation of the upper classes who boast that their condition is better than others, see Sellin, 242; Mays, 115.

13 Note the technical use once again of עבר ("to cross the border into another state"); see Amos 5:5. For the phrase עִבְרוּ . . . וּרְאוּ ("cross over . . . and look"), compare Jer 2:10.

14 G, *πάντες* incorrectly reads כֻּלָּנָה. However, in Gen 10:10, Masoretic וְכַלְנֵה should be repointed to וְכֻלָּנָה ("and all of them [that is, all the previously mentioned cities] are in the land of Shinar"). See E. A. Speiser, *Genesis: Introduction, Translation and Notes* (AB 1; Garden City, NY: Doubleday, 1964) 67; W. F. Albright, "The End of Calneh in Shinar," *JNES* 3 (1944) 254–55.

15 For citations and spellings of *Kullani*, see S. Parpola, *Neo-Assyrian Toponyms* (AOAT 6; Neukirchen-Vluyn: Neukirchener Verlag, 1970) 206, 213. See also J. D. Hawkins, "Assyrians and Hittites," *Iraq* 36 (1974) 81–83; Na'aman, "Letter," 37. The spelling *Kullania* in economic and administrative documents and letters reflects the pronunciation of the name during the neo-Assyrian period. The place-name כלנה also appears in Aramaic script in an inscription from Tel Taiyanat; see M. Abu Taleb, *Investigations in the History of North Syria 1115–717 B.C.* (Diss., Ann Arbor, 1973) 139 and n 59, cited by Y. Ikeda, *The Kingdom of Hamath and Its Relation with Aram and Israel* (Diss., Hebrew University, 1977) 38 n 123 (Heb.). See also P. Artzi, "Kalneh," *EM* 4.185–86 (Heb.); and J. D. Hawkins, "Ḫattin," *RLA* 4/2–3 (1973) 160–62; idem, "Kullani(a)," *RLA* 6/3–4 (1981) 305–6; idem, "Kinallua," *RLA* 5 (1976–1980) 476–80.

in Aramaic as עמק = *el-ʿAmq,* north of the bend of the Orontes), a late-Hittite state on the Lower Orontes Valley. Shalmaneser III of Assyria claimed victory over the kingdom of Pattin in 858, and in the years 857 and 853, he received tribute from this kingdom. Except for the reference of "a king of עמק," as one of the north Syrian states allied against Zakir of Hamath in the opening decades of the eighth century, nothing else is recorded about the kingdom from 824 to 745. It then reappears in Assyrian sources in conjunction with the campaigns of Tiglatpileser III. Kullani, the capital, after revolting, was conquered in 739 (note the Eponym Chronicle for 738 = "Kullani was captured"), and the land was reconstructed as an Assyrian province. The name "Kullani" was then extended to refer to the entire province and thus became identical with the territory of the former kingdom of Pattin/Unqi.[16]

"And go from there to Hamath Rabbah." Hamath, modern *Ḥamā,* was an important Syrian city-state on the middle Orontes, bordered on the north by Arpad and Ḫ/Pattin and on the south by Damascus.[17] Shalmaneser III also had military encounters with this kingdom. In 853 he was confronted at Qarqar on the Orontes by a coalition of the "twelve kings of the sea coast" led by Adadidri (= Ben Hadad) of Damascus and Irḫuleni, king of Hamath. Although the Assyrian monarch reports a victory, his repeated campaigns against similar coalitions in 849, 848, and 845 witness against his exaggerated claims.[18] These Hamathite campaigns, which resulted in the capture of several cities of the kingdom, are represented on his bronze gate reliefs. Sometime during the first quarter of the eighth century, a coalition of north Syrian monarchs led by Ben Hadad, son of Hazael, laid seige to Hamath. Zakir, king of Hamath, the successor to Irḫuleni, succeeded in withstanding the attack and erected a stele in commemoration of this event.

In the same campaign mentioned previously in connection with the defeat of Kullani, Tiglatpileser III also confronted the "nineteen provinces of Hamath," which joined the revolt against Assyria under the leadership of Azriyau.[19] The cities were annexed and reconstituted as Assyrian provinces. Eni-ilu, king of Hamath, who was not mentioned as participating in the actual battle, appears in a list of tributaries in 738 and was left in control of a very much reduced Hamath.

The name Hamath Rabbah (חֲמַת רַבָּה), "Hamath the Great," appears only here.[20] It probably was used to differentiate it from another Hamath, Hamath Zobah (חֲמַת צוֹבָה), of 2 Chr 8:3.[21] The two sites originally were most likely two different geographical units that together comprised the entire kingdom of Hamath: Hamath Rabbah, the northern part, and Hamath Zobah, the southern part. Like Kullani, the name Hamath Rabbah may have originally designated the capital city and was

16 Na'aman, "Letter"; Hawkins, cited in n 15.

17 For Hamath, see Ikeda, *Kingdom;* J. D. Hawkins, "Hamath," *RLA* 4/1 (1972–1975) 67–70; A. de Maigret, *Le citadella aramaica di Hama. Attività, funzione e comportemento* (Orientis Antiqui Collectio 15; Rome: Centro per le Antichità e la Storia dell'Arte del Vicino Oriente, 1979). For the name, see Ikeda, *Kingdom,* 50–51.

18 See *ANET,* 278–79.

19 *ANET,* 282. See also H. Tadmor, "Azriyau of Yaudi," in *Studies in the Bible* (ed. C. Rabin; Scripta Hierosolymitana 8; Jerusalem: Magnes, 1961) 232–71; Na'aman, "Letter."

20 For similar designations, for example, צִידוֹן רַבָּה, Josh 11:8; 19:28 = Akk. *Ṣidunu rabû* ("Sidon the Great"), as contrasted to *Ṣidunu ṣeḫru* ("Sidon the Small"); for example, Luckenbill, *Annals,* 29:41. So, too, Ugar. *'udm rbm* ("Udum the great"), *CTA* 14:iii:108–9; and Egyptian, *ʿrd rbt,* ("Arad the great"), in Shishak's (Shoshenk) inscription. See B. Mazar, "The Campaign of Pharaoh Shishak to Palestine," in SVT 4 (Leiden: Brill, 1957) 64. See, too, "Great *ʿpr*" and "Small *ʿpr*" in the list of Thutmose III. See Simons, *Handbook,* 115–19, numbers 53 and 54.

In Mesopotamian literature, compare the use of Sum. gal = Akk. *rabû,* with the cities Sippar, A. Ungnad, *VAS* 6 (Leipzig, 1908) 87:6; see R. Harris, *Ancient Sippar: A Demographic Study of an Old Babylonian City (1894–1595 B.C.)* (Istanbul: Nederlands Historisch-Archaeologisch Instituuts, 1975) 13; Der, L. W. King, CT 13,42; 20,30; Arrapḫu, E.-R. Lacheman, *Excavations at Nuzi VI, The Administrative Archives* (HSS 15; Cambridge: Harvard University, 1955) 150:7. Compare also *Ḫatti rabīti* in the inscriptions of Tiglatpileser I as the name of Carchemish and Melid. See H. Tadmor, "A Note on the Saba'a Stele of Adad-nirari III," *IEJ* 19 (1969) 47 n 13, and his reconstructed reading of the stele.

21 See also חַמַּת in Naftali, Josh 19:35.

subsequently extended to represent the entire kingdom or was itself the name of the great state of Hamath. (In 720, when Sargon II destroyed the kingdom of Hamath, he turned its capital into a new Assyrian province called "Hamath.")[22]

Thus commentators conclude that the references here in Amos are to the campaigns of Tiglatpileser III, which brought about the demise of these two kingdoms. The passage is then interpreted as a warning: Are you any stronger or more secure than they? Yet even they were overwhelmed and laid waste. Ergo, Israel can no longer afford the luxury of relaxing complacently in the false confidence of total security. They, too, will soon experience the bite of the Assyrian teeth. However, if this interpretation were correct, that is, if the historical references are to this specific period, it must be recalled that Tiglatpileser III also intervened at this very time into the politics of Israel. He imposed tribute in 738 upon *Me-ni-ḫi-im-me* ^{al}*Sa-me-ri-na-a-a*, "Menahem the Samarian."[23] Later he "overwhelmed" Menahem and placed *A-ú-si-*' ("Hosea") upon the throne of northern Israel. In 733 Dor, Megiddo, and Gilead were reconstituted into Assyrian provinces, and Israel thereby became constricted to a small Assyrian vassal kingdom in the hill country of Samaria.[24] What effect then would such a historical comparison have upon the people precisely at this time? For all intents and purposes, they were already no better off than these other defeated kingdoms. The threatened analogy simply would not be relevant or meaningful. Why should they fear that the same fate would overtake them as the others, if they were already experiencing the Assyrian onslaught?

If the intended comparison to the other kingdoms was made while Israel was luxuriating in good fortune, prosperity, and security, however, while they were still enjoying the dolce vita described in the following verses, then the poignancy of the prophet's words would constitute an ominous threat against their presumed confidence in immunity from all foreign incursions. It stands to reason, therefore, that the verse must precede the western campaigns of the Assyrian king and thus should not be considered a later addition to the text of Amos.

Although the exact historical references implied in this verse may never be known, the prophet is obviously relating to a period of time when these kingdoms had suffered defeats or incursions into their territories. Although the Assyrian campaigns of Shalmaneser III did occur some one hundred years before the time of Amos, they may still have been recalled in the days of the prophet. Even closer in time was the coalition referred to against Zakir, king of Hamath. In any case, the message was clear enough to the people of Israel. Those mighty kingdoms, although more powerful than Israel, still suffered defeats. How much more so, then, Israel!

(Another possibility is to interpret this verse as an additional example of Amos's literary penchant for citing the exact words of those whom he is accusing [see Amos 2:12; 4:1; 6:13]. The passage could then be understood as a direct quotation of the boastful reply that the leaders [referred to in v 1] give to their fellow Israelites who come to them for advice. These braggarts insist that they are superior to all other kingdoms and thus have nothing to fear.)[25]

"Go down to Gath of the Philistines" (גַּת־פְּלִשְׁתִּים).[26] The addition "of the Philistines" is most likely meant to specify which of the several cities named Gath the prophet had in mind. (See Gath-Hepher, Josh 19:13; 2 Kgs 14:25; Gath-Rimmon, Josh 19:45; 21:24, 25; 1 Chr 6:54; Gittaim, 2 Sam 4:3; Neh 11:33.) The reference here may be to the fall of Gath under the Aramean

22 Ikeda, *Kingdom*, 38.

23 For a date of 738 for the verse in Amos, see Na'aman, "Letter," 37.

24 *ANET*, 283–84.

25 See Sellin^{2}, 242; Maag, *Text*, 39; Amsler; Mays; Gottwald, *Kingdoms*, 110–11. See, by contrast, Soggin, 105: "The discourse may simply refer to the political and economic decadence of the two places without as yet raising the problem of their final fall."

26 For the perplexing problem of identification, see B. Mazar, "Gath and Gittaim," *IEJ* 4 (1954) 227–35, esp. 231; A. Rainey, "The Identification of Philistine Gath," in Eretz Israel 12 (*Nelson Glueck Memorial Volume*; ed. B. Mazar et al.; Jerusalem: Israel Exploration Society, 1975) 63*–76*, especially 73*.

Several commentators delete this stich referring to Gath; for example, Robinson-Horst; Weiser; Snaith. Rudolph, 216 n 2a, cites three reasons for its deletion.

attack led by Hazael (2 Kgs 12:18)[27] or to its capture by King Uzziah of Judah, who pulled down its walls (2 Chr 26:6), but not, as mentioned previously, to the advance on the Philistine coast by Tiglatpileser III in 734.

Also note that the selection of these various kingdoms also serves another purpose, a literary one: The kingdoms cited are located both to the north and south of Israel, thereby constituting a geographical merism. Israel, despite its unwarranted confidence, is no stronger or greater than any other kingdom in the area. They therefore should take warning from the fate that befell these other nations and not rely on the present military victories of Jeroboam II as a panacea for all their internal ills.

■ **3** The[28] proud, insolent upper class, either by apotropaic exorcising gestures[29] or by a mental attitude,[30] "thrust off" and push away (הַמְנַדִּים)[31] the thought of any such "day of disaster" (לְיוֹם רָע),[32] otherwise referred to by Amos as יוֹם ה׳ ("the Day of the Lord") in 5:18, 20, and יוֹם מַר ("a bitter day") in 8:10. Feeling secure and reveling in their present life style of pleasure and luxury (immediately described in detail),[33] they simply do not face, or do not wish to face, reality.[34] However, in their attempt to ward off the forthcoming national catastrophe, they paradoxically and antithetically "bring near" (וַתַּגִּשׁוּן),[35] שֶׁבֶת חָמָס. This perplexing unique phrase still defies a clear explanation. G, σαββάτων ψευδῶν ("false sabbaths") and V, *solio iniquitatis* ("throne of iniquity") both confirm the Masoretic text, although their translations are unacceptable (especially G's repointing, שַׁבָּת).[36] The crux lies in the understanding of the first word, שֶׁבֶת. Some interpret it as a substantive from the root ישב ("to sit"), meaning a "seat,"[37] "session,"[38] or "throne" of "violence" (חָמָס). This, in turn, is supposed to refer to a "rule" or "reign" of violence of a king or judge, whether of Israel or a foreign nation.[39] Although some have compared this expression with כִּסֵּא הַוּוֹת, "a seat of injustice" (Ps 94:20),[40] the use of שֶׁבֶת in such an

27 See Haran, "Rise and Decline," 269 n 1.

28 The הוֹי-cry of v 1 continues here; see ibn Ganaḥ, *Haschoraschim*, 496. According to Gordis ("Studies," 242), הוֹי was lost here due to haplography.

29 See Sellin; Maag, *Text*, 87, 171–72, 209; Amsler.

30 For example, Hammershaimb, 99.

31 The root נדה appears once more in the *piʿel* in Isa 66:5: "Your kinsmen who hate you, who spurn you (מְנַדֵּיכֶם) because of my name." Interdialectal etymological cognates of the Hebrew are Ugar. *ndy*—for a discussion of this verb, see P. Bordreuil and A. Caquot, "Les textes en cunéiforms alphabétiques," *Syria* 57 (1980) 346–47, who translate "repousser" ("drive away")—and Akk. *nadû* ("to throw"), *CAD, N*, I.68ff. From this root is derived the postbiblical term נִידּוּי: "one who is pushed off/driven away = excommunicated." Compare also the Akkadian cognate equivalent *ukkušu*, "to drive off" (from *akāšu*), in somewhat similar contexts; *CAD, A*, I.264.

There seems to be a close relationship between נדה and נדד, especially in Job 18:18: "They thrust him from light to darkness and expel him (יְנִדֻּהוּ) from the world." Budde ("Amos," 123) actually revocalizes the verb in Amos to מְנַדִּים, deriving it from the verb נדד. See also Rudolph, 216.

M. Dahood ("*Nādâ*, 'to hurl' in Ex 15, 16," *Bib* 43 [1962] 249 n 2) translates "who try to escape from," interpreting the ל as in Ugaritic, "from." Tur-Sinai, *Peshuṭo*, 466, seeking a direct parallel to the second stich, traces the verb back to the Arabic and Syriac root, דנא ("to draw near"), revocalizing by metathesis to הַמַּדְנִים.

G, οἱ εὐχόμενοι ("they make a vow" [in order to prevent the day of calamity]) is probably based on a Heb. הַמְנַדְּרִים. However, Heb. נדר never appears elsewhere in the *piʿel;* all of its occurrences are in the *qal.* Moreover, such a reading destroys the intended antithesis of the verbs.

32 For examples of ל with the accusative, see *GKC*, 117n. For the analogous יוֹם רָעָה ("day of calamity, disaster"), see Jer 17:17, 18; 51:2; Pss 27:5; 41:2; Prov 16:4; Eccl 7:14. Heb. יוֹם רָע appears only here. Its Akkadian interdialectal semantic and partial etymological equivalent, *ūmu lemnu,* means "unlucky/unhappy day." See *CAD, L*, 122, l c 3′, l d 2′, for examples. For a possible contextual analogy, compare *ana lemni šuātu šūtuqimma ana amēli u bitišu [la ṭeḫê]* ("In order to avert that evil and that it [may not approach] the man or his house"); *Or* 34 (1965) 125 no. 10:5.

33 Ibn Ganaḥ, *Haschoraschim*, 496.

34 See Amos 9:10.

35 Note the grammatical shift from the participial form to the direct second-person plural. See also Amos 5:18. There is no need to emend to וַיַּגִּישׁוּן; against Wolff, 272.

36 This reading is accepted by Hoffmann, "Versuche," 114; Tur-Sinai, *Peshuṭo*, 466.

37 See 1 Kgs 10:19, שֶׁבֶת ("seat"). See Ps 122:5, "thrones of judgment" (כִּסְאוֹת לְמִשְׁפָּט).

38 See *NJPS*.

39 Wellhausen, 85; Wolff, 272.

extended meaning is unparalleled, and would, in any case, be a very awkward way to express such a thought.

Another suggestion is to derive the substantive from the root שׁבת ("to cease") and to interpret the expression as "ein gewaltsames Ende" ("a violent end").[41] Although the grammatical form is attested,[42] the derived meaning would be very forced because it would then have to be translated as a "cessation of violence,"[43] which is simply not what the prophet had in mind. The derivation of שׁבת from Arab. وثبة *(waṯbat),* "assault" (root *wṯb*), is suggestive[44] but unparalleled in biblical Hebrew. Thus many commentators resort to conjectural emendations: שֶׁבֶר וְחָמָס ("calamity and violence");[45] שֹׁד וְחָמָס ("rapine and violence");[46] (see Amos 3:10); שְׁנַת חָמָס ("a year of lawlessness").[47]

Whatever the exact meaning of this enigmatic expression is, the intention of the prophet is clear: The leaders of the north are directly responsible for precipitating and accelerating the very misfortune that they claim will never overtake them. Note how they express themselves with these very same words when they polemicize against Amos: "All the sinners of my people shall perish by the sword, who boast, 'Never shall evil (רָעָה) overtake us (תַּגִּישׁ) or come near to us'!" (9:10).

■ **4** There now commences a unique detailed description of the indolent, carefree life of the wealthy class in Samaria. Amos seems to have had occasion to witness their behavior at first hand and thus is able to provide with great accuracy a marvelous satire of their comfortable, indulgent life style. These upper-class citizens of the northern empire "stretch out, lolling and sprawling (סְרֻחִים)[48] on their couches (עַרְשׂוֹתָם) and on their beds of ivory" (מִטּוֹת שֵׁן).[49] And so, en passant, one also hears of their expensive taste in furniture.[50] "Beds of ivory" (mentioned only here in the Bible) are those whose frames are inlaid with ivory designs. Similar beds are documented in Akkadian sources, *eršu šinni;*[51] and just such a bed was among the gifts that Hezekiah, king of Judah, presented to Sennacherib.[52]

These epicurean gourmets dine on nothing less than chateaubriand, on the most tender, tastiest, and choicest of meats: "on lambs (כָּרִים)[53] from the flock[54] and on

40 See Ps 74:20, "haunts of lawlessness" (נְאוֹת חָמָס).

41 Rudolph, 215, 216.

42 Prov 20:3.

43 See Gottwald, *Kingdoms,* 110.

44 J. Reider, "Etymological Studies in Biblical Hebrew," *VT* 2 (1952) 122.

45 Nowack; Weiser.

46 Marti.

47 *KB,* 947; Maag, *Text,* 37–38; Amsler. Another suggestion is שֵׁבֶט חָמָס, "the staff (= rule) of lawlessness."

48 For סרח ("flowing, spreading"), applied only in Amos to describe human beings (6:7), see Exod 26:12, 13; Ezek 17:6; 23:15. Its homonym, סרח, meaning "to stink, to become spoiled, ruined," appears once in the Bible, Jer 49:7. The latter, which became prevalent in postbiblical Hebrew, underlies the sexual interpretation of this verse in the Babylonian Talmud, Shabbath 62b and Kiddushin 71b.

49 For the parallel pair מִטָּה and עֶרֶשׂ, see comments on 3:12. Note the assonance of the recurrent sibilants in this colon.

50 See B. Mazar, ed., *Views of the Biblical World* (4 vols.; Jerusalem and Ramat Gan: International Publishing Company, 1960) 3.238–39 (Heb.); K. Kenyon, *Royal Cities of the Old Testament* (New York: Schocken, 1973) 71–89; N. Avigad, "Samaria," *Encyclopedia of Archeological Excavations in the Holy Land* (2 vols.; ed. B. Mazar; Jerusalem: Israel Exploration Society and Masada Press, 1970) 2.527–38 (Heb.), English translation, *Encyclopedia of Archaeological Excavations in the Holy Land* (4 vols.; ed. M. Avi-Yonah and E. Stern; Jerusalem: Masada Press, 1975–1978) 4.1032–50; *ANEP,* 140. For בָּתֵּי הַשֵּׁן ("houses of ivory"), see Amos 3:15.

51 See *CAD, E,* 315–16, for references. See also Salonen, *Die Möbel,* 110, 123ff., 132, and index. Note also previous comments to 3:12.

52 Luckenbill, *Annals,* 34 iii 43; *ANET,* 288. A bed of wood overlaid with ivory was also discovered in a tomb at Salamis, in Cyprus, dating to about 800 B.C.E. See V. Karageorghis, *Excavations in the Necropolis of Salamis III* (Nicosia: Department of Antiquities of Cyprus, 1973) 87–97.

53 Compare for possible cognates, Ugar. *kr, CML,* 145; and Old Akk. *kirru, CAD, K,* 410–11, "a breed of sheep?" For a possible semantic equivalent, see Ugar. *imr. bpḫd, KTU,* 17:V:17, which has been translated, "a lamb from the flock." See B. Margalit, "Lexicographical Notes on the *AQHT* Epic (Part 1; *KTU,* 1.17–18)," *UF* 15 (1983) 80.

54 Heb. צאן = Phoen. צאן *(KAI,* 26 A III 9) = Moab. צאן *(KAI,* 181:31) = Ugar. *ṣin* *(UT,* 2137) = Akk. *ṣenu* *(CAD, Ṣ,* 128–31).

calves[55] from the feeding stall" (מַרְבֵּק). The מַרְבֵּק are the stalls where the animals were confined (Arab. *rabaqa*, "to tie up") in order to be fed for fattening.[56] For עֶגְלֵי מַרְבֵּק ("stall-fed calves"), see also 1 Sam 28:24; Jer 46:21; Mal 3:20.[57]

■ **5** The sumptuous banquets are accompanied by the strains and tunes of appropriate background music—dining to the lilt of musical airs.[58] The precise activity referred to by the hapax legomenon verb פרט is still open to question. Some understand it to be the manner by which one plays the musical instrument, that is, "plucking"[59]—"They pluck on the strings of the lute." Others, relying on V[60] and a Samaritan root,[61] translate, "They sing songs to the sound of the lute." A variant line of exegesis interprets this verb to mean "to howl."[62] A tradition recorded in the works of some of the medieval exegetes defines the root to mean "to improvise"; compare also Arab. *fāriṭ*:[63] "They improvise or extemporize melodies to the tune of the lute."[64]

Another problem of exegesis arises in the second colon. The prophet continues to satirize their penchant for musical diversions and says that "Like David (כְּדָוִיד),[65] they חָשְׁבוּ לָהֶם musical instruments" (כְּלֵי־שִׁיר).[66] But what is the exact nuance of the Hebrew expression חשב ל? Although several suggestions have been offered, the most commonly accepted is "They invent[67] musical instruments like David." There is no reason to reject the veracity of this tradition connected with David,[68] even though it appears outside Amos only in postexilic sources; see Neh 12:36, בִּכְלֵי־שִׁיר דָּוִיד ("with

55 Heb. עֵגֶל = Ugar. *ʿgl*, *UT*, 1811.

56 See *AuS*, II.143; VI.178–79, 256.

57 For a reconstructed Ugaritic semantic parallel (*RŠ*, 24.252 = *Ug* V (1968), 151, No. 2, lines 9–10) to Amos 6:4b, 6, see S. Gevirtz, "Naphtali in the 'Blessing of Jacob,'" *JBL* 103 (1984) 516–17.

58 See Isa 5:12: "who, at their banquets, have lyre and lute (נֶבֶל), timbrel, flute, and wine."

59 W. Gesenius, *Hebräisches und aramäisches Handwörterbuch über das Alte Testament* (Leipzig: Vogel, [17]1921) 659. See Heb. פֶּרֶט, in Lev 19:10, פֶּרֶט כַּרְמְךָ ("the fallen fruit of your vineyard"). (Compare Akk. *parāṭu*, "to break/tear off.") Both G, οἱ ἐπικροτοῦντες, and S, דְנָקְשִׁין, render "to beat," whereas T translates דִמְנַגְּן ("they play"). For the basic meaning, "to separate," in Hebrew roots that begin with the first two letters פר, see Kutscher, *Words*, 106 (Heb.).

60 V, *qui canitis.* Rashi, following Menahem ben Saruq (*Maḥberet*, 145), combines the two by explaining the verb as "clipping the words in detail; all in accordance with the melody of the instrument, either to raise or lower (the voice)." See ibn Ezra. See, too, M. Pope, *Song of Songs: A New Translation with Introduction and Commentary* (AB 7c; Garden City, NY: Doubleday, 1977) 214: "They chant to the tune of the lyre." Compare the Karaite commentator, Daniel al-Kūmissi, *Commentarius in Librum Duodecim Prophetarum* (ed. I. D. Markin; Jerusalem: Meqisey Nirdamim, 1957), who relates it to Arab. *ʾafraṭ* (on p. 36).

61 See J. Montgomery, "Notes from the Samaritan: The Root פרט—Amos 6:5," *JBL* 25 (1906) 51–52: "God, let us give him praise; God, let us sing (נפרט) to him all songs; God, let us raise to him shouts; God, let us lift to him paeans," citing M. Heidenheim, *Bibliotheca Samaritana* (4 vols.; Leipzig: Schulze, 1885) 2.110, L1, line 14. See also Tur-Sinai's note in Eliezer ben Iehuda's *A Complete Dictionary of Ancient and Modern Hebrew* (16 vols.; Jerusalem and Tel-Aviv: LaʿAm, 1980) 10.5162 n 6 (Heb.); compare Kimchi.

62 So Wolff, 276; Rudolph, 217.

63 See ibn Ganaḥ, *Haschoraschim*, 412; Moses ibn Ezra, *Sepher Shirath Yisrael* (ed. B. Z. Halpern; Leipzig: A. Y. Stikel, 1924) 42 (Heb.); for the Arabic root, see *KB*, 910. For other medieval interpretations, see Kimchi (*Radicum Liber*, 299), who, as one of three possibilities, suggests "to begin, open."

64 For עַל־פִּי, see פֶּה, *KB*, 866, C; but all the examples cited there mean "according to" and not "to the tune/sound of." For נֶבֶל, see comments on Amos 5:23; and see also O. Keel, *Die Welt der altorientalischen Bildsymbolik und das Alte Testament* (Zürich, Einsiedeln and Köln: Benzinger Verlag, 1972) 465ff.

65 The word כְּדָוִיד does not belong to the first colon, contrary to Procksch; Neher, *Amos*, 105; and D. N. Freedman, *The New World of the Old Testament* (inaugural lecture, San Anselmo, CA: San Francisco Theological Seminary, 1968) 9. Any emendation of the name is totally unwarranted, against H. J. Elhorst, "Miscellen 3: Amos VI,5," *ZAW* 35 (1915) 62–63: כַּד וְיָד, with "pitcher and hand" they keep beat to the music (a proposal that Rudolph, 217, terms "mehr witziger als richtiger" ["more clever than correct"]). The *plene* spelling דָּוִיד, although prevalent in later biblical literature, is already found in Hos 3:5, contrary to Wolff, 273. See D. N. Freedman, "The Spelling of the Name 'David' in the Hebrew Bible," in *Biblical and Other Studies in Honor of Robert Gordis* (ed. R. Ahroni) = *HAR* 7 (1983) 89–104. Freedman states that because the name David appears about 285 out of 1073 times spelled with four letters, *dwyd*, this spelling is sufficient "to war-

the musical instruments of David"); 1 Chr 23:5, בַּכֵּלִים אֲשֶׁר עָשִׂיתִי לְהַלֵּל ("with instruments I devised for singing praises"); and 2 Chr 29:26, 27, כְּלֵי דָוִיד ("the instruments of David").

Other proposals are: "They think that their musical instruments are like David's";[69] "they account themselves musicians like David";[70] "they highly esteem musical instruments like David";[71] and, if the preposition עַל ("upon") in the first colon functions as a double-duty word implicit in the second colon, "They improvise for themselves [on or upon] instruments like David."[72] According to the last interpretation, Amos is charging the revelers with devising new songs with instrumental accompaniment.[73] It is also possible, moreover, to attach כְּדָוִיד metrically with the first colon (against the Masoretic division) with the same meaning. Despite the difficulties inherent in this verse, the intent of the prophet is clear. He is heaping scorn upon the reputed musical accomplishments of those who would compare themselves with David, "the sweet singer of Israel" (2 Sam 23:1).

■ **6** After censuring their culinary and musical pamperings, Amos now proceeds to satirize their excessiveness in

rant the designation of alternate official spelling" (p. 89). He dates those with the three-letter spelling, *dwd,* to the First Temple period, and the others to the Second Temple period. As for the longer spelling in Amos and Hosea, "while technically anachronistic [they] nevertheless reflect the date of publication of the composite work" (p. 100).

66 See Hammershaimb, 101, who proposes the reading כָּל־שִׁיר ("all sorts of songs"); see already Nowack. Another emendation is that of P. Lohmann, "Einige Textkonjekturen zu Amos," *ZAW* 32 (1912) 275–76, מִלֵּי שִׁיר ("the words of the songs"; note, however, that מִלָּה is an Aramaic loanword). Rudolph's suggestion (215, 217) to read מִכְּלֵי שִׁיר (the מ omitted by haplography), "they consider themselves like David: perfect singers," is simply un-Hebraic. The expression כְּלֵי שִׁיר ("musical instruments"), although appearing only in Chronicles (1 Chr 15:16; 16:42; 2 Chr 5:13; 7:6; 23:13; 34:12; see also כְּלִי־נֶבֶל, Ps 71:22; כְּלֵי נְבָלִים וּכִנֹּרוֹת, 1 Chr 16:5), need not be necessarily late.

67 For חשב ("to devise"), see, for example, Exod 31:4; 35:32; Ps 40:18; Prov 16:30; 2 Chr 2:13. Compare Wolff, 246. T translated the verb אַתְקִינוּ ("they prepare"). See also Sir 47:13 (Heb.).

68 For an early dating of the traditions concerning David, Psalms, and psaltery, see N. M. Sarna, "Psalms, Book of," *EncJud* 13.1313–14; idem, "The Psalm Superscriptions and the Guilds," in *Studies in Jewish Religious and Intellectual History Presented to Alexander Altmann on the Occasion of His Seventieth Birthday* (ed. S. Stein and R. Loewe; Birmingham: University of Alabama, 1979) 281–300. See, too, Weiss, *MiShut,* 36–38 (Heb.). This tradition is also reflected in Psalm 151 from Qumran: "I said to myself, my hands have made a harp (יָדַי עָשׂוּ עוּגָב), my fingers a lyre" (אֶצְבְּעוֹתַי כִּנּוֹר). See J. A. Sanders, *The Dead Sea Psalms Scroll* (Ithaca: Cornell University, 1967) 96–97, col. xxviii, lines 4–5. Compare similarly G (Ps 151:2): "My hands made a harp (*αἱ χεῖρές μου ἐποίησαν ὄργανον*) and my fingers fashioned a lyre" (*οἱ δάκτυλοί μου ἥρμοσαν ψαλτήριον*). The Greek verb in the second colon may have been supplied by the translators for the sake of balance, or may reflect an original עִצְּבוּ ("fashioned"), (whose letters by metathesis resemble those of the word for "fingers," אֶצְבָּעוֹת).

69 For other proposals, including his own, see Rudolph, 217. A very interesting suggestion, "play on," has been offered by Barstad (*Religious Polemics,* 127 n 3), based on Arab. *ḥasaba ʿalā* and referring to *Bibliotheca Geographorum Arabicorum* (ed. M. J. de Goeje; London, 1892) 7.123, lines 13ff.

70 *NJPS.* Compare Kimchi; Ehrlich, *Mikrâ,* 3.412; idem, *Randglossen,* 5.244–45.

71 R. Gordis, "Studies in the Relationship of Biblical and Rabbinic Hebrew," in *Louis Ginzberg Jubilee Volume on the Occasion of His Seventieth Birthday* (ed. S. Lieberman, S. Zeitlin, S. Spiegel, and A. Marx; New York: Jewish Theological Seminary, 1946) 178, based on Rabbinic Hebrew חשב ("to regard highly, esteem"), which is also found in Isa 13:17: "who do not value silver"; Isa 53:3: "We held him of no account"; Mal 3:16: "who esteem his name"; idem, "Studies," 243.

72 D. N. Freedman, "But Did King David Invent Musical Instruments?" *The Bible Review* 1 (1985) 49–51.

73 The suggestion is very plausible even if one does not accept Freedman's remarks that the songs themselves were "scurrilous, obscene, or blasphemous, and possibly all three."

drinking:[74] "They imbibe from (שׁתה בּ־)[75] bowls of wine."[76] Although the substantive מִזְרָק ("bowl") appears thirty-one times in the Hebrew Bible in connection with sacred vessels,[77] the prophet may have selected this specific word here not only for its cultic connotations[78] (see next verse), but also for the size of the bowl described,[79] that is, referring to the quantity and abundance of wine imbibed and the manner in which they conducted their excessive drinking exercises. *De gustibus est disputandum.*

Amos continues his biting description by mocking and scoffing at their indulgent habit of "anointing themselves (יִמְשָׁחוּ) with the choicest of oils" (רֵאשִׁית שְׁמָנִים). Because biblical Hebrew distinguishes between the two verbs, משׁח and סוך, "to anoint"—the former in cultic contexts, the latter in secular ones[80]—it is possible, if one follows the interpretation of מִזְרָק as bowls used in a ritual setting, to relate the use of משׁח here to a cultic practice that the elite of Samaria were apparently following, that is, the *marzeaḥ* institution (see next verse). Treating themselves in a cultic fashion, they, the "choicest of nations" (רֵאשִׁית הַגּוֹיִם), anoint themselves with only the "choicest of oils" (רֵאשִׁית שְׁמָנִים).[81] For רֵאשִׁית שְׁמָנִים, compare the Akkadian interdialectal cognate and semantic equivalents, *šamnu rēštu*[82] and *šamnu rūštu*[83] ("best/finest oil"). Compare, in particular, *šamnam rūštim tapšušini* ("You anointed me with the finest of oils").[84]

The application of oil to the head and body for cosmetic, hygienic, and therapeutic purposes is well documented throughout the ancient Near East.[85] Oil also

74 For the connection of music, singing, and the drinking of wine, all destined to come to an end, see Isa 24:7–9: "The new wine fails, the vine languishes, and all the merry-hearted sigh. Stilled is the merriment of timbrels, ended the clamor of revelers, stilled the merriment of lyres. They drink their wine without song; liquor tastes bitter to the drinker."

75 For שׁתה בּ־, where the בּ is instrumental, see Gen 44:5; so, too, in Aram. Dan 5:2, 3, 23. For the same idiom in Ugaritic, *šty b-*, see, for example, *CTA* 4:iii:16. It, too, is usually followed by the term for a drinking vessel, for example, *ks* ("cup"), *krpn* ("goblet"). Rudolph, 218, by contrast, emphasizing the satire, interprets the בּ here literally as "in" the bowls, due to their size; he also compares the French expression, *boire dans.*

76 G, τὸν διυλισμένον οἶνον ("refined/strained wine") refers to the quality, not the quantity, of the wine, and probably reflects a Hebrew expression יַיִן מְזֻקָּק (see Isa 25:6).

77 See concordances; *KB,* 537. Compare A. M. Honeyman, "The Pottery Vessels of the Old Testament," *PEQ* 71 (1939) 79–90 (especially 83–84, and pl. xix, fig. 6). For מִזְרָק in conjunction with wine, see Zech 9:15. R. D. Barnett ("Assurbanipal's Feast," in Eretz Israel 18 [*Nahman Avigad Volume;* ed. B. Mazar and Y. Yadin; Jerusalem: Israel Exploration Society, 1985] 6* n 30) suggests that it is to be identified with the type of bowl called a *phialē* in Greek.

78 So Ehrlich (*Randglossen,* 5.245), who reads בְּמִזְרָקַי ("from my bowls"); see, for example, van Gelderen, Deden, Frey—profanation of cultic vessels (see Dan 5:2); and, for example, Sellin²; and Maag, *Text,* 39, 161, 163, who relate it to a cultic meal. So, too, Barstad, *Religious Polemics,* 127 n 5.

79 So, too, Kimchi; Wolff, 276; Soggin, 105; Rudolph, 215, 220. Wolff remarks, "No doubt one normally drank from a 'goblet' rather than from such a bowl. If the society accused by Amos nevertheless used bowls for drinking, its intemperance is thereby exposed." For reference to possible pictures of such "chalice" bowls, see Wolff, 276 nn 37, 38. For another example of drinking out of large pots and flagons, but this time associated with the god Baal, see *CTA* 3:i:9–17.

80 See E. Kutsch, *Salbung als Rechtsakt im alten Testament und im alten Orient* (BZAW 87; Berlin: Töpelmann, 1963) 7, 9 n 50. For three rare exceptions of the use of משׁח that do not refer to the anointing of the body, see 2 Sam 1:21; Isa 21:5; Jer 22:14. Contrast, for example, Exod 30:31–32 with 2 Sam 14:2.

81 For רֵאשִׁית ("finest, choicest"), see comments to Amos 6:1. See also Cant 4:14, "all the choice perfumes" (כָּל־רָאשֵׁי בְשָׂמִים). Note the assonance of the letter שׁ: השׁתים . . . ראשׁית שׁמנים ימשׁחו.

82 See *AHw,* 3.972:4; 3.973:4b.

83 *AHw,* 3.996:1.

84 AbB 4, 142, 12 in F. R. Kraus, *Briefe aus dem Berliner Museum* (Leiden: Brill, 1974).

85 See S. M. Paul, "Exod 21:10—A Threefold Maintenance Clause," *JNES* 28 (1969) 48–53; and idem, *Studies in the Book of the Covenant in the Light of Cuneiform and Biblical Law* (SVT 18; Leiden: Brill, 1970) 56–61. See E. Lipiński, "Eshmun, 'Healer,'" *AION* 33 (1973) 161–83, especially 170–74; A. Ohry and A. Levy, "Anointing with Oil: An Hygienic Procedure in the Bible and in the Talmud," in *Proceedings of the Second International Symposium on Medicine in the Bible and Talmud, Jerusalem 18–20, 1984* = *Koroth* 9 (1985) 173–96.

frequently occurs together with wine in descriptions of the enjoyable pleasures of life, for example, Pss 23:5; 104:15; Prov 21:17; Cant 1:2–3; 4:10; Eccl 9:7–8.

In contrast, the abstinence from joy and delight during periods of mourning and sadness is characterized by one's refraining from the use of these two pleasure-bringing commodities. Compare Dan 10:3: "I ate no tasty food, nor did any meat or wine enter my mouth. I did not anoint myself." So, too, in the literary genre of the curse, compare Mic 6:15, ". . . You have trod olives, but have no oil for rubbing; and new wine, but have no wine to drink." The same applies outside Israel, both in times of joy and in times of sorrow. For the former, compare the description of Esarhaddon's festive banquet prepared in celebration of the dedication of his new palace: "With grape-wine and sesame-wine I 'sprinkled their hearts'; with choicest oils I drenched their foreheads."[86] For the latter, compare the Jews' expression of sorrow over the destruction of their temple in Elephantine in the fifth century B.C.E. Writing to the Persian governor of Judea, they lament, "We do not anoint ourselves with oil, and we drink no wine."[87]

Note that during approximately the same period when Amos was delivering his oracles against northern Israel, there is evidence from Samaria itself for the employment of this "finest oil." This documentation is gleaned from the Samarian ostraca, where the expression שמן רחץ ("oil for washing/cleansing"), variously translated as "refined oil" or "washed oil," occurs a dozen times.[88]

After this detailed epicurean list of the joie de vivre of the leaders of the northern kingdom, Amos drives home his essential point with a characteristic surprise ending. While devoting themselves to all their creature comforts of personal pleasures and delights—banqueting and imbibing, music making and cosmetic ointments—they nevertheless remain totally indifferent, apathetic, and oblivious to the perilous situation of Israel: They "remain unconcerned over (נֶחְלוּ) the ruin (שֵׁבֶר) of Joseph." There is no reason to regard this last phrase as being secondary, associating "the ruin of Joseph" to the period between 738 and 733 B.C.E.[89] According to the prophet, Israel, despite (and because of) the self-indulgent attitude of its leaders and their false confidence of security anchored in their bon vivant life style, is actually on the brink of impending disaster. Amos's contention is that this type of living, with its concomitant lack of care and concern for the rest of the people, is the very beginning and cause of the devastation and ruin of Joseph (= Israel).[90]

The verb נֶחְלוּ, which is the *niphʿal* of the root חלה, basically means "to be sick," and then develops the meaning "to be sick about, grieved over, worried and concerned about." Thus 1 Sam 22:8: "No one is concerned (חֹלֶה) about me."[91] (Compare similarly the same

86 Esarhaddon, Prism A 6:34–40, in D. D. Luckenbill, *Ancient Records of Assyria and Babylonia* (Chicago: University of Chicago, 1927) 2.269–70. For a relief depicting banqueteers, see *ANEP*, 637.

87 Cowley, *Aramaic Papyri*, 31:20; compare 30:20–21. See also E. Lipiński, "North-West Semitic Inscriptions," in OLP 8 (Leuven: Institut voor Orientalistiek, 1977) 85–86.

88 *Samarian Ostraca* 16–21, 53–55, 59. For some of these ostraca, see Gibson, *Hebrew and Moabite Inscriptions*, 9–11, and his remark on p. 8. For the original publication of the ostraca, see G. A. Reisner, *Israelite Ostraca from Samaria* (Cambridge, 1924, n.p.). See E. Lipiński, "North-West," 85, "oil for cleaning, toilet oil." See also A. Parrot (*Samaria: The Capital of the Kingdom of Israel* [tr. S. H. Hooke; Studies in Biblical Archeology 7; New York: Philosophical Library, 1958] 75), who draws attention to the fact that the sixty-five ostraca were invoices accompanying taxes dispatched by overseers to royal storehouses. The dues were recorded as paid in wine and oil, and "wine and oil are the two products coupled together by Amos." See, too, L. E. Stager, "The Finest Oil in Samaria," *JSS* 28 (1983) 241–45, who describes the method of extracting this "finest oil" and translates the expression "washed oil," which, according to him, refers to "the technical process by which the oil was produced and implies the high quality of the product." He, too, says it was also employed for anointing purposes. Compare V. Sasson ("*šmn rḥṣ* in the Samaria Ostraca," *JSS* 26 [1981] 1–5).

89 Against Wolff, 277.

90 See also Amos 5:15.

91 See also Isa 57:10: "Though wearied by much travel, you never said, 'I give up!' You found gratification for your lust, and so you never cared" (חָלִית). Compare M. Weinfeld, "The Covenant of Grant in the Old Testament and in the Ancient Near East," *JAOS* 90 (1970) 187.

semantic development in Akkadian, in which the verb *marāṣu* ["to be sick"] also means "to be concerned about, care for";[92] for example, *šumma ina kittim aḫi atta u tamarraṣa;* "If you really are my brother and are concerned about me, [send me barley].")[93] The selection of this verb along with its object שֶׁבֶר ("ruin") is very apt. This substantive is occasionally paired with the noun מַכָּה ("wound"), where the latter is described as being נַחְלָה ("severe, painful, grievous"), which is also derived from the *niphʿal* of the very same root, חלה (see Jer 10:19; 14:17; 30:12; Nah 3:19). Note, moreover, the opposite of this expression in biblical Hebrew. Just as there is a connection between "being sick over" the "break, ruin" (שֶׁבֶר) of the people, so, too, one also speaks of the "curing" (רפא) of this "calamity" or "break" (שֶׁבֶר). Compare Jer 6:14; 8:11: "They offer healing (וַיְרַפְּאוּ) offhand for the wounds (שֶׁבֶר, literally, "break, disaster, ruin") of my people," and by extension Ps 60:4: ". . . Mend (רְפָה) its fissures (שְׁבָרֶיהָ) for it [the land] is collapsing."

■ **7** Amos concludes his "woe"-oracle with a clever and sarcastic paronomasia that creates a literary inclusio for the entire pericope. His sardonic parody is directed against the elitist leaders who deem themselves the "choicest" (רֵאשִׁית, v 1) of the nations and pamper themselves with the "choicest" (רֵאשִׁית, v 6) of oils. The prophet ironically assures them that in the near future[94] they shall continue to maintain their "choice" position—"at the head (בְּרֹאשׁ)[95] of the exiles!" The headstrong leaders, who considered themselves רֵאשִׁית הַגּוֹיִם, shall retain primacy of position, as they advance headway into exile, בְּרֹאשׁ גֹּלִים.[96] Because they are the ultimate cause of the ruin of Joseph, they shall be "honored" by being the first in judgment as well. Amos once again concludes a literary unit on the ominous tones of exile and deportation (for example, 5:27; 6:14; 7:17).

The exile shall terminate all their bacchanalian behavior: "Spent will be the sprawlers' spree."[97] Note the alliterative hissing effect of the sibilants, וְסָר מִרְזַח[98] סְרוּחִים, and the twofold repetition of the two letters סר.[99] The סְרוּחִים ("sprawlers") are those who, mentioned in v 4, loll about dining and drinking. Their wining shall give way to whining.

The מַרְזֵחַ,[100] occurring once more in Jer 16:5 in the context of a funeral feast, is a religious institution documented from the Ugaritic texts of the fourteenth century B.C.E., from eighth-century Samaria (Amos), seventh-century Judah (Jeremiah), a fifth-century Aramaic ostracon from Elephantine, a third- or second-century Phoenician inscription from the Sidonian colony at Piraeus (96 B.C.E.) and the Punic sacrificial tariff from Marseilles, first-century C.E. Nabatean inscriptions from Petra and Oboda (Avdat), Palmyrene dedicatory inscriptions and tesserae (from the first to third centuries C.E.) decorated with banquet scenes with inscriptions mentioning *mrzḥ*,[101] and later Rabbinic sources.[102] It appears, finally, on the sixth-century Madeba map[103] describing the site of Baal-Peor where the pagan licentious celebration described in Num 25:1–9 took place: ΒέτοΜαρσεα ἡ κ(αὶ) Μαιουμας ("Beth Marzeah [= בֵּית מַרְזֵחַ] alias Maioumas [= מיומס])."[104]

Most of the descriptive information comes from the

92 *CAD, M,* I.269ff.

93 AbB, 1 89:20 in F. R. Kraus, *Briefe aus dem British Museum (CT 43 und 44)* (Leiden: Brill, 1964).

94 Heb. לָכֵן עַתָּה. Once again the announcement of punishment is introduced by לָכֵן; compare Amos 3:11; 4:12; 5:11, 16; 7:14. Heb. עַתָּה may be temporal, for example, Wolff, 273; Harper; van Gelderen; or consequential, for example, Rudolph, 215.

95 See ibn Ezra. See also 1 Sam 9:22, "at the head of the guests" (בְּרֹאשׁ הַקְּרוּאִים).

96 Note the clever pun in Hebrew: the רֵאשִׁית הַגּוֹיִם will be בְּרֹאשׁ גֹּלִים.

97 See Rudolph's (215) deft translation: "da schwindet des Schwadronieren der Schwelger" ("there disappears the swagger of sybarites"); and idem, 221: "dann ist es aus mit Saus und Braus" ("then away, the gay life"); Duhm, "Anmerkungen": "da verlernen das Lärmen die Lümmel" ("lost the loudness of louts"); Wolff, 273: "and suppressed will be the spree of the sprawlers."

98 For the punctuation מִרְזַח from מַרְזֵחַ, see מִשְׁבַּר, Hos 13:13, and the *nomen rectum* מַשְׁבֵּר, 2 Kgs 19:3 = Isa 37:3; and מִרְבַּץ, Ezek 25:5 from מַרְבֵּץ, Zeph 2:15.

99 For Heb. סור ("to come to an end"), see, for example, Exod 8:25; Lev 13:58; Judg 16:17; Isa 14:25.

100 See J. Braslavi, "Jeremiah 16:5; Amos 6:7," *BM* 48 (1971) 5–16 (Heb.), for a summary of the various sources from Ugarit through the Rabbinic midrashim and medieval Jewish commentators.

101 For the ever-burgeoning bibliography and the citations from the texts, see O. Eissfeldt, "Etymologische und archäologische Erklärung alttestamentlicher Wörter, *OrAnt* 5 (1966) 166–71, reprinted in

idem, *Kleine Schriften zum Alten Testament* (Tübingen: J. C. B. Mohr, 1968) 4.286–90; L. R. Fisher, "Two Projects at Claremont," *UF* 3 (1971) 31; P. D. Miller, "The *MRZḤ* Text," in *The Claremont Ras Shamra Tablets* (ed. L. R. Fisher; AnOr 48; Rome: Pontifical Biblical Institute, 1971) 37–49; M. Dahood, "Additional Notes on the *MRZḤ* Text," in *The Claremont Ras Shamra Tablets,* 50–54; reviewed by M. Heltzer in *IEJ* 22 (1972) 54–55; A. Rainey, "Gleanings from Ugarit," in Israel Oriental Studies 3 (Tel Aviv: Tel Aviv University, 1973) 56; and idem, *A Social Structure of Ugarit: A Study of West Semitic Social Stratification during the Late Bronze Age* (Jerusalem: Bialik Institute, 1967) 71–72, 125–26 (Heb.); J. C. Greenfield, "The *Marzeaḥ* as a Social Institution," *AcAn* 22 (1974) 451–55; T. L. Fenton, "The Claremont *'MRZḤ'* Tablet, Its Text and Meaning," *UF* 9 (1977) 71–75; B. Halpern, "A Landlord-Tenant Dispute at Ugarit?" *MAARAV* 2/1 (1979) 121–40; Pope, *Song of Songs,* 211–21, 228–29; and idem, "A Divine Banquet of Ugarit," in *The Use of the Old Testament in the New and Other Essays: Studies in Honor of William Franklin Stinespring* (ed. J. M. Efird; Durham: Duke University, 1972) 170–203; J. Sasson, "On M. H. Pope's *Song of Songs,*" *MAARAV* 1 (1978–1979) 177–96, esp. 188–90; B. Margalit, "The Ugaritic Feast of the Drunken Gods: Another Look at RŠ 24.258 (*KTU* 1.114)," *MAARAV* 2 (1980) 98–105; R. E. Friedman, "The *MRZḤ* Tablet from Ugarit," *MAARAV* 2 (1980) 187–206; B. Porten, *Archives from Elephantine: The Life of an Ancient Jewish Military Colony* (Berkeley and Los Angeles: University of California, 1968) 179–86; M. Dietrich and O. Loretz, "Der Vertrag eines *mrzḥ*—Klubs in Ugarit: Zum Verständnis von *KTU* 3.9," *UF* 14 (1982) 71–76.

Barstad (*Religious Polemics,* 128–42) translates and comments upon the pertinent texts from the different cultures and provides bibliographical references to their publication and studies based upon them. Add also N. Avigad and J. C. Greenfield, "A Bronze *phialē* with a Phoenician Dedicatory Inscription of the Fourth Century," *IEJ* 32 (1982) 118–29. The inscription pertains to two drinking cups that were offered למרזח שמש ("to the *marzeaḥ* of Shamash"). For the Palmyrene evidence, see also J. Teixidor, "Le thiase de Belastor et de Beelshamen d'après une inscription récemment découverte à Palmyre," *CRAIBL* (1981) 306–14. R. D. Barnett ("Assurbanipal's Feast," in Eretz Israel 18 [*Nahman Avigad Volume;* ed. B. Mazar and Y. Yadin; Jerusalem: Israel Exploration Society, 1985] 1*–6*) suggests that the banquet scene of Assurbanipal from Nineveh depicts the king celebrating a *marzeaḥ* ritual. For the scene itself, see J.-M. Dentzer, *Le motif du banquet couché dans le proche-orient et le monde grec du VIIe au IVe siècle avant J.C.* (Rome: Pontifical Biblical Institute, 1982).

102 Babylonian Talmud, Moʿed Qat. 28b; Ketuboth 69a; Jerusalem Talmud, Berachoth, III, 6a; Lev. Rab. 5:3; Num. Rab. 10:3; Sifre Num. 131; Koh. Rab. to Eccl 7:1; Yalk. Sam. 134; Est. Rab. 1:10; Targum Sheni to Esth 1:3. These sources reflect the two meanings of both mourning and feasting.

103 Kutscher, *Words,* 6–7 (Heb.). See also V. R. Gold, "The Mosaic Map of Madeba," *BA* 21 (1958) 50–71; and R. M. Good, "The Carthaginian Mayumas," *Studi Epigrafici e Linguistici sul Vicino Oriente Antico* 3 (1986) 241–45.

104 The etymology of the word is still unclear. O. Eissfeldt ("Etymologische und archäologische Erklärungen alttestamentlicher Wörter," 166–71) distinguished between two homonyms, רזח I, "to hail/shout"; and רזח II, "to bind together," and related מַרְזֵחַ to the former, that is, the similar feature between lamentation and celebration being the shouting. (See already David Kimchi, who cites his father, Joseph, both on this verse and in his *Sepher Haschoraschim,* רזח, 350; and ibn Ganaḥ, *Haschoraschim,* 476.) Greenfield *("Marzeaḥ")* and Pope *(Song of Songs),* however, do not find this etymology convincing. The latter (as well as Braslavi, "Jeremiah 16:5 and Amos 6:7," *BM* 48 [1971] 12–13) suggests connecting it to an Arabic root, *rzḥ* ("to fall down from fatigue and remain prostrate without power to rise"). The former, noting that there is no unified spelling of the word in the Akkadian texts from Ugarit *(marziʾu, marzaʾu, marziḫu),* suggests that it is a loanword, probably from a non-Semitic language. For other comments, see Porten, *Archives,* 180; R. Meyer, "Gegensinn und Mehrdeutigkeit in der althebräischen Wort- und Begriffsbildung," *UF* 11 (1979) 601–12.

It has also been suggested that the noun appears in Ebla. See G. Pettinato, *Testi amministrativi della biblioteca L. 2769. Materiali epigrapici di Ebla* (Napoli: University di Napoli, 1980) 2.46, rev. I, 1–2: *in* ud *mar-za-u*$_9$ ("on the day of his *marzeaḥ*"). See also M. Dahood, "The Minor Prophets and Ebla," in *The Word of the Lord Shall Go Forth: Essays in Honor of David Noel Freedman in Celebration of His Sixtieth Birthday* (ed. C. L. Meyers and M. O'Connor; Winona Lake, IN: Eisenbrauns, 1983) 54.

Ugaritic[105] and Palmyrene sources. The chronological difference between these two main records of documentation spans approximately one and a half millennia. The *marzeaḥ* institution, however, must have developed different aspects in the various periods and places where it is attested, and in many of the texts only a very partial and scanty picture is available. Studies of the institution have pointed out both its cultic and social dimensions. The *marzeaḥ* was a *thiasos* (this is G's translation of the term in Jeremiah) dedicated to a god *(mrzḥ 'lm),* often related to memorial rites to insure the beatification of members after death and was characterized by sacred banquets of eating and drinking that lasted several days. It was a religious and social association, at the head of which stood a symposiarch (Ugar. *rb. mrzḥ;* Aram. *rb mrzḥ';* Palmyrene-Greek bilingual, *συμποσίαρχη*), whose members (Ugar. *mt.mrzḥ;* Phoen. *bny mrzḥ;* Aram. *ḥbry' mrzḥ'*) belonged to the wealthier class possessing houses[106] and vineyards. This, of course, is of significance, because members of the upper-class society of Samaria are the very ones who are being denounced in Amos's oracle. Moreover, in light of the much later evidence from Palmyra that associates the *marzeaḥ* with reclining, eating, drinking, and anointing with oil, it can be safely said that the description given by the prophet in these verses is none other than a detailed account of the very activities that took place during the *marzeaḥ* itself. However, "the prophet was not interested solely in the religious side of the practices for the condemnation is aimed at the conspicuous consumption on the part of the wealthy burghers of Samaria."[107] Amos, who severely condemns the wealthy "cows of Bashan" and those whose opulence was obtained at the expense of the exploitation and oppression of others, once again attacks the elite class[108]—this time in the midst of their very festal celebrations.[109]

105 See *RŠ* 24.258.15–21, where El visits his *mrzḥ,* eats, drinks, becomes inebriated, befouls himself, and suffers from hallucinations. See M. Pope ("Divine Banquet") who, according to Greenfield *("Marzeaḥ"),* has exaggerated the licentious nature of the *marzeaḥ.*

106 See *RŠ* 15.88, *bīt* lú-meš*mar-za-i;* 15.70, also mentions a *marzeaḥ* house. On *rb mrzḥ'* in CIS 2.476, see F. Zayadine, "A Nabatean Inscription from Beida," *ADAJ* 21 (1976) 139–42.

107 Greenfield, *"Marzeaḥ,"* 453. See also P. J. King, "The *Marzeaḥ* Amos Denounces—Using Archaeology to Interpret a Biblical Text," *BAR* 15 (1988) 34–44.

108 There is no support whatsoever for assuming that the "banquet is condemned for connections with non-Yahwistic deities"; against Barstad, *Religious Polemics,* 141.

109 Many commentators transpose the expression "oracle of the Lord, the God of Hosts" from the middle of v 8 to the end of v 7; for example, Wolff, 273; Rudolph, 215, 218.

6 Doom and Destruction for the City and Its Inhabitants

8 Sworn has my Lord God by himself
—declares the Lord, the God of Hosts:
I loathe the pride of Jacob,
And I detest his fortresses.
I shall deliver over the city and all that is in it.
9 And if ten people are left in one house, they shall die.
10 And when one's kinsman and embalmer carry the remains out of the house, and he calls to the one at the rear of the house, "Are there any more with you?" he will reply, "None." And he shall say, "Hush!" For one must not invoke the name of the Lord.
11 For, lo, the Lord commands:
And he will smash the large house to bits
And the small house to splinters.

■ **8** This next literary unit (vv 8–11) is introduced by an oath of the Lord, "by his life" = himself (בְּנַפְשׁוֹ),[1] which potently expresses and stresses the implacable and irreversible nature of the impending punishment.[2] Many commentators unnecessarily transpose the following expanded oracle formula, "declares the Lord, the God of Hosts" (נְאֻם־ה׳ אֱלֹהֵי צְבָאוֹת), to the end of the preceding pericope, v 7.[3] Its position here, however, functions both as a reinforcement of the severity of the oath formula itself and, in addition, serves as the opening of an expanded literary inclusio that concludes in v 14 on the identical four words, נְאֻם־ה׳ אֱלֹהֵי הַצְּבָאוֹת.

The Lord swears "I loathe (מְתָאֵב)[4] the pride of Jacob and I detest (שָׂנֵאתִי)[5] his fortresses." "The pride of Jacob" (גְּאוֹן יַעֲקֹב)[6] refers to the arrogance of the people, who boast of their invincible superiority as witnessed in their economic prosperity,[7] their fortresses (אַרְמְנוֹת)[8] (see 3:9–11), and their military arrogance anchored in the victories of Jeroboam II. It is a fitting descriptive term to portray their entire luxurious style of living and outlook on life, as described in vv 1–6. They fervently believe

1 This oath formula appears again in Jer 51:14. It is a variant of כִּי נִשְׁבַּעְתִּי ("By myself I swear"); compare, for example, Gen 22:16; Isa 45:23; Jer 22:5; 49:13. It has been suggested (see Wolff, 281–82 n 8) that נִשְׁבַּע בְּנַפְשׁוֹ may have been related originally to the Akkadian oath ritual, *napištam lapātum* ("to touch the throat"), known especially from Mari treaty documents. For the idiom, see *CAD, N*, I.303, and *L*, 84–85, 201. This is a gesture whereby the party taking the oath touches his throat, symbolic of cutting the throat (as an animal would be cut in the covenant rite) if he does not abide by the conditions of the treaty. If correct, נֶפֶשׁ would then retain here its original meaning, "throat"; for example, Judg 12:3; 1 Sam 28:21; Jonah 2:6; Pss 69:2; 124:4–5 (compare Akk. *napištum, CAD, N*, I.303–4; Ugar. *npš, UT*, 1681).

2 For two other oath formulas, see Amos 4:2; 8:7.

3 See previously; so also Ehrlich, *Randglossen*, 5.245.

4 This hapax legomenon is a biform of the root תעב. For a similar interchange, see גאל = געל ("to be defiled, polluted"), for example, Isa 59:3; Zeph 3:1; Mal 1:7, 12; Lam 4:14. It has also been explained as an aural error based on the weakening of the gutterals. See also G. Garbini, "Note semitiche II," *Ricerche linguistiche* 5 (1962) 179–81. The proposal of M. Dahood, "Amos 6.8 *mᵉtāʾēb*," *Bib* 59 (1978) 265–66, to divide the verb into two nouns, is totally unacceptable.

5 For the paired terms שׂנא and תעב, see Amos 5:10. See also Ps 119:163; Prov 6:16.

6 See also Amos 8:7; Nah 2:3. For גָּאוֹן coupled with the names of other nations, see n 10.

7 For the arrogance of the southern kingdom, characterized by their reliance on material objects, see Isa 2:7ff. For Isaiah, human arrogance was the quintessence of idolatry.

8 For the recurrent motif of אַרְמְנוֹת ("fortresses") in Amos, see especially chapters 1—2.

that because they are the most favored nation (3:2; 6:1), no evil could overtake them (9:10). This expression is actually applied favorably to northern Israel itself in Ps 47:5 (a northern Psalm):[9] "He [=God] chose our heritage for us, the pride of Jacob (גְּאוֹן יַעֲקֹב) whom he loved." "The pride of Jacob"[10] must have been a current slogan or shibboleth in Samaria, a context Amos radically objects to and sets up to ridicule. The Lord takes no pride in their "pride," but totally abhors and abominates it.[11]

Thus the forthcoming punishment, "I shall deliver over (וְהִסְגַּרְתִּי) the city and all that is in it." The "city" (עִיר, most likely referring to the capital city, Samaria)[12] and "all that is in it" (וּמְלֹאָהּ, literally, "its fullness,"[13] referring to its populace as well as to its accumulated wealth) will be surrendered completely (הסגיר)[14] to enemy forces. Note once again, however, that Amos maintains the anonymity of the conqueror. The end shall ignominiously dawn upon the empire of Israel.

■ **9** From the wide-lens description of the surrender of the city to an unidentified enemy, Amos now focuses a closeup on the fate of the few surviving individuals.[15] Even if after this wholesale submission (and decimation) of the population there should yet remain alive a small number of people ("ten," עֲשָׂרָה)[16] who gather together in one of the remaining houses[17] for protection, even they, the last of the survivors, shall die.[18] Two of the prophet's recurring themes occur here together: the impossibility of escape (compare 2:13–16; 5:19; 9:1–4) and the nebulous and ominous effect of leaving the exact nature of the catastrophe unspecified. All that can be said is that he is alluding to some horrible disaster that will strike the remaining remnant as they are huddling together in a single house.[19]

■ **10** The closeup picture now further zooms in on what actually takes place within that very house and, in addition, records a very remarkable dialogue. The initial words of this verse, however, are beset with multiple

9 See Ginsberg, *Israelian Heritage,* 33–34: This is another example where "Amos refutes the conclusions of his Israelian hosts from the salvation history they keep repeating (Amos 2:10, 9, 11ff.; 3:1–2; 5:25; 9:7–8)." He adds that this "looks uncannily like a deliberate contradiction of Ps 47:5."

10 A. Caquot ("Le Psaume 47 et la Royauté de YAHWE," *RHPR* 39 [1959] 319) has suggested that גְּאוֹן refers to the capital of the nation; see Jer 13:9 (Judah); Hos 5:5; 7:10; Nah 2:3; Ps 47:5 (Israel); Zech 10:11 (Assyria); Isa 13:19 (Chaldeans); Isa 16:6; Jer 48:29 (Moab); Ezek 32:12 (Egypt); Zech 9:6 (Philistines). Compare Jer 13:9 (Jerusalem). See the reservation of Lipiński (*La Royauté,* 413 n 5) relating to Amos.

11 See Prov 8:13: "To fear the Lord is to hate evil; I hate (שָׂנֵאתִי) pride (גֵּאָה), arrogance (גָּאוֹן) . . .;" *NJPS.*

12 For "city" referring to the capital city of a country, see S. M. Paul, "Jerusalem—A City of Gold," *IEJ* 17 (1967) 263 and n 27. For other identifications of עִיר as Jerusalem, see S. Lieberman, *Tosefta Ki-Fshuṭah: A Comprehensive Commentary on the Tosefta,* Part III, *Order Moʿed* (8 vols.; New York: Jewish Theological Seminary of America, 1962) 62 (Heb.). For Mesopotamian references, see W. W. Hallo, "Antediluvian Cities," *JCS* 23 (1970) 60.

13 This phrase is unique to Amos. Compare the similar expressions הַיָּם וּמְלֹאוֹ ("the sea and all within it"), Isa 42:10; Pss 96:11; 98:7; 1 Chr 16:32; אֶרֶץ וּמְלֹאָהּ ("the earth and all within it"), Deut 33:16; Isa 34:1; Jer 8:16; 47:2; Ezek 12:19; 19:7; 30:12; 32:15; Mic 1:2; Ps 24:1; תֵּבֵל וּמְלֹאָהּ ("the world and all within it"), Pss 50:12; 89:12.

14 See Lam 2:7 and the notes to Amos 1:6, 9. See also Deut 32:30, "Unless their Rock had sold them, the Lord had given them up" (הִסְגִּירָם).

15 Rudolph (221) transposes v 11 before v 9 to preserve an ongoing description relating to a "house," in vv 9–10. However, the present order is much more effective. Even those few who survive the main onslaught and gather for protection in a house will be decimated. The prophet then, by means of a literary concatenation, continues the motif of "houses." Rudolph also drew attention to the interesting fact that there is no *Athnach* in v 9. The verse is in prose narrative.

Greenfield ("*Marzeaḥ,*" 453) made the interesting suggestion that vv 9–10 reflect the previously mentioned מַרְזֵחַ institution in its role as a funerary cult (see Jer 16:5). Amos, however, may very well be parodying this institution by announcing the impending death of the inhabitants and giving a description of the burial procedures.

16 See Gen 18:32; Isa 6:13; so, too, Rudolph, 224. Others interpret "ten" as representing a large number of people; see ibn Ezra; Kimchi. Ten, of course, is one of the numbers in the Bible that expresses completeness. See Avishur, "Forms," 1–55 (Heb.).

17 Note the recurring key word בַּיִת ("house"), which appears five times in vv 9–11.

18 See Ehrlich, *Mikrâ,* 3.412. He reads יָמֻתוּ instead of וָמֵתוּ.

19 The prophet may have in mind slaughter in warfare

difficulties, and solutions of all sorts abound.[20] Because the singular suffix of the verb, וּנְשָׂאוֹ (literally, "and someone shall carry him"), has no antecedent, and because it is followed by two substantives, almost all commentators accept the plural translation of G, *καὶ λήμψονται*, which presupposes וְנָשְׂאוּ ("and they shall take/carry"). But who are the "they" referred to in these next two nouns, and what is the meaning of the perplexing hapax legomenon וּמְסָרְפוֹ? Relying on the established meaning of "father's brother" for Heb. דּוֹד, some have explained מְסָרְפוֹ as the "mother's brother." This is primarily based on Karaite sources, but the existence of such a word has been contested.[21] Most exegetes, however, interpret the root סרף as a variant of שׂרף ("to burn"), which would literally mean "the one who burns him." This is then related either to the custom of burning aromatic spices in honor of the dead or to the practice of burning corpses at the time of a plague in order to restrict the danger of infection. The problem is that the former is attested only in connection with burial ceremonies for royalty (see Jer 34:5; 2 Chr 16:14; 21:19),[22] and the latter is an often cited but unproven assumption.[23] Moreover, this would be the sole example for the existence of such a variant spelling for the extremely common verb שׂרף, which, it should be emphasized, never appears elsewhere in the *piʿel*.[24] To obviate these difficulties, some have suggested a minor graphic emendation, along with a metathesis of the letters, and read מְסַפְּדוֹ/מְסַפִּידוֹ ("his mourner").[25] Others, basing themselves on the assumption that the nouns in question pertain not to the people who are tending the victims but rather to the receptacles in which the dead are carried, revocalize דוֹד to דּוּד ("pot")[26] or plural דְּוָדִים/דּוּדִים ("pots").[27]

There is, however, another very plausible way to interpret the hapax legomenon מְסָרְפוֹ, which fits the context admirably.[28] In Rabbinic Hebrew is the noun שְׂרָף (normal spelling, otherwise סְרָף), "resin," which is used in connection with the resin of various trees and spices. From this noun is derived a denominative verb that means "to smear with resin." Thus סֵירְפָה בִּשְׂרָף ("if he covered it [the handle of a saw] with resin"; Tosephtah Mikvaoth 6 [7] 21). See also Samaritan Aramaic, in which the verb סרף is a *vario lectio* for Hebrew סוּךְ ("to anoint") in Deut 28:40. The מְסָרֵף would then be the one whose profession is to anoint the dead

or the devastating pestilence that accompanies sieges and military attacks.

20 Rudolph's emendation, וְנִשְׁאַר נִשְׁאָר ("But if one should be left over") is unsupported and unnecessary; see also Sellin.

21 See Yehuda ibn Quraish (a contemporary of Saadiah Gaon), cited in ibn Ezra (who, incidentally, does not accept this interpretation); and Daniel al-Ḳumissi, ibn Ganaḥ, *Haschoraschim*, 37, 347; and Kimchi. B. Felsenthal ("Zur Bibel und Grammatik"—Zur Erklärung von Amos 6:10," in *Semitic Studies in Memory of Alexander Kohut* [ed. G. A. Kohut; Berlin: Calvary, 1897] 133–37) favors this interpretation, but see the criticisms of G. R. Driver ("A Hebrew Burial Custom," *ZAW* 66 [1954] 314–15), who claims that philologically Felsenthal's suggestion is impossible. T, קָרִיבֵיהּ ("his relative") is followed by Rashi.

22 Correctly, Rudolph, 222. See also Babylonian Talmud, Avodah Zarah 2b: "They burn (incense) for kings and heads of governments."

23 The case of Saul is a rare exception, for his body was already mutilated, 1 Sam 31:12–13.

24 Heb. שָׂרַף in Lev 10:16 is not a *piʿel* but an archaic passive *qal*. T translates, מִיְקִידָה ("from the fire") to which see the objection of ibn Ezra.

25 For example, Nowack; Tur-Sinai, *Peshuṭo*, 467–68.

26 Or (וֹ)יְדִיד ("[his] friend"); Tur-Sinai, *Peshuṭo*, 467–68.

27 For various suggested emendations, see Rudolph (222), who adds his own to the variegated list; see also Wolff, 280, relying on a difficult reconstruction based on G's translation.

28 See G. R. Driver, "A Hebrew Burial Custom," *ZAW* 66 (1954) 314–15, and esp. Y. Kutscher, "Lexicographical Problems of Rabbinic Hebrew: He Who Anoints the Dead with Resin," *Leš* 21 (1957) 251–55 (Heb.), reprinted in idem, *Hebrew and Aramaic Studies* (ed. Z. Ben-Hayyim, A. Dotan, and G. Sarfatti; Jerusalem: Magnes, 1977) 338 (Heb.). According to Driver, the tragedy is "not that the proper rites were neglected, but that the old [his uncle with the apothecary] buried the young, instead of the young burying the old." This, however, is not implied anywhere in the text. Driver thinks that this practice is also referred to in 1 Sam 31:12, again without any further proof. In lieu of the explanation offered previously there is no reason to conjecture that the first two letters here, ומ, should be parsed as the conjunctive *waw* with *mem* enclitic; against G. A. Rendsburg, "Eblaite *Ù-MA* and Hebrew *WM*," in *Eblaitica: Essays on the Ebla Archives and Eblaite Language* (ed. C. H. Gordon, G. A. Rendsburg, and N. H. Winter; Winona Lake, IN: Eisenbrauns, 1987) 1.39.

with סֶרֶף, most likely aromatic spices. This is a very well known custom attested from the Mishnaic period: "They may make ready [on the Sabbath] all that is needful for the dead and anoint (סָכִין) and wash it" (Mishnah Shabbath 23:5).[29] Compare also Matt 26:6–12 (= Mark 14:3–8 = John 12:3–7), as well as Mark 16:1; Luke 24:1; and John 19:39–40: "And then came also Nicodemus . . . and brought a mixture of myrrh and aloes. . . . Then they took the body of Jesus and wound it in linen clothes with the spices as is the manner of the Jews to bury."

The passage here is thus describing how the dead man's kinsman (דּוֹדוֹ)[30] and the one who is responsible for the proper last burial rites of anointing the body (מְסָרְפוֹ) are carrying the corpse out of the house. The corpse is referred to *pars pro toto* by the "bones" or the "limbs" (עֲצָמִים) of the body.[31] This same semantic development exists in several Aramaic dialects, where the cognate טמי (= עטמי), "bones," designates a dead body.[32] In Akkadian, as well, the interdialectal etymological equivalent, *eṣemtu* ("bones"), may also refer specifically to the remains of the dead.[33] Compare, for example, *pān nakrišu pagaršu linnadīma liššûni eṣemtašu* ("May his corpse be cast before his enemy, and may they carry off his bones").[34] The Akk. *liššûni* (from *našû*, "to carry") *eṣemtašu* = Heb. נָשְׂאוּ עֲצָמָיו. The only remains of Israel are their remains (that is, their corpses).

A unique dialogue now ensues between the two who are engaged in removing the corpses from the stricken house. One calls out to the other, who is[35] found "at the rear (יַרְכְּתֵי)[36] of the house," and asks, "Are there any more with you?" which can be understood as either "Are there any more corpses?"[37] or "Are there any more alive there besides you?"[38] The latter responds in the negative, "None" (אָפֶס). The former then cautions the latter to refrain from any further conversation by a direct command, "Hush!" (הַס; see 8:3). The imperative of this verb (הסה) is associated in some passages with the fear and trembling accompanying a theophany, for example, Hab 2:20; Zeph 1:7; Zech 2:17.[39] Here, too, it is employed as a warning to avoid any and all possible dread consequences that may be brought on by the presence of the Deity if the dialogue continues. It acts as a "countercharm" with a "preventative thrust."[40] The last clause, which gives the reason for this command to remain silent, has been explained in two slightly different ways. Some interpret בְּשֵׁם ה' as an oath in the vocative, "In the name of the Lord, do not continue to speak!"[41] A preferable possibility is to base the interpretation on the well-attested idiom, לְהַזְכִּיר בְּשֵׁם ("to invoke the name [of the Deity]").[42] The fear is that the Lord's name may be invoked in this dreadful place of death, with concomitantly dangerous consequences for all those yet alive. "[Do not say another word or you, too, may be struck down,] for one must not invoke the name of the Lord [in

29 See also Maimonides, *Mishneh Torah:* "Laws of Mourning," 4:1.

30 See Lev 10:4–5. After Aaron's two sons, Nadab and Abihu, were killed by a "fire that came forth from the Lord," Moses told "Mishael and Elzaphan, sons of Uzziel the uncle (דֹּד) of Aaron, 'Come forward and carry (שְׂאוּ) your kinsmen away from the front of the sanctuary to a place outside the camp.'"

31 See Gen 50:25; Exod 13:19; Ezek 6:5 (עַצְמוֹת). There is a slight difference in nuance, however, between the regular Hebrew plural, עֲצָמוֹת, and the much less attested עֲצָמִים. Whereas the former means "bones," the latter several times refers to "limbs." See, for example, Judg 19:29, וַיְנַתְּחֶהָ לַעֲצָמֶיהָ ("and they cut her up limb by limb"); Ezek 24:4, מִבְחַר עֲצָמִים ("best cuts," literally, "limbs"); Eccl 11:5, "Just as you do not know how the life-breath passes into the limbs (עֲצָמִים) within the womb of the pregnant woman."

32 See Y. Kutscher, "Lexicographical Problems," 251–55.

33 *CAD, E,* 342 1b. See also Ugar. *ʿṣm, UT,* 1841.

34 M. Streck, *Assurbanipal und die letzten assyrischen Könige bis zum Untergang Nineveh's* (VAB 7; Leipzig: Hinrichs, 1916) 22 ii 117; 28 iii 64.

35 For לַאֲשֶׁר ("he who"), Rudolph (222) reads לַנִּשְׁאָר ("to the one who remains").

36 Compare Akk. *arkatu* ("near side [of a building]"), *CAD, A,* II.274. See *KB,* 419. See also 1 Kgs 6:16.

37 Tur-Sinai, *Peshuṭo,* 468. See Hammershaimb, 103–4.

38 Most commentators.

39 For another cultic setting, see Neh 8:11. For a similar apocopated imperative formation of a ל"ה verb, see, for example, נַס ("test"), from the root נסה, Dan 1:12.

40 S. Niditsch, *The Symbolic Vision in Biblical Tradition* (HSM 30; Chico, CA: Scholars, 1983) 40. See also Amos 8:3.

41 Thus Ehrlich, *Mikrâ,* 3.412: "Schweig, bei dem Namen JHVHes!" He does not, however, repeat this interpretation in *Randglossen.*

42 Josh 23:7; Ps 20:8. See also Exod 23:13; Isa 26:13; 48:1. See W. Schottroff, *"Gedanken" im alten Orient und im alten Testament: Die Wurzel zākar im semitischen Sprachkreis* (WMANT 15; Neukirchen-Vluyn:

a house where pestilence has struck].” Such an invocation may be fatal for all survivors.

■ **11** After describing the dread destiny and doom of the inhabitants within the house, the next verse,[43] linked to the previous verse by the catchword בַּיִת, further explicates the fate of the “houses” themselves. Both the “large” and “small”[44] houses shall be smitten[45] to “bits” (רְסִיסִים)[46] and “splinters” (בְּקִעִים).[47] By the employment of a merism, the prophet foretells the total imminent destruction of the northern kingdom. The Lord issues the command,[48] but once again the one who receives the order to execute the judgment is left unidentified.[49]

Neukirchener Verlag, 1967) 250–51, 395. Many interpret the כִּי as the explanation of the prophet.

Heb. שֵׁם and זֵכֶר are a word pair found in several different types of parallelism; see Exod 3:15; Isa 26:8; 48:1; Pss 9:6–7; 135:13; Prov 10:7; Job 18:17. The cognate pairs appear similarly in Akk., *šumu–zikru;* Phoen. שם–סכר; and Aram. שם–זכר. For references, see Avishur, “Word Pairs,” 38–39.

43 Heb. כִּי־הִנֵּה forms the transition between the two passages and introduces the conclusion of the unit. See similarly כִּי הִנְנִי (v 14), which also serves as the introduction of the concluding unit of this chapter. There is no need to transfer this verse before v 9; against Rudolph, 221.

44 For גָּדוֹל–קָטָן as a merism, see Gen 19:11; Esth 1:5, 20. The “large” and “small” houses do not refer to the kingdoms of Israel and Judah; against T and many modern commentators, for example, Wellhausen, Procksch, Harper.

45 For the verb נכה, see Amos 3:15 (referring specifically to houses) and 9:11.

46 With this meaning, the noun is a hapax legomenon. For the verb, see Ezek 46:14. See otherwise Cant 5:2.

47 See Isa 22:9, “breeches (בְּקִיעֵי) in the city of David.”

48 See Amos 9:9, for the same construction.

49 See, for example, Amos 3:11; 4:2–3; 5:2–3; 6:7, 14; 7:17; 8:4.

6 Perversion of the Moral Order and "Pride Goes before Ruin"

12 Can horses gallop over rocks?
Can one plow the sea with oxen?
Yet you have turned justice into a poison herb
And the fruit of righteousness to wormwood.
13 You who rejoice over Lo-dabar,
Who boast, "Have we not by our own strength
Captured Karnaim for ourselves!"
14 But, lo, I am raising up against you,
O house of Israel, a nation
—declares the Lord, the God of Hosts,
And they will oppress you
From Lebo-hamath to Wadi Arabah.

■ **12** This brief utterance in the form of a rhetorical question[1] was appended here because of its affinities to the preceding pericopes. It employs the homonymic catchword ראשׁ, familiar from Amos 6:1, 6, 7, with, of course, an entirely different meaning; nevertheless, the intended concatenation is obvious. Moreover, there is a remarkable audible similarity between two of the nouns here and two in the prior verse: רְסִסִים-סוּסִים and בְּקִעִים-בְּקָרִים—with only one consonant difference in each of the pairs. The comparison is so deceptive that some have even emended these two substantives to conform exactly with those in v 12.[2] Although such forced exegesis is totally unwarranted, the external resemblance does help explain the present positioning of the verse.

Once again Amos resorts to the sapiential style of the rhetorical double question (הֲ . . . אִם) to convey cogently his conviction, this time by comparing the actions of animals and their handlers with human behavior: "Can horses gallop over rocks?"[3] Is it possible for horses, who were primarily employed for martial activities (see 2:15), to run upon rocky terrain, cliffs, and mountainsides? Obviously not, for the rocks would ruin their hooves, injure them, and prevent them from all further effectiveness.

The second of the two queries, however, presents a problem. The answer to the question as posed by the Masoretic text—"Can one plough with oxen (בַּבְּקָרִים)?"—is self-evident and natural. Of course one can and one does—which, of course, would undermine the prophet's very intention and defeat his purpose. Amos is obviously drawing upon imagery familiar to him and his audience in order to make exactly the opposite point. The answer he expects is unmistakably a negative one. Hence, most commentators accept the redivision of the letters בבקרים[4] to בְּבָקָר יָם ("[Can one plough] the sea with oxen?").[5] Such a question is preposterous and ridiculous, for it contradicts the natural order of things.[6] (Another suggested proposal to accentuate the

1 For other rhetorical questions, see Amos 2:11; 3:3–8; 5:18, 25; 6:2; 8:8.

2 See Ehrlich, *Randglossen*, 5.246–47; Tur-Sinai, *Peshuṭo*, 468.

3 Note the sequence of the letter *samech*, בסלע סוסים.

4 The plural בְּקָרִים is rare, appearing only twice elsewhere, Neh 10:37; 2 Chr 4:3. Because the singular, בָּקָר, is itself a collective, the plural form has been questioned by many commentators.

5 Ever since J. D. Michaelis, *Deutsche Übersetzung des Alten Testaments* (Göttingen: Vandenhoeck & Ruprecht, 1772).

6 Sellin's objection that this is "eigentlich zu platt" ("really too insipid") has been correctly countered by Rudolph, 226, "das Gleichnis kann gar nicht platt genug sein" ("the image can by no means be insipid enough").

nonsensicalness of this rhetorical question is to assume an ellipsis and supply the object from the first stich: "And do oxen [בְּקָרִים] plough upon the rocks?" [בַּסֶּלַע].)[7] Inane and insane! Yet this is the very demented and deranged manner in which the people are acting, totally bereft of reason. What is absurd in the animal world has become fact in Israel's world.[8] For they[9] "have turned justice into a poison herb (רֹאשׁ)[10] and the fruit of righteousness (וּפְרִי צְדָקָה)[11] to wormwood" (לַעֲנָה).[12] The perversion of justice (see Amos 5:7) is the perversion of the basic rules and standards of the human race and will eventually lead to disastrous results. One cannot upset the natural or the moral order with impunity.

■ **13** The background to these next two verses[13] reflects the period of the military incursion of Jeroboam II into Transjordan (see 2 Kgs 14:25). The two specific conquests cited by Amos reflect by their very names his sarcastic reaction to their joy in military victories.[14] The first, לֹא דָבָר ("Lo-dabar"), otherwise written לֹא דְבָר (2 Sam 17:27); לוֹ דְבָר (2 Sam 9:4, 5); or לִדְבִר, probably to be vocalized לִדְבָר (Josh 13:26), is generally identified with Tell 'el-Ḥammeh, north of the Jabbok River in the Ammonite territory of the northern part of Gilead.[15] The vocalization לֹא דָבָר, which appears only here, is an intentional paronomastic parody. For Amos their rejoicing over (הַשְּׂמֵחִים לְ־)[16] the fall of Lo-dabar is equated with their rejoicing over לֹא דָבָר, literally, "Nothing."

The second site, קַרְנָיִם, Karnaim,[17] is located in central Bashan, in Aramean territory. It is identified with Sheikh es-Saʿad on a northern tributary of the middle Yarmuk River, some four kilometers north of Tell ʿAstarah, biblical Ashtaroth. Referring to this conquest, the prophet resorts to one of his favorite devices, that of directly quoting the people themselves:[18] "Have we not by our own strength captured Karnaim for ourselves!" The haughty arrogance of their military superiority resounds throughout their self-praise: "Have we not by

7 Both these proposals are preferable to the suggestion אִם יַחֲרֹשׁ כַּבָּקָר רֵים ("[Can] the wild bull [plow] like the ox?"). See Rudolph, 225–26. The suggestion of M. Dahood ("'Can One Plow without Oxen?' [Amos 6,12]: A Study of *ba-* and *ʿal*," in *The Bible World: Essays in Honor of C. H. Gordon* [ed. G. Rendsburg; New York: Ktav, 1980] 13–23) to translate the preposition בְּ as "without" is totally unattested. A. Cooper ("The Absurdity of Amos 6:12a," *JBL* 107 [1988] 725–27, relying on the comments of Eliezer de Beaugency, *Kommentar zu Ezechiel und den XII kleinen Propheten* [ed. S. Poznański; Warsaw: Mekize Nirdamin, 1910] 151, who relates the animals to Israel's armies and the enemies to the "rock") goes on to emend the colon and translates, "Does a wild ox (רֵים—see already Sellin and Rudolph) plow in the valley?" (בַּבִּקְעָה). He then interprets סֶלַע as the Edomite Sela and בִּקְעָה as Beqaʿ in Lebanon. There is, however, no support for his emendation. Kimchi resolves the problem by an ellipsis "Does a man plow with oxen upon a rock?" But he, too, is constrained to introduce "a man" into the text. For another proposal, see O. Loretz, "Amos VI 12," *VT* 39 (1989) 240–41.

8 Compare Isa 1:3; Jer 8:7; 13:23.

9 Note the chiastic word order in the Hebrew text.

10 For רֹאשׁ, see Feliks, *Plant World,* 197–98 (Heb.). For the pair רֹאשׁ and לַעֲנָה, see Deut 29:17; Lam 3:19 (opposite order). Compare a similar image in Hos 10:4. See, for example, Melamed, "Break-up," 209 (Heb.).

11 The expression is unique to Amos. Compare Prov 11:30, "The fruit of the righteous (פְּרִי צַדִּיק) is a tree of life." For the opposite פְּרִי־כַחַשׁ, "the fruits of treachery," see Hos 10:13.

12 For לַעֲנָה, see Feliks, *Plant World,* 180, 200.

13 Several commentators suggest that this is a new oracle that began with a "woe" (הוֹי) cry; for example, Maag, *Text,* 42; Amsler; Robinson-Horst; Rudolph, 225, 226.

14 For territories in Bashan and Gilead during the reign of Jeroboam II, see 1 Chr 5:16–17.

15 For the site, see Z. Kallai, "לֹא דבר," *EM* 4.409–10 (Heb.); M. Metzger, "Lodebar und der Tell el-Mghannije," *ZDPV* 76 (1960) 97–102; S. Mittmann, "Beiträge zur Siedlungs und Territorial-geschichte des nördlichen Ostjordanlandes," *TLZ* 94 (1969) 391.

16 For the expression שמח ל־, see Isa 14:8; Obad 12; Mic 7:8; Pss 35:19, 24; 38:17; Job 21:12. All citations (except the last) imply a jeering glee.

17 For the site, see B. Oded, "Qarnaîm," *EM* 7.277–78 (Heb.); U. Kellerman, "ʿAštārōt–ʿAšterōt, Qarnayim–Qarnayim," *ZDPV* 97 (1981) 46–47, 50. See Gen 14:5; 1 Macc 5:26, 43–44; 2 Macc 12:21, 26. After the Assyrian conquest by Tiglatpileser III, Karnaim became the capital city of the Assyrian province Qarnina/Qarnini. See E. Forrer, *Die Provinzeinteilung des assyrischen Reiches* (Leipzig: Hinrichs, 1920) 62–63.

18 For other quotations, see Amos 2:12; 5:14; 6:2; 8:8, 14; 9:10. See Wolff, *Zitat,* 15, 58, 74.

our own strength" (הֲלוֹא בְחָזְקֵנוּ)[19]—not with the aid of any divine intervention—"captured (לָקַחְנוּ)[20] Karnaim (קַרְנָיִם)[21] for ourselves (לָנוּ)!" Because Karnaim is by its very name a dual form of קֶרֶן ("horn"), and because horns symbolize power and strength, the conquest of "Double-Horn"[22] would be a further demonstration of their overwhelming military prowess. Yet, in the eyes of the prophet, all their boastful bravado and braggart blustering over the conquests of sites from the south, in the land of the Ammonites, to the north, in the territory of Arameans, amount to one grand "Nothing." For Amos their panegyrical preening pride pompously precedes their precipitous fall. The chapter thus draws to a conclusion on the same theme on which it began: the self-confidence and braggadocio of the northern kingdom. "Pride goes before ruin, arrogance, before failure" (Prov 16:18).

■ **14** If they can boast of their military conquests, the Lord can respond in kind and go even one better: "But, lo, I am raising up against you" (כִּי הִנְנִי מֵקִים עֲלֵיכֶם)—and suddenly, before the actual threat is personified, the declaration is interrupted by an intermezzo containing an epithet of the God of Israel[23] that depicts him precisely as a military commander, "God of Hosts" (אֱלֹהֵי הַצְּבָאוֹת).[24] This is yet another example of the deliberate use of delayed response in the rhetoric of Amos.[25] He intentionally withholds for a few seconds longer the full impact of his words in order to heighten the tension and fear of his listeners. Here, moreover, the verbal expression itself can paradoxically be initially interpreted positively or negatively. For לְהָקִים עַל in a positive context, "to raise up for," compare Jer 6:17; 23:4. For its negative connotation, "to raise up against," compare 2 Sam 12:11; Isa 29:3; Ezek 26:8. Thus the slight delay succeeds momentarily in leaving the people hanging in suspense.

But not for long: The Lord, the military leader, "God of Hosts," is raising up *against* them "a nation" (גּוֹי).[26] Once again a nation—undefined, unspecified, and unidentified—will execute the divine judgment upon Israel; compare Amos 3:11.[27] Amos, prophesying prior to the westward expansion of Tiglatpileser III, does not and cannot identify the enemy as Assyria, which never appears in any of his oracles.[28]

This anonymous and inimical nation shall lead a counterattack that will more than offset Israel's present conquests: "They will oppress (לָחֲצוּ)[29] you from Lebo-hamath to Wadi Arabah." The two geographical loci refer to the northern and southern boundaries of the northern kingdom.[30] Lebo-hamath (לְבוֹא חֲמָת)[31] is one of the regular expressions for the northern frontier of Israel; see Num 13:21; 34:8; Josh 13:5; Judg 3:3; 1 Kgs 8:65; 2 Kgs 14:25; 1 Chr 13:5. It is located in northern Lebanon, south of Kadesh. The other site, "the Brook

19 For הֲלֹא as an emphatic, see Amos 5:20. Note, too, the intended verbal play and alliteration: . . . הֲלוֹא לֹא (דָבָר).

20 For לקח ("to capture" [a place]), see Deut 3:8; and in reference to people, see Amos 9:3. See also the Akkadian interdialectal etymological and semantic equivalent, *leqû; CAD, L,* 144–45.

21 Note the intended alliteration of the threefold repetition of the suffix נו, one after the other, בחזקנו לקחנו לנו; and the thrice-repeated letter ק: בחזקנו לקחנו . . . קרנים.

22 For prophetic paronomasia on geographical sites, see especially Mic 1:10–15. See S. Vergon, "Micah 4:14," *BM* 66 (1976) 392–401, esp. 398 n 47 (Heb.). For the phenomenon in general, see Weiss, *MiShuṭ,* 162–89 (Heb.). See also I. H. Eybers, "The Use of Proper Names as a Stylistic Device," *Semitics* 2 (1971–72) 82–92.

23 This expanded oracle formula is not a secondary insertion but part and parcel of the unique literary style of Amos; against Wolff, 286. For a discussion of the expression itself, see Wolff, 287–88. It appears nine times in the book with slight differences of formulation. See also O. Eissfeldt, "Jahwe Zebaoth," in idem, *Kleine Schriften zum Alten Testament* (6 vols.; Tübingen: J. C. B. Mohr, 1979) 3.105; B. N. Wambacq, *L'épithète divine Jahvé Ṣᵉba'ôt: Étude philologique, historique et exégétique* (Bruges: de Brouwer, 1947).

24 Compare also the context, for example, Amos 5:27; 6:8; 9:5.

25 See, for example, Amos 4:12.

26 See Deut 28:49; Jer 5:15.

27 See comments to Amos 3:11.

28 See Kaufmann, *Toledoth,* 6.87.

29 This is a regular expression for an enemy attack and oppression. See Exod 3:9; Judg 2:18; 4:3; 6:9; 1 Sam 10:18; 2 Kgs 13:4, 22; Jer 30:20; Ps 106:42.

30 The phrase מִ(ן) . . . (וְ)עַד ("from . . . to") is one of the ways to express the demarcation of borders in biblical Hebrew; see, for example, Deut 3:16; 11:24; Josh 13:6, 26; 2 Sam 20:2; as well as Amos 8:12. It is also found in the Aramaic Sefire inscription, *KAI,* 222 B 9–10: "From (מן) ʿArqu to (ועד) Ya'di . . . from (מן) Lebanon to (ועד) Yabrud . . . from (מן) the Valley to

(Wadi) of the Arabah" (נַחַל הָעֲרָבָה), appears only here.[32] It is in the vicinity of the northern end of the Dead Sea, often called "the Sea of the Arabah" (יָם הָעֲרָבָה); see Deut 3:17; 4:49; Josh 3:16; 12:3; 2 Kgs 14:25. It is usually identified either with Wādī 'el-Qelt or Wādī Kefrein.[33] The enemy, envisioned as attacking from the north, shall completely overrun the entire kingdom of Israel. Thus measure for measure: because Israel boasted of individual conquests in the north and south (v 13), the enemy's onslaught shall be a total invasion into all of Israelite territory, from north to south. The wording here of the boundaries of Israel is almost identical to the prophecy of Jonah son of Amittai in 2 Kgs 14:25, describing the conquests of Jeroboam II: "It was he who restored the territory of Israel from Lebo-hamath to the Sea of the Arabah." Here is the reverse: All land previously restored and gained shall be lost. It has been correctly stated that Amos "hier antithetisch auf die Heilsweissagung jenes Propheten Jona b. Amittai anspiele" ("here is antithetically alluding to the prophecy of salvation of that prophet, Jonah ben Amittai").[34]

By the employment of the concluding epithet, נְאֻם־ה׳ אֱלֹהֵי (הַ)צְבָאוֹת, the verse concludes on exactly the same words as found in v 8, forming thereby an editorial inclusio. (Note, too, that in both instances the phrase appears within the middle of the verse.) The entire chapter itself creates, as presently compiled, one grand inclusio. For just as the prophet commenced his charge against the aggrandized self-confidence of the leaders of Samaria, so here he concludes by attacking the overbearing arrogance of the population in general. Just as the former will eventually lead to the punishment of exile, with the elite in the lead (v 7), so here, too, the oracle concludes with the description of all of northern Israel being entirely overrun by an enemy (v 14).[35] Moreover, herein lies one final connection, a very ironic one: The enemy who will exact the judgment is called simply גּוֹי ("a nation"). This nameless גּוֹי shall bring about the demise of Israel, the "prime of nations," גּוֹיִם.

(ועד) KTK." For text and translation, see Fitzmyer, *Sefire*, 16–17. See also M. Saebø, "Grenzbeschreibung und Landideal im alten Testament, mit besonderer Berücksichtigung der *min-ʿad* Formel," *ZDPV* 90 (1974) 14–37. Compare, too, the Akkadian interdialectal equivalents, *ištu . . . adi* ("from . . . to"), which appear alongside place-names; for example, TCL, 11 156 r. 9, 14 in C.-F. Jean, *Contrats de Larsa* (Paris: Geuthner, 1926).

31 For the site, present-day Lebwe, see B. Mazar, "Lebo Hamath," *EM* 4.416–18 (Heb.). See also B. Mazar, "Lebo-Hamath and the Northern Border of Canaan," *Bulletin of the Jewish Palestine Exploration Society* 12 (1946) 91–102 (Heb.), reprinted in idem, *Cities and Districts in Eretz-Israel* (Jerusalem: Bialik, 1975) 167–81 (Heb.); R. de Vaux, "Le pays de Canaan," *JAOS* 88 (1968) 23–29; M. Weinfeld, "Bᵉrît—Covenant vs. Obligation," *Bib* 56 (1975) 126–27. For a suggested historical background, see J. A. Soggin, "Amos VI:13–14 und I:3 auf den Hintergrund der Beziehungen zwischen Israel und Damaskus im 9. und 8. Jahrhundert," in *Near Eastern Studies in Honor of William Foxwell Albright* (ed. H. Goedicke; Baltimore and London: Johns Hopkins University, 1971) 433–41.

32 For the site, see M. Broshi, "The Brook of the Arabah," *EM* 5.810 (Heb.). It is not to be confused with נַחַל הָעֲרָבִים ("Wadi of the Willows") between Moab and Edom (Isa 15:7), as G translates here. See Rudolph, 226.

33 See Wolff, 289.

34 Rudolph, 228, quoting O. Eissfeldt ("Amos und Jona in volkstümlicher Überlieferung," in ". . . *Und Fragten nach Jesus": Festschrift Ernst Barnikol* [Berlin: A. Töpelmann, 1964] 9–13, reprinted in idem, *Kleine Schriften zum Alten Testament* [6 vols.; Tübingen: Mohr, 1962–1979] 4.137–42). Gordis ("Studies," 248) calls it a "sardonic parody of II Kings 14.25."

35 This oracle, unlike the above, does not end with the threat of exile. For here there is put into effect the poetic law of talion: They, who boasted of their territorial expansion through military conquest, shall be oppressed in their very own territory from north to south by an enemy military conquest.

Excursus: The Visions in Amos

The five visions occupy an important part of the Book of Amos and have been the subject of intensive investigation.[1] Scholarly opinion, however, is still seriously divided over some of the basic issues concerning the interpretation of the visions: Do the first two reflect the commissioning of the prophet?[2] Do the visions (the first two or four) date from the beginning of his career,[3] and/or do they reflect successive stages in his prophetic mission?[4] Are the five a single unified composition, or does the fifth vision constitute an independent entity?[5] Is there any discernible order in the arrangement of the visions?[6]

As to the first question, that the initial visions pertain to his prophetic call is highly unlikely. Not only is Amos not given any prophetic charge, but, even more significantly, he is already functioning as a

1 Among the many studies that may be cited, see S. Amsler, "La parole visionnaire des prophètes," *VT* 31 (1981) 359–63; G. Bartczek, *Prophetie und Vermittlung. Zur literarischen Analyse und theologischen Interpretation des Visionsberichte des Amos* (Europäische Hochschulschriften XXIII/120; Frankfurt: Peter Lang, 1980); G. Brin, "The Visions of Amos (7:1—8:3): Studies in Structures and Ideas," in *Isac Leo Seeligmann Volume: Essays in the Bible and the Ancient World* (3 vols.; ed. A. Rofé and Y. Zakovitch; Jerusalem: E. Rubinstein, 1983) 2.275–90 (Heb.).; A. Guillaume, *Prophétie et divination chez les Semites* (Paris: Payot, 1950) 182ff.; F. Hesse, *Die Fürbitte im Alten Testament* (Unpub. diss., Erlangen, 1949); F. Horst, "Die Visionsschilderungen der alttestamentlichen Propheten," *EvT* 20 (1960) 193–205; B. O. Long, "Reports of Visions among the Prophets," *JBL* 95 (1976) 353–66; Niditsch, *Vision;* Reventlow, *Amt,* 30–56; I. P. Seierstad, *Die Offenbarungserlebnisse der Propheten Amos, Jesaja und Jeremia: Eine Untersuchung der Erlebnisvorgänge unter besonderer Berücksichtigung ihrer religiössittlichen Art und Auswirkung* (Oslo: Dybwad, 1965) 52–59, 82–91; M. Sister, " Die Typen der prophetischen Visionen in der Bibel," *MGWJ* 78 (1934) 399–430; reprinted and tr. as "Types of Prophetic Visions in the Bible," in *LeToldoth HaḤevrah VeHasifruth* (Tel Aviv: Seminar HaKibbutzim, 1962) 116–43 (Heb.); B. Uffenheimer, *The Visions of Zechariah: From Prophecy to Apocalyptic* (Jerusalem: Kiryat Sepher, 1961) 139–41 (Heb.); Watts, *Vision,* 27–50; Z. Weisman, "Patterns and Structures in the Visions of Amos," *BM* 39 (1969) 40–57 (Heb.); Würthwein, "Amos-Studien," 10–52, especially 28–35. For pertinent additional biography for each one of the visions themselves, see the corresponding textual notes.

2 For those who consider them to be his prophetic call, see, for example, Wellhausen, 88; Budde, "Amos," 65; Weiser, *Profetie,* 72ff.

3 See Seeligmann, "History," 125–32 (Heb.); Haran, *Ages and Institutions,* 340 (Heb.); idem, "Amos," 273 (Heb.); Zakovitch, *For Three,* 186 (Heb.). According to this interpretation, all the other oracles are subsequent to the visions and presuppose the divine decision of punishment. See, however, Reventlow, *Amt,* 21, 36ff.; V. Herntrich, *Amos der Prophet Gottes* (Göttingen: Vandenhoeck & Ruprecht, 1941) 70.

Not only the time of the oracles but also their original position is disputed. According to Baumann *(Der Aufbau),* they belong to chapter 6; Sellin (156ff.) places them after 9:10; Marti, after 9:7; Budde, "Amos," at the beginning of the book.

4 See especially Weiser (*Profetie,* 71ff.), who states that the visions belong to his preprophetic stage; and Würthwein ("Amos-Studien") from his *Nabi* stage. For criticism of these views, see Reventlow, *Amt,* 33–34, 55, 112; Watts, *Vision,* 28ff., 48–49 n 8; B. Uffenheimer, *The Visions of Zechariah: From Prophecy to Apocalyptic* (Jerusalem: Kiryat Sepher, 1961) 140 (Heb.).

5 Most commentators separate the fifth vision from the previous four. The first four are then interpreted as a single composition. See, for example, Brin, "Visions," 283 (Heb.); Haran, *Ages and Institutions,* 328–29, 331, 347; Reventlow, *Amt,* 30–31, 43, 48, 112; Kapelrud, *Central Ideas,* 51–53.

Some exegetes, however, assume that after the first three visions and the encounter with Amaziah, the priest of Bethel (7:12–17), Amos was expelled from Bethel. See, for example, Gordis, "Composition," 248–51; Watts, *Vision.* Compare, however, Long, "Reports," 360; Haran, "Amos," 274. According to Brin ("Visions," 283–85), the change in the third and fourth visions reflects different periods in the history of the people. The first two mirror the past sins of the people, which the Lord forgave. The next pair relate to the condition of the present (and the near future), which the Lord will no longer condone. The four are thus interpreted as a historical essay and not as one-time events. For the view of past and present in the visions, compare also McKeating, 52–53; Ward, *Amos,* 55–57.

For the integrality of the fifth vision with the previous four, see Sister, "Types," 119; Weisman, "Patterns and Structures," 41–42; Weiser, *Profetie,* 70–77, 248–52.

6 For the interpretation of the visions as reflecting the seasons of the calendar year, see S. Talmon, "The Gezer Calendar and the Seasonal Cycle of Ancient Canaan," *JAOS* 83 (1963) 177–87, reprinted and tr. in *BM* 29 (1967) 3–17, especially 11–12 (Heb.): the locusts at the beginning of spring; the heat of the fire

prophet as evidenced by his interceding on behalf of Israel in order to revoke the imminent divine chastisement. As for the contention that his motivation for intervention is that "Jacob" (= Israel) will otherwise not survive because it is so "small" (קָטֹן, Amos 7:2, 5) and that this "smallness" refers to the period prior to the territorial expansion of King Jeroboam II,[7] it is totally unfounded and is based, moreover, on an incorrect understanding of the meaning of קָטֹן.[8] Neither do his visions reflect different periods or stages in his prophetic career. The two primary roles of the prophet—the intercessor who defends his people and the messenger who delivers God's pronouncement of the forthcoming catastrophe[9]—are the raison d'être of his call and characterize his mission throughout his ministry. Thus there is no reason to assume that these visions are the direct inspiration for his oracles against the nations in chapters 1 and 2, which themselves need not reflect the initial period of his mission.[10] The visions could actually have occurred at any time during his lifetime.

Although on formalistic, stylistic, and contextual grounds, the five visions may be divided into three separate literary units—the first pair, the second pair, and the fifth[11]—nevertheless, they appear to form a unified composition in which an internal order may be perceived. Ideationally they are a single unit, tied together not only by formal literary characteristics but also by a graduated development of severity. The punishment in the first vision is executed only against the agricultural land; in the second vision, the soil as well as the underground sources of water are desiccated; the sanctuaries and the "house" of Jeroboam are the targets of the threat in the third vision; and in the fourth vision, the entire nation is visited with a devastating decimation, whose ultimate inescapability is dramatically portrayed in the final vision. As the severity of destruction increases, moreover, the response of the prophet decreases: in the first two visions he responds with an entire sentence; in the next pair, with only a word or two; and in the last he remains entirely silent. Furthermore, the unity of the visions may also be vouched for by their very number, five, which plays an important role in the Book of Amos. There are five visions that correspond numerically (and partially thematically)[12] to the punishments recorded in Amos 4, where the refrain, וְלֹא־שַׁבְתֶּם עָדַי נְאֻם־ה' ("and yet you did not turn back to me, declares the Lord"), is repeated five times, in vv 6, 8, 9, 10, and 11. Compare also the pentad of curses and threats in Amos 7:17 and the fivefold theme of inescapability in Amos 9:2–4.

The visions have often been studied synchronically[13]—defined in terms of their types, forms, structures, and themes—as well as diachronically.[14] The affinities of the symbolic visions to the interpretation of dreams in the ancient Near East and the way the symbol relates to its meaning have also been duly noted.[15] "Dreams are thought to be an avenue of direct communication with the deity which as such is often considered to have theological standing as waking visions."[16]

The following brief comments (which are to be supplemented by the textual analysis of the individual

at the beginning of summer; the basket of dry fruits at the end of the summer. The third vision, however, is not dated "seasonally." The fifth reflects the earthquake. See also Cripps, 99; Hammershaimb, 107–8.

7 Thus Haran, *Ages and Institutions.*

8 See commentary at this verse.

9 See Paul, "Prophets," 1169–71.

10 Seeligmann, "History"; Zakovitch, *For Three.*

11 See Sister, "Types."

12 For the relation between the visions and the punishments recorded in chapter 4, see Haran, *Ages and Institutions,* 331; Brin, "Visions," 287–90; Ward, *Amos,* 55–57. Neither the five punishments of chapter 4 nor the first two visions effected any change in the conduct of the people. Thus the inevitable was about to occur, as reflected in 4:13 and the next three visions.

13 See most of the bibliographical references in n 1.

14 Niditsch, *Vision.*

15 See A. L. Oppenheim, *The Interpretation of Dreams in the Ancient Near East* (Transactions of the American Philosophical Society 46/3; Philadelphia: The American Philosophical Society, 1959) 179ff.

16 Oppenheim, *Interpretation,* 238. For dream omina outside Mesopotamia, see A. Volten, *Demotische Traumdeutung (Papyrus Carlsberg No. XIII–XIV 7)* (Analecta Aegyptica 3; Copenhagen: Munksgard, 1942) 60ff. (Egyptian); Artemidorus Daldianus, *Onirocriticon Libri* V (ed. R. A. Pack; Leipzig: Teubner, 1963) 4.80 (Greek); Babylonian Talmud, Berachoth 55a–57a (Jewish).

For the connection between visions and prophetic symbolic acts, see Reventlow, *Amt,* 44ff. The interpretation of the symbol has the power to initiate and effectuate that which is predicted. See also Paul, "Prophets," 1162–63; Niditsch, *Vision,* 247.

visions themselves) are meant to call attention to the internal structure and connections in style, thought, and content among the five visions, which are here categorized under three subgroupings: one and two, three and four, and five. First, the first four visions occur in pairs of two each. As is well known, the repetition underlies their importance as well as authenticates their veracity. The message of the Deity is conveyed by reiteration, employing a different symbol yet without a change of meaning. Compare likewise the two dreams of Joseph (the sheaves and the sun, moon, and eleven stars; Gen 37:5–9) and the two of Pharaoh (the two sets of seven cows and ears of grain; Gen 41:1–7). Joseph makes this very clear when he says to Pharaoh, "Pharaoh's dreams are one and the same: God has told Pharaoh what he is about to do" (Gen 41:25). "As for Pharaoh having had the same dream twice, it means that the matter has been determined by God, and that God will soon carry it out" (Gen 41:32). This phenomenon is also documented in extrabiblical sources.[17] Compare the Gilgamesh Epic, in which the presaged arrival of Enkidu, Gilgamesh's future bosom friend, is announced by a double dream. In each dream strange objects (first a meteorite of Anu and then, in the second dream, an axe of mysterious appearance) fall from the sky, land in the city of Uruk, and cause the inhabitants to gather around them in wonder and admiration.

The first four visions (with a slightly abbreviated formula in the third)[18] share a common opening formula, כֹּה הִרְאַנִי אֲדֹנָי ה׳ וְהִנֵּה ("This is what my Lord God showed me"; Amos 7:1, 4, 7; 8:1). The first two visions, introduced by a participial form, center around different "agents" of God's wrath (the locusts and the fire) who are described as "devouring/consuming" (7:2, 4). This threat leads to an outcry from the prophet, who immediately intercedes to plead for Israel's survival: "How will Jacob survive? He is so small" (מִי יָקוּם יַעֲקֹב כִּי קָטֹן הוּא) in 7:2, 5. God, in turn, then revokes his decision: "The Lord relented concerning this. 'It shall not come to pass [either],' said my Lord [God]" (נִחַם ה׳ עַל־זֹאת [גַּם־הִיא] לֹא תִהְיֶה אָמַר [אֲדֹנָי] ה׳) in 7:3, 6.

These two dynamic visions are entirely clear, and their severity is understood by Amos, who needs no explanation to clarify God's plan (compare likewise the dreams of Joseph). They are interconnected by the addition in the second vision of the two words, גַּם־הִיא ("This one [shall not come to pass] either"; v 6). However, whereas in v 3 of the first vision Amos pleads, סְלַח־נָא ("Pray forgive"), that is, annul the guilt and the punishment entirely, in the second, by the mere fact of its repetition, the prophet comes to realize that all he can do is beseech God to חֲדַל־נָא ("Refrain"; v 5), that is, stop this impending disaster.[19] He invokes God's attribute of mercy, which eventually overcomes his attribute of justice.

The next pair of visions, the third and fourth, also have a common stylistic structure. After the presentation of the symbolic vision,[20] both continue with the question of the Deity, who now initiates the dialogue: "And the Lord asked me, 'What do you see, Amos?'" (וַיֹּאמֶר ה׳ אֵלַי מָה־אַתָּה רֹאֶה עָמוֹס), 7:8; 8:2. The prophet responds (וָאֹמַר) by merely naming the object seen. Then the Lord replies (וַיֹּאמֶר אֲדֹנָי/ה׳) by interpreting the symbol and adds, "I will pardon them no more" (לֹא־אוֹסִיף עוֹד עֲבוֹר לוֹ). This is followed by a poetic description of the forthcoming destructive punishment (7:9; 8:3).[21]

These two visions relate directly to the first pair as is evident from the Lord's statement, "I will pardon them no more," that is, as he had done the first two times. However, the differences are also very evident. Here

17 Oppenheim (*Interpretation,* 208), in addition to the two dreams of Gilgamesh (215, 246–48), brings examples from other cultures for the repetition of dreams as indicative of stress, clarity, and authentication.

18 According to G and some manuscripts of V, however, the third vision shares a similar formulaic introduction. Some commentators assume that this reading is original and that the abbreviated Masoretic text was caused by haplography; see, for example, Haran, *Ages and Institutions,* 328 n 18.

19 See Wolff, 303: "The first petition aims at Israel's guilt, pleading that it be washed away and that all reason for the punishing intervention thus be removed. The second petition has in view only Yahweh's punishment . . .: may this precise form of destruction not occur! . . . There is no forgiveness of guilt; there is only delay of punishment. Amos wins forbearance, not pardon."

20 See Wolff, 294; they are images, not scenes.

The fact that God initiates the dialogue and interprets the visions is very significant. According to L. Eslinger ("The Education of Amos," in *Biblical and Other Studies* [ed. R. Ahroni; *HAR* 11 (1987) 41]), it is "a development in God's rhetorical strategy for convincing Amos about the necessity of judgment." See similarly F. Landy, "Vision and Poetic Speech in Amos," in the same volume, 228: "Thus God steals the initiative in the dialogue, effectively depriving Amos of the possibility of intercession."

21 These poetic descriptions are integral to the text and are not a later interpolation. See commentary; compare Haran, *Ages and Institutions,* 328 n 17; Niditsch, *Vision,* 244.

the images (כְּלוּב קָיִץ אֲנָךְ,) are static, not dynamic; the speakers are reversed: God initiates the dialogue; the meaning of the symbol in the vision, which is not understood by the prophet, is interpreted by the Deity in a surprisingly paradoxical fashion, either by a paronomastic word association[22] (קַיִץ-קֵץ, "singly heard, doubly meant")[23] or by an idea association (אֲנָךְ, "destructively meant"; compare Pharaoh's dreams); Amos makes no attempt at intervention or intercession; the divine decision is now irrevocable. God's retributive justice has overcome his mercy.

The fifth vision, except for the employment of the verb ראה—here in the *qal* and not in the *hiphʿil* as in the other four—is totally different in form and style. There is no similar opening or concluding formula; the prophet is only a witness to a scene in which the sole "object" seen is the Lord himself;[24] there is no dialogue, and thus no interpretation is necessary. The dénouement, described by five successive threats, has arrived. This vision is the finale. The disaster is definitive and decisive.

22 Niditsch, *Vision*, 31–32. Horst ("Visionsschilderungen") calls Amos 7:7–9 a "Wortspielvision" ("paronomastic vision"), and 8:1–3, "Assonanzvision" ("assonance vision"). Long ("Reports") designates 7:1–6 as "dramatic word visions" and 7:7–9 and 8:1–2 as "oracle visions." For similar paronomastic associations in Mesopotamian dreams, see Oppenheim, *Interpretation*, 241, 272: "If a man in his dream eats a raven *(aribu)*: income *(irbu)* will come in." "If in his dream they gave him fir *(miḫru)* wood, he will have no rival" *(māḫiru)*. See also W. Farber, "Associative Magic: Some Rituals, Word Plays, and Philology," *JAOS* 106 (1986) 447–49. For this linguistic phenomenon in Egypt, see Volten, *Demotische Traumdeutung*, 60ff.; in Greece, Artemidorus, ch. LXXX (book 4); in Israel, Babylonian Talmud, Berachoth 55a–57a.

23 Niditsch, *Vision*, 38.

24 Note that the Lord also appears in the third vision, but the emphasis there is entirely upon the אֲנָךְ.

7

First Three Visions: Prophetic Intercession and the Die is Cast

1 **This is what my Lord God showed me: Lo, he was creating locusts just when the late-sown crops were beginning to sprout—the late-sown crops are after the king's mowing.**
2 **And when it finished consuming the herbage of the land, I said, "O my Lord God, please pardon! How can Jacob survive? He is so small."**
3 **The Lord relented concerning this. "It shall not happen," said the Lord.**
4 **This is what my Lord God showed me: Lo, my Lord God was summoning a judgment by fiery heat; it consumed the great deep and was consuming the fields.**
5 **I said, "O my Lord God, please cease! How can Jacob survive? He is so small."**
6 **The Lord relented concerning this. "This too shall not happen," said my Lord God.**
7 **This is what he showed me: Lo, my Lord was standing by a wall of *ʾanak,** with *ʾanak** in his hand.**
8 **And the Lord asked me, "What do you see, Amos?" "*ʾAnak,**" I replied. And my Lord declared, "Lo, I am setting *ʾanak** in the midst of my people Israel. I will pardon them no more.**
9 **The high places of Isaac shall become desolate,**
The sanctuaries of Israel shall be ruined.
And I will rise against the house of Jeroboam with the sword."

*** Hebrew obscure**

■ **1** The initial first-person prophetic vision is a report of an event: an attack of locusts. The prophet is given a preview (כֹּה הִרְאַנִי)[1] of this plague that the Lord[2] was "creating" (יוֹצֵר)[3] to unleash against the crops.[4] The locusts are referred to here by the collective term גֹּבַי. The same designation also appears in Nah 3:17, גּוֹב גּוֹבָי (see, too,

1 For this introductory expression, see also Amos 7:4, 7; 8:1. Compare, too, 2 Sam 15:25; 2 Kgs 8:10, 13; Ezek 11:25.

2 Some have suggested that וְהִנֵּה should be read וְהִנֵּהוּ (a case of haplography): "And behold he (= God)"; for example, Weiser, *Profetie,* 15. There is no reason to delete אֲדֹנָי, against Marti; Weiser, *Profetie,* 15.

3 In light of G, ἐπιγονή ("offspring"; see also T, בִּרְיַת ["formation"] and S, בְּרִיתָא), several commentators propose reading יְצַר ("generating of/formation") instead of יוֹצֵר, for example, Wellhausen and Sellin. However, Ehrlich (*Mikrâ,* 3.413), as well as *KB* (410), suggests that the Greek actually reflects an original יוֹצֵא and not יְצַר (*KB* presents both possibilities). Others have suggested that יוֹצֵר should be interpreted as a noun (and not as a participle), meaning a "swarm/group assembly"; see ibn Ezra's citing of a previous authority (which he does not accept); and Kimchi, who brings this as the first of several possibilities. There is, however, no support for this.

4 The subject of the participle is the prior mentioned substantive אֲדֹנָי, which, according to biblical syntax, need not be repeated (compare Amos 7:4); see *GKC,* 116s. Compare also the following visions in which verbal forms follow הִנֵּה: v 4, קֹרֵא; v 7, נִצָּב. A further example of this syntactical construction is found in Isa 29:8: "Like one who is hungry and dreams he is eating (וְהִנֵּה אוֹכֵל) . . . ; like one who is thirsty and dreams he is drinking" (וְהִנֵּה שֹׁתֶה). In both cases וְהִנֵּה אוֹכֵל and וְהִנֵּה שֹׁתֶה refer back to the one who is dreaming.

Isa 33:4, גֵּבִים)[5] and may refer to the larva stage directly after hatching.[6]

The plague of locusts, forming and swarming in front of the very eyes of the prophet, takes place at the time when the "late-sown crops (הַלֶּקֶשׁ)[7] were beginning to sprout"[8] (בִּתְחִלַּת עֲלוֹת). These late-sown crops are the harvest produce engendered by the "late spring rains" (מַלְקוֹשׁ),[9] during the months of March and April. They are also referred to in the Gezer Calendar as ירחו לקש ("the two months of late sowing," that is, the months of Shebat and Adar).[10] They consist of nongrain crops such as vegetables and onions. If a locust plague attacks in the late spring, the results are extremely deleterious. At the time when the late sowing is beginning to sprout, the earlier sowing, the grain crop, is already well advanced. Thus, the locusts would devastate not only the late crop but also the more developed, but as yet unreaped, earlier crop—spelling a total agricultural catastrophe. If the locust invasion were a bit earlier, when the late crop had not yet sprouted,[11] this future harvest would remain untouched and unharmed and subsequently could be reaped; if the locusts came a bit later, the first crop would already have been harvested. Either way, earlier or later, at least one crop could have been saved. However, an attack precisely at this late-spring season of the year would consume both crops and culminate in a disastrous year of famine.

The last words of this verse[12] are usually interpreted as an explanatory gloss defining precisely the meaning of the hapax legomenon, לֶקֶשׁ:[13] "The late sowing is after the king's mowing" (גִּזֵּי הַמֶּלֶךְ).[14] However, they are more likely an additional description of the exacerbating situation, relating that whatever there was to reap before the locust assault had already been harvested for the king. It is probably a reference to some royal prerogative of reaping (for example, fodder for horses) that took place toward the end of the late-rain season. Thus the locust attack was "experienced" at the very time not only

5 For locusts, see Y. Palmoni, "Locust," *IDB* 3.144–48; compare Y. Feliks, *Animals in the Bible* (Tel Aviv: Sinai, 1956) 422–24 (Heb.). For this specific form of locust, see also Arab. *ǧābi'*; late Heb. and Aram. גּוֹבִי, גּוֹבָא, גּוֹבַאי. Compare Babylonian Talmud, Ḥullin 65a, "Locust (אַרְבֶּה) is גּוֹבַאי." See also Mishnah Berachoth 6:3. The name הגבה also appears on a seal as a patronymic accompanied by a pictorial illustration of its meaning, a locust. See N. Avigad, "A Hebrew Seal with a Family Emblem," *IEJ* 16 (1966) 50–53. T translates the last two words of Nah 3:15: "They shall devour you (יְחַסְלוּנִיךְ) like גּוֹבָא." The root חסל also designates another form of locust, חָסִיל; see 1 Kgs 8:37; Isa 33:4; Joel 1:4; 2:25; Ps 78:46; 2 Chr 6:28.

6 See Hammershaimb, 108.

7 See *AuS* I.411–12; VI.178, 212; E. Power, "Note to Amos 7, 1," *Bib* 8 (1927) 87–92. For the verb לקש, see Job 24:6: "They harvest (יִקְצֹרוּ) fodder in the field, and they glean the late grapes (יְלַקֵּשׁוּ) in the vineyards of the wicked." It also appears in Rabbinic Hebrew and Aramaic. Tur-Sinai (*Peshuṭo*, 469) suggests that לֶקֶשׁ itself was a type of locust, "perhaps even the source of Latin, *locusta.*" In the light of all the other Semitic analogues, this is unnecessary. Compare, too, Arab. *laqasa* ("to be late") and Syr. *leqsa* ("late-growing grass"). For the term *laqši/laqsi* in Palestinian Arabic to describe the late corn crop sown between the twentieth of January up until the end of February, see Power, "Note," 87–92.

8 See T, צִמּוּחַ. For עלה ("to grow, sprout") see, for example, Gen 40:10; Isa 5:6; Prov 24:31; Job 5:26.

9 So most commentators.

10 For the Gezer Calendar, see *KAI*, 1.182. These two months follow the two months of אסף ("gathering in the fruit crop"), that is, Tishri-Marheshvan; and זרע ("grain"), that is, Kislev-Tebeth.

11 Compare Exod 9:31–32 (as a result of the plague of hail): "Now the flax and barley were ruined, for the barley was in the ear and the flax was in bud; but the wheat and millet were not hurt, for they ripen late."

12 Several commentators read וְהַלֶּקֶשׁ instead of וְהִנֵּה־לֶקֶשׁ; for example, Ehrlich, *Randglossen*, 5.247; Sellin.

13 So Power, "Note," 89; Rudolph, 229; Wolff, 291–92. Some (including Hoffmann, Wellhausen, Löhr, Cheyne, Marti; for citations, see Harper, 160) have suggested that G, βροῦχος ("larva") may reflect an underlying Heb. יֶלֶק, another form of locust, which supposedly represents a later stage of growth after the גּוֹבִי (compare Joel 1:4). See Gordis, "Studies," 254.

14 This hapax legomenon does not refer to sheepshearing (for example, Gen 31:19; 38:12–13; Deut 18:4; Job 31:20), which takes place in the beginning of the summer, but to the mowing of grass (T, שִׁחֲתָא) in late spring. Compare Ps 72:6a: "Let him [= the king] be like rain that falls on a mown field" (גֵּז). This is the only biblical attestation of such a royal prerogative. See *AuS*, I.411–12. The reference in 1 Kgs 18:5 is to a different situation altogether, that is, an exceptional case of a famine year. Although there is a form of locust that is called גַּזִּין (see Babylonian Talmud, Shabbath 106b, and Rashi's commentary, in situ),

when both crops could not be salvaged but also after the king had taken his first share of the extant agricultural produce. For the nation the effect would be devastating and crippling.

Locusts are one of the classical biblical plagues, an instrument of the Lord's curse; see, for example, Exod 10:12ff.; Deut 28:42; Joel 1:4–12. So, too, in Mesopotamian sources where the onslaught of locusts is described literally as an invasion, *tibūt erbim*[15] ("an invasion of locusts"), which devours the country's crop: *erbu itebbīma še᾿i ebūrim ikkal* ("Locusts will invade and devour the barley crop");[16] *ebūr māti erbu ikkal* ("Locusts will eat the country's harvest").[17] The spring season is the time of their attack: "Like a spring *(ša pān šatti)* invasion of countless locusts."[18] In talmudic times, locusts are listed as one of the disasters for which the ram's horn is sounded and a public fast held (Mishnah Taʿanith 3:5).

■ **2** The prophet goes on to report that the locusts had completely destroyed all of the vegetation and crops: "When[19] it finished consuming[20] (וְהָיָה אִם־כִּלָּה לֶאֱכוֹל) the herbage of the land (עֵשֶׂב הָאָרֶץ)." Heb. עֵשֶׂב הָאָרֶץ is the comprehensive term employed to express plant growth necessary for man and animal.[21] The grain, vegetables, and fodder were entirely consumed by this invasion. Compare the plague in Exod 10:15, in which the locusts are similarly described as having "devoured all the herbage in the land" (וַיֹּאכַל אֶת־כָּל־עֵשֶׂב הָאָרֶץ).[22] In both accounts, moreover, the disastrous effects of the locust attack are followed by the direct intercession of the prophet—there Moses, here Amos—who pleads, "O my Lord God, please pardon" (סְלַח־נָא). The appellation אֲדֹנָי ה׳ is frequently found in the language of both prayers and lamentations.[23] Here it serves as the introduction to the brief supplication of the prophet, who petitions the Lord to pardon and forgive his people. The sum and substance of this plea, however, lies in the correct understanding of the verb סָלַח.[24] In the Bible, it

this does not fit the context here, against Budde, "Amos," 67–68; Cripps.

15 For locusts as a plague, see *CAD, E,* 257, c; for the different varieties of locusts, see *CAD, E,* 258; Landsberger, *Fauna,* 18ff., 121ff. For an "invasion of locusts," see Goetze, *Omen Texts,* 9 r 27; 11 iii 26: 18, 21.

16 *ABL,* 1214, r 12.

17 TCL 6, 1, r 20 in F. Thureau-Dangin, *Tablettes d'Uruk à l'usage des prêtres du temple d'Anu au temps des Séleucides* (Paris: Guethner, 1922). Note the paronomasia of *ebūr(u)* ("harvest") and *erbu* ("locust") in this and the above passage.

18 OIP, 2, 43:56 in Luckenbill, *Annals.*

19 Heb. אִם here has a temporal connotation, "when"; see, for example, Gen 38:9; Num 36:4; Isa 24:13. Compare Rashi and Kimchi. For a somewhat similar syntactical construction, see 1 Sam 1:12. Nevertheless, the style is a bit cumbersome and difficult. See n 20.

20 Many have accepted the slight emendation and redivision of the letters, וַיְהִי הָא מְכַלָּה ("And when it [= the locusts] was finishing . . ."), suggested by C. C. Torrey, "On the Text of Amos 5:26; 6:1, 2; 7:2," *JBL* 19 (1894) 83, for example, Wellhausen, Sellin, Driver, and Hammershaimb. Rudolph (229) accepts the suggestion of J. Huesman ("The Infinitive Absolute and *waw* + Perfect," *Bib* 37 [1956] 433), who points the verb as an infinitive absolute, וְהָיֹה, which would be equivalent to וַיְהִי but would not entail emending the text. See also Gese, "Komposition," 76 n 3 (who does not emend the text). According to this view, the locusts had not yet completed devouring the crops. Thus there still remained some time for the prophetic intercession. However, because this all takes place in a vision, one need not subject the contents of the vision to the needs of temporal necessity. See I. P. Seierstad, "Erlebnis und Gehorsam beim Propheten Amos," *ZAW* 52 (1934) 31–32; Reventlow, *Amt,* 51 (who also reads וַיְהִי). Note that Amos intercedes as well in the second vision (Amos 7:4–5) only after the action described is already completed; against Sellin.

21 See also Wolff, 297; compare Joel 1:4–12. The expression עֵשֶׂב הָאָרֶץ also appears in Ps 72:16; Job 5:25; see Gen 1:12. Compare the Akkadian equivalent, *šammi erṣeti, LKA,* 25 II 4. Akk. *šammu* also refers to more than mere grass. See *AHw,* 3.1156–57. Similarly, Heb. עֵשֶׂב הַשָּׂדֶה (for example, Gen 2:5; 3:18; Exod 10:15) is the cognate of Akk. *šammi ṣeri,* for example, *RA* 58 (1964) 73 E 11; *BoSt* 8, 32, 62; 50, 28 in E. F. Weidner, *Politische Dokumente aus Kleinasien, die Staatsverträge in akkadischer Sprache aus dem Archiv von Boghazköi* (Leipzig: Hinrichs, 1923).

22 The description of the locusts "devouring the herbage of the land"—which is unique to these two books—may point to yet another influence of the Book of Exodus upon Amos. See previously Amos 3:14.

23 See Wolff, 297. It repeatedly appears in the visions: Amos 7:1, 4, 5; 8:1.

24 Compare Ugar. *slḫ npš, UT,* 1757. See B. A. Levine, "Ugaritic Descriptive Rituals," *JCS* 17 (1963) 107; P. Xella, *I Testi Rituali di Ugarit* (Studi Semitici 54;

occurs only when the Deity is the subject or object and refers to an absolute and total pardon of sin.[25] Man may "forgive" (מחל) individual wrongdoings, but only God can grant complete "pardon" (סלח). The prophet's petitionary plea is that Israel's guilt (which is not directly mentioned, but is the basic assumption underlying the divine punishment) be completely expurgated. He requests an unconditional pardon. As such there would be no need to punish Israel anymore.

He then explicates his entreaty with the following words: "How[26] can Jacob[27] survive[28] (מִי יָקוּם יַעֲקֹב)? He is so small" (כִּי קָטֹן הוּא).[29] Note that Amos's appeal is not based on the hope of the possible repentance of the people. He does not call upon the traditional guarantees of salvation, nor does he cite the Lord's promises to the patriarchs. The prayer, moreover, is not even motivated by a reminder of Israel's election.[30] For the prophet the special status of Israel does not serve as a pretext for any favored treatment or privilege, but is rather the basis for judgment (compare Amos 3:2). Nevertheless, he immediately intercedes. The prophet, by resorting to the power of prayer, attempts to offset the nation's threatened doom. (Compare, for example, Gen 18:25; 20:7; Exod 32:11–14; Num 11:2; 14:13–20; 1 Sam 7:5–9; 12:19, 23; 15:11; Jer 4:10; 7:16; 11:14; 14:7–9; 15:1, 11; 18:20; Ezek 9:8; 11:13.) One of the most basic and prime functions of the prophet is to serve as an advocate for his people and to defend them by acting as an intercessory mediator between them and the Lord.[31] The prophet's duty is to represent the nation's cause by "standing in the breach" in times of ultimate danger (see Ezek 13:5; 22:30; Ps 106:23). Amos does not shirk from this onerous task for a moment and immediately becomes the attorney for the accused party. His intercession is predicated upon the quality of mercy inherent within the nature of the God of Israel. Jacob, the northern kingdom, is too small and helpless[32] (קָטֹן)[33] to survive such a catastrophe. The entire country would be ruined by such

Rome: Centro di Studi Semitici, Universita di Roma, 1981) 54, 56–57.

25 Note (in addition to the many references in the concordances) especially Exod 34:9; Num 14:19, where Moses, in his role as prophetic intercessor and covenantal mediator, appeals to the Lord with the same plea, סלח. See also J. Milgrom, "Vertical Retribution: Rumination on *Parashat Shelaḥ*," *Conservative Judaism* 34 (1981) 15.

26 For מִי as an interjection, "How," see also Ruth 3:16. See, too, Kimchi. It has also been suggested for Deut 33:11b, where the Samaritan reads מִי for the Masoretic מִן. Another possibility is to relate it to its later usage in Rabbinic Hebrew as an interrogative; see Gordis ("Studies," 255), who interprets it as an Aramism: "Will Jacob survive, for he is so small?" See Jastrow, *Dictionary*, 770.

27 יַעֲקֹב is one of the prophet's favorite names for northern Israel, for example, 3:13; 6:8; 7:5; 8:7; 9:8. There is no reason to assume that it refers here to both the northern and southern kingdoms; against Rudolph, 231 n 4. In the first two oracles Amos refers to "Jacob"; in the second two, to "Israel." According to Brin ("Visions," 284), the former reflects the past; the latter, the present.

28 For קום ("to endure, survive"), see 1 Sam 13:14; 24:21; Nah 1:6. (Compare also the Canaanite loanword in Mari, *qamat*, ARM, X:15. See W. von Soden, "Ugaritica V—Rezensionsartikel (I). Bemerkungen zu einigen literarischen Texten in akkadischer Sprach aus Ugarit," *UF* 1 [1969] 189–95; W. H. P. Römer, *Frauenbriefe über Religion, Politik, und Privatleben in Mari* [AOAT 12; Kevelaer: Bulzon und Bercker, 1971] 26.) There is thus no reason to emend to יָקִים, based on G, τίς ἀναστήσει τὸν Ιακωβ ("Who will raise up Jacob?"); against W. Brueggemann ("Amos' Intercessory Formula," *VT* 19 [1969] 393ff.), who interprets the phrase as "a disputation word, i.e., a rhetorical question which argues a court case."

29 The כִּי particle here may be interpreted as the emphatic כִּי. For its employment as an emphatic, see J. Muilenburg, "The Linguistic and Rhetorical Usages of the Particle *ki* in the Old Testament," *HUCA* 32 (1961) 145, 156.

30 See Vollmer, *Rückblicke*, 51.

31 See Paul, "Prophets," 1150–75. Because Amos already acts as an intercessor, the visions cannot have predated his call to prophecy; against Weiser, *Profetie*.

32 See the similar syntactical construction in Prov 22:22, כִּי דַל־הוּא ("because he is poor").

33 Heb. קָטֹן has also been interpreted in an economic sense; see Ehrlich, *Randglossen*, 5.247–48. See Hammershaimb, 109: "poor and ill-provided with resources, so that a catastrophe of this sort would mean their ruin"; see also Sellin. This has nothing to do with the size of the country, or whether or not the visions preceded the military conquests and territorial expansion of Jeroboam II; against Haran, "Rise and Decline," 266–97, esp. 272–78 (Heb.); idem, "Amos," 273 (Heb.). See, too, Rudolph, 231 n 5. In Rabbinic Hebrew קָטֹן also means "insignificant," similar to זְעֵיר in Aramaic. See S. Lieberman, "A Tragedy or a Comedy," *JAOS* 104 (1984) 318.

a plague. Amos does not say that they are worthy to be pardoned but relies entirely upon the pathos of God—appealing to him and praying that the attribute of mercy will overcome that of justice. The Lord has declared that he is a God who is "compassionate and gracious, slow to anger, rich in steadfast kindness, extending kindness to the thousandth generation, forgiving iniquity, transgression, and sin . . ." (Exod 34:6–7; compare Num 14:18).

■ **3** Intercession prevails. Israel is spared this time because the Lord consents to accept the prophetic plea. He "relented" and renounced (נִחַם עַל)[34] the punishment that was seen in the vision. For נִחַם עַל, in reference to the Lord's changing his decision and not executing a predicted calamity, see Exod 32:12, 14; Jer 18:8; Joel 2:13; Jonah 3:10; 4:2. (The variant נִחַם אֶל appears in 2 Sam 24:16; Jer 26:3, 13, 19; 42:10.) One of the prime attributes of the God of Israel is his willingness (at times) to relent and renounce. The Lord's compassion and mercy now overcome his justice and judgment. The gates of repentance still remain open.[35] However, there is no indication that he has *pardoned* his people as Amos had requested. The Lord does not respond here as he did to Moses, who (after the incident of the spies) prayed, "Pardon (סְלַח) the iniquity of this people. . . . And the Lord replied, 'I pardon, as you have asked'" (סָלַחְתִּי כִּדְבָרֶךָ), Num 14:19–20. In the response to the first vision, God relents but does not pardon. The guilt of Israel has not been expunged; only the punishment has been offset and postponed. All that the Lord promises is that "it shall not happen." Amos has obtained a reprieve, not a pardon.

■ **4** The second vision shares several basic characteristics with the first one. They both commence with a formal introductory presentation of the vision itself: כֹּה הִרְאַנִי אֲדֹנָי ה׳[36] וְהִנֵּה, followed by a participle (קֹרֵא/יוֹצֵר), whose subject, the Lord, is drawn from the introductory clause. In both visions the object that is seen (locusts, fire) causes devastating results by "devouring and consuming" (אָכְלָה, וַתֹּאכַל, לֶאֱכוֹל). This disastrous scene is followed by Amos's intercessory prayer, which, except for the change in the appeal itself (חֲדַל, סְלַח), is motivated by the very same words he employed in his first plea (כִּי קָטֹן הוּא). Both visions then conclude with the Deity renouncing his decision (נִחַם עַל . . . לֹא תִהְיֶה). Nevertheless, the vision itself is new, the punishment is intensified, and the prophet's outcry is slightly, but significantly, different.

"This is what my Lord God showed me: Lo, my Lord God was summoning (קֹרֵא). . . ."[37] The next two words, לָרִב בָּאֵשׁ, have been interpreted in various ways. Many have suggested that קֹרֵא לָרִב בָּאֵשׁ should be translated "was summoning to contend by fire."[38] This would mean that the Lord was calling forth a legal contest to contend with his people and judge them with the punishment of fire.[39] See Isa 66:15–16: "See the Lord is coming with

According to Brin ("Visions," 279), it refers to the "weak" part of the society, the poor and destitute.

Brueggemann ("Amos' Intercessory Formula," *VT* 19 [1969] 393ff.), however, suggests that the word "small" should be understood in the context of covenant liturgy and lawsuit. He states that it refers to one who "lacks the legal credentials to make a claim for himself and . . . who is totally dependent on another for his position or power which is not his right but a gift granted to him" (p. 387). He connects this with the use here of "Jacob," which, according to him, is a "theological" appeal to the patriarchal tradition. "The covenant people is still totally dependent upon Yahweh" (p. 388). This is thus an intercessory prayer reminding the Lord of his obligation and commitment to Israel. He also relates this unilateral action to the southern covenant tradition. See D. N. Freedman, "Divine Commitment and Human Obligation," *Int* 18 (1964) 419–31.

See also the study of E. Jacob, "Prophètes et intercesseurs," in *De la Tôrah au Messie: Études d'exégèse et d'herméneutique bibliques offertes à Henri Cazelles* (ed. J. Doré, P. Grelot, and M. Carrez; Paris: Desclée, 1981) 205–17, esp. 210–11.

34 The verb in these passages does not mean "to repent." See the remarks of Ehrlich, *Randglossen*, 5.248. Heb. נִחַם here is a *niphʿal.* G, by translating the verb as an imperative, *μετανόησον* (= Heb. הִנָּחֵם; "Repent") interprets v 3a as the conclusion of Amos's prayer.

35 Compare the message of the Book of Jonah. See also Jer 18:7–10.

36 Tur-Sinai (*Peshuṭo,* 470) again reads here וְהִנֵּהוּ.

37 Compare also 2 Kgs 8:1; Ps 105:16, where the Lord "summons" (קרא) a famine; and Jer 25:29; Ezek 38:21—"the sword." See also Amos 5:8; 9:6 for the similar construction קרא ל . . . ו.

38 Many commentators.

39 See J. Limburg, "Amos 7:4: A Judgment with Fire?" *CBQ* 35 (1973) 346–49.

fire. . . . For with fire will the Lord contend" (בָּאֵשׁ ה' נִשְׁפָּט). The Heb. רִב (written without a *yod* also in Exod 23:2; Prov 25:8; Job 13:6 [plural]; 29:16; 31:13) is a technical term that signifies a legal disputation in which Israel is put on trial for the crimes it has committed. This is a well-known motif and pattern in prophetic literature.[40] The problem is, however, that in just such instances the next word, introduced by the particle ־בּ, should point to the party accused, for example, Gen 31:36; Judg 6:32; Hos 2:4.[41] But here בָּאֵשׁ does not refer to the accused against whom God is contending but rather to the means whereby he is about to execute his judgment.

Thus many emendations have been offered in order to resolve this difficulty:[42] God is summoning לַהֲבוֹת אֵשׁ (Ps 29:7); לַבַּת־אֵשׁ (Exod 3:2); לַהַב אֵשׁ (Isa 29:6; 30:30; 66:15; Joel 2:5); שְׁבִיב אִשּׁוֹ (Job 18:5; see Dan 3:22; 7:9; Sir 8:10; 45:19); all denoting a "flame" or "spark of fire." Another suggestion relates the expression לָרִב בָּאֵשׁ to a controversial hapax legomenon in Ugaritic, *d̠bb*, which, because of its paired parallelism with *ʾist*, is presumed somehow to be related to "fire."[43] The tortuous assumption is that the original reading in Amos was לדבב אש, which became corrupted to לרבב אש and was subsequently divided incorrectly to לרב באש. However, it is doubtful whether Ugar. *d̠bb*, whose exact meaning itself is still unclear, would be transcribed into Hebrew with a ד because Ugar. *d̠* normally appears as a ז.

Two additional, plausible suggestions are an alternate word division, reading לִרְבִב אֵשׁ ("a rain of fire"),[44] or an assumed dittography of the letter ב, that is, לָרֹב אֵשׁ ("a mighty fire/strong blazing heat").[45]

Although the difficulty of interpretation still exists, clearly the rod of God's wrath in this vision is אֵשׁ, which most likely refers to a scorching, burning "heat"[46] that "devours" both the land and sea and results in a deadly famine and drought. Compare similarly Joel 1:19–20: "To you, O Lord, I call. For blazing heat (אֵשׁ) has consumed (אָכְלָה) the pastures in the wilderness and scorching heat (לֶהָבָה) has devoured all the trees of the countryside. The very beasts of the field cry out to you. For the water courses are dried up and blazing heat (אֵשׁ) has consumed (אָכְלָה) the pastures in the wilderness." (Compare also Joel 2:3.)[47]

In the present vision this fiery heat is seen as drying up the "great deep" (תְּהוֹם רַבָּה), that is, the cosmic deep,

40 For literature on the רִיב, see H. B. Huffmon, "The Covenant Lawsuit in the Prophets," *JBL* 78 (1959) 285–95; J. Harvey, "Le '*rib*-Pattern.' Requisitore prophétique sur la rupture de l'alliance," *Bib* 43 (1962) 172–96; idem, *Le plaidoyer prophétique contre Israël après la rupture de l'alliance* (Travaux de recherche 22; Bruges and Paris: Desclée de Brouwer, 1967); Sinclair, "Courtroom Motif," 351–53; S. Amsler, "Le thème du procès chez les prophètes d'Israël," *RTP* 24 (1974) 116–31.

41 For example, Wolff, 292; Hammershaimb, 110. The latter connects בָּאֵשׁ with קָרָא, "He called to the fire"; לָרִיב is interpreted absolutely, "to judgment." Both the syntax and קָרָא ־בּ ("call to"), however, are very difficult to accept.

42 For the various suggested emendations, see Harper; S. Talmon, "The Ugaritic Background of Amos 7:4," *Tarbiz* 35 (1965–1966) 301–3 (Heb.).

43 Talmon, "The Ugaritic Background." The text in question is *CTA*: 30:42–43: *mḫšt.klbt.ʾilm.ʾišt* ("I smote the bitch of El, Fire"); *klt.bt.ʾil.d̠bb* ("I destroyed the daughter of El, *d̠bb*"). For the various interpretations of *d̠bb*, see Talmon. It should be noted, however, that in the corresponding cola different powers are mentioned each time.

44 See M. Krenkel ("Zur Kritik und Exegese der kleinen Propheten," *ZWT* 14 [1866] 271), followed and expanded by Hillers ("Amos 7:4," 221–25) and accepted by Wolff, 293, 298. This reading preserves the consonantal text. Although in Hebrew the substantive is found only in the plural, רְבִיבִים (Deut 32:2; Jer 3:3; 14:22; Mic 5:6; Pss 65:11; 72:6), it appears in Ugaritic also in the singular, both *rbb* and *rb*, in parallelism with *ṭl* ("dew"); *CTA* 19:44: *bl ṭl bl rbb*. (It has been suggested by Hillers ["Amos 7:4," 224 n 6] and others that the singular form is found once in the Bible, in Job 36:28b, but this is still questionable.) Hillers also brings references to the destruction of a sea monster by lightning in Hittite and Greek literature. This motif is further developed by Miller, "Fire," 256–61.

45 So Ehrlich, *Mikrâ*, 3.413, and *Randglossen*, 5.248. Elsewhere Heb. רֹב, of course, almost always refers to a multiple quantity. See n 50.

46 Ehrlich, *Randglossen*, 5.248: "eine starke Feuersglut, eine grosse Dürre" ("a strong blazing heat, a great dryness"). See already ibn Ezra and Kimchi.

47 The motif of אֵשׁ ("fire") recurrently appears in Amos: 1:4, 7, 10, 12, 14; 2:2, 5; 5:6.

which according to biblical cosmogony lies beneath the earth and is the source of all the springs and rivers.[48] The imagery here is drawn from the ancient Near Eastern mythological tale of the primeval conflict between the Deity and the primordial monster of the subterranean ocean. In many of these descriptions, supernatural fire appears as one of the weapons employed by the Deity. This motif of a god wielding fire against his enemies is transferred in the Bible from the realm of mythology to that of prophetic imagery.[49] The term "great"[50] also describes the "deep" (תְּהוֹם רַבָּה) in Gen 7:11; Isa 51:10; Ps 36:7; and Ps 78:15, where the plural form appears, תְּהֹמוֹת. The connection between the Deity's primordial victory over the mammoth maritime monster of the deep and the drying up of its waters appears clearly in Isa 51:9–10, "It was you who hacked Rahab in pieces, that pierced the Dragon. It was you who dried up the Sea, the waters of the great deep" (תְּהוֹם רַבָּה).[51]

This blazing fire and heat consumes not only the sources of water but all the "fields" (חֵלֶק)[52] as well. The repetition of the verb אכל ("to consume"; תֹּאכַל–אָכְלָה)[53] relates first to the water supply and then to all the tillable land, thereby expressing a merism for total desiccation.[54] The consequences of the second vision are therefore even more severe than those of the first.[55]

■ **5** The prophetic intercession, although similarly motivated as before, is distinguished here by a change in the plea itself. In place of "pardon" (סְלַח), the prophet beseeches the Lord, "cease" (חֲדַל).[56] The supplication to

48 See O. Kaiser, *Die mythische Bedeutung des Meeres in Ägypten, Ugarit und Israel* (BZAW 78; Berlin: Töpelmann, 1959) 45–49.

49 See Hillers ("Amos 7:4") and Miller ("Fire") for additional evidence for the significance of fire in the mythology of the ancient Near East and the motif of the gods using it as a weapon against their enemies. See also Limburg, "Amos 7:4."

50 Heb. רַב means "many," but in Ugar. "great." See M. D. Cassuto, *The Goddess Anat: Canaanite Epics of the Patriarchal Age* (tr. I. Abrahams; Jerusalem: Magnes, 1971) 35.

51 An additional reason for the use of רַבָּה here may be for paronomasia; both רב and רבה appear in the same sentence. This was already alluded to by Ehrlich, *Mikrâ*, 3.413.

52 Because of the assumed "weakness" of the imagery, two alternative suggestions have been made. Ehrlich (*Mikrâ*, 3.413, and *Randglossen*, 5.248) reads וְאָכְלָה אֹתָהּ חָלָק ("und frass ihn [den grossen Ocean] kahl, d. i., wasserleer machen") ("and consumed it [the great ocean] completely, that is, to make dry"). Tur-Sinai (*Peshuṭo*, 470) emends to וְאָכְלָה אֹתָהּ לַחֵךְ, based on 1 Kgs 18:38: "Then fire (אֵשׁ) from the Lord descended and consumed (וַתֹּאכַל) . . . ; and it licked up (לִחֵכָה) the water (הַמַּיִם) that was in the trench." Both are unnecessary. Other commentators follow a variant reading of G, τὴν μερίδα κυρίου (= Heb. חֵלֶק ה׳, "the Lord's portion," that is, the land of Israel); see Deut 32:9. This, however, is acknowledged as a later addition. See J. Ziegler, *Die Einheit der Septuaginta zum Zwölfprophetenbuch* (lectures delivered at Braunsberg, Staaliche Akademie, 1934–1935) 198.

For חֵלֶק ("field") see 2 Kgs 9:10, 36, 37, all connected with יִזְרְעֶאל, "the field of Jezreel." Heb. חֵלֶק (see also חֶלְקָה) is most likely related by metathesis to Akk. *eqlu* ("field") and Aram. חַקְלָא. See also Hos 5:7.

53 See M. Held, "The *YQTL-QTL (QTL-YQTL)* Sequence of Identical Verbs in Biblical Hebrew and Ugaritic," in *Studies and Essays in Honor of Abraham A. Neuman* (ed. M. ben Horin, B. D. Weinryb, and S. Zeitlin; Leiden: Brill, 1962) 281–90; idem, "The Action-Result (Factitive Passive) Sequence of Identical Verbs in Biblical Hebrew and Ugaritic," *JBL* 84 (1961) 272–82. See also S. Gevirtz, "Evidence of Conjugational Variation in the Parallelization of Selfsame Verbs in the Amarna Letters," *JNES* 32 (1973) 99–104; M. D. Cassuto, "Il palazzo di Baʿal nella tavola II AB di Ras Shamra," *Or* 7 (1938) 288–89. In Ugaritic, see *CTA*, 3 B ii 40–41; 4 vi 38–40; 19 iii 114–15.

54 Rudolph (232), following Hitzig and others, remarks that וְאָכְלָה in distinction from וַתֹּאכַל connotes incomplete action. So, too, Wolff, 293: "It devoured the great abyss, and it was about to devour the acreage."

Note that the same sequence of striking first the food and then the water supplies is followed in the first two plague curses of Amos 4.

55 See Gese, "Komposition," 76: "Die zweite Vision ist eine Steigerung dieser Vegetationsbedrohung" ("The second vision is an intensification of the threat against the vegetation"). He also views the first two visions as "a pair threatening the totality of destruction" (p. 77).

For the cosmic dimensions of this vision, see also Robinson-Horst, 198; Reventlow, *Amt*, 39; Maag, *Text*.

56 For the absolute use of חדל, see Jer 40:4; 41:8; Ezek 3:27. T and S harmonized the two visions by translating here "Pardon" (שְׁבוֹק).

cease and resist[57] relates to the execution of the punishment; it is not a prayer for total forgiveness. Amos pleads with God that he desist from the disastrous plague foreseen in the vision. Because his first appeal for complete pardon was not granted, Amos can only attempt now to rely upon God's attribute of mercy and kindness.

■ **6** Once again Amos is successful in his role as intercessor: this punishment "too (גַּם־הִיא) shall not happen."[58] "Dieses Auch untermalt nicht nur die stetige Bereitschaft des Amos . . . sondern vor allem die göttliche Langmut" ("This 'too' emphasizes not only the constant readiness of Amos . . . but in particular the divine forbearance").[59] Once more punishment is annulled; but pardon is not granted.

There appears to be an analogy here between the visions and the plague curses of chapter 4. In both instances Israel initially had the opportunity to forestall future punishment by changing their conduct. Because the plagues proved ineffectual, however, the people were destined to face ultimate consequences (4:12). So, too, the first two visions, even though they were not actualized because of prophetic intercession, should have served as dire harbingers of what was in store for them if they remained adamant and obdurate. Because they did not mend their ways, however, the concomitant catastrophes that appeared in the prophet's visions would no longer be delayed. The Lord could be beseeched no more. The execution of punishment becomes irretrievable and irrevocable.

■ **7** The third and fourth visions share the same introductory clause with the first two visions: כֹּה הִרְאַנִי[60] . . . וְהִנֵּה[61]. Their connection with the first two is also indicated by their identical concluding clause, "I will pardon them no more" (לֹא־אוֹסִיף עוֹד עֲבוֹר לוֹ, 7:8; 8:2), where "no more" refers directly to the double reprieve granted above: twice yes; a third and fourth time, no. These latter two visions, however, do not present action events in which the prophet is witness to wholesale destruction but rather describe images that are to be interpreted symbolically. The prophet, unaware of the symbolic significance of what he sees, is then apprised by the Lord of the punishment inherent within the vision.

In the third vision Amos beholds "the Lord standing by[62] a wall of אֲנָךְ, with אֲנָךְ in his hand." The perplexing problem is the interpretation of the word אֲנָךְ, which appears four times in this vision but nowhere else in the entire Bible. The substantive אֲנָךְ is a loanword from Akk. *annaku,* "tin."[63] Thus the usual meaning "plumb

57 See Rudolph, 233; it refers to the cessation of that which is already happening.

58 For the sequence of זֹאת followed by הִיא, see Ps 118:23.

59 Rudolph, 233.

60 Once again Tur-Sinai *(Peshuṭo)* suggests reading וְהִנֵּהוּ. The variant G reading ἀνήρ ("man"; "And behold there was a man") was most likely influenced by Zech 1:8; 2:5. It is accepted, however, by Reventlow (*Amt,* 37), who also compares Ezek 40:3ff.; see also Soggin, 115. G. R. Driver's resort here to his hypothesis of abbreviations—'א = אֲדֹנָי misunderstood as 'א = אִישׁ—is very farfetched ("Abbreviations in the Masoretic Text," *Textus* 1 [1960] 130).

61 Harper, Cripps, Robinson, and Wolff (299) insert יהוה with G and V immediately after הִרְאַנִי, as in Amos 7:1, 4. The Hebrew text in this verse has אֲדֹנָי after הִנֵּה. This vision has an abbreviated introduction, just כֹּה הִרְאַנִי ("Thus he showed me"). The lack of stereotypic uniformity is characteristic of the style of Amos. See comments to chapters 1 and 2. The pattern of the third and fourth visions—presentation of a vision, initial description, question posed by God to the prophet, the latter's reply repeating the description, followed by the Deity's explanation—is common to Jer 1:11–12, 13–19; 24:1ff. See Niditsch (*Vision,* 23–24) for this literary tradition.

62 Heb. נִצָּב עַל may mean "standing upon" or "standing near"; for the latter, for example, Gen 18:2; 24:13; see also Amos 9:1. See M. Weinfeld ("Ancient Near Eastern Patterns in Prophetic Literature," *VT* 27 [1977] 186), who draws attention to a pattern in dream revelations in Mari in which a figure in a vision "stands up" (Akk. *izziz*) beside the seer; for example, ARM X 51:9.

63 See *CAD, A,* II.127–30. This was definitively determined by B. Landsberger, "Tin and Lead—The Adventures of Two Vocables," *JNES* 24 (1965) 285–96. (Thus Wolff's statement, 300, is completely incorrect.) See also Z. Schneider ("Looking for the Source of Tin in the Ancient Near East," *Qadmoniot* 15 [1982] 98–102 [Heb.]), who cites many recent studies in the English bibliography at the end of his article. He does not refer, however, to the passage in

line,"[64] which is set against the wall to measure its straightness, must now be discarded. The word simply does not mean "lead" and thus cannot be a "plumb" line, which, of course, exacerbates the difficulty. There is no such thing as a "tin" line, and a "wall of tin" does not exist. Walls are constructed of many elements, for example, stone or various metals, but not of tin. Tin, moreover, is not attested as a decorative plating or embossing for walls. Faced with such imponderables, scholars have made various proposals (even before the meaning "tin" was clarified). Some suggest that the first אֲנָךְ is a dittography of the second (which many assumed incorrectly to mean "plumb line") and therefore delete it: "The Lord was standing on/by a wall" (חוֹמָה).[65] Others prefer the reading אֶבֶן ("stone") for אֲנָךְ and see the Lord standing on a "wall of stone."[66] A few exegetes maintain the reading אֲנָךְ but interpret it not as "tin" but either metaphorically as a perpendicular wall[67] or conjecturally as some type of instrument (pickax, crowbar),[68] which is employed in the demolishing of the wall: "The Lord is standing on a wall destined for the pickax, and in his hand is a pickax." With this meaning, however, the prophet would have had some inkling of the destructive nature of the instrument and would have responded accordingly. He would not have needed any divine exegesis. However, neither here nor in the fourth vision is he the least aware of the exact nature or the function of the object he sees.

If one then returns to the only established and documented meaning of the noun אֲנָךְ ("tin"), how then can the scene be interpreted? It certainly does not imply that if "Yahweh is able to commandeer such an immense amount of that strategic metal for manufacturing bronze weaponry against Israel, then Israel is lost indeed."[69] The word refers to tin and not to bronze, and weapons are not made out of tin per se. Moreover, there is no indication in the vision that this tin is alloyed with another metal to produce arms.[70] Furthermore, the

Amos. To his bibliography may also be added R. J. Forbes, *Studies in Ancient Technology* (9 vols.; Leiden: Brill, 1964) 9.124–60, and J. E. Dayton, "The Problem of Tin in the Ancient World," *World Archeology* 3 (1971) 49–70. See also J. D. Muhly, *Copper and Tin: The Distribution of Mineral Resources and the Nature of the Metals Trade in the Bronze Age* (Transactions of the Connecticut Academy of Arts and Sciences 43; New Haven: Yale University, 1973) 243.

64 Lat. *plumbum* = "lead." This is the standard exegesis of the passage; see 2 Kgs 21:13; Isa 28:17; 34:11; Lam 2:8. It was understandable prior to Landsberger's study; however, now it is no longer warranted. The assumed expanded interpretation "lead ⟩ lead weight ⟩ plumb line" seems to be attested only from medieval times. See A. Condamin ("Le prétendu 'fils à plomb' de la vision d'Amos," *RB* 9 [1900] 586–94), who translates "weapon." Compare G. Brunet, "La vision de l'étain: réinterprétation d'Amos 7:7–9," *VT* 16 (1966) 387–95, esp. 388. A plumb line, of course, serves the opposite purpose. It is used in construction to determine perpendicularity and is not employed for destructive purposes. All walls would be constructed with such an instrument. However, in this expression אֲנָךְ would have to refer to the material of which the wall was constructed and not the means by which it was constructed. In biblical Hebrew the word for "lead" is עֹפֶרֶת, which is a loanword from Akk. *abāru;* see B. Landsberger, "Einige unerkannt gebliebene oder verkannte Nomina des Akkadischen," *WZKM* 56 (1960) 117; idem, "Tin and Lead," 285ff.; and the word for "tin" is בְּדִיל, which is a loanword from Sanskrit, *pātīra.* Note that the same meaning, "plummet," has been suggested for the latter in the passage Zech 4:10, הָאֶבֶן הַבְּדִיל. However, this is very problematic.

65 For example, Oort, "Amos," 121; Weiser, *Profetie;* Harper; Robinson-Horst; Cripps; Hammershaimb, 111.

66 For example, Wellhausen; Sellin²; Maag, *Text;* Seierstad, *Offenbarungserlebnisse,* 54 n 2; Tur-Sinai, *Peshuṭo,* 470; Wolff; Rudolph, 234. Although these commentators did not note it, such an expression does appear in Akk. *dūr-abni* ("a wall of stone"). See *CAD, D,* 193. Others have suggested emending חוֹמָה to חֵמַת ("glowing [tin]"), for example, van Hoonacker; H. Junker, "Text und Bedeutung der Vision Amos 7:7–9," *Bib* 17 (1936) 359–64. The latter then relates this to the molten lead poured down a criminal's throat to execute the capital punishment of burning in talmudic times. This is totally unnecessary and unsupported by the present text, as is also the suggestion of A. Bruno (*Das Buch der Zwölf. Eine rhythmische und textkritische Untersuchung* [Stockholm: Almquist & Wiksell, 1957] to read מַחְתַּת ("a pan").

67 See Reventlow, *Amt,* 40.

68 See Rudolph (234, 235), who adds correctly that this image cannot be interpreted as a test, that is, testing the straightness of the wall. Because in the first two visions Israel has already been found worthy of punishment, no further proof is required.

69 Brunet ("Vision"), who concludes that אֲנָךְ becomes synonymous with "sword." See also Gese,

symbol is not dependent upon its assumed immense quantity.

Another suggested approach to the understanding of the text is as follows:[71] When walls of metal are mentioned in ancient Near Eastern texts, they occasionally bear a metaphorical or symbolical dimension. Thus in Egyptian texts Seti I is portrayed as a "wall of bronze for Egypt with crenellations of flint" and "a great wall of copper," which protects his soldiers. His son, Rameses II, while addressing his troops before the battle of Qadesh, describes himself as "your wall of iron." In an Akkadian text from El Amarna, Abimilki of Tyre addresses Pharaoh, "You are the sun which rises over me and a wall of bronze *(dūr siparri)* erected for me."[72] Similarly in the Bible, the Lord promises Jeremiah that he will be unassailable against the attacks of the people, because he is making him "a fortified city, and an iron pillar, and bronze walls" (חֹמוֹת נְחֹשֶׁת; Jer 1:18; compare Jer 15:20). Compare likewise the symbolic siege of Jerusalem constructed by the prophet Ezekiel (4:3), which also employs the image of an "iron wall" (קִיר בַּרְזֶל). (Compare 2 Macc 11:9.) If, then, walls of iron and bronze symbolize strong fortified walls, a wall of tin would be the very opposite. This metal is a symbol of softness, uselessness, and perishability[73] (if not alloyed with another metal). Thus in this vision the "wall" of Israel is portrayed as being extremely weak, not durable, and on the verge of being demolished. The probability still very likely exists that there is more in this vision (a possible double entendre on אֲנָךְ?) than meets the eye, and thus it is no wonder that the prophet, as well as his exegetes, remains baffled by its symbolism.

■ **8** The abbreviated dialogue now commences. The prophet, unaware of the symbolic significance of the אֲנָךְ and the perishable wall of tin, when questioned by the Deity, "What do you see?" can only respond by calling the item by its name,[74] "אֲנָךְ."[75] It is now the Lord's turn to supply the necessary explanation.[76] He declares that he is "setting אֲנָךְ in the midst of my people Israel. I will pardon them no more."

The applying of אֲנָךְ apparently refers here symbolically to the execution of judgment.[77] See 2 Kgs 21:13; Isa 28:17; 34:11; Lam 2:8, where קַו ("measuring line") and/or מִשְׁקֹלֶת ("weights") symbolize the meting out of judgment and retribution[78] as the plan of God's action.[79]

"Komposition," 80–81.

70 See the study by J. Ouellette, "Le mur d'étain dans Amos, VII, 7–9," *RB* 80 (1973) 321–31. Brunet ("Vision") and A. Condamin ("Le prétendu 'fil à plomb' de la vision d'Amos," *RB* 9 [1980] 586–94) also interpret the image symbolically, relating to war and destruction. Tin, however, being a very soft metal, must be alloyed with other metals for any practical (and martial) use. As Ouellette correctly points out, however, there is nothing in the text to lead one to interpret that the tin here is alloyed for the fabrication of arms. (See also A. Malamat, "Tin Inventory," *IEJ* 21 [1971] 31–38.)

71 The quotations are cited from J. Ouellette ("Le mur d'étain," 324f.), and from A. R. Millard ("King Og's Bed and Other Ancient Ironmongery," in *Ascribe to the Lord: Biblical and Other Studies in Memory of Peter C. Craigie* [ed. L. Eslinger and G. Taylor; JSOT Supp 67; Sheffield: JSOT, 1988] 490), who cites additional Egyptian and Hittite references. Ouellette himself leaves the problem unresolved (pp. 328, 330), as does W. L. Holladay, "Once More אֲנָךְ = 'Tin,' Amos VII 7–8," *VT* 20 (1970) 492–94. See also C. van Leeuwen, "Quelques problèmes de traduction dans les visions d'Amos chapitre 7," in *Übersetzung und Deutung: Studien zu dem Alten Testament und seiner Umwelt, A. R. Hulst gemidmet von Freunden und Kollegen* (ed. H. A. Brongers and others; Nijkerk: Callenbuch, 1977) 103–12; and H. S. Mackenzie, "The Plumb-Line: Amos VII:8," *ExpTim* 60 (1949) 159.

72 *EA*, 147:53. For examples from classical literature, see Gese, "Komposition," 80–81 n 18.

73 B. Landsberger, "Tin and Lead," 287.

74 See Jer 1:11; 24:3; Zech 5:2.

75 The attempt to discover here onomatopoeia based on the Hebrew roots אנח/אנק ("to sigh") is very tortuous and unconvincing; against Horst, "Visionsschilderungen," 201, and Gese, "Komposition," 81–82.

76 For the question-answer dialogue as characterizing a didactic style, see P. Volz, *Der Prophet Jeremiah* (KAT 10; Leipzig: Deichert, 1928) 9; Wolff.

77 Ehrlich, *Randglossen*, 5.249; see T, "Behold I shall exact judgment" (עָבִיד דִּין).

78 It does not refer to "testing," as it is already clear from the first visions that Israel is guilty. No more proof is necessary.

79 Budde's suggestion ("Amos," 76) to read בְּקִרֹת ("in the walls") instead of בְּקֶרֶב ("in the midst of") has been accepted by Sellin², Deden, Maag *(Text)*, Robinson-Horst, and Rudolph (234) as referring to the "wall" (חוֹמָה) mentioned in the previous verse. This emendation, however, is superfluous. Not only is the Hebrew word for "wall" different, but there is no

The divine resolve is one of demolition, but it is a very painful decision.[80] Those about to be punished are still called by the Lord, "my people Israel" (עַמִּי יִשְׂרָאֵל).[81] "Israel" here, as always in Amos, refers to the northern kingdom. They are still his beloved chosen people. With them he contracted a covenant (3:2). But precisely for that reason they are being punished. Israel has failed to live up to its covenantal responsibility and has thus forfeited its rights of election and selection. Thus God declares, "I will pardon them no more." This time he neither relents nor changes his decision.

At this dramatic juncture Amos refrains from responding and interceding, as he had done in the first two visions. He asks neither for pardon nor for cessation of the impending punishment. Having heard the Lord's explanation and decision, he realizes that the die is cast; intervention is no longer feasible or possible. The delaying of punishment has come to an end. The divine decree is now final and absolute and precludes any possibility of prophetic intercession. When the Lord refuses to "pass by" (עבר ל), that is, pardon[82] his people, he will ultimately "pass through" them (עבר בְּקִרְבְּ, 5:17).[83] In this vision not a messenger or an agent of the Deity (the plagues of locusts, fire/heat) appears, but the Lord himself, who is about to render judgment.[84] This appearance may also help explain why Amos does not even attempt to intercede.[85]

■ **9** The specific details of the imminent punishment are now delineated.[86] The mainstays of Israel's existence—both cultic (its sites of worship) as well as secular (its reigning dynasty)—are destined for extermination.[87]

The "high places" (בָּמוֹת) that "shall become desolate" (נָשַׁמּוּ) do not refer to unauthorized sites of worship of the Lord or to high places that served as centers for idol worship.[88] They are the legitimate sacrificial high places that existed all over the country prior to the reforms of Hezekiah and Josiah (2 Kgs 18:3–6; 22—23). Before that time there was nothing objectionable about the worship of the Deity at these cultic sites (for example, 1 Sam 9:12; 1 Kgs 3:4). Here, however, they represent, along with the "sanctuaries of Israel" (מִקְדְּשֵׁי יִשְׂרָאֵל) that "shall be ruined" (יֶחֱרָבוּ),[89] the entire religious establishment that Amos time and again censures and condemns (see 3:14). The prophet refers to them as the "high places of Isaac," written יִשְׂחָק instead of the usual יִצְחָק. Compare also v 16 (where the order Israel-Isaac is chiastically

need to demand an exact one-to-one relation between the visions and their explanations. Of course, according to Rudolph's explanation of אֲנָךְ as an instrument of destruction, the demolition of the walls becomes self-evident.

80 Also Rudolph, 236.

81 See Amos 7:15.

82 Although עבר ל designating "pardon" does not appear elsewhere, the similar expression עבר עַל is found in Mic 7:18; Prov 19:11. See Crenshaw ("Theophanic Tradition," 200–215, esp. 206–7) for the phrase עבר ל as part of theophanic vocabulary. For the meaning "to forgive" see Sellin; Würthwein, "Amos-Studien," 30; Harper, 166; Cripps, 226; Lindblom, *Prophecy*, 338.

83 See Exod 12:12.

84 In the first two visions, Amos pleads that Israel *could* not survive. In the second two, the Lord declares that Israel *should* not survive. See Mays, 132–33.

85 See Würthwein, "Amos-Studien," 32. He suggests (p. 34) that "es ist dieser Wandel in Jahwe selber, der den Unterschied zwischen den beiden ersten und den folgenden Visionen bedingt" ("It is this change in Yahweh himself which causes the difference between the first two and the following visions"). However, Weiser (*Profetie*, 270), Lehming ("Erwägungen," 145–69), and Reventlow (*Amt*, 33) propose a change within the prophet. Compare the latter, "Der Wandel erklärt sich aus einem veränderten Gotterserleben des Propheten" ("The change is accounted for by the prophet's varying experience of the Deity").

86 Several commentators (for example, Weiser, *Profetie;* Watts, *Vision*, 41; Wolff) contend that v 9 is a later addition. See, however, the cogent rebuttals of Rudolph, 237, 239 n 7; and Gese, "Komposition," 78: "Das formale Argument, dass die Vision rein weiteres Drohwort enthalten dürfe, ist angesichts der letzten Vision—vgl. ix 2ff.—hinfällig" ("The formal argument that the vision absolutely must contain an additional threat is, in view of the last vision [cf. 9:2ff.], untenable").

87 Note the chiastic structure of the first two stichs and the repetition of the letter מ in the first two words of the verse (וְנָשַׁמּוּ בָּמוֹת).

For the combination of the destruction of the secular institutions along with the cultic, see also Amos 3:14–15.

88 See Sellin²: "Einfach alle heiligen Höhen des Landes, ohne jeden tadelnden Nebengedanken an eine Illegitimität" ("Simply all the high places of the land without any censuring second thoughts about their illegitimacy"). Cf. Hammershaimb, 112.

89 For שמם parallel to חרב, see Isa 49:19; 61:4; Ezek 6:6; 36:4, 35; Zeph 3:6. For the "laying waste" (שמם)

reversed); Jer 33:26; Ps 105:9.[90]

Along with the cultic establishment, the "house of Jeroboam" (בֵּית יָרָבְעָם), that is, the dynasty of the northern kingdom, will also fall by the sword.[91] No enemy is mentioned as executing this judgment. It will be put into operation by the Lord himself: "I will rise up against" (וְקַמְתִּי עַל)[92] the royal house. The threat actually materialized a bit later when Zechariah, the son of Jeroboam II, was assassinated (2 Kgs 15:10), thus ending the dynasty that "was in accord with the word that the Lord had spoken to Jehu: 'Four generations of your descendants shall occupy the throne of Israel'" (2 Kgs 15:12).

For a striking similarity to the vocabulary and the threats of punishment in this verse, compare Lev 26:30–33, "I will destroy your high places (בָּמֹתֵיכֶם) . . . , and I will make your sanctuaries desolate (וַהֲשִׁמּוֹתִי אֶת מִקְדְּשֵׁיכֶם) . . . , and I will unsheath the sword (חֶרֶב) against you."

---

of "shrines" (מִקְדָּשִׁים), see Lev 26:31; and "high places" (בָּמוֹת), see Ezek 6:6. For the parallelism of בָּמָה and מִקְדָּשׁ, see Isa 16:12.

90 According to J. Blau ("Polyphony in Biblical Hebrew," *Proceedings of the Israel Academy of Sciences and Humanities* 6 [1977–1982] 105–83), "שׂחק is an early dialectic form, arising from *ḏḥq when ḏ still existed, and was excluded from early literary language to enter literary Hebrew at a comparatively late period only." F. M. Cross explains it by the "dissimilation of emphatics as in Aramaic and according to the rule in Akkadian" (written communication). For other suggested explanations, see references in *KB*, 408, entry יִצְחָק. It should be noted that the root צחק ("laugh") with a צ appears, outside the Pentateuch, only in Judg 16:25; Ezek 23:32. The spelling שׂחק, however, never appears in the Pentateuch, but is found thirty-five times in the Prophets and Writings. Thus שׂחק eventually replaced צחק. The proper name יִצְחָק, however, still appears throughout the entire Bible. Check concordances for references. The spelling יִשְׂחָק is also found in the Damascus Covenant, 3:3.

For various suggestions to explain the reference to "Isaac" (which is one of the designations of the northern kingdom; see v 16), see Wolff, 301–2; Rudolph, 237. See also A. van Selms, "Isaac in Amos," in *Studies in the Books of Hosea and Amos (Die Ou Testamentiese Werkgemeenskap in Suid Afrika, 7th and 8th Congresses* (Poteschstroom: Rege-Pers Beperk, 1964–1965) 157–65, esp. 158; and M. Moreshet, "Micah 3:12 = Jeremiah 26:18," *BM* 31 (1967) 123–26 (Heb.).

91 "Sword" (חֶרֶב) of course symbolizes war (see 1:11; 4:10; 7:9, 11, 17; 9:1, 4, 10). Note the homonymic wordplay in this verse on the verbal root חרב ("to be reduced to ruins") and חֶרֶב ("sword"). Heb. חֶרֶב is a concatenous key word in this chapter appearing in vv 9, 11, 17.

92 For קוּם עַל, see, for example, Judg 9:43; Isa 14:22; Ps 124:2. Note how the figure בַּיִת ("house" = dynasty) also continues the building imagery of the vision.

Note that the first two verbs in this verse are passive, while the third, with God as its subject, is active.

7

Amaziah Versus Amos

10 Amaziah, the priest of Bethel, sent this message to Jeroboam king of Israel: "Amos has conspired against you in the midst of the house of Israel. The country cannot endure all his words.
11 "For thus Amos has said, 'By the sword shall Jeroboam die, and Israel shall surely be exiled from its own land.'"
12 Amaziah then said to Amos, "Seer, depart quickly to the land of Judah! Earn your living there! And there prophesy!
13 "But at Bethel never prophesy again! For it is the king's sanctuary, and it is the state temple."
14 Amos in turn replied to Amaziah, "I was not a prophet nor was I a member of a prophetic guild. I was a herdsman and a tender of sycamore figs.
15 "But the Lord took me away from the flock, and the Lord said to me, 'Go, prophesy to my people Israel.'
16 "So now hear the word of the Lord. You say, 'Do not prophesy against Israel and do not preach against the house of Isaac.'
17 "Therefore, this is what the Lord has said: 'Your wife shall become a public harlot; your sons and daughters shall fall by the sword; your land shall be divided up with a measuring line; you yourself shall die on unclean land; and Israel shall surely go into exile away from its land.'"

The series of visions is interrupted here by the narration of a dramatic encounter that takes place between the acknowledged head of the institutional religion, the priest Amaziah, and the representative of the Deity, the prophet Amos.[1] This cause célèbre, which initiates a chain of conflicts between priest and prophet,[2] provides the sole biographical data concerning Amos outside the superscription of the book. It was inserted here directly after the third vision on the basis of the catchword principle ("Jeroboam"),[3] for these are the only two literary units in the entire book where King Jeroboam II is mentioned by name (7:9 and 7:10, 11) and where an oracle is delivered against the royal dynasty.

The episode is divided into three scenes, which are

1 See the felicitous description of this narrative given by S. Spiegel, *Amos versus Amaziah* (Essays in Judaism Series 3; New York: Jewish Theological Seminary, 1957).

2 See Jer 20:1–6, Jeremiah versus Pashur; and Jer 29:24–32, Jeremiah versus Zephaniah, son of Maaseiah. See Paul, "Prophets," 1173.

3 Although almost all commentators agree that this is the reason for the present position of this pericope, some suggest that originally it was located elsewhere. See, for example, Gressmann (*Prophetie,* 330) and Budde ("Amos," 77), who place it after Amos 1:1–2; Duhm ("Anmerkungen," 15), after chapter 6; Cripps (311), after chapter 3; Sellin (190ff.), after 9:10; and Marti (150–51, 211), after 9:7. Zakovitch (*For Three,* 187–88), by contrast, argues for the correctness of its present position on the basis of the three-four literary pattern, in which the fourth differs from the first three. See also G. M. Tucker ("Prophetic Authenticity: A Form-Critical Study of Amos 7:10–17," *Int* 27 [1973] 423–34), who suggests that the setting here is a controversy among later hearers who "in the face of opposition" attempt to authenticate his prophecies. For the different opinions as to its original position,

comprised almost entirely of direct quotations. First Amaziah reports an oracle of Amos to Jeroboam II and accuses the prophet of conspiracy against the king (vv 10–11). The priest then commands Amos to leave Bethel, bans his further prophesying there, and orders him to return to Judah, where he may continue to make his living as a prophet (vv 12–13). Amos thereupon responds that he is not a prophet by profession, but a herdsman and a tender of sycamore trees. The reason he is in Bethel is because the Lord had commissioned him to prophesy there (vv 14–16). He continues with an oracle of judgment against the priest (the only oracle against a specific individual in the entire book), his family, and the people of Israel as a whole (v 17).

Although this confrontation may very well have put an end to the prophet's involvement in the affairs of Israel, there is no further indication of his expulsion or deportation. Thus there is no convincing reason to assume that the following oracles in chapters 8 and 9 were subsequently delivered in Judah.[4]

■ **10** Amaziah, the (high-)priest of Bethel,[5] sends a message to Jeroboam II, king of Israel, that Amos is conspiring (קָשַׁר)[6] against him and that the country[7] can no longer tolerate the oracles he is uttering. At Bethel,[8] linked by tradition to both Abraham (Gen 12:8; 13:3ff.) and Jacob (Gen 28:11ff.; 31:13; 35:1), Jeroboam I, after the secession of the northern kingdom, established one of his two religious centers to compete with Jerusalem as state sanctuaries (1 Kgs 12:26–33). The shrine at Bethel was therefore directly identified as the king's sanctuary and the temple of the kingdom.

Amaziah, as the official representative of the state priesthood, reports to the king of an alleged political conspiracy inspired by Amos to overthrow the government. For the king there would be ample reason to fear such possible treason. Not only did the preclassical prophets on several different occasions instigate insurrections[9] but also the dynasty of Jehu, to which Jeroboam II belonged, actually came into power as a result of a prophetic conspiracy incited by the prophet Elisha and his followers (2 Kgs 9:1–10). Prudence would obviously be the better part of valor.

Although there was not, of course, any direct instigation against the king himself, the oracle of Amos could be interpreted as a cause for sedition that could undermine the present dynasty.[10] Amaziah exploits this

see Gordis, "Composition," 249–50. For another study of this pericope, see G. Pfeifer, "Die Ausweisung eines lästigen Ausländers, Amos 7:10–17," *ZAW* 96 (1984) 112–18.

4 In contradiction of Gordis, "Composition," 247ff.; Watts, "The Origin of the Book of Amos," *ExpTim* 66 (1955) 109–12; idem, *Vision,* 31–35.
For an entirely different approach, see C. Hardmeier ("Old Testament Exegesis and Linguistic Narrative Research," *Poetics* 15 [1986] 89–109), who applies basic insights of empirical linguistic research to historical-exegetical narrative analysis.

5 For a similar semantic construction found on a Hebrew seal, a personal name followed by כהן דאר, "priest of Dor," see N. Avigad, "The Priest of Dor," *IEJ* 25 (1975) 101–5.

6 Heb. קָשַׁר ("to bind, conspire"). Compare similarly Akk. *rakāsu* ("to bind, conspire") and *rikiltu* ("conspiracy"); *AHw* 2.945–47, 984. According to Y. Hoffman ("Did Amos Regard Himself as a Nabi?" *VT* 27 [1977] 209–12), the expression קָשַׁר עַל refers only to local residents in the Bible and not to those who came from another place; see 1 Kgs 16:16, 20; 2 Kgs 10:9; 15:5, 25, 30.

7 The expression בְּקֶרֶב בֵּית יִשְׂרָאֵל ("within the house of Israel") is another link with the previous pericope, בְּקֶרֶב עַמִּי יִשְׂרָאֵל ("to [literally, "within"] my people Israel") in v 8. Both ibn Ezra and Kimchi interpret בְּקֶרֶב as "openly, publicly."

8 For Bethel, see *IDB* 1.391–93; J. L. Kelso, "Bethel (Sanctuary)," in *The Archaeological Encyclopedia of the Holy Land* (ed. A. Negev; Jerusalem: Thomas Nelson, 1986) 56–57.

9 See 1 Kgs 11:29–39; 19:15–18. See Paul ("Prophets," 1157–58) for further examples.

10 Amos had not actually delivered prophecies against King Jeroboam. Only once, in 7:9, does he declare, "I will rise against the house of Jeroboam with the sword." These words, however, were not meant to incite an insurrection but were referring to the forthcoming divine punishment upon the dynasty. Nevertheless, they could easily be taken out of context and intentionally reinterpreted. See Babylonian Talmud, Pesaḥim 87b; ibn Ezra; Kimchi; Zakovitch, *For Three,* 192, 195.

possibility and declares that the limit of tolerance has passed, for the state of the nation is at stake. The country, pictured as one grand receptacle, can no longer "contain" (לְהָכִיל)[11] his prophecies.[12] The king cannot remain indifferent to this threat; there are too many tragic precedents to take into serious consideration.

■ **11** Amaziah now cites two utterances of Amos: Jeroboam shall die "by the sword" (בַּחֶרֶב)[13] and "Israel shall surely be exiled" (גָּלֹה יִגְלֶה).[14] Although the first statement is undocumented, it can obviously be derived from v 9, where the threat of death "by the sword" is leveled by the Deity against the dynasty of Jeroboam. Obviously, the king himself would be included in such a punishment.[15] However, the context there is not one of insurrection or conspiracy but is an oracle of judgment directed against Israel, its shrines, and its dynasty. The second statement, that is, exile, however, is very well attested throughout the oracles of Amos; see 4:2–3; 5:5, 26–27; 6:7; 9:4.

What is important, however, is what Amaziah does not report. First, he does not state that these oracles were "the word of the Lord," but rather that they were the words of Amos (כֹּה אָמַר עָמוֹס). It is made to sound as though the prophet were speaking on his own initiative and not delivering a divine message. He also omits the most important factor—the reason for such threats, that is, that the punishment is a consequence of the sins of the people. He is totally concerned with the social and political impact of the oracles and does not refer at all to their basis or origin. Last, he makes no mention of the threats against the "high places" and "sanctuaries" that comprised two-thirds of Amos's oracle of punishment (v 9). Amaziah deftly omits all that would be of direct concern to himself, that is, the cultic establishment, and concentrates on matters of significance to the king and the people per se. He has, so to speak, no direct vested interests—or so he presents the message to the king, concealing his own personal motives.

■ **12** Scene two in this dramatic tête-à-tête resumes a bit later[16] with the words of Amaziah. The question arises as to why there is no report of a response or reaction from the king.[17] Did he find no reason to trouble himself about such an incident and therefore refrained from sending a reply? Did Amaziah act on his own authority even before he received an answer? Or was he carrying out a royal order on the authority of the king, whose response was omitted from the text? Because there is no way of decisively deciding the issue, it must remain an enigma. For the narrator reporting the incident, it obviously was not imperative to inform his audience as to the exact turn of events. What was important was the ensuing dialogue between the priest and prophet.

Amaziah turns to Amos, whom he addresses as a "seer" (חֹזֶה). Some commentators assume that this is a derogatory term[18] and that the priest is actually mocking Amos by calling him a "seer" and not a "prophet." The possibility should also be considered, however, that this specific address may have been selected because the incident is reported and inserted within the section of the vision reports.[19] The title itself is perfectly legitimate and acceptable. It is first applied to Gad in 2 Sam 24:11, when he is called the "seer" of David. (See, too, 1 Chr

11 For Heb. לְהָכִיל ("to bear, contain"), see, for example, Jer 6:11; 10:10; Joel 2:11. Compare, Akk. *kullu, CAD, K,* 511–12. Note the alliteration, . . . לֹא־תוּכַל לְהָכִיל . . . כָּל, and the paronomasia, תוּכַל לְהָכִיל; see similarly 2 Chr 7:7.

12 Heb. דְּבָרָיו ("his words") refers to "his prophecies."

13 Note the prepositioning in the Hebrew text of the word בַּחֶרֶב for emphasis.

14 Note the chiastic order of the Hebrew and the emphatic absolute infinitive. These exact words are repeated in 7:17. Cf. L. Rost, "Zu Amos 7:10–17," in *Festgabe für Theodor Zahn* (Leipzig: Deichert, 1928) 229–36.

15 Because Jeroboam II actually died a peaceful death (2 Kgs 14:29), this would be an instance of an unfulfilled prophecy, which paradoxically accentuates its authenticity.

16 Wolff (310) remarks that there is a fifty-kilometer distance from Bethel to Samaria, the king's residence, and that the answer must have come days later. That is assuming, of course, that there was a response.

17 See the commentaries for various conjectural suggestions.

18 See Ehrlich, *Mikrâ,* 3.414; Marti, 212; Fosbroke, 835; S. Cohen, "Amos *Was* a Navi," *HUCA* 32 (1961) 177; J. L. Crenshaw, *Prophetic Conflict: Its Effect upon Israelite Religion* (BZAW 124; Berlin: Töpelmann, 1971) 67; *KB,* 289.

19 See Driver; Mays, 136; Harper, 170; Cripps, 230.

21:9; 2 Chr 29:25.) On the interchangeability of "seer" and "prophet," note that Gad is also called a נָבִיא ("prophet") in 1 Sam 22:5; and in 2 Sam 24:11, he merits a dual title, both נָבִיא and חֹזֶה. According to the Book of Chronicles, several other kings had men at court who were called "seers": 1 Chr 25:5, Heman was a seer for David; 2 Chr 9:29, Jedo for Jeroboam I; 2 Chr 12:15, Iddo for Rehoboam (compare 2 Chr 13:22, where he is called a "prophet"); 2 Chr 19:2, Jehu the son of Hanani for Jehoshaphat (compare 1 Kgs 16:7, 12, where he is called a "prophet"); 2 Chr 33:18, anonymous men for Manasseh; and 2 Chr 25:15, Asaph, Heman, and Jeduthun for Josiah.[20] Although חֹזֶה may be employed within a negative framework (see Mic 3:7), it appears in a positive context alongside נָבִיא in 2 Sam 24:11; 2 Kgs 17:13; Isa 29:10; and is set in parallelism with yet another term, רֹאֶה (in the plural), in Isa 30:10. Moreover, it was not confined to Israel alone but is also attested in the early eighth-century Aramaic inscription of Zakir, king of Hamath, a contemporary of Amos: "I lifted up my hands to Baalshamayn, and Baalshamayn answered me and spoke to me through seers (חזין) and diviners"[21]—again without any derogatory overtones. It is also found in the first line of the text from Deir ʿAlla (also contemporaneous to Amos) relating to Balaam, the "seer of the gods" (חזה אלהן).[22] Note, too, that Amos in his response (v 14) does not deny that he is a חוֹזֶה but emphatically declares that he is not a נָבִיא, which provides a somewhat oblique identification of the two terms.[23]

Amaziah, after addressing Amos as a "seer," then commands him, "לֵךְ בְּרַח־לְךָ[24] to the land of Judah." The verb ברח, which is usually translated as "flee," can also mean "depart quickly."[25] Moreover, because of the addition of the ethical dative[26] לְךָ ("for yourself"), many commentators understand the words of Amaziah as friendly, well-meaning counsel or as an expression of personal good will given in an attempt to save the prophet, whose life was in dire jeopardy.[27] This suggestion finds support in the very same advice that Isaac gives his son Jacob in Gen 27:43. Others interpret the words as

20 Z. Zevit ("A Misunderstanding at Bethel—Amos VII 12–17," *VT* 25 [1975] 783–90), on the basis of a suggestion alluded to by Paul ("Prophets," 1155), interprets the term here to apply to a court prophet. However, Amos is anything but a court prophet in northern Israel, for he does not enjoy royal patronage, and his role in Judah is totally unknown. Zevit (789) suggests that if the term was borrowed "as a semantic calque, the source langauge was Aramaic."

21 *KAI*, I.202:12.

22 J. Hoftijzer and G. van der Kooij, *Aramaic Texts from Deir ʿAlla* (Documenta et Monumenta Antiqua XIX; Leiden: Brill, 1976). For its date, see J. Naveh, "The Date of the Deir ʿAlla Inscription in Aramaic Script," *IEJ* 17 (1967) 256–58. See also A. Caquot and A. Lemaire, "Les textes araméens de Deir ʿAlla," *Syria* 54 (1977) 189–208. For later discussions and an updated bibliography, see Weinfeld, "Balaam," 141–47; A. Rofé, *"The Book of Balaam"* (Jerusalem: Simor Ltd., 1979) 59–70 (Heb.); H. Ringgren, "Balaam and the Deir ʿAlla Inscription," in *Isac Leo Seeligmann Volume: Essays on the Bible and the Ancient World* (ed. A. Rofé and Y. Zakovitch; Jerusalem: E. Rubinstein, 1983) 3.93–98; A. Lemaire, "L'inscription de Balaam trouvée à Deir ʿAlla: épigraphie," in *Biblical Archaeology Today: Proceedings of the International Congress on Biblical Archaeology, Jerusalem, April, 1984* (Jerusalem: Israel Exploration Society, 1985) 313–25, with extensive bibliographical references on pp. 322–23 n 4; also in this volume, B. A. Levine, "The Balaam Inscription from Deir ʿAlla: Historical Aspects," 326–39. The identity of the language is still the subject of debate among scholars; most tend toward Aramaic, a few favor Ammonite, and according to J. A. Hackett ("The Dialect of the Plaster Text from Deir ʿAlla," *Or* 53 [1984] 57–65), it is a Transjordanian Canaanite dialect.

23 See Mays, 136; Rudolph, 255; Wolff, 358, 361; R. Rendtorff, "נָבִיא in the Old Testament," *TDNT* 6.810; Morgenstern, "Amos Studies IV," 296; Lindblom, *Prophecy*, 183.

24 The two verbs here (לֵךְ, בְּרַח) are constructed as an asyndetic parataxis. For the two as syndetic parataxis, see Judg 9:21; and in parallelism, see Ps 139:7.

25 Rudolph (249), who compares Exod 14:5; Num 24:11; Isa 48:20; Cant 8:14. For another interpretation, "escape by stealth," see H. Rabin, "*BĀRIaḤ*," *JTS* 47 (1946) 38–41.

26 *GKC*, 119s.

27 See van Hoonacker; Robinson-Horst; Sellin; van Gelderen; Weiser, *Profetie;* Budde, "Amos"; Cripps, 231; Mays, 136; Wolff, 311; Würthwein, "Amos-Studien," 20–21. In contrast, see Pfeifer, "Ausweisung," 112–13.

an expression of ironical condescension.[28] Note, however, that the exact phrase also appears in the Balaam episode, when Balak addresses him, ". . . I called you to damn my enemies, and instead you have blessed them these three times! Back with you (בְּרַח־לְךָ) to your own place at once!" (Num 24:10–11). Note the similarities: an individual, who delivers the word of the Lord in a place other than his homeland, is charged by the authorities to return to his geographical point of origin. Both are recognized as men who deliver oracles but whose oracles are not desired, desirable, or acceptable. Their legitimacy is not questioned; they are simply persona non grata. They are both explicitly and succinctly demanded to leave but in a manner that befits the position they hold. Thus rather than voicing genuine personal concern or belittlement, the expression seems to be the correct manner and proper protocol for the deportation of a VIP (very important prophet).[29]

Amaziah follows up his expatriation order with a bit of a taunt: "Earn your living there" (אֱכָל־שָׁם לֶחֶם, literally, "eat your bread")[30] in Judah, in your own native habitat. That a prophet may prophesy for profit is amply attested on several occasions. Remuneration for "services" rendered may amount to as little as a quarter of a shekel (1 Sam 9:8); ten loaves of bread, some wafers, and a jug of honey (1 Kgs 14:3); twenty loaves of barley bread and some fresh grain on the stalk (2 Kgs 4:42); or as much as forty camel-loads of the rich bounty of Damascus (2 Kgs 8:9). Although the charge is not unprecedented,[31] the payment of a fee for an oracle is not to be found among the classical prophets. Only false prophets still accept perquisites for their oracles; see Mic 3:5; Ezek 13:19.

Amaziah does not deny the legitimacy of Amos to function as a prophet, neither does he challenge the authenticity of his oracles, nor does he categorically prohibit him from delivering the words of God—which, of course, he could not do. His only demand and command is that Amos cease from delivering his prophecies in the northern kingdom. He twice reiterates that Amos can continue his prophetic activity "there" (שָׁם), in Judah.[32] There his words would be welcomed. The determining factor is the place itself: Judah, yes; Bethel, no! There in the southern kingdom any calamity portended for northern Israel, its king, and dynasty would be well received, and he could continue totally unhindered. But not in Bethel.[33] Too much was at stake to

28 So Rudolph, 255. See G. A. Smith, *The Book of the Twelve Prophets* (New York: A. C. Armstrong, ^{2}1928) 116.

29 Because Amaziah says בְּרַח לְךָ and not שׁוּב ("Return!"), H. Schmidt (*Der Prophet Amos* [Tübingen: Mohr, 1917] 5–6; and "Die Herkunft des Propheten Amos," in *Beiträge zur alttestamentliche Wissenschaft: Karl Budde zum siebzigsten Geburtstag* [ed. K. Marti; BZAW 32; Giessen: Töpelmann, 1920] 158–71, esp. 170) suggested that one may conclude that Amos was not from Tekoa in Judah but from a northern Tekoa. So, too, Graetz; Marti; Oort, "Amos"; Haran, "Amos," 272; and S. N. Rosenbaum, "Northern Amos Revisited: Two Philological Suggestions," *Hebrew Studies* 18 (1977) 132–48. See already Kimchi on Amos 1:1. However, as the parallel situation with Balaam demonstrates, one may command another to "return" to his homeland by the words לֵךְ בְּרַח.

30 This is the only example of this idiom. Compare, however, Akk. *akalam akālu* ("to eat bread" = sustenance), *CAD, A,* I.246–51; and *akālu* ("to provide for oneself"), *CAD, A,* I.245f. Soggin (127) suggests that Amos may have "eaten at the temple table and had been expelled by the priest, hence the sarcastic invitation."

31 See J. B. Curtis, "A Folk Etymology of *Nābî*," *VT* 29 (1979) 491–93, esp. 492.

32 Note as well that both the roots נבא and מלך, as well as the construct of the substantive בֵּית, appear twice in vv 12–13.

33 See Würthwein ("Amos-Studien," 21–22), who emphasizes that the entire encounter was not a personal one but that Amaziah was acting in his official capacity. (So, too, Reventlow, *Amt*, 22–23.) His conclusion, however, that Amos's being a "Nabi" and his commission to deliver prophecies of disaster do not belong to the same period of his life (p. 27)—the former preceding the latter in Amos's career—and his subsequent division of the oracles into these two assumed stages of development in the prophet's life—with the first visions and the oracles against the nations representing the first stage—is artificial and totally unsubstantiated. See A. H. J. Gunneweg ("Erwägungen zu Amos 7, 14," *ZTK* 57 [1960] 1–16), who correctly states, "Dieses Amt [נָבִיא] muss die Funktion der Heils-*und* der Unheilsverkündigung gehabt haben" ("This office [נָבִיא] must have had the function of proclaiming both salvation and doom"). Reventlow (*Amt,* 13ff.), however, also correctly criticizes Würthwein, "dass die Unterscheidung zwischen Heilspropheten = Kultnebiim = Berufspropheten und freien Schriftpropheten = Unheilsverkündern gar nicht möglich ist" (p. 20) ("that the distinction between prophets of salvation = cult

allow his words to go unchecked.

■ **13** Note how the beginning of this verse contrasts with the end of the former one: Amos may "prophesy" (תִּנָּבֵא) in Judah (v 12), but he may "never prophesy" (. . . לֹא לְהִנָּבֵא) in Bethel. The expression "never [prophesy] again" (לֹא־תוֹסִיף עוֹד) creates another associative linkage of this narrative account with the third and fourth visions, for in both (7:8; 8:2) the identical phrase reappears, לֹא־אוֹסִיף עוֹד.[34] Amaziah proceeds to present two reasons[35] for his order restraining Amos from delivering oracles.[36] First of all, Bethel is the "king's sanctuary" (מִקְדַּשׁ־מֶלֶךְ), a hapax legomenon designating it as the personal sanctum sanctorum of the king's cultic activities. (Compare 1 Kgs 12:32–33.) Furthermore, it is also the בֵּית מַמְלָכָה. This hapax legomenon has been interpreted in two different ways. It may refer to the "royal palace," that is, the "residence" (בַּיִת) of the king. Compare 1 Chr 1:18: "Then Solomon resolved to build a House (בַּיִת) for the name of the Lord and a royal palace (וּבַיִת לְמַלְכוּתוֹ) for himself." It is linguistically well attested that late biblical Hebrew מַלְכוּת replaces earlier מַמְלָכָה.[37] Thus בֵּית מַמְלָכָה is the exact equivalent of בֵּית (הַ)מַּלְכוּת, for which see also Esth 1:9; 2:16; 5:1; and in Aramaic, בֵּית מַלְכוּ ("royal residence," Dan 4:27); see Dan 4:26, הֵיכַל מַלְכוּתָא ("the royal palace").[38]

However, because royal residences are known to have existed only in Samaria (1 Kgs 21:1),[39] the phrase בֵּית מַמְלָכָה here may also possibly mean "the temple of the king"—the national, state temple.[40] For בַּיִת ("temple"), see, for example, 1 Kgs 6:1–3; 7:50; 2 Chr 1:18; 29:3.[41] Bethel would then represent both the private and public sanctuary and/or temple of both the king and all of northern Israel. According to either interpretation, it would be off-limits to Amos on two counts.[42] Amos, according to Amaziah, has set himself up directly against the state authority.

■ **14** Act three, scene one[43] begins[44] with Amos's twofold response (וַיַּעַן)[45] to Amaziah's charges. The exact nuance

prophets = professional prophets, on the one hand, and free literary prophets = messengers of doom, on the other, is entirely impossible"), but reaches his own wrong conclusion in assuming that Amos was a cult prophet. According to Tucker ("Authenticity"), these verses reflect an independent tradition about Amos, whose setting is a controversy over the "authority and validity" of the prophet's oracles, and whose purpose was "to authenticate" his prophecies "in the face of opposition" (p. 433). The narrator employs language familiar from other prophetic calls in order to confirm the prophet's authority.

34 This is in addition to the mentioning of the name of Jeroboam, as cited previously, and the reference to "sanctuary"—מִקְדְּשֵׁי יִשְׂרָאֵל (v 9), מִקְדַּשׁ־מֶלֶךְ (v 13).

35 Note the emphatic prepositioning of בֵּית־אֵל, which is an accusative of place. See *GKC*, 118d–g.

36 Amos had previously upbraided the people for prohibiting the prophets from delivering oracles (2:12). Now he himself is experiencing this very same restriction, this time from the religious establishment.

37 See A. Hurvitz, *The Transition Period in Biblical Hebrew: A Study in Post-Exilic Hebrew and Its Implications for the Dating of the Psalms* (Jerusalem: Mosad Bialik, 1972) 81 and n 28 (Heb.).

38 Compare Akk. *bīt šarri*, "royal residence," *CAD, B*, 289–90.

39 See Paul, "Amos III 15," 358–60.

40 See Hoffmann, "Versuche," 119; Driver; Hammershaimb, 116; Cripps, 232; Wolff, 306, 311; Rudolph, 249; M. Weinfeld, "Zion and Jerusalem as Religious and Political Capital: Ideology and Utopia," in *The Poet and the Historian: Essays in Literary and Historical Biblical Criticism* (ed. R. E. Friedman; HSS 26; Chico, CA: Scholars, 1983) 75–115, esp. 90, 93ff.

41 Compare also Akk. *bītu*, "temple," *CAD, B*, 286–89.

42 Note the twice-repeated use of the root מלך, referring to Bethel.

43 On the structure of the pericope Amos 7:10–17, see Tucker, "Authenticity," 423–34.

44 For an extensive bibliographical list of earlier studies, see H. H. Rowley, "Was Amos a Nabi?" in *Festschrift Otto Eissfeldt* (ed. J. Fück; Halle an der Salle: Niemeyer, 1947) 191–98. See also Würthwein, "Amos-Studien," 16ff.; A. van Hoonacker, "Miscellenées bibliques III. Le sens de la protestation d'Amos VII 14–15," *ETL* 18 (1941) 65–67. This is not, however, Amos's "call to prophetic service," for example, Watts, *Vision*, 9ff.; Seierstad, *Offenbarungserlebnisse*, 41; V. Herntrich, "Das Berufungsbewusstein des Amos," *CuW* 9 (1933) 161–76; J. Hempel, "Berufung und Bekehrung" in *Festschrift Georg Beer zum 70. Geburtstag* (ed. A. Weiser; Stuttgart: Kohlhammer, 1935) 41f.; S. Mowinckel, "Die Offenbarungserlebnisse der Propheten Amos, Jesaja und Jeremia," *NorTT* 49 (1948) 120–28. See also R. Bach, "Erwägungen zu Amos 7, 14," in *Die Botschaft und die Boten. Festschrift für Hans Walter Wolff* (ed. J. Jeremias and L. Perlitt; Neukirchen-Vluyn: Neukirchener Verlag, 1981) 203–16.

45 The verb ענה at times also functions as a technical reply to an accusation, for example, Prov 15:28; Job 9:3, 14, 15, 32; 16:3. See Harper, 174; *KB*, 806.

of his reply, however, still baffles the exegetes, who have resorted to many (at times ingenious and inventive) suggestions to unravel the meaning of Amos's self-justification. The basic problem lies in the apparent contradiction between his denial of being a prophet (לֹא־נָבִיא אָנֹכִי) and the ensuing verse in which Amos acknowledges that God selected him to prophesy to Israel.[46] The first part[47] of his response (vv 14–15) consists of three nominal clauses, two negative and one positive (v 14), each one of which contains an emphatic first-person subject, אָנֹכִי, "I."[48] Nominal sentences, however, are neutral in reference to time, which can only be determined by either the context of the passage (which here is ambiguous) or by the tense of other verbs that appear in the contiguous verses[49] (here, too, the situation is equivocal). If one refers to Amos 7:13a, the passage should be translated in the present tense; if one relies on Amos 7:15, then the past tense would be correct. Hence the dilemma: Is Amos denying that he *is* not or *was* not a prophet, nor a son of a prophet (בֶּן־נָבִיא), that is, belonging to a group or guild of prophets?[50]

In a tortuous attempt to resolve the problem of a contradiction with v 15 (where Amos definitely declares that he was sent to prophesy), some commentators have suggested that Amos is not denying at all that he is or was a prophet but is asserting exactly the opposite, that he *is* a prophet. Thus Driver[51] interprets the sentence as a rhetorical question: "Do you suppose that I am not a true prophet because I am a seasonal laborer? Why the Lord called me. . . ." So, too, Ackroyd,[52] but without the tones of indignation: "Am I not a prophet . . . ?" Translating any sentence as a rhetorical question without any clear contextual guidelines, however, is extremely hazardous. Even if this were possible, it would then clearly imply that Amos is admitting that he is also a son of a prophet, "a member of a prophetic guild," which is obviously totally untenable.[53] If he is declaring that he is a prophet, why does he need to add that he also has a

46 See Gunneweg ("Erwägungen," 1–16), who notes on page 6, "dass sich seiner Erwiderung gar nicht gegen diese bestimmte Bezeichnung seiner Person [חוֹזֶה] richtet und dass der Ton gar nicht auf diesem 'Nabi' liegen kann" ("that his reply is in no way directed against this specific designation of his person [חוֹזֶה] and that the emphasis can in no way be placed on this 'Nabi'").

47 According to Zevit ("Misunderstanding," 783–90, esp. 783–84), Amos's reply in vv 14–15 contains a response to each of the four distinct points found in Amaziah's remarks. See his chart on p. 784.

48 Thus the suggestion of O. Loretz ("Die Berufung des Propheten Amos [7,14–15]," *UF* 6 [1974] 487–88) to delete אָנֹכִי in 7:14 on metrical grounds is unacceptable.

49 See *GKC*, 141:3f, "To what period of time the statement applies must be inferred from the context."

50 Heb. בֵּן in this context does not imply physical descent but belonging to and/or being a member of a certain group. So Wellhausen; Marti; Harper; Nowack; Sellin; Neher, *Amos;* Baumann, "Einzelheit," 62; Fosbroke; E. Vogt, "*Waw* Explicative in Amos VII,14," *ExpTim* 68 (1956–1957) 301–2; Lehming, "Erwägungen," 145–69; Weiser, *Profetie;* Cripps; Wolff; Rudolph; see *GKC*, 128 v. Compare also Ezra 2:42, בְּנֵי הַשֹּׁעֲרִים ("the gatekeepers," literally, "belonging to the guild of gatekeepers"); Neh 12:28, בְּנֵי הַמְשֹׁרְרִים ("the companies of singers," that is, "belonging to the guild of singers"). Note, however, that this is the sole occurrence of this expression in the singular. In all other passages it appears in the plural, בְּנֵי הַנְּבִיאִים; see 1 Kgs 20:35; 2 Kgs 2:3, 5, 7, 15; 4:1, 38; 5:22; 6:1; 9:1. Compare, however, Neh 3:8, בֶּן הָרַקָּחִים ("belonging to the guild of the perfumers"). Akk. *māru* ("son") is also employed in the exact same manner. See *CAD, M*, I.314–15. This verse in Amos is the last reference to this group, which existed some 120 years in the northern kingdom (from King Ahab of Israel onward). See also J. G. Williams ("The Prophetic 'Father': A Brief Explanation of the Term 'Sons of the Prophets,'" *JBL* 85 [1966] 344–48), who suggests that the "sons of the prophets" were those who "devoted themselves to Yahweh's service under a prophet who was 'the prophet' and their spiritual father" (p. 344).

51 G. R. Driver, "Amos 7:14," *ExpTim* 67 (1955–1956) 91–92: "הֲלוֹא, 'Is it not,' has an affirmative force . . . the interrogative becomes asseverative"; idem, "*Waw* Explicative in Amos VII,14," *ExpTim* 68 (1956–1957) 302. For his later opinion, see "Affirmation by Exclamatory Negation" (in *The Gaster Festschrift* [*JANESCU* 5; New York: Columbia University, 1973] 107–8), in which he suggests that the negative לֹא acquires an affirmative sense in interrogative sentences, that is, "surely."

52 P. R. Ackroyd, "Amos 7:14," *ExpTim* 68 (1956–1957) 94.

53 J. MacCormack, "Amos 7:14a, 'I Was (Am) No Prophet, Neither Was (Am) I a Prophet's Son,'" *ExpTim* 67 (1955–1956) 318; Cohen, "Amos," 175–78.

secular profession?[54] By stating that he has such a vocation, Amos clarifies that, contrary to whatever Amaziah may think, he does not earn his livelihood by delivering oracles.

Cohen[55] attempts to solve the enigma of vv 14 and 15 by interpreting the first לֹא as an emphatic negative, referring to Amaziah's charge that Amos was a חֹזֶה: "No! [= "I am not a חֹזֶה!"] I am indeed a prophet, but not a 'son of a prophet.'" According to Zevit,[56] who accepts this punctuation, Amos is emphasizing that he is not a prophet enjoying royal patronage (חֹזֶה)[57] but "an independent prophet—my own man." Amos is thereby identifying himself with those who preceded him as נְבִיאִים. Hoffman[58] attacked this manner of exegesis linguistically and contextually. According to him, לֹא is never employed absolutely as an independent clause to express denial. Although Zevit subsequently countered Hoffman on this point and brought some examples to support this "exegetical probability" (for example, Num 22:30b; Judg 12:5b),[59] Hoffman's other criticisms are still valid. He correctly noted that the repetition of the subject אָנֹכִי points to "two parallel negative sentences, rather than a positive statement followed by a negative one."[60] Furthermore, it is patently clear that Amos's response, which reappears in Zech 13:5, was understood as a denial: "And he will declare, 'I am not a prophet; I am a tiller of the soil.'" The following two affirmative statements identifying Amos's secular profession (בּוֹקֵר, בּוֹלֵס שִׁקְמִים), which also include the same emphatic subject, אָנֹכִי, are obviously presented as a contrast to his double denial, לֹא־נָבִיא אָנֹכִי וְלֹא בֶן־נָבִיא. Hoffman concludes that the issue remains a paradox, reflecting "a very serious inner conflict and his [Amos's] ambiguous feelings regarding his own identity."[61] Amos felt different from previous נְבִיאִים, but not entirely detached from them.

Another approach, but in the same direction, was offered by Richardson,[62] who interprets the first לֹא not as a negative but as an asseverative, vocalizing לָא, "I am surely a prophet, but not a member of a prophetic guild." Although there are some sporadic examples of an emphatic *lamed* in biblical Hebrew,[63] the obvious symmetry and parallelism between the first and second לֹא clauses raise serious obstacles to this exegesis.[64] Moreover, Amos, after asserting who he is not, continues by declaring his profession. This would be totally superfluous if he had already positively stated that he was a prophet.

Tur-Sinai[65] obviates the issue by translating אָנֹכִי as "at the time when," which is a very dubious solution. Watts[66] bypasses the problem by emphasizing the mood and not the tense: "No prophet did I choose to be! Nor did I seek to become one of the prophetic guild." This approach, as well, is fraught with many difficulties.

Most commentators accept that Amos unequivocally denies that he is to be categorized as a prophet. Nevertheless, even within this general consensus, several different ways to understand the verse still exist. Some interpret the *waw* before the second denial as a *waw explicativum*:[67] "I am not a prophet, that is, not a professional prophet."[68] If this were Amos's intention, he would obviously confound any audience, listening or

54 Rudolph, 350.
55 Cohen, "Amos," 175–78.
56 Zevit, "Misunderstanding," 783–84.
57 Ibid., 786, who follows a suggestion made by Paul, "Prophets," 1155.
58 Hoffman, "Amos," 209–12.
59 Zevit, "Expressing Denial in Biblical Hebrew and Mishnaic Hebrew and in Amos," *VT* 29 (1979) 505–9.
60 Hoffman, "Amos," 210.
61 Ibid., 212.
62 H. N. Richardson, "A Critical Note on Amos 7:14," *JBL* 85 (1966) 89.
63 For example, Isa 32:1. For other suggested examples, see Jer 49:25; Ps 89:19. The emphatic use of *lamed* is also attested in Ugaritic and Akkadian.
64 See Wolff, 306.
65 Tur-Sinai, *Peshuṭo*, 473, who compares Gen 24:27, 45, and interprets the verse in Amos as referring to the past tense.
66 Watts, *Vision*, 12. See also Gunneweg, "Erwägungen": "I did not make myself a prophet nor choose this calling for myself." See already the comments of Abarbanel.
67 See *GKC*, 154a, note 1b, which calls it a *wāw copulativum;* and *KB*, 248, 5.
68 Baumann, "Einzelheit," 62; E. Vogt, "*Waw* Explicative," 301–2; idem, "Recensiones," *Bib* 38 (1957) 472–73; Rudolph, 257.

reading. How would they ever decipher his meaning: "I am no prophet in the sense that you think I am, namely a member of a prophetic guild"?[69] Furthermore, Amaziah never charged or insinuated that Amos was a member of such a professional group. Another proposal that has been raised is that what Amos is denying is that "I am neither the head (נָבִיא) nor a member (בֶּן־נָבִיא) of such a guild."[70] Such a terminological distinction, however, is simply unfounded.[71] Others suggest that there is no difference between the two terms and assume that Amos is expressing an emphatic denial by means of synonymous repetition[72]—extremely dubious—or by an a fortiori argument;[73] such a syntax, however, is attested only in postbiblical Hebrew.[74]

The most commonly accepted approach to avoid a contradiction with v 15 is to interpret the nominal sentence as an absolute negation that is expressed either in the present[75] or past tense. Those who prefer the present tense (which is supported by V, *sum,* "I am") note that if the past were intended, the verb הָיִיתִי ("I was") would have been written.[76] This, however, is incorrect, for in nominal sentences the past can be expressed without the addition of this verb. An additional argument employed by those who favor the present tense is that there is no contradiction with v 15.[77] Amos is only repudiating the assertion that he is a prophet by profession and a member of a prophetic guild. These are no grounds, however, to interpret נָבִיא here as a "prophet by profession."

Those who favor the past tense[78] (see G, ἤμην, "I was") place the entire emphasis on the Lord's initiative. The cause for the radical change was divine constraint (see 3:8). Amos's prophetic activity was not by choice: "I was not a prophet nor a son of a prophet," until that dramatic moment when the Lord took me and charged me to prophesy against Israel. With this interpretation, too, a problem still exists. If Amos declares that he formerly was not a prophet but now is one, does it not follow that he is also admitting that as he was formerly not a "son of a prophet," he now is one? Does this also imply that he no longer makes his living, as he used to, by practicing his secular profession?[79] Wolff states that there is no intention to contrast then and now. Amos merely wishes to correct Amaziah's assessment and distinguishes between the office and the act, "between a prophet by office and one called by Yahweh," that is, temporarily a messenger of Yahweh.[80]

69 See Driver, "Amos 7:14," 91–92.

70 H. Schmid, "'Nicht prophet bin ich, noch bin ich Prophetensohn.' Zur Erklärung von Amos 7, 14a," *Judaica* 23 (1967): 68–74. See also S. Abramski's comments ("'I Am Not a Prophet or a Son of a Prophet,'" in *Studies in the Bible Dedicated to the Memory of U. Cassuto on the 100th Anniversary of His Birth* [Jerusalem: Magnes, 1987] 64–68 [Heb.]); he explains that Amos is separating himself from the former prophets, who were involved in palace conspiracies.

71 See also J. G. Williams ("The Prophetic 'Father': A Brief Explanation of the Term 'Sons of the Prophets,'" *JBL* 85 [1966] 344–48), who remarks that the head of such a group is called אָב, "father."

72 Thus Cripps.

73 So M. Weiss, *The Bible from Within: The Method of Total Interpretation* (Jerusalem: Magnes, 1984) 105.

74 For example, Babylonian Talmud, Avodah Zarah 50b.

75 For example, Nötscher; Maag, *Text,* 51; Baumann, "Einzelheit," 62; Deden; Fosbroke; Neher, *Amos,* 20–21; Hentschke, *Stellung,* 149–52; Lehming, "Erwägungen," 145–69; R. Smend, "Das Nein des Amos," *EvT* 23 (1963) 416–18; Hammershaimb, 117.

76 Cripps, 233. However, on p. 232 he translates it as a past tense.

77 Harper, 171.

78 For example, Rowley, "Was Amos a Nabi?" 194–95; Würthwein, "Amos-Studien," 17, 22–23; G. Quell, *Wahre und falsche Propheten: Versuch einer Interpretation* (BFCT 46/1; Gütersloh: Bertelsmann, 1952) 139–40; Gunneweg, "Erwägungen"; Mays, 138; H. Junker, "Amos, der Mann, den Gott mit unwiderstehlicher Gewalt zum Propheten machte," *TTZ* 65 (1956) 321–28; Kapelrud, *Central Ideas,* 7; J. MacCormack, "Amos 7:14a," 318; Reventlow, *Amt,* 20; Robinson-Horst; Osty; R. E. Clements, *Prophecy and Covenant* (ed. C.F.D. Monte; SBT 43; London: SCM, 1965) 36–37; Amsler; Tucker, "Authenticity"; R. Smend, "Das Nein des Amos," *EvT* 23 (1963) 416–18; Soggin, 128. So, already, ibn Ezra, quoting Rabbi Moses HaParsi; and Kimchi.

79 Rudolph, 256.

80 Wolff, 312–13.

If an unambiguous solution were available, the problem would have been resolved ages ago. In the meantime one must opt for that interpretation that, within the vast profusion of possibilities, makes the best sense. Amos is obviously denying that he is a professional prophet and that he makes his living by such a calling. He is also asserting that his present prophetic activity is due entirely to his being selected by the Lord, who commanded him to address northern Israel. Thus, although he formerly had no connections with any prophets or prophetic guilds, he now is a prophet of Yahweh, and Yahweh's authority supersedes Amaziah's.

Amos continues his self-justification by stating that he has his own vocation—he is both a בּוֹקֵר and a בּוֹלֵס שִׁקְמִים—and thus has no need to resort to delivering oracles for his livelihood as Amaziah insinuated. Both terms for his profession, however, are enigmatic hapax legomena.

The first, בּוֹקֵר, is commonly interpreted as a denominative from בָּקָר ("cattle") and is variously translated as a "herder of cattle, herdsman, cattle/livestock breeder."[81] The problem is that in the superscription to the book, Amos 1:1, Amos is called a נוֹקֵד ("a herdsman of sheep") and not a breeder of cattle. Moreover, in the following verse here, he declares that the Lord took him from following the צֹאן, a term that refers to "flocks, sheep and/or goats" but is never applied to cattle.[82] In order to avoid this apparent contradiction, many commentators simply resort to emending בּוֹקֵר to נוֹקֵד,[83] a fine example of unnecessary harmonization.

Others, who accept the correctness of the spelling בּוֹקֵר, attach an entirely different meaning to it. They assume that it refers either to a supervisory official appointed by the owners of herds in order to inspect the flocks and to collect the owner's portion of the levy[84] or that it has a cultic meaning, a hepatoscoper, that is, one who practices divination by inspecting the livers of sacrificial animals.[85] Both these latter suggestions have been correctly criticized and refuted.[86]

The "problem" can be resolved, however, by realizing that the contradiction between נוֹקֵד and בּוֹקֵר simply does not exist.[87] First, נוֹקֵד, as seen previously in connection

81 Most commentators and dictionaries. So, too, α', σ', θ', βουκόλος ("[cattle] herdsmen"), and similarly V, *armentarius*.

82 See dictionaries and concordances; compare Gen 12:16; Num 22:40.

83 For example, Harper, 168 (with a long list of those who preceded him); Mays, 138; Cripps, 234; Hammershaimb, 117; Maag, *Text*, 50; Snaith. The completely different reaction of scholars to G's translation here, αἰπόλος ("goatherd"), is interesting to note. According to Hammershaimb, this reading favors emending the text to נוֹקֵד, but according to Wolff (307) it is reason not to emend. The Greek was most likely influenced by the following צֹאן. Only T renders both nouns by the same translation, מָרֵי גִּיתִי/גִּתִּין ("owner of herds").

84 See Tur-Sinai (*Peshuṭo*, 450), who relies on Old Babylonian documents and relates the word to Heb. מְבַקֵּר ("inspector"); see *KB*, 144. See also Neher, *Amos*, 20–21.

85 See M. Bič, "Der Prophet Amos—Ein Haepatoskopos?" *VT* 1 (1951) 293–96. Compare, however, the criticism of A. Murtonen, "The Prophet Amos—A Hepatoscoper?" *VT* 2 (1952) 170–71; and Bič's rejoinder, "*Maštîn Beqîr*," *VT* 4 (1954) 413–14 n 4. See already A. Haldar (*Associations of Cult Prophets among the Ancient Semites* [Uppsala: Almquist and Wiksells, 1940] 79, 112) and J. A. Montgomery (*Record and Revelation: Essays on the Old Testament* [ed. H. W. Robinson; Oxford: Clarendon, 1938] 22) for a cultic interpretation of נוֹקֵד. J. Gray (*Legacy of Canaan: The Ras Shamra Texts and Their Relevance to the Old Testament* [SVT 5; Leiden: Brill, 1957] 156; and idem, *I and II Kings: A Commentary* [OTL; Philadelphia: Westminster, 1963] 431, 434) translates נוֹקֵד as "a hepatoscopist." See comments to Amos 1:1 for the background of this mistranslation. See also T. J. Wright, "Did Amos Inspect Livers?" *AusBR* 23 (1975) 3–11.

86 For additional criticism, see H. J. Stoebe, "Der Prophet Amos und sein bürgerlicher Beruf," *WuD* 5 (1957) 160–81, esp. 169ff.

87 Other emendations such as בּוֹצֵר, "owner of a wine press" (L. Goldschmidt, cited in Speier, "Bemerkungen," 308); "vinegleaner" (Cohen, "Amos," 178 n 9); or דּוֹקֵר, "piercer," interpreting the *waw* before בּוֹלֵס as a *waw explicativum*, "but I am a piercer and tender of sycamore figs" (L. Zalcman, "Piercing the Darkness at *bôqēr* [Amos vii 14]," *VT* 30 [1980] 252–55) are totally without justification. The last also relates G's translation of Amos 1:1, ἐν νακκαριμ, to Heb. נוֹקְדִים ("borers, piercers"). Some have drawn attention to the use of the verbal root בקר in connection with flocks in Ezek 34:11–12. However, this is

with its Akkadian interdialectal cognate and semantic equivalent, *nāqidu*, is an all-embracing term that may refer to either a breeder of cattle or herdsman of sheep and goats.[88] בּוֹקֵר, moreover, may denote one who owns cattle and, as such, would not preclude one who also tends sheep and goats.[89]

The designation of his other vocation also contains a unique word; he calls himself a "בּוֹלֵס of sycamore trees" (שִׁקְמִים).[90] The tree, whose growth is dependent upon a warm climate, is not found in the vicinity of Tekoa but does grow in the lowlands by the Mediterranean coast and in the Jordan Valley (see 1 Kgs 10:27; Ps 78:47; 1 Chr 27:28). Heb. בּוֹלֵס is a denominative from the Semitic root, בלס, which in Arabic, *balasu*, refers to a species of figs, and in Ethiopic, *balasa*, is applied to both figs and sycamores.[91] Hence all exegetes agree that בּוֹלֵס describes one who has something to do with the fruit of the sycamore tree, *Ficus sycamorus*.[92] The versions interpret the verb as referring to the activity of "scraping" (G, κνίζων); "nipping" (θ', χαράσσων); or "pinching" (V, *vellicans*) the fig fruit of the sycamore. (See σ' ἔχων, "owner.") This process of incising the fig hastens its ripening by increasing the ethylene production and also removes the infestation of the insect *Sycophaga crassipas*. If the fruit were not treated in such a manner, it would dry up and become inedible. Such a procedure is well attested in early documents, Egyptian reliefs, and contemporary Egypt.[93] The fig "cannot ripen unless it is scraped, but they scrape it with iron claws; the fruits thus scraped ripen in four days."[94] The tree can thus produce "seven crops of extremely juicy figs in a summer."[95] Modern experiments have confirmed that when these figs are gashed on the fifteenth to the twentieth day of the month, their ripening is accelerated to three or four days, and they are not plagued by insects.[96]

Because this activity does not demand total month-long attention, there is no difficulty in Amos's practicing both vocations.[97]

---

most likely an instance of homonyms.

88 See comments to Amos 1:1. See also P. C. Craigie ("Amos the *nōqēd* in the Light of Ugaritic," *SR* 11 [1982] 29–33), who contends that in Ugaritic it refers to "sheep managers . . . , a status higher than simple shepherds," and that the "office was not sacral."

89 See H. J. Stoebe, "Der Prophet Amos und sein bürgerlicher Beruf," *WuD* 5 (1957) 177; S. Segert, "Zur Bedeutung des Wortes *nōqēd*," in *Hebräische Wortforschung: Festschrift zum 80. Geburtstag von Walter Baumgartner* (ed. B. Hartmann and others; SVT 16; Leiden: Brill, 1967) 279–83; Rudolph, 250; Wolff, 313; Soggin, 129.

90 See Y. Feliks, *Plant World*, 52–55; J. Braslavi, "Amos—*Noqed, Boker* and *Boles Shikmim*," *BM* 31 (1967) 87–101 (Heb.); Y. Ziv, "Amos 7:14," *BM* 92 (1982) 49–53 (Heb.); Y. Galil, "The Almond Tree in the Culture of Israel," *Teva we'Aretz* 8 (1966) 306–18; 338–55 (Heb.).

91 See *KB*, 129. See also ibn Ezra and Kimchi.

92 See, in addition to the standard commentaries, the comprehensive study of T. J. Wright, "Amos and the 'Sycamore Fig,'" *VT* 26 (1976) 362–68. See also L. Keimer, "Eine Bemerkung zu Amos 7:14," *Bib* 8 (1927) 441–44. Wright's suggestion that α's translation ἐρευνῶν ("searcher, examiner") was based on a reading בּוֹלֵשׁ (known from later Rabbinic Hebrew) rather than בּוֹלֵס (see Zalcman, "Piercing the Darkness," 254 n 11) finds support in Leviticus Rabbah 10:2; Ecclesiastes Rabbah 1:2; and the commentaries of Rashi and Kimchi. Compare Rashi on 7:14: "בּוֹלֵס is like בּוֹלֵשׁ, except that Amos stammered in his speech"; see also Kimchi. See, too, P. Haupt, "Was Amos a Sheepman?" *JBL* 35 (1916) 280–87, esp. 282: "A pricker am I, a piercer of sycamores," relating בלס to Syr. *pĕlaš* and Akk. *palāšu*. For the latter, see *AHw*, 2.815, "durchbohren" ("to pierce").

93 For prooftexts and pictures, see Wright, "Amos." See also Mishnah Shebiʿith 2:5.

94 Theophrastus (372–287 B.C.E.), *Enquiry into Plants and Minor Works on Odours and Weather Signs* (tr. A. Hort; Loeb Classical Library; 2 vols.; London: Heinemann, 1966) 1.IV, ii:1, p. 293.

95 Pliny the Elder, *Natural History* (tr. H. Rackham, W. H. S. Jones and D. E. Eichholg; Loeb Classical Library; 10 vols.; London: Heinemann, 1945) XIII.xiv:57 (4.133). For the same situation in modern Israel, see J. Galil and D. Eisikowitch ("Flowery Cycles and Fruit Types of *Ficus Sycomorus* in Israel," *The New Phytologist* 67 [1968] 752–55), who discovered that the sycamore trees may bear fruit six times a year by the process of vegetative parthenocarpy.

96 J. Galil, "An Ancient Technique for Ripening Sycamore Fruit in East-Mediterranean Countries," *Economic Botany* 22 (1968) 178–90.

97 T. J. Wright ("Amos and the Sycamore Fig," *VT* 26 [1976] 362–68), however, suggests that the connection between the two professions was based on providing fodder for his animals. (See already the comments of Salomon ibn Parchon of the twelfth century in W. Bacher, "Salomon ibn Parchon hebräische Wörterbuch II," *ZAW* 2 [1891] 44, who relates

■ **15** Amos continues[98] by explaining that the radical metamorphosis in his life occurred while he was engaged in his secular vocation[99] and was due entirely to the divine call.[100] It was the Lord, whose name he emphatically states twice,[101] who "took me (וַיִּקָּחֵנִי)[102] away from the flock" (מֵאַחֲרֵי הַצֹּאן) and invested him with the divine charge to "go (לֵךְ),[103] prophesy to (הִנָּבֵא אֶל)[104] my people Israel" (עַמִּי יִשְׂרָאֵל).[105] Note that his call, לֵךְ הִנָּבֵא, recalls Amaziah's command, לֵךְ בְּרַח. The commissioning pattern itself is very similar to David's: "I took you (לְקַחְתִּיךָ) from the pasture, from following the flock (מֵאַחַר הַצֹּאן) to be ruler of my people Israel" (. . . עַמִּי יִשְׂרָאֵל) (2 Sam 7:8); and "He chose David his servant and took him (וַיִּקָּחֵהוּ) from the sheepfolds (מִמִּכְלְאֹת צֹאן). He brought him from following (מֵאַחַר) the nursing ewes to tend his people (עַמּוֹ) Jacob, Israel (יִשְׂרָאֵל) his very own" (Ps 78:70–71). In all three passages God "takes" (לקח), that is, selects, the chosen individual (David, Amos) from following the flock (מאחר[י] הַצֹּאן) and charges him with his new task concerning his people, Israel.

Amos, the prophetic messenger, was sent to deliver oracles to northern Israel, here called by the Lord עַמִּי ("my people"), a term implying endearment and yearning that is also linked to covenantal terminology. For Amos the divine charge completely annuls the charges of Amaziah.

■ **16** Act three, scene two opens (וְעַתָּה)[106] with Amos shifting from the defensive—his self-justification speech—to the offensive with a pronouncement of an oracle of judgment.[107] The prophet will yet have the last word. He commences with a summons to "hear" (שְׁמַע, v 16a), continues with an indictment against the priest in the form of a direct quotation[108] (v 16b, אַתָּה אֹמֵר, "You say"), which is followed by the messenger formula (v 17a), introducing a series of curses pronounced upon Amaziah, his family, and Israel in toto (v 17b–e). The wording of the messenger formula, moreover, sharply contrasts what Amaziah says (אַתָּה אֹמֵר) with what the Lord says (כֹּה־אָמַר ה'). The latter constitutes a direct antithesis to the former.

Amos quotes Amaziah as commanding him, "Do not prophesy against (עַל)[109] Israel and do not (תַטִּיף) preach against the house of Isaac."[110] Although the quote is not

---

בלם to a Mishnaic root, "to mix.") The figs that are not ripened by gashing are not palatable and thus may be used for fodder. He translates בּוֹלֵס as a "gatherer of figs."

98 Note the chiastic relationship between vv 14 and 15. In the former there first appears the key root "prophesy," followed by reference to his secular vocation. The latter verse then commences by mentioning this activity, followed by the divine charge to "prophesy."

99 Except for Amos 1:1, there are no other references to his vocation or to his call.

100 Compare also the call of Elisha, 1 Kgs 19:19–21.

101 Other twice-repeated terms are שָׁם, v 12, and the double negative and positive structure of v 14.

102 Heb. לקח also has overtones of "to take by force" (see ibn Ezra and Kimchi) and "to select, elect." For the latter, see Ps 78:70, where it is parallel to בָּחַר בְּ־ ("chose").

103 Compare similarly Isaiah's commission, where the command "go" (לֵךְ) also appears, Isa 6:9.

104 The attempt to distinguish between the noun נָבִיא in the former verse and the verb הִנָּבֵא here is totally without basis, contrary to Jepsen; Lehming, "Erwägungen," 153; Würthwein, "Amos-Studien," 24ff.; Hentschke, *Stellung*, 151–52.

For הִנָּבֵא אֶל interchanging with הִנָּבֵא עַל (v 16), see Ezek 37:4, 9. Some, for example Marti and Cripps, have suggested that הִנָּבֵא אֶל, similar to הִנָּבֵא עַל, should be translated "against." However, אֶל itself can also mean "against." See Isa 2:4: "Nation shall not take up sword against (אֶל) nation."

105 Herein lies yet another key word connection with the pericopes immediately preceding and following. In all three, vv 8 and 15 and 8:2, there appears עַמִּי יִשְׂרָאֵל.

106 See Cripps (237), who explains the use of וְעַתָּה as the "drawing of a practical conclusion." Cross also notes that it is used as the "opening of the main part of a letter, distinguishing the preliminary from the substance" (written communication).

107 See Mays, 139.

108 See Amos 4:1; 6:13.

109 The change from אֶל (v 15) to עַל may be intentional. The Lord commanded Amos to prophesy "to" (אֶל) Israel. According to Amaziah, however, he is prophesying "against" (עַל) Israel. See Wolff, 315; Amsler, 325; Pfeifer, "Ausweisung," 114. However, as noted previously, אֶל and עַל freely interchange, and אֶל itself may also mean "against."

110 The rare spelling יִשְׂחָק constitutes another connection with the above vision: v 9, בָּמוֹת יִשְׂחָק; v 16, בֵּית יִשְׂחָק.

exact, if one is to judge solely from the present text of the confrontation, it does convey the specific intention of the priest who prohibited Amos from continuing to deliver any further oracles in Bethel (v 13). The exact nuance of the verb נטף, which occurs in four other passages pertaining to prophecy (Ezek 21:2, 7, both times as here, in parallel with הִנָּבֵא; and Mic 2:6, 11),[111] is still open to question. The basic meaning of the root in the *qal* is to "drip"; see Judg 5:4; Joel 4:18; Ps 68:9; Prov 5:3; Job 29:22; Cant 4:11; 5:5, 13; so, too, in the *hiphʿil* in Amos 9:13. It therefore is usually interpreted as the "dripping" or "driveling" of spittle or saliva from the mouth, which presumably characterized the slaver of the ecstatic prophets.[112] The verb, however, is not always used in a contemptuous or pejorative sense. Witness especially the two verses cited from Ezekiel in which the Lord employs this very word when he orders the prophet to deliver his oracles. The verb thus may be translated "to preach, proclaim,"[113] with its positive or negative implications determined by the context itself.

■ **17** The finale is reached with an impassioned fivefold curse[114] uttered by Amos in the name of the Lord. Because Amaziah was attempting to interfere with God's plans, he becomes the target of divine maledictions.[115] The first curse[116] is leveled against Amaziah's wife: "Your wife shall become a public harlot" (בָּעִיר תִּזְנֶה).[117] It does not mean that she will be ravished[118] but rather that she will be shamed and disgraced into plying the profession of a prostitute in order to make her living, and this she will do "publicly." For בָּעִיר, "in the town," = "in public,"[119] see Deut 22:23, where the contrast is between בָּעִיר and בַּשָּׂדֶה ("in the open field"; v 25). A similar curse is found in the treaty of the Assyrian king Asshur-nirari V (who applies it to males):[120] "May Mati'ilu become like a prostitute *(Mati'ilu lu ḫarimtu)* and his soldiers women. May they receive gifts like a prostitute in the square of their city" *(kīma ḫarimtu ina ribēt ālišun[u nid]nu limḫuru).*[121]

111 For Micah, see A. S. van der Woude, "Micah in Dispute with the Pseudo-Prophets," *VT* 19 (1969) 247–48. See also the Damascus Document 1:14; and Deir ʿAlla, col. 2, lines 35–36 (see n 22 for bibliography).

112 So, for example, Cripps (237), who compares Heb. ערף ("to drip"); Deut 32:2; 33:28; Harper (172), who relates it to the words that "refreshingly drop like dew, or better, the flow of prophetic speech when in ecstasy"; Hammershaimb, 118 n 2, "stream of speech"; Wolff, 315, "describes impassioned discourse" and also refers to IQpHab 10:9, מטיף הכזב ("lying prophet," literally, "the spewer of lie"); Rudolph, 251.

113 See W. Zimmerli, *Ezekiel 1: A Commentary on the Book of the Prophet Ezekiel, Chapters 1—24* (tr. R. E. Clements; Hermeneia; Philadelphia: Fortress, 1979) 422–23.

114 This is yet another example of the employment of the pentad in Amos. See also the fivefold recurrent refrain, וְלֹא־שַׁבְתֶּם עָדַי נְאֻם־ה׳ ("Yet you did not turn back to me"), Amos 4:6, 8, 9, 10, 11; the five visions in chapters 7–9; and Amos 9:2–4. Therefore, there is no justification for transposing the last stich of this verse to the end of v 9, contrary to Zakovitch, *For Three,* 191, 192–93. See n 129.

115 Note that כֹּה־אָמַר ה׳ is in poignant contrast to אַתָּה אֹמֵר (v 16). For the curses, see also P. D. Miller, Jr., *Sin and Judgment in the Prophets: A Stylistic and Theological Analysis* (SBLMS 27; Chico, CA: Scholars, 1982) 25.

116 In all the curses, the person or object cursed is prepositioned for the sake of emphasis. Note the same order of curses—wife, children, property—in Wiseman, *Vassal Treaties,* 61, lines 428–30.

117 For זנה ־ב, see Ezek 16:17. Note the bitter irony in the light of Lev 21:7.

118 The curse does not pertain to the ravishing of his wife (contrary to, for example, Harper, 173; Rudolph, 251; see Isa 13:16; Zech 14:2) and thus should not be emended on the basis of Lam 5:11, as suggested by some commentators. See Riessler; Cripps, 237; and *NJPS.* So, too, the readings תַּזְנֶה, *hiphʿil* (van Hoonacker) and תֻּזְנֶה, *hophʿal* (Hoffmann, "Versuche," 119) are unnecessary.

The interpretation of עִיר as meaning "enemy," suggested by Speier ("Bemerkungen," 309, citing G. R. Driver), is totally unnecessary. See already the objections of Harper (169) to a similar proposal by Hoffmann ("Versuche," 119).

119 Once it is understood that בָּעִיר means "publicly," there is no reason to declare the term "remarkably pale," as does Wolff, 307. This nuance was already observed by Ehrlich, *Randglossen,* 5.249–50. See also Seeligmann, "Terminologie," 259.

120 See E. F. Weidner, "Der Staatsvertrag Aššurnirâris VI. von Assyrien mit Mati'ilu von Bît-Agusi," *AfO* 8 (1932–1933) 25, rev. v 9–11.

121 Compare also the theme of a harlot in the judgment oracle of Tyre in Isa 23:15–18: ". . . For she [Tyre] shall resume her fee-taking and play the harlot with all the kingdoms of the world, on the face of the earth" (v 17).

For a series of threatened punishments against

Next in line for execration are his "sons and daughters [who] shall fall by the sword" (בַּחֶרֶב).[122] With his heirs slain, the end of Amaziah's line is foretold. He who accused Amos of prophesying the end of Jeroboam's house is cursed in turn by the death of his own offspring.

There then follows an imprecation against his land, which "shall be divided up (תְּחֻלָּק) with a measuring line" (בַּחֶבֶל).[123] For a similar figure of speech, see Mic 2:4–5: "Our field is allotted/divided up (יְחַלֵּק) to a rebel. Truly none of you shall cast a lot cord (חֶבֶל) in the assembly of the Lord!" (This phrase means that no one will cast a measuring line on a piece of land, thus acquiring title to it; see Ps 16:6.)[124] Conversely, in Ps 78:55: "He expelled nations before them, settled the tribes of Israel in their tents, allotting them their portion by the line" (בְּחֶבֶל).[125] Thus the loss of his property spells the end of his inheritance.[126] Both heirs and heritage are to be (ex)terminated.

And as for Amaziah himself, "You yourself shall die on unclean land" (אֲדָמָה טְמֵאָה). "Unclean land" refers to any foreign soil where the Lord of Israel is not present.[127] It applies to Assyria: "They shall not be able to remain in the land of the Lord. But Ephraim shall return to Egypt and shall eat unclean food (טָמֵא) in Assyria" (Hos 9:3); as well as to Babylonia: "'So,' said the Lord, 'shall the people of Israel eat their bread, unclean (טָמֵא), among the nations to which I will banish them'" (Ezek 4:13). The passage that best defines exactly what is meant by such a concept is found in Josh 22:19: "If it is because the land of your holding is unclean (טְמֵאָה), cross over into the land of the Lord's own holding, where the Tabernacle of the Lord abides."

Such a punishment is extremely severe and belittling to a priest, for he thereby becomes contaminated, polluted, and must suffer the indignity of eating "unclean" food in "unclean" land. He who attempted to hinder Amos from fulfilling his calling shall, in turn, be deprived of his very own calling, a very fitting "Entsprechungsstrafe" ("matching punishment").[128] The curses that previously were directed against the nation—war and exile—are here concentrated upon Amaziah and his family.

The fifth malediction[129] links the deportation of Amaziah to the exile of Israel as a whole. Once again the recurrent theme of exile[130] is inveighed against the corporate body of Israel. Amos appears to be quoting Amaziah, who quoted Amos, for these are the exact words that appear in v 11, וְיִשְׂרָאֵל גָּלֹה יִגְלֶה מֵעַל אַדְמָתוֹ.

houses, fields, and wives, as a result of the enemy's conquest, see Jer 6:12.

122 Thus another connection with the previous pericope, בַּחֶרֶב, v 9. What was formerly predicted for the house of Jeroboam is now pointedly directed personally against the house (that is, sons and daughters) of Amaziah. See also Pfeifer, "Ausweisung," 116 n 19.

123 For חֶבֶל with this meaning, see also 2 Sam 8:2; Zech 2:5. Note that in Akkadian, as well, words for "rope" also indicate a "measuring cord"; see *eblu* (= Heb. חֶבֶל), *CAD, E,* 15 and *ašlu, CAD, A,* II.447–48. For the curse of an enemy dividing up one's possessions, see Wiseman, "Vassal Treaties," line 430, "May a foreign enemy divide your possessions."

124 See footnote in *NJPS.* Note that in the next verse on Micah 2:6, there appears the very same verb נטף as in Amos: "'Stop preaching!' They preach. 'That's no way to preach.'"

125 The translation of the cola is inverted by *NJPS* for clarity. For the idiom, see also Job 21:17. See also M. Held, "Hebrew *maʿgāl:* A Study in Lexical Parallelism," *JANESCU* 6 (1974) 114 n 78.

126 See Haran, *Temples,* 120 n 14.

127 For the same idea, see also Deut 4:28; 1 Sam 26:19; Jer 16:13; Ps 137:4. Kaufmann (*Toledoth,* 1.606–8, 612–23) relates this concept to the popular religion and also distinguishes between the Lord's "province of dominion," which has no territorial limits, and his "province of favor," that is, Israel, where he reveals himself and confines his cultic sanctity.

128 Rudolph, 259.

129 There is no reason to assume that this last colon is an "interpretive addition," contrary to Wolff, 307. See also L. Rost, "Zu Amos 7:10–17," in *Festgabe für Theodore Zahn* (Leipzig: Deichert, 1918) 229–36, esp. 231ff.; Pfeifer, "Ausweisung," 114–15. The irony here is that Amos repeats the very words that appear in the indictment against him, which are an actual quote taken from his oracles. See also n 114 for the pentad.

130 Note that אֲדָמָה appears three times in this one verse.

Note, however, that Amos neither identifies the country to which Amaziah and Israel will be deported, nor does he mention the name of the enemy who will wield the "sword" and drive Israel into exile. Both remain anonymous, still beyond the chronological-political ken of the prophet.[131]

131 See comments on Amos 5:27. Note that the attempt to stop a prophet from delivering oracles occurs several other times in the Bible, and on each occasion the parties involved are the targets of the maledictions of the prophet or the Deity. Compare Jer 11:21–23; 18:18–23; 20:1–6; Mic 2:6–11. There are also several similarities between the curses in these passages and the ones here in Amos.

8 Fourth Vision: Doomsday and Mass Carnage

1 **This is what my Lord God showed me: Lo, a basket of summer fruit.**
2 **And he asked, "What do you see, Amos?" I replied, "A basket of summer fruit." Then the Lord said to me, "The summary hour is at hand for my people Israel. I shall pardon them no more.**
3 **And the singing women of the palace shall wail on that day—declared my Lord God: 'So many corpses! Strewn everywhere! Hush!'"**

■ **1** The fourth vision has been aptly called a "word-play vision."[1] It resembles the third vision in its four-part structure: vision, the Lord's question, the prophet's answer, the interpretation of the Deity. It differs, however, in several details: the Lord does not appear; the participle construction characteristic of the first three visions (Amos 7:1, 4, 7) is absent;[2] the introductory question is abbreviated ("And he said" in 8:2, as compared to "And the Lord said to me" in 7:8); and it concentrates not on the symbolic significance of the object seen but on a homonymic wordplay.

In this vision Amos is shown a כְּלוּב קָיִץ. The Hebrew noun כְּלוּב is also found in Jer 5:27 and Sir 11:28, where it designates a cage for birds.[3] Here, however, it represents a basket, possibly of wickerwork.[4] קָיִץ refers to the type of fruit contained within the basket, that is, "fresh figs," which are harvested at the end of the "summer" (קָיִץ), during the months of August and September.[5] This ripened summer fruit appears also in 2 Sam 16:1, 2; Isa 16:9; 28:4; Jer 40:10, 12; 48:32; Mic 7:1. Compare Jer 8:20. Compare also the eighth and last month of the agricultural year in the Gezer Calendar, which is called ירח קץ (line 7), "month of summer fruit," corresponding to the late summer and early autumn harvest of fruit.[6]

■ **2** As in vision three, Amos, upon questioning, identifies the object he sees without hesitation. What could be ominous about a basket of ripe figs?[7] However, this time the word for "summer fruit," קָיִץ, constitutes a paronomasia on its homonym, קֵץ ("final hour, hour of doom"). Although the respective roots of these two nouns are

1 Wolff, 213; Horst, "Visionsschilderungen," 201–2, designates it as a "Wortspielvision," "Assonanzvision" ("wordplay vision," "assonance vision"). Compare also the treatment of Niditsch, *Vision,* 34–41.

2 In this vision "attention is fixed from the outset on the crucial object"; Wolff, 318. No other figure is seen.

3 It appears also in El Amarna as a Canaanite gloss, *kilūbu,* to Akk. *ḫuḫāru,* "bird trap"; *EA,* 74:46; 79:36; 81:35; 105:9; 116:18; all in letters of Rib-Addi.

4 See W. Baumgartner, "Alttestamentliche Wortforschung. Die Etymologie von hebräischen *k^e^lūb,* Korb," *TZ* 7 (1951) 77–78. The expression is unique to Amos.

5 See J. Löw, *Die Flora der Juden* (4 vols.; Wien: Löwit-Kohut Foundation, 1924) 1.239–40; Dalman, *AuS,* 1/1.7–8; 1/2. 556ff.; M. Haran, "Food and Drink," *EM* 4.546 (Heb.). Compare El Amarna Canaanite *qēṣu,* VAB 2,131 15 in J. A. Knudtzon, *Die El-Amarna-Tafeln* (2 vols.; Aalen: Otto Zeller, 1964); and Ugar. *qẓ, UT,* 2224. Akk. *ebūru* also means "main crop" and "summer crop"; see *CAD, E,* 19–20.

6 For the Gezer Calendar, see *KAI,* 1,182:7. According to S. Talmon ("The Gezer Calendar and the Seasonal Cycle of Ancient Canaan," *JAOS* 83 [1963] 177–87), this would represent the last of the cycle of seasons: Amos 7:1, the "late planting" (לֶקֶשׁ) of the late spring; Amos 7:4, midsummer heat (אֵשׁ); Amos 8:1, ripened summer fruit (קָיִץ) at the end of the summer. B. D. Rahtjen ("A Critical Note on Amos 8:1–2," *JBL* 83 [1964] 416–17) also drew attention to the Gezer Calendar but assumed that its last line, ירח קץ, actually literally influenced Amos's play on words—meaning "summer fruit" and "the end." See also R. B. Coote, "Ripe Words for Preaching: Connotative Diction in Amos," *Pacific Theological Review* 8 (1976) 13–19. Niditsch (*Vision,* 34–35) translates "harvest basket."

7 Ripe fruit is normally an occasion for rejoicing, signaling the harvest festival.

different (קַיִץ, derived from the root קיץ [compare Aram. קיט; Arab. *qaiẓ;* Syr. *qaiṭā*], and קֵץ from קצץ, "to cut off" [compare Aram. כצץ; Ugar. *qṣṣ;* Arab. *qaṣṣa*]), they resemble each other in orthography and even in pronunciation. This can now be substantiated from the Samarian ostraca, which provide rare evidence for the unique dialect of northern Israel. In Samaria diphthongs were monophthongized. Thus the word for "wine" was spelled ין (see the expression נבל ין, "a jug of wine") and was pronounced יֵן in northern Israel (even when not in the construct state) and not יַיִן, as in the Hebrew dialect of Judah.[8] Amos, therefore, while addressing his northern audience, affected their very own dialectal pronunciation in order to heighten the similarity of sounds. By pronouncing both substantives as קֵץ, he produced a very poignant and powerful paronomasia.

The message then is clear: The "final hour is at hand"; doom is coming.[9] (For the expression בָּא קֵץ/קֵץ בָּא, see also Gen 6:13; Jer 51:13; Ezek 7:2, 6; Lam 4:18.) Yet in Amos's characteristic style the final hour still remains undefined. There is no explication as to how the end will take place. There is no mention of when the Lord will bring about doomsday. All that is said is that "the summary hour is at hand for my people Israel."[10] How? What? Where?—an enigmatic, suspenseful, tension-ridden mystery!

Note nevertheless that the next stage in the progressive intensification of the visions has been reached. Now the final hour is at hand, not merely for the cultic and royal institutions, but for the entire nation, "my people Israel"—"I shall pardon them no more" (לֹא־אוֹסִיף).[11]

■ **3** The third vision concluded with a description of the punishment in store for the shrines, sanctuaries, and the house of Jeroboam (Amos 7:9). The fourth one, which envisages a wholesale decimation of the people, ends on the dire tones of a funerary lamentation bemoaning the mass carnage.[12] "On that day" (בַּיּוֹם הַהוּא)[13] of retribution, "wailing and howling" (וְהֵילִילוּ)[14] will be heard issuing forth from the palace. The cries of woe shall be intoned by the שִׁירוֹת. This hapax legomenon[15] refers to the "singing women" of the palace who intone the dirges. Songstresses are mentioned several other times in the Bible. In both 2 Sam 19:36 and Eccl 2:8, they appear along with male singers as part of the personnel of the royal court, and in 2 Chr 35:25, they along with their male counterparts participate in the lamentations over

8 See Kutscher, *Words,* 34. See also Ugar. *qẓ*, "summer," *UT,* 2224; *yn,* "wine," *UT,* 1093; and Heb. קֵץ, "summer fruit," in the Gezer Calendar. See, too, L. Rost, "Bemerkungen zu Sacharja 4," *ZAW* 63 (1951) 216 n 4. See, in addition, the comments of Gese, "Komposition," 79.

For a review of the many suggestions previously offered to explain the connection symbolically between קַיִץ and קֵץ, see S. E. Loewenstamm, "כְּלוּב קָיִץ: A Remark on the Typology of the Prophetic Vision (Amos 8:1–3)," *Tarbiz* 34 (1964–1965) 319–22 (Heb.). Loewenstamm carefully criticizes the various proposals and then offers one of his own. He compares the dream of Alexander the Great reported by Artemidorus, *Dream Interpretations,* 4:24, in which Alexander, during his siege of Tyre, sees in his dream a "satyr dancing on his shield" (*σάτυρον ἐπὶ τῆς ἀσπίδος αὐτοῦ παίζοντα*). The dream is then interpreted by dividing the word *σάτυρος* into two separate words, *σὴ Τύρας* ("Tyre is yours"). Loewenstamm suggests that the idea of the final hour (קֵץ) so perturbed and disturbed Amos that it led to this vision. Thus the explanation of the vision is not based on a play of words but on the revealing of the idea that underlies the actual vision.

9 Heb. קֵץ eventually becomes an apocalyptic term representing the final hour of destruction or redemption. See its use throughout Dan 8—12 and in the literature of Qumran.

10 See Amos 7:15, עַמִּי יִשְׂרָאֵל.

11 R. B. Coote (*Amos among the Prophets: Composition and Theology* [Philadelphia: Fortress, 1981] 15–16) interprets אוֹסִיף here as a sound play on the substantive אָסִיף, another term for "harvest" in biblical Hebrew (see Exod 23:16; 34:22), which also appears in the Gezer Calendar (line 1), "two months of אסף" ("ingathering"). Israel is about to be "harvested, gathered in."

12 There is no reason to assume that this verse is secondary; against, for example, Weiser; Wolff.

13 "That day," that is, "the Day of the Lord"; see 2:16; 8:9, 13; 9:11. Note that the exact same expression, בַּיּוֹם הַהוּא נְאֻם אֲדֹנָי ה׳, appears in Amos 8:9.

14 For wailing in funerary rites, see, for example, Jer 4:8; 25:34; Mic 1:8; Zeph 1:10–11.

15 Some (for example, Sellin) have suggested the repointing שָׂרוֹת, "princesses" (a word also not attested in the Bible). Ehrlich (*Randglossen,* 5.250) proposes the emendation קִירוֹת ("walls") without citing G, *τὰ Φατνώματα* ("coffers in a ceiling"); so already Dahl. Much closer to the Masoretic text would be שׁוּרוֹת, a Hebraized form of the Aramaic word for "walls" (שׁוּרַיָּא/ה), for example, Ezra 4:12, 13, 16. This is also the interpretation given by R.

the king of Judah: "Jeremiah composed laments for Josiah which all the singers, male and female, recited in their laments for Josiah." In all three passages, however, the word for "female singers" is שָׁרוֹת, which leads many exegetes to repoint שִׁירוֹת in this verse to שָׁרוֹת.[16] Nevertheless, שִׁירוֹת may be a dialectical feminine plural of the masculine singular שִׁיר, which also once refers to a "singer"; see Ezek 33:32: "To them you [the prophet] are just a singer (שִׁיר) of bawdy songs, who has a sweet voice and plays skillfully."[17] In either case the substantive constitutes a catchword with v 10 of the next literary unit, which describes the "songs" (שִׁירֵיכֶם) being changed into "dirges."

The whining is occasioned by the dreadful sight of heaps of corpses strewn all about. The prophet does not indicate the cause of their death, whether by pestilence or by the hand of some enemy. He only gives utterance to his horror at this wholesale death scene in short apocopated ejaculations:[18] "So many corpses![19] (רַב הַפֶּגֶר) Strewn[20] everywhere! (בְּכָל־מָקוֹם[21] הִשְׁלִךְ) Hush!" (הָס).[22] Masses of bodies are cast about unburied or disinterred. Because the greatest ignominy and disgrace is not to be brought to a proper burial, all the prophet can utter is הָס ("Hush"), for under such dire circumstances one must be extremely careful not to mention the name of God (see 6:10). The cry here may also carry overtones of an anticurse charm intended to ward off any further disaster.[23] The fourth vision concludes on a demand and command for utter silence.

Gordis, *The Book of Job: Commentary, New Translation, and Special Studies* (Moreshet 2; New York: Jewish Theological Seminary of America, 1978) 371–72; idem, "Studies," 255. The word also appears in 2 Sam 22:30b = Ps 18:30b: "With my God, I can scale a wall" (שׁוּר); and possibly in Gen 49:22b (according to some exegetes), "Its branches run over a wall" (שׁוּר). The passage would then refer to the "wailing of the walls." For inanimate objects as the subjects of the verb ילל ("wailing"), see Isa 14:31 ("gate"); Isa 23:1, 14 ("boats"); and Zech 11:2 ("cedars" and "the oaks of Bashan"). Compare a somewhat similar image in Hab 2:11: "For a stone shall cry out from the wall, and a rafter shall answer it from the woodwork."

16 For example, Weiser; Hammershaimb; Rudolph, 238; Wolff, 317; Soggin, 118. See also B. Vawter, "Prophecy and the Redactional Question," in *No Famine in the Land: Studies in Honor of John L. McKenzie* (ed. J. W. Flanagan and A. W. Robertson; Missoula, MT: Scholars, 1975) 128.

17 This interpretation of שִׁיר has also been suggested for Cant 1:1, "The Song of Solomon's singers" (שִׁירִים), but this is very unconvincing.

18 These are the actual words of the wailing, weeping, and whining women. For wailing and mourning, see Amos 8:10.

19 Heb. פֶּגֶר is a collective; see 1 Sam 17:46; Nah 3:3. Compare Akk. *pagru* ("corpse"), *AHw*, 2.809. See Sefire I B 30; II B 11, for a similar curse in Aramaic.

20 For the "strewing" (הִשְׁלִיךְ) of corpses, see Josh 8:29; 10:27; 1 Kgs 13:24, 25, 28; 2 Kgs 9:25, 26; Jer 14:16; Ezek 16:5; see also Isa 14:19; 34:3; Jer 22:19; 36:30; and, of course, Amos 4:3. The corpses were left without proper burial. For this curse in the Bible and in Mesopotamia, see Hillers, *Treaty Curses*, 68–69. For the similar use of the Akkadian interdialectal semantic equivalent, *nadû* ("to throw out a corpse") see *CAD, N*, I.73–74.

The verb reappears in Amos 8:11, forming another linking device between the two independent pericopes.

21 So most commentators pointing the verb as a *hophʿal* perfect instead of the Masoretic *hiphʿil*, הִשְׁלִיךְ. See also the Karaite commentator, Daniel al-Ḳumissi, 38. Rudolph (238) suggests reading the infinitive absolute, הַשְׁלֵךְ. There is no need to emend to the first person, אַשְׁלִיכֵם ("I shall cast them out"), as suggested by Procksch.

22 This is the proper division of the text. The Masoretic cantillation, however, connects הָס with the preceding verb. Ehrlich (*Mikrâ*, 3.415; *Randglossen*, 5.250) begins the next verse with the interjection הָס. For הָס, see, too, Amos 6:10, where the context also pertains to a funeral setting.

23 Compare Niditsch (*Vision*, 40): "It has the same effect as saying 'God forbid' after hearing of some horrible event." It is "preventative magic." See also Sellin, 295–307.

8 Unscrupulous Traders in Grain and Human Traffic

4 Hear this, you who trample upon the needy,
exterminating the poor of the land,
5 Saying, "When will the new moon be over, so
that we may sell corn; and the Sabbath, so
that we may open the grain(bins)"—
making the ephah small and the shekel
large,
and distorting with false scales,
6 buying the poor for silver,
the needy for a perquisite—
"That we may sell the chaff of the wheat."
7 The Lord has sworn by the pride of Jacob:
I will never forget any of their actions.
8 On account of this shall not the earth quake,
And all who dwell on it mourn,
And all of it surge like the Nile,
And swirl and subside like the Nile of Egypt?

Amos 8:4–14 consists of a series of oracles that has been inserted between the fourth and fifth visions. (See the insertion of Amos 7:10–17 between the third and fourth visions.) The first oracle, vv 4–8,[1] commences with the familiar herald's summons (see 3:1; 4:1; 5:1) addressed to the upper classes who, in the marketplace, market upon the weaker and poorer members of society. Amos, as part of his charge, resorts to his familiar strategy of citing the actual words of the accused in order to provide firsthand self-incriminating testimony.[2] His indictment, vv 4–6[3] (similar in several details to the vices enumerated in 2:6–7), is characterized by a string of infinitives and followed by an oath in which the Lord swears never to forget their manner of acting (v 7). In v 8 he resorts once more to one of his favorite stylistic devices, a rhetorical question,[4] which picturesquely describes the nature of the forthcoming punishment.

■ **4** Amos confronts the accused directly in the marketplace and commences his following judgment oracle with a general comprehensive indictment: "Hear this[5] [that is, both the accusation and the threat of punishment], you who trample upon (הַשֹּׁאֲפִים)[6] the needy." The next colon continues with an infinitive construct coordinated with the preceding participial phrase by means of a copula, וְלַשְׁבִּית[7], "to make cease/annihilate the poor of the land" (עֲנִוֵּי־אָרֶץ [*Q* עֲנִיֵּי־]).[8] Although this construction is unusual,[9] it is not unique (see Jer 17:10; 44:19); thus there is no reason to resort unequivocally to emendation. Nevertheless, an ingenious proposal offered by Ginsberg should be duly noted and seriously considered.[10] He first

1 Several commentators, however, suggest that v 8 is an independent oracle artificially attached to v 7 by the words הַעַל זֹאת ("on account of this"). Watts (*Vision*, 40ff.), however, considers all of chapter 8 as "a clearly formed literary unit." Whatever the number of oracles here, there is no reason whatsoever to deny their authenticity as does Wolff (325, 333), who attributes them to the "school [or] disciples of Amos." See, instead, Rudolph (262 n 1), who correctly criticizes Wolff by stating that Amos would indeed be very "ausdrucksarm" ("poor of expression") if all these were to be deleted. For other views concerning the understanding of this pericope, see M. Krause, *Das Verhältnis von sozialer Kritik und kommender Katastrophe in der Unheilsprophezeiungen des Amos* (Diss., Hamburg, 1972) 35–36; M. Fendler, "Zur Sozialkritik des Amos. Versuch einer wirtschafts- und sozialgeschichtlichen Interpretation alttestamentlicher Texte," *EvT* 33 (1973) 40; B. Lang, "Sklaven und Unfreie im Buch Amos (II 6, VIII 6)," *VT* 31 (1981) 482–88; R. Kessler, "Die angeblichen Kornhändler von Amos VIII 4–7," *VT* 39 (1989) 13–22.

2 See 2:12; 4:1; 5:14; 6:13; 8:14; 9:10.

3 Note that these verses open and close on the theme אֶבְיוֹן.

4 For other rhetorical questions, see 2:11; 3:3–8; 5:18, 25; 6:2, 12; 9:7.

5 See Hos 5:1; Joel 1:2; Mic 3:9.

6 See comments to Amos 2:7.

7 This is a contracted *hiph'il* infinitive: לַשְׁבִּית = לְהַשְׁבִּית. See Isa 23:11, לַשְׁמִד; Jer 37:12, לַחֲלִק; Ps 26:7, לַשְׁמִעַ. For the syncopation of the ה, see *GKC*, 53q.

8 For other interchanges of עָנָו and עָנִי, see Isa 32:7; Pss

suggests repointing the consonants ולשבת as a substantive, וְלַשַּׁבָּת, "and on every shabbath."[11] He then retroverts the Greek expression, not represented in the Masoretic text,[12] εἰς τὸ πρωὶ, to לַשַּׁחַר (although the Greek usually represents בֹּקֶר, it may also reflect שַׁחַר), which he takes as a graphic corruption of לַחֹדֶשׁ ("on every new moon"). If this textual reconstruction is correct, the initial verse would then contain the very two key words of the detailed accusation found in v 5: "You who on every *new moon* crush the needy and on every *sabbath,* the humble of the land."

■ **5** In order to provide decisive incriminating evidence, Amos resorts to a favorite tactic—direct citation of their very own words:[13] "When will the new moon be over,[14] so that we may sell corn; and the sabbath, so that we may open the grain(bins)." From the quotation one gets a rare glimpse into the religious practice of northern Israel during the mid-eighth century: on the new moon[15] and sabbath,[16] work actually ceased and trade stopped. In their eager desire to continue their corrupt business practices, the businessmen could not wait until these two holidays were over so that they could resume their everyday "wheeling and dealing." The indictment is leveled against those who combine strict ritual performance with daily acts of dishonesty.

"The new moon" (הַחֹדֶשׁ), a prominent religious festival throughout the biblical period,[17] is also mentioned by two other somewhat contemporary prophets, Isa 1:13, 14; Hos 2:13. Although cessation from work on

9:13, 19; 10:12; Prov 3:34; 14:21; 16:19; Job 24:4. For the form and vocalization, see Delekat, "Wörterbuch," 46–47. See also Harper (177): "The emphasis here is on the low and miserable social state of the poor for which either form would be a correct expression." For the parallelism of עָנִי and אֶבְיוֹן, see Isa 29:19. See also comments on Amos 2:7.

9 *GKC,* 114p.

10 H. L. Ginsberg, "Some Notes on the Minor Prophets," in Eretz Israel 3 (*M. D. U. Cassuto Memorial Volume;* ed. B. Mazar and others; Jerusalem: Israel Exploration Society, 1954) 83 (Heb.).

11 Already suggested by Hoffmann, "Versuche," 120.

12 This is not a dittography of the preceding participle, οἱ ἐκτρίβοντες ("those grinding down"), against A. Hirscht ("Textkritische Untersuchungen über das Buch Amos," *ZWT* 44 [1903] 11–73) but reflects an additional word that was present in the Hebrew *Vorlage* of G. Rudolph (261), however, suggested that the Greek translators read הַשְּׁכֵּם for הַשּׁ(אֲ)פִים; see *BH*³ and *BHS*⁴ to Jer 48:33. Note, with or without the possible addition of לַשַּׁחַר, the alliteration of the letter ש in this verse.

13 See 2:13; 4:1; 6:13; 8:14; 9:10. Note here, as well, the alliterative repetition of the letter ש in four consecutive words: חדש, נשבירה, שבר, שבת.

14 For Heb. עבר in the context of the "passing" of time, see, for example, Gen 50:4; 1 Kgs 18:29; Cant 2:11. Compare also the Akkadian interdialectal semantic equivalent, *etēqu; CAD, E,* 387–88.

15 For the new moon, see Y. Licht, "New Moon/ Month," *EM* 3.40–41 (Heb.); A. Caquot, "Remarques sur la fête de la 'neoménie' dans l'ancien Israël," *RHR* 158 (1960) 1–18; W. W. Hallo, "New Moons and Sabbaths: A Case Study in the Contrastive Approach," *HUCA* 48 (1977) 1–18. S. E. Loewenstamm ("Ostracon 7 from Arad, Attesting the Observance of the New-Moon Day?" *BM* 66 [1976] 330–32 [Heb.]) suggests, on the basis of an ostracon, that the storehouses normally remained closed on the first of the month, thus bringing another eighth-century attestation (see also 2 Kgs 4:23) for the religious significance and popular observance of the new moon. B. Halevy's ("When Will the New Moon Pass?" *BM* 66 (1976) 333–46 [Heb.]) suggestion to translate יַעֲבֹר as "to come" is unfounded. It is followed, however, by Vesco, "Amos," 502.

Akk. *arḫu,* similar to Heb. חדש, also means "new moon, first of the month," as well as "month." See *CAD, A,* II.259–62. For the frequent cultic sequence: new moon *(arḫu),* seventh day *(sebûtu)*—followed by the fifteenth day *(šapattu)*—see, for example, *Atrahasis* I 206–7. See W. G. Lambert and A. R. Millard, *Atra-Ḫasis: The Babylonian Story of the Flood* (Oxford: Clarendon, 1969) 56.

16 For the sabbath, see J. Tigay, "Sabbath," *EM* 7.504–17 (Heb.); M. Greenberg, "Sabbath," *EncJud* 14.558–62; N.-E. A. Andreasen, *The Old Testament Sabbath: A Tradition-Historical Investigation* (SBLDS 7; Missoula, MT: Scholars, 1972).

17 See Num 10:10; 28:11–15; 29:6; 1 Sam 20:5, 18, 24, 27, 34; 2 Kgs 4:23; Isa 1:13, 14; 66:23; Ezek 45:17; 46:1, 6; Hos 2:13; Ps 81:4; Neh 10:34; 1 Chr 23:31.

that day may be inferred from such passages as 1 Sam 20:5; 2 Kgs 4:23; Ezek 46:1, 3, it is clearly cited only here. Preexilic evidence for the שַׁבָּת is also found in 2 Kgs 4:23 (see Exod 23:12; 34:21). Commercial activity was forbidden on that day along with many other prohibitions (see Jer 17:21–27; Neh 13:15–22). The two holidays are often paired together, for example, 2 Kgs 4:23; Isa 1:13–14; Hos 2:13. Once again Amos cites the scrupulous religious observance of northern Israel. Along with the bringing of sacrifices (4:4–5), they punctiliously observe both the new moon and sabbath.

Nevertheless, they begrudge and resent this moratorium: "Time is money"; and they wish to "sell grain (וְנַשְׁבִּירָה שֶּׁבֶר) and offer wheat for sale," literally, "open (storebins)[18] of grain" (וְנִפְתְּחָה־בָּר). Heb. שֶׁבֶר refers to "grain rations," for example, Gen 42:1–2; 43:2. The denominative verb שבר in the *qal* means "to buy" (for example, Gen 41:57; 42:2–3) or "to sell grain" (Gen 41:56); and in the *hiphʿil* "to sell grain" (for example, Gen 42:6; Prov 11:26). For the interchangeability of שֶׁבֶר and בָּר, see Gen 42:1–3, 25–26.[19]

Amos then further delineates their unethical business practices by describing their corrupt employment of false weights and measures: "making the ephah small (לְהַקְטִין אֵיפָה)[20] and the shekel large" (וּלְהַגְדִּיל שֶׁקֶל). They sell short measures of grain and use oversize weights for payment.[21] Their ephah, a unit of dry measure a bit over thirty-nine liters, was smaller than standard, and their shekel, the basic unit of weight a bit over eleven grams, was heavier than standard.[22] "Short measures, top prices." Even the very scales themselves were tampered and rigged: "distorting with false scales" (וּלְעַוֵּת מֹאזְנֵי מִרְמָה).[23] The buyer was always deceived—he received too little and paid too much.[24]

Honest scales, weights, measures, and balances are strictly demanded throughout the Bible; see, for example, Lev 19:35–36; Deut 25:13–15; Ezek 45:10–11; Prov 16:11. Dishonest ones are reprimanded, for example, Hos 12:8; Prov 11:1; 20:23. Note that in these last three passages the same expression, מֹאזְנֵי מִרְמָה ("false balances"), appears. See similarly Mic 6:11, אַבְנֵי מִרְמָה ("false stones") and מֹאזְנֵי רֶשַׁע ("wicked balances"). For the ephah, see Mic 6:10, אֵיפַת רָזוֹן זְעוּמָה ("the accursed short ephah").

The use and misuse of weights and measures are common themes in ancient Near Eastern literature. In

18 See T, אוֹצָרִין, and G, θησαυροὺς ("store/treasure houses"). See Gen 41:56: "When the famine became severe in the land of Egypt, Joseph laid open (וַיִּפְתַּח) all that was within, and rationed out grain (וַיִּשְׁבֹּר) to the Egyptians."

19 See Dalman, *AuS*, III.161. See also J. Klein ("שבר רעבון [Gen 22:19] in the Light of an Old Babylonian Parallel," in *The Proceedings of the Sixth World Congress of Jewish Studies* [Jerusalem: World Union of Jewish Studies, 1977] 1.237–44), who compares the expression "grain-(ration) for one's hunger" to its Akkadian semantic equivalent, *šē nebrītim*.

20 This is the only occurrence of the *hiphʿil* of the verb קטן in the Bible. For the construction לְהַקְטִין as equivalent to a gerundive in this sentence, see *GKC*, 114o. Heb. אֵיפָה ("ephah") is a loanword from Egyptian *jpt*.

21 Compare similarly in Mesopotamia, for example, *Šurpu* VIII: 65, *šiqlu ṣeḫru* and *šiqlu rabû* ("small [and] large sheqel"). So, too, *Šurpu* II:37, *ina ṣiḫirti ittadin ina rabīti imdaḫar* ("He sold with a small [measure], but purchased with a large [one]"). For the Akk. idiom *nadānu u maḫāru* ("to do business"), see *CAD*, *M*, I.57–58. See also *Šurpu* VIII: 64, and *PBS* 2/2 12:16. For the *Šurpu* texts, see E. Reiner, *Šurpu, A Collection of Sumerian and Akkadian Incantations* (*AfO* Beiheft 11; Graz: Selbstverlag des Herausgebers, 1958).

22 For the basic weights and measures and their relative ratios, see O. R. Sellers, "Weights and Measures," *IDB* 4.828ff.; E. Stern, "Weights and Measures," *EncJud* 16.375–87; R. B. Y. Scott, "Weights and Measures in the Bible," *BA* 22 (1959) 22–40; reprinted in *The Biblical Archeologist Reader III* (ed. E. F. Campbell, Jr., and D. N. Freedman; Garden City, NY: Doubleday, 1970) 345–58.

23 The verb עות ("to distort") is used only here in reference to weights. Compare also Akk. *ṣaliptu*, "tricky," *CAD*, *Ṣ*, 72–73, in connection with weights and balances.

24 Fixed weights and measures were also included in the *mīšaru*-reform proclamations; compare, for example, the Edict of Ammiṣaduqa and the Prologue to the laws of Ur Nammu. See J. J. Finkelstein, "The Laws of Ur Nammu," *JCS* 22 (1968–1969) 67, 142–49.

Egypt, see, for example, The Instruction of Amen-em-Opet, XVI.XVII.18–22, "Tamper not with the scales, nor falsify the *kite*-weights, nor diminish the fractions of the corn measure. . . . Do not lean on the scales nor falsify the weights"; compare XVIII.1–4.[25] It is also very prevalent in Mesopotamian texts.[26]

■ **6** These unscrupulous traders in grain also trade in human traffic: "Buying the poor for silver, the needy for a perquisite." Although the expression has already appeared in 2:6, this passage is not to be deleted.[27] There the vice was selling (מכר) the poor into debt slavery;[28] here it refers to the actual buying (קנה) of human beings. For a trifle they purchase the impoverished who cannot afford to buy their own barest necessities.

In an inclusio Amos now recounts another ruse of their fraudulent business practices.[29] They boast that they "sell the chaff of the wheat"[30] (וּמַפַּל בַּר נַשְׁבִּיר).[31] They market the lowest quality of grain for their insatiable gain. They refuse even to forgo the selling of refuse.[32]

■ **7** As in Amos 4:2 and 6:8, an oath dramatically introduces the declaration of the forthcoming punishment. The Israelites' corrupt and malevolent practices evoke an equally vehement reaction on the part of the Deity. The arrogant quotation of the entrepreneurs receives its due response in the words of the Lord, who swears, "I will never forget[33] (אִם־אֶשְׁכַּח לָנֶצַח)[34] any of their actions!" (כָּל־מַעֲשֵׂיהֶם).[35] The only difficulty in the verse is the exact meaning of the expression "the pride of Jacob" (גְּאוֹן יַעֲקֹב)[36] by which God swears. Because otherwise the Lord swears only "by himself" (6:8) or "by his holiness" (4:2), some have interpreted "the pride of Jacob" as a divine epithet, comparing 1 Sam 15:29, נֵצַח יִשְׂרָאֵל ("the

25 For Amenemopet, see R. Anthes, *Lebensregeln und Lebensweisheit der Alten Ägypter* (AO 32/2; Leipzig: Hinrichs, 1933).

26 See "The Šamas Hymn," *BWL*, 132:107–18: "The merchant who [practices] trickery as he holds the balances, who uses two sets of weights thus lowering the. . . . The honest merchant who holds the balances [and gives] good weight. . . . The merchant who practices trickery as he holds the corn measure, who weighs out loans (of corn) by the maximum standard, but requires a large quantity in repayment. . . . The honest merchant who weighs out loans (of corn) by the maximum standard. . . ." See also p. 321 and notes there to this text.

See also the Sumerian hymn to Nanše, which was already compared to this verse in Amos by S. N. Kramer and M. Weinfeld ("Sumerian Literature and the Book of Psalms—An Introduction to Comparative Research," *BM* 57 [1974] 149–50 [Heb.]). Compare *Šurpu* II:42, *zibānit la kitti iṣṣabat* ("He holds an untrue balance [but did not hold the true balance]"); and VIII:64, 67; *CAD, Z, zibānitu*, 99–100. See, too, Driver and Miles, *Babylonian Laws*, 1.180–84.

27 In contradiction to, for example, Wellhausen, Nowack, and Marti. See Rudolph, 263.

28 See comments on Amos 2:6.

29 Many commentators, however, transpose this stich from the end of the verse to the beginning, for it is a logical and thematic continuity of the previous verse. See, for example, Wolff, 322; Rudolph, 261. They did not notice the inclusio pattern here.

30 Note that in this expression the prophet combines two of the key words of the former verse chiastically: the verb לְהַשְׁבִּיר and the noun בַּר. For the expression itself, see Gen 42:3. For בַּר, see Amos 5:11.

31 Heb. מַפָּל ("refuse"; from the root, נפל, "to fall") is a hapax legomenon in this context. The only other time it appears it is related to the "layers of flesh" of the mythological animal described in Job 41:15. G, καὶ ἀπὸ παντὸς (a translation of Heb. וּמִכָּל ["and from every"]), did not recognize this rare substantive.

32 Compare T, וּמַהֲמַת עֲבוּרָא נְזַבֵּין ("that we may sell the refuse of wheat"). For Aram. המם, which has been related to Akk. *ḫimmatu* ("sweepings, refuse"), *CAD, Ḫ*, 191, from *ḫamāmu / ḫummumu* ("to collect, gather up small particles"), *CAD, Ḫ*, 59, and Arab. *ḥmm* ("to sweep"), see N. M. Waldman, "Rabbinic Homilies and Cognate Languages," in *Gratz College Anniversary Volume, 1895–1970* (ed. I. D. Passow and S. T. Lachs; Philadelphia: Gratz College, 1971) 272. The difficulty of Akk. *ḫ* = Aram. ה still remains, although one can suggest as a comparison Akk. *ḫurdu* ("reed mat"), which in the Aramaic of the Babylonian Talmud becomes הורדא/הודרא. See S. A. Kaufman, *The Akkadian Influences on Aramaic* (Assyriological Studies 19; Chicago and London: University of Chicago, 1974) 57, 142 n 18.

33 See Pss 74:19; 137:5.

34 For this elliptical use of אם as an oath-particle, see *GKC*, 149b.

35 G, τὰ ἔργα ὑμῶν ("your doings") = Heb. מַעֲשֵׂיכֶם.

36 The expression also appears in Nah 2:3 and Ps 47:5. See n 41.

Glory of Israel")[37] and Mic 5:3, בִּגְאוֹן שֵׁם ה' אֱלֹהָיו ("By the power of the name of the Lord his God").[38] However, neither passage is analogous to Amos. Furthermore, this expression, which does not appear anywhere else as a divine epithet, is employed by the prophet himself when he describes the overbearing and overvaunting arrogance of Jacob (6:8).[39] Thus Amos may very well be phrasing the oath in an ironic manner.[40] The Lord swears by the very attribute of the people that he has formerly condemned (6:8), that is, by the same pride and arrogance that are exhibited in their very words cited in the previous verses.[41]

■ **8** The forthcoming punishment, which describes the cosmic consequences of Israel's immoral behavior, is introduced by means of a rhetorical question[42] (הַעַל),[43] whose second word, זֹאת, creates an inclusio with the beginning of the oracle (v 4). God's wrath shall be concretized by the convulsion of the earth's surface: "On account of this (זֹאת) shall not the earth quake (תִרְגַּז) and all who dwell on it mourn?"[44] An earthquake[45] is a familiar portent of the anger of the Lord (see, for example, Hab 3:6; Zech 14:4, 5) and often is expressed by the verb רגז (see, for example, 1 Sam 14:15; Joel 2:10; Ps 77:19; Prov 30:21). This terrestrial upheaval with all its concomitant destruction and tragedy shall result in the mourning of the entire population.[46]

The convulsion of the earth is then potently and picturesquely portrayed by means of a simile drawn from the annual inundation of the Nile.[47] Shall it not all "surge like the Nile (כָּאֹר),[48] and swirl (וְנִגְרְשָׁה)[49] and

37 See Mays, 145.

38 See Wolff, 328. Some, for example, Kimchi and Meṣudot, have interpreted גָּאוֹן as referring to the Temple; see Ezek 24:21. Others, including Sellin² and Deden, have suggested the emending of the particle ב to ל: "The Lord has sworn against the pride of Jacob." It may also be construed as having objective force, that is, "that in which Jacob takes pride," and thus referring to the Lord (Cross, written communication).

39 See comments to the verse.

40 The ironic sense has been suggested by several commentators, for example, Fey, *Amos und Jesaja*, 37; Wolff, 238; Rudolph, 264. There is no reason whatsoever to attribute this oath formula to the "school of Amos" (against Wolff, 328), as is correctly refuted by Rudolph, 264 n 4. Nor is this oath "equally remarkable by its blandness" (against Wolff, 324). See also Rudolph, 264.

41 Ginsberg (*Israelian Heritage*, 33–34) suggests that Ps 47 is a "*probable* Israelian psalm." He then proposes that the expression "Pride of Jacob" may very well be part of Amos's refutation of "the conclusions of his Israelian hosts from the salvation history they keep repeating (Amos 2:9, 10, 11ff.; 3:1–2; 5:25; 9:7–8)." See 6:8, a verse that Ginsberg says "looks uncannily like a deliberate contradiction of Ps 47:5."

For an attempt to discover an analogous structure between 8:7–14 and 9:1–15, see D. A. Garrett, "The Structure of Amos as a Testimony to Its Integrity," *JETS* 27 (1984) 275–76.

42 For other rhetorical questions in Amos, see 2:11; 3:3–8; 5:18, 25; 6:2, 12; 9:7.

43 The interrogative הַעַל (which appears seven other times in the Hebrew Bible, usually as an introduction to a punishment—see concordances) was probably selected here also because of the verb עָלְתָה, which appears later in the verse. The verbal root עלה reappears as well in v 10 in conjunction with עַל (וְהַעֲלֵיתִי עַל) and thereby creates a recurring sound pattern in the pericope.

44 See, too, Amos 9:5; compare Hos 4:3 (for the root אבל and כָּל־יוֹשֵׁב בָּהּ). For another context, see Ps 24:1, הָאָרֶץ . . . וְישְׁבֵי בָהּ ("the earth . . . and its inhabitants"). The mourning motif connects this with the fourth vision, 8:3, as well as with the next unit, 8:10.

45 This earthquake confirmed Amos's prediction and is recorded in the superscription to his book, 1:1. There is no reason to deny this as being a "declaration" of a future earthquake, against Rudolph, 264.

46 Just as both nature and the people themselves will experience God's wrath, so, too, in the next two verses, both the elements of nature (v 9) and the people (v 10) will feel the effects of God's punishment.

47 For the rising of the Nile in another context, see Jer 46:7–8, describing the onslaught of the army of Pharaoh Necho, king of Egypt: "Who is this that rises like the Nile, like streams whose waters surge? It is Egypt that rises like the Nile, like streams whose waters surge, that said, 'I will rise; I will cover the earth; I will wipe out towns and those who dwell in them.'" Hillers (*Treaty Curses*, 70–71) connects both passages in Amos and Jeremiah to the treaty curse of flood.

48 Heb. כָּאֹר ("like the light"), a copyist's error for כַּיְאֹר, was most likely influenced by the next verse, בְּיוֹם אוֹר. Heb. יְאֹר is an Egyptian loanword, *jrw*, which in Egyptian originally designated the Nile and then was expanded to apply to other rivers. For its denoting a river in Mesopotamia, see Dan 12:5, 6, 7. There is no

subside (*K* ונשקה, *Q* וְנִשְׁקְעָה)[50] like the Nile (כַּיאוֹר) of Egypt?" The picture of the waters in upheaval—swelling, surging, sinking—vividly portray the rise and fall of the earth's surface during an earthquake. The verb used to describe the tossing, swirling, and surging of the sea, גרש,[51] is also found in Isa 57:20: "The wicked are like the troubled (נִגְרָשׁ) sea, which cannot rest, whose waters toss up (וַיִּגְרְשׁוּ) mire and mud"; and in Ezek 27:28: "At the outcry of your pilots, the billows (מִגְרְשׁוֹת) shall heave." It is also attested in the Hodayoth Psalms from Qumran[52] and in Rabbinic Hebrew.[53]

For yet another vivid description of the trembling of the earth's surface, see Isa 24:18b–20: "And the earth's foundations tremble. The earth is breaking, breaking. The earth is crumbling, crumbling. The earth is tottering, tottering. The earth is swaying like a drunkard. It is rocking to and fro like a hut. Its iniquity shall weigh it down; and it shall fall, to rise no more."

---

reason to view with suspicion the twice-repeated reference to the Nile in this verse and in Amos 9:5. See Horst, "Doxologien," 48. See also comments to Amos 5:9. G erroneously read כָּלָה ("annihilation"), συντέλεια, for Heb. כֻּלָּהּ ("all of it"). The error recurs in 9:5.

49 Heb. נִגְרְשָׁה is not an explanatory or supplementary gloss to נִשְׁקְעָה, contradicting many commentators (for example, Nowack; Elhorst; Oort, "Amos"; Oettli, "Amos und Hosea"; Graetz; Harper, 176; Wolff, 322; Rudolph, 262) who rely on the fact that G has only one verb here, καταβήσεται ("to sink"), and that the additional verb is missing in the similar citation in 9:5. Delekat ("Wörterbuch," 22–23) also misinterpreted the meaning of the verb as "verebben" ("to die down"), which, in turn, influenced Rudolph's exegesis.

50 The *qre* is correct, וְנִשְׁקְעָה. The *ketib*, ונשקה, is an obvious example of an aural error that led to the omission of the letter ע. Although this verse reappears in 9:5, where the verb is in the *qal*, שָׁקְעָה, there is no need to emend the *niph'al* (נִשְׁקְעָה), otherwise unattested, to the *qal*.

51 The substantive גֶּרֶשׁ ("crop"), Deut 33:14, may also be related to this root. See *KB*, 197.

52 See IQH 2:13; 3:32; 8:15.

53 See Sifre Deut., 39; Yalkut Shimoni, 809: "You might suppose the (rain) water will stir up (גּוֹרְשִׁים)." Compare also Samaritan גְּרוּשָׁה ("waves"); A. E. Cowley, *The Samaritan Liturgy* (Oxford: Clarendon, 1909) 262, 263. The correct meaning of this verb was already noted by ibn Ganaḥ, *Haschoraschim*, 101. See also H. Yalon, Review of Sukenik's *Dead Sea Scrolls*, *Kiryath Sepher* 26 (1950) 246 (Heb.); and esp. Blau ("Homonyme," I.242–48), who also compares Arab. *baḥr mašgūr*, "wallendes Meer" ("an undulating sea").

8
Solar Eclipse and Mourning Rites

9 **And on that day**
—declared my Lord God—
I will make the sun set at noon
And I will darken the earth in broad daylight.
10 **I will transform your festivals into mourning**
And all your songs into dirges.
I will put sackcloth on all loins
And on every head baldness.
I will make it like mourning for an only child,
And the end of it like a bitter day.

■ **9** This new literary unit (vv 9–10)[1] commences with the stock phrase בַּיּוֹם הַהוּא ("On that day"),[2] an expression that usually refers to the day of judgment and punishment; see 2:16; 8:3, 13.[3] The oracle constitutes, moreover, a natural and logical continuation of the prior pericope. In the previous verses, there was a vivid description of the convulsion and upsurging of the terrestrial world; here the focus is on the celestial world. Thus, the entire cosmos becomes a participant in the outpouring of the Lord's wrath when he comes to punish his people, Israel. For a similar combination of the dual motifs of earthquake and eclipse, see Joel 2:10: "Before them earth trembles (רָגְזָה), heaven shakes. Sun and moon are darkened and stars withdraw their brightness."

The eclipse is directly brought about by the Deity: "I will make the sun set (וְהֵבֵאתִי)[4] at noon, and I will darken the earth[5] (לָאָרֶץ) in broad daylight" (בְּיוֹם אוֹר).[6] The darkness caused by the eclipse[7] is part of the vocabulary of the Day of the Lord (see 5:18, 20)[8] and has already been mentioned by Amos in one of his doxologies, 5:8. Eclipses were considered portents of disaster throughout the entire ancient world because they were seen as

1 Note the parallel literary structure between the units following the fourth and fifth visions. After each vision comes an independent pericope, 8:8; 9:7–10, followed by two further pericopes beginning first with בַּיּוֹם הַהוּא (8:9; 9:11) and then הִנֵּה יָמִים בָּאִים נְאֻם ה׳ (8:11; 9:13).

2 The exact same expression, בַּיּוֹם הַהוּא נְאֻם אֲדֹנָי ה׳, appears in 8:3.

3 It may, however, also introduce an oracle of salvation; see 9:11. Compare similarly הִנֵּה יָמִים בָּאִים ("Behold days are coming") for punishment in 8:11 and for salvation in 9:13. Note that in 8:9 the oracle begins (second word) and concludes (last word but one) with the substantive יוֹם, which also appears at the end of the next verse, v 10. This becomes a concatenous key word for the next two oracles as well, vv 11, 13.

4 This is the sole occurrence of the *hiphʿil* of בוא in connection with astral bodies. For the curse of darkness in Mesopotamia, see, for example, Wiseman, *Vassal Treaties,* 59, lines 423–24. A corrected reading of these lines *(niṭil inīkunu liššima)* should now be translated, "May he deprive you of the light of your eyes (so that) they will wander about in darkness." See also the list in Hillers, *Treaty Curses,* 17 n 19. Compare Deir ʿAlla I,6–7 and Amos 5:18.

5 Compare Akk. *adāru,* A, 2, "to become obscured (said of heavenly bodies)"; *naʾduru* ("to become eclipsed"); see *CAD, A,* I.104, 107; and *adirtu,* A ("darkness"), 126–27; *ādiru,* A ("darkening"), 127–28.

6 "In broad daylight," literally, "on a day of light." The expression is found only here. For אוֹר ("light" = "sunlight"), see Zech 14:6a. See also Isa 60:19; Jer 31:35. Compare the Sumerian/Akkadian description, *ša ūmu namri ana ikleti taškunu* ("You who turn the bright day into darkness"), in Reisner, *Hymnen,* 77:20f. Akk. *ūmu namri* = Heb. יוֹם אוֹר. For other examples, see *CAD, I/J,* 61, *ikletu.*

7 For other references to eclipses, see, for example, Isa 13:10; 50:3; Joel 3:3–4; 4:15. For other citations, see Harper, 180–81. According to the Assyrian eponym lists, there was an eclipse on February 9, 784, and on June 15, 763. For the eponym lists, see A. Ungnad, "Eponymen," *RLA* 2 (1938) 412–57.

For a symbolic image of an eclipse portending sudden misfortune for a woman blessed with multiple children, see Jer 15:9, "She who bore seven is forlorn, utterly disconsolate; her sun has set while it is still day. . . ."

8 For the theme of darkness in descriptions of the Day of the Lord, see Weiss, "Origin," 34–35.

reflexes of the anger of the gods. Compare in Mesopotamia: "An eclipse of the moon [Akk. *attalû*] took place on the fourteenth, and this occurrence of an eclipse is ill-portending" [Akk. *maruṣ*];[9] *ṣiriḫtu nissati u bikîti ana Sin ina antallî našû* ("They sing dirges, wailings, and laments for Sin during the eclipse").[10] Just as the above announcement of doom is followed by the theme of mourning in v 8 (אָבַל), so here, as well, mourning (אֵבֶל) and mourning rites follow the eclipse.

Note should also be made of the juxtaposition of the themes of an eclipse and loss of prophecy here (vv 11–12) and in Mic 3:5–7 (false prophets).

■ **10** As the earthquake results in mourning and lamentation, so, too, the aftermath of the eclipse:[11] "I will transform (הָפַכְתִּי)[12] your festivals (חַגֵּיכֶם) into mourning (לְאֵבֶל) and all your songs (שִׁירֵיכֶם)[13] into dirges" (לְקִינָה). (The mourning and lamentation motif connects these literary units with the fourth vision, 8:3.) The religious festivals marked by singing and rejoicing (see 5:21, 23; חַג and שִׁיר)[14] shall turn into occasions for mourning and threnodies (see 5:1, 16–17; 8:3).[15] These, in turn, will be accompanied by the customary mourning practices:[16] "I will put[17] sackcloth (שָׂק) on all your loins and on every head baldness" (קָרְחָה). For these two rites as an expression of a national calamity and disaster,[18] see, for example, Isa 3:24; 15:2–3; 22:12; Jer 48:37; Ezek 7:18; 27:31. The pain and sorrow, moreover, will be so intense that it can be compared only to[19] the "mourning for an only child" (אֵבֶל יָחִיד),[20] symbolic of the greatest and most

9 See *CAD, A,* II.505–9, *attalû* ("lunar or solar eclipse"), for this and other examples. For eclipses in Mesopotamia, see O. Neugebauer, *Astronomical Cuneiform Texts: Babylonian Euphemerides of the Seleucid Period for the Motion of the Sun, the Moon, and the Planets* (London: Humphries, 1955); M. Kudlek and E. H. Mickler, *Solar and Lunar Eclipses of the Ancient Near East from 3000 B.C. to 0 with Maps* (AOAT Supp. 1; Neukirchen-Vluyn: Neukirchener Verlag, 1971). The latter dates the eclipses one year later than the dates cited in n 7 above.

10 See BRM, 4, 6:44 in Clay, *Epics;* and *CAD, B, bikîtu,* 225; *N,* II.*nissatu,* A, 274–75. See also *ša nissati* ("wailer"), *N,* II.275 (and *ša bikîti,* "wailer"). Akk. *nasāsu* means "to sing, wail, complain"; *CAD, N,* II.23–24.

11 For the similar concurrence of these phenomena in Mesopotamia, see, for example, "When the lunar eclipse begins, the lamentation priests put on a linen garment. With their rent garments, they cover their heads, while they sing dirges, wailings, and laments for Sin during the eclipse"; BRM 4, 6:44. For citation, see n 10.

12 Note the intended irony; just as Amos accuses them of having turned (הַהֹפְכִים) justice and righteousness into wormwood (Amos 5:7), so shall the Lord now punish them by "turning" (הָפַכְתִּי) their festivals to mourning. This "reversal" continues the theme of the previous verse, in which the Deity causes a reversal in the natural order.

13 This would include a cessation of their secular songs (see 6:5) and rejoicing as well. Compare similarly, for example, Jer 7:34; 16:9; 25:10; Ezek 26:13; Lam 5:15. For the root שִׁיר, see also Amos 8:3. For the curse of the removal of joyful sounds, see Hillers, *Treaty Curses,* 57–58.

14 See Isa 30:29: "For you, there shall be singing (הַשִּׁיר) as on a night when a festival (חַג) is hallowed; there shall be rejoicing as when they march with flute to the Rock of Israel on the Mount of the Lord."

15 See *ANET,* 462:358–60 (Lamentation over Ur): "Thy song has been turned into weeping. . . . Thy . . . music has been turned into lamentation."

16 See Kutsch, "'Trauerbräuche,'" 25–42. The shaving of the head was a mourning practice prohibited by the Torah in Lev 21:5 (for the priests) and in Deut 14:1 (for all of Israel). The law, however, was mostly honored in the breach; see Isa 22:12; Jer 16:6; Ezek 27:31; Mic 1:16; and the practice was considered divinely or prophetically acceptable.

17 Only here is the verb העלה used in connection with sackcloth and baldness.

18 For a pictorial presentation of women wearing sackcloth around their loins, see the Ahiram sarcophagus in *ANEP,* 459. See also *ANET,* 461:298, for the tearing of hair as part of mourning rites, and *ANET,* 56:291, 384:59, for the wearing of sackcloth. See, too, Cowley, *Aramaic Papyri,* 30:19–21. Compare U. M. D. Cassuto, "The Death of Baal," *Tarbiz* 13 (1940–1941) 178–79 (Heb.).

19 The text reads literally: "I will make it (וְשַׂמְתִּיהָ) like mourning for an only child." The third-person singular pronominal suffix is employed here as a neuter pronoun. See *GKC,* 135p. "It" has been explained as referring to the earth (see vv 8, 9d), *NJPS;* the occasion itself, Cripps, 248; the day, Sellin; the grievous event, Hammershaimb, 126; v 10 as a whole; or the total situation, Wolff, 322.

Compare Akk. *bikîtum šakānum* ("to set up a lament"); *CAD, B,* 225.

20 In the expression אֵבֶל יָחִיד, יָחִיד functions as an objective genitive; see *GKC,* 128b.

grievous of all misfortunes; see Jer 6:26[21] and Zech 12:10. The entire tragedy[22] is then dolefully designated as "a bitter day" (כְּיוֹם מָר);[23] for "bitter" is the weeping (see Isa 33:7), the crying (see Ezek 27:30), and the mourning (see Ezek 27:31).

Note that the two other passages that pertain to the death of an only child, Jer 6:26 and Zech 12:10, also conclude on the same note of the stark "bitterness" of the tragedy—Jer 6:26: "Daughter that is my people, put on sackcloth (שָׂק) and strew dust on yourselves! Mourn, as for an only child (אֵבֶל יָחִיד); wail bitterly (מִסְפַּד תַּמְרוּרִים)"; Zech 12:10: "Wailing over them as over an only son (הַיָּחִיד) and showing bitter grief (וְהָמֵר עָלָיו כְּהָמֵר) as over a firstborn."

After describing the cosmic catastrophe of v 9, the prophet now focuses on its effects, both the cessation of festivals and each individual person's outward expression of mourning and inner anguish of bereavement.[24]

For יָחִיד, compare the Akkadian interdialectal cognate and semantic equivalent, *ēdu* ("only child"). See the proper names *Ēdu-eṭir* ("Save the only child!"); *Ēdu-šalim* ("Keep the only child safe!"). See *CAD, E,* 37, a, 2.

21 The expression אֵבֶל יָחִיד is found only in Jeremiah and Amos. The root אבל is a key term in Amos; it appears twice in this verse and once in v 8. Note also that the verb עלה also appears in Amos 8:8 and in this verse.

22 The text reads "All of it (אַחֲרִיתָהּ, literally, "the end of it") as on a bitter day." For אַחֲרִית, see Amos 4:2; 9:1. Note, interestingly enough, that אַחֲרִיתָהּ always appears in passages with negative overtones; see Isa 47:7; Jer 5:31; Prov 5:4; 14:12, 13; 16:25; 20:21; 25:8; Lam 1:9.

23 The particle כ in the expression כְּיוֹם מָר may be a *kaph energeticus,* that is, "a very bitter day." Contrast יוֹם אוֹר at the end of the previous verse. Gordis ("Studies," 257) suggests that this is a technical term either for the day of death or for burial.

24 See R. Alter, *The Art of Biblical Poetry* (New York: Basic Books, 1985) 73–74.

8 The Inaccessibility of God

11 Lo, days are coming—declares my Lord God—
when I will cast famine on the land, not
hunger for bread or thirst for water, but
rather for hearing the words of the Lord.
12 They shall stagger from sea to sea,
And from north to east.
They shall roam all over, seeking the word of the Lord,
But they shall not find it.

■ **11** This next oracle of doom, commencing with הִנֵּה יָמִים בָּאִים ("Lo, days are coming"),[1] portrays an entirely different type of judgment.[2] Whereas the earthquake and eclipse are signs of God's active intervention in upsetting the laws of nature, the present pericope describes the opposite situation, that is, the total absence of the Deity. A famine and drought[3] will plague the population[4]—not for food and water but "for hearing the words of the Lord."[5] They will not suffer from want of physical nourishment but from spiritual deprivation. God's anger is manifested in his silence (see, for example, Mic 3:4). Those who up until now had refused to listen to the words of the Lord shall henceforth be deprived of his word.[6] The dialogue is ended. The inaccessibility of God, that is, the absence of prophecy depriving man of the divine word, is regarded throughout the Bible as a dire portent of God's wrath (compare 1 Sam 14:37; 28:6, 15–16). It is often threatened by the prophets, for example, Jer 18:18; Ezek 7:26; Mic 3:6–7; and actually materialized in Lam 2:9 (see Ps 74:9).[7]

■ **12** Thus begins their desperate but futile search for divine guidance.[8] Amos depicts their roaming and roving, tottering and tumbling quest by two verbs, נוע and שׁוט. The former often describes an unsteady swaying and staggering movement.[9] Compare the following

1 See also Amos 4:2 and, in an oracle of salvation, 9:13. Here it is situated between the two other oracles of doom that commence with (וְהָיָה) בַּיּוֹם הַהוּא, vv 9, 13.

2 No part of this verse need be deleted, as is arbitrarily suggested by many commentators; nor should it be interpreted as a Deuteronomistic addition.

3 Both together (creating a merism) are very often mentioned throughout the Bible as divine punishments. They are also the subjects of the first two visions, and are coupled together in 4:6–7.

4 The verbal expression here is וְהִשְׁלַחְתִּי בְּ־ ("I will send . . ."). In all other passages in which the verb appears in the *hiphʿil,* the Deity is the subject, and the object is either a plague (Exod 8:17; Lev 26:22; Ezek 14:13) or an enemy (2 Kgs 15:37). Compare the Akkadian interdialectal semantic equivalent, *nadû,* which is also employed in the context of "inflicting a disease or a calamity." See *CAD, N,* I.88, 2k). For example, *ana mātišu ḫušaḫḫa liddi* ("May he [Šamaš] inflict a famine on his country"). So, too, *nibrītu liddû* ("May they inflict famine/hunger"), *CAD, N,* II.203. Akk. *ana X ḫušaḫḫam / nibrītam nadû* = Heb. הִשְׁלִיךְ רָעָב בְּ־.

5 There is no reason to read the singular דְּבַר ה׳ ("the word of the Lord") for the plural דִּבְרֵי ה׳, despite G, λόγον κυρίου; V, *verbum Domini;* T, פִּתְגָמָא דַה׳; and the singular in v 12. The plural is itself well established; see, for example, Jer 36:11; 37:2; 43:1. For other examples of Amos's style of antithetical parallelism, see 5:2, 4–5, 14, 18, 20; 9:4.

6 See Kimchi. Such a punishment underlies the oracle in Isa 6:9–10 and is possibly alluded to in Isa 8:16–17. Compare also Prov 1:24ff. For the combination of "bread" and the word of the Lord, see Deut 8:3.

7 This is also the way in which Kaufmann (*Toledoth,* 8.378ff.) interprets the final cessation of prophecy in Israel.

8 There is no reason whatsoever to consider this verse in its entirety or its second half as a later gloss; against Marti; Nowack; Sellin; Duhm, "Anmerkungen"; Oort, "Amos"; Wellhausen; Löhr, *Untersuchungen;* Wolff, 322, 330.

9 This is how Amos describes the actual search for water in time of drought in 4:8. (See Ps 59:16.) He also aptly applies this verb twice in 9:9. See below.

picture of an earthquake in Isa 24:20a: "The earth is swaying (נוֹעַ תָּנוּעַ) like a drunkard. It is rocking to and fro like a hut." Compare Isa 29:9b: "They are drunk, but not from wine. They stagger (נָעוּ), but not from liquor."[10] Compare the fumbling and stumbling of the blind in Lam 4:14: "They stumble (נָעוּ) blindly through the streets." The latter, in turn, refers to wandering and perambulating over distant areas. See the references to the "eyes of the Lord ranging over the entire earth" in Zech 4:10 (מְשׁוֹטְטִים); 2 Chr 16:9 (מְשֹׁטְטוֹת). See also 2 Sam 24:2: "The king said to Joab, his army commander, 'Make the rounds (שׁוּט) of all the tribes of Israel, from Dan to Beersheba." (Compare v 8: "They traversed [וַיָּשֻׁטוּ] the whole country.")[11]

This frustrating ranging and racing to and fro will drive them eventually from one end to another of the northern kingdom: "From sea to sea (מִיָּם עַד־יָם),[12] and from north to east." The description of "from sea to sea," that is, from west to east (or vice versa) will lead them from the Mediterranean to the Dead Sea (or vice versa).[13] Compare somewhat similarly Joel 2:20: "I will drive the northerner [that is, the locusts] far from you; I will thrust it into a parched and desolate land. Its van to the Eastern Sea [that is, the Dead Sea], and its rear to the Western Sea [that is, the Mediterranean Sea]." See also Zech 14:8. Because the direction "south" is missing in this partial geographical merism, some have sought to emend one of the references of יָם ("sea," that is, the Dead Sea on the east) to דָּרוֹם, "south,"[14] thereby avoiding, on the one hand, a double reference to the east, and encompassing, on the other hand, all four points of the compass.[15] Its absence, however (if it is missing),[16] may not be accidental. The south is precisely where Judah is located, and this southern prophet most surely believes that there in Judah, at least, one can surely "find" the words of God.[17] Yet anywhere they wander and any-

10 See Ps 107:27a: "They reeled and staggered (וַיָּנוּעוּ) like a drunken man."

11 See the activity of Satan, Job 1:7; 2:2, and the search for manna, Num 11:8. See also Jer 49:3: "And run to and fro (וְהִתְשׁוֹטַטְנָה) in the sheepfolds"; Dan 12:4: "Many will range far and wide (יְשֹׁטְטוּ)" because Daniel is commanded (v 4) to "keep the words secret and seal the book until the time of the end"; and Jer 5:1. See similarly the Aramaic curse in Sefire I, A:24: "And may his seven daughters go looking for food (בשׁט לחם) but not. . . ." See Weinfeld, *Deuteronomy,* 125 n 5; A. Lemaire, "Sfire I A 24 et l'araméen *št*'," *Henoch* 3 (1981) 161–70.

12 For this phrase in the context of the boundaries of a world empire, see Zech 9:10; Ps 72:8. See also Mic 7:12. It belongs to the imperial typology of the ancient Near East, found in royal hymns as well as in Egyptian and Assyrian royal display inscriptions. See M. Weinfeld, "The Extent of the Promised Land—The Status of Transjordan," in *Das Land Israel in biblischer Zeit* (ed. G. Strecker; Göttinger Theologische Arbeiten 25; Göttingen: Vandenhoeck & Ruprecht, 1983) 66, 73, and nn 47–49; idem, "Zion and Jerusalem as Religious and Political Capital: Ideology and Utopia," in *The Poet and the Historian: Essays in Literary and Historical Biblical Criticism* (ed. R. E. Friedman; HSS 26; Chico, CA: Scholars, 1983) 97–98. See already Gressmann, *Der Messias,* 19, citing J. G. Eichhorn; and A. Alt, "Das Grossreich Davids," in *Kleine Schriften zur Geschichte des Volkes Israel* (3 vols.; München: C. H. Beck, 1953) 2.75.
The expression "from sea to sea" takes on further poignant significance as a double entendre. They cannot quench their "thirst" even when they reach the waters of the sea.

13 For example, Marti; Sellin; Robinson-Horst; Weiser, *Profetie;* and Maag, *Text* suggest from the Mediterranean Sea to the Kinnereth. Ibn Ezra and Kimchi interpret "from the Mediterranean to the Red Sea." Cross queries whether it might not be even more expansive—from "Mediterranean to Persian Gulf"—as the Dead Sea is not as far east as the Transjordanian tribes (written communication).

14 For example, Budde, "Amos," 94; Sellin; *NJPS.* Perles (*Analekten,* 55) emended the first מִיָּם to מִתֵּימָן, "from the south."

15 Compare, however, Ps 107:3, ". . . from east and west, from the north and from the sea." From this passage, Seidel ("Four Prophets," 229 n 110) assumed that the Dead Sea also demarcated the southern boundary.

16 The boundaries, of course, are those of the northern kingdom; against Nowack; Marti; Harper; Maag (*Text,* 55); and Wolff (331) who interpret the boundaries as being worldwide, similar to Zech 9:10 and Ps 72:8.

17 So Rudolph, 267.

where they roam in their frantic pursuit in "seeking the word of the Lord"[18] will be of no avail, for "they shall not find it."[19]

18 Although the specific phrase לְבַקֵּשׁ אֶת־דְּבַר־ה׳ is found only here, analogous expressions occur in Ezek 7:26 (וּבִקְשׁוּ חָזוֹן מִנָּבִיא, "They shall seek vision from the prophet") and Mal 2:7 (וְתוֹרָה יְבַקְשׁוּ מִפִּיהוּ, "And men seek rulings from his [that is, the priest's] mouth"). Moreover, the prophet may have selected the verb בקשׁ, and not דרשׁ, because the former, at times, also implies seeking after that which is lost.

19 Compare similarly Hos 5:6: "Then they will go with their sheep and cattle to seek the Lord (יֵלְכוּ לְבַקֵּשׁ אֶת־ה׳), but they will not find him" (וְלֹא יִמְצָאוּ). See also Cant 3:2; 5:6, for the same sequence of the verbs בקשׁ and לא מצא: "I searched for him, but found him not." See, too, Josh 2:22; 1 Sam 10:21; 2 Sam 17:20; 2 Kgs 2:17; Isa 41:12; Ezek 26:21; Ps 37:36; Eccl 7:28; 12:10; Esth 2:23; 2 Chr 15:4.

See also the discussion of this passage by M. Weiss (*HaMiqra,* 112–15 and nn on 224–26 [Heb.]; 188–94 [Eng.]), who surveys the many interpretations of this verse before offering his own. He suggests that מִיָּם עַד־יָם relates both to the ends of the earth (not merely to Israel) and to the forthcoming motif of lack of water.

Note that according to the unusual Masoretic division of this verse (adopted in this translation) the verb יְשׁוֹטְטוּ is attached to the second colon and not to the first. This is followed by several commentators, including Weiser, Robinson-Horst, Bič, and Hammershaimb. Many others (such as Cripps; Maag, *Text;* Amsler; Mays; Wolff; Rudolph), however, connect it to the prior colon in order to establish a chiastic parallelism. See Weiss, *HaMiqra,* 125, 228; 3d ed., 241–42 (Heb.); 254 (Eng.).

8 **Condemnation of Popular Oath Formulae**

13 **On that day the beautiful maidens and the**
young men
Shall faint from thirst—
14 **They who swear by the guilt of Samaria,**
Who say, "By the life of your god, Dan!"
And "By the life of the way* of Beer-sheba!"
They shall fall and never rise again.

***Hebrew obscure**

■ **13, 14b** "On that day" (בַּיּוֹם הַהוּא) begins a new oracle[1] that has been attached here because of the catchword צָמָא ("thirst")[2] (v 11). Even though in its present position it appears to provide a climax to the previous oracle, that is, the total spiritual collapse of those who have not been able to discover the word of God, in its original context, it most likely referred to a physical thirst and described the outcome of such a drought inflicted upon them as punishment (see 4:8). The flower of youth, the strongest and the most beautiful of both the young females (הַבְּתוּלֹת הַיָּפוֹת)[3] and males (הַבַּחוּרִים)[4] shall languish away and faint (תִּתְעַלַּפְנָה)[5] from thirst (בַּצָּמָא).[6]

Thematically, the end of v 14 also belongs here.[7] They who have become enervated "shall fall and never rise again" (וְנָפְלוּ וְלֹא־יָקוּמוּ עוֹד). Note that almost the very same expression, נָפְלָה לֹא־תוֹסִיף קוּם, appears in 5:2, where it also refers to Israel,[8] which is designated by the same epithet, בְּתוּלָה, in the context of a funerary lament. The expression לֹא . . . עוֹד reiterates the conclusion of the third and fourth visions in 7:8; 8:2. The oracles contained in 8:4–14 give concrete expression to the inevitable end that is in store for Israel.

■ **14** The reason for the threatened punishment now follows.[9] The indicted are those who are found guilty of swearing by three different oath formulae. The perplexing puzzle is to whom are these oaths sworn. Are they references to foreign gods—indicating the existence of syncretistic worship in the northern kingdom—or are they various appellations of the God of Israel, relating either to the form of his worship or to the various shrines

1 Almost all modern commentators.

2 Thus the emendation (הָ)אַמִּיצִים ("strong" [young men]), based on a metathesis of the letters צמא in order to create a corresponding adjective to יָפוֹת ("beautiful" [young women]), is totally unfounded as well as unsupported by the versions; against Sellin; Maag, *Text,* 54; Morgenstern, "Amos Studies IV," 305. Not only does it destroy the catchword principle so frequent in Amos but also it removes the reason for their fainting. Heb. אמץ, in addition, never appears in parallel to יפה. See also Wolff, 323. In contrast, Löhr *(Untersuchungen),* Duhm ("Anmerkungen"), Harper (180), Robinson-Horst, and Weiser all incorrectly omit the word בַּצָּמָא.

3 For בְּתוּלָה, see also Amos 5:2. For the meaning of this substantive, see S. M. Paul, "Virgin, Virginity," *EncJud* 16.160–61.

4 For בַּחוּרִים, see 4:10. Together the two form a merism. For the unusual sequence of the female בְּתוּלָה/וֹת preceding the male (בָּחוּר(ים, see Jer 31:13; Lam 1:18; 2:21.

5 The *hithpaʿel* of עלף appears again with this meaning in Jonah 4:8. L. Sabottka (*Zephanja: Versuch einer Neuübersetzung mit philologischem Kommentar* [BibOr 25; Rome: Pontifical Biblical Institute, 1972] 61 n 205) suggests that this form (as well as תִּתְמוֹגַגְנָה, Amos 9:13) is an iterative *hithpaʿel.* (Cross understands the form of the verb here as a reflexive; written communication.) In Gen 38:14 the verb refers to "wrapping/covering oneself up"; compare Arab. *ġlf* II ("to cover, veil"). For the connection of covering and fainting, compare Arab. *ġušiya ʿalayhi* ("he was covered over = he fainted"). See Hammershaimb, 127. For the rare usage of a feminine verb preceding both a feminine and masculine subject, see Gen 33:7; Num 12:1; Judg 5:1. In these passages it is occasioned by the feminine subject that immediately follows the verb. For the languishing away and fainting from physical hunger and thirst, see Lam 2:11–12, 19. The verb employed there is עטף, which also means "to cover over"; see Pss 65:14; 73:6. See, however, *KB* (770), who distinguish between the two verbs.

6 The particle ב signifies "because of"; see, for example, Isa 50:1; Hos 12:13; Jonah 1:12, 14.

7 See Nowack; Marti; Sellin; and Rudolph, 269.

8 See also 9:11, in which the same two roots reappear.

9 Some, however, consider this to be a new woe oracle, reading הוֹי הַנִּשְׁבָּעִים.

and sanctuaries from Dan to Beer-sheba where his worship took place[10]—but in a manner totally unacceptable to the prophet?

"They who swear by (הַנִּשְׁבָּעִים בְּ־)[11] אַשְׁמַת of Samaria"[12]—those who favor the syncretistic approach favor reading here אֲשִׁימַת שֹׁמְרוֹן ("Ashimah of Samaria").[13] This suggestion is tempting because it involves only a revocalization of the letters and would create a very biting paronomastic double entendre in Hebrew: The worship of אֲשִׁימַת שֹׁמְרוֹן ("Ashimah of Samaria") is אַשְׁמַת שֹׁמְרוֹן ("the guilt of Samaria"). The problem is that the worship of the deity Ashimah was introduced into the northern kingdom by the resettled foreign population of Hamath only after its destruction in 722 B.C.E. (2 Kgs 17:30).[14] This, of course, does not present any difficulty to the majority of commentators who consider the entire verse to be a later interpolation. However, this is by no means certain nor is it necessary.[15]

---

10 See Cripps, 253; Harper, 184; Rudolph, 270. See also Cross, "Aramaic Stele," 393.

11 Heb. נִשְׁבַּע בְּ־ ("to swear by"); see, for example, Deut 6:13; 10:20; Jer 12:16. By introducing the verse with this verb, Amos creates both a paronomasia with the last cultic site, בְּאֵר־שָׁבַע, and a literary inclusio.

12 Note the alliterative repetition of the letters שׁ in the first three words of the verse and שׁם in the second and third words.

For studies on the oath, see J. Pederson, *Der Eid bei den Semiten* (Strassburg: K. I. Trübner, 1914); F. Horst, "Der Eid im Alten Testament," *EvT* 17 (1957) 366–84; reprinted in idem, *Gottes Recht: Studien zum Recht im Alten Testament* (ed. H. W. Wolff; TBü 12; München: Kaiser, 1961) 292–314; and also idem, "Eid. II. Im AT," *RGG*³ Band 2 (1958) 349–50; M. R. Lehmann, "Biblical Oaths," *ZAW* 81 (1969) 74–92; M. san Nicolò, "Eid," *RLA* 2 (1938) 305–15. See also n 22.

13 Many commentators. For the root אשם in connection with idolatry, see Hos 13:1; 2 Chr 24:18; 33:23 (see v 22). There is no reason to deny the reading of MT based on the unfounded supposition that the word was "probably not in use as early as in the time of the prophet Amos"; against Barstad, *Religious Polemics.*

For the syncretistic worship of the deity אשמביתאל, Eshembethel, at Elephantine, see Porten, *Archives,* 160–73; idem, "The Religion of the Jews of Elephantine in Light of the Hermopolis Papyri," *JNES* 28 (1969) 118–21; Cowley, *Aramaic Papyri,* 70. The divine name appears in the Elephantine Papyrus, 22.124. For an extensive survey of the various possible derivations of the name of this deity and for the subject of "double-deities," see Barstad (*Religious Polemics,* 167–78), who concludes that Ashima is the female counterpart of the male deity Ashim attested in Elephantine (in Aramean personal names) and in Phoenicia, and that this deity was the city goddess of Samaria.

However, note that the element אשם in Elephantine may be understood as a hypostasis, an Aramaic form of שֵׁם ("name") with a prosthetic *aleph.* See Soggin, 140, and n 8 on that page. There would then be no connection whatsoever with the deity אֲשִׁימָא. For other discussions, see J. Gray, *I and II Kings* (OTL; Philadelphia: Westminster, 1963) 595–96; idem, "Ashimah," *IDB* 1.252; S. E. Loewenstamm, "The Religion of the Jews at Elephantine," *EM* 3.443–44 (Heb.); J. E. Wansbrough, "Antonomasia: The Case for Semitic *'ṮM,*" in *Figurative Language in the Ancient Near East* (ed. M. Mindlin, M. J. Geller, and J. E. Wansbrough; London: School of Oriental and African Studies, 1987) 103–16. According to Soggin (140), the Heb. ת represents the archaic termination in *-t.*

14 See Mays, 149; Cross ("Aramaic Stele," 393) states, "It is precarious to read *'ašîmā'* (in Amos 8:14)." See, however, the very forced attempt of Barstad (*Religious Polemics,* 167–78) to prove that the introduction of the goddess Ashima after the fall of Samaria is "totally unhistorical" (161–62).

15 Another suggestion is to interpret אַשְׁמַת שֹׁמְרוֹן as a dysphemism for אֲשֵׁרַת שֹׁמְרוֹן ("Asherah of Samaria"; see 1 Kgs 16:33; 2 Kgs 17:16), for example, Hitzig-Steiner; Budde, "Amos," 97; Maag, *Text,* 55–56, 128–29. This proposal, which was discounted by most scholars, becomes more intriguing after the discovery of the inscriptions from Kuntillet ʿAjrud and Khirbet el-Qom, which mention אשרה in blessing formulae. See n 19. In 2 Chr 24:18, the worship of הָאֲשֵׁרִים (and הָעֲצַבִּים) is called אַשְׁמָתָם ("their guilt"). For a study of the term Asherah, see E. Lipiński, "The Goddess Atirat in Ancient Arabia, in Babylon, and in Israel," in OLP 3 (Leuven: Institut voor Orientalistiek, 1972) 100–119. See also W. G. Dever, "Recent Archaeological Confirmation of the Cult of Asherah in Ancient Israel," *Hebrew Studies* 23 (1982) 37–43; J. Day, "Asherah in the Hebrew Bible and Northwest Semitic Literature," *JBL* 105 (1986) 385–408; W. A. Maier, *'Ašerah: Extrabiblical Evidence* (HSM 36; Atlanta: Scholars, 1986); P. K. McCarter, Jr., "Aspects of the Religion of the Israelite Monar-

By contrast, "the guilt/sin of Samaria" may very well refer to the worship of the Lord at the national sanctuary of Samaria in Bethel with its image of a calf.[16] Hosea (8:6) also mentions the "calf of Samaria" (עֵגֶל שֹׁמְרוֹן), which he, on another occasion (10:8a), alludes to as the "sin of Israel": "Ruined shall be the shrines of [Beth-] Aven [that is, Bethel], that sin of Israel." The golden calf is also called חַטַּאתְכֶם ("your sin") in Deut 9:21. Obviously the pejorative term is employed ironically in Amos, for the prophets often inject their own contemptuous and cynical invectives into quotes that they ascribe to the people.[17] Compare Isa 44:19: "They do not give thought, they lack the wit and judgment to say: 'Part of it I burned in a fire; I also baked bread on the coals; I roasted meat and ate it. Should I make the rest an abhorrence (לְתוֹעֵבָה)? Should I bow to a block of wood?'" The prophet simply introduced a cacophemism for idolatry into their imagined declaration. Amos likewise is probably asserting that the people sin and incur guilt by worshiping the Lord in this manner.[18] Compare the expression יהוה שמרן ("Yahweh of Samaria"), referring to Yahweh as he was worshiped in Samaria, which appears in inscriptions from Kuntillet ʿAjrud: "I have blessed you by Yahweh of Samaria and by his asherah" (ליהוה שמרנ ולאשרתה).[19]

A second oath formula is "By the life of your god, Dan!" (חֵי אֱלֹהֶיךָ דָּן). The oath by the god of Dan most likely refers as well to the worship of the Lord in the form of a bull image set up in Dan (as well as in Bethel) by Jeroboam I (1 Kgs 12:28–30).[20] According to Amos

chy: Biblical and Epigraphic Data," in *Ancient Israelite Religion: Essays in Honor of Frank Moore Cross* (ed. P. D. Miller, Jr., P. D. Hanson, and S. D. McBride; Philadelphia: Fortress, 1987) 143–49; and S. Olyan, *Asherah and the Cult of Yahweh in Israel* (Atlanta: Scholars, 1988).

16 For example, Rudolph, 270. See also Harper, 184; van Hoonacker, 227; Hammershaimb, 128. Wellhausen's emendation to read אֵל בֵּית־אֵל ("the god [= calf] of Bethel," 93) was followed by Marti, 219–20; Nowack, 163; Sellin, 215–16.

17 See Wolff, *Zitat,* 70–71.

18 See Hammershaimb, 128. For swearing by the deity worshiped in the cult, see Hos 4:15.

19 Many scholars have investigated the perplexity of this inscription and its theological implications. See M. Weinfeld, "A Sacred Site of the Monarchic Period," *Shnaton* 4 (1980) 280–84 (Heb.); J. A. Emerton, "New Light on Israelite Religion: The Implications of the Inscriptions from Kuntillet ʿAjrud," *ZAW* 94 (1982) 2–20: ". . . though the unity of Yahweh may not have been denied, his cult took a variety of local forms." M. Gilula ("To Yahweh Shomron and His Asherah," *Shnaton* 3 [1978–1979] 129–37 [Heb.]) suggests that there were two Yahwistic traditions in Israel: that of "Yahweh Ṣᵉbaoth," associated with first Shiloh and then Jerusalem, and "Yahweh of Samaria," which was the tradition of the northern tribes.

See also n 15, esp. Day, "Asherah," 391–94. In addition to these, see A. Angerstorfer, "Ašerah als 'Consort of Jahwe' oder Aširtah?" BN 17 (1982) 7–16; P. Beck, "The Drawings from Ḥorvat Teiman (Kuntillet ʿAjrud)," *Tel Aviv* 9 (1982) 3–68; W. G. Dever, "Asherah, Consort of Yahweh? New Evidence from Kuntillet ʿAjrud," *BASOR* 255 (1984) 21–37; Z. Meshel, *Kuntillet ʿAjrud: A Religious Centre from the Time of the Judean Monarchy on the Border of Sinai* (Catalogue 175 of the Israel Museum; Jerusalem: Israel Museum, 1978); idem, "Did Yahweh Have a Consort?" *BAR* 5 (1979) 24–35. For a similar formula in an inscription from Cave II at Khirbet el-Qom, see A. Lemaire, "Les inscriptions du Khirbet el-Qom et l'Ashérah de Yhwh," *RB* 84 (1977) 595–608; S. Mittmann, "Die Grabinschrift des Sängers Uriahu," *ZDPV* 97 (1981) 143–44; J. Naveh, "Graffiti and Dedications," *BASOR* 235 (1979) 27–30; Z. Zevit, "The Khirbet el-Qom Inscription Mentioning a Goddess," *BASOR* 255 (1984) 45–46.

For a similar construction, see Ugar. *ʾaṯrt ṣrm* ("Asherah of Tyre"), *CTA,* 14:iv:198, 201. For other examples, see McCarter in n 15.

20 For example, Cripps, 253–54; Mays, 150; Hammershaimb, 128; Wolff, 331; Rudolph, 270. Note that excavations at Dan have uncovered a bilingual inscription in Greek and Aramaic from the late third or first half of the second century B.C.E.: "To the God Who Is in Dan." See A. Biran, "To the God Who Is in Dan," in *Temples and High Places in Biblical Times* (ed. A. Biran; Jerusalem: Keter, 1981) 142–51. Dan was a sacred site from the tenth century B.C.E. to the third or fourth century C.E. See also Biran, "The Temenos at Dan," in Eretz Israel 16 (*Harry M. Orlinsky Volume;* ed. B. A. Levine and A. Malamat; Jerusalem: Israel Exploration Society, 1982) 15–43 and plates כ־יג (Heb.); idem, "An Incense Altar and Other Discoveries at Dan," *Qadmoniot* 19 (1986) 31–40 (Heb.). For studies of the calf cult at Dan, see S. B. Gurewicz, "When Did the Cult Associated with the 'Golden Calves' Fully Develop in the Northern Kingdom?" *AusBR* 2 (1952) 41–44; O. Michel, O. Bauernfeind, and O. Betz, "Der Tempel der goldenen Kuh," *ZNW* 49 (1958) 197–212; J. Dus, "Die

such a cult is actually a defection from the true worship of the Deity. Thus he disdainfully derides it as an oath to "your god." Note, too, that the vocalization of the oath formula is חֵי,[21] which is employed for all oaths other than those taken in the name of the Lord; the latter oaths are vocalized חַי.[22]

The third oath formula is "By the life of the way of Beer-sheba!" (חֵי דֶּרֶךְ בְּאֵר־שָׁבַע). Once again the prophet recalls the participation of northern Israel in the cult that took place in Judah at Beer-sheba; see 5:5. The correct interpretation of the oath taken in the name of "דֶּרֶךְ Beer-sheba," however, is very problematical. Some suggest reading דֹּדְךָ[23] (literally, "your uncle" or "your darling"), which is extended to mean "your patron deity/your tutelary god."[24] This line of exegesis is ultimately derived from G's translation, ὁ θεός σου ("your god"), which was assumed to be an inner Greek error for ὁ θεῖος σου ("your uncle").[25] However, such an expanded semantic development from "uncle" or "kinsman" to "patron deity" is totally unattested in the Bible. Two other suggestions involve only a different vocalization of the letters דרך. One proposal is to read דֹּרְךָ ("your assembly"),[26] a meaning based on Ugaritic; compare *dr bn ʾilm* ("And all the assembly *[dr]* of the sons of El/the gods").[27] Even in Ugaritic, however, the substantive *dr* appears only in a context in which reference is made specifically to gods.[28] More significant and decisive is the fact that דוֹר never refers to an "assembly" or a "pantheon" in Hebrew. A similar criticism may be leveled against the other proposal, relating Heb. דַּרְכְּךָ to Ugar. *drkt* ("dominion, strength, might"),[29] applied here as an epithet of the deity.[30] Such a meaning, although often

Stierbilder von Bethel und Dan und das Problem der Moseschar," *AION* 18 (1968) 105–37; H. Donner, "'Hier sind deine Götter, Israel,'" in *Wort und Geschichte. Festschrift für K. Elliger zum 70. Geburtstag* (ed. H. Gese and H. P. Rüger; AOAT 18; Neukirchen-Vluyn: Neukirchener Verlag, 1973) 45–50. The phrase itself may have been patterned after the expression אֵלֶּה אֱלֹהֶיךָ יִשְׂרָאֵל ("These are your gods, O Israel") in Exod 32:4; 1 Kgs 12:28. Compare also Neh 9:18.

21 See Gen 42:15, 16; 1 Sam 1:26; 17:55; 20:3; 25:26; 2 Sam 14:19; 15:21; 2 Kgs 2:2, 4, 6; 4:30; and the next phrase in Amos. The only exception is Dan 12:7.

22 See the manifold references in *KB*, 295. For its occurrence in two ostraca from Lachish, see *KAI*, I.193:9; 196:12. For this specific oath formula, see M. Greenberg ("The Hebrew Oath Particle *ḤAY/ḤĒ*," *JBL* 76 [1957] 34–39), who interprets the noun "life" as being in the construct state, "by the life of Yahweh." See also H.-J. Kraus, "Der lebendige Gott. Ein Kapitel biblischer Theologie," *EvT* 27 (1967) 169–200; M. Z. Segal, "On the Structure of Oaths and Vows in Hebrew," *Leš* 1 (1928–1929) 215–27 (Heb.).

Note that the common word for "oath" in Akkadian, *nišu*, literally means "life"; *CAD*, *N*, II. *nišu* A, 290ff. Thus *niš ili* ("an oath by the god") literally refers to the "life of the god" (= Heb. חֵי אֱלֹהֶיךָ).

23 For example, K. Galling, "Bethel und Gilgal II," 38; see already Hoffmann, "Versuche," 123; Oettli, *Amos und Hosea;* Marti, 220; Nowack, 163–64; Maag, *Text,* 55–56; Deden; Snaith; Osty; Markert, *Struktur;* van Hoonacker, 277; Sellin, 216–17; Robinson-Horst, 102, 104; Hammershaimb, 129–30.

24 The often cited reference to the meaning of the root in the Mesha inscription (*KAI*, I.181:11–12) is still very much debated and cannot be used as evidence here. For a partial bibliography, see Wolff, 323 *y*. See also A. J. Bjoerndalen, *Untersuchungen zur allegorischen Rede der Propheten Amos und Jesaja* (BZAW 165; Berlin and New York: de Gruyter, 1986) 260.

25 See Rudolph (268), who cites Wutz (in *Duodecim prophetae* [ed. J. Ziegler; SVT 13; Göttingen: Vandenhoeck & Ruprecht, 1963, ²1967]) but rejects the suggestion.

26 F. J. Neuberg, "An Unrecognized Meaning of Hebrew *DÔR*," *JNES* 9 (1950) 215–17. So, too, P. R. Ackroyd, "The Meaning of Hebrew דוֹר Reconsidered," *JSS* 13 (1968) 4. Compare D. N. Freedman and J. Lundbom, "*dôr*," *TWAT* II (1977) 187. They make totally unconvincing references to Pss 49:20; 84:11.

27 *KAI*, I.26:3, 19.

28 So, too, Wolff, 324. Rudolph, 268.

29 Ugar. *drkt* / / *mlk;* see *UT*, 702. For references in Ugaritic, see R. E. Whitaker, *A Concordance of the Ugaritic Literature* (Cambridge: Harvard University, 1972) 189.

30 See S. Bartina, "'Vivit Potentia Beer-Seba!' Amos 8:14," *VD* 34 (1956) 202–10; E. Jacob, *Ras Šamra-Ugarit et l'Ancien Testament* (Cahiers d'Archéologie Biblique 12; Paris: Delachaux & Niestlé, 1960) 66; Amsler, 237; Soggin, 140; Barstad, *Religious Polemics,* 195 (who compares Ugar. *bʿlt drkt,* in *RŠ* 24.252).

cited for many biblical passages,[31] is still very dubious for Hebrew.[32]

Thus, until a more convincing interpretation is suggested, one is left to surmise that Heb. דֶּרֶךְ ("way, path")[33] may refer to the taking of an oath by the life of the "way," that is, by the "pilgrimage to Beer-sheba."[34] Although such an oath is unattested in the Bible, comparison has often been made to the Muslim custom of swearing by the pilgrimage route to Mecca. This, too, for Amos is naught but apostasy. The oath formulae of northern Israel that encompass, as a merism, the shrines from Dan to Beer-sheba are all proscribed and censured by the prophet. Thus, they all "shall fall and never rise again."[35] Their collapse will be total; see 5:2.

31 Especially by M. Dahood in many places, for example, "Ugaritic *DRKT* and Biblical *DEREK*," *TS* 15 (1954) 627–31. For the literature pro and con on the identification, see Barstad, *Religious Polemics,* 194 n 284. This meaning is found (but very rarely) in Rabbinic literature. See E. Y. Kutscher, *Hebrew and Aramaic Studies* (ed. Z. Ben-Hayyim, A. Dotan, and G. Sarfatti; Jerusalem: Magnes, 1977) 345–46 (Heb.), citing S. Lieberman, "Forgotten Meanings," *Leš* 32 (1968) 90–92 (Heb.).

32 See Hos 10:13, where Heb. דַּרְכְּךָ (// גִּבּוֹרֶיךָ, "warriors") is translated by G as *ἐν τοῖς ἅρμασίν* ("in your chariots" = Heb. בְּרִכְבְּךָ).

33 For other earlier suggested emendations, see Harper, 191. Gordis ("Studies," 259) suggests vocalizing דָּרַךְ ("He who dwells in your midst").

34 See Wolff, 332; Rudolph, 268, 270–71. See also E. Würthwein ("Erwägungen zu Psalm CXXXIX," *VT* 7 [1957] 173ff.), who interprets it as "the practice of the cult." For literature on the sanctuary at Beer-sheba, see n 39 to Amos 5:5. For the popular etymology of the site Beersheba relating to the taking of an oath, see Gen 21:31.

35 There is no reason to transfer these words to the beginning of the verse; against Marti, 219; Nowack, 163; Sellin, 215; Maag, *Text,* 56; Robinson-Horst, 102; Rudolph, 268. For the opposite image employing the same two verbs, נפל and קום, see Amos 9:11.

9

Fifth Vision: Inescapability from Divine Judgment

1 I saw my Lord standing by the altar, and he said,
"Strike the capital so that the doorjambs tremble,
And *. . . all of them.
I shall slay them to the very last man with the sword.
No fugitive shall escape,
No survivor slip away.
2 If they dig down to Sheol,
From there my hand shall take them.
And if they climb up to heaven,
From there I will bring them down.
3 If they hide on the summit of Carmel,
There I will search and seize them.
And if they conceal themselves from my sight
At the bottom of the sea,
From there I shall command the serpent to bite them.
4 And if they go into captivity before their enemies,
There I will command the sword to slay them.
I will fix my eye upon them
For evil and not for good.
5 The Lord, God of Hosts, is he
Who touches the earth and it quavers,
And all who dwell on it mourn.
All of it surges like the Nile
And subsides like the Nile of Egypt.
6 Who built his upper chambers in heaven,
And founded his vault on the earth.
Who summons the waters of the sea,
And pours them over the face of the land.
The Lord is his name!

***Hebrew obscure**

The fifth vision[1] differs from the previous four in several aspects. The Lord does not make the prophet see (הִרְאַנִי, Amos 7:1, 4, 7; 8:1) but is himself seen (רָאִיתִי אֶת אֲדֹנָי). No object bearing a symbolic significance is present. No dialogue takes place between the Deity and Amos, but only one extended monologue in which the Lord issues a command and then proceeds to delineate its devastating consequences.[2] The fifth vision, moreover, constitutes the climactic conclusion of the prior four. Whereas the fourth announced the "end" of Israel (8:2), the fifth describes the coup de grâce in minute detail. Whereas the third and fourth pertained to the inalterability of destruction, the final vision adds the dimension of the absolute inescapability from the forthcoming disaster.

1 According to some commentators (for example, G. Fohrer, "Die Gattung der Berichte über symbolische Handlungen der Propheten," *ZAW* 64 [1952] 115; reprinted in idem, *Studien zur alttestamentliche Prophetie [1949–1965]* [BZAW 99; Berlin: Töpelmann, 1967] 107; and Reventlow, *Amt*, 48–50), this scene is interpreted as a symbolic act and not as a vision. See, however, Wolff, 337; Rudolph, 243.

2 There are also no opening or closing formulae.

The vision centers about *the* altar, most likely the one located in the main shrine of Bethel.[3] The presence of the Deity at this sacred site would lead one initially to anticipate a favorable reaction to the cultic proceedings, indicating that the offerings upon the altar were favorably accepted. Yet Amos, once again in his penchant for paradox and surprise, turns the tables on his audience by overturning the altar. The Lord's presence now is a guarantee not of protection but of destruction. The cultic shrine and the worshipers are the object of God's wrath, and both are destined for annihilation.[4]

■ **1** Amos sees the Lord[5] "standing by[6] (נִצָּב עַל) the altar."[7] The use of the definite article ("*the* altar"; הַמִּזְבֵּחַ) leads one to understand that the vision centered about the main altar in the shrine of Bethel,[8] most likely at the time of some major holiday when throngs of worshipers would be present at this central cultic site.

The prophet overhears the Lord giving the following order: "Strike (הַךְ)[9] the capital (הַכַּפְתּוֹר)[10] so that the doorjambs tremble." To whom is this second-person command directed? The ambiguity and lack of clarity allow for several possibilities of interpretation. It may have been addressed to the prophet[11] or to one of the heavenly host.[12] Other commentators, basing their analyses on the following first-person verb אֶהֱרֹג ("I shall kill"), relate the action directly to the Lord himself. They therefore suggest reading either וַיַּךְ ("And he smote")[13] or (assuming a haplography) the infinitive absolute, הַכֵּה,[14] or an emphatic, הַכֵּה אַכֶּה ("I shall smite").[15]

The "capital" (כַּפְתּוֹר)[16] refers to the spherical knobs at

3 Most commentators. It does not refer to Jerusalem (contrary to T; Procksch; Neher, *Amos;* Weiser, *Prophetie,* 188), or to a sanctuary on Mt. Carmel (contrary to K. Galling, "Der Gott Karmel und die Ächtung der fremden Götter," in *Geschichte und Altes Testament: Albrecht Alt zum siebzigsten Geburtstag* [ed. G. Ebeling; Tübingen: Mohr (Siebeck), 1953] 119).

4 Rudolph (244) interprets this as a chiastic reshaping of Amos 7:9. The initial threat of the latter passage, which was directed against all the cultic sites (v 9a), is here concentrated upon the one main sanctuary, and the threat of the "sword" (v 9b) is here extended from the royal house to the entire population.

For an attempt to discover a parallel structure between Amos 9:1–15 and 8:7–14, see D. A. Garrett, "The Structure of Amos as a Testimony to Its Integrity," *JETS* 27 (1984) 275–76.

5 See 2 Chr 18:18. Unlike the first four visions in which Amos was shown the vision, here, in the fifth and final one he sees it himself (רָאִיתִי).

6 Heb. נִצָּב עַל can mean "standing by" (see, for example, Gen 24:13, 43; 28:13; Exod 7:15; Num 23:3, 6, 17) or "standing on" (see, for example, Exod 33:21; 34:2). Compare the similar expression עמד על in 1 Kgs 13:1: "While Jeroboam was standing on the altar (עֹמֵד עַל) at Bethel." (Note the comment in *NJPS:* "standing on, i.e., at the top of the steps or ramp.") Compare, too, the third vision in which Amos also sees the Lord, נִצָּב עַל, in 7:7.

7 When the Lord is seen on high, in his temple (Isa 6:1) or in heaven (1 Kgs 22:19), the final judgment is nigh.

8 Herein lies an associative connection with the end of chapter 8, which also pertains to central shrines. The identification with Bethel is the commonly accepted interpretation. For an extrabiblical vision that takes place in a temple, see *ina bīt Itur-Mer īmur ummami* ("He saw [the vision] in the temple of Itur-Mer as follows"), ARM, X 10:6–7.

9 Heb. הַךְ is an apocopated singular imperative from the root נכה; compare הַט (from נטה) Pss 17:6; 119:36; and נַס (from נסה), Dan 1:12. For this verb in Amos, see also 3:15; 6:11.

10 G's reading, *τὸ ἱλαστήριον* ("the mercy seat") = Heb. הַכַּפֹּרֶת (a metathesis of the last two letters of הַכַּפְתֹּר), is not to be preferred. The prophet is expressing, by means of the words הַכַּפְתּוֹר and הַסִּפִּים, a merism, that is, from top to bottom—the entire temple. For these two nouns, see also Zeph 2:14b: "The jackdaws and owls roost on its capitals (בְּכַפְתֹּרֶיהָ) . . . and the raven [croaks] on the threshold" (בַּסַּף). Heb. הַכַּפְתּוֹר was chosen not only because architecturally it is the correct word but also because of the ensuing catchword association with כַּפְתּוֹר ("Caphtor") in v 7.

11 For example, van Hoonacker; Neher, *Amos;* Reventlow, *Amt,* 48–49.

12 For example, Hitzig-Steiner; Keil; Harper, 188; Theis-Lippel; Driver, 202; Gese, "Komposition," 83.

13 For example, Marti; Robinson-Horst; Weiser, *Profetie,* 42; Amsler; Hammershaimb, 131; Wolff, 334. These commentators then transpose וַיֹּאמֶר to follow הַסִּפִּים.

14 For example, Duhm, "Anmerkungen."

15 For example, Budde, "Amos," 101; Sellin[2]; Rudolph, 241; Soggin, 120.

16 The noun is usually interpreted as a collective singular; see, for example, Harper, 188; Hammershaimb, 131. Gese ("Komposition," 83 n 26), however, interpreting the singular literally, refers it to "die Spitze des Tempels, sozusagen um das Akroterion, den obersten Teil der Tempelfassade" ("the pinnacle of the Temple, so to speak the acroter, the highest section of the Temple façade"). See also

the heads of the columns of the pillars[17] that uphold the roof of the shrine. They are smitten with such force that the "doorjambs" (הַסִּפִּים)[18] of the temple "tremble" (וְיִרְעֲשׁוּ).[19] The entire temple, from top to bottom, is in convulsion. The destruction of the shrine would naturally shatter the faith of those who put their hope and trust in the security of the cult. (See 3:14; 5:21–23.)[20]

The next phrase remains a *crux interpretum*. The first word, וּבְצַעַם, is a *qal* second-person singular imperative[21] with a third-person plural suffix.[22] The problem, however, is how to interpret the meaning of the verb. There is a Hebrew root בצע that belongs to the vocabulary of weaving. It refers technically to "cutting off the thread" and, by extension, to the thread of life.[23] See Isa 38:12b: "My life is rolled up like a web and cut (יְבַצְּעֵנִי, literally, "and he cuts me") from the thrum." It comes to signify "to cut down/off," that is, "to kill." See Job 27:8a: "What hope has the impious man when he is cut down" (יִבְצָע; some suggest reading the *puʿal*, יְבֻצַּע); and Job 6:9: "Would that God consented to crush me, loose his hand and cut me off" (וִיבַצְּעֵנִי). If this were the intention here, the following בְּרֹאשׁ would not make much sense. To whom or to what would the verbal suffix "them" refer? The only antecedents in the sentence are the previously mentioned capital and doorjambs; this verb simply does not apply to them, even if one interprets רֹאשׁ as the "heads" of the capitals (1 Kgs 7:16).[24] However, כַּפְתּוֹר represents the top of the columns, and thus רֹאשׁ would be superfluous. The emending of the verb to the first person,[25] (אֲבַצְּעֵ(ם) ("I shall cut [them] off"; corresponding

Wolff, 339.

17 See the decoration on the golden lampstands in Exod 25:31ff.

18 See Isa 6:4, in which the corresponding verb is וַיָּנֻעוּ ("and they shook"). For a comparison of the two, see M. Kaplan, "Isaiah 6:1–11," *JBL* 45 (1926) 251–59. Rudolph (241) suggests adding וְיִפֹּל הַסִּפּוּן ("and let the ceiling fall"). For הַסִּפֻּן, see 1 Kgs 6:15. See already van Hoonacker and Osty. The addition, however, is totally unnecessary. For סַף, see also Judg 19:27; 1 Kgs 14:17.

Heb. סִפִּים is still translated in several different ways. See *KB*, 720, סַף, II. For the Akkadian interdialectal semantic and etymological equivalent, *sippu*, see A. Salonen, *Die Türen des Alten Mesopotamien* (Annales Academiae Scientiarum Fennicae B124; Helsinki: Suomalaisen Tiedeakatemia, 1961) 62ff.; *CAD, S*, 300–303, "doorframe, doorjambs." For analogous examples from Akkadian texts, see *amaḫḫaṣ sippama ušbalkat dalāti* ("I will smash the doorframe and dislodge the doors"), *CT* 15, 45:18; *sippam iʾbutu igārum irtūt* ("They demolished the doorframe; the wall shook") *CAD, A*, I.42, 1a); *I/J*, 38, 1), cited from the Gilgamesh Epic. A *sippum* is found on both the right and left sides of the door or gate: for example, referring to the sheep's liver, *[si]ppi abullim i[mittum si]ppi abullim šumēlum*, YOS 10, 29:8 in Goetze, *Omen Texts*. Goetze (*The Laws of Eshnunna* [AASOR 31; New Haven: ASOR, 1956] 99–100) refers it to "the stone doorjambs together with the threshold and the lintel [which] form the frame of the door." For a suggested (but very questionable) example from Mari of two opposite parts of a city gate, see ARM, X 9:12–13, 15, where along with the *sippu* there appears *rūšum*, which P.-R. Berger ("Die Alašia-Briefe, Ugaritica 5, Noug. *Nrn.* 22–24," *UF* 1 [1969] 221) regards as West Semitic *rôʾš* ("head"). However, most relate the latter to *rūšu* ("dirt"). See J. M. Sasson, "An Apocalyptic Vision from Mari? Speculations on ARM X:9," *M.A.R.I.* 1 (1982) 154, g, and 156; and *CAD, S*, 301.

19 The pointing וְ indicates the result of the blow. Because the verb רעשׁ is very often employed in connection with earthquakes, several exegetes interpret this vision as symbolic of an earthquake and refer back to Amos 1:1. See Weiser, *Profetie*, 188; Robinson-Horst, 104; Fosbroke, 845; Maag, *Text*, 45; Wolff, 339; Rudolph, 245; Soggin, 120.

20 For a different interpretation, see J. Ouellette, "The Shaking of the Thresholds in Amos 9:1," *HUCA* 43 (1972) 23–27.

21 For example, ibn Ganaḥ; Kimchi.

22 The punctuation בְּצַעַם and not בְּצָעֵם (see Num 11:28, כְּלָאֵם) or בָּצְעֵם (see Prov 3:3, קָשְׁרֵם) remains problematic. See *GKC*, 61g; otherwise, *BLe*, 51a. See M. L. Margolis, "Notes on Semitic Grammar," *AJSL* 19 (1902–1903) 45–48.

23 See Arab. *baḍaʿa* ("to cut") and Old South Arab. *bḍʿ* ("to slay," esp. with a sword, and "strip"). See W. W. Müller, "Altsüdarabische Beiträge zum Hebräischen Lexikon" *ZAW* 75 (1963) 307; *KB* (141) also cites a possible example from Ugaritic.

24 So Cripps, 256; Harper, 188. According to Gese ("Komposition," 84 n 30), the expression should be translated "an ihrer aller Spitze" ("on the head of all of them"); see Deut 20:9; 2 Chr 13:12.

25 Or אֲבַצַּע without the suffix; see Marti; Maag, *Text*, 45; Wolff, 334; Soggin, 120.

to the following first person, אֶהֱרֹג) still leaves בְּרֹאשׁ unresolved. Because the plural suffix of the verb must refer, however, to the people gathered at the sanctuary—and not to the capital and doorjambs, as the following כֻּלָּם ("all of them") and אַחֲרִיתָם ("the remainder of them") clearly indicate—several commentators favor emending בְּרֹאשׁ to בְּרַעַשׁ ("by an earthquake"), that is, "I shall cut them (אֲבַצְּעֵם) all off by an earthquake."[26] This, however, is forcing the issue. Does the prophet actually have an earthquake in mind? If so, can one employ the verb בצע in connection with an earthquake? It is, moreover, very difficult to dismiss the reading בְּרֹאשׁ for two reasons, both literary. First is the pervasive catchword principle that Amos continually employs. Just as כַּפְתּוֹר reverberates in v 7, so, too, רֹאשׁ reappears in v 3. Second, it is very possible to interpret בְּרֹאשׁ as a paired correlative term with the following אַחֲרִיתָם; compare the expression רֵאשִׁית–אַחֲרִית.[27] (It is also tempting to interpret רֹאשׁ and אַחֲרִית as an additional veiled personification and amplification of the paired כַּפְתּוֹר and סִפִּים. Just as the temple is about to be destroyed entirely, from top to bottom, so, too, the people, from their רֹאשׁ ["heads," that is, their leaders] to their אַחֲרִית [all the "residue," that is, the "rest" of the population].)[28] Once this skillful wordplay of the prophet is noted, there is no need to resort to the other suggested emendation of converting בְּרֹאשׁ by metathesis to a verb, אֶשְׁבֹּר ("I shall break"), and וּבְצָעֵם to a noun, וּבְעֵצִים ("and with beams/rafters," literally, "wood"): "I shall smash all of them to pieces with the rafters"[29] (that will fall from the ceiling when the temple collapses).[30]

Although the difficulty of the exact interpretation remains, the sense of the verse is still clear—the destruction will be total and comprehensive: "all of them" (כֻּלָּם) shall perish. Whatever remnant (אַחֲרִית)[31] shall remain (see 4:2), "I shall slay . . . with[32] the sword; no fugitive shall escape (יָנוּס), no survivor (פָּלִיט) slip away" (יִמָּלֵט).[33] Once again Amos accentuates the inescapability from divine judgment. The finality of doom looms on the horizon for all; see 2:14–16; 5:18–20. Here it is pronounced precisely at the time when the people gather to worship the Lord and thereby emphasizes that salvation cannot be found through the cult or at the cultic centers.

■ **2** After the general, all-inclusive introduction, there follows a vivid description of the frantic and frenetic flight of the people to escape divine retribution.[34] No

26 For example, Weiser, *Profetie,* 143; Marti; Reventlow, *Amt,* 48; Maag, *Text,* 45; Soggin, 120. Rudolph (241–42) suggests reading וּבִצְּעָם, interpreting the passage to mean "[des Lebens] beraubt werden [sie alle]" ("[all of them] were deprived [of life]").

27 See Deut 11:12; Isa 46:10; Job 8:7; 42:12; Eccl 7:8.

28 The suggestion is raised as part of the interpretation of Ehrlich, *Mikrâ,* 3.417; and idem, *Randglossen,* 5.253. (See already Kimchi.) He vocalizes the letters בצעם as a noun, בִּצְעָם, "so soll ihre Gewinnsucht (בֶּצַע) auf ihrer aller Haupt kommen" ("so shall their greed boomerang against them"). In *Randglossen,* however, he interprets בֶּצַע as "Ende," citing Jer 51:13, and translates, "ebenso soll ihr Ende bei ihrer aller Führern anfangen" ("just so shall their end [the people's] begin with all their leaders").

29 See Sellin. For "beams/rafters," he compares 1 Kgs 15:22, but the substantive עֵצִים there simply means "timber."

30 F. Horst (*Hiob* [BKAT 16/1; Neukirchen-Vluyn: Neukirchener Verlag, 1960] 196) suggests that רֹאשׁ here means "poison": "I will make an end of them all with poison." However, this interpretation is totally incompatible with the present context.

31 See Gese, "Beiträge," 436–37; Rudolph, "Schwierige Amosstellen," in *Wort und Geschichte: Festschrift für Kurt Elliger zum 70. Geburtstag* (ed. H. Gese and H.-P. Rüger; AOAT 18; Neukirchen-Vluyn: Neukirchener Verlag, 1973) 162, and his commentary, 241–42.

32 Note the inclusio formed by the verb הרג and the noun חֶרֶב in vv 1 and 4. For בַּחֶרֶב, see again v 10. See N. W. Lund, *Chiasmus in the New Testament: A Study in Formgeschichte* (Chapel Hill: University of North Carolina, 1942) 86–87.

33 For the pairing of the verbs נוס and מלט, see also Amos 2:14–16; 1 Sam 19:10; Jer 46:6; 48:6, 19. The first stich employs the repetition of the root נוס: יָנוּס . . . נָס ; the second, however, alters the verb and noun, יִמָּלֵט . . . פָּלִיט because there is no noun formation derived from the verb מלט in the Bible. Nevertheless, both expressions are alliterative.

For Heb. פלט, see Ugar. *plṭ* ("to save"), *UT,* 2048. See also J. Nougayrol, "Textes Suméro-Accadiens des Archives et Bibliothèques, privées d'Ugarit," in *Ugaritica V* (ed. C. F. A. Schaeffer and others; Mission de Ras Shamra 16; Paris: Guethner, 1968) 243, 20: *pu-la-ṭu = šūzubu* (Akk.), "to save." Both Heb. מלט and פלט may be related to Akk. *bulluṭu* ("to save/keep alive").

34 Compare similarly *ABL,* 350:2–7: "No sooner had he defeated them, than they renewed hostilities. But when overtaken by the oaths of the king, my lord, whoever has escaped from the sword will die of hunger" *(ša lapan namṣari ušēzibu ina bubūtu imâti).*

place in the universe, however, is beyond the absolute control and authority of the Lord. They are not beyond his reach no matter where they may hide or to where they may flee. They soon will comprehend that the Lord will apprehend them even in the remotest recesses of the world. In five conditional (אִם) sentences highlighted by a fivefold repetition of מִשָּׁם, "from there" (= everywhere),[35] Amos unconditionally declares that all possible escape routes are blocked off.

First, "If they dig down (יַחְתְּרוּ בְ־)[36] to Sheol, from there my hand shall take them."[37] If they make an arduous attempt to dig their way into the netherworld, into Sheol, it will be of no avail. Although at times Sheol is considered beyond the limits of God's reach and one cannot pray to him from that nether region (see, for example, Isa 38:18; Ps 6:6; 88:6, 11–13; 115:17),[38] nevertheless it is clearly affirmed here that the Lord's sovereignty extends even to this subterranean domain. See similarly 1 Sam 2:6; Hos 13:14; Ps 49:16; Prov 15:11;[39] note that in the passages from Hosea and Psalms the phrase יַד שְׁאוֹל, "the clutches (literally, "the hand") of Sheol" appears. In the present verse the prophet may be skillfully alluding to and punning upon this expression. The Lord does not say that *he* will capture them even there, but that his "hand" (יָד) will retrieve them.[40] Thus the יָד of the Lord will snatch them from the יָד of Sheol—but not in order to save them.

Second, completing this merism is the polar vertical opposite direction:[41] "If they climb up to heaven, from there I will bring them down." For שְׁאוֹל and שָׁמַיִם in antithetical parallelism, see Isa 14:13–15; Ps 139:8; Job 11:8.[42] No matter how high they ascend, they will be overtaken. Compare Jer 51:53; Obad 4. For the employment of the verbal opposites עלה and ירד, see Isa 14:13–15; Jer 48:5; Pss 104:8; 107:26; and for the polar substantives, see Jer 48:5.

Attention is usually drawn to the parallel in Ps 139:7–12:[43] "Where can I escape from your spirit? Where can I flee from your presence? If I ascend to heaven, you are there. If I descend to Sheol, you are there too. If I take wing with the dawn to come to rest on the western horizon[44] even there your hand will be guiding me; your right hand will be holding me fast. If I say, 'Surely darkness will conceal me, night will provide me with cover,' darkness is not dark for you; night is as light as

35 For other pentads, see the fivefold repetition of the refrain וְלֹא שַׁבְתֶּם עָדַי נְאֻם־ה׳, Amos 4:6–11; 7:17; and 7—9, the five visions. The two final stichs of v 1 along with these create a heptad here. The use of anaphora, מִשָּׁם, confirms "the fact of God's ineluctable presence in all conceivable corners of creation" (Alter, *Art*, 75).

36 Heb. חָתַר בְּ־ always implies strenuous activity, whether "breaking into," as here and Job 24:16 (read כַּבָּתִּים for בָּתִּים), or "breaking through," Ezek 8:8; 12:5, 7, 12.

37 For the verb לקח, see 6:13.

38 See Kaufmann, *Toledoth*, 2.544–48.

39 There is no need to relate this idea solely to the realm of wisdom literature, as do Terrien ("Amos and Wisdom," 110–11) and Wolff (340).

40 See *ašar marqītišunu qātī ikšussunūti* ("My hand reached them in the place where they had taken refuge"); M. Streck, *Assurbanipal und die letzten assyrischen Könige bis zum Untergang Niniveh's* (VAB 7; Leipzig: Hinrichs, 1916) 74 IX 41. Akk. *qātī ikšussunūti* = Heb. יָדִי תִּקָּחֵם.

41 This then continues the top-to-bottom image of the previous verse. Note, too, the assonance of הַשָּׁמַיִם and מִשָּׁם.

42 Compare similarly Isa 7:11, reading שְׁאֹלָה ("to Sheol") for שְׁאָלָה ("ask"), with the Greek versions α', σ', and θ', εἰς ᾅδην ("into Hades"). So, too, in Akkadian, in which *šamû* ("heaven") and *erṣetu* ("netherworld") function as the semantic and partially etymological cognates of the Hebrew. See *EA*, 264:17, in the following note. Compare likewise S. Langdon, *Babylonian Penitential Psalms to Which Are Added Fragments of the Creation Epic from Kish* (Paris: Guethner, 1929) 31–32. When Adad is angry and roars, not only the heaven, earth, and hills quake, but *ilū ša šamê ana šamê itelû* ("the gods of heaven ascend to heaven") and *ilūh ša erṣetim ana erṣetim iterbu* ("the gods of the netherworld enter the netherworld").

43 See *EA*, 264:15–19: "Even if we were to ascend to heaven *(nitelli ana šamê)*, if we were to descend to the netherworld *(nurrad ina erṣetim)*, our head is in your hands." In this text as well, the context is the impossibility of escape (here, from the king).

44 Note that here, too, there is a reference to the sea, יָם, as there is in the next verse of Amos.

day. Darkness and light are the same."[45] These verses also give vivid expression to the omnipresence of the Lord. Here they reiterate the theme of the absolute inescapability from the punishment of the Lord, a motif also found in Amos 2:14–16; 5:19.

■ **3** After describing that escape is totally impossible anywhere in the cosmos (neither in Sheol below nor in heaven above), Amos continues by denying them even the security of the most secluded and inaccessible places on earth—mountains above and sea below. Third, "If they hide on (יֵחָבְאוּ בְּ־)[46] the summit of Carmel (הַכַּרְמֶל בְּרֹאשׁ),[47] there I will search[48] and seize them." Neither the lofty summit of Mount Carmel (1,800 feet above sea level), nor its dense forests, nor its multiple caves[49] will prevent the Lord from apprehending the fugitives. Note the chiastic structure of this verse in relation to the former one.

Fourth, should one opt to conceal oneself from the sight of the Lord[50] in some cavernous submarine site at the bottom of the sea,[51] from there God will command his servant, the mythological dragon of chaos whom he defeated in primeval times[52] and turned into his obedi-

45 See H. Hommel, "Das religionsgeschichtliche Problem des 139. Psalms," *ZAW* 47 (1929) 110–24.

46 For חבא ב־, see, for example, Josh 10:16, 17; 2 Sam 17:9.

47 For רֹאשׁ הַכַּרְמֶל, see also the beginning of the book, 1:2. The expression appears also in 1 Kgs 18:42. Heb. בְּרֹאשׁ here is linked by the catchword principle to בְּרֹאשׁ in v 1. See previously.

48 Even the Lord must first "search them out" when hidden in such remote recesses.

49 See Kimchi. For Mount Carmel, the mountain range on the northernmost coastal plain of Israel, see Z. Kallai, "Carmel," *EM* 4.324–29 (Heb.); G. W. Van Beek, "Carmel, Mount," *IDB* 1.538. Crenshaw (*Hymnic Affirmation,* 133) makes the interesting observation that the Carmel may also have been chosen because it projects into the Mediterranean, which provides the point immediately preceding the next place of "refuge," the sea. For additional support to this suggestion, see (the problematic verse) Jer 46:18: "As surely as Tabor is among the mountains and Carmel is by the sea" (וּכְכַרְמֶל בַּיָּם).

Reference to the "promontory" (רֹאשׁ) of Mount Carmel may be already found in an Egyptian inscription of Thutmose III from the mid-fifteenth century B.C.E. (ראש קדש, "sacred promontory"), most likely referring to the Carmel; see Simons, *Handbook,* 27ff., no. 48; and in an Assyrian inscription from the Neo-Assyrian period where reference is made to *Baʿal raʾsi.* See E. Michel, "Die Assur-Texte Salmanassars III," *WO* 2 (1954–1959) 38–39. For this identification, see A. T. Olmstead, "Shalmaneser III and the Establishment of the Assyrian Power," *JAOS* 41 (1921) 372. See also M. Avi-Yonah, "Mt. Carmel and the God of Baalbek," *IEJ* 2 (1952) 121; Y. Aharoni, *The Settlement of the Israelite Tribes in Upper Galilee* (Jerusalem: Magnes, 1957) 122, 130 (Heb.); and idem, *The Land of the Bible. A Historical Geography* (tr. A. F. Rainey; London: Burns & Oates, 1967) 56–57. See also M. C. Astour, "Carmel, Mount," *IDBSup* 141.

50 Heb. מִנֶּגֶד עֵינַי ("from my eyes") is not an addition (against Wolff, 335), as the catchword עֵינַי ("my eye") in the next verse and in the next pericope, v 8, clearly demonstrate. Verses 3 and 4 are patterned in a chiastic fashion. See comments to v 4.

For a similar statement employing the same verb, לְהִסָּתֵר ("to conceal oneself"), and the expression נֶגֶד עֵינָי, see Jer 16:17: "For my eyes (עֵינַי) are on all their ways. They are not hidden (נִסְתְּרוּ) from my presence. Their iniquity is not concealed from my sight" (מִנֶּגֶד עֵינָי). For the theme of the "eyes of the Lord," see 2 Chr 16:9, and see notes to Amos 9:8 for references and bibliography.

51 Heb. קַרְקַע הַיָּם (literally, "the floor of the sea") appears only here. Note again the catchword principle of the noun יָם ("sea") with 8:12. In both sections there is a description of a futile search (for the word of God or for the security of concealment). Here again is another merism of polar opposites. For the phenomenon of merism, see J. Krašovec, *Der Merismus im Biblisch-Hebräischen und Nordwestsemitischen* (BibOr 33; Rome: Pontifical Biblical Institute, 1977).

52 For the primordial battle between the Lord and the sea serpent along with its ancient Near-Eastern antecedents, see U. Cassuto, "Israelite Epic Poetry," in idem, *Studies on the Bible and Ancient Orient: Biblical and Canaanite Literatures* (2 vols.; tr. I. Abrahams; Jerusalem: Magnes, 1972) 2.62–90 (Heb.); T. L. Fenton, "Differing Approaches to the Theomachy Myth in Old Testament Writers," in *Studies in Bible and the Ancient Near East, Presented to Samuel E. Loewenstamm on His Seventieth Birthday* (ed. Y. Avishur and J. Blau; Jerusalem: E. Rubinstein, 1978) 337–81 (Heb.). See also S. Ahitub and S. A. Loewenstamm, "*nāḥāš,*" *EM* 5.821–22 (Heb.).

ent subordinate servant,[53] to dispatch him with his deadly poisonous bite.[54] Note, however, that the Lord does not say that he will personally seize the one who flees to the bottom of the sea. In this remote domain he assigns the sea monster to execute his retributive punishment. Compare, too, the following verse in which another agent of the Deity, the sword, also serves his bidding.[55]

No place is hidden from the omnipresent scrutiny of the Lord. See Jer 23:24: "'If a man enters a hiding place, do I not see him?' says the Lord. 'For I fill both heaven and earth,' declares the Lord."[56]

■ **4** Fifth, and finally, after exhausting all possible vertical realms of escape, from zenith to nadir, the scene switches to the horizontal dimension—even the farthest distance abroad shall be of no avail.[57] Should they deceive themselves into thinking that their sole source of rescue would be paradoxically to "go into captivity" (יֵלְכוּ בַשְּׁבִי),[58] even "there I will command the sword to slay them." For those who naively think that safety lies in fleeing the borders of Israel into an alien land and thereby being beyond the reach of the Lord, there comes a rude awakening. No geographical realm is beyond the sovereignty of the God of Israel, whose absolute control extends over all nations. He has at his disposal "the sword,"[59] which will execute his vengeance no matter how far they may be driven into captivity.[60]

Note should be made here of two literary devices employed by the prophet. First, the mention of the sword that will "slay them" (הַחֶרֶב וַהֲרָגָתַם) forms an inclusio with the first verse of this chapter (בַּחֶרֶב אֶהֱרֹג). Second, this verse is chiastically arranged in relation to the former verse. Verse 3 begins by stating that no one can hide from the eyes (עֵינַי) of the Lord and then continues, מִשָּׁם אֲצַוֶּה אֶת־הַנָּחָשׁ וּנְשָׁכָם ("From there I shall command the serpent to bite them"). Verse 4 then picks up this latter phrase, מִשָּׁם אֲצַוֶּה אֶת־הַחֶרֶב וַהֲרָגָתַם ("There I will command the sword to slay them"), and continues with the former motif of the "eye" of the Lord (וְשַׂמְתִּי עֵינִי[61] עֲלֵיהֶם).

In the final stich[62] Amos once again employs language with a surprising switch of meaning. Elsewhere in the Bible the expression שִׂים עַיִן עַל ("to place one's eyes upon") is always employed in a positive context for the benefit of the party involved. See Gen 44:21; Jer 24:6; 39:12; 40:4. Here, however, when God fixes his eye upon them, it is not to look upon them favorably, but for evil (לְרָעָה וְלֹא לְטוֹבָה).[63] No one can avert the Deity's "evil eye" or destructive gaze;[64] see Amos 9:8.

■ **5** For the third time[65] a hymnic doxology of judgment[66]

53 See Jonah 2:1, 11.
54 See Amos 5:19; Jer 8:17.
55 Note that first the Lord himself is said to capture the fugitives; then he must search them out; and finally he is aided by his agents, snake and sword.
56 See also Prov 5:21; 15:3, 11.
57 See also Rudolph, 246.
58 For the expression לָלֶכֶת בַּשְּׁבִי, see, for example, Deut 28:41; Jer 20:6; 22:22; Ezek 30:18; Lam 1:5.
59 See 4:10. For the personification of the sword, see Isa 34:5, 6; Jer 47:6; Ezek 14:17; 32:11; Hos 11:6.
60 Once again the theme of captivity appears—but here as part of the people's strange strategy to escape from the wrath of the Lord.
61 There is no need to punctuate the noun as a plural, as is done by G; compare the singular in Jer 24:6; 40:4. For the key word "eye(s)" of the Lord, see vv 3, 4, 8; and for "commanding" (צוה), see vv 3, 4, 9.
62 Just as the series of plague curses concludes with a dramatic finale (4:12), so here, too, after the fivefold declaration of inescapability, the prophet concludes with a final all-embracing statement. Note that he first introduces the totality of the catastrophe in v 1, continues by spelling out in detail the ways in which it will be accomplished, and then gives a closing, summarizing statement.
63 This characteristic style of Amos of emphasizing his point by stating it twice, both positively and negatively, is also found in 5:4–5, 14, 18, 20; 8:11 (see also 5:2). For the same expression, see Jer 21:10; 39:16; 44:27; and for its opposite, see Jer 24:6.
64 Compare Akk. *ini ša ana marušti/lemutti ippalsūka* ("Eyes which look evilly upon you") CT, 17,33:26. The exact Akkadian cognate of Heb. לָשִׂים עַיִן, *inu šakānu*, also appears in several texts. For examples, see *AHw*, 3.1135,4γ. For the "evil eye," Akk. *īnu lemnu/lemuttu*, see *CAD*, *I/J*, 155–56.
65 See 4:13; 5:8–9.
66 See pp. 152–53. For reconstructions of this hymn (almost all superfluous), see Gaster, "Hymn," 23–26; Watts, "Old Hymn," 30–39; and Crenshaw, *Hymnic Affirmations*, 60 n 48.

glorifies the majesty of the Lord, affirming that he has the consummate power to carry out his threats of retributive punishment and chastisement just described.[67] Amos commences his recital of God's sovereignty over nature by describing an earthquake and its concomitant results:[68] "The Lord, God of Hosts,[69] is he who touches the earth and it quavers" (וַתָּמוֹג).[70] When the Lord merely touches the earth,[71] it quivers and quakes, shatters and shakes. As a result "all who dwell on it mourn" (וְאָבְלוּ כָּל־יוֹשְׁבֵי בָהּ).[72] This terrestrial convulsion is likened once again to the swelling and subsiding of the Nile in Egypt (see 8:8).[73] The cosmic upheaval of both land and sea[74] are by-products of the theophany of the Deity who appears in order to execute judgment.

■ **6** Amos continues his praise of God by extolling him as the creator, "who built his upper chambers (מַעֲלוֹתָו)[75] in heaven and founded his vault (אֲגֻדָּתוֹ) on the earth." The Lord's dwelling place in heaven[76] is pictured as a vault[77] firmly bound together and overarching the earth.[78] From there he "summons the waters of the sea and pours them over the face of the land" (see 5:8).[79] Note that the two sites of refuge to where those who are attempting in

67 Most commentators once again assume that this doxology is an interpolation or an "interpretative insertion"; for example, Wolff, 341. See, however, Hammershaimb, 133: "It is unjustifiable in principle to declare *a priori* that Amos cannot have written these verses, because they interrupt the preaching of judgment . . . or because they are divergent in style." See also Farr ("Language," 323): "Obviously then, the collectors did not think that these passages had no logical connection with the context. Why should not Amos have quoted this psalm, and for the same reason—to underline Yahweh's majesty and power?"

68 Maybe having reference to 9:1?

69 For this epithet of the Deity, see p. 156. See Rudolph, 242. The verse begins with a *casus pendens* introduced by *waw* (Cross, written communication).

70 For the verb מוג, see *KB*, 526. The verb is pointed as a pausal form. See *BLe*, 56u. Compare G, καὶ σαλεύων αὐτήν ("and he who makes it shake"). It describes the reeling and undulating motion of the earth also in Pss 46:7; 75:4. In Nah 1:5 it is parallel to רָעֲשׁוּ ("quake"). Two of the roots in this verse in Amos, מוג and ישב, reappear in vv 13–14.

71 So, too, when he touches the mountains, "they smoke"; Pss 104:32; 144:5.

72 See 8:8, where the passage is worded in the singular. Compare now the text Mur XII (88) 8:15, which also has the singular in this verse, identical to Amos 8:8 (אבל . . . יושב). See P. Benoit, J. T. Milik, and R. de Vaux, *Les grottes de Murabbaʿât* (DJD 2/1; Oxford: Clarendon, 1961) 183, 188. For the same expressions, see also Hos 4:3; compare Isa 24:4, 6.

73 G, συντέλεια αὐτῆς, erroneously interpreted כלה as כָּלָה ("annihilation"), instead of the Masoretic כֻּלָּהּ ("all of it"). The same error occurs in Amos 8:8. Heb. מִצְרַיִם ("Egypt") reappears in v 7 as an associative catchword.

74 For the triad of earth, sky, and water (vv 5–6) in a doxology, see Isa 40:12; Job 9:5–6.

75 Heb. מַעֲלוֹת elsewhere refers to "steps"; see, for example, Exod 20:23; 1 Kgs 10:19, 20; 2 Kgs 9:13; Neh 3:15. Thus some, for example, Rosenmüller, interpret the reference here to steps in a multistoried heaven. Most, however, delete the first *mem* as a dittography and read עֲלִיֹּתָו (or singular, עֲלִיָּתוֹ, "his upper chamber," as G, ἀνάβασιν αὐτοῦ, and V, *ascensionem suam*) "his upper chamber(s)"; see 1 Kgs 17:19, 23; Ps 104:3, 13; Neh 3:31, 32; for example, Wellhausen; Oort, "Amos"; Graetz; Nowack; Elhorst; Oettli, *Amos und Hosea;* Marti; Harper, 187; Horst, "Doxologien," 48; Hammershaimb, 134; Gaster, "Hymn"; Wolff, 336; Rudolph, 242; Soggin, 121. Some exegetes nevertheless leave the Masoretic text intact and still translate "upper chambers"; for example, Driver and van Hoonacker. The scroll Mur XII (88) 8:16 also attests Hebrew, מַעֲלוֹתָו.

Note the repetition of the key root, עלה, in vv 2, 5, 7.

76 See Ps 104:3. See also Isa 66:1; Pss 103:19; 115:3, 16.

77 Heb. אֲגֻדָּה refers to that which is firmly held together (see later Hebrew and Aramaic אגד); for example, a "bunch" of hyssop, Exod 12:22; a "company" of soldiers, 2 Sam 2:25; "cords" of the yoke (or lawlessness), Isa 58:6. Only here does it refer to the tightly fitted vault of heaven otherwise called רָקִיעַ or חוג. See Prov 8:27: "I was there when he set the heavens in place; when he fixed the horizon (חוג) upon the deep." See also Isa 40:22; Job 26:10.

For the corresponding Akkadian terms, *šipik/šupuk šamê/burūmê* and *markas šamê/burūmê,* see *CAD, B,* 344–45 and *CAD, M,* I, 283, 4a. Akk. *markasu,* derived from *rakāsu* ("to bind together"), seems to be very closely related.

78 Gaster ("Hymn") derives the root from a purported Arab. *ʾajd* ("foundation of a building"). This is also the meaning of Akk. *šipku/šupku;* see n 77.

79 See comments on 5:8. See also B. Z. Luria ("'Who Calls the Waters of the Sea and Spills Them on the Face of the Earth' [Amos 5:8; 9:6]," *BM* 101 [1984–1985] 259–62 [Heb.]), who interprets this as a tidal wave accompanying an earthquake.

vain to flee from the hand of the Lord, "heaven" (שָׁמַיִם) and "sea" (יָם)[80] (vv 2, 3), both appear in this verse.[81] Because God is extolled as controlling all realms, escape is totally impossible. The Lord who dwells on high[82] can apprehend those who brazenly seek to scale heaven for asylum.

The hymn concludes as it began, with the personal name of Yahweh, the God of Israel, thereby creating a literary inclusio.

80 This clear reference to יָם would lend credence to the originality of the passage here. There is thus no decisive reason to view it as an addition from 5:8.

81 And by allusion, the "land" (אֶרֶץ, which appears three times in these two verses) of the enemy, where even in captivity they shall be overtaken by the sword.

82 See *ANEP*, 529.

9 Destined for Decimation

7 **Are you not like the Ethiopians to me, O Israelites?**
—declares the Lord.
Of course I brought Israel up from the land of Egypt,
But so, too, the Philistines from Caphtor
And the Arameans from Kir.
8 **Lo, the eyes of my Lord God are upon the sinful kingdom.**
I will destroy it from the face of the earth,
But I will not totally destroy the house of Jacob
—declares the Lord.
9 **For, lo, I will give an order**
And shake the house of Israel
Among all the nations,
As one shakes with a sieve
And not even one pebble falls to the ground.
10 **They shall die by the sword,**
All the sinners of my people
Who vaunt, "Never shall disaster
Come near or overtake us!"

■ **7** This new literary unit commences with a double rhetorical question,[1] introducing a disputation saying[2] whose purpose is to contradict the popular belief that Israel, precisely because of its exodus from Egypt, occupies a privileged place before God.[3] The Lord himself absolutely denies and refutes this assumption of a superior status. In the eyes of the sovereign of history, who has absolute sway over all the nations of the world and personally directs their destinies, Israel has no more initial claim to preference than any other people. He declares first that the "Israelites" (בְּנֵי יִשְׂרָאֵל) are just like the "Ethiopians" (כִּבְנֵי כֻשִׁיִּים).[4] The Ethiopians, dwelling in Nubia, are not referred to disdainfully[5] because of their color[6] or their slave status,[7] but for the remote distance of their land from Israel.[8] Compare especially Isa 18:1–2: "Ah, land . . . beyond the rivers of Nubia (כּוּשׁ)! Go, swift messengers, to a nation far and remote, to a people thrust forth and away—a nation of gibber and chatter—whose land is cut off by streams . . . !"[9] Even the most inaccessible nation is still under God's surveillance and sovereignty, as is Israel.

Yet Yahweh is the Lord not only of those who live in

1 For other rhetorical polemical questions, a favorite device of the prophet, see Amos 3:3–8; 5:20; 6:2, 12; 8:8. Here, however, the words are the Lord's, not the prophet's.

2 See Wolff, 156, 345; Vollmer, *Rückblicke,* 33. Heb. הֲלוֹא functions, at times, as the introduction to a disputation saying; see Amos 5:20; see also Isa 10:8, 9, 11; Mal 2:10. For this verse, see also H. Gese, "Das Problem von Amos 9,7," in *Textgemäss: Aufsätze und Beiträge zur Hermeneutik des Alten Testaments: Festschrift für Ernst Würthwein zum 70. Geburtstag* (ed. A. H. J. Gunneweg and O. Kaiser; Göttingen: Vandenhoeck & Ruprecht, 1973) 33–38; Vollmer, *Rückblicke,* 33–37.

3 This is yet one more example of the overturning and refuting of a popular belief; see, for example, Amos 5:18–20.

4 This is the only place in the Bible where the Ethiopians (Nubians) are called בְּנֵי כֻשִׁיִּים (see 1 Chr 1:9 [twice], בְּנֵי כוּשׁ). This specific title was selected in order to match the corresponding בְּנֵי יִשְׂרָאֵל. Note also the pointing כֻּשִׁיִּים and פְּלִשְׁתִּיִּים, both appearing only here (otherwise, כּוּשִׁים and פְּלִשְׁתִּים). Same point, same pointing. For this vocalization of the plural of nouns whose singular ends in ִי. (see עִבְרִיִּים, Exod 3:18), see *GKC,* 87a. This ending, however, is usually contracted.

5 See Num 12:1.

6 See Jer 13:23. See Wellhausen, 94.

7 See 2 Sam 18:21; Jer 38:7.

8 See Esth 1:1; 8:9. See Fosbroke, 848; Vollmer, *Rückblicke,* 31 n 110; Soggin, 143; Rudolph (273–74), who compares the reference in Homer, *Odyssey* I, 23 to the Ethiopians as ἔσχατοι ἀνδρῶν ("the most

distant lands but also of those who live in the closest proximity to Israel, their very neighbors and classic enemies.[10] Just as he evinces no favoritism ethnically or geographically, so he shows no preference historically or politically. In the second rhetorical question, Israel is equated with its Philistine and Aramean foes, to the west and east,[11] both of whom have witnessed comparable feats of the Lord's power. For God brought not only Israel out of Egypt[12] but also the Philistines out of Caphtor (כַּפְתּוֹר)[13] and the Arameans from Kir.[14] These two nations, too, have experienced their own exoduses,[15] staged and directed by the very same Deity. The deliverance from Egypt, historically speaking, affords no special assurance or preference for Israel, for it is not unique.[16] It is merely another example of the Lord's universalistic impartiality. The fact is not debated; contrarily, the historical traditions of these other two nations provide similar data. What is objected to are the theological conclusions that Israel has repeatedly, and incorrectly, drawn from this event. Election is not predicated upon exodus.[17] If it is a sign of salvation

remote of mankind"). Hoffman (*Doctrine of Exodus,* 36 n 37), however, suggests that the reference here is to the Nubian dynasty that at that time ruled Egypt.

9 See notes in *NJPS.*

10 Note the chiastic structure of the two strophes: בְּנֵי כֻשִׁיִּים (= nations)/ בְּנֵי יִשְׂרָאֵל (Israelites)—יִשְׂרָאֵל (Israel)/ פְּלִשְׁתִּיִּים, אֲרָם (= nations). This structure may continue into the next verse, where the מַמְלָכָה חַטָּאָה ("the sinful kingdom") signifies any political entity, followed once again by the specific mention of Israel, called בֵּית יַעֲקֹב ("house of Jacob").

11 See the oracles against the nations where the Arameans and Philistines are also juxtaposed (1:3–5, 6–8); see also Isa 9:11; Ezek 16:57. This symmetry creates one grand inclusio for the entire book.

12 See Amos 2:10; 3:1. For the associative catchword, מִצְרַיִם ("Egypt"), see v 5.

13 See J. C. Greenfield, "Caphtor," *IDB* I.534; B. Mazar, "Caphtor," *EM* 4.236–38 (Heb.). For the connection of the Philistines with Crete, see Jer 47:4; Ezek 25:16; Zeph 2:5. See also T. Dothan (*The Philistines and Their Material Culture* [New Haven: Yale University; Jerusalem: Israel Exploration Society, 1982]), who discusses the complicated issue of the Philistine origins in the first chapter of her book. Others identify Caphtor with Cappadocia, as in G and other ancient versions here. See G. A. Wainwright, "Caphtor-Cappadocia," *VT* 6 (1956) 199–210; idem, "The Septuagint's Καππαδοκία for Caphtor," *JJS* 7 (1956) 91–92; idem, "Some Early Philistine History," *VT* 9 (1959) 73–84; F. Cornelius, "Genesis 14," *ZAW* 72 (1960) 5 n 16; J. J. Prignaud, "Caftorim et Kerétim," *RB* 71 (1964) 215–29. Cornelius suggests the reading כַּפְתּוּךְ for כַּפְתּוֹר. This Aramaic form for the Greek word "Cappadocia" appears in the Genesis Apocryphon (XXI:23), for אֶלָּסָר ("Ellasar"), Gen 14:1, 9. See J. A. Fitzmyer, *The Genesis Apocryphon of Qumran Cave I* (BibOr 18; Rome: Pontifical Biblical Institute, 1971) 159–60. However, as mentioned previously, כַּפְתּוֹר exemplifies the catchword principle, relating to its homonym in v 1.

For the suggested identification in Cyprus (southern and eastern part of the island), see J. Strange, *Caphtor/Keftiu. A New Investigation* (Acta Theologica Danica 14; Leiden: Brill, 1980). For references to כַּפְתּוֹר in other languages, see *KB,* 471.

14 See Amos 1:5. Just as the Lord has brought them forth from Kir, so will he exile them back to Kir; see 2 Kgs 16:9. For Kir, see C. H. Gordon, "Kir, 2," *IDB* 3.36.

15 This is a rare example of the preservation of non-Israelite historical traditions. The migration of the Philistines took place some one-half millennium earlier! For the Arameans, see A. Malamat, "Aram, Arameans," *EncJud* 3.252–56. See also C. H. Gordon's review of A. Malamat's *The Arameans in Aram Naharaim and the Rise of Their States* (Jerusalem: Israel Exploration Society, 1952) (Heb.), in *JBL* 74 (1955) 289.

16 What is unique is the binding of Israel into a covenantal relationship, postexodus. See 3:2. See M. Weinfeld ("The Awakening of National Consciousness in Israel in the Seventh Century B.C.," in *ʿOz Le-David: Collected Readings in Bible Presented to David ben Gurion on His Seventy-seventh Birthday* [ed. Y. Kaufmann and others; Jerusalem: Kiryat Sepher, 1964] 396–420 [Heb.]), who distinguishes between recognition (ידע) and selection. Because the condition of 3:2 has not been fulfilled, Israel is now classed in the same category as all the other nations, without any special benefits. See also J. J. Collins, "History and Tradition in the Prophet Amos," *ITQ* 41 (1974) 125–26. Soggin (143) remarks, "If in 3:2 the election is connected with greater responsibility, here it is dissociated from all privileges over against the other people." For another view, see W. Vogels, "Invitation à revenir à l'alliance et universalisme en Amos IX, 7," *VT* 22 (1972) 223–39.

17 Once again (see 3:1–2) the prophet downplays the significance of the exodus motif, which, although highly regarded in the north, originally was of no significant theological importance in Judah. See

history, so is it for the others as well. However, the exodus, qua exodus, is not a unique event and grants them no special priority or immunity.

There may be, moreover, an additional dimension to this comparison. True, the Lord did deliver these other two nations from their respective countries. Did this, however, save them from ultimate destruction? Of course not. Because immunity was not granted them, why then to Israel? As the Lord shares his grace equally, so does he exact punishment from all guilty nations (v 8).

■ **8** After the polemical disputation comes the ultimate verdict, which also serves as the denouement to the entire book.[18] The Lord of Israel, who has absolute sovereignty over the entire universe, decrees the destinies of all nations in accordance with strict moral criteria. Any and every nation that does not abide by his ethical standards, irrespective of its early "salvation history," is condemned to annihilation. The "eyes of my Lord God" (עֵינֵי אֲדֹנָי ה׳)[19] that scour the universe are set against any "kingdom" (בַּמַּמְלָכָה)[20] that is "sinful" (הַחַטָּאָה),[21] and he will totally "destroy[22] it from the face of the earth" (וְהִשְׁמַדְתִּי אֹתָהּ מֵעַל פְּנֵי הָאֲדָמָה).[23] The Heb. מַמְלָכָה refers here to a political entity, that is, kingdom (= nation), and not to the royal house.[24]

There is, however, one reservation, and it is introduced by the rare expression אֶפֶס כִּי—a reservation but not a contradiction. Although every sinful *nation* will be destroyed (and the nation Israel is, of course, by definition, included in this category), the "house of Jacob" (בֵּית יַעֲקֹב), that is, the *people* of northern Israel,[25] he "will

---

Ginsberg, *Israelian Heritage,* 1–2, 27, 33–34; and Hoffman, *Doctrine of Exodus,* 32–38.

18 This epilogue is usually considered to consist of three separate oracles. See, for example, Marti, 224; Koehler, 154–55; Maag, *Text,* 61–62; Weiser, *Profetie,* 204; Reventlow, *Amt,* 94–95; Amsler, 245–46. This, of course, is a literary division and does not refer to the arguments for or against their authenticity. For various opinions, see Hasel, *Remnant,* 207–8 n 300.

19 For the expression עֵינֵי ה׳, which appears many times in the Bible, consult the concordances. A. L. Oppenheim ("The Eyes of the Lord," *JAOS* 88 [1968] 173–80, reprinted in *Essays in Memory of E. A. Speiser* [ed. W. W. Hallo; AOS 53; New Haven, CT: American Oriental Society, 1968] 175) suggests that the same term in Zech 4:10 and 2 Chr 16:9 has "a double function: on one hand they act in accordance with what the 'eyes of the king' are supposed to do, namely, to spot misdeeds, report them to the authority and bring about swift punishment of the culprit; on the other hand, they are spoken of by the seer [Hanani in Chronicles] as if their purpose were rather to bring comfort to the pious and as if they were charged with his protection." He sees here "a transfer of a political institution [which he previously described from Egyptian, Mesopotamian, and Persian documentation as a royal 'secret service'] to a theological level." This dual function, even if not related to a "secret service," is already apparent in our present verse, to which he makes no reference. For Akkadian texts referring to the eyes of the king upon his subjects, see, for example, *EA,* 264:15; *ABL,* 498, r. 11.

Note the concatenous use of the substantive עַיִן in vv 3, 4, 8, linking the first two literary pericopes of chapter 9. See also the use of רָעָה in vv 4 and 10b. There is no reason to emend the text to read עֵינַי ("my eyes"), contrary to, for example, Robinson-Horst, 106.

20 Because the first part of this verse is a direct continuation of v 7, the intent is the total control of the Lord over all the nations. Thus the "sinful nation" referred to is not to be interpreted as Israel (as supposedly contrasted to Judah; against, for example, Rashi; ibn Ezra; Kimchi; Wellhausen, 95; Harper, 193; Watts, *Vision,* 48 n 4; Soggin, 144; but generically to any and every nation that does not meet God's moral standards. See, for example, Cripps, 264; van Gelderen; Driver, 224; Budde, "Amos," 110–11; Robinson-Horst, 107; Cramer, 46; Sellin², 268; Amsler.

For the political term מַמְלָכָה, see also Amos 7:13. Note also the chiastic structure of this verse as compared to v 7.

21 Heb. חַטָּאָה is a feminine adjectival form of *חַטָּא (found only in the plural, for example, Gen 13:13). It is to be distinguished from the substantive חֲטָאָה, for example, Gen 20:9.

22 For the verb הִשְׁמִיד, see Amos 2:9.

23 See Deut 6:15; 1 Kgs 13:34; and similarly Josh 23:15. For the switch from a third- to first-person address (so common in prophetic literature), see also Amos 8:11.

24 See also Rudolph, 276; against, for example, Weiser, *Profetie;* U. Kellermann, "Der Amosschluss als Stimme deuteronomistischer Heilshoffnung," *EvT* 29 (1969) 171; Wolff, 348.

25 "The house of Jacob" (בֵּית יַעֲקֹב) refers to the people of northern Israel in the Book of Amos (see 3:13; for יַעֲקֹב alone, see 7:3, 6) and not to Judah and, as such, is synonymous with his frequent use of בֵּית יִשְׂרָאֵל

not totally destroy" (לֹא הַשְׁמֵיד אַשְׁמִיד).[26] A remnant of the ethnic unit of Israel will survive.[27] That this remnant is not to be understood as a secondary redaction or a later interpolation[28] can be shown syntactically and contextually. As for syntax, in all the other passages where the expression appears, it functions as an integral contrasting continuation to that which immediately precedes it; Num 13:27–28: ". . . We came to the land you sent us to; it does indeed flow with milk and honey, and this is its fruit. However (אֶפֶס כִּי) the people who inhabit it are powerful and the cities are fortified and very large . . ."; Deut 15:3–4: "You may dun the foreigner; but you must remit whatever is due you from your kinsmen. However (אֶפֶס כִּי) there shall be no needy among you . . ."; Judg 4:9: "'Very well, I [Deborah] will go with you [Barak],' she answered. 'However (אֶפֶס כִּי), there will be no glory for you in the course you are taking, for then the Lord will deliver Sisera into the hands of a woman . . .'"; 2 Sam 12:13–14: ". . . And Nathan replied to David, 'The Lord has remitted your sin; you shall not die. However (אֶפֶס כִּי), since you have spurned the enemies of the Lord by this deed, the child about to be born to you shall die.'" Compare somewhat similarly the end of the Phoenician inscription of Azitawadda from Karatepe: "Whoever shall wipe out the name of Azitawadda from this gate and put down his own name . . . , let [the gods] wipe out that ruler and that king and that man. . . . However (אֶפֶס), the name of Azitawadda shall endure forever like the name of sun and moon."[29] All these references clearly demonstrate that the phrase is not a subsequent addition to the text but rather an integral component part characterizing a contrasting element to the prior statement.

As for context itself, the political entity, the *nation* of Israel (as well as all other immoral nations) shall be destroyed, but the *people* of Israel shall not be totally eradicated. This is further elucidated by the next verse, which describes the selective sifting of the moral from the immoral. This, moreover, is decisive, for v 9 is a direct continuation of v 8b and not 8a,[30] once again proving the originality of this clause within its present context.[31] Although the Lord will exact strict judgment against the nations of the world, his other attribute, that of mercy, will prevail when dealing with the "house of Jacob."

■ **9** By the employment[32] of metaphorical imagery familiar to the prophet from his agricultural and pastoral milieu,[33] Amos proceeds to describe the process of the partial annihilation of the population of the northern kingdom. The Lord will "give an order (מְצַוֶּה)[34] and shake (וַהֲנִעוֹתִי)[35] the house of Israel among all the

("house of Israel"). For בֵּית יַעֲקֹב as an epithet of the people, see, for example, Isa 2:5, 6; 10:20; 14:1; Jer 2:4; Ezek 20:5; Obad 17, 18. Amos first mentions בֵּית יַעֲקֹב, then בֵּית יִשְׂרָאֵל (v 9), and finally עַמִּי, "my people" (v 10).

26 This is a very unusual way of constructing the negative of the infinitive absolute. "The regular place of the negative is between the intensifying infinitive absolute and the finite verb" (*GKC,* 113v). The two other exceptions—where the negative precedes the infinitive absolute and the finite verb—are Gen 3:4 and Ps 49:8. For the infinitive absolute written fully, הַשְׁמֵיד, *ṣere* with a *yodh,* see *GKC,* 53k. The verb appears in one other passage, Amos 2:9, where once again it is employed twice.

27 For example, 5:3, 16.

28 So most commentators, for example, Wellhausen, 95; Marti; Nowack; Sellin, 268; Maag, *Text;* Kapelrud, *Central Ideas;* Weiser, *Profetie,* 201; Harper, 187; Cripps, 265; Amsler; Wolff, 346. See, however, Rudolph, 275.

29 See F. Rosenthal's translation in *ANESTP,* 654. It appears in col. IV, lines 2–3. For the literary genre of this blessing and its antecedents, see S. M. Paul, "Psalm 72:5—A Traditional Blessing for the Long Life of the King," *JNES* 31 (1972) 251–55.

30 See Rudolph, 276.

31 The phrase נְאֻם־ה' does not always conclude a literary unit in the Book of Amos; see 2:11; 3:10; 4:6, 8, 9, 10; 9:7, 13. It does function as a conclusion, however, in 2:16; 3:15.

32 The initial words, כִּי־הִנֵּה, do not necessarily indicate the beginning of a new literary unit; see 4:2, 13; 6:11, 14. Heb. כִּי may also be a כִּי-*energeticus.*

33 See also 2:13; 3:3–5, 12; 6:12.

34 See similarly 6:11, כִּי־הִנֵּה . . . מְצַוֶּה וְ.

35 The same root, נוע, which characterizes a shaking and shaky movement, is also used to describe other punishments in 4:8; 8:12. See, too, Gen 4:14; Num 32:13; Pss 59:12; 109:10. Only in Amos, however, is it related to the movement of a sifting-sieving process. The verb appears twice in this verse; compare הַשְׁמִיד, which appears thrice in the former verse.

nations,[36] as one shakes[37] (יָנוֹעַ)[38] with a sieve[39] and not even one pebble (צְרוֹר)[40] falls to the ground." The root צוה is another connecting link between the first two literary units:[41] In v 3, the Lord "commands" the "snake" to be his instrument of punishment, and in v 4 the "sword" fulfills this function. Here the image centers around a sieve.[42] Amos is apparently referring to a large meshed sieve that retains the useless straw, stones, and earth but allows the corn, smaller grains, and fine sand to pass through. The useless coarse rubbish, that is, the guilty, shall be held fast in the sieve, shortly to be cut off by the sword (v 10). However, the fine particles, that is, the righteous, shall slip safely through the perforations in the sieve—only to be dispersed throughout the nations.[43] A shaking, sieving, sifting, screening process will take place. A remnant will remain[44] but in exile.[45] Once again no one will escape punishment.

■ **10** The metaphor of the sifting process is now partially interpreted. The rubbish left in the sieve represents "all the sinners of my people"[46] (כֹּל חַטָּאֵי[47] עַמִּי), who shall subsequently "die by the sword."[48] The entire nation shall not be annihilated (see v 8b) but only those who are found to be guilty. Once again the instrument of destruction will be the sword (see 4:10; 7:9, 17; 9:1, 4—the references in the last two form part of the catchword principle connecting this pericope with the previous one). The executioner who will wield the sword is again left unidentified, as is usual throughout the Book of Amos.[49]

There then follows an exact quotation from those who

36 This is not a later interpolation; against, for example, Cripps, 265; Wolff; Rudolph, 272. See Hammershaimb, 139. It continues the prophet's thought of the Lord of Israel as master over all the nations. It is integral to the outlook of Amos, who so often envisions exile among the nations as being the forthcoming destiny of Israel. For the motif of "all the nations" (כָּל־הַגּוֹיִם), see v 12.

37 This is the only example of the *niph'al* of the root נוע. For the impersonal *niph'al*, see *GKC*, 121a–b.

38 Some add the word בַּר ("corn") before בַּכְּבָרָה ("sieve"), which was supposedly omitted by haplography; see, for example, V, *triticum* ("wheat"); Budde, "Amos," 111; *NJPS*.

39 Heb. כְּבָרָה is a hapax legomenon, and the exact type and size of the sieve is still in dispute. The interpretation followed here is "a coarse sieve for cleansing grain of straw and stones, or sand of pebbles and shells," *NJPS*. Others interpret it as a fine-meshed sieve that allows the dust and chaff to fall through, retaining only the best corn; see, for example, Kimchi; ibn Ezra; Driver, 268; Robinson-Horst, 107.

For a similar image, see Sir 27:4: "In the shaking of a sieve the refuse remains." See S. Krauss, *Talmudische Archäologie: Grundriss der Gesamtwissenschaft des Judentums* (3 vols.; Hildesheim: Georg Olms, 1966) 1.99, 288 n 156, 455 nn; Dalman, *AuS*, I.552; III.142ff. See P. Volz, "Zu Am 9:9," *ZAW* 38 (1919–1920) 105–11, and all modern commentaries. The word also appears in Rabbinic sources. See Mishnah Ohiloth 18:2. Whether or not a similar image is employed in Isa 30:28 is subject to doubt because the key word there may be related to Arab. ناف, *nāf* ("yoke"). See H. L. Ginsberg, "An Obscure Hebrew Word," *JQR* 22 (1931–1932) 143–45, and *NJPS*. The word also appears in Ugaritic, *kbrt*, in the Baal epic, *CTA* 6:v:16. See A. Caquot, M. Sznycer, and A. Herdner, *Textes ougaritiques, Tome I: Mythes et legendes* (Littérature anciennes du Proche-Orient 7; Paris: Cerf, 1974) 267, and note g; *CML*, 79.

40 Heb. צְרוֹר (see also 2 Sam 17:13; Prov 26:8) is also subject to various different interpretations. *KB*, 987, II, צְרוֹר, translates the word "Stein" based on G, λίθος ("stone") to 2 Sam 17:13; or "Steinchen" based on α', ψηφίον ("pebble"), and V, *lapillus* ("pebble") to Amos 9:9. See also T, אֶבֶן ("stone"). For a study of the two, see S. Avizur, *Implements for Harvesting* (Tel Aviv: HaMaḥon LeYediat HaAreṣ, 1966) 75–85 (Heb.).

41 See also the next verse and v 4 for the catchwords חֶרֶב and רָעָה.

42 Once again Amos draws his analogy from the realm of agriculture with which he was familiar.

43 See also Kaufmann, *Toledoth*, 6.89 n 46 (Heb.).

44 Again the recurrent motif of a remnant.

45 Again the recurrent motif of exile.

46 Even though they are "sinners," they still are called "my people"; see 7:8, 15; 8:2. The attempt to deny the authenticity of this verse on the basis of the absence of the word "Israel" after "my people" is totally unfounded; against H. W. Hoffmann, "Zur Echtheitsfrage von Amos 9, 9f.," *ZAW* 82 (1970) 121–22.

47 The key term חטא is also found in v 8a.

48 The verse is not a later addition or interpretation, as most suggest, but the conclusion of the unit that began with v 7. See Rudolph (277), who points out that in other places Amos also announces punishment for specific groups of people, clearly implying that he does make a differentiation. See 3:11f.; 4:2f.; 5:11f.; 6:7.

49 See, for example, 6:14.

are destined for decimation. Amos again resorts to his familiar rhetorical device of citing the actual words of those whom he condemns, thereby confirming their guilt and providing firsthand incriminating evidence to justify their forthcoming punishment (see 4:1; 6:13; 8:14).[50] Their sin is rooted in their brazen and unabashed arrogance. Their insolent remark may be interpreted in two different ways, dependent on whether the verbs are understood as third-person feminine singulars with הָרָעָה[51] (see 3:6) as the subject, or as second-person masculine singulars with the Lord as the subject. If the former (which most exegetes favor): "Never shall disaster (הָרָעָה) come near or overtake us!"[52] If the latter: "Never shall you [Lord] allow the disaster to overtake or come near to us."[53] The latter, of course, is not only boldly arrogant but also has clear overtones of a challenge.

50 See especially Wolff, 349. See also Isa 5:19; 9:10; 28:14–15.

51 Again another key word; see v 4. This is already alluded to in Amos 6:3. Note, too, the root נגש, which also appears in v 13.

52 See, for example, T; G; Rashi; Wellhausen; Nowack; Driver; Oort, "Amos"; Oettli, *Amos und Hosea;* Marti; Harper, 196, 200; Cripps, 269; Maag, *Text,* 59–60; Amsler; Hammershaimb, 140. Most commentators then revocalize the two verbs (which are in the *hiphʿil*) to the *qal,* תִּגַּשׁ, and *piʿel,* תְּקַדֵּם. However, the verbal forms need not be changed, even if הָרָעָה is the subject. See *GKC,* 53c. The *hiphʿil* of קדם appears one other time in the Masoretic text, Job 41:3. It is also very possible that the vocalization תַּגִּישׁ influenced that of תַּקְדִּים, thus harmonizing both verbs. H. Yalon ("Studies in Biblical Hebrew: הפעיל–קל," *Leš* 2 [1930] 120 [Heb.]) suggests that תַּגִּישׁ is an archaic remnant of a future *qal.*

53 See Wolff (344), who adds that בַּעֲדֵינוּ "suggests the idea of surrounding someone," comparing Ps 139:11; Job 1:10; Lam 3:7. See, too, Rudolph (272), who also interprets the words as being directly addressed to God. He translates בַּעֲדֵינוּ as "uns zugut" ("in our favor"). For בְּעַד with the meaning of "schutzend um ⟩ zugunsten von, für" ("protecting ⟩ for the benefit of ⟩ for"), see *KB,* 135. Another interpretation of this word has been suggested by Th. Riedel ("Miscellen. Amos 9:10," *ZAW* 20 [1900] 332) and Budde ("Amos," 113), who read בְּעֹדֵינוּ ("while we are still alive"). For this meaning of עוֹד, see Pss 104:33; 146:2 (and also suggested for Ps 103:5).

9

Future Restoration and Blessings of Bounty and Security

11 On that day
I will raise up the fallen booth of David.
I will repair its breaches
And its ruins I will restore,
And I will rebuild it as in the days of old.
12 So that they shall possess the remnant of Edom
And all the nations over whom my name has been called
—declares the Lord, who will do this.
13 Lo, days are coming
—declares the Lord—
When the plowman shall draw near the reaper,
And the treader of grapes him who sows the seeds.
The mountains shall drip fresh wine,
And all the hills shall wave [with grain].
14 I will restore my people Israel:
They shall rebuild desolate cities and inhabit them,
They shall plant vineyards and drink their wine,
They shall cultivate gardens and eat their fruits.
15 And I shall plant them on their own soil,
And they shall never again be uprooted
From the soil I have given them
—said the Lord your God.

Introductory Comments to the Epilogue

The authenticity of the last section of the book has been seriously doubted by most commentators ever since Wellhausen's famous remark that Amos 9:11–15 is "Rosen und Lavendel statt Blut und Eisen" ("roses and lavender instead of blood and iron").[1] There is common agreement among most commentators that the last verses are from the hand of an exilic or postexilic theologian-redactor who, from his own Judean point of view, bore tidings of consolation and salvation to his people. The arguments for the lateness of the pericope are based on linguistic and ideological grounds,[2] all of which, however, are seriously open to question.

1 Wellhausen, 96. The underlying false assumption, as stated by Wellhausen referring to Amos 9:8–15, is that a prophet who has constantly delivered oracles of "Unheil" ("disaster") could and would not end on a note of "Heil" ("salvation"). See also Reventlow, *Amt,* 102ff. For a comprehensive bibliography on the subject, emphasizing those who ascribe all or part of the epilogue to Amos, see Hasel, *Remnant,* 473, 207–8 n 300. See also K. Seybold, *Das davidische Königtum im Zeugnis der Propheten* (FRLANT 107; Göttingen: Vandenhoeck & Ruprecht, 1972) 17–19, and Wagner, "Überlegungen," 653–70, esp. 661–63, 669 n 18.

2 See Duhm, "Anmerkungen"; Marti; Guthe; Nowack; Weiser; Harper, 195f.; Cripps, 167–77; Cramer, 177ff.; Maag, *Text,* 246ff.; Wolff, 352–53; U. Kellermann, "Der Amosschluss als Stimme deuteronomistischer Heilshoffnung," *EvT* 29 (1969) 169–83. See 175 n 20 in Kellermann for those who defend its authenticity, including Koenig; Staerk; von Orelli; Gressmann, *Profetie;* Koehler; Sellin; van Hoonacker; Osty; Rinaldi; Neher, *Amos;* Maag, *Text;* Reventlow, *Amt,* 92ff.; Haran, "Amos," 281–82 (Heb.). See, too, Hammershaimb, 136–38; Rudolph, 280, 285–86; Benson, "Mouth of the Lion," 209–11. For linguistic similarities between these verses and the rest of the book, see, moreover, Kaufmann, *Toledoth,* 6.88 n 45.

Exegetes have claimed that linguistically there are many affinities to late biblical Hebrew in this section. They first cite the use of *scriptio plene,* especially in the name David, דָּוִיד (v 11). However, this is precisely the way in which David's name is spelled in Amos 6:5, a verse whose authenticity is not debated. As Rudolph has remarked, the entire subject of *plene*-writing in the books of the Minor Prophets is "eine unerklärte Marotte" ("an inexplicable whim"),[3] which cannot be used for the purpose of dating. As for the phrase הִנֵּה יָמִים בָּאִים ("behold, days are coming"; v 13), it is found in other passages of Amos that are not considered to be late.[4] The expression כִּימֵי עוֹלָם (v 11), moreover, already appears in Mic 7:14,[5] where it is explained by the next verse, v 15 (see similarly Mic 5:1). The substantive הֲרִיסֹת ("ruins"; v 11), a hapax legomenon, is patterned on a *qatilat(u)* construction, which, although well attested in later biblical Hebrew, is already found in earlier Hebrew.[6] The idiom שׁוּב שְׁבוּת, which has nothing to do with "captivity," is now documented in the contemporary mid-eighth-century Aramaic treaty from Sefire.[7]

The ideological "proofs" are also unsubstantiated. The argument that the "abruptness of transition" to a picture of restoration unaccompanied by an announcement of destruction, as well as the emphasis upon material blessings devoid of moral-ethical requirements, point to a late dating[8] completely misinterprets the purport of the prophetic pronouncements. Punishment for punishment's sake is not the prophetic ideal. The prophet's chastisement is meant to serve as a transitional stage to a period of future restoration, at least for the surviving remnant. Because the previous pericope described the sifting of the "wheat from the chaff," it is now followed by a series of unconditional promises of bliss and salvation, comprising themes characteristic of this literary genre that portray the happy future of those who will not be cut off by the sword.[9] Amos no longer conditions his promises upon a possible אוּלַי ("perhaps"), as in 5:15, for the people addressed in this prophecy are those who have already survived divine retribution. The restoration stems from the remnant.

Amos, the prophet whose roots are in Judah, focuses upon the restoration of the Davidic dynasty and kingdom,[10] an ideal already present in Hos 2:2; 3:5. Although this theme becomes very popular in later prophetic writings (for example, Ezek 37:16ff.), its roots are early. He describes the future of Israel as a return to the halcyon golden age of David and Solomon and then continues with promises of territorial expansion encompassing the boundaries of those former days, along with the blessings of agricultural bounty and security[11]—all

3 Rudolph, 286. See also Botterweck ("Authentizität," 188), who adds the cautious reminder that these texts were constantly being recopied.

4 For example, 4:2.

5 See also Mal 3:4. See similarly Deut 32:7; Isa 63:9.

6 See *BLe,* 471, for examples.

7 See Fitzmyer, *Sefire,* 100, III:24–25.

8 See Harper, 195.

9 Rudolph, 285, 286.

10 See von Rad, *Theology,* 138; Fey, *Amos und Jesaja,* 54; Gottlieb, "Amos und Jerusalem," 455–57; E. Rohland, *Die Bedeutung der Erwählungstradition Israels für die Eschatologie der alttestamentlichen Propheten* (Unpub. Diss., Heidelberg, 1956) 230–33.

11 See Weinfeld ("Mesopotamian Prophecies," 263–76 [Heb.]), who points out that a similar picture of restoration after destruction is present in Mesopotamian "prophetic" texts, where many of the same motifs as those found in Amos also appear. For the texts and their analysis, see A. K. Grayson and W. G. Lambert, "Akkadian Prophecies," *JCS* 18 (1964) 7–30; W. W. Hallo, "Accadian Apocalypses," *IEJ* 16 (1966) 231–42; R. D. Biggs, "More Babylonian 'Prophecies,'" *Iraq* 29 (1967) 117–32; R. Borger, "Gott Marduk und Gott-König Šulgi als Propheten. Zwei prophetische Texte," *BO* 28 (1971) 3–21; H. Hunger and S. A. Kaufman, "A New Akkadian Prophecy Text," *JAOS* 95 (1975) 371–75; A. K. Grayson, "The Dynastic Prophecy," in *Babylonian Historical-Literary Texts* (Toronto Semitic Texts and Studies 3; Toronto and Buffalo: University of Toronto, 1975) 24–37; S. A. Kaufman, "Prediction, Prophecy and Apocalypse in the Light of New Akkadian Texts," in *Proceedings of the Sixth World Congress of Jewish Studies* (Jerusalem: World Union of Jewish Studies, 1977) 1.221–28. See also P. Höffken, "Heilszeitherrschererwartung im babylonischen Raum," *WO* 9 (1977) 57–71; H. Ringgren, "Akkadian Apocalypses," in *Apocalypticism in the Mediterranean World and the Near East* (ed. D. Hellholm; Tübingen: Mohr, 1983) 379–86. The motifs of Davidic kingship, extended boundaries, agricultural fertility, the return to former secure times, and the ingathering of exiles are predominant in other

characteristic of the period of the United Kingdom.[12]

■ 11 The initial phrase בַּיּוֹם הַהוּא ("on that day")[13] is a neutral term that may introduce an oracle of judgment, for example, Amos 8:3, 9, 13, or one of salvation, for example, Isa 11:10, 11; 12:1; 27:2; Zeph 3:16, as it does here. It does not necessarily indicate a later addition or the work of a redactor; see Amos 2:16; 8:3, 13; and Zech 12:8, 9, 11; 13:1, 2, 4.

In a series of unconditional promises, the Lord first declares the restoration of the Davidic dynasty/kingdom: "On that day I will raise up[14] the fallen booth of David" (סֻכַּת דָּוִיד הַנֹּפֶלֶת). This hapax legomenon image of the "booth" (סוּכָּה) rather than the "house" (בַּיִת)[15] of David and the participle הַנֹּפֶלֶת ("fallen") have caused many difficulties to interpreters and have been used as a historical argument against the authenticity of the verse. The reference here, however, is not to the later destruction of Jerusalem in 587/6 B.C.E. but rather to the "fallen" or "falling"[16] state of the Davidic empire,[17] which was the concomitant result of the rupture of the United Kingdom.[18] The division of the kingdom was a momentous and tragic occurrence in the history of early Israel (see Isa 7:17), hence the description of a "fallen booth," that is, a dilapidated, unstable, precarious state of affairs. Yet the time will come when this condition will be repaired and restored.[19] The Lord announces that he will "repair its breaches"[20] (וְגָדַרְתִּי אֶת פִּרְצֵיהֶן)[21] and "will restore its ruins"[22] (וַהֲרִסֹתָיו אָקִים).[23] "I will rebuild it (וּבְנִיתִיהָ)[24] as in the days of old" (כִּימֵי עוֹלָם).[25] The phrase כִּימֵי עוֹלָם, already attested in Mic 7:14, is a nostalgic

prophetic biblical oracles of the future blissful times as well.

12 See J. Mauchline, "Implicit Signs of Persistent Belief in the Davidic Empire," *VT* 30 (1970) 287–303, esp. 291.

13 Note that the verse begins and ends on the same word, יוֹם, forming an internal inclusio. See also Amos 2:10. These verses are all considered genuine passages of Amos.

14 Note the twofold repetition of אָקִים ("I will raise up"). For the recurrence of the roots נפל and קום together, see Amos 5:2; 8:14.

15 Many see here a reflection of the prophecy of Nathan, 2 Sam 7:5, 7, 11, 13, 27. Note the recurring theme בנה ("to [re]build") in these verses, and the verbal root לְהָקִים ("to establish"), 2 Sam 7:12. If the word "house" were written, it would have been interpreted only as referring to the Davidic "house" (= dynasty). For "booth" as a symbol of the United Kingdom, see also Wagner, "Überlegungen," 661–62.

16 Context alone determines the temporal sense of this *qal* active participle; see *GKC*, 116d. See G, *τὴν πεπτωκυῖαν*; V, *quid cecidit;* T, דְנָפְלַת; S (all perfect tense). For those who translate the participle adjectivally, see, for example, Duhm, "Anmerkungen," 30; Cramer, 48; Hasel, *Remnant,* 208. See also Wagner, "Überlegungen," 661. Budde ("Amos," 115–16) already commented that the verb means "falling/fallen" and not destroyed. See also Maag, *Text,* 215.

17 For the Davidic kingdom, see T, מַלְכוּתָא דְבֵית דָוִד ("the kingdom of the house of David"); Rashi; Kimchi. For those who relate this image to the division of the United Monarchy and its subsequent gradual disintegration, that is, "falling/fallen" state, see, for example, Reventlow, *Amt,* 133; Hasel, *Remnant,* 211 and n 313; see p. 474 for others of the same view. Maag (*Text,* 246ff.) points out that most of the motifs identifiable with exilic and postexilic texts are absent here; for example, there is no reference to sin and its expiation or to the return of the exiled population. K. Seybold (*Das davidische Königtum im Zeugnis der Propheten* [FRLANT 107; Göttingen: Vandenhoeck & Ruprecht, 1972] 17–19, 60–67) also finds the arguments for a later dating mostly insufficient. He interprets the pericope as a criticism against Jeroboam II for his aspirations to restore the Davidic empire. For connections of Amos with the David traditions, see Gottlieb, "Amos und Jerusalem," 430–63. The suggestion of H. N. Richardson ("*Skt* [Amos 9:11]: 'Booth' or 'Succoth'?" *JBL* 92 [1973] 375–81), interpreting the reference to the city of Succoth in Transjordan (identified with tell Deir ʿAlla), was already refuted by Hasel, *Remnant,* 474.

18 See the note of M. Weinfeld and F. M. Cross in the latter's article "The Priestly Tabernacle in the Light of Recent Research," in *Temples and High Places in Biblical Times* (ed. A. Biran; Jerusalem: Keter, 1981) 177 n 31: "Amos 9:11 and Isaiah 16:5 preserve memories of the Davidic Tent of Yahweh. The expression *sukkat David* in Amos 9:11 refers on the surface to the Davidic Dynasty to be restored. This 'rebuilding' may refer to the rule again over the North (and the old empire). . . . [The prophet] is drawing on the typology between the dynasty and the dynastic shrine—the Tent of Yahweh."

19 For a messianic interpretation, see Babylonian Talmud, Sanhedrin 96b–97a, and the citation of this verse in the writings from Qumran, Damascus Covenant 7:16 and *4QFlor* (174)1.12–13. See J. M. Allegro, *Qumran Cave 4* (DJD 5; Oxford: Clarendon, 1968) 1.53.

reflection upon the ideal period of the Davidic empire.[26]

■ **12** This verse, too, has been questioned on several grounds. It is assumed that v 12 does not follow smoothly upon v 11 and that both the plural verb (יִירְשׁוּ) without any direct antecedent and the specific mention of the nation of Edom point to a later addition.[27] However, this verse should be interpreted as the direct continuation of the former one. After the reestablishment of the Davidic dynasty domestically, the next stage (לְמַעַן)[28] in the program of restoration, "as in the days of old," shall be the reassertion of its authority over all the nations that formerly were under its suzerainty, which will lead to the reemergence of the extensive Davidic empire. The plural verb יִירְשׁוּ ("so that they shall possess") may refer to the future rulers of the Davidic dynasty.[29]

According to most scholars, the singular mention of Edom[30] alludes directly to the time of the destruction of Jerusalem (587/6 B.C.E.) and the subsequent exilic period, when hostility toward that nation was prevalent; see Isa 63:1–6; Ezek 32:29; Obad 9ff.; Mal 1:3–4.[31] However, see the comments made about the oracle against Edom (Amos 1:11–12) concerning the long history of rivalry between the two nations. Furthermore, Rudolph[32] has drawn particular attention to the expression "the rest (= remnant) of Edom" (שְׁאֵרִית אֱדוֹם).[33] The Davidic empire will be reestablished over all the nations[34] and over the rest of Edom, implying that only part of Edom was presently in its possession. What then could possibly be the political-historical background of such a statement? In exilic and postexilic times, the opposite situation prevailed, that is, southern Judah was in Edomite possession. Thus there may be an allusion here to the regaining of part of Edom, the port of Elath, which was incorporated during the reign of Uzziah (2 Kgs 14:22; 2 Chr 26:2) but was subsequently lost by Ahaz (2 Kgs 16:6). This reference to the partial subjugation of Edom, therefore, in Rudolph's opinion, is an important indication for the authenticity of the passage.

For the motif of the future reunification of the northern and southern kingdoms, see also Isa 11:13–14; Jer 31:6; Ezek 37:15–28; Hos 2:2. For a somewhat similar theme in Mesopotamian "prophetic" texts, see Weinfeld, "Mesopotamian Prophecies," 267.

20 The suffixes seem to be in total disarray, singular and plural intermixing with masculine and feminine. Many commentators harmonize by reading all the suffixes as feminine singular, ־ֶיהָ, referring back to סֻכָּה.

21 See Isa 58:12; Ezek 13:5; 22:30. For the opposite, see Isa 5:5; Pss 80:13; 81:41; Eccl 10:8. This is another example of the reversal of Israel's destiny; see Amos 4:3.

22 See Rudolph, 279.

23 See Isa 49:19, הֲרִסֻתֵךְ. For the Qumran reading, הרוסתך, in IQIs[a], see Kutscher, *Language,* 283. Note the chiastic structure of the first two stichs.

24 For הרס, the opposite of בנה, see Jer 1:10; 24:6; 42:10; 45:4; Prov 14:1; Job 12:14. For Heb. בנה ("to rebuild" or "to repair"), see v 14; 1 Kgs 16:34; Mic 7:11 (לִבְנוֹת גְּדֵרָיִךְ, "to repair your walls"); Neh 2:17; 2 Chr 33:16. The root בנה appears also in the next pericope, v 14.

25 See Mal 3:4. The phrases יְמֵי עוֹלָם and יְמוֹת עוֹלָם also occur; see n 5. For a similar expression, כִּימֵי־קֶדֶם ("as in former days"), see Isa 51:9; Jer 46:26. See also Lam 2:17; 5:21.

26 See E. Rohland, *Die Bedeutung*, 232; H.-P. Müller, *Ursprünge und Strukturen alttestamentlicher Eschatologie* (BZAW 109; Berlin: Töpelmann, 1969) 213–14.

27 See, along with most commentaries, Wolff, 351.

28 Heb. לְמַעַן, for example, Gen 12:13; Deut 29:18; Jer 7:18; 27:10, 15; Hos 8:4; Amos 2:7; Mic 6:16, indicates the result of the former action.

29 See Hammershaimb, 140–41; Rudolph, 281. See also J. Halevy, "Recherches bibliques: Le livre d'Amos," *RevSém* 11 (1903) 298–99. See also Marti; Nowack; Driver; Robinson-Horst; Cramer; Cripps; Weiser, *Profetie;* Maag, *Text;* Snaith, *Text of Amos;* Amsler. Another solution to the problem is to relate the plural יִירְשׁוּ to אֲשֶׁר נִקְרָא שְׁמִי עֲלֵיהֶם and not to the subdued nations: "So that they over whom my name is called [= Israel] shall possess"; for example, Kimchi; Ehrlich, *Mikrâ,* 3:418; idem, *Randglossen,* 5.256.

30 Note G, *τῶν ἀνθρώπων* ("of men") = Heb. אָדָם, an error for אֱדוֹם.

31 Most commentators.

32 Rudolph, 282. It should also be noted that Edom is mentioned three times in the oracles against the nations: Amos 1:6, 9, 11. This would add an inclusio structure to the beginning and ending of the entire Book of Amos.

33 See the analogous expression, שְׁאֵרִית פְּלִשְׁתִּים ("the remnant of the Philistines"), Amos 1:8; and שְׁאֵרִית יוֹסֵף ("the remnant of Joseph"), Amos 5:15.

34 Although the *nota accusativi,* אֶת, is not repeated, the expression "all the nations" is not dependent upon שְׁאֵרִית ("the rest of"), as is the preceding אֱדוֹם; against Keil; van Gelderen; Neher, *Amos,* 173–74. See Rudolph, 279.

The "remnant" will yet be "possessed" by the reemergent Davidic kingdom.

The Davidic empire will also rule once again over all those nations "over whom my name has been called" (אֲשֶׁר נִקְרָא שְׁמִי עֲלֵיהֶם). This idiom, נִקְרָא שֵׁם עַל, denotes ownership and the act of possession.[35] The nations conquered by David are regarded as the Lord's possessions. Israel's wars are the wars of their God, and David conducted the battles of Israel at the Lord's command[36] (see 2 Sam 5:25; 8:6, 14), "who will do this" (עֹשֶׂה זֹאת)[37]—a note of reassurance that the Lord both announces and executes his prediction.

This unit thus refers to Israel (and Judah) as well as to the other nations, analogous to the beginning of the book, forming an overarching inclusio. According to Cross, moreover, "the recovery of the Davidic empire complements the condemnation of the nation states of the Davidic empire (Amos 1:3—2:3)" (written communication).

■ **13** This pericope directly follows upon the previous one.[38] After describing the political renewal of the Davidic kingdom and its territorial expansion, there next ensues a vivid picture of the forthcoming unconditional blessing[39] of abundant fertility[40] that will be bestowed upon the land.[41] In the "coming days" (הִנֵּה יָמִים בָּאִים),[42] the crops will be so bountiful that the "reaper" (קוֹצֵר)[43] will not complete his work before the "plowman" (חוֹרֵשׁ)[44] "shall draw near" him (נִגַּשׁ בְּ־).[45] During the normal agricultural cycle, there is a time lapse of about half a year between plowing and reaping.[46] The reaping of barley[47] begins during Passover in April[48] and that of wheat during the holiday of Pentecost, fifty days later in May.[49] The season of plowing, however, commences only after the first rains in October-November. Now, due to the boon of crops and harvests, the respective agricultural activities will take place continuously without the usual interval of six months.[50]

Furthermore, because of the vintage crop, the

35 See, for example, Deut 28:10; 2 Sam 12:28; Isa 4:1; 63:19; Jer 7:10; 15:16.

36 Similarly in Mesopotamian war annals, the king wages war in the name of his god. See B. Albrektson, *History and the Gods: An Essay on the Idea of Historical Events as Divine Manifestations in the Ancient Near East and Israel* (Coniectanica Biblica Old Testament Series 1; Lund: Gleerup, 1963).

37 For Heb. עֹשֶׂה, see Amos 4:13; 5:8. See Mal 3:17, 21. The combination of זאת with the verb עשה also appears in Amos 4:12.

38 See Rudolph, 283, contrary to most commentators. Note also the literary motifs common to these two units and Joel 4:18–19. In the latter, as well, the fertility of the future age is found in conjunction with the destruction of Israel's enemies, Egypt and Edom. For a thorough analysis of this verse, see M. Weiss, "These Days and the Days to Come according to Amos 9:13," in Eretz Israel 14 (*H. L. Ginsberg Volume;* ed. M. Haran and others; Jerusalem: Israel Exploration Society, 1978) 69–73 (Heb.). It has been overlooked by almost all exegetes that two key verbs in this verse, מוג and נגשׁ ־ב, appear in vv 5 and 10, respectively, adding the important dimension of the catchword association to the authenticity of the passage. See also Watts, *Vision,* 25f.; Reventlow, *Amt,* 90ff.

39 This differs from Lev 26:4–13, where the blessings are dependent upon obedience to the laws (Lev 26:3).

40 For the recurring motif of fertility in future days, see Isa 29:17; 32:15; 41:18–19; 51:3; 55:13; Jer 31:12–14; Ezek 34:26–27; 36:8–11; 47:1–12; Hos 2:23–24; Joel 2:19, 21–26; 4:18; Zech 8:12. For the assumed connection of a return to the primeval fertility of Eden in this verse, see the criticism of Weiss, "Days," 70 n 12.

For the direct relationship between political success and agricultural abundance in ancient Near Eastern literature, see the works cited by Rudolph, 283 n 13; and Weiss, "Days," 69–70 n 11. See also Ps 72:16 (within the context of the entire psalm).

41 This then is a reversal of the agricultural blights referred to previously; see 4:9; 5:11.

42 This phrase may precede oracles of punishment (for example, Amos 4:2; 8:11) as well as salvation (for example, Jer 16:14). It does not always designate a new literary section; see Amos 4:2.

43 Compare El Amarna Canaanite, *kaṣāru, EA,* 244, 14. The verbs קצר and חרש appear together in 1 Sam 8:12; Hos 10:13; and the substantives, קָצִיר ("harvest time") and חָרִישׁ ("plowing time"), in Gen 45:6; Exod 34:21; 1 Sam 8:12. See Avishur, "Word Pairs," 18. The Akkadian semantic equivalent is *ēṣidu* ("harvester, reaper"); *CAD, E,* 349–50.

44 Compare Akk. *errēšu* ("tenant farmer, cultivator"); *ērišu* ("plowman"), *CAD, E,* 301, 304; Ugar. *ḥrt, UT,* 905; and El Amarna Canaanite, *a/iḫrišu, EA,* 226, 11.

45 Heb. נגשׁ in the *nipḥ'al* followed by the particle ב appears only here but occurs twice in the *qal,* Isa 65:5; Job 41:8.

46 Ploughing and reaping designate the two opposite ends of the agricultural year. See *AuS,* II.177, 198; IV.368f.

47 See Gezer Calendar, line 4, ירח קצר שערם ("the

"treader of grapes" (וְדֹרֵךְ עֲנָבִים),[51] who presses the grapes (by foot) during the months of August and September,[52] will not finish his work before he "who sows the seeds" (מֹשֵׁךְ הַזָּרַע)[53] commences his rounds in November-December. Instead of the usual time gap of one to two months, these agricultural laborers will find themselves plying their chores simultaneously.

Compare similarly the image that appears in Mesopotamian "prophetic" texts: *dīš kuṣṣi ana ebūri dīš ebūri ana kuṣṣi uštabarra* ("The winter grass/vegetation will last until the summer grass/vegetation; the summer vegetation will last until the winter vegetation").[54]

The image of copious and fruitful fertility continues in the second half of the verse. The vineyards planted upon the mountain slopes (see 2 Chr 26:10)[55] will produce such an enormous quantity of wine that "the mountains shall drip fresh wine" (וְהִטִּיפוּ הֶהָרִים עָסִיס).[56] They will ripple and flow with the newly fermented wine (עָסִיס),[57] recalling the image of Israel as a land "flowing with milk and honey" (see Exod 3:17; 13:5)—and here with wine. At the same time, "the hills" (הַגְּבָעוֹת)[58] shall תִּתְמוֹגַגְנָה. This verb in the *hithpolel*[59] derived from the root מוג has been explained in several different ways. The usual interpretation is "to melt," that is, the hills shall melt from the teeming measures of wine that will flow over

month of the barley harvest"). See Gibson, *Hebrew and Moabite Inscriptions*, 2–3.

48 See Lev 23:10; 2 Sam 21:9; 2 Kgs 4:42.

49 See Exod 23:16; 34:22.

50 Other commentators (for example, Rashi, Harper, Driver, Nowack) interpret the image to mean that even before the ploughing is completed, the harvesting will begin. This then would refer not to the abundance of the crops but to their miraculously rapid ripening. See, however, Weiss ("Days," 69 n 9) for objections to this interpretation. He points out that the word order would then have to be reversed, וְנִגַּשׁ קוֹצֵר בַּחוֹרֵשׁ; that the parallel colon also refers only to abundance and not to ripening; and that throughout the verse the motif of fertility is described in a natural rather than miraculous manner. For the usual comparison of this verse with Lev 26:5, see the significant differences in imagery and ideology cited by Weiss ("Days," 70–71).

51 Heb. דֹּרֵךְ עֲנָבִים is a hapax legomenon. There are, however, several other similar phrases: דֹּרֵךְ (בְּ)גַת ("treads in a press"), Isa 63:2; Lam 1:15; Neh 13:15; דֹּרֵךְ יְקָבִים ("treads winepresses"), Job 24:11; דֹּרֵךְ יַיִן בַּיְקָבִים ("treads wine in the presses"), Isa 16:10; דֹּרֵךְ פּוּרָה ("treads winepresses"), Isa 63:3; דֹּרֵךְ זַיִת ("treads olives"), Mic 6:15.

52 See *AuS*, IV.372.

53 The expression is found only here. Heb. מֹשֵׁךְ is a denominative verb derived from the noun מֶשֶׁךְ ("leather bag, pouch") (compare Akk. *mašku*, *CAD*, *M*, I.376–79; Ugar. *mtk*, *UT*, 440), which also appears in Ps 126:6, "seed bag" (מֶשֶׁךְ הַזָּרַע); and Job 28:18a, "a pouch of wisdom (מֶשֶׁךְ חָכְמָה) is better than rubies." This was already interpreted correctly by ibn Ezra on Ps 126:6; ibn Ganaḥ, *Haschoraschim*, 276, entry משך; L. Köhler, "Hebräische Vokabeln II," *ZAW* 55 (1937) 161–62; T. H. Robinson, "New Light on the Text and Interpretation of the Old Testament Supplied by Recent Discoveries," *ZAW* 73 (1961) 267 n 9; Maag, *Text*, 161; Rudolph, 279; Weiss, "Days," 71; *KB*, 574b; and H. Yalon, *Quntreisim* 2 (Jerusalem: Wahrman, 1938–1939) 80 n 5 (Heb.). Compare also Akk. *mazrû* ("sowing basket") *CAD*, *M*, I.439.

54 See also Borger, *Inschriften*, 93, 13ff.; and for other examples, see *CAD*, *D*, 164; *E*, 20. The comparison was already noted by Weinfeld ("Mesopotamian Prophecies," 266), who also cites *JCS* 18 (1964) 7ff., Text A, obv. III, 7; *BiOr* 28 (1971) 11, III: 8–9. The example quoted in the commentary is taken from C. Virolleaud, *L'astrologie chaldéene: Le livre intitulé "enuma (Anu) ilu Bêl"* (Paris: Guethner, 1908) 20:96f.; see, too, TCL 6 16:50 in F. Thureau-Dangin, *Tablettes d'Uruk à l'usage des prêtres du temple d'Anu au temps des Séleucides* (Paris: Guethner, 1922).

55 See M. Zohary, *Plant Life of Palestine: Israel and Jordan* (New York: Ronald, 1962) 299ff. (Heb.).

56 See Joel 4:18 for the same imagery. The relationship between the verses in Joel and Amos has often been noted. There is no reason to assume, however, that one borrowed from the other.

57 See Isa 49:26; Joel 1:5; 4:18; Cant 8:2. Compare the description of fertility after Baal's revival and return in the Baal epic, *CTA*, 6:iii:6–7, 12–13, *šmm.šmn.tmṭrn nḫlm. tlk.nbtm* ("The heavens rained with oil, and the brooks flowed with honey").

58 For הָרִים and גְּבָעוֹת in synonymous parallelism (some twenty-seven times), see, for example, Deut 33:15; Isa 30:17; 41:15; 54:10; Jer 4:24; Joel 4:18; Mic 6:1; Nah 1:5; Hab 3:6; Ps 114:4, 6; Prov 8:25; Cant 2:8; 4:6.

59 See, too, Nah 1:5; Ps 107:26. Note also the use of this root in v 5.

them.[60] However, because the entire verse appears to be constructed chiastically[61]—the theme of wine that ends the first colon is resumed at the beginning of the next colon—it is also possible that the activity being described here refers to the produce of the first part of the first colon, that is, grain. Thus a more likely translation would be "and all the hills shall wave [with grain]."[62]

■ **14** The plethora of blessings promised for the future age continues with a first-person divine address announcing a threefold auspicious reversal of Israel's fortune. The technical expression for this grand metamorphosis is וְשַׁבְתִּי שְׁבוּת (literally, "I shall turn a turning"), which means that Israel will be restored to its former state (of well being).[63] This idiom, when properly understood, should no longer be denied to Amos, as many exegetes claim. It can be traced back to preexilic times[64] and is also documented in the contemporary eighth-century Aramaic inscription from Sefire (III 24–25): וכעת השבו אלהן שיבת ב[ית אבי] ("But now, the gods have brought about the return of the hou[se of my father . . .]").[65]

The restoration of Israel's fortune and prosperity now refers to a triad of activities that will be blessed with fruition (thus continuing the motif of the previous verse): "They shall rebuild (בָּנוּ)[66] desolate cities (עָרִים נְשַׁמּוֹת)[67] and inhabit them," reversing the former futility curse, 5:11.[68] "They shall plant (וְנָטְעוּ)[69] vineyards (כְּרָמִים) and drink their wine." This blessing, too, is the direct antithesis of 5:11; see also 4:9.[70] For the joint blessing of rebuilding cities and planting vineyards, see Isa 65:21; Jer 29:5; Ezek 28:26 (where it is also followed by the

60 Most commentators and translations. Others (for example, Weiser, *Profetie;* Hammershaimb, 136; Rudolph, 279, 284) interpret the verb to mean "soften." Rudolph compares the *polel*-form תְּמֹגְגֶנָּה in Ps 65:11b: "You soften it with showers." This would mean that the wine flowing down the slopes so softens them that they are always in a fertile state. For other opinions, see Weiss, "Days," 72 n 35. L. Sabottka (*Zephanja: Versuch einer Neuübersetzung mit philologischem Kommentar* [BibOr 25; Rome: Biblical Institute Press, 1972] 61 n 205) suggests that this verb (as well as תִּתְעַלַּפְנָה, Amos 8:13) is a durative *hithpael,* "beständig fliessen" ("constantly flowing").

61 So, too, Rudolph, 283–84.

62 See *KB,* 526a; see, too, *NJPS* and *NEB.* For the sense of a waving, shaking movement, see Nah 1:5; Ps 107:26. According to Alter (*Art,* 157), "Momentarily invoking the language of apocalypse [cf. the same verb in Nah 1:5], the poet has swung the vision of global destruction around to its exact antithesis." This antithetical image he renders as "dissolving in sweet abundance" (117).

63 The expression appears in several variant forms: שׁוּב שְׁבִית, Ezek 16:53; Zeph 2:7; Pss 85:2; 126:4; שׁוּב שְׁבוּת, Deut 30:3; Jer 29:14; 30:3, 18; 31:22; 48:47; Ezek 29:14; Hos 6:11; Zeph 3:20; Pss 14:7; 53:7; Job 42:10; לְהָשִׁיב שְׁבוּת, Jer 32:44; 33:7, 11, 26; 49:6, 39; Ezek 39:25; Joel 4:1; Lam 2:14. In some of these passages there is an interchange between שְׁבוּת and שְׁבִית. Only in Job 42:10 is it applied to an individual; in all the other passages the reference is to the nation. For studies of the expression, see E. L. Dietrich, שוב שבות. *Die endzeitlich Wiederherstellung bei den Propheten* (BZAW 40: Giessen: Töpelmann, 1925); W. L. Holladay, *The Root Šûbh in the Old Testament* (Leiden: Brill, 1958) 113; R. Borger, "Zu שוב שבו/ית," *ZAW* 66 (1954) 315f.; A. Soggin, "*ŠWB, šûb,* zurückkehren," *THAT* II, 886ff. In none of the above passages does it have anything whatsoever to do with the returning from captivity. The root of the noun is the same as the verb שׁוּב. See Hammershaimb, 143.

Note the use of the root שׁוּב here and repeatedly at the beginning of the book in the preface to the oracles against the nations, אֲשִׁיבֶנּוּ.

64 See Rudolph (285), who states that the expression surely "auf alle Fälle vorexilisch ist" ("is in any case preexilic").

65 Fitzmyer, *Sefire,* 100, iii:24–25. See Greenfield, "Stylistic Aspects," 4.

66 See v 11.

67 So, too, Isa 54:3; Jer 33:10. Compare the Akkadian parallel found in the Mesopotamian "prophetic texts," *šūšub namê nadûte* ("to cause abandoned sites to be inhabited"). See *CAD, A,* II.408, already noted by Weinfeld, "Mesopotamian Prophecies," 267.

68 See comments to that verse.

69 Compare the use of this root in v 15.

70 For the corresponding curses, see Deut 28:30, 39; Zeph 1:13. See Hillers, *Treaty Curses,* 29, 35–36, 41, 55. The two terms בַּיִת and כֶּרֶם often appear paired together; see Deut 20:5–6; 28:30; Josh 24:13; Isa 5:9–10; 65:21; Jer 35:7; Ezek 28:26; Eccl 2:4. In Amos 5:11 and 9:14 there appears the similar sequence of four verbs: בנה, ישב, נטע, and שתה.

promise of secure dwelling as in Amos); Ps 107:26–27. Last, but not least, "They shall cultivate gardens (עָשׂוּ גַנּוֹת)[71] and eat their fruits" (פְּרִיהֶם).[72] For this very same blessing, see Jer 29:5, 28.

■ **15** The oracle of unconditional and unqualified promise for the future blissful state of Israel concludes with the devoutly sought wish—the permanent possession of the land of Israel. Israel never again will be driven out of the promised land.

The final boon is expressed once again in the agricultural imagery so characteristic of Amos:[73] "I shall plant them (וּנְטַעְתִּים)[74] on their own soil, and they shall never again be uprooted from the soil (וְלֹא יִנָּתְשׁוּ עוֹד מֵעַל אַדְמָתָם)[75] I have given them" (אֲשֶׁר־נָתַתִּי לָהֶם).[76] Israel is pictured as a tree[77] permanently planted, never again to be uprooted. Once again the prophet literally reverses the destiny of Israel (see 5:2).

The oracle then ends on the reassuring direct second-person note, "said the Lord your God."[78]

71 See Eccl 2:5 for the same idiom. For גַּן ("garden") and כֶּרֶם ("vineyard") together, see Amos 4:9. For the Akkadian interdialectal equivalent, *kirâm epēšu* ("to prepare a field or garden for cultivation, to cultivate"), see *CAD, E,* 230, 5′.

72 In the Jeremiah passages the final noun appears with feminine suffixal endings, פְּרִיהֶן, פִּרְיָן. In the verse of Amos the masculine suffix is incongruous with the female antecedent גַּנּוֹת, derived from גַּנָּה.

For the phrase אָכַל פְּרִי ("to eat the fruits"), which appears twenty-one times in the Bible, see the concordances.

73 This follows immediately upon the imagery of vv 13–14.

74 For similar imagery of planting, see Jer 24:6; 32:41; 42:10. See also 2 Sam 7:10; Isa 60:21; Jer 2:21; 31:27. See, too, Hos 2:25. For the opposite, see Jer 45:4. See R. Bach, "Bauen und Pflanzen," in *Studien zur Theologie der alttestamentlichen Überlieferungen* (ed. R. Rendtorff and K. Koch; Neukirchen-Vluyn: Neukirchener Verlag, 1961) 7–32; T. Frymer-Kensky, "The Planting of Man: A Study in Biblical Imagery," in *Love and Death in the Ancient Near East: Essays in Honor of Marvin H. Pope* (ed. J. H. Marks and Robert M. Good; Guilford, CT: Four Quarters, 1987) 129–36. See also Amos 9:14.

75 For this expression, see Deut 29:27; 1 Kgs 14:15; Jer 12:14; 2 Chr 7:20. For נתשׁ as the opposite of נטע, see also Jer 1:10; 18:7, 9.

Note the twofold repetition of אַדְמָתָם ("their land") in this verse. Note also the apparently intended allusion (in reverse) to 5:2.

76 See Rudolph (285) for criticism against an alleged Deuteronomic origin for this expression.

77 See Ps 80:9. Note the similar sounding נְטַעְתִּי(ם) and נָתַתִּי. See also the use of the same verb immediately above in v 14.

78 G's reading, ὁ θεὸς ὁ παντοκράτωρ (= Heb. אֱלֹהֵי־(הַ)צְּבָאוֹת), harmonizes with the other concluding phrases of Amos 3:13; 4:13; 5:8 (G), 14, 15, 16, 27; 9:5, 6 (G). The Masoretic reading is unique to this verse; see Isa 54:6; 66:9.

Bibliography
Indices

The bibliography has been divided into a number of categories. Each volume or article is cited only once, under a single category. Many of the works have usefulness beyond the category under which they are listed, and the reader is advised to consult the complete bibliography.

1. Commentaries

Abarbanel, D. Y.
Commentary to the Latter Prophets (Jerusalem: Elisha, 1957) (Heb.).

al-Ḳumissi, D.
Commentarius in Librum Duodecim Prophetarum (ed. I. D. Markin; Jerusalem: Mekize Nirdamim, 1957).

Amsler, S.
Osée, Joël, Abdias, Jonas (CAT XIa; Neuchâtel/Paris: Delachaux & Niestle, 1965; Genève: Labor et Fides, ²1982) 157–247.

Anderson, B. W.
The Eighth Century Prophets Amos, Hosea, Isaiah, Micah (Philadelphia/London: SPCK, 1979).

Andersson, C. H.
Commentarius in Amos (Gotha, 1954).

Augé, R.
Profetes Menors (La Bíblia 16; Barcelona: Monestir de Montserrat, 1957).

Auld, A. G.
Amos (Sheffield: JSOT, 1986).

Bartina, S.
The Book of Amos (Madrid, 1968).

Baur, G.A.L.
Der Prophet Amos erklärt (Giessen, 1847).

Beaugency, E.
Kommentar zu Ezechiel und den XII kleinen Propheten (ed. S. Poznański; Warsaw: H. Eppelberg, 1914) (Heb.).

Beck, E.
Gottes Traum. Eine menschliche Welt: Hosea, Amos, Micha (Stuttgarter Kleiner Kommentar AT 14; Stuttgart: Katholische Bibelwerk, 1972).

Beek, M. A.
Amos. Een inleiding tot het verstaan der Profeten van het OT (Lochem: De Tijdstroom, 1947).

Bella, B. M.
Amos (Hermeneia Palaias Diathekes 1; Athens: Aster, 1947) (Greek).

Bewer, J. A.
The Book of the Twelve Prophets (Harper's Annotated Bible Series; 2 vols.; New York: Harper and Brothers, 1949).

Bič, M.
Das Buch Amos (Berlin: Evangelische-Verlagsanstalt, 1969).

Bleeker, L.H.K.
De Kleine Profeten, I: Hosea, Amos (Tekst en Uitleg 1/2; Groningen: J. B. Wolters, 1932).

Brillet, G.
Amos et Osée (Témoins de Dieu 3; Paris: Cerf, 1944).

British and Foreign Bible Society
The Book of Amos (Translator's Old Testament; London: British and Foreign Bible Society, 1976).

Bruno, A.
Das Buch der Zwölf. Eine rhythmische und textkritische Untersuchung (Stockholm: Almquist & Wiksell, 1957).

Burrons, W. O.
Amos with Introduction, Notes and Maps (1898).

Canney, M. A.
"Amos," *A Commentary on the Bible* (ed. A. S. Peake; New York: Thomas Nelson and Sons, 1920) 547–54.

Ceuppens, P. F.
De Kleine Profeten (Bruges: de Brouwer, 1924).

Chajes, H. P.
Biblia Hebraica—Liber duodecim prophetarum (ed. A. Kahana; Kiev: A. Kahana, 1906; rep. Jerusalem: Mekor, 1969) (Heb.).

Cooke, G. A.
The Book of Amos, with Notes by E. A. Edghill (London: Methuen, 1914).

Copass, B. A.
Amos (Nashville: Broadman, 1939).

Coppens, J.
Les Douze Petits Prophètes (Bruges: de Brouwer; Louvain: Publications Universitaires, 1950).

Cramer, K.
Amos. Versuch einer theologischen Interpretation (BWANT 3/15; Stuttgart: Kohlhammer, 1930).

Cripps, R. S.
A Critical and Exegetical Commentary on the Book of Amos (London: SPCK, 1920; ²1955).

Dahl, J.C.W.
Amos neu übersetzt und erläutert (Göttingen: Vandenhoeck & Ruprecht, 1795).

Deden, D.
De Kleine Profeten mit de Grondtekst vertaald en uitgelegd (2 vols.; Roermond en Maaseik: Romen & Zonen, 1953).

Deissler, A.
Zwölf Propheten: Hosea, Joel, Amos (Die Neue Echter Bibel; Würzburg: Echter, 1981).

Delcor, M.
Les Petits Prophètes I: Amos (La Sainte Bible 8/1; Paris: Letouzey & Ané, 1961).

Driver, S. R.
The Books of Joel and Amos (The Cambridge Bible for Schools and Colleges; Cambridge: Cambridge University, 1915, ²1934).

Edghill, E. A.
The Book of Amos (Westminster Commentaries; London: Longmans Green, ²1926).
Ehrlich, A. B.
Randglossen zur Hebräischen Bibel (7 vols.; Leipzig: Hinrichs, 1912) 5.227–56.
Idem
Mikrâ ki-Pheschutô (6 vols.; New York: Ktav, 1969) 3.401–18 (Heb.).
Elhorst, H. J.
De Profetie van Amos (Leiden: Brill, 1902).
Elliger, K.
Das Buch der Zwölf Kleinen Propheten II (Göttingen: Vandenhoeck & Ruprecht, 1950).
Ewald, H.
Die Propheten des Alten Bundes. Band I (5 vols.; Göttingen: Vandenhoeck & Ruprecht, 1867–69).
Fosbroke, H.E.W.
The Book of Amos: Introduction and Exegesis (The Interpreter's Bible; New York/Nashville: Abingdon, 1956) 6.761–853.
Frey, H.
Das Buch des Ringens Gottes um seine Kirche. Der Prophet Amos (Die Botschaft des Alten Testaments 23/1; Stuttgart: Calwer, 1958, ²1965).
Garland, D. E.
Amos, A Study Guide (Study Guide Series; Grand Rapids: Zondervan, 1974).
Graetz, H.
Emendationes in plerosque Sacrae Scripturae Veteris Testamenti Libros (ed. G. Bacher; 3 vols.; Breslau: Schottlaender, 1893).
Gressmann, H.
Die älteste Geschichtsschreibung und Prophetie Israels (*SAT* 2/1; Göttingen: Vandenhoeck & Ruprecht, 1910, ²1921).
Grosch, H.
Der Prophet Amos. Handbücherei für des Religionsunterricht (Gütersloh: Gerd Mohn, 1969).
Gunning, J. H.
De Godspraken van Amos, Vertaald en Verklaard (Leiden: Brill, 1885).
Guthe, H.
"Der Prophet Amos," HS 2/4 (ed. E. Kautzsch and A. Bertholet; Tübingen: J.C.B. Mohr [Siebeck], ⁴1923) 30–47.
Gwynn, R. M.
The Book of Amos (Cambridge: Cambridge University, 1927).
Ḥacham, A.
Minor Prophets (*Da'at Miqra* 10; Jerusalem: Mosad HaRav Kook, 1973) (Heb.).
Hailey, H. A.
A Commentary on the Minor Prophets (Grand Rapids: Baker Book House, 1970).
Hammershaimb, E.
Amos Fortolket (Kjøbenhavn: Nyt Nordisk Forlag, 1946, ²1958, ³1967); English tr. *The Book of Amos: A Commentary* (tr. J. Sturdy; Oxford: Basil Blackwell, 1970).
Harper, W. R.
A Critical and Exegetical Commentary on Amos and Hosea (ICC; Edinburgh: T. & T. Clarke, 1905).
Hartung, K.
Der Prophet Amos, nach dem Grundtexte erklärt (Biblische Studien [Freiburg] 3/4; Freiburg: Herder, 1898).
Hauret, C.
Amos et Osée (VS 5; Paris: Beauchesne, 1970).
Hayes, J. H.
Amos. The Eighth-Century Prophet: His Times and His Preaching (Nashville: Abingdon Press, 1988).
Henderson, E.
The Book of the Twelve Minor Prophets (Andover, MA: W. F. Draper; New York: Sheldon, 1846).
Herntrich, V.
Amos der Prophet Gottes (Wege in der Bibel 4; Göttingen: Vandenhoeck & Ruprecht, 1941).
Hesselberg, H.
Die Zwölf Kleinen Propheten ausgelegt (Königsbergen: A. W. Unzer, 1838).
Hitzig, F., and H. Steiner
Die Zwölf Kleinen Propheten erklärt (Leipzig: Hirzel, ⁴1881).
Honeycutt, R. L.
Amos and His Message. An Expository Commentary (Nashville: Broadman, 1963).
Horton, R. F., and S. R. Driver
The Minor Prophets (Edinburgh: T.C. & E.C. Jack, 1904–1906).
How, J.C.H.
Joel and Amos (Smaller Cambridge Bible for Schools; Cambridge: Cambridge University, 1910).
ibn Ezra, A.
See *Miqra'oth Gedoloth.*
Jensen, J.K.R.
Amos og Hosea (Kjøbenhaven, 1914).
Jepsen, A.
Die Zwölfprophetenbuch übersetzt und ausgelegt (Leipzig/Hamburg: Gustav Schloessmanns, 1937).
Justi, K.W.
Amos neu übersetzt und erläutert (Leipzig, 1820).
Juynboll, T.G.J.
Disputatio de Amoso (Leiden, 1828).
Keil, C. F.
Biblischer Commentar über Die Zwölf Kleinen Propheten (*BC* 3/4; Leipzig: Dörffling & Franke, ³1888).
Kelley, P. H.
The Book of Amos: A Study Manual (Grand Rapids, 1966); re-released under the title *Amos: Prophet of Social Justice* (Grand Rapids: Baker Book House, 1974).
Kimchi, D.
See *Miqra'oth Gedoloth.*

King, P. J.
"Amos," *The Jerome Biblical Commentary* (ed. R. E. Brown, J. A. Fitzmyer, and R. E. Murphy; London: Chapman; Englewood Cliffs, NJ: Prentice Hall, 1968); 245–52; ([2]1971) 655–73.
Idem
Amos, Hosea, Micah: An Archaeological Commentary (Philadelphia: Westminster, 1988).
Klausner, J.
The Book of Amos (Tel Aviv: Yizreel, 1943) (Heb.).
Knabenbauer, J.
Commentarius in Prophetes Minores (Cursus Scripturae Sacrae 2/24–25; Paris: Lethielleux, 1886).
Knapp, C.
Amos and His Age (London: Thomas Murby, 1923).
Koehler, L.
Amos der älteste Schriftprophet (Zürich: Rascher, 1920).
Koenig, A.
Die Profeet Amos: Koort Verklarings oor die Ou Testament (Kaapstad: N. G. Kerk–Uitgewers, 1974).
Kraeling, E. G.
Commentary on the Prophets (2 vols.; Camden, NJ: T. Nelson, 1966).
Kroeker, J.
Die Prophetie oder das Reden Gottes. Die vorexilischen Propheten, I. Amos und Hosea (Giessen/Basel, 1932).
Kutal, B.
Libri prophetarum Amos et Abdiae (Commentarii in Prophetas Minores 3; Olmütz: Lidové, Zavody Tiskarské é Nakladatelské, 1933).
Laetsch, T.F.K.
The Minor Prophets (St. Louis: Concordia, 1956).
Lehrman, S. M.
"Amos," *The Twelve Prophets* (Soncino Books of the Bible; ed. A. Cohen; London/Jerusalem/New York: Soncino, 1974).
Lindhagen, C.
Profeten Amos (Stockholm: Verbum, 1971).
Lockert, E.
Le Prophète Amos (Paris: Coveslant, 1909).
Macpherson, A.
Amos and Hosea: Prophets 1 (Scripture Discussion Commentary 2; Chicago: ACTA Foundation, 1971) 1–34.
McKeating, H.
The Books of Amos, Hosea, Micah (Cambridge Bible Commentary on the NEB; Cambridge: Cambridge University, 1971).
Marsh, J.
Amos and Micah: Introduction and Commentary (Torch Bible Commentaries; London: SCM, 1965).
Marti, K.
Das Dodekapropheton erklärt (KAT 23; Tübingen: Mohr [Siebeck], 1904).
Martin-Achard, R.
Amos—L'homme, le message, l'influence (Genève: Labor et Fides, 1984).
Martin-Achard, R., and S. P. Re'emi
A Commentary on the Book of Amos (tr. G.A.F. Knight; Edinburgh: Handsel, 1984).
Mays, J. L.
Amos: A Commentary (OTL; Philadelphia: Westminster, 1969).
Meṣudoth
See *Miqra'oth Gedoloth.*
Miqra'oth Gedoloth
[The Rabbinic Bible], commentaries of Rashi, Abraham ibn Ezra, David Kimchi, & Meṣudoth (New York: Pardes, 1961).
Monloubou, J.
Amos et Osée (Paris: Cerf, 1964).
Motyer, J. A., and D. Guthrie
Amos: New Bible Commentary (London: Tyndale Press, [3]1970).
Mowinkel, S., and N. Messel
De Senere Profeter Oversatt (Det Gamle Testamente 3; Oslo: H. Aschehoug [W. Nygaard], 1944).
Naastepad, T.J.M.
Amos (Kampen: Kok, 1976).
Nötscher, F.
Zwölfprophetenbuch oder Kleine Propheten (Echter Bibel; Würzburg: Echter, [2]1948).
Nowack, W.
Die Kleinen Propheten übersetzt und erklärt (*HKAT* 3/4; Göttingen: Vandenhoeck & Ruprecht, [3]1922).
Osty, C. E.
Amos-Osée traduits (*SBJ*; Paris: Cerf, 1952, [2]1960).
Procksch, O.
Die Kleinen Prophetischen Schriften vor dem Exil (Stuttgart: Deichert [Scholl], 1910, [2]1929).
Pusey, E. B.
The Minor Prophets, Vol. II Amos (London: J. H. & J. Parker, 1906).
Rashi
See *Miqra'oth Gedoloth.*
Refer, K.
Amos. Die Worte des Propheten übersetzt und gedeutet (München, 1927).
Reuss, E.
Das Alte Testament übersetzt, eingeleitet und erläutert. II: Die Propheten (Braunschweig: Schwetschke & Sohn, 1892).
Ridderbos, J.
De Kleine Propheten. Eerste Deel: Hosea, Joel, Amos (3 vols.; Kampen: Kok, 1932).
Riessler, P.
Die Kleinen Propheten oder das Zwölfprophetenbuch, nach dem Urtext übersetzt und erklärt (Rottenburg a. N.: Bader, 1911).
Rinaldi, G.
I Propheti Minori. Fasc. 1. Introduzione Generale, Amos (3 vols.; La Sacra Biblia; Torino/Roma: Marietti, 1952).
Robinson, H. W.
Amos. Hebrew Text (London: SPCK, 1923).

Robinson, T. H., and F. Horst
Die Zwölf Kleinen Propheten (HAT 1/14; Tübingen: Mohr, ^{2}1954; ^{3}1964).
Rosenmüller, E.F.K.
Scholia in Vetus Testamentum. Partis septimae Prophetas minores continentis, Vol. 2. Amos, Obadias et Jonas (Leipzig: J. A. Barthii, 1827).
Rudolph, W.
Joel–Amos–Obadia–Jonah (KAT 23/2; Gütersloh: Gerd Mohn, 1971).
Ruiz, G.
Don Isaac Abrabanel y su Commentario al Libro de Amós (Madrid: UPCM, 1984).
Idem
Commentarius hebreos medievalis al libro de Amós (Rashi, A. 'ibn 'Ezra, Beaugency, D. Kimḥi, J. 'ibn Caspi) (Madrid: UPCM, 1984).
Rusche, H.
Das Buch Amos erläutert (Düsseldorf: Patmos, 1975).
Ryan, D.
Amos (New Catholic Commentary on the Holy Scriptures; London: Nelson, 1969).
Schegg, P.
Die Kleinen Propheten. Erster Teil: Osee–Michaeas (Regensburg: Georg Joseph Manz, 1854, ^{2}1862).
Schlier, J.
Die Zwölf Kleinen Propheten: Ein Wegweiser zum Verständnis des Prophetenwörte für die Gemeinde (Stuttgart: Liesching, 1861).
Schmidt, H.
Der Prophet Amos (Tübingen: Mohr, 1917).
Schumpp, M.
Das Buch der Zwölf Propheten (Herders Bibel Kommentar 10/2; Freiburg i. B.: Herder, 1950).
Sellin, E.
Das Zwölfprophetenbuch übersetzt und erklärt (KAT 12; 2 vols.; Leipzig: Deichert [Scholl], 1922; ^{2}1929; ^{3}1930).
Smith, G. A.
The Book of the Twelve Prophets (2 vols.; The Expositor's Bible, 8th Series; New York: A. C. Armstrong, ^{2}1928).
Snaith, N. H.
Notes on the Hebrew Text of Amos (2 vols.; London: Epworth, 1945–46).
Idem
Amos, Hosea, and Micah (Epworth Preacher's Commentaries; London: Epworth, 1956).
Soggin, J. A.
Il Profeta Amos. Traduzione e commento (Studi Biblici 61; Brescia: Paideia, 1982); English tr. *The Prophet Amos* (tr. J. Bowden; London: SCM, 1987).
Solari, J. K.
"Amos, book of," *The New Catholic Encyclopedia* (New York: McGraw Hill, 1967).
Staerk, W.
Amos–Nahum–Habakuk herausgegeben (Ausgewählte poetische Texte des Alten Testaments 2; Leipzig: Hinrichs, 1908).
Stave, E.
De Mindre Profeterna (Uppsala, 1912).
Strange, M.
The Books of Amos, Osee and Micah, With a Commentary (Pamphlet Bible Series 26; New York: Paulist Press, 1961).
Sutcliffe, E. F.
The Book of Amos (London: Burns, Oates and Washbourne, 1939).
Theiner, J. A.
Die Zwölf Kleineren Propheten in der Art und Weise des von Brentano Dereserischen Bibelwerks übersetzt und erklärt (Leipzig: Teubner, 1828).
Theis, J., and J. Lippl
Die Zwölf Kleinen Propheten (HS 8/3/1; 2 vols.; Bonn: Hanstein, 1937; ^{2}1938).
Touzard, J.
Le livre d'Amos (Paris: Bloud, 1909).
Trochon, M.
Les petites Prophètes (Paris: Lethielleux, 1883).
Tur-Sinai, N. H.
Peshuṭo shel Miqra (6 vols.; Jerusalem: Kiryat Sepher, 1967) 3/2, 450–77 (Heb.).
Uffenheimer, B.
Commentary to Amos, in the revised edition of S. L. Gordon, *Biblical Commentaries, Minor Prophets*, vol. 1 (Tel Aviv: S. L. Gordon, 1968) (Heb.).
Umbreit, F.W.C.
Practischer Commentar über die Propheten des alten Bundes: Kleinen Propheten (Hamburg: R. Perthes, 1843).
Valeton, J.J.P.
Amos en Hosee een hoofdstuk uit de Geschiedenis (Nijmegen: H. Ten Hoet, 1894); German tr. *Amos und Hosea* (tr. F. K. Echternacht; Giessen: J. Ricker, 1898).
van Andel, J.
De Kleinen Profeten (Leeuwarden, 1881, Kampen: Kok, ^{2}1912).
van Gelderen, C.
Het Boek Amos (Commentar op het Oude Testament; Kampen: Kok, 1933).
van Hoonacker, A.
Les douze petits Prophètes, traduits et commentés (ÉBib; Paris: Gabalda, 1908).
Varadi, M.
Il profeta Amos (Florence: Casa Editrice Israel, 1947).
Veldkamp, H.
De Boer van Tekoa (Franeker: T. Wever, 1940).
von Orelli, C.
Die Zwölf Kleinen Propheten (München: Beck, ^{3}1908).
Weiser, A., and K. Elliger
Das Buch der Zwölf Kleinen Propheten (ATD 24/1; Göttingen: Vandenhoeck & Ruprecht, ^{4}1963; ^{5}1967).

Wellhausen, J.
Die Kleinen Propheten übersetzt und erklärt (Berlin: Reiner, ^{3}1898; Berlin: de Gruyter, ^{4}1963).
Werner, H.
Amos (Exempla Biblica 4; Göttingen: Vandenhoeck & Ruprecht, 1969).
Williams, A. L.
Joel and Amos: The Minor Prophets Unfolded (Cambridge: Cambridge University, 1918).
Wolff, H. W.
Dodekapropheton 2, Joel und Amos (BKAT 14,2; Neukirchen-Vluyn: Neukirchener Verlag, 1969); English tr. *Joel and Amos* (tr. W. Janzen, S. D. McBride, Jr., and C. A. Muenchow; ed. S. D. McBride, Jr.; Hermeneia: A Critical and Historical Commentary on the Bible; Philadelphia: Fortress, 1977).

2. Studies on Amos

Albert, E.
"Einige Bemerkungen zu Amos," *ZAW* 33 (1913) 265–69.
Allen, L. C.
"Amos, Prophet of Solidarity," *Vox Evangelica* 6 (1969) 42–53.
Alonso, D. J.
"El nuevo tipo de profecia que inicia Amos," *CB* 23 (1966) 36–42.
Amsler, S.
"Amos, prophète de la onzième heure," *TZ* 21 (1965) 318–28.
Idem
"La parole visionnaire des prophètes," *VT* 31 (1981) 359–63.
Andersen, F. I., and A. D. Forbes
The Computer Bible. Vol. VI: *A Synoptic Concordance to Hosea, Amos, Micah* (Wooster, OH: Biblical Research Associates, 1975).
Andrews, M. E.
"Hesiod and Amos," *JR* 23 (1943) 194–205.
Asen, B. A.
Amos' Faith: A Structural-Developmental Approach (diss.; St. Louis University, 1980).
Atger, J. F.
"Le message d'Amos," *Christianisme Social* 74 (1966) 303–12.
Auber, A.
Les expériences religieuses et morales du prophète Amos (Genève, 1911).
Balla, E.
Die Droh- und Scheltworte des Amos (Leipzig: Edelmann, 1926).
Barackman, P. F.
"Preaching from Amos," *Int* 13 (1959) 273–85.
Bartczek, G.
Prophetie und Vermittlung. Zur literarischen Analyse und theologischen Interpretation der Visionsberichte des Amos (Europäische Hochschulschriften 23/120; Frankfurt a. M.: Peter Lang, 1980).
Baumann, E.
"Eine Einzelheit," *ZAW* 64 (1952) 62.
Baumann, F., and K. Naef
Amos. Eine Botschaft aus alter Zeit für uns moderne Menschen (Zürich, 1962).
Beek, M. A.
"Ein Erdbeben wird zum prophetischen Erleben," *ArOr* 17/1 (1949) 31–40.
Bennett, F. W.
Devotional Studies in Amos (Grand Rapids: Baker Book House, 1966).
Berridge, J. M.
"Zur Intention der Botschaft des Amos. Exegetische Überlegungen zu Amos 5," *TZ* 32 (1976) 321–40.
Idem
"Jeremia und die Prophetie des Amos," *TZ* 35 (1979) 321–41.
Bjoerndalen, A. J.
"Jahwe in den Zukunftsaussagen des Amos," *Die Botschaft und die Boten: Festschrift für Hans Walter Wolff zum 70. Geburtstag* (ed. J. Jeremias and L. Perlitt; Neukirchen-Vluyn: Neukirchener Verlag, 1981) 181–202.
Blaquart, J. L.
"Parole de dieu et prophètes d'Amos à Ezechiel," *Point* 24 (1977) 15–30.
Blechmann, M.
Das Buch Amos in Talmud und Midrasch (diss.; Würzburg, 1937).
Boehmer, J.
"Die Eigenart der prophetischen Heilspredigt des Amos," *TSK* 76 (1903) 35–47.
Idem
"Amos nach Gedankengang und Grundgedanken," *Nieuwe Theologische Studiën* 10 (1927) 1–7.
Boer, P.A.H.
"Amos," *Zeist* (1964) 91–95.
Botterweck, J. G.
"Zur Authentizität des Buches Amos," *BZ* 2 (1958) 176–89.
Brandt, T.
Die Botschaft des Amos (Leipzig, 1931).
Braslavi, J.
"The Lions of the Desert of Teqoa in the Book of Amos," *BM* 32 (1967) 56–64 (Heb.).
Bright, J.
"Amos," *Dictionary of the Bible* (ed. F. C. Grant and H. H. Rowley; Edinburgh: T. & T. Clark, ^{2}1963) 27–29.
Idem
"A New View of Amos," *Int* 25 (1971) 355–58.
Brin, G.
"The Visions in the Book of Amos (7:1—8:3): Studies in Structure and Ideas," *Isac Leo Seeligmann Volume: Essays in the Bible and the Ancient World* (ed. A. Rofé and Y. Zakovitch; 3 vols.; Jerusalem: E. Rubinstein,1983) 2.275–90 (Heb.).

Brown, H. C.
The Positive Elements in the Preaching of Amos (diss.; Southern Baptist Theological Seminary, 1954).
Brueggemann, W.
"Amos' Intercessory Formula," *VT* 19 (1969) 385–99.
Bruston, E.
"Messages prophétiques: I. Le message d'Amos," *ETR* 7 (1932) 158–72.
Budde, K.
"Zur Geschichte des Buches Amos," *Studien zur Semitischen Philologie und Religionsgeschichte: Julius Wellhausen zum Siebzigsten Geburtstag* (ed. K. Marti; BZAW 27; Giessen: Töpelmann, 1914) 65–77.
Idem
"Zum Text und Auslegung des Buches Amos," *JBL* 43 (1924) 46–131; 44 (1925) 63–122.
Carlsen, B. H.
"Amos in Judeo-Persian," *Acta Iranica* 23 (1984) 73–112.
Carlson, A.
"Profeten Amos och Davidsriket," *Religion och Bibel* 25 (1966) 57–78.
Cazelles, H.
"À propos de quelques textes difficiles relatifs à la justice de dieu dans l'Ancien Testament," *RB* 58 (1951) 159–88.
Charue, A.
"Les diatribes d'Amos," *CollNam* 31 (1937) 237–47.
Cheyne, T. K.
"Amos," *Encyclopaedia Biblica: A Critical Dictionary of the Literary, Political and Religious History of the Bible* (ed. T. K. Cheyne; London, 1899) 1.147–58.
Collins, J. J.
"History and Tradition in the Prophet Amos," *ITQ* 41 (1974) 120–33; rep. in *The Bible in Its Literary Milieu* (ed. V. L. Tollers and J. R. Maier; Grand Rapids: Wm. B. Eerdmans, 1979) 121–33.
Coote, R. B.
"Ripe Words for Preaching Connotative Diction in Amos," *Pacific Theological Review* 8 (1976) 13–19.
Idem
Amos among the Prophets: Composition and Theology (Philadelphia: Fortress, 1981).
Cornell, C.
"Das Targum zu den Propheten," *ZAW* 7 (1887) 196–97.
Cox, D.
"Inspired Radicals: The Prophets of the Eighth Century," *SBFLA* 25 (1975) 90–103.
Craghan, J. F.
"The Prophet Amos in Recent Literature," *BTB* 2 (1972) 242–61.
Idem
"Traditions and Techniques in the Prophet Amos," *BiTod* 60 (1972) 782–86.
Crenshaw, J. L.
"*YHWH Ṣᵉba'ôt Šᵉmô*: A Form-Critical Analysis," *ZAW* 81 (1969) 156–75.
Idem
"Popular Questioning of the Justice of God in Ancient Israel," *ZAW* 82 (1970) 380–95.
Crocetti, G.
"'Cercate me e vivrete.' La ricerca di Dio in Amos," *Quaerere Deum* (ed. G. Danielli; Atti della XXV Settimana Biblica; Brescia: Paideia, 1980) 89–105.
Crocker, P.
"History and Archeology in the Oracles of Amos," *Buried History: A Quarterly Newsletter of the Australian Institute of Archaeology* 23 (1987) 7–15.
Crook, M. B.
"Did Amos and Micah Know Isa. 9:2–7 and 11:1–9?" *JBL* 73 (1954) 144–51.
Danson, J. M.
"Amos," *ExpTim* 11 (1899–1900) 442–46.
Davidson, A. B.
"The Prophet Amos," *The Expositor, Third Series* 5 (1887) 161–79.
Davies, G. H.
"Amos—The Prophet of Re-Union," *ExpTim* 92 (1981) 196–200.
Desnoyers, L.
"Le prophète Amos," *RB* 26 (1917) 218–46.
Dijkema, F.
Die Prophétie des Amos (1929).
Idem
"Le fond des prophéties d'Amos," *OTS* 2 (Leiden: Brill, 1934) 18–34.
Dines, J.
"Reading the Book of Amos," *ScrB* 16 (1986) 23–32.
Dinur, B. Z.
"Jeroboam, Son of Joash, and His Conquests," *BM* 20–21 (1964) 3–24 (Heb.).
Döller, J.
"Vom 'Überschüssigen' bei Amos," SMBO 28 (1907) 413–15.
Donner, H.
"Die soziale Botschaft der Propheten im Lichte der Gesellschaftsordnung in Israel," *OrAnt* 2 (1963) 229–45.
Duhm, B.
"Anmerkungen zu den Zwölf Propheten, 1. Buch Amos," *ZAW* 31 (1911) 1–18.
Dumeste, M. L.
"La spiritualité des prophètes d'Israël, 1: Le message de prophète Amos," *VSpir* 74 (1945) 834–52; 75 (1946) 424–35.
Dusterdieck, F.
"Beiträge zur Erklärung des Propheten Amos," *TSK* 22 (1849) 869–914.
Eissfeldt, O.
"Amos und Jonah in volkstümlicher Überlieferung," "*. . . Und Fragten nach Jesus:" Festschrift*

Ernst Barnikol (Berlin: Töpelmann, 1964) 9–13; rep. in *Kleine Schriften zum Alten Testament* (6 vols.; Tübingen: Mohr, 1962–1979) 4.137–42.

Elliger, K.
"Hamath," *BHH* 2.630.

Idem
"Lodebar," *BHH* 2.1101.

Engnell, I.
"Amos," SymBu 1 (1948) 59–63.

Eslinger, L.
"The Education of Amos," *Biblical and Other Studies* (ed. R. Ahroni; *HAR* 11; Columbus: The Ohio State University, 1987) 35–57.

Eubanks, S. W.
Amos: Artist in Literary Composition (diss.; Southern Baptist Seminary, 1943).

de Ferriol, S. L.
El Yahve de Amos (Trabajos Monográficos, 3; Buenos Aires: Universidad de Buenos Aires, 1987).

Fey, R.
Amos und Jesaja, Abhändigkeit und Eigenständigkeit des Jesaja (WMANT 12; Neukirchen-Vluyn: Neukirchener Verlag,1963).

Francisco, C. T.
"Teaching Amos in the Churches," *RevExp* 63 (1966) 413–25.

Idem
"Expository Outline of the Prophecy of Amos," *RevExp* 63 (1966) 427–28.

García de la Fuente, O.
"La búsque da de Dios según el profeta Amós," *Augustinanium Roma* 12 (1972) 257–76.

Garrett, T. S.
"The Structure of Amos as a Testimony to Its Integrity," *JETS* 27 (1984) 275–76.

Gemser, B.
"Die godsgetuientis van Amos," *HTSt* 1 (1944) 9–21.

Idem
"Amos in sy dadikse omgewing en bedryf," *HTSt* 1 (1944) 49–58.

Gese, H.
"Kleine Beiträge zum Verständnis des Amosbuches," *VT* 12 (1962) 417–38.

Gilead, H.
"Amos—Amongst the Herdsmen from Tekoa," *BM* 54 (1973) 375–81 (Heb.).

Giles, T.
"An Introductory Investigation of Amos by Means of the Model of the Voluntary Social Movement," *Proceedings, Eastern Great Lakes and Midwest Biblical Societies* 8 (1988) 135–53.

Givati, M.
"The Shabbat of the Prophet Amos," *BM* 69 (1977) 194–98, 278–79 (Heb.).

Glueck, J. J.
"Three Notes on the Book of Amos," *Studies in the Books of Hosea and Amos: Die Ou Testamentiese Werkgemeenskap in Suid Afrika: 7th and 8th Congresses* (Potchefstroom: Rege-Pers Beperk, 1964–1965) 115–21.

Gordis, R.
"Studies in the Book of Amos," *American Academy for Jewish Research Jubilee Volume (1928–29 / 1978–79)* (ed. S. A. Baron and J. E. Barzilay; *PAAJR* 46–47; New York: American Academy for Jewish Research, 1980) 201–64.

Gottlieb, H.
"Amos und Jerusalem," *VT* 17 (1967) 430–63.

Gunning, J. H.
De Godspraken van Amos: Vertaald en Verklaard (Leiden: Brill, 1885).

Idem
"Een Nieuwe Amos," *ThSt* 18 (1900) 193–225.

Halevy, J.
"Recherches bibliques: Amos," *REJ* 44 (1902) 14ff.

Idem
"Recherches bibliques: Le livre d'Amos," *RevSém* 11 (1903) 1–31, 97–121, 193–209, 289–300; *RevSém* 12 (1904) 1–18.

Haran, M.
"The Rise and Decline of the Empire of Jeroboam ben Joash," *VT* 17 (1967) 266–97; tr. of "The Rise and Fall of the Empire of Jeroboam II," *Zion* 31 (1966–1967) 18–38 (Heb.).

Idem
"The Period of Amos' Prophecies," *Ages and Institutions in the Bible* (Tel Aviv: Am Oved, 1972) 268–347 (Heb.).

Idem
"Amos," *EM* 6.271–87 (Heb.).

Harper, W. R.
The Utterances of Amos Arranged Strophically (Chicago, 1898; Biblical World Reprints, Edinburgh: T. & T. Clark, ²1901).

Haupt, P.
"Was Amos a Sheepman?" *JBL* 35 (1916) 288–90.

Hermando, E.
"Pueblo de Dios y convivencia humana (Amos–Oseas)" *LuVitor* 24 (1975) 385–411.

Herntrich, V.
"Das Berufungsbewusstsein des Amos," *CuW* 9 (1933) 161–76.

Idem
Amos, der Prophet Gottes (Wege in des Bibel 4; Göttingen: Vandenhoeck & Ruprecht, 1941).

Heschel, A. J.
"Amos," *The Prophets* (New York: Harper & Row, 1962) 27–38.

Hirscht, A.
"Textkritische Untersuchungen über das Buch Amos," *ZWT* 44 (1903) 11–73.

Hoffman, Y.
"A North Israelite Typological Myth and a Judean Historical Tradition. The Exodus in Hosea and Amos," *VT* 39 (1989) 169–82.

Hoffmann, G.
"Versuche zu Amos," *ZAW* 3 (1883) 87–126, 279f.
Hogg, H. W.
"The Starting Point of the Religious Message of Amos," *Transactions of the Third International Congress for the History of Religion* (ed. P. S. Allen and J. de M. Johnson; Oxford: Clarendon, 1908) 1:325–27.
Honeycutt, R. L., Jr.
Amos and His Message (Nashville: Broadman, 1963).
Idem
"Amos and Contemporary Issues," *RevExp* 63 (1966) 441–57.
Idem
"The Lion Has Roared!" *SWJT* 9 (1966) 27–35.
Horst, F.
"Die Visionsschilderungen der alttestamentlichen Propheten," *EvT* 20 (1960) 193–205.
Howard, J. K.
Amos among the Prophets (London: Pickering & Inglis, 1967).
Howie, C. G.
"Expressly for Our Time: The Theology of Amos," *Int* 13 (1959) 273–85.
Hunter, A. V.
Seek the Lord! A Study of the Meaning and Function of the Exhortations in Amos, Hosea, Isaiah, Micah and Zephaniah (Baltimore: St. Mary's Seminary and University, 1982).
Hyatt, J. P.
"The Book of Amos," *Int* 3 (1949) 338–48.
Igleheart, J. H.
Education and Culture in the Book of Amos: A Re-evaluation (diss.; University of Kentucky, 1974).
Irwin, W. A.
"The Thinking of Amos," *AJSL* 49 (1932–1933) 102–14.
Jackson, J. J.
"Amos and His Environment," *Proceedings of the Eastern Great Lakes and Midwest Biblical Societies* 5 (1985) 81–86.
Jacob, E.
"Prophètes et intercesseurs," *De la Tôrah au Messie: Études d'exégèse et d'herméneutique bibliques offertes à Henri Cazelles* (ed. J. Doré, P. Grelot, and M. Carrez; Paris: Desclée, 1981) 205–17.
Janssen, H.
"Amos und Amasja," *Schrift* 52 (1977) 132–37.
Jimenez, C.
Relecturas de Amos-Isaias (diss.; Jerusalem, 1973).
Junker, H.
"Amos und die 'opferlose Mosezeit,'" *TGl* 27 (1935) 686–95.
Idem
"Amos, der Mann, den Gott mit unwiderstehlicher Gewalt zum Propheten machte," *TTZ* 65 (1956) 321–28.
Kaiser, W. C., Jr.
"The Davidic Promise and the Inclusion of the Gentiles (Amos 9:9–15 and Acts 15:13–18): A Test Passage for Theological Systems," *JTS* 20 (1977) 97–111.
Kapelrud, A. S.
"God as Destroyer in the Preaching of Amos and in the Ancient Near East," *JBL* 71 (1952) 33–38.
Idem
Central Ideas in Amos (Skrifter utgitt av det Norske Videnskaps—Akademi i Oslo 2; Oslo: Aschenoug, 1956, ^{2}1961).
Idem
"Profeten Amos og hans yrke," *NorTT* 59 (1958) 76–79.
Idem
"Amos/Amosbuch," *BHH* 1.85–87.
Idem
"New Ideas in Amos," SVT 15 (Leiden: Brill, 1966) 193–206.
Karlsbad, I. Z.
Die Propheten Amos und Hosea (Frankfurt a. M.: J. Kaufmann, 1913).
Kaufmann, Y.
Toledoth Ha-Emunah Ha-Yisrealith (8 vols.; Jerusalem and Tel Aviv: Dvir, 1957) 6.56–92 (Heb.).
Idem
The Religion of Israel: From the Beginnings to the Babylonian Exile (tr. and abridged by M. Greenberg; Chicago: University of Chicago, 1960) 363–68.
Keller, C. A.
"Notes bibliques de prédication des textes du prophète Amos," *VC* 60 (1961) 390–98.
Kelley, P. H.
"Contemporary Study of Amos and Prophetism," *RevExp* 63 (1966) 375–85.
Kelso, J. L.
"Amos, A Critical Study," *Bibliotheca Sacra* 85 (1928) 53–63.
Kida, K.
Die Entstehung der prophetischen Literatur bei Amos (diss.; München, 1973).
King, P. J.
"The Great Eighth Century," *Bible Review* 5 (1989) 22–33, 44.
Koch, K.
Die Profeten I: Assyrische Zeit (Stuttgart/Berlin/Köln/Mainz: Kohlhammer, 1978); English tr. *The Prophets* (tr. M. Kohl; Philadelphia: Fortress, 1983) 36–75.
Koch, R.
Amos: Untersucht mit den Methoden einer strukturalen Formgeschichte. Teil 1: Programm und Analyse. Teil 2: Synthese. Teil 3: Schlüssel (AOAT 30; Neukirchen-Vluyn: Neukirchener Verlag, 1976).
Köhler, L.
"Amos," SThZ 34 (Zürich, 1917) 10–21; 68–79; 145–57; 190–208.

Idem
"Amos—Forschungen von 1917 bis 1932," *TRu* 4 (1932) 195–213.
Komlos, Y.
"On the Exegesis of Targum Jonathan to Amos," *Arameans, Aramaic, and the Aramaic Literary Tradition* (ed. M. Sokoloff; Bar-Ilan Studies in Near Eastern Languages and Cultures; Ramat Gan: Bar-Ilan University, 1983) 7–9 (Heb.).
Kuntz, M.
Ein Element der alten Theophanieüberlieferung und seine Rolle in der Prophetie des Amos (diss.; Tübingen, 1968).
Kusznitski, S.
Joel, Amos, Obadja, qua aetate et quibus de rebus sint locuti (diss.; Breslau; Vratislaviae: F. W. Jungfer, 1872).
Labuschange, C. J.
"Amos' Conception of God and the Popular Theology of His Time," *Studies in the Books of Hosea and Amos: Die Ou Testamentiese Werkgemeenskap in Suid Afrika: 7th and 8th Congresses* (Potchefstroom: Rege–Pers Beperk, 1964–1965) 122–33.
Landy, F.
"Vision and Poetic Speech in Amos," *Biblical and Other Studies* (ed. R. Ahroni; *HAR* 11; Columbus: The Ohio State University, 1987) 223–46.
Leahy, M.
"The Popular Idea of God in Amos," *ITQ* 22 (1955) 68–73.
Lehming, S.
Offenbarung und Verkündigung. Studien zur Theologiegeschichtlichen Bedeutung des Verhältnis von Berufung und Theologie bei Amos und Hosea (diss.; Kiel,1953).
Idem
"Erwägungen zu Amos," *ZTK* 55 (1958) 145–69.
Levey, S. H.
"Amos in the Rabbinic Tradition," *Tradition as Openness to the Future: Essays in Honor of Willis W. Fisher* (ed. F. O. Francis and R. P. Wallace; Lanham, MD: University Press of America, 1984) 55–69.
Lofthouse, W.
"The Call of Amos," *The Expositor* 24 (1922) 45–51.
Löhr, M.
Untersuchungen zum Buch Amos (BZAW 4; Giessen: Töpelmann, 1901).
Long, B. O.
"Reports of Visions among the Prophets," *JBL* 95 (1976) 353–66.
Loss, N. M.
"Uso e valore dei nomi di dio e dei nomi del populo nel libro di Amos," *Salesianum* 41 (1979) 425–40.
Maag, V.
Text, Wortschatz und Begriffswelt des Buches Amos (Leiden: Brill, 1951).
Idem
"Amos/Amosbuch," *RGG*³ (1957) 1.328–31.
McCullough, W. S.
"Some Suggestions about Amos," *JBL* 72 (1953) 247–54.
Mamie, P.
"Le livre d'Amos. Les châtiments et le 'reste d'Israël,'" NV 37 (1962) 217–23.
Margolis, M.
"Notes on Some Passages in Amos," *AJSL* 17 (1900–1901) 171.
Markert, L.
Struktur und Bezeichnung des Scheltworts: Eine gattungskritische Studie anhand des Amosbuches (BZAW 140; Berlin: de Gruyter, 1977).
Idem
"Amos/Amosbuch," *Theologische Realenzyklopädie* (ed. G. Krause and G. Müller; Berlin/New York, 1978) 2.471–87.
Martin-Achard, R.
"La prédication d'Amos: Remarques exégètiques et homilétiques," *ETR* 41 (1966) 13–19.
Idem
Amos. L'homme, le message, l'influence (Publications de la Faculté de Théologie de l'Université de Genève 7; Genève: Labor et Fides, 1984).
Matheson, G.
"Studies in the Minor Prophets. III: Amos," *The Expositor, 2d Series* 3 (1882) 338–52.
Mauchline, J.
"Implicit Signs of a Persistent Belief in the Davidic Empire," *VT* 20 (1970) 287–303.
Mays, J. L.
"Words about the Words of Amos. Recent Study of the Book of Amos," *Int* 13 (1959) 259–72.
Meinhold, J.
Studien zur Israelitischen Religionsgeschichte. Band I, Der Heilige Rest, Teil I: Elias, Amos, Hosea, Jesaja (Bonn: Weber's Verlag, 1903).
Michel, D.
"Amos," *Israels Glaube im Wandel* (Berlin: Verlag Die Spur Dorbandt, 1968) 179–209.
Miller, C. H.
"Amos and Faith Structures: A New Approach," *BiTod* 19 (1981) 314–19.
Miller, P. W.
"Amos," *EvQ* 12 (1940) 48–59.
Mitchell, H. G.
"The Idea of God in Amos," *JBL* 7 (1887) 131–40.
Idem
Amos, An Essay in Exegesis (Boston: N. J. Bartlett, ²1900).
Moffatt, J.
"Literary Illustrations of Amos," *The Expositor* 9 (1915) 272–88.
Monloubou, L.
"Amos," in "Prophètes d'Israël," *IDBSup* 8 (1972) 706–24.

Montgomery, J. A.
"Notes on Amos," *JBL* 23 (1904) 94–96.
Moreno, C. A.
"Amos," TV 4 (1963) 25–35.
Morgenstern, J.
"Amos Studies I," *HUCA* 11 (1936) 19–140.
Idem
"Amos Studies II: The Sin of Uzziah, the Festival of Jeroboam and the Date of Amos," *HUCA* 12/13 (1937–1938) 1–53.
Idem
"Amos Studies III: The Historical Antecedents of Amos' Prophecy," *HUCA* 15 (1940) 59–304.
Idem
"Amos Studies IV: The Addresses of Amos—Text and Commentary," *HUCA* 32 (1961) 295–350.
Idem
"The Universalism of Amos," *Essays Presented to Leo Baeck on the Occasion of His Eightieth Birthday* (ed. N. Bentwich and others; London: East and West Library, 1954) 106–26.
Motyer, J. A.
"The Day of the Lion"—The Message of Amos (The Voice of the Old Testament; Leicester/Downers Grove: Inter-Varsity, 1974).
Mousset, P.
"La pédagogie d'un prophète Amos," *Catechistes* 27 (1956) 267–73.
Mowinckel, S.
"Amos-Boken. Oversaettelse med Tekstkritiek Kommentar," *NorTT* 28 (1927) 1–31.
Idem
"Die Offenbarungserlebnisse der Propheten Amos, Jesaja, und Jeremia," *NorTT* 49 (1948) 120ff.
Neher, A.
Amos. Contribution à l'étude du prophètisme (Paris: Vrin, 1980, ²1981).
Niditsch, S.
The Symbolic Vision in Biblical Tradition (HSM 30; Chico, CA: Scholars, 1983).
Oettli, S.
Amos und Hosea. Zwei Zeugen gegen die Anwendung der Evolutionstheorie auf die Religion Israels (BFCT 5/4; Gütersloh: Bertelsmann, 1901).
Ogden, D. K.
A Geography of Amos (diss.; Utah, 1982).
O'Neill, D.
The Attitudes of Amos, Hosea, Jeremiah and Deutero-Isaiah Concerning the Man / God Relationship (diss.; Michigan, 1979).
Oort, H.
"De profeet Amos," *ThT* 14 (1880) 114–58.
Idem
"Het Vaderland van Amos," *ThT* 25 (1891) 121–26.
Orlinsky, H. M., and M. Weinberg
"Notes on Some *Masora Parva* of Amos," *Sefarad* 46 (1986) 381–90.
Osswald, E.
Urform und Auslegung im masoretischen Amostext. Ein Beitrag zur Kritik an der neueren traditionsgeschichtlichen Methode (diss.; Jena, 1951). Review in *TLZ* 80 (1955) 179.
Overholt, T. W.
"Commanding the Prophets: Amos and the Problem of Prophetic Authority," *CBQ* 41 (1979) 517–32.
Owens, G. G.
"Exegetical Studies in the Book of Amos," *RevExp* 63 (1966) 429–40.
Paton, L. B.
"Did Amos Approve the Calf-Worship at Bethel?" *JBL* 13 (1894) 80–90.
Pfeifer, C. J.
"Amos the Prophet: The Man and His Book," *BiTod* 19 (1981) 295–300.
Pfeifer, G.
"Amos und Deuterojesaja denkformenanalytisch verglichen," *ZAW* 93 (1981) 439–443.
Idem
"'Ich bin in tiefe Wasser geraten, und die Flut will mich ersäufen' (Psalm LXIX 3)—Anregungen und Vorschläge zur Aufarbeitung wissenschaftlicher Sekundärliterature," *VT* 37 (1987) 327–39.
Polley, M. E.
Amos and the Davidic Empire (New York/Oxford: Oxford University, 1989).
Prado, J.
"Amos, Amos Libro de," *Enciclopedia de la Biblia* (Barcelona: Garriga, 1963) 1.435–40.
Praeger, M.
"Amos, der Hirte aus Teqoa," *Bibel und Liturgie* 36 (1962–1963) 84–96, 164–72, 243–55, 295–308.
Praetorius, F.
"Zum Texte der Amos," *ZAW* 34 (1914) 42–44.
Idem
"Bemerkungen zu Amos," *ZAW* 35 (1915) 12–25.
Idem
Textkritische Bemerkungen zum Buche Amos (Berlin: von Reuther & Reichard, 1918) 1248–62.
Idem
Die Gedichte des Amos. Metrische und textkritische Bemerkungen (Halle: Niemeyer, 1924).
Procksch, O.
Die Geschichtsbetrachtung bei Amos, Hosea, und Jeremia (diss.; Königsberg, 1901).
Reimann, P. A.
"Models of Exegesis," *Int* 25 (1971) 198–201.
Reventlow, H. G.
Das Amt des Propheten bei Amos (FRLANT 80; Göttingen: Vandenhoeck & Ruprecht, 1962).
Richardson, H. N.
"Amos's Four Visions of Judgment and Hope," *Bible Review* 5 (1989) 16–21.
Ridderbos, N. H.
"Beschouwingen naar aanleding van Wolffs 'Die Stunde des Amos,'" GTT 72 (1972) 1–18.

Idem
Het Godswoord der Propheten. I. Van Elia tot Micha (Kampen: Kok, 1980) 98–159.
Riedel, W.
"Bemerkungen zum Buche Amos," *Alttestamentliche Untersuchungen* 1 (Leipzig: Deichert, 1902) 19–36.
Rieger, J.
Die Bedeutung der Geschichte für die Verkündigung des Amos und Hosea (Giessen: Töpelmann, 1929).
Rinaldi, G.
"Due note ad Amos," *RSO* 28 (1953) 149–52.
Roberts, J.J.M.
"Recent Trends in the Study of Amos," ResQ 13 (1970) 1–16.
Robscheit, H.
"Die Thora bei Amos und Hosea," *EvT* 10 (1950–1951) 26–38.
Rosenbaum, S. N.
"Northern Amos Revisited: Two Philological Suggestions," *Hebrew Studies* 18 (1977) 132–40.
Rothstein, G.
"Amos und seine Stellung innerhalb des Prophetismus," *TSK* 78 (1905) 323–58.
Routtenberg, H. J.
Rabbinic Interpretation of Amos (diss.; Boston, 1943).
Idem
Amos of Tekoa: A Study in Interpretation (New York/Washington/Hollywood: Vantage, 1971).
Rudolph, W.
"Gott und Mensch bei Amos—Anmerkungen zu Weiser's *Amosbuch*," *Imago Dei: Beiträge zur theologischen Anthropologie: Gustav Krüger zum siebzigsten Geburtstag* (ed. H. Bornkamm; Giessen: Töpelmann, 1932) 19–31.
Idem
"Schwierige Amosstellen," *Wort und Geschichte: Festschrift für Karl Elliger zum 70. Geburtstag* (ed. H. Gese and H.-P. Rüger; AOAT 18; Neukirchen-Vluyn: Neukirchener Verlag, 1973) 157–62.
Sampsey, J. R.
"Notes on Amos," *RevExp* 30 (1933) 284–95.
Sansoni, C.
"Amos: Uomo del suo Tempo," *BeO* 10 (1968) 253–65.
Sasowski, B.
"Dann wende Ich das Schicksal meines Volkes. Die Verheissung des kommenden Heils," *Gericht und Umkehr: Die Botschaft des Propheten Amos = BK* 22/4 (1967) 116–19.
Scharbert, J.
"Die prophetische Literatur. Der Stand der Forschung," *ETL* 44 (1968) 346–406.
Schaumberger, J. R.
"Grundgedanken und Charakterbild des Propheten Amos," *Kirche und Kanzel* 14 (1931) 1–16.
Scherb, D.-A.
Introduction aux prophéties d'Amos. Essai d'interprétation des chapitres VII, VIII, et IX (thesis; Straatsburg, 1869).
Schmidt, H.
"Die Herkunft des Propheten Amos," *Beiträge zur alttestamentliche Wissenschaft: Karl Budde zum siebzigsten Geburtstag* (ed. K. Marti; BZAW 34; Giessen: Töpelmann, 1920) 158–71.
Schmidt, W. H.
"'Suchet den Herrn, so werdet Ihr leben.' Exegetische Notizen zum Thema 'Gott Suchen' in der Prophetie," *Ex Orbe Religionum: Studia Geo. Widengren* (ed. C. J. Bleeker and others; Studies in the History of Religions 21; Leiden: Brill, 1972) 127–40.
Schottroff, W.
"Amos—das Porträt eines Propheten," *Stimme der Gemeinde* 24 (1972) 113–15; 145–46; 193–96; 225–27; 289–92.
Idem
"Der Prophet Amos," *Der Gott der kleinen Leute* (ed. W. Schottroff and W. Stegemann; München: Kaiser, 1979) 39–66.
Schultes, J. L.
Herr ist sein Name. Ein Arbeitsheft zum Buch Amos (Gespräche zur Bibel 9; Klosterneuburg: Österreichisches Katholisches Bibelwerk, 1979).
Schuman, N. A.
"Amos on de traditie," *Amos, Een Aanklacht de profeet en Zijn betekenis nu* (Amsterdam: Vrije Universiteit, 1979) 27–29.
Schuurmans, S.J.K.
"Het Vaterland van Amos," *Theologische Studiën* 7 (1889) 222–28.
Sedding, E. D.
The Eyes of the Lord. The Message of Amos (London: SPCK, 1946).
Seesemann, O.
Israel und Juda bei Amos und Hosea (diss.; Leipzig, 1898).
Seidel, M.
"Four Prophets Who Prophesied at the Same Time," *Ḥiqrē Mikra* (Jerusalem: Mosad HaRav Kook, 1978) 195–238 (Heb.).
Seierstad, I. P.
"Amosprophetien: i ljoset av nyare gransking," *TTKi* 2 (1931) 117–27.
Idem
"Erlebnis und Gehorsam beim Propheten Amos," *ZAW* 52 (1934) 22–41.
Idem
Die Offenbarungserlebnisse der Propheten Amos, Jesaja und Jeremia: Eine Untersuchung der Erlebnisvorgänge unter besonderer Berücksichtigung ihrer religiössittlichen Art und Auswirkung (Oslo: Dybwad, 1946, [2]1965).
Idem
"Oplenelse oglydighet hosprofeten Amos," *Budskapet: Et utvalg au gammeltestamentlige artikler* (Oslo: Universitets forlaget, 1971) 77–97.

Shea, W.
"Amos's Geographic Horizon," *Studies in the Books of Hosea and Amos: Die Ou Testamentiese Werkgemeenskap in Suid Afrika: 7th and 8th Congresses* (Potchefstroom: Rege–Pers Beperk, 1964–1965) 166–69.
Shoot, W. B., Jr.
The Fertility Religions in the Thought of Amos and Micah (diss.; California, 1951).
Sicre, J. L.
Los dioses olvidados. Poder y riqueza en los profetas preexilicos (Estudios de Antiguo Testamento 1; Madrid: Ed. Cristiandad, 1979) 109–16.
Sievers, E., and H. Guthe
Amos, metrisch bearbeitet (Abhandlungen der Philologisch-historischen Klasse der Königl. Sächsischen Gesellschaft der Wissenschaften 23/3; Leipzig: Teubner, 1907).
Sievi, J.
"Weissage über mein Volk Israel. Der Prophet Amos—Zeit, Persöhnlichkeit, Botschaft," *Gericht und Umkehr: Die Botschaft des Propheten Amos* = BKAT 22 (1967) 110–23.
Sister, M.
"Die Typen der prophetischen Visionen in der Bibel," *MGWJ* 78 (1934) 399ff; rep. and tr. as "Types of Prophetic Visions in the Bible," *LeToldoth HaḤevrah VeHasifruth Bitqufath HaMiqra'* (Tel Aviv: Seminar HaKibbutzim, 1962) 116–43 (Heb.).
Smart, J. D.
"Amos," *IDB* 1.116–21.
Smend, R.
Review of H. G. Reventlow, *Amt*, in *TLZ* 88 (1963) 662–63.
Idem
"Das Nein des Amos," *EvT* 23 (1963) 404–23.
Smith, G. V.
The Book of Amos (Grand Rapids: Zondervan, 1988).
Smith, R. L.
"The Theological Implications of the Prophecy of Amos," *SWJT* 9 (1966) 49–56.
Speier, S.
"Bemerkungen zu Amos," *VT* 3 (1953) 305–10.
Idem
"Bemerkungen zu Amos, II," *Homenaje a J. M. Millás-Vallicrosa* (ed. R. Almagià and M. Almagro; Barcelona, 1956) 2.365–72.
Staehelin, J. J.
Bermerkungen über Amos und Hosea (Basel, 1842).
Staples, W. E.
"Epic Motifs in Amos," *JNES* 25 (1966) 106–12.
Steinmann, J.
"Le prophétisme biblique des origines à Osée," LD 23 (Paris: Cerf, 1959) 139–86.
Stephany, M.
"Character und zeitliche Aufeinanderfolge der Drohsprüche in der Prophetie des Amos," *CuW* 7 (1931) 281–89.
Stoebe, H. J.
"Der Prophet Amos und sein bürgerlicher Beruf," *WuD* 5 (1957) 160–81.
Idem
"Geprägte Form und geschichtlich individuelle Erfahrung im A.T.," SVT 17 (Leiden: Brill, 1969) 212–19.
Idem
"Überlegungen zu den geistlichen Voraussetzungen der Prophetie des Amos," *Wort—Gebot—Glaube: Beiträge zum Theologie des Alten Testaments. Walter Eichrodt zum 80. Geburtstag* (ed. H. J. Stoebe; ATANT 59; Zürich: Zwingli, 1970) 209–25.
Stuhlmueller, C.
"Amos, Desert-Trained Prophet," *BiTod* 1 (1962–1963) 224–30.
Szabó, A.
"Textual Problems in Amos and Hosea," *VT* 25 (1975) 500–24.
Taylor, J.
"Amos," *A Dictionary of the Bible Dealing with Its Language, Literature, and Contents including Biblical Theology* (ed. J. Hastings; New York, 1919) 1.85–88.
Tietsch, A.
"Die Botschaft des Amos," *Die Zeichen der Zeit* 26 (1972) 211–17.
Trapiello, J. G.
"Situación Histórica del Profeta Amós," *EstBíb* 26 (1967) 249–74.
Tromp, N. J.
"Amos—Profetie als Kritische Funktie," *Ons Geestelijk Leven* 48 (1971) 294–302.
Idem
"Vraagtekens bij Amos," *Amos, Een Aanklacht de profeet en Zijn betekenis nu* (Amsterdam: Vrije Universiteit, 1979) 30–40.
Tromp, N. J., and D. Deden
De profeet Amos (Boxtel: Katholich Bijbelstichting, 1971).
Tsim, S.
"HaHatafah L'ahduth Ha-Umah Binevuoth Amos veHoshea," *Sefer Schmuel Tsim* (Jerusalem: Kiryat Sepher, 1958) 15–17 (Heb.).
Tuschen, W.
Die historischen Angaben im Buche des Propheten Amos (diss.; Freiburg, 1951).
Tweedie, A.
A Sketch of Amos and Hosea: Their Message and Their Times (Edinburgh: W. Blackwood & Sons, 1916).
Uffenheimer, B.
"Amos and Hosea—Two Directions in Israel's Prophecy," *Zer Li-Gevurot. The Zalman Shazar Jubilee Volume: A Collection of Studies in Bible, Eretz Yisrael, Hebrew Language, and Talmudic Literature* (ed. B. Z. Luria; Jerusalem: Kiryat Sepher, 1973) 284–320 (Heb.); tr. and abridged in *Dor LeDor* 5 (1976) 101–10.

Idem
"Mythological and Rationalistic Thought in Hosea and Amos," *Studies in the Minor Prophets* (ed. B. Z. Luria; Jerusalem: Kiryat Sepher, 1981) 155–79 (Heb.).
Valeton, J.J.P.
"Onderzoek naar den leeftijad van Joel vooral met het oog op zijne verhouding tot Amos," *Studien* 1 (1875) 122–45.
van der Wal, A.
"Amos, een paar Notities," *Amos, Een Aanklacht de profeet en Zijn betekenis nu* (Amsterdam: Vrije Universiteit, 1979) 5–26.
Idem
Amos. Een systematische literatuurlijst (Amsterdam: Vrije Universiteit, 1981); English tr. *Amos: A Classified Bibliography* (Amsterdam: Free University, 1983, ³1986).
Idem
"The Structure of Amos," *JSOT* 26 (1983) 107–13.
van der Wal, A., and E. Talstra
Amos: Concordance and Lexical Surveys (Amsterdam: VU Uitgeverij/Free University Press, 1984).
van der Woude, A. S.
"Three Classical Prophets—Amos, Hosea, Micah," *Israel's Prophetic Tradition: Essays in Honour of Peter R. Ackroyd* (ed. R. Coggins, A. Phillips, and M. Knibb; Cambridge: Cambridge University, 1982) 32–57.
van Gelderen, C.
"Amos te Bethel," *Almanak van het Studentencorps aan de Vrije Universiteit* (Amsterdam: Vrije Universiteit, 1911) 229–46.
van Hoonacker, A.
"Notes d'exégèse sur quelques passages difficiles d'Amos," *RB* 14 (1905) 163–87.
van Leeuwen, C.
"De 'kleine profeten' in het onderzoek van de laaste tien jaar," NGTT 28 (1947) 113–29.
Idem
"De Heilsverwachting bij Amos," *Vruchten van de Uithof: Studies opgedragen aan Dr. H. A. Brongers* (Utrecht: Theological Institute, 1974) 71–87.
van Steenbergen, N.
Motivation in Relation to the Message of Amos (diss.; Los Angeles, 1953).
van Zyl, A. H.
"Die Sondebesef bij Amos," NGTT 9 (1968) 69–82.
Vaux, R. de
"Le 'Reste d'Israël' d'après les prophètes," *RB* 42 (1933) 526–39.
Vawter, B.
Amos, Hosea, Micah, with an Introduction to Classical Prophecy (Wilmington: Michael Glazier, 1981).
Veldkamp, H.
Paraphrase van het boek van der profeet Amos en van het boek van den profeet Obadjah (Franeker: T. Wever, 1940).
Vienney, A. B.
Amos de Tékoa, son époque et son livre (Montauban, 1899).
Vischer, W.
"Amos, citoyen de Téqoa," *ETR* 50 (1975) 133–59.
Vollborn, W.
Innerzeitliche oder endzeitliche Gerichtserwartung: Ein Beitrag zu Amos und Jesaja (Kiel: Schmidt & Klaunig, 1938).
Vollmer, J.
Geschichtliche Rückblicke und Motive in der Prophetie des Amos, Hosea und Jesaja (BZAW 119; Berlin: de Gruyter: 1971).
de Waard, J., and W. A. Smalley
A Translator's Handbook on the Book of Amos: Helps for Translators (New York: United Bible Societies, 1979).
Wagner, S.
"Überlegungen zur Frage nach den Beziehungen des Propheten Amos zum Südreich," *TLZ* 96 (1971) 653–70.
Ward, J. M.
Amos and Isaiah: Prophets of the Word of God (Nashville/New York: Abingdon, 1969).
Idem
"Amos," *IDBSup* 21–23.
Warmuth, G.
Das Mahnwort. Seine Bedeutung für die Verkündigung der vorexilischen Propheten Amos, Hosea, Micha, Jesaja und Jeremia (diss.; Kiel, 1977).
Watts, J.D.W.
"The Origin of the Book of Amos," *ExpTim* 66 (1955) 109–12.
Idem
Vision and Prophecy in Amos (Leiden: Brill, 1958).
Idem
"Amos, the Man and His Message," *SWJT* 9 (1966) 21–26.
Idem
"Amos, the Man," *RevExp* 63 (1966) 387–92.
Idem
Studying the Book of Amos (Nashville: Broadman, 1966).
Weippert, H.
"Amos: Seine Bilder und ihr Milieu," *Beiträge zur prophetischen Bildsprache in Israel und Assyrien* (ed. H. Weippert, K. Seybold, and M. Weippert; Orbis Biblicus & Orientalis 64; Freiburg CH: Universitätsverlag; Göttingen: Vandenhoeck & Ruprecht, 1985).
Weiser, A.
Die Profetie des Amos (BZAW 53; Giessen: Töpelmann, 1929).
Idem
"The Background of the Prophecies of Hosea and Amos," *Sinai* 31 (1952) 253–64 (Heb.).
Weisert, A.
"Die Berufung des Amos," TBü (1928) 177–82.

Weisman, Z.
"Patterns and Structure in the Visions of Amos," *BM* 39 (1970) 40–57 (Heb.).
Idem
"Stylistic Parallels in Amos and Jeremiah: Their Implications for the Composition of Amos," *Shnaton* 1 (1975) 129–49 (Heb.).
Welch, C.
"Amos," *Kings and Prophets of Israel and Judah* (London: Lutterworth, 1952) 108–29.
White, K. O.
The Doctrine of God in Amos with Its Complications (diss.; Southern Baptist Theological Seminary, 1934).
Whitford, J. B.
"The Visions of Amos," *Bibliotheca Sacra* 83 (1913) 109–22.
Williams, D. L.
"The Theology of Amos," *RevExp* 63 (1966) 393–403.
Willi-Plein, I.
Vorformen der Schriftexegese innerhalb des Alten Testaments. Untersuchungen zum literarischen Werden der auf Amos, Hosea und Micha zurückgehenden Bücher im hebräischen Zwölfprophetenbuch (BZAW 123; Berlin/New York: de Gruyter, 1971).
Winter, A.
"Analyse des Buches Amos," *TSK* 83 (1910) 323–74.
Wolfe, R. E.
Meet Amos and Hosea, The Prophets of Israel (New York/London: Harper and Brothers, 1945).
Wolff, H. W.
Die Stunde des Amos. Prophetie und Protest (München: Kaiser, 1969).
Idem
"Das Ende des Heiligtums in Bethel," *Archäologie und Altes Testament: Festschrift für Kurt Galling zum 8. Januar 1970* (ed. A. Kutschke and E. Kutsch; Tübingen: Mohr, 1970) 287–98.
Woodward, B. F.
A Study of the Norms of Indictment in Amos (diss.; Union Theological Seminary, 1970).
Wright, S. L.
"O homem de Deus e o homem do rei," *RevT* 2 (1986) 37–42.
Würthwein, E.
"Amos-Studien," *ZAW* 62 (1950) 10–52, rep. in *Wort und Existenz. Studien zum Alten Testament* (Göttingen: Vandenhoeck & Ruprecht, 1970) 68–110.
Yeiven, S.
"The Social, Economic, and Political Situation according to Amos and Hosea," *Studies in the Minor Prophets* (ed. B. Z. Luria; Jerusalem: Kiryat Sepher, 1981) 97–111 (Heb.).
Yoshida, H.
"Prophecy and Salvation, in the Case of Amos," *Kiyo: Meiji Gakuin University Christian Research Institute Bulletin* 14 (1981) 27–47.
Zeijdner, H.
"Iets over den profeet Amos," *Stemmen voor Waarheid en Vrede* 20 (1886) 531–59.
Idem
"Nog iets over den profeet Amos," *Stemmen voor Waarheid en Vrede* 27 (1890) 613–34.
Zobel, H.-J.
"Prophet in Israel und in Judah. Das prophetische Verständnis des Hosea und Amos," *ZTK* 82 (1985) 281–99.

3. Composition and Redaction

Baumann, E.
Der Aufbau der Amosreden (BZAW 7; Giessen: Töpelmann, 1903).
Budde, K.
"Zur Geschichte des Buches Amos," *Studien zur semitischen Philologie und Religionsgeschichte: Julius Wellhausen zum siebzigsten Geburtstag* (ed. K. Marti; BZAW 27; Giessen: Töpelmann, 1914) 63–77.
Caspari, W.
"Wer hat die Aussprüche des Propheten Amos gesammelt?" *NKZ* 25 (1914) 701–15.
Coulot, C.
"Propositions pour une structuration du livre d'Amos au niveau rédactionnel," *RevScRel* 51 (1977) 169–86.
Crüsemann, F.
"Kritik an Amos im deuteronomistischen Geschichtswerk. Erwägungen zu 2 Könige 14, 27," *Probleme biblischer Theologie: Gerhard von Rad zum 70. Geburtstag* (ed. H. W. Wolff; München: Kaiser, 1971) 57–63.
Day, E., and W. H. Chapin
"Is the Book of Amos Post-Exilic?" *AJSL* 18 (1902) 65–93.
Fuhs, H. F.
"Amos 1:1. Erwägungen zur Tradition und Redaktion des Amosbuches," *Bausteine Biblischer Theologie: Festgabe für G. J. Botterweck* (ed. H. J. Fabry; Bonner biblische Beiträge 50; Bonn: Hanstein, 1977) 271–90.
Gese, H.
"Komposition bei Amos," SVT 23 (Leiden: Brill, 1981) 74–95.
Gordis, R.
"The Composition and Structure of Amos," *HTR* 33 (1940) 239–51.
Jozaki, S.
"The Secondary Passages of the Book of Amos," *Kwansei Gakuin University Annual Studies 4* (Nishinomiya: Kwansei Gakuin University, 1956) 25–100.

Kellermann, U.
"Der Amosschluss als Stimme deuteronomistischer Heilshoffnung," *EvT* 29 (1969) 169–83.
Koch, K.
Amos. Untersucht mit den Methoden einer strukturalen Formgeschichte (AOAT 30; Neukirchen-Vluyn: Neukirchener Verlag, 1976).
Krause, H. H.
"Der Gerichtsprophet Amos, ein Vorläufer des Deuteronomisten," *ZAW* 50 (1932) 221–39.
Lust, J.
"Remarks on the Redaction of Amos 5:4–6, 14–15," *Remembering All the Way* (ed. A. S. van der Woude; *OTS* 21 [Leiden: Brill, 1981]) 129–54.
Melugin, R. F.
"The Formation of Amos: An Analysis of Exegetical Method," SBLASP 1 (ed. P. Achtemeier; Missoula, MT: Scholars Press, 1978) 369–91.
Schmidt, W. H.
"Die deuteronomistische Redaktion des Amosbuches," *ZAW* 77 (1965) 168–93.
Smalley, W. A.
"Recursion Patterns and the Sectioning of Amos," *BT* 30 (1979) 118–27.
Spreafico, A.
"Amos: Struttura formale e spunti per una interpretazione," *RivB* 29 (1981) 147–76.
Waller, H. S.
The Unity of the Book of Amos (diss.; Southern Baptist Seminary, 1948).
Weimar, P.
"Der Schluss des Amos-Buches. Ein Beitrag zur Redaktionsgeschichte des Amos-Buches," BN 16 (1981) 60–100.

4. Covenant and Law

Amsler, S.
"Le thème du procès chez les prophètes d'Israël," *RTP* 24 (1974) 116–31.
Bach, R.
"Gottesrecht und weltliches Recht in der Verkündigung des Propheten Amos," *Festschrift für Günther Dehn* (ed. W. Schneemelcher; Neukirchen-Vluyn: Verlag der Erziehungsvereins, 1957) 23–34.
Barth, K.
"Gerichtsbotschaft des Propheten Amos," *KD* 4/2 (1955) 502–9.
Bright, J.
Covenant and Promise: The Future in the Preaching of the Preexilic Prophets (London: SCM, 1977) 83–87.
Brueggemann, W.
"Amos 4:4–13 and Israel's Covenant Worship," *VT* 15 (1965) 1–15.
Buis, P.
"Les formulaires d'alliance," *VT* 16 (1966) 396–411.
Clements, R. E.
Prophecy and Covenant (ed. E.F.D. Monte; SBT 43; London: SCM, 1965).
Dion, P. E.
"Le message moral du prophète Amos s'inspirait-il du 'droit de l'alliance'?" *ScEs* 27 (1975) 5–34.
Dürr, L.
"Altorientalisches Recht bei den Propheten Amos und Hosea," *BZ* 23 (1935–1936) 150–57.
Fensham, F. C.
"Common Trends in Curses of the Near Eastern Treaties and *Kudurru*-Inscriptions Compared with Maledictions of Amos and Isaiah," *ZAW* 75 (1963) 155–75.
Feuillet, A.
"L'universalisme et l'alliance dans la religion d'Amos," *BVC* 17 (1957) 17–29.
Fishbane, M.
"The Treaty Background of Amos 1:11 and Related Matters," *JBL* 89 (1970) 313–18.
Gerstenberger, E.
"Covenant and Commandment," *JBL* 84 (1965) 38–51.
Harvey, J.
"Le '*rib*-pattern,' réquisitoire prophétique sur la rupture de l'alliance," *Bib* 43 (1962) 172–96.
Idem
Le plaidoyer prophétique contre Israël après la rupture de l'alliance (Travaux de recherche 22; Bruges/Paris: de Brouwer, 1967).
Hillers, D. R.
Treaty Curses and the Old Testament Prophets (BibOr 16; Rome: Pontifical Biblical Institute, 1964).
Idem
Covenant: The History of a Biblical Idea (Baltimore: Johns Hopkins University, 1969).
Huffmon, H. B.
"The Covenant Lawsuit in the Prophets," *JBL* 78 (1959) 285–95.
Idem
"The Treaty Background of Hebrew *yada'*," *BASOR* 181 (1966) 31–37.
Huffmon, H. B., and S. B. Parker
"A Further Note on the Background of Hebrew *yada'*," *BASOR* 184 (1966) 36–38.
Kalluveettil, P.
Declaration and Covenant: A Comprehensive Review of Covenant Formulae from the Old Testament and the Ancient Near East (AnBib 88; Rome: Pontifical Biblical Institute, 1982).
Keel, O.
"Rechttun oder Annahme des drohende Gerichts?" *BZ* 21 (1977) 200–18.
Limburg, J.
The Lawsuit of God in the Eighth-Century Prophets (diss.; Union Theological Seminary, 1969).

McCarthy, D. J.
Treaty and Covenant: A Study in Form in the Ancient Oriental Documents and the Old Testament (AnBib 21a; Rome: Pontifical Biblical Institute, 1978).
Noth, M.
"Die mit des Gesetzes Werken umgehen, die sind unter dem Fluch," *Gesammelte Studien zum Alten Testament* (München: Kaiser, 1960) 155–71; English tr. "For All Who Rely on Works of the Law Are under a Curse," *The Laws in the Pentateuch and Other Studies* (tr. D. R. Ap-Thomas; Philadelphia: Fortress, 1967) 118–31.
O'Rourke-Boyle, M.
"The Covenant Lawsuit of the Prophet Amos III:1—IV:13," *VT* 21 (1971) 338–62.
Perlitt, L.
Bundestheologie im Alten Testament (WMANT 36; Neukirchen-Vluyn: Neukirchener Verlag, 1969).
de Roche, M.
"Yahweh's *RÎB* Against Israel: A Reassessment of the So-Called 'Prophetic Lawsuit' in the Preexilic Prophets," *JBL* 102 (1983) 563–74.
Seeligmann, I. L.
"Zur Terminologie für das Gerichtsverfahren im Wortschatz des biblischen Hebräisch," *Hebräische Wortforschung: Festschrift zum 80. Geburtstag von Walter Baumgartner* (ed. B. Hartmann and others; SVT 16; Leiden: Brill, 1967) 251–78.
Seilhamer, F. H.
"The Role of Covenant in the Mission and Message of Amos," *A Light unto My Path: Old Testament Studies in Honor of Jacob M. Myers* (ed. H. N. Bream, R. D. Heim, and C. A. Moore; Gettysburg Theological Studies 6; Philadelphia: Temple University, 1974) 435–51.
Sinclair, L. A.
"The Courtroom Motif in the Book of Amos," *JBL* 85 (1966) 351–53.
Vattioni, F.
"La terminolgie dell'alleanza," *Riblos Press* 6/4 (1965) 112–16.
Wijngaards, J.
Vazal van Jahweh (Baarn: Bosch & Keuning, 1965).
Zimmerli, W.
"Das Gottesrecht bei den Propheten Amos, Hosea, und Jesaja," *Werden und Wirken des Alten Testaments: Festschrift für Claus Westermann zum 70. Geburtstag* (ed. R. Albertz and others; Göttingen: Vandenhoeck & Ruprecht, 1980) 216–35.

5. Cult

Barstad, H. M.
The Religious Polemics of Amos (SVT 34; Leiden: Brill, 1984).
Bentzen, A.
"The Ritual Background of Amos 1:2—2:16," *OTS* 8 (Leiden: Brill, 1950) 85–99.
Byron, H. L.
A Study in Amos' Attitude toward the Cult (diss.; 1964).
Garcia-Treto, F. O.
"The Three Day Festival Pattern in Ancient Israel," *Trinity University Studies in Religion* 9 (1967–1969) 19–30.
Gottlieb, H.
"Amos og Kulten," *DTT* 30 (1967) 65–101.
Hentschke, R.
Die Stellung der vorexilischen Schriftspropheten zum Kultus (BZAW 75; Berlin: Töpelmann, 1957).
Hermisson, H. J.
Sprache und Ritus im altisraelitischen Kult: Zur "Spiritualisierung" der Kultbegriffe im Altem Testament (WMANT 19; Neukirchen-Vluyn: Neukirchener Verlag, 1965).
Hertzberg, H. W.
"Die prophetische Kritik am Kult," *TLZ* 75 (1950) 219–60.
Hyatt, J. P.
The Prophetic Criticism of Israelite Worship (Cincinnati: Hebrew Union College, 1963).
Jeremias, J.
Kultprophetie und Gerichtsverkündigung in der späten Königszeit Israels (WMANT 35; Neukirchen-Vluyn: Neukirchener Verlag, 1970).
Kaupel, H.
"Gibt es opferfeindliche Stellen im Alten Testament?" *TGl* 17 (1925) 172–78.
Maigret, J.
"Amos et le sanctuaire de Bethel," *BTS* 47 (1962) 5–6.
Oettli, S.
"Der Kultus bei Amos und Hosea," *Griefswalder Studien . . . Festschrift Hermann Cremer* (ed. G. A. Kohut; Gütersloh, 1895) 1–34.
Press, R.
"Die Gerichtspredigt der vorexilischen Propheten und der Versuch einer Steigerung der kultischen Leistung," *ZAW* 70 (1958) 181–84.
Rector, L. J.
"Israel's Rejected Worship: An Exegesis of Amos 5," ResQ 21 (1978) 161–75.
Rendtorff, R.
"Priesterliche Kulttheologie und prophetische Kultpolemik," *TLZ* 81 (1956) 339–42.
Sant, C.
"Religious Worship in the Book of Amos," *Melita Theologica* 3 (1950) 75–93; 4 (1951) 34–48.
Schulz, A. C.
Amos and the Popular Religion in Israel (diss.; Northern Baptist Theological Seminary, 1953).
Sekine, M.
"Das Problem der Kultpolemik bei den Propheten," *EvT* 28 (1968) 605–9.
Vuilleumier-Bessard, R.
La tradition cultuelle d'Israël dans la prophétie d'Amos

et d'Osée (Cahiers Théologiques 45; Neuchâtel/ Paris: Delachaux & Niestlé, 1960).

Würthwein, E.
"Kultpolemik oder Kultbescheid?" *Tradition und Situation. Studien zur alttestamentlichen Prophetie: Festschrift für A. Weiser* (ed. E. Würthwein and O. Kaiser; Göttingen: Vandenhoeck & Ruprecht, 1963) 115–31, rep. in *Wort und Existenz: Studien zum Alten Testament* (Göttingen: Vandenhoeck & Ruprecht, 1970) 144–60.

6. Day of the Lord

Carniti, C.
"L'espressione 'Il Giorno di JHWH': Origine ed Evoluzione Semantica," *BeO* 12 (1970) 11–25.

Černý, L.
The Day of Yahweh and Some Relevant Problems (Práce Z Vědeckých Ústarů 53; V Praze: University Karlovy, 1948).

Eppstein, V.
"The Day of Yahweh in Jes. 4:23–28," *JBL* 87 (1968) 93–97.

Everson, A. J.
"The Days of Yahweh," *JBL* 93 (1974) 329–37.

Idem
"Day of the Lord," *IDBSup* 209–10.

Fensham, F. C.
"A Possible Origin of the Concept of the Day of the Lord," *Biblical Essays: Die Ou Testamentiese Werkgemeenskap in Suid Afrika: 9th Congress* (Potchefstroom: Rege-Pers Beperk, 1966) 90–97.

Fohrer, G.
"Der Tag JHWHs," Eretz Israel 16 (*Harry Orlinsky Volume*; ed. B. A. Levine and A. Malamat; Jerusalem: Israel Exploration Society, 1982) 43*–50*.

Gray, J.
"The Day of Jahweh in Cultic Experience and Eschatological Prospect," *SEÅ* 39 (1974) 5–37.

Hélewa, F. J.
"L'origine du concept prophétique du 'Jour de Yahvé,'" *EphCarm* 15 (1964) 3–36.

Hoffman, Y.
"The Day of the Lord as a Concept and a Term in the Prophetic Literature," *ZAW* 93 (1981) 37–50.

Klein, R. W.
"The Day of the Lord," *CTM* 39 (1968) 517–25.

Largement, R.H.L.
"Le jour de Yahweh dans le contexte oriental," *Sacra Pagina* 1 (1959) 259–66.

Ne'eman, P.
"The Day of the Lord in Literary Prophecy," *BM* 34 (1968) 57–70 (Heb.).

Rappel, D.
"'Day of the Lord' in the Bible," *Studies in the Minor Prophets* (ed. B. Z. Luria; Jerusalem: Kiryat Sepher, 1981) 78–85 (Heb.).

Schnunk, K.
"Strukturlinien in der Entwicklung der Vorstellung vom 'Tag Jahwes,'" *VT* 14 (1964) 319–30.

Idem
"Der 'Tag Jahwehs' in der Verkündigung der Propheten," *Kairos* 11 (1969) 14–21.

Semen, P.
"Sensul expresiei 'Iom Iahve,'" *Studii Teologice* 30 (1978) 149–61.

Trapiello, J. G.
"La nocien del 'Dia de Yahve' en el Antiguo Testamento," *CB* 26 (1969) 331–36.

van Leeuwen, C.
"The Prophecy of the *Yôm YHWH* in Amos V:18–20," *Language and Meaning* (*OTS* 19; Leiden: Brill, 1974) 113–34.

von Rad, G.
"The Origin of the Concept of the Day of Yahweh," *JSS* 4 (1959) 97–108.

Idem
Old Testament Theology (2 vols.; New York/London: Harper & Row, 1975) 2.119–25.

Weinfeld, M.
"The Concept of the Day of the Lord and the Problem of Its *Sitz im Leben*," *Studies in the Minor Prophets* (ed. B. Z. Luria; Jerusalem: Kiryat Sepher, 1981) 55–76 (Heb.).

Idem
"Aspirations for the Kingdom of God in the Bible and Their Reflection in Jewish Liturgy—The Essence of the Concept of the 'Day of the Lord,'" *Messianism and Eschatology: A Collection of Essays* (ed. Z. Barag; Jerusalem: Zalman Shazar Center, 1983) 73–96 (Heb.); rep. and tr. in *Studies in the Bible* (ed. S. Japhet; Scripta Hierosolymitana 31; Jerusalem: Magnes, 1986) 341–72.

Weiss, M.
"The Origin of the 'Day of the Lord'—Reconsidered," *HUCA* 37 (1966) 29–72.

7. Doxologies

Berg, W.
Die sogenannten Hymnenfragmente im Amosbuch (Europäische Hochschulschriften 23/45; Bern/ Frankfurt: M. Lang, 1974).

Bergler, S.
Die hymnischen Passagen und die Mitte des Amosbuchen. Ein Forschungsbericht (diss.; Tübingen, 1979).

Booij, P.
"Vertaalproblemen in de Amos-doxologieën," *Beginnen bij de letter beth* (1985) 90–97.

Carny, P.
"Amos 4:13—A Doxology?" *HaZvi Israel: Studies in the Bible Dedicated to the Memory of Israel and Zvi Brodie* (ed. J. Licht and G. Brin; Tel Aviv: Tel Aviv University School of Jewish Studies, 1976) 143–50 (Heb.).

Idem
"Doxologies—A Scientific Myth," *Hebrew Studies* 18 (1977) 149–59.
Condamin, A.
"Les chants lyriques des prophètes," *RB* 10 (1901) 352–76.
Crenshaw, J. L.
"The Influence of the Wise Upon Amos—The 'Doxologies of Amos' and Job 5:9–16; 9:5–10," *ZAW* 79 (1967) 42–52.
Idem
"Amos and the Theophanic Tradition," *ZAW* 80 (1968) 203–15.
Idem
"*Wedōrēk 'al-bāmôtê 'areṣ*," *CBQ* 34 (1972) 39–53.
Idem
Hymnic Affirmation of Divine Justice: The Doxologies of Amos and Related Texts in the O.T. (SBLDS 24; Missoula, MT: Scholars, 1975).
Crüsemann, F.
Studien zur Formgeschichte von Hymnus und Danklied in Israel (WMANT 32; Neukirchen-Vluyn: Neukirchener Verlag, 1969).
Foresti, F.
"Funzione semantica dei brani participali di Amos: 4,13; 5,8s.; 9,5s.," *Bib* 62 (1981) 169–84.
Frost, S. B.
"Asseveration by Thanksgiving," *VT* 8 (1958) 380–90.
Gaster, T. H.
"An Ancient Hymn in the Prophecies of Amos," *Journal of the Manchester University Egyptian and Oriental Society* 19 (1935) 23–26.
Grimm, K. J.
Euphemistic Liturgical Appendices in the Old Testament (Baltimore: Johns Hopkins University; Leipzig: Hinrichs, 1901).
Horst, F.
"Die Doxologien im Amosbuch," *ZAW* 47 (1929) 45–54, rep. in *Gottes Recht: Studien zum Recht im Alten Testament* (ed. H. W. Wolff; München: Kaiser, 1961) 155–66.
Koch, K.
"Die Rolle der hymnischen Abschnitte in der Komposition des Amos-Buches," *ZAW* 86 (1974) 504–37.
Oort, H.
"De Echtheid van Amos 4:13; Amos 5:8,9; Amos 9:5,6," *ThT* 25 (1891) 125–26.
Story, C.I.K.
"Amos—Prophet of Praise," *VT* 30 (1980) 67–80.
Vaccari, A.
"Hymnus Propheticus in Deum Creatorem," *VD* 9 (1929) 184–88.
van Leeuwen, C.
"De 'Lofprijzingen' in Amos," *Rondom het Woord* 13 (1971) 255–64.
von Rad, G.
"Das theologische Problem des Alttestamentlichen Schöpfungsglaubens," *Werden und Wesen des Alten Testaments* (ed. J. Hempel, F. Stummer, and P. Volz; BZAW 66; Berlin: Töpelmann, 1936) 138–47.
Idem
"Gerichtsdoxologie," *Schalom: Studien zu Glaube und Geschichte Israels: Alfred Jepsen zum 71. Geburtstag dargebracht von Freunden, Schülern und Kollegen* (ed. K.-H.Bernhardt; Arbeiten zur Theologie 1/46; Stuttgart: Calwer Verlag, 1971) 45–79; rep. in *Gesammelte Studien zum Alten Testament* (TBü 48; München: Kaiser, 1973) 245–54.
Wambacq, B. N.
L'épithète divine Jahvé Ṣᵉba'ôt (Bruges: de Brouwer, 1947).
Watts, J.D.W.
"An Old Hymn Preserved in the Book of Amos," *JNES* 15 (1956) 33–39.

8. Early Christian Interpretation

Abel, F. M.
"Parallelisme exégétique entre S. Jerome et S. Cyrille d'Alexandrie," *RB* 50 (1941) 94–119, 212–30.
Bouwman, G.
Das Julian von Aeclanum Kommentar zu den Propheten Osee, Joel und Amos. Geschichte der Exegese (AnBib 9; Rome: Pontifical Biblical Institute, 1958).
Braun, M. A.
"James' Use of Amos at the Jerusalem Council: Steps Towards a Possible Solution of the Textual and Theological Problems," *JETS* 20 (1977) 113–21.
Cyril of Alexandria
Commentarius in Amos prophetam. Opera Omnia 4. (ed. J.-P. Migne; *PG* 71; 1859) col. 407–582.
Julien of Eclane
Pseudo-Rufin d'Aquilée Commentarius in Oseam, in Joel, in Amos (ed. J.-P. Migne; *PG* 21; 1849) col. 1057–1104.
Kelly, J. G.
"The Interpretation of Amos 4:13 in the Early Christian Community," *Studies in Honor of J. P. Brennan* (ed. R. F. McNamara; New York, 1976) 60–77.
Moreau, M.
"Sur un commentaire d'Amos, *De Doctrina Christiana* IV, VII, 15–21; sur Amos VI, 1–6," *Bible de Tous les Temps* 3 (1986) 313–22.
Rahmer, M.
"Die hebräischen Traditionen in den Werken des Hieronymus. Die Commentarien zu den XII Kleinen Profeten, III. Amos," *MGWJ* 42 (1898) 1–16, 97–107.

Richard, E.
"The Creative Use of Amos by the Author of Acts," *NovT* 24 (1982) 37–53.
Smythe, H. R.
"The Interpretation of Amos 4,13 in St. Athanasius and Didymus," *JTS* 1 (1950) 158–68.
Theodore of Mopsueste
In Amosum prophetam commentarius (ed. J.-P. Migne; *PG* 66; 1864) col. 241–304.
Idem
"In Amos 2,3–5," *Theodori Mopsuesteni fragmenta syriaca* (ed. E. Sachau; Leipzig: Englemann, 1869).
Theodoret of Cyr
Commentarius in Amos prophetam. Opera Omnia 2 (ed. J.-P. Migne; *PG* 81; 1864) col. 1663–1708.

9. Eschatology

Baumgartner, W.
"Kennen Amos und Hosea eine Heilseschatologie?" (diss.; Zürich, 1913) = SThZ 30 (1913) 30–42, 95–124, 152–70.
Benson, A.
"From the Mouth of the Lion: The Messianism of Amos," *CBQ* 19 (1957) 199–212.
Brooke, G. J.
"The Amos-Numbers Midrash (CD 7 13b–8 1a) and Messianic Expectation," *ZAW* 92 (1980) 397–404.
Caspari, W.
"Erwarten Amos und Hosea den Messias?" *NKZ* 41 (1930) 812–24.
Dietrich, E. L.
שוב שבות. *Die endzeitlich Wiederherstellung bei den Propheten* (BZAW 40; Giessen: Töpelmann, 1925).
Gressmann, H.
Der Ursprung der israelitisch-jüdischen Eschatologie (FRLANT 6; Göttingen: Vandenhoeck & Ruprecht, 1905).
Herrmann, S.
Die prophetischen Heilserwartungen im Alten Testament: Ursprung und Gestaltwandel (BWANT 85; Stuttgart: Kohlhammer, 1965).
Hoffman, Y.
"'בַּיּוֹם הַהוּא' and 'אַחֲרִית הַיָּמִים,' Their Relation to Eschatological Passages in the Bible," *BM* 71 (1978) 438–44 (Heb.).
Müller, H.-P.
Ursprünge und Strukturen alttestamentlicher Eschatologie (BZAW 109; Berlin: Töpelmann, 1969).
Preuss, H. D.
Jahweglaube und Zukunftserwartung (BWANT 87; Stuttgart/Berlin: Kohlhammer, 1968).
Rohland, E.
Die Bedeutung der Erwählungstradition Israels für die Eschatologie der alttestamentlichen Propheten (diss.; Heidelberg, 1956).
van Leeuven, C.
"De Heilsverwachting bij Amos," *Vruchten van de Uithof: Studies opgedragen aan Dr. H.A. Brongers* (Utrecht: Theological Institute, 1974) 71–87.
Weinfeld, M.
"Mesopotamian Prophecies of the End of Days," *Shnaton* 3 (1979) 263–76 (Heb.).

10. Ethics

Alger, B.
"The Theology and Social Ethic of Amos," *Scripture* 17 (1965) 109–16, 318–28.
Amsler, S.
"Amos et les droits de l'homme," *De la Tôrah au Messie: Études d'exégèse et d'herméneutique bibliques offertes à Henri Cazelles* (ed. J. Doré, P. Grelot, and M. Carrez; Paris: Desclée, 1981) 181–87.
Bailey, J. G.
"Amos Preacher of Social Reform," *BiTod* 19 (1981) 306–13.
Bohlen, R.
"Zur Sozialkritik des Propheten Amos," *TTZ* 95 (1986) 282–301.
Bonora, A.
Amos. Il profeta della giustizia (Brescia: Paideia, 1975).
Idem
"Amos diffensore del diritto e della guistizia," *Testimonium Christi Scritti in onore de Jacques Dupont* (Brescia: Paideia, 1985) 69–90.
Botterweck, G. J.
"'Sie verkaufen den Unschuldigen um Geld.' Zur sozialen Kritik des Propheten Amos," *BibLeb* 12 (1971) 215–31.
Idem
"Die soziale Kritik des Propheten Amos," *Das Amt des Bischofs. Eine Festgabe für den Erzbischof von Köln—Joseph Kardinal Höffner* (ed. W. Mogge; Köln: Bachem, 1971) 39–58.
Causse, A.
"Les prophètes et la crise sociologique de la religion d'Israël," *RHPR* 12 (1932) 97–110.
Fabian, N.
Protest gegen Ausbeuter: Amos sozialkritische Ansätze in der alttestamentlichen Prophetie-dargestellt am Propheten Amos (Pfeiffer Werkbücher 118; Münster i. W.: Pfeiffer, 1973).
Fendler, M.
"Zur Sozialkritik des Amos: Versuch einer wirtschafts-und sozialgeschichtlichen Interpretation alttestamentlicher Texte," *EvT* 33 (1973) 32–53.
Finley, T. J.
"An Evangelical Response to the Preaching of Amos," *JETS* 28 (1985) 414–20.
Gelin, A.
Les pauvres de Yahvé (Témoins de Dieu 14; Paris: Cerf, 1953).

de Geus, J. K.
"Die Gesellschaftskritik der Propheten und die Archaeologie," *ZDPV* 98 (1982) 50–57.
Gutierrez, R. C.
La justicia social en los profetas del siglo VIII: Amos, Oseas, Isaias, y Miqueas (Lizentiatsarbeit; Fribourg, 1970).
Hardmeier, C.
"Die judäische Unheilsprophetie. Antwort auf einen Gesellschafts-und Normwandel im Israel des 8. Jahrhunderts vor Christus," *Der altsprachliche Unterricht* 26 (1983) 20–44.
Hoppe, L. J.
Being Poor: A Biblical Study (Good News Studies 20; Wilmington: Michael Glazier, 1987).
Howington, N. P.
"Toward an Ethical Understanding of Amos," *RevExp* 63 (1966) 405–12.
Huey, F. B., Jr.
"The Ethical Teaching of Amos: Its Content and Relevance," *SWJT* 9 (1966) 57–67.
Huffmon, H. B.
"The Social Role of Amos' Message," *The Quest for the Kingdom of God: Studies in Honor of G. E. Mendenhall* (ed. H. B. Huffmon, F. A. Spina, and A.R.W. Green; Winona Lake, IN: Eisenbrauns, 1983) 109–16.
Humbert, P.
"Un héraut de la justice, Amos," *RTP* 5 (1917) 5–35.
Idem
"Quelques aspects de la religion d'Amos," *RTP* 17 (1929) 241–55.
Kee, A.
"Amos and Affluence," *The Furrow* 38 (1987) 151–61.
Kelley, P. H.
Amos: Prophet of Social Justice (Grand Rapids: Baker Book House, 1974); originally published as *The Book of Amos: A Study Manual* (1966).
Koch, K.
"Die Entstehung der sozialen Kritik bei den Propheten," *Probleme biblischer Theologie: Gerhard von Rad zum 70. Geburtstag* (ed. H. W. Wolff; Münich: Kaiser, 1971) 236–57; rep. in *Das Prophetenverständnis in der deutschsprachigen Forschung seit Heinrich Ewald* (ed. P.A.H. Neumann; Wege der Forschung 307, 1979) 565–93.
Kraus, H.-J.
"Die prophetische Botschaft gegen das soziale Unrecht Israels," *EvT* 15 (1955) 295–307.
Krause, M.
Das Verhältnis von sozialer Kritik und kommender Katastrophe in den Unheilsprophezeiungen des Amos (diss.; Hamburg, 1972).
Kuschke, A.
"Arm und Reich im Alten Testament, mit besonderen Berücksichtigung der nachexilischen Zeit," *ZAW* 57 (1939) 31–57.
Laridon, V.
"Amos, genuinae religionis defensor ac propheta iustitiae socialis," *Collationes Brugenses et Gandavenses* 47 (1951) 405–10; 48 (1952) 3–7, 27–31.
Lattes, D.
"Amos, prophète de la justice," *Madregoth* 1 (1940) 23–31.
Levin, S.
"The Idea of Social Justice in the Prophecies of Amos and First Isaiah," *Sefer Neiger* (ed. A. Biran and others; Jerusalem: Kiryat Sepher, 1959) 120–33 (Heb.).
Limburg, J.
The Prophets and the Powerless (Atlanta: John Knox, 1977).
McFadyen, J. E.
A Cry for Justice: A Study in Amos (New York: Charles Scribner's Sons, 1912).
Monloubou, J.
Amos et Osée, Sainteté de Justice, Sainteté d'Amour (Paris: Editions Fleurus, 1964).
Prado, J.
Amos. El Profeta pastor: Introducción, versión y commentario teológico popular (Biblia y Predicacion 2; Madrid: El Perpetuo Socorro, 1950).
Randellini, L.
"Ricchi e Poveri nel libro del Profeta Amos," *SBFLA* 2 (1951–1952) 5–86.
Idem
"Il Profeta Amos Defensore dei Poveri," *Bullettino del l'Anicizia Ebraico-Cristiana de Firenze* 6 (1971) 35–43.
Rinaldi, G.
"Il profeta del 'guidizio,'" *Studi . . . B. Biondi* (Milan: Giuffré, 1966) 417–23.
Schwantes, M.
Das Recht der Armen, Beiträge zur Biblischen Exegese und Theologie 4 (Bern/Frankfurt, a. M.: Peter Lang, 1977) 87–99.
Sowada, J.
"Let Justice Surge Like Water. . . ," *BiTod* 19 (1981) 301–5.
Spiegel, S.
Amos Vs. Amaziah (Essays in Judaism 3; New York: Jewish Theological Seminary, 1957).
Thompson, C. L.
The Ideological Background and Analysis of Economic Injustice in the Book of Amos (diss.; Southern Baptist Theological Seminary, 1956).
Thorogood, B.
Guia del libro de Amos. El profeta de la justicia social (Theological Education Fund Study Guide 4; Madrid: SPCK, 1974); English tr. *A Guide to the Book of Amos* (Theological Education Fund Study Guide 4; London: SPCK, 1977).

Tourn, G., and A. Soggin
Amos, Profeta della guistizia (Torino: Claudiana, 1972).
van der Ploeg, J.
"Les pauvres d'Israël et leur piété," *OTS* 7 (Leiden: Brill, 1950) 236–70.
van Leeuwen, C.
Le dévelopement du sens social en Israël avant l'ère chrétienne (Studia Semitica Neerlandica 1; Assen: Van Gorcum, 1959).
Vesco, J.-L.
"Amos de Téqoa, défenseur de l'homme," *RB* 87 (1980) 481–513.
Wanke, G.
"Zu Grundlagen und Absicht prophetischer Sozialkritik," *KD* 18 (1972) 2–17.
Wigley, A. L.
Amos and Social Righteousness (1947).

11. Forms of Speech and Language

Avishur, Y.
"The Forms of Repetition of Numbers Indicating Wholeness (3,7,10)—in the Bible and in Ancient Semitic Literature," *Beer-Sheva* 1 (1973) 1–55 (Heb.).
Idem
"Patterns of the Double Rhetorical Question," *Zer Li-Gevurot. The Zalman Shazar Jubilee Volume: A Collection of Studies in Bible, Eretz Yisrael, Hebrew Language, and Talmudic Literature* (ed. B. Z. Luria; Jerusalem: Kiryat Sepher, 1973) 421–64 (Heb.).
Bjoerndalen, A. J.
Untersuchungen zur allegorischen Rede der Propheten Amos und Jesaja (BZAW 165; Berlin/New York: de Gruyter, 1986).
Blank, S. H.
"Irony by Way of Attribution," *Semitics* 1 (1970) 1–6.
Carrier, A. S.
"The Hapax Legomena of the Minor Prophets," *Hebraica* 5 (1888–1889) 131–36.
Casanowicz, I. M.
"Paronomasia in the Old Testament," *JBL* 12 (1893) 105–67.
Clifford, R. J.
"The Use of *HÔY* in the Prophets," *CBQ* 28 (1966) 458–64.
Crenshaw, J. L.
"Impossible Questions, Sayings, and Tasks," *Gnomic Wisdom* (ed. J. D. Crossan; *Semeia* 17; Chico, CA: Scholars, 1980) 19–34.
Curtis, J. J.
An Application of the Syntax of the Hebrew Verbs to the Writings of Amos (diss.; Southern Baptist Seminary, 1949).
Doron, P.
"Paronomasia in the Prophecies to the Nations," *Hebrew Studies* 10/11 (1979–1980) 36–43.
Eybers, I. H.
"Some Examples of Hyperbole in Biblical Hebrew," *Semitics* 1 (1970) 38–49.
Idem
"The Use of Proper Names as a Stylistic Device," *Semitics* 2 (1971–1972) 82–92.
Farr, G.
"The Language of Amos, Popular or Cultic?" *VT* 16 (1966) 312–24.
Freedman, D. N.
"Deliberate Deviation from an Established Pattern of Repetition in Hebrew Poetry as a Rhetorical Device," *Proceedings of the Ninth World Congress of Jewish Studies: Division A: The Period of the Bible* (Jerusalem: World Union of Jewish Studies, 1986) 1.45–52.
Gerstenberger, E.
"The Woe-Oracles of the Prophets," *JBL* 81 (1962) 248–63.
Gevirtz, S.
Patterns of the Early Poetry of Israel (Studies in Ancient Oriental Civilization 32; Chicago: University of Chicago, 1963).
Ginsberg, H. L.
"Towards the History of the Graded Number Sequence," *Minḥa LeDavid: Dedicated to David Yellin* (Jerusalem: Va'ad HaYovel, 1935) 78–82 (Heb.).
Gordis, R.
"A Rhetorical Use of Interrogative Sentences in Biblical Hebrew," *AJSL* 49 (1933) 212–17.
Idem
"The Heptad as an Element of Biblical and Rabbinic Style," *JBL* 62 (1943) 17–26.
Haran, M.
"Biblical Studies: The Literary Applications of the Numerical Sequence x/x+1 and Their Connections with the Patterns of Parallelism," *Tarbiz* 39 (1970) 109–36 (Heb.) = "The Graded Numerical Sequence and the Phenomenon of 'Automatism' in Biblical Poetry," SVT 22 (Leiden: Brill, 1972) 238–67.
Hardmeier, C.
"Old Testament Exegesis and Linguistic Narrative Research," *Poetics* 15/1–2 (1986) 89–109.
Hehn, F.
"Zur Bedeutung der Siebenzahl," BZAW 41 (Giessen: Töpelmann, 1925) 128–36.
Held, M.
"Rhetorical Questions in Ugaritic and Biblical Hebrew," Eretz Israel 9 (*W. F. Albright Volume*; ed. A. Malamat; Jerusalem: Israel Exploration Society, 1969) 71–79.
Hillers, D. R.
"*Hoy* and *Hoy*-Oracles. A Neglected Syntactic Aspect," *The Word of the Lord Shall Go Forth: Essays in Honor of D. N. Freedman* (ed. C. L. Meyers and M. O'Connor; American Schools of Oriental Research Special Volumes, 1; Winona Lake, IN: Eisenbrauns, 1983) 185–88.

Jahnow, H.
Das hebräische Leichenlied im Rahmen der Völkerdichtung (BZAW 36; Giessen: Töpelmann, 1923).
Janzen, W.
"*ĂSRÊ* and *HÔI* in the Old Testament," *HTR* 62 (1969) 432–33.
Idem
Mourning Cry and Woe Oracle (BZAW 125; Berlin: de Gruyter, 1972).
Kohata, A. F.
"A Stylistic Study in the Metaphors of Amos," *The Bible, Its Thoughts, History and Language: Essays in Honor of Masao Sekine* (ed. S. Arai; Tokyo: Yamamoto Shoten, 1972) 147–61.
Kraft, C. E.
"Strophic Structure in the Book of Amos," *JAOS* 59 (1939) 421.
Krašovec, J.
Der Merismus im Biblisch-Hebräischen und Nordwestsemitischen (BibOr 33; Rome: Pontifical Biblical Institute, 1977).
Krause, H.-J.
"hôj als prophetische Leichenklage über das eigene Volk im 8. Jahrhundert," *ZAW* 85 (1973) 15–46.
Landy, F.
"Vision and Poetic Speech in Amos," *Biblical and Other Studies* (ed. R. Ahroni; *HAR* 11; Columbus: The Ohio State University, 1987) 223–46.
Lemcke, G.
Die Prophetensprüche des Amos und Jesaja, metrisch-stilistisch und literarisch-aesthetisch betrachtet (Breslau: Buchdruckerei H. Fleishmann, 1914).
Lewis, R. L.
The Persuasive Style and Appeals of the Minor Prophets Amos, Hosea, and Micah (diss.; Ann Arbor, MI, 1959).
Limburg, J.
"Sevenfold Structure in the Book of Amos," *JBL* 106 (1987) 217–22.
Lindblom, J.
"Die literarische Gattung der prophetischen Literatur," *UUÅ* (1924) 66–97.
Loewenstamm, S. E.
"Studies in the Stylistic Patterns of Biblical and Ugaritic Literature," *Leš* 32 (1968) 27–36 (Heb.).
Idem
"The Phrase 'X (or) X Plus One' in Biblical and Old Oriental Laws," *Bib* 53 (1972) 543.
Melamed, E. Z.
"Break-up of Stereotype Phrases as an Artistic Device in Biblical Poetry," *Studies in the Bible* (ed. C. Rabin; Scripta Hierosolymitana 8; Jerusalem: Magnes, 1961) 115–63; rep. in *Studies in the Bible Presented to Professor M. H. Segal* (ed. J. M. Grintz and J. Liver; Publications of the Israel Society for Biblical Research 17; Jerusalem: Kiryat Sepher, 1964) 188–219 (Heb.).
Newman, L. I.
Studies in Biblical Parallelism. Part 1: Parallelism in Amos (University of California Publications in Semitic Philology 1/2; University of California, 1918).
Noy, H.
"Prophecy, Rhetoric, and Interpretation," *BM* 32 (1967) 128–32 (Heb.).
Rabin, C.
"The Language of Amos and Hosea," *Studies in the Minor Prophets* (ed. B. Z. Luria; Jerusalem: Kiryat Sepher, 1981) 115–36 (Heb.).
Ramsey, G. W.
"Speech—Forms in Hebrew Law and Prophetic Oracles," *JBL* 96 (1977) 45–48.
Roth, W.M.W.
"The Numerical Sequence *x/x+1* in the Old Testament," *VT* 12 (1962) 300–311.
Idem
Numerical Sayings in the Old Testament (SVT 13; Leiden: Brill, 1965).
Rüger, H. P.
"Die gestaffelten Zahlensprüche der alten Testaments und aram. Achikar 92," *VT* 31 (1981) 229–34.
Sauer, G.
Die Sprüche Agurs (BWANT 84; Stuttgart: Kohlhammer, 1963).
Stuart, D. K.
Studies in Early Hebrew Meter (Missoula, MT: Scholars, 1976).
Super, A. S.
"Figures of Comparison in the Book of Amos," *Semitics* 3 (1973) 67–81.
van der Merwe, B. J.
"A Few Remarks on the Religious Terminology in Amos and Hosea," *Studies in the Books of Hosea and Amos: Die Ou Testamentiese Werkgemeenskap in Suid Afrika: 7th and 8th Congresses* (Potchefstroom: Rege-Pers Beperk, 1964–1965) 143–52.
de Waard, J.
"The Chiastic Structure of Amos 5:1–17," *VT* 17 (1977) 170–77.
Walker, L. L.
"The Language of Amos," *SWJT* 9 (1966) 37–48.
Wanke, G.
"אוֹי und הוֹי," *ZAW* 78 (1966) 215–18.
Weiss, M.
"The Pattern of Numerical Sequence in Amos: For Three . . . and For Four," *Tarbiz* 36 (1967) 307–18 (Heb.) = "The Pattern of Numerical Sequence in Amos 1—2. A Re-Examination," *JBL* 86 (1967) 416–23.
Williams, J. G.
"The Alas-Oracles of the Eighth Century Prophets," *HUCA* 38 (1967) 75–91.
Idem
"Irony and Lament: Clues to Prophetic

Consciousness," in *Semeia* 8 (Missoula, MT: Scholars, 1977) 51–74.
Zakovitch, Y.
"For Three . . . and for Four": The Pattern of the Numerical Sequence in the Bible (2 vols.; Jerusalem: Mekor, 1979) (Heb.).
Zobel, H. J.
"HÔY," TDOT 3 (1978) 359–65.

12. Oracles against the Nations

Bartlett, J. R.
"The Land of Seir and the Brotherhood of Edom," *JTS* 20 (1969) 13–18.
Idem
"The Brotherhood of Edom," *JSOT* 4 (1977) 2–27.
Barton, J.
Amos' Oracles against the Nations. A Study of Amos 1,3—2,5 (SOTSMS 6; Cambridge: Cambridge University, 1980).
Beaucamp, E.
"Amos I—II. Le *Pesha'* d'Israël et celui des nations," *ScEs* 29 (1969) 435–41.
Bentzen, A.
"The Ritual Background of Amos i 2—ii 16," *OTS* 8 (Leiden: Brill, 1950) 85–99.
Christensen, D. L.
"Studies in the Oracles against the Nations: Transformations of the War Oracle in Old Testament Prophecy," *HTR* 65 (1972) 592–93.
Idem
Transformation of the War Oracles in Old Testament Prophecy: Studies in the Oracles against the Nations (Missoula, MT: Scholars, 1975).
Cohen, S.
"The Political Background of the Words of Amos," *HUCA* 36 (1965) 153–60.
Crenshaw, J. L.
Review of J. Barton, *Amos' Oracles against the Nations*, *CBQ* 44 (1982) 475–77.
Fensham, F. C.
"The Treaty between the Israelites and the Tyrians," in SVT 17 (Leiden: Brill, 1969) 71–87.
Fritz, V.
"Die Fremdvölkersprüche des Amos," *VT* 37 (1987) 26–38.
Geyer, J. B.
"Mythology and Culture in the Oracles against the Nations," *VT* 36 (1986) 129–45.
Gordis, R.
"Edom, Israel and Amos. An Unrecognized Source for Edomite History," *Essays on the Occasion of the Seventieth Anniversary of the Dropsie College (1909–1979)* (ed. A. I. Kautsch and L. Nemoy; Philadelphia: Dropsie University, 1979) 109–32.
Gosse, B.
"Le recueil d'oracles contra les nations du livre d'Amos et l'histoire deutéronomique,'" *VT* 38 (1988) 22–40.
Haran, M.
"Observations on the Historical Background of Amos 1:2—2:6," *BIES* 30 (1966) 56–69 (Heb.) = *IEJ* 18 (1968) 201–12.
Hayes, J. H.
The Oracles against the Nations in the Old Testament: Their Usage and Theological Importance (diss.; Princeton Theological Seminary, 1964).
Idem
"The Usage of Oracles against Foreign Nations in Ancient Israel," *JBL* 87 (1968) 81–92.
Höffken, P.
Untersuchungen zu den Begründungselementen der Völkerorakel der Alten Testament (diss.; Bonn, 1977).
Hoffman, Y.
The Prophecies against Foreign Nations in the Bible (Tel Aviv: HaKibbutz HaMeuhad, 1977) (Heb.).
Idem
"From Oracle to Prophecy: The Growth, Crystallization, and Disintegration of a Biblical Gattung," *JNSL* 10 (1982) 75–81.
Jones, G. H.
An Examination of Some Leading Motifs in the Prophetic Oracles against Foreign Nations (Bangor, 1970).
Knierim, R. P.
"'I Will Not Cause It to Return' in Amos 1 and 2," *Canon and Authority: Essays in Old Testament Religion and Theology* (ed. G. W. Coats, and B. O. Long; Philadelphia: Fortress, 1977) 163–75.
Luria, B. Z.
"The Prophecies unto the Nations in the Book of Amos from a Historical Point of View," *BM* 54 (1973) 287–301 (Heb.); rep. in *Studies in the Minor Prophets* (ed. B. Z. Luria; Jerusalem: Kiryat Sepher, 1981) 199–219 (Heb.).
McAlpine, T. H.
"The Word against the Nations," SBT 5/1 (1975) 3–14.
Margulis, B. B.
Studies in the Oracles against the Nations (diss.; Brandeis University, 1967).
Marti, K.
"Zur Komposition von Amos 1,3—2,3," *Abhandlungen zur Semitischen Religionskunde und Sprachwissenschaft: W. W. G. von Baudassin zum 26. September 1917 überreicht von Freunden und Schülern* (ed. W. Frankenberg and Fr. Küchler; BZAW 33; Giessen: Töpelmann, 1918) 323–30.
Muntingh, L. M.
"Political and International Relations of Israel's Neighboring Peoples according to the Oracles of Amos," in *Studies in the Book of Hosea and Amos: Die Ou Testamentiese Werkgemeenskap in Suid Afrika: 7th and 8th Congresses* (Potchefstroom: Rege–Pers Beperk, 1964–1965) 134–42.
Osborn, A. R.
"The Responsibility of Privilege," *Biblical Research* 16 (1931) 574–78.

Paul, S. M.
"A Literary Reinvestigation of the Oracles against the Nations of Amos," *De la Tôrah au Messie: Études d'exégèse et d'herméneutique bibliques offertes à Henri Cazelles* (ed. J. Doré, P. Grelot, and M. Carrez; Paris: Desclée, 1981) 189–204.
Pfeifer, G.
"Die Fremdvölkersprüche des Amos—Spätere *Vaticinia Ex Eventu?*" *VT* 38 (1988) 230–33.
Priest, J.
"The Covenant of Brothers," *JBL* 84 (1965) 400–406.
Rudolph, W.
"Die angefochtenen Völkersprüche in Amos 1 und 2," *Schalom. Studien zu Glaube und Geschichte Israels: Alfred Jepsen zum 71. Geburtstag* (ed. K.-H. Bernhardt; Arbeiten zur Theologie 1/46; Stuttgart: Calwer Verlag, 1971) 45–79.
Schoville, K. N.
"A Note on the Oracles of Amos against Gaza, Tyre, and Edom," SVT 26 (Leiden: Brill, 1974) 55–63.
Idem
"The Sins of Aram in Amos 1," *Proceedings of the 6th World Congress of Jewish Studies* (Jerusalem: World Congress of Jewish Studies, 1977) 1.363–75.
Soper, B. K.
"A New Interpretation of Amos 1,3 etc.," *ExpTim* 71 (1959–1960) 86–87.
Toy, C. H.
"The Judgment of Foreign Peoples in Amos i:3—ii:3," *JBL* 25 (1906) 25–28.
Tur-Sinai, N. H.
"King and Princes—Amos and His Prophecy against the Nations," *HaLashon VeHasefer* (3 vols.; Jerusalem: Bialik, 1954) 1.81–91 (Heb.).
Ulrichsen, J. H.
"Oraklene i Amos 1,3ff.," *NorTT* 85 (1984) 39–54.
Weiss, M.
"The Pattern of the 'Execration Texts' in the Prophetic Literature," *IEJ* 19 (1969) 150–57.
Zorell, F.
"Zu Amos 1,3.6. usw.," *Bib* 6 (1925) 171–73.

13. Septuagint and Vulgate

Arieti, J. A.
A Study in the Septuagint of the Book of Amos (diss.; Stanford, 1972).
Idem
"The Vocabulary of Septuagint Amos," *JBL* 93 (1974) 338–47.
Auer, F. X.
Vulgatastudien an Hand der Kleinen Propheten, I. Teil: Osea bis Micha (diss.; Breslau, 1942).
Bosshardt, E.
"Septuagint Codices V. 62 and 147 in the Book of Amos," *JBL* 58 (1939) 331–47.
Dingermann, F.
Masora—Septuaginta der kleinen Propheten (diss.; Würzburg, 1948).
Fischer, J.
"Einige neue Beobachtungen zur LXX des Buches Amos," *ATR* (1923) 245–47.
Highfield, H.
"Gleanings from the Septuagint," *ExpTim* 38 (1926–1927) 44–45.
Howard, G.
"Some Notes on the Septuagint of Amos," *VT* 20 (1970) 108–12.
Idem
"The Quinta of the Minor Prophets. A First Century Septuagint Text?" *Bib* 55 (1974) 15–22.
Idem
"Revision toward the Hebrew in the Septuagint Text of Amos," Eretz Israel 16 (*Harry M. Orlinsky Volume*; ed. B.A. Levine and A. Malamat; Jerusalem: Israel Exploration Society, 1982) 125–33.
Johnson, S. E.
The Septuagint Translator of Amos (diss.; Chicago, 1936).
Kraft, R. A.
"P. Oxy. VI 846 (Amos 2, Old Greek) Reconsidered," *BASP* 16 (1979) 201–204.
Meinhold, J., and H. Lietzmann
Der Prophet Amos. Hebräisch und Griechisch (Kleine Texte für theologische und philologische Vorlesungen und Übungen 15/16; Bonn: Marcus and Weber, 1905).
Muraoka, T.
"Is the Septuagint Amos VIII:12—IX:10 a Separate Unit?" *VT* 20 (1970) 496–500.
Oesterly, W.O.E.
Studies in the Greek and Latin Versions of the Book of Amos (Cambridge: Cambridge University, 1902).
Rahmer, M.
Die Hebräische Traditionen in den Werken des Hieronymus. 2. Theil: Die Commentarien zu den XII Kleinen Propheten. III. Amos (Berlin: Poppelauer, 1902).
Sawyer, H.F.A.
"'Those Priests in Damascus': A Possible Example of Anti-Sectarian Polemic in the Septuagint-Version of Amos 3:12," *ASTI* 8 (1970–1971) 123–30.
Seboek, M.
Die Syrische Übersetzung der Zwölf kleinen Propheten und ihr Verhältnis zu dem Masoretischen Text und zu den Älteren Übersetzungen, namentlich dem LXX und den Targum (diss.; Leipzig, 1887).
Tov, E.
"Loan-Words, Homophony, and Transliterations in the Septuagint," *Bib* 60 (1979) 216–36.
Treitel, L.
"Wert und Bedeutung der LXX zu den Zwölf Kleinen Propheten," *MGWJ* 73 (1929) 232–34.

Turner, P.D.M.
"Anoikodomein and Intra-Septuagintal Borrowing," *VT* 27 (1977) 492–93.
Idem
"Two Septuagintalisms with STHRIZEIN," *VT* 28 (1978) 481–82.
Vater, J. S.
Amos übersetzt und erläutert mit Beifügung des Hebräischen Textes und des Griechischen des Septuaginta (Halle: Hemmerde & Schwetschke, 1810).
Vollers, K.
"Das Dodekapropheton der Alexandriner," *ZAW* 3 (1883) 219–72.
de Waard, J.
"A Greek Translation-Technical Treatment of Amos 1:15," *On Language, Culture and Religion: In Honor of Eugene A. Nida* (ed. M. Black and W. A. Smalley; Approaches to Semiotics 56; Den Hague: Mouton, 1974) 111–18.
Idem
"Translation Techniques Used by the Greek Translators of Amos," *Bib* 59 (1978) 339–50.
Ziegler, J.
Die Einheit der Septuaginta zum Zwölfprophetenbuch (Lectures delivered at Braunsberg, Staatliche Akademie: 1934–1935).
Idem
"Studien zur Verwertung der Septuaginta im Zwölfprophetenbuch," *ZAW* 60 (1944) 107–30.
Idem, ed.
Duodecim Prophetae (Septuaginta Vetus Testamentum 13; Göttingen: Vandenhoeck & Ruprecht, 1963, [2]1967).

14. Verses

1:1

Bič, M.
"Der Prophet Amos—Ein Haepatoskopos?" *VT* 1 (1951) 293–96.
Idem
"*Maštîn BᵉQîr*," *VT* 4 (1954) 411–16.
Budde, K.
"Die Überschrift des Buches Amos und des Propheten Heimat," *Semitic Studies in Memory of Rev. Dr. Alexander Kohut* (ed. G. A. Kohut; Berlin: Calvary, 1897) 106–10.
Craigie, P. C.
"Amos the *noqed* in the Light of Ugaritic," *SR* 11 (1982) 29–33.
Dietrich, M., and O. Loretz
"Die ugaritische Berufsgruppe der *NQDM* und das Amt des *RB NQDM*," *UF* 9 (1977) 336–37.
Fuhs, H. F.
"Amos 1,1. Erwägungen zur Tradition und Redaktion des Amosbuches," *Bausteine Biblischer Theologie. Festgabe für G. J. Botterweck* (ed. H.-J. Fabry; BBB 50; Bonn: Hanstein, 1977) 271–89.
Isbell, C. D.
"A Note on Amos 1:1," *JNES* 36 (1977) 213–14.
Klein, S.
"תקוע in Galilea," *MGWJ* 67 (1922) 270–73.
Luria, B. Z.
"Teqoa—The City of Amos," *Sepher E. Auerbach* (ed. A. Biram; Jerusalem: Kiryat Sepher, 1956) 104–15 (Heb.).
Meek, T. J.
"The Accusative of Time in Amos 1:1," *JAOS* 61 (1941) 63–64, 190–91.
Murtonen, A.
"The Prophet Amos—A Hepatoscoper?" *VT* 2 (1952) 170–71.
Peiser, F. E.
"שנתים לפני הרעש—Eine Philologische Studie," *ZAW* 36 (1916) 218–24.
Segert, S.
"Zur Bedeutung des Wortes *nōqēd*," *Hebräische Wortforschung: Festschrift zum 80. Geburtstag von Walter Baumgartner* (ed. B. Hartmann and others; SVT 16; Leiden: Brill, 1967) 279–83.
Soggin, J. A.
"Das Erdbeben von Amos 1,1 und die Chronologie der Könige Ussia und Jotham von Judah," *ZAW* 82 (1970) 117–21.
Stamm, J. J.
"Der Name des Propheten Amos und sein sprachlicher Hintergrund," *Prophecy: Essays Presented to Georg Fohrer on His Sixty-fifth Birthday, 6 September 1980* (ed. J. A. Emerton; BZAW 150; Berlin/ New York: de Gruyter, 1980) 137–42.
Wright, T. J.
"Did Amos Inspect Livers?" *AusBR* 23 (1975) 3–11.
Yamashita, T.
"Noqed," *Ras Shamra Parallels: The Texts from Ugarit and the Hebrew Bible* (ed. L. R. Fisher; AnOr 50; Rome: Pontifical Biblical Institute, 1975) 2:63–64.

1:2

Bertholet, A.
"Zu Amos 1:2," *Theologische Festschrift G. Nathanael Bonwetsch zu seinem 70. Geburtstag* (Leipzig: Deichert, 1918) 1–12.
Budde, K.
"Amos 1:2," *ZAW* 30 (1910) 37–41.
Loewenstamm, S. E.
"Some Remarks on Biblical Passages in the Light of Their Akkadian Parallels," *Bible Studies, Y. M. Grintz in Memoriam* (ed. B. Uffenheimer; *Te'uda* 2; Tel Aviv: Tel Aviv University, 1982) 187–96 (Heb.).
van Leeuwen, C.
"Amos 1:2—Epigraphe du livre entier ou introduction aux oracles des chapitres 1–2?" *Verkenningen in een Stroomgebied: proeven van oudtestamentisch onderzoek* (*Studies in Honor of M. A. Beek*; ed. M. Boertien; Amsterdam, 1974) 93–101.

Weiss, M.
"On the Traces of a Biblical Metaphor," *Tarbiz* 34 (1964–1965) 107–28, 211–23, 303–18 (Heb.).
Idem
"Methodologisches über die Behandlung der Metapher, dargelegt an Amos 1:2," *TZ* 23 (1967) 1–25.

1:2–2:16

Beaucamp, P.-E.
"Amos I–II, Le Pesha d'Israël et celui des nations," *ScEs* 29 (1969) 435–41.
Idem
"Amos 1–2: O Peshà de Israël e o das Naciones," *Atualidades Bíblicas: Miscelânea em memória de Frei João José Pedreira de Castro, O.F.M.* (ed. S. Voigt and F. Vier; São Paolo: Editôra Vozes, 1971) 325–30.
Bentzen, A.
"The Ritual Background of Amos i 2—ii 16," *OTS* 8 (Leiden: Brill, 1950) 85–99.
Christensen, D. L.
"The Prosodic Structure of Amos 1—2," *HTR* 67 (1974) 427–36.
Condamin, A.
"Amos 1:2—3:8, Authenticité et structure poétique," *RevScRel* 20 (1930) 298–311.
Pfeifer, G.
"Denkformenanalyse als exegetische Methode, erläutert an Amos 1,2—2,16," *ZAW* 88 (1976) 56–71.

1:3

Soggin, A.
"Amos 6:13–14 und 1:3 auf dem Hintergrund der Beziehungen zwischen Israel und Damaskus im 9. und 8. Jahrhundert," *Near Eastern Studies in Honor of W. F. Albright* (ed. H. Goedicke; Baltimore/London: Johns Hopkins University, 1971) 433–41.
Soper, B. K.
"For Three Transgressions and for Four. A New Interpretation of Amos 1:3, etc.," *ExpTim* 71 (1959–1960) 86–87.
Zorell, F.
"Zu Amos 1:3, 6, usw.," *Bib* 6 (1925) 171–73.

1:3–2:3

Marti, K.
"Zur Komposition von Amos 1:3—2:3," *Abhandlungen zur Semitischen Religionskunde und Sprachwissenschaft: W. W. G. von Baudissin zum 26. September 1917* (BZAW 33; Giessen: Töpelmann, 1918) 323–30.
Paul, S. M.
"Amos 1:3—2:3: A Concatenous Literary Pattern," *JBL* 90 (1971) 397–403.

1:3–2:6

Barré, M. L.
"The Meaning of *l' 'šybnw* in Amos 1:3–2:6," *JBL* 105 (1986) 611–31.
Knierim, R.
"'I Will Not Cause It to Return' in Amos 1 and 2," *Canon and Authority: Essays in Old Testament Religion and Theology* (ed. G. W. Coats and B. O. Long; Philadelphia: Fortress, 1977) 163–75.

1:3–2:8

Segert, S.
"A Controlling Device for Copying Stereotype Passages (Amos I 3—II 8, VI 1–6)," *VT* 34 (1984) 481–82.

1:4

Höffken, P.
"Eine Bemerkung zum 'Haus Hasaels' in Amos 1:4," *ZAW* 94 (1982) 413–15.

1:5

Eitan, I.
"Biblical Studies II: Stray Notes to Minor Prophets (Amos 1:5, 8)," *HUCA* 14 (1939) 6.
Malamat, A.
"Amos 1:5 in the Light of the Til Barsip Inscriptions," *BIES* 16 (1951) 42–45 (Heb.) = *BASOR* 129 (1953) 25–26.
Tsumura, D. T.
"'Inserted Bicolon,' The AXYB Pattern in Amos I 5 and Psalm IX 7," *VT* 38 (1988) 234–36.
Winckler, H.
"Einzelnes. Am 1,5—Am 1,6.9," *Alttestamentliche Untersuchungen* (Leipzig: Pfeiffer, 1892) 183–84.

1:6

Grintz, Y. M.
"Because They Exiled a Whole Exile to Deliver to Edom," *BM* 32 (1967) 24–26 (Heb.); rep. in *Moṣa'ey Doroth* (Tel Aviv: Tel Aviv University, 1969) 354–56 (Heb.).
Haupt, P.
"Scriptio Plena des emphatischen *la*- im Hebräischen," *OLZ* 10 (1907) 308.
Idem
"Heb. *galûṯ šōlemâ*, a Peaceful Colony," *JBL* 35 (1916) 288–92.
Zorell, F.
"Zu Amos 1:3, 6, usw.," *Bib* 6 (1925) 171–73.

1:8

Eitan, I.
"Biblical Studies II: Stray Notes to Minor Prophets (Amos 1:5, 8)," *HUCA* 14 (1939) 6.

1:9

Priest, J.
"The Covenant of Brothers," *JBL* 84 (1965) 400–406.

1:9–10

Cazelles, H.
"L'arrière-plan historique d'Amos 1:9–10," *Proceedings of the Sixth World Congress of Jewish Studies* (3 vols.; Jerusalem: World Union of Jewish Studies, 1977) 1.71–76.
Müller, H.-P.
"Phönizien und Juda in exilisch-nachexilischer Zeit," *WO* 6/2 (1971) 189–204.

1:11

Barré, M. L.
"Amos 1:11 Reconsidered," *CBQ* 47 (1985) 420–27.

Coote, R. B.
"Amos 1:11: *RḤMYW*," *JBL* 90 (1971) 206–8.

Fishbane, M.
"The Treaty Background of Amos 1,11 and Related Matters," *JBL* 89 (1970) 313–18.

Idem
"Additional Remarks on *RḤMYW*," *JBL* 91 (1972) 391–93.

Sperber, D.
"Varia Midrashica IV. 1: Esau and His Mother's Womb—A Note on Amos 1:11," *REJ* 137 (1978) 149–53.

1:13

Burn, P.
"Conjectures on Some Minor Prophets," *ExpTim* 38 (1926–1927) 377–78.

Cogan, M.
"'Ripping Open Pregnant Women' in Light of an Assyrian Analogue," *JAOS* 103 (1983) 755–57.

Reider, J.
"Etymological Studies in Biblical Hebrew (Amos 1:13)," *VT* 4 (1954) 276–95.

1:15

Puech, E.
"Milkom, le dieu Ammonite, en Amos 1:15," *VT* 27 (1977) 117–25.

2:1

Braslavi, J.
"*dwd h'ṣym, 'ṣmwt lsyd, msrpwt syd*," *BM* 13 (1962) 34–36 (Heb.).

2:2

Praetorius, F.
"Zum Texte des Amos," *ZAW* 34 (1914) 42.

Winckler, H.
"Einzelnes. Am 2,2," *Alttestamentliche Untersuchungen* (Leipzig: Pfeiffer, 1892) 184.

2:6

Box, G. H.
"Amos II, 6 and VIII, 6," *ExpTim* 12 (1900–1901) 377–78.

Gordis, R.
"*Na'alam* and Other Observations on the Ain Feshka Scrolls," *JNES* 9 (1950) 44–47.

Lang, B.
"Sklaven und Unfreie im Buch Amos (II, 6; VIII, 6)," *VT* 31 (1981) 482–86.

Speiser, E. A.
"Of Shoes and Shekels (1 Samuel 12:3; 13:21)," *BASOR* 77 (1940) 15–20; rep. in *Oriental and Biblical Studies. Collected Writings of E. A. Speiser* (ed. J. J. Finkelstein and M. Greenberg; Philadelphia: University of Pennsylvania, 1967) 151–59.

2:6-8

Beek, M. A.
"The Religious Background of Amos 2:6–8," *OTS* 5 (Leiden: Brill, 1948) 132–41.

2:6-16

Happel, O.
"Amos 2:6–16 in der Urgestalt," *BZ* 3 (1905) 355–67.

Schwantes, M.
"Profecia e Organização: Anotações à luz de um texto (Am 2, 6–16)," *EstBíb* 5 (1985) 26–39.

2:7

Bewer, J. A.
"Critical Notes on Amos 2:7 and 8:4," *AJSL* 19 (1902–1903) 116–17.

Idem
"Note on Amos 2:7a," *JBL* 28 (1909) 200–202.

Bronznick, N. M.
"More on *HLK 'L*," *VT* 35 (1985) 98–99.

Delekat, L.
"Zum hebräischen Wörterbuch," *VT* 14 (1964) 44–45.

Ginsberg, H. L.
"Some Notes on Minor Prophets," Eretz Israel 3 (*U.M.D. Cassuto Memorial Volume*; ed. B. Mazar and others; Jerusalem: Israel Exploration Society, 1954) 83–84 (Heb.).

Orlinsky, H. M., and M. Weinberg
"The Masorah on ענוים in Amos 2:7," *Estudios Masoréticos (V Congreso de la IOMS) Dedicados a Harry M. Orlinsky* (ed. E. F. Tejero; Textos y Estudios "Cardenal Cisneros" 33; Madrid: Institut "Arias Montano," 1983) 25–35.

Paul, S. M.
"Two Cognate Semitic Terms for Mating and Copulation," *VT* 32 (1982) 492–94.

Torczyner, H.
"Dunkle Bibelstellen. Am. 2:7," *Vom Alten Testament: Karl Marti zum siebzigsten Geburtstag* (ed. K. Budde; BZAW 41; Giessen: Töpelmann, 1925) 278–79.

Torrey, C. C.
"Notes on Amos 2:7, 6:10, 8:3, 9:8–10," *JBL* 15 (1896) 151–54.

Zolli, I.
"Note Esegetiche (Amos 2:7a)," *RSO* 16 (1936) 178–83.

2:8

Dahood, M. J.
"To Pawn One's Cloak," *Bib* 42 (1961) 359–66.

Joüon, P.
"Notes de lexicographie hébraïque. 9. ענושים = exaction," *MUSJ* 4 (1910) 9.

Oesterley, W.O.E.
"Pledged Clothes," *ExpTim* 13 (1901–1902) 40–41.

2:9

Ginsberg, H. L.
"'Roots Below and Fruit Above' and Related Matters," *Hebrew and Semitic Studies Presented to G. R. Driver* (ed. D. W. Thomas and W. D. McHardy; Oxford: Clarendon, 1963) 72–76.

Noth, M.
"Der Gebrauch von אמרי im alten Testament," *ZAW* 58 (1940–1941) 182–89.

2:10

Hobbs, T. R.
"Amos 3:1b and 2:10," *ZAW* 81 (1969) 384–87.

2:11

Weiss, M.
"'And I Raised Up Prophets from amongst Your Sons'—A Note about the History and Character of Israelite Prophecy," *Isac Leo Seeligmann Volume: Essays in the Bible and the Ancient World* (ed. A. Rofé and Y. Zakovitch; 3 vols.; Jerusalem: E. Rubinstein, 1983) 1.257–74 (Heb.).

2:13

Farmer, G.
"Note on the Emendation of Amos ii,13 (A.V.) proposed in Q.S., 1912, p. 102," *PEFQS* (1912) 159.

Gese, H.
"Kleine Beiträge zum Verständnis des Amosbuches," *VT* 12 (1962) 417–38.

Joüon, P.
"Notes de lexicographie hébraïque. 7. עוק = osciller," *MUSJ* 4 (1910) 8.

Müller, H.-P.
"Die Wurzeln עיק, יעק, und עוק," *VT* 21 (1971) 556–64.

Wetzstein, J. G.
"Briefliche Bemerkungen von Consul Dr. J. G. Wetzstein," *ZAW* 3 (1883) 278–79.

Wilbers, H.
"Étude sur trois textes relatifs à l'agriculture: Isa 28:27–28; Amos 2:13; 9:9," *MUSJ* 5 (1911–1912) 269–82.

2:13–16

Richardson, H. N.
"Amos 2:13–16: Its Structure and Function in the Book," in SBLASP I (Missoula, MT: Scholars, 1978) 361–67.

2:14–16

Rendtorff, R.
"Zu Amos 2:14–16," *ZAW* 85 (1973) 226–27.

2:16

Winckler, H.
"Einzelnes. Am 2,16," *Alttestamentliche Untersuchungen* (Leipzig: Pfeiffer, 1892) 184–85.

Chapters 3—6

Jörg, J.
"Amos 3—6. Beoachtungen zur Entstehungsgeschichte eines Prophetenbuches," *ZAW* 100 (1988) 123–37.

3:1

Hobbs, T. R.
"Amos 3:1b and 2:10," *ZAW* 81 (1969) 384–87.

3:1–2

Boehmer, I.
"Ad Amos 3, 1–2," *Teologisk Tidsskrift* 4 (1929) 96–98.

Janssen, H.
Voorliefde en verantwoordelijkheid—Een eksegetische studie over Amos 3,1–2 en 9,7 (Utrecht: Theological Institute, 1975).

3:1–15

Gitay, Y.
"A Study of Amos's Art of Speech: A Rhetorical Analysis of Amos 3:1–15," *CBQ* 42 (1980) 293–309.

3:2

Katzoff, L.
"Noblesse Oblige," *Dor le-Dor* 16 (1987–1988) 213–16.

Vriezen, T. C.
"Erwägungen zu Amos 3:2," *Archäologie und Altes Testament: Festschrift für Kurt Galling* (ed. A. Kuschke and E. Kutsch; Tübingen: Mohr, 1970) 255–58.

3:3

Thomas, D. W.
"Note on נועדו in Amos 3:3," *JTS* 7 (1956) 69–70.

3:3–8

Baumgartner, W.
"Amos 3,3–8," *ZAW* 33 (1913) 78–80.

Daiches, S.
"Amos III, 3–8," *ExpTim* 26 (1914–1915) 237.

Eichrodt, W.
"Die Vollmacht des Amos. Zu einer schwierigen Stelle im Amosbuch 3:3–8," *Beiträge zur alttestamentlichen Theologie: Festschrift für Walther Zimmerli zum 70. Geburtstag* (ed. H. Donner; Göttingen: Vandenhoeck & Ruprecht, 1977) 124–31.

Gese, H.
"Kleine Beiträge zum Verständnis des Amosbuches," *VT* 12 (1962) 417–38.

Holwerda, B.
De Exegese van Amos 3,3–8 (Kampen: Kok, 1948).

Junker, H.
"'Leo rugiet, quis non timebit? Deus locutus est, quis non prophetabit?' Eine textkritische und exegetische Untersuchung über Amos 3:3–8," *TTZ* 59 (1950) 4–13.

Mittmann, S.
"Gestalt und Gehalt einer prophetischen Selbstrechtfertigung (Amos 3,3–8)," *TQ* 151 (1971) 134–45.

Paul, S. M.
"Amos 3:3–8: The Irresistible Sequence of Cause and Effect," *Biblical and Other Studies in Honor of Robert Gordis* (ed. R. Ahroni; *HAR* 7; Columbus: The Ohio State University, 1983) 203–20.

Pfeifer, G.
"Unausweichliche Konzequenzen. Denkformenanalyse von Amos III 3–8," *VT* 33 (1983) 341–47.

Renaud, B.
"Genèse et Théologie d'Amos 3,3–8," *Mélanges Bibliques et Orientaux en l'Honneur de M. Henri Cazelles* (ed. A. Caquot and M. Delcor; AOAT 212;

Neukirchen-Vluyn: Neukirchener Verlag, 1981) 353–72.
Schenker, A.
"Zur Interpretation von Amos 3,3–8," *BZ* 30 (1986) 250–56.
Shapiro, D. S.
"The Seven Questions of Amos," *Tradition* 20 (1982) 327–31.
3:4
Ashbel, D.
"Notes on the Prophecy of Amos: 'Does a Lion Raise His Voice from His Lair Unless He Has Caught Something?'" *BM* 25–26 (1965) 106–7 (Heb.).
Braslavi, J.
"'Does a Lion Roar in the Forest When He Has No Prey?'" *BM* 30 (1967) 12–16 (Heb.).
3:5
Ashbel, D.
"Notes on the Prophecy of Amos: 'Does a Bird Fall into a Trap . . .?'" *BM* 25–26 (1966) 103–4 (Heb.).
Gehman, H. S.
"Notes on מוקש," *JBL* 58 (1939) 277–81.
3:6
Mulder, M. J.
"Ein Vorschlag zur Übersetzung von Amos III 6b," *VT* 34 (1984) 106–8.
3:9
Joüon, P.
"Notes de lexicographie hébraïque. 12. מהומה pour *מאומה dans Ez. 22:5; Am. 3:9; Prov. 15:16," *MUSJ* 10 (1925) 16–17.
Winckler, H.
"Einzelnes. Am 3,9," *Alttestamentliche Untersuchungen* (Leipzig: Pfeiffer, 1892) 185.
3:9–11
Pfeifer, G.
"Die Denkform des Propheten Amos (III:9–11)," *VT* 34 (1984) 476–81.
3:11
Pelser, H. S.
"Amos 3:11—a Communication," *Studies in the Books of Hosea and Amos: Die Ou Testamentiese Werkgemeenskap in Suid Afrika: 7th and 8th Congresses* (Potchefstroom: Rege-Pers Beperk, 1964–1965) 153–56.
3:12
Gese, H.
"Kleine Beiträge zum Verständnis des Amosbuches," *VT* 12 (1962) 417–38.
Guillaume, A.
"Hebrew Notes: Amos 3,12," *PEQ* 79 (1947) 42–44.
Loretz, O.
"Vergleich und Kommentar in Amos 3:12," *BZ* 20 (1976) 122–25.
Moeller, H. A.
"Ambiguity of Amos 3:12," *BT* 15 (1964) 31–34.
Pfeifer, G.
"'Rettung' als Beweis der Vernichtung (Amos 3,12)," *ZAW* 100 (1988) 269–77.
Rabinowitz, I.
"The Crux at Amos III:12," *VT* 11 (1961) 228–31.
Reider, J.
"דמשק" in Amos 3:12," *JBL* 67 (1948) 245–48.
3:12–15
Mittmann, S.
"Amos 3:12–15 und das Bett der Samarier," *ZDPV* 92 (1976) 149–67.
3:13
Praetorius, F.
"Zum Texte des Amos," *ZAW* 34 (1914) 42–44.
3:15
Glanzman, G. S.
"Two Notes: Amos 3:15 and Hosea 11:8–9," *CBQ* 23 (1961) 227–33.
Paul, S. M.
"Amos III 15—Winter and Summer Mansions," *VT* 28 (1978) 358–60.
Schlesinger, S.
"Zu Am. 3, 15," *MGWJ* 67 (1923) 137.
4:1
Barstad, H. M.
"Die Basankühe in Amos 4:1," *VT* 25 (1975) 286–97.
Jacobs, P. F.
"'Cows of Bashan'—A Note on the Interpretation of Amos 4:1," *JBL* 104 (1985) 109–10.
Maisler, B.
"Die Landschaft Basan im 2. Vorchr. Jahrtausend," *JPOS* 9 (1929) 80–87.
Mazar, E.
"Archeological Evidence for the 'Cows of Bashan Who Are in the Mountain of Samaria,'" *Festschrift Reuben R. Hecht: Studies in Honor of His 70th Birthday* (ed. B. Akzin and others; Jerusalem: Koren Publishers, 1979) 151–57.
4:1–3
Bauer, L.
"Einige Stellen des Alten Testaments . . . Amos 4:1–3," *TSK* 100 (1927–1928) 437–38.
Watts, J.D.W.
"A Critical Analysis of Amos 4:1ff.," SBLASP 108 (Missoula, MT: Scholars, 1972) 489–500.
Williams, A. J.
"A Further Suggestion about Amos IV 1–3," *VT* 29 (1979) 206–11.
4:2
Luria, B. Z.
"Amos 4:2," *BM* 30 (1967) 6–11 (Heb.).
Paul, S. M.
"Fishing Imagery in Amos 4:2," *JBL* 97 (1978) 183–90.
Praetorius, F.
"Zum Texte des Amos," *ZAW* 34 (1914) 42–43.
Schwantes, S. J.
"Note on Amos 4:2b," *ZAW* 79 (1967) 82–83.

Zolli, E.
"Amos 4:2b," *Anton* 30 (1955) 188–89.

4:3

Freedman, D. N., and F. I. Anderson
"*Harmon* in Amos 4:3," *BASOR* 198 (1970) 41.

Glueck, J. J.
The Verb פרץ in the Bible and in the Qumran Literature," *RevQ* 5 (1964–1965) 123–27.

4:4

Barth, C.
"Theophanie, Bundschliessung und neuer Anfang am Dritten Tage," *EvT* 28 (1968) 521–33.

4:4–13

Brueggemann, W.
"Amos 4:4–13 and Israel's Covenant Worship," *VT* 15 (1965) 1–15.

4:6

Dahood, M.
"Hebrew-Ugaritic Lexicography V," *Bib* 48 (1967) 421–38.

Goldman, M. D.
"The Root '*NQY*,'" *AusBR* 4 (1954–1955) 49–55.

4:6–12

Crenshaw, J. L.
"A Liturgy of Wasted Opportunity (Amos 4:6–12; Isa. 9:7–10; 4; 5:25–29)," *Semitics* 1 (1970) 27–37.

4:6–13

Rudolph, W.
"Amos 4:6–13," *Wort-Gebot-Glaube: Beiträge zum Theologie des Alten Testaments, Walter Eichrodt zum 80. Geburtstag* (ed. H. J. Stoebe; ATANT 59; Zürich: Zwingli, 1970) 27–38.

Tsvi, C.
"Notes on the Books of the Prophets," *Sinai* 33 (1957) 270–74 (Heb.).

Weiser, A.
"Zu Amos 4:6–13," *ZAW* 46 (1928) 49–59.

4:10

Speier, S.
"Did Rashi Have a Different Vorlage in Amos 4,10 Than Is Found in the Usual Edition?" *Leš* 33 (1969) 15–17 (Heb.).

4:12

Ramsey, G. W.
"Amos 4:12—A New Perspective," *JBL* 89 (1970) 187–91.

Youngblood, R.
"לקראת in Amos 4:12," *JBL* 90 (1971) 98.

4:13

Coppens, J.
Amos IV 13. Een Nieuwe Lezing (Mendelingen van de Koninklijke Vlaamse Academie voor Wetenschappen, Letteren in Schonekunsten van Belgie Klasse der Lettern 14/4; Brussels, 1952).

Devescovi, U.
"Camminare sulle altare," *RivB* 9 (1961) 235–42.

Köhler, L.
"Die Morgenröte im alten Testament," *ZAW* 44 (1926) 56–59.

Mowinckel, S.
"The Verb שׂיח and the Nouns שׂיח, שׂיחה," *ST* 15 (1961) 1–10.

Müller, H.-P.
"Die hebräische Wurzel שׂיח," *VT* 19 (1969) 361–71.

5:1–17

Berridge, J. M.
"Die Intention der Botschaft des Amos. Exegetische Überlegungen zu Amos 5," *TZ* 32 (1976) 321–40.

Tromp, N. J.
"Amos V 1–17. Towards a Stylistic and Rhetorical Analysis," *Prophets, Worship, and Theodicy* (*OTS* 23; Leiden: Brill, 1984) 56–84.

de Waard, J.
"The Chiastic Structure of Amos V: 1–17," *VT* 27 (1977) 170–77.

Wilcke, D. W.
"Two Perspectives (Amos 5:1–17)," *CurTM* 13 (1986) 89–96.

5:4–6

Hesse, F.
"Amos 5:4–6, 14f.," *ZAW* 68 (1956) 1–17.

Lust, J.
"Remarks on the Redaction of Amos V 4–6, 14–15," *Remembering All the Way* (ed. A.S. van der Woude; *OTS* 21; Leiden: Brill, 1981) 129–54.

5:4–15

Neubauer, K. W.
"Erwägungen zu Amos 5:4–15," *ZAW* 78 (1966) 292–316.

5:6

Tawil, H.
"Hebrew הצלח / צלח, Akkadian *ešēru* / *šūšuru*. A Lexicographical Note," *JBL* 95 (1976) 405–13.

5:6–7

Ciric, I.
"Zu Amos 5:6 und 7," *BZ* 8 (1910) 133–34.

5:7

Watts, D. W.
"Note on the Text of Amos V:7," *VT* 4 (1954) 215–16.

5:7–17

Gese, H.
"Kleine Beiträge zum Verständnis des Amosbuches," *VT* 12 (1962) 417–38.

5:8

Eitan, I.
"Biblical Studies II: Stray Notes to Minor Prophets," *HUCA* 14 (1939) 6.

Luria, B. Z.
"'Who Calls the Water of the Sea and Spills Them on the Face of the Earth' (Amos 5:8; 9:6)," *BM* 101 (1984–1985) 259–62 (Heb.).

5:9

Driver, G. R.
"Two Astronomical Passages in the Old Testament," *JTS* 4 (1953) 208–12.

Montgomery, J. A.
"Notes on the Old Testament (6. מבליג, Amos 5:9)," *JBL* 31 (1912) 143.

Yellin, D.
"Forgotten Meanings of Hebrew Roots in the Bible. 4. בלג," *Jewish Studies in Memory of Israel Abrahams* (ed. D. Wright; New York: Jewish Institute of Religion, 1927) 441–58.

Zalcman, L.
"Astronomical Illusions in Amos," *JBL* 100 (1981) 53–58.

5:11

Dietrich, M., and O. Loretz
"Ug. *'*BŠ*, *ṮBŠ*, hebr. **ŠBS* (Am. 5,11) sowie ug. *ṮŠY* und *ŠBŠ*," *UF* 10 (1978) 434–35.

Fenton, T. L.
"Ugaritica—Biblica," *UF* 1 (1969) 65–70.

5:13

Jackson, J. J.
"Amos 5,13: Contextually Understood," *ZAW* 98 (1986) 434–35.

Maag, V.
"Zur Übersetzung von *Maśkil* in Amos 5.13, Ps 47.8, und in den Überschriften einiger Psalmen," SThU 12 (1943) 108–15.

Ruiz, G.
"Amos 5:13: Prudencia en la denuncia Profetica?" *CB* 25 (1973) 347–52.

Sellin, E.
"Drei umstrittene Stellen des Amosbuches," *ZDPV* 52 (1929) 141–48.

Smith, G. V.
"Amos 5:13—The Deadly Silence of the Prosperous," *JBL* 107 (1988) 289–91.

van der Wal, A.
"Amos 5.13—Een omstreder texst," *NorTT* 41 (1987) 89–98.

5:14

Burais, T.
"Amos 5:14," *ST* 19 (1967) 492–503.

5:14–15

Hesse, F.
"Amos 5:4–6, 14f.," *ZAW* 68 (1956) 1–17.

Lust, J.
"Remarks on the Redaction of Amos V 4–6, 14–15," *Remembering All the Way* (ed. A. S. van der Woude; *OTS* 21; Leiden: Brill, 1981) 129–54.

5:15

Neubauer, K. W.
Der Stamm חנן *im Sprachgebrauch des AT* (diss; Berlin, 1964).

5:16–17

Joüon, P.
"Notes de critique textuelle—Amos 5:16–17," *MUSJ* 4 (1910) 30.

5:17

Hauan, M. J.
"The Background and Meaning of Amos 5:17B," *HTR* 79 (1986) 337–48.

5:18–20

Hirota, K.
An Interpretation of Amos 5, 18–20 (Tokyo: St. Paul's/Rikkyo University, 1978).

Smelik, K.A.D.
"The Meaning of Amos V 18–20," *VT* 36 (1986) 246–48.

5:18–27

Vaikinger, J. G.
"Erklärung schwieriger Stellen des alten Testamentes. V. Amos 5, 18–27," *Archiv für Wissenschaftliche Erforschung des Alten Testaments* 1 (1870) 486–88.

5:21

Kutsch, E.
"Die Wurzel עצר im Hebräischen," *VT* 2 (1952) 57–69.

5:21–27

Sacon, K. K.
"Amos 5, 21–27—An Exegetical Study," *The Bible, Its Thoughts, History and Language: Essays in Honor of Masao Sekine* (ed. S. Arai; Tokyo: Yamamoto Shoten, 1972) 278–99.

Würthwein, E.
"Amos 5:21–27," *TLZ* 72 (1947) 143–52; rep. in *Wort und Existenz: Studien zum Alten Testament* (Göttingen: Vandenhoeck & Ruprecht, 1970) 55–67.

5:22

Loretz, O.
"*Šlm* in Am. 5,22 und das *šlmjm* Opfer," *UF* 13 (1981) 127–31.

5:23–24

Hyatt, J. P.
"The Translation and Meaning of Amos 5,23–24," *ZAW* 68 (1956) 17–24.

5:25

Dobbie, R.
"Amos 5:25," *Transactions of the Glasgow University Oriental Society* 17 (1957–1958) 62–64.

5:25–26

van der Woude, A. S.
"Bemerkungen zu einigen umstrittenen Stellen im Zwölfprophetenbuch. Amos 5:25–26," *Mélanges Bibliques et Orientaux en l'Honneur de M. Henri Cazelles* (ed. A. Caquot and M. Delcor; AOAT 212; Neukirchen-Vluyn: Neukirchener Verlag, 1981) 485–90.

Williamson, H. A.
"Rendering of Amos V, 25–26," *ExpTim* 36 (1924–1925) 430–31.

5:25–27

Erlandsson, S.
"Amos 5,25–27, ett crux interpretum," *SEÅ* 33 (1968) 76–82.

Schmidt, N.
"On the Text and Interpretation of Amos 5:25–27," *JBL* 13 (1894) 1–15.

5:26
Artzi, P.
"Sikkuth and Chiun," *EncJud* 14.1531.
Borger, R.
"Amos 5,26, Apostelgeschichte 7,43 und Šurpu II, 180," *ZAW* 100 (1988) 70–81.
Burrows, E.
"Cuneiform and the Old Testament: Three Notes (I. *Sakkūt* in Amos)," *JTS* 28 (1926–1927) 184–85.
Driver, G. R.
"Glosses in the Hebrew Text of the Old Testament," *L'Ancien Testament et L'Orient* (ed. G. Ryckmans; Leuven: Universitaires Instituut voor Orientalisme, 1957) 140–43.
Fenton, T. L.
"Sikkuth," *EM* 5.1037 (Heb.).
Gevirtz, S.
"A New Look at an Old Crux: Amos 5:26," *JBL* 87 (1968) 267–76.
Graf, K. H.
"Über Amos V,26," *Archiv für Wissenschaftliche Erforschung des Alten Testaments* 2 (1870) 93–96.
Isbell, C. D.
"Another Look at Amos 5:26," *JBL* 97 (1978) 97–99.
Loretz, O.
"Die babylonischen Gottesnamen *Sukkut* und *Kajjamanu*. Ein Beitrag zur jüdischen Astrologie," *ZAW* 101 (1989) 286–90.
Muss-Arnolt, W.
"Amos V, 26 (21–27)," *The Expositor*, Sixth Series, (1900) 2, 414–28.
Speiser, E. A.
"Note on Amos 5:26," *BASOR* 108 (1947) 5–6.
Torrey, C. C.
"On the Text of Amos V.26, VI.1–2, VII. 2," *JBL* 13 (1894) 61–63.
5:26–27
von der Osten-Sacken, P.
"Die Bücher der Tora als Hütte der Gemeinde—Amos 5,26f. in der Damaskusschrift," *ZAW* 91 (1979) 423–35.
6:1
Holladay, W. L.
"Amos VI 1B: A Suggested Solution," *VT* 22 (1972) 107–10.
Praetorius, F.
"Zum Texte Amos," *ZAW* 34 (1914) 43.
6:1–2
Torrey, C. C.
"On the Text of Amos V.26, VI.1–2, VII.2," *JBL* 13 (1894) 61–63.
6:1–6
Segert, S.
"A Controlling Device for Copying Stereotype Passages (Amos I 3—II 8, VI 1–6)," *VT* 34 (1984) 481–82.
6:2
Daiches, S.
"Amos VI.2," *ExpTim* 26 (1914–1915) 562–63.
6:4
Cohen, A.
"*Shen*," *BM* 23 (1978) 237–38 (Heb.).
6:4–7
Dentzer, J.-M.
"Aux origines de l'iconographie du banquet couché," *RArch* (1971) 215–58.
King, P. J.
"The *Marzeaḥ* Amos Denounces—Using Archaeology to Interpret a Biblical Text," *BAR* 15 (1988) 34–44.
6:5
Cheyne, T. K.
"The Witness of Amos to David as a Psalmist," *ExpTim* 9 (1897–1898) 334.
Elhorst, H. J.
"Miscellen 3: Amos VI, 5," *ZAW* 35 (1915) 62–63.
Freedman, D. N.
"But Did King David Invent Musical Instruments?" *Bible Review* 1 (1985) 49–51.
Lohmann, P.
"Einige Textkonjekturen zu Amos," *ZAW* 32 (1912) 274–77.
Montgomery, J. A.
"Notes from the Samaritan. 2. The Root פרט—Amos 6:5," *JBL* 25 (1906) 51–52.
6:6
Dahm, U.
"Zur Text- und Literarkritik von Amos 6,6a," BN 31 (1986) 7–10.
6:7–8
Braslavi, J.
"Jeremiah 16:5 and Amos 6:7," *BM* 48 (1971) 5–16 (Heb.).
Dahood, M.
"Amos 6,8 *m^{e}tā'ēb*," *Bib* 59 (1978) 265–66.
Eissfeldt, O.
"Etymologische und archäologische Erklärung alttestamentlicher Wörter," *OrAnt* 5 (1966) 165–76; rep. in *Kleine Schriften zum Alten Testament* (6 vols.; Tübingen: Mohr, 1962–1979) 4.285–96.
Idem
"מרזח and מרזחא 'Kultmahlgenossenschaft' im spätjüdischen Schrifttum," *Kleine Schriften zum Alten Testament* (6 vols.; Tübingen: Mohr, 1962–1979) 5.136–42.
Garbini, G.
"Note semitiche II," *Ricerche linguistiche* 5 (1962) 179–81.
Greenfield, J. C.
"The *Marzeaḥ* as a Social Institution," *AcAn* 22 (1974) 451–55.
Kutscher, Y.
Words and Their History (Jerusalem: Kiryat Sepher, 1968) 4–6 (Heb.).

Loretz, O.
"Ugaritisch-biblisch *mrzḥ* Kultmahl, Kultverein in Jer 16,5 und Am 6,7. Bemerkungen zur Geschichte des Totenkultes in Israel," *Künder des Wortes. Beiträge zur Theologie der Propheten: Joseph Schreiner zum 60. Geburtstag* (ed. L. Ruppert, P. Weimar, and E. Zenger; Würzburg: Echter, 1982) 87–93.

Meyer, R.
"Gegensinn und Mehrdeutigkeit in der althebräischen Wort- und Begriffsbildung," *UF* 11 (1979) 601–12.

Pope, M. A.
"Le *MRZḤ* à l'Ugarit et ailleurs," *Annales Archéologiqus Arabes Syriennes* 28/30 (1978–1980) 141–43.

6:9–10

Box, G. H., and W.O.E. Oesterley
"Amos VI, 9 and 10," *ExpTim* 12 (1900–1901) 235–36.

Lohmann, P.
"Einige Textkonjekturen zu Amos," *ZAW* 32 (1912) 276–77.

6:10

Ahlström, G. W.
"King Josiah and the *DWD* of Amos vi.10," *JSS* 26 (1981) 7–9.

Driver, G. R.
"A Hebrew Burial Custom," *ZAW* 66 (1954) 314–15.

Felsenthal, B.
"Zur Bibel und Grammatik—Zur Erklärung von Amos 6:10," *Semitic Studies in Memory of Alexander Kohut* (ed. G. A. Kohut; Berlin: Calvary, 1897) 133–38.

Kutscher, Y.
"Lexicographical Problems of Rabbinic Hebrew: 'He Who Anoints the Dead with Resin,'" *Leš* 21 (1957) 251–55 (Heb.); rep. in *Hebrew and Aramaic Studies* (ed. Z. Ben-Hayyim, A. Dotan, and G. Sarfatti; Jerusalem: Magnes, 1977) (Heb.).

Torrey, C. C.
"Notes on Amos 2,7; 6,10; 8,3; 9,8–10," *JBL* 15 (1896) 151–54.

6:11

Praetorius, F.
"Zum Texte des Amos," *ZAW* 34 (1914) 44.

6:12

Cooper, A.
"The Absurdity of Amos 6:12a," *JBL* 107 (1988) 725–27.

Dahood, M.
"'Can One Plow Without Oxen?' (Amos 6:12). A Study of *ba-* and *'al*," *The Bible World: Essays in Honor of C. H. Gordon* (ed. G. Rendsburg and others; New York: Ktav, 1980) 13–23.

Loretz, O.
"Amos VI 12," *VT* 39 (1989) 240–41.

6:13

Metzger, M.
"Lodebar und der Tell el-Mghannije," *ZDPV* 76 (1960) 97–102.

6:13–14

Soggin, J. A.
"Amos VI,13–14 und I,3 auf dem Hintergrund der Beziehungen zwischen Israel und Damaskus im 9. und 8. Jahrhundert," *Near Eastern Studies in Honor of W. F. Albright* (ed. H. Goedicke; Baltimore/London: Johns Hopkins University, 1971) 433–41.

6:14

Eissfeldt, O.
"Der Zugang zu Hamath," *OrAnt* 10 (1971) 269–76.

Mazar, B.
"Lebo-Hamath and the Northern Border of Canaan," *Bulletin of the Jewish Palestine Exploration Society* 12 (1946) 91–102 (Heb.); rep. in *Cities and Districts in Eretz-Israel* (ed. B. Mazar; Jerusalem: Bialik, 1975) 167–81 (Heb.).

7:1

Power, E.
"Note to Amos 7:1," *Bib* 8 (1927) 87–92.

Talmon, S.
"The Gezer Calendar and the Seasonal Cycle of Ancient Canaan," *JAOS* 83 (1963) 177–87; rep. and tr. in *BM* 29 (1967) 3–17 (Heb.).

van Leeuwen, C.
"Quelques problèmes de traduction dans les visions d'Amos chapitre 7," *Übersetzung und Deutung: Studien zu dem Alten Testament und seiner Umwelt, A. R. Hulst gewidmet von Freunden und Kollegen* (ed. H. A. Brongers and others; Nijkerk: Callenbuch, 1977) 103–12.

7:1–3

Ḥayuth, T. P.
"Amos' First Vision," *Hagoren* 5 (1936) 43–55 (Heb.).

7:1—8:3

Brin, G.
"The Visions of Amos (7:1–8:3): Studies in Structures and Ideas," *Isac Leo Seligmann Volume: Essays in the Bible and the Ancient World* (ed. A. Rofé and Y. Zakovitch; 3 vols.; Jerusalem: E. Rubinstein, 1983) 2. 275–90 (Heb.).

7:2

Mitchell, H. G.
"והיה of the Past," *JBL* 33 (1914) 48–55.

Montgomery, J. A.
"Notes on Amos," *JBL* 23 (1904) 95.

Rinaldi, G.
"Mi (Mj)," *BeO* 9 (1967) 118.

Seidel, T.
"Heuschreckenschwarm und Prophetenintervention. Textkritische und syntektische Erwägungen zu Amos 7,2," BN 37 (1987) 129–38.

Torrey, C. C.
"On the Text of Amos V,26; VI,1–2; VII,2," *JBL* 13 (1894) 61–63.

7:4

Hillers, D. R.
"Amos 7:4 and Ancient Parallels," *CBQ* 26 (1964) 221–25.

Limburg, J.
"Amos 7:4, A Judgment with Fire?" *CBQ* 35 (1973) 346–49.

Montgomery, J. A.
"Notes on Amos," *JBL* 23 (1904) 95–96.

Praetorius, F.
"Zum Texte des Amos," *ZAW* 34 (1914) 44.

Talmon, S.
"The Ugaritic Background of Amos 7:4," *Tarbiz* 35 (1965–1966) 301–3 (Heb.).

7:4-6

Ḥayuth, T. P.
"Amos' Second Vision," *Hagoren* 6 (1936) 77–87 (Heb.).

7:7-8

Holladay, W. L.
"Once More, אנך = 'tin,' Amos VII,7–8," *VT* 20 (1970) 492–94.

7:7-9

Brunet, G.
"La vision de l'étain, réinterpretation d'Amos VII,7–9," *VT* 16 (1966) 387–95.

Condamin, A.
"Le prétendu 'fil à plomb' de la vision d'Amos," *RB* 9 (1900) 586–94.

Cornet, P. B.
"Une 'crux' Amos VII, 7–9: אנך = bélier," *Études Franciscaines* 2 (1951) 61–83.

Ellenbogen, M.
Foreign Words in the Old Testament, Their Origin and Etymology (London: Luzac, 1962) 31–32.

Junker, H.
"Text und Bedeutung der Vision Amos 7:7–9," *Bib* 17 (1936) 359–64.

Landsberger, B.
"Tin and Lead: The Adventures of Two Vocables," *JNES* 24 (1965) 285–96.

Ouellette, J.
"Le mur d'étain d'Amos VII:7–9," *RB* 80 (1973) 321–31.

Rinaldi, G.
"De III et IV Visione Libri Amos," *VD* 17 (1937) 82–87, 114–16.

7:8

Mackenzie, H. S.
"The Plumb-Line (Amos 7:8)," *ExpTim* 60 (1949) 159.

Rinaldi, G.
"La parola *'anak*," BibOr 4 (Rome: Pontifical Biblical Institute, 1962) 83–84.

7:9

van Selms, A.
"Isaac in Amos," *Studies in the Books of Hosea and Amos: Die Ou Testamentiese Werkgemeenskap in Suid Afrika 7th and 8th Congresses* (Potchefstroom: Rege–Pers Beperk, 1964–1965) 157–65.

7:9-17

Ackroyd, P. R.
"A Judgment Narrative between Kings and Chronicles? An Approach to Amos 7:9–17," *Canon and Authority: Essays in Old Testament Religion and Theology* (ed. G. W. Coats and B. O. Long; Philadelphia: Fortress, 1977) 71–87.

Idem
Studies in the Religious Tradition of the Old Testament (London: SCM, 1987) 196–208.

7:10-17

Bjoerndalen, A. J.
"Erwägungen zur Zukunft des Amazja und Israels nach der Überlieferung Amos 7:10–17," *Werden und Wirken des Alten Testaments: Festschrift für Claus Westermann zum 70. Geburtstag* (ed. R. Albertz and others; Göttingen: Vandenhoeck & Ruprecht, 1980) 236–51.

Mallau, H. H.
"Las reacciones frente a los mensajes profeticos y el problema de la distincion entre profetas verdaderos y falsos. A proposito de Amos 7:10–17," *RivB* 34 (1972) 33–39.

Pfeifer, G.
"Die Ausweisung eines lästigen Ausländers. Amos 7:10–17," *ZAW* 96 (1984) 112–18.

Rost, L.
"Zu Amos 7:10–17," *Festgabe für Theodor Zahn* (Leipzig: Deichert, 1928) 229–36.

Stoebe, H. J.
"Noch einmal zu Amos VII,10–17," *VT* 39 (1989) 341–54.

Tucker, G. M.
"Prophetic Authenticity: A Form-Critical Study of Amos 7:10–17," *Int* 27 (1973) 423–34.

Utzschneider, H.
"Die Amazjaerzählung (Am 7,10–17) zwischen Literatur und Historie," BN 41 (1988) 76–101.

7:12-15

Hauret, C.
"La vocation d'un prophète. Am 7:12–15," *15e Dimanche ordinaire. Assemblées du Seigneurs* 2/46 (1974) 30–35.

7:12-17

Zevit, Z.
"A Misunderstanding at Bethel. Amos VII,12–17," *VT* 25 (1975) 783–90.

7:14

Abramski, S.
"'I Am Not a Prophet or a Son of a Prophet,'" *Studies in Bible Dedicated to the Memory of U. Cassuto on the 100th Anniversary of His Birth* (ed. S. E.

Loewenstamm; Jerusalem: Magnes, 1987) 64–68 (Heb.).
Ackroyd, P.
"Amos 7:14," *ExpTim* 68 (1956–1957) 94.
Ashbal, D.
"Notes to the Prophecy of Amos," *BM* 25–26 (1966) 103–7 (Heb.).
Bach, R.
"Erwägungen zu Amos 7, 14," *Die Botschaft und die Boten: Festschrift für Hans Walter Wolff* (ed. J. Jeremias and L. Perlitt; Neukirchen-Vluyn: Neukirchener Verlag, 1981) 203–16.
Bartina, S.
"Hiéndo los higos de los sicomoros," *EstBíb* 25 (1966) 349–54.
Bič, M.
"Der Prophet Amos—Ein Haepatoskopos?" *VT* 1 (1951) 293–96.
Idem
"*Maštîn Bᵉ Qîr*," *VT* 4 (1954) 413–15.
Braslavi, J.
"Amos—*Noqed, Boker,* and *Boles Shikmim*," *BM* 31 (1967) 87–101 (Heb.).
Cohen, S.
"Amos *Was* a Navi," *HUCA* 32 (1961) 175–78.
Danell, G. A.
"Var Amos verkligen en nabi?" *SEÅ* 16 (1951) 7–20.
Driver, G. R.
"Amos 7:14," *ExpTim* 67 (1955–1956) 91–92.
Idem
"*Waw* Explicative in Amos VII,14," *ExpTim* 68 (1956–1957) 302.
Idem
"Affirmation by Exclamatory Negation," *The Gaster Festschrift = JANESCU* 5 (ed. D. Marcus and others; New York: Columbia University, 1973) 107–14.
Galil, J.
"An Ancient Technique for Ripening Sycamore Fruit in East-Mediterranean Countries," *Economic Botany* 22 (1968) 178–90.
Galil, J., and D. Eisikowitch
"Flowery Cycles and Fruit Types of *Ficus Sycamorus* in Israel," *The New Phytologist* 67 (1968) 752–55.
Gunneweg, A.H.J.
"Erwägungen zu Amos, 7,14," *ZTK* 57 (1960) 1–16.
Haupt, P.
"Was Amos a Sheepman?" *JBL* 35 (1916) 280–87.
Herntrich, V.
"Das Berufungsbewusstsein des Amos," *CuW* 9 (1933) 161–76.
Hoffman, Y.
"Did Amos Regard Himself as a Nabi?" *VT* 27 (1977) 209–12.
Humbert, P.
"Amos VII, 14," *OLZ* 20 (1917) 296–98, 350; 21 (1918) 31.
Kapelrud, A. S.
"Propheten Amos og hans yrke," *NorTT* 59 (1958) 76–79.
Keimer, L.
"Eine Bemerkung zu Amos 7,14," *Bib* 8 (1927) 441–44.
MacCormack, J.
"Amos 7:14a, 'I Was (Am) No Prophet, Neither Was (Am) I a Prophet's Son,'" *ExpTim* 67 (1955–1956) 318.
Murtonen, A.
"The Prophet Amos—A Hepatoscoper?" *VT* 2 (1952) 170–71.
Richardson, H. N.
"A Critical Note on Amos 7,14," *JBL* 85 (1966) 89.
Roberts, J. J.
"A Note on Amos 7:14 and Its Context," ResQ 8 (1965) 175–78.
Rowley, H. H.
"Was Amos a Nabi?" *Festschrift Otto Eissfeldt* (ed. J. Fück; Halle: Niemeyer, 1947) 191–98.
Schmid, H.
"'Nicht prophet bin ich, noch bin ich Prophetensohn.' Zur Erklärung von Amos 7, 14a," *Judaica* 23 (1967) 68–74.
Smend, R.
"Das Nein des Amos," *EvT* 23 (1963) 404–23.
Spiegel, S.
Amos vs. Amaziah (Essays in Judaism Series 3; New York: Jewish Theological Seminary of America, 1957); rep. in *The Jewish Expression* (ed. J. Goldin; New Haven, CT: Yale University, 1957) 40–47.
Stoebe, H. J.
"Der Prophet Amos und sein bürgerlicher Beruf," *WuD* 5 (1957) 160–81.
Treu, U.
"Amos 7,14, Schenute und der Physiologos," *NovT* 10 (1968) 234–40.
Vanden Oudenrijn, F. A.
"L'expression 'fils des prophètes' et ses analogies," *Bib* 6 (1925) 165–71.
Vogt, E.
"Recensiones," *Bib* 38 (1957) 472–73.
Idem
"*Waw* Explicative in Amos VII,14," *ExpTim* 68 (1957) 301–2.
Weiser, A.
"Die Berufung des Amos," *TBl* 7 (1928) 177–82.
Weiss, M.
HaMiqra Kidmuto (Jerusalem: Bialik, 1967) 71–74, 262–63 ([3]1987) 180–86 (Heb.); English tr. *The Bible from Within: The Method of Total Interpretation* (Jerusalem: Magnes, 1984) 102–6, 417–21.
Weitz, Y.
"Amos—*Noqed, Boker,* and *Boles Shikmim*," *BM* 33 (1968) 141–44 (Heb.).
Wright, T. J.
"Amos and the Sycamore Fig," *VT* 26 (1976) 362–68.

Zalcman, L.
"Piercing the Darkness at *bôqēr* (Amos vii 14)," *VT* 30 (1980) 252–53.
Zevit, Z.
"Expressing Denial in Biblical Hebrew and Mishnaic Hebrew, and in Amos," *VT* 29 (1979) 505–10.
Ziv, Y.
"Amos 7:14," *BM* 92 (1982) 49–53 (Heb.).

7:14–15

Loretz, O.
"Die Berufung des Propheten Amos (7, 14–15)," *UF* 6 (1974) 487–88.
van Hoonacker, A.
"Miscellenées bibliques. III. Le sens de la protestation d'Amos VII, 14–15," *ETL* 18 (1941) 65–67.

7:15a

Schult, H.
"Amos 7:15a und die Legitimation des Aussenseiters," *Probleme biblischer Theologie: Gerhard von Rad zum 70. Geburtstag* (ed. H. W. Wolff; München: Kaiser, 1971) 462–78.

7:16

Winckler, H.
"Einzelnes. Am 7,16," *Alttestamentliche Untersuchungen* (Leipzig: Pfeiffer, 1892) 185.

Chapter 8

Casalis, G.
"Du texte au sermon. 12: Amos 8," *ETR* 46 (1971) 113–24.

8:1–2

Baumgartner, W.
"Alttestamentliche Wortforschung: Die Etymologie von hebräischen k^{e}*lūb*, Korb," *TZ* 7 (1951) 77–78.
Rahtjen, B. D.
"A Critical Note on Amos 8:1–2," *JBL* 83 (1964) 416–17.

8:1–3

Loewenstamm, S. E.
"'כלוב קיץ': A Remark on the Typology of the Prophetic Vision (Amos 8:1–3)," *Tarbiz* 34 (1964–1965) 319–22 (Heb.).

8:3

Torrey, C. C.
"Notes on Amos 2,7; 6,10; 8,3; 9,8–10," *JBL* 15 (1896) 151–54.

8:4

Bewer, J. A.
"Critical Notes on Amos 2:7 and 8:4," *AJSL* 19 (1902–1903) 116–17.
Lohmann, P.
"Einige Textkonjecturen zu Amos," *ZAW* 32 (1912) 274–75.

8:4–7

Desrousseaux, L.
"Acheter le malheureux pour un peu d'argent," *25e Dimanche ordinaire. Assemblées du Seigneur* 56 (1974) 56–61.
Kessler, R.
"Die angeblichen Kornhändler von Amos VIII 4–7," *VT* 39 (1989) 13–22.
Schultes, J. L.
"Gott redet auch durch sein Schweigen. Bibel Meditation zu Amos 8:4–7, 11–12," *Bibel und Liturgie* 48 (1975) 256–59.

8:5

Givati, M.
"The Sabbath in the Words of the Prophet Amos," *BM* 69 (1977) 194–98 (Heb.).
Halevy, B.
"When Will the New Moon Pass?" *BM* 66 (1976) 333–46, 493 (Heb.).
Loewenstamm, S. E.
"Ostracon 7 from Arad, Attesting the Observance of the New-Moon Day," *BM* 66 (1976) 330–32 (Heb.).

8:6

Box, G. H.
"Amos II, 6 and VIII, 6," *ExpTim* 12 (1900–1901) 377–78.
Lang, B.
"Sklaven und Unfreie im Buch Amos (II, 6; VIII, 6)," *VT* 31 (1981) 482–86.

8:11–12

Haag, E.
"Das schweigen Gottes. Ein Wort des Propheten Amos (Am 8,11–2)," *BibLeb* 10 (1969) 157–64.
Rusche, H.
"Wenn Gott sein Wort entzieht. Meditation zu Amos 8,11–12," *BibLeb* 10 (1969) 219–21.
Schultes, J. L.
"Gott redet auch durch sein Schweigen. Bibel Meditation zu Amos 8:4–7, 11–12," *Bibel und Liturgie* 48 (1975) 256–59.
Speidel, K.
"Hunger nach Gottes Wort—Meditation zu Amos 8:11–12," *Gericht und Umkehr. Die Bostchaft des Propheten Amos* = BKAT 22 (1967) 120–22.
Szwarc, U.
"Thirst after God's Word—Exegetic-Theological Analysis of the Text of Amos 8, 11–12," *Rocjniki Teologiczns-Kanoniczne* 27 (1980) 43–51.

8:11–13

Albert, E.
"Einige Bemerkungen zu Amos," *ZAW* 33 (1913) 270–71.

8:14

Ackroyd, P. R.
"The Meaning of Hebrew דור Reconsidered," *JSS* 13 (1968) 3–10.
Bartina, S.
"Vivit Potentia Beer-Seba! (Am 8,14)," *VD* 34 (1956) 202–10.
Freedman, D. N., and J. Lundblom
"*dôr*," *TWAT* II (1977) 187.

Neuberg, F. J.
"An Unrecognized Meaning of Hebrew *DÔR*," *JNES* 9 (1950) 215–17.

Winckler, H.
"Zum A.T.—Amos 8:14," *Altorientalische Forschungen* 1 (1894) 194–95.

9:1

Gese, H.
"Kleine Beiträge zum Verständnis des Amosbuches," *VT* 12 (1962) 417–38.

Ouellette, J.
"The Shaking of the Thresholds in Amos 9:1," *HUCA* 43 (1972) 23–27.

9:3

MacLagan, P. J.
"Amos 9.3," *ExpTim* 26 (1914–1915) 237.

9:6

Luria, B. Z.
"'Who Calls the Water of the Sea and Spills Them on the Face of the Earth' (Amos 5:8; 9:6)," *BM* 101 (1984–1985) 259–62 (Heb.).

Praetorius, F.
"Zum Texte des Amos," *ZAW* 34 (1914) 44.

Rinaldi, G.
"Sull'uso de *'gdh* (*'ăguddâ*) nell'AT," BibOr 24 (1985) 202–4.

Winckler, H.
"Einzelnes. Am 9,6," *Alttestamentlische Untersuchungen* (Leipzig: Pfeiffer, 1892) 185.

9:7

Delcor, M.
"Les Kerethim et les Cretois," *VT* 28 (1978) 409–22.

Fang, C.
"Universalism and the Prophet Amos," *Collectanea Theologica Universitatis Fujen* 5/20 (1974) 165–71.

Feuillet, A.
"L'universalisme et l'alliance dans la religion d'Amos," *BVC* 17 (1957) 17–29.

Gese, H.
"Das Problem von Amos 9:7," *Textgemäss: Aufsätze und Beiträge zur Hermeneutik des Alten Testaments: Festschrift für Ernst Würthwein zum 70. Geburtstag* (ed. A.H.J. Gunneweg and O. Kaiser; Göttingen: Vandenhoeck & Ruprecht, 1979) 33–38.

Janssen, H.
Voorliefde en verantwoordelijkheid—Een eksegetische studie over Amos 3,1–2 en 9,7 (Utrecht: Theological Institute, 1975).

Nogah, R.
"'Are You Not Like the Ethiopians unto Me,'" *BM* 89/90 (1982) 174–82 (Heb.).

Prignaud, J.
"Caftorim et Kerétim," *RB* 71 (1962) 215–29.

Strange, J.
Caphtor/Keftiu. A New Investigation (Acta Theologica Danica 14; Leiden: Brill, 1980).

van Wyk, W. C.
"Die Kusiete in Amos 9:7," *HTSt* 22 (1967) 38–45.

Vogels, W.
"Invitation à revenir à l'alliance et universalisme en Amos IX:7," *VT* 22 (1972) 223–39.

Wainwright, G. A.
"Caphtor—Cappadocia," *VT* 6 (1956) 199–210.

9:7-15

Florival, E.
"Le jour du jugement (Amos 9,7–15)," *BVC* 8 (1954–1955) 61–75.

9:8-10

Torrey, C. C.
"Notes on Amos 2,7; 6,10; 8,3; 9,8–10," *JBL* 15 (1896) 151–54.

9:8-15

Bernard, M.
"Exegetical Study, Amos 9,8–15," *Ministry* 9 (1969) 22–26.

McCullough, W. S.
"Some Suggestions about Amos," *JBL* 72 (1953) 247–54.

9:9

Volz, P.
"Zu Amos 9:9," *ZAW* 38 (1919–1920) 105–11.

Wilbers, H.
"Étude sur trois textes relatifs à l'agriculture: Isa 28:27–28; Amos 2:13; 9:9," *MUSJ* 5 (1911–1912) 269–82.

9:9-10

Hoffmann, H. W.
"Zur Echtheitsfrage von Amos 9:9f.," *ZAW* 82 (1970) 121–22.

9:10

Reidel, W.
"Miscellen. 7. Amos 9:10," *ZAW* 20 (1900) 332.

9:11

Richardson, H. N.
"*Skt* (Amos 9:11): 'Booth' or 'Succoth'?" *JBL* 92 (1973) 375–81.

9:11-12

Galling, K.
"Die Ausrufung des Namens als Rechtsakt in Israel," *TLZ* 81 (1956) 65–70.

9:11-15

Kellermann, U.
"Der Amosschluss als Stimme deuteronomistischer Heilshoffnung," *EvT* 29 (1969) 169–83.

9:12

Lohfink, N.
"Die Bedeutung von Heb. ירש Qal und Hif.," *BZ* 27 (1983) 14–33.

9:13

Weiss, M.
"These Days and the Days to Come According to Amos 9:13," Eretz Israel 14 (*H. L. Ginsberg Volume*; ed. M. Haran and others; Jerusalem: Israel Exploration Society, 1978) 69–73 (Heb.).

9:14

Baumann, E.
"שׁוּב שְׁבוּת. Eine exegetische Untersuchung," *ZAW* 47 (1929) 17–44.

Dietrich, E. L.
שׁוּב שְׁבוּת. *Die Endzeitliche Wiederherstellung bei den Propheten* (BZAW 40; Giessen: Töpelmann, 1925).

Holladay, W. L.
The Root Šûbh in the Old Testament (Leiden: Brill, 1958).

Preuschen, E.
"Die Bedeutung von שׁוּב שְׁבוּת im alten Testament," *ZAW* 15 (1985) 1–74.

Soggin, J. A.
"*ŠWB, šûb*, zurückkehren," *THAT* II (1976) 886–87.

15. Wisdom Literature

Baumgartner, W.
"The Wisdom Literature," *The Old Testament and Modern Study: A Generation of Discovery and Research* (ed. H. H. Rowley; Oxford: Clarendon, 1951) 210–37.

Crenshaw, J. L.
"The Influence of the Wise upon Amos—The 'Doxologies of Amos' and Job 5:9–16; 9:5–10," *ZAW* 79 (1967) 42–52.

Idem
"Amos and the Theophanic Traditions," *ZAW* 80 (1968) 203–15.

Idem
"Methods in Determining Wisdom Influence upon Historical Literature," *JBL* 88 (1969) 129–42.

Idem
"Prolegomenon," *Studies in Ancient Israelite Wisdom* (New York: Ktav, 1976) 1–45.

Hermisson, H. J.
Studien zur israelitischen Spruchweisheit (WMANT 28; Neukirchen-Vluyn: Neukirchener Verlag, 1968) 88–89.

Kahlert, H.
"Zur Frage nach der 'geistigen Heimat' des Amos. Eine Prüfung der These von H. W. Wolff," DBAT 4 (1973) 1–12.

Lindblom, J.
"Wisdom in the Old Testament Prophets," *Wisdom in Israel and in the Ancient Near East: Presented to Prof. H. H. Rowley by the Society for Old Testament Study* (ed. M. Noth and D. W. Thomas; SVT 3; Leiden: Brill, 1955) 192–204.

McKane, W.
Prophets and Wise Men (SBT 44; London: SCM, 1965).

McKenzie, J. L.
"Reflections on Wisdom," *JBL* 86 (1967) 1–9.

Murphy, R. E.
"Assumptions and Problems in Old Testament Wisdom Research," *CBQ* 29 (1967) 408–17.

Idem
"The Interpretation of Old Testament Wisdom Literature," *Int* 23 (1969) 289–301.

Idem
"Thesis and Hypothesis," *Israelite Wisdom: Theological and Literary Essays in Honor of Samuel Terrien* (ed. J. G. Gammie and others; New York: Scholars, 1978) 35–42.

Schmidt, H. H.
"Amos. Zur Frage nach der 'geistigen Heimat' des Propheten," *WuD* 10 (1969) 85–103.

Scott, R.B.Y.
"The Study of the Wisdom Literature," *Int* 24 (1970) 20–45.

Terrien, S.
"Amos and Wisdom," *Israel's Prophetic Heritage: Essays in Honor of James Muilenburg* (ed. B. W. Anderson and W. Harrelson; New York: Harper & Brothers, 1962) 108–15; rep. in *Studies in Ancient Israelite Wisdom* (ed. J. L. Crenshaw; New York: Ktav, 1976) 448–55.

Whybray, R. N.
The Intellectual Traditions in the Old Testament (BZAW 135; Berlin/New York: de Gruyter, 1974).

Wolff, H. W.
Amos' geistige Heimat (WMANT 18; Neukirchen-Vluyn: Neukirchener Verlag, 1964); English tr. *Amos the Prophet: The Man and His Background* (tr. F. R. McCurley; Philadelphia: Fortress, 1973).

Zimmerli, W.
"Ort und Grenze der Weisheit im Rahmen der alttestamentlichen Theologie," *Gottes Offenbarung: Gesammelte Aufsätze zum Alten Testament* (TBü 19; München: Kaiser, 1963) 300–315; English tr. "The Place and Limit of Wisdom in the Framework of Old Testament Theology," *SJT* 17 (1964) 146–58.

16. Other Works Cited

Aalen, S.
Die Begriffe 'Licht' und 'Finsternis' im Alten Testament, im Spätjudentum und im Rabbinismus (Oslo: Dybwad, 1951).

Abou-Assaf, A., P. Bordreuil, and A. R. Millard
La statue de Tell Fekherye et son inscription bilingue assyro-araméenne (Études Assyrologiques 7; Paris: Editions Recherche sur les civilisations, 1982).

Abramson, S.
"On the Hebrew in the Babylonian Talmud," *Archive of the New Dictionary of Rabbinic Literature* (ed. M. Z. Kaddari; Ramat-Gan: Bar-Ilan University, 1974) 2. 9–15 (Heb.).

Abu Taleb, M.
Investigations in the History of North Syria 1115–717 B.C. (diss.; Ann Arbor, MI, 1973).

Ackroyd, P. R.
"Samaria," *Archaeology and Old Testament Study: Jubilee Volume of the Society for Old Testament Study 1917–1967* (ed. D. W. Thomas; Oxford: Clarendon, 1967) 343–54.
Adamiak, R.
Justice and History in the Old Testament: The Evolution of Divine Retribution in the Historiographies of the Wilderness Generation (Cleveland: John T. Zubal, 1982).
Aharoni, Y.
"On Some Animals Mentioned in the Bible," *Osiris* 5 (1938) 461–78.
Idem
The Settlement of the Israelite Tribes in Upper Galilee (Jerusalem: Magnes, 1957).
Idem
The Land of the Bible: A Historical Geography (tr. A. F. Rainey; London: Burns and Oates, 1967).
Idem
"Tel Beersheba," *IEJ* 23 (1973) 254–56.
Idem
"The Horned Altar at Beersheba," *BA* 37 (1974) 2–6.
Ahitub, S.
"Ekron," *EM* 6.339–43 (Heb.).
Idem
"Teman," *EM* 8.524–25 (Heb.).
Albrektson, B.
History and the Gods: An Essay on the Idea of Historical Events as Divine Manifestations in the Ancient Near East and Israel (Coniectanca Biblica Old Testament Series 1; Lund: Gleerup, 1963).
Albright, W. F.
"The End of Calneh in Shinar," *JNES* 3 (1944) 254–55.
Idem
Review of B. N. Wambacq, *L'épithète divine Jahvé Ṣᵉba'ôt: Étude philologique, historique et exégétique* (Bruges: de Brouwer, 1947), *JBL* 67 (1948) 377–81.
Idem
"The High Place in Ancient Palestine," SVT 4 (Leiden: Brill, 1957) 242–58.
Idem
"A New Archaeological Interpretation," *BASOR* 163 (1961) 36–54.
Idem
Yahweh and the Gods of Canaan: A Historical Analysis of Two Contrasting Faiths (Garden City, NY: Doubleday, 1968).
Idem
"Some Comments on the Amman Citadel Inscription," *BASOR* 198 (1970) 38–40.
Allegro, J. M.
Qumrân Cave 4 (DJD 5; Oxford: Clarendon, 1968).
Alt, A.
Kleine Schriften zur Geschichte des Volkes Israel (3 vols.; München: C. H. Beck, 1953, 1959).
Idem
"Die Wallfahrt von Sichem nach Bethel," *Kleine Schriften zur Geschichte des Volkes Israel* (3 vols.; München: C. H. Beck, 1953) 1.79–88.
Idem
"Das Grossreich Davids," *Kleine Schriften zur Geschichte des Volkes Israel* (3 vols.; München: C. H. Beck, 1953) 2.66–75.
Idem
"Neue Assyrische Nachrichten über Palästina," *Kleine Schriften zur Geschichte des Volkes Israel* (3 vols.; München: C. H. Beck, 1953) 2.226–41.
Idem
"Menschen ohne Namen," *Kleine Schriften zur Geschichte des Volkes Israel* (3 vols.; München: C. H. Beck, 1959) 3.198–213.
Alter, R.
"Biblical Type-Scenes and the Uses of Convention," *Critical Inquiry* 5 (1978) 368ff.
Idem
The Art of Biblical Poetry (New York: Basic Books, 1985).
Amit, Y.
"Nazarites for Life—The Evolution of a Motif," *Studies in Judaica* (*Te'udah* 4; ed. M. A. Freidman and M. Gil; Tel Aviv: Tel Aviv University, 1986) 23–36 (Heb.).
Andersen, B. W.
"Hosts, Hosts of Heaven," *IDB* 1.654–56.
Anderson, G. W., ed.
Tradition and Interpretation: Essays by Members of the Society for Old Testament Study (Oxford: Clarendon, 1979).
Andreasen, N.-E. A.
The Old Testament Sabbath: A Tradition-Historical Investigation (SBLDS 7; Missoula, MT: Scholars, 1972).
Angerstorfer, A.
"Ašerah als 'Consort of Jahwe' oder Aširtah?" BN 17 (1982) 7–16.
Anthes, R.
Lebensregeln und Lebensweisheit der alten Ägypter (AO 32/2; Leipzig: Hinrichs, 1933).
Artemidorus, D.
Onirocriticon Libri V (ed. R. A. Pack; Leipzig: B. G. Teubner, 1963) (Greek).
Artzi, P.
"Kalneh," *EM* 4.185–86 (Heb.).
Idem
"Sikkuth and Chiun," *EncJud* 14.1531.
Astour, M. C.
"Carmel, Mount," *IDBSup* 141.
Idem
"Un texte d'Ugarit récemment découvert et ses rapports avec l'origine des cultes bachiques grecs," *RHR* 164 (1963) 1–15.
Idem
"Two Ugaritic Serpent Charms," *JNES* 27 (1968) 13–36.

Idem
"The Rabbeans: A Tribal Society on the Euphrates from Yahdun-Lim to Julius Caesar," *SMSR* 2 (1978) 1–12.
Avigad, N.
"Shomron," *EM* 8.148–62 (Heb.).
Idem
"Some Unpublished Ancient Seals," *BIES* 25 (1961) 241 (Heb.).
Idem
"Seals of Exiles," *IEJ* 15 (1965) 222–32.
Idem
"A Hebrew Seal with a Family Emblem," *IEJ* 16 (1966) 50–53.
Idem
"A Group of Hebrew Seals," Eretz Israel 9 (*W. F. Albright Volume;* ed. A. Malamat; Jerusalem: Israel Exploration Society, 1968) 1–9 (Heb.).
Idem
"The Priest of Dor," *IEJ* 25 (1975) 101–5.
Idem
"Samaria," *Encyclopaedia of Archeological Excavations in the Holy Land* (ed. M. Avi-Yonah and E. Stern; 4 vols.; London: Oxford University; Jerusalem: Masada, 1975–1978) 4.1032–50.
Avigad, N., and J. C. Greenfield
"A Bronze *phialē* with a Phoenician Dedicatory Inscription of the Fourth Century," *IEJ* 32 (1982) 118–29.
Avishur, Y.
"Pairs of Synonymous Words in the Construct State (and in Appositional Hendiadys) in Biblical Hebrew," *Sem* 2 (1971–1972) 17–81.
Idem
"Word Pairs Common to Phoenician and Biblical Hebrew," *UF* 7 (1975) 13–47.
Idem
"The Construct State of Biblical Synonyms Employed in Early Hebrew Poetry," *BM* 66 (1976) 412–57 (Heb.).
Idem
The Construct State of Synonyms in Biblical Rhetoric: Studies in the Stylistic Phenomenon of Synonymous Word Pairs in the Construct State (Jerusalem: Kiryat Sepher, 1977) (Heb.).
Idem
Phoenician Inscriptions and the Bible: Studies in Stylistic and Literary Devices and Selected Inscriptions (2 vols.; Jerusalem: E. Rubinstein, 1979) (Heb.).
Idem
"Breakup of Stereotype Phrases as a Literary Stylistic Pattern in Biblical Poetry," *Studies in Rabbinic Literature, Bible, and the History of Israel, Dedicated to Prof. E. Z. Melamed* (ed. Y. D. Gilat and others; Ramat-Gan: Bar-Ilan University, 1982) 20–42 (Heb.).
Avi-Yonah, M.
"Mt. Carmel and the God of Baalbek," *IEJ* 2 (1952) 118–24.
Avi-Yonah, M., and E. Stern, eds.
Encyclopaedia of Archeological Excavations in the Holy Land (4 vols.; London: Oxford University; Jerusalem: Masada, 1975–1978).
Avizur, S.
Implements for Harvesting (Tel Aviv: HaMaḥon LeYediat HaAreṣ, 1966) (Heb.).
Bach, R.
"Bauen und Pflanzen," *Studien zur Theologie der alttestamentlichen Überlieferungen* (ed. R. Rendtorff and K. Koch; Neukirchen-Vluyn: Neukirchener Verlag, 1961) 7–32.
Idem
Die Aufforderungen zur Flucht und zum Kampf im alttestamentlichen Prophetenspruch (WMANT 9; Neukirchen-Vluyn: Neukirchener Verlag, 1962).
Bacher, W.
"Salomon ibn Parchon hebräische Wörterbuch II," *ZAW* 2 (1891) 35–99.
Bächli, O.
"Zur Lage des alten Gilgal," *ZDPV* 83 (1967) 64–71.
Baillet, M., J. T. Milik, and R. de Vaux
Les "Petites Grottes" de Qumran (DJD 3/1; Oxford: Clarendon, 1962).
Bardtke, H.
"Der Erweckungsgedanke in der exilisch-nachexilischen Literatur des Alten Testaments," *Von Ugarit nach Qumran: Beiträge zur alttestamentlichen und altorientalischen Forschung. Otto Eissfeldt zum 1. September 1957* (ed. J. Hempel and L. Rost; BZAW 77; Berlin: Töpelmann, 1958) 9–24.
Idem
"Altisraelitische Erweckungsbewegungen," *Near Eastern Studies in Honor of William Foxwell Albright* (ed. H. Goedicke; Baltimore/London: Johns Hopkins University, 1971) 17–34.
Barnett, R. D.
"Assurbanipal's Feast," Eretz Israel 18 (*Nahman Avigad Volume;* ed. B. Mazar and Y. Yadin; Jerusalem: Israel Exploration Society, 1985) 1*–6*.
Barrick, W. B.
"The Meaning and Usage of *RKB* in Biblical Hebrew," *JBL* 101 (1982) 481–503.
Bauer, B.
"Music in the Bible," *EncJud* 12.559–66.
Idem
"Nebel," *EM* 5.767–71 (Heb.).
Idem
"The Biblical *Nebel*," *Yuval* 1 (1968) 89–161.
Baumgärtel, F.
"Die Formel *ne'um jahwe*," *ZAW* 73 (1961) 227–90.
Beaugency, E.
Kommentar zu Ezechiel und den XII kleinen Propheten (ed. S. Poznański; Warsaw: Eppelberg, 1914) (Heb.).

Beck, P.
"The Drawings from Horvat Teiman (Kuntillet 'Ajrud)," *Tel Aviv* 9 (1982) 3–68.

Begrich, J.
"Die priestliche Thora," *Werden und Wesen des Alten Testaments. Vorträge gehalten auf der Internationalen Tagung alttestamentlicher Forscher zu Göttingen von 4—10. September 1935* (ed. P. Volz, F. Stummer, and J. Hempel; BZAW 66; Berlin: Töpelmann, 1936) 63–88.

Idem
Gesammelte Studien zum Alten Testament (TBü 21; München: Kaiser, 1964).

ben Iehuda, E.
Thesaurus totius hebraitatis et veteris et recentioris (Jerusalem: Hemda Ben-Yehuda, 1908–1951) (Heb.); rep. *A Complete Dictionary of Ancient and Modern Hebrew* (16 vols.; Jerusalem/Tel Aviv: La'Am, 1980) (Heb.).

ben Saruq, M.
Sepher HaMaḥberet (ed. Y. Philipawaski; Yadenburg, 1854) (Heb.).

Benoit, R., J. T. Milik, and R. de Vaux
Les grottes de Murabb'ât (DJD 2/1; Oxford: Clarendon, 1961).

Bentzen, A.
Introduction to the Old Testament (2 vols.; Copenhagen: Gad, [2]1952).

Benz, F. L.
Personal Names in the Phoenician and Punic Inscriptions: A Catalog, Grammatical Study and Glossary of Elements (Studia Pohl 8; Rome: Pontifical Biblical Institute, 1972).

Berger, P.-R.
"Die Alašia-Briefe, Ugaritica 5, Noug. *Nrn.* 22–24," *UF* 1 (1969) 217–21.

Bergman, G., H. Ringgren, and B. Lang
"*zbḥ*," *TWAT* II (1977) 509–31.

Bernhardt, K.-H.
"Beobachtungen zur Identifizierung moabitischen Ortslagen," *ZDPV* 76 (1960) 136–58.

Bewer, J. A.
"Lexical Notes," *AJSL* 17 (1900–1901) 168.

Biggs, R. D.
"More Babylonian 'Prophecies,'" *Iraq* 29 (1967) 117–32.

Biran, A.
"An Israelite Horned Altar at Dan," *BA* 37 (1974) 106–7.

Idem
"Tell er-Ruqeish to Tell er-Ridan," *IEJ* 24 (1974) 141–42, pl. 24–25.

Idem
"To the God Who Is in Dan," *Temples and High Places in Biblical Times* (ed. A. Biran; Jerusalem: Keter, 1981) 142–51.

Idem
"The Temenos at Dan," Eretz Israel 16 (*Harry M. Orlinsky Volume*; ed. B. A. Levine and A. Malamat; Jerusalem: Israel Exploration Society, 1982) 15–43 (Heb.).

Idem
"An Incense Altar and Other Discoveries at Dan," *Qadmoniot* 19 (1986) 31–40 (Heb.).

Bjoerndalen, A. J.
"Zu den Zeitstufen der Zitatformen 'כה אמריי' im Botenverkehr," *ZAW* 86 (1974) 393–403.

Black, H.
"The Penalty of Privilege," *Expositor* (1894) 317–19.

Blau, J.
"Über Homonyme und angeblich Homonyme Wurzeln, I," *VT* 6 (1956) 242–48; part II, *VT* 7 (1957) 100–101.

Idem
"On Polyphony in Biblical Hebrew," *Proceedings of the Israel Academy of Sciences and Humanities* 6 (1977–1982) 105–83.

Bodreuil, P., and A. Caquot
"Les textes en cunéiformes alphabétiques découverts en 1978 à Ibn Hani," *Syria* 57 (1980) 343–73.

Boecker, H. J.
Redeformen des Rechtslebens im alten Testament (WMANT 14; Neukirchen-Vluyn: Neukirchener Verlag, 1963).

Borger, R.
"Zu שוב שבו/ית," *ZAW* 66 (1954) 315–16.

Idem
Die Inschriften Asarhaddons Königs, von Assyrien (*AfO* Beiheft 9; Graz: im Selbstverlag des Herausgebers, 1956).

Idem
"Die Aussprache des Gottesnamens Ninurta," *Or* 30 (1961) 203.

Idem
"Zu den Asharhaddon Verträge aus Nimrud," *ZA* 54 (1961) 173–96.

Idem
Keilschrifturkunden. Einleitung in die Assyrischen Königsinschriften. Erster Teil: Das Zweite Jahrtausend vor Chr. (Leiden/Köln: Brill, 1964).

Idem
"Gott Marduk und Gott-König Šulgi als Propheten. Zwei prophetische Texte," *BO* 28 (1971) 3–21.

Botterweck, G. J.
"*'bywn*," *TWAT* 1 (1973) 38–43.

Botterweck, G. J., and B. Kedar-Kopfstein
"*ḥag*," *TWAT* II (1977) 73.

Bowman, R. A.
"Ben-hadad," *IDB* 1.381–82.

Idem
"Hazael," *IDB* 2.538.

Braslavi, J.
"Lions in the Bible," *Sefer Shemu'el Yevin* (ed. S. Abramski and others; Jerusalem: Kiryat Sepher, 1970) 90–125 (Heb.).

Brenner, A.
Colour Terms in the Old Testament (JSOT Supplement Series 21; Sheffield: JSOT, 1982).
Bright, J.
Jeremiah: Introduction, Translation and Notes (AB 21; Garden City, NY: Doubleday, 1965).
Idem
A History of Israel (Philadelphia: Westminster, [3]1981).
Brinkman, J. A.
"Appendix: Mesopotamian Chronology of the Historical Period," in A. Leo Oppenheim, *Ancient Mesopotamia: Portrait of a Dead Civilization* (Chicago: University of Chicago, 1964) 335–52.
Broshi, M.
"The Brook of the Arabah," *EM* 5.810 (Heb.).
Buber, M.
The Prophetic Faith (New York: Harper and Brothers, 1960).
Buhl, F.
Geschichte der Edomiter (Leipzig: Edelmann, 1893).
Buttenweiser, M.
The Prophets of Israel from the Eighth to the Fifth Century: Their Faith and Their Message (New York: Macmillan, 1914).
Cagni, L.
L'Epopea di Erra (Studi Semitici 34; Rome: Instituto di Studi del Vicino Oriente, 1964).
Idem
The Poem of Erra: Sources from the Ancient Near East (Malibu: Undena, 1977).
Caquot, A.
"Le Psaume 47 et la royauté de YAHWE," *RHPR* 39 (1959) 311–37.
Idem
"Remarques sur la fête de la 'neoménie' dans l'ancien Israël," *RHR* 158 (1960) 1–18.
Caquot, A., and A. Lemaire
"Les textes araméens de Deir 'Alla," *Syria* 54 (1977) 189–208.
Caquot, A., M. Sznycer, and A. Herdner
Textes ougaritiques, Tome I: Mythes et Légendes (Littératures anciennes du Proche-Orient 7; Paris: Cerf, 1974).
Cassuto, U.M.D.
"Il palazzo di Ba'al nella tavola II AB di Ras Shamra," *Or* 7 (1938) 265–90.
Idem
"The Death of Baal," *Tarbiz* 13 (1940–1941) 169–80 (Heb.).
Idem
The Goddess Anat: Canaanite Epics of the Patriarchal Age (tr. I. Abrahams; Jerusalem: Magnes, 1971).
Idem
"Biblical and Canaanite Literature," *Tarbiz* 13 (1942) 203–5 (Heb.); rep. in *Studies on the Bible and Ancient Orient: Biblical and Canaanite Literatures* (2 vols.; Jerusalem: Magnes, 1972–1979) 2.20–55 (Heb.).
Idem
"Israelite Epic Poetry," *Studies on the Bible and Ancient Orient: Biblical and Canaanite Literatures* (2 vols.; Jerusalem: Magnes, 1979) 2.62–90 (Heb.).
Idem
Biblical and Oriental Studies (tr. I. Abrahams; 2 vols.; Jerusalem: Magnes, 1973, 1975).
de Castellione, G.
Alexandreis (ed. M. L. Colker; Padova: Antenori, 1978).
Cathcart, K. J.
Nahum in the Light of Northwest Semitic (BibOr 26; Rome: Pontifical Biblical Institute, 1973).
Cazelles, H.
"The Problem of the Kings in Osée 8:4," *CBQ* 11 (1949) 14–25.
Idem
"À propos de quelques textes difficiles relatifs à la justice de dieu dans l'Ancien Testament," *RB* 58 (1951) 159–88.
Idem
"De l'idéologie royale orientale," *The Gaster Festschrift* (*JANESCU* 5; ed. D. Marcus; New York: Columbia University, 1973) 59–73.
Chiera, E.
Excavations at Nuzi I. Texts of Varied Contents (HSS 5; Cambridge: Harvard University, 1929).
Civil, M.
"New Sumerian Law Fragments," *Studies in Honor of Benno Landsberger on His Seventy-fifth Birthday, April 21, 1965* (ed. H. G. Güterbock and T. Jacobsen; Assyriological Studies 16; Chicago: University of Chicago, 1965) 1–12.
Clay, A. T.
Documents from the Temple Archives of Nippur Dated in the Reigns of Cassite Rulers (BE Series A; CT 15; Philadelphia: University of Pennsylvania, 1906).
Idem
Legal Documents from Erech Dated in the Seleucid Era, 312–65 B.C. (BRM 2; New York: privately printed, 1913).
Idem
Neo-Babylonian Letters from Erech (YOS 3; New Haven, CT: Yale University, 1919).
Idem
Epics, Hymns, Omens, and Other Texts (BRM 4; New Haven, CT: Yale University, 1923).
Cogan, M.
"A Technical Term for Exposure," *JNES* 27 (1968) 133–35.
Idem
Imperialism and Religion: Assyria, Judah and Israel in the Eighth and Seventh Centuries B.C.E. (Society of Biblical Literature Monograph Series 19; Missoula, MT: Scholars, 1974).
Cohen, A.
"Uses of Language in the Books of the Prophets," *BM* 25–26 (1966) 123–26 (Heb.).

Cohen, C.
"Hebrew *tbh*, Proposed Etymologies," *JANESCU* 4 (1972) 37–45.
Idem
"The Legend of Sargon and the Birth of Moses," *JANESCU* 4 (1972) 46–51.
Cohen, H. R.
Biblical Hapax Legomena in the Light of Akkadian and Ugaritic (SBLDS 37; Missoula, MT: Scholars, 1975).
Cohen, S.
"Bashan," *IDB* 1.363–64.
Idem
"Gilead," *IDB* 2.397–98.
Collins, T.
Line-Forms in Hebrew Poetry. A Grammatical Approach to the Stylistic Study of the Hebrew Prophets (Studia Pohl Series Maior 7; Rome: Pontifical Biblical Institute, 1978).
Cornelius, F.
"Genesis 14," *ZAW* 72 (1960) 1–17.
Cowley, A. E.
The Samaritan Liturgy (Oxford: Clarendon, 1909).
Idem
Aramaic Papyri of the Fifth Century B.C. (Oxford: Clarendon, 1923).
Craig, J. A.
Assyrian and Babylonian Religious Texts (4 vols.; Leipzig: Hinrichs, 1895).
Crenshaw, J. L.
Prophetic Conflict. Its Effect upon Israelite Religion (BZAW 124; Berlin: de Gruyter, 1971).
Cross, F. M.
"A New Qumran Biblical Fragment Related to the Original Hebrew Underlying the Septuagint," *BASOR* 132 (1953) 15–26.
Idem
"The Divine Warrior in Israel's Early Cult," *Biblical Motifs: Origins and Transformations* (ed. A. Altmann; Studies and Texts 3; Cambridge: Harvard University, 1966) 11–30.
Idem
"Epigraphic Notes on the Amman Citadel Inscription," *BASOR* 193 (1969) 13–19.
Idem
"The Stele Dedicated to Melcarth by Ben-hadad of Damascus," *BASOR* 205 (1972) 36–42.
Idem
Canaanite Myth and Hebrew Epic: Essays in the History of the Religion of Israel (Cambridge: Harvard University, 1973).
Idem
"The Ammonite Oppression of the Tribes of Gad and Reuben: Missing Verses from I Samuel 11 in 4QSamuel[a]," *The Hebrew and Greek Texts of Samuel* (Proceedings of International Organization of Septuagint and Cognate Studies; ed. E. Tov; Vienna/Jerusalem: Academon, 1980) 105–19. Reprinted in *Historiography and Interpretation: Studies in Biblical and Cuneiform Literature* (ed. H. Tadmor and M. Weinfeld; Jerusalem: Magnes, 1983) 148–58.
Idem
"The Priestly Tabernacle in the Light of Recent Research," *Temples and High Places in Biblical Times* (ed. A. Biran; Jerusalem: Keter, 1981) 169–80.
Idem
"A New Aramaic Stele from Taymā'," *A Wise and Discerning Heart: Studies Presented to Joseph A. Fitzmyer, S.J., in Celebration of His Sixty-fifth Birthday* (ed. R. E. Brown and A. A. Di Lella) = *CBQ* 48 (1986) 387–94.
Crowfoot, J. W., and G. M. Crowfoot
Early Ivories from Samaria: Samaria-Sebaste II (London: Palestine Exploration Fund, 1938).
Idem
Samaria-Sebaste III: The Objects from Samaria (London: Palestine Exploration Fund, 1957).
Curtis, J. B.
"A Folk Etymology of *Nâbî*," VT 29 (1979) 491–93.
Dahood, M.
"Ugaritic *DRKT* and Biblical *DEREK*," *TS* 15 (1954) 627–31.
Idem
"The Value of Ugaritic for Textual Criticism," *Bib* 40 (1959) 160–70.
Idem
"Textual Problems in Isaiah," *CBQ* 22 (1960) 400–9.
Idem
"*Nādâ*, 'to hurl' in Ex. 15,16," *Bib* 43 (1962) 248–49.
Idem
"Denominative *riḥḥam*, 'to conceive, enwomb,'" *Bib* 44 (1963) 204–5.
Idem
Psalms 1:1—50, Introduction, Translation and Notes (AB 16; Garden City, NY: Doubleday, ^{2}1966).
Idem
Psalms 2:51—100, Introduction, Translation and Notes (AB 17; Garden City, NY: Doubleday, 1968).
Idem
"Additional Notes on the *MRZḤ* Text," *The Claremont Ras Shamra Tablets* (ed. L. R. Fisher; AnOr 48; Rome: Pontifical Biblical Institute, 1971) 50–54.
Idem
Psalms 3:101—150, Introduction, Translation and Notes (AB 17a; Garden City, NY: Doubleday, 1974).
Idem
"The Minor Prophets and Ebla," *The Word of the Lord Shall Go Forth: Essays in Honor of D. N. Freedman* (ed. C. L. Meyers and M. O'Connor; Winona Lake, IN: Eisenbrauns, 1983) 47–67.

Dajani, R. W.
"The Ammonite Theatre Fragment," ADAJ 12–13 (1967–1968) 65–67.
Dalman, G.
Arbeit und Sitte in Palaestina (7 vols.; Hildesheim: G. Olms, 1964).
Danell, G. A.
Studies in the Name Israel in the Old Testament (Uppsala: Appelbergs, 1946).
David, M.
"Deux anciens termes bibliques pour la gage," *OTS* 2 (1943) 79–86.
Day, J.
"Asherah in the Hebrew Bible and Northwest Semitic Literature," *JBL* 105 (1986) 385–408.
Dayton, J. E.
"The Problem of Tin in the Ancient World," *World Archeology* 3 (1971) 49–70.
Deimel, A.
Pantheon Babylonicum (Rome: Pontifical Biblical Institute, 1914).
Delekat, L.
"Zum hebräischen Wörterbuch," *VT* 14 (1964) 7–66.
Deller, K.
Review of A. Salonen, *Die Möbel des alten Mesopotamien nach sumerisch-akkadischen Quellen* (Annales Academiae Scientiarum Fennicae B 127; Helsinki: Suomalainen Tiedeakatemia, 1963), in *Or* 33 (1964) 99–103.
Dentzer, J.-M.
Le motif du banquet couché dans le proche-orient et le monde grec du VIe au IVe siècle avant J.C. (Rome: École Francaise de Rome, 1962).
Dever, W. G.
"Recent Archaeological Confirmation of the Cult of Asherah in Ancient Israel," *Hebrew Studies* 23 (1982) 37–43.
Idem
"Asherah, Consort of Yahweh? New Evidence from Kuntillet 'Ajrud," *BASOR* 255 (1984) 21–37.
Devescovi, U.
"Caminare sulle Altare," *RivB* 9 (1961) 235–42.
Dietrich, E. K.
Die Umkehr im alten Testament und im Judentum (Stuttgart: Kohlhammer, 1936).
Dietrich, F.
"Beiträge zur biblischen Geographie. 2: Qerijjoth in Moab," *AWAT* 1 (1870) 320–37.
Dietrich, M., and O. Loretz
"Der Vertrag eines *mrzḥ*—Klubs in Ugarit: Zum Verständnis von *KTU* 3:9," *UF* 14 (1982) 71–76.
Diman (Haran), M.
"An Archaic Remnant in Prophetic Literature," *BIES* 13 (1946–1947) 7–16 (Heb.).
Dommerhausen, W.
"*ḥll*," *TWAT* II (1977) 972–81.
Donner, H.
"'Hier sind deine Götter, Israel,'" *Wort und Geschichte: Festschrift für K. Elliger zum 70. Geburtstag* (ed. H. Gese and H. P. Rüger; AOAT 18; Neukirchen-Vluyn: Neukirchener Verlag, 1973) 45–50.
Donner, H., and W. Röllig
Kanaanäische und Aramäische Inschriften (3 vols.; Wiesbaden: Harrassowitz, 1966–1969).
Dossin, G.
Lettres de la première dynastie babylonienne (TCL 18; Paris: Geuthner, 1934).
Idem
"Une révélation du dieu Dagan à Terqa," *RA* 42 (1948) 316–20.
Idem
"L'inscription de fondation de Iaḫdun-Lim, roi de Mari," *Syria* 32 (1955) 1–27.
Dothan, T.
The Philistines and Their Material Culture (New Haven, CT/London: Yale University; Jerusalem: Israel Exploration Society, 1982).
Driver, G. R.
"Studies in the Vocabulary of the Old Testament, 2, 3," *JTS* 32 (1931) 250–57; 361–66.
Idem
"Confused Hebrew Roots," *Occident and Orient. Being Studies in Semitic Philology and Literature, Jewish History and Philosophy and Folklore in the Widest Sense. In Honor of Haham M. Gaster's 80th Birthday* (ed. B. Schindler and A. Marmorstein; London: Taylor's Foreign, 1936) 73–75.
Idem
"Linguistic and Textual Problems: Minor Prophets I," *JTS* 39 (1938) 154–66.
Idem
"Linguistic and Textual Problems: Minor Prophets II," *JTS* 39 (1938) 260–73.
Idem
"Difficult Words in the Hebrew Prophets," *Studies in Old Testament Prophecy Presented to Professor Theodore H. Robinson* (ed. H. H. Rowley; Edinburgh: T. & T. Clark, 1950) 52–72.
Idem
"Babylonian and Hebrew Notes," *WO* 2 (1954) 19–26.
Idem
"Reflections on Recent Articles," *JBL* 73 (1954) 131–36.
Idem
"Abbreviations in the Massoretic Text," *Textus* 1 (1960) 112–31.
Idem
"A Confused Hebrew Root (דמם,דמה,דום)," *Sefer N. H. Tur-Sinai* (ed. M. Haran and B. Z. Luria; Jerusalem: Kiryat Sepher, 1960) 1*–11*.
Driver, G. R., and J. C. Miles
The Babylonian Laws: Edited with Translation and Commentary (2 vols.; Oxford: Clarendon, 1952).

Duhm, B.
Die Theologie der Propheten als Grundlage für die innere Entwicklungsgeschichte der israelitischen Religion (Bonn: Marcus, 1875).
Dumbrell, W. J.
"The Role of Bethel in the Biblical Narratives," *Australian Journal of Biblical Archaeology* 2 (1974) 65–76.
Dus, J.
"Die Stierbilder von Bethel und Dan und das Problem der Moseschar," *AION* 18 (1968) 105–37.
Ebeling, E.
"Ein Heldenlied auf Tiglatpileser I," *Or* 18 (1949) 30–39.
Idem
Die akkadische Gebetsserie 'Handerhebung' (Berlin: Akademie Verlag, 1953).
Ebeling, E., F. Köcher, and L. Rost
Literarische Keilschrifttexte aus Assur (Berlin: Akademie Verlag, 1953).
Edelman, D.
"The Meaning of *qiṭṭar*," *VT* 35 (1985) 395–400.
Edzard, D. O.
"Altbabylonisch *nawûm*," *ZA* 53 (1959) 168–73.
Eisenbeis, W.
Die Wurzel šlm im Alten Testament (BZAW 113; Berlin: de Gruyter, 1969).
Eissfeldt, O.
Molk als Opferbegriff im Punischen und Hebräischen und das Ende des Gottes Moloch (Halle: Niemeyer, 1935).
Idem
"Die älteste Bezeugen von Baalbek aus Kultstätte," *FuF* 12 (1936) 51–53.
Idem
"Philister und Phönizer," *AO* 34 (1936) 31–36.
Idem
Ras Schamra und Sanchunjaton (Halle: Niemeyer, 1939).
Idem
Kleine Schriften zum Alten Testament (6 vols.; Tübingen: Mohr, 1962–1979).
Idem
"Jahwe Zebaoth," *Kleine Schriften zum Alten Testament* (6 vols.; Tübingen: Mohr, 1962–1979) 3.103–23.
Idem
"*NUAḤ*, sich vertragen," *Kleine Schriften zum Alten Testament* (6 vols.; Tübingen: Mohr, 1962–1979) 3.124–28.
Idem
The Old Testament: An Introduction (tr. P. R. Ackroyd; New York/Evanston: Harper & Row, 1965).
Eitan, I.
"Biblical Studies II—Stray Notes to Minor Prophets," *HUCA* 14 (1939) 1–22.
Ellermeier, F.
Prophetie in Mari und Israel (Herzberg am Harz: Jungfer, 1968).
Ellis, M. de J.
"Taxation in Ancient Mesopotamia: The History of the Term *miksu*," *JCS* 26 (1974) 211–50.
Idem
Agriculture and the State in Ancient Mesopotamia: An Introduction to Problems of Land Tenure (Occasional Publications of the Babylonian Fund 1; Philadelphia: University of Pennsylvania Museum, 1976).
Emerton, J. A.
"New Light on Israelite Religion: The Implications of the Inscriptions from Kuntillet 'Ajrud," *ZAW* 94 (1982) 2–20.
Engnell, I. E.
"The 'Ebed Yahweh Songs and the Suffering Messiah in Deutero-Isaiah," *BJRL* 31 (1948) 54–93.
Eph'al, I.
"Gaza," *EM* 6.116–21 (Heb.).
Erman, A., and H. Ranke
Ägypten and ägyptisches Leben im Altertum (Tübingen: J.C.B. Mohr [Siebeck], 1923).
Fabry, H.-J.
"*dal*," *TWAT* II (1977) 221–44.
Fales, F. M.
"Accadico e aramaico: livelli dell' interferenza linguistica," *Vicino Oriente* III (1980) 243–67.
Falk, Z. W.
Hebrew Law in Biblical Times (Jerusalem: Wahrmann Books, 1964).
Idem
"Zum jüdischen Bürgschaftsrecht," *RIDA*[3] 10 (1963) 43–54.
Farber, W.
"Associative Magic: Some Rituals, Word Plays, and Philology," *JAOS* 106 (1986) 447–49.
Feliks, J.
The Animal World of the Bible (Tel Aviv: Sinai, 1954) (Heb.).
Idem
The Plant World of the Bible (Ramat-Gan: Bar Ilan University, 1968) (Heb.).
Fenton, T. L.
"*Sikkuth*," *EM* 5.1037 (Heb.).
Idem
"The Claremont '*MRZḤ*' Tablet, Its Text and Meaning," *UF* 9 (1977) 71–75.
Idem
"Differing Approaches to the Theomachy Myth in Old Testament Writers," *Studies in the Bible and the Ancient Near East, Presented to Samuel E. Loewenstamm on His Seventieth Birthday* (ed. Y. Avishur and Y. Blau; Jerusalem: E. Rubinstein, 1978) 337–81 (Heb.).
Finet, A.
"Citations littéraires dans la correspondence de Mari," *RA* 68 (1974) 35–47.

Finkelstein, J. J.
"The Middle Assyrian *Šulmānu*-Texts," *JAOS* 72 (1952) 77–80.
Idem
"The Laws of Ur Nammu," *JCS* 22 (1968–1969) 66–82.
Finkelstein, L., ed.
Siphre ad Deuteronomium (New York: Jewish Theological Seminary of America, 1969) (Heb.).
Fisher, L. R.
"Two Projects at Claremont," *UF* 3 (1971) 25–32.
Fitzmyer, J. A.
The Aramaic Inscriptions of Sefîre (BibOr 19; Rome: Pontifical Biblical Institute, 1967).
Idem
The Genesis Apocryphon of Qumran Cave I (BibOr 18A; Rome: Biblical Institute Press, [2]1971).
Fohrer, G.
"Neuere Literatur zur alttestamentlichen Prophetie," *TRu* 19 (1951) 314–15; continuation, "2. Teil. Literatur von 1940–1950," *TRu* 20 (1952) 258–62; second edition of part 2, *TRu* 45 (1980) 193–225.
Idem
"Die Gattung der Berichte über symbolische Handlungen der Propheten," *ZAW* 64 (1952) 101–20; rep. in *Studien zur alttestamentlichen Prophetie (1949–1965)* (BZAW 99; Berlin: Töpelmann, 1967) 92–112.
Idem
"Remarks on Modern Interpretation of the Prophets," *JBL* 80 (1961) 312–14.
Idem
"Zehn Jahre Literatur zur alttestamentlichen Prophetie (1951–1960), Fortsetzung," *TRu* 28 (1962) 284–88.
Idem
Das Buch Hiob (KAT 16; Gütersloh: Gerd Mohn, 1963).
Idem
"Prophetie und Magie," *ZAW* 78 (1966) 40–42; rep. in *Studien zur alttestamentliche Prophetie (1949–1965)* (BZAW 99; Berlin: Töpelmann, 1967) 242–64.
Idem
Introduction to the Old Testament (tr. D. E. Green; Nashville: Abingdon, 1968).
Idem
"Zion-Jerusalem im Alten Testament," *Studien zur alttestamentlichen Theologie und Geschichte (1949–1966)* (BZAW 115; Berlin: Töpelmann, 1969) 195–241; English tr. "Zion-Jerusalem in the Old Testament," *TDNT* 7.293–319.
Idem
Die Propheten des 8. Jahrhunderts (*Die Propheten des Alten Testaments*; 7 vols.; Gütersloh: Mohn, 1974) 1.22–55.
Forbes, R. J.
Studies in Ancient Technology (9 vols.; Leiden: Brill, 1964).
Forrer, E.
Die Provinzeinteilung des assyrischen Reiches (Leipzig: Hinrichs, 1920).
Fraenkel, S.
Die Aramäischen Fremdwörter im Arabischen (Leiden: Brill, 1886).
Frankena, R.
Tākultu. De sacrale maaltijd in het assyrische ritueel (Leiden: Brill, 1953).
Idem
"Some Remarks on a New Approach to Hebrew," *Travels in the World of the Old Testament: Studies Presented to M. A. Beek on the Occasion of His Sixty-fifth Birthday* (ed. N.S.H.G. Heerma van Voss, Ph.J.J. Houwinkten, and N. A. vam Uchelen; Studia Semitica Neerlandica 16; Assen: Van Gorcum, 1974) 41–49.
Idem
Briefe aus dem Berliner Museum (AbB 6, Leiden: Brill, 1974).
Fredriksson, H.
Jahwe als Krieger. Studien zum alttestamentlichen Gottesbild (Lund: Gleerup, 1945).
Freedman, D. N.
"Divine Commitment and Human Obligation," *Int* 18 (1964) 419–31.
Idem
"Isaiah 42,13," *CBQ* 30 (1968) 225–26.
Idem
The New World of the Old Testament (inaugural lecture, San Anselmo, CA: San Francisco Theological Seminary, 1968).
Idem
"The Burning Bush," *Bib* 50 (1969) 246.
Idem
"Prolegomenon," to G. B. Gray, *The Forms of Hebrew Poetry* (New York: Ktav, 1972) vii–lvi.
Idem
"The Spelling of the Name 'David' in the Hebrew Bible," *Biblical and Other Studies in Honor of Robert Gordis* (ed. R. Ahroni; *HAR* 7; Columbus: Ohio State University, 1983) 89–104.
Friedman, R. E.
"The *MRZḤ* Tablet from Ugarit, *MAARAV* 4 (1979–1980) 187–206.
Friedman, S. Y.
"Law of Increasing Numbers in Mishnaic Hebrew," *Leš* 35 (1971) 117–29, 192–206 (Heb.); rep. in *Studies in Mishnaic Hebrew* (ed. M. Bar-Asher; Jerusalem: Hebrew University, 1980) 2.299–326 (Heb.).
Friedrich, J.
Die hethitischen Gesetzen (Documenta et Monumenta Orientis Antiqui 7; Leiden: Brill, 1959).

Frisch, A.
"The Number One Hundred in the Bible," *BM* 102 (1985) 435–40 (Heb.).
Frymer-Kensky, T.
"The Planting of Man: A Study in Biblical Imagery," *Love & Death in the Ancient Near East: Essays in Honor of Marvin H. Pope* (ed. J. H. Marks and R. M. Good; Guilford, CT: Four Quarters Publishing Company, 1987) 129–36.
Fulco, W. J.
The Canaanite God Rešep (AOS 8; New Haven, CT: American Oriental Society, 1976).
Gadd, C. J., and L. Legrain
Ur: Royal Inscriptions (2 vols.; London: The Trustees of the Two Museums, 1928).
Galil, Y.
"The Almond Tree in the Culture of Israel," *Teva we'Aretz* 8 (1966) 306–18, 338–55 (Heb.).
Galling, K.
Die Erwählungstradition Israels (BZAW 48; Giessen: Töpelmann, 1928).
Idem
"Bethel und Gilgal," *ZDPV* 66 (1943) 140–55.
Idem
"Bethel und Gilgal, II," *ZDPV* 67 (1944–1945) 21–43.
Idem
"Der Charakter der Chaosschilderung in Gen 1:2," *ZTK* 47 (1950) 145–57.
Idem
"Der Gott Karmel und die Ächtung der fremden Götter," *Geschichte und Altes Testament: Albrecht Alt zum siebzigsten Geburtstag* (ed. G. Ebeling; Tübingen: Mohr, 1953) 105–25.
Idem
"Der Ehrenname Elisas und die Entrückung Elias," *ZTK* 53 (1956) 129–48.
Garbini, G.
"Un nuovo sigillo aramaico-ammonita," *AION* 17 (1967) 251–56.
Garsiel, M.
Midrashic Name Derivations in the Bible (Ramat Gan: Revivim, 1987) (Heb.).
Gaster, T. H.
"A Canaanite Magical Text," *Or* 11 (1942) 41–79.
Idem
Myth, Legend and Custom in the Old Testament (New York/Evanston: Harper & Row, 1969).
Geiger, A.
Urschrift und Übersetzungen der Bibel (Frankfurt: Verlag Madda, ²1928).
Geller, S.
Die sumerisch-assyrische Serie Lugal-e ud me-lam-bi nirgál (AOTU I/4; Leiden: Brill, 1917) 255–361.
Gerleman, G.
"Contributions to the Old Testament Terminology of the Chase," *Bulletin de la Société Royale des Lettres de Lund* (Kungl Humanistiska Vetenskapssamfundet I Lund Årsberattelse 1945–1946; Lund: Gleerup) 4.79–90.
Gerleman, G., and E. Ruprecht
"*drš*," *THAT* 1 (1975) 460–67.
Gesenius, W.
Hebräisches und aramäisches Handwörterbuch über das Alte Testament (Leipzig: Vogel, 1899; ¹⁷1921).
Gevirtz, S.
"West-Semitic Curses and the Problem of the Origins of Hebrew Law," *VT* 11 (1961) 137–58.
Idem
"Evidence of Conjugational Variation in the Parallelization of Selfsame Verbs in the Amarna Letters," *JNES* 32 (1973) 99–104.
Idem
"Naphtali in the 'Blessing of Jacob,'" *JBL* 103 (1984) 513–21.
Gibson, J.C.L.
Textbook of Syrian Semitic Inscriptions: Volume I—Hebrew and Moabite Inscriptions (Oxford: Clarendon, 1971).
Idem
Textbook of Syrian Semitic Inscriptions: Volume II—Aramaic Inscriptions Including Inscriptions in the Dialect of Zendjirli (Oxford: Clarendon, 1975).
Idem
Textbook of Syrian Semitic Inscriptions: Volume III—Phoenician Inscriptions, Including Inscriptions in the Mixed Dialect of Arslan Tash (Oxford: Clarendon, 1982).
Gilula, M.
"To Yahweh Shomron and His Asherah," *Shnaton* 3 (1978–1979) 129–37 (Heb.).
Ginsberg, H. L.
"An Obscure Hebrew Word," *JQR* 22 (1931–1932) 143–45.
Idem
The Legend of King Keret: A Canaanite Epic of the Bronze Age (*BASOR* Supplementary Studies 2–3; New Haven, CT: Yale University, 1946).
Idem
"An Unrecognized Allusion to Kings Pekah and Hosea of Israel (Isa 8:23)," Eretz Israel 5 (*Benjamin Mazar Volume*; ed. M. Avi-Yonah; Jerusalem: Israel Exploration Society, 1958) 61*–65*.
Idem
"Hosea's Ephraim, More Fool than Knave. A New Interpretation of Hosea 12:1–14," *JBL* 80 (1961) 339–47.
Idem
Koheleth Interpreted: A New Commentary on the Torah, the Prophets and the Holy Writings (Tel Aviv/Jerusalem: Newman, 1961) (Heb.).
Idem
"Contributions to Biblical Lexicography," *Hanoch Yalon Jubilee Volume: On the Occasion of His Seventy-fifth Birthday* (ed. S. Lieberman and others; Jerusalem: Kiryat Sepher, 1963) 167–73 (Heb.).

Idem
"From Isaiah's Diary," *'Oz LeDavid: Collected Readings in Bible Presented to David ben Gurion on His Seventy-seventh Birthday* (ed. Y. Kaufmann and others; Jerusalem: Kiryat Sepher, 1964) 335–50 (Heb.).

Idem
The Israelian Heritage of Judaism (Texts and Studies of the Jewish Theological Seminary of America 24; New York: Jewish Theological Seminary of America, 1982).

de Goeje, M. J., ed.
Bibliotheca Geographorum Arabicorum (London, 1892).

Goelz, F.
"Vom biblischen Sinn des Sabbat," *Theologische Beiträge* 9 (1978) 243–56.

Goetze, A.
Old Babylonian Omen Texts (YOS 10; New Haven, CT: Yale University; London: Cumberledge, 1947).

Idem
The Laws of Eshnunna (AASOR 31; New Haven, CT: ASOR, 1956).

Idem
Kleinasien (Handbuch der Altertumswissenschaft 3/1.3 [Kulturgeschichte des Alten Orients] 3.1; München: Beck, ^{2}1957).

Gold, V. R.
"Tekoa," *IDB* 4.527–29.

Idem
"Teman," *IDB* 4.534–35.

Idem
"The Mosaic Map of Madeba," *BA* 21 (1958) 50–71.

Good, E. M.
Irony in the Old Testament (Philadelphia: Westminster, 1965).

Good, R. M.
"The Just War in Ancient Israel," *JBL* 104 (1985) 385–400.

Idem
"The Carthaginian Mayumas," *Studi Epigrafici e Linguistici sul Vicino Oriente Antico* 3 (1986) 99–114.

Gordis, R.
"Some Hitherto Unrecognized Meanings of the Verb *Shub*," *JBL* 52 (1933) 153–62.

Idem
"Studies in the Relationship of Biblical and Rabbinic Hebrew," *Louis Ginzberg Jubilee Volume: On the Occasion of His Seventieth Birthday* (2 vols.; ed. S. Lieberman and others; New York: American Academy for Jewish Research, 1946) English Section, 173–99.

Idem
The Book of Job: Commentary, New Translation and Special Studies (Moreshet 2; New York: Jewish Theological Seminary of America, 1978).

Idem
"On 'מֵרַחֵם בֶּן בִּטְנָהּ' in Isa. 49:15," *Tarbiz* 53 (1983–1984) 31 (Heb.).

Gordon, C. H.
"Kir, 2," *IDB* 3.36.

Idem
Introduction to Old Testament Times (Ventor, NJ: Ventor Publishers, 1953).

Idem
"Ugarit as a Link between Greek and Hebrew Literature," *RSO* 29 (1954) 161–69.

Idem
Review of A. Malamat, *The Arameans in Aram Naharaim and the Rise of Their States* (Jerusalem: Israel Exploration Society, 1952) (Heb.) in *JBL* 74 (1955) 289.

Idem
"New Directions," *BASP* 15 (1978) 59–66.

Idem
"Assymetric Janus Parallelism," Eretz Israel 16 (*Harry M. Orlinsky Volume;* ed. B. A. Levine and A. Malamat; Jerusalem: Israel Exploration Society, 1982) *80–*81.

Gössmann, F.
Planetarium Babylonicum, oder: Die sumerisch--babylonischen Stern-Namen (ed. P. A. Deimel; Šumerisches Lexikon IV/2; Rome: Pontifical Biblical Institute, 1950).

Idem
Das Era Epos (Würzburg: Augustinus Verlag, 1955).

Gottwald, N. K.
All the Kingdoms of the Earth: Israelite Prophecy and International Relations in the Ancient Near East (New York/London: Harper & Row, 1964).

Gowan, D. E.
"The Beginnings of Exile-Theology and the Root *GLH*," *ZAW* 87 (1975) 204–7.

Gradwohl, R.
Die Farben im Alten Testament: Eine Terminologische Studie (BZAW 83, Berlin: Töpelmann, 1963).

Graetz, H.
Emendationes in plerosque Sacrae Scripturae Veteris Testamenti libros, fasc. 2 (ed. G. Bacher; Breslau: Schottlaender, 1893).

Gray, J.
"Ashimah," *IDB* 1.252.

Idem
Legacy of Canaan: The Ras Shamra Texts and Their Relevance to the Old Testament (SVT 5; Leiden: Brill, 1957, ^{2}1965).

Idem
1 and 2 Kings (OTL; Philadelphia: Westminster, 1963).

Grayson, A. K.
"The Dynastic Prophecy," *Babylonian Historical-Literary Texts* (Toronto Semitic Texts and Studies 3; Toronto/Buffalo: University of Toronto, 1975) 24–37.

Grayson, A. K., and W. G. Lambert
"Akkadian Prophecies," *JCS* 18 (1964) 7–30.
Greenberg, M.
"Oaths," *EncJud* 12.1295–98.
Idem
"Sabbath," *EncJud* 14.558–62.
Idem
"The Hebrew Oath Particle *ḤAY/ḤĒ*," *JBL* 76 (1957) 34–39.
Idem
"Some Postulates of Biblical Criminal Law," *Yehezkel Kaufmann Jubilee Volume: Studies in Bible and Jewish Religion Dedicated to Yehezkel Kaufmann on the Occasion of His Seventieth Birthday* (ed. M. Haran; Jerusalem: Magnes, 1960) 20–27.
Idem
Ezekiel 1—20: A New Translation with Introduction and Commentary (AB 22; Garden City, NY: Doubleday, 1983).
Greenfield, J. C.
"Caphtor," *IDB* 1.534.
Idem
"Stylistic Aspects of the Sefire Treaty Inscriptions," *AcOr* 29 (1965) 1–18.
Idem
"Some Aspects of Treaty Inscriptions in the Bible," *Fourth World Congress of Jewish Studies* (Jerusalem: World Union of Jewish Studies, 1967) 1.117–19.
Idem
"Scripture and Inscription: The Literary and Rhetorical Element in Some Early Phoenician Inscriptions," *Near Eastern Studies in Honor of William Foxwell Albright* (ed. H. Goedicke; Baltimore/London: Johns Hopkins University, 1971) 253–68.
Idem
"The Background and Parallel to a Proverb of Ahiqar," *Hommages à André Dupont-Sommer* (ed. A. Caquot and M. Philonenko; Paris: Adrien-Maisonneuve, 1971) 49–59.
Greenfield, J. C., and A. Shaffer
"Some Observations on the Akkadian-Aramaic Bilingual from Tell-Fekherye," *Shnaton* V–VI (1978–1979) 119–29 (Heb.); English tr. "Notes on the Akkadian-Aramaic Bilingual Statue from Tell Fekherye," *Iraq* 45 (1983) 109–16.
Gressmann, H.
Der Ursprung des israelitisch-judäischen Eschatologie (FRLANT 6; Göttingen: Vandenhoeck & Ruprecht, 1905).
Idem
"Hadad und Baal nach den Amarnabriefen und nach ägyptischen Texten," *Abhandlungen zur Semitischen Religionskunde und Sprachwissenschaft* (ed. W. Frankenberg and F. Küchler; BZAW 33; Giessen: Töpelmann, 1918) 191–216.
Idem
Die älteste Geschichtschreibung und Prophetie Israels (von Samuel bis Amos und Hosea) (*SAT* 2/1; Göttingen: Vandenhoeck & Ruprecht, [2]1921).
Idem
Altorientalische Bilder zum Alten Testament gesammelt und beschrieben (Berlin/Leipzig: de Gruyter, [2]1927).
Idem
Der Messias (FRLANT 43; Göttingen: Vandenhoeck & Ruprecht, 1929).
Gruber, M. I.
"Mourning," *EncJud* 10.485–87.
Idem
Aspects of Nonverbal Communication in the Ancient Near East (2 vols.; Studia Pohl 12/1–2; Rome: Pontifical Biblical Institute, 1980).
Idem
"'Will a Woman Forget Her Infant?' Isa 49:15," *Tarbiz* 51 (1981–1982) 491–92 (Heb.).
Idem
"The Many Faces of Hebrew נשא פנים, 'Lift Up the Face,'" *ZAW* 98 (1983) 252–60.
Guillaume, A.
"Hebrew Notes," *PEQ* 79 (1947) 42–44.
Idem
Prophétie et divination chez les Semites (Paris: Payot, 1950).
Idem
Hebrew and Arabic Lexicography (Leiden: Brill, 1965).
Gunkel, H.
Die Propheten (Göttingen: Vandenhoeck & Ruprecht, 1917).
Idem
Einleitung in die Psalmen. Die Gattungen der religiösen Lyrik Israels (Göttingen: Vandenhoeck & Ruprecht, 1953).
Idem
"Propheten II: Seit Amos," in *RGG*[1], IV, 1866–1886, rep. in *RGG*[2] 4, 1538–54; tr. and rep. as "The Israelite Prophecy from the Time of Amos," *Twentieth Century Theology in the Making* (tr. R. A. Wilson; ed. J. Pelikan; New York: Harper & Row, 1969) 48–75.
Idem
Genesis (Göttingen: Vandenhoeck & Ruprecht, 1970).
Gunneweg, A.H.J.
"Religion oder Offenbarung. Zum hermeneutischen Problem des alten Testaments," *ZTK* 74 (1977) 151–78.
Gurewicz, S. B.
"When Did the Cult Associated with the 'Golden Calves' Fully Develop in the Northern Kingdom?" *AusBR* 2 (1952) 41–44.
Gurney, O. R.
"The Sultantepe Tablets IV: The Cuthean Legend of Naram-Sin," AnSt 5 (1955) 93–113.
Hackett, J. A.
"The Dialect of the Plaster Text from Tell Deir 'Alla," *Or* 53 (1984) 57–65.

Haldar, A.
Associations of Cult Prophets among the Ancient Semites (Uppsala: Almquist & Wiksells, 1940).
Idem
"Tradition and History," *BO* 31 (1974) 26–37.
Haller, M.
"Edom im Urteil der Propheten," *Vom Alten Testament: Karl Marti zum siebzigsten Geburtstag* (ed. K. Budde; BZAW 41; Giessen: Töpelmann, 1925) 109–17.
Hallo, W. W.
"From Qarqar to Carchemish: Assyria and Israel in the Light of New Discoveries," *BA* 23 (1960) 34–61; rep. in *The Biblical Archeologist Reader* (ed. E. F. Campbell and D. N. Freedman; Garden City, NY: Doubleday, 1962) 2:152–88.
Idem
"Accadian Apocalypses," *IEJ* 16 (1966) 231–42.
Idem
"Antediluvian Cities," *JCS* 23 (1970) 57–67.
Idem
"New Moons and Sabbaths: A Case-Study in the Contrastive Approach," *HUCA* 48 (1977) 1–18.
Hallo, W. W., and J. J. A. van Dijk
The Exaltation of Inanna (YNERS 3; New Haven, CT/London: Yale University, 1968).
Halpern, B.
"A Landlord-Tenant Dispute at Ugarit?" *MAARAV* 2/1 (1979) 121–40.
Hammond, P. C.
"New Light on the Nabateans," *BAR* 7 (1981) 22–41.
Haran, M.
"Food-Drink," *EM* 4.543–48 (Heb.).
Idem
"Tithe," *EM* 5.206–8 (Heb.).
Idem
"Nazirites," *EM* 5.795–99 (Heb.).
Idem
"The Uses of Incense in the Ancient Israelite Ritual," *VT* 10 (1960) 113–29.
Idem
Ages and Institutions in the Bible (Tel Aviv: Am Oved, 1972) (Heb.).
Idem
Temples and Temple Service in Ancient Israel: An Inquiry into the Character of Cult Phenomena and the Historical Setting of the Priestly School (Oxford: Clarendon, 1978).
Hareuveni, E.
"Studies in the Names of the Flora of Israel," *Leš* 2 (1929) 176–83 (Heb.).
Harris, R.
Ancient Sippar: A Demographic Study of an Old Babylonian City (1894–1595 B.C.) (Istanbul: Nederlands Historisch-Archaeologisch Instituuts, 1975).
Harris, Z.
A Grammar of the Phoenician Language (AOS 8; New Haven, CT: American Oriental Society, 1936).
Harrison, R. K.
Introduction to the Old Testament (Leicester: Inter-Varsity, 1969).
Hasel, G. F.
The Remnant: The History and Theology of the Remnant Idea from Genesis to Isaiah (Andrews University Monograph Studies in Religion 5; Berrien Springs, MI: Andrews University, 1972).
Idem
"Semantic Values of Derivatives of the Hebrew Root *Š'R*," *AUSS* 2 (1973) 152–59.
Haupt, P.
Akkadische und sumerische Keilschrifttexte (Leipzig: Hinrichs, 1882).
Idem
"Eine altestamentliche Festliturgie für den Nikanortag," *ZDMG* 61 (1907) 275–97.
Idem
"Ur of the Chaldees," *JBL* 36 (1917) 99.
Hawkins, J. D.
"Hammath," *RLA* 4/1 (1972) 67–70.
Idem
"Hattin," *RLA* 4/2–3 (1973) 160–62.
Idem
"Assyrians and Hittites," *Iraq* 36 (1974) 81–83.
Idem
"Kinallua," *RLA* 5 (1976–1980) 476–80.
Idem
"Kullani(a)," *RLA* 6/3–4 (1981) 305–6.
Heer, L. G.
"The Servant of Baalis," *BA* 48 (1985) 169–72.
Heidenheim, M.
Bibliotheca Samaritana (Leipzig: Schulze, 1885).
Heider, G. C.
The Cult of Molek—A Reassessment (*JSOT* Supplement 43; Sheffield: JSOT Press, 1985).
Heintz, J.-G.
"Oracles prophétiques et 'guerre sainte' selon les archives royales de Mari et l'ancien Testament," SVT 17 (Leiden: Brill, 1968) 112–38.
Held, M.
"The *YQTL-QTL* (*QTL-YQTL*) Sequence of Identical Verbs in Biblical Hebrew and Ugaritic," *Studies and Essays in Honor of Abraham A. Neuman* (ed. M. ben Horin, B. D. Weinryb, and S. Zeitlin; Leiden: Brill, 1962) 281–90.
Idem
"The Action-Result (Factitive-Passive) Sequence of Identical Verbs in Biblical Hebrew and Ugaritic," *JBL* 84 (1965) 272–82.
Idem
"The Root *ZBL/SBL* in Akkadian, Ugaritic and Biblical Hebrew," *Essays in Memory of E. A. Speiser* (ed. W. W. Hallo; New Haven, CT: Yale University, 1968) = *JAOS* 88 (1968) 90–96.
Idem
"Rhetorical Questions in Ugaritic and Biblical Hebrew," Eretz Israel 9 (*W. F. A. Albright Volume;*

ed. A. Malamat; Jerusalem: Israel Exploration Society, 1969) 71–79.

Idem
"Studies in Biblical Homonyms in the Light of Akkadian," *JANESCU* 3 (1970–1971) 46–55.

Idem
"Hebrew *ma'gāl*: A Study in Lexical Parallelism," *JANESCU* 6 (1974) 107–16.

Idem
"Studies in Biblical Lexicography in the Light of Akkadian," Eretz Israel 16 (*Harry M. Orlinsky Volume*; ed. B. A. Levine and A. Malamat; Jerusalem: Israel Exploration Society, 1982) 76–85 (Heb.).

Idem
"Studies in Biblical Lexicography in the Light of Akkadian, Part II," *Studies in Bible, Dedicated to the Memory of U. Cassuto on the 100th Anniversary of His Birth* (ed. S. E. Loewenstamm; Jerusalem: Magnes, 1987) 104–26 (Heb.).

Heller, H.
"New Biblical Interpretations," *Zvi Karl Memorial Volume* (ed. A. Weiser and B. Z. Luria; Jerusalem: Kiryat Sepher, 1960) 48–53 (Heb.).

Heltzer, M.
Review of L. R. Fisher, *The Claremont Ras Shamra Tablets* (AnOr 48; Rome: Pontifical Biblical Institute, 1971) in *IEJ* 22 (1972) 254–55.

Hempel, J.
"Jahwegleichnisse der israelitischen Propheten," *ZAW* 42 (1924) 74–104.

Idem
"Berufung und Bekehrung," *Festschrift Georg Beer zum 70. Geburtstag* (ed. A. Weiser; Stuttgart: Kohlhammer, 1935).

Hendel, R. S.
"The Flame of the Whirling Sword: A Note on Genesis 3:24," *JBL* 104 (1985) 671–74.

Herdner, A.
Corpus de tablettes en cunéiform alphabétiques découvertes à Ras Shamra-Ugarit de 1929 à 1939 (Paris: Geuthner, 1963).

Hermisson, H.-J.
"Die Kennenzeichen der hebräischer Poesie," *TRu* 21 (1953) 97–129, 324.

Herrmann, W.
"Jahwes Triumph über Mot," *UF* 11 (1979) 371–77.

Hertzberg, H. W.
"Die prophetische Botschaft vom Heil," *NKZ* 43 (1932) 511–34.

Herzog, Z.
"Israelite Sanctuaries at Arad and Beer-Sheba," *Temples and High Places in Biblical Times* (ed. A. Biran; Jerusalem: Keter, 1981) 120–22.

Herzog, Z., A. F. Rainey, and S. Moskowitz
"The Stratigraphy of Beer-sheba and the Location of the Sanctuary," *BASOR* 225 (1975) 49–58.

Hesse, F.
Die Fürbitte im alten Testament (Erlangen, 1949).

Hillers, D. R.
"A Note on Some Treaty Terminology in the Old Testament," *BASOR* 176 (1964) 46–47.

Hilprecht, H. V.
Old Babylonian Inscriptions Chiefly from Nippur (BE Series A; CT 1; Philadelphia: University of Pennsylvania, 1893).

Hirschberg, H. H.
"Some Additional Arabic Etymologies in Old Testament Lexicography," *VT* 11 (1961) 373–85.

Höffken, P.
"Heilszeitherrschererwartung im babylonischen Raum," *WO* 9 (1977) 57–71.

Idem
"Zu den Heilszusätzen in der Völkerorakelsammlung des Jeremiabuches," *VT* 27 (1977) 398–412.

Hoffman, D. Z.
Leviticus (2 vols.; Jerusalem: Mosad HaRav Kook, [2]1976) (Heb.).

Hoffman, Y.
"Edom as the Symbol of Wickedness in Prophetic Literature," *Bible and Jewish History: Studies in Bible and Jewish History Dedicated to the Memory of Jacob Liver* (ed. B. Uffenheimer; Tel Aviv: Tel Aviv University, 1972) 76–89 (Heb.).

Idem
"Two Opening Formulae in Biblical Style," *Tarbiz* 46 (1977) 157–80 (Heb.).

Idem
The Doctrine of Exodus in the Bible (Tel Aviv: Tel Aviv University, 1983) (Heb.).

Hoffner, H.
Alimenta Hethaeorum. Food Production in Hittite Asia Minor (AOS 55; New Haven, CT: American Oriental Society, 1974).

Hoftijzer, J., and G. van der Kooij
Aramaic Texts from Deir 'Alla (Documenta et Monumenta Orientis Antiqui 19; Leiden: Brill, 1976).

Holladay, W. L.
The Root ŠÛBH in the Old Testament: With Particular Reference to Its Usages in Covenantal Contexts (Leiden: Brill, 1958).

Homer
The Iliad (tr. A. T. Murray; Loeb Classical Library; London: Heineman, 1960).

Idem
The Odyssey (tr. A. T. Murray; Loeb Classical Library; London: Heineman, 1985).

Hommel, H.
"Das religiongeschichtliche Problem des 139. Psalms," *ZAW* 47 (1929) 110–24.

Honeyman, A. M.
"The Pottery Vessels of the Old Testament," *PEQ* 71 (1939) 76–90.

Horn, S. H.
"Ammon, Ammonites," *IDBSup* 20–21.

Idem
"The Amman Citadel Inscription," *BASOR* 193 (1969) 2–13.
Idem
"A Seal from Amman," *BASOR* 205 (1972) 43–45.
Horst, F.
"Der Eid im Alten Testament," *EvT* 17 (1957) 366–84; rep. in *Gottes Recht: Studien zum Recht im Alten Testament* (ed. H. W. Wolff; TBü 12; München: Kaiser, 1961) 292–314.
Idem
"Eid. II. Im AT," *RGG*³, 2 (1958) 349–50.
Idem
Hiob (BKAT 16/1; Neukirchen-Vluyn: Neukirchener Verlag, 1960).
Houtman, C.
"De jubelzang van de struiken der wildernis in Psalm 96:12b," *Loven in geloven: Festschrift H. N. Ridderbos* (Amsterdam: Franeker, 1975) 151–74.
Huesman, J.
"The Infinitive Absolute and *waw* + Perfect," *Bib* 37 (1956) 410–34.
Huffmon, H. B.
Amorite Personal Names in the Mari Texts: A Structural and Lexical Study (Baltimore: Johns Hopkins University, 1965).
Humbert, P.
La "terou'a": Analyse d'un rite biblique (Neuchâtel: Secrétariat de l'Université, 1946).
Idem
"Emploi et portée du verbe *bārā* (créer) dans l'Ancien Testament," *TZ* 3 (1947) 401–22; rep. in *Opuscules d'un Hébraïsant* (Neuchâtel: Secrétariat de l'Université, 1958) 146–65.
Idem
"Emploi et portée bibliques du verbe *yāṣar* et de ses dérivés substantifs," *Von Ugarit nach Qumran. Beiträge zur Alttestamentlichen und Altorientalischen Forschung* (ed. J. Hempel and L. Rost; BZAW 77; Berlin: Töpelmann, 1958) 82–88.
Idem
"Dieu fait sortir," *TZ* 18 (1962) 357–61.
Hunger, H., and S. A. Kaufman
"A New Akkadian Prophecy Text," *JAOS* 95 (1975) 371–75.
Hurvitz, A.
"The Chronological Significance of 'Aramaisms' in Biblical Hebrew," *IEJ* 18 (1968) 234–40.
Idem
The Transition Period in Biblical Hebrew. A Study in Post-Exilic Hebrew and Its Implications for the Dating of the Psalms (Jerusalem: Bialik, 1972) (Heb.).
Idem
"Wisdom Vocabulary in the Hebrew Psalter: A Contribution to the Study of 'Wisdom Psalms,'" *VT* 38 (1988) 41–51.
Hyatt, J. P.
The Prophetic Criticism of Israelite Worship (Cincinnati: Hebrew Union College, 1963).
ibn Ezra, M.
Sepher Shirath Yisrael (ed. B. Z. Halpern; Leipzig: A. Y. Stikel, 1924) (Heb.).
ibn Ganaḥ, Y.
Sefer HaRiqmah (2 vols.; Jerusalem: Academy for the Hebrew Language, 1964) (Heb.).
Idem
Sepher Haschoraschim (ed. W. Bacher; Berlin: H. Itzkowski, 1896) (Heb.).
Ikeda, Y.
The Kingdom of Hamath and Its Relations with Aram and Israel (diss.; Hebrew University, 1977) (Heb.).
Isbell, C. D.
Corpus of the Aramaic Incantation Bowls (SBLDS 17; Missoula, MT: Scholars, 1975).
Jacob, E.
Ras Šamra-Ugarit et l'Ancien Testament (Cahiers d'Archéologie Biblique 12; Paris: Delachaux & Niestlé, 1960).
Jacobsen, T.
Toward the Image of Tammuz and Other Essays on Mesopotamian History and Culture (ed. W. Moran; HSS 21; Cambridge: Harvard University, 1970).
Jastrow, M.
Dictionary of the Targumim, the Talmud Bavli and Yerushalmi, and the Midrashic Literature (2 vols.; New York: Putnam, 1950).
Jean, C.-F.
Contrats de Larsa (Paris: Guethner, 1926).
Jenni, E.
"*Yôm*," *THAT* 1² (1975) 707–26.
Jeremias, J.
Theophanie. Die Geschichte einer alttestamentlichen Gattung (WMANT 10; Neukirchen-Vluyn: Neukirchener Verlag, 1965).
Kahle, W.
Der Kleine Brehm: Das gesamte Tierreich in allgemeinverständlicher Darstellung (Berlin: Vögels, 1933).
Kaiser, O.
Die mythische Bedeutung des Meeres in Ägypten, Ugarit und Israel (BZAW 78; Berlin: Töpelmann, 1959).
Kallai, Z.
"Carmel," *EM* 4.324–29 (Heb.).
Idem
"Lo Debar," *EM* 4.409–10 (Heb.).
Kallner-Amiran, D. H.
"A Revised Earthquake Catalogue of Palestine," *IEJ* 1 (1950–1951) 223–46; *IEJ* 2 (1952) 48–65.
Kapelrud, A. S.
"Tyre," *IDB* 4.721–23.
Kaplan, M.
"Isaiah 6:1–11," *JBL* 45 (1926) 251–59.
Karageorghis, V.
Excavations in the Necropolis of Salamis III (Nicosia: Department of Antiquities of Cyprus, 1973).
Kasowski, C. J.
Thesaurus Mishnae (4 vols.; Jerusalem: Jewish Theological Seminary of America, 1957).

Kassis, H. E.
"Gath and the Structure of the 'Philistine' Society," *JBL* 84 (1965) 259–71.

Katzenstein, H. J.
"Tyre," *EM* 6.698–707 (Heb.).

Idem
The History of Tyre: From the Beginning of the Second Millennium B.C.E. until the Fall of the Neo-Babylonian Empire in 538 B.C.E. (Jerusalem: Schocken Institute, 1973).

Kaufman, S. A.
The Akkadian Influences on Aramaic (Assyriological Studies 19; Chicago/London: University of Chicago, 1974).

Idem
"Prediction, Prophecy and Apocalypse in the Light of New Akkadian Texts," *Proceedings of the Sixth World Congress of Jewish Studies* (Jerusalem: World Union of Jewish Studies, 1977) 1:221–28.

Kaufmann, Y.
The Book of Judges (Jerusalem: Kiryat Sepher, 1962) (Heb.).

Kautzsch, E.
"*ṣᵉbāʼôth*," *RE* 3/21 (1908) 620–27.

Kautzsch, E., and A. E. Cowley
Gesenius' Hebrew Grammar (Oxford: Clarendon, ²1957).

Kedar-Kopfstein, B.
"*ḥag*," *TWAT* 11 (1977) 730–44.

Keel, O.
Die Welt der altorientalischen Bildsymbolik und das Alte Testament (Zürich/Einsielden/Köln: Benzinger Verlag, 1972).

Keller, C. A.
"Über einige alttestamentliche Heiligtumslegende, I," *ZAW* 67 (1955) 162–68.

Kellermann, D.
"*ḥmṣ*," *TWAT* II (1977) 1061–68.

Idem
"ʻAštārōt-ʻAštᵉrōt, Qarnayim-Qarnayim," *ZDPV* 97 (1981) 45–61.

Kelso, J. L.
"Bethel (Sanctuary)," *IDB* 1.391–93.

Kenyon, K.
Royal Cities of the Old Testament (New York: Schocken, 1973).

Kessler, W.
"Aus welchen Gründen wird die Bezeichnung 'Jahweh Zebaoth' in der späteren Zeit gemieden?" *Gottes ist der Orient: Festschrift für Otto Eissfeldt zu seinen 70. Geburtstag am 1. September 1957* (Berlin: Evangelischer Verlag, 1959) 79–83.

Kimchi, D.
Radicum Liber (= *Sepher Haschorachim;* Berlin: G. Bethge, 1847; rep. Jerusalem, 1967) (Heb.) Photocopy.

King, L. W.
The Seven Tablets of Creation: Or the Babylonian and Assyrian Legends Concerning the Creation of the World and of Mankind (Luzac's Semitic Text and Translation Series 13; 2 vols.; London: Luzac, 1902).

Idem
Cuneiform Texts from Babylonian Tablets in the British Museum, Volume 15: Old Babylonian Legends (CT 15; London: The British Museum, 1902)

Kinnier-Wilson, J. V.
"The Kurba'il Statue of Shalmaneser III," *Iraq* 24 (1962) 90–115.

Kitchen, K. A.
"The Philistines," *Peoples of Old Testament Times* (ed. D. J. Wiseman; Oxford: Clarendon, 1973) 53–78.

Idem
The Third Intermediate Period in Egypt, 1110–650 B.C. (Warminster: Aris & Phillips, 1973).

Kittel, R.
Geschichte des Volkes Israel. 3. Bd.: Die Zeit der Wegführung nach Babel und die Aufrichtung der neuen Gemeinde (3 vols.; Stuttgart: Kohlhammer, 1923).

Klein, J.
"שבר רעבון (Gen 22:9) in the Light of an Old Babylonian Parallel," *The Proceedings of the Sixth World Congress of Jewish Studies* (Jerusalem: World Union of Jewish Studies, 1977) 1:237–44.

Knierim, R.
"Das erste Gebote," *ZAW* 77 (1965) 20–39.

Idem
"*pšʻ*," *THAT* II (1972) 488–95.

Knudtzon, J. A.
Die El-Amarna-Tafeln (VAB 2/2; 2 vols.; Aalen: Otto Zeller, 1964).

Koch, K.
"*ṣdq*," *THAT* II (1976) 507–30.

Idem
Die Propheten I: Assyrische Zeit (Urban-Taschenbücher 280; Stuttgart: Kohlhammer, 1978).

Köcher, F.
Literarische Texte in akkadischer Sprache (*KUB* 37; Berlin: Akademie Verlag, 1953).

Idem
"Ein spätbabylonischer Hymnus auf den Tempel Ezida in Borsippa," *ZA* 53 (1959) 236–40.

Koehler, L.
Hebrew Man (tr. P. R. Ackroyd; Nashville: Abingdon, 1956).

Köhler, L.
"Hebräische Vokabeln II," *ZAW* 55 (1937) 161–62.

Koldeway, R., and F. Wetzel
Die Königsburgen von Babylon (*WVDOG* 54; Leipzig: Hinrichs, 1931).

Idem
Die Königsburgen von Babylon, II. Teil: Die Hauptburg und der Sommerpalast Nebukadnezars im Hügel Babil (*WVDOG* 55; Leipzig: Hinrichs, 1932; rep. Osnabrück, 1969).

Kraeling, C. H.
"Music in the Bible," *Ancient and Oriental Music* (ed. E. Wellesz) = *New Oxford History of Music* (London: Oxford University, 1954) 1.283–319.
Kraeling, E. G.
Aram and Israel: Or the Arameans in Syria and Mesopotamia (Columbia University Oriental Studies 13; New York: AMS, 1918).
Idem
The Brooklyn Museum Aramaic Papyri: New Documents of the Fifth Century B.C. from the Jewish Colony at Elephantine (New Haven: Yale University, 1935).
Kramer, S. N., and Weinfeld, M.
"Sumerian Literature and the Book of Psalms—An Introduction to Comparative Research," *BM* 57 (1974) 136–60 (Heb.).
Krašovec, J.
Antithetic Structure in Biblical Hebrew Poetry (SVT 35; Leiden: Brill, 1984).
Kraus, F. R.
Briefe aus dem British Museum (CT 43 und 44) (AbB 1; Leiden: Brill, 1964).
Kraus, H.-J.
"Gilgal. Ein Beitrag zur Kultusgeschichte Israels," *VT* 1 (1951) 181–99.
Idem
Gottesdienst in Israel. Grundriss einer Geschichte des alttestamentlichen Gottesdienstes (München: Chr. Kaiser, [2]1962).
Idem
"Der lebendige Gott. Ein Kapitel biblischer Theologie," *EvT* 27 (1967) 169–200.
Idem
Psalmen 1—63 (BKAT XV/1; Neukirchen-Vluyn: Neukirchener Verlag, 1972).
Krauss, S.
Talmudische Archäologie. Grundriss der Gesamtwissenschaft des Judentums (3 vols.; Hildesheim: George Olms, 1966).
Krenkel, M.
"Zur Kritik und Exegese der kleinen Propheten," *ZWT* 14 (1866) 266–81.
Küchler, F.
Beiträge zur Kenntnis der assyrisch-babylonischen Medizin (Assyriologische Bibliothek 18; Leipzig: Hinrichs, 1904).
Kudlek, M., and E. H. Mickler
Solar and Lunar Eclipses of the Ancient Near East from 3000 B.C. to 0 with Maps (AOAT Supplement 1; Neukirchen-Vluyn: Neukirchener Verlag, 1971).
Kuschke, A.
"Zweimal *ḳrjtn*," *ZDPV* 77 (1961) 24–34.
Idem
"Horonaim and Qiryathaim. Remarks on a Recent Contribution to the Topography of Moab," *PEQ* 99 (1967) 104–5.
Kutsch, E.
"Die Wurzel *'ṣr* im Hebräischen," *VT* 2 (1952) 57–69.
Idem
Salbung als Rechtsakt im alten Testament und im alten Orient (BZAW 87; Berlin: Töpelmann, 1963).
Idem
"'Trauerbräuche' und 'Selbstminderungsriten' im Alten Testament," *Drei Wiener Antrittsreden* (*ThSt* 78; Zürich: EVZ-Verlag, 1965) 25–42.
Kutscher, E. Y.
The Language and Linguistic Background of the Isaiah Scroll (Jerusalem: Magnes, 1959, Heb.; English tr., Leiden: Brill, 1974).
Idem
"Mittelhebräisch und jüdisch-aramäisch im neuen Köhler-Baumgartner," *Hebräische Wortforschung: Festschrift zum 80. Geburtstag von Walter Baumgartner* (ed. B. Hartmann and others; SVT 16; Leiden: Brill, 1967) 158–75.
Idem
Words and Their History (Jerusalem: Kiryat Sepher, 1968) (Heb.).
Idem
Hebrew and Aramaic Studies (ed. Z. Ben-Hayyim, A. Dotan, and G. Sarfatti; Jerusalem: Magnes, 1977) (Heb.).
Kutscher, R.
"A New Inscription from Amman," *Qadmoniot* 17 (1972) 27–28 (Heb.).
Labuschagne, C. J.
"Ugaritic *BLT* and *BILTÎ* in Isa X 4," *VT* 14 (1964) 97–99.
Idem
"The Emphasizing Particle גם and Its Connotations," *Studia Biblica et Semitica: Theodoro Christiano Vriezen qui munere professoris theologiae per XXV annos functus est* (Wageningen: Voenman & Zonen, 1966) 193–203.
Lacheman, E. R.
Excavations at Nuzi VI: The Administrative Archives (HSS 15; Cambridge: Harvard University, 1955).
Lambdin, T. O.
"Egyptian Loan Words in the Old Testament," *JAOS* 73 (1953) 145–55.
Lambert, W. G.
"Nebuchadnezzar, King of Justice," *Iraq* 24 (1965) 1–11.
Idem
Babylonian Wisdom Literature (Oxford: Clarendon, 1967).
Idem
"A Neo-Babylonian Tammuz Lament," *Studies in Literature from the Ancient Near East, by Members of the American Oriental Society Dedicated to Samuel Noah Kramer* (ed. J. M. Sasson) = *JAOS* 103/1 (1983) 211–15.
Lambert, W. G., and A. R. Millard
Atra-Ḫasis: The Babylonian Story of the Flood (Oxford: Clarendon, 1969).
Landes, G. M.
"Ammon, Ammonites," *IDB* 1.108–14.

Idem
"Rabbah," *IDB* 4.1–3.
Idem
"Rabbah," *IDBSup* 724.
Landsberger, B.
"Bemerkungen zu San Nicolò und Ungnad, Neubabylonische Rechts- und Verwaltungsurkunden, Bd. II.2," *ZA* 39 (1929–1930) 277–94.
Idem
Sam'al: Studien zur Entdeckung Ruinenstätte Karatepe (Ankara: Turkische historische Gesellschaft, 1948).
Idem
The Series Ḫar-ra = ḫubullu Tablets I-IV (*MSL* 5; Rome: Pontifical Biblical Institute, 1957).
Idem
"Einige unerkannt gebliebene oder verkannte Nomina des Akkadischen," *WZKM* 56 (1960) 109–29.
Idem
The Fauna of Ancient Mesopotamia (*MSL* 8; 2 vols.; Rome: Pontifical Biblical Institute, 1962).
Idem
"Tin and Lead—The Adventures of Two Vocables," *JNES* 24 (1965) 285–96.
Lang, B.
"The Social Organization of Peasant Poverty in Biblical Israel," *JSOT* 24 (1982) 47–63.
Idem
Monotheism and the Prophetic Minority: An Essay in Biblical History and Sociology (The Social World of Biblical Antiquity 1; Sheffield: Almond, 1983).
Langdon, S.
Die neubabylonischen Königsinschriften (VAB 4; Leipzig: Hinrichs, 1912).
Idem
Babylonian Liturgies: Sumerian Texts from the Early Period and from the Library of Ashurbanipal (Paris: Guethner, 1913).
Idem
Babylonian Penitential Psalms to Which Are Added Fragments of the Creation Epic from Kish (Oxford Editions of Cuneiform Texts 6; Paris: Guethner, 1927).
Langlemet, F.
Gilgal et les récits de la transversée du Jourdain (Cahiers de la Revue Biblique 11; Paris: Gabalda, 1969).
Layard, A. H.
Inscriptions in the Cuneiform Character from Assyrian Monuments (London: Longman & Pickering, 1851).
Lehmann, M. R.
"Biblical Oaths," *ZAW* 81 (1969) 74–79.
Lemaire, A.
"Les inscriptions du Khirbet el-Qom et l'Ashérah de Yhwh," *RB* 84 (1977) 595–608.
Idem
"Sfire I A 24 et l'araméen *št'*," *Henoch* 3 (1981) 161–70.
Idem
"L'inscription de Balaam trouvée à Deir 'Alla: épigraphie," *Biblical Archaeology Today. Proceedings of the International Congress on Biblical Archaeology, Jerusalem, April, 1984* (Jerusalem: Israel Exploration Society, 1985) 313–25.
Levine, B. A.
"Ugaritic Descriptive Rituals," *JCS* 17 (1963) 105–11.
Idem
In the Presence of the Lord: A Study of Cult and Some Cultic Terms in Ancient Israel (SJLA 5; Leiden: Brill, 1974).
Idem
"The Balaam Inscriptions from Deir 'Alla: Historical Aspects," *Biblical Archaeology Today. Proceedings of the International Congress on Biblical Archaeology, Jerusalem, April, 1984* (Jerusalem: Israel Exploration Society, 1985) 326–39.
Levine, B. A., and J.-M. de Tarragon
"'Shapshu Cries Out in Heaven': Dealing with Snake-Bites at Ugarit (*KTU* 1.100, 1.107)," *RB* 95 (1988) 481–518.
Lewis, B.
The Sargon Legend (Cambridge, MA: American Schools of Oriental Research, 1980).
Licht, Y.
"New Moon/Month," *EM* 3.40–41 (Heb.).
Idem
The Thanksgiving Scroll: A Scroll from the Wilderness of Judea (Jerusalem: Bialik, 1957) (Heb.).
Lichtenstein, M.
"A Note on the Text of I Keret," *JANESCU* 2 (1970) 94–100.
Lieberman, S.
Tosefta Ki-Fshuṭah: A Comprehensive Commentary on the Tosefta, Part 3, Order Mo'ed (New York: Jewish Theological Seminary of America, 1962) (Heb.).
Idem
"Forgotten Meanings," *Leš* 32 (1968) 89–102 (Heb.).
Idem
Greek in Jewish Palestine: Studies in the Life and Manners of Jewish Palestine in the 2nd-4th Centuries C.E. (New York: Jewish Theological Seminary of America, 1972).
Idem
"A Tragedy or a Comedy," *JAOS* 104 (1984) 315–19.
Lindblom, J.
Prophecy in Ancient Israel (Philadelphia: Fortress, 1965).
Lipiński, E.
La Royauté de Yahwé dans la Poésie et le Culte de l'Ancien Israël (Bruges: Paleis der Academiën, 1968).

Idem
"The Goddess Atirat in Ancient Arabia, in Babylon, and in Israel," in OLP 3 (Leuven: Institut voor Orientalistiek, 1972) 100–119.
Idem
"Eshmun, 'Healer,'" *AION* 33 (1973) 161–83.
Idem
"*SKN* et *SGN* dans le sémitique-occidental du nord," *UF* 5 (1973) 191–207.
Idem
"North-West Semitic Inscriptions," OLP 8 (Leuven: Institut voor Orientalistiek, 1977) 81–117.
Lods, A.
Histoire de la littérature hébraïque et juive depuis les origines jusqu'à la ruine de l'état juif (Paris: Payot, 1950).
Loewenstamm, S. E.
"Ben-hadad," *EM* 2.155–58 (Heb.).
Idem
"*bq'h*," *EM* 2.311 (Heb.).
Idem
"Hazael," *EM* 3.87–88 (Heb.).
Idem
"The Religion of the Jews at Elephantine," *EM* 3.347–444 (Heb.).
Idem
"*mry'*," *EM* 5.455–56 (Heb.).
Idem
"Oath," *EM* 7.479–91 (Heb.).
Idem
Review of R. de Vaux, *Les institutions de l'Ancien Testament I* (Paris, 1958), in *Kiryat Sepher* 34 (1958) 48 (Heb.).
Idem
"The Shaking of Nature at the Time of the Manifestation of the Lord," *'Oz LeDavid: Collected Readings in Bible Presented to David ben Gurion on His Seventy-seventh Birthday* (ed. Y. Kaufmann and others; Jerusalem: Kiryat Sepher, 1964) 508–20 (Heb.).
Idem
The Tradition of the Exodus in Its Development (Jerusalem: Magnes, 1965) (Heb.).
Idem
"Isaiah I 31," *VT* 22 (1972) 246–48.
Idem
"Some Remarks on Biblical Passages in the Light of Their Akkadian Parallels," *Biblical Studies: Y. M. Grintz in Memoriam* (*Te'uda* 2; ed. B. Uffenheimer; Tel Aviv: Tel Aviv University, 1982) 187–96 (Heb.).
Loewenstamm, S. E., and S. Ahitub
"*nāḥāš*," *EM* 5.821–22 (Heb.).
Löw, I.
Die Flora der Juden (4 vols.; Wien: Löwit-Kohut Foundation, 1924).
Luckenbill, D. D.
The Annals of Sennacherib (OIP 2; Chicago: University of Chicago, 1924).
Idem
Ancient Records of Assyria and Babylonia: Volume 2, Historical Records of Assyria from Sargon to the End (2 vols.; Chicago: University of Chicago, 1927).
Lund, N. W.
Chiasmus in the New Testament: A Study in Formgeschichte (Chapel Hill: University of North Carolina, 1942).
Luzzato, S. D.
Il profeta Isaia (Padova: Bianchi, 1867) (Heb.).
Lyon, D. G.
Keilschrifttexte Sargon's Königs von Assyrien (722–705 v. Chr.) (Leipzig: Hinrichs, 1883).
Maag, V.
"Jahwäs Heerscharen," *Festschrift für Ludwig Köhler zu dessen 70. Geburtstag* (ed. W. Baumgartner; SThU 19; Bern, 1954) 27–52.
Maass, F.
"*ḥll*," *THAT* I (1975) 570–75.
McCarter, P. K. Jr.
"The Balaam Texts from Deir 'Allā: The First Combination," *BASOR* 239 (1980) 49–60.
Idem
1 Samuel: A New Translation with Introduction, Notes, and Commentary (AB 8; Garden City, NY: Doubleday, 1980).
Idem
2 Samuel: A New Translation with Introduction, Notes, and Commentary (AB 9; Garden City, NY: Doubleday, 1984).
Idem
"Aspects of the Religion of the Israelite Monarchy: Biblical and Epigraphic Data," *Ancient Israelite Religion. Essays in Honor of Frank Moore Cross* (ed. P. D. Miller, Jr., P. D. Hanson, and S. D. McBride; Philadelphia: Fortress, 1987) 137–55.
MacDonald, M. D.
The Prophetic Oracles Concerning Egypt in the Old Testament (diss.; Baylor University, 1978).
McKay, J. W.
Religion in Judah under the Assyrians 732–609 B.C. (SBT 2/26; London: SCM, 1973).
Maier, W. A.
'Ašerah: Extrabiblical Evidence (HSM 37; Atlanta: Scholars, 1986).
de Maigret, A.
Le citadella aramaica di Hama. Attività funzione e comportemento (Orientis Antiqui Collectio 15; Rome: Centro per le Antichità e la Storia dell'Arte del Vicino Oriente, 1979).
Maisler, B.
"Phoenician Inscriptions from Byblos," *Leš* 14 (1946) 166–81 (Heb.).
Idem
"A Study of Biblical Personal Names," *Leš* 15 (1947) 37–44 (Heb.).

Malamat, A.
"Aram, Arameans," *EncJud* 3.252–56.
Idem
"Prophecy in the Mari Documents," Eretz Israel 4 (*Yitzhak Ben-Zvi Volume;* ed. H. Z. Hirschberg and B. Mazar; Jerusalem: Israel Exploration Society, 1956) 74–84 (Heb.).
Idem
"Mari and the Bible," *JAOS* 82 (1962) 143–50.
Idem
"Tin Inventory," *IEJ* 21 (1971) 31–38.
Idem
"Arameans," *Peoples of Old Testament Times* (ed. D. W. Thomas; Oxford: Clarendon, 1973) 134–55.
Mandelbaum, B., ed.
Pesikta de Rav Kahana (2 vols.; New York: Jewish Theological Seminary of America, 1961) (Heb.).
Margalit, B.
"A Ugaritic Psalm (*RŠ* 24.252)," *JBL* 89 (1970) 292–304.
Idem
"Weltbaum und Weltberg in Ugaritic Literature: Notes and Observations on RŠ 24, 245," *ZAW* 86 (1974) 1–23.
Idem
"The Early Israelite Epic and the Origin of Biblical Eschatology," *Ḥeqer VeIyyun BeMadaei HaYahaduth: Sifruth, Miqra VeLashon* (Haifa: University of Haifa, 1976) 162–76 (Heb.).
Idem
"The Ugaritic Feast of the Drunken Gods: Another Look at RŠ 24.258 (KTU 1.114)," *MAARAV* 2 (1980) 65–120.
Idem
"Lexicographical Notes on the *AQHT* Epic (Part 1 *KTU* 1. 17–18)," *UF* 15 (1983) 65–103.
Margolis, M. L.
"Notes on Semitic Grammar," *AJSL* 19 (1902–1903) 45–48.
Marzal, A.
Gleanings from the Wisdom of Mari (Studia Pohl 11; Rome: Pontifical Biblical Institute, 1976).
Mauchline, J.
"Implicit Signs of Persistent Belief in the Davidic Empire," *VT* 30 (1970) 287–303.
May, H. G.
"Archer," *IDB* 1.208.
Mayer, R.
"Sünde und Gericht in der Bildersprache der vorexilischen Prophetie," *BZ* 8 (1964) 22–44.
Mazar, B.
"Caphtor," *EM* 4.236–38 (Heb.).
Idem
"Gē-HaMelech," *EM* 2.479–80 (Heb.).
Idem
"Lebo' Ḥamath," *EM* 4.416–18 (Heb.).
Idem
"Sela," *EM* 5.1050–51 (Heb.).
Idem
"Gath and Gittaim," *IEJ* 4 (1954) 227–35; rep. in *Cities and Districts in Eretz-Israel* (Jerusalem: Mosad Bialik, 1975) 101–9 (Heb.).
Idem
"The Campaign of Pharaoh Shishak to Palestine," SVT 4 (Leiden: Brill, 1957) 57–66.
Idem, ed.
Views of the Biblical World (4 vols.; Jerusalem/Ramat Gan: International Publishing, 1960) (Heb.).
Idem
The Kingdoms of Israel and Judah (ed. A. Malamat; Jerusalem: Israel Exploration Society, 1961) (Heb.).
Idem
"The Philistines and the Rise of Israel and Tyre," *Proceedings of the Israel Academy of Sciences and Humanities*, I (Jerusalem: Israel Academy of Sciences and Humanities, 1967) 7–16; rep. in *Canaan and Israel: Historical Essays* (Jerusalem: Mosad Bialik, 1974) 152–73 (Heb.).
Idem, ed.
Encyclopedia of Archaeological Excavations in the Holy Land (2 vols.; Jerusalem: Israel Exploration Society, 1970) (Heb.).
Meier, G.
"Die Zweite Tafel der Serie *bīt mēseri*," *AfO* 14 (1941) 137–52.
Meinhold, J.
Studien zur israelitischen Religionsgeschichte. I: Der heilige Rest. 1. Elias Amos Hosea Jesaja (Bonn: Weber's, 1903).
Meissner, B.
Assyriologische Forschungen, I (AOTU 1/1; Leiden: Brill, 1918).
Mendelsohn, I.
Slavery in the Ancient Near East: A Comparative Study on Slavery in Babylonia, Assyria, Syria, and Palestine, from the Middle of the Third Millennium to the End of the First Millennium (New York: Oxford University, 1949).
de Mertzenfeld, C. D.
Inventaire commenté des ivoires phéniciens et apparentés, découvertes dans la proche orient (Paris: deBoccard, 1954).
Meshel, Z.
Kuntillet ʿAjrud: A Religious Centre from the Time of the Judean Monarchy on the Border of Sinai (Catalogue No. 175 of the Israel Museum; Jerusalem: Israel Museum, 1978).
Idem
"Did Yahweh Have a Consort?" *BAR* 5 (1979) 24–35.
Michaelis, J. D.
Deutsche Übersetzung des Alten Testaments (Göttingen: Vandenhoeck & Ruprecht, 1772).
Michel, E.
"Die Assur-Texte Salmanassars III," *WO* 2/1 (1954) 27–45.

Michel, O., O. Bauernfeind, and O. Betz
"Der Tempel der goldenen Kuh," *ZNW* 49 (1958) 197–212.
Milgrom, J.
"Nazirites," *EncJud* 12.907–9.
Idem
"Did Isaiah Prophesy during the Reign of Uzziah?" *VT* 14 (1964) 178–82.
Idem
Studies in Levitical Terminology I: The Encroacher and the Levite, The Term 'Aboda (University of California Publications in Near Eastern Studies 14; Berkeley/Los Angeles: University of California, 1970).
Idem
"The Missing Thief in Leviticus 5:20ff.," *RIDA* 3e série 22 (1975) 71–85.
Idem
Cult and Conscience: The Asham and the Priestly Doctrine of Repentance (SJLA 18; Leiden: Brill, 1976).
Idem
"Vertical Retribution: Rumination on *Parashat Shelaḥ*," *Conservative Judaism* 34 (1981) 11–16.
Millard, A. R.
"Kings Og's Bed and Other Ancient Ironmongery," *Ascribe to the Lord: Biblical and Other Studies in Memory of Peter C. Craigie* (ed. L. Eslinger and G. Taylor; *JSOT* Supplemental Series 67; Sheffield: JSOT, 1988) 481–92.
Miller, J. M., and J. H. Hayes
A History of Ancient Israel and Judah (Philadelphia: Westminster, 1986).
Miller, P. D., Jr.
"Fire in the Mythology of Canaan and Israel," *CBQ* 27 (1965) 256–61.
Idem
"Animal Names as Designations in Ugaritic and Hebrew," *UF* 2 (1970) 177–86.
Idem
"The *MRZḤ* Text," *The Claremont Ras Shamra Tablets* (ed. L. R. Fisher; AnOr 48; Rome: Pontifical Biblical Institute, 1971) 37–49.
Idem
The Divine Warrior in Early Israel (HSM 5; Cambridge: Harvard University, 1973).
Idem
Sin and Judgment in the Prophets: A Stylistic and Theological Analysis (Society of Biblical Literature Monograph Series 27; Chico, CA: Scholars, 1982) 21–25.
Mittmann, S.
Beiträge zur Siedlungs-und Territorialgeschichte des nördlichen Ostjordanlandes (Wiesbaden: Harrassowitz, 1970).
Idem
"Die Grabinschrift des Sängers Uriahu," *ZDPV* 97 (1981) 143–44.
Montgomery, J. A.
Aramaic Incantation Texts from Nippur (Philadelphia: University of Pennsylvania Museum, 1913).
Moran, W.
"The Ancient Near Eastern Background of the Love of God in Deuteronomy," *CBQ* 25 (1963) 77–87.
Idem
"A Note on the Treaty Terminology of the Sefîre Stelas," *JNES* 22 (1963) 173–76.
Moreshet, M.
"Micah 3:12 = Jeremiah 26:18," *BM* 31 (1967) 123–26 (Heb.).
Morgenstern, J.
"The Loss of Words at Ends of Lines in Manuscripts of Biblical Poetry," *HUCA* 25 (1954) 41–83.
Idem
"Jerusalem 485 B.C.," *HUCA* 28 (1957) 42–43.
Mowinckel, S.
Psalmenstudien: Das Thronbesteigungsfest Jahwäs und der Ursprung der Eschatologie II (6 vols.; Kristiania: Dybwad, 1922).
Idem
Psalmenstudien: Die technischen Termini in den Psalmenüberschriften IV (6 vols.; Kristiania: Dybwad, 1923).
Idem
Psalmenstudien: Segen und Fluch in Israels Kult und Psalmdichtung V (6 vols; Kristiania: Dybwad, 1924).
Idem
Die Sternnamen im alten Testament = NorTT 29 (1928).
Idem
Prophecy and Tradition: The Prophetic Books in the Light of the Study of the Growth and History of the Tradition (Oslo: Dybwad, 1946).
Idem
He That Cometh (tr. G. W. Anderson; Oxford: Blackwell, 1956).
Idem
"Jahwes dag," *NorTT* 59 (1958) 1–56.
Idem
"Drive and/or Ride in O.T.," *VT* 12 (1962) 278–99.
Muffs, Y.
Studies in the Aramaic Legal Papyri from Elephantine (Studia et documenta ad iura orientis antiqui pertinentia, 8; Leiden: Brill, 1969).
Muhly, J. D.
Copper and Tin. The Distribution of Mineral Resources and the Nature of the Metals Trade in the Bronze Age (Transactions of the Connecticut Academy of Arts and Science 43; New Haven, CT: Yale University, 1973) 155–535.
Muilenburg, J.
"The Site of Ancient Gilgal," *BASOR* 140 (1955) 11–27.

Idem
"The Linguistic and Rhetorical Usages of the Particle *ki* in the Old Testament," *HUCA* 32 (1961) 135–60.
Müller, H.-P.
"Die kultische Darstellung der Theophanie," *VT* 14 (1964) 183–91.
Idem
"Phönizien und Juda in exilisch-nachexilischer Zeit," *WO* 6 (1971) 189–204.
Müller, W. W.
"Altsüdarabische Beiträge zum Hebräischen Lexikon," *ZAW* 75 (1963) 304–16.
Munn-Rankin, J. M.
"Diplomacy in Western Asia in the Early Second Millennium B.C.," *Iraq* 18 (1956) 68–100.
Murphy-O'Connor, J.
"The Essenes in Palestine," *BA* 40 (1977) 100–24.
Na'aman, N.
"Sennacherib's 'Letter to God' on His Campaign to Judah," *BASOR* 214 (1974) 25–39.
Napier, B. D.
"The Omrides of Jezreel," *VT* 9 (1959) 366–78.
Naveh, J.
"The Data of the Deir 'Alla Inscription in Aramaic Script," *IEJ* 17 (1967) 256–58.
Idem
"Graffiti and Dedications," *BASOR* 235 (1979) 27–30.
Negev, A., ed.
The Archaeological Encyclopedia of the Holy Land (Jerusalem: Steimatzky, 1986).
Neufeld, E.
"Inalienability of Mobile and Immobile Pledges in the Laws of the Bible," *RIDA* 9 (1962) 33–44.
Neugebauer. O.
Astronomical Cuneiform Texts: Babylonian Euphemerides of the Seleucid Period for the Motion of the Sun, the Moon, and the Planets (London: Humphries, 1955).
Noth, M.
"Edomites," *RGG*³, 2, 309.
Idem
Die israelitischen Personennamen im Rahmen der gemeinsemitischen Namengebung (BWANT 3/10; Stuttgart: Kohlhammer, 1928).
Idem
"Remarks on the Sixth Volume of Mari Texts," *JSS* 1 (1956) 322–33; rep. in *Aufsätze zur biblischen Landes- und Altertumskunde* (ed. H. W. Wolff; 2 vols.; Neukirchen-Vluyn: Neukirchener Verlag, 1971) 2.234–44.
Idem
"Gilead und Gad," *ZDPV* 75 (1959) 14–73; rep. in *Aufsätze zur biblischen Landes- und Altertumskunde* (ed. H. W. Wolff; 2 vols.; Neukirchen-Vluyn: Neukirchener Verlag, 1971) 1.489–543.
Nougayrol, J.
"Textes hépatoscopiques d'époque ancienne conservés au musée du Louvre," *RA* 38 (1941) 67–88.
Idem
"Guerre et paix à Ugarit," *Iraq* 25 (1963) 110–23.
Idem
"Textes Suméro-Accadiens des Archives et Bibliotèques Privées d'Ugarit," *Ugaritica* V (ed. C.F.A. Schaeffer and others; *MRŠ* 16; Paris: Geuthner 1968) 1–446.
Obermann, J.
"Two Magic Bowls: New Incantation Texts from Mesopotamia," *JAOS* 57 (1940) 1–31.
O'Connor, M.
"Northwest Semitic Designations for Elective Social Affinities," *JANESCU* 18 (1986) 66–80.
Oded, B.
"Ammon, Ammonites," *EM* 6.254–71 (Heb.).
Idem
"Qarnāîm," *EM* 7.277–78 (Heb.).
Idem
"Keriyot," *EM* 7.269–70 (Heb.).
Idem
Mass Deportations and Deportees in the Neo-Assyrian Empire (Wiesbaden: Ludwig Reichert, 1979).
Ohry, A., and A. Levy
"Anointing with Oil: An Hygienic Procedure in the Bible and in the Talmud," *Proceedings of the Second International Symposium on Medicine in the Bible and Talmud, Jerusalem 18–20, 1984 = Koroth* 9 (1985) 173–96.
Olmstead, A. T.
"Shalmaneser III and the Establishment of the Assyrian Power," *JAOS* 41 (1921) 345–82.
Idem
History of the Persian Empire (Achaemenid Period) (Chicago: University of Chicago, 1948).
Olshausen, J.
Die Psalmen erklärt (Leipzig: Hirzel, 1853).
Olyan, S.
Asherah and the Cult of Yahweh in Israel (Society of Biblical Literature Monograph Series 34; Atlanta: Scholars, 1988).
Oppenheim, A. L.
The Interpretation of Dreams in the Ancient Near East (Transactions of the American Philosophical Society 46/3; Philadelphia: American Philosophical Society, 1959).
Idem
"The Eyes of the Lord," *JAOS* 88/1 (1968) 173–80; simultaneously published as a separate volume entitled *Essays in Memory of E. A. Speiser* (ed. W. W. Hallo; AOS 53; New Haven, CT: Yale University, 1968)
Orlinsky, H. M.
"The Plain Meaning of *Ruaḥ* in Gen.1:2," *JQR* 58 (1957) 174–82.

Palmoni, Y.
"Locust," *IDB* 3.144–48.
Parpola, S.
Neo-Assyrian Toponyms (AOAT 6; Neukirchen-Vluyn: Neukirchener Verlag, 1970).
Idem
"The Forlorn Scholar," *Language, Literature, and History: Philological and Historical Studies Presented to Erica Reiner* (ed. F. Rochberg-Halton; New Haven, CT: American Oriental Society, 1987) 257–78.
Parrot, A.
Le Palais (*Mission archéologique de Mari II*; 2 vols.; Paris: Geuthner, 1958).
Idem
Samaria: The Capital of the Kingdom of Israel (tr. S. H. Hooke; Studies in Biblical Archeology 7; New York: Philosophical Library, 1958).
Paul, S. M.
"*ṣlmwt*," *EM* 6.735–36 (Heb.).
Idem
"Euphemism and Dysphemism," *EncJud* 6.959–61.
Idem
"Prophets and Prophecy," *EncJud* 13.1150–75.
Idem
"Virgin, Virginity," *EncJud* 16.160–61.
Idem
"Jerusalem—A City of Gold," *IEJ* 17 (1967) 259–63; abridged and rep. as "Jerusalem of Gold—A Song and an Ancient Crown," *BAR* 3 (1977) 38–41.
Idem
"Cuneiform Light on Jer 9, 20," *Bib* 49 (1968) 373–76.
Idem
"The Image of the Oven and the Cake in Hosea VII 4–10," *VT* 18 (1968) 114–20.
Idem
"Sargon's Administrative Diction in II Kings 17:27," *JBL* 88 (1969) 73–74.
Idem
"Exodus 21:10—A Threefold Maintenance Clause," *JNES* 28 (1969) 48–53; rep. in *Studies in the Book of the Covenant in the Light of Cuneiform and Biblical Law* (SVT 18; Leiden: Brill, 1970) 56–61.
Idem
Studies in the Book of the Covenant in the Light of Cuneiform and Biblical Law (SVT 18, Leiden: Brill, 1970).
Idem
"Psalm 72:5—A Traditional Blessing for the Long Life of the King," *JNES* 31 (1972) 351–55.
Idem
"מַשָּׂא מֶלֶךְ שָׂרִים": Hosea 8:8–10 and Ancient Near Eastern Royal Epithets," *Studies in Bible and the Ancient Near East, Presented to Samuel E. Loewenstamm on His Seventieth Birthday* (2 vols.; ed. Y. Avishur and Y. Blau; Jerusalem: E. Rubinstein, 1978) 309–17 (Heb.); English tr. in *Studies in the Bible* (ed. S. Japhet; Scripta Hierosolymitana 31; Jerusalem: Magnes, 1986) 193–204.
Idem
"Unrecognized Biblical Legal Idioms in the Light of Comparative Akkadian Expressions," *RB* 86 (1979) 231–35.
Pederson, J.
Der Eid bei den Semiten (Strassburg: K. I. Trübner, 1914).
Perles, F.
"Ergänzungen zu den 'Akkadischen Fremdwörtern,'" *OLZ* 21 (1918) 70.
Idem
Analekten zur Textkritik des Alten Testaments (Leipzig: Engel, 1922).
Pettinato, G.
Testi amministravi della biblioteca L. 2769. Materiali epigrapici di Ebla (Napoli: Universitá di Napoli, 1980).
Idem
The Archives of Ebla (Garden City, NY: Doubleday, 1981).
Pfeiffer, R. H.
"The Polemic against Idolatry in the Old Testament," *JBL* 33 (1924) 229–40.
Idem
Introduction to the Old Testament (New York: Harper, 1948).
Pinches, T. G.
The Cuneiform Inscriptions of Western Asia: Volume 5, A Selection from the Miscellaneous Inscriptions of Assyria and Babylonia (series ed. H. C. Rawlinson; London: The British Museum, 1909).
Pitard, W. T.
Ancient Damascus (Winona Lake, IN: Eisenbrauns, 1987).
Pliny the Elder
Natural History (tr. H. Rackham, W.H.S. Jones, and D. E. Eichholg; 10 vols.; Loeb Classical Library; London: Heineman, 1938–1962).
Pope, M.
"Oaths," *IDB* 3.575–77.
Idem
"A Divine Banquet at Ugarit," *The Use of the Old Testament in the New and Other Essays: Studies in Honor of William Franklin Stinespring* (ed. J. M. Efird; Durham, NC: Duke University, 1972) 170–203.
Idem
Job: Introduction, Translation and Notes (AB 15; Garden City, NY: Doubleday, [3]1973).
Idem
"Notes on the Rephaim Texts from Ugarit," *Essays on the Ancient Near East in Memory of Jacob Joel Finkelstein* (ed. M. Ellis; Hamden, CT: Archon Books, 1977) 163–82.

Idem
Song of Songs: A New Translation with Introduction and Commentary (AB 7c; Garden City, NY: Doubleday, 1977).
Porten, B.
Archives from Elephantine: The Life of an Ancient Jewish Military Colony (Berkeley/Los Angeles: University of California, 1968).
Idem
"The Religion of the Jews of Elephantine in Light of the Hermopolis Papyri," *JNES* 28 (1969) 118–21.
Postgate, J. N.
Neo-Assyrian Royal Grants and Decrees (Studia Pohl Series Maior 1; Rome: Pontifical Biblical Institute, 1969).
Idem
Taxation and Conscription in the Assyrian Empire (Studia Pohl Series Maior 3; Rome: Pontifical Biblical Institute, 1974).
Pritchard, J. B.
The Ancient Near East in Pictures Relating to the Old Testament (Princeton, NJ: Princeton University, 1954, ^{2}1969).
Idem
The Ancient Near Eastern Texts Relating to the Old Testament (Princeton, NJ: Princeton University, ^{3}1969).
Procksch, O.
"Textual notes to Librum XII prophetarum," BH^{3} (ed. Rudolph Kittel; Stuttgart: Württembergische Bibelstalt, ^{3}1937).
Puech, E.
"Sur la racine *ṣlḥ* en hébreu et en araméen," *Sem* 21 (1972) 5–17.
Puech, E., and A. Rofé
"L'inscription de la citadelle d'Amman," *RB* 80 (1973) 531–41.
Quell, G.
Wahre und falsche Propheten: Versuch einer Interpretation (BFCT 46/1; Gütersloh: Bertelsmann, 1952).
Rabin, C.
"*BĀRI^{a}Ḥ*," *JTS* 47 (1946) 38–41.
Idem
The Zadodite Documents (Oxford: Clarendon, ^{2}1958).
Idem
"An Arabic Phrase in Isaiah 21:11–12," *Studi sull'Oriente e la Biblia offerti al P. Giovanni Rinaldi* (ed. G. Buccelati; Genova: Ed. Studio e vita, 1967) 303–9.
Radau, H.
Letters to Cassite Kings from the Temple Archives of Nippur (BE 17/I; Philadelphia: University of Pennsylvania, 1908).
Rainey, A.
A Social Structure of Ugarit: A Study of West Semitic Social Stratification during the Late Bronze Age (Jerusalem: Bialik, 1967) (Heb.).
Idem
"Gleanings from Ugarit," *Israel Oriental Studies* 3 (Tel Aviv: Tel Aviv University, 1973) 34–62.
Idem
"The Identification of Philistine Gath," Eretz Israel 12 (*Nelson Glueck Memorial Volume*; ed. B. Mazar and others; Jerusalem: Israel Exploration Society, 1975) 63*–76*.
Raitt, T. M.
"The Prophetic Summons to Repentance," *ZAW* 83 (1971) 30–49.
Ravn, O. E.
Herodotus' Description of Babylon (tr. M. Tovborg-Jensen; Kjøbenhaven: Nyt Nordisk, 1942).
Rawlinson, G.
The Five Great Monarchies of the Eastern World (3 vols.; New York: Dodd, 1870, ^{2}1881).
Raymond, P.
L'eau, sa vie et sa signification dans l'Ancien Testament (SVT 6; Leiden: Brill, 1958).
Reider, J.
"Etymological Studies in Biblical Hebrew," *VT* 2 (1952) 113–30; *VT* 4 (1954) 276–95.
Idem
"Contributions to the Scriptural Text," *HUCA* 24 (1952–1953) 85–106.
Reiner, E.
"Deux fragments du Myth de Zû," *RA* 48 (1954) 145–48.
Idem
Šurpu: A Collection of Sumerian and Akkadian Incantations (AfO Beiheft 11; Graz: Im Selbstverlag des Herausgebers, 1958).
Reisner, G. A.
Sumerisch-babylonische Hymnen nach Thontafeln griechischer Zeit (Berlin: W. Spemann, 1896).
Idem
Israelite Ostraca from Samaria (Cambridge, 1924).
Rendsburg, G. A.
"Janus Parallelism in Gen 48:26," *JBL* 99 (1980) 291–93.
Idem
"Eblaite *Ù-MA* and Hebrew *WM*," *Eblaitica: Essays on the Ebla Archives and Eblaite Language* (ed. C. H. Gordon, G. A. Rendsburg, and N. H. Winter; Winona Lake, IN: Eisenbrauns, 1987) 1.33–41.
Rendtorff, R.
"נָבִיא in the Old Testament," *TDNT* 6.796–812.
Idem
Studien zur Geschichte des Opfers im Alten Israel (WMANT 24; Neukirchen-Vluyn: Neukirchener Verlag, 1967).
Reventlow, H. G.
Wächter über Israel: Ezechiel und seine Tradition (BZAW 82; Berlin: Töpelmann, 1962).

Reviv, H.
A Commentary on Selected Inscriptions from the Period of the Monarchy in Israel (Jewish Historical Sources 1; Jerusalem: The Historical Society of Israel, 1975) (Heb.).
Richardson, H. N.
"Threshing," *IDB* 4.636.
Richter, G.
Erläuterungen zu dunklen Stellen in den kleinen Propheten (Gütersloh: Bertelsmann, 1914).
Richter, W.
"Zu den 'Richtern Israels,'" *ZAW* 77 (1965) 40–72.
Idem
Recht und Ethos: Versuch einer Ortung des weisheitlichen Mahnspruches (SANT 15; München: Kösel, 1966).
Ringgren, H.
Israelitische Religion (Der Religionen der Menschheit 26; Stuttgart: Kohlhammer, 1963); English tr. *Israelite Religion* (tr. D. E. Green; London: SPCK, 1969).
Idem
"Akkadian Apocalypses," *Apocalypticism in the Mediterranean World and the Near East* (ed. D. Hellholm; Tübingen: Mohr, 1983) 379–86.
Idem
"Balaam and the Deir 'Alla Inscription," *Isac Leo Seeligmann Volume: Essays on the Bible and the Ancient World* (3 vols.; ed. A. Rofé and Y. Zakovitch; Jerusalem: E. Rubinstein, 1983) 3:93–98.
Robinson, T. H.
"New Light on the Text and Interpretation of the Old Testament Supplied by Recent Discoveries," *ZAW* 73 (1961) 265–69.
Rofé, A.
"*The Book of Balaam*" (Jerusalem: Simor Ltd., 1979) (Heb.).
Römer, W.H.P.
Frauenbriefe über Religion, Politik, und Privatleben in Mari (AOAT 12; Kevelaer: Bulzon und Bercker, 1971).
Rosenthal, F.
"Rescensiones," *Or* 16 (1947) 401–2.
Rost, L.
"Bemerkungen zu Sacharja 4," *ZAW* 63 (1951) 216–21.
Rost, P.
Die Keilschrifttexte Tiglat-Pilesers III (Leipzig: Pfeiffer, 1893).
Roux, G.
Ancient Iraq (London: Allen & Unwin, 1964).
Rudolph, W.
Jeremia (HAT 1/12; Tübingen: Mohr, 1958).
Rylaarsdam, J. C.
"Nazirite," *IDB* 3.526–27.
Sabottka, L.
Zephanja: Versuch einer Neuübersetzung mit philologischem Kommentar (BibOr 25; Rome: Pontifical Biblical Institute, 1972).
Saebø, M.
"Grenzbeschreibung und Landideal im alten Testament mit besonderer Berücksichtigung der *min-'ad* Formel," *ZDPV* 90 (1974) 14–37.
Saggs, H. W. F.
"The Nimrud Letters—II: Relations with the West," *Iraq* 17 (1955) 21–50.
Idem
The Might That Was Assyria (London: Sidgwick & Jackson, 1984).
Salonen, A.
Die Wasserfahrzeuge in Babylonien (StudOr 8/4; Helsinki: Societas Orientalis Fennica, 1939).
Idem
Die Türen des alten Mesopotamien (Annales Academiae Scientiarum Fennicae B 124; Helsinki: Suomalainen Tiedeakatemia, 1961).
Idem
Die Möbel des alten Mesopotamien nach sumerisch-akkadischen Quellen (Annales Academiae Scientiarum Fennicae B 127; Helsinki: Suomalainen Tiedeakatemia, 1963).
Idem
Die Hausegeräte der alten Mesopotamier nach sumerisch-akkadischen Quellen (Annales Academiae Scientiarum Fennicae B 139 & B 144; Helsinki: Suomalainen Tiedeakatemia, 1965–1966).
Idem
Die Fussbekleidung der alten Mesopotamier nach sumerisch-akkadischen Quellen (Annales Academiae Scientiarum Fennicae B 157; Helsinki: Suomalainen Tiedeakatemia, 1969).
Idem
Die Fischerei im alten Mesopotamien nach sumerisch-akkadischen Quellen (Annales Academiae Scientiarum Fennicae B 166; Helsinki: Suomalainen Tiedeakatemia, 1970).
Idem
Vögel und Vogelfang im alten Mesopotamien (Annales Academiae Scientiarum Fennicae B 180; Helsinki: Suomalainen Tiedeakatemia, 1973).
Sanders, J. A.
The Dead Sea Psalms Scroll (Ithaca: Cornell University, 1967).
Idem
The Psalm Scrolls of Qumran Cave 11 (IIQPs) (DJD 4; Oxford: Clarendon, 1981).
San Nicolò, M.
"Eid," *RLA*, II (1938) 305–15.
Idem
"Materialen zur Viehwirtschaft in den neubabylonischen Tempeln," *Or* 17 (1948) 273–93.
Sarna, N. M.
"Psalms, Book of," *EncJud* 13.1313–14.
Idem
"The Psalm Superscriptions and the Guilds," *Studies in Jewish Religious and Intellectual History Presented to Alexander Altmann on the Occasion of His Seventieth Birthday* (ed. S. Stein and R. Loewe;

Birmingham: University of Alabama, 1979) 281–300.
Sasson, J. M.
The Military Establishments at Mari (Studia Pohl 3; Rome: Pontifical Biblical Institute, 1969).
Idem
"On M. H. Pope's *Song of Songs*," *MAARAV* 3 (1979–1980) 177–203.
Idem
"An Apocalyptic Vision from Mari? Speculations on ARM X:9," *M.A.R.I.* 1 (1982) 151–67.
Sasson, V.
"*šmn rḥṣ* in the Samaria Ostraca," *JSS* 26 (1981) 1–5.
Schaeffer, C.F.A.
"Les fouilles de Minet-el-Beida et de Ras Shamra. Quatrième campagne," *Syria* 14 (1933) 93–127, pl. 9–17.
Scheil, V.
Textes élamites-sémitiques (Paris: Leroux, 1908).
Schmidt, W. H.
Die Schöpfungsgeschichte der Priesterschaft (WMANT 17; Neukirchen-Vluyn: Neukirchener Verlag, ²1967).
Schmökel, H.
"Gotteswort in Mari und Israel," *TLZ* 76 (1951) 53ff.
Schmuttermayr, G.
"*RḤM*—Eine lexikalische Studie," *Bib* 51 (1970) 499–532.
Schneider, Z.
"Looking for the Source of Tin in the Ancient Near East," *Qadmoniot* 15 (1982) 98–102 (Heb.).
Schnutenhaus, F.
"Das Kommen und Erscheinen Gottes im Alten Testament," *ZAW* 76 (1964) 1–22.
Schottroff, W.
"Gedenken" im alten Orient und im alten Testament. Die Wurzel zakar im semitischen Sprachkreis (WMANT 15; Neukirchen-Vluyn: Neukirchener Verlag, 1964).
Schramm, W.
Einleitung in die Assyrischen Königsinschriften. Zweiter Teil, 934–722 v. Chr. (Leiden/Köln: Brill, 1973).
Schroeder, O.
Kontrakte der Seleukidenzeit aus Warka (Leipzig: Hinrichs, 1916).
Idem
Keilschrifttexte aus Assur historischen Inhalts (WVDOG 37; Leipzig: Hinrichs, 1922).
Schwarzwald, O. R.
"Complementary Distribution and Shift in the Syntax of 'Who' Abstract," *BM* 76 (1978) 81–88 (Heb.).
Scott, R.B.Y.
"Weights and Measures in the Bible," *BA* 22 (1959) 22–40; rep. in *The Biblical Archeologist Reader* (ed. E. F. Campbell, Jr., and D. N. Freedman; Garden City, NY: Doubleday, 1970) 3.345–58.
Seeligmann, I. L.
"On the History and Nature of Prophecy in Israel," in Eretz Israel 3 (*Dedicated to the Memory of M.D.U. Cassuto 1883–1951*; ed. J .W. Hirschberg and others; Jerusalem: Israel Exploration Society, 1954) 125–32 (Heb.).
Idem
"Lending, Pledge, and Interest in Biblical Law and Biblical Thought," *Studies in Bible and the Ancient Near East Presented to Samuel E. Loewenstamm on His Seventieth Birthday* (2 vols.; ed. Y. Avishur and Y. Blau; Jerusalem: E. Rubinstein, 1978) 183–205 (Heb.).
Segal, M. H.
"On the Structure of Oaths and Vows in Hebrew," *Leš* 1 (1928–1929) 215–27 (Heb.).
Idem
"On the Poetical Forms of Ancient Proverbial Literature," *Tarbiz* 1 (1930) 1–19 (Heb.).
Idem
"A Study of the Forms of Biblical Poetry," *Tarbiz* 18 (1947) 142–45 (Heb.).
Segert, S.
"Die Sprache der moabitischen Königsinschrift," *ArOr* 29 (1961) 197–267.
Sekine, M.
"Vom Verstehen der Heilsgeschichte," *ZAW* 75 (1963) 145–54.
Sellers, O. R.
"Weights and Measures," *IDB* 4.828–39.
Sellin, E., and G. Fohrer
Introduction to the Old Testament (tr. D. E. Green; Nashville/New York: Abingdon, 1968).
Seux, M.-J.
Épithètes Royales Akkadiennes et Sumériennes (Paris: Letouzey & Ané, 1967).
Seybold, K.
Das davidische Königtum im Zeugnis der Propheten (FRLANT 107; Göttingen: Vandenhoeck & Ruprecht, 1972).
Shea, W. H.
"The Form and Significance of the Eblaite Letter to Hamazi," *OrAnt* 23 (1984) 143–58.
Simons, J.
Handbook for the Study of Egyptian Topographical Lists Relating to Western Asia (Leiden: Brill, 1937).
Smith, G. A.
The Cuneiform Inscriptions of Western Asia. Volume 3, A Selection from the Miscellaneous Inscriptions of Assyria (series ed. H. C. Rawlinson; London: The British Museum, 1870).
Smith, M.
"On Burning Babies," *JAOS* 95 (1975) 477–79.
Smith, R. H.
"Abram and Melchizedek (Gen 14:18–20)," *ZAW* 77 (1965) 129–53.
Soggin, J. A.
"Der prophetische Gedanke über den heiligen Krieg, als Gericht gegen Israel," *VT* 10 (1960) 79–

83; English tr. "The Prophets on Holy War as Judgment against Israel," *Old Testament and Oriental Studies* (BibOr 20; Rome: Pontifical Biblical Institute, 1975) 67–71.

Idem
"*šûb*," *THAT* II (1976) 884–91.

Idem
"Osservazioni sulla radici *špṭ* e sul termine *šopᵉṭim* in ebraico biblico," *OrAnt* 19 (1980) 57–59.

Sokoloff, M.
The Targum to Job from Qumran Cave XI (Bar-Ilan Studies in Near Eastern Language and Culture; Ramat-Gan: Bar-Ilan University, 1974).

Sollberger, E.
Corpus des inscriptions "royales" présargoniques de Lagaš (Genève: Droz, 1956).

Speiser, E. A.
Genesis: Introduction, Translation and Notes (AB 1; Garden City, NY: Doubleday, 1964).

Sperber, A.
The Bible in Aramaic: Based on Old Manuscripts and Printed Texts (5 vols.; Leiden: Brill, 1959–73).

Spiegel, J.
"Der 'Ruf' des Königs," *WZKM* 54 (1957) 191–203.

Stager, L. E.
"The Finest Olive Oil in Samaria," *JSS* 28 (1983) 241–45.

Steinspring, W. F.
"Ekron," *IDB* 2.69.

Idem
"Gath," *IDB* 2.255–56.

Idem
"Gaza," *IDB* 2.357–58.

Stendebach, F. J.
"Altarformen im kanaanäisch-israelitischen Raum," *BZ* 20 (1976) 180–96.

Stern, E.
"Rabbah, Rabbath Ammon," *EM* 7.315–19 (Heb.).

Idem
"Weights and Measures," *EncJud* 16.375–87.

Sternberg, M.
The Poetics of Biblical Narrative: Ideological Literature and the Drama of Reading (Indiana Literary Biblical Series; Bloomington: Indiana University, 1985).

Streck, M.
Assurbanipal und die letzten assyrisichen Könige bis zum Untergang Nineveh's (VAB 7; Leipzig: Hinrichs, 1916).

Stuart, D. K.
Studies in Early Hebrew Meter (Missoula, MT: Scholars, 1976).

Tadmor, H.
"Jeroboam, Son of Joash," *EM* 3.775–77 (Heb.).

Idem
"Chronology," *EM* 4.245–310 (Heb.).

Idem
"The Campaigns of Sargon II of Assur: A Chronological-Historical Study," *JCS* 12 (1958) 33–39.

Idem
"Azriyau of Yaudi," *Studies in the Bible* (ed. C. Rabin; Scripta Hierosolymitana 8; Jerusalem: Magnes, 1961) 232–71.

Idem
"The Southern Border of Aram," *IEJ* 12 (1962) 114–22.

Idem
"The Assyrian Campaigns to Philistia," *The Military History of the Land of Israel in Biblical Times* (ed. Y. Liver; Jerusalem: Israeli Defense Forces Publishing House, 1964) 261–85 (Heb.).

Idem
"Philistia under Assyrian Rule," *BA* 29 (1966) 86–102.

Idem
"Fragments of a Stele of Sargon II from the Excavations of Ashdod," Eretz Israel 8 (*E. L. Sukenik Memorial Volume*; ed. N. Avigad and others; Jerusalem: Israel Exploration Society, 1967) 241–45 (Heb.).

Idem
"A Note on the Saba'a Stele of Adad-nirari III," *IEJ* 19 (1969) 46–48.

Idem
"The Aramaization of Assyria: Aspects of Western Impact," *Mesopotamien und seine Nachbarn: Politische und Kulturelle Wechselbezeihungen im Alten Vorderasien* (Berliner Beiträge zum Vorder Orient 1 = *Comptes Rendus de la XXV Rencontre Assyriologique Internationale*; ed. H.-J. Nissen and J. Renger; 2 vols.; Berlin: Dietrich Heimer, 1982) 2.449–70.

Talbert, R. M.
"Ben-hadad," *IDBSup* 95.

Tallqvist, K. L.
Akkadische Götterepitheta (StudOr 7; Helsinki: Academic Bookshop, 1938).

Talmon, S.
"Synonymous Readings in the Textual Traditions of the Old Testament," *Studies in the Bible* (ed. C. Rabin; Scripta Hierosolymitana 8; Jerusalem: Magnes, 1961) 335–83.

Idem
"The 'Desert Motif' in the Bible and in Qumran Literature," *Biblical Motifs. Origins and Transformation* (ed. A. Altmann; Studies and Texts 3; Cambridge: Harvard University, 1966) 31–63.

Idem
"*Har* and *Midbār*: An Antithetical Pair of Biblical Motifs," *Figurative Language in the Ancient Near East* (ed. M. Mindlin, M. J. Geller, and J. E. Wansbrough; London: School of Oriental and African Studies, 1987) 117–42.

Idem
"The Book of Daniel," *The Literary Guide to the Bible* (ed. R. Alter and F. Kermode; Cambridge: Collins, 1987) 347–49.

Teixidor, J.
"Le thiase de Bêlastor et de Beelshamên d'après une inscription récemment découverte à Palmyre," *CRAIBL* (1981) 306–14.
Theophrastus
Enquiry into Plants and Minor Works on Odours and Weather Signs (tr. A. Hort; Loeb Classical Library; 2 vols.; London: Heineman, 1916).
Thompson, H. O., and F. Zayadine
"The Tell-Siran Inscription," *BASOR* 212 (1973) 5–11.
Thompson, R. C.
The Reports of the Magicians and Astrologers of Nineveh and Babylon (Luzac's Semitic Text and Translation Series 6 & 7; 2 vols.; London: Luzac, 1900).
Idem
The Prisms of Esarhaddon and Ashurbanipal Found at Nineveh, 1927–8 (London: The British Museum, 1931).
Thureau-Dangin, F.
Lettres et contrats de l'époque de la première dynastie babylonienne (Paris: Guethner, 1910).
Idem
Une relation de la huitième campagne de Sargon (TCL 3; Paris: Guethner, 1912).
Idem
Rituels accadiens (Paris: Leroux, 1921).
Idem
Tablettes d'Uruk à l'usage des prêtres du temple d'Anu au temps des Séleucides (TCL 6; Paris: Guethner, 1922).
Thureau-Dangin, F., and M. Dunand
Til-Barsib (Bibliothèque Archéologique et Historique 23; Paris: Guethner, 1936).
Tigay, J. H.
"Dirge," *EM* 7.125–44 (Heb.).
Idem
"Sabbath," *EM* 7.504–17 (Heb.).
Toombs, L. E.
"Traps and Snares," *IDB* 4.687–88.
Torczyner, N. H.
"Presidential Address," *JPOS* 16 (1936) 6–7.
Tournay, J. R.
"Un cylindre babylonien découvert en Transjordanie," *RB* 74 (1967) 248–54.
Tremayne, A.
Records from Erech, Time of Cyrus and Cambyses (538–521 B.C.) (YOS 7; New Haven, CT: Yale University, 1952).
Tsevat, M.
"The Neo-Assyrian and Neo-Babylonian Vassal Oaths and the Prophet Ezekiel," *JBL* 78 (1959) 199–204.
Idem
"Isaiah I 31," *VT* 19 (1969) 261–63.
Tsumura, D. T.
"Janus Parallelism in Nah 1:8," *JBL* 102 (1983) 109–11.
Tucker, G. M.
"Prophetic Speech," *Int* 32 (1978) 31–45.
Tur-Sinai, N. H.
The Book of Job (Tel Aviv: Yavneh, 1954) (Heb.).
Uffenheimer, B.
The Visions of Zechariah: From Prophecy to Apocalyptic (Jerusalem: Kiryat Sepher, 1961) (Heb.).
Ungnad, A.
"Eponymen," *RLA* 2 (1938) 412–57.
van Beek, G. W.
"Carmel, Mount," *IDB* 1.538.
van der Woude, A. S.
"Micah in Dispute with the Pseudo-Prophets," *VT* 19 (1969) 244–60.
Vattioni, F.
"I Sigilli Ebraici," *Bib* 50 (1969) 43–45.
Vaughan, P. H.
The Meaning of 'Bāmâ' in the Old Testament: A Study of Etymological, Textual and Archaeological Evidence (SOTSMS 3; Cambridge: Cambridge University, 1974).
de Vaux, R.
"Le 'reste d'Israël' d'après les prophètes," *RB* 42 (1933) 526–39; rep. in *Bible et Orient* (Cogitatio fidei 24; Paris: Cerf, 1967) 25–39; English tr. "The Remnant of Israel According to the Prophets," *The Bible and the Ancient Near East* (tr. J. McHugh; Garden City, NY: Doubleday, 1971) 15–30.
Idem
"La quatrième campagne de fouilles a Tell-el-Far'ah, près Naplouse," *RB* 59 (1952) 551–83, pl. 10–20.
Idem
Ancient Israel: Its Life and Institutions (tr. J. McHugh; New York/Toronto/London: McGraw-Hill, 1961).
Idem
Les sacrifices de l'Ancien Testament (Cahiers de la Revue Biblique 1; Paris: Gabalda, 1964).
Idem
"Le pays de Canaan," *JAOS* 88 (1968) 23–29; rep. in *Essays in Memory of E. A. Speiser* (ed. W. W. Hallo; New Haven: Yale University, 1968) 23–29.
Idem
"Téman, ville ou région d'Edom?" *RB* 76 (1969) 379–85.
Idem
"El-Far'a, Tell, North," *Encyclopedia of Archaeological Excavations in the Holy Land* (ed. M. Avi-Yonah and E. Stern; 4 vols.; London: Oxford University, 1976) 2.395–404.
Vawter, B.
"Prophecy and the Redactional Question," *No Famine in the Land: Studies in Honor of John L. McKenzie* (ed. J. W. Flanagan and A. W. Robertson; Missoula, MT: Scholars, 1975) 127–39.
Vergon, S.
"Micah 4:14," *BM* 66 (1976) 392–401 (Heb.).

Vermeylen, J.
"Prophètes de la conversion et traditions sacrales," *RTL* 9 (1978) 5–32.
Vetter, D.
"שחת, *šḥt*, pi/hi, 'verderben,'" *THAT* II. 892.
Virolleaud, C.
L'astrologie chaldéene. Le livre intitulé "enuma (Anu) iluBêl" (Paris: Guethner, 1908).
Vogt, E.
"'Ihr Tisch werde zur Falle' (Ps 69, 23)," *Bib* 43 (1962) 79–82.
Volten, A.
Demotische Traumdeutung (Papyrus Carlsberg No. XIII–XIV 7) (Analecta Aegyptiaca 3; Kjøbenhaven: Munksgaard, 1942).
Volz, P.
Die vorexilische Jahweprophetie und der Messias (Göttingen: Vandenhoeck & Ruprecht, 1897).
Idem
Der Prophet Jeremiah (KAT 10; Leipzig: Deichert, 1928).
von Oppenheim, M. F.
Der Tell Halaf: Eine neue Kultur im ältesten Mesopotamien (Leipzig: Brockhaus, 1931).
von Rad, G.
Theologie des Alten Testaments (2 vols.; München: Kaiser, 1960); English tr. *Old Testament Theology* (tr. D.M.G. Stalker; 2 vols.; New York/Evanston: Harper & Row, 1962/1965).
Idem
Gesammelte Studien zum Alten Testament (2 vols.; TBü 8, 48; München: Kaiser, ^{4}1971–73).
von Soden, W.
"Verkündigung des Gotteswillen durch prophetisches Wort in den altbabylonischen Briefen aus Mari," *WO* 1/5 (1950) 397–403.
Idem
Assyrisches Handwörterbuch (3 vols.; Wiesbaden: Harrassowitz, 1959–1981).
Idem
"Licht und Finsternis in der sumerischen und babylonisch-assyrischen Religion," *Studium Generale* 13 (1960) 647–53.
Idem
"Aramäische Wörter in nA, nB, und spB Texten. Ein Vorbericht, I," *Or* 35 (1966) 1–10; 37 (1968) 261–71; 46 (1977) 183–97.
Idem
"Zur Herkunft von hebr. *'ebjōn*, 'arm,'" MIO 15 (1969) 322–26.
Idem
"Ugaritica V—Rezensionsartikel (I). Bemerkungen zu einigen literarischen Texten in akkadischer Sprach aus Ugarit," *UF* 1 (1969) 189–95.
Vriezen, T. C.
Die Erwählung Israels nach dem Alten Testament (ATANT 24; Zürich: Zwingli, 1953).
Wagner, S.
"*drš*," *TWAT* II (1977) 313–29.
Wainwright, G. A.
"The Septuagint's Καππαδοκία for Caphtor," *JJS* 7 (1956) 91–92.
Idem
"Some Early Philistine History," *VT* 9 (1959) 73–84.
Waldman, N.
"Rabbinic Homilies and Cognate Languages," *Gratz College Anniversary Volume, 1895–1970* (ed. I. D. Passow and S. T. Lachs; Philadelphia: Gratz College, 1971) 269–73.
Idem
"Words for 'Heat' and Their Extended Meanings," *Gratz College Annual of Jewish Studies* 3 (ed. I. D. Passow and S. T. Lachs; Philadelphia: Gratz College, 1974) 43–49.
Wambacq, B. N.
L'épithète divine Jahvé Seba'ôt: Étude philologique, historique et exégétique (Bruges: de Brouwer, 1947).
Wansbrough, J. E.
"Antonomasia: The Case for Semitic *'ṮM*," *Figurative Language in the Ancient Near East* (ed. M. Mindlin, M. J. Geller, and J. E. Wansbrough; London: School of Oriental and African Studies, 1987) 103–16.
Ward, W. A.
"Notes on Some Semitic Loan Words and Personal Names," *Or* 32 (1963) 413–36.
Watson, W.G.E.
Classical Hebrew Poetry (*JSOT* Supplement Series 26; Sheffield: JSOT, 1984).
Weidner, E. F.
Politische Dokumente aus Kleinasien. Die Staatsverträge in akkadischer Sprache aus dem Archiv von Boghazköi (Leipzig: Hinrichs, 1923).
Idem
"Altbabylonische Götterlisten," *AfO* 2 (1924–1925) 1–18.
Idem
Eine Beschreibung des Sternenhimmels aus Assur,"*AfO* 4 (1927) 73–85.
Idem
"Der Staatsvertrag Aššurnirâris VI. von Assyrien mit Mati'ilu von Bît-Agusi," *AfO* 8 (1932–1933) 17–27.
Idem
Die Inschriften Tukulti-Ninurtas I. und seiner Nachfolger (*Afo* Beiheft 12; Graz: Selbstverlag des Herausgebers, 1959).
Weidner, E. F., E. Ebeling, and B. Meissner
Die Inschriften der altassyrischen Könige (Altorientalische Bibliothek 1; Leipzig: Quelle & Meyer, 1926).
Weinfeld, M.
"The Change in the Conception of Religion in Deuteronomy," *Tarbiz* 31 (1962) 1–17 (Heb.).
Idem
"The Awakening of National Consciousness in Israel in the Seventh Century B.C.," *'Oz Le-David:*

Collected Readings in Bible Presented to David ben Gurion on His Seventy-seventh Birthday (ed. Y. Kaufmann and others; Jerusalem: Kiryat Sepher, 1964) 396–420 (Heb.).

Idem
"The Period of the Conquest and of the Judges as Seen by the Earlier and the Later Sources," *VT* 17 (1967) 93–113.

Idem
"The Covenant of Grant in the Old Testament and in the Ancient Near East," *JAOS* 90 (1970) 184–203.

Idem
"הַבְּרִית וְהַחֶסֶד," *Leš* 36 (1972) 85–105 (Heb.).

Idem
"בְּרִית," *TWAT* I (1972) 781–808 = *TDOT* II, 253–97.

Idem
Deuteronomy and the Deuteronomic School (Oxford: Clarendon, 1972).

Idem
"The Worship of Molech and the Queen of Heaven and Its Background," *UF* 4 (1972) 133–54.

Idem
"The Royal and Sacred Aspects of the Tithe in the Old Testament," *Beer-Sheba* I (1973) 122–31 (Heb.).

Idem
"'Rider of the Clouds' and 'Gatherer of the Clouds,'" *The Gaster Festschrift* (*JANESCU* 5; ed. D. Marcus and others; New York: Columbia University, 1973) 421–26.

Idem
"Covenant Terminology in the Ancient Near East," *JAOS* 93 (1973) 190–99.

Idem
"*B*^{e}*rît*—Covenant versus Obligation," *Bib* 56 (1975) 120–28.

Idem
"Ancient Near Eastern Patterns in Prophetic Literature," *VT* 27 (1977) 178–95.

Idem
"'They Fought from Heaven'—Divine Intervention in Ancient Israel and in the Ancient Near East," Eretz Israel 14 (*H. L. Ginsberg Volume*; ed. M. Haran and others; Jerusalem: Israel Exploration Society, 1978) 23–30 (Heb.); English tr. "Divine Intervention in War in Ancient Israel and in the Ancient Near East," *History, Historiography and Interpretation. Studies in Biblical and Cuneiform Literature* (ed. H. Tadmor and M. Weinfeld; Jerusalem: Magnes, 1983) 121–47.

Idem
"Divine War in Israel and the Ancient Near East," *Studies in the Bible and the Ancient Near East, Presented to Samuel E. Loewenstamm on His Seventieth Birthday* (2 vols.; ed. Y. Avishur and Y. Blau; Jerusalem: E. Rubinstein, 1978) 171–81 (Heb.).

Idem
"Burning Babies in Ancient Israel," *UF* 10 (1978) 411–13.

Idem
"Mesopotamian Prophecies of the End of Days," *Shnaton* 3 (1979) 263–76 (Heb.).

Idem
"A Sacred Site of the Monarchic Period," *Shnaton* 4 (1980) 280–84 (Heb.).

Idem
"The Balaam Oracle in the Deir 'Alla Inscription," *Shnaton* 5–6 (1981–1982) 141–47 (Heb.).

Idem
"Further Remarks on the 'Ajrud Inscriptions," *Shnaton* 5–6 (1981–1982) 237–39 (Heb.).

Idem
"Instructions for Temple Visitors in the Bible and in Ancient Egypt," *Egyptological Studies* (ed. S. Israelit-Groll; Scripta Hierosolymitana 28; Jerusalem: Magnes, 1982) 224–50.

Idem
"Justice and Righteousness in Ancient Israel against the Background of 'Social Reforms' in the Ancient Near East," *Mesopotamien und seine Nachbarn: Politische und Kulturelle Wechselbeziehungen im Alten Vorderasien* (2 vols.; Berliner Beiträge zum Vorderen Orient 1 = *Comptes Rendus de la XXV Rencontre Assyriologique Internationale*; ed. H.-J. Nissen and J. Renger; Berlin: Dietrich Heimer, 1982) 2:491–519.

Idem
"The Extent of the Promised Land—The Status of Transjordan," *Das Land Israel in biblischer Zeit* (ed. G. Strecker; Göttinger Theologische Arbeiten 25; Göttingen: Vandenhoeck & Ruprecht, 1983) 60–75.

Idem
"Zion and Jerusalem as Religious and Political Capital: Ideology and Utopia," *The Poet and the Historian: Essays in Literary and Historical Biblical Criticism* (ed. R. E. Friedman; HSS 26; Chico, CA: Scholars, 1983) 75–115.

Idem
"Desecrating, Treading Down and Trampling," *Hebrew Language Studies Presented to Professor Ze'ev Ben-Ḥayyim* (ed. M. ben Asher and others; Jerusalem: Magnes, 1983) 196–200 (Heb.).

Idem
Justice and Righteousness in Israel and the Nations. Equality and Freedom in Ancient Israel in Light of Social Justice in the Ancient Near East (Jerusalem: Magnes, 1985) (Heb.).

Idem
"The Aramaic Text (in Demotic) from Egypt on Sacrifice and Morality and Its Relationship to Biblical Texts," *Shnaton* 9 (1987) 179–89 (Heb.).

Idem
"Initiation of Political Friendship in Ebla and Its Later Developments," *Wirtschaft und Gesellschaft*

von Ebla (Heidelberger Studien zum Alten Orient; ed. H. Hauptmann and H. Waetzoldt; Heidelberg: Heidelberger Orientverlag, 1988) 2.345–48.
Weingreen, B. J.
"Rabbinic-Type Glosses in the Old Testament," *JSS* 19 (1957) 142–62.
Weippert, N.
"'Heiliger Krieg' in Israel und Assyrien: Kritische Anmerkungen zu Gerhard von Rads Konzept des 'Heiligen Krieges' im alten Israel," *ZAW* 84 (1972) 460–93.
Weiser, A.
"Zur Frage nach den Beziehungen der Psalmen zum Kult: Die Darstellung der Theophanie in den Psalmen und im Festkult," *Festschrift Alfred Bertholet zum 80. Geburtstag* (ed. W. Baumgartner and others; Tübingen: Mohr, 1950) 513–31.
Idem
"The Exodus from Egypt in the Prophets," *Sinai* 41 (1957) 342–47 (Heb.).
Weisman, Z.
"The Institution of the Nazirites in the Bible—Its Types and Roots," *Tarbiz* 36 (1966–1967) 207–20 (Heb.).
Weiss, R.
MiShuṭ BaMiqra (Jerusalem: E. Rubinstein, 1977) (Heb.).
Idem
Studies in the Text and Language of the Bible (Jerusalem: Magnes, 1981) (Heb.).
Weissbach, F. H.
Babylonische Miscellen (*WVDOG* 4; Leipzig: Hinrichs, 1903).
Westermann, C.
"Die Begriffe für Fragen und Suchen im Alten Testament," *KD* 6 (1960) 2–30; rep. in *Forschung am Alten Testament: Gesammelte Studien* II (TBü 55; München: Kaiser, 1974) 162–90.
Idem
Grundformen prophetischer Rede (München: Kaiser, 1960); English tr. *Basic Forms of Prophetic Speech* (tr. H. C. White; Philadelphia: Westminster, 1967).
Whitaker, R. E.
A Concordance of the Ugaritic Literature (Cambridge: Harvard University, 1972).
Wiesner, J.
Fahren und Reiten im Alteuropa und im alten Orient (AO 38/2–4; Leipzig: Hinrichs, 1939).
Wijngaards, J.
"הוציא and העלה: A Twofold Approach to the Exodus," *VT* 15 (1965) 91–102.
Wilcke, C.
Das Lugalbandaepos (Wiesbaden: Harrassowitz, 1969).
Williams, J. G.
"The Prophetic 'Father': A Brief Explanation of the Term 'Sons of the Prophets,'" *JBL* 85 (1966) 344–48.
Wilson, R.
"An Interpretation of Ezekiel's Dumbness," *VT* 22 (1972) 91–104.
Winckler, H.
Die Keilschrifttexte Sargons (Leipzig: Pfeiffer, 1889).
Winward, S.
A Guide to the Prophets (Atlanta: John Knox, 1969, ^{2}1976).
Wiseman, D. J.
"Haza'el," *RLA* 4 (1975) 238–39.
Idem
"The New Stele of Aššur-naṣir-pal II," *Iraq* 14 (1952) 24–44.
Idem
Chronicles of Chaldaean Kings (626–556 B.C.) in the British Museum (London: The British Museum, 1956).
Idem
"A Fragmentary Inscription of Tiglath-Pileser III from Nimrud," *Iraq* 18 (1956) 117–29.
Idem
"The Vassal-Treaties of Esarhaddon," *Iraq* 20 (1958) i-ii, 11–99; plates 1–12, 1–53.
Wiseman, Z.
"The Biblical Narrative, Its Types and Roots," *Tarbiz* 36 (1967) 207–20 (Heb.).
Wolff, H. W.
Das Zitat im Prophetenspruch (BEvT 4; München: Kaiser, 1937); rep. in *Gesammelte Studien zum Alten Testament* (TBü 22; München: Kaiser, 1964) 36–129.
Idem
"Das Thema 'Umkehr' in der alttestamentlichen Prophetie," in *Gesammelte Studien zum Alten Testament* (TBü 22; München: Kaiser, 1964) 130–52.
Wörterbuch der aegyptischen Sprache
(Berlin: Akademie Verlag, 1982).
Wright, G. E.
"The Nations in Hebrew Prophecy," *Encounter* 26 (1965) 225–37.
Wright, W.
A Grammar of the Arabic Language (Cambridge: Kaisler, 1951).
Würthwein, E.
"Erwägungen zu Psalm CXXXIX," *VT* 7 (1957) 163–82.
Xella, P.
I testi rituali di Ugarit—I (Studi Semitici 54; Roma: Centro di Studi Semitici; Universitá di Roma, 1981).
Xenophon
Anabasis I–VII (tr. C. L. Brownson; Loeb Classical Library; London: Heineman, 1922).
Idem
Cyropaedia II (tr. W. Miller; Loeb Classical Library; London: Heineman, 1914).
Yadin, Y.
Hazor II: An Account of the Second Season of Excavations, 1956 (Jerusalem: Magnes, 1960).

Idem
The Art of Warfare in Biblical Lands in the Light of Archaeological Study (2 vols.; New York/Toronto/London: Weidenfeld & Nicolson, 1963).
Idem
"Beer-Sheba: The High Place Destroyed by King Josiah," *BASOR* 222 (1976) 5–17.
Yalon, H.
"Studies in Biblical Hebrew: *qal-hiph'il*," *Leš* 2 (1930) 113–26 (Heb.).
Idem
Quntreisim 2 (Jerusalem: Wahrman, 1938–1939) (Heb.).
Idem
Review of Sukenik's *Dead Sea Scrolls*, in *Kiryath Sepher* 26 (1950) 246 (Heb.).
Idem
Studies in the Hebrew Language (Jerusalem: Bialik, 1971) (Heb.).
Yamashita, T.
"Professions," *Ras Shamra Parallels: The Texts from Ugarit and the Hebrew Bible* (ed. L. R. Fisher; AnOr 50; Rome: Pontifical Biblical Institute, 1975) 41–68.
Yaron, R.
Introduction to the Law of the Aramaic Papyri (Oxford: Clarendon, 1961).
Idem
"Notes on Aramaic Papyri, II," *JNES* 20 (1961) 127–30.
Idem
The Law of the Elephantine Documents (Jerusalem: Mif'al HaShichpul, 1968) (Heb.).
Yeivin, S.
"Agriculture," *EM* 6.35 (Heb.).
Idem
"Judahite-Israelite Relations during Jehu's Dynasty," *Studies in Honor of Mordechai Zer Kavod* (ed. H. Gevaryahu and others; Jerusalem: Kiryat Sepher, 1968) 367–81 (Heb.).
Idem
"Work," *EM* 4.1016 (Heb.).
Yeivin, S., and S. E. Loewenstamm
"Gilead," *EM* 2.512 (Heb.).
Yellin, D.
"Forgotten Meanings of Hebrew Roots," *Leš* 1 (1929) 5–26 (Heb.).
Zayadine, F.
"A Nabatean Inscription from Beida," ADAJ 21 (1976) 139–42.
Zeijdner, H.
"Bijdragen tot de Tekstkritiek op het O.T.," *ThSt* 4 (1886) 196–204; 6 (1888) 247ff.
Zevit, Z.
"The Khirbet el-Qom Inscription Mentioning a Goddess," *BASOR* 255 (1984) 45–46.
Zimmerli, W.
Geschichte und Tradition von Beersheba im Alten Testament (Giessen: Töpelmann, 1932).
Idem
Ezekiel 2 (BKAT XIII/2; Neukirchen-Vluyn: Neukirchener Verlag, 1969).
Idem
"Vom Prophetenwort zum Prophetenbuch," *TLZ* 104 (1979) 481–96.
Idem
Ezekiel I: A Commentary on the Book of the Prophet Ezekiel, Chapters 1–24 (tr. R. E. Clements; ed. F. M. Cross and Klaus Blatzer; Hermeneia: A Critical and Historical Commentary on the Bible; Philadelphia: Fortress, 1979).
Idem
Ezekiel II: A Commentary on the Book of the Prophet Ezekiel, Chapters 24–48 (tr. R. E. Clements; ed. F. M. Cross and Klaus Blatzer; Hermeneia: A Critical and Historical Commentary on the Bible; Philadelphia: Fortress, 1983).
Zimmerli, W., and J. Jeremias
The Servant of the Lord (SBT 20; London: SCM, 1957).
Zimmern, H.
Die Beschwörungstafeln Šurpu (Leipzig: Hinrichs, 1896).
Idem
Beiträge zur Kenntnis der babylonischen Religion (Leipzig: Hinrichs, 1901).
Zohary, M.
Plant Life of Palestine: Israel and Jordan (New York: Ronald, 1962).
Zurro, E.
"Disemia de *brḥ* y paralelismo bifronte en Job 9:25," *Bib* 62 (1981) 546–47.

1. Passages

a / Hebrew Bible

b / New Testament

c / Apocrypha

d / Qumran

e / Josephus

f / Rabbinic Literature

g / Targumim

h / Greek and Roman Literature

i / Cuneiform Literature

j / Ugaritic Literature

k / Northwest Semitic and Aramaic Inscriptions

l / Egyptian Literature

2. Authors

McFadyen, J. E.
318
McKane, W.
336
McKay, J. W.
197 n. 87; 354
McKeating, H.
222 n. 5; 300
Mackenzie, H. S.
235 n. 71; 332
McKenzie, J. L.
336
MacLagan, P. J.
335
Macpherson, A.
301
Maier, W. A.
269 n. 15; 354
de Maigret, A.
202 n. 17; 354
Maigret, J.
314
Maimonides
151 n. 116; 216 n. 29
Maisler, B.
51 n. 72; 327; 354
Malamat, A.
40 n. 69; 50 n. 62; 51 n. 71; 53 n. 100; 54 n. 104; 55 n. 116; 134 n. 82; 135 n. 83; 235 n. 70; 283 n. 15; 324; 355
Mallau, H. H.
332
Mamie, P.
307
Mandelbaum, B.
79 n. 359; 355
Margalit, B.
52 n. 86; 185 n. 23; 205 n. 53; 211 n. 101; 355
Margolis, M.
165 n. 61; 307
Margolis, M. L.
120 n. 62; 275 n. 22; 355
Margulis, B. B.
9; 9 nn. 34, 35, 36, 37, 38, 39, 40; 19 n. 120; 25 n. 161; 49 n. 44; 54 n. 107; 89 n. 457; 321
Markert, L.
90 n. 464; 104 n. 1; 271 n. 23; 307
Marsh, J.
301
Marti, K.
16 nn. 89, 97; 17 n. 107; 36 n. 39; 41 n. 77; 50 n. 60; 51 n. 78; 55 n. 115; 80 n. 367; 93 n. 488; 100 n. 4; 107 n. 14; 109 nn. 23, 27; 121 n. 67; 122 n. 75; 126 n. 37; 135 n. 88; 142 nn. 25, 26; 144 n. 47; 145 n. 56; 147 n. 75; 148 n. 82; 150 n. 105; 151 n. 119; 166 n. 72; 171 n. 122; 193 n. 57; 194 n. 62; 199 n. 2; 205 n. 46; 222 n. 3; 226 n. 2; 227 n. 13; 238 n. 3; 240 n. 18; 242 n. 29; 244 n. 50; 249 n. 104; 259 n. 27; 265 n. 8; 266 nn. 13, 16; 268 n. 7; 270 n. 16; 271 n. 23; 272 n. 35; 274 n. 13; 275 n. 25; 276 n. 26; 280 n. 75; 284 n. 18; 285 n. 28; 287 n. 52; 288 n. 2; 291 n. 29; 300; 321; 324
Martin-Achard, R.
301; 307
Marzal, A.
134 nn. 82, 83; 355
Matheson, G.
307
Mauchline, J.
290 n. 12; 307; 355
May, H. G.
97 n. 518; 355
Mayer, R.
142 n. 29; 355
Mays, J. L.
1 n. 2; 16 n. 91; 17 nn. 102, 103, 106, 107, 108; 18 n. 112; 19 nn. 120, 121; 21 n. 136; 30 n. 192; 33 n. 1; 36 n. 39; 41 n. 78; 45 n. 5; 47 n. 25; 49 n. 50; 50 n. 60; 51 n. 78; 55 n. 115; 57 n. 132; 58 n. 150; 63 n. 200; 77 nn. 335, 344; 78 n. 346; 80 n. 363; 81 n. 376; 83 n. 392; 90 nn. 464, 465; 105 nn. 2, 4; 112 n. 54; 113 n. 58; 143 n. 35; 176 n. 172; 201 n. 12; 203 n. 25; 236 n. 84; 240 n. 19; 241 nn. 23, 27; 246 n. 78; 247 n. 83; 249 n. 107; 260 n. 38; 267 n. 19; 269 n. 14; 270 n. 20; 301; 307
Mazar, B.
16 n. 90; 51 n. 72; 61 n. 185; 63 nn. 205, 206; 202 n. 20; 203 n. 26; 205 n. 50; 221 n. 31; 283 n. 13; 331; 355
Mazar, E.
327
Meek, T. J.
323
Meier, G.
168 n. 89; 355
Meinhold, J.
74 n. 291; 142 n. 25; 307; 322; 355
Meissner, B.
70 n. 253; 355; 364
Melamed, E. Z.
28 n. 175; 74 n. 298; 219 n. 10; 320
Melugin, R. F.
90 n. 464; 105 n. 3; 313
Mendelsohn, I.
56 n. 132; 355
de Mertzenfeld, C. D.
162 n. 34; 355
Meshel, Z.
270 n. 19; 355
Messel, N.
301
Meṣudoth
260 n. 38; 301
Metzger, M.
219 n. 15; 331
Meyer, R.
211 n. 104; 331
Michaelis, J. D. 218 n. 5; 355
Michel, D.
307
Michel, E.
278 n. 49; 355
Michel, O.
270 n. 20; 356
Mickler, E. H.
263 n. 9; 352
Miles, J. C.
84; 84 n. 414; 85 n. 415; 119 n. 44; 259 n. 26; 342
Milgrom, J.
36 n. 35; 83 n. 402; 84; 84 nn. 404, 405, 406, 413; 92 n. 480; 117 n. 16; 125 n. 21; 129 n. 7; 140 n. 16; 190 n. 12; 229 n. 25; 356
Milik, J. T.
47 n. 32; 59 n. 156; 280 n. 72; 338; 339
Millard, A. R.
30 n. 194; 146 n. 64; 235 n. 71; 257 n. 15; 336; 352; 356
Miller, C. H.
307
Miller, J. M.
1 n. 3; 356
Miller, P. D., Jr.
9 n. 46; 49 nn. 45, 48; 129 n. 4; 211 n. 101; 231 n. 44; 232 n. 49; 250 n. 115; 356
Miller, P. W.
307
Mitchell, H. G.
163 n. 41; 307; 331
Mittmann, S.
104 n. 1; 109 n. 23; 121 n. 68; 219 n. 15; 270 n. 19; 326; 327; 356
Moeller, H. A.
120 n. 59; 121 n. 73; 327
Moffatt, J.
307
Monloubou, J.
301; 307; 318
Montgomery, J. A.
24 n. 156; 206 n. 61; 247 n. 85; 308; 329; 330; 331; 332; 356
Moran, W.
15 n. 82; 61 n. 181; 62 nn. 189, 197; 66 n. 229; 356
Moran, W. L.
134 n. 82; 135 n. 83
Moreau, M.
316
Moreno, C. A.
308
Moreshet, M.
237 n. 90; 356
Morgenstern, J.
17 n. 107; 19 n. 120; 20 n. 126; 40 n. 72; 41 n. 77; 50 n. 60; 51 n. 78; 74 n. 291; 100 n. 4; 147 n. 75; 150 n. 109; 164 n. 47; 190 n. 20; 241 n. 23; 268 n. 2; 308; 356

3. Names and Subjects

In the design of the visual aspects of *Hermeneia,* consideration has been given to relating the form to the content by symbolic means.

The letters of the logotype *Hermeneia* are a fusion of forms alluding simultaneously to Hebrew (dotted vowel markings) and Greek (geometric round shapes) letter forms. In their modern treatment they remind us of the electronic age as well, the vantage point from which this investigation of the past begins.

The Lion of Judah used as visual identification for the series is based on the Seal of Shema. The version for *Hermeneia* is again a fusion of Hebrew calligraphic forms, especially the legs of the lion, and Greek elements characterized by the geometric. In the sequence of arcs, which can be understood as scroll-like images, the first is the lion's mouth. It is reasserted and accelerated in the whorl and returns in the aggressively arched tail: tradition is passed from one age to the next, rediscovered and re-formed.

"Who is worthy to open the scroll and break its seals. . . ."
Then one of the elders said to me
"weep not; lo, the Lion of the tribe of David,
the Root of David, has conquered,
so that he can open the scroll and
its seven seals."
Rev. 5:2, 5

To celebrate the signal achievement in biblical scholarship which *Hermeneia* represents, the entire series will by its color constitute a signal on the theologian's bookshelf: the Old Testament will be bound in yellow and the New Testament in red, traceable to a commonly used color coding for synagogue and church in medieval painting; in pure color terms, varying degrees of intensity of the warm segment of the color spectrum. The colors interpenetrate when the binding color for the Old Testament is used to imprint volumes from the New and vice versa.

Wherever possible, a photograph of the oldest extant manuscript, or a historically significant document pertaining to the biblical sources, will be displayed on the end papers of each volume to give a feel for the tangible reality and beauty of the source material.

The title-page motifs are expressive derivations from the *Hermeneia* logotype, repeated seven times to form a matrix and debossed on the cover of each volume. These sifted-out elements will be seen to be in their exact positions within the parent matrix. These motifs and their expressional character are noted on the following page.

Horizontal markings at gradated levels on the spine will assist in grouping the volumes according to these conventional categories.

The type has been set with unjustified right margins so as to preserve the internal consistency of word spacing. This is a major factor in both legibility and aesthetic quality; the resultant uneven line endings are only slight impairments to legibility by comparison. In this respect the type resembles the handwritten manuscripts where the quality of the calligraphic writing is dependent on establishing and holding to integral spacing patterns.

All of the type faces in common use today have been designed between A.D. 1500 and the present. For the biblical text a face was chosen which does not arbitrarily date the text, but rather one which is uncompromisingly modern and unembellished so that its feel is of the universal. The type style is Univers 65 by Adrian Frutiger.

The expository texts and footnotes are set in Baskerville, chosen for its compatibility with the many brief Greek and Hebrew insertions. The double-column format and the shorter line length facilitate speed reading and the wide margins to the left of footnotes provide for the scholar's own notations.

Kenneth Hiebert

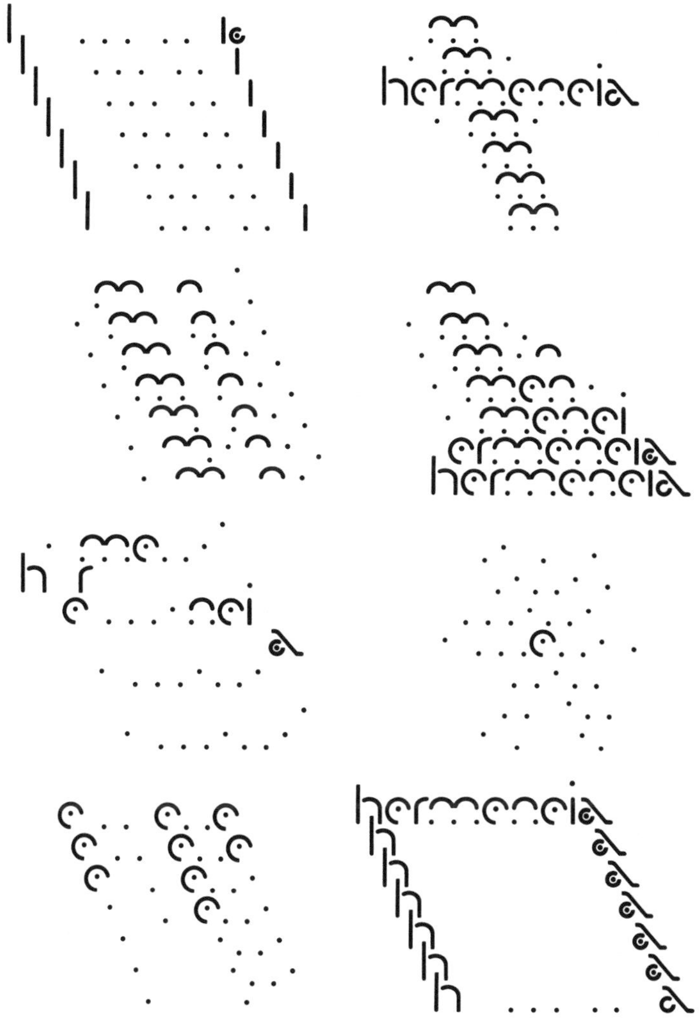

Category of biblical writing, key symbolic characteristic, and volumes so identified.

1
Law
(boundaries described)
- Genesis
- Exodus
- Leviticus
- Numbers
- Deuteronomy

2
History
(trek through time and space)
- Joshua
- Judges
- Ruth
- 1 Samuel
- 2 Samuel
- 1 Kings
- 2 Kings
- 1 Chronicles
- 2 Chronicles
- Ezra
- Nehemiah
- Esther

3
Poetry
(lyric emotional expression)
- Job
- Psalms
- Proverbs
- Ecclesiastes
- Song of Songs

4
Prophets
(inspired seers)
- Isaiah
- Jeremiah
- Lamentations
- Ezekiel
- Daniel
- Hosea
- Joel
- Amos
- Obadiah
- Jonah
- Micah
- Nahum
- Habakkuk
- Zephaniah
- Haggai
- Zechariah
- Malachi

5
New Testament Narrative
(focus on One)
- Matthew
- Mark
- Luke
- John
- Acts

6
Epistles
(directed instruction)
- Romans
- 1 Corinthians
- 2 Corinthians
- Galatians
- Ephesians
- Philippians
- Colossians
- 1 Thessalonians
- 2 Thessalonians
- 1 Timothy
- 2 Timothy
- Titus
- Philemon
- Hebrews
- James
- 1 Peter
- 2 Peter
- 1 John
- 2 John
- 3 John
- Jude

7
Apocalypse
(vision of the future)
- Revelation

8
Extracanonical Writings
(peripheral records)

P. xxvi: The subtitle of the Willi-Plein *Vorformen* should read *Werden der auf Amos, Hosea und Micha zurückgehenden Bücher im hebräischen Zwölfprophetenbuch.*

P. xxvii: The fragments of a leather scroll of Amos are reproduced with permission of the Israel Antiquities Authority, not the publisher.

P. 5, 2d col., line 17: The doxology 5:8 should be deleted.

P. 14, 2d col., line 22: the word "have" should read "provide."

P. 15, 1st col., line 15: The sentence should read: "So I captured it [Nebo] and slayed all, seven thousand men . . . , and women . . . , and young women,[84] for I had devoted it to destruction for (the god) Ashtar-Chemosh."

P. 15, n. 84: Read *KAI,* I. p. 33, 181; . . .

P. 23, 2d col., lines 18–21: "wept" should read "weeps," *diku* should read *dikū,* and *šunullu* should read *šunūlū.*

P. 24, n. 156, last line: "and 105" should read "ll. 4–5."

P. 28, 2d col., line 20: The reference to Pss 6:14 should be deleted.

P. 33: Footnote 5 should read: This in no way needs to be interpreted as being of "lowly birth" or of "obscure origin," see Koehler, 35; Terrien, "Amos and Wisdom," 114 n 13.

P. 38, 2d col., lines 17–18: *irubbu* should read *irubbū* and *itarruru* should read *itarrurū.*

P. 38, n. 56: "however" should read "too," and [*itarraru*] should read [*itarrarū*].

P. 39, n. 56 (continued): *inuššu* should read *inuššū.*

P. 39, n. 57: Read *EA* 147:13–15. See also *CAD,* . . .

P. 47, 2d col., line 12: Transliteration should read: *dāiš kullat nakirī.*

P. 49, 2d col., lines 24–27: Transliterations should read: *dūršu ekallīšu u nišišu ina išātu iqtali* and *nakru ana dalat abullija išāta inaddīma ana libbi āli* . . .

P. 50, 1st col., line 28: The year 849 B.C.E. should also be included.

P. 50, n. 64: Read *KAI,* I. p. 37, 201, 1–3; . . .

P. 50, n. 65: Read *KAI,* I. p. 37, 202, A 4.

P. 51, n. 71: Read *RLA,* 4.238–39, . . .

P. 51, n. 73: Lines 9–10 should read as follows: "2 Sam 20:1, בֶּן־יִשַׁי // דָּוִד; Num 23:18, // בָּלָק בְּנוֹ צִפֹּר; Ugar. *bʿl // bn dgn, CTA* 14:ii77–79—the . . ."

P. 52, 1st col., lines 2–3: Read "the analogous terms מֶלֶךְ (1:15), שׁוֹפֵט and שָׂרִים (1:15, 2:3). . . ."

P. 52, n. 90: Read *KAI,* I. p. 5, 24:13–14: . . .

P. 52, n. 91: Read *KAI,* I. p. 1, 1:2. . . .

P. 57, n. 140: Read *KAI,* I. p. 5, 26:2–5; . . .

P. 58, n. 151, line 22 of 2d col.: "Citizens" should replace "sons," and transliteration should read *šitti mārī.*

P. 58, n. 151, line 24 of 2d col.: Transliteration should begin *šittat nišī* . . . and end *ipparšidū.*

P. 58, n. 153, line 5: Read Moabite, Mesha Stele, *KAI,* I. p. 33; 181:7, "And Israel perished" . . .

P. 60, n. 173: Read *KAI,* I. p. 3, 14; . . .

P. 61, n. 184: "H. Goetze" should read "A. Goetze."

P. 62, 1st col., line 10: *raksu* should read *raksū.*

P. 62, n. 190: *inscriptiones* should read *inscriptions,* and "Geneva" should read "Genève."

P. 65, n. 216: Read *KAI,* I. p. 33, 181:17; . . .

P. 68, 2d col., line 7: Transliteration should begin *ušarriṭi*

P. 68, 2d col., line 12: "mother's" should read "mothers'."

P. 70, n. 253, line 6: Transliteration should read *rigim ummānīja galtu kima ᵈAdad ušašgim.*

P. 70, n. 258: Read OIP 2.45 v 77; . . .

P. 72, n. 268: Read *KAI,* II. p. 179.

P. 73, 2d col., last line: "northeast" should read "northwest."

P. 73, n. 287, line 2 of 2d col.: "Keriyot" should read "Keriyoth."

P. 73, n. 289: Read *KAI,* I. p. 33, 187; . . .

P. 73, n. 290: Read Fitzmyer, *Genesis Apocryphon,* 62, 147.

P. 75, n. 301 (continued): Pfeifer title should begin "Ich bin in teife . . ." and end "Sekundärliteratur."

P. 75, n. 311: The reference Hos 4:6; 8:1 should be deleted.

P. 77, n. 333, line 3: Read "נִפְּלוֹ, with 1 Sam 29:3, נָפְלוֹ. . . ."

P. 77, n. 344, line 7: Read *ammar šēni ammar.* . . .

P. 78, n. 350: Add "Compare Isa 1:15."

P. 79, n. 355, lines 5–6: Translation should read "I am the dust beneath the feet of the king."

P. 85, 1st col., line 2: The first LH reference should read (LH 113).

P. 88, 2d col., line 9: *išīhuma ikbiru* should read *išīhūma ikbirū.*

P. 88, n. 451: Read See *CAD, A,* I.354–55.

P. 88, n. 452: "Luzatto's" should read "Luzzato's"

P. 89, 1st col., line 11: Transliteration should begin *ʾl ykn lm.* . . .

P. 94, 1st col., line 26: Transliteration should read *niphʿal.*

P. 95, 2d col., lines 10–11: Read "רֹכֵב הַסּוּס,); v 16 . . ."

P. 106, 1st col., line 1: Add reference 6:1–6.

P. 106, n. 10, line 3 from the bottom: *akâlime* should read *akālime.*

P. 107, n. 15: "Theis-Lippel" should read "Theis-Lippl."

P. 108, n. 19: Read *KAI,* I. p. 2, 13:5.

P. 110, n. 31: See also Mic 5:7.

P. 110, n. 33: "Theis-Lippel" should read "Theis-Lippl."

P. 111, n. 41, line 5: *iṣṣabatuni* should read *iṣṣabatūni.*

P. 111, n. 41, line 10: *arrutu* should read *arrūtu.*

P. 114, n. 66: Rudolph title should begin "Und. . . ."

P. 118, 1st col., line 2: Add Amos references 4:12; and 13.

P. 120, 1st col., line 9: *ikkimu* should read *ikkimū.*

P. 121, n. 71, line 7: phrase should read "which it transliterated incorrectly as ἱερεῖς. . . ."

P. 124, 2d col., line 3: read מִזְבַּח for מִזְבֵּחַ.

P. 124, n. 12: "Ahroni" should read "Aharoni."

P. 125, n. 25: Read *KAI,* I. p. 40, no. 216:15–20; . . .

P. 126, n. 29, line 7: "Tell Babel" should read "Tell Babil."

P. 127, n. 39: The first sentence should be deleted.

P. 129, 2d col., line 9: At paragraph's end, add "So, too, 4Q xii[c]."

P. 129, n. 12: See v 2 and Ruth 1:8.

P. 134, n. 81: At note's end, add "See *CAD, S,* 418, b."

P. 135, n. 88, line 7 of 2d col.: Add "*UT* 2117." between sentences.

P. 135, n. 94 *[ik]kisu* should read *[ik]kisū.*

P. 141, n. 19: *quṭṭuru* should read *qutturu.*

P. 143, n. 33: "C. Y. Kasovsky" should read "C. J. Kasovsky."

P. 144, n. 42, line 11: *akalim* should read *akalē* and *amât* should read *amuʾat.*

P. 144, n. 44: Read *KAI,* I. p. 34, 182.

P. 145, n. 50, line 11: Note should include "So, too, ibn Ganaḥ, *Sefer HaRiqmah,* p. שכה, lines 4–5."

P. 145, n. 58: All text except the first sentence should be deleted.

P. 148, n. 86: *bu ʾšū* should read *bu ʾšu.*

P. 148, n. 87: Read *KAI,* I. p. 37, 37, text 202.

P. 149, n. 99: Note should include "Compare Arab. *ʾūd,* 'wood'."

P. 150, n. 106: "Bertelsman" should read "Bertelsmann."

P. 150, n. 111: "*Mikrâ,* 3.409; idem," should be deleted.

P. 154, 1st col., line 5: "Gen. 1–3" should be "Gen. 1–2."

P. 154, 2d col., lines 17–18: "expression of thought" should be "speech."

P. 154, n. 147, line 5: *šāre* should be *šārī,* and *sibittišunu* should be *sibittišun.*

P. 155, n. 153, lines 4–5: Should read "dawn who appears in a Ugaritic text, *KTU.* . . ."

P. 155, n. 154, line 1: Should read "See the reference to ibn Ganaḥ in H. L. Ginsberg, "An Unrecognized . . ."

P. 155, n. 154, line 5: reference should be to n r, not par. r.

P. 161, 1st col., line 19: Should read "May a thousand houses turn into one house."

P. 161, n. 20, line 1: "Any" should be "every."

P. 161, n. 22, line 2: Compare also Isa 6:13.

P. 162, n. 33: *balaṭa* should read *balāṭa,* and *tuttā* should read *tutta.*

P. 163, 2d col., line 2: Compare to Amos 4:4.

P. 166, 2d col.: Note reference 73 should move to line six, after the word "participle."

P. 166, n. 77, line 1: Read "For הפך ל- . . . ." Also, in line 6, *nabalkatum* should read *nabalkutum.*

P. 166, n. 78: "Zohari" should read "Zohary."

P. 167, n. 82, line 1: *mēšaru* should read *mīšaru.*

P. 167, n. 85, line 15: "2:6–7" should read "2:6–8."

P. 168, n. 89, line 15: *Sumerisches* should read *Šumerisches.*

P. 173, n. 134: See the Marseilles Tariff, *KAI,* I. p. 15, 69: 3, 6, 10, 17, 18, 20, 21; see also 75:2; 119:5; and in the plural, p. 16, 74:1. . . .

P. 175, n. 165, line 2: "ʾEbed" should read "ʿEbed."

P. 176, n. 171: *dumāmu* should read *damāmu.*

P. 176, n. 172, line 13: "G. Lust" should read "J. Lust."

P. 177, n. 182: Read *KAI,* I. 26, p. 6, II:17.

P. 178, n. 187: “Rabbi Ashi” should read “Rabbi Assi.”

P. 179, n. 197: Read Mishnah Taʿanith, 2:1.

P. 179, n. 205, line 4: *ilsa* should read *ilsâ.*

P. 179, n. 205, line 11: Read “I:84,” not “I:133, 84.”

P. 183, n. 9, line 7: “Z. Barag” should read “Z. Baras.”

P. 185, n. 22, line 8: Read “לָמָּה־זֶּה, . . .”

P. 186, n. 33: Read “Heb. בא ב־ means . . . .”

P. 186, n. 40, line 9: Read “lines 6–7.”

P. 189, n. 9: Reference should read “1 Kgs 8:2, 65.”

P. 191, n. 29: Read *βοσκηθήσονται.*

P. 192, n. 49, line 4: “a disappointing stream” should read “a spring that fails” and reference should change to Jer 15:18.

P. 195, n. 72, lines 13–14: Read *Die sumerisch-babylonischen Stern-Namen* (ed. P. A. Deimel; Šumerisches . . .

P. 196, n. 75, line 1: Read *Ραιφάν.*

P. 196, n. 75, line 3: Read *Καιφάν.*

P. 196, n. 78, line 2: Transliteration should read “*Nannaru* (variant *[ka]kkabšu*).”

P. 196, n. 78, line 3: translation should read “the moon (variant: his star)”

P. 196, n. 81, 2d para.: Read *KAI,* I. p. 45–46, 228:2, 3ff.; 229:3, . . .

P. 199, 1st col., line 6: Reference should be (5:23; 6:5).

P. 200, n. 8: *ăsarīdu* should read *ăsaridu.*

P. 205, 2d col., line 15: “such a bed was” should read “such beds were.”

P. 205, n. 54: *ṣenu* should read *ṣēnu.*

P. 206, n. 60, line 10: “Kumissi” should read “Ḳumissi.”

P. 206, 2d col., line 10: Read “expression חשב ל־?”

P. 210, 2d col., line 13: Read “מַרְזֵחַ, . . .”

P. 210, 2d col., lines 16–17: Read “sixth century Judah . . .”

P. 210, 2d col., line 20: “(96 B.C.E.)” should be deleted.

P. 215, n. 24, line 1: *piʿel* should read *puʿal.*

P. 217, n. 42: date of Neukirchener Verlag should be 1964, not 1967.

P. 222, n. 1, line 23: 1965 should be ^{2}1965.

P. 225, n. 22, line 9: *(aribu)* should read *(āribu)*

P. 227, n. 10: Read *KAI,* I. p. 34, 182.

P. 228, n. 21, lines 7–11: *ṣeri* should read *ṣēri,* and Weidner title should read *Politische Dokumente aus Kleinasien. Die Staatsverträge in akkadischer Sprache aus dem Archiv von Boghazköi.*

P. 230, n. 37, line 4: Read “קרא ל־ . . . ו.”

P. 231, 1st col., line 15: Read “לַהֲבוֹת אֵשׁ. . . .”

P. 231, n. 44: add to end: For a “rain of fire,” see Gen 19:24; Ezek 38:22.

P. 234, n. 66, line 5: There should be no hyphen in *dūr abni.*

P. 236, 1st col., line 21: Read “(עבר ל־), . . .”

P. 236, n. 82, line 1: Read “עבר ל־.”

P. 236, n. 82, line 5: Read “עבר ל־.”

P. 236, n. 88, line 2: The last word should read “seine.”

P. 241, n. 21: *KAI,* I. p. 37, 202:12.

P. 242, n. 29: K. Marti reference should be BZAW 34.

P. 243, 2d col., line 8: phrase should read "Samaria (1 Kgs 16:24), and Jezreel (1 Kgs 21:1) . . ."

P. 249, n. 102: Note should include "Compare Num 18:6."

P. 250, 2d col., lines 16 and 18: *ḫarimtu* should read *ḫarīmtu.*

P. 250, 2d col., line 19: *limḫuru* should read *limḫurū.*

P. 253, n. 5, line 1: "J. Löw" should read "I. Löw."

P. 253, n. 6: Read *KAI,* I. p. 34, 182:7.

P. 254, 1st col., lines 1–2: Read "Aram. קִיטָא; . . ."

P. 254, n. 10: Reference should read Amos 7:8, 15.

P. 256, 2d col., line 12: Reference: Job 5:11 should be included.

P. 259, 1st col., line 2: Reference should read XVII: 18–22.

P. 259, 1st col., line 5: Reference should read XVIII:4–XIX:3.

P. 259, n. 26, lines 17–18: *iṣṣabat* should read *iṣ[ṣabat],* and "hold" should read "h[old]."

P. 261, n. 49, line 8: Reference should read ("Wörterbuch," 11–13).

P. 261, n. 53, line 1: Reference should read "Yalkut Shimoni, 859."

P. 262, n. 4, line 5: *īnīkunu* should read *ēnēkunu.*

P. 262, n. 4, line 7: phrase should read "(so that) you will wander . . ."

P. 262, n. 6, lines 5, 7: *namri* should read *namru.*

P. 263, 1st col., line 4: *nissati* should read *nissāti.*

P. 263, n. 17: Compare Lev 19:19; Ezek 44:17.

P. 270, n. 20, line 15: Read *Qadmoniot* 19 (1986) 27–31 (Heb.).

P. 271: note 27 should read: "*CTA* 32.1.25, 27.30.1-2."

P. 274, n. 12: "Theis-Lippel" should read "Theis-Lippl."

P. 275, n. 18, line 19: *butu* should read *butū.*

P. 277, n. 42, line 13: *ilūh* should be *ilū,* and *īterbu* should be *īterbū.*

P. 279, n. 64: *īni* should read *īnī.*

P. 283, n. 13, line 16: "1964" should be "1962."

P. 284, n. 25, line 3: "7:3, 6" should be "7:2, 5."

P. 285, n. 32: Phrase should read: "see 4:2. Heb. כִּי may also be a כִּי *energeticus*; see 4:13; 6:11, 14."

P. 286, n. 37: Sentence should begin: "See also Nah 3:12 for the *niphʿal* of the root . . ."

P. 287, 1st col., line 5: Reference should read "(see 2:12; 4:1; 5:14; 6:13; 8:5, 14)."

P. 290, n. 13: Amos reference should be 2:9-10.

P. 291, n. 24, line 5: Reference should read "2 Chr 33:15."

P. 292, n. 43: First line should be deleted.

P. 292, n. 44, line 3: "and the El Amarna Canaanite gloss, *ḫarāšu, EA,* 226, 11."

P. 294, n. 60, line 13: *hithpael* should read *hithpaʿel.*

P. 294, n. 63, line 9: "in all the other passages" should read "in most other passages."

P. 294, n. 63: *endzeitlich* should read *endzeitliche.*

P. 303, 2d col.: "Botterweck, J. G." should read "Botterweck, G. J."

P. 307, 1st col.: "Labuschange" should read "Labuschagne."

P. 308: Page numbers for Niditsch are 21–41.

P. 310: Page numbers for Sister (1934) should be 399–430.

P. 310: Within the Stoebe (1970) reference, "*Walter*" should read "*Walther.*"

P. 312: Within the Weisman reference, "Structure" should read "Structures."

P. 314: Hermisson title should read "Alten," not "Altem."

P. 315, 2d col.: Weinfeld, M. *Idem*, "Z. Barag" should read "Z. Baras."

P. 316: von Rad 1973 should end 2. 245–54.

P. 320: Janzen reference should begin "*ĂŠRÊ* . . .

P. 325: Lang (beneath 2:6) page numbers should be 482–88.

P. 328: In Rudolph (beneath 4:6-13), "*Walter*" should read "*Walther.*"

P. 330: In Eissfeldt *Idem*, "and" should be "und."

P. 334: Lang (beneath 8:6) page numbers should be 482–88.

P. 334: In Speidel (beneath 8:11–12), *Bostchaft* should read *Botschaft*.

P. 337, 2d col.: "Andersen, B. W." should read "Anderson, B. W."

P. 339: In Bjoerndalen, read 'כה אמר יי׳'.

P. 339, 2d col.: "Bodreuil" should read "Bordreuil."

P. 342: In Dossin (1948), page numbers should be 125–34.

P. 344: Frankena (1953) should be 1954.

P. 349, 2d col.: "Hoffman, D. Z." should read "Hoffmann, D. Z."

P. 352: Lambert (1965), volume number should be 27, not 24.

P. 354: Loewenstamm (1964) *Collected Readings* should read *Collected Studies*.

P. 355: Mazar *Idem* "Sela" should be "Selaᶜ."

P. 362, 1st col.: "Steinspring" should read "Stinespring."

P. 366, 1st col.: "Weippert, N." should read "Weippert, M."

P. 395: First reference beneath Ta'anith should be 2:1.

P. 398: First reference beneath *UT* should be deleted.

P. 399: Missing from or changed in the index:

Deir ᶜAlla

I:1	241 n. 22
I:6-7	186, n. 40, 262 n. 4

Delete entry for line 7.

KAI

I.1:2	52 n. 91
I.26:2–5	57 n. 140
I.181:7	58 n. 153
I.181:12–13	73
I.181:15–17	15 n. 84
I.181:17	65
I.182:4–5	144 n. 44
I.202	148 n. 87

P. 405: 1st col.: "Gitay, B." should read "Gitay, Y."